ENCYCLOPEDIA OF
AFRICAN HISTORY

ENCYCLOPEDIA OF AFRICAN HISTORY

VOLUME 1
A–G

Kevin Shillington, Editor

Fitzroy Dearborn
An Imprint of the Taylor & Francis Group
New York • London

Published in 2005 by
Fitzroy Dearborn
Taylor & Francis Group
270 Madison Avenue
New York, NY 10016

10 9 8 7 6 5 4 3 2

Library of Congress Cataloging-in-Publication Data
    Encyclopedia of African history / Kevin Shillington, editor.
        p. cm.
      Includes bibliographical references and index.
      ISBN 1-57958-245-1 (alk. paper)
      1. Africa—History—Encyclopedias. I. Shillington, Kevin.

    DT20.E53 2004
    960'.03—dc22   2004016779

CONTENTS

LIST OF ENTRIES A–Z

(with chronological sublistings within nation/group categories)

VOLUME 1

VOLUME 2

LIST OF ENTRIES: THEMATIC

Iron Age to End of Eighteenth Century: North Africa

Iron Age to End of Eighteenth Century: Western Africa

Beginnings of European Imperialism

The "Scramble"

Postcolonial Africa

Modern Cities of Historical Importance

Algiers
Antananarivo
Bamako
Beira Corridor
Blantyre
Brazzaville
Bulawayo
Cairo
Cape Town
Casablanca
Conakry
Dakar
Dar es Salaam
Douala
Durban
Freetown
Harare
Ibadan
Johannesburg
Kampala
Kano
Khartoum
Kinshasa
Kumasi
Lagos
Libreville
Lomé
Lubumbashi
Luanda
Lusaka
Maputo
Mogadishu
Monrovia
Port Harcourt

Pretoria
Tangier
Tripoli
Tunis
Yaoundé
Zanzibar (City)

Historiographical Surveys
Historiography of Africa
Historiography of Western Africa, 1790s–1860s
History, African: Sources of

Outlines of Regional History
Eastern Africa
Northern Africa
Southern Africa

Pan-African Comparative Topics and Debates
Art and Architecture, History of African
Community in African Society
Diaspora: Historiographical Debates
Geography, Environment in African History
Labor: Cooperative Work
Language Classification
Mosque, Sub-Saharan: Art and Architecture of
Political Systems
Production and Exchange, Precolonial
Religion, History of
Women: History and Historiography
World History, Africa in

INTRODUCTION

African history as a modern academic discipline came of age in the 1950s, the decade of African nationalism that saw the parallel emergence of African institutions of higher education on the continent. The true origins of African higher education can be traced back many centuries to the Islamic universities of North Africa, Timbuktu, and Cairo, while the origins of recorded history itself are to be found in the scrolls of ancient Egypt, probably the oldest recorded history in the world. Beyond the reaches of the Roman Empire in North Africa, the tradition of keeping written records of events, ideas, and dynasties was followed, almost continuously, by the priests and scholars of ancient, medieval, and modern Ethiopia. Meanwhile, preliterate African societies recorded their histories in the oral memories and ancestral traditions that were faithfully handed down from generation to generation. Sometimes these were adapted to suit the political imperatives of current ruling elites, but as the modern academic historian knows only too well, the written record is similarly vulnerable to the interpretation of the recorder.

Before the European incursion at the end of the nineteenth century, literate Africans in western and southern Africa had appreciated the importance of recording oral traditions and writing the history of their own people. Following the colonial intrusion, however, Europeans took over the writing of African history, and interpreted it primarily as a timeless backdrop to their own appearance on the scene. They brought with them not only the social Darwinism of the imperial project, but also the perspective of their own historical traditions. Thus, early colonial historians saw an Africa of warring "tribes" peopled by waves of migration, such as Roman imperialists had seen and conquered in Western Europe some 2000 years earlier. To these historians, African peoples had no history of significance and were distinguished only by a variety of custom and tradition. Any contrary evidence of indigenous sophistication and development was interpreted as the work of outside (by implication, northern Eurasian) immigration or influence. The origins of Great Zimbabwe (a Shona kingdom founded between 1100 and 1450), originally believed by European colonial historians to be non-African despite much evidence to the contrary, proved to be the most notorious and persistent of these myths. Despite early academic challenges, these European-constructed myths about Africa's past exerted a dominant influence on approaches to African history until well into the second half of the twentieth century.

Encouraged and supported by a handful of European and North American academics, pioneering Africans seized the opportunities offered by the newly open academic world that emerged after World War II. So began the mature study of African history, which established the subject as a modern, respected, academic discipline. The fruits of this discipline were summarized in two major collective works, written and published primarily in the 1970s and 1980s, the *Cambridge History of Africa* (8 volumes, 1975–1986) and the *UNESCO General History of Africa* (8 volumes, 1981–1993).

The present *Encyclopedia of African History* builds upon this tradition, and in doing so provides a new reference resource on the history of the African continent and an up-to-date survey of the current state of scholarship at the turn of the new millennium. Unlike other reference works that do not treat North Africa together with Sub-Saharan Africa, the coverage of this encyclopedia is that of the whole continent, from Morocco, Libya, and Egypt in the north to the Cape of Good Hope in the south, and includes the surrounding islands, from Cape Verde in the west to Madagascar, Mauritius, and Seychelles in the east. Covering the history of the continent as a diverse whole—with complementary and competing cultural forces from north to south and east to west—reflects the direction toward which contemporary scholarship of African history has moved in recent years. It is an indispensable feature of this work that students can find African history presented with a view to the continent in its entirety.

The historical periods covered are also unique for a reference work. This encyclopedia does not chop African history into discrete and seemingly unrelated periods. To allow students to find the interlinking histories of continuity and change, the periods included in this encyclopedia range from the earliest evolution of human beings on the continent to the new millennium. Approximately one-third of the encyclopedia covers the history of Africa to the end of the eighteenth century, a fascinating period of rich cultural achievements and profound historical developments that occur in the time before the Roman Empire through the European Middle Ages and beyond. Students can find information about the emergence of foraging and food-producing societies, the flowering of the great Egyptian civilization, and the development of other, less obviously dramatic, civilizations in the savannas and forests in all regions of Africa. Attention is paid both to indigenous developments and to the impact of outside influences and intrusions, including the spread of Islam and the slave trade in all its forms, to provide students with the dynamic cultural context of the continent within the many forces shaping human history. Most of the remaining two-thirds of this encyclopedia details the history of each region from the precolonial nineteenth century, through the twentieth-century colonial period that defined the modern states, and takes the user into the postcolonial contemporary period, and the dawn of the new millennium.

How to Use this Book

The *Encyclopedia of African History* is organized into a series of free-standing essays, most of them approximately 1,000 words in length. They range from factual narrative entries to thematic and analytical discussions, and combinations of all these. There are, in addition, a number of longer essays of about 3,000–5,000 words, which analyze broader topics: regional general surveys, historiographical essays, and wide historical themes, such as the African Diaspora, African Political Systems, and Africa in World History. The encyclopedia takes a broadly African viewpoint of the history of the continent, where this is appropriate, and as far as possible provides the reader with a reliable, up-to-date view of the current state of scholarship on the full range of African history. Where debates and controversies occur, these are indicated and discussed. As far as possible, this book takes the history of Africa up to the present, at least to the opening years of the twenty-first century. Thus topics such as Nigeria's Fourth Republic or the civil war and demise of Charles Taylor as president of Liberia are put into their historical context, as are themes such as the disease pandemics of malaria and HIV/AIDS.

Perhaps the most significant feature of the encyclopedia is the easily accessible A-to-Z format. The titles of the essays are organized for easy reference into composite articles on the major regions, states, themes, societies, and individuals of African history. Within these multiple-entry composites, the essays are organized in a broadly chronological order: thus Egypt under the Ottomans precedes Egypt under Muhammad Ali. Cross-referencing in the form of *See also*'s at the end of most entries refers the reader to other related essays. Blind entries direct readers to essays listed under another title; for example, the blind entry "Gold Coast" refers the reader to the entry on Ghana's colonial period. In addition, a full index is provided for reference to those items and individuals that are mentioned within essays but do not appear as head words in their own right. A list for Further Reading at the end of each entry refers the reader to some of the most recent work on the subject.

Other special features include 100 specially commissioned maps, one for each of the 55 modern states, and a further 45 specially designed historical maps, indicating such important features as the Languages of Africa, the New Kingdom of Ancient Egypt, the Songhay Empire, and the Peoples of the East African Savanna in the Eighteenth Century. I researched widely in other people's work for the material for these historical maps, in particular Ajayi and Crowder's *Historical Atlas of Africa* (1985), the various works of the late David Beach for the Zimbabwe Plateau of the fifteenth to eighteenth centuries, and the work of Jan Vansina for the peoples of the Congolese forest of Equatorial Africa by the early nineteenth century. I should like to take this opportunity to thank Catherine Lawrence for drawing the maps and for her patience with my not-infrequent editorial interventions. Any errors of interpretation, however, particularly in the historical maps, must remain mine alone. In addition, 103 illustrations are dispersed throughout, many of them not previously published in a work of this nature.

The encyclopedia consists of nearly 1,100 entries. The original list of entry topics was devised by the editor with the advice of a panel of 30 advisers, all of them established specialists in a particular field of African history, and some with decades of experience, not only in the teaching, researching, and writing of African history, but also in the editing and publication of large collaborative volumes. The final decision on the selection or omission of topics remained, however, my own.

A total of 330 authors have contributed the entries to this encyclopedia, and approximately 130 of them are African. About half of the latter are currently working in African universities, and the remainder overseas, mostly in North American universities, but also in Europe, India, and Australia. A number of entries from Francophone West Africa, Madagascar, France, and Belgium have been translated from their original French.

Acknowledgments

This encyclopedia has taken considerably longer than originally planned, both to write and prepare for publication. Anybody who has worked on collaborative projects, even on a small scale, knows only too well how delays quickly get built into the system. I am grateful for the patience of advisers and contributors, many of whom have inevitably been asked to add last-minute updating to their entries. I am particularly grateful for the help, guidance, and encouragement I received from our team of eminent advisers in the early stages. In addition, the commitment to the project by the large number of contributors was always an inspiration to me, and the whole project is greatly indebted to that handful of contributors who responded so willingly to appeals for yet more work to be produced on short notice. My thanks to Kristen Holt and her team at Routledge Reference, New York, who took up the project at a late stage, trusted my judgment, and completed the work expeditiously. Special acknowledgment, however, is due to the originator of the concept, Mark Hawkins-Dady of Fitzroy Dearborn Publishers, who first proposed the project to me, and then, through several years of inspiring and industrious work, saw it through, almost to its final stages. Without him, this book would not have happened. Finally, I dedicate this book to Pippa, my wife, always an inspiration in my work.

Kevin Shillington
Editor

A

'Abd Allah ibn Yasin: Almoravid: Sahara

Most accounts of the origins of the Almoravids indicate that ibn Yasin (d.1059) was dispatched as a religious instructor to the western Sahara by his master, Wajjaj b. Zallu, at the request of the Sanhaja leader Yahya ibn Ibrahim. The Sanhaja tribes of the region had only been recently Islamicized, and their knowledge of Muslim dogma and rituals was limited. Ibn Yasin was entrusted with the mission of spreading the Islamic creed and helping wipe out unorthodox religious practices among the Berbers of the western Sahara.

The brand of Islam preached by ibn Yasin was based on a strict application of Qur'anic injunctions and a literal interpretation of the sacred text. Among the first measures he adopted after settling among the Sanhaja were the imposition of Islamic law (*Shari'a*) in all spheres of life, the introduction of a public treasury, and the levying of the tithe (*'ushr*). He also adopted Malikism as the officially-endorsed legal practice. Ibn Yasin adhered to a rigorous spiritual code dominated by asceticism and self-discipline and demanded absolute obedience from his followers, the growing religious community later known as the Almoravids.

The term *Almoravid*, a deformation of the Arabic *murabit*, has long been the subject of controversy among historians. The prevalent view is that it derives from *ribat*, a type of fortified convent, and referred to the religious compound where ibn Yasin allegedly sought refuge, together with his closest followers, after a disagreement with one of the Sanhaja chiefs. Some scholars, however, dispute this interpretation and claim that the term *murabit* does not refer to the legendary island retreat founded by ibn Yasin according to some sources. It would be connected, rather, with the Qur'anic root *rbt*, commonly translated as "wage holy war (jihad)," but also "perform good deeds." Supporters of this version also point out that the term *Almoravid* is clearly linked to the name given by Wajjaj b. Zallu, ibn Yasin's mentor, to the residents of the ascetic lodge set up by the former in the Sus region: the so-called *dar al-murabitin*.

The reform movement inspired by the teachings of ibn Yasin spread rapidly due to the support of Sanhaja chiefs. The three main branches of the Sanhaja, namely the Massufa, Lamtuna, and Guddala, had just been united into a loose confederation under the command of Yahya b. Ibrahim. Mostly nomads, they made a precarious living by engaging in pastoralism and often supplemented their income by charging protection dues to the caravans that circulated along the Saharan trade routes. Natural adversity, in the form of a prolonged drought in Mauritania, and the new religious ardor instilled into them by ibn Yasin's reformist message, prompted the Sanhaja to seek alternative sources of income that ultimately entailed wresting control of trans-Saharan commerce from their immediate competitors.

Before the advent of the Almoravids in the first half of the eleventh century, the Sanhaja had only played an ancillary role in the trade links between southern Morocco and Ghana and the western Sudan. They had been passive witnesses of the intense commercial exchanges taking place through their territory without gaining any profit from them. Control of the trade routes was in the hands of the Soninke state in Ghana, in the south, and of Zanata Berbers—a rival tribal group—in the north. The first Almoravid campaigns were aimed, therefore, at occupying the main commercial centers. Sijilmasa, the northern terminus of the caravan trade and ruled by the Maghrawa, a Zanata clan, since 970, was seized by ibn Yasin in 1053, apparently with the acquiescence of the local population. The following year, the Almoravids conquered Awdaghust, an important commercial center, especially in salt coming from Ghana, and virtually the other end of the Saharan trade.

Once control of the commercial routes had been consolidated, the Almoravids turned their attention to other areas of southern Morocco with obvious economic appeal: the pastures of the Draa and the Sus valleys. This period of quick military expansion was marred, however, by infighting within the Almoravid ruling elite. During Yahya b. Ibrahim's lifetime, the Almoravid polity had a de facto dual leadership: Yahya exercised political power and oversaw military campaigns while ibn Yasin had authority over religious and legal matters. After the death of his royal protector, ibn Yasin fell in disgrace and went into exile, probably around 1052–1053. He soon gained favor, however, among the new Almoravid leadership, this time dominated by the Lamtuna chiefs Yahya b. 'Umar and his brother Abu Bakr.

Yahya b. 'Umar died in 1056 trying to quell the rebellion of the Guddala, one of the original components of the great Sanhaja confederation who resented the new status quo. Although not entirely subdued, a modus vivendi was agreed upon whereby, although nominally autonomous, the Guddala agreed to end their resistance and participate in further expeditions. Once order in the royal household was restored, military activity soon resumed. Abu Bakr b. 'Umar seized the Draa Valley and, after arduous negotiations, ibn Yasin managed to secure the submission of the Masmuda of the High Atlas and the Sus in 1058. After the initial resistance of local people, the town of Aghmat Warika was also occupied and the allegiance of recalcitrant notables secured through the marriage of Abu Bakr, the Almoravid *amir*, and Zaynab, the widow (or daughter, according to some sources) of one of its chiefs. Unhindered access to the plains of the Tansift valley was now possible. The Almoravids' northward expansion was two-pronged: on the one hand, through the central plateau where the future capital, Marrakesh, was to be erected and, on the other, along the Atlantic coast. The region of Tamesna, dominated by a heretical sect known as the Barghawata, resisted Almoravid penetration fiercely. In fact, their first incursions in the area were successfully repelled, and ibn Yasin died in one of them in 1059.

FRANCISCO RODRIGUEZ-MANAS

See also: **Yusuf ibn Tashfin: Almoravid Empire: Maghrib: 1070–1147.**

Further Reading

Brett, M. "Islam in North Africa," in P. Clarke (ed.), *The World's Religions. Islam*, London: 1990, pp. 23–47.
Levtzion, N. "'Abd Allah b. Yasin and the Almoravids," in J.R. Willis (ed.), *Studies in West African Islamic History. I: The Cultivators of Islam*, London: 1979, pp. 78–112.
Meier, F. "Almoraviden und Marabute," *Die Welt des Islams*, 21 (1981), 80–163.
Moraes Farias, P.F. de. "The Almoravids: Some Questions Concerning the Character of the Movement during Its Period of Closest Contact with the Western Sudan," *Bulletin de l'Institut Francais d'Archeologie Orientale*, 29 (1967), 794–878.
Norris, H.T. "New evidence on the life of 'Abdallah b. Yasin and the origins of the Almoravid movement," *Journal of African History*, 12.2 (1971), 255–268.
Norris, H.T. *Saharan Myth and Saga*, Oxford: 1972.

'Abd al-Mu'min: Almohad Empire, 1140–1269

The circumstances surrounding 'Abd al-Mu'min's accession to power after the death of ibn Tumart, founder of the Almohad movement, are still unknown. 'Abd al-Mu'min did not belong to one of the so-called Almohad tribes (the first to embrace the Mahdi's doctrine), and furthermore, other members of ibn Tumart's "entourage" occupied a higher rank and could have claimed rights of succession. It seems, however, that the fact that he was a relative outsider was an asset rather than a liability, and he was viewed as a compromise candidate among Masmuda chiefs. The support of Abu Hafs 'Umar al-Hintati, one of the Mahdi's closest confidants, seems to have been crucial in ensuring that his rise to power progressed smoothly. But loyalty toward the new leader was lukewarm at this early stage, and 'Abd al-Mu'min had to prove both his political acumen and military skill.

His first military campaigns were aimed at occupying the mountain ranges and encircling the Almoravid capital, avoiding direct clashes on the plains, where the Sanhaja cavalry was proving unbeatable. Control of the Anti- and High Atlas left the regions of Sus and the Draa valley clearly exposed; their populations did not fail to observe the potential danger and recognized Almohad authority. Further north, the conquest of the Middle Atlas and the Tafilalt in 1140–1141 led to the occupation of the Rif, the Taza region, and the Mediterranean littoral. 'Abd al-Mu'min's military ambitions were not confined to the western Maghrib; he wished to unify all the lands of North Africa between Tunisia and southern Morocco under a single command.

The first serious confrontation with the Almoravid army took place near Tlemcen in 1145, and resulted in the defeat of the ruling dynasty and the death of its *amir*, Tashfin b. 'Ali. This event signaled the inexorable decline of the Almoravids. In less than two years the main cities of Morocco—Fez, Meknes, and Sale—were taken. Marrakesh fell in 1147, after a prolonged siege. Once control of Morocco had been achieved, 'Abd al-Mu'min turned his attention to

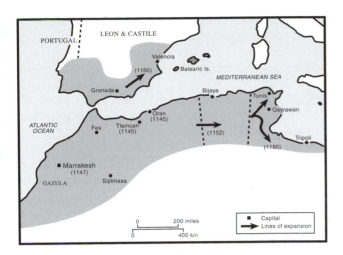

Almohads, c.1140–1269.

The reign of Abu Yusuf Ya'qub al-Mansur (1184–1199) was equally turbulent. As soon as he became caliph, one of the longest anti-Almohad rebellions broke out in the eastern fringes of the empire. Its leaders belonged to a family of former Almoravid officials, the Banu Ghaniyya, who had settled in Tunisia after being expelled from the Balearic Islands, where they had served as governors. The unrest increased even further as a result of attempts, on the part of local Sanhaja, to revive the Hammadid kingdom in eastern Algeria. The seizure of Bougie in 1184 put an end to Sanhaja ambitions. The Banu Ghaniyya insurrection was more difficult to check for two reasons: a) long distances forced the Almohads to rely on the navy and, although they could take coastal towns quite easily, they could not pursue their punitive strikes further inland, precisely where the rebels sought refuge, and b) the Banu Ghaniyya managed to obtain the support of the Arab tribes of the region, such as the Judham and Riyah, thus notably increasing their military capability. The defeat of 'Ali ibn Ghaniyya near Gafsa in 1187 was a severe blow to the rebels, but it did not seal their fate. His descendants managed to regroup their troops and establish a new base in the central Maghrib. They even occupied the town of Sijilmasa during the reign of Muhammad al-Nasir (1199–1214) but were finally crushed in the Libyan region of Jabal Nafusa in 1209–1210. Reprisals against the Arab tribes of Ifriqiya had important repercussions, especially in the demographic make-up of North Africa. They were "evicted" and resettled in the region of Tamesna, on the Atlantic coast of Morocco. This measure was not only momentous demographically, but also politically. From then onward, Almohad caliphs partly recruited their armies from these Arab contingents, to counterbalance the weight of Berber tribes, notorious for their volatility.

Defeat by the Christians in the battle of Navas de Tolosa (Spain) in 1212 was the first sign of the process of imperial fragmentation. Military weakness, infighting within the ruling elite, and the abandonment of the Almohad doctrine by al-Ma'mun (1227–1232) marked the first half of the thirteenth century, ultimately leading to the dissolution of the empire into three political entities, roughly equivalent to present-day Morocco, Algeria, and Tunisia.

FRANCISCO RODRIGUEZ-MANAS

See also: Ibn Tumart, Almohad Community and.

Tunisia (known in Arabic sources as Ifriqiya). The Norman kingdom of Sicily did not conceal its territorial ambitions in the area, and the Almohad caliph saw this campaign as a kind of jihad. The Qal'a, the capital of the Hammadi kingdom, was captured in 1152. The Arab tribes that had assisted the local Sanhaja Berbers were pushed back toward the region of Setif in 1153. The eastern campaign had to be interrupted, however, because various outbreaks of dissent in Morocco required the attention of the caliph. It was resumed in 1159. The last remnants of the Zirid kingdom were suppressed and the Normans, then occupying Mahdiyya and other coastal enclaves, were repelled.

The creation of a North African empire was the paramount objective of 'Abd al-Mu'min's foreign policy. This goal was hindered, however, by the impossibility of concentrating military efforts on this campaign. Instability in Morocco as a result of sporadic rebellions, mostly instigated by the Almohad hierarchy, and the perennial issue of the war in Muslim Spain meant that imperial troops had to fight on several fronts at the same time. Domestic policy was not exempt from difficulties, either. The caliph's attempts to turn the empire into a hereditary monarchy proved successful, but he was forced to make important concessions to the Almohad chiefs. 'Abd al-Mu'min's successors (sayyids) served as provincial governors, but their decisions were closely monitored by advisers selected from among the Almohad shaykhs.

'Abd al-Mu'min's heir, Abu Ya'qub Yusuf (1163–1184), spent most of his reign fighting disgruntled opponents. In fact, he was unable to take the caliphal title until 1168, after two years of trying to quell the rebellion of the Ghumara in the Rif mountains. His campaigns in Spain had more immediate results and culminated in the defeat of ibn Mardanish, the last of the pro-Almoravid rebels, in 1165.

Further Reading

Abun-Nasr, J.M. *A History of the Maghrib in the Islamic Period*, Cambridge, 1987.

Hopkins, J.F.P. "The Almohad Hierarchy," *Bulletin of the School of Oriental and African Studies*, 16 (1954), 93–112.

Hopkins, J.F.P. *Medieval Muslim Government in Barbary until the Sixth Century of the Hijra.* London, 1958.

Laroui, A. *The History of the Maghrib: An Interpretive Essay.* Princeton, 1977.

'Abd al-Qadir (1832–1847)

Amir of Mascara

'Abd al-Qadir, who led a mid-nineteenth century revolt against France, is considered by modern-day Algerians as the greatest hero in their country's struggle for liberation. Early in life, 'Abd al-Qadir ibn Muhyi al-Din quickly acquired a reputation for piety, good manners, and intelligence. His father, Muhyi al-Din ibn Mustafa al-Hasani al-Jaza'iri, was a local religious leader, the head of a Sufi brotherhood, and director of a local religious school, or *zawiyah*. In 1830, when 'Abd al-Qadir was twenty-two years old, French forces invaded Algeria on the pretext of avenging the dishonor suffered by the French consul when the *dey* struck him in the face with a fly whisk during a disagreement about France's debt to Algeria (though in fact, the French invasion had much more to do with diverting the attention of the French from the domestic problems caused by their own inept kings). Then nominally controlled by the Ottoman Empire (in the person of the *dey*, or governor), Algeria was already deeply divided between those supporting the *dey* (mainly the Turkish Janissaries, responsible for choosing the *dey* and keeping him in power, a group of local elites of mixed Turkish and Algerian descent known as the Koulouglis, and a number of tribal elites), and the mass of Algerians, who opposed the government of the *dey* and who had begun launching a series of minor revolts in the early nineteenth century.

These divisions resulted in a government incapable of combating the French invasion; instead, opposition was organized by religious brotherhoods like that led by Muhyi al-Din. However, Muhyi al-Din was not a young man, and in 1832, one year after French forces occupied the port city of Oran, he engineered the election of his son, 'Abd al-Qadir, to take his place as head of the brotherhood (and hence, of the opposition). In this position, 'Abd al-Qadir took responsibility for organizing opposition to the French in Oran and in nearby Mostaganem, calling for a jihad (holy war) against the invaders. He also took the title of *amir al-mu'manin* (commander of the faithful), a title symbolic of the role religion played in his military exploits. An effective military leader, his campaigns forced the French to sign the Treaty of Desmichels in 1834. This treaty gave the young leader control of the area around Oran. Three years later, in the Treaty of Tafna, 'Abd al-Qadir scored another success. Since the signing of the previous treaty, the *amir* had managed to expand the amount of territory under his control (including occupying the towns of Médéa and Miliana, located south and southwest of Algiers, respectively), had defeated the French forces under the command of General Camille Trézel at Macta, and had further mobilized Algerian support of his movement. The 1837 treaty gave 'Abd al-Qadir further control of areas near Oran and control of the Titteri region.

After 1837, the *amir* spent two years consolidating his new state. Governing at times from Mascara and at times from the fortress of Tiaret, 'Abd al-Qadir established a model administration in which equal taxation and legal equality, fixed salaries for officials, and the absence of tribal privilege were prominent features. He expanded educational opportunities for his people, which helped spread ideas of nationalism and independence. Although he functioned as an absolutist leader, 'Abd al-Qadir was willing to employ anyone he deemed qualified, including foreigners and religious minorities. With the occasional help of such advisers, the *amir* organized a permanent regular army of approximately 2,000 men; when the need arose it could be supplemented by tribal recruits and volunteers. His military was supported by fortified towns such as Boghar, Taza, Tiaret, Sebdou, and Saga located in the interior, where they were safe from attacks launched from French-controlled territory near the coast.

The *amir* also continued in his quest to gain more territory for his new state. He began occupying all areas in the interior not already occupied by the French military, expanding eastward to the border of the territory governed by the *bey* of Constantine, taking revenge against the Koulouglis in Zouatna who supported the French, and pushing to the south, where he successfully challenged the authority of al-Tijini, the leader of the southern oases, destroying his capital and winning the allegiance of the Saharan tribes. In the span of about one year, 'Abd al-Qadir had asserted his control over a sizeable portion of Algeria: across the mountainous Kabylie region in the north and from the Biskra oasis to the border of Morocco in the south.

Conditions changed in 1841, however, when a new governor-general arrived from Paris. General Thomas-Robert Bugeaud was no stranger to Algeria nor to 'Abd al-Qadir, having defeated the *amir* five years earlier in a battle at Sikkah; he had spent the interim developing ideas for more effective techniques of irregular warfare which he anticipated using against the Algerian opposition upon his return. Bugeaud's arrival in Algeria in 1841 signaled a change in French policy toward *occupation totale*. No longer was it sufficient for French forces to hold the coastal regions of Algeria, now they were to take the interior as well. This new policy clearly meant that 'Abd al-Qadir's budding state must be crushed. In 1841, the *amir*'s fortified towns were destroyed, and the *amir* himself was left without a home base from which to counteract the French attacks. Bugeaud's armies set about conquering the interior, systematically taking district after district and establishing army posts and regular mounted patrols in areas they occupied. This systematic conquest carried a high price for the Algerian population, as French military action became increasingly brutal. Villages and homes were burned, crops destroyed, and all types of civilians killed during the conquest of the interior.

Seeking refuge briefly with the sultan of Morocco after 1842 (who helped channel British arms to the *amir* for use against the French), 'Abd al-Qadir quickly returned to Algeria and launched a new campaign against French forces in the interior. However, the *amir* lost the support of Morocco two years later, when the sultan's forces were drawn into the conflict and soundly defeated by Bugeaud at the battle of Isly in 1844 (Bugeaud earning the title *Duc d'Isly* in consequence). The withdrawal of Moroccan support (accompanied by orders from the sultan that the *amir* be imprisoned if caught trying to enter Morocco) seriously damaged 'Abd al-Qadir's campaigns. The *amir*'s power base had all but eroded; though supported in spirit by many Algerians, he had neither territory nor weapons to effectively challenge the French, and in 1847, was forced to surrender to the French armies under the command of General Christophe-Louis-Leon Lamorcière. After his surrender, the *amir* was sentenced to exile in Damascus, where he died in 1883.

Though his movement was defeated by the French, and though France's policy of total colonization in Algeria had by 1870 essentially eradicated all vestiges of a separate Algerian national identity, the *Amir* 'Abd al-Qadir remains a national hero. The short-lived state he established in the mid-nineteenth century, with its ideals of equality, piety, and independence, was idealized in the popular imagination and served as a rallying cry for the long and difficult process of Algerian liberation in the mid-twentieth century.

AMY J. JOHNSON

See also: **Algeria: Conquest and Resistance, 1831–1879; Algeria: Government and Administration, 1830–1914.**

Biography

'Abd al-Qadir was born in 1808 near the city of Mascara in northwestern Algeria. In 1832, his father Muhyi al-Din ibn Mustafa al-Hasani al-Jaza'iri, the head of a Sufi brotherhood, engineered the election of his son to take his place as head of the brotherhood. Al-Qadir led military campaigns in France, resulting in treaties in 1834 and 1837, in which he was ceded territory. In 1841, al-Qadir's towns were destroyed, in renewed attacks from the French. He sought refuge in Morocco after 1842, returned to Algeria, and launched a new campaign against French forces in the interior. He was defeated at the battle of Isly in 1844, and forced to surrender to the French in 1847. Al-Qadir was sentenced to exile in Damascus, where he died in 1883.

Further Reading

Aouli, Smail, Randame Redjala, and Philippe Zoummeroff. *Abd el-Kader*. Paris: Fayard, 1994.

Abazah, Nizar. *Al-Amir Abd al-Qadir al-Jazairi: al-alim al-mujahid*. Bayrut, Lubnan: Dar al-Fikr al-Muasir; Dimashq, Suriyah; Dar al-Fikr, 1994.

Blunt, Wilfrid. *Desert Hawk; Abd el Kader and the French Conquest of Algeria*. London: Methuen, 1947.

Churchill, Charles Henry. *The Life of Abdel Kader, Ex-Sultan of the Arabs of Algeria*. London: Chapman and Hall, 1867.

Clancy-Smith, Julia. *Rebel and Saint*. Berkeley: University of California Press, 1994.

Danziger, Raphael. *Abd al-Qadir and the Algerians: Resistance to the French and Internal Consolidation*. New York: Holmes and Meier Publishers, 1977.

Ibn al-Tuhami, Mustafa. *Sirat al-Amir Abd al-Qadir wa-jihadihu*. Bayrut, Lubnan: Dar al-Gharb al-Islami, 1995.

King, John. "'Arms and the Man': Abd el-Kader," *History Today*, vol. 40 (August 1990), 22–28.

'Abd el-Krim: *See* Morocco: Resistance and Collaboration, Bu Hmara to Abdelkrim (Ibn 'Abd el-Krim).

Abdile Hassan: *See* Somalia: Hassan, Muhammad Abdile and Resistance to Colonial Conquest.

Abdlekrim: *See* Morocco: Resistance and Collaboration, Bu Hmara to Abdelkrim (Ibn 'Abd el-Krim).

Abolition: *See* Slavery, Abolition of: East and West Africa; Slavery: Atlantic Trade: Abolition: Philanthropy or Economics?

'Abouh, Muhammad
Egyptian Scholar and Reformer

Muhammad 'Abouh (1849–1905) is regarded as the most important and influential proponent of Islamic modernism in the nineteenth and twentieth centuries.

During the course of his student days at al-Azhar, 'Abouh came into contact with Jamal al-Din al-Afghani (1839–1897), a Persian who advocated a program of Muslim self-strengthening based on Muslim political unification and religious reform. He was particularly attracted to al-Afghani's idea that Muslims had an obligation to foster those elements within the Islamic heritage, which encouraged an ethos of activism and progress in the socioeconomic and political realms. Encouraged by al-Afghani's activist example, 'Abouh joined the mounting protest that arose among sectors of the Egyptian population in reaction to the political autocracy of Egypt's rulers and to Europe's growing influence over Egypt's financial affairs. Although mistrustful of radical solutions to Egypt's political and economic problems, the tide of events eventually prompted him to support the measures of rebel army colonel Ahmad 'Urabi, who early in 1882 succeeded in establishing a new government that was protective of Egypt's national sovereignty.

'Abouh, however, paid for his support of the 'Urabi government. After Britain invaded Egypt in September 1882 in order to restore the khedive's power and thereby secure its interests in the country, he was sentenced to exile. He traveled first to Beirut and in 1884 joined al-Afghani in Paris. In Paris the two founded and edited a journal called al-'Urwa al-Wuthqa (The Firm Bond; a reference to the Quran), which called upon Muslims worldwide to liberate themselves from European imperialism and the despotic governments under which many of them lived. The journal, which lasted only eight months, had a profound effect on many Muslim writers and activists of the era, including the Syrian Rashid Rida, who became 'Abouh's biographer and one of his most important disciples. In 1885 'Abouh returned to Beirut and took up a teaching post at the Sultaniyya school, where he delivered a series of lectures on theology that were published in 1897 as Risalat al-Tawhid (Discourses on Unity), one of the most influential theological works of Islamic modernism.

In 1888, six years after the commencement of Britain's occupation of Egypt, the khedive Tawfiq granted 'Abouh the right to return to his homeland and, in recognition of his talents, allowed him to enter into public service. 'Abouh was initially appointed Qadi (judge) in the native tribunals, which tried cases involving Egyptians according to the new codes of positive law. In 1890 he was made counselor to the court of appeals and in 1892 was instrumental in establishing the Muslim Benevolent Society for the benefit of Egypt's poor. In 1895 he was asked to set up a council for the reform of al-Azhar's administration and curriculum, a project that was only partially successful due to the opposition he encountered from that institution's conservative scholars ('ulama). The apogee of 'Abduh's career came in 1899 when he was appointed mufti, which made him the authoritative interpreter of Islamic law (Shari'a) throughout Egypt.

'Abouh's elevation to positions of influence and authority within Egypt's educational and legal institutions provided him with the opportunity to express more freely than had hitherto been possible his ideas concerning the reform of Islam. At issue for 'Abouh were the implications of the rapid economic, social, and political change that had taken root in Egypt since the early decades of the nineteenth century. Although 'Abouh recognized the importance of modernization to the advancement of Egypt and other Muslim countries, he also understood the necessity of linking the processes of change with the true principles of Islam. In 'Abouh's view, unless Muslims of the modern era made an accommodation with the novel circumstances of the modern age, Islam's relevance, both at the level of individual faith and as a worldly force, would continue to diminish. 'Abouh's response to the threat of modernity was to go behind the established edifice of medieval theology and law to Islam's first sources, the Quran and the prophetic Sunna (example), and to fashion from these an ethical understanding of Islam that advanced the common good (maslaha). 'Abouh's interpretive efforts were guided by a belief in the compatibility of reason and revelation: wherever there appeared to be a contradiction between the two, he used reason to interpret scripture. His method led him to identify certain Quranically-based concepts with modern institutions. Thus he equated ijma', the principle of legal consensus, with public opinion, and shura, consultation with the elders, with modern forms of consultative government. While such identifications point to the apologetic nature of 'Abouh's reformism, 'Abouh himself conceived his project as deriving from the pious example of the early generations of Muslims, al-Salaf al-Salih, whose faith and practice derived from the essential principles of the Quran and Sunna alone.

The chief organ of 'Abouh's views in his later years was the Manar Quranic commentary, which first appeared in 1897 and continued after his death under the editorship of Rashid Rida. Unlike traditional Quran exegeses, the Manar commentary was written in a style designed to be understood by ordinary people, and focused on practical matters of guidance rather than on grammatical usage and theological controversy, as had been the norm. During his lifetime, 'Abouh influenced many Muslim scholars. In addition to Rashid Rida, these included the Algerian 'Abd al-Hamid ibn Badis (1889–1940), who met 'Abouh during the latter's visit to Algiers and Constantine in 1903, and the Moroccan scholar Shu'ayb al-Dukkali (1878–1937).

JOHN CALVERT

See also: **Egypt: Salafiyya, Muslim Brotherhood; Religion, Colonial Africa: Islamic Orders and Movements.**

Biography

Born in the village of Mahallat Nasr in the Nile Delta, Muhammad 'Abouh received his early instruction at the Ahmadi mosque in Tanta and then attended Cairo's al-Azhar, the preeminent center of learning in the Sunni Muslim world, where he evinced an interest in mysticism. After concluding his studies in 1877 he embarked on a short-lived career as a teacher. He simultaneously held positions at al-Azhar, the Khedival School of Languages, and Dar al-'Ulum, the teachers' college that had been established a few years earlier to train "forward looking" Arabic language instructors for the emergent system of government schools. In 1879 'Abouh was forced to step down from his posts at Dar al-'Ulum and the language school by the khedive Tawfiq, who appears to have been wary of his ideas concerning religion and politics. However, due to the intervention of a liberal government ministry, he was allowed the following year to assume the editorship of the official government gazette *al-Waqa'i al-Misriyya* (Egyptian Events). He was exiled in 1882, but allowed to return to Egypt in 1888. He died in 1905.

Further Reading

Adams, Charles C. *Islam and Modernism in Egypt.* London, New York: Oxford University Press, 1933.

Amin, Osman. *Muhammad 'Abouh,* Charles Wendell, trans. Washington, DC: American Council of Learned Societies, 1953.

Hourani, Albert. *Arabic Thought in the Liberal Age, 1798–1939,* 2nd edition, London: Cambridge University Press, 1987.

Kerr, Malcolm. *Islamic Reform: The Political and Legal Theories of Muhammad 'Abouh and Rashid Rida,* Berkeley: University of California Press, 1966.

Abu Madian, al-Shadhili, and the Spread of Sufism in the Maghrib

Mysticism manifested itself in Islam as Sufism, of which there were two schools, the one of Bestami, the other of Junaid. Whereas the pantheism of the former could not be harmonized with Islamic *tawhid* (the unity of God), the latter could. It was not until the twelfth century, however, that the Sufism of Junaid's school, acceptable to Islamic orthodoxy, was institutionalized in a rite, the Qadiriyya *tariqa*, by 'Abd al-Qadir al-Jilani (1077–1166) of Baghdad. The harmonization embodied in the Qadiriyya *tariqa* was probably not without the influence also of Islam's greatest theologian, Abu Hamid al-Ghazzali (d.1111), the "father of the church in Islam," in whom "orthodoxy, philosophy and mysticism found a happy combination," having "reconciled sufism, with its many unorthodox practices, with Islam, and grafted mysticism upon its intellectualism" (Hitti 1968a: 431, 436; Hitti 1968b: 163).

Islam Sufism penetrated the Maghrib in the late tenth or early eleventh century. One of its earliest exponents in the Maghrib was Abu Imran ibn 'Isa, an *alim* of Fez, who went to Baghdad at about the end of the tenth century and returned to Qairawan, where he taught Sufism of the Junaid's school. This was disseminated in Morocco in the twelfth century by, among others, Ali ibn Hirzihim and Abu Median, a scholar and a holy man (*wali*) of repute in Fez, but originally from Seville in Spain; he is credited with having introduced to Morocco the Qadiriyya *tariqa*, whose founder, Abd al-Qadir al-Jilani, he had met in Baghdad. An Idrisid sharif and pupil of these two teachers, 'Abd al-Salam ibn Mashish adopted Sufism in the twelfth century and became the second "pole" of western Islam; western Islam acknowledges 'Abd al-Qadir al-Jilani as its first "pole." (The "pole," namely *qutb*, the "pivot of the universe," is regarded as the greatest saint of his time, occupying the highest point in the mystic hierarchy). Maghribian Sufism did not become institutionalized in a rite until the thirteenth century, when another Idrisid sharif and pupil of 'Abd al-Salam ibn Mashish, 'Abd al-Salam al-Shadhili, founded the Shadhiliyya *tariqa*; he is the third "pole" of western Islam. The Shadhiliyya, like the Qadiriyya in the east, became the chief vehicle for the transmission of Junaid's school of Sufism in the west. The Shadhiliyya is also the first indigenous Sufi order in the Maghrib, the Qadiriyya being an import from the east.

The foregoing illustrates the seminal role of the Idrisids, the sharifian family of Fez, in the development and institutionalization of Sufism in the Maghrib. In the years of political obscurity following the demise of the Idrisid state in northern Morocco, the Idrisids seemed to have found a new vocation in the pursuit of mysticism and its propagation.

Before the sixteenth century, however, Sufism commanded a severely circumscribed following in the Maghrib. The religious ferment generated by the "national" uprising against Portuguese imperialism in Morocco was to benefit the Sufi movement in the Maghrib, serving as the catalyst for its popularization. It was under a new guise, however, the Jazuliyya *tariqa*, founded by Muhammad ibn Sulaiman al-Jazuli, that Shadhilism was propagated in Morocco and in the rest of the Maghrib from the sixteenth century onward. Al-Jazuli is the fourth "pole" of western Islam and the author of a popular mystic "guide manual," *Dala 'il al-Khairat*. Jazulism may thus be regarded as the latter-day reincarnation of Shadhilism; it has provided the doctrinal basis of the majority of the *zawiya-s* in Morocco, and it is from al-Jazuli that the founders of these *zawiya-s* trace their spiritual descent (*silsila*).

A characteristic Maghribian variety of Sufism is maraboutism, which may be described as the "Islamicization" of the prevalent tradition of hagiolatry, or saint-worship. It is in Morocco that this Maghribian species of Sufism is most pronounced; indeed, it has been remarked that "Islam in Morocco is characterized by saint-worship to a greater degree than perhaps in any other country" (Hitti 1968a: 437).

B.A. MOJUETAN

Further Reading

Abun-Nasr, J.M. *The Tijaniyya: A Sufi Order in the Modern World*. London: Oxford University Press, 1965.
Arbery, A.J. *Sufism*. London: Allen and Unwin, 1950.
Hitti, P.K. *History of the Arabs*. London: Macmillan, 1968.
Hitti, P.K. *Makers of Arab History*. London: Macmillan, 1968.
Mojuetan, B.A. *History and Underdevelopment in Morocco: The Structural Roots of Conjuncture*. Hamburg: Lit Verlag, 1995 (published for the International African Institute, London).

Abuja

Abuja is Nigeria's Federal Capital Territory. It was chosen as Nigeria's new capital in 1976 by a panel headed by Justice Akinola Aguda as an alternative to Lagos, which suffered from heavy congestion problems. Situated north of the confluence of the Benue and Niger Rivers, Abuja is centrally located; this has earned it the appellation "Center of Unity." The city, which is about 8,000 square kilometers, was carved out from the Niger, Plateau, and Kogi states of Nigeria.

Originally inhabited by the Gwari, Gwandara, and Bassa peoples, it was founded by the Hausa ruling dynasty of Zaria in approximately the fifteenth century. Most of the area covered by the new Federal Capital Territory did not come under the control of the Fulani jihadists of the nineteenth century. Even though subjected to several raids, the area known today as Abuja was never really "Islamicized," as the topography assisted the anti-Fulani resistance. However, with the advent of colonialism, the area was brought under the political suzerainty of the Sokoto caliphate. Although its inhabitants were predominantly practitioners of African

traditional religion, a good number of them later embraced Islam and Christianity, during the colonial era.

The vegetation of Abuja is largely that of a guinea Savanna. More than 85 per cent of its traditional population are farmers. These features of Abuja remained primary, until it was chosen as the site for Nigeria's new capital.

The transfer of Nigeria's seat of power to Abuja took place in December 1991. This was effected after the attempt to topple General Ibrahim Babangida, through a coup carried out by Major Gideon Okar and his cohorts on April 22, 1990. The coup attempt resulted in the attack and partial destruction of Dodan Barrack, the then-Nigerian seat of power in Lagos. The feeling of insecurity engendered by the coup must have contributed to the need to quickly move from Lagos. The haste that accompanied this movement significantly increased the pace of construction of the new capital city of Abuja. The amount of resources committed to it, coupled with the speed of work, made it one of the most quickly developed state capitals in the world.

Twice the size of Lagos, Abuja was planned to accommodate a population of 3.1 million people when fully developed. From its inception, Abuja was supposed to create a greater sense of unity among Nigerians. All residents of the city could, therefore, claim citizenship of the Federal Capital Territory. It was also to afford the authorities the opportunity of rectifying the inadequacies of Lagos, such as persistent accommodation and traffic jam problems.

Throughout the 1990s, Abuja witnessed a significant influx of people from across the country. This is due primarily to the movement of most government ministries into the city. Currently, it is mainly populated by civil servants and a fast-growing business community. The return of Nigeria to democratic rule in April 1999 has further consolidated Abuja as a center of unity. The convergence of politicians from different parts of the country has finally settled the question of its acceptance.

Abuja is one of the most beautiful cities in Africa. Some of the main settlement centers are Bwari, Garki, Gwagwa, Gwgwalada, Karo, Kubwa, and Kuje. The beauty of Abuja is enhanced by its relatively new buildings, modern architectural styles, elaborate road network, and the parks and gardens that dot the city.

Apart from the numerous federal government ministries and offices, and the growing number of business establishments, other major features of Abuja are the presidential villa (Aso Rock), the Economic Community of West African States Secretariat, the International Conference Center, Nnamdi Azikiwe International Airport, three five-star hotels (NICON,

Sofital, and Sheraton), the University of Abuja, and the National Assembly Complex.

C.B.N. OGBOGBO

See also: **Nigeria: Colonial Period: Federation; Nigeria: Gowon Regime, 1966–1975; Nigeria: Second Republic, 1979–1983.**

Further Reading

Fejokwu, Lawrence (ed.). *Nigeria, a Viable Black Power: Resources, Potentials, and Challenges.* Lagos: Polcom Press, 1996.

Udo, R.K., and Mamman, A.B. (eds.). *Nigeria: Giant in the Tropics,* vol. 2. Lagos: Gabumo Publishing Co., 1993.

Accra

Like many of the important coastal towns of Ghana, Accra began as an offshoot of a key inland capital, but geography and history combined to bring about the break between parent and offspring earlier than was the case elsewhere. Archaeological evidence indicates that in the late sixteenth century the Ga people, who had been moving into the area of grassy plains south of the Akwapem escarpment, established Ayawaso, or what Europeans came to know as Great Accra. Initially, the Ga were reluctant to allow Europeans to establish permanent settlements on the coast, but in 1649 they allowed the Dutch West India Company to establish Fort Crèvecoeur at "Little Accra." Then, the Danes established Christiansborg Castle at the settlement of Osu, two miles to the east of the Dutch fort in 1661. Eleven years later the English company, the Royal African Company, began construction of James Fort at the village of Tsoco, half a mile to the west of Fort Crèvecoeur.

According to Ga traditions, the coastal area was settled sometime during the reign of Okai Koi (1610–1660); the settlement of the region probably took place as a more gradual series of migrations. In 1680–1681 the Akwamu invaded and destroyed Great Accra. Fifty years later the Akyem defeated the Akwamus, and shortly after, in 1742, the Asante conquered this area and incorporated it into the southern provinces of their empire. The result was that the connection between inland capital and the coastal settlement was broken early. Nevertheless, a centralized state did not develop on the coast largely due to the presence of competing European trading companies in this area. Even in the nineteenth century Accra remained divided into three distinct towns (Ussher Town, or Kinka, James Town, or Nleshi, and Osu), which in turn were divided into their own *akutsei,* or quarters. It was not until 1867 that the British finally acquired all of the forts in this area of the coast and brought these towns under one administration.

Connections with Europeans enhanced the powers of various *mantses,* the rulers of towns and quarters, with the *mantse* of the Abola *akutso* as *primus inter pares.* However, this ordering was fiercely contested at times and was to remain a central issue of twentieth-century political life. Contributing to these tensions was the history of invasions and conquests that made this one of the most culturally heterogeneous areas of the coast. Apart from Ga there were Adangme, Allada, Akwams, Akyem, Fante, and Asante. There were also people from what was to become Nigeria, and freed slaves from Brazil continued this influx in the nineteenth century. Undoubtedly it was the Akan element that was most important and contributed to an Akanization of Ga institutions. For example, Ga patrilineal systems of inheritance came to intermingle with Akan matrilineal inheritance.

The extension of European rule was challenged, as opposition in 1854 to a British attempt to introduce a poll tax indicated. Only after two bombardments from the sea were the British able to regain control of the areas around their forts. Nevertheless, in 1877 the British relocated their capital of the colony from Cape Coast to Accra. The area was healthier and the open plains of its hinterland made expansion much more possible than was the case for cramped, hilly Cape Coast. These benefits compensated for the harbor conditions, among the roughest on the coast, and the area's susceptibility to earthquakes as the devastating 1862 tremor indicated. At that time Accra was already the largest trading town on the coast with a population of about 20,000. Initially growth was slow, but by 1921 the population was more than 38,000.

In 1894 Accra was the first town in the Gold Coast to get a municipal council. The combination of house rates and an African minority on this body contributed to making it extremely unpopular. Not until 1898 could three Africans be persuaded to accept nomination. Plague and yellow fever scares in the early twentieth century transformed the council into even more of an arm of government, and African participation remained limited. These epidemics also stimulated growth outside of the original, congested areas of settlement. The plague scare of 1908 resulted in the establishment of new suburbs such as Kole Gonno, Riponsville, Kansehie, and Adabraka. From the 1870s British officials had been moving to Victoriaborg to escape the congestion of Osu. The yellow fever outbreak of 1910 resulted in the establishment of the Ridge residential area somewhat further inland.

There were also extensive infrastructure improvements. In 1907 construction of a breakwater for the harbor began. In 1909 work began on a railway line to Nsawam that was to reach Kumasi in 1923. The Weija reservoir was opened to serve Accra with pipe-borne water in 1914, and two years later the town was supplied with electricity. Compensating local chiefs for the land required for these projects inevitably resulted in bitter litigation, and much of Accra's political life was linked to this growth of the city. In the 1920s infrastructure development continued, the most notable being the building of the Korle Bu Teaching Hospital (1923), and the Prince of Wales College at Achimota (1927).

By the 1930s Accra was the center of the colony's political life. The National Congress of British West Africa (established in 1920) was dormant, but new political organizations came into being, such as J.B. Danquah's Gold Coast Youth Conference (1930 and 1937), the Central National Committee (1934) that organized protest against the "Obnoxious Ordinances," and the Sierra Leonian I.T.A. Wallace-Johnson's West African Youth League (1935). Under the editorship of Nigerian Nnamdi Azikiwe, it had the first regular daily newspaper (*The African Morning Post*—1934). The town doubled in size, with new-comers arriving from different regions of the colony and other areas of West Africa. A serious earthquake in 1939 caused considerable property damage and spurred the government to develop housing estates in the suburbs that contributed to the town's spatial expansion.

After World War II, Accra became the center of nationalist activity. It was here, in 1948, that the anti-inflation campaign initiated by the Accra chief Nii Bonne began. Shortly after, a march of ex-servicemen ended in shootings and general looting of stores. Building on these events, in 1949 Kwame Nkrumah announced at Accra's Arena meeting ground the founding of the Convention People's Party, which eight years later was to lead Ghana to independence. As the colony advanced toward independence, Accra's expansion also followed at a hectic pace. A 1954 estimate put the population at just under 200,000 with an annual growth rate of close to 10 per cent. Areas like Adabraka that had been distinct suburbs were now linked to the center, and in 1961 Kwame Nkrumah declared Accra a city.

The population of what is now known as Greater Accra is estimated to be more than two million, and the city, with its many suburbs, extends more than eight miles inland. In 1961 an artificial harbor was built at Tema, 25 kilometers to the east, to solve Accra's harbor problems. More recently there has been considerable highway building to ease traffic congestion in this rapidly expanding city. Administering this large area is the Accra Metropolitan Assembly, which traces its origins back to the Town Council of 1898.

ROGER GOCKING

See also: **Ghana Empire: Historiography of Origins; Ghana, Empire of: History of; Ghana (Republic of): 1800–1874; Ghana (Republic of): Colonization and Resistance, 1875–1901; Ghana (Republic of): Nationalism, Rise of, and the Politics of Independence; Ghana, Republic of: Social and Economic Development: First Republic.**

Further Reading

Acquah, Ione. *Accra Survey: A Social Survey of the Capital of Ghana*, 1958. Reprint, Accra[-]Tema: Ghana Universities Press, 1972.

Field, Margaret J. *Social Organization of the Ga People*. London: Crown Agents for the Colonies, 1940.

Gocking, Roger. *Facing Two Ways: Ghana's Coastal Communities Under Colonial Rule*. Lanham, MD: University Press of America, 1999.

Kilson, Marion. *African Urban Kinsmen: The Ga of Central Accra*. London: C. Hurst, 1974.

Parker, John. "Ga State and Society in Early Colonial Accra, 1860–1920s." Ph.D. diss., School of Oriental and African Studies, London University, 1995.

Pellow, Deborah. *Women in Accra: Options for Autonomy*. Algonac, MI: Reference Publications, 1977.

Achaempong: *See* Ghana, Republic of: Achaempong Regime to the Third Republic, 1972–1981.

Achebe, Chinua

Albert Chinualomogu Achebe is generally considered to be the most widely read African writer. Chinua Achebe, as he first started to call himself on entering university, grew up at a time when the two different lifestyles—that of the more traditional Igbo people and that of those who had converted to Christianity—still coexisted; his work is influenced by both. While his exposure to the fables of his indigenous background is omnipresent in his writing, his family's Christian background enabled him to attend one of the prestigious colleges of colonial Nigeria. He later continued his education at Ibadan University, where he soon switched to literature, having started as a medical student.

Achebe's literary ambition was first nurtured when he read Joyce Cary's *Mister Johnson* (1939) while at university. Achebe found the depiction of Africa in a novel written by somebody whose knowledge of African cultures and languages was only that of an outsider grossly inappropriate. While the positive reception of that novel surprised Achebe, it also encouraged him to start work on what later became a series of novels describing the changes in Igbo communities as a result of the confrontation with European traditions. Achebe has commented repeatedly on his reasons for writing these novels. In "The Novelist As Teacher" (included in *Hopes and Impediments*), he argues that his aim is to present to his African readers texts that show that Africa's past "was not one long night of savagery" (p. 45). According to Achebe, pride in the historical achievements of African societies can, for example, be based on the wealth of knowledge passed on in the form of oral traditions, for instance in proverbs. In another essay included in the same book, Achebe heavily criticizes the subliminal racism in Joseph Conrad's work, most notably in *Heart of Darkness* (1902).

Alongside his essays, it is mostly his fictional writing, primarily his first three novels, which have won Achebe a lasting reputation. The relationship between traditional and newly adopted customs forms a common theme in Achebe's texts. Opposing the dissolving of all traditions, Achebe pleads for a combination of the positive features of both old and new; thus an incorporation is preferable to a revolution. In his first novel, *Things Fall Apart* (1958), he describes life in an Igbo village where the customs are still intact. However, life changes drastically with the arrival of missionaries, whose questioning of such practices as the abandonment of twins wins them support among some members of the community. Soon the village deteriorates into a state of instability. *No Longer at Ease* (1960) concentrates on contemporary Nigeria and the difficulties that people have to face when they return to Nigeria after studying abroad. The Western habits and values they have adopted prove inappropriate when applied to life in postindependence Nigeria. In the novel, a young man returns from Britain, where his village had paid for him to study, and finds work in an office. Both the wish of his village that he should return the money that paid for his studies, and his parents' disapproval of his choice of wife, who is an untouchable, put more pressure on the tragic protagonist than he can handle. He accepts a bribe and as a consequence loses his job. In *Arrow of God* (1964), set between the first two novels and completing what is often called Achebe's "African Trilogy," a village chief-priest is looking for a way to combine his own beliefs with the new ideology of British colonialism. Despite his effort, this protagonist, too, fails tragically.

Achebe's fourth novel, *A Man of the People* (1966), won attention for the fact that in it Achebe predicted the military coup that coincided with its publication. It is a bitter satire on the poor moral state of the governing classes of newly independent African nations.

A refusal to think and argue in terms of binary oppositions is another constant theme in Achebe's texts. He argues that claims to absolute truths—a European tradition—are mostly futile. This attitude might also explain why, after initial interest in the new idea, Achebe sided with numerous other Anglophone writers in criticizing the predominantly Francophone *Négritude* movement, which emphasized African culture to the exclusion of foreign elements. There too, Achebe sees himself in the role of the mediator.

With the secession of Biafra in 1967, Achebe became actively involved in the political future of the Igbo people, whose independence from Nigeria he supported. Following Biafra's unconditional surrender in 1970, Achebe left Nigeria for the United States, where, between 1972 and 1976, he taught at various universities. During these tumultuous years Achebe found himself unable to work on more extensive texts, and instead concentrated on shorter writings. He completed various political, didactic, and literary essays, as well as short stories, poetry, and books for children. Through his involvement with Heinemann Publishers and its "African Writers Series," which he edited from 1962 to 1972, Achebe was of crucial importance for the then still young tradition of African writing. Together with the poet Christopher Okigbo, who died in August 1967, Achebe also published a journal, *Okike*, devoted to new African writing.

Achebe sees the role of the writer in contemporary African societies as mostly didactic. Accordingly, he opposes any view of art as an exclusively aesthetic medium. His continuing involvement with the struggles of Nigeria features prominently in his *The Trouble with Nigeria* (1983), which attempted to inform voters about the state of their country and government, as well as in his intellectual biography, *Home and Exile* (2000), which includes detailed commentaries on Achebe's early experiences with literature. In the ongoing debate about whether a truly African literature should be written in African languages, Achebe believes that the colonial languages can be an element that supports the unity of the newly independent nations of Africa by offering a single language within a multilingual nation.

GERD BAYER

See also: **Soyinka, Wole K.**

Biography

Albert Chinualumogu Achebe was born on November 15, 1930, in Ogidi, an Igbo community in eastern Nigeria. He was educated at Ibadan University, where he switched to literature, having started as a medical student. After graduation, he worked as a teacher. In 1954, he took employment with the Nigerian Broadcasting Corporation. Following Biafra's unconditional surrender in 1970, he left Nigeria for the United States. Between 1972 and 1976, he taught at various universities.

He was paralyzed in a serious car accident in 1990. Currently, he teaches at Bard College in New York state.

Further Reading

Achebe, Chinua. *Things Fall Apart*. London: William Heinemann, 1958, New York: Astor Honor, 1959.

Achebe, Chinua. *No Longer at Ease*. London: William Heinemann, 1960, New York: Obolensky, 1961.

Achebe, Chinua. *Arrow of God*. London: William Heinemann, 1964, New York: John Day, 1967.

Achebe, Chinua *A Man of the People*. London: William Heinemann, and New York: John Day, 1966.

Achebe, Chinua. *Morning Yet on Creation Day*. London: Heinemann Educational Books, and Garden City, NY: Anchor Press/Doubleday, 1975.

Achebe, Chinua. *The Trouble with Nigeria*. London: Heinemann Educational Books, 1983.

Achebe, Chinua. *Anthills of the Savanna*. London: William Heinemann, 1987, New York: Doubleday, 1988.

Achebe, Chinua. *Hopes and Impediments: Selected Essays*. London: William Heinemann, and New York: Doubleday, 1988.

Achebe, Chinua. *Home and Exile*. Oxford and New York: Oxford University Press, 2000.

Carroll, David. *Chinua Achebe*. New York: Twayne, 1970.

Ezenwa-Ohaeto. *Chinua Achebe: A Biography*. Oxford: James Currey, and Bloomington: Indiana University Press, 1997.

Innes, Catharine Lynnette. *Chinua Achebe*. Cambridge and New York: Cambridge University Press, 1990.

Killam, G.D. *The Novels of Chinua Achebe*. New York: Africana Publishing Corporation, 1969.

Lindfors, Bernth (ed.). *Conversations with Chinua Achebe*. Jackson: University Press of Mississippi, 1997.

Wren, Robert M. *Achebe's World: The Historical and Cultural Context of the Novels of Chinua Achebe*. Washington, DC: Three Continents Press, 1980.

Acheulian: *See* Olduwan and Acheulian: Early Stone Age.

Adal: Ibrahim, Ahmad ibn, Conflict with Ethiopia, 1526–1543

By the beginning of the sixteenth century, political, military, commercial, and religious conflict between Christian Ethiopia and the Muslim regions flanking its southern and eastern borders was long-standing and followed an established pattern in which the Christian kingdom invariably held the advantage. This was principally due to its political cohesion in comparison to the Muslim states which, although led by the Walasma dynasty, ranged over such a vast area occupied by disparate peoples that they lacked both a reliable communications system and a cohesive political focus. Gradually, however, the balance of power began to shift in favor of the Muslim regions. As Islamization proceeded in the lands to the south and east of the central Ethiopian highlands and also in Nubia to the north, the Christian kingdom became increasingly isolated. The growing power of the Ottoman Turks, who conquered Egypt in 1517, further increased this isolation and threatened Christian Ethiopia's access to the northern port of Massawa on the Red Sea coast. Control of the southern trade routes running through Adal to the port of Zeyla and the Gulf of Aden consequently became an issue of ever more pressing importance to the Christian kings, especially as firearms imported through Zeyla were far more difficult for them to obtain than for the Muslim rulers situated nearer the coast.

However, the Muslim states could not make use of these developments to pose a serious threat to their Christian neighbor while they continued to lack a strong, unifying leadership that could overcome the conflicting interests of merchants and warmongers and bring together often fiercely independent, nomadic peoples in a common cause. These divisions were aggravated by the waning authority of the Walasma dynasty, which was challenged by various ambitious military leaders, the most successful of whom was Ahmad ibn Ibrahim.

Ahmad seized his opportunity in 1526 when the Walasma sultan, Abu Bakr, was killed. He installed the sultan's brother as a puppet ruler and made the wealthy commercial city of Harar his power base. Assuming the title of imam (in this context meaning the elected leader of the *jihad* or holy war), he set about both tempting and

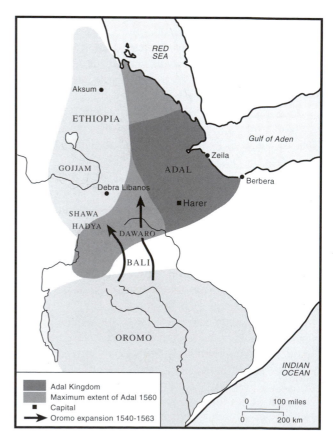

Adal, fifteenth–sixteenth centuries.

coercing the neighboring Afar and Somali pastoralists into an alliance against the Christian kingdom. Islam as a conquering force in the Horn of Africa had now acquired what previously it had lacked; a charismatic military leader with the ability to unite fragmented Muslim communities under the banner of holy war.

Preliminary hostilities were limited to border skirmishes and raids. Far more extensive operations began in 1529 when the Christian king, Lebna Dengel (1508–1540), suffered a major defeat in battle. According to custom, however, the Muslim forces subsequently dispersed and returned home with their booty, thereby failing to consolidate their victory. This was clearly not enough for Ahmad, whose ultimate aim was to occupy permanently the regions he conquered and convert the local populations to Islam. At first his followers refused to leave their homes and settle in recently subjugated lands but, as the Muslims made ever deeper incursions into the Christian kingdom, it became obvious that settlement was the only practical option. By 1532 almost all of the southern and eastern provinces of the kingdom had been overrun, and by 1533 Ahmad's forces had reached as far north as Amhara and Lasta. Two years later the final stage of the conquest was launched against the most northerly province of Tigray. But here, despite support from Ahmad's Turkish allies, the Muslim advance faltered. The main reason for this seems to have been one of logistics. In the mountainous, in the rugged terrain of Tigray, Ahmad's lines of supply and communication were probably stretched beyond their limit and without this backup the Muslim troops had no choice but to turn back.

Although the failure to conquer Tigray was a setback, it was not a decisive one. By this stage the Christian kingdom had already virtually ceased to exist, and Lebna Dengel, with the remnants of his followers, was reduced to nothing more than a fugitive in what had once been his own realm. In 1535, in desperation, he sent for help to the Portuguese. As a Christian ally with trading interests in the Horn of Africa, Portugal could reasonably be expected to send military assistance, but it was only in 1541, by which time Lebna Dengel had died and been succeeded by his son, Galawdewos (1540–1559), that a Portuguese contingent of 400 men finally reached Massawa. The arrival of these well-armed Portuguese soldiers raised the morale of the beleaguered Christian resistance and together they were able to inflict considerable damage on Ahmad's troops. However, it was not until 1543, when the imam was killed in battle, that the Christian side was able to gain the upper hand. Without their charismatic leader, the cause for which the Muslim forces had fought so long collapsed, although not quite entirely. Fighting continued sporadically until 1559, but it became increasingly clear that both sides were exhausted and unable to inflict any further serious damage on each other.

Inevitably this conflict had many consequences. In the long term, the most significant was that it facilitated the migration of Oromo pastoralists into the Ethiopian region, a process that was to continue for many years and was ultimately to have a much more profound and lasting impact than Ahmad's holy war. For the Christian kingdom, Portugal's intervention proved to be a mixed blessing. Although it promoted much needed contact with the wider Christian world, it also ushered in a period of intense religious disagreement between the exponents of Roman Catholicism and orthodox Ethiopian Christianity. The short-term consequences were only too obvious to see. The war left both sides depopulated, severely impoverished, and politically weakened. In fact, so devastating was this damage, it helped to ensure that Muslim and Christian never confronted each other in the Horn of Africa in such a destructive way again.

CAROLINE ORWIN

See also: **Ethiopia: Muslim States, Awash Valley: Shoa, Ifat, Fatagar, Hadya, Dawaro, Adal, Ninth to Sixteenth Centuries; Ethiopia: Portuguese and, Sixteenth–Seventeenth Centuries; Religion, History of.**

Further Reading

Pankhurst, Richard. *The Ethiopians.* Oxford, England, and Malden, MA: Blackwell, 1998.

Marcus, Harold G. *A History of Ethiopia.* Berkeley, Los Angeles, London: University of California Press, 1994.

Taddesse Tamrat. "Ethiopia, the Red Sea and the Horn," in *The Cambridge History of Africa,* vol. 3 (*c.*1050–*c.*1600), Roland Oliver (ed.), Cambridge, England: Cambridge University Press, 1977.

Trimingham, John Spencer. *Islam in Ethiopia.* London: Oxford University Press, 1952; 2nd edition, London: Frank Cass, 1965.

Conti Rossini, Carlo (ed. and trans.). "Storia di Lebna Dengel re d'Etiopia sino alle prime lotte contro Ahmad ben Ibrahim/nota di Conti Rossini Carlo," estratto dei *Rendiconti della Reale Accademia dei Lincei* (Roma: Tipografia della Reale Accademia dei Lincei, September 1894).

Cuoq, Joseph. *L'Islam en ethiopie des origines au XVIe siècle.* Paris: Nouvelles editions Latins, 1981.

Hassen, Mohammed. *The Oromo of Ethiopia: A History 1570–1860.* Cambridge, New York, Port Chester, Melbourne, Sydney: Cambridge University Press, 1990.

Addis Ababa

Addis Ababa is the capital city of Ethiopia. It is one of the fastest growing cities, with a population of approximately 3.5 million people.

The establishment of the town by King Menelik II in 1886 ended a period of shifting Ethiopia's capital, foremost for military reasons. Menelik's wife, Queen Taytu, played a crucial role in the founding of Addis

Ababa. She preferred the mild climate of the Finfinne plains to adjacent hilly Entoto, a rather inaccessible, cold, and windy summit that located the then capital city a few hours journey to the north. In 1886, with Menelik away battling in Harar, Taytu camped at Filwoha ("hot-spring"). She decided to build a house north of the hot springs. Queen Taytu settled fully in 1887, after Menelik's return in March of that year, and gave it the name Addis Ababa ("New Flower"), possibly due to the presence of the mimosa trees. Officially the name of the capital city changed from Entoto to Addis Ababa in 1906.

Menelik's generals were allocated land around the royal camp. Each resided in a *safar* (encampment area), which brought together relatives, servants, soldiers, and priests linked to this person. Rivers and valleys separated *safars*. As a result, Addis Ababa became a spacious city, and many hours were needed to traverse the town, especially during the rains.

In 1889, shortly before Menelik's coronation as emperor, construction of the royal palace started. A fire in 1992 destroyed the palace but was soon rebuilt. Because of the 1889–1892 famine, many countryside people sought refuge in Addis Ababa. Another period of immigration followed the 1896 battle of Adwa, where Menelik's forces defeated an invading Italian army. After the war the nobility settled in Addis Ababa; so did foreign advisors, traders, businessmen, and diplomats. This boosted the rise of Addis Ababa from a military camp to an important civilian settlement. Plastered huts and wooden constructions replaced tents. The *gebbi* (palace complex) was extended, bridges were built, and Italian prisoners of war constructed modern roads. The settling by archbishops of the Ethiopian Orthodox Church made Addis Ababa an important religious center.

By 1900–1901, Menelik started building Addis Alem, ("New World") approximately 60 kilometers to the west. Yet Menelik decided to keep Addis Ababa alive; the heavy investments in public and private facilities, and the c.1894 introduction of the fast-growing Australian Eucalyptus tree saved the city. Within five years, this tree attains a height of more than twelve meters, albeit at the cost of high water consumption. It gave Addis Ababa the nickname Eucalyptopolis.

The first decades of the twentieth century saw the building of the Bank of Abyssinia, the first hotel, the first modern school, the capital's first hospital, a brickmaking factory, a hydroelectric power station and the Djibouti railway track reaching Addis Ababa by 1917. The initial growth of Addis Ababa was largely unplanned. The main advantage of this "spontaneous growth" was the absence of specific quarters (rich versus the poor, foreigners versus Ethiopians), as often witnessed in African cities that developed under colonial rule.

By the mid-1930s, Addis Ababa was Ethiopia's largest city, with a population of approximately 300,000 people. Thus it was a natural target for colonization by Italian dictator Benito Mussolini in 1935. He sought revenge for the Adwa humiliation and wanted to establish an Italian East African empire with Addis Ababa as administrative center. Emperor Haile Selassie I, the successor to Menelik, had left shortly before the Italian occupation.

The discussion whether to abandon Addis Ababa was renewed, but Mussolini decided to retain it. The authorities accepted an Italian plan that emphasized the "prestige of the colonizer." It projected two residential areas in the east and south of the city for the exclusive use of Italians, one for officials, the other for "ordinary" Italians. Ethiopians were to be moved to the west, as was the main market (Arada), which was transferred from St George's Cathedral to an area known as Mercato, the largest open-air market in Africa, still in use today.

The equestrian statue of Menelik II, pulled down by the Italians, and the removal of the Lion of Judah statue, were restored after the patriots and Allied Forces defeated the Italians in April 1941. Several streets were renamed in honor of Allied leaders (such as Churchill Street). Although the planned settlement of thousands of ordinary Italians in Addis Ababa never materialized, the Italian occupation resulted in dozens of European-style offices, shops, and houses as can still be witnessed, for example, in the piazza area of the city. After the Italians left, the Ethiopian elite took over their legacy of improved housing and amenities.

Except for the division of Addis Ababa into ten administrative districts (*woredas*) the post-Italian years witnessed a continued growth without any structured town planning. The Abercrombie Plan of 1956 (Abercrombie had been responsible for town planning in greater London) was an attempt to guide the growth of Addis Ababa. However, this plan—containing satellite towns and ring roads—did not materialize, nor did the 1959 redrafting attempt by a British consulting group.

In the late 1950s and early 1960s, Addis Ababa witnessed the construction of a number of much larger and modern buildings: the Africa Hall, Addis Ababa City Hall, Jubilee palace (now National palace), and a Hilton Hotel. A French city plan (1965) guided this construction boom period. By now Ethiopia's capital was recognized as the unofficial capital of Africa. Haile Selassie's pan-African diplomacy was rewarded when the city was chosen in 1963 as headquarters of the Organization of African Unity (OAU).

Due to the Ethiopian revolution of 1974, however, the capital witnessed the deposition of Haile Selassie and the coming to power of Mengistu Haile Mariam.

His policy of movement restriction and land reform slowed down the urbanization process until 1991. During this period more than one-third of the city's forests were destroyed with little attempt at reforestation. The Derg regime introduced *kebeles*, a kind of neighborhood cooperative of urban dwellers. In the 1980s, house cooperatives were installed to address poor living conditions and new neighborhoods created at the city's boundary. The most notable physical development was the erection of monuments to celebrate the revolution, among them the vast Revolution Square designed by an Hungarian planner. It was renamed Meskal Square after the collapse of the Derg regime in 1991.

Another plan, the Addis Ababa Master Plan, was developed from 1984 to 1986. It was a joint undertaking by the government of Ethiopia and the government of Italy, in collaboration with the Venice School of Architecture. A new boundary of the city was defined, but only approved in 1994. The master plan gave an ideal vision of the future city, but lacked practical applications of the ideas presented.

After the removal of the Derg regime, Ethiopia was subdivided in fourteen regions, of which Addis Ababa was named Region 14. Private initiative was, within certain limits, promoted resulting in the construction of new office buildings and apartments. In the 1995 constitution of the "Federal Democratic Republic of Ethiopia," Addis Ababa was given the status of a self-governed city and the Region 14 administration transformed into the Addis Ababa city government. It initiated the Office for the Revision of the Addis Ababa Master Plan (ORAAMP).

By early 1998 the city administration produced the "5-year Action Plan for the City of Addis Ababa." Citywide discussions and deliberations were held on the document. A new city charter, master plan, and urban management system have been operational since 2001. Among the major achievements have been the Dire Water Dam and the Ring Road project. Yet, there has been a lack of job creation, handling of garbage collection and other sanitation projects, and especially the housing policy of raising rents, bulldozing slum areas, and its investment policies have been criticized.

The challenges facing Addis Ababa are enormous, starting from the provision of fundamental city services like trash collection, access to clean water, employment, housing, transportation, and so on. The city's new administration, which took office in 2003, has indicated to establish counsels in partnership with all stakeholders to address these difficulties in a transparent way. This should realize the vision statement "Addis 2010 a safe livable city," which portrays Addis Ababa as an effective center for national economic growth and as Africa's diplomatic capital.

MARCEL RUTTEN AND TEREFE DEGEFA

Further Reading

Addis Ababa City Government. *City Development Plan 2001–2010*, Addis Ababa, Ethiopia, 2002.

Dierig, S. *Urban Environmental Management in Addis Ababa: Problems, Policies, Perspectives, and the Role of NGOs*, Institut für Afrika-Kunde, Hamburg African Studies, 8, 1999.

Garretson, P.P. *A History of Addis Abäba from Its Foundation in 1886 to 1910*. Aethiopische Forschungen 49, Wiesbaden: Harrassowitz Verlag, 2000.

Hagos, A. *The Impact of Migration on Primate City Growth in Ethiopia*. Proceedings of the National Conference on Urban and Regional Development Planning and Implementation in Ethiopia, February 7–10, 1996, Addis Ababa, 1997.

Hancock, G., R. Pankhurst, and D. Willets. *Under Ethiopian Skies*, chap. 3: "The City and the Wilderness." Nairobi: Camerapix Publishers, 1997.

Pankhurst, R. "The History of Säwan Towns from the Rise of Menilek to the Founding of Addis Ababa," in: *Modern Ethiopia—from the Accession of Menilek II to the Present*. Joseph Tubiana (ed.). Rotterdam: A.A. Balkema, 1980.

Works and Urban Development Bureau. *Addis Ababa and Prevailing Problems and Prerequisites Required from Clients*, Addis Ababa: Public Relations Service, 2000.

Afonso I: *See* Kongo Kingdom: Afonso I, Christianity, and Kingship.

African Development Bank

The African Development Bank (ADB) promotes the economic development and social progress of its member countries in Africa. It operates on the basic principle of providing long-term finance for projects that are bankable and developmental. Historically, the ADB was seen as the single most important institution that could fill the gap in the financial systems of African countries. However, some criticisms, fueled by periods of poor performance, have been leveled against the ADB.

The bank was conceived in 1963 by the Organization of African Unity; it started functioning in 1966, with its headquarters in Abidjan, Côte d'Ivoire. The Secretariat of the United Nations Economic Commission for Africa, together with a nine-member committee of experts from member states, engineered the original agreement of establishment, though the bank is not formally associated with the United Nations. Its aim was to promote African self-reliance through the provision of nonconcessional loans (English and Mule 1996).

The bank's operations were restricted by the weak capacity of African members to honor financial subscriptions, so membership was opened to non-African countries in 1983, which raised the borrowing capacity of the ADB by 200 per cent. This occurred despite concerns of turning the ADB into a World Bank or an IMF, bodies which enforce free market development ideology (Ruttan 1995). Now two-thirds of the shares are owned by the African members. Shareholders include the 53 countries in Africa and 24 countries in the Americas, Europe, and Asia. The United States, with 5.9 per cent of shares, is the third largest shareholder in the ADB Group, behind Nigeria and Egypt. The U.S. is also the largest shareholder among ADB's non-African shareholders. The wealthier member countries provide guarantees that enable the bank to borrow money on international bond markets at favorable interest rates, which the bank passes on to its poorer African borrowers. Loans are made through two windows: the African Development Bank hard loan window, which lends at market rates to lower and middle income developing countries in Africa, and the African Development Fund, which makes concessional loans at below market rates, or interest-free loans to Africa's poorest countries. The African Development Fund is financed by regular cash infusions from the wealthier member countries.

Although nonregional members provide the bulk of the bank's resources, African members continue to retain control on both boards of directors by limiting the voting power of nonregional members to 50 per cent and 33–36 per cent, respectively. Between 1985 and 1992, the ADB group's share of total disbursements to Africa, mostly in the form of nonconcessional loans, grew substantially from 2.7 per cent to 8.1 per cent. Yet with the entrenchment of the African debt crisis, arrears began to rise, demand for nonconcessional lending fell, the ADF dried up, and the net income of the ADB group began to plummet.

The ADB's main functions are lending, the provision of guarantees, cofinancing to the public sector, and lending and equity investments to the private sector for projects developed in its African member countries. The ADB is second only to the World Bank in the project-lending field in Africa. Project loans are generally awarded to governments and government-owned institutions. Government loan recipients use the bulk of these funds to conduct procurement activities that result in contract awards to private companies from ADB member countries. The ADB has six associated institutions through which public and private capital is channeled: the African Development Fund, the Nigeria Trust Fund, the Africa Reinsurance Corporation (Africare), the Société Internationale Financière pour les Investissements et le Développement en Afrique (SIFIDA), the Association of African Development Finance Institutions (AADFI), and Shelter-Afrique. The bank's other principal functions are: to provide technical assistance for the preparation and execution of development projects and programs, to promote investment of public and private capital for development purposes, to respond to requests for assistance in coordinating development policies and plans of member countries, and to give special attention to national and multinational projects and programs that promote regional integration.

The bank's operations cover the major sectors, with particular emphasis on agriculture, public utilities, transport, industry, the social sectors of health and education, poverty reduction, environmental management, gender mainstreaming, and population. The loan disbursement of the ADB historically goes to the agricultural sector (31 per cent), public utilities (23 per cent), transport (19 per cent), and industry (14 per cent) (English and Mule 1996). Most bank financing is designed to support specific projects, but it also provides program, sector, and policy-based loans to enhance national economic management. The bank's highest policy-making body is its board of governors, which consists of one governor for each member country.

In early May 1994, a consultancy report by David Knox sharply criticized the bank's management. He identified numerous management problems: lack of accountability, boardroom squabbles, allegations of corruption and fraud, and a top-heavy bureaucracy (Adams and Davis 1996). One symptom of this bureaucracy is that about half of its $28 billion in loans have been disbursed to only seven countries (Egypt, Nigeria, Morocco, Zaïre/Congo, Tunisia, Algeria, and Côte d'Ivoire). The bank has another forty-six borrowing members. In recent years, it has lent money at commercial rates to countries such as Zaïre/Congo and Liberia that were either too poor, or too torn by conflict, to have any hope of paying the loans back. An estimated 40 per cent of the bank's projects have been unsuccessful.

In August 1995, Standard and Poor's, one of the world's foremost credit rating agencies, downgraded the ADB's senior long-term debt. The downgrade made it more expensive for the bank to borrow money on international markets, rocking the bank's already precarious financial foundation, and threatening the bank's very survival. Since 1995, the ADB, under the new leadership of President Omar Kabbaj, has been undertaking a comprehensive program of institutional reforms to ensure its operations get results and restore the confidence of shareholders and the support of development partners (Herrling 1997). However, the question of reform raises the prospect of the bank losing its "African character" and becoming a replica of the World Bank, enforcing (via policy-based lending) the donor-driven policy agenda of structural adjustment programs (English and Mule 1996). In 1997, the bank's authorized capital totaled about $23.3 billion. The ABD's major operational objectives continue into the new millennium; it aims to meet the demand for project investments (especially given the low level of production capacity and socioeconomic infrastructure prevalent in Africa), and promote private sector development and regional integration. The bank's concern for poverty reduction and human resource development constitute high priority areas, along with the strengthening of production capacity and socioeconomic infrastructure.

CAMILLA COCKERTON

See also: **Currencies and Banking; Organization of African Unity (OAU) and Pan-Africanism; World Bank, International Monetary Fund, and Structural Adjustment.**

Further Reading

Adams, Patricia, and Andrea Davis. "On the Rocks: The African Development Bank Struggles to Stay Afloat," *Multinational Monitor*, 17(July–August), 1996: 7–8: 30–34.

African Development Bank. *African Development Report.* New York: Oxford University Press, various years.

Boas, Morten. "Governance as Multilateral Development Bank Policy: The Cases of the African Development Bank and the Asian Development Bank," *European Journal of Development Research*, 1998, 10: 2: 117–134.

Culpeper, R. "Regional Development Banks: Exploiting Their Specificity," *Third World Quarterly*, 1994, 15: 3: 459–482.

English, E. Philip, and Harris M. Mule. *The Multilateral Development Banks, Vol. 1: The African Development Bank.* Ottawa: The North-South Institute, 1996.

Mingst, Karen. *Politics and the African Development Bank.* Boulder, CO: Westview Press, 1992.

African National Congress: *See* South Africa: African National Congress.

Industrial and Commercial Workers Union: *See* South Africa: Industrial and Commercial Workers Union.

African Union: *See* Organization of African Unity (OAU) and Pan-Africanism.

Africanus, Leo
Traveler and Writer

Little is known of the life of this Moroccan traveler, in spite of his well-established fame. All details of his vicissitudes before his arrival in Rome are based upon the few autobiographical notes in his surviving geographical work. Even during his stay in Italy, he did not leave many traces in the contemporary documents. Hence it has been suggested that no Leo Africanus ever existed and his description of Africa was composed by a Venetian ghostwriter, according to Italian reports from the Barbary Coast. This interpretation is too rigid but it contains a grain of truth. Leo Africanus is a somewhat mythical character, and much of our conventional knowledge of his life rests on speculations made by his enthusiastic admirers.

Africanus was born in Granada. The exact date is unclear, but it took place after the city had surrendered to Spaniards in 1492. His parents, however, moved soon to Morocco. They settled in Fez where their son received a sound education. In 1507–1508, Leo Africanus is said to have performed the first of his great voyages, visiting the eastern Mediterranean. His reason for undertaking this journey is unknown; it is not even certain that he actually went on this journey. In the winter of 1509–1510, Leo, who (according to his own words) was at that time sixteen years old, accompanied one of his uncles in a diplomatic mission to Timbuktu. Two years later he allegedly revisited Timbuktu, though this time on personal affairs. From Timbuktu, he is claimed to have extended his travels to other parts of the Sudanic Africa; thence to Egypt, returning in Fez in 1514.

Thereafter, Leo Africanus devoted himself to a vagabond life. During his Moroccan adventures, he was often accompanied by a sharif who was rebelling against the Wattasid sultan of Fez. This person might have been Ahmad al-Araj, the founder of the Sadid dynasty, who had become in 1511 the ruler of southern Morocco and gained much popularity by his fighting against the Portuguese. From Morocco, Leo extended his wanderings to Algeria and Tunisia, including a visit to Constantinople, possibly his second. In the spring of 1517, he appeared in Rosetta where he witnessed the Ottoman conquest of Egypt. He then continued to Arabia. Leo was returning Tunis, perhaps from a pilgrimage to Mecca, when he fell into the hands of Christian corsairs, near the island of Crete in June 1518. For a long time it was believed that Leo was captured near the island of Djerba, off the Tunisian coast, but recent research by Dietrich Rauchenberger has proven this unlikely.

Initially, Leo was taken to Rhodes, but he was soon transferred to Rome, where he was presented to Pope Leo X Medici (1513–1521), who was planning a crusade to northern Africa. From the pope's point of view, the appearance of a learned Moor who was willing to collaborate with him and his counselors by providing them with accurate information of northern Africa, was certainly like a gift from heaven. In Rome, he was freed and given a pension. Moreover, he converted to Christianity and was baptized at St. Peter's on January 6, 1520, receiving the name Johannes Leo de Medicis, or Giovanni Leone in Italian, according to his noble patron, or Yuhanna 'l-Asad al-Gharnati, as the man preferred to call himself in Arabic.

Leo Africanus left Rome for Bologna in 1522. The reason for this move was probably that the new pope, Hadrian VI (1522–1523), the former imperial viceroy of Spain, was suspicious about the presence of a converted Morisco at the papal court. Another reason was certainly the outbreak of plague that killed nearly half of Rome's population by the end of 1523. While in Bologna, he put together an Arabic-Hebrew-Latin medical vocabulary, of which the Arabic part has survived. This manuscript, now preserved at the Escorial library, contains Leo's autograph, which is one of few surviving sources for his original Arabic name: al-Hasan b. Muhammad al-Wazzan.

Africanus returned to Rome in early 1526, living there under the protection of the new Medici Pope Clement VII (1523–1534). Nothing is known of his final years with certainty. According to Johann Albrecht von Widmanstetter, who had arrived in Italy in 1527 to study Oriental languages, the man (whom he called Leo Eliberitanus) had left Rome shortly before the sack of the city in May 1527. Subsequently he went to Tunis where he is believed to have passed away around 1550. This information can be considered reliable, for Widmanstetter was moving in the circles where Leo Africanus was remembered well. Considering, however, that Leo had forsaken Christianity, he hardly wanted to witness the Spanish conquest of Tunis in 1535. Against this background, Raymond Mauny's speculation that Leo Africanus spent the remaining years of his life in Morocco sounds reasonable.

Upon his return to Rome, Africanus completed his magnum opus on African geography, according to his own words, on March 10, 1526. It was believed that Leo composed his work first in Arabic, translating it afterward into Italian. This hypothesis rested on the claim by Paul Colomiés, according to whom Leo's original manuscript had belonged to the Italian humanist Gian Vincenzo Pinelli (1535–1601), whose collection forms the core of the Bibliotheca Ambrosiana in Milan. The Ambrosiana possesses an anonymous Arabic manuscript containing a description of Africa but it is not written by Leo Africanus. It is now considered that Leo wrote his work directly in rather corrupted Italian, though he certainly relied upon Arabic notes that he might have composed during his travels.

An Italian manuscript version of Leo's geographical work was unexpectedly found in 1931 and purchased by the Biblioteca Nazionale in Rome. The style in this manuscript (entitled *Cosmographia & geographia de Affrica*) differs greatly from that of the Italian printed edition, but the manuscript represents clearly the original text written by Leo and that was later adopted by his Italian publisher. The manuscript is still unpublished, except for the sections and fragments describing the Sahara and Sudanic Africa, which were published by Rauchenberger with German translation.

Leo's geographical work was printed at Venice, bearing the title *Delle descrittione dell' Africa*, in 1550. It was incorporated in the first volume of the anthology of travels and discoveries, *Delle navigationi et viaggi*, edited by Giovanni Battista Ramusio (1485–1557). When and how Ramusio had obtained Leo's original manuscript is a mystery. The anthology was an immediate success and several reprints were called for. Subsequently, Leo's text was translated into major European languages, which made it available for the ever-widening audience. French and Latin versions were both published in 1556; an English in 1600; a Dutch in 1665. These translations were, however, of a poor quality, being arbitrarily abridged and including many errors. The Latin version, especially, which was the most popular, contains many grave mistranslations.

Modern times have produced further translations of Leo's text. A German version appeared in 1805; an updated English version, based upon the earlier translation, in 1896; an updated French version in 1896–1898. A scholarly annotated, new French translation, based upon Ramusio's printed text and superficially compared to the Italian manuscript version, was published in 1956. An Arabic translation from the French edition of 1956 appeared in Morocco in 1982.

A reason for the popularity of Leo's work was the lack of available rival sources for African geography. The Portuguese had put the coasts of Africa adequately on the map, but their access to the interior was checked by local resistance and the lethal endemic diseases. Also, most of the Portuguese chronicles describing their discoveries in Africa were not printed. According to a contemporary reader, Leo Africanus discovered a new world for Europeans, like Columbus "discovering" America. It is even suggested that Shakespeare modeled the character of Othello on Leo Africanus. The *Descrittione* maintained its authoritative position in the European geography of Africa until the early nineteenth century explorers brought more reliable information of the Niger and the adjacent regions. In the historiography of western Africa, Leo's influence lasted much longer, till the early twentieth century. Leo's *Descrittione* has justly been characterized as the final contribution of Islamic learning to European civilization.

Despite its title, the *Descrittione* is not a comprehensive exposition of African geography. The emphasis is on the Barbary Coast; especially on Morocco, which had become Leo's native land. The description of the city of Fez alone takes as much space as the sections reserved for Tunisia and Libya. As to the rest of the continent, Leo's knowledge was limited to Sudanic Africa; he wrote nothing about the Guinea Coast, Congo, or Christian Ethiopia, which were at that time familiar to European readers from the Portuguese reports. The section describing Sudanic Africa is the shortest, and there is nothing that would prove that it was based upon the author's own observations. Leo could have derived all the information from Arab traders and West African pilgrims, whom he had met during his wanderings in northern Africa. Leo's view on Sudanic Africa is strongly Islamic, and he claimed that the blacks had been uncivilized savages until they were subjugated and educated by the Muslim Berbers of the Sahara in the twelfth century. He also pictured Timbuktu as a center of West African gold trade. This image turned, in the hands of his later copyists in Europe, into a vision of an African Zipangu, which had an important impact in the beginning of the exploration of West African interior at the end of the eighteenth century.

According to internal references, Leo was planning to supplement his *Descrittione* with two volumes, one describing Europe and another the Middle East. Nothing came of this plan. He also wrote, or at least intended to write, an exposition of Islamic faith, and a treatise of North African history. Neither of these two works, if he ever completed them, has survived. Besides his magnum opus, Leo wrote a biographical work of Islamic and Jewish philosophers, which he completed in Rome in 1527. This work was published in Latin translation in 1664, in Zürich, by Johann Heinrich Hottinger under the title *Libellus de viris quibusdam illustribus apud Arabes*, and later in 1726 by J.A. Fabricius in Hamburg. Leo also made an Arabic translation of the Epistles of St. Paul, which is now preserved at the Biblioteca Estense in Modena.

PEKKA MASONEN

See also: **Europe: Explorers, Adventurers, Traders; Historiography of Africa.**

Further Reading

Fisher, Humphrey J. Leo Africanus and the Songhay Conquest of Hausaland, *IJAHS*, xi, 1978, pp. 86–112.

Masonen, Pekka. Leo Africanus: The Man with Many Names, Al-Andalus – Magreb. *Revista de estudios árabes e islámicos y grupo de investigación al-Andalus*. Magreb, vii–ix, facsimile 1 (2000–2001), pp. 115–143.

Afrikaans and Afrikaner Nationalism, Nineteenth Century

Exactly *when* Afrikaner nationalism originated has been the subject of debate between traditional Afrikaner historians and more recent commentators. Traditional Afrikaner historians saw the nineteenth-century trekker states of the interior as expressions of a national self-awareness that could be traced back to Hendrik Bibault's declaration of his identity as an "Africaander" in 1707. However, more recent commentators, such as L.M. Thompson and T.R.H. Davenport, destroyed much of the nationalist mythology surrounding the Great Trek, and identified Afrikaner nationalism as a phenomenon commencing only in the last quarter of the nineteenth century. Early Afrikaner historians such as Gustav Preller had depicted the trek as a modern-day reenactment of the biblical exodus from Egypt, with the Boers as God's elect escaping from the bondage of the British pharaoh to the "Promised Land" of the highveld, where they became a people bound to God by a covenant (sworn by Boer leaders before confronting the Zulu army at the battle of Blood River in 1838), and dedicated to the spread of Christian enlightenment (as proclaimed in the Retief manifesto of 1837).

In his *Political Mythology of Apartheid*, Leonard Thompson demonstrated that many of these notions only took shape half a century or so later: the Day of the Covenant (December 16) commemorating the Blood River victory was celebrated as a religious occasion only after the renewal of the covenant, when the independence of the British-controlled Transvaal was proclaimed at Paardekraal in December 1880. The concept of the Boers as God's chosen people planted in Africa by God was the product of the strong neo-Calvinist influence within the Dutch Reformed Church in the 1880s and 1890s, becoming the prevailing ideology only after World War I. The early trekker states themselves seem to have lacked many of the attributes of modern nation-states, built as they were around individual Boer leaders and their followers, with the minimum of formal political institutions: the personalized and highly factional nature of Transvaal politics delayed the acceptance of a constitution for the whole country until 1860, while the development of a viable governmental system there had to await the rise of Kruger and the restoration of Transvaal independence in 1881.

Davenport has made a strong case for placing the emergence of Afrikaner nationalism at a much later stage than the trek, and in the British-controlled Cape Colony rather than the Boer republics. He presents it as, initially, the reaction of the Cape Dutch elite to the imperial annexation of the Kimberley diamond-fields at the expense of the Orange Free State Boers (1871), and to the way in which the English language had become "the hallmark of breeding" in the Cape's urban centers. In the mid-1870s, the neo-Calvinist minister Rev. S.J. du Toit launched the *Genootskap van Regte*

Afrikaners (Society of True Afrikaners) in the country town of Paarl, dedicated to winning acceptance for Afrikaans, the *patois* of the common Afrikaner people (in contrast to High Dutch), and a language that he declared had been given to Afrikaners by God. In 1876, he produced a history of South Africa, written in "the language of our people," followed by a newspaper, *Die Afrikaanse Patriot*, and talked about setting up separate Afrikaner institutions such as banks, a dream that was to achieve reality after World War I. *Genootskap's* anti-imperial political agenda led to the creation of the *Afrikaner Bond* in 1880, proclaiming the goal of a united South Africa with its own flag. By 1883, forty-three Bond branches had been set up in the Cape and the interior republics, but the association of the Bond with Joubert and Reitz, Kruger's opponents, led to its early demise in the newly-independent Transvaal. Thereafter, the opening of the Witwatersrand gold fields in 1886 and the resulting urbanization of Afrikaners, many lacking the necessary industrial skills, provided a seedbed for later radical nationalism, forced into rapid growth by the South African War (1899–1902).

Meanwhile, in the Cape itself, Jan Hofmeyr's Boeren Beschirmings Vereeniging (Farmers Protection Association), formed in 1878 to protest a new excise duty on spirits that hit the farming industry, succeeded in taking over control of the Bond, and steered it in a less exclusivist direction. The Bond now welcomed all those white people, English as well as Dutch/ Afrikaans-speaking, who saw themselves as "South Africans," and significantly muted its opposition to imperial rule. Politically more astute than du Toit, Hofmeyr saw the electoral virtue of seeking to unite the farming interest irrespective of language in the Cape legislature, and was to win a position strong enough for him to act as kingmaker, most notably in 1890, when he offered the support Cecil Rhodes needed to form his first ministry. In exchange, Hofmeyr secured special favor for white farmers. The Afrikaner nationalist cause lost ground as a result of Hofmeyr's more moderate approach. It was the more "polite" High Dutch of the elite, rather than the Afrikaans of the common people, that secured acceptance for use in the assembly (1882), and Hofmeyr decided to throw in his lot with Rhodes when Kruger attempted to thwart his plans for expansion to the north at the end of the 1880s. The Jameson Raid (December 1895) eventually brought the alliance with Rhodes to an end, although—ironically—du Toit remained a supporter of the disgraced premier. The remaining years of peace saw the Bond in an increasingly equivocal position. On the one hand, Milner cast doubt on its loyalty to the imperial cause and accused it of undue sympathy for its republican cousins, thus placing the Bond on the defensive—although in reality, it had little patience with many of Kruger's policies such as the Uitlander franchise. On the other, it sought to be an effective spokesman for the Afrikaner (as well as the wider farming) interest. The Afrikaner nationalist cause was the main casualty, with the Bond becoming set even more firmly into the stance of moderation Hofmeyr had imposed on it after becoming its leader. Its fortunes thus revived only after the traumas of the South African War and its aftermath.

MURRAY STEELE

See also: **Cape Liberalism, Nineteenth Century; Jameson Raid, Origins of South African War: 1895–1899; Kruger, Paul; South Africa: Confederation, Disarmament and the First Anglo-Boer War, 1871–1881; South African War, 1899–1902.**

Further Reading

Davenport, Thomas. *The Afrikaner Bond: The History of a South African Political Party, 1880–1911.* Cape Town and New York: Oxford University Press, 1966.

Davenport, Thomas, and Saunders, Christopher. *South Affica— A Modern History.* Basingstoke: Macmillan, and New York: St. Martin's Press, 2000.

De Klerk, Willem. *The Puritans in Africa: A Story of Afrikanerdom.* London: Rex Collings, 1975.

Elphick, Richard, and Giliomee, Hermann. *The Shaping of South African Society, 1652–1840.* Middletown, CT: Wesleyan University Press, 1989 (2nd edition).

Thompson, Leonard. *The Political Mythology of Apartheid.* New Haven, CT, and London: Yale University Press, 1985.

Thompson, Leonard. *A History of South Africa.* New Haven, CT, and London: Yale University Press, 1990.

Aghlabid Amirate of Ifriqiya (800–909)

The Abbasid caliph assigned Ibrahim ibn Aghlab, his governor of the Mzab oases in the Sahara, the task of quelling an uprising in the province of Ifriqiya in 800. In return, Ibrahim secured an acknowledgment of autonomy in civil and military affairs for himself and his heirs, contingent only on the submission of an annual tribute to the caliph recognizing him as the spiritual head of the Muslim community. Since the Abbasids were no longer able to exert effective control over Ifriqiya in any event, they viewed such nominal influence as preferable to none at all.

The Aghlabid *amirs* encountered problems from the outset. They were contemptuous of Ifriqiya's Berber majority, but also alienated the influential religious leaders of Qairawan, who vehemently objected to the Aghlabid habit of levying non-Quranic taxes. The rulers' adherence to the Hanafi school of Islamic jurisprudence favored in Baghdad, rather than the Maliki school that predominated in North Africa, constituted a further irritant until they adopted the views of their subjects in this sensitive matter. The subsequent entrenchment of Maliki practices gave the population of Ifriqiya an identity that differentiated it from the peoples of the Middle East.

The Aghlabid army consisted of Arabs from the Middle East, slave troops, and mercenaries. The fractious nature of this institution prompted the *amirs* to engineer overseas adventures—epitomized by the conquest of Sicily, begun in the 820s—that minimized the army's opportunity to meddle in political activities. After pushing the Byzantines out of Sicily, the Aghlabids used the island as a springboard for attacks on the Italian mainland. They portrayed these expeditions as jihads, thereby emphasizing their commitment to Islam and legitimizing their rule.

Hostilities were not permitted to jeopardize commerce. Although Aghlabid raiders preyed on Christian shipping in Sicilian and Italian waters, they rarely attacked vessels trading with Muslims and some southern Italian communities even allied with the Aghlabids. Religious critics of the dynasty questioned the wisdom of such linkages, but could not deny that substantial economic benefits flowed from its cultivation of Mediterranean trade. The *amirs* also augmented Qairawan's religious importance by turning the city into a major entrepôt whose merchants shipped slaves and other Sub-Saharan commodities to lucrative Middle Eastern markets. Revenues amassed through conquest and trade financed both rural improvements and urban growth. The Aghlabids oversaw the construction of extensive irrigation canals and reservoirs that heightened agricultural productivity and supported increasing urbanization. To guarantee the security of coastal towns and villages, the rulers built *ribats*, or fortified mosques, at key points along the shoreline.

Except for the mercantile elite, the Aghlabid rulers made little effort to foster the development of close ties with their subjects. The reign of Ibrahim II (875–902) demonstrated the importance not only of guarding against potential threats from external enemies, but also of maintaining the allegiance of the sedentary population. Doing so required the pursuit of sound economic policies and the exertion of sufficient strength to protect settled areas from nomadic incursions. Despite a sequence of climatic disasters and inadequate harvests during his reign, Ibrahim II levied high taxes to finance the construction of the royal city of Raqqada, near Qairawan. This extravagant project created antagonisms that not even his notable victories in Sicily could offset. Indeed, Ibrahim's overseas activities drew troops from Ifriqiya's western frontiers just as a serious threat was emerging there. Shi'ite propagandists won support among many Berbers by sowing dissatisfaction with the Abbasids and the

Aghlabids, both representatives of Islam's Sunni establishment. The individualistic nature of the Berbers predisposed them to appeals against authority, but the frequently deplorable treatment the Aghlabids had accorded them increased their susceptibility and many Berbers embraced Shi'ite Islam.

Despite their disengagement from Ifriqiya's affairs, the Abbasids realized that Ibrahim II could not surmount this challenge and that the continuation of his reign provided the Shi'ites with a choice target. They encouraged his relatives to demand Ibrahim's abdication. His successor's opposition to the Maliki legal school—which may have been intended to tighten the province's links with Baghdad—deprived him of local support and precipitated his assassination. The last Aghlabid ruler, Ziyadat Allah III (903–909), gained power by murdering relatives who opposed him. His actions not only weakened family solidarity, but also lent credence to accusations of immorality that the Shi'ites had leveled at the Aghlabids from the start of their campaign.

As Aghlabid fortunes ebbed in the early tenth century, those of the Shi'ites rose. Led by Abu Abdallah, the Berbers won a string of victories. These successes swelled their ranks, often with Berbers motivated more by materialistic concerns than moral or religious ones. The Aghlabids hesitated to seek the help of Baghdad, fearing that the Abbasids might take advantage of their weakness to reassert direct control over Ifriqiya. The rout of the Aghlabid army at al-Urbus in 909 signaled the dynasty's end. Ziyadat Allah III fled to Egypt, leaving Ifriqiya open to his enemies.

Aghlabid efforts to build a viable autonomous entity foundered on the dynasty's failure to forge durable links with the local populace. Extensive overseas campaigns supplied the revenue for the region's economic development, but the ill-considered practices of Ibrahim II weakened the ties between rulers and ruled. To many of their subjects, the Aghlabids' extravagant lifestyle emphasized their lack of interest in the people of Ifriqiya. When an alternative to the dynasty arose, many Aghlabid subjects, especially the Berbers from the fringes of the territory, supported it. Yet Shi'ite doctrines and rituals never took root in Ifriqiya, suggesting that the movement's attraction rested primarily on the framework it provided for political protest. Irritation with the rulers had grown so acute that any force capable of ousting them—even one based on a sect with little acceptance in Ifriqiya—gained followers. The Aghlabids fell because Abu Abdallah's Berber forces defeated them repeatedly on the battlefield, but a more fundamental cause of their collapse lay in their subjects' conviction that they had nothing to lose, and perhaps much to gain, in any political restructuring of the province.

KENNETH J. PERKINS

Further Reading

Le Tourneau, Roger. "La révolte d'Abu Yazid au Xème siècle," *Cahiers de Tunisie*, 1 (1953): 103–125. ["The Revolt of Abu Yazid in the Tenth Century"].

Talbi, Mohamed. "Law and Economy in Ifriqiya (Tunisia) in the Third Islamic Century: Agriculture and the Role of Slaves in the Country's Economy," in *The Islamic Middle East, 700–1900: Studies in Economic and Social History*, Avram Udovitch (ed.), Princeton, NJ: Darwin Press, 1981.

Agriculture, Cash Crops, Food Security

The majority of African nations became independent in the late 1950s and early 1960s. In the immediate postcolonial period, most African nations chose mixed economies, with a concentration on industrial development, education, and expansion of their economies. Financing for these projects would come not only from revenue generated from agriculture, but also from foreign aid. Countries such as Mali, Ghana, and Guinea changed dramatically to revolutionary socialism in the early 1960s, and Nyerere's Tanzania adopted *ujamaa* or African socialism in the 1970s in the Arusha Declaration. Ujamaa was a unique socialist concept, which recognized the specificity of the African reality and experience. It focused on self-reliance through a process of villagization. The idea was to create cooperative villages where the means of production would be communally owned and directed by the village cooperative.

In spite of the different ideological directions of postcolonial African leaders, they all did not pay much attention to modernizing and diversifying the agricultural sector of their economies. Furthermore, African postcolonial regimes placed little emphasis on food production. To be sure, African leaders, both civilian and military, saw agriculture as a vehicle for generating much-needed surplus in the form of taxes to finance industrial development. Furthermore, the marketing

Sowing maize, Eritrea. Note the use of a camel for plowing. © Friedrich Stark/Das Fotoarchiv.

boards, which had been set up in the colonial period to stabilize cash crop prices, were continued in the post-colonial period and became instruments for appropriating surplus revenue. The surplus revenue has been used to provide social services, educational institutions, and infrastructure for the large cities to the neglect of the rural areas.

Among the reasons for the low priority given to agriculture in the 1960s was the assumption that industrialization was the most appropriate way to bring about rapid economic growth, structural change, and economic independence. In the late 1950s and early 1960s, however, there was a significant decline in the prices of agricultural commodities. Declining revenues from agricultural exports combined with ambitious programs of industrialization and inefficient bureaucracies engendered growing deficits in both government budgets and balance of payments. In order to be able to finance their development programs, African economies resorted to obtaining loans from international financial houses, which would result in a significant debt problem.

In the last two decades of the twentieth century, almost all African governments shifted from industrialization, export promotion, and agricultural transformation to espousing the multiple goals of food self-sufficiency, improved nutrition, diversification of their economies, and increased income and social services.

One of the most formidable challenges faced by postcolonial, Sub-Saharan Africa has been lack of food security. From the early 1970s through the 1990s, Sub-Saharan Africa's food sector was been characterized by a decline in per capita food production. In the last ten years Sub-Saharan Africa has had the largest growth of population in the Third World and the slowest growth of food production. Sub-Saharan Africa moved from an exporter to a significant importer of basic food staples. Final exports of basic food staples by Sub-Saharan Africa in the period from 1966 to 1970 were an average of 1.3 million tons a year. In fact, between 1961 and 1980, almost half of the countries in Sub-Saharan Africa gained annual increases of about 2 per cent. Eastern and southern Africa accounted for more than half of the total increase in food production in Sub-Saharan Africa, central Africa accounted for about a quarter, and West Africa was responsible for a little less than a quarter.

But this promising trade situation changed dramatically because production could not keep pace with the rise in demand. Consequently, net imports increased to ten million tons by the mid-1980s. For example, in West Africa, food exports, primarily groundnuts, declined, while food imports tripled. Structural constraints, ineffective government policies, changing environmental conditions, and the scourge of pests and insects have adversely affected food security in Sub-Saharan Africa.

For example, cereal production in Tanzania plummeted because of drought in major parts of the country in the early 1970s and early 1980. The case of Sudan illustrates the inability of a country to harness its agricultural resources to stimulate economic growth and ensure food security. In the mid-1970s, it was hoped that the Sudan would get economic aid from the Middle East to develop its huge reserves of uncultivated land to become a major supplier of grain to the region. But in the 1980s Sudan's food imports amounted to $30 million.

During the 1970s, several Sub-Saharan African countries launched accelerated food production programs to reverse the long decline in food production per capita and to reduce dependence on food imports. For example, when Ghana inaugurated its "Operation Feed Yourself" in 1972, the government stated that the decline of food production was attributable to the higher priority given to cocoa and palm oil. In the early stages of the program, the government placed emphasis on large-scale farms, which did not result in any significant increase in food production. Nigeria also inaugurated a similar program christened "Green Revolution" in the 1980s. In the immediate postcolonial period, Nigeria was a net exporter of food, primarily oil palm and groundnuts, but by the early 1970s, Nigeria was importing food. Nigeria imported 1.4 million tons of basic staples in 1977, and by 1981 the figure had reached $1.3 billion.

Although these programs were intended to increase smallholder food production by enlarging peasant access to improved seeds, fertilizers, and other modern inputs at subsidized rates, the results were not encouraging. These programs failed to achieve their ambitious targets because of an unwieldy, bureaucratic organization, bad planning and implementation, lack of involvement by peasant farmers, and mismanagement.

There were, however, some exceptions to this rather dismal situation. Among the success stories on the food production front in the 1980s were food programs in Malawi and Zimbabwe. For example, in 1980, Zimbabwe exported 500,000 tons of maize. Also, Zimbabwe had a record maize crop of 215 million tons in 1981 and about one million tons was available for export. Although Zimbabwe was a net exporter of food in the 1980s, it was also characterized by a lack of the infrastructure for sustained food production by smallholders.

The structural policy failures of the 1970s and the worldwide recession of the early 1980s, resulted in a steady economic decline, and finally in a severe economic crisis. This made several African countries adopt the Structural Adjustment Programs (SAPs) initiated by the World Bank and the International Monetary Fund (IMF). SAPs were designed to diversify and rehabilitate African economies by stimulating domestic production in the agricultural, manufacturing, and industrial sectors. Furthermore, it was hoped that by generating internal production through the utilization of local raw materials, the balance of payments deficit would reduce and there would be a diminution of Africa's dependence on foreign imports. The SAPs also strove to deregulate the economy by removing administrative encumbrances and reducing the stranglehold of government on the economy. This new economic philosophy would effect liberalization of trade, privatization, and the fostering of a market economy.

Despite the improvement in the economic performance of many African countries in relation to food security since 1983, there are still a number of structural constraints and long-term challenges such as 1) a still high inflation rate, 2) a still high external debt burden, 3) an agricultural production that was still well below potential, and 4) still high prevalent rates of poverty and food insecurity. In order to cope with the above-mentioned structural bottlenecks and long-term challenges, African countries have continued to intensify their macroeconomic reforms.

For example, with regard to agriculture, the government of Ghana launched the Medium Term Agricultural Development Program (MTADP), 1991–2000. One of the main objectives of the MTADP was the provision of food security for all Ghanaians by way of adequate and nutritionally balanced diets at affordable prices. However, agricultural output and performance during this period was weak. The Accelerated Agriculture Growth and Development Strategy has been adopted as a new strategy for the period 1997–2007. The primary goal of this strategy is to increase the annual growth rate in agriculture to 6 per cent by 2007. Also in Malawi, specific projects such as Rural Financial Service and the Agricultural Services Project have supplemented the structural adjustment program. One of the new directions in most African countries regarding food security is the placing of greater reliance on the private sector and their grassroots organization while reducing the role of the public sector, especially in the direct production and marketing activities of agricultural inputs and outputs.

EZEKIEL WALKER

See also: **Development, Postcolonial: Central Planning, Private Enterprise, Investment; Egypt, Ancient: Agriculture; Lesotho (Basutoland): Peasantry, Rise of; Tanzania (Tanganyika): Arusha Declaration; World Bank, International Monetary Fund, and Structural Adjustment.**

Further Reading

Mellor, John, Christopher Delgado, and Malcolm Blackie (eds.). *Accelerating Food Production in Sub-Saharan Africa*, Baltimore, MD: Johns Hopkins University Press, 1987.

Berry, Sara. *No Condition Is Permanent: The Social Dynamics of Agrarian Change in Sub-Saharan Africa*, Madison: University of Wisconsin Press, 1993.

Pinstrup-Andersen, Per. *Government Policy, Food Security, and Nutrition in Sub-Saharan Africa*, Ithaca, NY: Cornell University Press, 1989.

Sijm, Johannes. *Food Security and Policy Interventions in Sub-Saharan Africa: Lessons from the Past Two Decades*, Amsterdam: Thesis Publishers, 1997.

Ahidjo, Ahmadou (1924–1989)
Politician and Cameroon's First President

To some, Ahmadou Ahidjo was an opportunist who found himself at the right place at the right time and, given the opportunity, did not hesitate to take advantage of his situation and outmaneuver his contemporaries. To others, he was an able leader who succeeded in molding the vastly diverse peoples of Cameroon into a united, stable, and prosperous country. He was the first president of Cameroon and served in that position for twenty-four years. He left office on his own accord, unlike many of his contemporaries, who were forced from power by coups d'état.

He worked in various parts of the country as a radio technician for several years before entering politics. He began his career as a radio technician in the Yaounde Broadcasting Station in 1943. He was then transferred to Bertoua in the eastern part of Cameroon to begin the first radio station in the region. After Bertoua, he was sent to Mokolo in the north for a similar task. In 1944, Ahidjo was made head of the Garoua radio station. The position was a very important position because Garoua was the headquarters of the northern region of Cameroon and the center of most activities in the region. He made the best use of his stay in his hometown to lay the foundation for his political career.

Ahidjo's political career began in earnest in 1946 when he was elected to the First Consultative Assembly of the then East Cameroon, created after the war in response to French Africa's support for Charles de Gaulle's Free French Movement during World War II. In 1952, when the French government replaced the Consultative Assembly with the Territorial Assembly, Ahidjo was reelected into that body. The French National Assembly passed the *loi cadre* ("enabling law") in June 1956, granting East Cameroon self-government and its own assembly. On December 23 of that year, Ahidjo was elected to the newly created East Cameroon Legislative Assembly. In February of 1957, Ahidjo organized the northern representatives of the assembly into a voting bloc called Union Camerounaise (UC). In 1958, after the fall of the government headed by Andre Marie Mbida, Ahidjo, who had been vice premier and whose party controlled thirty-one of the seventy seats in the assembly, was asked to form a new government. No new elections were held again until after East Cameroon became independent on January 1, 1960. Ahidjo became president by default and the country took the name the Republic of Cameroon.

On February 11, 1961, British-administered Southern Cameroon opted to reunite with the Republic of Cameroon in a United Nations-supervised plebiscite. Ahidjo became president of the new entity that was created from the union of the two territories, called the Federal Republic of Cameroon. The country's federal structure was changed in 1972 to a unitary system, called the United Republic of Cameroon. In 1982, Ahidjo suddenly resigned from office and handed power to his constitutionally designated and hand-picked prime minister, Paul Biya. Biya was from the Beti ethnic group in the south of Cameroon and also a Christian. But Ahidjo still kept his position as president of the ruling party after his resignation. Not long thereafter, friction erupted between him and Paul Biya, with Biya accusing him of meddling in state affairs. Ahidjo saw it differently, arguing that as head of the country's sole party (Cameroon National Union), he had the final say on state matters. Biya won out in the struggle that ensued. In 1983, the Biya government accused Ahidjo of plotting to overthrow Biya. But before the plot was made public, Ahidjo resigned his position as president of the party and left the country, entering a self-imposed exile.

In April 1984, members of the republican guards, who had been responsible for presidential security under Ahidjo and then Biya, attempted to overthrow the Biya government, without success. Ahidjo, who was implicated in this effort, was tried in absentia and given a death sentence, which was later commuted to life imprisonment. In 1989 he suffered a heart attack and died in Senegal.

Ahidjo was a contradictory figure, commanding respect and love within some segments of the population, earning hatred and repugnance from others. He brought stability to Cameroon, a diverse and multicultural country of more than 200 ethnic groups, two colonial cultures, and a north-south division along geographic as well as religious, cultural, and educational lines. His success at achieving national unity, however, came at a high cost in terms of democracy. Individual liberties, press freedom, human rights, and other democratic norms, including the right to organize and participate in political activities within the framework of free, fair, and competitive elections, were done away with under his rule. He imprisoned and even eliminated individuals that he considered a threat to his regime. In 1966, he officially made Cameroon a one-party system with his Cameroon National Union party as the sole political party.

Under Ahidjo's leadership, the Cameroonian economy experienced unprecedented growth. He emphasized food and cash crop agriculture in his economic policy while pursuing an industrial policy that was built on medium-size import substitution industries. This paid off as income levels rose and Cameroon moved from being a low-income to a middle-income developing country. Cameroon under his rule also became one of the few African countries to be self-sufficient in food production.

MOSES K. TESI

See also: **Cameroon: Independence to the Present; Cameroon: Rebellion, Independence, Unification, 1960–1961.**

Biography

Born in the northern city of Garoua in 1924 to Fulani parents. In 1932, at age eight, entered the Garoua regional primary school. Joined the veterinary service in Maroua after failing to pass the final examination to graduate from primary school in 1938. After repeating the final year of primary school, he graduated and went on to Yaoundé Higher School, graduating in 1942. Completed a six-month training in Douala to be a radio technician in 1943. Named president of the Republic of Cameroon (former East Cameroon) on January 1, 1960. Named president of the Federal Republic of Cameroon (later the United Republic of Cameroon) in 1961, created when Southern Cameroon opted to reunite with the Republic of Cameroon In 1982, resigned and handed power to his prime minister, Paul Biya. Accused of plotting to overthrow Biya in 1983. Left the country in self-imposed exile. In 1989, suffered a heart attack and died in Senegal.

Further Reading

Gaillard, P. *Ahmadou Ahidjo*, Paris: Jeune Afrique, 1994.
Johnson, Willard. *The Cameroon Federation*, Princeton, NJ: Princeton University Press, 1970.
LeVine, Victor T. *Cameroon: From Mandate to Independence*, Berkeley and Los Angeles: University of California Press, 1964.

Ahmad Bey: *See* **Tunisia: Ahmad Bey and Army Reform.**

Ahmad al-Mansur: *See* **Morocco: Ahmad al-Mansur and Invasion of Songhay.**

Ahmad ibn Ibrahim: *See* **Adal: Ibrahim, Ahmad ibn, Conflict with Ethiopia, 1526–1543.**

Aid, International, NGOs, and the State

Nongovernmental organizations (NGOs) have been instrumental in providing a wide range of aid to African countries. Mostly multinational in composition, they operate with the consent of host governments. They are a diverse group of largely voluntary, nonmembership support organizations that work with communities to provide technical advice and economic, social, and humanitarian assistance to address development issues. In Africa, some of their specific developmental objectives include tackling poverty, providing financial credit and technical advice to the poor, empowering marginal groups, challenging gender discrimination, and delivering emergency relief.

NGOs can be professional associations, religious institutions, research institutions, private foundations, or international and indigenous funding and development agencies. The NGOs are usually either international or indigenous organizations; most of the indigenous organizations are community-based grassroots and service-based organizations.

Some well-known NGOs in Africa are the Catholic Relief Services, the Salvation Army, CARE, World Vision, Save the Children, Ford Foundation, and Oxfam. Some NGOs focus on particular issues; for example, the International Planned Parenthood Federation, the Population Council, and Family Planning International Assistance address population issues, while the Red Cross and Medecins Sans Frontieres (Doctors Without Borders) deliver humanitarian aid.

The number of NGOs has accelerated recently. For example, the number of NGOs registered with the United Nations jumped from 48 in 1989 to 1,300 in 1994. Numbers of NGOs within each country vary; for example, Kenya has more than 400 NGOs, while Ethiopia has less than 50 (Bratton 1989). The principal reason for the recent boom in NGOs is that Western governments, not just private donations, finance them (*The Economist* 2000). For example, of Oxfam's $162 million income in 1998, a quarter ($24.1 million) was given by the British government and the European Union. Medecins Sans Frontieres receives 46 per cent of its income from government sources.

NGOs play an important role in the social and economic development of Africa in directing government aid and setting policy. The present prominence of NGOs in development thinking stems from economic constraints on state activity, the propensity of donors to channel aid through the voluntary sector, and a set of beliefs about the relative efficiency and effectiveness of NGOs (Curtis 1994). Donors increasingly see NGOs as a means of filling gaps in weak, ineffective government programs, and have begun to call for more NGO involvement in programs that have traditionally been implemented through government organizations (Bebbington and Farrington 1993).

Some African governments have instituted coordinating bodies to supervise NGO activity. Some examples of these coordinating bodies include the Voluntary Organizations in Community Enterprise, the Council for Social Development in Zambia, the Permanent Secretariat of NGOs in Burkina Faso, and the Council of NGO Activity in Togo.

The relationship between NGOs and states is highly variable and contentious. Ndegwa (1994) argues that NGOs have contributed to the wider political reform movement in Kenya by successfully repelling controlling legislation of their activities in 1990. Ndiaye (1999) maintains that NGOs and grassroots organizations such as village self-help groups, women's organizations, and peasant associations have been highly effective in Africa. However, many discussions of NGOs overoptimistically assess their effectiveness as agents of grassroots change and agricultural development, and NGOs' rhetoric of democratic participation exceeds reality (Bebbington and Farrington 1994).

In some cases, NGOs are becoming instruments of Western government foreign policy (*Economist* 2000). In 1999, the U.S. Congress passed a resolution to deliver food aid to rebels in southern Sudan via USAID and some Christian NGOs. Other NGOs are directly intervening in African politics. For example, UNICEF brought about a peace deal between Uganda and Sudan, and the Italian Catholic lay community of Sant' Egidio helped to end thirteen years of civil war in Mozambique in 1992.

Some authors identify negative relationships between NGOs and African states. Beinart (1994) argues that NGOs in Somalia in the 1980s condoned and engaged with corrupt networks and repressive strategies to win government approval. These policies decimated civil society and eventually led to civil war. Only one NGO, a small Australian agency called Community Aid Abroad, spoke out and left the country in protest against Muhammad Siad Barré's human rights record in 1989. In South Africa, Johnson (1998) claims that NGOs undermined democracy. The United States Agency for International Development (USAID) funded the National Democratic Institute (NDI) apparently to promote multiparty democracy in South Africa, and the NDI has been linked with communists. And the Ford Foundation supported a bill that would give the South African government broad powers over all nongovernmental organizations.

Other researchers argue that NGOs undermine governments. By filling a void in terms of additional investments, capital, and services to rural areas, NGOs undermine the ability of governments to perform as effective leaders and policymakers.

Partnerships between international, national, and indigenous NGOs are growing, with increasing calls for African states to encourage growth and interaction among NGOs (e.g., Chazan 1992; Kingman 1994). For example, the Forum of African Voluntary Development Organizations, formed in 1987, encourages NGOs to exchange ideas, share their expertise and resources, support local initiatives, and establish effective channels of communication and partnerships with governments and intergovernmental organizations. An increasing number of NGOs collaborate with the World Bank to address rural development, population, health, and infrastructural issues that are relevant to the human dimensions of its structural adjustment programs. Several NGOs also have consultative status with the United Nations Economic and Social Council.

There are numerous successful cases of NGOs working closely together and with governments, in particular in times of crisis in Africa. For example, during the Ethiopian famine in 1984 and 1985, the United Nations coordinated the relief program. The Ethiopian government's Relief and Rehabilitation Commission and sixty-three NGOs distributed basic food rations to more than seven million people. Since the early 1990s it has been widely suggested that development strategies would benefit from increased collaboration between government and NGOs. This suggestion has come from various points across the ideological spectrum, from NGO activists and radical economists to the new right and the multilateral institutions. They claim that NGO involvement ought to increase the impact of programs in grassroots development and poverty alleviation, and contribute to the democratization of the development process.

CAMILLA COCKERTON

Further Reading

Bratton, M. "The Politics of Government-NGO Relations in Africa," *World Development*, 1989, 17: 4: 569–587.

Curtis, Donald. *Non-Governmental Organisations and the State in Africa: Rethinking Role in Sustainable Development*, London: Royal African Society, 1994.

Johnson, R.W. "Destroying South Africa's Democracy: USAID, the Ford Foundation, and Civil Society," *The National Interest*, 53 (fall), 1998, 19–29.

Ndegwa, Stephen N. "Civil Society and Political Change in Africa: The Case of Non-Governmental Organizations in Kenya," *International Journal of Comparative Sociology*, 2000, 41: 4: 381.

Ndiaye, Serigne M. "Promoting Rural Community Development in Africa: State Versus Grassroots Organizations," *The Journal of Social, Political, and Economic Studies*. 24 (spring), 1999, 1: 65–67.

"Sins of the Secular Missionaries." *The Economist Magazine*, January 29, 2000.

AIDS: *See* Epidemics: Malaria, AIDS, Other Disease: Postcolonial Africa.

Air, Sultanate of

Traditionally, the largest Tuareg political unit is the group under the leadership of a supreme chief, known as the *amenukal* or sultan. He is also traditional leader of the drum-groups (descent-based clans) within the larger political group. In Air, the Amenukal is more often called the sultan of Air in Agadez. In the past, the sultan of Air was considered supreme chief with superior judicial rights and also war leader of the whole group. But the authority was somewhat limited, and quarrels between the various drum-groups within a larger confederation were very frequent.

The people who are placed under the sultan of Air are called the Kel Amenukal ("People of the Sultan"), and are predominantly pastoralists, with some sedentary or semi-sedentary groups also among them. They are comprised of Itesen, Kel Faday, Kel Ferwan, and Kel Geres (though the latter now live outside Air, to the south in the Hausa borderlands).

Accounts of the history and origin of the sultanate have different variants. These are connected to the relationships among the various Tuareg precolonial drum-groups and confederations, and also to their relationships with neighboring peoples. The first sultan of Air was Yunus. He was succeeded by his nephew, Akkasan (Hamani 1989:146). There is vagueness and dispute concerning his precise genealogy preceding this, but these feminine names clearly indicate the initial importance of at least the Berber matrilineal type of descent and succession. The *Agadez Chronicle*, a compilation of Arabic manuscripts kept by the current sultan, dates the establishment of the Air sultanate as in 1405 BCE. Before that time, it was said in oral and chronicle traditions, anarchy reigned over the country.

Despite disagreements and uncertainty surrounding the origin of the Air sultanate, most traditions now agree on the existence of a situation of crisis in Air toward the end of the fourteenth century. The Itesen were the most powerful of the Tuareg groups, but their supremacy was not uncontested. Certain factions refused to obey their leader, Aghumbulu, and these troubles caused them to search for a supreme arbitrator from outside. The document *Kitab Asi Sultanati Ahyar I*

reports that the Isandalan, after the out-migration of the Gobirawa (proto-Hausa, Sudanic farming) populations who had earlier lived in Air, had no designated sultan. "Their [The Itesens'] social state was like that of Arabs, and like the Arabs, there were only elder judges to adjudicate among them. This situation obliged them to look for a sultan" (Hamani 1989: 137–138). This document continues to relate the story of five groups going to Aghram Sattafan to find a sultan and transporting him to the country of Tadaliza.

Traditions indicate the marginal but prestigious position of the sultan in Air Tuareg society. Whether his reputed descent from the sultan of Constantinople is literally "true" or mythical/symbolic, the point is that this legend is in effect a metaphor that endows him with spiritual, as well as secular, creativity and power, and conveys his ability to mediate in disputes from outside the local descent and alliance system of the noble clans. From this perspective, of viewing the lines of "myth/history" as continued and blurred rather than discrete, one can understand why the noble drum-groups still elect as heir to the sultanate a son of a concubine of Sudanese origins, rather than the son of a Tuareg wife from among his sons.

The first sultans were installed in the southern parts of Air, in the rocky mountainous zones, indicating that their Tuareg drum-groups had not yet come out of the massif into Agadez and needed a leader there, near them, in the Itesan region, near the caravan passage points. The proximity to Agadez soon became important, however. War (victory of the Kel Taghazart Zigrat over the Tasannagat) caused the royal family to leave the mountainous zones and move closer to the town's security and centrality to trade routes (Hamani 1989:147). Agadezian traditions state that Sultan Yusuf was the first sultan of Air to be installed in Agadez. This move was also a response to other, wider events and conditions during the fifteenth century in the region extending between Middle Niger and Lake Chad. In the Chad region there was the renaissance of the Sayfawa and a new expansionist Bornu kingdom. To the west of Bornu, the Hausa lands attained political and economic complexity: a new dynasty appeared in Katsina with Muhammad Korau, and by the middle of the century, Katsinawa merchants were present in Agadez. A trading connection was solidly established between Hausa country and North Africa by the Air.

At the junction of these events, the installation of the first Sultan Yusuf in Agadez took place. Djibo Hamani analyzes oral traditions' accounts of the installation of the first sultanate, as recorded in the *Tarikh Asli Wilayat Amir Abzin VIII* in Agadez, obtained from Sarkin Makada Kutuba, as follows: in the sixteenth century there were wars against Tigidda. Following the death of a co-leader, Al Ghadil against Tigidda, war continued until the day when they called in Aligurran, the Tuareg mythical ancestor who in local legends inscribed the Tifinagh (Tamajaq alphabet) writings on the Saharan rock art. They made him a large lance, of gold and copper, and performed rituals. Aligurran divined by throwing this lance, from Tadaliza (where one still sees his footprint), to where it fell: at the place where the palace of the sultan would be built. The day after this lance-throwing, all the Tuareg mounted donkeys, oxen, camels, and horses, and they left in search of the lance. They found it near a stream with many euphorbia (a type of plant). The people gave cries of joy, cut the euphorbia in their enthusiasm, and constructed the palace. Then they went to search for the sultan and installed him. The Tuareg who were with the sultan built themselves small dwellings and occupied them (Hamani 1989:155–156).

On the surface, this tradition appears to imply that the sultan leadership of Tadaliza wished to escape from Tigidda to find a better leverage point for maximizing their chances for success against Tigidda. But the end of the text contradicts this idea: Kutuba related how, after some time, the Tuareg, who came from the sultan's installation, said: "Agadez is not a place where one can install (a sultan); it is a place of visiting, a place for the Maggades (Agadezian people, of Songhay origin) and the Arabs." So they got up and left the town, leaving their slaves in their homes. When they came in from the desert to see the sultan, they lodged with their slaves, but did not have their own homes in Agadez. Thus the nomadic Tuareg saw their own homes as outside of Agadez. Indeed, a similar pattern persisted in Agadez in the 1970s: many nomads at that time still tended to reside outside the town, coming into it only for trading and other business and lodging with clients and formerly servile families who resided there.

In precolonial eras, the sultan was the main arbitrator and judge in disagreements between the different Tuareg groups, whose supreme chiefs were installed by him. But he could not meddle in their internal affairs, and rarely was so influential that he could stop the frequent disputes and battles. Since the French colonial administration, the power of individual drum-chiefs has diminished, while that of the sultan of Air has increased, now backed by central state coercion. During the French subjugation of the Tuareg regions of the Sahara, Sultan Tegama was involved in much Tuareg resistance. In more recent times, the sultan of Agadez became a liaison between the independent nation-state central government in Niamey, the capital of present-day Niger, and local government: he was placed in charge of tax collection and school registration. The current sultan of Air was caught up in the 1990–1995 armed conflict between Tuareg separatist/nationalist rebels and the central state government of Niger. Many

Tuareg cultural events have shifted from the sultan's palace near the Agadez mosque, their former place of performance, to the newly-constructed Maison des Jeunes (Youth House) on the outskirts of the town. The sultan now spends much of his time in Niamey.

SUSAN RASMUSSEN

See also: **Tuareg.**

Further Reading

Barth, Heinrich. *Travels and Discoveries in North Central Africa, 1–5*, London: Longman, Brown, Green, 1857–59.
Nicolaisen, Johannes. *Ecology and Culture of the Pastoral Tuareg*, Copenhagen: Royal Museum, 1963.
Norris, H.T. *The Tuareg: Their Islamic Legacy and Its Diffusion in the Sahel*, Wilts, England: Aris and Philips, Ltd., 1975.
Palmer, H.R. *Sudanese Memoirs*, Lagos: Government Printer, 1928.

Aja-Speaking Peoples: Aja, Fon, Ewe, Seventeenth and Eighteenth Centuries

The Aja (Adja), the Fon, and the Ewe are often classified together in the historical literature under blanket terms such as the Aja, the Aja-Ewe, or more recently, the Gbe. Although distinct from each other, the Aja, the Fon, and the Ewe share a common set of cultural beliefs and practices, their languages all belong to the Kwa subgroup of the Niger-Congo language family, and they have a collective history of migrations from areas to the east of their present locations. These migrations originated from Ketu, a walled city in present-day southeastern Benin, probably in the fifteenth century, according to oral traditions.

During the seventeenth century, the migrations entered their final phase, and the Aja, the Fon, and the Ewe each settled into the areas that they inhabit today: the Aja and Fon in southern Bénin, with small populations of each in southern Togo and southwestern Nigeria, and the Ewe in southeastern Ghana and southern Togo. Flanked by the Akan to the west and the Yoruba to the east, this stretch of West Africa was referred to as the "Slave Coast" by European cartographers by the end of the century.

There was a series of migrations out of the Aja kingdom of Allada, located on the coast of present-day Benin, due to a succession dispute in the early seventeenth century. The migrants settled in a plateau area of woodland savanna about sixty miles north of the coast, established the kingdom of Dahomey in the 1620s, and eventually became known as the Fon. The kingdom gradually expanded into areas to the south and southeast of Abomey, the capital of Dahomey. But, throughout the seventeenth century, the most powerful local polities were Allada and Hweda, another coastal Aja kingdom that was later superseded by the town of Ouidah (Whydah), both of which conducted trade directly with European merchants. Furthermore, Dahomey was a tributary state of its powerful neighbor to the east, the Yoruba kingdom of Oyo.

Under King Agaja (1708–1740), Dahomey came to dominate most of the Aja kingdoms, including Allada, Hweda, Grand Popo (Popo), and Jakin, by the 1740s. Concerned with Dahomey's growing power, Oyo attacked the Fon kingdom four times between 1726 and 1730. As a result, Agaja agreed to continue to pay an annual tribute and to recognize Oyo's control over Porto Novo (in present-day Benin).

The central kingdom of Dahomey became the most powerful state between the Volta and the Mono Rivers. Dahomey was one of the biggest suppliers of slaves in West Africa and derived most of its revenues from that trade. During the early eighteenth century, the trade in slaves to the French, the English, the Portuguese, and the Dutch at Ouidah, controlled by Abomey, increased dramatically.

Further to the west, the Ewe split into three distinct groups after their dispersal from Notsé, a walled-town in central Togo. The first traveled in a northwesterly direction and settled the upland and valley regions and founded, among others, the towns of Hohoe, Kpandu, and Peki (in present-day Ghana), as well as Kpalimé (Togo). Ho and surrounding towns (Ghana) were settled by the Ewes, who migrated westward from Notsé. Finally, the third group moved toward the southwest and settled along the coast and founded the towns of Be (which includes what is presently Lomé, the capital of Togo) and Anlo (Ghana), among others. After arriving in these locations in the mid-seventeenth century, the Ewe were soon joined by other immigrants from west of the Volta River, including speakers of the Ga, Akan, and Guang languages. In addition, it is assumed that speakers of the Central-Togo languages (also known as the Togo Remnant languages) were indigenous to the central and northern areas settled by the Ewe and other migrant groups.

The Ewe-speaking region (often referred to as Eweland) was comprised of numerous chieftaincies and small states. Chieftaincies existed at the town level, while several towns together constituted a state, presided over by a paramount chief, who was elected on a patrilineal basis, from one or two lineages of the founding families, and advised by a council of elders. Although each of the Ewe polities was independent of the others, their shared linguistic, cultural, and historical ties served to foster a common identity.

The areas inhabited by the Ewe, particularly the northern part, were drastically affected by the slave trade in the eighteenth century. Highly decentralized and thus lacking an organized military defense, the Ewe were attacked by nearby powerful states, particularly those of the Akan, and sometimes participated in the slave trade themselves. Various Ewe groups repeatedly battled one another for prominence in the local slave trade. During the 1680s, for example, the Anlo Ewe and the Ge Ewe fought several wars in their attempts to wrest control of this trade from each other.

Several Ewe groups also allied themselves with non-Ewe. The longest-lasting of these alliances was between the Anlo Ewe and the Akan state of Akwamu, who together waged war against other Ewe polities in the 1730s. By the end of the eighteenth century, the Anlo Ewe state had become a local power based on its position within the regional trading network, particularly due to its commerce with the Danes at the coast, who built a fort at Keta in 1784.

In the early eighteenth century, the Akwamu subjugated the Ewe towns of Ho, Kpandu, and Peki. The Akwamu were forced to retreat from this area in 1730 after their conquest by the Akyem, another expansionist Akan state, who themselves were defeated in 1742 by the Asante. By the mid-eighteenth century, Asante assumed its place as the dominant economic and military power in the region west of Dahomey.

DENNIS LAUMANN

Further Reading

Amenumey, D.E.K. *The Ewe in Pre-Colonial Times: A Political History with Special Emphasis on the Anlo, Ge, and Krepi*, Accra: Sedco Publishing, 1986.

Bay, Edna G. *Wives of the Leopard: Gender, Politics, and Culture in the Kingdom of Dahomey*, Charlottesville: University of Virginia Press, 1998.

Boahen, A. Adu. "The states and cultures of the lower Guinea coast," UNESCO General History of Africa, Vol. 5, *Africa from the Sixteenth to the Eighteenth Century*, B.A. Ogot (ed.), Berkeley: University of California Press, 1992: 399–433.

Greene, Sandra E. *Gender, Ethnicity, and Social Change on the Upper Slave Coast: A History of the Anlo-Ewe*, Portsmouth, NH: Heinemann, 1996.

Law, Robin. *The Slave Coast of West Africa 1550–1750: The Impact of the Atlantic Slave Trade on an African Society*, Oxford: Clarendon Press, 1991.

Aja-Speaking Peoples: Dahomey, Rise of, Seventeenth Century

Throughout the seventeenth century, the Aja lived in the southern third of the modern Republic of Benin. The Aja kingdom, known as Dahomey, was created by a ruling dynasty of the Fon or Aja, during the second half of the seventeenth century. This dynasty ruled Dahomey until the end of the nineteenth century. The kingdom began as a vassal or tributary state of the Yoruba kingdom of Oyo. It became independent in 1818. Under the leadership of King Gezo (1818–1858), and King Glele (1859–1889), Dahomey developed into one of the most efficient indigenous African states in history.

Dahomey began as an offshoot of Allada. A branch of the Allada dynasty set out, with several hundred followers, to conquer the stateless and leaderless people who lived on the Abomey plateau. Dahomey, by contrast, was a centralized state with a well organized, disciplined, and hierarchically arranged military machine. By the late seventeenth century, Dahomey was in command of the coastal hinterland, which it raided at will to collect slaves. The Dahomey also broke away from the parent Aja kingdoms because they wanted to trade with European merchants. The other Aja kingdoms refused to trade with Europeans, yet European power was growing. As European power grew the Aja kingdoms declined. Public order was threatened, and good government declined. The European presence created new difficulties for the Aja. The Dahomey believed that by working with Europeans solutions to these problems would evolve.

Dahoman kings were not absolute monarchs; they consulted frequently with the Great Council and the council of ministers, as well as distinguished merchants and soldiers. Representatives of most interest groups had access to the king and could influence him. Dahomey's rulers rose to power through courage in battle and success in war.

Dahoman officials were appointed, transferred, and dismissed by the king. Conquered states formed integrated provinces within the kingdom. Neither vassal kings nor separate laws were recognized. The king and his council of advisors dominated hereditary aristocrats. The *mingi* served as the king's chief magistrate and police chief. The *meu* collected taxes for the king and acted as minister of finance. The *topke* served as minister of agriculture, and the *yevogan* acted as foreign minister and handled external affairs for the Dahomey. His duties included supervision of seaports, such as Whydah, overseas trade, and European relations. Female officials, known as *naye*, served in each province as the king's special envoys. They inspected male officials' work, and reported any irregularities directly to the king. Dahomey developed a special class of fierce female warriors. They joined the army to protect their children from Yoruba slave trading cavalry. On a continent where women are usually subservient and deferential to men, this marked an extraordinary development. The British explorer, Sir Richard Burton, called these female soldiers Amazons and created a legend.

The civil service planned and managed the economy for the king. Farm production allowed for the support of all royalty, the elite, the urban craft population, the army, and a surplus cash crop for sale. During crop shortages, the government forced specific regions to produce more of it. An annual census counted all livestock. The state collected income tax, custom duties, and road tolls to generate operating revenue. Rental of royal estates created additional wealth. This revenue, together with guns and ammunition, became the foundation for their power and their freedom. Without these, Dahomey would become a victim of neighboring kingdoms' slave raids.

Oyo frequently raided Dahomey and forced the Dahomans to pay the Yoruba tribute, in the form of an increased but tragic flow of slaves. Historians estimate that Allada and Whydah exported more than 20,000 slaves a year between 1680 and 1730 (Oliver 1981: 99). African city-states, such as those created by the Aja, saw the slave trade as a peripheral issue. Their goal was power and territorial expansion. To achieve this they needed guns from Europe and horses from the north. Northern Hausa city-states captured and trained horses. They demanded slaves in payment for their horses. Europeans, likewise, demanded slaves as payment for guns. As Aja power grew, Dahomey kept an increasing number of slaves who were put to work on farms, which supported the urban population. Slave agricultural villages emerged in areas around cities. Taxes and tribute from an expanding tributary region soon exceeded the slave trade in value. More and more people were needed to man Dahomey's expanding armies. Slave soldiers grew in importance. The neighboring Yoruba city-state of Benin restricted the sale of slaves to Europeans. Agricultural expansion required their labor at home. Slave status did not carry the stigma it had in the Americas and Europe. Few Africans realized that fellow Africans sold into slavery in the America's faced permanent bondage. They thought of slavery as Europeans think of serfdom. Tradition demanded the adoption of loyal slaves into the master's family. Commonly, rewards of land and freedom followed the master's death (Davidson 1961: passion.) Descendants of slaves easily assimilated into society as members of one social class or another.

Dahomans are often portrayed as bloodthirsty savages because of mass killings. This view is inaccurate. Indirectly, European slave traders caused mass murders. Dahomey gathered together large numbers of slaves at special coastal bulking stations. Here they waited for European slave ships that visited every month or so. European slave traders preferred to buy entire shiploads of slaves, rather than buy slaves in lots from different ports. Europeans tried to give Dahoman kings sufficient time to collect an entire shipload of slaves before visiting their ports. Often Europeans miscalculated how long it would take Dahomans to gather a shipload of slaves. If European slave traders waited too long, then slaves at coastal bulking stations exhausted local food supplies. Dahoman kings devised massive ritual murders, rather than watch slaves die of starvation. The kings viewed these killings as humanitarian. To justify these acts to their people they claimed that such rituals were required to guarantee their continued strength, vitality, and courage to rule. In time, this became part of their tradition. On several occasions, European slave traders pulled into port too late to buy the slaves Dahomey collected for them, but soon enough to witness the bloody ritual murders, not realizing that their demand for slaves helped to cause such horrors.

The need for defense against nearby slave raiding states and the need to collaborate with Europeans to guarantee the safety of Dahomey's children caused the formation of this great state in the seventeenth century. Its armies pushed out in all directions, trying to create buffers to safeguard the state. The state first broke through to, and captured, slave ports in an effort to end the slave trade. The need to acquire guns and ammunition from Europeans caused the reversal of this policy.

The Dahomey state reached its pinnacle between 1790 and 1858. In 1818 its armies won independence from Oyo and ravaged surrounding areas for slaves to work palm oil plantations. By 1850, the palm oil trade supplanted the slave trade as the dominant trade relationship binding Dahomey and Europe. The decline and abolishment of the slave trade eased pressures upon Dahomey to defend itself. Today, the modern nation of Benin occupies Dahomey's territory plus additional lands to its north.

DALLAS L. BROWNE

See also: **Yoruba-Speaking Peoples; Yoruba States (Other Than Ife and Oyo).**

Further Reading

Afigbo, A.E., E.A. Ayandele, R.J. Gavin, J.D. Omer-Cooper, and R. Palmer. *The Making of Modern Africa*, vols. 1 and 2, Harlow: Longman, 1968.

Cornevin, Robert. *Le Dahomey*, Paris: Presses universitarires de France, 1965.

Davidson, Basil, F.K. Buah, and J.F. Ade Ajayi. *A History of West Africa to the Turn of the Nineteenth Century*, New York: Anchor Books, Doubleday and Company, 1965.

Davidson, Basil. *Black Mother: The Atlantic Slave Trade*, Boston: Little, Brown, and Company, 1961.

Fage, J.D. *A History of West Africa.* Cambridge: Cambridge University Press, 1969.

Fage, J.D. *A History of Africa.* Routledge. London. 1978.

Harris, Joseph. *The African Presence in Asia.* Evanston, IL: Northwestern University Press, 1971.

Manning, Patrick. *Slavery, Colonialism, and Economic Growth in Dahomey, 1640–1960*, Cambridge: Cambridge University Press, 1982.

Murphy, E. Jefferson. *History of African Civilization*, New York: Dell Publishing Company, 1972.

Oliver, Roland, and Anthony Atmore. *The African Middle Ages: 1400–1800*, Cambridge: Cambridge University Press, 1981.

Tidy, Michael, and Donald Leeming. *A History of Africa: 1800–1914*. London: Hodder and Stoughton, 1980.

Akan and Asante: Farmers, Traders, and the Emergence of Akan States

The Akan people, who comprise close to 60 per cent of the modern nation of Ghana, have a richly textured history, which can be traced back to at least 1500 BCE. They possess a common language that is called *Twi*, a lineage system based on the matriclan, and common religious beliefs based on worship of the supreme being, *Onyame*, although the names of secondary deities may vary from place to place. How and when the Akan people coalesced from disparate local origins into the large, identifiable ethnolinguistic subgroup that is today classified as part of the greater Kwa subfamily of West African languages is uncertain. Whereas older formulations suggested origins of the Akan from more distant parts of Africa (perhaps as far east as the Nile Valley), the most up-to-date archaeological and linguistic research points to local origins near the present-day frontiers of Ghana and the Côte d'Ivoire. Today the Akan, or Twi-speaking peoples, occupy the southern half of Ghana, and also parts of Togoland and the southeastern corner of the Côte d'Ivoire. Their closest neighbors are the Ga-Andangme peoples of southeastern Ghana. They are bounded on the east by the Ewe peoples and on the north by the Guan-speaking peoples. Some of the major linguistic and political subdivisions of the Akan are Akyem, Akuapem, Asante, Assin-Twifo, Wassa, Fanti-Agona, Ahanta, Wassa, Nzema, and Sefwi/Aowin.

It would appear that, from at least medieval times, the people later called the Akan were living in small

The Akan of Ghana. A group of village elders in the Akan region from the 1970s. © Raymond E. Dumett.

chiefdoms in the forests and coastlands of what is now Ghana. According to most local traditions, as well as early European sources, the original heartland of the Akan people was called "Accany," an area that was roughly congruent with the modern Akan states of Adanse (in southern Asante), plus Assin and Twifo. Early Dutch maps of the seventeenth century sometimes show a "Great Akani"; but it is difficult to know if this was a true state, a league of chieftaincies, or simply a broad geographic or cultural expression. Simultaneously, the period 1000 to 1500 also witnessed the organization of towns and pre-states on the northern fringes of the Akan cultural area. Bono-Manso (in the Brong region), which became the early hub of a northern trading network appears to have been the first entity where the well-known royal regalia of all future states—the golden stool, golden sword, and the mace—were conceived and then diffused further south.

It would be a mistake to speak of the early Akan simply, or even mainly, as farmers, even though that is their main reputation today. From the earliest times of recorded history, it is clear that the Akan exhibited entrepreneurial skills in a diverse range of economic activities. To express this diversity a better term would be farmers/hunters/fishermen/gold miners and long-distance traders. It is important to point out that in most districts before the twentieth century a majority of the Akan states were sparsely populated, and so the demands on the land for intensive food crop cultivation were not great. Forests blanketed much of the land, and villages with extensive cleared land fields were few and far between. Most cultivated family plots surrounding characteristic *nkuro*, or hamlets, were small, dispersed, and difficult for strangers to discern. Modern specialists estimate that the average size of family forest farms in Asante was about 2.5 acres (or one hectare). Early sources indicate that in the precolonial period interior markets were rare, that the wants of most people were relatively simple and based on subsistence production; and that, therefore, the agricultural requirements for the most common staples—bananas, plantains, plus native yams—were not overwhelming. People supplemented their diet with protein derived from considerable time spent in forest hunting (deer and "bush puppies"), river fishing, and foraging (for example, forest snails were a significant food item).

The inception of the Atlantic overseas trade constituted a major watershed in the life of the Akan people. Trading contacts, with European oceanic traders—first the Portuguese and later the Dutch and English—brought economic betterment for some and with it social change. The opportunities for profit from trade drew upcountry people to the coast, stimulating population growth; and this gradually transformed, in some cases, what had previously been villages into trading towns, near the European trading forts and the offshore roadsteads for passing ships. Documents speak of a constant coming and going of producers and traders into such coastal towns as Saltpond, Cape Coast, El Mina, and Axim. Although most transactions continued to be in gold dust or by barter, there was a gradual monetization of the local economy based on the introduction of European coins. Although slave labor was common, both at the European trading factories and under indigenous African entrepreneurship, opportunities for artisanship led to experience and local traditions in the skilled trades, such as carpentry, stoneworking, and blacksmithing.

The other major development, which gained force in the late 1600s, was the growth of state formation among major Akan subgroups. States and kingdoms grew slowly out of earlier family, lineage, and village organizations and were often the product of alliances and confederations of chieftaincies. It should be noted that the Akan states were seldom defined by rigid territorial boundaries: the power of a paramount ruler over subordinated kings and chiefs was highly flexible, and it depended on the dynamism of the particular man holding office. Often a state's power extended along major trade routes, and was felt mainly in the towns and villages along those routes, like the nodes in a spider's web. It is clear, however, that the great expansion of Atlantic commerce in which imported firearms and other manufactured products were exchanged, first for gold and later, and most substantially for slaves, ran parallel to, and, indeed, was a prime causal factor in the expansion of the great Akan forest kingdoms, such as Akwamu, Denkyera, Gyaman, and, above all, Asante. In each of these states complex, centralized administrative cadres developed.

Modern Akan nationalism evolved slowly out of a mixture of Western-style education and a reaction against British colonial rule. Under the leadership of both traditional kings and chiefs, plus the westernized elite of the central coastal districts, the Fante Confederation (1868–1873) reflected a strong attempt by the coastal Akan to establish their own self-governing institutions and also to provide a counterweight to the great inland power of Asante. The inability of British officials at the time to perceive the worth of this organization as an early building block for democratic nationhood constituted one of the great missed opportunities of colonial rule. Another Akan-based proto-nationalist movement was the Gold Coast Aborigines Rights Protection Society of 1897, which successfully blocked efforts by colonial officials to bring all exploitable mineral and forests lands under government control.

Throughout their history, the Akan people have displayed remarkable entrepreneurial capabilities. Gold mining—both small-scale/artisanal and capitalistic/mechanized—has been a continuing major theme up to the present day. But by the second half of the nineteenth century, these qualities were also evinced in their responsiveness to price incentives for the production of palm oil and palm kernels, in the development of the export trade in wild rubber, in the exploitation of local mahogany forests, initially in the southwestern region and later in Asante and the Brong-Ahafo region; and, above all, in the famous cocoa-growing revolution. Research by Polly Hill and by Gareth Austin has underscored the great abilities of Akan cocoa farmers from Akwapim, Akyem, and Asante in adapting traditional socioeconomic institutions and in perfecting growing, drying, and distribution methods to meet the demands of the world market in the development of Ghana's primary export industry of the twentieth century.

RAYMOND E. DUMETT

Further Reading

Anquandah, James. *Rediscovering Ghana's Past*. Essex, UK: Harlow, 1982.

Hill, Polly. *The Migrant Cocoa Farmers of Southern Ghana*. Cambridge, 1963.

Kea, Ray A. *Settlements, Trade, and Politics in the Seventeenth-Century Gold Coast*. Baltimore, MD, 1982.

Lentz, Carola, and Nugent, Paul. *Ethnicity in Ghana: The Limits of Invention*. New York, 2000.

McCaskie, Thomas C. *State and Society in Pre-colonial Asante*. Cambridge, 1995.

Osei-Kofi, E. *The Family and Social Change in Ghana*. Goteborg, 1967.

Sarbah, John Mensah. *Fanti Customary Laws*. London, 1904.

Wilks, Ivor. *Asante in the Nineteenth Century*. Cambridge, 1975.

Akan States: Bono, Dankyira, Wassa, Akyem, Akwamu, Fante, Fifteenth to Seventeenth Centuries

The Akan constitute the largest single ethno-cultural group of Ghana, forming about 50 per cent of its population. They consist today of the Akyem, Asante, Assin, Akuapem, Akwamu, Bono or Bron, Denkyira, Etsi, Fante, Gyaaman, Kwahu, Twifo, and Wassa.

At one time it was thought that the Akan migrated from the north and east, from ancient Ghana, Mesopotamia, Egypt, or Libya. However, on the basis of archaeological, linguistic, ethnic, and oral evidence, it seems likely that the Akan evolved in Ghana in the Adansi-Amansie region by about 1000.

The first Akan state to emerge was Bono (capital Bono-Manso), southwest of the Black and White Volta and east of the important Mande or Dyula trading center of Begho (Nsoko), and north of the forest region. It was founded in the late fourteenth or early fifteenth century with a view to tapping the Banda gold fields and controlling the trade routes linking the areas of the Niger bend, the Sahara, and Hausaland to the north and the Akan gold and kola-producing forest regions to the south. The rapid development of the state is attributed to two of its early kings, Ameyaw and Obunumankoma, during the second half of the fifteenth century. By the third decade of the seventeenth century, Bono had developed into a large, wealthy, and cultured kingdom; this is borne out by the fact that Bono is clearly indicated on a map drawn on Christmas Day 1629 by a Dutch cartographer at Moure in Asebu on the coast.

The other Akan states of Denkyira, Wassa, Akyem, Akwamu, Fante, and Kwahu developed during the sixteenth and seventeenth centuries.

According to oral tradition, Fante was founded by the Borebore Fante, who migrated from Tekyiman, first to Kwaaman and then to Mankessim. Fante had become well established by the time the Portuguese appeared on the coast in the 1470s. Unlike many of the Akan emigrants, the Borebore Fante did not establish different states or kingdoms, but all settled together at Mankessim about ten miles from the coast in five different quarters, namely, Kurentsi Aman, Anaafo, Bentsi, Edumadze, and Nkusukum. By the beginning of the sixteenth century, the government of that state was not monarchical (unlike neighboring Akan states). The state did have one head, but he was referred to in the European records as *Braffo* and not *Ohene* of Fante, and that office rotated among the *Braffo* of the different quarters of the city-state.

The founders of the present three Akyem states, Akyem Abuakwa, Akyem Kotoku, and Akyem Bosome with their capitals of Kyebi, Akyem Oda, and Akyem Swedro, respectively, belong to the Asona and Agona clans, and originated in the Adansi area from where they migrated to found these states. Since these states appear on the 1629 map as well established, it is not unreasonable to conclude that they were founded during the second half of the sixteenth century. By the time of that map, Akyem Abuakwa—from its capital at Banso—was dominating that Pra-Birem area, and must have established control over the trade routes and the gold-producing districts of the area. By the end of the seventeenth century, Akyem Abuakwa had grown into a large, rich, and centralized kingdom and one of the leading producers of gold in the country, ruled by "the king. . . who may be called an Emperor."

The Agona founders of Akyem Kotoku also migrated from Adansi about that same time as the Abuakwa, first to Ahwiren near Bekwai, and from where they settled finally at Adupon near Dwansa on the Konongo-Agogo road by about the end of the sixteenth century. By the middle of the seventeenth century, they had succeeded in establishing the Kotoku state in the present Asante-Akyem area between the Pra and Lake Bosumtwi. The Agona founders of Bosome also migrated with their kinsmen, the Kotoku, to Ahwiren and thence to Kotoku Omanso on Lake Bosomtwe. They remained on the lake as a small state, becoming a tributary state first of Denkyira during the second half of the seventeenth century, and then of Asante throughout the eighteenth century.

While the Akyem states were emerging in the Adansi/Pra-Birem areas, Denkyira and Akwamu were also rising in the west and east. The founders of Denkyira were members of the Agona clan, which evolved in the Adansi area near Akrokyere and from where they migrated southwestward to settle at Banso or Abankeseeso in the rich gold-producing Oda-Ofin basin. It has now been established that, as in the case of the Akyem states, the foundation of Denkyira was laid toward the end of the sixteenth century. It was not until the second half of the seventeenth century that the state rapidly expanded and conquered all the pre-Asante states including Adansi to the northeast, part of present Ahafo area to the northwest, Wassa and Aowin to the west, and Twifo and Assin and even Fetu to the south. By the end of the seventeenth century, Denkyira had developed into a large and rich empire dominating the southwestern part of the country.

While Denkyira was emerging in the west, the Aduana state of Akwamu was rising in the east. According to oral tradition, they migrated from the early Akan state of Twifo and settled at Asamankese from where they later migrated eastward and founded their second capital, Nyanoase, near Nsawam. Its foundation, like that of the Akyem states, probably took place during the second half of the sixteenth century.

The second phase of Akwamu's expansion began after 1600 and ended in about 1670. It was during this period that Akwamu expanded northwestward to the Atewa hills and Anyinam, northward to the border of Kwahu, and eastward by conquering the predominantly Guan principalities of Tafo, Aburi, Equea, Aberadi, Late, and Kamana. The final phase began in 1677 and ended in 1700. The Akwamu defeated the Ga kingdom, the Adangbe Ladoku kingdom, and the Agona state, and crowned its successes with the capture of Christiansborg Castle in 1693. By the end of the seventeenth century, the small inland Aduana state of Asamankese had been converted into the largest Akan kingdom (if not empire), dominating southeastern Ghana.

In the southwestern part of the country, a similar political revolution was taking place in the rise and growth of Wassa. There are now three Wassa states, Wassa Amenfi, Wassa Fiase, and Wassa Mpoho with their capitals Akropon, Benso, and Mpoho, respectively. It appears, however, that until the eighteenth century there was only a single Wassa state. The founders of this Asona state, like their Abuakwa kingsmen, evolved in the Adansi area and while the latter migrated eastward, the former turned southwestward, possibly through Twifo-Heman to Nerebehi. Since Wassa was well-known to the Portuguese as a rich gold-producing state by the early decades of the sixteenth century, and in fact, the Portuguese sent an ambassador to the king's court in 1520, it would appear that the founders of Wassa migrated from the Adansi area much earlier than the Asona of Abuakwa, probably during the second half of the fifteenth century. During the second half of the seventeenth century, the Wassa rulers continued their expansionist activities southward toward the coast, and by the end of that century Wassa was dominating southwestern Ghana and had become the leading producers of gold in the country.

It is evident from the above that by the end of the seventeenth century, a veritable political revolution had taken place in the Akan areas of southern Ghana. In place of the forty or so small states and principalities in place prior to the sixteenth century, just a few large kingdoms, or rather empires, had emerged.

There are several reasons for these developments. All these states were founded in the gold-producing regions through which the important trade routes passed. Enlightened and courageous leadership, which all these states enjoyed, also played a key role. The third and undoubtedly the most important reason was the use of firearms in warfare at this time. It is evident from Dutch and English records that from the 1640s onward, the Europeans began to sell firearms to the local rulers; by the 1660s and 1670s, guns and gunpowder had become the main imports into the country. Since these inland states emerged in the gold-producing areas of the country, they were able to accumulate the greatest quantities of firearms. The introduction of firearms was linked to a great increase in the number of war captives, which led to the replacement of the gold trade by the notorious slave trade as the principal economic activity of these states in the following century.

A. ADU BOAHEN

Further Reading

Boahen, Albert Adu. *Topics in West African History*. London: Longman, 1966.

"The states and cultures of the lower Guinea coast," in Ogot, Bethnel Allan (ed.), *UNESCO General History of Africa, Vol. 5, Africa from the Sixteenth to the Eighteenth Century*. London: Heinemann, 1992.

Daaku, Kwame Yeboah. *Trade and Politics on the Gold Coast, 1600–1720.* Oxford: The Clarendon Press, 1976.

Warren, Dennis M. *The Akan of Ghana.* Accra: Pointer Ltd., 1973.

Akan States: Eighteenth Century

The history of the Akan states in the eighteenth century can be divided into three phases: 1700 to 1730, 1730 to 1750, and 1750 to 1800. During the first decade of the eighteenth century, the states of Akwamu, Akyem Abuakwa, and Denkyira attained their widest territorial expansion, mainly through conquests. The Akwamu continued their expansionist activities eastward under their famous King Akonno. In 1702, he launched a campaign to suppress the resistance in Ladoku and pushed across the Volta and occupied Anlo, and conquered the inland Ewe states of Peki, Ho, and Kpando. He then recrossed the Volta and conquered Kwahu between 1708 and 1710. These conquests brought Akwamu to its widest territorial extent and the apogee of its fame and glory.

The two Akyem states also attained the peak of their power during this period. After suffering defeat at the hands of the Asante in 1702, which led to the migration of the Kotoku across the Pra to Da near Afosu, the two Akyem states inflicted a decisive defeat on the Asante in 1717, during which they ambushed and killed the great Asantehene Osei Tutu. In 1730, both of them also invaded and defeated Akwamu, moving across the Volta to their present location. They took over the Akwamu lands, the greatest portion of which went to Akyem Abuakwa. Thus, by the middle of the eighteenth century, Akyem Abuakwa had become the second largest of the Akan states in southern Ghana. It was also during this period that, in reaction to the increasing threat to their middleman role, the Fante launched a series of campaigns and conquered the coastal states of Fetu, Aguafo, and Asebu between 1702 and 1710, and Agona in 1724. By the end of the third decade, the Fante controlled the entire stretch of the coast from the mouth of the Pra to the borders of the Ga kingdom to the east.

The final political change, which in fact amounted to a veritable revolution, was the arrival in Ghana of Asante, with its dramatic defeat and overthrow of the powerful state of Denkyira at the famous battle of Feyiase near Kumasi in October 1701, under the leadership of King Osei Tutu. Immediately after that victory, Osei Tutu attacked the Akyem states for assisting Denkyira. In 1711, he turned his attention northward and conquered Wenkyi, sacking its capital Ahwenekokoo, hoping to gain control of the trade routes leading to Bono and the important Dyula trading center of Begho. Osei Tutu marched southward, and between 1713 and 1715 conquered Twifu, Wassa, Aowin, and Nzema. In 1717 Osei Tutu turned eastward and attacked the two Akyem states, which ended in his defeat and death. But that time, Asante had replaced Akyem and Akwamu as the largest of the Akan states.

How can this dramatic emergence of the Asante state be accounted for? The first reason was the creation of not just a new Asante state, the Asanteman, but also of a new nation, Asantefoo, by Osei Tutu and his friend and adviser, Okomfo (Prophet) Anokye. They did this by uniting all the preexisting states within a 30 mile radius of Kumasi and endowing it not only with a new constitution with the Oyoko clan of Osei Tutu as its royal family, a federal governing council, a new common capital, Kumasi, and a national annual festival. But the most effective device that they used was the creation of the famous golden stool, Sika Agua Kofi, which Okomfo Anokye is believed to have conjured down from the sky and which was accepted as embodying the soul of the nation, to be preserved and guarded at all costs. These factors endowed this young nation-state with a sense of destiny that has ensured its survival to this day. Osei Tutu also provided it with leadership and inspiration, which was further enhanced by the more effective application of the new military technology in the form of firearms, which the Asante were able to acquire in large quantities because of their great wealth derived from their rich gold mines, trading activities, and tributes, and which made their armies virtually invincible.

The period from 1730 to 1750 saw even more revolutionary changes than before. After three years of internal instability, Opoku Ware succeeded Osei Tutu. He began his wars with attempts to suppress the revolts against Asante rule by Akyem, Wassa, Aowin, and Denkyira with an attack on Akyem in 1720–1721. He then turned westward and beat back an invasion of Kumasi by Ebrimoro, the king of Aowin. Opoku Ware moved northward and attacked and defeated the ancient and famous kingdom of Bono in 1723–1724, and invaded Wasa again in 1726. It was as a result of this defeat that Ntsiful I (*c.*1721–1752) moved the capital of Wassa from the north to Abrade near the coast, where it remained until the nineteenth century. Opoku Ware overran western Gonja and Gyaaman in 1732, Banda in 1740, the Akyem states of Akyem Abuakwa and Kotoku in 1742, and eastern Gonja and Dagomba in 1744. By the time of his death in 1750, Opoku Ware had proved more than a worthy successor of Osei Tutu and had converted Asante into a sprawling empire extending over an area wider than modern Ghana and including all the existing Akan states with the sole exception of Fante. Using experts, craftsmen, and musicians captured or recruited from the conquered Akan states, Osei Tutu and Opoku Ware brought the Akan monarchical civilization to its fruition, marked today by its gold regalia and ornaments, colorful *kente* cloth, beautiful music and dance forms, and impressive and elaborate court ceremonies.

The history of the Akan states during the second half of the eighteenth century is essentially the history of the determination of the Asante to preserve their huge empire, the determination of the Akan vassal states (especially Denkyira, Wassa, Twifu, and Akyem Abuakwa) to regain their independence, and the desire of the Fante to retain and safeguard their independent existence. Thus in 1760, 1776, and 1785, the Asante moved their troops to suppress the rebellions of the Wassa. In 1765, 1767, and 1772–1773, Akyem also revolted. The Asante won a victory over the Akyem in 1765 and 1767, but they were defeated in 1772.

Of all the Akan states, it was only Fante that remained outside the control and domination of the Asante in the eighteenth century, and Fante was able to achieve this mainly through diplomacy and especially the support of the British. After the defeat of the Akyem states by the Asante in 1742, the Fante felt so threatened that they worked hard to form an alliance consisting of Kommenda, Abrem, Fetu, Akwamu, Assin, Wassa, and Denkyira, which imposed a blockade on the trade with Asante. So successful was this blockade that no Asante could trade on the Fante coast from 1742 until 1752. By that time, the Fante were feeling the negative consequences of this blockade, and so secretly allied with the Asante in 1759. But they broke with the Asante in 1765 and formed a new alliance with Wassa, Twifo, and Akyem, and only the intervention of the British prevented a clash between the two groups. In 1772 the Asante threatened to invade the Fante for refusing to hand over some Asante hostages; only the intervention of the British, who had by then adopted the policy of supporting the Fante to prevent the Asante from becoming masters of the entire stretch of the coast of Ghana, deflected a potential conflict. Thus by 1775 peaceful relations were ensured between Asante and Fante and trade was flourishing, and this continued until 1785 when Wassa revolted, which was effectively suppressed. Wassa remained a unified state until the 1820s, when it broke into the present Wassa Fiase and Wassa Amenfi states.

To summarize, by the end of eighteenth century, the Asante empire was still intact and dominating all the Akan states except Fante, which succeeded through diplomacy and the support of the British to maintain its sovereign and independent existence until the early nineteenth century, when it was finally incorporated into the Asante empire.

A. ADU BOAHEN

See also: **Akan and Asante: Farmers, Traders, and the Emergence of Akan States; Akan States; Ghana (Republic of) (Gold Coast): Colonial Period: Administration**

Further Reading

Addo-Fening, Robert. *Akyem Abuakwa 1700–1943 from Ofori Panin to Sir Ofori Atta.* Trondheim: Department of History, Norwegian University of Science and Technology, 1997.

Boahen, Albert Adu. "The states and cultures of the lower Guinea coast," in Ogot, Bethnel Allan (ed.), *UNESCO General History of Africa*, Vol. 5, *Africa from the Sixteenth to the Eighteenth Century.* London: Heinemann, and Paris: UNESCO, and Berkeley: University of California Press, 1993.

Dumett, Raymond E. *El Dorado in West Africa: The Gold-Mining Frontier, African Labour and Colonial Capitalism in the Gold Coast, 1875–1900.* Athens: Ohio University Press, and London: James Currey, 1998.

Fynn, John Kerson. *Asante and its Neighbours, 1700–1807.* London: Longman, 1971.

Akhenaten
Egyptian Pharaoh

King of the Eighteenth Egyptian Dynasty, Akhenaten reigned from approximately 1360 to 1343BCE. Akhenaten is notable for having briefly replaced the entire Egyptian pantheon with a single deity, the Aten, the physical manifestation of the sun. It is now argued that the basis of the cult was the deification, while still alive, of Akhenaten's father, Amenhotep III, as the living Aten. Certainly, the whole cult of the Aten was centered on the royal family, and it was possible to worship the deity only through his representative on Earth, the king.

Akhenaten was born with the name Amenhotep, which he continued to bear for the first five years of his reign as the fourth king of that name. It is possible that up to the first twelve years of the reign were spent ruling jointly with his father, with Egypt's principal religious capital remaining at Thebes. Here, a large temple to the Aten was built behind that of Amun-Re,

The ruins of the North Palace at Amarna. The city contains many of the best preserved examples of Egyptian domestic architecture. The buildings were largely of mud brick, with a few stone elements such as column bases (shown) and door lintels. Photo © Aidan Dodson

king of the gods, of Karnak. However, in his fourth year Amenhotep IV decided to seek a unique cult center for the Aten, establishing a new city called Akhetaten (modern Tell el-Amarna), roughly halfway between Thebes and the civil capital, Memphis. At the same time, he changed his name from Amenhotep ("Amun is satisfied") to Akhenaten ("Effective Spirit of the Aten").

It is often suggested that these moves were a reaction against the growing power of the Amun priesthood, with a move toward a more democratic form of religion. However, this is at best an oversimplification, at worst completely inaccurate. The intimate links between the king and the Aten, particularly if the latter was to all intents and purposes Amenhotep III, certainly heavily reinforced the royal household's position at the center of both political and religious power. However, the divine king had always held a central role, and one should be careful of making too many assumptions about the motivations of ancient individuals, records of which have not survived.

As to the supposedly democratic nature of the cult, it is a telling fact that the focus of devotion in private household shrines at Amarna was a single stela showing the royal family in the act of worship. This provides a strong suggestion that an ordinary person's access to the god was limited, at the very best.

Akhenaten had two known wives. The senior was Nefertiti; nothing is known of her origins, but it is possible that she was the daughter of a general named Ay. The suggestion that she was a princess from the north Syrian state of Mitanni, who joined the king's harem in a diplomatic union, has now been almost entirely discredited. The junior wife was Kiya; her origins are likewise obscure, and it is not impossible that she was the Mitannian lady. Nefertiti bore her husband six known children, all girls: Meryetaten, Meketaten, Ankhesenpaaten, Neferneferuatentasherit, Nefernefer-ure, and Setpenre. In addition, a son named Tutankhu-aten is recorded in an inscription originally from Amarna. However, his mother is not known.

The city of Akhetaten was built on a virgin site on the east bank of the Nile. The royal residence was at the north end of the area, while the private residential suburbs extended around the central city, where lay the palace, temples, and government offices. The city limits, delineated by a series of fifteen large boundary stelae, also embraced a large swathe of agricultural land on the west bank. The tomb-chapels of the nobility were cut into the eastern cliffs behind the city, with the royal cemetery placed at the end of a 5 km-long wadi, running into the eastern desert.

The city site has been excavated since the 1890s, primarily by German and British teams. A large quantity of clay tablets inscribed in Mesopotamian cuneiform script, which represent letters received from other great powers as well as from vassals, was found at the site. These have been used to argue for a decline in Egyptian power in Syria-Palestine during Akhenaten's reign, exacerbated by willful neglect on the part of the king. Given problems in ordering many of the letters, and the fact that this is the only extant archive of this kind known from Egypt, one needs to be careful in drawing such conclusions. Old views as to Akhenaten's alleged pacifism are also made problematic by the survival of fragments showing the king (and the queen) smiting Egypt's enemies.

The Aten faith is well summarized in the so-called Hymn to the Aten, inscribed in a number of private tomb-chapels. Its universalist outlook and structure have been likened to some of the Hebrew Psalms. There is no evidence for direct links between these two texts; rather, they are manifestations of a cultural milieu that was common across the Near East during the late Bronze Age.

Soon after his twelfth reignal year, which may also have seen his transition to sole rule following the death of Amenhotpe III, Akhenaten's daughter, Meketaten, died. Also, the king took a new coruler, initially named Smenkhkare, later Neferneferuaten. Since Nefertiti disappears from the record at the same time, it has been suggested that one or both of these names refer to her as female king. However, there is clear evidence that the name Smenkhkare was borne by a male, married to Princess Meryetaten, while a set of inscriptions showing a transitional titulary, halfway between those associated with the names Smenkhkare and Neferneferuaten, indicate that we actually have a single individual (probably Akhenaten's eldest son), who subsequently changed his name.

Smenkhkare/Neferneferuaten seems to have died before Akhenaten. To the last months of the reign should probably be dated Akhenaten's attack on polytheistic monuments, particularly involving the destruction of the names and images of Amun, whose continued worship had been supported by the dead coruler.

Akhenaten died in his seventeenth regnal year, and was succeeded by his probable younger son, Tutankhaten, married to his third daughter. Under the tutelage of the generals Ay and Horemheb (both later kings), the religious status quo was restored by the middle of the ten-year reign of Tutankhamun (as he was renamed). It is likely that directly after Tutankhamun's death, Akhenaten's tomb at Amarna was desecrated, its furnishing destroyed, and the king's mummy burned.

AIDAN DODSON

See also: **Egypt, Ancient: New Kingdom and the Colonization of Nubia; Egypt, Ancient: Religion.**

Further Reading

Aldred, Cyril. *Akhenaten and Nefertiti*. New York: The Brooklyn Museum, 1973.

Aldred, Cyril. *Akhenaten, King of Egypt*. London and New York: Thames and Hudson, 1968; as *Akhenaten, Pharaoh of Egypt*. London and New York: Thames and Hudson, 1988.

Arnold, Dorothea. *The Royal Women of Amarna: Images of Beauty from Ancient Egypt*. New York: The Metropolitan Museum of Art, 1996.

Dodson, Aidan. "Kings' Valley Tomb 55 and the Fates of the Amarna Kings," *Amarna Letters* 3 (1994): 2–103.

Gabolde, Marc. *D'Akhenaton à Toutânkhamon* [From Akhenaten to Tutankhamun]. Lyon: Université Lumiére-Lyon 2, 1998.

O'Connor, David, and Eric H. Cline (eds.). *Amenhotep III: Perspectives on His Reign*. Ann Arbor: University of Michigan Press, 1998.

Redford, Donald B. *Akhenaten, the Heretic King*. Guildford and Princeton, NJ: Princeton University Press, 1984.

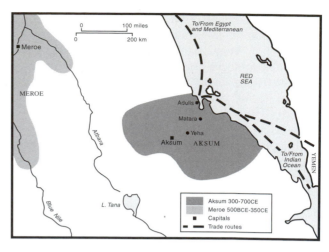

Aksum, fourth–seventh centuries.

Aksum, Kingdom of

Aksum was the principal metropolis of a major polity that arose during the early centuries CE in the highlands of northern Ethiopia (Tigray) and southern Eritrea. The development of sociopolitical complexity in this region may be traced directly to the first half of the last millennium BCE, although its economic foundations are of even greater antiquity.

The period during which the formative processes of Aksumite civilization must have taken place remains very poorly understood. Within the relevant area, virtually no archaeological sites have been investigated that clearly date to the last few centuries BCE or the first century CE. There is no indication of human settlement at the actual site of Aksum itself until the first century CE, which is also the date of the *Periplus of the Erythraean Sea*, a trader's handbook to the Red Sea and India Ocean coastlands which refers to the port of Adulis near modern Massawa in Eritrea and to "the people called Aksumites." By the third century CE, Aksum was capital of a powerful centralized kingdom, controller of abundant resources, ruler of extensive territories, trading extensively and, by *c.*270, issuing its own coinage, which circulated both locally and internationally.

By this time the rulers of Aksum were designated kings. Inscriptions of the early fourth century imply that they personified the power and achievements of the state. These inscriptions boast wide-ranging military conquests and extraction of tribute. Largely because of their personalized grandiloquence, we know very little about the mechanisms by which the royal authority was implemented, or how it was transmitted from one generation to another. There are hints that Aksum may at times have been ruled through a dual kingship. Contemporary foreign records and subsequent Ethiopian traditions both indicate that kingship

may have been hereditary through the male line, although it is hard to confirm whether these hints reflect ancient Aksumite reality rather than transferred assumptions based on foreign or subsequent practice. It is, however, incontrovertible that Aksum rapidly established itself in nominal control (however exercised) of extensive territory and thereby acquired very substantial human and material resources. These territories appear to have comprised much of the modern Eritrea apart from the extreme north and west, as well as the greater part of what is now Tigray region in Ethiopia, their southerly extent remaining poorly understood. At times, Aksumite political authority extended eastward across the Red Sea to the Yemeni highlands and, less certainly, westward as far as the Nile valley. Whether or not Aksum finally conquered Meroe in the fourth century, as is often suggested, there can be little doubt that it was the rise of Aksum that led to the economic decline of its Nilotic neighbor.

Aksumite royal inscriptions mention the taking of numerous captives. Slaughter is not specifically mentioned; indeed, it is claimed that the captives were maintained by their conquerors. This is in accord with the archaeological evidence, which indicates that a huge labor force was available at Aksum for processing raw materials and for erecting grandiose monuments. The extent to which these people were temporarily or perpetually slaves remains unknown.

There is reliable archaeological evidence of a substantial population enjoying a high level of material prosperity. At and around Aksum there are remains of stone buildings where a tall central structure is surrounded by an extensive walled court and ranges of rooms. In the older literature, these buildings are often referred to as "palaces," but the less committal "elite structures" is probably a preferable designation. The largest and most elaborate of these structures was that in western Aksum, known as Ta'akha Maryam. Those for which archaeological dating evidence is available were probably erected during the fifth or sixth centuries; we do not know whether similar structures existed in earlier times. However, by about the second century CE, burials were accompanied by grave goods of varying richness, some of great abundance, which indicates unequal access to resources.

Although until recently archaeologists and historians have placed almost exclusive emphasis on international aspects of the Aksumite economy, there can in fact be little doubt that this economy was locally based on the productivity of the land and indigenous Ethiopian agriculture. Recent research has indicated that, while sheep and goats were herded, cattle was the dominant domestic species being used both for food and for traction. Donkeys and chickens were also available. Inscriptions indicate that the herds were augmented by capture and tribute in the course of military campaigns. The range of cultivated crops was remarkably similar to that exploited in the region during more recent times, including wheat, barley, teff, finger millet, and sorghum as well as chick peas, noog, and linseed. Cereals thus predominated, including varieties originating in the Near East as well as local domesticates. Oil was obtained from linseed and from the locally domesticated noog. Traces have also been recovered of grapes and cotton; in neither case can one be certain whether the plants were grown locally or their produce imported from elsewhere. Grape vines were, however, known to the ancient Aksumites, being represented in contemporary artworks; and rock-cut tanks in the vicinity may have been used for making wine.

It has long been recognized that the Aksumites imported luxury goods from a wide range of sources, the evidence being both documentary and archaeological. The items concerned included glassware, beads, metals, textiles, wine and, probably, olive oil. What has only recently become apparent is the extent to which these imports provided stimuli for local production: glass vessels were, for example, made in imitation of foreign forms, Aksumite metalwork displayed great technological and artistic sophistication, while wine was probably obtained from local as well as imported sources.

The *Periplus of the Erythraean Sea* states that ivory was a major Aksumite export in, it would appear, the first century CE; and archaeological evidence now confirms this for later times also. A tomb of the late third century has yielded quantities of finely turned and carved ivory in the form of boxes, decorative panels, and furniture-components that are interpreted as having formed parts of an elaborate chair or throne. At workshops on the outskirts of Aksum highly standardized flaked stone tools were used in enormous numbers to process raw material, perhaps ivory or timber.

Gold may have been another significant export. From about the third quarter of the third century it was used to produce coins, Aksum being the only polity in Sub-Saharan Africa to have produced its own coinage in ancient times. Denominations were struck in gold, silver, and copper, those in the two less valued metals being frequently elaborated by the application of gilding to particular parts of the design. Aksumite gold coins are found only rarely in Ethiopia and Eritrea but are more frequent overseas, notably in Yemen and India; significantly, they almost invariably bear Greek inscriptions. This, and the fact that their weight was apparently based on standards prevailing in the eastern Roman Empire, suggests that they were primarily intended for international circulation. By contrast, coins in silver and copper are much more common on Aksumite sites and bear inscriptions in the local Ge'ez language, as befits media whose circulation was largely internal. Study of Aksumite coinage, which bears the names of successive rulers, permits an ordering of the various issues and of the rulers named in their inscriptions. It is not easy, however, to correlate the names on the resultant "king-list" with those preserved in traditional sources, the only undoubted links being provided by kings Ezana in the mid-fourth century and Kaleb early in the sixth.

Study of Aksumite coinage throws considerable light on several other aspects of its parent civilization: art styles, metallurgy, regalia, and religion. In the last-named instance, it provides a clear indication of the adoption of Christianity at Aksum during the reign of Ezana, an event also recorded in surviving Aksumite stone inscriptions, in Roman historical records, and (less directly) in Ethiopian historical tradition. Prior to this event, which probably took place around 340CE, the Aksumite rulers adhered to the polytheistic practices of earlier centuries which had much in common with those prevailing in South Arabia and were reflected in the use of the crescent-and-disc symbol on the earliest Aksumite coins. This symbol was replaced, during the reign of Ezana, by the Christian cross. The cross was subsequently accorded greater prominence in coinage design, sometimes accompanied by an inscription indicating the gradual adoption of the new religion through the Aksumite countryside.

The adoption of Christianity exerted a powerful influence over the subsequent history of Aksum, which came to be regarded by Roman and Byzantine emperors as a potential ally both in doctrinal controversies and in political maneuvers. Much of the Ethiopian and Eritrean highlands has remained a staunchly Christian area ever since; the Ethiopian Orthodox Church traces its origin and its authority to Aksum, which is to this day a place of unparalleled sanctity. The Cathedral of Maryam Tsion (Saint Mary of Zion) at Aksum was first built in ancient times. There is controversy whether this took place during the reign of Ezana or, rather later, during that of Kaleb. In any event, it took the form of a five-aisled basilica that survived, doubtless modified, until the sixteenth century; the huge plinth on which it stood may still be seen.

Apart from church buildings, none of which can so far be dated with any precision, it is only in the burial customs of the elite that the impact of Christianity's advent may be discerned in the Aksumite archaeological record. The most famous monuments that have survived from ancient Aksum are the huge monolithic stelae, carved in representations of multistoried buildings; one, which still stands, is 23 m high and weighs approximately 150 tons. Another, which probably fell and broke while being erected, would have been 30 m high and more than 500 tons in weight. It may be the largest single monolith that people anywhere have ever attempted to erect. These stelae were quarried about 4 km distant from the site where they were erected. Their extraction, carving, transport, and erection would have required enormous investment of labor. The largest stela was intended to mark a pair of tombs, at least one being a monumental structure of great complexity and magnificence. There can be little doubt that the other great stelae were likewise tomb-markers and that these tombs, being by far the grandest such monuments at Aksum, were those of the kings. The largest stelae and their associated tombs probably date from the third and fourth centuries, immediately prior to the advent of Christianity under Ezana. Later elite tombs were of distinct types, lacking stelae, although other elements of their design show continuity with earlier practice.

Use of upright stones as grave markers has been widespread through much of northeastern Africa over several thousands of years. Aksumite sites illustrate one specialized local manifestation of this tradition. The custom was followed at several levels of Aksumite society, the elaborate (probably royal) examples just described being contrasted with shaft or simple pit-graves marked with plain or undressed smaller stelae. There is corresponding variation in the quantity and elaboration of the associated grave goods.

This funerary evidence for socioeconomic stratification is paralleled by the domestic architecture. Aksumite "palaces" or elite structures have been noted above; they utilized the same materials and stone-dressing of a similar quality to that employed for the finest funerary monuments. In no case, unfortunately, has archaeological evidence been reported that would permit a confident assessment of the purposes to which these buildings were put. They may, however, be contrasted with other buildings, erected on a smaller scale using only undressed stone with or without supporting timbers, which are associated with farming pursuits and/or small-scale craft industry. It seems likely that the actual dwellings of the lowest strata in Aksumite society have not yet been unearthed; they are, however, probably represented by clay models of small thatched houses.

Our knowledge of Aksumite art is restricted by the limited survival of material. With the exception of funerary monuments, most surviving Aksumite architecture is poorly preserved and difficult to date. Religious buildings of this period have been little investigated, and it is probable that few if any have survived except in severely modified form. The original cathedral at Aksum is known only from accounts that were committed to writing many centuries after the building was constructed. Such accounts mention the existence of rich and elaborate mural decoration, no physical trace of which has survived. Likewise, ancient accounts mention the existence of large metal statues but, with the exception of a stone base recorded in 1906, no archaeological confirmation has been preserved.

Domestic and portable artifacts are better known. Pottery was, as elsewhere in Sub-Saharan Africa, exclusively hand made, without use of a wheel. The elaborately decorated wares known as "Classical Aksumite" are mainly known from funerary contexts of the third-fourth centuries; doubt remains of the extent to which such vessels were the prerogative of the elite and/or reserved for interment with the dead. Elaborate painted decoration has been preserved in certain circumstances, almost invariably in tombs, but may have been widespread. Many of the vessels from tombs are small and poorly fired, with soft fabric that contrasts markedly with that recovered on domestic occupation sites. The full significance of this variation vis-a-vis chronology, status, and function cannot be understood until further excavations have been undertaken and published. Pottery of particular interest includes bowls in the foot of which stand molded figures of yoked oxen, and jars with necks modeled in representation of female heads whose elaborate hairstyles strongly resemble those favored in the area today.

It may be assumed that most domestic pottery was produced close to its area of use, although it has not yet proved possible to undertake the detailed fabric studies necessary to confirm this. At least some finer and smaller vessels were, however, transported over considerable distances. Although some Aksumite pottery was slipped and finely burnished, true glazes occur only on vessels (mostly wheel-thrown) that were imported from beyond the Aksumite polity. Imported pottery may be divided between vessels that came to Aksum primarily as containers for some foreign commodity, and those that were brought as luxury items in their own right.

Examples of the two categories are large amphorae from Cyprus and/or Syria, which contained wine or olive oil, and the fine red-ware bowls of African red-slip ware made in the Mediterranean regions of North Africa. The former, once their contents had been decanted or consumed, were often reused for a variety of purposes, while the characteristic shapes of the latter were imitated by Aksumite potters.

Quantities of glass vessels and beads are found on Aksumite sites, particularly but by no means exclusively in elite tombs. It was often assumed that all this material was imported and, indeed, very close parallels for some may be recognized at sites around the eastern Mediterranean. However, parallels for other items have proved extremely hard to find; and certain vessels, although closely resembling Mediterranean counterparts, display idiosyncratic features. The suspicion that some of these items may have been produced in Aksum, perhaps by reworking imported glass that may have been broken in transit, has recently been confirmed by the recovery of raw glass in an industrial area of Aksum, providing clear evidence that some glass was worked there. Such a practice was by no means unique to Aksum, being attested, for example, at several broadly contemporary sites in the Sudanese Nile valley. It is not yet possible clearly to distinguish all imported glass vessels from those that were produced locally, but it is clear that both categories are represented.

Gold, silver, ferrous, and cuprous metals are well represented in the Aksumite archaeological record. They were clearly worked with considerable skill: in addition to the basic smelting and forging, techniques for which we have evidence include welding, riveting, production of even-thickness plates, drilling, perforating, casting, polishing, plating (including both annealing and mercury gilding), and enameling. Despite the recovery of slag and crucible fragments, no extensive Aksumite metalworking site has yet been located. Wherever they were, such sites and their associated debris must have been very substantial and their operation must have involved much labor and fuel. Quarrying must have involved the use of large numbers of iron wedges, none of which have yet been found. The sheer scale of Aksumite metallurgy indicates that it was largely local, involving production of utilitarian and luxury goods: a few imported luxury items have nonetheless been recognized.

Alongside the technological sophistication represented by the working of metal, ivory, and glass, it is important to recognize that the Aksumites continued to make and to use flaked stone tools in continuation of traditions practiced in the area for many centuries, if not millennia, previously. This, and the agricultural base on which the civilization's prosperity

ultimately depended, emphasize the local roots of ancient Aksum.

When considering imports, it is essential to include the less tangible as well as those directly represented in the archaeological record. Here must be included Christianity itself, which came in later Aksumite times to occupy a major place in state and popular affairs that continued for many hundreds of years after the decline of Aksum. From the third century, Aksum's aspirations to membership of the eastern Mediterranean world were symbolized by the use of Greek in stone inscriptions and by the issue of coinage.

Although there are major gaps in research coverage, it is possible to suggest some changing patterns in Aksumite material imports. In the third and early fourth centuries, glass and occasional pieces of metalwork are represented, pottery from outside the Aksumite hegemony being effectively absent. By the sixth century, however, glazed pottery was imported from Mesopotamia and Egypt, amphorae and their contents from Cyprus/Syria and the northern Red Sea, and bowls from North Africa. Aksum's exports are less easy to recognize in the archaeological record of recipient countries, but gold coins in both Yemen and southern India/Sri Lanka indicate the scale of dispersal. Ivory cannot yet be traced to its original source, but it is tempting to attribute the decline of its price in the Roman Empire during the late third century, and its sudden scarcity from the early seventh, to the fluctuating fortunes of Aksum's export trade.

The decline of Aksum is a topic surrounded by controversy. Ethiopian tradition is often interpreted as indicating its survival as a political capital into the tenth century; and the Aksumite coinage was formerly interpreted as having continued until that date. More detailed study has, however, suggested a significantly shorter coinage chronology that has recently received support from radiocarbon dates for late Aksumite occupation. It now appears that issue of the coinage ceased around the early seventh century and that by or even shortly before that time the scale of human settlement at Aksum sharply declined. Two factors may have contributed independently to this decline. Locally, the scale of the area's exploitation during the previous half-millennium must have had a great impact on the essentially fragile environment: reduced availability of timber for construction and fuel would have reduced availability and increased the cost of metal and numerous other commodities; increased runoff and soil erosion would have reduced agricultural productivity and predictability, affecting not only the overall prosperity and physical well-being of the population but also the availability of labor for prestige projects. Internationally, the rapid expansion of Islamic control of the lands bordering the Red Sea, most notably the conquest of Egypt in 642, effectively cut Aksum's link with the long-distance trade on which its prosperity had partly depended.

For centuries thereafter, the peoples of highland Ethiopia developed their predominantly Christian traditions on an island surrounded by Islam, maintaining only tenuous links with their coreligionists around the Mediterranean. It is in the architecture and other accoutrements of medieval Ethiopian Christianity that the legacy of ancient Aksum may be most clearly seen. Churches both built (as at Debra Damo) and rock-cut (as at Lalibela), display the timber-frame construction attested in the Aksum "palaces" and represented on the carved stelae.

DAVID W. PHILLIPSON

See also: **Ethiopia: Aksumite Inheritance.**

Further Reading

Munro-Hay, S.C. *Aksum: An African Civilisation of Late Antiquity.* Edinburgh: Edinburgh University Press, 1991.

Phillipson, D.W. *The Monuments of Aksum.* Addis Ababa and London: Addis Ababa University Press and British Institute in Eastern Africa, 1997.

Phillipson, D.W. *Ancient Ethiopia.* London: British Museum Press, 1998.

Akwamu: *See* **Akan States: Bono, Denkyira, Wassa, Akyem, Akwamu, Fante, Fifteenth to Seventeenth Centuries.**

Akyem: *See* **Akan States, Bono, Denkyira, Wassa, Akyem, Akwamu, Fante, Fifteenth to Seventeenth Centuries.**

'Alawite Dynasty: *See* **Morocco: Maraboutic Crisis, Founding of the 'Alawite Dynasty.**

Alcohol: Popular Culture, Colonial Control

Alcohol has always played an important role in African societies, but its functions and significance began to change with the advent of colonial rule. European colonizers attempted to control the production and consumption of alcohol to increase revenue, engineer social development, and suppress what they viewed as a potential source of rebellion, especially within the rapidly expanding labor force of the mining compounds and urban areas. New forms of popular culture, centered on the trade and social relations of drinking establishments, developed as a form of adaptation and resistance to colonial attempts to control every aspect of African life, including work and leisure time.

By the start of the colonial period, a variety of alcoholic drinks were found throughout Africa. More common to non-Muslim, Sub-Saharan areas for religious reasons, these included palm wine, fermented honey and fruit drinks, and beers made from maize, sorghum, bananas, or millet. Alcohol had both ritual and social significance and was used for many different occasions, including initiation rites, weddings, funerals, work meetings, and planting and harvest festivals. It also served as a fine to be paid for social infractions, as a method to confer honor, and as a means to spend an evening of leisure. The right to drink was usually reserved as a privilege of male elders, and drunkenness was regarded as disgraceful.

From the early days of colonial rule, officials saw alcohol as a cause of disrespect, indolence, and criminality. The 1890 Brussels Convention and the 1919 Convention of St. Germain-en-Laye banned the importation of European liquor into "prohibition zones," areas beyond the coast where the liquor trade had not yet been established, and restricted the importation of "trade spirits" in tropical Africa. Some laws, like the East Africa Liquor Ordinance of 1902, went even further by attempting to prohibit all locally produced intoxicating liquors. This proved unenforceable and was followed by the 1930 Native Liquor Ordinance delegating authority to district commissioners to closely supervise legal brewing and thus allow regulation and taxation. Measures such as this became even more common with the development of European controlled urban and industrial areas.

With the rise of the mining industry in South Africa, officials used alcohol as a magnet to draw and keep workers from rural areas, creating a close association between wage employment and drinking. Composed largely of young, male migrants, usually separated from their families, the workforce turned to drinking as a prominent form of leisure. The bar or pub became a focal point of this activity, especially after they were paid their wages, which in some cases were made in drink vouchers. This not only encouraged consumption, but also offered a form of European management over where Africans could drink. But government officials sought further control over African drinking habits, which they blamed for low productivity, high absenteeism, and unacceptable accident rates. They developed the "Durban system," a series of liquor restrictions designed to give local governments a monopoly over the production of local spirits and then sell them exclusively in municipal beer halls. This not only gave the state a means to shape urban, working-class leisure activities, but it also helped to secure the funds needed to enforce segregationist policies and remove

African alcohol consumption from the view of whites. In a limited sense, the Durban system was successful. By the late 1930s it had spread throughout the Union of South Africa. But the shift in drinking patterns and locales also helped to bring about new forms of popular culture. The workers developed *shebeens*, illegal drinking establishments serving local brews, to take the stress off their daily jobs. Within the *shebeens*, *marabi* culture thrived and new dance and music forms emerged, such as South African jazz, *marabi* music, and *isicathamiya*. Despite the perceived success of the Durban system, drinking patterns of Africans were never totally under white control, and the private and illegal trade in alcoholic drinks flourished.

Alcohol was also very important to colonial rule in the Gold Coast, or Ghana, where liquor taxes accounted for up to 40 per cent of government revenue in 1913. The enforcement of new liquor laws throughout the 1920s, however, led to a sharp drop in revenue and a rise in the production of local gin, *akpeteshie*. Drinking places associated with the consumption of *akpeteshie* became common and new forms of music, dance, and theater developed into a growing and dynamic popular culture. Acoustic guitar highlife and "concert parties" incorporated rural and urban aspects and met the social needs of new urban, working-class immigrants. Restrictive liquor laws in the 1930s attempted to quell, or at least limit, these cultural forms, but were largely unsuccessful because of the rapid growth of local drinking places and the production of *akpeteshie*, which became a symbol of resistance to colonial rule. Like the *shebeens* and *marabi* culture in South Africa, *akpeteshie* and the popular culture associated with it developed into a political issue and raids on illegal establishments inspired resentment and anger among Africans, often ending in violence and bloodshed.

The colonial state attempted to control the production and consumption of alcoholic beverages in Africa by promoting European distilled beverages, implementing liquor duties, and attempting to outlaw the local production of traditional brews. Control of alcohol consumption, however, was an area where colonial powers were destined to fail because of their dependence on African labor, and the rise of illegal drinking places and new popular culture forms. The role of alcohol in urban and industrial drinking locales differed markedly from that in rural communities as alcohol became available to a wider range of age and gender groups. Urban industrial drinking culture shaped new notions of leisure, community, and resistance, providing escape from the atmosphere of control exemplified in the workplace and acted as a means to cope with the harsh demands of everyday life.

STEVEN J. SALM

Further Reading

Ambler, Charles. "Drunks, Brewers, and Chiefs: Alcohol Regulation in Colonial Kenya, 1900–1939," in *Drinking: Behavior and Belief in Modern History*, Susanna Barrows and Robin Room (eds.). Berkeley: University of California Press, 1991.

Crush, Jonathan, and Charles Ambler (eds.). *Liquor and Labor in Southern Africa*. Athens: Ohio University Press, and Pietermaritzburg: University of Natal Press, 1992.

Karp, Ivan. "Beer Drinking and Social Experience in an African Society: An Essay in Formal Sociology," in *Explorations in African Systems of Thought*, Ivan Karp and Charles S. Bird (eds.). Bloomington: Indiana University Press, 1980.

la Hausse, Paul. *Brewers, Beerhalls, and Boycotts: A History of Liquor in South Africa*. Johannesburg: Ravan Press, 1988.

Pan, Lynn. *Alcohol in Colonial Africa*. Helsinki: Finnish Foundation for Alcohol Studies, and Uppsala: The Scandinavian Institute of African Studies, 1975.

Alexandria

Alexandria, now second only to Cairo in terms of size and importance in Egypt, has historically been considered a city somewhat separate from the rest of Egypt. In late antiquity, Alexandria came to be known as a Mediterranean, rather than an Egyptian, city; the phrase *Alexandria ad Aegyptum* (Alexandria next to, or adjacent to, Egypt) illustrates this sense of separation. Perhaps best known today for its beaches and its thriving port and industries, Alexandria's history is a rich one.

The city was founded by Alexander the Great in 332BCE, when the Macedonian conqueror seized Egypt from Persian control. Alexander wanted a new capital city, one that would link Egypt to the Mediterranean. Alexandria was established as Egypt's new capital, and it remained so until the Arab invasions in the mid-seventh century. The city also was to serve Alexander as a naval base from which to control the Mediterranean.

Less than one hundred years after its founding, Alexandria was already known as a center of learning, science, and scholarship. Under the Ptolemaic dynasty (which ruled Egypt from 305BCE until the death of Cleopatra VII in the year 30), the city flourished and earned the nickname "the center of the world." Ptolemy I, also known as Ptolemy Sater (savior), who had ruled Egypt from Alexander's death in 323BCE before being crowned officially in 305BCE, began the construction of Alexandria's famous library. The Library of Alexandria was the most famous library of the ancient world, and it was founded with the purpose of collecting the entire body of Greek knowledge. Here, on papyrus scrolls and vellum, works of literature, poetry, medicine, science, and philosophy, among other subjects, were collected and housed; Ptolemy I contributed his own history of Alexander's campaigns to

Pharos of Alexandria (reconstruction after Adler). One of the Seven Wonders of the World. Built by Sostratus of Cnidus for Ptolemy II of Egypt, c.280BC on the island of Pharos in the harbor of Alexandria. Anonymous. © Foto Marburg/Art Resource, New York.

the hundreds of thousands of volumes stored there. The library was part of a larger complex founded by Ptolemy I: the Mouseion, or museum, the city's research center, which hosted such luminaries as Euclid, Archimedes, Herophilous, Erasistratus, and Eratosthenes. Alexandria also became a center of Jewish learning; it is believed the translation of the Old Testament from Hebrew to Greek (the Septuagint) was produced here.

Under Ptolemy II, the city gained one of what were to become known as the seven wonders of the ancient world: the Pharos, or lighthouse at Alexandria. The approximately 350-foot-high lighthouse was an engineering wonder for its time. Situated on the island of Pharos in the city's harbor, the lighthouse was built by Sostratus of Cnidus and stood for centuries. Records indicate the lighthouse survived until the twelfth century, but by the mid-fifteenth had become so dilapidated that the Mamluke sultan Qait Bey built a fortress atop the ruins. Like the lighthouse, neither the Mouseion nor the library survived into modern times. The Mouseion complex, including the library, was destroyed by civil war under the Roman emperor Aurelian in 272; a companion library, housed in a separate complex, was destroyed by Christians in 391.

Alexandria is also well known for its association with Cleopatra VII, the Egyptian queen and last of the Ptolemies, who in that city wooed and won Julius Caesar, claiming to have borne him a son. After Caesar's death, Cleopatra conspired with Marc Antony against Caesar's grandnephew Octavian. The unsuccessful conspiracy foundered in 30BCE when Octavian gained control of Alexandria and Egypt, adding them to the Roman world, and both Antony and Cleopatra committed suicide.

The Roman period in Alexandria (30BCE–313) brought changes to the city, principal among them religious conflict. Alexandria was said to be one of the cities where Saint Mark had preached in the first century; as such it was a stronghold of Christianity in the region, and Christian and Jewish communities alike resisted Rome's attempts to impose its own pagan religion upon the city. Persecution of Christians in Alexandria reached a high point under the emperor Diocletian, who is believed to have been responsible for the deaths of almost 150,000 Christians. Even after the emperor Constantine made Christianity the official religion of the Roman Empire, religious conflict continued in the city. This time, conflict arose over issues of doctrine, specifically, the nature of Jesus and his role within the Trinity. The Alexandrian church also found religious doctrine a way to assert its independence from Constantinople (from which it was governed following the division of the Roman Empire in 364CE). Declaring its belief in monophysitism (the idea that Jesus had a single divine nature despite taking on human form), the Alexandrian church held fast to this belief even after the Council of Chalcedon rejected the view in 451. This atmosphere of dissatisfaction with Byzantine rule contributed to the ease with which Arab armies took the city in 642.

After the Arab conquest of the city, Alexandria declined in importance. The Arab conqueror, Amr ibn al-'As, chose to found the new city of al-Fustat (later part of Cairo), which became the political and economic center of Egypt. Yet despite its being overshadowed by the new capital, Alexandria remained an important trading center, particularly for textiles and luxury goods.

Although the Ottoman conquest of Egypt occurred in 1517, little changed in Alexandria. Trade continued, but the city's waterways were allowed to become laden with silt. The gradual decline of Alexandria continued unabated; when Napoleon's troops arrived in Egypt in 1798, the "center of the world" had become a small fishing village with a population of under 5,000.

Muhammad 'Ali, the Ottoman governor of Egypt who came to power in the early 1800s, revived the city. 'Ali's desire to make Egypt into a modern nation meant Alexandria's return to relative prominence. Egypt needed a seaport, both for commercial and military reasons, and Alexandria was deemed suitable. The opening of the Mahmudiyya canal in 1820 linked Alexandria to the Nile, and thus to Cairo. European advisers and aid helped build a harbor, docks, and an arsenal; many Europeans stayed and took up residence in the revitalized city, helping to increase the population of Alexandria to more than 200,000. Alexandria became an important banking center in the mid-1800s as well. Alexandria also profited from Egypt's cotton industry boom in the 1860s (a result of the Civil War in the United States), the opening of the Cairo railway in 1856, and the opening of the Suez Canal in 1869. British shelling of the city in response to a nationalist revolt against the authority of the khedive Tewfiq (and against foreign influence in Egypt) by army colonel Ahmad 'Urabi resulted in heavy damage; rioting and looting worsened the situation, and the British used the opportunity to seize control of Egypt (which they retained until formal independence in 1922).

Alexandria was a key base of operations for the Allied forces in both world wars. In World War I it was the main naval base in the Mediterranean; in World War II it was nearly taken by German armies and was frequently a target of bombing raids. Alexandria played an important role in the Egyptian revolution and the government of Gamal Nasser as well. It was from Alexandria that King Farouk sailed into Italian exile in 1952, and the sequestrations of property after the 1956 Suez War, or Tripartite Aggression (of Israel, France, and Britain against Egypt after 'Abd el-Nasr's nationalization of the Suez Canal) served as the impetus for many minorities and foreign residents to leave the city. These sequestrations were followed by a series of nationalizations in the 1960s that were designed to further "Egyptianize" the country, and more foreigners deserted Alexandria.

While the city lost much of its international character after the revolution, it nonetheless benefited from Nasser's industrialization plans. Food processing and textile manufacturing industries in Alexandria grew rapidly. The port of Alexandria became extremely important during the 1967 war with Israel, when the Suez Canal was temporarily closed; the diversion of goods from Port Said to Alexandria swamped the port, and Egyptian president Anwar el-Sadat's policy of economic liberalization (*infitah*) begun in 1974 further increased the amount of goods coming into the city, straining its capacity. Encouraged by Sadat's economic policies, the merchants of Alexandria began demanding more financial independence from the government. The Sadat years also witnessed the discovery of offshore and onshore natural gas reserves (in Abu Qir Bay and at Abu Mai in the delta region near the city), which in turn fostered further industrial development, particularly in petrochemicals, iron, and steel. Attempts have been made in recent years to revive Alexandria's international character—the establishment of a free trade zone in al-Amiriyyah, the reopening of the stock exchange, and plans for improvements in the city's infrastructure are all designed to resurrect some of the city's lost glory. Nonetheless, it is safe to say that Alexandria is no longer *ad Aegyptum*, but instead has become a part of Egypt.

AMY J. JOHNSON

See also: **Egypt: Muhammad Ali, 1805–1849: State and Economy; Egypt, Ancient: Ptolemaic Dynasty: Historical Outline; Egypt, Ancient: Roman Conquest and Occupation: Historical Outline; Egypt: World War II And.**

Further Reading

Abdel-Salam, Hassan. "The Historical Evolution and Present Morphology of Alexandria, Egypt," *Planning Perspectives*, vol. 10, no. 2 (1995), pp. 173–198.

Empereur, Jean-Yves, trans. Margaret Maehler. *Alexandria Rediscovered*. London: British Museum Press, 1998.

Fraser, P.M. *Ptolemaic Alexandria*. Oxford: Clarendon Press, 1972.

Haas, Christopher. *Alexandria in Late Antiquity: Topography and Social Conflict*. Baltimore, MD: Johns Hopkins University Press, 1997.

Haag, Michael. *Alexandria*. Cairo: The American University in Cairo Press, 1993.

Marlowe, John. *The Golden Age of Alexandria*. London: Gollancz, 1971.

Reimer, Michael J. *Colonial Bridgehead: Government and Society in Alexandria*. Boulder, CO: Westview Press, 1997.

Saad El-Din, Morsi. *Alexandria: The Site and the History*. New York: New York University Press, 1993.

Alexandria and Early Christianity: Egypt

Early Egyptian Christianity (like Egypt as a whole in the period from 100 to 450CE) reflects sharp differences between its urban and rural expressions. Alexandria was a vast Greek-speaking cosmopolitan city, with a substantial Jewish community, and a hub of the Roman imperial system. Its famous library and imperially patronized museum helped make it one of the main intellectual and cultural centers of the Hellenistic world. Alexandrian Christianity was Greek-speaking, and it developed an intellectual tradition that made it one of the principal foci of Christian theological activity. But Alexandria had a massive hinterland, not only in the Nile Delta but also in the lands beyond, watered by the Nile and shading off into desert, supporting a large rural population engaged in agriculture. This population spoke Coptic (in several dialects), a language derived from old Egyptian, with a script derived from Greek. Ethnically, the population was descended from the old Egyptians, with an admixture of the darker-skinned peoples long resident in Egypt and known to the Hebrews as Cushites; the traditional religion was also derived from old Egypt. A vigorous vernacular Christianity grew up in these rural areas, and produced at least one innovation that spread across the Christian church at large, and helped to ensure the survival of Christianity in Egypt to the present day. The two Christian streams were never wholly separated. Alexandria and its hinterland were interdependent in the social, economic, and political spheres, and, in a period of rapid social change and increasing urbanization, townsfolk were often transplanted villagers. A single church structure linked Alexandria and the rest of Egypt, with all Egyptian bishops recognizing the leadership of the see of Alexandria, and its bishop as patriarch and coordinator.

Christian Origins

The New Testament writings speak of Jesus being taken to Egypt as a refugee child, but the origins of Christianity, urban or rural, are obscure. The Acts of the Apostles mentions a learned Alexandrian Jew called Apollos who became a notable Christian teacher, and some have attributed to him the anonymous Epistle to the Hebrews, since its style of argument is consonant with what we know of Alexandrian Jewish writing; but all references to Apollos locate his activity outside Egypt. In any case, Christianity probably entered Alexandria through its large Jewish community; church tradition from the fourth century attributes the foundation of the church to the Gospel writer Mark. The tract known as the Epistle of Barnabas, variously dated between 70 and 138, is probably Alexandrian. It reflects intense controversy between Christians and traditional Jews over the right use of Scripture; the author may himself have been Jewish. Fragments of an early Gospel, otherwise unknown, have been found in Egypt, but the first named Egyptian Christian writers (all using Greek) belong to the Gnostic wing of Christianity, which produced a radically Hellenistic interpretation of the Christian message, distancing it from the synagogue. There are also works of Gnostic tendency, purporting to represent the words of Jesus, most notably the Gospel of Thomas, found in Coptic translation. None of these works necessarily represents the ethos of Alexandrian Christianity of the time as a whole, but they do reflect the intellectual challenges that the Greek tradition in Alexandria presented for Christianity, and perhaps a reaction against an earlier period when Christianity was presented in essentially Jewish terms.

Clear evidence of an organized Alexandrian church appears around 180 (though its origins must be much earlier), with a bishop and twelve presbyters. Public preaching was hardly possible where Christianity was not a legal religion, and a key to Christian expansion lay in its teachers, resembling those of a philosophical school. The catechetical school of Alexandria, first heard of about this time, not only prepared enquirers for baptism, but presented Christianity in terms of the Greek intellectual tradition. Successive leaders of the school were Pantaenus, a converted Stoic philosopher, Clement, also a converted philosopher, of Athenian origin, and Origen, born of Christian parents around 185, who studied under Ammonius Saccas and other Alexandrian philosophical luminaries. Much of the writing of Clement and of Origen survives. Clement saw philosophy as part of a divine educational process to prepare humanity for Christianity, and the Christian life as a school of perfection. Origen was the most prodigious scholar of early Christianity, pioneering new forms of learned activity such as textual criticism and systematic theology, extending others such as the biblical commentary, and engaging with the whole range of Greek thought and science. Origen left for Caesarea after a dispute with his bishop, but Alexandria was his intellectual home. Like Clement he drew on the Platonism already used by the Alexandrian Jewish scholar Philo to present biblical teaching, and, like Philo, used allegorical exegesis of the Old Testament, thus maintaining the link between Christianity and Israel that more radical Gnostics rejected.

Origen's work underlies much of the theology of the third, fourth, and fifth centuries. The first major theological crisis, subsequent to the toleration of Christianity in 313, arose when an Alexandrian presbyter, Arius, produced a theory of the divine "sonship" which, (though this was probably not his intention) could be interpreted as making Christ a sort of demigod. Denounced by his bishop, Alexander, Arius found support elsewhere in the Greek world. The creed of the Council of Nicea (325CE) established the position generally regarded as orthodox, which was elaborated by the Alexandrian theologian and future bishop Athanasius (295–373). Both sides could claim to be drawing on Origen's legacy. Alexandrian theology continued to focus on the full divinity of Christ, and (perhaps assisted by Coptic spirituality) on the union of the divine and human in Christ—an emphasis later visible when a majority in the Egyptian church adopted a Monophysite form of theology.

Up to 313, Alexandrian Christianity suffered periodic violence, sometimes severe, from the Roman state. Origen became head of the catechetical school at a young age because his seniors were dead or dispersed. Persecution sometimes strengthened bonds; for instance, it drove Bishop Dionysius from Alexandria, but brought him into contact with rural Christians and provided missionary opportunities with non-Christians.

Coptic Christianity

Still less is known of Christian origins in the Coptic-speaking areas, where the literary sources are more sparse. The evidence suggests a background of regressive taxation with traditional temples used as tax collection points, administrative corruption and oppression, and abandonment of agricultural land. The earliest literature in Coptic consists of magical formulae. By the third century this gives way to the Bible translated into the Sahidic dialect of Upper Egypt, suggesting a steady spread of Christianity there. The earliest evidence of its nature comes in the story of Antony, born to Christian parents, wealthy by local standards, some 60 miles south of modern Cairo around 251. From his life as written by Athanasius, we gather that by about 270 (still in the age of persecution), Christianity was well established and organized in this rural community on the Nile. Antony evidently rejected Greek education and, seeking to be a radical disciple of Christ, sold his land to devote himself to following Christ's example. At first he emulated earlier holy men who had lived outside their villages, valued as sources of advice and wisdom. He next took the unusual step of moving into deserted areas, even tombs, recognized as the abode of demonic powers. His spiritual combats were interpreted as demonstrating Christ's triumph over the demons in their own territory. Others followed his example and sought his advice, until desert areas once left to demons could be described as a city full of those praising Christ.

Antony, who lived to a great age and gained significant celebrity, did not organize his disciples, believing that Scripture and spiritual conversation provided guidance enough. Organization was the contribution of Pachomius, a former soldier (c.290–346), who formed communities living under strict discipline to imitate Christ's life and seek perfection. Rural communities saw holy men and women as sources of counsel, power, and protection; the monasteries of Pachomius, numerous and often large, also became important economic units. They could be the landlords of share-cropping peasants, and places of supply and refuge in hard times. Antony and Pachomius, the principal figures of Coptic Christianity, were pioneers of the monastic movement that spread throughout early Christianity and took different forms elsewhere. In Egypt it helped to shape the self-understanding of a whole community.

Coptic Christianity was essentially rural. Antony and Pachomius understood the peasant worldview and the place of spiritual powers within it. It was also a vernacular movement. Antony refused the entry to cosmopolitan society that Greek education offered, and Pachomius eschewed use of it. In its origins the movement was not literary; some of Antony's letters have survived, but the early Coptic literature is essentially practical; its business is the spiritual life. As Greek works of theology or spirituality were translated, Coptic became a literary language for the first time. Meanwhile, Coptic Christianity developed a distinctive oral genre of its own. Sayings of the "Desert Fathers," often vivid, pithy, or gnomic, were treasured, collected, and translated into Greek and even Latin. They form perhaps the first literary expression of rural Africa, an early example of collected proverbial lore.

Coptic Christianity was charismatic, its leading figures subject to visions and extraordinary experiences. (Pachomius was credited with second sight and accused by more conventional churchmen of witchcraft.) This Christianity was radical, and honed under hard conditions. It produced single-minded dedication, and a capacity for extreme behavior. In the politico-theological battles of Alexandria, the passionate intensity of the desert monasteries was often a decisive—and sometimes an explosive—factor.

Christianity, in elevating the status of Coptic and giving a voice to its rural population, helped to shape a new Egyptian identity, capable of resisting Roman attempts to establish a single religious discourse throughout the empire. Between the mid-fifth century and the Arab conquest, this came to be expressed in explicitly Monophysite form, and reinforced the political and economic alienation of Egypt from the imperial center.

ANDREW F. WALLS

See also: **Monophysitism, Coptic Church, 379–640.**

Further Reading

Haas, Christopher. *Alexandria in Late Antiquity.* Baltimore, MD: Johns Hopkins University Press, 1997.

Pearson, Birger A. *Earliest Christianity in Egypt.* Claremont, CA: Institute for Antiquity and Christianity, 1997.

Pearson, Birgir A., and J.E. Goehring. *The Roots of Egyptian Christianity.* Philadelphia: Fortress, 1986.

Sellers, R.V. *Two Ancient Christologies.* London: SPCK, 1954.

Algeria: Algiers and Its Capture, 1815–1830

Although the regency of Algiers had declined considerably from its peak in the sixteenth and seventeenth centuries, when its corsairs had raided for slaves as far afield as southern Ireland and the English Channel, it was still strong enough in the early nineteenth century to capture ships belonging to weaker Christian states and hold their crews for ransom or to get undertakings that annual tribute would be paid. Not surprisingly, the regency was seen as a continued and nagging threat to naval commerce in the western Mediterranean. However, the port of Algiers was sufficiently well-fortified to repel most attacks, and even when its armaments were systematically destroyed by Lord Exmouth's fleet in August 1816, the regency was able quickly to repair the damage once the British had left. All together, it survived a total of seventeen separate operations mounted between 1541 and July 1830, when it finally capitulated to France.

This French military action was the culmination of a lengthy and at times tangled sequence of events going back over thirty years. In 1796/1797, the financially-pressed directorate government had purchased wheat

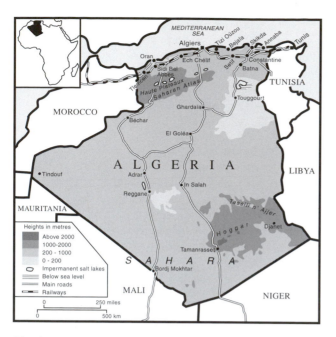

Algeria.

on credit at allegedly inflated prices through the agency of the Bacri and Busnach families, who dominated Algiers's foreign trade. In 1801 France set aside just over half of what was claimed (eight million francs), a sum that was held on account in Marseilles. By 1819, interest on the debt had increased the due amount to fourteen million francs, but after negotiation, Hussein, the *dey* of Algiers, declared himself satisfied with an offer of seven million. Later, he asked the French government to advance a part of this sum to himself to clear a debt the families owed him personally, a request rejected as inadmissible under French law. The *dey* then asked for the full amount to be paid, and tried to get the French consul, Pierre Deval, recalled as he believed the consul had personally influenced his home government to take a negative stance. Finally, on April 30, 1827, Deval was received in audience by the irritated Hussein, who asked him why he had not received a reply. The consul then made slighting remarks about the *dey*'s status as compared with that of his king, adding that it was useless/pointless (*inutile*) to expect a reply. Infuriated, the *dey* told him that the audience was at an end. Accounts vary as to what happened next: either he tapped Deval on the arm with his flywhisk to indicate that business had ended, or he struck him angrily once (or even three times, according to some authorities) on the sleeve with what is described as a flyswatter.

Whatever the *dey*'s intentions, Charles X's restoration government took this incident as a grave insult to the French monarch and sent him an ultimatum that, among other things, required the *dey* to make a public

apology and salute a French flag to be hoisted over the Algiers forts. Hussein refused to comply, and a French naval blockade was set in place on June 16. Some desultory and indecisive naval action ensued, and in January of the following year, new and less stringent conditions were offered to the *dey*, again in vain. Over the next eighteen months, the increasingly ineffective blockade continued, until Charles's final ministry, led by Polignac, was appointed in August 1829. Polignac suggested a Muslim solution to the problem, inspired by an offer from Mehemet Ali, ruler of Egypt, to send an army (financed by France) overland to supplant the *dey* and bring "piracy" and slavery to an end. However, the French military influenced the king to reject this proposal as logistically impractical. In February 1830, Polignac finally grasped the nettle, and with the king's approval, decided upon direct military action against the regency. A force of 37,000 soldiers, supported by 27,000 naval personnel, was placed under the command of General Bourmont and dispatched from Toulon to secure a beachhead at Sidi Ferruch, west of Algiers, as a prelude to a land-borne assault on the *dey*'s stronghold. This less direct approach, starting with a virtually unopposed landing, and culminating after a campaign lasting only three weeks in a successful attack on the port's less formidable landward defenses, is usually credited to the French restoration government's strategists, although the initial plan had in fact been drawn up by Napoleon in 1808, after an extensive reconnaissance, but postponed following complications in Europe. Algiers port surrendered on July 5, and other coastal towns submitted or were reduced over the next few months. The *dey*, plus the bulk of the Turkish military elite, were expelled, and the local population was informed that the French had freed them from tyranny.

The restoration government's intentions for Algiers were unclear, from the implementation of the blockade to the final victory. British hostility, rooted in its historical mistrust of its rival's ambitions in the Mediterranean, and expressed in tacit support for the *dey*'s obduracy, had inclined Polignac and his predecessors to hide behind generalities and high-sounding rhetoric: Polignac made great play of France's Christian and humanitarian purpose in seeking to rid "civilized" nations of the curses of piracy, slavery, and demands for tribute, and had even suggested the possibility of an international conference to determine Algiers's future (not followed up by his successors). Also, he seemed to have contemplated handing it back to its Ottoman overlords, an option that ran contrary to the actual situation on the ground with Bourmont's expulsion of the Turks. However, Charles X, who had seen the value of a successful military campaign as a means of restoring his waning prestige at home, had few doubts: as he told the British ambassador on July 20,

1830: "In taking Algiers, I considered only France's dignity; in keeping or returning it, I shall consider only her interests." The 1830 revolution, which swept him from power a few days later, aborted this process, and left his Orleanist successors with a choice that was more likely to favor retention because of the costs and prestige of military victory, as set against the uncertainty that would follow a departure from Algiers.

MURRAY STEELE

Further Reading

Bertier de Sauvigny, Guillaume de. *The Bourbon Restoration.* Philadelphia: University of Pennsylvania Press, 1966.

Heggoy, Alf. *The French Conquest of Algiers, 1830: An Arab Oral Tradition.* Athens: Ohio University Center for International Studies, 1986.

Perkins, Roger, and Douglas-Morris, Kenneth. *Gunfire in Barbary: Lord Exmouth's Battle with the Corsairs of Algiers in 1816.* Havant, Hants: Mason, 1982.

Spencer, William. *Algiers in the Age of the Corsairs.* Norman: University of Oklahoma Press, 1976.

Valensi, Lucette. *On the Eve of Colonialism: North Africa Before the French Conquest,* trans. Kenneth Perkins. New York: Africana Publishing, 1977.

Algeria: Conquest and Resistance, 1831–1879

At the end of May 1830, a French military expedition under the command of the minister of war, Comte de Bourmont, left for Algeria. The French troops landed in June at Sidi Ferruch, a small coastal town west of Algiers. Facing the weak and less organized army of the *dey*, they were able to rapidly crush it and capture Algiers on July 5. This French conquest of Algeria seemed to have taken place for a number of reasons, ranging from those viewed as trivial causes to those dictated by important political and economic considerations.

One reason was a financial dispute originating in France's failure to honor its debt to the regency of Algiers. Unsatisfied by the arguments of the French consul about this issue in a meeting in April 1827, the *dey*, Hussein, used his fly-whisk to strike his host's shoulder to signify the end of their discussion. This incident, known as the coup d'éventail, was viewed by French officials as a major diplomatic affront, particularly when the *dey* refused to apologize. Considering France's prestige and honor affected as a result, the decision was taken to send a punitive military expedition.

But the incident was not so decisive in itself as to justify a military invasion. Other motives can be adduced to account for the French venture. These had more to do with domestic problems and were not openly stated. The regime of Charles X, king of France (1824–1830), was experiencing internal difficulties and its popularity was declining. The idea of engaging in a military invasion of Algeria seemed a good oppor-

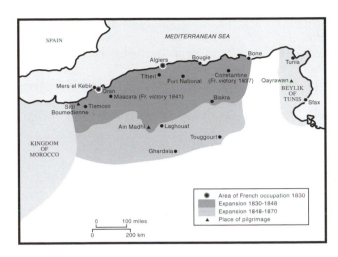

Algeria, nineteenth century.

tunity to divert attention from prevailing domestic political discontent. A military victory would then enhance the regime's popularity and ensure its success in the elections of July 1830. However, the revolt that ensued ended Charles's reign, and he was replaced by the "July Monarchy" of King Louis Philippe.

It is also worth mentioning that certain local economic and commercial circles, especially from Marseille, were supporting, if not putting pressure on, the French government to conquer Algeria. This was because their trade had stagnated during the three-year period (1827–1830) that France blockaded Algiers. The conquest would therefore help restore, and even promote, the affected trade exchanges.

In sum, at an early stage the occupation was not the outcome of a colonial policy thought through and carefully elaborated, but was largely a reaction to external and internal events and, at the same time, an attempt to rescue the regime of the restoration Bourbon monarchy and enhance its popularity.

After the occupation of Algiers and other coastal cities, there was no immediate resolve on the part of the French to engage in a full-scale expansion into other parts of the territory. Instead, they were officially content with what they considered as limited occupation, until the end of 1840. But in reality this did not prevent French military command in Algeria from attempting on several occasions to extend the occupation beyond the areas under their direct authority. To oppose this foreign invasion, resistance movements emerged. The first attempts to contest the French military presence in Algeria came from two leaders: in the east Hadj Ahmed, *bey* of Constantine (1826–1837), and in the west Amir 'Abd al-Qadir, proclaimed *amir* by tribes in the region of Mascara in September 1832.

In the eastern province of Algeria, Ahmed Bey refused the French demand to submit to their authority.

Rather, after 1830 he started transforming the whole area under his authority into an independent province with its own government, currency, and flag. This annoyed the French, and under the leadership of Marshal Bertrand Clauzel (governor-general in Algeria, 1835–1837), an attack was launched on Constantine in 1836. It ended in a total failure and disaster for the French troops, who suffered the loss of a thousand of their 7,400-man expedition. A second offensive, commanded by General Comte Damrémont, who replaced Clauzel, was successful; the city was captured in October 1837. Ahmed Bey fled to the south and continued the struggle, though he was more weakened and isolated as time went on.

In the western part of Algeria, 'Abd al-Qadir was able to unite various tribes to resist the French occupation. He also succeeded in creating an autonomous state in the region he controlled. In 1834, the treaty signed with the French General Louis Alexis Desmichels stipulated that the *amir* enjoyed sovereignty over western Algeria and recognized him as the commander of the faithful. His position was strengthened further when, in 1837, he signed an agreement with General Thomas Bugeaud, who had already defeated him at the battle of the River Sikkak in July 1836. Called the Treaty of Tafna, it redefined and extended the area under 'Abd al-Qadir's sovereignty, to include more than two-thirds of Algeria's territory. This enabled him to extend his authority into the eastern region and to strengthen his position in the west and center.

Toward the end of 1839, a violation of the territory under his control caused him to declare a state of war and to invade the plain of the Mitidja, the main area of French settlement. This led France to end its so-called official policy of limited occupation and reinforce its military presence in Algeria. Having decided on all-out war, General Bugeaud, commanding one-third of the total French army force (more than 100,000 men), was assigned the task of waging the war against 'Abd al-Qadir. Gradually the latter's territory was reoccupied by the French. Becoming aware of the fact that it was more and more difficult to continue the fight, he decided to surrender to the French in December 1847. He was detained in France until 1852. After his release he settled in Damascus.

The defeat of 'Abd al-Qadir did not mark the end of resistance. Popular movements contesting the French occupation and its administration continued until the beginning of the twentieth century. The inhabitants of the Zaatcha, an oasis near Biskra in the southeast, fought the French troops until their resistance was crushed in 1849. The invasion of eastern Kabylie in 1851 was also met with strong opposition. After successive expeditions, this region was brought under control in 1857. However, the rebellion in the whole region of Kabylie was not completely suppressed until its leader, Mohamed el-Mokrani, was killed in action in May 1871. After this rebellion, other uprisings of smaller scale took place: El-Amri in 1876 and the Aures in 1879. However, the southern region of Oran was to witness another serious insurrection led by Cheikh Bouamama (1881–1883).

Unlike the resistance led by 'Abd al-Qadir on a large scale, these revolts and uprisings, with the exception of the significant rising of el-Mokrani, were generally isolated and ineffective. It was not until 1954 that Algeria was to experience the start of a great insurrection on a national scale.

AHMED AGHROUT

See also: **'Abd al-Qadir; Algeria: Algiers and Its Capture, 1815–1830; Algeria: Government and Administration, 1830–1914; Algeria: War of Independence, 1954–1962.**

Further Reading

Ageron, Charles-Robert. *Modern Algeria: A History from 1830 to the Present*, Michael Brett (trans., ed.). London: Hurst, 1991.

Ageron, Charles-Robert. *Les Algériens musulmans et la France 1871–1919*. Paris: Presses Universitaires de France, 1968.

Clancy-Smith, Julia. *Rebel and Saint: Muslim Notables, Populist Protest, Colonial Encounters (Algeria and Tunisia, 1800–1904)*. Berkeley and Los Angeles: University of California Press, 1994.

Danziger, Raphael. *Abd al-Qadir and the Algerians: Resistance to the French and Internal Consolidation*. New York: Holmes and Meier, 1977.

Gallissot, René. "Abdel Kader et la nationalité algérienne: Interprétation de la chute de la Régence d'Alger et des premières résistances à la conquête française (1830–1839)," *Revue Historique*, 2 (1965): 339–368.

Heggoy, Alf Andrew. *The French Conquest of Algiers, 1830: An Algerian Oral Tradition*. Athens: Ohio University Center for International Studies, 1986.

Julien, Charles-André. *Histoire de l'Algérie contemporaine: La Conquête et les débuts de la colonisation 1827–1871*. Paris: Presses Universitaires de France, 1964.

Mahsas, Ahmed. *Le Mouvement révolutionnaire en Algérie*. Paris: L'Harmattan, 1979.

Ruedy, John. *Modern Algeria: The Origins and Development of a Nation*. Bloomington: Indiana University Press, 1992.

Thomas, Ann. "Arguments for the Conquest of Algiers in the Late 18th and Early 19th Centuries," *Maghreb Review*, 14/1–2 (1989): 108–118.

Von Sivers, Peter. "Insurrection and Accommodation: Indigenous Leadership in Eastern Algeria, 1840–1900," *International Journal of Middle East Studies*, 6/3 (1975): 259–275.

Algeria: Government and Administration, 1830–1914

The administration of Algeria between 1830 and 1914 falls into two phases: the first (1830–1870), primarily military and monarchist in character, reflecting the aggressive nature of the colonial occupation; and the second (1870–1914), civilian and pro-settler, reflecting the growing ascendancy of the local French *colons* over the Paris bureaucracy.

Following its capture of Algiers in July 1830, the French army established an administration, the legitimacy of which was confirmed after some hesitation by the incoming Orleanist monarchy. Under a succession of military governors-general, reporting to the French war ministry, the bridgehead at Algiers was extended through various expedients, including treaties with local rulers and piecemeal conquest, throughout the 1830s. The pace of this expansion quickened under Thomas-Robert Bugeaud (1841–1848), who defeated France's erstwhile ally Abdel-Qadir after a long campaign, and in 1844 established the colony's administrative basis: coastal areas of European settlement, organized on a civil basis; and in the interior, predominantly Arab/Berber areas under military governance. In these latter districts, existing *bureaux arabes* were formalized as administrative structures, with military officers "advising" traditional authorities, reportedly in a rather directive fashion. Meanwhile, those areas settled by Europeans developed along more metropolitan lines. In the wake of the 1848 revolution, and the renewed impetus given to assimilation policies, three *départements* (Algiers, Oran, and Constantine) were formed and given direct representation in the French parliament for the brief life of the Second Republic (1848–1852).

France's Algerian policy underwent several shifts during the Second Empire (1852–1870). Bugeaud's aggressive expansionist policy was continued by General Randon, later Napoleon III's minister of war, who extended the practice of *cantonnement*, of taking for the state tribal land that was apparently unused. Napoleon then abolished the governor-generalship in 1858, and created a ministry for Algeria and the colonies, run by his nephew. His visit to the colony in 1860 brought about another policy change, with the restoration of the governor's post, reporting directly to the emperor himself. However, the most radical turn occurred in 1863 when, influenced by his visit and his counselor, Ismaïl Urbain (a Muslim convert), he declared the colony to be an "Arab kingdom" (*arabe royaume*), with himself as protector equally of Muslims and Europeans, whom he regarded as equal partners in the state. Although his declaration greatly angered the *colons*, his policy differed in method rather than spirit from that of earlier assimilationists: a hybrid local government system (*communes mixtes*) was set up to bring Arabs and Berbers (meaning "Algerians") into the French system, while in July 1865, a decree was introduced allowing naturalization only if Muslim civil status was set aside. The principle behind this legislation

survived until World War II and ironically undermined its intrinsically assimilationist purpose, as few Muslims were prepared to reject Islamic values: only 1,557 Muslims had been granted French citizenship up to 1913.

The emperor's final attempt at liberalism, a constitution that would have allowed Muslims to participate in elections to a new assembly in Paris, was aborted by the 1870 revolution. The Third Republic's new parliamentary structure effectively excluded the Muslim majority, while rewarding the *colons* for their traditional republican loyalty. They were given direct representation in the assembly and senate, while the three *départements* became overseas provinces of France, separated from it only by an accident of geography. As a further mark of this administrative assimilation, in 1871, Algerian affairs were placed under the corresponding metropolitan ministries (*rattachements*), a policy that turned the governor-general into a minor functionary. Civil administration was progressively extended with the confiscation of tribal land after the 1871 revolt and the resulting spread of white settlement into the interior: *communes mixtes* were transformed into *communes de plein exercice*, corresponding to their metropolitan equivalent. Especially in urban areas, the *communes* were dominated by *colons*, who jealously guarded their exclusive right to elect their own mayors. The *bureaux arabes*, with their essentially paternalist attitude toward native Algerians, were eventually restricted to the military districts of the south (*communes indigènes*), much to *colon* satisfaction. After some years of formulation, the *code d'indigénat* was formally adopted in 1881, giving district officials powers to punish Muslims (with the exception of a privileged elite) without due legal process. Legal discrimination was matched by the imposition of the *arabes impôts*, a wide range of taxes imposed on native Algerians for such items as plows and date palms, and who in consequence were paying 70 per cent of all direct taxes in 1909, despite their general impoverishment. In summary, the *colons* saw assimilation as a process related to their exclusive political (and economic) needs, and one from which Muslim Algerians were excluded. This was an assumption from which the local administration rarely dissented in the period up to 1914.

The only major exception took place in the mid-1890s, when in response to *colon* high-handedness, Governor-General Jules Cambon succeeded in getting the *rattachement* system abolished in 1896, thus strengthening his own position: thereafter, Algeria came under the interior ministry. Cambon himself paid the penalty for this intervention: Étienne, the Algerian-born leader of the colonial lobby in the French assembly, secured his recall. The next stage in the reform process ironically gave back to the *colons* more than they had lost. In 1898 anti-colonial deputies complaining about the heavy cost of Algeria to the exchequer managed to obtain a separate budget for the colony, with a view to curtailing metropolitan expenditure. A complicated mechanism to advise the governor-general, the *délégations financières* (made up of three panels, two *colons* and one Muslim), was set up. Following *colon* protests, this body eventually secured actual control over more than four-fifths of the budget—a situation unmatched in the French empire—and gave the local settlers a wide measure of control over the allocation of services between themselves and the Muslim majority, even though they had only an advisory voice in the governor-general's superior council. Thus, despite fitful attempts to protect the interests of the Muslim majority, colonial reformers were unable to achieve much before 1914, leaving the *colons* in a position of considerable influence over all levels of administration in Algeria.

MURRAY STEELE

Further Reading

Ageron, Charles-Robert. *Modern Algeria: A History from 1830 to the Present*. London: Hurst and Co., and Trenton, NJ: Africa World Press, 1991.

Amin, Samir. *The Maghreb in the Modern World* Harmondsworth, England: Penguin Books, 1970.

Confer, Vincent. *France and Algeria: The Problem of Civil and Political Reform, 1870–1920*. Syracuse, NY: Syracuse University Press, 1966.

Martin, Jean. *L'Empire Renaissant, 1789–1871*. Paris: Denoël, 1987.

Roberts, Stephen. *The History of French Colonial Policy, 1870–1925*. London: Cass and Hamden: Archon Books, 1963 (reprint of London: P.S. King, 1929 edition).

Algeria: Muslim Population, 1871–1954

A series of calamities struck the Algerian Muslim population between 1867 and 1871. Already pushed onto marginal territory by French land confiscation, they were acutely vulnerable to the drought that hit in 1867–1868. Then, on the heels of France's defeat by the Germans in 1870, there was a large-scale uprising centered in the mountains of eastern Algeria led by Muhammad al-Mokrani. The French army crushed that revolt and still more land was confiscated. French refugees from Alsace and Lorraine, the provinces annexed by Germany, contributed to increased European presence in Algeria.

The 1870s and 1880s were in many ways the darkest decades in the experience of the Muslims of colonial Algeria. Europeans dominated politics at the local level. The government decreased funding for the Islamic courts and the three government schools that trained Muslim judges and interpreters. The settler-dominated

Tuareg Chiefs in Algiers, 1930s, during the celebrations for the 100th anniversary of the French occupation of Algeria. © SVT Bild/Das Fotoarchiv.

commercial agricultural economy expanded, especially after a blight hit French vineyards. It was during these years that there occurred the last of the desperate rural revolts, notably that of the Awlad Sidi Shaykh along the Moroccan frontier.

By the mid-1880s the situation began to change. As nationalist French politicians called for a war of revenge against Germany they realized that Algerian Muslims constituted a possible source of military manpower. But conscription would require political concessions. There were periodic waves of emigration by Algerian Muslims to the territory of the Ottoman empire that caused embarrassment for France in the Middle East.

Within Algeria, urban Muslim leaders took a more active role, protesting repressive measures and defending Muslim interests. The French metropolitan government saw the need to accommodate these leaders. In 1891, a new governor more sympathetic to Muslim interests, Jules Cambon, was appointed by Paris. He took measures to respond to the grievances of the Muslim urban leaders. There were expanding opportunities for Muslims within the French school system.

The rural Muslim population, however, lived in desperate poverty. A local rebellion around the settler village of Margueritte in 1900 dramatized their plight. The rebels' trial, held in France, proved a forum for exposing the injustices that led to the outbreak.

The French parliament finally passed a conscription law in 1911, drawing support from a small, French-educated Muslim elite. The conscription system was in place by the outbreak of World War I. Though there were incidents of resistance, many young Algerian men found in military service or wage labor in wartime France an alternative preferable to a life of poverty and humiliation in Algeria.

At the end of the war, with the inspiration of U.S. President Woodrow Wilson's call for self-determination, there was a brief upsurge of Muslim political activity in Algeria, focused on Emir Khalid, a grandson of nineteenth-century resistance hero Abd al-Qadir. But the movement lacked the ability to withstand harassment and manipulation by colonial authorities. More durable was the current of labor migration to France. This emigrant community proved the seedbed for Algerian nationalist politics. Messali Hajj, a wartime conscript who returned to France as a worker, emerged as leader of the North African Star, the first organization to clearly advocate independence.

Within Algeria, Islamic associations sprang up, concerned mainly with providing Algerian Muslim youth with a modern-style Arabic-Islamic education. They coalesced into the Association of Algerian Ulama in 1931, led by Abd al-Hamid Bin Badis, scion of an influential family in the city of Constantine.

There was some hope for political reform within Algeria, first in 1927 under liberal Governor Maurice Violette, and again at the time of the Popular Front government in France in 1936. But these efforts, which would have granted full political rights only to a minority of French-educated Muslims and army veterans, were resisted vociferously by settlers, many of them drawn to the racist ideologies of the European right.

With the fall of France in May 1940 Algeria came under the rule of the pro-Nazi Vichy regime. Prominent Muslim religious and political activists were arrested and interned. But in late 1942 British and American forces took over Algeria, bringing in their tow the Free French forces led by Charles de Gaulle. He recruited Algerian Muslim troops who fought loyally for his cause. Muslim leaders now set their aim on ambitious changes, embodied in the Manifesto of Liberty. They called for full political equality for Muslims and autonomy for Algeria. The war, which brought trade to a standstill, left most Algerian Muslims in deepening poverty. It also made them aware that a re-ordering of global power relations was in the making, one in which France would have a secondary role.

Demonstrations in favor of the manifesto were scheduled for V-E Day (May 8, 1945). The goal was to convince the British and Americans of the widespread popularity of the nationalist cause. Muslim leaders, warned by French authorities, called off demonstrations in most localities, but they went ahead in the small eastern city of Setif. Demonstrators unfurled the Algerian flag, and shots were fired. In the ensuing repression an estimated 50,000 Muslims were killed.

In the wake of these events the French government began one final effort at reform. In 1947 a new legal framework was established for Algeria that for the first time made Algerian Muslim representation possible in the French parliament. But the French administration in Algeria rigged elections in favor of its own malleable protégés.

The nationalists themselves were divided between moderates, led by Ferhat Abbas, and militant nationalists under Messali Hajj. There was a failed attempt in 1949 to launch an uprising. Then in 1954 the victory of the Viet Minh over the French at Dien Bien Phu helped convince a group of young nationalists that the time was ripe for armed struggle. They met in the summer and laid plans for an insurrection that was to begin on All Saints Day, November 1, 1954.

ALLAN CHRISTELOW

See also: **Algeria: European Population, 1830–1954.**

Further Reading

Christelow, Allan. *Muslim Law Courts and the French Colonial State in Algeria*. Princeton, NJ: Princeton University Press, 1985.

Kaddache, Mahfoud. *Histoire du nationalisme algérien: question nationale et politique algérien*. Algiers: SNED, 1980.

Meynier, Gilbert. *L'Algérie révélée*. Geneva: Droz, 1981.

Algeria: European Population, 1830–1954

White settlement in Algeria started immediately after the capture of Algiers in July 1830, at a time when the new Orleanist government in Paris was debating whether or not to withdraw, and on the initiative of Clauzel, the local military commander. By the time the decision to stay was taken, in 1833, some 10,000 settlers (*colons*—alternatively, *pieds noirs*) had established themselves in urban centers such as Algiers and Oran, and also on the fertile Mitidja plain. Although a succession of official settlement schemes organized by Clauzel, Bugeaud (the best-known of Algeria's early administrators), and Randon, failed, a flood of settlers arrived in the colony, seeking a fresh start in an area conveniently close to the European states of the western Mediterranean. Initial conditions were harsh, and the death rate high, inspiring the contemporary rueful comment that "the cemeteries are the only colonies that continually prosper in Algeria." Nevertheless, the white population steadily rose: 1840: 25,000; 1848: 110,000; 1860: 205,000; 1880: 376,000; 1896: 578,000—making Algeria second only in size to South Africa as a colony of white settlement.

The success of this colonization was underwritten by a series of expensive wars of conquest, and later punitive confiscation of land as a reprisal for rebellion, official decrees from 1844 onward giving the state control of allegedly "unused" tribal land, and in 1873, an endeavor to spread the benefits of "civilization" by introducing individual tenure, which ironically led to many indigenous Algerians having to sell off land to pay for the surveying costs involved. Through these and other processes the white rural population acquired about 40 per cent of Algeria's arable land, mostly located in the more fertile coastal areas.

The character of this rural settlement was essentially peasant. Successive administrators from Clauzel onward had favored the *petit-colon* peasantry over the plantation system (g*rands domaines capitalistes*) of other French colonies. Conservative administrators saw this as a solution to the impoverishment of French rural communities, especially in the south, while those appointed by republican regimes regarded the *colons* as reliable allies against royalists and the military. With the exception of a short period toward the end of the Second Empire (1852–1870), when Napoleon III proclaimed an Arab kingdom and halted land grants to settlers, this *petit-colon* policy continued until the economic dislocation following World War I. Algeria became the home of French peasant farmers seeking better opportunities abroad, joined by a substantial number of Spanish and Italian peasants similarly escaping from rural hardship. The size of this foreign element caused some concern in Paris, but they were soon assimilated into the French *colon* population, a process assisted by a decree in 1889 that automatically naturalized them, unless they requested otherwise. From 1878 to 1904, European peasant proprietors were able to obtain free grants of land, provided they occupied holdings for three years and carried out prescribed levels of improvement. However, from an early stage the majority of *colons* lived in urban centers, where they were later joined by peasants unable to make a living from Algeria's often hostile environment, who drifted to the towns in search of employment. By 1900, Algeria had a large "poor white" population, generally urban-based and demanding special treatment because of their white (and French) identity. The pace of land consolidation in the countryside accelerated during the interwar (1918–1939) period, with a contracting number of successful vine and cereal farmers.

The *colons'* political ascendancy was secured in 1870, when in response to the Paris revolution they ejected the local imperial bureaucracy in Algiers and won from the new republican authorities a number of important changes, including direct representation in the French parliament (three senators and six deputies), and control over the coastal *communes* with directly elected mayors. The Algerian-born deputy, Eugène Étienne (1844–1921) became their main advocate, holding office in various ministries between 1887 and 1913, and leading the colonial group in the assembly. From 1900, the *colons* were able to exercise control over a substantial part of the local budget, a unique situation within the French empire at that time. The *colon* ascendancy established itself behind the banner of *Algérie Française*, perceived as an integral and inseparable part of France, and having no other credible identity; where the interests of the *colons*, long-term defenders of the French republic and French values, prevailed over those of the Muslim (Arab and Berber) majority.

From the start, the *colons* had opposed any liberal, or suggestion of liberal, policies toward the "lazy Arabs" (as they were termed). In 1918, they greeted with extreme hostility Georges Clemenceau's modest proposal to reward Algerians for their assistance to the war effort by giving the vote to certain elite Muslims without their having to set aside Muslim civil status, a sticking point for the overwhelming majority of Algerians. This was eventually abandoned for less contentious reforms. Leon Blum's attempt to revive the proposal and extend the vote to some 20,000 Muslims without sacrificing their Muslim civil status was again attacked by the *colons*, who joined hands with the French right to get the legislation (the Blum-Viollette Bill) thrown out by the senate in 1938. Although the wartime de Gaulle administration introduced this reform in 1944, the Algerian settlers were able, with the help of the postwar revival of French imperialism, to renew their ascendancy in 1947, when the Organic Law gave them an effective veto in the new Algerian assembly. Ostensible attempts to balance interests by having two electoral colleges, equal in size (one *colon* with a small number of elite Muslims; the other, entirely Muslim), were effectively undermined by the provision that a second vote, requiring an overall two-thirds, could be demanded if requested by at least a quarter of the assembly members. The value of this constitutional instrument was enhanced by a process of ballot rigging that ensured the victory of Muslim conservatives over most of their radical opponents in the second college. At the outbreak of the Algerian revolt in November 1954, the 910,000 *colons* had thus made *Algérie Française* into an apparently unchallengeable—and permanent—feature of French policy.

MURRAY STEELE

See also: **Algeria: Muslim Population, 1871–1954.**

Further Reading

Abun-Nasr, Jamil. *A History of the Maghrib*. Cambridge and New York: Cambridge University Press, 1971.

Ageron, Charles. *Modern Algeria: A History from 1830 to the Present*. London: Hurst and Co., and Trenton, NJ: Africa World Press, 1991.

Amin, Samir. *The Maghreb in the Modern World*. Harmondsworth, England: Penguin Books, 1970.

Behr, Edward. *The Algerian Problem*. London, Hodder and Stoughton, 1961, and Westport, CT: Greenwood Press (reprint), 1976.

Horne, Alistair. *A Savage War of Peace: Algeria 1954–1962*. London: Macmillan, 1977, and New York: Viking Press, 1978.

Algeria: Arabism and Islamism

The best known formulation of the Algerian national identity is that coined by Abd al-Hamid Ben Badis in 1936: "Arabic is our language, Islam is our religion, Algeria is our fatherland." This statement served as an inspiring rally cry for the revolution that led to Algeria's independence in 1962. But, in certain respects, it is a problematic proposition.

The political unit known as Algeria came into existence with the external catalyst of Ottoman intervention in the 1520s. Before then there had been distinct state traditions in eastern and western Algeria. These separate traditions were still evident in resistance movements to the French conquest in the 1830s and 1840s, split between that led by Abd al-Qadir in the west, and the one led by Hajj Ahmad Bey in the east. The frontiers of the modern Algerian state were created by French colonial armies as they penetrated far into the Sahara, a process not completed until the early twentieth century.

Linguistically the country is divided between speakers of Tamazigh or Berber dialects, in the Kabylia mountains near Algiers, in the Aurès mountains south of Constantine, and among the Tuareg of the far south, and speakers of Arabic dialects. Many Tamazigh speakers also speak Arabic. Algeria's colonial language, French, was and remains limited to written communication or formal speech.

Arabism, as a cultural movement, has meant the promotion of the modern written version of Arabic through the development of print publications and modern schools. These phenomena first emerged in the eastern Arab countries in the late nineteenth century. They did not take root in Algeria until the decade before World War I.

It was only after World War I that cultural Arabism took on a clearly anticolonial association. There were now full-fledged national movements in Egypt and Tunisia, and their published expression was largely in Arabic. With the collapse of the Ottoman empire Algerians who had been living in exile and had been immersed in the modern cultural developments of the Middle East returned to Algeria and took up teaching and journalism.

At the same time, French education, compulsory military service, and labor migration to France worked to create a growing knowledge of French among Algerians. Those who worked and studied in France formed social ties with French people, and some married French women. Algerian nationalists sensed that this erosion of cultural and social boundaries made it important to take measures to revive Algerian religious and linguistic identity. They began by forming local associations to support Arabic and Islamic schooling. In 1931, these associations coalesced into the nationwide Association of Algerian Ulama, led by Abd al-Hamid Ben Badis (1889–1940).

The Association of Ulama promoted the doctrines of the Salafiyya, a reform movement seeking to revive the pure, unified Islam of the religion's early days, rejecting the heterodox practices of the Sufis, and condemning their collaboration with colonial authorities. But the Sufi orders had been a key element in organized resistance to the French conquest in the nineteenth century. Some orders, especially the Rahmaniyya, had links with nationalist parties in the 1930s and 1940s, and developed their own network of modern Arabic Islamic schools. A problem facing the nationalist movement in the late 1940s and early 1950s was the failure to achieve a united front on a wide range of issues. The rivalry between Sufis and Salafis contributed to this failure to find consensus.

It was the establishment of an independent state in 1962 that consolidated the roles of Arabism and Islamism as mainstays of the Algerian national identity. During the war, the Algerians relied heavily on the political and financial support of other Arab countries, especially Egypt, where Arabism was a key element of President Gamal Abdel Nasser's program.

The new government of Algeria sought to strengthen its ideological and institutional foundations. During the war the Association of Ulama had all of its property confiscated and its schools closed down by the French. Thus they presented the dual advantage of espousing a unitary ideology and lacking an independent resource base. The Sufi orders were suspect because of their autonomy and their past links to the colonial authorities and traditional power holders.

Under President Houari Boumédienne (1965–1977), Ben Badis was elevated to the status of a national icon, and Salafi doctrine received strong official endorsement. But relatively few resources were channeled into building mosques or religious schools. Arabism proved of more practical relevance to state policy as secondary and higher education underwent extensive Arabization starting in the early 1970s.

This brought an influx of teachers from Arab east, many of whom came to Algeria because of difficulties with their own ministries of education due to their connections with the Society of Muslim Brothers. They helped to promote Islamist views among a new generation of students. In the early 1980s, the government of President Chadeli Benjedid made efforts to co-opt this new wave of Islamism with government support. But by the mid-1980s the growth of grassroots Islamic sentiment outstripped the regime's ability to manage the Islamist movement.

Meanwhile, the political appeal of Arabism had ebbed. Iraq's defeat in 1991 seemed to confirm the bankruptcy of Arabism, while the victory of rebels in Afghanistan lent credence to the power of Islamism. But there was a wide range of tendencies within Algerian Islamism regarding political strategy and the degree to which their views should be imposed on other Algerians.

When the military regime suppressed the Islamic Salvation Front in early 1992 it had little in the way of an ideological arsenal to combat it, only the fears of many Algerians that the more radical wing of the front would prevail. The brutal excesses of the Armed Islamic Groups (GIA) worked to reinforce these fears but also undermined confidence in the military regime's ability to protect Algerian citizens. The resignation of most Algerians to the election as president of the army's candidate, Abdelaziz Bouteflika, in May 1999 seemed to express a sense of exhaustion with conflict among nearly all segments of Algerian society. Disaffected with unitary nationalists and religious ideologies, Algerians may be prepared to come to terms with their own diversity.

ALLAN CHRISTELOW

See also: **Algeria: Ben Bella, Boumédienne, Era of, 1960s and 1970s; Algeria, Colonial: Islamic Ideas and Movements in; Algeria: Muslim Population, 1871–1954.**

Further Reading

Entelis, John P. *Algeria: The Revolution Institutionalized.* Boulder, CO: Westview Press, 1986.

Malley, Robert. *The Call from Algeria: Third Worldism, Revolution, and the Turn to Islam.* Berkeley: University of California Press, 1996.

Ruedy, John. *Modern Algeria: The Origins and Development of a Nation.* Bloomington: Indiana University Press, 1994.

Algeria, Colonial: Islamic Ideas and Movements in

The Algerian experience under French colonial rule (1830–1962) ranks as one of the most intense and difficult Muslim encounters with modern Europe. There were repeated rebellions and a large-scale influx of European settlers. Algerian Muslims were exposed to French schooling and compulsory military service, and large numbers of men traveled to France in search of work. The experience climaxed with a seven-year revolutionary conflict. The development of Islamic thought and movements in colonial Algeria reflects broader trends in the contemporary Islamic world, but also needs to be considered within the context of the Algerian historical experience.

When the Ottoman administration collapsed with the French conquest of Algiers in 1830, Algerian Muslims were faced with three choices: armed resistance, emigration to a Muslim territory, or living under French rule and attempting to preserve their identity and promote their interests within a colonial framework.

The foremost resistance leader was Abd al-Qadir whose family had a tradition of attachment to the Qadiriyya Sufi order. Their base was in the Eghris Plain near Mascara in western Algeria.

Between 1832 and 1847, Abd al-Qadir used his religious prestige and organizational skill to lead sustained resistance to the French. After his surrender in 1847 he was, contrary to French promises, interned in France. During his five-year captivity he entered into dialogue both with French Catholics and Saint Simonian apostles of a universal civilization based upon science and run by engineers.

In 1852, Abd al-Qadir went into exile in the East, first in Bursa, Turkey, then after 1854 in Damascus. Through the colonial period until World War I, many Islamic scholars chose not to live in Algeria under French rule and went into exile, some joining Abd al-Qadir in Damascus, others going to Morocco, Tunisia, Egypt, or the Hijaz. Abd al-Qadir himself continued to cultivate an intense mysticism, but also kept up his ties to the Saint Simonians, helping to gain Ottoman consent to Saint Simonian Ferdinand De Lesseps, project of building a canal through the isthmus of Suez. Politically, Abd al-Qadir maintained a studied ambivalence toward both French and Ottoman authority. After his death in 1882 his sons and grandsons split, some affirming loyalty to France, others to the Ottoman sultan.

Within Algeria, many Islamic leaders continued to advocate armed resistance. Sufi orders played a key role in organizing rebellions. But as rebellions throughout the mid-nineteenth century met with failure, others counseled a realistic approach, urging cooperation in order to secure Muslim cultural, political, and economic rights within the colonial order. Some advocated reform and self-strengthening of Muslim society. Advocates of this approach included al-Makki Bin Badis, a Muslim judge in Constantine, who had a major role in creating a merit-based Islamic judicial bureaucracy in the 1860s, and Abd al-Qadir al-Majjawi, a leading Islamic educator who promoted scientific study and reminded Algerians that earlier Islamic scholars had excelled in the sciences.

In the 1890s, as the French sought to expand their influence in Muslim territories in North and West Africa and the Middle East, they took a more benevolent attitude toward Islam in Algeria. French Islamic specialists worked closely with Algerian scholars and helped them to publish their work and gain scholarly recognition, as did Muhammad Ben Cheneb at the International Congress of Orientalists, held at Algiers in 1905. But the passage by the French parliament that same year of a law separating religion and state crippled efforts to promote a loyal colonial Algerian Islamic religious establishment.

The decade before World War I saw the emergence of voluntary associations among Algerian Muslims, some of them dedicated to promoting Arabic Islamic education in order to sustain the Algerian national identity in the face of assimilationist pressures. In the 1920s these efforts intensified with the return to Algeria of men who had studied in the Arab East: Abd al-Hamid Bin Badis, Tayyib al-Uqbi, and Bashir Ibrahimi. In 1931 they helped establish the Association of Algerian Ulama in order to coordinate promotion of efforts to provide modern-style Arabic Islamic education at a national level. While Bin Badis and Uqbi were inspiring religious figures, it was Ibrahimi, with the most experience with modern intellectual developments in the East, who was the chief educational theorist and organizer.

By the 1930s, a number of Algerians with both French and Islamic educational backgrounds had gone to study in France. The best known of these is Malek Bennabi (1905–1973). His experience as an Algerian Islamic intellectual in France continued themes seen earlier in the case of Abd al-Qadir. He became involved in relations with French student members of the lay religious organization, Catholic Action, and he pursued a scientific education, studying electrical engineering. In the process, he developed a philosophy that emphasized the need for religious revitalization and the intellectual discipline of modern science. He spoke disparagingly of the secular political ideologies popular among many of his fellow Algerian students. These were the key themes in his best-known work, *Vocation de l'Islam*, published in 1954.

When the British and Americans pushed Axis forces out of North Africa in 1943, Bashir Ibrahimi (1890–1965) took the helm of the Association of Algerian Ulama. As nationalist leaders formulated Algerian grievances in a national charter, Ibrahimi contributed the document's religious plank. He called for the French government to compensate the Algerian Muslim community for the loss of religious endowment properties they had confiscated in the 1830s, and for scrupulous application of the law separating religion and state—thus allowing Muslims free religious expression without government intervention. Except for minor concessions, the French rejected these demands. Frustrated, Ibrahimi went into exile in Cairo in 1952. Bennabi also went to Cairo, in 1954. Both spent the revolutionary years (1954–1962) in the Middle East where they were thoroughly exposed to the ideas of Arab nationalism and of the Muslim Brotherhood. Both men would return to Algeria after independence where they contributed to the complex task of articulating the role of Islam within postcolonial Algeria.

ALLAN CHRISTELOW

See also: **Algeria: Arabism and Islamism; Algeria: Muslim Population, 1871–1954.**

Further Reading

Christelow, Allan. *Muslim Law Courts and the French Colonial State in Algeria*. Princeton, NJ: Princeton University Press, 1985.

Clancy-Smith, Julia. *Rebel and Saint: Muslim Notables, Populist Protest, Colonial Encounters (Algeria and Tunisia, 1800–1904)*. Berkeley: University of California Press, 1994.

Algeria: Nationalism and Reform, 1911–1954

After the defeat of the Muslim Algerian armed rising in 1871, Algeria was resigned to being governed as three French departments (Algiers, Oran, and Constantine). Few Muslims were naturalized, as the conditions regarding "personal status" were unacceptable for practicing Muslims. Very few even received a French education. Among those who did, a protest movement grew up in the early twentieth century that sought true equality of rights between Muslims and French-Algerians, without insistence on conditions for citizenship contrary to Islam.

This loosely organized movement took the name Jeunes Algériens. Founded in 1909, it rarely had more than a thousand members. It fully accepted French rule and was rejected by some Muslims for that reason, besides being denounced by the French-Algerian lobby (powerful in Paris then as later). The Jeunes Algériens accepted compulsory military service. The hope was that military service would be rewarded with French citizenship. Many Algerians fought in World War I, and in 1919 thousands of Muslim Algerians received French citizenship and the right to vote.

The movement for rights under French rule was continued by people such as "Emir" Khaled (grandson of the nineteenth-century resistance leader Abd al-Qadir, and an officer in the French army), who was prominent in local politics in Algiers in 1919–1923, and Ferhat Abbas (1899–1985), a chemist of Sétif who became a prominent spokesman of the French-educated (or *évolué*) class in the 1920s and 1930s. Their proposals, if adopted, would have ended the colonial order in Algeria; but as they accepted French rule in principle, their views came to be rejected by many Algerians. In 1926 a radical nationalist party, the Etoile Nord Africaine (ENA), was founded in Paris, mainly supported by the thousands of Algerian workers in France. It was founded with the help of the French communist party, but under Ahmed Messali of Tlemcen (1898–1974), who became the ENA's secretary-general in 1926, it was a nationalist party which at first saw the communists as a useful ally but gradually parted company with them between 1928 and 1933. From the start the ENA called for independence for Algeria.

Active in France, the ENA was at first unable to operate in Algeria where radical anticolonial activity was firmly suppressed. However, French rule was increasingly rejected in another way in Algeria, by Muslims who adopted ideas of reform of Islam preached by Muhammad Abduh of Egypt and others. They challenged the depressed state of the Muslims and the Islamic faith under French rule, and denounced the Sufi *marabouts* who were venerated as saints and approved by the French but who, according to the reformers, led people into false ideas. The leader of this movement in Algeria, Abdelhamid Ben Badis (1889–1940), founded newspapers and then formed in 1931 an association of Muslim teachers or *ulama*, the Association des Oulémas Musulmans Algériens. It spread rapidly, founding many schools, and became a nationalist movement with its slogan "Algeria is my country, Arabic is my language, Islam is my religion."

In 1936 the ENA was allowed to organize in Algeria. Meanwhile, a Muslim congress, dominated by the *évolués* and the Oulémas, met in Algiers and put forward "assimilationist" demands including universal suffrage. While the ENA had for the moment stopped calling for independence, it disagreed with the congress's and the Oulémas's loyalism. It rejected as highly inadequate the new government's bill, the Blum-Violette bill, which would have extended citizenship initially to about 20,000 more Muslim Algerians. The bill failed owing to opposition from the French-Algerian lobby, and meanwhile, the French left-wing parties, including the communists in Algeria (where a separate Parti Communiste Algérien [PCA], was set up in 1936) and France, were turning against colonial nationalism because of the priority need to face the Nazi-fascist danger. Accordingly, the Popular Front government banned the ENA on January 27, 1937.

Messali founded a new party, the Parti du Peuple Algérien (PPA), in Paris on March 11, 1937. It called for self-government, plus major reforms, but not for independence. Messali and some fellow leaders of the party were arrested in Algiers in August 1937. While Messali served a two-year sentence the party's popularity increased. In contrast the Muslim congress declined, but Abbas founded a new Union Populaire Algérien (UPA) in 1938, with policies less assimilationist than those he had followed before. The PPA was banned on the eve of World War II, and soon afterward Messali was arrested again; he received a sixteen-year sentence in 1941.

In February 1943 Abbas joined fifty-five other *évolués* to draw up a "Manifesto of the Algerian People," calling for equality, agricultural reform, and free compulsory education; a supplement was added calling for an Algerian state. General Charles de Gaulle announced in December 1943 that the Muslim Algerian elite would be given full French citizenship rights. But leaders of that elite now wanted more, and on March 17, 1944, Abbas launched the Amis du Manifeste et de la Liberté (AML), which aimed ultimately to form an Algerian republic federated with France. Fiercely denounced by the settlers, Abbas was also rejected as too moderate by many ordinary Algerians; the PPA had continued underground, and its more militant views prevailed at the AML central conference in 1945. PPA followers were involved in protests at Sétif in May 1945 that led to riots and ferocious repression; Abbas was among thousands arrested.

The French government allowed Muslim Algerians to elect thirteen representatives to the constituent assembly. Abbas, released in March 1946, founded a new party, the Union Démocratique du Manifeste Algérien (UDMA); his candidates won most Muslim votes in the elections for a second constituent assembly in June 1946, and in August he submitted a proposal to the assembly for an Algerian republic federated to France. Instead of this, the national assembly of the Fourth French Republic adopted in September 1947 an Algeria statute that created an Algerian assembly with equal representation for the Muslim majority and the settler minority, and very limited powers; the rule of France and the settlers was little altered. Nationalists believing in peaceful progress were further frustrated when the elections to the Algerian assembly in April 1948 were rigged on a large scale.

Messali was freed in 1946. He organized a new party, the Mouvement pour le Triomphe des Libertés Démocratiques (MTLD), to replace the outlawed PPA. While Messali (called Hadj Messali after his Mecca Pilgrimage in 1951) was highly popular among Muslims, he had become more distant from his party while in prison, until eventually the MTLD split in 1952–1954. By then Messali, arrested during a triumphal tour of Algeria in 1952, had been confined by government order to the area of Niort in France. His influence was still great, but events were passing out of the hands of leaders like Messali and Abbas (who was a minor political player by then). In 1948 some younger activists in the MTLD formed the Organisation Secrète (OS) committed to armed action against the French rulers. It was broken up in the succeeding years, but some of its members were able to form the Comité Révolutionnaire de l'Unité et de l'Action (CRUA) in 1954. That small group, joined by a few others, became the Front de Libération Nationale (FLN), which initiated the efforts that launched the war of independence on November 1, 1954.

JONATHAN DERRICK

See also: **Algeria: Conquest and Resistance, 1831–1879; Algeria: European Population, 1830–1954; Algeria: Muslim Population, 1871–1954; Algeria: War of Independence, 1954–1962; Colonialism, Overthrow of: Nationalism and Anticolonialism; Colonialism, Overthrow of: Northern Africa.**

Further Reading

Abbas, F. *La nuit coloniale.* Paris: Julliard, 1962.
Abun-Nasr, J. *A History of the Maghrib.* Cambridge: Cambridge University Press, 2nd edition, 1975.
Berque, J. *French North Africa: The Maghrib between Two World Wars.* London: Faber and Faber, 1967.
Nouschi, A. *La nuisance du nationalisme algérien, 1914–1954.* Paris: Editions de Minuit, 1962.
Stora, B. *Messali Hadj, pionnier du nationalisme algérien.* Paris: L'Harmattan, 1986.

Algeria: War of Independence, 1954–1962

The Algerian War for Independence began on November 1, 1954, when the FLN (*Front de Libération Nationale,* or National Liberation Front), a group advocating social democracy with an Islamic framework, called upon all Algerians to rise up against French authority and fight for total independence for Algeria. The FLN had been created the same year by the Revolutionary Committee of Unity and Action (Comité Révolutionnaire d'Unité et d'Action, or CRUA), in an attempt to unite the various nationalist factions in Algeria and to formulate a plan of action for resistance to French rule. Resistance was to include two specific tactics. At home, the rebels were to use guerrilla warfare as their primary method of resistance, while internationally, the FLN launched a diplomatic campaign to gain support for Algerian independence (including mobilizing support in the United Nations and sending representatives to Bandung).

One of the most important of the rebel leaders was Ahmed Ben Bella. Ben Bella had been convicted of robbing the post office in Oran in 1950 (an undertaking designed to acquire funds for the emerging nationalist movement), and sent to prison. After serving two years of his sentence, Ben Bella escaped from prison and took refuge in Egypt, where he was received with open arms by Gamal 'Abd el-Nasr (after the Egyptian revolution in 1952), who promised support for the Algerian cause. Ben Bella, along with other revolutionary leaders outside Algeria, played a key role in founding the FLN in 1954; he also was instrumental in arranging arms shipments to the Algerian rebels.

In 1956, several key events took place. The French government, having been unable to stem the growing tide of violence in Algeria, began calling up reserves, resulting in a doubling of the French military presence in Algeria; by April there were almost half a million French troops in Algeria. The Soummam Conference, held in August and September 1956, resolved two important disputes within the FLN leadership (despite the fact that Ben Bella was not present at the conference, his absence being variously attributed to intentional efforts by other leaders to exclude him and to Ben Bella's inability to elude French security forces and reenter Algeria for the conference). The conference decided that political affairs were to take precedence over military matters and that internal action must have precedence over external action. The FLN also further organized itself in preparation for a new campaign against French control.

The new campaign began shortly after the Soummam Conference ended. On September 30, 1956, the FLN bombed two locations frequented by young French colonists, the Milk Bar and the Cafeteria, marking the beginning of the battle of Algiers. Ben Bella was kidnapped by French forces the following month and put in prison, where he remained until independence in 1962 (he then served as Algeria's prime minister from 1962 to 1963, and president from 1963 to 1965). In November 1956 the French military was distracted temporarily by other events in North Africa, as French and British forces landed in Egypt as part of the Suez War (following 'Abd el-Nasr's nationalization of the Suez Canal Company); they were forced by international events to withdraw in early 1957. In Algeria, 1957 began with a reaffirmation of the permanent linkage of France and Algeria by French Prime Minister Guy Mollet. In late January, a general strike called by the FLN in Algiers was broken by French forces, and in February the French succeeded in capturing another key rebel leader, Larbi Ben M'hidi, who died in custody a few days later. The battle of Algiers officially ended later that year with the capture of the head of the Algiers branch of the FLN, Yacef Saadi.

In Algeria, French settlers, unsatisfied with the French response to the rebellion, seized government buildings in Algiers in May 1958, prompting the French army to take full control of the government of Algeria until June 1. Charles de Gaulle, elected president of France in December 1958, was no stranger to Algeria, having set up a shadow government in Algiers in 1943–1944 during the German occupation of France in World War II. Though a new offensive against the FLN was launched in July 1959, de Gaulle offered Algeria self-determination in September, prompting French settlers to revolt once more against the French government in Algeria. The revolt was unsuccessful, as were peace talks between France and the FLN in June 1960.

Meanwhile, in France, pressure had been mounting for an end to the war in Algeria. A growing number of French citizens began criticizing the conduct of the war, and allegations of the widespread use of torture by the French military were made public; Henri Alleg's 1958 work, *La Question*, which gave a detailed account of torture during the battle of Algiers, was banned by the French government after it had sold some 65,000 copies. French citizens also aided the FLN by serving as couriers to transport funds from the Algerian expatriate community in France to the FLN in Algeria, by helping hide FLN members, and by helping smuggle FLN members across national borders. The Algerian rebels were supported by many intellectuals in France, including Jean-Paul Sartre, Simone de Beauvoir, André Breton, and André Masson. These were some of the members of a group of 121 intellectuals who in 1960 published the "Declaration of the Right to Refuse to Take up Arms" (also known as the 121 Manifesto), that recognized the right to resist involvement in the war through illegal means (such as desertion from the French army). By December 1960, international pressure was mounting as well, as the United Nations recognized Algeria's right to self-determination.

Negotiations began again in 1961. A national referendum was held in February 1961 in which the vast majority of Algerians voted in favor of independence. However, the referendum results prompted another settler revolt, this time led by a group called the Secret Army Organization (OAS). Peace talks held in mid-1961 at Evian failed, and in late 1961 and early 1962 more than 200 Algerians were killed in demonstrations in Paris. France and the FLN finally signed a cease-fire agreement in March 1962; three months later a truce was signed between the FLN and the OAS. The previous year's referendum results were subsequently approved, and on July 3, 1962, after 132 years of French domination, Algeria became officially independent.

The announcement of independence caused someone million European settlers to flee Algeria, fearing reprisals and the loss of their favored political and economic position. The Algerian war for independence

had lasted eight years. More than 8,000 villages had been destroyed in the fighting, some three million people were displaced, and more than a million Algerians and some 10,000 *colons* lost their lives.

AMY J. JOHNSON

Further Reading

Evans, Martin. *The Memory of Resistance: French Opposition to the Algerian War*. Oxford: Berg, 1997.
Fanon, Frantz. *A Dying Colonialism*. Haakon Chevalier (trans., ed.). New York: Grove Press, 1967.
Fanon, Frantz. *The Wretched of the Earth*. Constance Farrington (trans., ed.). New York: Grove Weidenfeld, 1991.
Maran, Rita. *Torture: The Role of Ideology in the French-Algerian War*. New York: Praeger, 1989.
Stone, Martin. *The Agony of Algeria*. New York: Columbia University Press, 1997.

Algeria: Ben Bella, Boumédienne, Era of, 1960s and 1970s

Ahmed ben Bella and Houari Boumédienne emerged from the war of 1954–1962 as the dominant figures who would control the newly independent state of Algeria. Ben Bella had fought for the Free French in Italy, but in 1947 he severed his links with the French to create the Organisation Secrète (OS), which advocated an Algerian armed struggle to achieve independence from France. In 1950 Ben Bella led an OS armed attack on the Oran post office to obtain money for the revolt; he was imprisoned by the French but escaped after two years. In 1954, with Belkacem Krim, Ben Bella formed the Comité Revolutionnaire pour l'Unité et l'Action (CRUA), which later became the Front de Libération Nationale (FLN).

At independence in 1962, the Gouvernement Provisoire de la Republique Algerienne (GPRA) was divided between Colonel Houari Boumédienne, who commanded the FLN army in Tunisia and was supported by Ben Bella, and the more moderate members of the GPRA. The possibility of a civil war between these two factions loomed briefly when the new government, then headed by Ben Youssef Ben Khedda, dismissed Boumédienne for plotting a coup. However, Boumédienne advanced on Algiers with his troops, Ben Khedda fled, and a new, more radical government was set up with Ben Bella as prime minister and Boumédienne as chief of staff. Elections on September 20, 1962, were won by the Ben Bella-Boumédienne faction.

These two contrasting characters left a profound imprint upon Algeria both during the struggle against the French, and in the years that followed independence. The chances of the two men working well together were slim, for they differed sharply in their approaches to government and its problems. Ben Bella was the more radical of the two, Boumédienne a greater pragmatist. Moreover, Ben Bella, despite his popularity, became increasingly dictatorial. He promised Algerian support to other revolutionary movements while simultaneously eliminating perceived political rivals. On June 19, 1965, to forestall Ben Bella's dictatorial behavior and his apparent intention of establishing a Marxist state (as well as to safeguard his own position), Boumédienne used the army, the loyalty of which he had retained, to mount a coup to depose Ben Bella. Thereafter, despite enjoying only limited popular support, the austere Boumédienne would rule Algeria as a socialist until his death in 1978. At first he set up a military Council of the Revolution and attempted to create a "true socialist society."

Ahmed Ben Bella was born in 1918, the son of a small businessman of Maghuia in the department of Oran. He served with distinction in the French Army, which he joined in 1937 and he was to win both the Croix de Guerre and the Medaille Militaire. In the later 1940s, however, ben Bella joined the Algerian nationalist underground movement and became one of its leading members. After the 1950 OS raid on the Oran post office, he spent two years in prison, before escaping. He moved to Egypt where he obtained support for the nationalists from the new government of Gamal Abdel Nasser. With others he was instrumental in creating the FLN, which launched its armed struggle against the French in 1954. Seen as a major threat to the French position in Algeria, Ben Bella was the target of two assassination attempts during 1956, in Cairo and Tripoli. He returned to Algeria in 1956 to negotiate peace terms with the French prime minister, Guy Mollet, but he was arrested by the French. He was imprisoned from 1956 to 1962, a fact that allowed him to keep his radical reputation intact. Upon his release from prison, and following the events of that year when Ben Bella and Boumédienne emerged as the new government, Ben Bella was elected unopposed to the presidency of Algeria in 1963.

As president, Ben Bella had to create a working state out of the ruins of a devastated country when almost all the French *colons* (settlers) had returned to France, decimating the class of skilled workers. One of Ben Bella's first political decisions was to set aside 25 per cent of the budget for education. He nationalized the huge farms of the former French settlers and embarked upon other agrarian reforms. He supported the anti-Zionist Arab states opposed to Israel. At the same time he tried to develop cultural and economic relations with France.

Ben Bella, whose humanist instincts appealed to the people, enjoyed great popularity; however, he tended to govern on a day-to-day basis and, crucially, he failed to obtain the full support of the army or the FLN. Following Boumédienne's coup of June 19, 1965, Ben

Bella was to be imprisoned for fifteen years and was only released on October 30, 1980, two years after Boumédienne's death.

In many respects, Boumédienne was the antithesis of Ben Bella. One of a family of seven children, Mohammed Ben Brahim Boukharouba was born on August 23, 1927, at Clauzel near Guelma. When he failed to obtain deferment from conscription into the French army so that he could continue his studies, Boumédienne fled to Egypt. In Cairo he forsook his studies to join Ben Bella and the other Algerian nationalists who were there and changed his name to Houari Boumédienne. Once the FLN had launched the armed struggle against the French in Algeria in 1954, Boumédienne pushed himself forward in search of a leadership role. He was given military and then guerrilla training in Egypt and Morocco respectively and by 1958 had been promoted to commander of the Armée de la Liberation Nationale (ALN) in the west while, by the end of the war, he had risen to the command of the ALN general staff.

Following independence in 1962, Boumédienne became involved in the power struggle between the old guard nationalists led by Ben Khedda and the radicals led by Ben Bella, with whom he had identified. After Ben Bella was elected prime minister (taking 90 per cent of the vote) on September 20, 1962, he appointed Boumédienne minister of defense. On September 15, 1963, Ben Bella became president; he made Boumédienne first deputy premier. Boumédienne also retained his post as minister of defense and army commander, which placed him in an exceptionally powerful and influential position. By 1964 Ben Bella began to see Boumédienne as a threat and attempted to downgrade his influence. He nominated Colonel Tahar Zbiri as chief of the army general staff but Zbiri entered into a secret pact with Boumédienne to allow him to keep control of the army. Then Ben Bella forced the minister of the interior, Ahmed Medeghri, who was a strong supporter of Boumédienne, to resign. Finally, when Boumédienne learned that Ben Bella intended to oust him from office during an Afro-Asian summit due to be held in Algeria during the summer of 1965, Boumédienne mounted his successful coup.

Boumédienne was to rule Algeria from 1965 until his death in 1978. He was a "hawk" in relation to both Israel and in the councils of OPEC, and he played a prominent role promoting the idea of a New International Economic Order (NIEO), which was one of the consequences of the rise of OPEC power in 1973–1974. At first Boumédienne ruled through a twenty-six-member revolutionary council, but following a coup attempt against him in 1967 he ruled directly.

Austere and Spartan in his personal life, Boumédienne's principal source of support was the army.

Although he was a socialist and introduced a range of socialist measures he was neither extreme nor doctrinaire. He argued that people did not need speeches but wanted "bread, shoes, and schools."

GUY ARNOLD

See also: **Algeria: Bendjedid and Elections, 1978–1990; Algeria: War of Independence, 1954–1962.**

Further Reading

Ageron, Charles-Robert. *Modern Algeria: A History from 1830 to the Present.* London: Hurst, 1991.

Arnold, Guy. *Wars in the Third World since 1945* (2nd edition). London: Cassell, 1995.

Pickles, Dorothy. *Algeria and France: From Colonialism to Cooperation.* New York: Praeger, 1963.

Quandt, William B. *Revolution and Political Leadership: Algeria, 1954–1968.* Cambridge, MA.: Massachusetts Institute of Technology, 1969.

Algeria: Bendjedid and Elections, 1978–1990

Conquered by France in the 1830s and formally annexed in 1842, Algeria achieved independence as a result of a nationalist guerrilla struggle that commenced in 1954 and ended with the withdrawal of the French in July 1962. However, the group that took power, the National Liberation Front (FNL), was handicapped by deep divisions, especially between commanders of the nationalist army and the predominantly civilian political leadership headed by Ahmed Ben Bella. Although the latter was elected to a five-year presidential term in 1963, his lack of popularity within the armed forces led to a military coup d'état, led by Colonel Houari Boumedienne, in June 1965. Following his accession to power, Boumedienne assumed power as the leader of the National Council of the Algerian Revolution.

During the 1960s and 1970s, Algeria embarked on a socialist development strategy (land reform, nationalization of the oil industry, and an "agricultural revolution"), and between 1962 and 1988 the country had a single-party political system. The Algerian people took part in three major referendums in 1976, which not only confirmed Boumedienne in power, but also approved a new constitution and committed the country to a socialist development path. However, Boumedienne died soon after, in December 1978. He was briefly replaced by assembly president Rabah Bitat, who soon gave way to Colonel Chadli Bendjedid following a national election in February 1979. Bendjedid was unopposed in his reelection bid in January 1984. However, his government was shortly beset by a host of problems.

In the 1980s, with the economy in rapid decline, demands grew for more political and cultural freedoms. The growing importance of cultural demands was reflected in the rise of a movement of the minority Berber people as well as the emergence of fundamentalist Islamist groups. Economic decline helped stimulate the growth of an Islamist opposition to the Chadli Bendjedid government. The Islamists advocated a reversal of Algeria's modernization path under the FLN government, arguing for a culturally authentic replacement based upon the tenets of Islam and embodied in *shari'a* (Islamic law) to replace Algeria's French-influenced civil code. The Islamists pushed for reforms based on Islamic principles, including a strict dress code for women, increased religious broadcasts on radio and television, and the banning of public consumption of alcohol. Initially ignored by the Bendjedid government, the Islamists began to take over state-controlled mosques and to install their own preachers. Conflict erupted on several university campuses at this time between Islamists and secular students. The state's response was to clamp down on the Islamists by arresting the main leaders.

Economic concerns and the political problems posed by the Islamists led to growing tension within the government. While political infighting limited the effectiveness of reform efforts, critics charged that many of those entrenched in positions of power were reluctant to surrender economic and social privileges. Pent-up anger and frustration erupted into rioting in the capital city, Algiers, in early 1988, quickly spreading to other urban centers. These events shattered Algeria's reputation as an "oasis of stability" in an otherwise turbulent region. More than 500 people died when the armed forces opened fire on demonstrators in Algiers, while more than 3,000 were arrested. Following these events, President Bendjedid adopted a conciliatory attitude, converting what could have been a challenge to his authority into a mandate for sweeping economic and political change. A referendum in November 1988 led to voters overwhelmingly approving a constitutional amendment that reduced the FLN's political dominance. Henceforward the prime minister would have greater responsibility and would be responsible to the national assembly. Benjedid appointed a new prime minister, Kasdi Merbah, who quickly announced a new cabinet with many new faces, while agreement was reached that future elections would allow the participation of non-FLN candidates. In December 1988 Benjedid secured a third five-year term in office, achieving an overwhelming mandate in a presidential election in which he was the sole candidate.

The constitution was liberalized in February 1989; from that point on, multiparty elections were to be the chief mechanism for choosing popular representatives. The first polls under the new regime, at municipal and provincial levels, took place in June 1990. These elections highlighted the growing political importance of the Islamists. During the preceding few years the Islamist movement had been building its strength. Initially rather fluid and nebulous, the 1988 riots had encouraged it to solidify into a variety of formal organizations, including political parties with religious, social, cultural, and political objectives. The largest party was the Islamic Salvation Front (FIS), followed by Hamas (*al-Haraka li-Mujtama' Islami* [Movement for an Islamic Society]) and the MNI (*La Mouvement de la Nahda Islamique* [Movement for Islamic Renewal]). Smaller groups included *Rabitat al-Da'wa al-Islamiyya* (League of the Islamic Call) and the Party of Algerian Renewal. While differing in their tactics to achieve the Islamic state, they agreed that Algeria's problems were caused by the public downgrading of Islam during decades of Western-style modernization.

The FIS emerged as the main political rival to the ruling FLN in the municipal and provincial elections of June 1990, taking control of more than 50 per cent of Algeria's municipalities and winning over 54 per cent of the vote. The FIS platform was that Algeria should at once replace Western-style pluralism and representative democracy, replacing it with rule on the basis of *sharir'a* law and *shura* (popular consultation). The FIS (along with *Hamas*, MNI, and the Party for Algerian Renewal) then took part in elections for the national assembly in December 1991, winning 188 of the 430 seats in the first round of voting (3.26 million of the 6.8 million votes cast [47.9 per cent]). This impressive result was achieved despite the fact that its leaders, Abassi Madani and Ali Belhadj, were in prison. The other Islamic parties did much less well in the election.

Following the elections the army forced President Bendjedid to resign, replacing him with a five-man collective presidency, the High Committee of State (Haut Comité d'Etat, HCE), chaired by Mohamed Boudiaf. Boudiaf was assassinated in June 1992. The FIS was banned and thousands of its activists and supporters incarcerated, while an estimated 80,000 to 100,000 people died in the ensuing civil war.

JEFF HAYNES

Further Reading

Entelis, John. "Civil Society and the Authoritarian Temptation in Algerian Politics: Islamic Democracy vs. the Centralized State, in A.R. Norton (ed.), *Civil Society in the Middle East*, vol. 2. Leiden/New York/Koln: E.J. Brill: 45–86.

Kapil, A. "Algeria's Elections Show Islamist Strength," *Middle East Report*, 20, 1990: 31–36.

Seddon, David. "Elections in Algeria," *Review of African Political Economy*, 54, 1990: 70–73.

Sutton, Keith. "Political Changes in Algeria. An Emerging Electoral Geography," *The Maghreb Review*, 17/1–2, 1992: 3–27.

Algeria: International Relations, 1962–Present

When the Front de Libération Nationale (FLN) took power in 1962, it embarked immediately on a determined and high-profile foreign policy that was to continue throughout the party's thirty years of rule. It was characterized by strong opposition to Western imperialism and colonialism, solidarity with other Arab, African, and Third World countries, defense of Third World economic interests, and sympathy for leftist and revolutionary movements and governments. But the FLN's desire to maintain good relations with France, despite the bloodshed and bitterness of the war of independence, modified its generally radical stance.

Algeria's foreign policy mirrored its socialist domestic policies (in October 1963, for example, the last remaining 5,000 French farms were nationalized). Relations were soured by that and other factors, and France began to impose restrictions on the Algerians' migration to France from 1964. But the two countries negotiated a revision of the oil exploitation agreements, and a new fifteen-year pact was signed in July 1965, a month after Algerian leader Ahmed Ben Bella was overthrown.

Colonel Houari Boumedienne's coup on June 19, 1965, came on the eve of a scheduled Afro-Asian People's Solidarity Organization conference, which was intended to be held in Algeria. The conference was postponed and then never held, and many of Ben Bella's Third World and nonaligned allies were angered by the coup. Eventually, Algeria's foreign policy initiatives were resumed much as before, implemented and defended by Abdelaziz Bouteflika, foreign minister under Boumedienne as under Ben Bella.

The main difference under Boumedienne was greater emphasis on the Arab world. Algerians were generally sympathetic to the cause of Palestine, and after the 1967 Arab-Israeli war Algeria was a leading advocate of an uncompromising stance against Israel.

Relations with neighbors in the Maghreb were more complicated. Treaties of "brotherhood, good neighborliness, and cooperation" were signed with Morocco in 1969 and Tunisia in 1970. But in the 1970s, Algeria and Morocco clashed severely when Morocco and Mauritania annexed Spanish Sahara (Western Sahara) against the opposition of the territory's nationalist leaders, the Polisario Front, which declared the independence of the Sahrawi Arab Democratic Republic (SADR). Algeria recognized the SADR; a prolonged breach between Algeria and Morocco followed. Tindouf in Algeria became the main base for the SADR government and guerrilla forces and the main concentration of Sahrawi refugees. French military aid to Mauritania in 1977–1978 added to tensions between Algeria and France.

For years France and Algeria quarreled over many issues and yet continued to work together. There were disputes over implementation of the 1965 oil and gas agreement, before Algeria asserted itself with the nationalization (on February 24, 1971) of oil and gas deposits and pipelines, and a 51 per cent takeover of French oil companies. Meanwhile, when France and Algeria clashed over Algerian wine exports, the USSR stepped in and offered to buy Algerian wine. This developed further the increasing economic ties with Moscow that had been growing, together with military ties, since Ben Bella's time. Despite large-scale Soviet military aid with equipment and training, Algeria remained resolutely nonaligned. However, in the Cold War it was considered pro-Soviet in U.S. eyes, and Algerian policy was often vocally anti-American, especially during the Vietnam War. However, Algeria sold natural gas to the U.S. and was able to mediate over the U.S. hostages in Iran (1979–1981).

Algeria and France had to work together, above all because of the large and increasing numbers of Algerian workers in France, useful to both countries but especially to countless Algerian families, through their remittances. They numbered about 820,000 by the late 1980s. Algeria was concerned about immigration restrictions, police harassment, and racist attacks and propaganda, but needed the labor migration to continue and negotiated with Paris on aspects of it. Despite the various disagreements, President Giscard d'Estaing of France visited Algeria in April 1975. After years of worsening relations, an improvement led to a visit by President François Mitterrand in November 1981, followed by an agreement on natural gas pricing in February 1982.

Algeria's assertion of state power over the oil and gas industry was followed by full support for OPEC's aggressive oil pricing policy started in 1973. This was in line with Algeria's consistent calls for an end to the economic inequality between developed and developing countries. Representatives of seventy-seven countries met in Algiers in 1967 and agreed on the Algiers Charter of the Economic Rights of the Third World, founding the "Group of 77," which still meets under that name (though its numbers have much increased).

The death of Houari Boumedienne on December 27, 1978, and the accession of President Bendjedid Chadli, did not affect the structure and policies of the FLN party or state. Bouteflika was replaced, after sixteen years, by Mohammed Seddick Ben Yahia (who was killed in an air crash, and then by Ahmed Taleb Ibrahimi until 1988. In February 1983 President Chadli Bendjedid met King Hassan and the border with Morocco was reopened, but only on May 16, 1988, were normal relations restored with Morocco, and even then suspicion continued as Algeria continued to back the Sahrawi republic.

President Bendjedid visited France in November 1983, declaring, "It is a new page which the Algerian people inaugurate with the French people." In fact many causes of discord continued, especially relating to the Algerians in France; in the early 1990s France drastically cut back on the issuing of visas for Algerians. French aid, however, continued, and Mitterrand visited in March 1989.

Bendjedid paid an official visit to the U.S. in April 1985. However, he backed Libya at the time of the U.S. air raid on Tripoli in 1986 and during the Chad civil war. Algeria maintained its militant stand on Palestine, denouncing Egypt for its peace treaty with Israel in 1979, and organizing an Arab summit to declare support for the Palestine Intifada starting in 1987. In November 1988, the Palestine National Council met in Algiers and declared the independence of Palestine.

The Gulf War and crisis of 1990–1991 aroused passions in Algeria, where public opinion strongly favored Iraq. Internal affairs preoccupied Algerians more than ever after the military takeover of January 1992, depriving the FIS (Front Islamique du Salut) of its expected general election victory, and the subsequent Islamist guerrilla action leading to years of civil war. But the war inevitably affected foreign relations.

France generally gave the Algerian government diplomatic support and, it was reported, some covert military aid also; it was more favorable to the government than other European Union (EU) members. But Algiers protested at French and other Western expressions of concern over the government's own crimes. In particular, it was angry at the meeting in Rome in early 1995 at which several parties operating legally in Algeria met the FIS and agreed on some points, and at some Western sympathy for that effort to end the crisis. The U.S. and Germany were criticized for giving asylum to top FIS leaders, and Britain for sheltering some other Algerian Islamists. For some years Algeria broke off relations with Sudan because of its government's support for the FIS. Meanwhile, in 1994, renewed tension with Morocco led to closing of the border until 2001.

When Bouteflika became president in 1999 he softened the attitude to foreign concern about human rights; the war had, in any case, declined in intensity by then. Bouteflika has become one of the most prominent African heads of state on the diplomatic scene, and the OAU summit of 1999 was held in Algiers. However, the Western Sahara issue remains unresolved.

JONATHAN DERRICK

Further Reading

Entelis, J.P., and P.C. Naylor (eds.). *State and Society in Algeria.* Boulder, CO: Westview Press, 1992, chapter 9 (P.C. Naylor, "French-Algerian Relations, 1980–1990"), and chapter 10 (R.A. Mortimer, "Algerian Foreign Policy in Transition").

Malley, R. *The Call from Algeria: Third Worldism, Revolution, and the Turn to Islam.* Berkeley: University of California Press, 1996.

Ottaway, D., and M. *Algeria: The Politics of a Socialist Revolution.* Berkeley: University of California Press, 1970.

Algeria: Islamic Salvation Front, Military Rule, Civil War, 1990s

In October 1988 riots by disaffected urban youth shook Algiers, the Algerian capital. Their anger stemmed from high unemployment and deteriorating living standards that had accompanied the decline of oil and gas revenues over the preceding four years. President Chadli Bendjedid called in the army to quash the riots. Then he launched a bold political opening. The FLN (National Liberation Front) lost the monopoly it had held since independence in 1962.

The most important, but by no means the only, new party to emerge was the Islamic Salvation Front, known by its French initials, FIS. Its strength derived from a multitude of local Islamic associations and informal networks. These had sprung up mainly since the late 1970s but the history of such associations can be traced back to the early twentieth century. It sought to fill a void left by the regime that had spent large sums on sprawling apartment complexes but gave little thought to providing religious infrastructure for rapidly growing cities.

The FIS drew its ideas in part from local Algerian currents of modern Islamic thought, particularly from Malik Bennabi (1905–1973), mentor of the movement's leader Abassi Madani. As a student in Paris in the 1930s, Bennabi had been impressed by the French lay religious movement Catholic Action. He saw in it an alternative to the political movements that usually attracted Algerian students. These he found flawed both by the boundless ambitions of their leaders and the mindless sloganeering of the followers.

The FIS was also influenced by transnational Islamic movements, particularly the Muslim Brotherhood. Algerian Islamic leaders living in Cairo had been in contact with this movement since the early 1950s. It provided a model for religious social action ranging from establishing prayer groups to providing charity, job finding, and health services. Official and private parties in Saudi Arabia and Kuwait had a long history of supporting this kind of activity in Algeria.

There was also a current within the Algerian Islamic movement that stressed armed struggle. There had been an Islamic guerrilla movement led by Mustafa Bouyali, brought to an end with his death at the hands of security forces in 1983. A number of Algerian Islamic militants had seen service with the *mujahidin* in Afghanistan.

The FIS view on politics was ambiguous. Some members argued that elections were a clever snare. The FIS's most popular preacher, the young Ali Ben Hajj, lashed out against party politics as running against the grain of Islam's unitary spirit, yet he spurred the party faithful forward into the electoral fray.

Many Algerians were disaffected with the military-dominated regime that had held sway since independence and so gave their support to the FIS in municipal elections in 1990. But they still worried that the FIS, as its critics argued, stood for "one man, one vote, one time," in other words using elections merely to legitimate establishment of a new authoritarian regime.

The emergence of the FIS as by far the most powerful in a field of otherwise small parties prompted both the FIS and its opponents in the regime to plot their next moves. Neither proved astute in this game. The regime attempted to tinker with electoral laws in order to favor the FLN. But the implementation of "first past the post" electoral rules would provide an even greater advantage to the FIS. As for the FIS leadership, they attempted to use popular demonstrations in June 1991 in order to pressure the regime to accepting a fast track toward presidential elections. But the top leaders were jailed, and the FIS did not have such overwhelming popularity that it could force their release.

Neither the FIS nor its regime opponents seemed to grasp the necessity of appealing to the numerous smaller parties, nor did they recognize the importance of Amazigh (Berber) particularism or of showing commitment to the right to free speech and political expression. Both sides contributed to reducing the political question to a choice between the regime and the FIS, leading to the regime outlawing the FIS in early 1992.

There ensued a civil war, with the FIS establishing a military wing, the Army of Islamic Salvation (AIS), and more radical Islamists forming the Armed Islamic Groups (GIA). Unable to rely on the largely conscript army to suppress the rebellion, the government turned to establishing local militias, known as "patriots," to suppress the Islamic rebels. The conflict produced numerous atrocities, some attributable to the rebels, some to government forces.

The regime sought to enhance its credibility by bringing back from exile in Morocco Mohammed Boudiaf, a founding father of the FLN, to serve as president. He was assassinated in June 1992. Some Algerians blamed the Islamists; others believed the killing was ordered by high-level officials fearful that they would become targets of his anti-corruption drive.

The first major efforts toward peace were facilitated by a group of Catholic peace activists, the Community of Sant' Egidio. They brought together parties ranging from the FIS to the Front of Socialist Forces (FFS), based in the Berber Kabylia region, to the FLN. The resulting platform established principles for a solution to the Algerian conflict, including respect for the right of free political expression. However, both the regime and the GIA rejected the platform and violence and repression continued.

In 1996 President Liamine Zeroual made his own bid to gain support of a wide coalition by holding elections. A new regime-sponsored party, the Democratic National Rally, came out on top, but moderate Islamic parties, those with mainly Berber constituencies, and others all won seats, and some were rewarded with subordinate roles in government.

By early 1998 the death toll had reached, by various estimates, from 60,000 to 100,000. But later that year violence began to subside and a cease-fire took hold between the AIS and the army. Zeroual announced his resignation and a presidential election to be held in April 1999. Several prominent candidates distanced themselves from the regime, including the liberal Mouluod Hamrouche, Hocine Ait Ahmed of the FFS, and Ahmed Taleb Ibrahimi, associated with the Islamists. The military made clear its preference for Abdelaziz Bouteflika, a former foreign minister. Sensing a rigged election, the other candidates withdrew, so that Bouteflika won without competition.

He began his presidency by announcing himself as the man who would restore peace to Algeria. He released thousands of Islamist detainees in July 1999. He also alleviated the widely resented military service obligation. Nevertheless, the future of democratic liberties in Algeria remains very uncertain.

ALLAN CHRISTELOW

See also: **Algeria: Arabism and Islamism; Algeria: Bendjedid and Elections, 1978–1990; Algeria, Colonial: Islamic Ideas and Movements in; Algiers.**

Further Reading

Labat, Séverine. *Les islamistes algériens: entre les urnes et le macquis.* Paris: Éditions du Seuil, 1995.

Martinez, Luis. *La guerre civile en Algérie.* Paris: Éditions Karthala, 1998.

Quandt, William. *Between Ballots and Bullets: Algeria's Transition from Authoritarianism.* Washington, DC: Brookings Institution Press, 1998.

Rouadjia, Ahmed. *Les frères et la mosquée, enquête sur le mouvement islamiste en Algérie.* Paris: Éditions Karthala, 1990.

Willis, Michael. *The Islamist Challenge in Algeria: A Political History.* Reading, UK: Ithaca Press, 1996.

Algiers

The city of Algiers stands on a bay marking roughly the midpoint of Algeria's coastline. It draws its Arabic name, al-Jaza'ir, from the islands in the bay. This was the site of a small Phoenician trading center, and later a Roman outpost named Icosium, which had fallen to ruins by the time the Muslim town was founded in the tenth century. Prior to the sixteenth century, the main centers of state formation in northwest Africa had lain in the fertile plains of what are now Morocco and Tunisia. Parts of Algeria alternately fell under the control of these states or asserted their autonomy from them.

A transformation of this pattern occurred in the sixteenth century. Muslims expelled from Spain (during the Reconquista) found refuge in Algiers, which they found a convenient base for corsair raids against Christian Spain. In response, the Spanish seized the islands in the bay and fortified them. The Muslims of Algiers called upon Turkish corsairs who held the port of Jijel to the east to come to their aid. By 1529 they succeeded in expelling the Spanish from their island fortress, which they then dismantled, using the rubble to create a breakwater. This made Algiers into an important all-weather port. The city became the capital of a new province under the sovereignty of the Ottoman sultan.

The population of Ottoman Algiers was diverse, composed of Turkish-speaking military personnel, Kulughlis (the offspring of Turkish soldiers and local

The harbor at Algiers, Algeria, 1930. © SVT Bild/Das Fotoarchiv.

women), an established Arabic-speaking urban population, slaves (drawn mainly from south of the Sahara), and a Jewish community. In addition there were temporary residents including merchants from the Mzab oasis, laborers from Biskra in the Sahara and from the nearby Kabylia mountains, and varying numbers of Christian captives hopefully awaiting redemption.

The wealth derived from corsairing made possible the emergence of a strong urban community. A substantial proportion of this wealth was invested in religious endowments, which came to own many of the houses and shops in the city. Rent from these properties supported the building and maintenance of mosques, Islamic education, charity for the holy cities of Mecca and Medina, and public services such as the provision of water.

The French conquest of 1830 altered the city, first politically, then physically. The Turkish military elite departed, and some of the city's Muslim population fled, eventually to other Muslim lands. The French seized the property of those who had departed, and also took ownership or religious endowment properties. The Katjawa Mosque became a cathedral, in spite of large-scale protests by the Muslim population. Algiers's covered market, together with its mosque, was destroyed to provide space for a large public square, the Place du Gouvernement, now the Place des Martyrs. Other buildings were leveled in order to straighten and enlarge streets.

But the French left untouched the Muslim neighborhoods known as the Kasbah, which climbed up a steep hill just beyond the Place du Gouvernement. They also refrained from destroying the New Mosque, which stood at the edge of the Place, facing the bay. It remains today a landmark in the heart of downtown Algiers.

By the 1860s, Algiers began to thrive as a center of colonial administration and as the main hub of an agricultural export economy. As the colony became more secure, new neighborhoods sprang up outside the walls. Europeans of French origin came to dominate the city, while immigrants of Spanish, Italian, and Maltese origin filled out the lower ranks of European society. The city's Muslims, barely a quarter of the total population by the end of the century, were largely impoverished. Yet there remained an elite who held government jobs or had carved out specialized niches in the economy, such as timber or tobacco.

After reaching a low point in the 1870s, the Muslim community of Algiers regained numbers and importance. Before World War I, they had founded their own newspapers and cultural associations. Following that war, Algiers was the base for the first major political challenge to colonialism led by Emir Khaled. By the 1940s Muslims were a major force in municipal politics,

a factor recognized by socialist mayor Jacques Chevallier, though the city failed to meet the rapidly growing needs of its Muslim population for housing and services. The result was a burgeoning expansion of *bidonvilles* (shanty towns) on the urban periphery.

In stylistic terms, the French oscillated between imposing their own architectural and planning norms and accommodating styles of local origin. In the interwar period, French modernist architect Le Corbusier fused enthusiasm for indigenous styles with modernism in plans for renovating downtown Algiers. Though these plans remained on paper, this penchant for fusion was revived in independent Algeria with the works of Fernand Pouillon.

With the outbreak of revolution in 1954, the special configuration of Algiers, with the impoverished Muslim Kasbah at its heart, had a major role in the unfolding of events. Protestors could mobilize in the Kasbah and in minutes reach the Place du Gouvernement. Bomb carriers could slip out and sow terror in the prime European commercial streets. Control of the Kasbah was the chief object of the "battle of Algiers" in 1956.

With Algerian independence in 1962 there was a massive exodus of the European and Jewish populations. Property abandoned by them fell under government control, and new Muslim tenants moved in. But physically, the existing city remained much as it had been. The most important new developments took place on the urban periphery: the university complex at Ben Aknoun, the international fair grounds at El Harrach, a Pouillon-designed luxury hotel on the beach at Sidi Ferruch, where the French had landed in 1830, and a towering monument to revolutionary martyrs built in the 1980s on the heights above the city.

Turbulence returned to the city in 1988 as angry urban youth, frustrated over deteriorating living conditions, rioted for several days in October. Algiers again became the setting of large-scale political demonstrations. Since the army's crackdown against the Islamic Salvation Front in 1992, Algiers has suffered great insecurity affecting above all the densely populated older quarters and sprawling apartment complexes on the city's outskirts. Private security forces provide relative security for the elite living in the tree-shaded villas of such hilltop neighborhoods as Hydra and El Biar.

ALLAN CHRISTELOW

See also: **Algeria: Algiers and Its Capture, 1815–1830.**

Further Reading

Çelik, Zenep. *Urban Forms and Colonial Confrontations: Algiers under French Rule.* Berkeley: University of California Press, 1997.

Friedman, Ellen G. *Spanish Captives in North Africa in the Early Modern Age.* Madison: University of Wisconsin Press, 1983.

Hegoy, Alf Andrew. *The French Conquest of Algiers, 1830: An Algerian Oral Tradition.* Athens: Ohio University Press, 1986.

Hoexter, Miriam. *Endowments, Rulers, and Community: Waqf al-haramayn in Ottoman Algiers.* Leiden: Brill, 1998.

Horne, Alistair. *A Savage War of Peace, 1954–1962.* New York: Viking, 1977.

Allada and Slave Trade

The Aja-speaking peoples are, historically speaking, cousins of the Yoruba, with whom they share many cultural affinities. Indeed, by the early eighteenth century, the most prominent of Aja states was Allada, bordering the old Oyo kingdom in the south. Although it was an inland kingdom, Allada maintained control over some coastal settlements (such as Jakin, Offra, and Huedah [Whydah]), where European traders were stationed. Thus, the most significant economic development in the old Aja kingdom of Allada in the late seventeenth and early eighteenth centuries was the growth in the volume of slaves that passed through. Essentially, the Allada kingdom received substantial revenue from its principal port towns such as Offra and Jakin, as well as the kingdom of Whydah (with capital and port at Sahe and Grehue, respectively), and Great Popo. During the Allada kingdom's peak, the slave trade was its steady source of revenue and accounted for most of its commercial activities. The income from the slave trade enabled Allada to meet its obligations to its overlord, the old Oyo kingdom to the north.

However, by 1724, a new kingdom had been fully developed out of Allada. This new kingdom was Dahomey, which sought to repudiate the age-long suzerainty of Oyo (the dominant military power in the area), and thus promote the independence of its Fon peoples. To consolidate its independence from the old Aja-state of Allada, Dahomey's most prominent ruler in its incipient years, Agaja Trudo, organized many wars of expansion and conquest around the Aja country, creating in the process a new power center at Abomey, its capital. This development led to the rise of an atmosphere of insecurity, which truncated the relative peace and economic boom of the societies in this area. It also sought to discourage the slave trade as a major economic activity of the new Dahomey kingdom. Not surprisingly, European slave traders, apprehensive about continued investment in an unfriendly environment marked by internecine strive and civil wars, shifted base to the east of Allada, where the old Oyo kingdom had encouraged the establishment of new centers of commerce such as Ardrah (Porto Novo) and Badagri. Thus, new slave ports were developed in these two towns, which formed new centers for slave trade activities by Europeans as well as the Yoruba,

who continued to attack the new Dahomey kingdom until the latter acknowledged Oyo suzerainty.

At the same time, the fortune of slave trade in the Aja-speaking areas continued to suffer as attention also shifted to Lagos (situated further east of Allada), which soon became, in the words of a contemporary visitor, a veritable slave emporium. Lagos became a natural successor to Allada in the slave trade era because of three major factors. First, Lagos had a natural seaport. Second, it was relatively peaceful prior to growth of the slave trade, which transformed it from neglected backwater of Yoruba land to a nascent coastal kingdom with a semi-divine kingship along the lines of other Yoruba kingdoms. Third, by the mid-eighteenth century (when Lagos became attractive to the slave traders of Allada, and then Ardrah and Badagry), Akinsemoyin, who had ascended the throne, had been a familiar figure in the Aja country and had been well-known to many of the European slave traders. Thus, the political and economic decline of Allada led to the growth of new slave ports and new centers of European influence on the West African coast.

The relevance of Allada in the history of the slave trade in West Africa began to wane from the mid-eighteenth century when Dahomey, despite its problems with Oyo, gained full ascendancy in the politics and economy of the area. Indeed, by the middle of the eighteenth century, Dahomey had brought the whole of the Aja region under its influence. Correspondingly, new ports such as Porto Novo, Badagry, and Lagos, which were developed as a result of Allada's decline, projected a new slave-driven economy with its attendant consequences on the politics, economy, and society of the area. Succession disputes became frequent among claimants to the throne, as it was obvious that whoever controlled the throne would control the economy. Such political disputes characteristically involved violence. It was not surprising, therefore, that demographic repositioning became frequent throughout the coastal areas, as people moved from one area to another in an attempt to avoid the negative consequences of wars and civil disorders. The turbulence of the early and mid-eighteenth century West African slave trading coast could be attributed to the collapse of Allada and the rise of Dahomey.

KUNLE LAWAL

See also: **Aja-Speaking Peoples; Dahomey: Eighteenth Century.**

Further Reading

Akinjogbin, I.A. *Dahomey and Its Neighbours, 1708–1818.* Cambridge, 1967.

Burton, R.F. *A Mission to Gelele, King of Dahomey.* London, 1864.

Dalziel, Archibald, *History of Dahomey.* London, 1973.

Law, R.C.C. "The Fall of Allada: An Ideological Revolution?" in *Journal of the Historical Society of Nigeria* (JHSN), vol. 5, no. 1, December 1969.

Newbury, C.W. *The Western Slave Coast and Its Rulers*. Oxford, 1961.

Verger, Pierre. *Trade Relations Between the Bight of Benin and Bahia*, Ibadan, 1976.

All-African People's Conference, 1958

Kwame Nkrumah, the prime minister of Ghana, declared on March 6, 1957, at the independence of his country that independence for the Gold Coast was meaningless unless it was linked with the total liberation of the African continent. Following Ghana's independence, Pan-Africanism became identified with Ghana under Nkrumah's leadership. From the time of the All-African People's Conference of December 1958, the drive of African colonial states for independence was interwoven with the drive for continental unity. The conference opened a new chapter in the relations between Africa and Europe when it called upon the colonial powers to apply the principle of self-determination to their African colonies.

Following an earlier meeting of independent African nations in Accra in April 1958, a preparatory committee consisting of Ethiopia, Ghana, Guinea, Liberia, Libya, Morocco, Tunisia, and the United Arab Republic prepared for a larger meeting of the African states in December 1958.

From December 5–13, 1958, 300 people representing political parties and trade union leaders from twenty-eight African countries met at Accra at the invitation of Kwame Nkrumah. There were also observers from Canada, China, Denmark, India, the Soviet Union, the United Kingdom. and the United States.

The meeting was attended by representatives from Angola, Basutoland, Belgian Congo, Cameroon, Chad, Dahomey, Ethiopia, French Somaliland, Nigeria, Northern Rhodesia, Nyasaland, French Central Africa, Senegal, Sierra Leone, South Africa, South West Africa, Tanganyika, Togoland, Tunisia, Uganda, and Zanzibar. All of these countries, except Ethiopia and Tunisia, were still under some form of colonial rule. Individual notable attendees included Felix Monmie of the Basutoland Congress Party, M. Roberto Holden from Angola, Horace M. Bond, president of Lincoln University, and Marguerite Cartwright, an African-American author and journalist.

The preparatory committee chose Tom Mboya, general secretary of the Kenya Federation of Labor as chairman of the conference. Mboya in his plenary address compared the conference to that of the Berlin Conference seventy-four years before and told the gathering that Africans were tired of being governed by other people. In his view, Africans should control their destiny, and he therefore appealed to the United States and the Soviet Union to avoid involving Africa in the Cold War. Mboya wanted the colonized states to acquire political power as quickly as possible and urged Africans to avoid Balkanization.

W.E.B. Du Bois, the prominent African-American who championed Pan-Africanism during the course of his long life, also addressed the plenary. Aged 91, and suffering from illness, his wife read his speech for him. Du Bois told the conference that Pan Africanism meant that each nation must relinquish part of its heritage for the good of the whole continent; in making such a sacrifice, the African people would lose nothing except their chains, and they would gain back their dignity.

During the working session of the conference, five committees discussed and passed resolutions concerning imperialism and colonialism, frontiers, boundaries and federations, racialism and discriminatory laws and practices, tribalism, religious separatism and traditional institutions, and a resolution on the establishment of a permanent organization.

The committee on imperialism resolved to see the end of economic exploitation and declared its support for freedom fighters in Africa. It called for independence for areas still under colonial rule and territories dominated by foreigners who had settled permanently in Africa like Kenya, Union of South Africa, Algeria, Rhodesia, Angola, and Mozambique. The committee on frontiers, boundaries, and federations was also interested in the ending of white settlement in Africa and deplored the alienation of land for colonial use and underlined the theme of a United States of Africa. The committee on racialism voted to abrogate diplomatic and economic relationship with territories like South Africa, the Portuguese territories, and Rhodesia that practiced racism. It further urged dismantling of the UN mandate that placed South West Africa under the Union of South Africa. The committee on tribalism, religious separatism, and traditional institutions viewed these elements as obstacles to the rapid liberation of Africa and urged that steps be taken for political organizations and trade unions to educate the masses. The committee on the establishment of the permanent organization wanted the All-African People's Conference to be put on a permanent basis with a professional secretariat at Accra. The organization was to promote understanding among Africans, accelerate liberties for Africans, mobilize world opinion against the denial of fundamental rights of Africans, and develop a feeling of community among Africans.

Kwame Nkrumah, the host of the conference, concluded his closing remarks by emphasizing that Africa's independence and the creation of an African community were of paramount importance and that future Africa's economic and social reconstruction should be on the basis of socialism. Tom Mboya, the chairman of the conference in his final address told the people that the problems facing the conference were colonialism and European minority elements in East and South Africa and that the attitude taken by Europeans to African freedom would determine if they would be driven to violence.

The conference had a tremendous impact on the African independence movement, and many of the delegates from the conference returned home to redouble their efforts for independence. Congolese Patrice Lumumba for example, had been a little-known delegate at the conference, but he returned home and addressed a mass meeting in Leopoldville. There is no doubt that the ideas people like Lumumba brought home hastened Belgian's granting of independence to the Congo. Many African nations were imbued with the ideas of the conference and the confidence it inspired, and by the end of 1960, eighteen additional African countries had attained their independence. More important, Pan-Africanism moved from the realm of idea to become a practical reality, and the discussion that followed the conference contributed to the formation of the Organization of African Unity.

EDWARD REYNOLDS

Further Reading

Esedebe, P. Olisanwuche. *Pan-Africanism, The Idea and Movement, 1776–1991.* Washington, DC: Howard University Press, 1994.

Geiss, Emanuel. "The Development of Pan Africanism," *Journal of the Historical Society of Nigeria,* no. 3 (1967).

Hanna, William John (ed.). *Independent Black Africa.* Chicago: Rand McNally and Company, 1964.

Thompson, Vincent B. *Africa and Unity: The Evolution of Pan–Africanism.* London: Longmans, 1969.

Almohad Empire: *See* **'Abd al-Mu'min: Almohad Empire, 1140–1269.**

Almoravid: *See* **'Abd Allah ibn Yasin: Almoravid: Sahara; Yusuf ibn Tashfin: Almoravid Empire: Maghrib: 1070–1147.**

Alwa: *See* **Nobadia, Makurra, and 'Alwa.**

Ambaquista: *See* **Angola: Ambaquista, Imbangala, and Long-Distance Trade.**

Anglo-Boer War: *See* **South African War, 1899–1902.**

Anglo-Boer War, First: *See* **South Africa: Confederation, Disarmament and the First Anglo-Boer War, 1871–1881.**

Anglo-Zulu War, 1879–1887

The Anglo-Zulu war marked the end of an independent Zulu kingdom and the forcible integration of the region and its people into the white settler-dominated capitalist political economy of South Africa. On December 11, 1878, the British high commissioner, Sir Bartle Frere, provoked the war by presenting the Zulu king, Cetshwayo KaMpande, with an untenable ultimatum demanding what was tantamount to the dismantling of his kingdom. Cetshwayo had no choice but to reject the unreasonable demands. Subsequently, for fear of the supposed threat that the Zulu posed to Britain's neighboring Natal colony, and under the pretext of border violations and Cetshwayo's refusal to comply with the ultimatum, British and Natal forces invaded Zululand on January 12, 1879. The war ended in British victory with the burning of Cetshwayo's royal homestead on July 4, 1879, and his capture on August 28 of that year. Thereafter, the British established their authority over the Zulu through the suppression of the Zulu monarchy, the political division of the territory, and the stationing of a British resident there. British domination culminated in the annexation of the former kingdom in 1887.

The war represents a classic case of British imperial intervention driven by grand colonial strategies, yet precipitated by local events. Moreover, it remains the hallmark of imperial conflict with powerful African states, and was distinguished by some of the most remarkable military successes and blunders in colonial Africa. The postwar colonial settlement, however, was an expedient marked by an equally remarkable Machiavellian quality. It divided the vestiges of the kingdom against itself and served British interests for the political subordination and fragmentation of Zululand.

Prior to 1879, the Zulu kingdom presented something of an obstacle to both imperial and Natal colonial designs on southeast Africa. A burgeoning Natal settler population sought to expand north to satisfy their desire for land and labor resources they believed were held by the Zulu monarchy. Moreover, by the 1870s, Natal officials felt supremely confident in their ability to manage Africans under the system of indirect rule devised by Sir Theophilus Shepstone, secretary for native affairs, although this was tempered by an almost paranoid fear of the military might of the Zulu. Much of this fear was fueled by a colonial mythology of Zulu military prowess developed since the days of Shaka and the establishment of the kingdom in the 1820s.

Nevertheless, Natal demands converged with imperial designs to precipitate the war. The consolidation of the Boer republic in the Transvaal to the northwest, and its encroachment onto Zulu lands threatened not only Zulu interests, but also British desires to contain the republicans as well as to protect Natal's obvious route to the interior. For Shepstone, and many of the British officials he influenced, the Zulu monarchy and military system were a menace. Moreover, Frere, beset by conflicts with other African states in the region, was determined to establish a confederation of Boer and British territories, thus creating a united white state and a uniform policy for Africans within it. To that extent, the conquest and annexation of Zululand was "inevitable" in the eyes of nervous colonial officials and calculating imperial agents.

Under the command of Lieutenant-General Sir Frederick Thesiger, second baron of Chelmsford, more than 17,000 troops invaded Zululand. Of these, less than half were white, including some 5,700 British regulars and the rest assorted colonials. More than 9,000 of the force were Africans of the Natal native contingent, which gives some indication of the divisions between African societies, and that black race unity against whites was a product of a terrified colonial imagination. The Zulu forces, which significantly outnumbered the invaders, and had the home-ground advantage, could not sustain the fighting. They did not make full advantage of outmoded firearms procured through trade, and they were constrained by Cetshwayo's defensive strategy. The Zulu king, baffled by British aggression, still hoped to negotiate an end to the hostilities. This may account for reports that the Zulu *impi* (army) simply melted away after heavy engagements, rather than take the offensive, although heavy casualties and the need to tend to cattle and crops were more probable factors. Nevertheless, the Zulu had put up a formidable resistance that tempered the peace in their favor.

The war itself was far from the easy romp of an industrialized nation over a traditional African military system hoped for by the British. Chelmsford's advance was hampered by poor organization, logistical problems of supply over difficult terrain, and more importantly, shrewd Zulu tactics. Overly sanguine about their chances for a short and successful war, myopic British officers discounted reports of Zulu forces where they were not expected. Chelmsford then broke a cardinal rule of engagement by splitting his forces. He took half his own column in pursuit of a small Zulu reconnaissance party, leaving the rest camped at Isandlwana. It was here, on January 22, 1879, that a force of some

20,000 Zulu struck their most telling blow of the war, annihilating more than a third of Chelmsford's force. Following this massacre, a Zulu reserve force under Cetshwayo's brother, Prince Dabulamanzi, then abandoned the defensive strategy to besiege the fortified depot at Rorke's Drift just inside Natal. A Welsh regiment of 150 men, demonstrating the deadly effect of modern weapons, put up a heroic defense inflicting 500 casualties out of an estimated 2,000–3,000 Zulu attackers. The British garrison lost only 17, but won 11 Victoria Crosses for heroism, the most ever awarded for a single engagement. The Zulu managed one more major victory, overwhelming a cavalry force at Hlobane. Thereafter, however, Zulu defenses fell away. British forces pressed on to take Cetshwayo's capital, Ondini. By September 1, British victory was assured.

At the end of the war, the Zulu retained their land and formal independence, but at the cost of their monarchy, military system, and political cohesion. Cetshwayo was exiled, and it was the ensuing British "settlement" of Zululand that ultimately caused the destruction of the kingdom. Sir Garnet Wolseley, the new high commissioner for southeastern Africa, influenced by practices elsewhere in the empire, and the decidedly anti-Zulu monarchist, Shepstone, devised the notorious division of the kingdom into thirteen chiefdoms. By recreating and exploiting long-standing divisions within Zulu society, local Natal officials supported compliant appointed and self-aggrandizing chiefs such as Zibhebhu kaMaphitha and the white chief, John Dunn, against remaining Zulu royalists.

The settlement failed, and the result was a protracted and bloody civil war. In the interim, Cetshwayo and his missionary allies, Bishop Colenso of Natal and his daughters, Frances and Harriette, successfully petitioned the British government, which now had flagging confidence in the settlement, for the restoration of the exiled king, albeit with drastically curtailed powers and territory. This and the imposition of British administrators and a reserve territory as buffer between the Zulu and Natal only served to exacerbate the violence. Both Cetshwayo and his rival Zibhebhu enlisted the aid of white mercenaries in continued fighting. After Cetshwayo's sudden death on February 8, 1884, it was his son and successor, Dinuzulu, who turned the tide of the civil war. He engaged a formidable force of Boers, who had been encroaching on Zululand for decades, to support the royal cause. The exorbitant price for their success was the unprecedented cession of vast Zulu lands to the Boers to the northwest and along the coast.

Faced with the rapidly deteriorating conditions and coupled with imperial anxieties over a Boer-German alliance, the British intervened. After recognizing limited Boer claims in the interior of Zululand, imperial authorities formally annexed the remaining territory in 1887. Thereafter, colonial officials intensified the integration of a devastated Zulu society into the ambit of the wider colonial political economy. Thus, the British finally crushed Zulu independence with an administration that retained only certain features of the preconquest kingdom. Furthermore, they imposed taxes paid for by migrant wage labor that redirected the productive forces away from the monarchy system to the service of the capitalist South African state.

ARAN S. MACKINNON

See also: **Cetshwayo; Natal, Nineteenth Century; Shaka and Zulu Kingdom, 1810–1840.**

Further Reading

Ballard, C.C. *John Dunn: The White Chief of Zululand.* Johannesburg: Ad Donker, 1985.

Brookes, E.H., and Webb, C. de B. *A History of Natal.* Pietermaritzburg: University of Natal Press, 1965.

Bryant, A.T. *A History of the Zulu and Neighbouring Tribes.* Cape Town: Struik, 1964.

Davenport, T.R.H. "The Fragmentation of Zululand, 1879–1918," *Reality,* 11/5 (1979): 13–15.

Duminy, A.H., and Ballard, C.C. (eds.). *The Anglo-Zulu War: New Perspectives.* Pietermaritzburg: University of Natal Press, 1981.

Duminy, A., and Guest, B. (eds.). *Natal and Zululand from Earliest Times to 1910.* Pietermaritzburg: University of Natal Press, 1989.

Emery, F. *The Red Soldier: Letters from the Zulu War, 1879.* London: Hodder and Stoughton, 1977.

Guy, J.J. *The Destruction of the Zulu Kingdom: the Civil War in Zululand, 1879–1884.* London: Longman, 1979; Johannesburg: Raven Press, 1982.

———, "A Note on Firearms in the Zulu Kingdom with Special Reference to the Anglo-Zulu War, 1879," *Journal of African History,* 12 (1971) 557–570.

Laband, J.P.C. *Fight Us in the Open: The Anglo-Zulu War Through Zulu Eyes.* Pietermaritzburg: Shuter and Shooter, 1985.

———, "Humbugging the General?: King Cetshwayo's Peace Overtures during the Anglo-Zulu War," *Theoria,* 67 (1986) 1–20.

Laband, J.P.C., and Thompson, P.S. (ed.). *Field Guide to the War in Zululand and the Defence of Natal, 1879* (revised edition). Pietermaritzburg: University of Natal Press, 1983.

Marks, S., and Rathbone, R. (eds.). *Industrialisation and Social Change in South Africa: African Class Formation, Culture, and Consciousness, 1870–1930.* London: Longman, 1982.

Morris, D.R. *The Washing of the Spears: A History of the Rise of the Zulu Nation under Shaka and Its Fall in the Zulu War of 1879.* New York: Simon and Schuster, 1965.

Welsh, D. *The Roots of Segregation: Native Policy in Colonial Natal, 1845–1910.* Cape Town: Oxford University Press, 1971.

Angola, Eighteenth Century

Although the first century of the Portuguese presence in Angola had been characterized by an aggressive policy of territorial expansion and political interference with Angola's neighbors, by the late seventeenth century these options were no longer available. Strong opponents, such as the kingdoms of Kasanje, Matamba-Ndongo, and Kongo had halted further expansion. Although Angola was primarily an exporter of slaves, it no longer obtained the slaves by direct capture as it had during most of the seventeenth century.

The only exception to this pattern was in the south, in the land behind the small outlying colony of Benguela. Founded in 1617, Benguela had not been as aggressive as the main colony, and during most of the seventeenth century had acted as more of a trading post than military base. In 1682, however, Benguela became involved in the politics of the central highlands with the establishment of a new fort at Caconda, and sent a number of expeditionary forces into the region between about 1715 and 1725. These, however, did not result in any further conquests.

Military policy in Angola focused largely on gaining control of the trade industry, both in order to tax it efficiently and to prevent it from being appropriated by non-Portuguese shippers. Policy changes in Lisbon freed governors' salaries from the slave trade, both reducing their incentive to conduct war and increasing their desire to control trade. Dutch merchants had been particularly problematic in the seventeenth century, especially those fixed along what Angolans called the "North Coast," the coast of Kongo and the smaller states north of the Zaïre River. In the eighteenth century French and English merchants joined them, encouraging trade to their ports across Kongo. Many Angolan merchants, anxious to avoid taxes and with long-established contacts in Kongo were willing to ship slaves to the northern regions—even from the heart of Angola itself.

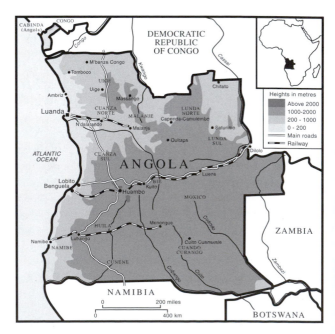

Angola.

Beginning especially after the Dutch were expelled from Angola in 1641, Brazilian commercial interests became more pronounced in Angola. Angola remained a major center for the slave trade, and much of its formal export trade was directed to Brazil. Merchant houses from Brazilian cities set themselves up in Luanda and even in the hinterland, competing with Portuguese interests, even as the governors and bishops were increasingly drawn from Brazil. In many respects, Angola was a subcolony of Brazil within the Portuguese empire.

For much of the early eighteenth century, Angola governors did not feel capable of enforcing their power fully, but dreamed of constructing posts and forts at key points on the "North Coast" in the "Dembos" regions and in the central highlands to channel all the trade to the coast. Military and financial resources to carry out such plans were lacking, however, and they had the often active resistance of Angolan settlers and the local allied African rulers who enjoyed the freedom of trade that Portuguese laxity allowed them.

The Portuguese government and army rested on a combination of resident settlers and alliances with local *sobas* (African rulers) who supplied troops for wars and porters for trade as part of their tribute arrangements. The Portuguese settlers were primarily landowners, whose estates were located along the Dande, Bengo, and Kwanza-Lukala rivers, and shipped a host of agricultural goods to Luanda to feed the hordes of slaves being exported from the colony. Provisioning the 10,000 to 15,000 slaves that passed through the city every year provided ample markets for this produce. In addition to agriculture, they or their agents, typically trusted slaves or clients called *pombeiros*, were engaged in trade, traveling to markets far from Angola (since the government banned whites from going into the interior). Settlers often married into the families of the *sobas*, and in many respects the rights and legal positions of the two groups became blurred. Equally frequently, the cultures of the two groups blended as well, Kimbundu being the most frequently spoken home language of settler and *soba* alike, while both also claimed competence in Portuguese. Christianity, the universal religion of all groups, included an ample mixture of elements from the Mbundu culture of the colony.

In the mid-eighteenth century the fortunes of the colony shifted, particularly as the Lunda empire, which had emerged in central Africa in the earlier eighteenth century sent armies to conquer the areas around the Kwango, disturbing political relations and sending thousands of slaves westward to the Atlantic ports. In addition, more powerful states came into being in the central highlands, especially Viye, Mbailundu, and Wambu. At this time, a new and aggressive governor, Francisco Innocenzo de Sousa Coutinho, arrived in Angola.

Sousa Coutinho and his successors sought to enforce more vigorous policies. He hoped to reunite Angola with Portugal and favor Portuguese interests against those of Brazil. Portuguese merchants arrived in the country in larger numbers, and the plans for new fiscal management were revived. He completed a new fort at Encoge intended to stop illegal trade across the Dembos, moved the fort at Caconda from the foothills of the central highlands to the heart of the highlands, opened an iron works, created a salt monopoly and many other programs intended to promote local industry and fiscal obedience. Later governors were equally aggressive, seeking to force the kingdoms of the central highlands into submission, and launching military campaigns to attempt to subdue the southern Kongo districts accused of supporting smuggling, and even far away Cabinda. At the same time they also sought to reinstate Portuguese culture and eliminate what they considered non-Christian elements from local religion.

In the end the more ambitious of the plans failed to achieve their objectives, being beyond the capabilities of the colony. Military campaigns proved expensive and disruptive, the forts were too difficult to supply against determined resistance, and even the large haul of captives for enslavements was impossible. Angola remained essentially one of several trading posts managing a sizable agricultural population that Portugal only partially controlled. Real control would await the last half of the nineteenth century.

JOHN THORNTON

See also: **Angola: "Scramble."**

Further Reading

Birmingham, David. *Trade and Conflict in Angola: The Mbundu and Their Neighbours under the Influence of the Portuguese, 1483–1790*. Oxford, 1966.

Miller, Joseph C. *Way of Death: Merchant Capitalism and the Angolan Slave Trade, 1730–1830*. Madison, WI: 1988.

Angola: Ambaquista, Imbangala, and Long-Distance Trade

Along the northern Angolan trade route, which led from Luanda into the interior, different communities had established themselves by the nineteenth century. They played a crucial role as intermediaries in the trade between the population groups in the interior further to the east and the Portuguese merchants in Luanda.

Two of the most important groups in the hinterland of Luanda and the Kwanza valley were the Imbangala at Kasanje, who settled outside the territory controlled by the Portuguese, and the Ambaquista, settling within the Portuguese colonial sphere. Contrary to central Angola, the area that was under direct Portuguese control stretched further inland and included portions where larger African populations had been living. Therefore, cultural contact was much more intense here than in other parts of Angola, and resulted in the creation of a mixed Afro-Portuguese settler community around the town of Mbaka, which was founded in 1618 and from which the name Ambaquista derives. This mixed population used both languages, Kimbundu and Portuguese, and at present, Eastern Kimbundu, which owes its existence to this intimate cultural contact, shows numerous vestiges of Portuguese. By the mid-nineteenth century the name Ambaquista (Mbakista) was in common use for this important branch of the Afro-Portuguese community.

Interestingly at a later stage, the fact that such mixed communities existed in Angola was used by the Portuguese as an argument to justify Portugal's colonial claims. They aimed at showing the close links between metropolitan Portugal and Angola, emphasizing the high degree of interaction between the European- and African-based populations. The Portuguese pointed at examples such as the Ambaquista in order to demonstrate that, as they claimed, Portugal's presence in Angola would necessarily lead to an acculturation of the African population. In the case of the Ambaquista, a far-reaching assimilation did in fact take place. Many European customs were adopted, and Portuguese influence was strong. Economically and politically the Ambaquista belonged to the colonial Angolan society, in contrast to their eastern neighbors, the Imbangala at Kasanje (Cassange). However, some observers from outside did not necessarily value these phenomena as a positive consequence of Portuguese colonialism. Toward the end of the nineteenth century, the strength of economically independent groups such as the Ambaquista was regarded as a potential threat to the new colonial policy.

Long before the nineteenth century, the Imbangala and the Ambaquista had both become involved in the slave trade, from which they had earned a good income. Due to their integration into the Luso-Angolan colonial society, the Ambaquista were able to adapt quickly to the changing economic situation after the slave trade was officially abolished.

In the case of the Imbangala, slavery had a much deeper impact on the sociopolitical system. In contrast to the Ambaquista, the Imbangala maintained political sovereignty until the mid-nineteenth century. Only when the slave trade had become insignificant, and this major source of revenue ceased to exist, did the system fail. Internal problems evolved because the position of the *kinguri*, the Imbangala king at Kasanje, depended on individuals who were loyal to him, rather than on the influential and antagonistic lineage elders who pursued their own policies and at times opposed royal decisions. As long as the *kinguri* was able to gather enough followers (usually slaves who lived in Kasanje in large numbers and did not belong to any of the powerful matrilineal clans because they were deprived of their social networks based on family ties), he was strong enough to counteract such secessionist tendencies. Furthermore, he gained a direct income from the slaves, whom he could also turn into material wealth by selling them to the slave traders from Luanda. Since in the nineteenth century the slave trade had decreased in importance, the position of the *kinguri* in the highly centralized state of Kasanje grew weak. Finally, the kingdom disintegrated and fell prey to the Portuguese advance to the east in the second half of that century.

Long-distance trade underwent radical changes in the nineteenth century because of the abolition process. Some of the effects were of equal significance for both the Ambaquista and the Imbangala, especially after the latter had come under direct Portuguese colonial administration. The coastal areas and the northern interior were confronted with a great number of dislocated people from the interior who had been brought there as slaves. The Portuguese government tried to encourage the production of new export goods. Soon coffee, palm oil, palm kernels, and groundnuts were produced on plantations in northern Angola. However, there was considerable competition by an emerging export-oriented African peasantry. Furthermore, other export goods, e.g., rubber, beeswax, and ivory, were more profitable. Unfortunately for the northern parts of Angola, these were provided mainly by the interior and transported via the central plateau toward the central Angolan ports. Thus, long-distance trade suffered more from the abolition process in the north than at the central route, where commercial interest shifted to the successful substitutes. In the north the cultivation of coffee, one of the major agricultural export goods in Angola, experienced a more difficult start, since world market prices went down in the later nineteenth century. Hence, the communities living in the Ambaka and the Kasanje regions needed to diversify more to cope with the changing situation. Economically, this led to a paradoxical situation: On the one hand, the north yielded less produce for export and thus the Ambaquista and the Imbangala, albeit economically successful, gained a smaller income than those participating in the central Angolan rubber trade. On the other hand, however, that was also, in part, an advantage, since economic activity centered increasingly around internal commerce, which would prove more stable in the long run. Also, in terms of general development this was rather favorable, since it went hand in hand with a slow infrastructure improvement that the central plateau only experienced when Portuguese settlers arrived in larger numbers.

AXEL FLEISCH

Further Reading

Birmingham, David. "Early African Trade in Angola and Its Hinterland" in *Pre-Colonial African Trade. Essays on Trade in Central and Eastern Africa before 1900*, Richard Gray and David Birmingham (eds.). London, New York, Nairobi: Oxford University Press, 1970.

Miller, Joseph C. "Slaves, Slavers, and Social Change in Nineteenth-Century Kasanje" in *Social Change in Angola*, Franz-Wilhelm Heimer (ed.). München: Weltforum Verlag, 1973.

Miller, Joseph C. "The Confrontation on the Kwango: Kasanje and the Portuguese, 1836–1858" in *I. Reunião de História de África. Relação Europa-África no 3° Quartel do Século XIX*, Maria Emília Madeira Santos (ed.). Lisbon: Centro de Estudos de Historia e Cartografia Antiga, 1989.

Angola: Chokwe, Ovimbundu, Nineteenth Century

Before the nineteenth century, the history of contact with the Portuguese and the degree of world market integration were rather different for the Chokwe and the Ovimbundu. Whereas the latter had been interacting directly with the Portuguese for a longer period, for the Chokwe the colonial encounter—in the form of direct contact with Portuguese military, traders, missionaries, and administrators—took place much later (notwithstanding the consequences of the advancing slaving frontier, which had been affecting the Chokwe at an earlier stage). However, in the nineteenth century, both groups became integrated into the Angolan economy on an increasingly global scale, taking on similar functions. For the Portuguese colonial economy, trade with Angola during the 1830s and 1840s was characterized mainly by the decrease in maritime slave exports. In the second half of the nineteenth century, trade with communities inland centered on rubber, ivory, and beeswax. These commodities were brought to the central Angolan coast by intermediaries. At first, Ovimbundu traders often called *ovimbali* dominated the trade in the central part of Angola serving Benguela.

Numerous Ovimbundu states had developed before the nineteenth century. These kingdoms occupying the central plateau in the hinterland of Benguela formed a network of political entities that had for a long time been marked by warfare and continuous raiding, as well as by the activities of the "barefoot-traders" serving as intermediaries between the producers in the interior and the Portuguese merchants along the coast. By the nineteenth century, significant changes led to new economic opportunities. Laws that prohibited the entry of Portuguese traders into the interior dating from the early seventeenth century were abrogated, and the number of Portuguese colonists (and with them, European influence) on the central plateau increased between 1770 and 1840. Some resident traders were considerably successful and established

themselves in close vicinity to the Ovimbundu kings to whom they paid tribute. Whereas before raiding had rendered this risky, the local authorities were now inclined to take advantage of the commercial opportunities that were due to the higher number of traders settling in their sphere of influence. Some of the coastal traders were absorbed into the inland communities. At the same time, the Ovimbundu themselves became more and more involved in trade, especially after the number of Portuguese residents decreased in the 1830s and 1840s due to the abolition of the slave trade. From the 1840s the Ovimbundu experienced a great commercial development, following the growing demand for ivory and other produce, which substituted for the slave trade.

It is important to note, however, that not all of the relatively small Ovimbundu kingdoms acted alike in this process. As a matter of fact, formerly more important kingdoms, such as Caconda, became less powerful, whereas Viye (Bié), Mbailundu (Bailundo), and Wambu (Huambo) grew in importance. The significance of the particular Ovimbundu kingdoms relied less on military strength than on commercial success. This became most obvious when the coffee prices on the world market dropped in the later nineteenth century, whereas the rubber export flourished. As a consequence, during this period the towns along the central coast became more significant for the Angolan export economy than Luanda. Toward the end of the nineteenth century, the Portuguese interest in central Angola as an area for European settlement grew fast and the number of Portuguese colonists from Europe rose sharply on the central plateau. With the influx of Portuguese settlers and in particular when the rubber boom came to an end, the African population in this area, largely Ovimbundu, faced a difficult situation. Those who had taken an active part as skilled employees or traders usually tried to find remunerated work, thus creating a labor force for the Portuguese settlers, whereas the larger part of the population took to small-scale farming and petty trade.

Contrary to the Ovimbundu traders, the Chokwe had not taken an active role in the commerce with the coast before the nineteenth century. Instead, they were affected by slave raids from their western neighbors. The nineteenth century saw a remarkably quick expansion of the Chokwe in the eastern half of present-day Angola. The changing European demand for African products initiated the success story of the Chokwe, who entered the long-distance commercial stage in the mid-nineteenth century. After Portugal had abolished its monopoly on ivory in 1830, prices went up 300 per cent. Wax exports rose even more drastically in the mid-nineteenth century, to the benefit of the Chokwe and Lucazi who had so far been excluded from active participation in long-distance trade. Being situated between the powerful Lunda empire and the well-established trade routes of the Ovimbundu and Imbangala, the Chokwe took advantage of the fact that their core land in present-day Moxiko provided large quantities of ivory and wax. The Chokwe relied on local products where their competitors, the Ovimbundu, spent some of the income gained by trade on the European goods they had already adopted, e.g., cloths, salt, metal knives. Therefore, the Chokwe could build up an arsenal of fire weapons within a relatively short time. This enabled them to hunt larger numbers of elephants and added to their commercial success. At the same time, they grew in military strength.

Both aspects had important consequences. Within a few years, the elephant population had been decimated in the Chokwe area. The Chokwe hunters came to an agreement with the Lunda who did not exploit ivory as a resource and allowed the Chokwe to enter their area in return for a share in the economic yield. However, shortly after the temporary hunting parties had begun, Chokwe started to build permanent settlements in this area. At the same time, they integrated women of other ethnic groups into their own. Intermarriage between ethnic groups was frequent, and the number of people regarding themselves as Chokwe increased rapidly. After the hunting grounds of the Lunda had also been emptied of elephants, the Chokwe tried a similar system with regard to their northeastern neighbors, the Luba. However, the Luba themselves hunted elephants, and the role of the Chokwe changed from that of producers to commercial intermediaries who traded in the goods they formerly produced. Hence they became competitors to the Imbangala and Ovimbundu traders.

From that point on, Chokwe were frequently to be seen at the coastal ports. The system of trade routes in the interior grew. The Chokwe bridged the two older latitudinal trade routes in a north-south direction. By the time elephant hunting became increasingly difficult, the rising demand for rubber once again changed the economic basis of the Angolan trade system. Due to the high world market prices, those participating in the trade of rubber experienced a material wealth unknown in these regions before. Both the Ovimbundu and the Chokwe had by now highly developed commercial skills and benefited from the rubber boom.

Unfortunately, the boom came to an end in 1910, and the Chokwe, who had changed their entire economic system within a relatively short time, were deprived of their major sources of income. The socioeconomic conditions that had led to population growth became less favorable. The Chokwe migrations once motivated by population growth now received further stimulus by the relative poverty that these people experienced after the breakdown of the rubber trade

and the appearance of the Portuguese military conquering southeastern Angola. At this stage the Chokwe could rely solely on subsistence farming, craftsmanship, and remunerated work, albeit to a lesser extent than the Ovimbundu.

AXEL FLEISCH

Further Reading

Birmingham, David. "Early African Trade in Angola and Its Hinterland," in *Pre-Colonial African Trade. Essays on Trade in Central and Eastern Africa Before 1900*, Richard Gray and David Birmingham (eds.). London, New York, Nairobi: Oxford University Press, 1970.

Clarence-Smith, W.G. "Portuguese Trade with Africa in the nineteenth Century: An Economic Imperialism (with an Appendix on the Trade of Angola)," in *Figuring African Trade. Proceedings of the Symposium on the Quantification and Structure of the Import and Export and Long-Distance Trade in Africa 1800–1913*. G. Liesegang, H. Pasch, and A. Jones (eds.). Berlin: Dietrich Reimer Verlag, 1986.

Miller, Joseph C. "Chokwe Trade and Conquest in the Nineteenth Century," in *Pre-Colonial African Trade. Essays on Trade in Central and Eastern Africa before 1900*. Richard Gray and David Birmingham (eds.). London, New York, Nairobi: Oxford University Press, 1970.

Angola: Slave Trade, Abolition of

At the beginning of the nineteenth century, most European nations started to implement bans on slave trading. Since the overseas commerce concerning Angola was focused almost solely on slaves, Portugal, given its dependence on the Angolan slave trade, lagged behind in implementing the ban. Throughout the nineteenth century Portugal was often viewed negatively for its reluctance to abolish its slave trade. However, there were also voices from within the Portuguese colonial system arguing against slavery, or at least demanding an end to the atrocities committed against African slaves.

In 1810, Portugal gave way to the pressure from Britain. Five years later, Portugal and Britain reached an abolition agreement. As a concession to the British, Portugal restricted its slave trade to the southern hemisphere. However, for a number of years Portugal refused to give up slave trading entirely. Portugal pointed out that Britain had also limited its traffic in slaves gradually, which had led to an increase in the number of slaves exported to its colonies in the years preceding the British ban on slave traffic. When Britain eventually abolished the transatlantic slave trade, a certain saturation of the labor force occurred in its colonies. In Brazil, the demand for slaves continued to be high, and Portugal had not experienced a similar restructuring from a mercantilist to an industrialized economy as had Britain in the early nineteenth century. Thus, the economic network between Angola, Brazil, and Portugal still relied to a large extent on the slave trade. Only in 1836 did a Portuguese decree finally prohibit the transatlantic slave trade altogether. Britain also influenced the Portuguese slave exports from Angola by exerting pressure on Brazil, which gained independence in 1822. Officially, Brazil suppressed the slave trade following a treaty with Britain from 1826, a prerequisite to recognizing Brazil's independence demanded by the British. In 1831 the first steps were taken toward setting up a system of punishment for captured slave traders.

Although slave trade was prosecuted as piracy, traffic in slaves continued. For Portugal, it was nearly impossible to enforce abolition laws in Angola, where slaves were the main economic resource, and influential merchants and slave dealers resisted the antislavery decrees issued from Portugal. The export of human beings went on for several years, particularly from the northern ports of Ambriz and Cabinda. In Britain, a humanitarian, antislavery lobby grew stronger, and eventually the British government decided to intervene again. Taking advantage of its economically stronger position and naval strength, Britain sent its navy to raid along the Angolan coast. In 1842 another treaty was signed between Britain and Portugal, in which the slave trade was declared piracy. Yet, the export traffic continued, supplying Brazil until 1853 and Cuba until the late 1860s. Thereafter, slaves were still exported from Angola to the islands of São Tomé and Príncipe. Since this type of slave traffic was intra-imperial, it did not necessarily fall under the regulation of the international treaties. When external pressure on Portugal grew, the slave deportations to the Portuguese Atlantic islands persisted under the guise of contract labor.

In the second half of the nineteenth century, Christian missionaries began to support abolitionism more unanimously than before. Whereas they had first been working among freed slaves along the African coast, they now started to found stations in many parts of the African interior where they found slavery to be widespread, even after it had been officially abolished. Their humanitarian wish to end slavery in all its forms was taken up by colonial politicians. During the Brussels Conference (1889–1890), the colonial powers used the widespread occurrence of slavery as a moral justification for the conquest of Africa. The Brussels Act, an international agreement against slave trade in any form, was reached in 1890. However, the colonial powers did not necessarily intend to effectively end slavery within a short time. Portugal feared political unrest, initiated by the considerable number of liberated slaves, that would result if slavery was abolished. Moreover, the work force was badly needed, compensations to former slave owners were costly, and the means of effective control inland were meager, thus hindering the enforcement of the regulations.

After a proposal in the Portuguese parliament that the children of slaves be considered free (1845), and a project for the gradual abolition of slavery in Portuguese Africa (1849), a limited abolition decree was introduced by Portuguese Prime Minister Sáda Bandeira in 1854. It encompassed clauses on all government slaves who were declared *libertos* ("freed slaves"). Often these changes did not affect the actual situation of the individuals. *Libertos* remained with their former owners as unpaid apprentices. Sáda Bandeira's decree further required that all slaves in private possession (approximately 60,000 individuals) be registered.

These measures met with protests from the colonists in Angola. One of the leading figures in the debate was António da Silva Porto, who welcomed the repression of traffic to foreign territories, but criticized the Portuguese government's decision to act not only against the slave trade, but also against the institution of slavery itself. Economic considerations stood behind such attitudes among Portuguese colonists in Angola. In 1869 a Portuguese decree abolished slavery. All slaves were to become *libertos*, a status that persisted until 1875. The abolition law from 1875 envisaged the complete freedom of all slaves in Angola in the year 1878. Again, Portugal was not able to enforce this law except in the coastal towns, and even there only to some extent. Slaves continued to be traded. Although officially slavery had been brought to an end in 1878, in many instances little changed for the affected population. In rural areas, the authorities either ignored the extent to which slavery occurred among the subjugated African peoples, or they were not capable of dealing with the matter. Former slaves were often kept as remunerated workers whose living conditions were not any better than before. Former slave traders in the interior still provided a labor force by contracting cheap workers. However, since freed slaves often preferred not to become part of the remunerated work force, but to engage in either small-scale trade or farming, a constant lack of cheap labor led to even harsher measures, such as an increase in forced labor. With the introduction of strict vagrancy laws, some officials considered any African not under contract a vagrant, and thus available for recruitment as cheap labor, either in the form of contract labor, or as forced labor. Under these circumstances, it can be argued that slavery and disguised forms of the slave trade continued to exist well into the twentieth century.

Axel Fleisch

Further Reading

Duffy, James. *Portuguese Africa*. London: Oxford University Press, and Cambridge, MA: Harvard University Press, 1959.

Manning, Patrick. *Slavery and African Life. Occidental, Oriental, and African Slave Trades*. Cambridge, England: Cambridge University Press, [African Studies Series 67], 1990.

Miers, Suzanne, and Richard Roberts (eds.), *The End of Slavery in Africa*. Madison: University of Wisconsin Press, 1988.

Miller, Joseph C. *Way of Death. Merchant Capitalism and the Angolan Slave Trade 1730–1830*. London: James Currey, 1988.

Angola: "Scramble"

In 1838, an intensified Portuguese expansion from the Angolan harbor towns began with the successive foundations of new military outposts, soon to be accompanied by settlements, both along the coast and further inland. Before this period, Portuguese merchants did not move inland on a regular basis to trade. Instead, African traders served as middlemen. In the nineteenth century, this began to change when prohibitive decrees by the Portuguese government were lifted, and military outposts in the interior seemed to favor settlement in these areas. However, trading inland was still a risky and costly enterprise because of tribute payments to the African authorities and enmity on the part of the African competitors. At the same time, military campaigns were necessary to bring a larger area under effective control and to subdue contraband along the Angolan harbors by means of controlling the immediate hinterland of these coastal spots, especially between Luanda and the mouth of the Congo River.

However, financing these measures turned out to be impossible. A hut tax was introduced to alleviate the precarious situation, but instead of yielding an increased revenue, it caused many Africans to migrate beyond the limits of the area brought under Portuguese control, and thus added to the relative depopulation formerly caused by the demand for slaves. From 1861 until approximately 1877, Portugal showed a limited interest in Angola, albeit with a few innovations, illustrated by several facts: the Portuguese withdrawal from frontier garrisons, a new policy introducing forced labor, and a concentration on the coastal towns.

Around 1877, Portuguese enthusiasm for the colonial endeavor increased again, especially in the cities of Portugal. In Portugal, an imperialist ideology became so inextricably associated with the late nineteenth-century nationalism that its repercussions lasted far into the twentieth century. It was, at least in part, such ideologies that instigated the renewed interest in the colonial empire.

The old idea of connecting the two largest territories in Africa upon which Portugal laid its claims, Angola and Mozambique, was taken up. Several overland expeditions between the Angolan hinterland and the southeastern African coast took place. The explorers who organized these expeditions produced a knowledge about Africa that was accessible to a broader public in Portugal. Matters concerning Angola became part of a more general concern for what was seen as a civilizing mission bestowed upon Portugal due to its longstanding history as a naval power. Such considerations were used to construe a political agenda. For Portugal the overseas possessions grew in importance not only because of the expected economic yields, but as a means of strengthening the nation's weak position in Europe. Portuguese politicians expressed their fear that unless imperialist claims succeeded, Portugal would face political insignificance.

Throughout the nineteenth century, Britain's informal hegemony on the African continent seemed largely uncontested. Ports in Angola were open to British traders, and Portugal's sovereignty near the mouth of the Congo River was violated.

However, the pace of appropriation accelerated when France became more influential as a colonial power and new participants in the "Scramble for Africa" appeared on the scene, among them the Belgian monarch King Leopold II (acting as a private entrepreneur), as well as Spain, Italy, and Germany. In the Anglo-Portuguese Treaty of 1884, Britain agreed to recognize Portuguese sovereignty on both sides of the mouth of the Congo River; in exchange, Britain would gain commercial privileges. The treaty was sharply criticized by other colonial powers. France as well as the Belgian king also demanded rights to the mouth of the Congo. The complicated situation called for diplomatic intervention. The German chancellor Bismarck organized the Congo-Conference, which was held in Berlin between November 1884 and February 1885. Apart from some areas of present-day Malawi, the mouth of the river Congo was again a heavily disputed issue. Finally, the earlier treaty was abandoned and Portugal retained a small enclave, Cabinda, north of the river Congo. To the south, the present coastline of Angola was regarded as the Portuguese sphere of influence.

The outcome of the Berlin Conference for Portugal was both disappointing and surprising. Although for some time Portugal sought (and was eventually to receive) support from France and Germany, who initially recognized Portuguese rights of sovereignty in the territories between Mozambique and Angola, the idea of linking the two territories overland had to be discarded in the end. Portugal was in no position to compete with Britain over what would become part of present-day Zambia and Zimbabwe. Nevertheless, taking into consideration Portugal's weak position, the territories it gained were considerable. At the time of the Berlin Conference, Portugal controlled barely 10 per cent of the overall territory of Angola.

Much remained to be done in order to meet the dictate that the colonizing nations were entitled to their claims only if they proved capable of effectively maintaining law and order within the respective borders. Lacking financial resources and manpower, it was difficult for Portugal to bring Angola under effective control. Portugal was eager to found police stations in the interior and to build forts along the boundaries of the prospective Angolan territory because Portugal not only had to suppress African resistance, but also to demonstrate to other colonial powers that it had, in fact, occupied the entire area delineated in successive bilateral treaties with Britain, France, Germany, Belgium, and the Union of South Africa. The "Lunda issue" concerning the border between northeastern Angola and the Congo Free State was first addressed in a treaty between Belgium and Portugal in 1891, and later determined in subsequent negotiations until 1927. Regulations concerning the border with the French and German territories to the north and south were installed in 1886, but it took until 1931 until the Kunene was finally accepted as the border between South West Africa (then under South African control) and Angola.

Negotiations with Britain were marked by increased hostility, especially after the British ultimatum to withdraw from the Shiré river in present-day Malawi under the threat of military measures in 1890. Only in 1915 were the eastern borders of Angola against Northern Rhodesia (now Zambia) determined, and the intention to link Angola and Mozambique was abandoned. Roughly at the same time, the Portuguese authorities had brought Angola under effective control.

AXEL FLEISCH

Further Reading

Abshire, D.M., and M.A. Samuels. *Portuguese Africa*. London: Pall Mall, 1969.

Duffy, James. *Portuguese Africa*. London: Oxford University Press, and Cambridge, MA: Harvard University Press, 1959.

Newitt, Malyn. *Portugal in Africa. The Last Hundred Years*. London: Hurst, 1981.

Wheeler, Douglas, and René Pélissier. *Angola*. New York, London: Pall Mall, 1971.

Angola: New Colonial Period: Christianity, Missionaries, Independent Churches

The Catholic Church has been present in Angola for more than 500 years, its first representatives having arrived with Portuguese explorers in 1492. But missionary activities were initially few and limited to the coast and the region along the Kwanza river. By the mid-nineteenth century, the church in Angola had almost vanished. When, in 1866, the first members of the Congregation of the Holy Ghost began their work in northern Angola, they had to "replant" the church. Soon they were followed by various other Catholic congregations and non-Catholic mission organizations.

The colonial authorities aimed at making the African people under their domination Portuguese in terms of culture, and therefore Catholic by religion. The Catholic Church was, therefore, considered a natural ally and aid of the government. The close relationship between the state and the Catholic hierarchy was later formalized in the concordat of 1940. However, since Portugal had to grant religious freedom in its territories (due to the Berlin Conference of 1884–1885), it tolerated, albeit grudgingly, non-Catholic missions from other Western nations. In order to control their work better, the government assigned a certain region to every mission. Belonging to one denomination rather than to another became, for the people of Angola, not so much a question of creed, but of geography. The missionary training and translation programs contributed to the perception of the existing ethnolinguistic differences as different identities; on the Protestant side, this resulted in a striking parallel between membership of an ethnic group and membership of a particular Christian denomination.

Particularly by providing health assistance and education, the churches came to represent the only positive aspect of colonialism, and people adhered to them in large numbers. Reliable statistics are not available, but one can say that in consequence of the various foreign and, later, Angolan missionary initiatives, roughly 80 per cent of the population are Christians, and two-thirds of that population is Catholic. Only very recently have Islamic missionary activities been undertaken, limited so far to the capital, Luanda.

In 1961, the Angolan war began as a struggle for independence. Many of its Angolan militants had been trained in mission schools, both Catholic and Protestant. The colonial authorities accused mainly the Protestants of subversive action. Some missions (the Baptist, the Methodist, the North Angola Mission) were closed down, their members persecuted and driven into hiding or exile. It is, however, an oversimplification to state that the decision whether to support the independence movements depended on whether one was Catholic or Protestant.

When independence was declared in 1975, it became obvious that the various political movements and factions were not prepared to join forces in the necessary task of nation-building, but were turning their aggression against each other in a struggle for power and its privileges. The anticolonial war became—in the context of the Cold War—an internationalized, civil war. The regional character of some Protestant denominations was now to have problematic consequences, as parties to the civil war politically exploited regional and ethnic factors. Some of the denominations were seen to be in too close an alliance with one of the belligerent parties, and the churches were thus partially paralyzed in their duty of promoting reconciliation.

The People's Movement for the Liberation of Angola (MPLA) succeeded in securing power and declared an organized independent Angola as a socialist people's republic. The churches were regarded by the MPLA as reactionary forces from the past and of no use to, if not dangerous for, the revolution. The process of the Africanization of the churches was accelerated by the exodus of most of the foreign mission personnel. The action of the churches was limited to the realm of the spiritual, since, with few exceptions, their medical and educational institutions were nationalized.

Nevertheless, toward the end of the 1980s, the government loosened its tight control on people identified with the churches and sought to establish more constructive relationships with them. Realizing the almost total loss of popular support, and threatened by an internal rival it could not overcome by military means, the MPLA calculated that it might be advantageous to have the churches as allies rather than as adversaries. A series of churches were officially recognized and received a judicial status. Some of the formerly nationalized institutions were handed back to the religious communities. The ruling party was strongly centralized and inclined to favor the Catholic Church.

In the authoritarian systems of Portuguese colonialism and state socialism, "African independent" Christianity hardly had space to develop. While in most surrounding countries African indigenous churches blossomed, Angola seemed an infertile soil for forms of Christianity that were not linked either to the Catholic Church or to a Western mission board and church. The most long-standing exceptions have been the Kimbanguist Church, spreading from Belgian Congo and then Zaïre, and the Tokoist Church, founded by a former member of the Baptist mission in northern Angola. The situation changed when the government abandoned its restrictive religious policy. Religious communities proliferated, many of them founded or established by former refugees returning from Zaïre.

The emerging African independent fellowships, many of them consisting of only a few dozen members, were responding not only to the need for a culturally African expression of faith. In more than thirty years of war, Angolan society has suffered a process of disintegration. The health and education systems have broken down, and the economy offers viable prospects for only a small minority linked to the power elite. In this context, churches function as networks of mutual assistance. In one way, the founding of a church became one of the strategies of economic survival, since it seemed to offer the possibility of establishing links with foreign partners and, by that means, gaining direct access to foreign assistance.

At the beginning of the twenty-first century, Angolan Christianity is a multifaceted reality. The Catholic Church, organized in twelve dioceses and led by the Episcopal Conference of Angola and São Tomé/CEAST, remains the largest body. Two umbrella organizations bring together the majority of the traditional and some of the independent non-Catholic churches: the Council of Christian Churches in Angola/CICA and the Association of Evangelicals in Angola/AEA.

BENEDICT SCHUBERT

See also: **Missionary Enterprise: Precolonial.**

Further Reading

CEAST – Episcopal Conference of Angola and São Tomé (ed.), *A Igreja em Angola entre a guerra e a paz. Documentos episcopais 1974–1978*, Luanda, edited by the CEAST, 1998.

Hastings, Adrian. *A History of African Christianity 1950–1975.* Cambridge, London, New York, etc.: Cambridge University Press, 1979, p.136–144, 202–223.

Henderson, Lawrence. *The Church in Angola. A River of Many Currents*, Cleveland, OH: Pilgrim Press, 1992.

Angola: New Colonial Period: Economics of Colonialism

The early 1890s were a time of renewed Portuguese expansion into the Angolan interior after the Berlin Congress of 1884–1885 obliged Portugal to show effective control of all areas for which it made colonial claims. A primary concern of the conference was to open up the continent's interior for commerce, and more fully, drive local African labor into the global market economy.

Much work was done during the first decades of the twentieth century to establish the economic infrastructure and tighten Portuguese control of Angola. New towns were established in the interior, and networks of roads and rails were developed after the mid-1920s.

The centerpiece of this development was construction of the Benguela Railway, completed in 1929, which was funded by British capital. Not only did it become the largest employer in Angola, it also provided the crucial connection between the copper mines of the Katanga province in Belgian Congo and Angola's port at Lobito, while also providing a route to deliver Portuguese settlers to the Angolan interior. Direct and indirect methods were derived to compel participation in the capitalist economy and labor market. The indirect pressure took the form of taxes, while the direct method was forced labor.

Three types of forced labor were imposed in Angola. The most severe was a form of modern slavery in which workers were shipped to São Tomé or

Principe for five years of hard labor on coffee and cocoa plantations, from which few returned. The second type of forced labor put people to work for major government and business enterprises throughout Angola. The colonial government contracted with major employers to provide required numbers of workers in exchange for substantial administrative fees paid by employers for this service. The third type of forced labor involved local service by men, women, and children on public works such as highway construction and maintenance, cultivation of gardens, building of houses, and other tasks determined by the local administrator. While exact numbers are impossible to determine, one estimate suggested that as late as 1954, almost 380,000 workers were subjected to forced labor. Despite some reforms in the 1940s and 1950s, forced labor was not abolished until 1962. The compulsory labor system played a great part in uniting Africans against Portuguese rule during the early liberation struggles.

In 1908 the "native tax" was instituted as another means to force Africans into the capitalist money economy and to raise revenue for the government. The tax had to be paid in Portuguese currency rather than traditional means of exchange such as shells, salt, calico, or cloth. The compulsion to pay money taxes brought local societies within the economic realm of the colonial powers.

In 1928 the annual tax for an African male in central Angola was the equivalent of 100 days pay for a contract laborer. By 1945 the tax had increased by 50 per cent. Many fled to neighboring countries rather than pay the tax. Those who could neither pay the tax nor flee were the most likely to be subjected to contract labor.

Between 1920 and 1960, the Angolan economy remained primarily agricultural. The emergence of coffee as a cash crop was perhaps the major economic development in the north between 1920 and 1960. While coffee production stood at only 3,000 to 4,000 tons annually in the first two decades of the twentieth century, by 1961 coffee exports had reached 118,000 tons. Between 1948 and 1961 the land area given over to coffee production grew from 120,000 to 500,000 hectares. In 1974 Angola stood as the second most important coffee grower in Africa and the third largest in the world. The coffee plantations enjoyed great economic success for their primarily settler owners, until disruption of most of Angola's agriculture during the civil war. Tens of thousands of Africans were displaced by European producers in townships across the coffee-producing areas. While coffee production brought great prosperity to the Portuguese and large profits to foreign investors, for Africans it created only great resentment directed against the government.

In addition, many Africans were forced from their subsistence lands to work on cotton plantations. In some areas African families were forced to grow cotton for no wages on prescribed plots of land. Their harvests were sold at below-market prices in order to subsidize the floundering urban-based textile industry. When plots ceased being productive, the African workers were forced to move to new ones, often great distances from their homes.

In central Angola, the development of corn and sisal as export crops likewise forced many subsistence farmers into wage labor. Corn exports expanded from zero in 1919 to 100,000 metric tons in 1950. Corn production, which took place on small family plots, greatly impoverished the region's already poor soils.

Production of crops such as coffee, corn, cotton, and sisal for export greatly diminished the land and labor available for subsistence activities. The minimal wages gained through contract labor could in no measure make up for the loss of subsistence production and goods. In addition the loss of community members to contract labor contributed to the deterioration of village life and the breakdown of kinship groups.

From 1920 to 1960 the government undertook a policy of colonization as white settlers were provided with free transportation, land, housing, animals, seeds, and technical advice.

Overall, Portugal invested little capital in Angola until after World War II.

Trade barely revived after the collapse of the rubber boom just before World War I. By the end of Portugal's republican period (1910–1926), Angola's finances were in serious trouble.

The Salazar regime's Colonial Act of 1930 placed strict financial controls on Angola's economy, bringing it into close alignment with policies being applied in Portugal. This policy shift was directed toward economic, political, and social integration of Portugal with its colonies. Protective trade barriers were erected and foreign investment capital was discouraged, except in the construction of the Benguela Railway and the exploration and mining of diamonds and later oil. This economic system was designed to allow Portugal to benefit from intensified exploitation of its colonies.

Angola became an overseas province (Ultramarine Province) of Portugal and a market for Portuguese goods, while also developing its own industries. By 1940 Portugal took in almost two-thirds of Angolan exports while supplying almost half of Angola's imports. These amounts were up from less than 40 per cent only a decade earlier. Angola's industries were largely reliant on Portugal for equipment and markets.

Postwar increases in the price of principal crops, especially coffee and sisal, encouraged the Portuguese government to invest in projects of infrastructure development in Angola. This included the construction of dams, transportation networks, and hydroelectric power stations in the 1950s. By the mid-1950s several mining operations had been developed for the extraction of iron ore, copper, and magnesium.

Diamonds were discovered in Luanda in 1912, and in 1917 the Diamond Company of Angola (Companhia de Diamantes de Angola, or Diamang) was formed as a monopoly with rights covering all of Angola. Capital was provided by British, Belgian, South African, and American firms with the Portuguese government holding 5 per cent of the shares. Diamond mining began in the 1920s.

Diamang, an exclusive concessionaire in Angola until the 1960s, employed almost 20,000 African workers and delivered massive investment and some social services in welfare, health, and education in the Luanda district. A condition for granting the exclusive concession was that the government would receive 40 per cent of Diamang's earnings. In 1954 the proportion was raised to 50 per cent. By 1960, diamond exports had reached almost $20 million per year, an increase five times over the value from the late 1930s.

In 1955, Petrofina struck oil in Benfica and sent the first shipment of crude petroleum for processing the following year. In 1957, the Companhia Concessionária de Petróleos de Angola (Petrangola) was founded with an investment from Petrofina, which also turned over one-third interest to the Portuguese administration in Angola. By 1974 there were at least thirty-three wells under exploration in northern Angola.

In 1966, extensive oil deposits were discovered off the coast of Cabinda by Cabinda Gulf Oil, a subsidiary of the U.S.-based Gulf Oil Company. By the early 1970s production from the Cabindan oil fields had reached almost 10 million tons of oil per year, making Angola the fourth largest oil producer in Africa, behind Libya, Algeria, and Nigeria. Between 1971 and 1974 oil revenues accounted for more than 40 per cent of Portugal's foreign earnings from Angola.

Oil provided Portugal with a major source of revenue to finance its wars against the independence movements in the colonies. Taxes and royalties from Gulf's operations provided almost half of the military budget of the Portuguese administration in Angola in the early 1970s. In 1972 alone, oil revenues provided 13 per cent of Angola's provincial budget and 60 per cent of its military expenditures.

In an attempt to stem potential uprisings, the Salazar regime initiated, in the early 1960s, a program of economic infrastructure development. Among the most important initiatives included expanding the paved road network by 500 per cent, developing domestic air routes, and making emergency aid available to coffee producers. Through reforms, including the abolition of compulsory labor and increased access to administrative positions for Africans, the Portuguese regime hoped to win greater loyalty among the civilian population. Compulsory cultivation of cotton was also abolished.

By 1965, growing defense expenditures related to Portugal's attempts to contain the liberation movements forced the Salazar government to allow foreign capital, especially from the U.S. and South Africa, into Angola. South African capital financed the building of the Cunene River Dam project along Angola's border with Namibia. This initiated a period of economic expansion and industrialization that was further propelled by increased military spending, which stimulated investment in communications and transportation infrastructure.

In 1972 the Portuguese national assembly redesignated Angola's status from an overseas province to an autonomous state. Angola was able to draft its own budget and collect its own taxes, but Portugal maintained a supervisory role with regard to the economy and administration. Expanded agricultural production and surpluses in coffee, iron ore, oil, and diamond exports continued into the early 1970s. Between 1965 and 1974, enormous productive growth was experienced in iron, diamonds, and manufacturing. This great economic expansion made Angola more economically valuable to Portugal than any of its other colonies in Africa. As a result Portugal became even more determined to oppose Angolan independence.

JEFF SHANTZ

Further Reading

Harsch, Ernest, and Tony Thomas. *Angola: The Hidden History of Washington's War*. New York: Pathfinder Press, 1976.

Heywood, Linda. *Contested Power in Angola, 1840s to the Present*. Rochester, NY: University of Rochester Press, 2000.

Hodges, Tony. *Angola: From Afro-Stalinism to Petro-Diamond Capitalism*. Oxford and Bloomington: James Currey and Indiana University Press, 2001.

Maier, Karl. *Angola: Promises and Lies*. Rivonia: William Waterman, 1996.

Martin, Phyllis. *Historical Dictionary of Angola*. Metuchen, NJ: Scarecrow Press, 1980.

Minter, William. *Portuguese Africa and the West*. Harmondsworth, England: Penguin Books, 1972.

Pitcher, M. Anne. "From Coercion to Incentives: The Portuguese Colonial Cotton Regime in Angola and Mozambique, 1946–1974," In *Cotton, Colonialism, and Social History in Sub-Saharan Africa*, Allen Isaacman and Richard Roberts (eds.). Portsmouth,: Heinemann, 119–143, 1995.

Wright, George. *The Destruction of a Nation: United States' Policy Toward Angola since 1945*. London: Pluto Press, 1997.

Angola: New Colonial Period: White Immigration, Mestiços, Assimilated Africans

The revival of Portuguese colonial expansion in the last twenty years of the nineteenth century produced a radical change in relations between resident whites and Angola's black "modern elites." Throughout the final years of the monarchy (to 1910), the short-lived republic (1910–1926), and the Salazarist dictatorship up to the 1961 revolts, the status of the "old" *assimilados*, or Creoles, *mestiços* (people of mixed race), and "new" *assimilados* (Africans who had passed the colonial "civilization test") was gradually eclipsed by the increasing wave of white Portuguese immigration. In conjunction with the repressive and exploitative nature of Portuguese imperial control, it was a material factor in the emergence of radical political movements in the 1950s, and their decision to use force against the Salazar regime in the 1960s.

At the end of the 1860s, there were only 3,000 resident whites in Angola, mostly officials, businessmen, and planters. Interior trade was dominated by the "old" *assimilado* families, culturally Portuguese, but otherwise black: *mestiços*, often acknowledged by their white fathers, who had secured sometimes important positions in government service and professions such as journalism. While it was certainly stratified, Angolan society prior to the new colonial period offered significant opportunities for nonwhites to advance on the basis of merit rather than race, opportunities that were to diminish as the old century gave way to the new.

The partition of Africa was the main harbinger of change. It galvanized Portugal into action to protect its African interests, generating an intense patriotism that expressed itself through the agency of the "Generation of 1895." From the start of the new century onward, Portuguese rule was extended over the hinterland, bringing the entire country under its control by 1920. Rural revolts, such as the Kongo hut tax rebellion of 1906–1913, were crushed. The main symbol of Portuguese control, the 1899 Labor Code, which required all nonassimilated Africans to work for six months each year, was imposed throughout the colony.

The overall effect of this consolidation of imperial control was the growth of white racism, influenced also by the contemporary and international current of social Darwinism, and assisted by the steady rise of white immigration into Angola. By 1950, the 78,000 whites then resident in Angola exceeded the *assimilado* and *mestiço* elements by a ratio of more than two to one, and were to more than double, to a total of 172,000, in 1960. The social class of the typical settler fell from the coffee planters of the monarchy to the lower middle-class civil servants of the republic, and thence to the peasants, often illiterate, planted in the countryside in the 1950s to establish a Portuguese presence. Creole coffee planters were displaced, while the "new" *assimilados* and *mestiços* were progressively frozen out of responsible civil service jobs, a process formalized by the 1929 decree restricting their advance to the level of clerk. The post-1950 flood of immigrants affected nonassimilated Africans (*indigenas*); the coffee boom of the 1940s and 1950s resulted in the expropriation of black-occupied land for white producers, while opportunities in the towns diminished with even semiskilled jobs being taken by Portuguese peasants who had given up on rural agriculture and become what amounted to a "poor white" population. By the late 1950s, a severe socioeconomic situation had developed in several towns, and particularly in Luanda: a lack of facilities, including adequate housing, and major unemployment that affected all racial groups (including whites), creating a potentially revolutionary situation.

Also, the political climate for the black elites worsened. There had been relative freedom of speech during the monarchy, although critics of Portuguese rule tended to publish their criticism in Lisbon rather than Luanda. At times, Portuguese sensitivities were very noticeable: the Angolan *mestiço* lawyer Fontes Pereira (1823–1891) lost his government post after making a negative remark about the monarchy's record of development in Angola over the previous three centuries. The new republic started with the best of intentions: the first major black organization, the *Liga Angolana* (1913), proclaiming a moderate, reformist message, was able to thrive. However, the white settlers in Angola influenced successive high commissioners to implement illiberal policies. With their approbation, Norton de Matos (1920–1923) proscribed the *Liga*, allegedly for subversive activities, in 1922. The ensuing Salazar period witnessed a general ban on all (including white) political activity, obliging organizations to transform themselves into "cultural clubs." After 1942, this ban was relaxed somewhat, allowing "loyal" blacks to operate within the straitjacket of the corporatist state. The postwar period saw the rapid growth of political activity, open and clandestine, in Angola itself and in Lisbon, where Angolan students met their peers from other Portuguese colonies, and came into contact with the underground Portuguese communist and socialist parties. Some radical activists made two approaches to the UN, in 1950 and 1955, expressing dissatisfaction with Portuguese rule, in the hope of some kind of international intervention. Following the failure of this and other reformist initiatives, radical politics moved in a revolutionary direction. The underground Angolan Communist Party, led by Agostinho Neto (1922–1979), and Mario de Andrade was formed in October 1955. Subsequently, two nationalist parties were set up in 1956: the multiracial MPLA (Popular Movement for the Liberation of Angola), also led by Neto, in which *mestiços* played an significant part; and Holden Roberto's predominantly Bakongo UPNA (Union of the People of Northern Angola), which adopted a more exclusive, "Africanist" stance. The Salazarist authorities infiltrated secret agents into the MPLA from 1957 onward, and, following riots in the adjacent Belgian Congo (January 1959), arrested more than a hundred political activists (including Neto) in two separate operations, thus setting the scene for the revolts of early 1961.

MURRAY STEELE

See also: **Angola: "Scramble"; Angola: MPLA, FNLA, UNITA, and the War of Liberation, 1961–1974.**

Further Reading

Clarence-Smith, Gervais. *The Third Portuguese Empire, 1825–1975: A Study in Economic Imperialism.* Manchester, England, and Dover, NH: Manchester University Press, 1975.

Duffy, James *Portugal in Africa*, Harmondsworth, England: Penguin Books, and Cambridge, MA: Harvard University Press, 1962.

Henderson, Lawrence. *Angola: Five Centuries of Conflict.* Ithaca, NY: Cornell University Press, 1979.

Messiant, Christine. "Angola: the challenge of nationhood" in David, Birmingham, and Phyllis Martin (eds.). *History of Central Africa: The Contemporary Years since 1960.* London and New York: Longman, 1998.

Newitt, Malyn. *Portugal in Africa: The Last Hundred Years.* London: C. Hurst, 1981.

Angola: Revolts, 1961

In Luanda, early in the morning on February 4, 1961, small bands of insurgents, numbering altogether approximately 180, attacked a police patrol, the prison, army and police barracks, and the radio station. Each of the attacks was repulsed and throughout the next two days armed white civilians inflicted reprisals in the *muceques*, the shanty neighborhoods surrounding the Angolan capital. In the absence of an anticipated insurrectionary response from Luanda's African population, the remaining insurgents fled the city to find refuge in the densely forested mountainous Dembos region, from which they would conduct intermittent guerrilla warfare against the Portuguese and rival insurgencies for the next fourteen years, until independence.

One month later, a much more formidable challenge to Portuguese rule arose in the north. In the weeks following the Luanda uprising, emissaries of revolt had been arriving in the villages of the Zaïre and Uige districts to mobilize support for a rebellion. On March 12, the first small-scale attacks on coffee plantations began, reaching a climax three days later. The rebels killed 250 Portuguese officials and farmers within the first week and 500 more over the next three months. At least as many plantation workers from southern Angola also died. As in Luanda, reprisals were led by a civilian militia, the *Corpos de Voluntarios*, but in this

case they considerably magnified the scope of the insurgent movement, claiming 20,000 victims and prompting a mass exodus of 250,000 refugees across the Congolese border and into isolated settlements (*sanzalas*) deep in the forest. In April, the revolt's leadership declared the inception of a second "guerrilla" phase, and in August the Portuguese army began a full-scale counteroffensive, entrenching a military conflict that would persist in Angola until the end of the century and beyond.

These two rebellions were organized by sharply contrasting movements. In Luanda, the uprising was inspired by the *Movimento Popular Libertaçao de Angola* (MPLA), formed from a cluster of Marxist and communist groups in December 1956. The MPLA's following and activities were largely confined to African *assimilados* and *mestiços*, relatively privileged subaltern groups in colonial society; both Methodist ministers and Catholic priests played an important role in its early history, and its leadership was dominated by a group of interrelated Creole families who had prevailed in Luanda's cultural politics for decades. Between March and June 1959, many of the MPLA's key adherents were arrested and detained by the PIDE, the secret police, including its president, Agostinho Neto, a medical doctor. Other leaders established themselves in exile; the planning of the February rebellion seems to have been local and prompted by further PIDE operations in the *muceques* in the previous month. Nominally a workers movement, there is little evidence that the MPLA enjoyed generalized support outside the home villages in which its leaders were "favorite sons."

Overseeing the northern insurrection was the *Uniao das Populacoes de Angola* (UPA), originally an irredentist Bakongo movement formed in 1954 with the ostensible aim of restoring the autonomy of the Congo kingdom, the boundaries of which had for 500 years straddled the Angolan/Belgian Congo border. In 1958, the UPA's leaders had been persuaded by their Baptist allies (Baptist missionaries were very influential among the Bakongo) as well as their contacts with Pan-African circles to drop their ethnoregional presumptions. From 1958, the key personality within the UPA was Holden Roberto, formerly a clerk in the Belgian administration (though of Angolan birth). Roberto had spent most of his life in the Congo, and the precipitate departure of the Belgian colonizers in the wake of the Leopoldville riots helped to convince him that the Portuguese would be similarly intimidated by an anticolonial revolt.

Roberto had little personal knowledge of conditions among the Bakongo on the Angolan side of the border, but both historical tradition and recent developments had created a receptive atmosphere for the UPA's activists. Many of the UPA partisans who appeared in the villages during February 1961 presented themselves not as sophisticated political cadres, but as prophets (*nqunzas*), holding services at which all in attendance drank a cup of holy water and paid 2.50 escudos. The authorities later found "fund registers" recording collections of 30,000 escudos at single meetings. The ritual echoed generations of Christian millenarian practices in the region. Millenarian traditions had an especial force in Bakongo society as a consequence of a centuries-old heritage of African syncretic Christianity as well as a colonial presence that had been especially prolonged and intrusive.

Reinforcing the cumulative influence of generations of millenarian imaginings, as well as the memory of a golden age of Bakongo statehood, were more immediate material setbacks. Portuguese sponsorship of white settlement into Zaïre and Uige districts after 1945 had resulted in the confiscation from the Bakongo of 360,000 acres of land, much of this dispossession illegal. As a consequence, about half the preexisting population of African smallholder coffee producers had been forced off the land, a process that had accelerated through the 1950s and that peaked at the end of the decade. As African purchasing power declined as a consequence of the loss of farm incomes, indebtedness to an increasingly rapacious class of Portuguese traders mounted. In 1960, the age of tax liability was lowered to sixteen and Bakongo men for the first time began to be forced into indentured labor contracts on settler-owned coffee plantations. Remaining African farmers had their livelihoods further threatened by the effects of Portugal's agreement to an international coffee quota system, which caused a sharp fall in coffee producer prices in 1960. Intensifying economic hardship and social resentment in Bakongo villages in early 1961 were fresh restrictions on slash and burn field clearance and cultivation. Unlike the cerebral Marxist modernizers of Luanda's Creole elite, the UPA's leadership of Bakongo businessmen was able to tap successfully popular predispositions for rebellion, recruiting a local layer of activism among African coffee farmers and thereafter acquiring a mass following in a social context characterized by material crisis and millennial expectation.

TOM LODGE

Further Reading

de Andrade, Mario, and Marc Ollivier. *The War in Angola*. Dar es Salaam: Tanzanian Publishing House, 1975.

Barnett, Don, and Roy Harvey (eds.). *The Angolan Revolution*: MPLA—Life Histories and Documents. Indianapolis, IN: Bobbs Merrill, 1972.

Bender, Gerald, *Angola under the Portuguese: The Myth and the Reality*. London: Heinemann, 1978.

Birmingham, David. "Angola Revisited," in *Journal of Southern African Studies*, 15, 1, October 1988, pp. 1–15.

Heimer, Franz-Wilhelm (ed.). *Social Change in Angola*. Munich: Welforum Verlag, 1973.

Angola: MPLA, FNLA, UNITA, and the War of Liberation, 1961–1974

In many respects, Angolan history forms part of the history of southern Africa. While most states in the rest of Africa became independent, in many southern African countries a reverse trend was visible: white rule became more entrenched. South Africa's apartheid system, Rhodesia's settler government, and Portuguese investments to expand their administrative and military system in the colonies were all aimed to prevent African independence. To interpret Angola's past in a southern African context, however, runs the risk of promoting reasoning from within a colonial framework. For the Angolan nationalist parties involved, relations within the central African context may have been just as important. Apart from contact with leaders from nations such as Tanzania, North African states, and other Portuguese-speaking colonies, the ties with independent Congo, Zaïre, and Zambia were crucial for the Angolan nationalist movements. These regional aspects can hardly be separated from the wider international scene. This was the age of the Cold War: the parties involved all had their own channels of support, such as China, the Soviet Union, or the United States. The complex linkages between local, regional, and international spheres set the stage for later developments after Angolan independence in 1975.

Many names from different epochs have been associated with the Angolan resistance against colonialism, such as Queen Njinga, who fought the Portuguese in the seventeenth century, Chief Mandume, who opposed colonial conquest at the beginning of the twentieth century, and the prophet António Mariano, who led Maria's War in January 1961.

The Luanda rising of February 1961 is generally taken as the beginning of the Angolan war of liberation. It started with Africans making an abortive attempt to release political prisoners, whereupon white immigrants entered the Luandan slums and engaged in a killing spree that left an unknown number of mostly educated Africans dead. A movement called MPLA (Popular Movement for the Liberation of Angola), which had been founded in 1956, was linked with the rising. Its leadership mostly consisted of Luandan *assimilados*, who, despite a Portuguese upbringing, were eager to explore their African background. Their poetry and protest, both with Marxist and *négritude* overtones, soon aroused the suspicion of the Portuguese police and many of them were detained, executed, or forced into exile. Some MPLA supporters were involved in the Luanda rising, but many MPLA leaders were in exile trying to create internal cohesion and to look for international support, neither of which proved an easy task.

Just a month after the Luanda rising, eruptions of violence occurred in the north of Angola, where immigrant plantation ownership led to the impoverishment of local entrepreneurs. Soon the coffee plantations became the scene of widespread murder and mutilation, with atrocities committed by all sides involved. Many people from the region fled to neighboring Zaïre, where some joined the FNLA (National Front for the Liberation of Angola). This movement was led largely by Baptists from the Angolan Kongo region, of whom Holden Roberto became the most prominent. The leadership stood close to the Kongo royalty, but concerns of local capitalist trade were equally important for its otherwise little-developed program. Soon relations between FNLA and MPLA became marked by fierce competition and fighting. While Holden Roberto managed to secure Zairian support and international recognition, the MPLA did not. In addition, the factions in the MPLA leadership faced sharp opposition from Viriato da Cruz and others against Agostinho Neto, the MPLA president. Internal strife was, however, not confined to the MPLA: in 1964 Jonas Savimbi left the Angolan government, which had been created in Kinshasa by Holden Roberto. Two years later he formed his own movement: the National Union for the Total Independence of Angola (UNITA).

Zambian independence changed the scene. After 1966 both UNITA and MPLA started guerrilla activities in the sparsely populated plains of eastern Angola neighboring Zambia. Portuguese retaliation was harsh, the border between Zambia and Angola was cleared, most of the inhabitants were herded into wired camps, and helicopters dropped bombs on both guerrillas and any remaining villagers. Cooperating with South African forces, the Portuguese managed to hold the towns, while the guerrilla movements held the countryside. With few strategic targets to be conquered or lost, the war became what Basil Davidson has called "a war for people" (1972). Using methods ranging from ideological explanation and material attraction to threat and abduction, the fighting parties tried to control as many civilians as they could.

The MPLA and UNITA never managed to face the Portuguese forces with a common front. To the contrary, the Portuguese were able to employ their mutual animosity to check guerrilla activities. None of the parties tolerated the presence of another group in its vicinity, and there is proof that during the final years of the war UNITA cooperated with the Portuguese to oust its rival. Furthermore, internal tensions mounted. In the MPLA the strained relations between learned political leaders from Luanda and local army leaders with little education proved too difficult a problem to overcome. A second internal crisis ensued: in 1973 both the "Active Revolt" and the "Eastern Revolt" nearly caused a split. The latter movement was led by chief commander of the eastern forces, Daniel Chipenda, who later assembled his followers, broke away from MPLA, and formed a southern branch of the FNLA.

In the meantime, the northern branch of the FNLA continued to gather support from African coffee planters who wished to safeguard their interests against white plantation holders. Increasing reliance on Western support and the capitalist ethos of FNLA diminished its revolutionary outlook. This did not prevent guerrilla actions, and in the northern region the FNLA was rather successful in this respect. With its regional base and interests, however, the FNLA only managed to expand to other areas on a limited scale. Furthermore competition with groups ready to negotiate with the Portuguese, a mutiny against the leadership suppressed with the aid of the Zairian government, and rivalry with MPLA did much to damage the party. Only with Zairian support the FNLA was able to remain a political and military force worth mentioning. In the oil-rich Cabinda enclave FNLA and MPLA interests clashed with FLEC (Cabindan Liberation Front), which sought Cabindan independence, both from Portugal and Angola. In this region fighting diminished.

In the east and south the war initiative shifted from this fighting party to that. On the whole the war slowly expanded and at times reached eastern Malange and the central highlands. Especially for UNITA, whose leadership mainly originated from the central highlands this was an important development. UNITA had started out with limited Chinese support, but on the whole had a far less developed structure outside Angola than FNLA and MPLA. Its leadership, in contrast to the other nationalist groups, largely operated from within Angola, especially after Savimbi had been expelled from Zambia in 1967. Due to its external contacts, MPLA troops were on the whole somewhat better armed and better trained than UNITA soldiers. Yet, they also suffered from a lack of supplies and their fragmented leadership was unable to provide the necessary coordination.

Attempts to unite the Angolan nationalist movements, sometimes initiated by the leaders of the movements themselves, sometimes led by African heads of state or the OAU, never succeeded: the Angolan liberation movement remained hopelessly divided. Yet despite the cleavages in the nationalist movement and Portuguese efforts to build up a decisive war machinery, the Portuguese forces were unable to wipe out the nationalist groups. Portugal spent nearly half of its annual budget on the war in the colonies, in 1969 alone it sent some 150,000 troops to Africa and lost an average of 100 soldiers and more than 200 civilians annually in Angola. When war-worn Portuguese soldiers and their commanders staged a coup in Lisbon in 1974, a new epoch in Angolan history started. The first war of liberation had come to an end; soon another would be fought. Hitherto the period between 1961 and 1974 has been studied largely in terms of the discussions on nationalism and liberation. This valid approach may be widened by detailing other aspects of the war, such as the interactions between local, regional, and international support networks, witchcraft accusations, magic and political power, the relations with the churches, mobility, containment and concepts of space, questions of morality, agency and gender. Although the available sources may not provide answers to all questions, many questions still remain to be asked.

INGE BRINKMAN

See also: **Neto, António Agostinho.**

Further Reading

Barnett, Don, and Roy Harvey. *The Revolution in Angola: MPLA, Life Histories and Documents.* Indianapolis, IN,: Bobbs-Merrill, 1972.

Birmingham, David. *Frontline Nationalism in Angola and Mozambique.* London: James Currey, and Trenton NJ: Africa World Press, 1992.

Davidson, Basil. *In the Eye of the Storm. Angola's People.* London: Longman, 1972.

Henderson, Lawrence W. *Angola. Five Centuries of Conflict.* Ithaca, NY, London: Cornell University Press, 1979.

Marcum, John A. *The Angolan Revolution: Vol. 1: The Anatomy of an Explosion (1950–1962),* Cambridge, MA, London: MIT Press, 1969.

Marcum, John A. *The Angolan Revolution. Vol. 2: Exile Politics and Guerrilla Warfare (1962–1976),* Cambridge, MA, London: MIT Press, 1978.

Angola: Independence and Civil War, 1974–1976

The military coup that overthrew the Portuguese government on April 25, 1974, led to a resurgence in organized African political activity in Portugal's colonies. However, Angola's natural resources, primarily oil and diamonds, also attracted the interest of external forces. Eventually, the Angolan civil war would be perceived by the global media as a microcosm of the Cold War.

Following the coup, Holden Roberto, the leader of the National Front for the Liberation of Angola (FNLA) in exile in Zaïre, assembled an army under the guidance of Chinese and Zairian instructors. The National Union for the Total Independence of Angola (UNITA), under the leadership of Jonas Savimbi, rapidly abandoned Maoist rhetoric and opened channels of communication with the Portuguese authorities. The socialist Popular Movement for the Liberation of Angola (MPLA), led by Agostinho Neto, was caught off guard by the April coup and beset by factionalism.

By September 1974 the MPLA had split into three factions. Daniel Chipenda's Revolta do Leste (Eastern Revolt) opened communications with the FNLA and UNITA. Two months earlier, UNITA had accepted a cease-fire agreement with the Portuguese. By October, the Neto-led MPLA and the FNLA had also come to terms with the colonial administration. The Chipenda defection led the MPLA to appeal to the Cuban government for assistance. In November, the Soviet Union, partly in response to Chinese assistance to the FNLA, began to provide support for the MPLA through the OAU Liberation Committee.

On January 3, 1975, Neto, Savimbi, and Roberto assembled in Mombasa to sign an accord pledging peaceful cooperation, the facilitation of national reconstruction, and the safeguarding of Angola's "territorial integrity." Two weeks later, the Alvor Agreement was signed by all three parties. The agreement declared that Cabinda, where the oilfields were situated and which had been the subject of a secessionist movement, was "an unalienable component part of Angola." November 11, 1975, was set as the date for independence, and the MPLA, the FNLA, and UNITA were recognized as "the sole legitimate representatives of the people of Angola." The agreement also constructed a coalition government made up of the three parties which was mandated to conduct legislative elections and draft a provisional constitution under the guidance of the high commissioner general.

American intervention focused on the Alvor attempt to create a viable Angolan polity. In late January 1975, the United States covertly provided the anticommunist FNLA with $300,000. Fighting erupted in Luanda, and Chipenda formally joined forces with the FNLA. In response to the U.S. intervention, the Soviet Union increased arms deliveries to the MPLA. Meanwhile, UNITA attempted to consolidate its position in the central highlands, while Savimbi traveled overseas in search of funding. In June, the three leaders attended talks in Kenya under the chairmanship of Jomo Kenyatta.

The FNLA, working closely with right-wing Portuguese elements, held the northern districts of Angola but were forced out of Luanda by the MPLA. Military advances by the MPLA, by now linked to leftists within the Portuguese administration, concerned the American government. On July 17, the U.S. provided increased funds to the FNLA and UNITA.

At the same time, the South African army was adopting positions on the Angola-Namibia border. Under the guise of pursuing South West Africa People's Organization (SWAPO) guerrillas, the South African troops made a number of sorties into Angola. The MPLA attempted to publicize these interventions but to no avail. As the FNLA and UNITA waited for the American-financed weapons to arrive, they turned to South Africa for assistance. On September 21, 1975, South African officials arrived in Silva Porto to help UNITA against the MPLA. On October 14, the South African army launched Operation Zulu, an armored force supported by helicopter gunships that moved rapidly up the Angolan coast, dislodging and expelling the MPLA army in its wake.

In Luanda, the MPLA were besieged on all sides. In the north, the FNLA prepared to strike, while in the south, the UNITA/South African forces were dominant. Cuba and the Soviet Union moved quickly to bolster the MPLA. The airlift of Cuban combat troops known as Operation Carlota started on November 7. Within days, the war began to turn in the MPLA's favor. The Portuguese administration fled Angola, and on November 11, independence was declared. The MPLA immediately announced the foundation of the People's Republic of Angola. In response, the FNLA and UNITA joined forces to establish the "Democratic People's Republic of Angola."

Following the public exposure of the South African intervention (November 22), support for UNITA began to ebb. On November 27, Nigeria recognized the MPLA government and offered them funding in a show of support. In the United States, Secretary of State Henry Kissinger's attempt to provide more money to the FNLA-UNITA alliance foundered in the Senate. The Tunney-Clark amendment (December 18) cut off any further covert aid.

Cuban reinforcements continued to pour into Angola. After the FNLA had been defeated in the north, Chipenda's FNLA in the south abandoned any pretense of organized warfare. Eventually, the Chipenda FNLA and UNITA fought each other, creating in the process a war within a war. The final blow for the anti-MPLA forces was the failure of the OAU to provide majority support for either a condemnation of the Cuban intervention or a tripartite political solution. On January 22, 1976, the South African force began to withdraw from Angola. By late February, the MPLA-Cuban army had defeated UNITA.

By mid-1976, the MPLA was well established as the governing party of Angola. Holden Roberto had returned to exile in Zaïre, and Jonas Savimbi and UNITA had retreated to their prior position as guerrillas. Savimbi, however, retained contacts with the South African army, contacts that would return to torment Angola in the future.

JAMES SANDERS

Further Reading

Guimaraes, Fernando Andresen. The Origins of the Angolan Civil War: Foreign Intervention and Domestic Political Conflict. London, Macmillan Press, 1998.
Legum, Colin, and Hodges, Tony. After Angola: The War over Southern Africa. London: Rex Collings, 1976.
Marcum, John A. The Angolan Revolution, Vol. 2. Exile Politics and Guerrilla Warfare (1962–1976). Cambridge, MA: MIT Press, 1978.
Stockwell, John. In Search of Enemies: A CIA Story, New York: W.W Norton, 1978.

Angola: Cold War Politics, Civil War, 1975–1994

Angola's national independence struggle became deeply entangled with both global Cold War politics and an increasingly bloody regional confrontation, as South Africa's white minority government attempted to halt the spread of African self-rule. The MPLA, while weakened by internal divisions, won crucial levels of external support on the eve of independence, first from Yugoslavia, then from Cuba, and finally from the Soviet Union. Slaves from Angola's shores had been shipped to Cuba in earlier centuries; hence there were strong historical links between the two countries. President Fidel Castro of Cuba made an early commitment to support the MPLA that brought in the Soviet Union superpower on its coattails. The United States placed its support behind the other two nationalist movements, UNITA and the FNLA. Herein were laid the seeds of an ongoing Cold War confrontation by proxy.

Into the midst of this cocktail of Cold War politics was added South Africa's efforts to maintain white minority rule by creating a cordon sanitaire around its borders. South Africa was determined to undermine the postindependence socialist government of the MPLA, which provided external bases for the nationalist movement of the South West African People's Organization (SWAPO), fighting for the independence of South West Africa (now known as Namibia), a territory under South African control, and of the African National Congress (ANC) fighting to overthrow the apartheid system in South Africa. The South African government joined the U.S. in actively supporting UNITA and the FNLA against the MPLA and its socialist bloc backers. Both SWAPO and ANC camps inside Angola were subjected to periodic attack, and the South African Defense Forces (SADF) fought alongside UNITA in battles with the Angolan government army.

Following the initial defeat of UNITA and the FNLA along with its western and South African supporters in 1976, and the consolidation of the MPLA government in Luanda, Angola entered into an extended period of civil war encouraged by the prevailing global and regional confrontations. The MPLA government declared itself a Marxist-Leninist regime and relied increasingly on Soviet bloc support along with significant aid from northern European social democracies. Angola's government was never a puppet of Moscow, but the heightening of Cold War confrontation with the election of President Ronald Reagan in the United States created an ever-deepening divide within Angolan politics.

Throughout the 1980s the civil war intensified, fueled by this Cold War proxy confrontation and South Africa's newly found position as the regional champion for "rolling back communism." The South African Defense Forces continually supplied UNITA with weapons and logistical support and brought their own troops in to fight alongside UNITA when MPLA government offensives were launched in the center and south of the country. UNITA paid for this support in part by killing elephants and exporting ivory along with precious hardwoods. The U.S. provided assistance to UNITA via the northern neighboring territory of Zaïre. Soviet Union and Cuban support bolstered the MPLA regime.

An attempted resolution to the multilayered conflict that had national, regional, and international dimensions began to unfold toward the end of the 1980s. United States policy under Assistant Secretary of State Chester Crocker was to link the withdrawal of the Cuban and Soviet presence in Angola, with South Africa moving toward granting independence for Namibia. This was finally achieved following a major battle at Cuito Cuanavale in southern Angola in 1988, when the SADF were obliged to withdraw. The U.S. had encouraged an aggressive South African "roll back" strategy, but after a decade, the South African military needed taming somewhat, to let the South African diplomats take the running. Hence the United States did not permit the use of all available military technology in that confrontation to enable the South African military to win. On the side of the Soviet Union and Cuba, they needed to be able to claim some shared success in achieving their policy aims as well as being given an opportunity to pull out.

The South African government agreed to free elections in Namibia, which brought a SWAPO government to power. Cuban and Soviet support to the MPLA government was withdrawn. The path was created for a new peace initiative to try to end the civil war. Finally, in 1992, the Bicesse Agreement was signed, leading up to a UN monitored peace process with an end to armed hostilities, and a democratic election took place in September 1992. The MPLA won a majority of the seats in the national assembly and Jose Eduardo dos Santos a majority of votes in the election for president, held in tandem. Savimbi and UNITA refused to accept the judgment of the international community that the elections were free and fair and Savimbi returned to war with a vengeance. By so doing, Savimbi revealed that he had deliberately misled the international community by failing to integrate his troops into the national army and demobilize the remaining forces. UNITA's hidden military forces struck swiftly and soon had nearly two-thirds of the national territory under its control.

BARRY MUNSLOW

See also: **Angola: Independence and Civil War, 1974–1976; Angola: MPLA, FNLA, UNITA, and the War of Liberation, 1961–1974; Savimbi, Jonas.**

Further Reading

Anstee, Margaret. *Angola. Orphan of the Cold War.* London: Macmillan, 1996.

Bloomfield, Richard (ed.). *Regional Conflict and U.S. Policy: Angola and Mozambique.* Algonac, MI: Reference Publications, 1988.

Crocker, Chester. *High Noon in Southern Africa: Making Peace in a Rough Neighbourhood.* New York and London: W.W. Norton, 1992.

Maier, Karl. *Angola: Promises and Lies.* London: Serif, 1996.

Martin III, James. *A Political History of the Civil War in Angola, 1974–1990.* New Brunswick, NJ: Transaction Publishers, 1992.

McCormick, Shawn. *The Angolan Economy. Prospects for Growth in a Postwar Environment.* Washington, DC: Center for Strategic and International Studies, 1994.

Minter, William. *Apartheid's Contras. An Inquiry into the Roots of War in Angola and Mozambique.* London and New Jersey: Zed Books, 1994.

Munslow, Barry, and Katherine O'Neil. "Ending the Cold War in Southern Africa," *Third World Quarterly*, 12/3–4 (1991): 81–96.

Pereira, Anthony, W. "The Neglected Tragedy: The Return to War in Angola 1992–1993," *Journal of Modern African Studies*, 31/2 (1994): 1–28.

Sogge, David. *Sustainable Peace. Angola's Recovery.* Harare: Southern African Research and Documentation Center, 1992.

Somerville, Keith. *Angola: Politics, Economics, and Society.* London: Francis Pinter, 1986.

Tvedten, Inge. *Angola. Struggle for Peace and Reconstruction.* Boulder, CO: Westview Press, 1997.

Windrich, Elaine. *The Cold War Guerrilla. Jonas Savimbi, the U.S. Media, and the Angolan War.* Westport, CT: Greenwood Press, 1992.

Angola: Civil War: Impact of, Economic and Social

Angola first entered into war in 1961, with the start of the anticolonial struggle, and war has continued into the twenty-first century. From 1975 onward, this took the form of a civil war, waged between the MPLA government and UNITA, with only two very brief periods of troubled peace in the 1990s.

Angola's rich natural resource base offered virtually limitless potential for economic development. War destroyed the opportunity for that potential to be realized in productive economic endeavors that would accelerate the social development of the country. Instead, agricultural and industrial production collapsed. Two nonrenewable resources, oil and diamonds, became the mainstay of the economy. By 1997, oil exports were worth 4.5 billion U.S. dollars, and diamond exports an estimated half a billion U.S. dollars. Following the withdrawal of the Portuguese colonial power in 1975, the MPLA government relied upon the country's oil revenues, while UNITA used the country's diamond revenues, as well as ivory exports, to fuel an ongoing civil war.

From 1975 to 1990 the war was essentially confined to the rural areas. The farmland being cultivated at the end of this period represented only one-quarter of that being cultivated in 1975, as a result of mine laying and general insecurity, with infrastructure, transport, and all forms of social provision being seriously disrupted. A massive rural population exodus occurred of internally displaced persons to the capital city of Luanda and to the provincial capitals. Over two decades of warfare since independence contributed to the urban population growing from 20 per cent to well over 50 per cent of the total population. In addition, refugees poured into neighboring countries, notably Zaïre (now Democratic Republic of Congo), and Zambia. By the mid-1990s, 1.2 million were refugees or internally displaced persons; there were 70,000 amputees and tens of thousands of street children. Agricultural production collapsed, as did industrial production.

Only 12 per cent of the economically active population are employed in the formal sector. Urban unemployment is more than 30 per cent, affecting women and youth in particular. This situation emerged as a combined result of the war, the state's misguided socialist, centralized economic planning, and the absence of effective management and education strategies. Oil revenues continually grew, however, alleviating the need for the government to seriously address economic renewal in the rest of the economy. By the late 1990s, oil accounted for about 90 per cent of government revenue and 95 per cent of export earnings. Angola went from being a food exporter at the time of independence, to becoming heavily reliant on food aid and imports. The petroleum sector remained relatively immune from the war as most of the production was offshore, benefiting from new deep water mining technologies.

Undoubtedly the main responsibility for the war lay with UNITA, which was able to obtain the backing of the South African government and its defense forces. UNITA's activities crippled the non-oil sectors, destroying the economy and people's livelihoods. As a result of the civil war, government expenditure was primarily targeted on defense, reaching a peak in 1993 of almost half of total official expenditure. Social sector expenditure was correspondingly squeezed. According to UNICEF, levels of social expenditure remain far below comparable levels in neighboring countries. As the radical socialist ideology of the government was gradually undermined, corruption and enrichment of the small elite around President Jose Eduardo dos Santos replaced the genuine social concerns of the MPLA government in the early years of independence. In spite of the oil and diamond wealth, the population sank into ever deeper levels of poverty.

One of the most serious economic impacts of the war was to compound the hyperinflation that resulted from the government's unrealistic economic policies as well as from UNITA's military activities. From independence to the beginning of the 1990s, the government maintained an official exchange rate of 30 kwanza to US$1. This artificially low exchange rate produced a parallel market exchange rate of 2,400 kwanza to US$1 in 1991. Goods were only available to the population on the parallel market, not in the state shops at artificially low controlled prices. By 1999, as a result of ongoing war and the government's refusal to adopt economic stabilization measures, US$1 on the parallel market was equal to 1.5 billion old kwanzas, or 1.5 million new kwanzas.

This MPLA government policy ensured a redistribution strategy from the poor to the rich. Those with assets, the rich, benefited from an increasing kwanza value for their assets, while those wishing to purchase assets, the poor, had to pay ever more. Wages remained appallingly low, based upon the unrealistic official rate of exchange. Public sector workers could not survive on their salaries; hence all pursued separate avenues of earning. Corruption thrived as a survival mechanism. Moral values deteriorated, spreading out from the top of the political system.

The dual exchange rate allowed the small ruling elite to profit from their privileged access to purchase dollars at the official rate of exchange and sell these for kwanzas on the parallel market at the far higher rate of exchange. Then the cycle of accumulation could begin once again for the elite, by exchanging the kwanzas for dollars at the beneficial official rate of exchange. This system provided a license to become rich for the few and a recipe for poverty for the many. Two-thirds of the urban population live below the poverty line, with one in ten living in extreme poverty.

The war not only destroyed the economic and social fabric of the country, it also offered the excuse for the government to resist economic reform. War also presented lucrative economic opportunities for the military leaders to enrich themselves. This took a variety of forms. Generals on both sides, the MPLA and UNITA, benefited from controlling some of the diamond mines, and selling diamonds illegally. Arms purchases allowed big "kick-backs," and military control of territory allowed taxation of any trade and commerce occurring within the area controlled.

The government has reaped the reward of the development of offshore deep water oil drilling technology, selling off concessions with high bonuses paid on signature of the concession by the foreign oil exploration companies. Since the mid-1980s the balance of payments was permanently in deficit, and arms and food imports were paid for by mortgaging future oil revenue. In the absence of an agreed structural adjustment program with the IMF and World Bank, the government was obliged to borrow money at extremely high levels of interest, further indebting the country.

BARRY MUNSLOW

See also: **Angola: Cold War Politics, Civil War, 1975–1994; Angola: Independence and Civil War, 1974–1976; Angola: MPLA, FNLA, UNITA, and the War of Liberation, 1961–1974; Angola: Peace Betrayed, 1994 to the Present.**

Further Reading

Maier, Karl. *Angola: Promises and Lies*. London: Serif, 1996.

Munslow, Barry. "Angola: The Politics of Unsustainable development," *Third World Quarterly* 20/3 (1999): 537–554.

Pereira, Anthony W. "The Neglected Tragedy: The Return to War in Angola 1992–1993," *Journal of Modern African Studies*, 31/2 (1994): 1–28.

Roque, Fatima Maura. *Building the Future in Angola*. Oeiras: Celta Editora, 1997.

Tvedten, Inge. *Angola. Struggle for Peace and Reconstruction*. Boulder, CO: Westview Press, 1997.

Angola: Peace Betrayed, 1994 to the Present

The Lusaka Protocol peace agreement between the MPLA and UNITA was signed on November 20, 1994. This followed two years of heavy fighting after UNITA's leader, Jonas Savimbi, refused to accept that he had lost the UN-supervised democratic elections of September 1992. The Lusaka Protocol followed earlier peace accords between the two parties, Alvor (1975) and Bicesse (1991), both of which were broken. Savimbi of UNITA did not attend the signing ceremony, which was taken as a bad omen. He was angered by the MPLA's final offensive on the eve of the signing, which led to the fall of Huambo, the principal city in the heartland of his Ovimbundu regional base in the central high plateau, which had great symbolic significance. Savimbi felt obliged to go along with the agreement because of reversals on the battlefield and

because of increasing international pressure. He was never committed to the Lusaka Protocol, regarding it as a capitulation if it were fully implemented.

Fundamentally, there was a basic lack of trust between the two protagonists, President Jose Eduardo dos Santos and Jonas Savimbi, given the extensive history of broken agreements and in particular Savimbi's unwillingness to accept his defeat in the national assembly and presidential elections of 1992, which were deemed to be free and fair by the international community. Savimbi never accepted the legitimacy of his defeat.

The implementation of the Lusaka Accords proceeded at a painfully slow pace. Not until May 1995 did dos Santos and Savimbi meet face to face. The UN Security Council only authorized the United Nations Angola Verification Mission III in February 1995, and the first Blue Helmet troops became operational in May. Delays occurred across all fronts against a backdrop of accusation and counteraccusation of cease-fire violations. The first critical issue was the quartering of UNITA troops, the engagement of an agreed number of these into a unified Angolan army, and the demobilization of the remaining UNITA forces. UNITA continuously delayed implementation, questioning the location of the sites, the inadequacy of the camps, and security issues. UNITA wanted the sites located in the areas of its dominance, the MPLA in areas further away from direct UNITA influence. Heavy laying of land mines, with bridges and air strips destroyed, all created delays in establishing the quartering areas. The actual quartering process only began exactly one year after the Lusaka Protocol was signed.

The agreed-upon process involved UNITA committing its troops and armaments into the quartering areas and the government withdrawing its troops into defensive positions and confining to barracks the Rapid Intervention Police known as the *ninjas*. In fact, UNITA never committed its core troops, instead recruiting young boys and civilians, then sending them into the camps with frequently old and unserviceable weapons. Formally the incorporation of UNITA generals into the new national army and the completion of UNITA's troop quartering was achieved in December 1996. Yet in the words of Paul Hare, the U.S. special representative until 1998 for the Angolan peace process: "The simple truth was that UNITA was never enamored with the Lusaka Protocol, especially the provision calling for the disarming of its troops. The problem was fundamental, as UNITA's military arm had formed the backbone and *raison d'être* of the movement since 1966."

In essence, Savimbi was simply not prepared to relinquish control of his military power base. This was linked to a second critical issue, the expansion of the state administration over the whole country. At the time of the peace agreement, the country was effectively divided between areas controlled by the government and those controlled by UNITA. The protocol had called for the free movement of goods and people, and this was only ever partially attained in certain areas of the country. When the government began in earnest to expand the state administration in 1997 and 1998, tensions began to erupt. UNITA complained of government police behaving like an occupying army, while the government saw its efforts to implement the agreement being blocked at every turn. Some of the pillaging by government police reflected personal survival strategies, as often they received neither their salaries nor supplies.

There was great expectation that the entry of UNITA deputies and ministers and vice-ministers into the Government of National Unity and Reconciliation (GURN) when this occurred in April 1997, would facilitate the peace process. UNITA provided four ministers and seven vice-ministers out of a total of twenty-eight ministers and fifty-five vice-ministers. At the inauguration ceremony, once again Savimbi refused to attend.

At the heart of the contestation was maintenance of the economic and political power bases of the rival leaders. The main flash point was the control of the diamond mining areas in the provinces of Lunda Norte and Lunda Sul in the northeast of the country. The MPLA relied upon its control of Angola's oil wealth to finance its power base, while UNITA controlled much of the diamond mining areas of the northern interior. The MPLA were keen to expand their control of the diamond areas and to restrict access to UNITA, thereby cutting off the financial resources for UNITA's military effort.

The critical issue was whether a compromise could be negotiated to leave UNITA front companies with guaranteed access to diamond revenues if UNITA fully implemented the peace agreement. In fact, UNITA hung on to its essential revenue source by going through the motions of the peace agreement while building up sufficient revenues from diamond production to reequip and upgrade its army to launch yet another major offensive intended to defeat the MPLA-dominated government. Diamond revenues also enabled UNITA to break United Nations sanctions imposed in a serious way from September 1998. Logistical access for UNITA rearmament was purchased by bribes paid to political and military leaders in neighboring countries.

The MPLA strategy, on the other hand, was to try to cut off UNITA's logistical access through those same neighboring countries. This strategy led to heavy Angolan government military commitments in the two northern bordering countries of the Democratic Republic of the Congo (formerly Zaïre), and Congo-Braazaville.

Dos Santos had supported the opposition forces of Laurent Kabila in his overthrow of President Mobuto of Zaïre in 1997. UNITA's friendly relationship with Mobuto had allowed Zaïre to be a resupply zone for the areas of Angola that UNITA controlled. Kabila failed to halt the use of his country for attacks by various groups against the neighboring states that had supported his successful military campaign, notably Uganda, Rwanda, and Angola. While Angola's government continued to support Kabila, Uganda and Rwanda grew impatient and launched a new offensive to oust Kabila. UNITA found new allies with Uganda and Rwanda, while the Angolan government, supported by the governments of Zimbabwe and Namibia, provided military support to Kabila in a new central African war that escalated regional tensions. These new regional dimensions of conflict fueled the breakdown of the peace agreement between the MPLA and UNITA.

In February 2002, Jonas Savimbi was killed during a skirmish with government forces. In April of that year, MPLA and UNITA signed a formal cease-fire, raising hopes that a lasting peace may be achieved.

BARRY MUNSLOW

See also: **Angola: Cold War Politics, Civil War, 1975–1994; Angola: Civil War: Impact of, Economic and Social; Angola: Independence and Civil War, 1974–1976; Angola: MPLA, FNLA, UNITA, and the War of Liberation, 1961–1974.**

Further Reading

Maier, Karl. *Angola: Promises and Lies*. London: Serif, 1996.
Pereira, Anthony W. "The Neglected Tragedy: The Return to War in Angola 1992–1993," *Journal of Modern African Studies*, 31/2 (1994): 1–28.
Tvedten, Inge. *Angola. Struggle for Peace and Reconstruction*. Boulder, CO: Westview Press, 1997.

Antananarivo

Located at the highest point (1,480 meters above sea level) of three ranges of hills forming a Y-shape, Analamanga dominated a plain, more than 200 meters below, that was floodable, being drained by the River Ikopa, and that was transformed over the centuries, through the irrigation policies of successive kings, into a set of rice-growing regions known as the Betsimitatatra. This immense space, undivided by canals, became one of the symbols of the unity of the kingdom, and of the alliance between the monarch (the rice) and the people (the water).

The migrants who entered Imerina before the end of the first millennium preferred to establish themselves relatively close to the lower ground, but control of a position as exceptional as Analamanga's attracted the interest of the Vazimba, who established their capital there by the end of the fourteenth century at the latest.

The site aroused the greed of the Andriana dynasty, who came from the east and arrived in the vicinity of Analamanga in the course of successive relocations of their capital. By the beginning of the seventeenth century, they were based to the northeast, at Ambohimanga. It was from there that the ruler Andrianjaka set out to conquer Analamanga, seizing the citadel and expelling the Vazimba kings. However, he chose not to live in their *rova* (the fortified enclosure in which the royal palaces stood), preferring a location slightly lower but further to the north, the cardinal direction associated with political power in the symbolic organization of space in Imerina. A moat formed part of the defensive complex and boundary, separating it from the residence of the Vazimba. While the Andriana *rova* was given the name Analamasina ("in the sacred forest"), Analamanga became Antananarivo. This place name, imposed by Andrianjaka, has traditionally been translated as "town (or village) of the thousand," meaning the settlers, but it may be a deformation of Antaninarivo, "in the land of the people," a meaning that would fit better with the purpose of the capital, conceived in the image of the kingdom.

In the early eighteenth century, Andrianampoinimerina, whose own capital was Ambohimanga, reunified Imerina, which had been divided into four kingdoms, and restored the political preeminence of Antananarivo. He too had free subjects settle there. Following the tradition of his ancestors, Andrianampoinimerina assigned to each territorial or status group a specific district within the moats or in the suburbs. The reallocation of these districts, which became *tanindrazana* (ancestral lands containing tombs), was carried out in relation to the *rova*, which was regarded as the central pillar structuring the space of the "great house," the kingdom itself.

Antananarivo clung to its rocks (forming today's Haute Ville [Upper City]) until the nineteenth century, when it became the capital of the kingdom of Madagascar. Then it spread onto the slopes to the west, which were sheltered from the winds, and onto the hills to the north, reaching Faravohitra, a suburb that was held in low esteem until the British missionaries began to favor it as a place of residence. They secured a privileged status for their district by constructing, between 1863 and 1872, a memorial church on the site of the martyrdoms under Ranavalona I, built on the initiative of James Sibree of the London Missionary Society. Their use of stone for this and other buildings led to an upheaval in the symbolism of Imerinian architecture, which had traditionally made a contrast between stone, the material of monuments to the dead, and vegetable matter, used for the residences of the living. Even the Manjakamiadana, the largest of the palaces in the *rova* (an ensemble almost completely destroyed by fire in November 1995), having been built of timber by

a Frenchman, Jean Laborde, was refitted in stone under the direction of James Cameron, a Scottish craftsman and missionary who departed from Madagascan tradition and conceived a model for residential building that was to be adopted by the elite. Even today, this model still gives the city its distinctive cachet, with its brick-built houses, each with a sloping roof, an upper story, a veranda, and several rooms, including a drawing room. The bourgeois homes of the colonial period may be distinguished by their more massive aspect, an arcade over the veranda, and the addition of a tower.

The colonial administration insisted on stamping a certain "Frenchness" on Antananarivo. It started with innovations in infrastructure, with paved roads, electric lighting, and sewers carrying drinking water, as well as with the laying out of the districts of the Ville Moyenne [Middle City] in the vicinity of the governor-general's headquarters. In 1924, the French architect and town planner Géo Cassaigne drew up the first programmatic plan for the layout, expansion, and embellishment of the capital. This plan paid special attention to the circulation of automobiles and the specialization of districts within the city; it also provided for garden suburbs for the Europeans and for "villages" for the natives, within a city where racial segregation had been unknown. However, material and financial constraints forced the abandonment of this plan.

Modern town planning in the Western style was adopted mainly in the Betsimitatatra, where the rice farms gave way to the Ville Basse [Lower City], which was given a park, squares, and other geometric open spaces. The buildings on this main axis, including the Hôtel de Ville [city hall], which was burned down at the time of the movement of May 1972, formed a homogeneous ensemble typical of the 1930s. The edges of the city held little interest for the administration, or for European speculators, and the less salubrious establishments were located there. In those valleys and parts of the plain that had not been cleared, residential districts were developed by the common people, beyond the reach of any planning controls. The hillsides were deficient in roads, yet they were more and more densely filled by the houses of the Madagascan petty and middle bourgeoisie.

The estates constructed in the suburbs under the city plan of 1956 only partially resolved the housing problems caused by the growth of the city, which had become especially rapid after World War II. Antananarivo also continued to expand into the Betsimitatatra, which became the site of major embankment operations after the serious flooding of 1959. The plain became the location of an administrative complex, with ministries, a hospital, and educational institutions, as well as more estates, but little was done to clear the ground, and, in the absence of policies for housing or credit, the municipality failed to prevent either illicit occupation or spontaneous settlement. The development in the last few decades of a great suburban sprawl has impeded the process of urban development. The implementation of a plan for Grand Tananarive [Greater Tananarive], extending as far as the ranges of hills several kilometers from the center of the city, is also expected to contribute to reducing congestion in the greater metropolitan region.

FARANIRINA RAJAONAH

See also: **Madagascar.**

Further Reading

Rajaonah, Faranirina. "Modèles européens pour une ville malgache: Antananarivo aux 19ème[-]20ème siècles," in *La ville européenne outre-mers: un modèle conquérant? (15ème–20éme siècles)*, Catherine Coquery-Vidrovitch and Odile Goerg (eds.). Paris: L'Harmattan, 1996 ["European Models for a Madagascan City: Antananarivo in the Nineteenth and Twentieth Centuries," in *The European City Overseas: A Conqueror's Model? The Fifteenth through the Twentieth Century*].

Rajaonah, Faranirina. *Élites et notables malgaches à Antananarivo dans la première moitié du 20ème siècle.* Doctoral thesis, Université de Lyon 2, 1996–1997 [*Elites and Notable Madagascarans of Antananarivo in the First Half of the Twentieth Century*].

Anticolonialism: *See* **Colonialism, Overthrow of: Nationalism and Anticolonialism.**

Anti-Slavery Movement

The anti-slavery movement in Western Europe stemmed from two main sources: evangelical Christianity in Great Britain and the ideals of the Enlightenment on the Continent. As early as 1744 John Wesley, founder of the Methodist Church, had written *Thoughts on Slavery*, one of the first influential tracts to condemn slavery on moral grounds. But the heart of the movement for legislative action in England stemmed from the leadership of three men. One was Granville Sharp, who had won the benchmark Mansfield decision in 1772 that slavery could not be sustained by law on English soil. Another was Thomas Clarkson, author of a *Summary View of the Slave Trade and the Probable Causes of Its Abolition* (1787). The third was William Wilberforce, a great parliamentary orator. Both Clarkson and Wilberforce were inspired by evangelical preachers at the University of Cambridge. Enlisting the support of other activists (including J. Stephen, T. Babbington, Z. Macaulay, and the former slave Olaudah Equiano), they formed the Anti-Slave Trade Society. The society, with its connection to the Methodist Church, effective organization, pamphleteering, and mass petitions to parliament, inspired other pressure groups focused on societal improvement during the age of reform.

Assisted by votes from the Irish bloc in the House of Commons, as well as behind-the-scenes support from politicians of the highest rank, such as William Pitt and Lord Grenville, the group succeeded in overcoming the entrenched power of the West Indies sugar lobby and opposition in the House of Lords to outlaw the slave trade (for British citizens) and, at the same time, to establish the Sierra Leone Colony in West Africa for freed slaves in 1807. Meanwhile, other nations prohibited the slave trade: Denmark in 1803, the United States in 1808, Sweden in 1813, and the Netherlands in 1814. During its radical phase (1793), the French National Assembly abolished both the slave trade and slavery, but slavery was reinstituted by Napoleon, and the institution was not finally abolished in the French West Indies until the 1840s. British diplomatic pressure and naval coercion would play a significant part in ending Brazil's participation in the slave trade in the 1850s.

Meanwhile, the British humanitarian movement had revived in the 1820s under T.F. Buxton, who founded the new Anti-Slavery Society, with a base at Exeter Hall, London, in 1823. The final end to slavery as an institution throughout the British Empire, ten years later, was preceded by extensive missionary activity in the West Indies, which roused British Caribbean slaves and led ultimately to rebellion (i.e., the Montego Bay uprising and the gruesome planter retribution of 1831, where upwards of 600 Africans were killed). These events once again stirred British public opinion and led to action. The final 1833 Emancipation Bill, drafted by James Stephen, Jr., and passed by the reformed 1832 parliament, had to be approved by the Jamaican legislature (on condition of compensation paid to slave owners, coupled with a lengthy seven-year apprenticeship for the ex-slaves), thus it was not immediately successful. A majority of ex-slaves, fueled by frustration and disappointment, would lead to further unrest and rebellion in Jamaica in the years ahead. The freeing of slaves would not be completed in a majority of the other European colonies of the Caribbean until forty years after the British effort. During this time, and up until the American Civil War in the 1860s, the British Anti-Slavery Society corresponded with kindred spirits in the U.S., led by William Lloyd Garrison, Frederick Douglass, and New England-based abolitionists.

Most of the great powers, including Britain, viewed African internal slavery (sometimes recast as "domestic servitude") in a different light from New World plantation slavery, and colonial governments proceeded slowly against it in order to avoid antagonizing African rulers and disrupting indigenous social structures. Still, British humanitarians vowed to stifle the inland slave trade and slave raiding. Buxton and the African clergyman, Samuel Ajayi Crowther, led the campaign for their replacement by "legitimate trade" (mainly the export of palm products), commencing with the River Niger expeditions of the 1840s and 1850s. The celebrated Victorian explorations and missionary activities of David Livingstone in east and southern Africa from 1841 to 1873 became a beacon for late nineteenth-century anti-slavery movements in Africa. But this also served as a prelude to, and a rhetorical cover for, imperialism and territorial annexations during the "scramble for Africa." French colonial policy regarding the ending of slavery in Africa (like that of nearly every other European nation) was uneven and marked by contradiction. At times nearly all the colonial powers were guilty of perpetuating servitude through harsh schemes for labor recruitment and the use of slaves as transport workers. The epitome of "abolitionist imperialism" in British colonial Africa was exemplified by the exploits of Frederick Lugard (c.1900), who used anti-slavery as a partial rationale for his military and territorial conquest of the northern Nigerian Muslim emirates.

Throughout the nineteenth and early twentieth centuries, Britain used its leverage with other nations to curb both the slave trade and slavery as an institution by diplomatic influence, colonial administration, the legal nonrecognition of slavery, and periodic naval and military actions. Over the last century African internal slavery slowly disappeared in most countries, owing to the assimilation of former slaves into their host societies. However, both slave raiding and use of slave labor have reared their heads again in modern times. The humanitarian abolitionist movement lives on today in the group Anti-Slavery International.

RAYMOND E. DUMETT

See also: **Crowther, Reverend Samuel Ajayi and the Niger Mission; Equiano, Olaudah; "Legitimate Commerce" and the Export Trade in the Nineteenth Century; Livingstone, David; Nigeria: Lugard, Administration, "Indirect Rule"; Slavery in African Society.**

Further Reading

Bolt, Christine, and S. Drescher. *Anti-Slavery, Religion, and Reform*. Folkestone, 1980.

Buxton, T.F. *The African Slave Trade and Its Remedy*. London, 1840.

Davis, David Brion. *The Problem of Slavery in the Age of Revolution*. Ithaca, NY, 1975.

Equiano, Olaudah. *The Interesting Life of O. Equiano or Gustavus Vasa, The African*. London, 1789.

Klein, Martin (ed.). *Breaking the Chain: Bondage and Emancipations in Modern Africa and Asia*. Madison, WI, 1993.

Knight, Franklin. *Africa and the Caribbean: The Legacies of a Link*. Baltimore, MD, 1979.

Lovejoy, P., and J. Hogendorn. *Slow Death for Slavery: The Course of Abolition in Northern Nigeria, 1897–1936*. Cambridge, England, 1993.

Miers, S., and Roberts (eds.). *The End of Slavery in Africa: Historical and Anthropological Perspectives*. Madison, WI, 1988.

Temperley, Howard. *British Anti-Slavery, 1833–1879*. London, 1972.

Anti-Slavery Squadron, Decline of Export Slave Trade, Nineteenth Century

The transatlantic trade in slaves dominated Euro-African relations from the late fifteenth through the early nineteenth centuries. It grew rapidly in volume and importance over the years, undergoing vast increases, especially from 1650 to 1850. Although the Portuguese were the leading slave traders in Africa in the fifteenth and sixteenth centuries, and although they were superseded later by the Dutch and the French, the English had, by the eighteenth century, become the main dealers in the nefarious trade. Ironically, Britain was also the nation that, toward the close of the eighteenth century and the beginning of the nineteenth, had spearheaded the anti-slavery movement, due to new socioeconomic attitudes toward Africa in general and West Africa in particular, which were then growing in several British circles.

In 1807 Britain abolished its slave trade. The British were by no means alone in outlawing the sea-borne trade: it appeared that opinion worldwide was turning against slavery, as reflected in the actions of other countries. Denmark, for instance, had abolished it in its areas of jurisdiction (including those in the Caribbean), while the United States, Sweden, and the Netherlands each independently enacted similar laws, which took effect in 1808, 1813, and 1814, respectively. However, the British campaign against the traffic in human beings was far more active and widespread than that of any other European nation; in addition to outlawing its own slave trade, the nation actively suppressed the slave trade of other nations.

By the beginning of the nineteenth century, the climate of public opinion in Britain was such that abolition became possible. Although it was 1833 before the British parliament passed an act (effective from 1834) outlawing the institution of slavery in all of Britain's imperial possessions, it had been illegal for British subjects to engage in the obnoxious trade since the Act of Abolition of 1807. Severe penalties were imposed on British subjects caught trading in slaves, and by 1824 such actions were punishable by death.

The road to abolition, however, was not an easy one. Even in 1807 there were still groups in Britain anxious to continue the slave trade. Measures taken by Britain were frustrated as substantial numbers of slaves were transported across the Atlantic after 1807. Several European nations and individuals derived their wealth from the trade and were therefore reluctant to support any move to suppress it. At the same time, new centers of demand for slaves developed, especially in Cuba and Brazil. The same went for the southern states of the U.S. While the British prohibition was stringently enforced in the British Empire, it was difficult to put into effect the new laws on an international scale without the full support of other nations.

To enforce the Abolition Act of 1807, Britain instituted an anti-slave trade squadron, as an arm of the royal navy, to patrol the West African waters, inspect ships, and seize any found to have slaves aboard. Slaves found in such captured ships were set free and settled in Freetown, Sierra Leone, the base of the squadron. The naval squadron undertook a blockade of the major slave trading ports. Between 1808 and 1830, British efforts at putting an end to the slave trade were concentrated on the activities of the anti-slave trade squadron, and this was quite active and widespread, producing some positive results.

Having hopefully abolished its own slave-trading practices, Britain shifted its attention toward securing the cooperation of others through a tortuous and protracted phase of international diplomatic bargaining. Its sustained pressure led to the passage of anti-slavery legislation by other principal slave-trading nations in Europe, North Africa, the Americas and the Middle East during the first three decades of the nineteenth century. This resulted in France outlawing its trade in 1818 and Brazil in 1825. Earlier, Portugal and Spain had initiated laws (in 1815 and 1817, respectively) which increasingly restricted their slave traders to the seas south of the equator, in return for British loans and financial subsidies.

Although the British government had succeeded in persuading other nations to enact laws banning slavery, by the 1820s it had become apparent that, apart from Britain itself, most of those other powers had not taken positive measures to enforce compliance with the laws. The next stage in the British campaign was thus devoted to efforts to get those states to agree to "reciprocal search treaties" granting the right of search of ships suspected of carrying slaves to all nations that were party to the treaty. At Freetown, after the granting of reciprocal search treaties, slave traders of any nation were brought to justice and their slaves set free by courts of mixed commission (that is, courts with judges of various European nationalities notably British, Spanish, and Portuguese).

The anti-slavery squadron failed to stop the transport of slaves to the Americas, but the presence of those royal naval patrols had a deterrent effect as it made the slave trade a risky venture. Between 1825 and 1865, for instance, no less than 1,287 slave ships were captured, from which about 130,000 slaves were released alive, even though nearly 1,800,000 slaves were still exported from West Africa alone about this same period. By the late 1860s (that is, more than fifty years after Britain passed the Act of Abolition), however, the slave trade overseas was no longer significant. At that time, the impact of the industrial revolution was being felt all over Europe and in the United States. On the other hand, Christian missionary enterprise and the new "legitimate commerce" (the African version of the pervasive mid-nineteenth-century British doctrine of free commodity trade) had gained a fairly strong footing in Africa. The quest for slaves, therefore, became increasingly anachronistic, thus complementing the efforts of the anti-slavery squadron to suppress the slave trade.

Be that as it may, following the stationing of the naval squadron, which undertook a blockade of the major slave trading ports in West Africa, a new European interest and influence began to develop. The concomitant weakening of the economic and political sovereignty of the coastal states gradually set in motion a chain of events that prepared the way for the eventual British and European occupation of the respective states starting in the late nineteenth century.

S. ADEMOLA AJAYI

See also: **Slavery: Atlantic Trade: Abolition: Philanthropy or Economics?; Slavery, Atlantic Basin in the Era of; Slavery: Atlantic Trade: Effects in Africa and the Americas.**

Further Reading

Coupland, Reginald. *The British Anti-Slavery Movement.* London, 1993.

Eltis, David. *Economic Growth and the Ending of the Trans-Atlantic Slave Trade.* New York, 1987.

Lovejoy, Paul E. *Transformation in Slavery: A History of Slavery in Africa.* Cambridge: Cambridge University Press, 1983.

Ransford, Oliver. *The Slave Trade: The Story of Trans-Atlantic Slavery.* London: John Murray Publishers, 1971.

Zeleza, Paul Tiyambe. *A Modern Economic History of Africa, vol. 1, The Nineteenth Century.* Dakar, Senegal, 1993.

Anywa: *See* **Nilotes, Eastern Africa: Western Nilotes: Shilluk, Nuer, Dinka, Anywak**

Aouzou: *See* **Chad: Libya, Aozou Strip, Civil War.**

Apartheid: *See* South Africa: Antiapartheid Struggle, International; South Africa: Antiapartheid Struggle: Townships, the 1980s; South Africa: Apartheid, 1948–1959; South Africa: Apartheid, Education and.

Arab and Islamic World, Africa in

Africa has long interacted with the Arab and wider Islamic worlds. Historically, Islam spread from the Middle East via North Africa to Sub-Saharan Africa in two main ways: first, by a series of jihads from the seventh and eighth centuries, and second, by trade in commodities and people from the ninth to the nineteenth centuries. Trade was focused on the eastern seaboard of Africa, beginning before and ending after the Western Europe and Americas centered trade on the west coast, which brought Christianity to Africa. The spread of Islam took about twelve centuries; by the nineteenth century the faith had spread throughout much of the African continent.

By the time that European colonialism came to an end in Africa, there was a Muslim presence in virtually all African countries. But because of European colonialism, during the first half of the twentieth century the pace of growth of Christianity generally outstripped that of Islam. The numbers of Christians increased from around 10 million in 1900 to more than 250 million by the 1990s, while the numbers of Muslims in Africa grew from about 34 million at the beginning of the twentieth century to around 300 million during the same period. The consequence was that, while many of Africa's Muslims live in North Africa, a substantial number also reside south of the Sahara. The continent is predominantly Muslim above the tenth parallel, a dividing line that cuts through the northern regions of Sierra Leone, Côte d'Ivoire, Ghana, Togo, Benin, Nigeria, Cameroon, Central African Republic, Ethiopia, and Somalia. The same line roughly separates Muslim from non-Muslim in Sudan and Chad.

In the late nineteenth century, the Muslim world experienced the slow demise of the Turkish Ottoman empire and the (near) contemporaneous emergence of Saudi Arabia as champion of Islamic reformist ambitions. During this time, the growth of Sufi brotherhoods in Africa led to the extension of Muslim networks throughout much of Africa and beyond, and the introduction of new modernizing ideas. African Muslims joined Sufi brotherhoods to further their own commercial networks and were often receptive to Islamic reformist ideas, as well as to Pan-Islamic ideals during the first half of the twentieth century.

The historical characteristics of the Arab/Islamic-African connection make the relationship between the two regions easy to trace but difficult to assess. Interactions between Islam and Africa began with the arrival of Arabs and the process of religious conversion. This was a process reflective of the "dominant Arab/dominated African" relationship, which was to become an unhappy component of some of Africa's historical development. Given the historical significance of slavery in Africa, the role of the Arabs in the region was hardly auspicious. This is not to diminish the impact of the effects of European colonial rule, for the latter tended to forge a closer link between the Arabs and the Africans, especially during the postindependence period as both regions fought the struggle against imperialism. Yet the years of colonial rule underlined the fact that divisions widely existed between Muslim Africans, often powerful in their communities, favored and patronized by some colonialists, and non-Muslim Africans who, often deeply resenting the burden of European colonial control, produced the great majority of African nationalist leaders after World War II.

In the postcolonial era, the sometimes uneasy relationship between Muslims and non-Muslims has significantly informed political developments in a number of African countries including Nigeria, Sudan, and Chad. Religious rivalry in such countries was informed by two main issues: first, putative or actual African membership of the wider Islamic community and, second, the role of Arab oil wealth in Africa's economic and social development.

Certain Arab or Muslim countries have sought to pursue foreign policy goals in Africa in recent years. The Iranian, Saudi Arabian, and Libyan governments have all been active in Africa since the 1970s, seeking to pursue strategic foreign policy goals that often had the impact of helping to stir up Arab-oriented discontent. Decades of oil revenues gave such states the financial ability to prosecute aggressive foreign policies in Africa, policies in which the separation of political, diplomatic, and religious goals was sometimes difficult to draw. For example, Iran's status as a predominantly Shi'ite country, when most African Muslims are Sunni, was partially offset for some African Muslim radicals (for example, in Nigeria) by its bona fide revolutionary credentials.

Also controversial in recent years was the role in Africa of the Organization of the Islamic Conference (OIC). The OIC was formed in Rabat in 1969, with the first conference held a year later in Jeddah, Saudi Arabia. The aim of the OIC was to promote Islamic solidarity and further cooperation among member states in the economic, social, cultural, scientific, and political fields. The OIC had fifty-three members in the late 1990s, half of which were African countries. However, in at least two African countries, Nigeria and Zanzibar (a part of the unified state of Tanzania), the issue of the country's membership was highly controversial. This was because Christians in both countries felt very strongly that membership of the OIC implied that each was a "Muslim country," a policy direction they wished strenuously to contest.

Another important area of Arab-Muslim/African interaction was the Arab Bank for Economic Development in Africa (BADEA). The idea of an Arab bank to assist in the economic and social development of all non-Arab African states was first discussed by the Arab heads of state during the Sixth Arab Summit at Algiers in 1973. The BADEA, with headquarters at Khartoum, Sudan, began operations in March 1975. Its main functions include the financing of development projects, promoting and stimulating private Arab investment in Africa, and supplying technical assistance. All member states of the Organization of African Unity, except Arab League participants, are eligible for funding. BADEA's lending to Arab countries, which regularly totaled more than $100 million annually in the early 1980s, dropped significantly in the second part of the decade as oil revenues fell; in 1988, only $35 million was loaned by BADEA. However, annual levels of loans grew again over the next few years to total $90 million in the mid-1990s.

The bank indicated at this time that it would like to increase funding levels to needy African countries, but was constrained by the adverse economic climate in most of them. The third Five-year Plan (1995–1999) aimed to increase the percentage of concessionary lending and refocus lending away from large infrastructural projects to smaller rural ventures, as well to health services and educational programs.

JEFF HAYNES

See also: **Islam: Eastern Africa; Religion, History of; Religion: Colonial Africa: Islamic Orders and Movements; Religion, Postcolonial Africa: Islam.**

Further Reading

Brenner, Louis (ed.). *Muslim Identity and Social Change in Sub-Saharan Africa*. London: Hurst and Co., 1993.

Deegan, Heather. *Third Worlds. The Politics of the Middle East and Africa*. London: Routledge, 1996.

El-Din, Khair Haseeb (ed.). *The Arabs and Africa*. London: Croom Helm, 1985.

Haynes, Jeff. *Religion and Politics in Africa*. London: Zed Books, 1996.

Lapidus, Ira. *A History of Islamic Societies*. Cambridge: Cambridge University Press, 1988.

Arab Bedouin: Banu Hilal, Banu Sulaym, Banu Ma'qil (Eleventh to Fifteenth Centuries)

The Fatimid rulers who had controlled Ifriqiya since the early tenth century shifted their political center eastward to the Nile Valley in the 960s, entrusting a vassal Berber group, the Zirids, with the administration of Ifriqiya. Within a century, however, the Zirids had proclaimed themselves independent rulers. The Fatimids' attention was then focused on the task of solidifying their position in the eastern Mediterranean, but they were unwilling to ignore the Zirids' defiance. In retaliation, they set in motion a process that punished their disloyal subordinates and simultaneously ameliorated a recurrent problem in Egypt. Bedouin tribes that had immigrated across the Red Sea to Upper Egypt as Islam expanded out of the Arabian Peninsula had long wreaked havoc in that region, frequently disrupting the agriculture on which Egypt's prosperity hinged. By forcing as many as a quarter of a million of these Arab nomads from the Banu Hilal, Banu Sulaym, and Banu Ma'qil confederations to leave the Nile Valley and migrate westward, the Fatimids avenged the Zirids' temerity and rid themselves of troublesome subjects. The Banu Sulaym resettled in Cyrenaica and Tripolitania, but the Banu Hilal and Banu Ma'qil pushed farther westward.

As the nomads poured into Ifriqiya, the Zirids at first tried to integrate them into their army, hoping to use them to quell the unrest triggered by economic deterioration in rural areas. Some Banu Hilal accepted the offer to join forces with the Zirids, but far more ignored it. As they overran the province's plains and steppes, the Zirids were compelled to mount a defense of their most valuable lands. In a pitched battle at Haidaran, northwest of Qairawan, in 1052, the bedouins routed the Zirid forces. More vulnerable than ever to the depredations of the nomads, the Zirids were powerless to prevent the Banu Hilal from sacking Qairawan in 1057. The city was already in the process of losing much of its economic vitality as a result of shifts in the trans-Saharan trade routes, but the departure of the Zirid court for Mahdiyya, on the coast, marked Qairawan's demise as Ifriqiya's political center of gravity. In the ensuing decades, many bedouin shaykhs carved out enclaves that they were able to govern independent of Zirid influence.

Other factions of the Banu Hilal continued to push into the central Maghrib, where some allied with the Hammadid dynasty that controlled the region. Like their Zirid relatives, however, the Hammadids were soon overwhelmed by the bedouins and retreated to the coastal city of Bajaia, replicating the Zirids' retreat to Mahdiyya. In the course of the twelfth century, the Banu Hilal who had remained in Ifriqiya were joined by bands of the Banu Sulaym who were beginning to enter the region from Tripolitania. In 1153, these groups united in an unsuccessful attempt to thwart the eastward advance of the Almohad empire. After their victory in a pitched battle near Setif in 1153, the Almohads deported thousands of the defeated bedouins to Morocco, incorporating them into their army. These bedouin contingents later participated in the Almohad campaign that brought Ifriqiya under the dynasty's control in 1160.

To the south, along the fringes of the Sahara, the Banu Ma'qil were also on the move during the twelfth century. Penetrating into eastern Morocco, they rapidly asserted their dominance over a swath of territory stretching from the Mediterranean southward to the oasis of Tafilalt. With the collapse of Almohad power in the second half of the thirteenth century, the Banu Ma'qil challenged the authority of the dynasty's successors, the Banu Marin. Recurrent conflicts marked the following two centuries of Marinid rule, after which the bedouins added the region around Marrakesh, much of the Middle Atlas, and parts of the Atlantic plain to their domain.

Students of Maghrib history have long debated the impact of this influx of bedouin groups. Ibn Khaldun, a fourteenth-century Tunisian scholar, compared the Banu Hilal to a swarm of locusts that destroyed everything in its path and showed particular contempt for sedentary, civilized society. But Ifriqiya was experiencing considerable turmoil even before these nomadic incursions. Shifting patterns of trade had already set in motion the province's economic decline, which was marked by the increasing marginalization of Qairawan. This situation increased the region's vulnerability to the bedouins, and they used it to their advantage, but they were neither the sole, nor even the primary, cause of Ifriqiya's ills. Even so, the bedouins never gained control of Qairawan, nor of any other important urban center, for any extended period. Indeed, because Qairawan's collapse required smaller provincial cities to explore new economic horizons, many of them enjoyed an era of prosperity following these events.

While not so catastrophic as their critics charged, the bedouin did have a pronounced impact throughout the Maghrib. Their presence raised the incidence of nomadism, inevitably menacing agricultural life. This was especially true in the interior, where agrarian activity was more fragile than along the coast. In the areas where their numbers were greatest, some previously sedentary Berbers turned to nomadism themselves. More importantly in the long run, the Banu Hilal, Banu Sulaym, and Banu Ma'qil swelled the Maghrib's small Arab population, although the Berbers continued to constitute the majority of the region's population. The bedouins' presence rendered the Arab customs and traditions that had overlain the Maghrib, especially its eastern and central portions, since the seventh century much more apparent. No general process of Arabization yet developed, but more Berbers were more intensively exposed to more Arabs than ever before. Finally, the bedouins' mastery of large areas of the deserts and the steppes combined with the already precarious conditions of the trans-Saharan trade to alter the commercial focus of the Maghrib from the interior of Africa to the Mediterranean. The transfer of the Zirid capital to Mahdiyya after the sack of Qairawan, the Hammadid shift to Bajaia, and the Almohad decision to site their eastern Maghrib headquarters at Tunis all suggested this reorientation.

KENNETH J. PERKINS

See also: **Ibn Khaldun: Civilization of the Maghrib.**

Further Reading

Brett, Michael. "Ibn Khaldun and the Arabisation of North Africa," *Maghreb Review*, 4 (1979): 9–16.

Idris, Roger. "L'invasion hilalienne et ses conséquences," *Cahiers de Civilisation Médiévale*, 11 (1968): 353–369. ["The Hilalian Invasion and Its Consequences"].

Jacques-Meunié, D. *Le Maroc saharien des origines à 1670*. Paris: Librairie Klincksieck, 1982. [Saharan Morocco and Its Origins to 1670].

Poncet, Jean. "Le Mythe de la 'catastrophe' hilalienne," *Annales Economies, Sociétés, Civilisations*, 22 (1967): 1099–1120. ["The Myth of the Hilalian 'Catastrophe'"].

Arabization: *See* Nubia: Banu Kanz, Juhayna, and the Arabization of the Nilotic Sudan (Fourteenth–Eighteenth Centuries)

Architecture: *See* Art and Architecture, History of African; Egypt, Ancient: Architecture.

Arma: *See* Songhay Empire: Moroccan Invasion, 1591.

Armies, Colonial: Africans in

European success in the African colonial wars was due largely to the ability of Europeans to recruit large armies of African troops. The availability of these African soldiers, it should be pointed out, was largely the result of the extraordinary flux that beset internal African politics in the nineteenth century, as empires expanded and retracted and smaller states rose and fell. The "peripheral flux" that stemmed from the decline of African states (and sometimes also their growth, as in the case of Samori's empire in Guinea) gave the European invaders the opportunity to insert themselves into local political disputes and, ultimately, to divide and conquer. But the benefit to the newcomers was even more direct than that. From out of the upheaval and civil war that afflicted African states, they were able to draw the manpower they needed to build their armies.

The European forces that took part in the conquest of Africa in the second half of the 1800s were very small because European imperial troops were needed elsewhere, colonial budgets were restrained, and the scale of warfare in Africa was considered modest. Additionally, fears of susceptibility to tropical diseases and a hostile climate also kept European armies in Africa small. Perhaps most importantly, European imperialists thought that colonies should bear a significant part of the burden for defense. Thus, although their numbers and the nature of their employment varied from one colonial army to another, large numbers of African soldiers were employed by each of the European powers. In their wars of conquest in Africa, David Killingray exaggerates only slightly when he asserts that:

> European empires in Africa were gained principally by African mercenary armies, occasionally supported by white or other colonial troops. In what Kipling described as "savage wars of peace" the bulk of the fighting was done by black soldiers whose disciplined firepower and organization invariably defeated numerically superior African armies.

Of the European powers involved in Africa, the French probably used the largest number of African troops, even though the African percentage of overall French troop strength in West Africa was lower than in the admittedly smaller *Schutztruppe* in German East Africa or *Force Publique* in the Congo Free State. From 1857, when the first battalion of Senegalese light infantry (*Tirailleurs Sénégalais*) was raised, up to World War I, the part played by African soldiers in the French forces in West Africa grew steadily. In 1910 there were 12,500 African soldiers in West Africa and the Congo-Chad region. British forces in tropical Africa also relied heavily on African troops. The 11,500 soldiers serving under the Union Jack in West Africa, East and central Africa, and northern Nigeria in 1902 included no more than 300 white officers and NCOs.

The Great War of 1914–1918 in Africa required an extensive infusion of military resources and manpower. Africa's greatest service to the war effort was as a source of military labor. Large areas were exploited, with the heaviest burden being borne by East and central Africa, and Egypt. The French conscripted more than 180,000 *Tirailleurs Sénégalais*, and many served on the western front. The performance of these troops is much debated, but their use was hotly contested everywhere. Europeans did not want African soldiers directly involved in "white man's wars." The Germans feared the "black barbarians" and reports of brutality by African soldiers. They argued it was one thing to recruit *askaris* as soldiers and carriers in East Africa, but quite a different matter to use these troops in Europe where they might be exposed to new political perceptions and expectations. For the same reasons, the South Africans refused to arm African soldiers during the conflict and kept them confined in separate compounds in France. European powers also worried that veterans would act as catalysts for resistance against white rule. World War I had a disastrous impact on Africa. The war pundits, related of tragedies the dispersed people, increased taxation, and reduced food surpluses. To these human disasters can be added the impact of the influenza pandemic of 1918–1919. Influenza carried into Africa by the routes of war reached most regions of the continent, hitting with great severity those areas already weakened from the effects of war.

World War II found African soldiers across the globe. After helping to defeat the Italians in Ethiopia in 1940, the King's African Rifles were sent to Burma to fight the Japanese. All together, some 166,000 African troops served Britain outside Africa during World War II. Around 141,000 black soldiers served in the French forces during the war; some defending the *metropole* in 1940. They spent the rest of the war in German prisons. World War II had a great effect on imperialism and thus on Africa. Africans had fought on behalf of the Allies, they had been educated by travel and by the army, they had enjoyed a higher standard of living than before, and they returned home to conditions that did not satisfy them. They had seen white men killed in battle, they had gained confidence from becoming proficient at the white man's weapons, and they had heard of the humiliation of Europeans in the Far East. Above all, the great British Empire, which had seemed so powerful only fifty years before, was quaking everywhere with protest. By 1959, European decolonization was underway.

Postcolonial Africa inherited European military institutions that stressed elitism and ethnic divisions. This tended to put the armed forces at odds with civilian governments and contributed to the endless cascade of military coups in Africa since independence. Contemporary African armies are struggling to restore the symbiosis between armies and the people that existed before the imperial conquest.

DEBORAH SCHMITT

See also: **Soldiers, African: Overseas.**

Further Reading

Echenberg, Myron. *Colonial Conscripts: The Tirailleurs Sénégalais in French West Africa, 1857–1960.* Portsmouth, NH: Heinemann, 1991.

Grundlingh, Albert. *Fighting Their Own War: South African Blacks and the First World War.* Johannesburg: Ravan Press, 1987.

Killingray, David, and Richard Rathbone (eds.). "Africa and the Second World War," *Journal of African History* 26 (1985): 287–288.

Killingray, David. "Colonial Warfare in West Africa, 1870–1914," *Imperialism and War*, J.A. De Moor and H.L. Wesseling (eds.). Leiden: Brill, 1989.

Killingray, David. "War and Society in Africa since 1800," *South African Historical Journal* 25 (1991): 131–153.

Vandervort, Bruce. *Wars of Imperial Conquest in Africa, 1830–1914*. Bloomington: Indiana University Press, 1998.

Arms, Armies: Postcolonial Africa

At independence, the states of Africa inherited the military structures established by the European colonialists. During both world wars, Africa had been a fertile recruiting ground for the Western powers. However, the permanent forces established in each colony were generally small in number and devoted primarily to internal control rather than defense against external aggression. This legacy is reflected in the composition and size of many of Africa's postcolonial armies. Generally speaking, they are small in number, averaging around 42,000 across the continent as a whole. Twenty-four Sub-Saharan African countries have militaries with a strength of less than 20,000. The majority of African armies are lightly equipped with regards to armor and artillery. Most contemporary African states are incapable of sustaining large-scale military operations without disastrous consequences for their economies and societies. There are exceptions to this general rule. Egypt, for example, is possessed of a large and sophisticated military machine as a consequence of its involvement in the politics of the Middle East. Other North African militaries are more numerous than their Sub-Saharan counterparts, but of debatable quality. Large forces and concentrations of equipment can also, by definition, be found in those states engaged in persistent internal or external conflicts, including Ethiopia, Eritrea, and Angola.

Despite being essentially configured for internal security tasks, African armies have been involved in a surprisingly large number of operations in neighboring states. Countries such as Morocco, Zaïre (now Democratic Republic of Congo), Tanzania, Nigeria, and Ghana are among the many states that have been involved in these interventions. Some of these operations have been for peacekeeping purposes under the auspices of organizations such as the Organization of African Unity (OAU) and the Economic Community of West African States (ECOWAS). For example, both Nigeria and Senegal contributed to the OAU's Inter-African Force in Chad in 1982, and Nigeria was the largest contributor to ECOMOG in Liberia. Other interventions have been motivated by self-interest, such as Tanzania's invasion of Uganda in 1979, which led to the overthrow of Idi Amin. A further category of interventions includes those that have been initiated in support of friendly regimes. Morocco's support of Mobutu in Zaïre in 1977 and 1978 falls into this group.

The armies of the minority regimes in Rhodesia and South Africa were constantly involved in raids on their neighbors. Their general level of success against guerrilla forces and other African armies helped them acquire a reputation for ruthless efficiency. For the South Africans, the shine was taken off this reputation to a degree when they suffered reverses at the hands of the Cubans in Angola in 1975. The long, drawn-out nature of these conflicts led to the development of a high level of skill within the ranks of both the government forces and their guerrilla opponents. This "professional" image survived the transition to majority rule. However, the Zimbabwean military has recently suffered a number of embarrassing setbacks in the Democratic Republic of the Congo. The South African National Defense Force's (SANDF) attempt at intervention in Lesotho in September 1998 became something of a fiasco. Together with the problems associated with restructuring this force in the post-apartheid era, this has led to questions being raised about the SANDF's professionalism and capabilities.

The military ethos, ceremonies, and uniforms of many African armies, and especially the attitudes of the officer corps, often reflect their colonial past. Many still receive their training from the former imperial power. Prior to 1989 several of the more radical African militaries received training and assistance from the USSR and its allies. African states have also sought training for their armies from other sources such as the United States, Israel, China, and North Korea.

The professionalism of Africa's militaries has been best by decades of political interference, ethnically based recruitment and promotion, corruption, and military coups. Many African armies reflect the fractured nature of the societies from which they are recruited. They can often give the appearance of being nothing more than a collection of armed groups whose loyalty is restricted to individual military or political leaders. The proliferation of "presidential guards" and special forces units, with their first call on resources, undermines the overall efficiency of the military. Often mired in the politics of the state, the officer corps is more often than not more interested in the acquisition of personal wealth rather than military skills. This decline has rendered many African armies incapable of their primary task of defending the state against either external or internal threats.

It is during periods of actual fighting that African armies tend to reinforce the negative image of them widely held outside the continent. Looting, cruelty to civilians, and the use of child soldiers have now become almost synonymous with African conflicts. The contest for the control of mineral resources, particularly diamonds, is at the heart of these contemporary wars, for example, in Angola, Sierra Leone, and the Democratic Republic of the Congo. The potential for acquiring wealth under these circumstances can serve to undermine military discipline and control. In several recent civil wars, particularly Sierra Leone, it has become almost impossible to distinguish between soldiers and rebels, leading to the emergence of so called "sobels." In Liberia, the looting by the peacekeepers became so notorious that local people said that the acronym ECOMOG actually stood for *Every Car Or Movable Object Gone.*" The failure of their militaries has led a number of regimes including Angola and Sierra Leone to seek the assistance of private security companies such as Executive Outcomes and Military Professional Resources, Inc. Such help as is provided almost inevitably comes with economic and political strings attached. The use of such "private" forces reflects a decline in the reliance placed by African states in their own armed forces.

Many of Africa's postcolonial military conflicts can be accurately described as "low tech" and often "low intensity." The principal casualties are usually civilians, often as the indirect result of the fighting, through such associated causes as famine or disease. Increasingly civilians are being seen as a target for armed forces. In Angola UNITA has used terror to force the rural population into government-held urban areas, thus increasing the burden on them. In Sierra Leone mutilation has been used to terrorize the civilian population into submission to the rebels. Across the continent children are press-ganged and forced to become combatants. Pitched battles between military forces are rare and often inconclusive. In the war in the Democratic Republic of the Congo, despite the intervention of the armies of a number of neighboring states, no military conclusion has been reached. Even when battle is joined with intensity, the tactical impasse remains unbroken. In the war between Ethiopia and Eritrea, World War I tactics and casualties have met late twentieth-century weaponry. Both sides have employed sophisticated weapons systems such as MIG fighters, together with mercenary pilots to fly them, yet after months of intense fighting the front lines have barely moved.

Africa as a whole has little in the way of an indigenous arms industry. The most obvious exception to this is South Africa. Here an arms industry was developed in response to the imposition of sanctions against the apartheid regime. The weapons developed were more suited to the terrain and budgets of Africa than many imports and the post-apartheid government has continued to seek export markets for this important industry.

During the Cold War the primary sources of arms for African states were the two superpower blocs. They, in their turn, were keen to support their clients and woo new allies. As a consequence Africa became an increasingly armed and militarized continent. This process was accelerated from the mid-1970s onward due to the revolutionary wars of liberation in southern Africa and the conflicts in the Horn of Africa. As superpower rivalry increased, so the USSR in particular poured increasing amounts of weaponry into its client states. Eastern Bloc weapons were particularly attractive to African states. They were cheap, designed for ease of use and maintenance, robust, capable of surviving any amount of abuse from soldiers, and did not require great technical expertise from their users. The classic example of all these features is the ubiquitous AK-47 Kalashnikov assault rifle. Since the end of the Cold War, Russia and other Eastern European countries have continued to export weapons to Africa in an effort to bolster their economies. The flood of small arms in particular, into Africa via both official and unofficial routes, has made them both cheap and readily available. This has contributed not only to levels of violence and instability but also—in no small measure—to the intractability of many contemporary African conflicts.

The majority of Africa's militaries are too weak and ill-equipped to effectively defend their countries from external attack. Fortunately, most African states face little in the way of serious external military threats. A side effect of the continent's economic problems is that African states lack the capacity to wage aggressive war. However, these economic factors also have a negative impact on their capacity to conduct peacekeeping operations. Despite these limitations Africa's politicians continue to involve themselves in the affairs of their neighbors, often with disastrous results.

Significant disarmament, especially of irregular forces, regulation of the arms trade, the exclusion of the military from politics, and an end to military adventurism continue to be top priorities for the continent.

GERRY CLEAVER

See also: **Armies, Colonial: Africans in; Soldiers, African: Overseas.**

Further Reading

Clapham, Christopher (ed.). *African Guerrillas*. Oxford: James Currey Ltd., 1998.

May, Roy, and Arnold Hughes. "Armies on Loan: Toward an Explanation of Transnational Military Intervention among Black African States: 1960–1985," in *Military Power and Politics in Black Africa*. S. Baynham, (ed.), London: Croom Helm, 1986.

The Military Balance 1998–1999. London: Brasseys/International Institute for Strategic Studies, 1998.

Turner, John. W. *Continent Ablaze: The Insurgency Wars in Africa 1960 to the Present.* London: Arms and Armour Press 1998.

Art and Architecture, History of African

In precolonial Africa, art was not created for its own sake but for social, political, or religious purposes. The human body, utilitarian objects, and architectural structures were adorned not only to enhance their visual appeal, but also to reflect taste and economic status. Sculptures and masks were used to mediate between the human and spirit worlds. As a result, the traditional African artist ignored imitative naturalism, emphasizing conceptual or symbolic representations in an attempt to capture the spiritual essence of a given subject. Once mistaken for a failed attempt to imitate nature accurately and hence called "primitive" by evolutionist-minded anthropologists and art historians, this conceptual approach ironically inspired the birth of modernist art at the beginning of the twentieth century, being canonized as the epitome of artistic creativity by Western artists such as Picasso and Matisse, among others, who had revolted against academic naturalism.

This new development had both positive and negative consequences for the study of African art. On the one hand, it eliminated the evolutionist prejudice against conceptual representations, obliging the art historian to research the *raison d'etre* for their creation, thus deepening our understanding of African aesthetics. On the other hand, it fostered a scholarly bias for Sub-Saharan African woodcarvings because of their seminal influence on art. The focus on the woodcarvings also marginalized significant artistic expressions in other materials within and from outside Sub-Saharan Africa. Further, it isolated the study of Sub-Saharan African art from those of northern, northeastern, and southern parts of the continent where different artistic traditions predominate, making it extremely difficult to pursue the type of interdisciplinary research that could have shed some light on the historical interactions as well as the extensive artistic exchanges among different groups during the precolonial period. It is gratifying to note, however, that some scholars are beginning to correct this anomaly by looking beyond the traditional boundaries previously set for African art and providing a broader geographical and historical coverage. Thanks to the new data from archeology, the prehistoric rock art, various eyewitness accounts by Arab and European visitors to the continent between the eleventh and nineteenth centuries, as well as the art works of African origin that had been preserved in European collections from the fifteenth century onward, it is now possible to attempt an overview of the artistic activities in the continent from the earliest times to the present, even if there are still several gaps in our knowledge.

The hundreds of thousands of rock paintings and engravings found all over the continent strongly indicate that art has played an important role in African cultures from time immemorial. At any rate, the oldest African rock paintings so far discovered come from the Apollo Cave 11 in Namibia, southwest Africa, and are dated to *c.*27,000BCE. Many of them are naturalistic drawings of animals such as antelopes, hippopotamuses, and rhinoceros rendered in charcoal on portable stones. Some paintings depict stylized human figures wearing what appear to be animal and bird masks either for ritual or hunting purposes. More complex representations, featuring animal and human figures in different styles, can be found everywhere in southern Africa, from Zimbabwe to the Cape, although their exact age cannot yet be ascertained. Most of them are thought to have been created by the ancestors of the present-day San, who still paint and engrave on rock walls in connection with rainmaking, healing, initiation, hunting, fertility, and shamanistic rituals. It may very well be that a good majority of the rock art found in the other parts of the continent had similar functions in the past.

Baule mask, wood, 47 cm, Côte d'Ivoire. Such masks fulfill the Baule's ideal of beauty. The Baule are an Akan-speaking people that settled in the Ivory Coast 200 years ago, and took up the mask traditions of neighboring Senufo, Guro, and Yaure. © Markus Matzel/Das Fotoarchiv.

Some of the most spectacular engravings and paintings have been discovered in the Sahara desert and North Africa. They are classified into five main periods. Those assigned to the Bubalus period (c.10,000BCE), the earliest, are distinguished by their emphasis on the naturalistic rendering of hunting scenes and wild game such as the buffalo, elephant, rhinoceros, hippopotamus, giraffe, and other animals. Several engravings depict the ram with collars and a disk on the head, suggesting either domestication or the association of the animal with supernatural forces.

The paintings of the Round Head period (c.9000BCE) occur mainly in the Tassili n'Ajjer. They are so called because the human figures in most of the paintings frequently have large and featureless heads. Some wear elaborate body adornment, feathered headdresses, masks, and tailed garments; but many are shown engaging in various activities, such as running, hunting, drumming, and dancing. The artists frequently combine the front and side views in the same figure.

The art of the Cattle/Pastoralist period (dated c.6000 and 3000BCE) seems to reflect the dawn of the African Neolithic because of its emphasis on sedentary life: there are representations of what appear to be huts and special enclosures for domesticated animals, especially sheep, goats, and cattle. Human beings are often depicted playing, herding cattle, courting, or fighting. The combination of frontal and side views in the same figure continues and is most conspicuous in the animal representations, which show the body in profile, and the horns from the front.

The paintings and engravings of the Horse period (dated to c.1200BCE) feature charioteers and horsemen rendered in the flying gallop style. The dating is partly based on the association of this style with the "People of the Sea" from the Aegean Islands who reportedly attacked ancient Egypt in the second millennium BCE.

The art of the Camel period is characterized by an emphasis on the animal, which is thought to have been introduced to Africa about 700BCE, although some scholars argue for a much later date. At any rate, the various archaeological excavations in the Sahara and North Africa, coupled with the representation of water-loving animals, such as buffalo, hippopotamus, rhinoceros, elephant, giraffe, sheep, goat, and cattle in the rock art, strongly indicate that the area once enjoyed a wetter climate and sustained a large number of people who hunted and eventually domesticated some of the animals depicted. A gradual decrease in the rainfall would seem to have caused the former inhabitants of the Sahara to flee to more hospitable regions along the Mediterranean coastline and the Nile valley, as well as to Sub-Saharan Africa, among other places.

That some of the founders of ancient Egypt were immigrants from the Sahara is suggested by the stylistic and thematic similarities between the prehistoric rock art of Sahara and ancient Egypt. For example, the frontal-cum-profile style that characterizes much of Saharan rock art would continue in ancient Egyptian art, along with the tradition of showing figures wearing tailed garments.

Through a combination of social, economic, political, and environmental factors, ancient Egypt soon developed into one of the most advanced civilizations in Africa. A belief in the supernatural and a quest for immortality shaped ancient Egyptian art and architecture. Huge and lavishly adorned temples, containing assorted sculptures and murals, were dedicated to the gods to secure their benevolence. As the living representatives of the gods on earth, the kings (pharaohs) wielded enormous spiritual and political powers, which were reflected in the gigantic monuments that they commissioned during their reigns to preserve their memory for posterity. Moreover, the bodies of deceased pharaohs were mummified and concealed beneath pyramids, massive tombs, and mortuary temples that were furnished with pottery, household and ceremonial utensils, elaborate works of art in wood, stone, ivory, brass, marble, glass, and metal, as well as biographical murals, all intended to ensure that the ka or life force of a departed king lived on and continued to enjoy the same amenities in the afterlife. Retinue burial was practiced in the early periods before being replaced with miniatures of servants, courtiers, and soldiers whose spirits were expected to wait on the departed king.

Nubia, another early African kingdom, developed in the Nile valley about the same time as ancient Egypt. Situated between present-day Darfur and Khartoum, it had a predominantly black population. The early arts of Nubia consist of decorated ceramics, clay figurines of humans and animals, jewelry, and beaded objects. Some Nubian kings were buried under huge circular mounds that were furnished, as in ancient Egypt, with artifacts for the use of the deceased in the afterlife. Although Nubian art and architecture had come under Egyptian influence as early as the third millennium BCE when the two nations traded with one another, this influence intensified between 1550 and 1100BCE, when the pharaohs subjugated Nubia and forced it to pay annual tributes. The Nubians, however, took advantage of the war between Libya and Egypt about 1100BCE not only to assert their political independence, but also to invade and impose Nubian rule on Egypt in the eighth century BCE. But following its defeat and expulsion from Egypt by the Assyrians (c.673BCE), the Nubian dynasty retreated to its homeland, establishing a new capital at Napata and later, further to the south, at Meroe, where Egyptian cultural and artistic influences continued.

The introduction and spread of Christianity in North Africa, Egypt, Nubia/Meroe, and Aksum/Ethiopia between the first and sixth centuries brought new art and architectural forms. Basilicas were built at Numidia, Tripolitania, Cyrenaica, Djemila, Leptis Magna, and other cities. Paintings, murals, mosaics, and sculptures with biblical themes adorned many of the basilicas. According to the Greek shipping handbook, the *Periplus of the Erythraean Sea*, published in the first century, Adulis, Aksum's capital city and main seaport, was the most important market for ivory in northeast Africa. It was also noted for the sale of high-quality crafts, weapons, incense, and herbal preparations. A booming economy spawned the construction of prestigious buildings, temples, tombs, and public monuments. In the fourth century, the Aksum king, Ezana, converted to Christianity and made it a state religion. But by the eighth century, Adulis had declined as a commercial center, necessitating the establishment of a new capital in what is now Ethiopia.

The ascension of the Zagwe dynasty in the twelfth century ushered in an era of economic development that peaked in the thirteenth century, when King Lalibela commissioned massive rock-cut churches, some adorned with murals in the Byzantine tradition and yet reflecting an Ethiopian identity.

In the meantime, a new religion called Islam had risen in the Arabian Peninsula about 632, sweeping through Egypt and North Africa and replacing the Christian basilicas with mosques and other forms of Islamic architecture, emphasizing the dome and minaret. The ancient traditions of sculpture in the region were soon replaced (though not completely) by the Islamic emphasis on the decorative arts.

Although it failed to penetrate the whole of Ethiopia and southern Nubia, Islam did succeed in spreading along the East African coastline, which had been participating in the Red Sea/Indian Ocean trade for several centuries, exporting slaves, ebony, ivory, rhino horns, gold, and leopard skins from the African interior to the Persian Gulf and Southeast Asia, and importing glazed porcelains, carnelian and glass beads, scents, weapons, fabrics, and food plants. As a result, big cities sprang up along the coast, from Mogadishu (Somalia) to Sofala (Mozambique) before the Islamic era. Between the tenth and fifteenth centuries, larger cities developed along the coastline and the neighboring islands, distinguished by their huge stone mansions, palaces, and mosques, which, though influenced by Arab models, still had significant African contributions in terms of craftsmanship and form.

This brings us to cultural developments in Sub-Saharan Africa. There is ample evidence that the inhabitants of the region interacted with their North African counterparts as far back as prehistoric times.

For example, pottery and ground stone implements, excavated from Iwo Eleru in southeastern Nigeria and dated to about the sixth millennium BCE, have strong affinities with materials from the "wet" Sahara period. Moreover, the rock paintings of Mauritania, Mali, Niger, northern Nigeria, and Chad, as well as the human and animal clay figurines found in a second millennium BCE context at Karkarichinka in the Tilemsi valley of northern Mali, are now widely regarded as evidence of the southern spread of ancient Saharan populations.

The oldest terracotta sculptures in Sub-Saharan Africa are those associated with the Nok culture of northern Nigeria, dated between about the sixth century BCE and CE200. They consist of human and animal representations, characterized by highly simplified and stylized features with an emphasis on spherical and cylindrical forms. The head almost always dominates the human body, recalling the figures in the paintings of the Round Head period of Saharan rock art. However, the Nok facial features are clearly delineated, while the eyes, nostrils are usually pierced. Also reminiscent of the Saharan rock art is the stylistic dichotomy in the rendering of the animal and human figures, the one being much more realistic than the other. The original context and cultural significance of the Nok terracottas are unknown, though the placement of clay and terracotta on ancestral altars and graves in many parts of the continent may imply that some of the former might have had a similar function. Other ancient terracotta sculptures in Sub-Saharan Africa have turned up at Ancient Djenne, Mali (tenth–sixteenth century), Komaland, Ghana (CEthirteenth–sixteenth century), Sao, Chad (CEtenth–sixteenth century), Yelwa, Nigeria (CEseventh century), Ife, Nigeria (CEtwelfth–fifteenth century), ancient Benin, Nigeria (CEthirteenth–nineteenth century) and Lydenburg, South Africa (CE500–700), among others.

Sculptures and ritual/ceremonial objects cast in gold, copper, brass, or bronze (by the lost wax technique) constitute another important category of African art. The earliest ones, so far, are from ancient Egypt and date from about the second millennium BCE. Those found in Nubia, Aksum, Meroe, Ethiopia, and many parts of North Africa belong to a later date. Although Arab visitors to the ancient kingdoms of Ghana and Mali between the ninth and fourteenth centuries observed the use of jewelry and ceremonial objects cast in gold, silver, and brass, the earliest bronze objects produced by the lost wax technique are from Igbo-Ukwu in southeastern Nigeria. Castings recalling the Igbo-Ukwu style have been found in several parts of eastern Nigeria, the lower Niger, and the Cameroon, suggesting that such objects were traded (as prestige items) across cultures in precolonial times.

Raw materials for casting were obtained either through local mining or from long-distance trade.

By the beginning of the twelfth millennium, the artists of the Yoruba kingdom of Ife had acquired knowledge of the lost wax technique, using it to cast highly naturalistic portraits of kings, queens, chiefs, and other notables. The technique was introduced to ancient Benin from Ife sometimes in the fourteenth century, where it was employed to cast assorted sculptures and commemorative plaques. Ancient castings in brass/bronze, copper, and gold have been found in other parts of Africa as well, especially among the Bamana and Dogon of Mali, Baule of Côte d'Ivoire, Asante of Ghana, the Fon of the Republic of Benin, the Bamum and Bamileke of the Cameroon, and the Kongo of the Democratic Republic of Congo (formerly Zaïre).

Although Sub-Saharan African artists carved in various materials such as stone, ivory, and bone, wood was undoubtedly the most popular medium of artistic expression in precolonial times because much of the continent lies in the tropics, and is dense with trees. Moreover, wood is easy to carve and hence affordable. The dryness of northern and northeastern Africa has enabled woodcarvings dating back to the second millennium BCE to survive in the Nile valley. The oldest specimen so far is a carved animal head found in 1928 on the bank of the Liavela river in central Angola and dated by radiocarbon analysis to the CEeighth century.

As noted earlier, much African woodcarving functioned in a religious context in the form of statues, masks, altar furniture, and ritual implements used in the veneration of deities and spirit forces. Others, such as carved posts and royal staffs, neckrests, containers, beds, thrones, and stools, functioned at the secular level either to project taste, reinforce high status/political power, or promote social and gender harmony. Thus, the artists of a given culture were trained in the past to work within a group style handed down from the past and aimed at creating a sense of oneness within the culture and at differentiating its art forms from those of neighbors. Yet certain more than fortuitous similarities are evident in the woodcarvings of west, central, equatorial, eastern, and southern Africa—especially in the conceptual approach and the emphasis on the head—similarities that underscore closer ethnic interactions in precolonial times.

In West Africa, the rise and fall of kingdoms (i.e., ancient Ghana, Mali, Songhay, Mossi, Asante, Oyo, Dahomey, and Benin) between the fourth and nineteenth centuries, the trans-Atlantic slave trade (CEfifteenth–nineteenth century), and the Fulani jihad of the nineteenth century, set into motion a series of population movements that not only relocated artistic styles, but also encouraged cultural and aesthetic exchanges among contiguous and far-flung groups. These factors would seem to be responsible for a certain formal and stylistic relationship between, say, the terracotta of ancient Djenne (CEtenth–sixteenth century), on the one hand, and the woodcarvings of the Tellem/Dogon, Bamana, Senufo, Mossi, Bwa, Nuna, Winiama, and Nunuma, on the other. A similar phenomenon occurred in central, equatorial, eastern, and southern Africa as a result of the various waves of Bantu migrations into the region from the Nigerian/Cameroon border in the early centuries of the Christian era. Little wonder, the heart-shaped face mask has a wide geographical distribution, stretching from southeastern Nigeria to equatorial and southern Africa. Recent archaeological excavations by Ekpo Eyo in Calabar have yielded pottery dated to the first century CE, displaying diamond and circular motifs commonly found in Kongo and Kuba art and suggesting some kind of genetic relationship, the exact nature of which is yet to be analyzed. Also contributing to the homogenization of forms and symbols in this region in precolonial times were interethnic marriages, trade in art works, and the military expansion associated with the Kongo, Luba, Lunda, Marawi, and Mutapa kingdoms.

Although stone sculptures were produced in many parts of Sub-Saharan African in precolonial times, they are few and far between. They range in style from the naturalistic and the semi-naturalistic (such as Ife, Esie, Igbajo, and Esure figures of southwestern Nigeria, (dating between the twelfth and nineteenth centuries) and the *mintadi* grave figures of the Kongo (dating to about the fifteenth or sixteenth century), to stylized representations (such as the *pondo* and *nomoli* ancestral figures of Sierra Leone dating about the fifteenth or sixteenth century). Others are anthropomorphized monoliths such as the ones from Zimbabwe (thirteenth–fifteenth centuries) and the *akwanshi* ancestral figures of the Ekoi-Ejagham (eighteenth century), who inhabit the Cross River region of the Nigerian-Cameroon border. The monoliths from Tondidarou in Mali (seventh century) are phallic in shape, while some of those from Zimbabwe are in the form of pillars and are adorned with reptiles and surmounted by bird motifs.

The use of stone and other durable materials for architecture in north and northeastern Africa and the Swahili coast has enabled many ancient structures in these areas to survive for centuries. On the other hand, the preponderant use of perishable materials for construction in many Sub-Saharan African cultures reduced the life span of most of the buildings, except in a few cases. In precolonial times, mud or clay were the most common materials for the wall, although they were sometimes mixed with palm oil, shea butter, or cow dung and other materials which served as bonding agents. The roof was normally covered with leaves or grasses.

This building practice continues to the present, co-existing with the use of modern construction materials and techniques. In the coastal or swampy areas (usually inhabited by fishermen), the predominant building type is the rectangular, gable-roofed structure with bamboo or wooden walls, constructed on stilts to prevent flooding. Moving away from the coast, one begins to encounter the rectangular, wattle-and-daub house. The wall is often made of interwoven branches or mangrove poles plastered with the brittle mud found in this area. But in the rainforest and tropical woodlands area, where the laterite soil has less water (and hence more plastic), the wattle is dispensed with. Frequently, four rectangular structures are grouped to form a courtyard which has a hole in the middle to drain out rain water. The houses of the Kuba and related groups who live along the Kasai and Sankuru rivers often have their walls adorned with woven mats. Among the Yoruba of southwestern Nigeria, a verandah usually runs along the courtyard supported by figurated posts.

In eastern central Africa, south of the Zambesi River, an area of open grassland and rock formations, the ruins of many ancient constructions with mortarless dry stone walling have survived at Bambandyanalo, Khami Leopard Kopje, Mapela, Mapungubwe, and Naletale, among others, dating between the twelfth and nineteenth centuries. The most advanced of the constructions is at Great Zimbabwe. Built by the Shona between the thirteenth and fifteenth centuries, it consists of three groups of structures: an enclosure with high stone walls that seems to have once doubled as a palace and temple, a collection of walls and enclosures, and what appears to be a rampant. Shona oral history and archaeological excavations reveal that the site and its surroundings were occupied by farmers and cattle herders who benefited from the long distance trade in gold and ivory between the Swahili coast and the African interior.

In the dry savannah region of West Africa, called the Sahel (the Arabic word for "shore" because this region adjoins the Sahara desert), round and rectangular houses often coexist; the flat, mud-plastered roof is common in this area. In the urban areas, rectangular forms outnumber the round ones. The principal building material here is *adobe*, that is, sun-dried blocks of clay mixed with dung or straw. Among the Hausa and Fulani, the walls of the houses are adorned with interlace designs in high relief, echoing the embroidery patterns found on dress, leatherwork, and carved doors, and reflecting Islamic influence from North Africa and the Near East. This influence can be traced back to the seventeenth century, when Arab and Berber merchants began to settle in the western Sudan and other parts of the Sahel, bringing with them different aspects of Islamic art and architecture.

Contemporary Developments

Today, the skyline of many African cities is dominated by Western-type architecture, such as high-rise buildings of concrete, steel, and glass. The beginnings of this phenomenon can be traced back to the fifteenth century, when European slave traders built temporary residences, castles, and forts along the African coast, from Cape Blanco in Mauritania to Mombasa in Kenya. The arrival of Dutch settlers at the Cape of Good Hope in 1652 began the gradual Westernization of the South African landscape that has transformed cities such as Cape Town and Johannesburg into the "concrete jungles" that they are today. The European colonization of the continent toward the end of the nineteenth century has since spread this Westernization process to virtually every nook and corner, resulting in a large-scale use of cement, burnt bricks, steel, glass, corrugated iron roof, and asbestos in contemporary building construction.

In precolonial Africa, the layout of a house or compound was determined by the social structure and the size of the family, its construction being a communal activity involving all members of a given family, assisted by friends, relatives, and some craftsmen. As a result, all buildings within a given culture tended to look alike, although economic status determined size and the degree of embellishment. European colonialism has changed all that by introducing the idea of an architect whose design must be approved by the government before a building could be erected, especially in the urban areas. Such a design usually reflects the individuality of the architect or his/her Western training. Urbanization has also disrupted village life, causing many to flee to the cities in search of modern education and better-paying jobs. The limited space of a rented city apartment discourages the African extended family residency pattern normally found in the traditional compounds. Admittedly, the nationalism generated by decolonization has led some African architects to seek inspiration from indigenous African architecture, yet the emphasis continues to be on international trends dictated by Western materials and spatial concepts.

A similar situation exists in the visual arts. Western education, coupled with large-scale conversion to Islam and Christianity since the turn of the twentieth century, has encouraged many urbanized Africans to abandon their traditional values, especially the ancient belief that art has the power to influence the spirit world. The Western-type art schools, a byproduct of colonialism, have introduced the concept of "art-for-art's-sake" and an imitative naturalism that stresses the cultivation of a personal idiom of expression, unlike in the precolonial period when the artists of a given culture were expected to conform to a group style inherited from the past, but which still allowed for individual and regional variations. Having lost many of their local patrons, many traditional artists now work for the tourist industry, mass-reproducing ancient forms and sometimes copying the styles of other ethnic groups (from African art books) in order to meet the high demand of the trade. In short, contemporary African art not only reflects the metamorphic changes precipitated by colonialism, urbanization, industrialization, and new socioeconomic forces, but also a frantic struggle to cope with them. Although its formative period was marked by a tendency to ape Western forms and styles—which turned off many art historians and collectors—the nationalism precipitated by political independence is galvanizing the search for an African identity. Conscious of their rich artistic heritage and its contributions to modern art, many formally and informally trained contemporary African artists are now digging back to their roots in an attempt to reconcile the present with the past so as to create new forms that will capture the spirit of the postcolonial era. Some seek inspiration from indigenous African sculptures, while others, especially those from Islamicized cultures, experiment with the nonfigurative, combining Arabic calligraphy with abstract forms. The growing international interest in the study and collection of contemporary African art is a testimony to its inventiveness and potential.

In summary, a survey of African art and architecture from the earliest times to the present reveals not only extensive interactions between northern and Sub-Saharan Africa dating back to prehistoric times, but also varying responses to external influences. The similarities are as significant as the differences. Hence the urgent need to integrate the art history of the entire continent in order to facilitate a more objective study of continuities and change in form, style, context, and meaning.

BABATUNDE LAWAL

Further Reading

Blair, Sheila S., and Jonathan M. Bloom. *The Architecture of Islam, 1250–1800*. New Haven, CT: Yale University Press, 1994.

Celenko, Theodore (ed.). *Egypt in Africa*. Indianapolis, IN: Indianapolis Museum of Art, 1996.

de Grunne, Bernard. *The Birth of Art in Black Africa: Nok Statuary in Nigeria*. Luxembourg: Baque Generale du Luxembourg, 1998.

Hackett, R. *Art and Religion in Africa*. London and New York: Cassell, 1996.

Lawal, Babatunde. "Yoruba-Shango Ram Symbolism: From Ancient Sahara of Dynastic Egypt?" in *African Images: Essays in African Iconology*, Daniel McCall and Edna Bay (eds.). New York: Africana Publishing Company, 1975.

Perani, J., and F.T. Smith, *The Visual Arts of Africa: Gender, Power, and Life Cycle Rituals*. Englewood Cliffs, NJ: Prentice-Hall, 1998.

Phillipson, David W. *African Archaeology* (2nd edition). Cambridge, England: Cambridge University Press, 1993.

Art, Postcolonial

In many African countries that attained independence around 1960, art was seen to play an important role in celebrating the new nation, expressing a new postcolonial identity, unifying fragmented ethnic entities, and asserting traditional African culture and values (Vogel 1994). This general sentiment was most systematically and saliently propagated in Senegal, where Leopold Senghor—poet, art collector, statesman, and the newly independent nation's first president—formulated the philosophy of *Négritude*. Deeply influencing artists in Senegal and beyond, *Négritude* became a discourse aimed at the rehabilitation of Africa and the search for a uniquely African identity. With the foundation of the École des Beaux Arts, Dakar soon became the African continent's first and most important center of postcolonial art production. Artists associated with the early days of the school include Ibou Diouf or Boubacar Coulibaly, who produced colorful oil paintings merging references to traditional African art (e.g., masks) with dynamic abstract shapes. Although art was soon considerably deprioritized, Dakar still holds an important position as a regional focal point, among other things hosting the Dakar Biennale.

Two opposing ideologies emerged in response to the challenge of finding a modern African form of expression: Some artists rejected foreign (colonial) styles, materials, and subjects in their search for an artistic language that was innately African. Others asserted their artistic freedom to make whatever art they chose, including works resembling European art (Vogel 1994). The latter approach is to be understood in the context of a tradition of marginalization due to the West's rejection of "derivative" work.

Négritude and the search for an innate "Africanness" strongly influenced the African art scene of the 1960s in the West African region and beyond. In Nigeria, for instance, artists from the Zaria Art Society (Uche Okeke, Demas Nwoko, and Bruce Onobrakpeya) developed the theory of "Natural Synthesis," which called for the merging of indigenous art traditions, forms and ideas with useful Western ones (Okeke 1999). Okeke's organic, lyrical drawings of the early 1960s, for instance, were influenced by *uli*, the local tradition of wall painting.

Mounting skepticism toward essentialist projects throughout the contemporary art world eventually lead to a shift away from the search for innate African identity toward a more universalist perspective and aesthetic, influenced by current theoretical discourses (especially on identity and postcolonialism) and the visual language of the international art world. A small elite of so-called *avant-garde* or "international" artists are now active participants in this arena, and some have moved to the West. On the whole, however, contemporary African art continues to be marginalized within a global art system.

Postcolonial African art is characterized by important regional differences, while simultaneously sharing significant similarities that tend to distinguish it from art produced in the West. Throughout postcolonial Africa, art has been shaped, to some degree, in relation to the respective country's history of colonialism. In some instances, entire genres have developed around the complex issue of dealing with this historical legacy, most notably the *Colonie Belge* theme that has become popular in the Democratic Republic of Congo (DRC). Other aspects of the colonial legacy include the shortage of higher education and artistic training opportunities, which have resulted in a large number of informally trained or autodidact artists with a limited aesthetic and conceptual range (e.g., Kivuthi Mbuno from Kenya, or sculptor Agbagli Kossi from Togo). Shortage or unattainability of (imported) art materials has produced a tradition of economizing materials, work on a small scale, and use of recycled materials (e.g., scrap metal sculptures by Calixte and Théodore Dakpogan from Benin, or Ndary Lô in Senegal). Art museums and galleries are virtually absent anywhere on the continent outside South Africa, and knowledge of contemporary Western art is at most available through photographs. Like traditional African art, contemporary art in postcolonial Africa is to a considerable degree functional, as it is expected to play a political, social, and moral role (Vogel 1994).

Despite these and other hurdles, the visual arts are flourishing throughout the African continent, and the repertoire of forms available to young artists in Africa is larger than ever before. The Cairo Biennale is Dakar's counterpoint for the north of Africa, but also the wider Mediterranean world. Historically, art in North Africa is influenced by Islamic traditions of visual representation, some incorporating calligraphy and showing a preference for abstraction. Artists such as Ibrahim El Salahi (Sudan), or Skunder Boghossian (Ethiopia), were regarded as pioneers, whose development of a new visual language have defined the modern art movement in their countries (Hassan 1995). The current generation of artists, exemplified by the colorful work of Rashid Diab or Hassan Ali Ahmed from Sudan, has developed a more universal aesthetic that merges Western, African, and Islamic influences and expresses cultural identity in a global context.

In the south, Johannesburg serves as an important hub of the contemporary postcolonial art world, and the city hosted two biennials in 1995 and 1997. In South Africa, postcolonialism can, in many respects, be equated with the post-apartheid era (since 1994). Historically, the country's art world with its various institutions and support structures has been highly developed, but until recently, this has mostly benefited white artists. Despite the fact that the legacy of the past still impacts on the current art scene, a number of young black artists (notably Sandile Zulu, Moshekwa Langa, and Kay Hassan) have ascended to the global stage of the international contemporary art world. For both black and white artists, the current emphasis is on issues of (often redefined) identity in a country in transformation.

African art is often classified into different genres or categories, but in reality the boundaries are often fluid and much dependent on context. International, "elite," or *avant garde* artists, such as Issa Samb (Senegal), David Koloane (South Africa), Antonio Ole (Angola), Abdoulaye Konate (Mali), Sane Wadu (Kenya), or Sokari Douglas Camp (Nigeria), one of the few female international artists, tend to have absorbed Western concepts of creative freedom and art as a means of self-actualization and expression of identity. Their work is either influenced by current theoretical discourses and aesthetic trends in the global art world, or—perhaps more often—perceived (by the West) to be allied to such trends and therefore worthy of attention and inclusion. Yet, unlike many of their Western counterparts, these artists rarely produce work of an intensely private, intimate, or autobiographical character. Like traditional African art, much of contemporary work appears to have a more public function, expressing collective concerns.

The Congolese artist Cheri Samba has in a sense become an international artist, but emerges from the genre of urban painters, of which the Congo region has a particularly strong tradition (as well as some parts of West and East Africa). Urban painters such as Cheik Ledy, Moke, or Tshibumba Kanda from the DRC produce realistically painted work in series for street sale to tourists and members of their own urban community. Although this type of art is market driven and commercial, it often serves an important societal function, containing moral or educational lessons, social or political commentary.

The genre of urban painting overlaps to some extent with various forms of tourist and popular art, which have received considerable scholarly and public attention lately. Examples include Nigerian truck paintings, vernacular sign painting in Ghana, religious murals in Senegal, hotel art in Ethiopia, or the famous coffins by the late Ghanaian sculptor and carpenter Kane Kwei and his son. Art in postcolonial Africa also includes a strong and continuing tradition of craft-making and production of traditional artifacts (masks, wood sculptures, pottery, beadwork, etc.) both for use by the community for ceremonial occasions and traditional practices and for sale to tourists. Especially the tourist wares have often been creatively developed in accordance with market forces to include more cosmopolitan imagery and incorporate new materials.

Much of African art either developed through the initiative of white artists, art teachers, or culture brokers, such as Uli and Georgina Beier in Nigeria, or in response to white patronage. Among the latter are the "primitive" paintings and prints produced by largely untrained members of San and Bushmen communities in Namibia, Botswana, and South Africa (e.g., Qwaa or Steffaans Hamukwaya), which have attracted much attention in the West. Certain sculptural traditions, notably the so-called Shona sculptures in Zimbabwe by artists such as Nicholas Mukomberanwa or Bernard Matemera, were initiated by white culture brokers for sale to mostly white patrons, but soon developed into a vibrantly creative and self-sustaining tradition. These sometimes monumental works—thematically inspired by traditional African stories and beliefs and formally derived from German Expressionism and early twentieth-century abstraction—tend to straddle the line between tourist art and "fine art."

The current interest in and scholarly research about art and artists in postcolonial Africa is a relatively recent phenomenon, which has emerged with the field of African art studies, informed by cultural studies and postcolonialism as major theoretical trajectories, and driven mostly by scholars and curators situated in the West. A truly African art historiography has yet to be written.

SABINE MARSCHALL

See also: **Négritude.**

Further Reading

Hassan, Salah. "The Modernist Experience in African Art," *Nka. Journal of Contemporary African Art*, spring/summer (1995): 30–33, 72.

Havell, Jane (ed.). *Seven Stories about Modern Art in Africa*. Paris and New York: Whitechapel, Flammarion, 1995.

Kasfir, Sidney Littlefield. *Contemporary African Art*. World of Art series, London and New York: Thames and Hudson, 1999.

Kennedy, J. *New Currents, Ancient Rivers: Contemporary African Artists in a Generation of Change*. Washington, DC, and London: Smithsonian Institution Press. 1992.

Magnin, André, and Jacques Soulillou (eds.). *Contemporary Art of Africa*. New York: Harry N. Abrams, 1996.

Nka. Journal of Contemporary African Art. New York: Nka Publications in conjunction with Africana Studies and Research Center: Cornell University, Ithaca, NY.

Okeke, Chika. "The Quest: from Zaria to Nsukka," in *Seven Stories about Modern Art in Africa*, Jane Havell (ed.). Paris, New York: Whitechapel, Flammarion, 1995.

Vogel, Susan (ed.). *Africa Explores: 20th Century African Art*. Centre for African Art: New York and Prestel: Munich, 3rd edition, 1994.

Williamson, Sue, and Ashraf Jamal, *Art in South Africa—the Future Present*. Cape Town and Johannesburg: David Philip, 1996.

Asante Kingdom: Osei Tutu and Founding of

Osei Tutu, ruler of Asante from 1701 to 1717, stands out as one of the most important figures in Asante history. He finalized the long task of nation building initiated by Twum and Antwi, the first two Asante rulers. With the support of his friend and lieutenant, Okomfo Anokye, Osei Tutu gave the Asante a capital, a constitution, a military machine that assured a long period of political stability, and a unifying element, the Golden Stool. The Asante great oath, *memeneda kromante*, which recalls the death of Osei Tutu, attests to his greatness and role in the development of the Asante nation.

Early Asante tradition records the sojourn of Osei Tutu in Denkyira, and later in Akwapim, where he met and became friends with Okomfo Anokye, a native of Awukugua, who was to become his most trusted counselor and lieutenant. Osei Tutu's sojourn in Denkyira and Akwamu not only introduced him to the politics of the two principal powers of the time, but more importantly, it emphasized for him the importance of the Atlantic trade at the coast for firearms.

On his return home to Asante after the death of his uncle, Obiri Yeboa, Osei Tutu, with the help and support of Okomfo Anokye, contributed to the growth of Asante in five main ways: he completed the union of Akan states that were within a twenty-five mile radius of Kumasi, provided the Asante union with a new capital, Kumasi,

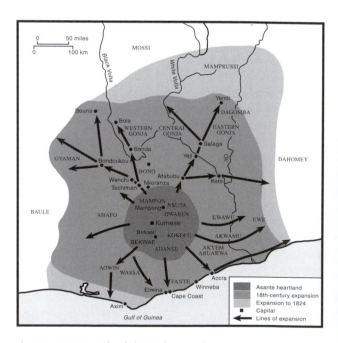

Asante, seventeenth–eighteenth centuries.

Akan figure made of gold. © Daniel Koelsche/Das Fotoarchiv.

and a national festival, the Odwira, provided the new union with a constitution, introduced a new military organization, and expanded the boundaries of the kingdom.

The elements of a union already existed before Osei Tutu became ruler of Asante. All the chiefs of the original *Amantoo* (nucleus of Asante empire), except the chief of Mampon, belonged to the Oyoko clan and thus the notion of brotherhood consistent with the Akan family system was maximized. Osei Tutu utilized this bond, and playing on the common fears and aspirations, he convinced the chiefs of the Amantoo states to recognize the Golden Stool as the soul, strength, and vitality of the Asante nation. The Golden Stool has, to this day, remained a symbol of Asante nationhood.

The Golden Stool, supposedly conjured from the sky by Okomfo Anokye, was believed to contain the spirit of the Asante nation. By astute statesmanship, and by playing upon the religious beliefs of the Asante, Osei Tutu and Okomfo Anokye invested a sense of collective destiny in the national consciousness. The various clans were thus linked in a mystical and religious bond whose physical manifestation was personified by the Golden Stool, which was displayed during festivals.

Moreover, the songs and recitals connected with the traditional history of Asante were couched in terms calculated to foster and perpetuate the notion of a community of origins and a common collective destiny. The most potent of these instruments, however, were the Asante army, the Golden Stool, the Odwira Festival, and the Asante Constitution.

After forging the union, Osei Tutu and Okomfo Anokye were determined that the Asante state should last, especially since Osei Tutu was familiar with the dissension that plagued Akwamu and Denkyira. To this end, a number of state-building instruments (some inherited, some created) were put to use to ensure this unity. Osei Tutu moved the capital from Kwaman to Kumasi. This was achieved through diplomacy and religious rituals designed to indicate the consent of the ancestral spirits.

Osei Tutu is also credited with devising a constitution for the Asante nation. This defined the hierarchy of authority in the Asante administrative system. At the head of the structure was the Asantehene, the political and spiritual head of Kumasi. Under the Asantehene were the chiefs of the Amantoo states. These chiefs attended the annual odwira festival, swore the oath of allegiance to the Asantehene, contributed regiments in times of war or emergency and gave up the right of declaring war. They also recognized the Asantehene's court as the court of appeal, and contributed to *apeatuo*, a national levy imposed for specific tasks. On the other hand, the Amanhene had the right to lands conquered before the union was forged, and had a say in the formulation of foreign policy.

Osei Tutu crystallized the spirit of aristocratic ranks by using different insignia and emblems in accordance with the levels of clan-family positions and dignities of the different chiefs. Therefore, Dwaben, Kumawu, Bekwae, and Mampon were ranked on almost the same level as the Asanthene himself.

The successful employment of the Asante in rapid territorial expansion suggests the existence of a highly developed system of military organization. The Asante national army was composed of a body of scouts (*nkwansrafo*), an advance guard (*twafo*), a main body (*adonten*), a personal bodyguard (*gyase*), a rear-guard (*kyidom*), and left (*benkum*) and right (*nifa*) wings, respectively. The effective coordination of these segments contributed to Asante successes in war. Each member state of the Union (Amantoo) was assigned a place in the military formation. The Mamponghehe was the commander-in-chief, the Essumengyahene was commander of the left wing, and the Krontihene, the commander of the right wing.

Osei Tutu used this effective military organization to deadly effect. He avenged the Asante defeat by the Dormaa, fought and defeated Denkyira between 1699 and 1701, and conquered Akyem and Offinso. He incorporated conquered states such as Amakom, Tafo, and Ofinso into the union. Asante forces commanded by Amankwa Tia crossed the Pra and campaigned in the Begho area. The Akyem had not been fully subdued, and Osei Tutu died in 1717 fighting against the Akyem.

By the end of his reign, Osei Tutu had completed the task of building an effective administrative system and expanding the empire, a process initiated by his predecessor.

EDMUND ABAKA

See also: **Akan and Asante: Farmers, Traders, and the Emergence of Akan States; Akan States.**

Further Reading

Boahen A. Adu. *Ghana: Evolution and Change.* London: Longman, 1975.

Boahen, A. Adu (with J.F. Ade Ajayi and Michael Tidy). *Topics in West African History*. Essex, England: Longman, 1986, (2nd edition).

Fynn, J.K. *Asante and Its Neighbours* 1700–1807. Longman: Northwestern University Press, 1993.

Wilks, Ivor. *Asante in the Nineteenth Century: The Structure and Evolution of a Political Order*. London: Cambridge University Press, 1975.

Wilks, Ivor. *Forests of Gold. Essays on the Akan and the Kingdom of Asante*. Athens: Ohio University Press, 1993.

Asians: East Africa

The origins of Asians in East Africa lie in the subjugation of India by the British and its incorporation into the British Empire. The subjugation of India initiated the Indian Diaspora, which led to the dispersal of Indians into the far-flung parts of the British empire where they were taken over as indentured labor. In East Africa Indians bought by the British worked as indentured labor on the construction of the East African railway in the late nineteenth century. In the early twentieth century many Gujarati (from Gujarat, a western Indian state) traders found their way into East Africa and joined Indian traders who were already resident in Zanzibar. Throughout the period of the Indian Diaspora, Indians in East Africa, as elsewhere, maintained close links with their homeland.

Although Indians became more populous in East Africa following the colonization of the region by the British, contact between East Africa and India goes back as far as the fifteenth century. For example, it is strongly suggested that in 1468, Vasco da Gama met a Cutchi-speaking Muslim ship captain who showed him the way to India. When the British colonized East Africa, they found the Cutchi speakers already present in East Africa. They were mainly traders, and they represented nearly twenty different groups, who were either Muslim or Hindu. A small group became Christian in the mid-twentieth century.

Another Indian community found in East Africa is that generally known as the Sikhs. These were a militant order, and the British used them in the colonial armies of East Africa to police the colonies. The Sikhs went to East Africa, Kenya in particular, as soldiers, and later as guards in the building of the East African railway. Other Sikhs went as professionals and skilled workers. The history of Sikhs in East Africa is that of a community that from the very beginning were among the most affluent people, since they easily became entrepreneurs in their new country.

Also common in East Africa are Asians commonly called Shia Muslims. These came to East Africa from India's Gujarati state. They came largely as part of the indentured labor community to build the East African railway in the 1890s and early twentieth century. Many stayed in Kenya after the completion of the railway. They became part of the backbone of the modern Indian business and trading community in Kenya and Uganda and Tanzania.

There are three clearly distinct Shia Muslim communities in East Africa: the Khoja Ismaili, Dawood Bohra, and Ithanashari. These groups resulted from schism within the Muslim sect over the years. Despite these differences, the Shia Muslims command a large share of the economic wealth of Kenya and the other East African countries of Tanzania and Uganda.

Apart from the Shia Muslims who came as indentured labor, there were also the Punjabi-speaking Asians, who included Muslims, Orthodox Hindus, Arya Samaj Hindus, Ahmadiyyas, and Sikhs. While it is generally true that Indians lived under conditions of appalling poverty in many places where they were taken as indentured labor, many easily transformed themselves within a few generations into a prosperous community. By sheer perseverance, labor, and thrift, these Indians transformed their social and economic conditions to affluence and prosperity. This transformation attracted resentment from the indigenous communities of East Africa.

In Kenya and Uganda the resentment against Indian traders was displayed through the policy of Africanization in trade and services. The policy was deliberately aimed at Indians who held British passports. By the late 1970s, economic stagnation and poverty among indigenous communities was blamed on Asian economic exploitation of the indigenous communities. Consequently, in 1972, Idi Amin of Uganda decided to expel all Asians from his country irrespective of their nationality. The expulsions of Asians from Uganda signified clear racial hatred of the Asian community by a state president. The expulsion of Asians from Uganda further weakened Asian confidence in East Africa as their new permanent home. The world condemned Idi Amin's action, but could not reverse the expulsions, which clearly showed the vulnerability of the Asian racial minority in a hostile environment.

Asians in East Africa are a resilient community, and within a few years they were able to overcome the difficulties caused by the expulsion. While some permanently left Uganda, others returned after the overthrow of Idi Amin and started all over again. It is also important to point out that Asians in East Africa are not just involved in business. They are also actively involved in politics, and in Kenya a number have held important political and ministerial positions. This development legitimizes their new nationality in their adopted countries of East Africa. Asians in East Africa are, for all practical purposes, as patriotic to their adopted countries as are the indigenous communities. However, as a racial minority, they are constantly discriminated against, and blamed for most economic problems experienced by the indigenous communities.

However, it is important to point out that after the independence of Kenya in 1963, and that of other East African countries, the Asians who chose to take up citizenship in the various countries were joined by more Asians. The Asians in business prefer to employ immigrants from India. This process contributed to the fast growth of the Indian population of East Africa. Some Asian immigrants to East Africa found that life was not at all easy in East Africa. Their hope of a better life in East Africa was shattered because they could not get the kinds of jobs they hoped to find in East Africa. East African countries receive more unskilled Asians from India than they can employ. The presence of these unskilled Asians generates racial conflict between communities.

Another source of conflict is the experience of Africans working for Asian employers as housemaids and those who work in Asian-owned businesses. Many complain of underpayment and poor conditions of service. On the other hand, Asians see Africans as being responsible for the many crimes committed against Asian businesspeople. The Kenya press, for example, observed that the 1990s have seen mounting tension between Africans and Asians. The source of the rising tension is high levels of unemployment among the Africans who, in turn, blame Asians for their plight.

BIZECK J. PHIRI

See also: **Kenya: Independence to the Present; Uganda: Amin Dada, Idi: Coup and Regime, 1971–1979.**

Further Reading

Bhatia, P. *Indian Ordeal in Africa*. Delhi: Vikas Publishing House, 1973.

Chattopadhyaya, Haraprasad. P. *Indians in Africa: A Social and Economic Study*. Calcutta: Bookland Private Limited, 1970.

Delf, G. *Asians in East Africa*. London: Oxford University Press, 1963.

Mangat, J.S. *A History of Asians in East Africa*. Oxford: Clarendon Press, 1969.

Tandon, Yash. "The Asians in East Africa in 1972," in Colin Legum (ed.), *Africa Contemporary Record: Survey and Documents 1972–1973*. London: Lex Collins, 1973.

Ateker: *See* Nilotes, Eastern Africa: Eastern Nilotes: Ateker (Karimojong).

Augustine, Catholic Church: North Africa

As church leader and theologian, St. Augustine (Aurelius Augustinus, 354–430) was the outstanding representative of the vigorous regional Christianity of the North African provinces in the Roman Empire—chiefly modern Tunisia and Algeria, but reaching also eastward into Libya and westward through Morocco. Here Latin-speaking Christianity emerged, exercising a formative influence on the church in the western empire even before Rome rose to ecclesiastical hegemony. Through his extensive writings, Augustine became one of the most influential Christians of all time.

The origins of Christianity in Roman Africa (which, in antiquity, did not include Egypt) are obscure. From the later second century, the works of Tertullian (*c.*60–*c.*225), effectively the creator of Christian Latin, reflect a vibrant church in and beyond Carthage (near modern Tunis), the Roman capital. Tertullian made important contributions to developing Christian doctrine, especially regarding the Trinity and the person of Christ (Christology), and helped stamp a distinctive ethos on the growing church. It was ethically and religiously rigorist—glorifying martyrdom and brooking no compromise with paganism—spiritually enthusiastic, and rhetorically confident.

Issues of church unity and discipline dominated the troubled career of Cyprian, bishop of Carthage (246–258), who died as a martyr. He bequeathed to Latin Christianity a tightly episcopal definition of the church expressed in potent utterances such as "no salvation outside the church." His refusal to recognize baptism given outside the boundaries of episcopal communion brought him into collision with Stephen, bishop of Rome. In Cyprian more clearly than any before him one recognizes the ecclesiastical counterpart to the Roman imperial official, an early harbinger of the medieval prelate.

Persecution, and varied responses to it, featured prominently in early North African Christianity. The *Passion of Perpetua and Felicity* (203) is an exquisitely feminine firsthand account of martyrdom in Carthage. The Great Persecution initiated by emperor Diocletian in 303 exposed deep-seated divisions over accommodation to Roman officialdom that led to schism and the formation of the Donatist counter-church. Its roots in earlier North African Christian tradition favored its rapid growth, and for most of the fourth century it held the edge over the Catholic Church.

This was so in Thagaste (modern Souk-Ahras in Algeria), where Augustine was born in 354 to Patrick and his zealously Christian wife, Monnica. Augustine's *Confessions*, a classic of Western Christian literature, a kind of spiritual autobiography written *c.*400 after he had become bishop of Hippo, credit Monnica's tenacity in his eventual baptism into the Catholic Church at Milan at Easter 387. His parents had him dedicated as an infant, but numerous twists and turns would mark his intellectual, moral, and religious pilgrimage, including a decade-long association with Manichaeism, a late, Persian form of gnosticism, until, outside Africa, the combined impact of Neopolatonism, the ascetic movement, and Bishop Ambrose brought him full circle, as it were, back to the religion of his childhood, in a famous conversion in a Milanese garden in August 386.

Returning to Africa in 388 after his mother's death, Augustine was able briefly to pursue a quasi-monastic calling as a Christian philosopher in Thagaste. But the clamant needs of the Catholic Church claimed him for the presbyterate (391), and then the episcopate (395) at Hippo Regius (modern Annaba, on the Algerian coast). There he remained, never leaving Africa again (he avoided sea travel), until his death in 430, with Hippo besieged by the Vandals, who would shortly oust Rome from power in North Africa. Most of Augustine's massive theological corpus was produced while he served as chief pastor and preacher of Hippo's Catholic community. He was inevitably a prominent figure in the town, in great demand as counselor, champion of the disadvantaged, troubleshooter, ombudsman, and trustee. In the wider region, with Bishop Aurelius of Carthage he spearheaded a final period of ascendancy for the Catholic Church before the Vandal takeover.

Augustine spoke only Latin (he never read Greek with ease). The whole story of Christianity in the North African littoral seems almost an aspect of the Roman presence. Yet Augustine provided Punic-speaking pastors within his diocese, and hasty judgments about the alleged failure of Christianity to indigenize itself in North Africa (relevant to an assessment of Donatism) must be resisted. Augustine's life and work not only summed up the era of the church fathers in the Latin West, but also witnessed the empire's accelerating terminal decline. The Gothic sack of Rome in 410 set Augustine writing his greatest work, *City of God* (413–422). The North African church always retained a degree of independence from papal pretensions.

Augustine's importance for African Christianity was manifold, although his greater influence lay beyond Africa. He promoted monasticism, running his episcopal residence as an ascetic seminary, producing numbers of clergy for other churches. He routed Manichaean spokesmen in debate, and against Manichaean teaching vindicated the Old Testament (in the process defending the just war), Christianized a Neoplatonic account of the nature of evil, and set out the relations between faith and reason. In an explicit change of mind, he provided the first extended Christian justification of state coercion of religious dissidents: the Donatists. This was in part a pragmatic move, for Donatism had remained largely impervious to Augustine's historical, biblical, and theological refutation of their case. Admitting Cyprian's error, he

argued for the recognition of Donatist baptism and ordination—but as valid only, not spiritually efficacious. The unity of a mixed church was preferable to a deluded quest for earthly purity. After the decision of a conference under an imperial commissioner went against the Donatists (411), Augustine was much involved in their compulsory absorption into the Catholic Church.

Augustine's anti-Pelagian theology dominated subsequent Western thought, but Pelagian teaching was never a force in Africa. In defense of infant baptism (for the remission of the guilt of original sin), and in rejection of false claims to moral competence and false aspirations to sinlessness, Augustine expounded humanity's dependence on grace (given only to the elect), and the inclusive embrace of the church. He orchestrated the African church's condemnation of Pelagian errors, which prevailed over a vacillating papacy.

DAVID WRIGHT

See also: **Donatist Church: North Africa; Monophysitism, Coptic Church, 379–640.**

Further Reading

Augustine. *City of God*. Several translations, including R.W. Dyson, Cambridge, England: Cambridge University Press, 1998.

Augustine. *Confessions*. Many translations, including Henry Chadwick, Oxford: Oxford University Press, 1992.

Barnes, Timothy D. *Tertullian: A Historical and Literary Study*, 2nd edition. Oxford: Oxford University Press, 1985.

Bonner, Gerald I. *St. Augustine of Hippo: Life and Controversies*. London: SCM, 1963.

Brown, Peter. *Augustine of Hippo: A Biography*. London: Faber; Berkeley: University of California Press, 1967.

Chadwick, Henry. *Augustine*. Oxford: Oxford University Press, 1986.

Cuoq, J. *L' Église d'Afrique du Nord des IIe au XIIe siècle*. Paris: Le Centurion, 1984.

Deane, Herbert A. *The Political and Social Ideas of St. Augustine*. New York and London: Columbia University Press, 1963.

Di Berardino, Angelo (ed.). *Patrology*, vol. 4, Westminster, MD: Christian Classics, 1988: 342–362 (for list of works, editions, translations).

Ferguson, Everett (ed.). *Encyclopedia of Early Christianity*, 2nd edition, 2 vols. New York and London: Garland, 1997.

Markus, Robert A. *Saeculum: History and Society in the Theology of St. Augustine*. Cambridge, England: Cambridge University Press, 1970.

Mayer, Cornelius (ed.). *Augustinus-Lexikon*. Basel and Stuttgart: Schwabe, 1986.

O'Meara, John J. *The Young Augustine*. London: Longmans, Green, 1954.

Raven, Susan. *Rome in Africa*, 3rd edition. London and New York: Routledge, 1993.

Sage, M.M. *Cyprian*. Cambridge, MA: Philadelphia Patristic Foundation, 1975.

TeSelle, Eugene. *Augustine the Theologian*. London: Burns and Oates, 1970.

Van der Meer, F. *Augustine the Bishop*. London: Sheed and Ward, 1961.

Awolowo, Obafemi (1909–1987)
Nationalist Leader

Obafemi Awolowo was a mission-educated Yoruba politician and nationalist leader who, during Nigeria's decolonization years, articulated and to a large extent successfully initiated movements that challenged British colonial monopolies of wealth and power. Although Awolowo's political education began early, through his exposure to nationalist politics and culture in southern Nigeria and India, his occupational activities as a money lender, public letter writer, and transport and produce merchant all exposed him to the vagaries of living in a colonial society. One of his first involvements as an activist was to help organize the Nigerian Produce Traders Association. He eventually became secretary of the Nigerian Motor Transport Union, and in 1937 basically single-handedly engineered a successful strike against an unjust and inequitable colonial law that had undermined the union's welfare.

Awolowo used his experiences as a trader and later a newspaper reporter to gain experience in colonial economic practices and to assist with the birth of a new liberal media. He was named secretary of the Ibadan branch of the country's foremost political party, the Nigerian Youth Movement (NYM), in June 1940 and led the agitation that reformed the Ibadan Native Authority Advisory Board in 1942. In 1944, as secretary of the Ibadan branch of the Nigerian Produce Traders Association, Awolowo successfully organized a mass protest involving more than 10,000 farmers against the government's ban on the exportation of palm kernel.

One of the earliest African politicians to critique the workings of the colonial administration in relation to indigenous political structures and economic responsibilities, Awolowo was also a pioneer in the postwar intellectual debates in favor of a new and appropriate constitution for a modern Nigeria. His trailblazing publication, *Path to Nigerian Freedom*, published in 1951, outlined the relevance of a local intelligentsia opposed to colonial conservatism within a postwar colonial political and economic setting. When the controversy concerning the form of Nigeria's constitution began in 1960, he had already been a dedicated federalist for more than eighteen years. His federalist philosophy was highly influenced by his familiarity and fascination with East Indian politics and political figures. While in London studying to be a lawyer, he had helped establish the Yoruba cultural organization *Egbe Omo Oduduwa* with the support of a corps of the wealthy Yoruba intelligentsia. These progressive groups exploited the rich combination of a western Nigerian cultural and economic setting to create a primarily Yoruba cultural and political interest association. The Awolowo-led group, combined with other Nigerian nationalist efforts, helped erode major exploitative colonial economic policies. At the same time, they found that appropriating certain aspects of those infrastructures was useful for shaping some of their own welfare and development programs. Their efforts undermined the waning colonial policies of "indirect rule" by obtaining the support of prominent traditional rulers of Yorubaland. Galvanized by educational, developmental, and welfare programs, the *Egbe* was able to cultivate a large following among the masses. On his return to Nigeria in 1947, Awolowo worked as a legal practitioner while also elevating his activities within the *Egbe*. In 1949, he started the *Nigerian Tribune*, a daily newspaper still in circulation, which served as the mouthpiece for his populist welfare programs. The paper became the main tool for defending Yoruban interests in the midst of emergent postwar interethnic nationalist rivalries. Backed by a combination of traditional Yoruba and Western communication media, Awolowo's emphasis on welfare policies and educational programs helped the Yoruba intelligentsia triumph over the conservative postwar initiatives of the British Colonial Office. In the country's transition to political independence, Awolowo's policies from his base in Nigeria's western region allowed a core number of his followers to impose their influence on the nation-building project.

In April 1951, Awolowo launched the Action Group (A.G.) political party, which displayed able and disciplined characteristics under his leadership. A year later, Awolowo was named the leader of government business and minister of local government and was elected into the then Western House of Assembly on the A.G. platform. At its peak, the A.G. arguably became the most efficiently run party in the history of modern democracy in Africa. The success of the party's economic and welfare initiatives saw a radical shift in the colonial-guided Africanization of the civil service and constitutional reforms in Nigeria. In 1954, with the introduction of the new constitution, Awolowo was named the first premier of the western region and minister of finance. During his term of office, he introduced a revolutionary program of free primary education. Under the postwar influence of British Fabian socialism and what Awolowo described as indigenous humanistic-guided responsibilities and duties, the A.G. launched major welfare programs centered around primary education, scholarship provisions for higher education, free healthcare, and the curbing of urban and rural unemployment. With a combination of stringent and disciplined policies, Awolowo was able to deliver a high-standard model in public affairs management. He and his party members later realized that there were financial hurdles of mountainous heights to overcome, especially without the financial and political clout of power at the center. In 1959, he contested federal elections in a bid to form government at the center, but he lost. Awolowo relinquished his premiership of the western region and moved to Lagos as the leader of the opposition. His attempts to extend his political and economic influence and projects nationwide were frustrated by colonial machinations, class conflicts, and interethnic rivalries within Yorubaland and Nigeria. In 1962, he was falsely charged with treasonable felony and sentenced to ten years' imprisonment. He was pardoned and freed from prison on July 31, 1966. In 1967, Awolowo was appointed federal commissioner for finance and vice chairman of the Federal Executive Council. In 1971, after realizing the limits of his influence on government policies, he resigned and returned to private law practice. In September 1978, Awolowo founded the social welfarist-oriented Unity Party of Nigeria and contested elections as president of Nigeria, but lost in a controversy-ridden election. He contested another equally troubled presidential election in 1983, though again he was defeated. This time, Awolowo retired from active political duties for good. He died on May 9, 1987, at age 78.

The popularity of the nationalist programs initiated by Awolowo's Action Group political party threatened colonial hegemonic designs in the decolonization era. They alienated the Yoruba intelligentsia from colonial authorities and conservative elites on one level and the less economically or materially endowed political associations on the other. The impact of Awolowo's legacy on Nigerian political and intellectual history is visible in the political terrain of southern Nigeria, a postwar political emphasis on welfare policies of free education as a tool for social, democratic, and economic development and national integration. In addition to the many intellectual and political protégés of Awolowo, who went on to adopt his policies and become successful politicians, are the progressive political associations and individuals who have invoked his name and philosophies to oppose feudalist unitary and military autocracy in Nigerian politics. In a contemporary era characterized by competing nationalist ideals, conflicts over the allocation of scarce resources draw attention to the federation's ability to instill power in the different nationalities so they may shape their own policies free from a powerful center, as well as carry out debates on the extent to which foreign capital should be allowed into the country. Such initiatives reveal the durability of Chief Obafemi Awolowo's

vision for the political future of Nigeria and Africa at large. Some of his major publications include: *Path to Nigerian Freedom* (1947); *Thoughts on Nigerian Constitution* (1966); *The Strategy and Tactics of the People's Republic of Nigeria* (1970); *Adventures in Power, Book One: My March Through Prison* (1985); *Adventures in Power, Book Two: The Travails of Democracy and the Rule of Law* (1987).

SAHEED A. ADEJUMOBI

See also: **Nigeria: Colonial Period: Intelligentsia, Nationalism, Independence.**

Biography

Born on March 6, 1909. Educated at Anglican and Methodist schools in his hometown, Ikenne, and at Baptists Boys' High School in Abeokuta, Western Nigeria. Enrolled in 1927 at Wesley College, Ibadan, to obtain training in shorthand and typing. In 1928, dropped out of college to take up a job as a schoolteacher in Abeokuta and Lagos. Returned to Wesley College in 1932 to assume a position as school clerk. In 1944, moved to Great Britain. Obtained a bachelor of commerce degree from the University of London. Studied law at the University of London and qualified as a barrister at law two years later. Called to the bar by the Honorable Society of the Inner Temple on November 18, 1946. Died May 9, 1987, at age 78.

Ayyubid Dynasty: *See* **Egypt: Ayyubid Dynasty.**

Azande: *See* **Central African Republic: Nineteenth Century: Gbaya, Banda, and Zande.**

Azania: *See* **Swahili: Azania to 1498.**

Azikiwe, Nnamdi (1904–1996)
Nigerian Nationalist and Politician

Nnamdi Azikiwe achieved academic distinction before turning to journalism. Moving from Nigeria to the Gold Coast (Ghana), he was editor of the *African Morning Post* for three years. A collection of his articles written for the *Post* was later published as *Renascent Africa*. His aim around this time, he wrote, was to shock Africa out of its stagnation and state of "arrested mental development" under British colonialism. Acquitted on a technicality from a charge of publishing a seditious article, he left for Nigeria in 1937 and set up Zik's Press, Ltd. In November of that year he published the first edition of the *West African Pilot*. Describing itself as "a sentinel of liberty and a guardian of civilization," the *Pilot* employed a sensational and pugnacious style, vaunting the achievements of Africans and criticizing the colonial government. Azikiwe also joined the Nigerian Youth Movement (NYM), the foremost nationalist body in the country, which won all three Lagos seats in the 1938 Legislative Council elections. Yet "Zik," as he was now widely known, soon found the NYM leaders, most of whom were older than himself, to be too moderate.

Zik established a good relationship before the outbreak of war in 1939 with Governor Sir Bernard Bourdillon, who helped him acquire government-controlled land for his printing presses and appointed him to several official committees. Yet a war against Nazi imperialism, which saw high inflation, inspired Zik to be far more critical of the British regime. The years 1944–1948 saw intense conflict in Nigeria, and Azikiwe was at its very heart. Bourdillon was replaced by the more astringent Sir Arthur Richards, and the new governor was determined to combat the growing nationalist movement around Azikiwe. Something of a personal vendetta developed between the two men.

In 1944 Azikiwe and the veteran nationalist Herbert Macaulay founded the National Council of Nigeria and the Cameroons (NCNC). Azikiwe was calling for self-government within fifteen years, while the new Richards Constitution, which was about to be inaugurated, though conceding an unofficial majority on the Legislative Council, was designed to conserve British control. In June 1945 Zik supported a "general strike" involving 30,000 workers, and in July the government banned two of his papers. A week later Zik alleged that he had discovered a government plot to assassinate him. These charges were not taken seriously in the Colonial Office. Zik, however, may well have taken the plot seriously. What is beyond doubt is that he used his journalistic skills to publicize his cause. A tall, handsome, and charismatic figure, and a superb orator, he had long been popular among the Igbo: now Zik became a hero to many.

Richards decided that Zik was "an irresponsible lunatic" and prosecuted the newspaper, the *Daily Comet*, of which Zik was managing director, for libel; but although its editor was imprisoned, Zik was untouched. The governor, however, took comfort that when he retired in 1947 his constitution was working reasonably well. Even Azikiwe, who won one of the Lagos seats, did not boycott the Legislative Council for long. Yet Richards's satisfaction was short-lived, for in August 1948 the British announced that the constitution was to be replaced (and within a few years the appointment of Nigerian ministers signaled internal self-government for Nigeria and the beginnings of speedy decolonization). Some historians have argued that Zik compelled the British to quicken the tempo of reform. Certainly the formation of the radical "Zikists" (originally a bodyguard of young men pledged to protect their hero during the assassination scare) was disquieting for the British, though they could make little of the philosophy of "Zikism," which lacked rigor. But the decision to scrap the Richards Constitution was made without any compulsion. The Accra riots of February 1948 produced a commission which called for extensive constitutional change in the Gold Coast, and it was judged in the Colonial Office that Nigeria had to keep in step.

Almost immediately Azikiwe began to be overshadowed. His very success in establishing himself as Nigeria's foremost nationalist, and in attracting huge personal publicity, produced a backlash from non-Igbos. Zik always insisted that he spoke for the whole of Nigeria, but early on the emirs of northern Nigeria repudiated him, and in 1941 he fell foul of the NYM. After the war the wider political scope offered by constitutional reform led rivals to the NCNC to appear, including the Action Group in the west and the Northern People's Congress. The dominance of the Nigerian federation by the latter was consequent upon the size of the northern region, and Zik had to be content with the position of premier of Eastern Nigeria from 1957 to 1959. An investigation by the Foster-Sutton Commission into his decision to invest £2 million of public money into the African Continental Bank, which led to his being mildly rebuked, had delayed regional self-government for a year. On independence in 1960 he was president of the Nigerian senate, and shortly thereafter governor-general, but these were largely honorific positions. Real power lay in the regions and with the federal prime minister.

After independence Zik helped to found the University of Nigeria at Nsukka, and after the coup of 1966 he was an adviser to the military government of the eastern region. He was a respected elder statesman until his death in 1996.

ROBERT PEARCE

See also: **Journalism, African: Colonial Era; Macaulay, Herbert; Nigeria: Colonial Period: Intelligentsia, Nationalism, Independence.**

Biography

Born in November 16, 1904, in Zungeru, in northern Nigeria. Educated at the schools in Calabar and Lagos before becoming a clerk in the treasury department in 1921. Stowed away on a ship bound for the United States in 1925. Studied political science, obtained a doctorate at the University of Pennsylvania for a dissertation later published as *Liberia in World Politics*. Lectured at Lincoln University before returning to West Africa in 1934. Rejected for the post of tutor at King's College in Lagos, he turned to journalism. Premier of Eastern Nigeria from 1957 to 1959. Named president of the Nigerian senate in 1960. Died May 11, 1996.

Further Reading

Azikiwe, Nnamdi. *My Odyssey*. London: Hurst, 1970.

Azikiwe, Nnamdi. *Zik: A Selection of the Speeches of Nnamdi Azikiwe*. London and New York: Cambridge University Press, 1961.

Coleman, James. *Nigeria: Background to Nationalism*. Berkeley and Los Angeles: University of California Press, and London: Cambridge University Press, 1958.

Jones-Quartey, K.A.B. *A Life of Azikiwe*. Harmondsworth, England: Penguin Books, 1965.

Pearce, R.D. "Governors, Nationalists, and Constitutions in Nigeria, 1935–1951," *The Journal of Imperial and Commonwealth History*, 9/3 (May 1981): 289–307.

B

Bagirmi, Wadai, and Darfur

Bagirmi (1522–1897)

Located southeast of Lake Chad, Bagirmi has a history marked by constant warfare to acquire slaves from its southern neighbors, while struggling to maintain its independence or to ameliorate its status as a tributary of Kanem-Bornu and Wadai to the north. According to tradition, Bagirmi emerged from the welter of village polities in north-central Africa about 1522. During the sixteenth century the sun kings, or *mbangs*, forged a recognizable state. Islam became the court religion, but the rural people continued to worship their traditional gods. The mbang consolidated the heartland of the state, reduced vulnerable neighbors to tributaries, and became an important provider of slaves for trans-Saharan trade. During the reign of Burkumanda I (1635–1665), Bagirmi established its influence as far north as Lake Chad. Slaves procured in the south were the fundamental commodity of the economy, whether as chattel for trans-Saharan trade, agricultural laborers on local estates, retainers for the mbang and *maladonoge*, or eunuchs for the Ottoman Empire.

The military and commercial hegemony of Bagirmi did not go unchallenged. Between 1650 and 1675, Bornu claimed sovereignty over Bagirmi, but it did not inhibit the mbang from sending raiding parties into Bornu. More successful was the claim of suzerainty by the *kolak* (sultan) Sabun of Wadai who, taking advantage of the decline of Bagirmi's power at the end of the eighteenth century, launched a brutal offensive in 1805, captured Massenya, the capital, slaughtered the mbang and his relatives, and decimated and enslaved the populace. Sabun's invasion was the beginning of a century of decline and disintegration, during which the armies of Wadai plundered with impunity. This period ended only in the 1890s with the invasion of the kingdom by the forces of the Sudanese freebooter, Rabih Zubayr.

In desperation the last mbang, Gaugrang II, sought to ally himself with the advancing French, but when he signed a treaty of protection with Commandant Emil Gentil in 1897, he in fact consigned the Kingdom of Bagirmi to its place as a footnote of history.

Darfur (1650–1916)

The sultanate was established by the Fur, a non-Arab people who inhabit the western Nile River Basin surrounding the mountain massif of Jabal Marra. Their origins are obscure, but as cultivators they long interacted with the Fazara nomads, the non-Arab Toubou, and Arabs from Upper Egypt. The original state founded by the Tunjur may have appeared as early as the fifteenth century, but the first historically recorded Fur sultan was Sulayman Solongdungu (*c.*1650–1680) who founded the Keira dynasty.

Although the royal house claimed an Arab heritage, it was probably more the result of intermarriage with Arabs from the Nile Valley whose holy men and merchants brought Islam to the court. Fur ritual and traditional beliefs, however, prevailed in the countryside. The successors of Sulayman are more obscure, but they seemed to have been preoccupied with unsuccessful attempts to extend their authority westward into Wadai and their unpopular enlistment of slave troops as an imperial guard from the equatorial south.

Frustrated in the west, the seventh sultan, Muhammad Tayrab (*r.*1752–1786), turned east to conquer Kordofan from the Funj sultanate of Sennar, opening the Fur to Islamic legal and administrative practices and Muslim merchants. As early as 1633 the Darb al-Arba'in (the Forty Days Road) was an established trans-Saharan route from Kobbei to Asyut in Egypt. The reign of Abd al-Rahman was the apogee of the Keira sultanate, symbolized by his founding the permanent capital at El Fasher in 1792.

In the nineteenth century, Darfur began a tempestuous passage through a period characterized by problems. In 1821 the forces of Muhammad 'Ali conquered the Funj Kingdom of Sennar and the Kordofan province of the sultanate of Darfur. Thereafter, the Keira sultanate in El Fasher continued an uneasy coexistence with the riverine Arabs on the Nile and the Turco-Egyptian government at Khartoum whose traders established their control over the traditional slaving regions of Darfur to the south in the Bahr al-Ghazal. In 1874 the head of the largest corporate slaving empire, Zubayr Pasha Rahma Mansur, invaded Darfur with his well-armed slave army, defeated and killed the Sultan Ibrahim Qarad at the Battle of al-Manawashi, and occupied El Fasher as a province of the Turco-Egyptian empire in the Sudan. In 1881 Muhammad Ahmad Al-Mahdi proclaimed his jihad against the Turco-Egyptian government. By 1885 his *ansar* had captured Darfur and destroyed Khartoum, ending their rule in the Sudan. Led by pretenders to the sultanate, the Fur resisted Mahdist rule in Darfur, the last of whom was Ali Dinar Zakariya. When the Anglo-Egyptian army defeated the forces of the Khalifa at the Battle of Karari in 1898 to end the Mahdists state, he restored his authority over the sultanate. For the next eighteen years Ali Dinar ruled at El Fasher, his independence tolerated by the British in Khartoum while the French advanced from the west, conquering Wadai in 1909. At the outbreak of World War I Ali Dinar allied himself with the Ottoman Empire, which precipitated the Anglo-Egyptian invasion of the sultanate. Ali Dinar was killed, and with him ended the kingdom of Darfur.

Wadai (c.Sixteenth Century–1909; Also Waday, Ouadai, Oueddai)

The kingdom of Wadai was founded by the Tunjur as they moved westward from Darfur. They were eventually driven farther west into Kanem by the Maba under their historic leader Ibrahim Abd al-Karim (*c.*1611–1655). He built his capital at Wara, introduced Islam, and founded the Kolak dynasty, which ruled Wadai until 1915.

After his death the history of Wadai was characterized by desultory civil wars, hostile relations with Darfur and Bornu, and the development of a hierarchical aristocracy. Islam was the state religion, but its dissemination among the cultivators and herders was casual, the subjects of the kolak observing their traditional religious practices. The resources of the state came from the trade in slaves and the ability of its slave-raiding expeditions to supply the trans-Saharan caravans. The expanding economy was accompanied by more able

sultans in the nineteenth century. 'Abd al-Karim Sabun (*r.*1805–1815) promoted Islam, controlled commerce, and equipped his army with chain mail and firearms to raid and plunder Baguirmi and Bornu. After his death, Wadai was plunged into internecine strife that enabled the Sultan of Darfur to intervene in 1838 and install the younger brother of Sabun, Muhammad al-Sharif (*r.*1838–1858), in return for loyalty and tribute. Muhammad al-Sharif did not remain a puppet. He formed a close alliance with Muhammad ibn 'Ali al-Sanusi, whom he had met in Mecca, embraced the Sanusi order, and profited from their control of the new eastern trade route through the Sanusi strongholds of Jalu and Kufra. He founded a new capital at Abeche (Abeshr), from which he tightly controlled the Sanusi merchants and their commerce. His successors, protected and prospered by their connections with the Sanusiyya, imported firearms that enabled them to expand their influence in Bornu and continue their intervention in Baguirmi.

In 1846 the sultan defeated the army of the *shehu* of Bornu, sacked the capital Kukawa, and enforced the tributary status of Bagirmi. Relations with Darfur degenerated into inconclusive *razzia* (raid and counterraid). Muhammad al-Sharif was succeeded by his two sons, 'Ali ibn Muhammad Sharif (*r.*1858–1874) and Yusuf ibn Muhammad Sharif (*r.*1874–1898), both of whom enjoyed long, stable, and prosperous reigns that enabled them to increase trade and expand the state. The death of Yusuf in 1898 ironically coincided with the return of 'Ali Dinar to El Fasher to rejuvenate the sultanate of Darfur and to intervene in the succession struggles in Wadai. His candidate, Ahmad al-Ghazali, was enthroned only to be assassinated and replaced by the Sanusi candidate, Muhammad Salih, the son of Yusuf, known as Dud Murra, "the lion of Murra." Dud Murra repaid the Sanusiyya by allowing free trade for Sanusi merchants. In 1906 the French initiated an aggressive policy against the Wadai complete with a puppet sultan, Adam Asil, a grandson of Sultan Muhammad al-Sharif. On June 2, 1909, Abeche fell to a French military column. Dud Murra fled to the Sanusiyya, Asil was proclaimed sultan, and the French prepared to conquer and confirm French sovereignty over the tributary vassals of Wadai.

ROBERT O. COLLINS

See also: **Central Africa, Northern: Slave Raiding.**

Further Reading

Bjørkelø, A. J. *State and Society in Three Central Sudanic Kingdoms: Kanem-Bornu, Bagirmi, and Wadai.* Bergen, Norway: University of Bergen Press, 1976.

Kapteijins, L., and J. Spaulding. *After the Millennium: Diplomatic Correspondence from Wadai and Dar Fur on the Eve of*

Colonial Conquest, 1885–1916. East Lansing: Michigan State University Press, 1988.

Lampen, G. D. "The History of Darfur." *Sudan Notes and Records* 31, no. 2 (1950): pp.177–209.

Lavers, J. E. "An Introduction to the History of Bagirmi c. 1500–1800." *Annals of Borno*, no. 1 (1983): pp.29–44.

Reyna, S. P. *Wars without End: The Political Economy of a Pre-Colonial African State.* Hanover, NH: University Press of New England, 1990.

Balewa, Alhaji Sir Abubakar (1912–1966)
Prime Minister of Nigeria

Sir Abubakar Tafawa Balewa was born in the village of Tafawa Balewa in the modern Bauchi area of northeastern Nigeria. He trained as a teacher, and was a respected member of the elite of the northern region of Nigeria after the end of World War II. He was a founding member of the conservative Northern Peoples' Congress, and acted as its vice president. Although he taught for many years, Balewa's importance in the political history of modern Nigeria was in the area of politics during the struggle for independence and immediately after, when he was Nigeria's first indigenous prime minister (1960–1966). Before independence, Balewa was appointed central minister of works, transportation, and prime minister in the era of the transfer of power (1952–1960).

To understand Balewa's importance in the politics of Nigeria in the 1950s and 1960s, it is necessary to appreciate the fact that he was a liberal politician within the conservative politics of the northern region in the wake of nationalism. Compared to his contemporaries—such as the late premier, Sir Ahmadu Bello, the Sardauna of Sokoto, and Alhaji Aliyu Makaman Bida, who were extremely northern-oriented in their political outlook and temperament—Balewa was capable of appreciating issues of national importance within the context of a Nigerian nation. It can be said with some authority that Balewa stood between the left-wing Northern Elements Progressive Union (NEPU) of Mallam Aminu Kano on the one hand and the extreme reactionary conservatives (of which the Sardauna was a leading spokesman) on the other.

Thus, not surprisingly, when the British colonial government had to make a decision as to who should lead the government of Nigeria as independence approached in the late 1950s, Balewa was the natural choice. He did not differ too significantly in his positions from the other emergent conservative northern elites on issues of core value to the northern region—primarily the preeminence of the north in national politics, and the north's control of the federal government. Balewa's Anglophilism was never in doubt. His accommodation of some issues that his colleagues from the conservative north considered as irritants, such as minority rights (including fundamental and human rights), endeared him to the decolonizing British as an ally in the impending transfer of power. Britain was able to offer unified support of Balewa for the position of prime minister because his was considered a good rallying point for divergent opinions within the emergent Nigerian nation, as he was respected by other political parties. Thus, in spite of the controversy that accompanied the 1959 federal elections heralding Nigeria's independence, Balewa was invited to form a new federal government.

In the first six years of independence, Balewa led Nigeria's federal government until a combination of factors culminated in a bloody military coup that not only terminated Balewa's government but his very life. It was during his period of rule that the midwest region was carved out of the old western region, a development seen by some as an attempt to undermine the electoral position of the Action Group, the ruling party in the west. These six years were also characterized by political crises exemplified by riots in central Nigeria by the Tiv, who were agitating against domination by the ruling Hausa-Fulani oligarchy, as well as against intolerance on the part of the ruling elites in Nigeria's various political regions. His government constantly faced allegations of corruption and high-handedness, but Balewa himself was considered to be above the fray, a gentleman with a pan-Nigerian outlook. A major reason for the mutiny undertaken by the army in January 1966 was the widespread allegation of election rigging that followed the chaotic western regional elections of October 1965. Balewa's decision to send the army to restore law and order was hardly accomplished when a section of the armed forces staged a coup d'état on January 15, 1966, during which Balewa was killed.

In foreign affairs, Balewa placed considerable weight on British colonial views of international affairs. In January 1966, however, Balewa convened and hosted an extraordinary session of the commonwealth heads of state to discuss the crisis arising from the Unilateral Declaration of Independence of the minority regime headed by Ian Smith in Southern Rhodesia (Zimbabwe). Balewa's respect for British ideals was not in doubt. Correspondingly, he was respected by the British official classes throughout his ascendancy in the government of colonial and independent Nigeria. In 1952, Balewa was named Officer of the British Empire, and in 1955 he was named Commander of the British Empire. At independence in 1960, the Queen of England conferred the title of Knight Commander of the British Empire on Balewa, who was also appointed a privy councillor in 1961.

KUNLE LAWAL

BALEWA, ALHAJI SIR ABUBAKAR (1912–1966)

See also: **Nigeria: Colonial Period: Intelligentsia, Nationalism, Independence; Nigeria: Federalism, Corruption, Popular Discontent: 1960–1966; Nigeria: Gowon Regime, 1966–1975; Zimbabwe (Rhodesia): Unilateral Declaration of Independence and the Smith Regime, 1966–1979.**

Biography

Sir Abubakar Tafawa Balewa was born in Tafawa Balewa village in the modern Bauchi area of northeastern Nigeria. Trained as a teacher. Served as Nigeria's first prime minister, 1960–1966. Died January 15, 1966, during a coup d'état.

Further Reading

Clark, T. *The Right Honourable Gentleman: The Biography of Sir Abubakar Tafawa Balewa.* Kaduna, Nigeria: Gaskiya Press, 1991.

Lawal, K. *Britain and the Transfer of Power in Nigeria, 1945–1960.* Lagos: LASU Press, 2000.

Bamako

Bamako (its name means "marshland of crocodiles" in the Bambara language) is the capital of independent Mali since 1960, and formerly the capital of colonial Soudan Français (French Sudan); today it has around 900,000 inhabitants.

By the time the French arrived in the nineteenth century, Bamako was already a multiethnic settlement that could trace its origins to some time between the fifteenth and seventeenth centuries, the period of its formal foundation by Séribadian Niaré, a Sarakollé. In the nineteenth century it was still no more than a small town surrounded by a defensive *tata* (adobe wall), but it had a degree of commercial importance, being located at the junction of routes among Sotuba, Segu, and Kangaba. The explorer Mungo Park visited Bamako twice, in 1795 and in 1805, and René Caillé referred to it in 1830.

At the time of the wars launched during the 1880s by the French army under Gallieni against the Tukulor ruler Ahmadu Seku, this small town was chosen as the base for a military post on the Niger River. The struggle against Samori Touré further enhanced its strategic importance. A treaty imposed on the chief Titi Niaré in 1883 provided for the building of a French fortress, and it was around this that the city rapidly expanded; the fortress was built on the right bank of the Niger, and a "village of liberty" was established close by as an enclave for freed prisoners, who formed a reservoir of labor for the French.

Bamako was, therefore, a colonial refoundation rather than a new foundation in the strict sense. Nevertheless, the colonists' choice of Bamako, particularly after it became the capital of French Sudan in 1908, was crucial to the development of the city, which continued at the expense of its rival Kayes, but also induced decline in secondary centers such as Gao or Timbuktu. During the first two decades of the twentieth century, Bamako experienced spectacular growth under the influence of two successive governors general, Trentinian and Clozel. Most of the government buildings were assembled on a single site on the hill of Koulouba during the first decade of the century, and the railway line from Dakar reached Koulokoro in 1904, while commercial buildings, the first residential quarters for Europeans, and the "native" districts were all established on the plain below. Educational and medical institutions gradually prevailed over military facilities, which were on the decline, since they were being relocated several miles away, at Kati. In fact, the fortress itself was destroyed in 1903. The main layout of the city center was designed under the terms of the development plan of 1923, with a network of major streets, a market, public buildings, a cathedral, and a zoo. The Niger still had to be crossed by ferry until 1929, when a submersible causeway to Sotuba was constructed. The European districts were given electricity and provided with street-cleaning services early in the 1930s.

Bamako "la coquette," as the city was known between the two world wars, had 20,000 inhabitants in 1930 and close to 40,000 by 1945. The exodus from the countryside, which began during the crisis of the 1930s, had a major impact on the capital of French Sudan. Its growth became explosive after World War II, and the city continued to acquire enhanced infrastructure and to be modernized, thanks to investments by the Fonds d'Investissement pour le Développement Economique et Social (Investment Fund for Economic and Social Development). However, its uncontrollable growth undermined the changes that were carried out during the 1950s.

Meanwhile, the capital also seemed to be increasingly explosive in the political and social sense. The congress that established the Rassemblement Démocratique Africain (African Democratic Rally) was held in Bamako in 1946 due to the influence of the nationalist leader of French Sudan, Fily Dabo Sissoko, and the city became a focus for African nationalism. The great strike by railway workers on the Dakar–Niger line in 1947 was to have a lasting impact on the city.

By the time Mali became independent, Bamako had a population of 100,000, and its relative lack of infrastructure was apparent despite the previous concerted efforts to expand it. The central districts inhabited by Europeans were almost unique in being provided with electricity, street cleaning, and other modern amenities such as a water supply, hospitals, and schools. The construction of the Vincent Auriol Bridge, which was completed in 1958, contributed to the development of the right bank of the Niger from that year onward.

The rise to power of Modibo Keita as president of an independent Mali (1960–1968) transformed the situation. He achieved a rapprochement with the Communist bloc (though, in spite of everything, he also maintained the link with France), and Mali became committed to nonalignment; these political orientations had their effects on the country's capital city. During the 1960s Mali received infrastructure from the Soviet Union and funds from the United Arab Republic, mainland China, and North Korea. At the same time, the new regime launched a campaign against people arriving in the city from the countryside, introducing a system of internal passports and organizing the compulsory return of young peasants to the provinces.

The policy of cooperation with the former colonial power, which was confirmed by the coming to power of Moussa Traoré in 1968, continued, despite these changes, to provide the French residents of the city with an important role in its development. Bamako was given guidelines for development, and its transformation continued, but from the middle of the 1970s a decline in urban investment, coupled with exponential growth of the population, which reached 800,000 in 1986, further aggravated the problems faced by the majority of its poorer inhabitants, while existing facilities and services declined. Social tensions found expression in such events as the uprising by secondary school students in Bamako in 1979–1980 and the sporadic student protests of the early 1990s. *Finye* (*The Wind*), a film directed by Souleymane Cissé, offers an outstanding view of the difficulties of life in the poorer districts of the Malian capital.

During the 1980s and 1990s, bilateral and multilateral aid became more diversified, with funds from the World Bank and the United States. Within the constraints of Mali's economic problems, there was a new emphasis on the development of the suburbs, such as Badalabougoue, that lie on the right bank of the Niger. A reallocation of resources in favor of such secondary settlements has been encouraged, within the framework of the Projet Urbain du Mali (Mali Urban Project), which is being implemented under the guidance of the United Nations, in order to counterbalance the predominance of the capital city.

SOPHIE DULUCQ

See also: **Mali.**

Further Reading

IDA, *Mali: Urban Development Project.* Washington, D.C.: United Nations, 1979.

Skinner, E. P. "Urbanization in Francophone Africa." *African Urban Quarterly* 1, nos. 3–4 (1986): 191–195.

Bambandyanalo: *See* **Iron Age (Later): Southern Africa: Leopard's Kopje, Bambandyanalo, and Mapungubwe.**

Banda: *See* **Central African Republic: Nineteenth Century: Gbaya, Banda, and Zande.**

Banda, Dr. Hastings Kamuzu (*c*.1896–1997)
Malawian Doctor and Former President

Hastings Banda, president of Malawi from July 1964 to May 1994, was born around 1896 near Mthunthama, Kasungu. In 1915 or 1916, he went to South Africa, where he took the middle name Kamuzu (*Kamuzu* meaning "little root").

Unlike most Nyasalanders who went to that part of Africa to seek employment, Banda planned to attend Lovedale College, founded by the Free Church of Scotland in the nineteenth century. He found employment at the Witwatersrand deep mine Boksburg, and for the first time was exposed to the rough life of a growing mining city. He was never to forget this experience and, when later he became head of state, would always oppose labor migration to South Africa on the grounds that, among other things, it rendered the migrants vulnerable to criminal elements and to venereal diseases from prostitutes in the cities.

Although he was fully employed, Banda's quest for further education remained prominent in his personal plan and to this end he enrolled at a local night school. In 1922, he joined the African Methodist Episcopal (AME) Church, and in November 1923 attended the church's annual meeting at Bloemfontein, where he met the American Bishop W. T. Vernon, who agreed to sponsor Banda's travel to the United States to pursue his education. By July 1925, Banda had raised the fare to board a ship for the New World.

Banda registered as a student at the AME Church's Wilberforce Institute, Ohio, graduating in three years. In 1932, he became a student at the Meharry Medical College in Nashville, Tennessee. After qualifying as a doctor in 1937, he went to Edinburgh, Scotland, where in 1938 he became a student at the School of Medicine of the Royal College of Physicians and Surgeons. Such additional qualifications were necessary for him to practice within the British Empire, his ambition being to return to Nyasaland as a medical missionary. However, even after satisfactorily completing his Edinburgh courses, it became clear to him that neither the Church of Scotland nor the colonial government in Zomba would allow him to work for them. During World War II, he worked in Liverpool and, after the war, established a thriving practice in London.

Postwar London was a hive of activity, especially among Africans working and studying in the United Kingdom; they included the future leaders Jomo Kenyatta, Kwame Nkrumah, and Seretse Khama. Increasingly, Banda became involved in Pan-African affairs, but he also became active in the Fabian Society and the British Labour Party.

In 1944, the Nyasaland African Congress (NAC) was formed, bringing together the various pressure groups, and Banda acted as its external advisor, regularly giving it financial assistance. He strongly campaigned against the Federation of the Rhodesias and Nyasaland and, when it was actually established in 1953, he left London for Kumasi, Ghana, where he continued to practice medicine. In 1957, the NAC became convinced that only Banda could lead the fight for decolonization, and they invited him to return home, which he did on July 6, 1958. Although most Nyasalanders had not heard of Banda before that year, the NAC had constructed a powerful image of him, presenting him as the only African able to deal effectively with Europeans given his education and experience of living in the West. Banda was welcomed back by large crowds as a messiah-like figure.

Within a few months of his arrival, the NAC was reorganized, and the political atmosphere became highly charged. In January and February 1959, riots and minor incidents took place in various parts of the colony and on March 3, Governor Robert Armitage declared a state of emergency. The NAC was banned, and Banda and many congressional leaders were imprisoned in Southern Rhodesia; hundreds of others were detained in various parts of the country—mainly at Kanjedza, Limbe.

Released on April 1, 1960, Banda took over the helm of the Malawi Congress Party (MCP), which had been formed while he was in detention. After constitutional talks in London attended by various political interests, Nyasaland held general elections in August 1961. The MCP was swept into power, and Banda became minister of agriculture, a position he sought because he viewed it as crucial to the development of the country. In January 1963, he became prime minister, and on July 6, 1964, Nyasaland attained independence and was renamed Malawi.

However, within two months, Prime Minister Banda was arguing with most of his cabinet over his style of leadership, and domestic and foreign policies, including Malawi's future relations with communist China and with the white-ruled regions of southern Africa. The "cabinet crisis" of 1964 was a turning point in Malawi's short postcolonial history, in that it turned Malawi into a full-fledged one-party state and Banda into a virtual dictator. With the rebelling ministers in exile in Zambia and Tanzania and, with a new cabinet of ministers, Banda's will was law. Political incarcerations increased. He dominated the print and broadcasting media and, on the economic front, he supervised the creation and expansion of Press Holdings, which had interests in a wide range of economic sectors. In 1971, he became life president of Malawi, and visited South Africa—the first African head of state to do so.

Banda's domination of Malawi continued throughout the 1970s and 1980s, as did abuse of human rights. However, with the demise of the Cold War, the Western powers that had supported Banda began to press for political reform and, by the early 1990s, aid was conditional on change. Within Malawi pressure mounted and, by the end of 1992, Banda was forced to accept the possibility of losing his position of power, a fact confirmed by a national referendum in June 1993. In the free general elections in May of the following year, the MCP lost, and Bakili Muluzi of the United Democratic Front replaced Banda as president. Aging and frail, he virtually retired from politics. He died on November 25, 1997, and received a state funeral on December 3.

OWEN J. M. KALINGA

See also: **Malawi: Independence to the Present; Malawi: Nationalism, Independence.**

Biography

Born about 1896 near Mthunthama, Kasungu, a primarily Chewa area bordering with the Tumbuka-speaking region conquered by the M'mbelwa Ngoni in the 1860s. Attended three local Free Church of Scotland schools. In 1914, passed the standard three examinations and either at the end of the following year or early in 1916 left Chilanga for South Africa. Registered as a student at the AME Church's Wilberforce Institute, Ohio, graduating in three years and, early in 1928, proceeded to Indiana University for premedical studies. Two years later, transferred to the University of Chicago at the suggestion of a professor of linguistics, who wanted Banda to be his research assistant in Bantu languages. In December 1931, awarded a Bachelor of Philosophy degree from the the University of Chicago, with a double major in history and politics. In 1932, became a student at the Meharry Medical College in Nashville, Tennessee. After qualifying as a doctor in 1937, went to Edinburgh, Scotland, and in 1938 became a student at the School of Medicine of the Royal College of Physicians and Surgeons. Returned to Malawi in 1958, and in January 1963 became prime minister. In 1971 was named life president. Lost the free general elections in 1994 to Bakili Muluzi. Died November 25, 1997, and received a state funeral on December 3.

Further Reading

Lwanda, J. L. *Kamuzu Banda of Malawi: A Study of Promise, Power and Paralysis*. Glasgow: Dudu Nsomba, 1993.

———. *Promises, Power Politics, and Poverty: Democratic Transition in Malawi 1961–1993*. Glasgow: Dudu Nsomba, 1996.

Phiri, K. M., and Kenneth R. Ross (eds.). *Democratization in Malawi: A Stocktaking*. Blantyre, Malawi: CLAIM, 1998.

Rotberg, R. I. *The Rise of Nationalism in Central Africa: The Making of Malawi and Zambia, 1873–1964*. Cambridge, Mass.: Harvard University Press, 1965.

Sanger, C. *Central African Emergency*. London: Heinemann, 1960.

Short, P. *Banda*. London: Routledge and Kegan Paul, 1974.

Williams, T. D. *Malawi: The Politics of Despair*. Ithaca, N.Y.: Cornell University Press, 1978.

Banking and Finance

The financial systems of African countries at the time of independence in the 1960s were dominated by foreign-owned and foreign-managed commercial banks. Other financial institutions, such as development banks, building societies, and agricultural or land banks were relatively small, with few resources and small portfolios of loans compared with those of the commercial banks. It was clear, therefore, that in the short and probably the medium term, significant domestic finance for development would have to come from the commercial banks.

In Anglophone Africa, these foreign-owned commercial banks were nearly all British and followed British banking practice. In particular, lending policy was to make short-term loans, largely to finance foreign trade and working capital; to take security; and largely to neglect medium- and long-term lending or investment in equity. Newly independent African governments also accused these banks of lending mainly to the expatriate business community. It appeared (rightly or wrongly) that African businesses, and individual Africans, had little or no access to commercial bank credit, and that this was both irrational and unjust.

Governments therefore intervened extensively in the financial sector, intending to create a financial system to support their development objectives. Intervention included takeover by governments (partial or complete) of foreign-owned commercial banks;

creating government-owned commercial banks from scratch; directing credit to favored sectors; creating government-owned development banks to provide long-term loans, in particular for industry and small-scale agriculture; creating government-owned development corporations to provide equity finance for both domestic and foreign investors; exchanging control regulations to limit the borrowing of foreign-owned businesses; and setting interest rates below market levels to encourage investment and reduce the costs of borrowers.

The regulation and supervision of financial institutions tended to be badly neglected—partly because the foreign-owned commercial banks clearly did not need supervision and partly because it was difficult for central banks to supervise government-owned financial institutions that were pursuing government development objectives—so that the buildup of bad debts in their loan portfolios was often ignored.

Not every country pursued all these interventions, and a minority of countries did not intervene in commercial bank ownership at all. Overall, however, a new type of commercial banking sector tended to emerge, with three distinct types of bank: the old expatriate banks, frequently with a much reduced share of the market (or no share at all in a few countries, including Ethiopia, Mozambique, and Tanzania); government-owned banks, which were dominant in some countries (including Ghana, Malawi, and Uganda) but had only a minority share of the market in others (including Kenya, Zambia, and Zimbabwe); and new indigenous or local banks, wholly owned and managed by local people (initially most notable in Kenya and Nigeria, to a lesser extent in Uganda and Zambia, and in Ghana, Ethiopia, and Zimbabwe in the mid-1990s).

Unfortunately, most local banks were licensed before the reform of banking legislation and the rehabilitation of bank supervision capacity. This proved extremely damaging, because the most common cause for local bank failures, of which there were many, had been uncontrolled insider lending (the lending of depositors' money to the directors and managers and to their businesses) which was only later made illegal. The survival of some local banks, despite inadequate legislation and supervision, suggested that better sequencing would sharply reduce the number of failures.

Those countries in which the economy had deteriorated most in the 1970s and 1980s tended also to be those in which the banking system was most decayed: government commercial banks with extremely high levels of bad debt (government commercial banks in Ghana, Uganda, and Tanzania; some of the Nigerian federal government banks and most of the Nigerian state banks, the Gambia, Malawi, and the smaller government bank in Kenya, had up to 80 per cent bad debts), and large numbers of local bank failures.

Reform of the larger failed government banks was difficult. Most of them had been recapitalized, and management reforms had been implemented, but reversing previous lending practice was difficult, and there was already evidence of some reformed banks building up new portfolios of bad debts. Only one country, Guinea, took the radical alternative action of closing down the country's whole (entirely government-owned) banking system and starting again.

Compounding the problem of banking reform was that financial liberalization and structural adjustment programs—usually introduced as part of International Monetary Fund and World Bank conditionality for loans and for support from other aid donors—included sharp increases in interest rates. Higher interest rates were intended to attract more deposits into the commercial banks, so that they could provide finance to businesses as the economy recovered. However, attracting more deposits into banks that were fundamentally insolvent, badly managed, and, in many cases, corrupt tended only to make things worse. In some countries it was also necessary to simultaneously reform the loss-making parastatal sector along with the banks in order that the banks might have profitable lending opportunities; this was exceptionally difficult.

A further problem was that some reformed banks had been, understandably, excessively cautious in making new lending decisions; the Ghana Commercial Bank, for example, had loans and advances in the early 1990s equivalent to only 8 per cent of its total assets, which created a shortage of credit because of its dominant position. On the other hand, it is notable that some of the economies that had recovered from economic disaster with some success (including Ghana) did not embark upon banking reform immediately, putting it aside for five to ten years. It could be argued, therefore, that economic recovery was possible (at least for some years) without reforming the banking system. Another positive factor was that most countries had introduced reformed banking legislation and supervision. It was important that these reforms were effective, because a repetition of past banking failures would be extremely expensive; rehabilitating the Tanzanian banking system, for example, cost more than 10 per cent of its gross domestic product.

CHARLES HARVEY

See also: **Debt, International, Development and Dependency; World Bank, International Monetary Fund, and Structural Adjustment.**

Further Reading

Brownbridge, M., and C. Harvey. *Banking in Africa: The Impact of Financial Sector Reforms since Independence.* Oxford: James Currey, 1998.

Fry, M. *Money, Interest and Banking in Economic Development.* Baltimore: Johns Hopkins University Press, 1988.

Kitchen, R. L. *Finance for the Developing Countries.* Chichester, England: Wiley, 1986.

Maxfield, S. *Gatekeepers of Growth: The International Political Economy of Central Banking in Developing Countries.* Princeton, N.J.: Princeton University Press, 1997.

Roe, A. R. "The Financial Sector in Stabilisation Programmes." Discussion paper no. 77. Warwick, Department of Economics, University of Warwick, 1988.

White, L. H. (ed.). *African Finance: Research and Reform.* San Francisco: ICS Press, 1993.

Bantu Cultivators: Kenyan Highlands

The Kenyan Highlands stretch across south-central Kenya; they are delimited in the south and north by arid zones, in the west by plains which extend to Lake Victoria, and in the east by the plateau east of Mount Kenya. The Rift Valley separates the Western Highlands, which are inhabited mostly by Southern Nilotic peoples of the Kalenjin group from the Central Highlands, which are home mainly to Bantu groups like the Igembe, Meru, Tharaka, Chuka, Embu, Mbeere, Kikuyu, and Taita. Major boundary landmarks of the Central Highlands are the Nyandarua (Aberdare) Range and Mount Kenya in the west and the Tana River in the northeast.

The Taita inhabit the upland valleys and slopes of the Dawida, Saghala, and Kasigau regions, where the fertile valley bottoms are exploited for the cultivation of bananas, sugarcane, and yams, and the higher regions for cattle raising. The Kikuyu, who live on top of the ridges of the Central Highlands, cultivate perennial crops such as arrowroot and sweet potato and also practice stock farming. The Embu live on the fertile and well-irrigated slopes of Mount Kenya above 1200 meters; and the Mbeere live in the lower dry savanna. While the Embu are well-positioned to practice intensive agriculture, the Mbeere grow drought-resistant field crops such as maize, millet, or sorghum in addition to raising cattle. The Chuka and the Meru are neighboring tribes of highland farmers on the northeastern slopes of Mount Kenya.

To date, no comprehensive picture has emerged from the scarce evidence available concerning the Iron Age history of these Bantu peoples. Such evidence comes chiefly from historical linguistics, archaeology, and oral history. Particularly problematic are the construction of a chronology of historical events and the establishment of synchronisms of historical findings across multiple disciplines. According to the leading hypothesis about the geographical origin of these peoples, whose languages belong to the Thagicu group of northeastern Bantu, they originally migrated into the Kenyan Highlands from Zaïre. Judging from percentages of shared cognates, the languages of today's highland Bantu must have begun developing from proto-Thagicu around the tenth century.

The Bantu peoples of the Central Highlands have no unitary myth of origin. The Chuka, Embu, Mbeere, and Kikuyu south of Mount Kenya maintain that they immigrated from Igembe/Tigania in the northern Meru region. In the early phase of the migration they were pastoralists and hunters, but after colonizing the higher forest regions of the Highlands they became agriculturalists. Kikuyu oral traditions maintain a record of age-groups going back into the past; thus counting back from today's age-groups, it could be argued that the Kikuyu left Igembe/Tigania in the fifteenth century and reached the northern part of their modern settlement areas in the early seventeenth century. The Meru claim to have migrated from an island called Mbwa, which several scholars believe is Manda Island, off the northern Kenyan coast. These migrations are estimated to have taken place in the first half of the eighteenth century. Oral traditions of various highland Bantu groups agree that the highlands were acquired by land purchase from southern Nilotic Okiek hunters.

In addition, the oral traditions of the Kikuyu, Chuka, and Embu recall the Gumba, a cattle-raising and iron-manufacturing people. The Gumba are said to have resisted the colonization of the highlands by the Kikuyu and were defeated by them only in the nineteenth century. The Kikuyu emphasize that they inherited their iron manufacturing techniques and their circumcision rites from the Gumba. Archaeological finds near Gatung'ang'a in central Kenya, which have been tentatively attributed to the Gumba, point to a population who raised cattle, worked iron, and used obsidian and Kwale-like pottery; the findings are dated to the twelfth–thirteenth and fifteenth–sixteenth centuries. The culture reflected in these material remains represents a mixture of elements of the later Stone Age and the Iron Age. If it was really a Bantu culture, it must have already been present in the highlands before the migrations mentioned in the traditions began.

Discrepancies become evident when one tries to align the findings of historical linguistics and oral traditions. On the one hand, the overall picture emerging from the oral traditions points to a variety of geographical origins for the migrations of the highland Bantu—regions as diverse as Igembe/Tigania, the coast, and Mount Kilimanjaro. On the other hand, the uniformity and present distribution of the so-called Thagicu languages suggest a single common center of dispersal in the highlands. Moreover, the circumcision terminology of the Kikuyu is borrowed from southern Cushitic languages; ironworking terminology, however, is of Bantu origin. This, coupled with the fact that

the origin myths of the various clans show substantial differences, leads to the conclusion that Kikuyu culture is an amalgam of different overlapping traditions. The explanation for the close linguistic relationship on the one hand and the variability of the migration legends on the other probably lies in the ecological and topographical diversity of the highlands. This can be illustrated in the sphere of political organization. The Kikuyu, for example, after taking possession of the highland ridges, developed localized lineages connected with particular ridges; each ridge is occupied by a certain group of lineages, inhabiting a fortified settlement. On the other hand, the main political and social organizational unit of the valley-dwelling Taita is the neighborhood, comprising a number of lineages having equal rights and living together in the same valley. Thus, local cultural institutions arose through adaptation to the respective ecological and topographical niches and through cultural convergence on a local scale. This could plausibly have engendered inconsistencies in the folk memory of origins and migrations.

Many of the "contradictions" outlined above will undoubtedly turn out to represent successive overlays of historical processes, if and when the problems of chronology and interdisciplinary synchronisms are solved.

REINHARD KLEIN-ARENDT

See also: **Iron Age (Later): East Africa.**

Further Reading

Fadiman, J. A. *When We Began There Were Witchmen: An Oral History from Mount Kenya.* Berkeley and Los Angeles: University of California Press, 1993.

Frontera, A. "The Taveta Economy in the Pre-Colonial Period." *Kenya Historical Review* 5, no. 1 (1977): 107–114.

Muriuki, G. *A History of the Kikuyu, 1500–1900.* Nairobi: Oxford University Press, 1974.

Mwaniki, H. S. Kabeka. *Embu Historical Texts.* Kampala, Nairobi: East African Literature Bureau, 1974.

Siiriäinen, A., "The Iron Age Site at Gatung'ang'a Central Kenya: Contributions to the Gumba Problem." *Azania*, no. 6 (1971): pp.199–225.

Spear, T. *Kenya's Past: An Introduction to Historical Method in Africa.* London: Longman, 1981.

Bantustans: *See* South Africa: Homelands and Bantustans.

Banu Hilal: *See* Arab Bedouin: Banu Hilal, Banu Sulaym, Banu Ma'qil.

Banu Kanz: *See* Nubia: Banu Kanz, Juhayna, and the Arabization of the Nilotic Sudan.

Banu Ma'qil: *See* **Arab Bedouin: Banu Hilal, Banu Sulaym, Banu Ma'qil.**

Banu Sulaym: *See* **Arab Bedouin: Banu Hilal, Banu Sulaym, Banu Ma'qil.**

Barbary Corsairs and the Ottoman Provinces: Algiers, Tunis, and Tripoli in the Seventeenth Century

The corsairs are the subject of legend. Inspired by seventeenth-century seafaring lore, the European fear of the Muslim corsairs represented a link to the era of the crusades, which persisted well into the modern period. The legend of Muslim cruelty and Christian suffering was at the heart of the Barbary legend. The corsairs, however, were not pirates; their raids on Christian shipping were legitimized by the holy war between Muslims and Christians, which had the support of the Ottoman and Christian European governments. The taking of Christian captives enabled the Ottoman provinces to exert pressure on European states, whether to raise ransom money or else regular subsidies to forestall Muslim raids upon European shipping. In some cases, a truce or a regular peace treaty could also be won as a result of corsair activity. It was also of course a means to liberate Muslims captured by Christian corsairs. In the North African ports, Christian captives were rarely objects of commerce, except by ransom, but while the wealthier captives could purchase exemption, those who were not ransomed were integrated into North African society as concubines, slave officials or skilled slaves in the service of the rulers.

In contradiction to the legend of Muslim piracy, the Ottoman provinces in North Africa were important trading partners with Europe, and the corsairs were the principal agents of interregional trade. This development came after the defeat of the Ottoman fleet at Lepanto in 1571, when the corsairs lost their strategic importance to the Ottoman Empire. However, the continuation of the naval war by independent corsair activity provided a means for the Ottoman provinces of North Africa to maintain a naval presence in the Mediterranean, as well as ensuring their share of Mediterranean commerce. At the same time the European states competed for control of the Mediterranean after 1571 and relied upon the facilities of the North African ports to provision and refit their fleets. In the course of the seventeenth century, the rivalries of the European states and the relative indifference of the Ottoman Empire enabled the corsairs to pursue regional, economic interests, which propelled the development of autonomous regimes in North Africa.

The port of Algiers underwent a phenomenal development during the seventeenth century, as it became both an important commercial and political center. Its prosperity was founded by the corsairs, who constituted a powerful corporation (*ta'ifa*) within the city, which acted as a check upon the corporate power of the militias (*ojak*). The corsairs controlled an equal share of the profits of seafaring with the leading officers of the militias, the *deys*, while the merchants of Algiers marketed the cargoes, as well as local wheat, wool, and leather, largely to a European market, through Marseilles intermediaries. The interdependence of Algeria and France, in particular, contradicts the legend of barbarous "piratical states" preying upon "civilized" Christian states. Instead, trade with France and other European states made Algiers a prosperous and cosmopolitan port in the seventeenth century, with a fleet numbering 75 ships in 1623 and a population that included Muslim Turks, Arabs, Berbers, and Andalusians (political refugees from Spain), as well as Christians, and Jews. The trend toward political autonomy began in 1659, when the Ottoman-appointed pasha, Ibrahim, attempted to tax subsidies paid by the Ottoman government to the corsairs. The corsairs and ojak revolted, but while the pasha was defeated and stripped of his powers, the revolt turned to the advantage of the ojak. Afterward, the ruler was a dey selected by janissary officers, rather than by the ta'fa, which was incorporated into the ojak by 1689.

The Tunisian economy was less dependent upon the corsairs than Algiers. The bulk of its exports were produced domestically for export to the Middle East and Europe. The Andalusians, of whom 60,000 had arrived in 1609, developed the olive oil industry. This export, alongside wheat, wool, leather, coral, and wax, as well as the manufacture of the fez (*shashiya*), constituted Tunisia's main sources of income. However, during the reign of Yusuf Dey (1610–1637), seafaring became an important state activity. The capture of ships provided income for the ruler, who took the captured ship and half its cargo (including captives), while the remainder was distributed among the corsairs. Unlike Algiers, however, the deys of Tunis did not have the backing of strong militia; therefore they were overwhelmed by an alliance of Tunisia's urban notables behind an administrative official, the bey. Murad Bey (*r.*1612–1631) thus secured appointment as pasha, which became hereditary in his family when the notables forced Yusuf Dey to appoint his son, Hammuda Bey (*r.*1631–1666), as his successor. Hammuda was officially invested with the title of pasha by the Ottoman sultan in 1657, which meant that the beys superseded the deys. Murad Bey (*r.*1666–1675) rebuilt the fleet, which amounted to 17 ships, and constructed a new palace for the Muradite dynasty on the western walls of the city. The last quarter of the century witnessed a period of political conflict between Murad's successors, until the situation was complicated further by a series of invasions by the Algerian ojak, in 1686, 1694, and 1705. The crisis was not resolved until 1710, when the Husaynid dynasty established its supremacy.

In Tripoli, Muhammad Saqizli Pasha (r. 1631–1649) extended Ottoman military authority over the surrounding Arab lineages as far as Cyrenaica and the Fezzan, which more firmly grounded Tripolitania as a territorial state. As an indicator that this expansion of the state was connected to commercial prosperity, a French consul, chosen and financed by the Marseilles chamber of finance, was sent to Tripoli in 1630. The consul represented commercial interests only; Tripoli continued to target European, including French, shipping, though England signed a treaty with Tripoli in 1675 to spare its ships from the corsairs. In Algiers, a treaty was made with France in 1670, which provoked war with England and Holland, indicating the development of a complex intercontinental system that cut across Christian and Islamic cultural frontiers. Likewise, Tripoli, Tunis, and Algiers tolerated a European consular and trading presence alongside the North African merchant communities resulting in a cosmopolitan urban culture that combined African, Ottoman, and European influences. This tends to contradict the legend of Muslim exclusivity, as well as religiously inspired hatred between Europeans and Muslims. Ottoman culture had an impact mainly upon the political elites, as some North Africans were integrated into Ottoman political culture, while at the same time the Ottomans were absorbed into the politics of the indigenous society, as is evident in the case of Tunisia.

JAMES WHIDDEN

See also: **Maghrib: Algiers, Tunis and Tripoli under the Deys, Husaynids, and Qaramanlis in the Eighteenth Century; Maghrib: Ottoman Conquest of Algiers, Tripoli, and Tunis.**

Further Reading

Abun-Nasr, J. M. *A History of the Maghrib.* London: Cambridge University Press, 1971.
Braudel, F. *La Mediterranee et le monde mediterraneen sous Phillipe II.* 2 vols. Paris: A. Colin, 1949.
Clissold, S. *The Barbary Slaves.* London: P. Elek, 1977.
Fisher, Sir Godfrey. *Barbary Legend: War, Trade, and Piracy in North Africa 1415–1830.* Oxford: Clarendon Press, 1957.
Julien, C.-A. *History of North Africa: From the Arab Conquest to 1830.* translated by John Petrie and edited by C. C. Stewart. New York: Praeger, 1970.
Laroui, A. *The History of the Maghrib.* Princeton, N.J.: Princeton University Press, 1977.
Valensi, L. *On the Eve of Colonialism: North Africa before the French Conquest,* translated by Kenneth J. Perkins. New York: Africana Publishing, 1977.

Basotho Kingdom: *See* **Moshoeshoe I and the Founding of the Basotho Kingdom.**

Basutoland: *See* **Lesotho (Basutoland): Colonial Period; Lesotho (Basutoland): Colonization and Cape Rule; Lesotho (Basutoland): Peasantry, Rise of.**

Baya: *See* **Central African Republic: Nineteenth Century: Gbaya, Banda, and Zande.**

Baya Revolt: *See* **Central African Republic: Colonial Period: Occupation, Resistance, Baya Revolt, 1928.**

Baybars: *See* **Egypt: Mamluk Dynasty: Baybars, Qalawun, Mongols.**

Bechuanaland Protectorate: *See* **Botswana: Bechuanaland Protectorate, Founding of: 1885–1899; Botswana (Bechuanaland Protectorate): Colonial Period.**

Bedouin: *See* **Arab Bedouin: Banu Hilal, Banu Sulaym, Banu Ma'qil.**

Beira Corridor

A major port and the capital of Sofala Province in central Mozambique, Beira was significant largely depending upon its ability to service the landlocked countries of the interior. The city is situated on the Mozambique Channel of the Indian Ocean at the mouths of the Pungue and Buzi rivers, and was founded on an old Muslim settlement. The beginnings of the modern city were established in 1889; it was to be the headquarters of the Companhia de Moçambique (Mozambique Company). In 1892 Cecil Rhodes's British South Africa Company began the construction of the railway from Beira to Umtali (later Mutare) in Rhodesia; this was completed in 1898, and the following year the line reached Salisbury (Harare), the capital of Rhodes's new colony. Nyasaland's right of access to the sea through Mozambique was recognized in the bilateral Anglo-Portuguese Treaty of 1890. The city celebrated its centenary in 1989 when, after a long period of decline due to the civil war in Mozambique, it at last appeared that a slow rejuvenation was underway, assisted by a large European Union loan to rehabilitate the port.

The city was controlled by the Companhia de Moçambique until 1942, when the administration was handed over to the Portuguese colonial authorities. British capital was an important factor in the development of Beira. British entrepreneurs led by Cecil Rhodes, British colonial officials, and the white settlers in the Rhodesias always saw Beira as a vital outlet for the British-controlled territories of the interior: Zambesia (later Northern Rhodesia, then Zambia), Southern Rhodesia (later Rhodesia, then Zimbabwe), and Nyasaland (Malawi), and Beira's prosperity depended upon its principal role as a port serving the interior.

Beira is a major rail terminus, with links extending to Zimbabwe, South Africa, Zambia, the Democratic Republic of Congo, and Malawi. In particular, it is the main and most convenient port for both Zimbabwe and Malawi. The principal exports passing through Beira are mineral ores, especially copper from Zambia and chromium from Zimbabwe, tobacco, food products, cotton, hides, and skins. Its major imports, again for the countries of the interior, are fuel oils, fertilizers, wheat, heavy machinery and equipment, textiles, and beverages. A separate fishing harbor was constructed in the early 1980s comprising canneries, processing plants, and refrigeration units. The Mozambique Channel is one of the world's richest fishing areas.

The population of Beira was approximately 300,000 at the beginning of the 1990s. The end of the civil war in Mozambique in 1992 saw Beira begin to recover as the country's second city and as a tourist destination. Prior to the escalation of the nationalist war against the Portuguese in the mid-1960s, Beira had derived much of its income from Rhodesian and South African (white) tourists who sought relaxation on its beaches, and the city had developed a number of hotels, restaurants, and nightclubs to cater to such visitors.

The short route of 250 kilometers, which connected Beira to Mutare in Rhodesia (Zimbabwe) and was that country's best route to the sea, came to be known as the Beira Corridor. The creation in 1953 of the Central African Federation led to an upsurge in trade and a consequent economic upswing in Beira, which was equidistant from London by either the Cape or Suez routes. This was to last until the Unilateral Declaration of Independence in 1965 imposed sanctions upon Rhodesia, including an oil blockade of Beira by Britain. Even so, as long as the Portuguese controlled Mozambique (which they did until their departure in 1975), Beira and the Beira Corridor played a crucial role in breaking international sanctions and allowing Rhodesia to export its minerals—especially chrome. By 1973, however, when it became clear that the nationalist Frente da Libertacao de Mocambique (Frelimo) forces were winning the war, and that the Beira Corridor was at risk of being shut down, Rhodesia developed a new railway to Beit Bridge in the south so as to link it into the South African network. From this time until the early 1990s, the fortunes of Beira declined, due to a number of circumstances.

First, from 1976 to 1980 the new government of Mozambique closed its borders with Rhodesia to deny the latter the use of its railways and ports. Second, once Rhodesia had become independent as Zimbabwe in 1980, the Beira Corridor was threatened by the insurgent anti-Frelimo forces of the Resistencia Nacional Mocambicana, so that its use was constantly interrupted. By this time the corridor provided a passage for the railway, a road, an oil pipeline, and overhead electric power lines, each within half a mile of the other. Only after the deployment of substantial numbers of Zimbabwean troops along the Beira Corridor during the latter part of the 1980s did the corridor begin to operate effectively again. Even so, as a result of war and neglect, the port of Beira had silted up so that it could only handle vessels of 5,000 tons or less. And only after 1992, when the civil war in Mozambique had come to an end, could the port of Beira and the corridor begin to handle substantial traffic again.

Throughout the years of confrontation between the "front line states" and South Africa (1965–1990) the fortunes of Beira fluctuated, depending upon the extent to which at any given time the Beira Corridor could be fully used. During the latter part of the 1980s Mozambique was at least able to attract substantial international aid for the rehabilitation of the Beira port, including $600 million provided by a Western (European) consortium. Following the end of the civil war in 1992 and Mozambique's abandonment of Marxism, international funds began to return to the country and Beira began to regain its place both as a vital port servicing much of southern Africa and as the second city of Mozambique.

GUY ARNOLD

See also: **Mozambique.**

Further Reading

Andersson, H. *Mozambique: A War against the People.* Basingstoke, England: Macmillan, 1992.

Arnold, G., and R. Weiss. *Strategic Highways of Africa.* London: Julian Friedmann, 1977.

Finnegan, W. *A Complicated War: The Harrowing of Mozambique.* Berkeley and Los Angeles: University of California Press, 1992.

Hall, M. "The Mozambique National Resistance Movement (RENAMO): A Study in the Destruction of an African Country." *Africa* 60, no. 1 (1990): 39–96.

Human Rights Watch. *Conspicuous Destruction—War, Famine and the Reform Process in Mozambique*. New York: Human Rights Watch, 1994.

Synge, R. *Mozambique: UN Peacekeeping in Action, 1992–1994*. Washington, D.C.: United States Institute of Peace, 1995.

Belgian Congo: *See* **Congo (Kinshasa), Democratic Republic of/Zaire: Belgian Congo: Administration and Society, 1908–1960; Congo (Kinshasa), Democratic Republic of/Zaire: Belgian Congo: Colonial Economy, 1908–1960; Congo (Kinshasa) (various).**

Bello, Alhaji (Sir) Ahmadu (1910–1966)
Northern Nigerian Politician

One of Nigeria's greatest politicians in the 1950s and 1960s, Alhaji (Sir) Ahmadu Bello, the *sardauna* of Sokoto was, in fact, the acknowledged political leader of Nigeria's northern region both in the devolution years (the 1950s) and immediately after independence in 1960. Bello was born in Sokoto in 1910 into the family of the great Islamic reformer of the early nineteenth century, Shaykh 'Uthman dan Fodio, whose Islamic movement brought about the creation of a new ruling elite in northern Nigeria. After his primary education in Sokoto, Bello proceeded to the Katsina Higher College for his secondary education, where he was a contemporary of Sir Abubakar Tafawa Balewa, Nigeria's first indigenous prime minister.

In 1933, Bello unsuccessfully contested the throne of the Sultan of Sokoto and settled for the office of the district head of a locality, Rabah, where his father Ibrahim—who was Fodio's grandson—had been chief. His regal and royal background seems to have determined his political worldview and role. At the commencement of Britain's devolution of power in Nigeria in the 1950s, Bello joined others to establish the Jammiyyar Mutanen Arewa, which metamorphosed into the Northern Peoples' Congress (NPC) in 1951, ostensibly to contest the first local elections of the decolonization years. He became the president general of the NPC and minister of local government, works, and community development, playing the role of its foremost spokesman and symbol. In 1954, he was appointed the first premier of northern Nigeria.

Thus, Bello was totally devoted to the cause of the people of the north because he thought that it was his inherited duty to be so. He was one of the most important indices in the determination of Britain's attitude toward Nigerian nationalism in the 1950. It is, therefore, not surprising that Macpherson (who was governor general in Nigeria, 1948–1954) saw Bello as being "too narrowly northern in his outlook" and thus not at a good rallying point for divergent opinions in Nigeria. But Bello himself never aspired to the direct physical control of Nigeria. He was contented in his roles of northern regional leader and president general of the NPC, which was the largest political party in the country. As late as 1965, Bello was quoted as saying that he would rather be called the sultan of Sokoto than the president of Nigeria.

Bello's extreme love for the north generated its own resentment from many of his political opponents in the other political regions. Without doubt, he commanded a lot of respect from friends and foes alike. His deep attachment to the north and the efforts that many of his political adversaries perceived to be an indirect attempt to utilize his political leverage within the ruling party to control the entire country further alienated him from non-northern regional political leaders of his time. Even within the north, Bello's influence and seeming omnipotence was opposed by the Tiv of Central Nigeria and the aristocracy in Kano, the north's leading commercial center. Such opposition was resisted and repressed harshly. Yet Bello was a man of considerable intellect who had a clear grasp of the northern political milieu. His strength appears to have been his ability to utilize human and material resources to achieve set goals for the overall benefit of his people.

Bello's importance in Nigeria's political history should be understood within the context of the subnationalism of the 1950s and early 1960s. Many of the enduring physical infrastructures in the entire northern Nigeria were planned by him. Among these were Ahmadu Bello University (appropriately named after him), the Bank of the North, and the Northern Nigerian Development Company, among others. The belief that the Sardauna was the most powerful politician in Nigeria, more powerful than the prime minister, led a group of army officers to the conclusion that once he was removed from the scene, Nigeria's multifaceted problems would have been solved. In January 1966, a group of army officers led by Major Chukwuma Nzeogwu attacked Bello's residence in Kaduna, and he was killed brutally. The political stature of the Sardauna remains intimidating in northern Nigerian politics; even after Bello's death, many politicians still use his name and politics as a basis of galvanizing political support in contemporary Nigeria.

KUNLE LAWAL

See also: **Nigeria: Colonial Period: Intelligentsia, Nationalism, Independence; 'Uthman dan Fodio.**

Biography

Born in 1910 in northern Nigeria; received a primary education in Sokoto, and attended Katsina Higher College. In 1954, appointed the first premier of Northern

Nigeria. In January 1966, a group of army officers led by Major Chukwuma Nzeogwu attacked his residence in Kaduna, and he was killed brutally.

Further Reading

Bello, Alhaji (Sir) Ahmadu. *My Life*. London: Oxford University Press, 1962.

Clark, T. *A Right Honourable Gentleman: The Life and Times of Alhaji Sir, Abubakar Tafawa Balewa*. Zaria, Nigeria: Huda Huda Press, 1991.

Lawal, K. *Britain and the Transfer of Power in Nigeria, 1945–1960*. Lagos: LASU Press, 2000.

Paden, Sir John. *The Biography of Alhaji (Sir) Ahmadu Bello*. Zaria, Nigeria: Huda Huda Press, 1986.

Ben Ali: *See* Tunisia: Ben 'Ali, Liberalization.

Benin, Empire: Origins and Growth of City-State

Forest areas east of the Volta and west of the Niger long served as refuge to numerous small groups of peoples. There is no written record of how some of these developed into important kingdoms; however, oral tradition, evaluated in the light of archaeological findings and linguistic evidence, has helped historians reconstruct the past.

The kingdom of Benin, in what is now southwestern Nigeria at the center of an area inhabited by a linguistically defined bloc known as the Edo-speaking peoples, was founded by one such group. At first family clusters of hunters, gatherers, and agriculturalists formed more complex societies centered on villages and organized by kinship along patrilineal lines. It seems that the components of social life—administration of justice, land rights, farming, and religious beliefs and rituals—were already in place.

Early in the second millennium of the common era, invaders from the grasslands of the Sudan moving south and southwest on horseback due to increasingly harsh climate conditions, or perhaps fleeing their own land's conversion to Islam, settled in the region and married daughters of local elders. Further development proceeded by agglomeration rather than conquest. Villages grew into towns surrounded by walls. The excavations by Graham Connah have shown that these walls were a honeycomb of linear earthworks defining territory rather than defensive fortifications. This suggests that Benin city may originally have been an aggregate of small settlements, each of which owed allegiance to the king, but had its own farmlands surrounded by its own walls and ditches. In the countryside around Benin City lies a complex of walls, the height and extent of which suggest that the region may already have had a large population.

Society was hierarchical, headed by a succession of kings, known as *ogiso*. The kingdom was divided into a number of tribute-paying units entrusted to chiefs responsible for their daily administration. The king was assisted by seven powerful nobles, the *uzama*, holders of hereditary positions. The king's palace represented temporal power and was also the center of spiritual forces.

This city-state was financed by tribute rather than trade. Its economy was largely agricultural, depending on yams and palm oil. Nevertheless, with urbanization traders and craftsmen became increasingly important. By the eleventh century the expansion of trade had major consequences for technological development, accumulation of wealth, and the structure of state institutions.

Cotton was already cultivated and woven by the tenth century. A regular northward trade in salt, cloth, metal, beads, and pottery was flourishing in the middle Iron Age. Ere, the second *ogiso* (tenth century), is believed to have introduced many symbols, such as human heads made of wood and terra cotta, used in a religious context. The development of sculpture seems to indicate that Benin society had, at the time of Ere, reached the point where it included spare manpower for pursuits not directly related to survival.

Clearly the use of copper in bronze and brass sculpture—which soon replaced the previously used wood and terra cotta—reveals the existence of a long-distance trade in luxury goods, since the nearest sources of copper were in the Saharan Aïr Massif and in the Sudan around Darfur. The quantity of copper items in Benin before 1300 indicates that trade was on a large scale and had already been in existence for a while. The technique of brass casting by the lost wax method in use in Benin, had probably been introduced to Ife by northerners who founded the city, and had spread from there. Until the fifteenth century, brass casting remained exclusively a palace art, producing sculptured heads and other cult objects for royal altars.

According to Benin tradition, around 1300 the Edo people felt that the ogiso was no longer an effective leader and asked Oluhe, king of Ife, the spiritual center of the region, to send them a king. He sent his son Oranmiyan, who stayed in Benin only long enough to father a child with a daughter of a local chief. Their son, Eweka I, became the first *oba* (king) of Benin. Oranmiyan thus headed a dynasty that was to last over six centuries, a fact that seems verifiable because Benin's oral tradition refers to the past in terms of dynastic time, relating significant events to the reigns of particular kings. Some historians have suggested that the tale of a marriage between Oranyan and a chiefly family of Benin may actually have been invented to disguise the fact that Benin was at that time conquered by outsiders who became its rulers. Groundless though the legend may be, its message seems clear. It asserts that the dynasty is of alien origin, but claims that it came to power by will of the Edo and was nurtured by their culture.

Royal power grew under Eweka I, whose reign was relatively peaceful. Division of labor in the town progressed and society became more stratified; but basic social and political organization did not change much since the uzama held on to their ancient rights and controlled Eweka I. The *oba* do not seem to have been able to assert their authority until the reign of Ewedo (*c.*1255). Aware of the symbolic significance of ritual changes, Ewedo began by forbidding the uzama to carry their ceremonial swords in his palace and to sit down in his presence. He then reorganized the army, and proceeded to deprive the uzama of their inherited right to hold national offices and to appoint persons of their choice to key positions. This enabled him to surround himself with administrators answerable to him alone.

There is archaeological evidence that Benin continued to grow with the expansion of long-distance trade during his reign. Indeed bronze sculptures became more numerous, and bronze was no longer used for altar pieces exclusively, but also for plaques set into palace walls or pillars of houses.

The medieval era of the kingdom of Benin ended with the accession to the throne of the most famous *oba*, Eware the Great (1440–1480), and the arrival of the Portuguese.

NATALIE SANDOMIRSKY

Further Reading

Ajayi, J.F. A., and Michael Crowder (eds.). *History of West Africa*, 2nd ed., vol. 1. London: Longman, 1976.

Boxer, C. R. *Four Centuries of Portuguese Expansion 1415–1825: A Succinct Survey*. Johannesburg: Witwatersrand University Press, 1961.

Bradbury, R. E. *The Benin Kingdom and the Edo-Speaking Peoples of South-Western Nigeria*. London: International African Institute, 1964.

Bradbury, R. E. *Benin Studies*. London: International African Institute and Oxford University Press, 1973.

Connah, G. *The Archaeology of Benin: Excavations and Other Researches in and around Benin City, Nigeria*. Oxford: Clarendon Press, 1975.

Fage, J. D. *The Cambridge History of Africa, c. 500 BC–AD 1050*, vol. 2. Cambridge: Cambridge University Press, 1978.

Hrbek, I. (ed.). *General History of Africa*, abr. ed., vol. 3, *Africa from the Seventh to the Eleventh Century*. London: James Currey, 1990.

Okpewho, I. *Once upon a Kingdom: Myth, Hegemony, and Identity*. Bloomington: Indiana University Press, 1998.

Oliver, R. (ed.). *The Cambridge History of Africa, from c. 1050 to c. 1600*, vol. 3. Cambridge: Cambridge University Press, 1977.

Oliver, R., and B. M. Fagan (eds.). *Africa in the Iron Age, c. 500 B.C. to A.D. 1400*. Cambridge: Cambridge University Press, 1970.

Benin, Empire: Oba Ewuare, Trade with the Portuguese

The kingdom of Benin, situated in the Yorubaland forest in present-day southwestern Nigeria, reached its zenith in the fifteenth and sixteenth centuries under the reigns of the *oba* (king) Ewuare (*r. c.*1440–1473), his son Ozolua (*r. c.*1481–1504), and his grandson Esigie (*r.*1504–1547).

Ewuare relied on his subjects' belief in the divine nature of kings to consolidate his power. The king was believed to influence the weather, fertility, harvests, and social harmony; he was sacred and feared. On this basis Ewuare instituted reforms aimed at diminishing the power of the *uzama*, hereditary chiefs who traditionally participated in the selection of the *oba*. He enacted a rule of primogeniture to eliminate their role in the process of succession to the throne. In time, the chiefs themselves adopted this rule, thereby impeding the development of large lineage support groups and further strengthening the *oba*. Ewuare, however, needed chiefs to supervise the day-to-day administration of the kingdom and to collect the tributes from villages, which constituted much of his revenues. To further dilute the uzama's authority he appointed additional "town" and "palace" chiefs, directly beholden to him.

The degree of the king's authority fluctuated for a century. However, palace skirmishes had little effect on the expansion of Benin's empire. During the dry season Ewuare and his successors regularly undertook campaigns to extend Benin's frontiers eastward to the

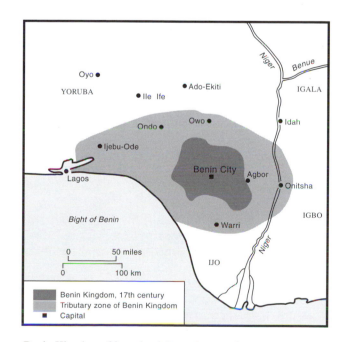

Benin Kingdom, fifteenth–eighteenth centuries.

Niger delta, southward to the sea, and westward into Yoruba country. These conquests have earned Ewuare the title of "Ewuare the Great" and his son that of "Ozolua the Conqueror."

During the century of expansion, the vitality and stability of the kingdom were displayed in many ways. Eware rebuilt the capital Benin City, dividing it into two sections—the larger for the bulk of the town's residents and the smaller for the royal palace and the elite. He also improved communications by ordering construction of broad avenues and smaller intersecting streets. In the sixteenth century, Benin was a city 25 miles in circumference, protected by walls and moats. The arts flourished. As trade brought more copper and brass into Benin, craftsmen refined casting techniques. They produced not only palace art and elaborate altar pieces, but also bronze bas-reliefs, representing the oba, his court, and his contacts with the Portuguese. As a historical record, these are reminiscent of Western Europe's medieval tapestries.

Tradition, perhaps alluding to Ruy de Sequeira's trip to Africa in 1472, credits Ewaure with having been the first oba of Benin in contact with the Portuguese, who were then exploring the region. It is likely that European goods reached Benin prior to the arrival of the Europeans themselves. It is known from writings of Portuguese eyewitnesses that upon arrival in Benin they found a large centralized state already involved in political and commercial relations with several—sometimes distant—areas.

The Portuguese were then the only Europeans seeking trade in the region. By the 1480s their policy was to make trade with the Guinean coasts a Portuguese monopoly. Their forts and ships in the region were meant to keep other Europeans out as much as to control Africans. The Portuguese thought that an alliance with Benin would offer them sizable markets for their own goods. Benin traded with Europeans to obtain guns, powder, metals, salt, and cloth in exchange for palm oil, ivory, cloth, beads, pepper, and slaves. Except for slaves, a natural by-product of the wars waged by Benin, the other exports do not seem to have come from local sources. Apparently one of the keys to Benin's wealth was its location at a junction of east-west and north-south trade.

Little of what Benin was exporting went to Europe: there was pepper at first (until the Portuguese succeeded in establishing their spice trade with Asia), and small numbers of slaves. Beads, cloth, and slaves the Portuguese also initially exchanged in African ports along the Gulf of Guinea for gold—the west African product they sought above all else at that time. However, the Portuguese interest in slaves grew steadily throughout the sixteenth century, first to supplement the labor force of Portugal itself and then to work in the newly developed Portuguese plantations on islands off the west African coast and in the Gulf of Guinea; but Benin never became deeply involved in the slave trade.

For the Portuguese, trade with Benin was complicated by the fact that the kingdom lay about 50 miles inland. In 1487 they built a fort at Ughoton (Gwato), which was as near as their ships could get to Benin City. To get there, they had to travel about 40 miles from the sea up treacherous rivers and could still reach the capital only by traveling 19 miles overland. Benin controlled river and land routes. Authority here depended on labor; the Portuguese were few and had to rely on local inhabitants for military support, fresh water, and provisions. They could trade at Benin only with the oba and his accredited agents on terms laid down by him. After about 30 years they found the oba's conditions, particularly the new ban on the export of male slaves, too onerous, and abandoned Ughoton. Later trade was conducted mainly by individual Portuguese merchants from Gulf of Guinea islands.

However, relations did not end when the Portuguese left Ughoton. It seems that both Africans and Europeans were investigating what they could gain from each other. In 1514 oba Esigie sent a delegation to Portugal, complaining about Portuguese slaving activities, but also asking for a Christian mission and firearms. What Benin needed from the Portuguese was, above all, firearms. King Manuel I was, however, reluctant to sell weapons to pagans. This request seemed to the Portuguese to be the opportunity they had been waiting for. Actually the oba was far less interested in Christianity than he was in obtaining firearms, and though he learned to speak Portuguese, permitted establishment of a Christian mission, and allowed his son Orhogba and some officials to be baptized, he did not accept baptism himself. By the middle of the century the Portuguese had virtually no contact with Benin.

NATALIE SANDOMIRSKY

See also: **Portugal: Exploration and Trade in the Fifteenth Century.**

Further Reading

Ajayi, J. F. A., and Michael Crowder (eds.). *History of West Africa*, 2nd ed., vol 1. London: Longman, 1976.

Boxer, C. R. *Four Centuries of Portuguese Expansion 1415–1825: A Succinct Survey*. Johannesburg: Witwatersrand University Press, 1961.

———. *Race Relations in the Portuguese Colonial Empire, 1415–1825*. Oxford: Clarendon Press, 1963.

Bradbury, R. E. *The Benin Kingdom and the Edo-Speaking Peoples of South-Western Nigeria*. London: International African Institute, 1964.

———. *Benin Studies*. London: International African Institute and Oxford University Press, 1971.

Dark, P. J. C. *An Introduction to Benin: Arts and Technology*. Oxford: Clarendon Press, 1973.

Egharevba, J. U. *A Short History of Benin*, 3rd ed. Ibadan, Nigeria: Ibadan University Press, 1960.

Hrbek, I. (ed.). *General History of Africa*, abr. ed., vol. 3, *Africa from the Seventh to the Eleventh Century*. London: James Currey, 1990.

Okudowa, A. I. (ed.). *Studies in Esan History and Culture: Evolution*. Benin City, Nigeria: Omo-Uwessan, 1998.

Oliver, R. (ed.). *The Cambridge History of Africa, from c. 1050 to c. 1600*, vol. 3. Cambridge: Cambridge University Press, 1977.

Ryder, A. F. C. *Benin and the Europeans, 1485–1897*. New York: Humanities Press, 1969.

Benin Kingdom: Nineteenth Century

By the nineteenth century, the Benin kingdom had begun to face a crisis of adaptation as a result of several internal and external factors. At the domestic level, Benin lacked strong and committed leadership. The incessant succession disputes for the throne, coupled with the civil wars they engendered, increased political and social instability in the kingdom. The reign of Oba Obanosa in 1804 was inaugurated by a civil war in which over one thousand people lost their lives. His successor, Oba Osemwede, had to engage his rival, Ogbebo, in a protracted, bloody, and destructive civil war. In the course of this civil war, Eredia-Uwa, as he was known before he became Oba Osemwede, has to flee to Ewokhimi in Ishan for safety. The auspicious intervention of Ogie, his cousin, tipped the scale in his favor and he eventually secured the throne. Odin-Ovba, who ascended to the Benin throne in 1848 as Oba Adolo, also had a troubled rule. Despite his accession to the Obaship, his implacable rival, Ogbewekon, remained. From Igueben, in Ishan, where he sought refuge, Ogbewekon instigated two rebellions against Adolo (in 1853 and 1854), both of which were crushed. It was only in 1880, upon the death of Ogbewekon, that Adolo could feel safe in his position. The reign of Oba Ovonramwen, the last of the nineteenth-century kings of Benin, is marked by his decision to execute some notable chiefs whom he claimed had opposed his succession to the throne.

Notwithstanding the debilitating impact and unrest brought about by these disputes and civil wars, the obas of this period, particularly Osemwede, Adolo, and Ovonramwen, still managed to make occasional attempts at asserting imperial control over Ekiti, Akure, and Owo in northeast Yoruba, parts of the Ishan county, and the western Igbo areas. Nonetheless, the last decade of the nineteenth century witnessed a considerable diminution of Benin's authority over its imperial domain. To a large extent, the kingdom had shrunk to virtually its heartland.

This latter development was due largely to external factors over which Benin had no control. As a result of the "Scramble" for Africa in the 1880s, Britain began signing treaties with the people of the Niger Delta. In 1885, the Niger Coast Protectorate was declared, but it was not until 1891 that the British decided to assert its control over the areas with the appointment of Claude Macdonald as commissioner and consul general. A number of vice consuls and other officials were also appointed. One vice consul, Gallwey, was given jurisdiction over the Benin rivers in the Western Delta of the Niger; Benin itself also came under his authority.

Up to this time, the obas of Benin had continued to run the sociopolitical and economic affairs of their kingdom unhindered. In matters of trade, the oba exercised royal monopoly over certain items of merchandise. He also set the terms by which non-Bini traders were to participate in trade within his domain.

This situation was to change for the worse for Benin with its incorporation as part of the Niger Coast Protectorate. European trade, which had earlier flourished in Benin up to the eighteenth century, had greatly declined by the first decades of the nineteenth century. Ughoton, Benin's foremost port, had ceased to be of any commercial relevance given its replacement by such Itsekiri coastal ports as Jakpa and Ebrohimi, founded by Chief Olumu in 1865. Backed by his powerful fleet, Olumu was able to dominate other rival Itsekiri houses and to control virtually all the trade on palm produce on the Benin rivers, enforcing his monopoly at its source in the hinterland. This situation led to a deterioration in the Benin-Itsekiri relationship, and even led to war, in which Benin supported Uwangue against the Olu of Itsekiri. Since Oba Osemwede lacked the resources to carry out a waterborne attack against the Olu, the most he could do was to place a curse on him. Through his strong-arm tactics, Olumu was able to establish himself firmly in the Benin rivers region, a fact that the British recognized when they appointed his son, Nana, governor in 1879. In 1884, the Itsekiri signed a protectorate treaty with the British that implied their loss of sovereignty. Thus the Itsekiri, who lived along the coast, exploited their strategic advantage by playing the role of middlemen between the Bini and the European traders at the coast.

The *oba* imposed dues on the Itsekiri, who had to pay a certain amount in goods before they were allowed to trade. Failure by the Itsekiri to meet their tax obligation meant stoppage of trade by the oba until the necessary conditions were fulfilled. In taking such action, the *oba* wanted to maximize his opportunities in the European trade.

Throughout the 1880s, European traders tried to convince the *oba* to abolish the dues imposed on non-Bini traders, but the *oba* refused to do so. In an attempt to gain access to the riches of the hinterland, Gallwey became more determined to sign a protection treaty with the Oba of Benin. After a prolonged delay, Oba Ovonramwen reluctantly granted him audience on March 1892, and the anticipated treaty was signed between Gallwey and the oba's chiefs. The oba was suspicious of the vice consul's intentions and personally refused to sign the treaty. The signing of the treaty was tantamount to accepting British rule. But whether the *oba* and his chiefs saw it in that light is a different matter. For the vice consul, the treaty provided a perfect excuse for interfering in the internal affairs—both political and economic—of Benin. Some of the provisions of the treaty infringed upon the entire social, political and economic foundation of Benin. For instance, it now became mandatory for the Oba of Benin to accept the advice of the consul in matters of internal and external policy. Trade restrictions were relaxed, and Christianity was forced upon Benin.

Consequently, between 1892 and 1896, European officials, traders and their Itsekiri middlemen attempted to force the *oba* into submission. The British conquest of Chief Nana in 1894 and Brass in 1895, and the accusation in 1896 that the *oba* had closed all the markets in this territory heightened the isolation, desperation, and sense of foreboding that hung over Benin.

In late 1896, the acting consul general, James R. I. Phillips, embarked upon a visit to the Oba of Benin to persuade him to lift the ban then placed on trade. Phillips's visit came at an awkward time, when the oba was observing the annual festivals and was therefore not receiving visitors; but nothing would detract Phillips from his stated objective. His foolhardiness was to cost him and his party of six Europeans and over two hundred carriers their lives at the hands of Benin soldiers who ambushed them on January 3, 1897. The incident presented the casus belli for the punitive expedition that sacked Benin on February 17, 1897. With this event, the Benin monarchy and the ancient kingdom came to an inglorious end. Oba Ovonramwen, the last of the nineteenth-century Benin kings, was exiled to Calabar, never to return. Thus, economic interests and a desire to dominate the oba prompted the British conquest of Benin.

J. O. Ahazuem

Further Reading

Akintoye, S. A. "The North-east Yoruba Districts and the Benin Kingdom." *Journal of the Historical Society of Nigeria*, no. 414 (1969): p.539–555.

Boisragon, A. *The Benin Massacre*. London: Methuen, 1898.

Bradbury, R. E. *The Benin Kingdom and the Edo-Speaking Peoples of South Western Nigeria*. London: Wightman Mountain, 1970

Egharevba, J. U. *A Short History of Benin*. Ibadan, Nigeria: Ibadan University Press, 1966.

Ryder, A. *Benin and the Europeans 1485–1897*. London: Longman, 1977.

Benin Kingdom: British Conquest, 1897

The kingdom of Benin was located in the western part of the Niger Delta. The population of the kingdom consisted of the Edo-speaking Bini people and was headed by the *oba*, the traditional ruler supported by a number of councils and societies consisting of chiefs and advisors.

The kingdom was one of the first on the coast to be encountered by Europeans in the late fifteenth century. The British had continuous contact with Benin. The late-nineteenth-century history of relations was strongly influenced by the consular authority and travelers' accounts. The former was the manifestation of Britain's informal empire in the region, first initiated on the island of Fernando Po in the 1840s and later entrenched in Lagos after 1851; it represented the policy that relied on individual authority and ill-defined political aims while emphasizing the economic advantages of free trade. Among travelers, it was the consul Richard Francis Burton who visited Benin in 1862 and presented, as later scholarship argues, a possibly distorted picture of human sacrifices and moral decay, a significant element in formulating the British image associated with the kingdom at the end of the nineteenth century.

The Niger Coast Protectorate, the other British territory besides the Royal Niger Company in the Niger Delta, was an administrative unit under the Foreign Office that had its headquarters in Old Calabar and some centers in coastal commercial depots like Warri and Sapele. The consular authority extended to the kingdom in 1892 when vice consul Gallwey completed a treaty with Oba Ovonramwen, who had been on the throne since 1888. As some scholars argue, Benin leaders most probably misunderstood the treaty. The British interpreted it as the formal submission of the kingdom to British economic requirements to allow free trade, thus bypassing the Bini middlemen in rubber and palm oil trade, a commodity that was in great demand in the European market after the Dunlop company's invention of the pneumatic tire in 1887. Based on the treaty, there was an increasing pressure from the protectorate to allow the activities of traders in Benin territory. At the same time, it seems, the oba and Benin leaders interpreted these as a growing tendency to penetrate into the kingdom and overthrow its government.

In the protectorate there existed a certain intention to break Benin's resistance by force, a tendency that had prevailed on the West African coast. In the few years preceding 1897, there was some correspondence between Ralph Moor, consul general of the protectorate and the Foreign Office, indicating his intention to use force against Benin as early as 1895. The Foreign Office turned down the initiative, which prevented both Moor and acting consul James R. Philips from advancing their position by achieving acts similar to those of Gallwey's mission. These personal career aspirations most probably played an important part in the expedition that was ambushed by Benin soldiers in January 1897 and resulted in the death of seven Europeans, including Philips. Although initially launched as a peaceful diplomatic envoy, Philips's mission was, on one hand, without Foreign Office authorization, an issue that was being lobbied by Moor in London. On the other hand, its clear aim was not defined and most certainly was not communicated to Benin authorities. The British party was told that they could not be seen by the oba as there was an important festival, the *Ague* celebrations, going on, during which outsiders were not allowed to see the ruler. Despite warnings, Philips continued his advance. Later investigations showed that Philips probably survived the attack and was taken to Benin City, where he probably either died of his wounds or, as contemporary claims asserted, was executed. Both Moor and Philips overstepped the limits of their authorities when the consul had planned a military action earlier and the acting consul initiated an unauthorized diplomatic mission. The Benin political and military leaders misunderstood the situation, as reports only reached them about the coming of a large party. Although it was not confirmed that they were armed, permanent fears previously induced them to defend the kingdom's independence against an upcoming attack.

The public uproar in England and the subsequent punitive expedition followed a swift wave of actions. In two months' time Benin City was captured by British troops, and the oba and most of his chiefs fled. The city was burned, and ivory was looted to compensate the cost of the expedition. Bronzes, some of the most exquisite and priceless pieces of art of royal Africa, were either sent to the British Museum or auctioned. Museums in Berlin and Vienna acquired a great number of treasures.

Accounts of the city presented images of human sacrifice and bloodshed that, in contemporary arguments, justified the arrival of the British. Alfred Turner was appointed to initiate British administration; his immediate policy was consolidation and the demonstration of peaceful intent, a move that was to bring success when the majority of Benin chiefs and the oba returned. Moor insisted on a trial of the chiefs who were considered to be responsible for the deaths in the

Philips party, as well as a trial of the *oba*. Two chiefs were sentenced to death, while the *oba* was dethroned and eventually deported to Tenerife.

Three war chiefs, including Ologbose, who had been sentenced to death for his participation in the ambush, put up stiff resistance around Benin city, which was only crushed by British military force as late as 1899. The death sentence of Ologbose marked the beginning of long consolidation, now under the amalgamated administration of the Southern Nigerian Protectorate. The native council, consisting of former members of the *oba's* court, acted as administrative middlemen for the colonial government. In 1914 the new *oba* was enthroned, representing the changed British policy in the region—an attempt to implement indirect rule.

The punitive expedition against the kingdom of Benin was in many ways a typical example of the British expansion policy in the 1890s and the 1900s in West Africa. Similar examples of small-scale campaigns directed against independent states and political units that resisted British interests could include examples like the Ijebu campaign in 1892, Jaja's deposition in 1894, or the Ashanti campaign in 1896. The consolidation of colonial southern Nigeria involved many similar actions, like the Aro campaign in 1902 up to 1911, a year when further similar unauthorized actions were prevented by legal measures. It was mostly the members of the previous administration of the protectorate, taken over by the colonial government, who carried out these highly controversial wars. Yet the looting of the Benin bronzes in the palace still remains a controversial issue as well as a bitter memory of 1897 and aggressive imperial conquest and subjugation.

LÁSZLÓ MÁTHÉ-SHIRES

Further Reading

Home, R. *City of Blood Revisited: A New Look at the Benin Expedition of 1897*. London: Rex Collings, 1982.

Igbafe, P. A. *Benin under British Administration: The Impact of Colonial Rule on an African Kingdom, 1897–1938*. London: Longman, 1979.

Igbafe, P. A. "The Fall of Benin: A Re-assessment." *Journal of African History*, no. 11 (1970): pp.385–400.

Omoregie, Osaren S. B. *Great Benin*. Benin City, Nigeria: Neraso, 1997.

Ryder, Alan Frederick Charles. *Benin and the Europeans 1485–1897*. Harlow, England: Longmans, 1969.

Benin (Republic of)/Dahomey: Colonial Period: Survey

The Republic of Benin is situated between Nigeria to the east and Togo to the west, along the west coast of Africa. Until 1975, Benin was known as the Republic

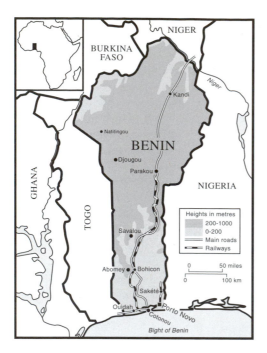

Benin.

of Dahomey. The name *Dahomey* derives from the precolonial Kingdom of Dahomey, which dominated the trade in slaves between the interior and the Atlantic coast until the end of the nineteenth century. To the northwest, Benin borders Burkina Faso (formerly Upper Volta), while to the northeast it shares a common border with the Niger Republic along the Niger River. The Atlantic coast forms Benin's southernmost limit. With an area of about 113,000 square kilometers, which extends in a north-south direction for approximately 700 kilometers, the modern state of Benin has a population of approximately 6.5 million. Among the largest ethnic groups are the Fon, Aja, and Gun. The population also comprises groups of Yoruba- and Ewe-speaking peoples.

Between the late seventeenth and nineteenth centuries, the slave-raiding exploits of the Kingdom of Dahomey dominated the political economy of the "Slave Coast" located between the Gold Coast (present-day Ghana) and the Bight of Benin, from which millions of African slaves were shipped across the Atlantic to the Americas. In addition to a standing army of men, the Kingdom of Dahomey was famous for its women soldiers. Dahomey emerged as a leading player in the coastal slave trade by defeating rival states, with the exception of Porto Novo, which became a French protectorate in 1863, hoping to deter Dahomey.

As the campaign against the slave trade and slavery spearheaded by Britain gathered momentum during the first half the nineteenth century, European abolitionists decried Dahomey for persistently dealing in slaves. In addition, European missionary and travel accounts recorded Dahomey's use of slaves in sacrificial ceremonies to pay homage to the ancestors of the royal family. Recent research, however, indicates that Dahomean leaders were not entirely negligent of respect for human life and made conscious effort to preempt wanton destruction of life. After the French invasion of 1892–1894, which paved the way for the establishment of colonial rule, the slave trade in Dahomey gradually ended as "legitimate" trade increasingly dominated the economy. Agricultural produce, especially palm oil and palm kernels, became the colony's main export.

French conquest led to the deposition of King Béhanzin and the annexation of Dahomey. A French-appointed successor, Agoliegbo, replaced the deposed king; Béhanzin was exiled to Martinique and subsequently died in Algeria, where he had been transferred in 1906. The war with the French decimated Dahomey's female army. Moreover, many slaves were set free following the French conquest. France also extended its jurisdiction into the hinterland so that the new colony occupied a much larger area than the erstwhile Dahomey Kingdom. As in other parts of Africa, the new frontiers resulting from the European "Scramble" for colonies cut across precolonial political and linguistic boundaries. Ewe-speaking peoples and other smaller ethnic groups were split between German Togoland to the west and the French-occupied Dahomey. Similarly, the Yoruba and Borgou states to the east were divided between Nigeria, which became a British colony, and Dahomey.

Colonial rule meant the effective end of Dahomey's political independence. Moreover, it led to the increasing penetration of French commercial interests and eventual domination of the economy. Local rulers, merchants (especially the displaced Afro-Brazilian commercial elite), and common people alike resented French colonial rule. Indeed, resistance to French colonialism in the form of revolts and strikes intensified during World War I, when Africans from all over French West Africa were recruited to fight for France in Europe. In addition, disputes over chieftaincy, some of which French colonial officials failed to resolve, and urban discontent only compounded the numerous problems the colonial regime encountered. In 1923, for example, mass demonstrations took place in Porto Novo (Benin's capital), a thriving coastal city during the colonial period. To a large degree, increasing taxes and dropping commodity prices aggravated discontent among the local population. Colonial administrators, however, downplayed the import of these factors and were quick to blame indigenous intellectuals and Islamic leaders as the chief instigators of local resistance.

In 1904, Dahomey became part of French West Africa, which stretched from the mouth of the Senegal River on the Atlantic coast to Lake Chad in the east. Colonial rule did not stimulate economic development in Dahomey. Instead, the colony's potential income subsidized the regional government of French West Africa headquartered in Dakar, Senegal. Deprived of opportunities to accumulate capital, the people of Dahomey resorted to popular protests, to which the colonial regime responded with characteristic force and brutality. French commercial interests monopolized the palm oil industry, the mainstay of Dahomey's economy during the colonial period. Of course, dependence on primary commodities meant that the colonial regime hardly attempted to stimulate industrial growth in Dahomey. Hampered by limited funds, the colonial government developed only infrastructure, such as roads and railway, to meet its own needs; it also constructed a seaport at Cotonou (Benin's largest city) to facilitate the exportation of local products. Despite an increase in the output of palm products, the cost of running the colonial administration increasingly outweighed the revenue from Dahomey's agricultural exports.

Because of its limited military presence in Dahomey, the French adopted a form of "indirect rule" to govern the southern part of the colony through local representatives, including *chefs de canton*, *commandants* (district officers), and a host of local auxiliaries—clerks, interpreters, nurses, and other medical personnel. African soldiers and the African commercial elite complemented the corps of local administrative personnel. With the chefs de canton at the helm of local administration, the commandants were in charge of forced labor recruitment, military conscription, and tax collection. A more direct system of rule was practiced in the northern part of the colony.

Dahomey's missionary and state schools produced a relatively high number of educated bureaucrats who served throughout French West Africa. Some of Dahomey's "expatriate" bureaucrats became more active in politics after World War II. Together with demobilized army veterans from the war, they made demands the French government found difficult to ignore. This led to the creation of a territorial assembly in 1946 and the election of Dahomean deputies to the French parliament in Paris. Among other things, Dahomey's emerging politicians were concerned about the recruitment of Dahomean soldiers for France's war in Indochina during the 1950s, forced labor, and, perhaps most important, decolonization. Significantly, the Loi Cadre of 1956 introduced more reforms by not only proclaiming a universal franchise but also expanding the powers of the territorial assembly. In 1958, Dahomey gained administrative autonomy within a French community of West African states (Guinea and Conakry opted out). Benin eventually gained independence from France on August 1, 1960, with Herbert Maga, a teacher from northern Benin who served in the French assembly, as its first president.

TAMBA M'BAYO

See also: **Anti-Slavery Movement; Benin Kingdom: Nineteenth Century.**

Further Reading

Akinjogbin, I. A. *Dahomey and Its Neighbours, 1708–1818*. Cambridge: Cambridge University Press, 1967.
Bay, E. G. *Wives of the Leopard: Gender, Politics, and Culture in the Kingdom of Dahomey*. Charlottesville: University of Virginia Press, 1998.
Decalo, S. *Historical Dictionary of Benin*. 3rd ed. Metuchen, N.J.: Scarecrow Press, 1995.
Eades, J. S., and C. Allen. *Benin*. Oxford: Clio Press, 1996.
Manning, P. *Slavery, Colonialism, and Economic Growth in Dahomey, 1640–1960*. Cambridge: Cambridge University Press, 1982.
Middleton, J. (ed.). *Encyclopedia of Africa South of the Sahara*. New York: Charles Scribner's Sons, 1997.

Benin (Republic of)/Dahomey: Independence, Coups, Politics

Under French influence since the mid-nineteenth century, the territory then known as Dahomey became self-governing within the French community in December 1958, before achieving full independence in August 1960. While electoral politics in the country had begun under French colonial rule, it did imply the dominance of one single political leader during the struggle for independence, unlike the situation in many other French colonies. This was a reflection of the fact that the country was divided into three spheres of influence largely corresponding to traditional loyalties according to regional, ethnic, or religious concerns, with leaders emerging that reflected such divides.

Between 1960 and 1972, mirroring such a state of affairs, personal and regional animosities generated five military coups d'état, interspersed with short-lived civilian governments. Overall, ten different heads of state served during this time. In an attempt to end a period of debilitating political turmoil, a military government was established in October 1972, evolving into a Marxist one-party system during 1972–1975. The government adopted a strongly Marxist orientation from the mid-1970s on, a shift in political orientation reflected in a change in the country's name to the People's Republic of Benin in late 1975.

The years of rule of General Mathieu Kérékou (1972–1990) were primarily notable for the creation of a top-down system under the political leadership of a single legal party, the Benin People's Revolutionary

Party (BPRP). However, the BPRP did not seem particularly revolutionary or popular, especially in the rural areas of the country, where 70 per cent of the population live. The consequence was that some rural communities, primarily comprising peasant farmers, were not well integrated into the formal polity, and, as a result, the central authorities were widely perceived as a form of alien colonialism.

During the 1980s, Kérékou's government privatized a number of state-run companies in an attempt to counter an economic situation characterized by high international indebtedness, serious state-level corruption, and economic problems. Reflecting a weak economic position, per capita gross domestic product was only US$380 in 1988. Economic problems led to wide-ranging austerity measures, which not only facilitated international aid agreements but also led to social unrest, culminating in the shift to democratic government.

Once again, in early 1990, a change in political orientation led to a change in the country's name, this time to the Republic of Benin. This alteration was delivered at the behest of the National Conference of Active Forces of the Nation, which also repudiated the Marxist-inspired constitution of August 1977. A multiparty constitution was approved by popular referendum in December 1990, and presidential and legislative elections then inaugurated Benin's second democratic experiment. This political liberalization provided an initial step toward a more democratic polity, with the political structure, formerly dominated by the only legal party, the BPRP, replaced by a highly fragmented party system with dozens of parties fighting for the allegiance of Benin's fewer than three million voters. Perhaps surprisingly, despite the plethora of parties, there were few preelection debates in 1991 about economic policy, with the competing parties failing to offer alternative economic or development agendas to the package of International Monetary Fund-sponsored economic reforms that was the price of continued foreign economic support.

Five years later, not much seemed to have changed: before and during the 1996 elections no substantive policy issues were publicly debated. This state of affairs was facilitated by the fact that the regime of Nicéphore Soglo, who had taken power in 1991, saw fit to ban all political transmissions and radio programs with a "political slant" on the grounds that they might not be in the "national interest." The outcome was that—despite ditching the one-party state dominated by the BPRP—the political system that took its place, despite a clear degree of political liberalization, was not one that seemed calculated to gain and keep the allegiance of Benin's voters. This was especially true in many rural areas that were notable, in many places,

for the virtual absence of modern amenities such as good roads, clean water, and the adequate provision of state-provided health, education, and welfare programs.

On the one hand, Benin's democratizing credentials were most clearly rooted in the fact that the country managed to hold two, orderly and relatively peaceful, rounds of free and fair parliamentary and presidential elections during the 1990s. While the parliamentary polls were inconclusive with, on both occasions, a large number of parties acquiring limited amounts of seats, the second presidential election of 1996 produced a second consecutive defeat for an incumbent president. By establishing the principle of alternation of leaders in office, this appeared to bode well for eventual democratic consolidation. The situation was given piquancy by the fact that Kérékou, the country's unelected president from 1972 to 1991, was chosen as president in the 1996 elections, having lost power five years earlier to Nicéphore Soglo.

At the end of the 1990s, Benin presented a politically complex mixture of continuity and change. Apparently, Kérékou was undeterred by this rich irony, for in the 1996 elections he was able successfully to present himself as the democratic alternative to Soglo, although he had support from all the dictators in the surrounding countries. The return of Kérékou to power emphasized how little had changed in the country politically, despite two recent democratic elections. While Soglo's administration had been successful in some ways (for example, in managing to reverse to some degree the dramatic economic decline under Kérékou), it had shown itself to be willing to rely too much on old-style dictatorial politics and, as a result, lost popular favor. As during Kérékou's two decades of rule, the timbre of politics under Soglo showed that political power was still largely a function of ethnic affiliation, with religious allegiance also an important factor in deciding which individuals enjoyed political power.

JEFF HAYNES

Further Reading

Allen, C. "Restructuring an Authoritarian State: 'Democratic Renewal' in Benin." *Review of African Political Economy*, no. 54 (1992): 42–58.

Decalo, S. "Benin: First of the New Democracies." In *Political Reform in Francophone Africa*, edited by J. F. Clark and D. E. Gadinier. Boulder, Colo.: Westview Press, 1997.

Heilbrunn, J. R. "Social Origins of National Conferences in Benin and Togo." *Journal of Modern African Studies* 31, no. 2 (1993): 277–299.

Robinson, P. "The National Conferences in Francophone Africa." *Comparative Studies in Francophone Africa* 34, no. 2 (1994): 575–610.

Ronen, D. "People's Republic of Benin: The Military, Marxist Ideology and the Politics of Ethnicity." In *The Military in African Politics*, edited by John Harbeson. New York: Praeger, 1978.

Benin, Republic of (Dahomey): Kérékou, Mathieu (1935–)

Former Military Leader and President of Benin

The adoption of the Marxist doctrine by Mathieu Kérékou in his first stint as ruler of Benin condemned his administration to utter contempt and a number of political problems. Kérékou, born on September 2, 1933, in Kouarfa village in the Vattitingou Local Government Area of the northeastern state of Atacora, Dahomey (the previous name of Benin), first assumed the mantle of leadership as president of the military revolutionary government and as head of state in 1972. There was nothing in Kérékou's education that suggested any exposure to or admiration for Marxism. On the contrary, the dominant field of his education was Western philosophy. He attended Saint-Louis Secondary School in Senegal; the Military Training College in Frejus, France; and Saint Raphaal Military School, also in France. In 1960, Kérékou joined the French army. The following year he enlisted in the Dahomeyan Army. He was made the aide-de-camp to Hubert Maga, Dahomey's first postindependence president. He held this post from 1961 to 1963, when Maga was overthrown by the army.

From the mid-1960s on, Kérékou became involved in the high-level corruption that characterized the political terrain in Dahomey. In 1967, he took part in the military coup that displaced President Christopher Soglo. Thereafter he became the chairman of the Military Revolutionary Council from 1967 to 1968. In 1968, a civilian government was restored under Emile-Dersin Zinsou, who was to serve as president of the republic for five years. Between 1970 and 1972, Kérékou was commander of the Quidah paratrooper unit and deputy chief of staff. In 1972 he was made minister of planning. Not content with being in the shadows, Kérékou led a coup in October 1972; for the next seventeen years, he was an absolute military dictator.

The president brought considerable change to the political and economic character of his country. In 1975, he changed the country's name from Dahomey to Benin. Communism became a state-approved ideology, and all foreign enterprises were nationalized; as a result, most foreign investors, particularly the Europeans and Lebanese, left the country.

As an absolute ruler, Kérékou dissolved all political structures and drove all democratic groups and every form of opposition underground with a ferocity that was uncommon even in Africa. Michael Aikpe, the man who had spearheaded the 1972 coup, met a tragic death in Kérékou's detention camp based on a trumped-up charge that he was having an affair with Kérékou's wife. In 1973, Majors Jean Baptiste Hacheme and M. Chabi Kao were jailed for dissidence. Two years later, Kérékou sentenced Captain Jamie Assogba and Betin Boma, former minister of finance, to death for opposing him. In October 1975, 11 others were sentenced to death for plotting against Kérékou.

By 1977, however, the opposition had had enough of Kérékou's antics. Exiles, aided by foreign mercenaries, landed at the Cotonou airport and attempted to seize power. The attempt failed, but it provided ample opportunity for Kérékou to clamp down on opposition; several exiled individuals were sentenced to death in absentia.

In 1979, Kérékou began to regard democratization as a viable option of political development. However, his initial attempt at democracy was to hold an election in which he was the only candidate. By 1989 the failure of his Marxist socialist doctrine was all too apparent; he had no option but to renounce it. Demand for reforms and unpaid back wages had led to serious disaffection among the people.

The unrelenting protest against Kérékou's regime crystallized into the convening of the 1990 Sovereign National Conference, which was mandated to work out a new modus operandi of governance. The conference, presided over by Dr. Nicéphore Soglo, an intellectual and former International Monetary Fund expert, was the first of its kind in Africa. Initially, Kérékou did everything he could to frustrate the convocation of the national conference, but it held against all odds. The constellation of interests and open agitation for a change in the political process eventually culminated in multiparty elections. In 1991, Kérékou was defeated and Soglo was sworn in for a five-year term as president.

The former president bowed out and went into a sort of voluntary political exile in his home region. In spite of his tyrannical antecedents, it is interesting that Kérékou refused to use the incumbency factor to his advantage during the process of transition to multiparty democracy. Indeed, he was credited with the wisdom of reading the trend of events correctly and so did not exploit it to perpetuate himself. Also curious was the fact that, although Kérékou was an absolute ruler for seventeen years, his people never associated him with affluence. He lived a simple life in and out of office.

Five years after he was rejected by his people, Kérékou, who had been popularly called "the Tiger of Atakora," reappeared on the political scene. His return was as dramatic as his exit had been. In the 1996 presidential elections he presented himself as a candidate. In the first round of the elections neither Soglo, who was seeking reelection, nor Kérékou received the necessary 53 per cent of the vote. A runoff election was held in March 1996, at which time Kérékou received 54 per cent of the vote and thus declared the president elect. But the incumbent president, after alleging electoral irregularities, refused to concede defeat to the former dictator. The matter was then referred to the Constitutional Court, which upheld the result of the runoff elections and declared Kérékou the winner and president elect. On April 4, 1996, in a colorful ceremony that Soglo refused to attend, Kérékou was sworn in as the democratically elected president of Benin.

OLUTAYO ADESINA

Biography

Born on September 2, 1933 in Kouarfa village in the Vattitingou Local Government Area of the northeastern state of Atacora. Attended Saint-Louis Secondary School in Senegal; Military Training College in Frejus, France; and Saint Raphael Military School, also in France. Joined the French army in 1960. Enlisted in the Dahomeyan Army in 1961. Acted as aide-de-camp to Hubert Maga, Dahomey's first postindependence president, from 1961 to 1963, until Maga was overthrown by the army. Participated in the military coup that displaced President Christopher Soglo in 1967. Acted as chairman of the Military Revolutionary Council from 1967 to 1968. Commander of the Quidah paratrooper unit and deputy chief of staff from 1970 to 1972. Made minister of planning in 1972. Led a coup in October 1972, named president of the Military Revolutionary Government and head of state. In 1991, lost democratic elections to Nicéphore Soglo. Stood in next elections, won, and was named president in 1996.

Further Reading

Foltz, W. *From French West Africa to the Mali Federation*. New Haven, Conn.: Yale University Press, 1965.
Post, K. W. J. *The New States of West Africa*. Harmondsworth, England, 1964.
Suret-Canale, J. *French Colonialism in Tropical Africa*. London, 1971.
National Concord (Lagos), May 27, 1996.
Nzouankey, Jacques M. "The Role of the National Conference in the Transition to Democracy in Africa: The Cases of Benin and Mali." Issue 21 (1–2).

Benin, Republic of (Dahomey): Democratization, National Conference and, 1990s

In 1991, Benin began to institutionalize democracy and the rule of law. Prior to this, there were no developmental prerequisites for liberal democracy in that country which, for almost two decades, had been ruled under the tyranny of one man, Mathieu Kérékou. Since his ascension to power, Kérékou had not only instituted an authoritarian rule but had also privatized political power. Benin (formerly Dahomey) had achieved political independence in 1960.

Between 1963, when the first military coup occurred, and 1972, when Kérékou came to power, Dahomey was characterized by political intrigue, mistrust, and instability. The coup led by Kérékou in 1972 was the country's sixth. Between 1972 and 1990, Kérékou held on tightly to the reins of government, brooking no opposition and trampling at will on fundamental human rights. Unfortunately for his people, the period of his reign as an autocratic ruler coincided with the era of the Cold War, when global society tolerated behavior that patently disregarded conventional notions of the rule of law, democracy, and civilized governance. Kérékou (who adopted Marxism as an official state ideology) became a living example of the "sit-tight" school of African leaders. From time to time Kérékou not only succeeded in containing pressures for reforms but also succeeded in establishing the trappings, but not the substance, of democracy. He created an avenue for himself to hold on to political power with the aid of the country's sole ruling party, the Parti de la Revolution Populaire du Benin. His mock attempt at democratizing in 1979 consisted of an election in which he was the only presidential candidate. A similar situation occurred in 1984. But by 1989 things changed.

With the end of the Cold War, Kérékou and other African leaders like him were forced to come to terms with the requirements of the new international order. As demands for democratization and multiparty structures increased in the 1990s, autocracy and dictatorships began to succumb to pressures both domestic and international. Benin was one of the first countries where the demand for fundamental changes became highly vociferous and potent.

The events that turned Benin into an autocratic state were unparalleled even by West African standards. The ferocity with which Kérékou drove all opposition underground effectively silenced any attempts at reform. Even when the opposition succeeded in mustering enough clout to launch a foreign mercenary-aided invasion of Benin in 1977 to topple Kérékou, the reprisals taken by the government against all opposition effectively silenced dissent.

The lack of a competitive spirit in both the economy and politics pushed Benin to the brink of disaster. By December 1989, the failure of Kérékou's Marxist-oriented strategy was all too apparent. The country's foreign debt stood at $1 billion, with nothing to show for it. Left with no option other than to liberalize the economy, Kérékou renounced Marxism as an official state ideology in 1989.

The renunciation of Marxism and the relaxing of state control over the lives of the citizenry allowed thousands of disgruntled people to openly voice their grievances for the first time. Public servants, employees of the private sector, and teachers who were owed several months of back wages spilled into the streets demanding not only payment but also political reforms in the hope that a change in government would also lead to a better economic future. The looming chaos prompted a group of concerned legislators and citizens led by Robert Dossou, the dean of the faculty of law at the Université Nationale du Benin, to meet with Kérékou and to advise him that it was only through a de-monopolization of the political terrain, a general amnesty, and an end to all repressive measures that the impending national calamity could be averted. President Kérékou accepted the new challenges and agreed to a multiparty state.

Kérékou presented a decree inaugurating and empowering a committee of eight ministers, headed by Dossou, to convene an assembly of "forces vives de la nation, quelles que soient leurs affinites" (all living forces of the nation whatever their political persuasion) to take part in the construction of a new democratic process. In the aftermath of this decree, a national preparatory committee for the conference was set up and vested with the power to set the agenda for the conference, identify the interest groups, and recommend the number of delegates. The committee came up with a list of 488 delegates representing all shades of opinion in Benin.

In February 1990, a constitutional conference was convened. Those present, representing a variety of opinions, were united by a common goal: to reform the system and remove the incumbent. The conference came up with a series of guidelines for the new political process. It voted into law a constitution that limited the age of the president to between 40 and 70 years. It, delegated powers to the High Council of the Republic, and an interim administration was mandated to conduct elections.

As a result of the new liberal climate, by the time the multiparty elections were held on March 28, 1991, there were as many as 13 political parties. Kérékou was defeated by Nicéphore Soglo, who was sworn in for a five-year term. The victory of the prodemocracy factions in Benin effectively demonstrated the capability of a national conference to engender a sustainable democracy; the situation in Benin was to serve later as a model for other African nations.

The inability of Soglo to actually reform the economy of the hapless country was, however, to cost him his exalted position after his first term. In a surprising development, Soglo lost the presidency to Mathieu Kérékou in the 1996 presidential election. Although neither Soglo nor Kérékou could muster the required 53 per cent of the votes, Kérékou went on to win the runoff election with 54 per cent. The government, however, contested the provisional results of the election as published by the National Independent Electoral Commission, citing irregularities; nevertheless, the Constitutional Court declared Kérékou the winner, and he was sworn in on April 4, 1996, as the second democratically elected president of Benin. Benin thus symbolized not only a sincere attempt at democratic transition in Africa, but a landmark victory for democracy in the Third World.

OLUTAYO ADESINA

Further Reading

Diamond, L. *Developing Democracy: Toward Consolidation.* Baltimore: Johns Hopkins University Press, 1999.

Nzouankey, J. M. "The Role of the National Conference in the Transition to Democracy in Africa: The Cases of Benin and Mali" Issue, 21 (1–2), 1993.

Omitoogun, W., and Kenneth Onigu-Otite. *The National Conference as a Model for Democratic Transition: Benin and Nigeria.* Ibadan, Nigeria: IFRA/African Book Builders, 1996.

Benue Valley Peoples: Jukun and Kwarafa

The Nigerian Middle Belt is home to numerous ethnic groups, the most notable of which are the Nupe, Baruba, Idoma, Tiv, Ebira, Igala, Chamba, and Jukun. Of these groups, the most enigmatic is the Jukun, who have been associated with the establishment of the powerful but ephemeral state of Kwararafa. Kwararafa became famous in Nigerian history because, between the sixteenth and the eighteenth centuries, it was a terror to the Hausa states and Borno. However, the identification of Jukun with Kwararafa has been questioned, largely because the term *kwararafa* means nothing to present-day Jukun, who have virtually no memories of their allegedly martial past. The weight of evidence seems to indicate that *kwararafa* was a generic term used by the Islamic peoples of the Central Sudan to refer to non-Muslim peoples from the south.

Today, over a dozen ethnic groups, scattered over a wide area of northern and central Nigeria, claim ancestral linkages with the Kwararafa. This could mean that Kwararafa was a confederacy. At the core of this were the Hausa-speaking Kutumbawa-Abakwariga, as well as the Arago, Kalam, Gwana, Pindiga, Kona, Kundi, and Jukun. The location of the capital, like the membership of the confederacy, appeared to have oscillated with the vicissitudes of the confederacy and the location of the particular group or groups dominant in it. Organized for specific purposes such as defense and trade, the confederacy had no clearly defined frontier or permanent geographical location, established no lasting hegemony over the peoples they conquered, and disbanded once their specific aims had been achieved. They left behind no histories or chronicles. Therefore, much of what we know today about them comes from the records of their enemies. The reconstruction offered here is based on the creative use of other sources, such as the chronicles of successor states and peoples, and the historical analysis of spirit masquerades and shrines as well as of political and biological totems.

Pioneering studies by J. B. Webster (1976, 1993) and others show that four phases are discernible in Kwararafan history. The first began with its establishment, around the year 1000, at Santolo, on the southern bank of the Hadeija River, east of Lake Chad. By 1380, the center of the confederacy had moved to Tagara, north of the Gongola-Hawal confluence. Ruled by a Kutumbawa dynasty, Kwararafa rivaled and competed with the Hausa Habe states—especially Kano—for the control of Saharan trade. Commercial and religious antagonisms soon developed into confrontations. In these early encounters, the Habe states appeared to have had the upper hand. According to a Katsina account, Korau, the ruler of Katsina, waged a war against the Kwararafa in 1260. A century later, it was the turn of Kano, whose rulers Yaji (1349–1385), and Kanajegi (1390–1410) successfully compelled the Kwararafa to submit to an annual tributary payment that included, among other things, 200 slaves. Further, defeated in battle by Queen Amina of Zaria, the Kwararafa paid tribute to Zaria for most of the fifteenth century. Their devastating defeat by Bornu, between approximately 1462 and 1495, dramatically brought this first phase of Kwararafan history to a close. Thereafter, the capital shifted to Biepi, on the southern bank of the Benue River.

In the meantime, refugees fleeing from the forces of Islam in the northern states flooded the Kwararafa region, transforming the confederacy into a bastion of traditionalism. Active engagement in both Saharan and Atlantic commerce made this second phase, which ended with the ascension of King Kenjo in about 1610, one of prosperity. With their control of the salt supply of the Benue Valley, they traded this essential but scarce commodity for horses to build up their army, as well as for slaves in order to gain access to European commodities on the coast. Calabar, on the Atlantic coast, became known as the port of Kwararafa.

Increased wealth and a demographic upsurge permitted the establishment of a powerful cavalry army. This would, over the course of the next two centuries (c.1610–1790), enable the Kwararafa to maintain its independence in addition to inflicting a series of spectacular defeats on the Hausa and Kanuri states and rivals to the north. Zaria was the first to be reduced to tributary status. Between 1582 and 1703, Kano came

under repeated attacks, as its army watched helplessly while a new and reinvigorated Kwararafan army ravaged through the heart of the Hausa country. Katsina, situated farther to the north, did not escape the Kwararafan depredations. By 1680, Kwararafa was at the peak of its power when it once again swept through the Hausa country and its army reached the gate of Ngazargamu, the capital of the Borno empire, which it sacked, putting its ruler to death. Borno, however, soon rallied and the Kwararafan were repulsed.

It was during the final phase of this era of conquest that Kwararafan history began to merge into Jukun history. Now situated in the Benue Valley, Kwararafa began to experience waves of Jukun migrations, and the Jukun before long became the dominant group in the region. Internal dissension and unabated external attacks, combined with natural disasters such as drought, contributed to Kwararafa's decline. The Chamba drove Adi Matswen, generally acknowledged as the last king of the Kwararafa, from his capital at Uka. He fled north across the Benue, establishing a new capital at Wuse.

By 1820, a Jukun dynasty based at Wukari, south of the Benue, had taken control of what was left of the Kwararafa state. With this transformation, the martial state of Kwararafa had finally come to an end. The Jukun inherited the political power of Kwararafa, but not its martial tradition. The far-flung confederacy had become the homogeneous Jukun kingdom of Wukari. Kwararafa under the Jukun ceased to be a warrior state; extant accounts portray the new state as a pacifist and religious one, made up of a collection of unwarlike people solely and strictly devoted to the maintenance of their innumerable religious cults and the veneration of their sacred kings, a people whose prestige and continuing legitimacy depended on their successful performance of their main ritual function, which was to guarantee good harvest and good health for the people.

FUNSO AFOLAYAN

See also: **Hausa Polities: Origins, Rise; Kano; Niger Delta and Its Hinterland: History to Sixteenth Century; Niger Delta and Its Hinterland: Peoples and States to 1800.**

Further Reading

Fremantle, J. M. *Gazetteer of the Northern Provinces of Nigeria*, vol. 2: *The Eastern Kingdoms* (1920). Reprint, London: Frank Cass, 1972.

Isichei, E. *A History of Nigeria*. London: Longman, 1983.

Low, V. N. *Three Nigerian Emirates: A Study in Political History.* Evanston, Ill.: Northwestern University Press, 1972.

Meek, C. K. *A Sudanese Kingdom: An Ethnographic Study of the Jukun-Speaking Peoples of Nigeria* (1931). Reprint, London, University Press, 1968.

Miller, J. "The Biu Plateau: Establishing a Chronology and Linkages between Bura-Babur and Kwararafa." M.A. thesis, Dalhousie University, 1984.

Palmer, H. R. *Sudanese Memoirs*. 3 vols. Lagos, 1928.

Sargent, R. A. "Politics and Economics in the Benue Basin c. 1300–1700." Ph.D. thesis, Dalhousie University, 1984.

Webster, J. B. "Dating, Totems and Ancestor Spirits: Methods and Sources in Oral History." *Journal of Social Studies* (Malawi), no. 5 (1976).

———. "Kwararafa: The Traditional Face of the Coin." In *Fundamentals of African History*, edited by Apollos Nwauwa and Bertin Webster. Halifax, Dalhousie University Press, 1993.

Berbers: Ancient North Africa

At the dawn of the first millennium BCE, a new cultural development began in the Maghrib as Phoenicians from Tyre, now organized into a robust mercantile civilization, began to settle along the North African coast. The emergence of Phoenician and Roman culture in North Africa created patterns still apparent in the landscapes and societies of the Maghrib: a littoral civilization connected with the exterior Mediterranean world; an interior Maghrib, Berber and largely contained within itself. In antiquity (which in North Africa dates from c.1000BCE to the advent of the Arabs in the late 600s CE), a series of external cultures—Phoenician, Greek, Roman, and in many ways, a separate Christian one—built a succession of cultural overlays that fused Berber society and culture with their own. Our knowledge of the Berbers comes largely from accounts (often fragmentary) of them filtered through Punic and Roman histories.

What unfolds is the development of three cultures: (1) the mercantile Mediterranean civilizations of the littoral, which, depending upon their levels of power and defensive organization, had varying reach into the Maghribi interior and fused Berber culture to their own within their perimeter of rule and formed part of the great interconnective cultures of the day; (2) a series of indigenous Berber societies, eventually recognized mostly as kingdoms, the most important of which are the Numidians and the Mauri of Mauritania, who surrounded the Mediterranean civilizations and interpenetrated their histories and who seem to have had levels of organization that competed directly with the Mediterranean cultures; and (3) peoples deeper in the Maghrib (the Atlas mountains and the desert fringe), also Berber, who lay outside the framework of the Mauri, Numidians, and others, whose ethnic names occasionally surface in history and about whose social organization and history we know almost nothing.

Greek and Latin traditions place the earliest Phoenician arrivals (in search of gold and silver) outside the Strait of Gibraltar at Gades (Cadíz) in Spain and Lixus (Larache) in Morocco toward the end of the twelfth century BCE. But the focus of Phoenicia in North Africa became the settlement at Carthage, founded along the Bay of Tunis sometime around 800BCE. Here civilization was to flourish for 1500 years, first in its Phoenician form—or as it is called in North Africa, Punic (after their culture) or Carthaginian (after the city)—and then, after the destruction of Carthage at the hands of Rome in 146BCE, in a synthesis of Punic and Roman cultures. In and around the Phoenician and then Roman settlements, the original North Africans merged with the new, creating a new society in place.

East of the Gulf of Sirte, a similar phenomenon took place as Greek settlements were implanted in Cyrenaica, so named after their principal city, Cyrene, in the land of the people the Greeks consistently identified as Libyans of different, known tribes. From 639BCE on and the arrival of the first colonists from the Greek island state of Thera, Greek settlements grew in size and scope, absorbing "Libyan" (read: Berber) elements into their culture, which was primarily focused on agriculture and noted for their monopoly export of silphion, an elusive and extinct native plant of the desert steppes used widely in the Mediterranean world for culinary and medicinal purposes. The Greeks of the Pentapolis, or "Five Cities," as Cyrenaica was often known, were annexed by Ptolemy I of Egypt in 322BCE and by Rome in 74BCE. Here, as throughout much of North Africa to the west, a thorough synthesis of local and Berber cultures emerged that lasted throughout antiquity.

In the Maghrib, the Berber kingdoms of Numidia (Latin *Numidae*; Greek *Nomades*, and the origin of the word *nomad*)—which extended westward from the boundary of Carthage to the Moulouya River in Morocco; and Mauritania, land of the Mauri, who were in northwest Morocco beyond the river—enter history in a significant way at the time of the First (241–237BCE) and Second Punic Wars (218–202BCE).

By the time of Roman friction with Carthage, the Numidians were divided into two kingdoms, the Masaeylii in the west, with their capital at Siga (at the mouth of the Oued Tafna in Algeria) and the Maseylies in the east, whose capital was Cirta (Constantine). The long-lived king of the Maseylies, Masinissa (d.148BCE), seeking expansion of territory, fought against first Carthage and then Rome in Spain; he made a secret alliance with the Roman commander and conqueror of Carthaginian territories in Spain, Scipio, to secure his throne against challengers at home. At the Battle of Zama (northern Tunisia) in 202, ending the Second Punic War, Masinissa gained all of Numidia. Masinissa's continued aggressions against Carthage, now prohibited from making war, led to Carthaginian attempts to rearm itself and the subsequent Roman declaration of war against Carthage and its complete destruction in 146.

For the next 150 years, North Africa was largely left to itself, and Phoenician culture continued, and even expanded, among the North African population. Punic alphabetic writing was appropriated by the Berbers at some point, and used in different styles, of which only the archaic *tifnagh* script of the Tuareg persists to the present.

Rome declared the realm of Carthage the new province Africa (named after its indigenous people), constructed the *fossa regia* (royal ditch) to demarcate its boundary with Numidia, and intended to leave the rest of the Maghrib to itself. As time passed, however, internecine Numidian politics led to Roman intervention against Jugurtha, grandson of Masinissa, and the eventual division of Numidia into two parts, east and west. Numidia subsequently became involved in the Roman civil wars between partisans of Marius and Sulla, and then between Caesar and Pompey, and in 46BCE when Caesar invaded the province of Africa, held by the Pompeians, he did so by invading from the territory of the Mauritanians; upon his victory, eastern Numidia was annexed to the province of Africa, which then became Africa Nova. Africa Nova was subsequently enlarged with the absorption of Western Numidia and the previously independent cities of Tripolitania.

At the time of Jugurtha, the Mauritanian king Bocchus, deeply involved with the Numidian royal family, betrayed Jugurtha and made a separate peace with Rome in 105BCE. Mauritania then, too, became involved in the civil wars of Rome, and the kingdom was annexed to Rome by Caesar Octavian in 33BCE and then reformulated as a client-kingdom in 25BCE with Juba II of Numidia as king. Juba, son of an opponent of Caesar, had been brought up in Octavian's household in Rome. He established a new capital at Caesarea (Cherchel, Algeria) and received as consort the daughter of Antony and Cleopatra, Selene. Juba's long reign (*d. c.*23) was marked by his deep scholarly interests. Juba wrote a compendium in Greek (which is long lost) on the geography of Africa and Asia. He sent missions to distant territories and left his kingdom to his son, named Ptolemy in honor of his mother's Egyptian-Macedonian heritage. Caligula convoked Ptolemy to Rome in 40BCE, however, and murdered him, annexing Mauritania in the bargain. This brought all of the coastal Maghrib, Tripolitania, and Cyrenaica under direct Roman control, where it remained in varying size and administrative arrangements until the collapse of Roman power in the early 400s.

The littoral populations of northern Africa, already profoundly influenced by Punic civilization, underwent a gradual Romanization. Rome expanded agriculture and trade; the cities of North Africa expanded in number and size. Roman settlers were encouraged to populate the provinces of Africa and Numidia, and considerable flow of people entered and exited North Africa to move across the mercantile and administrative arteries of empire. Wheat and olive oil were exported in large quantities, leading to the naming of North Africa as the "granary of Rome." Latin replaced Punic as the vernacular in the cities; in the countryside, Berber held sway. Roman life reached a high point, both in wealth and geographic control, under rule of the emperors of the Severi (193–235), themselves a dynasty of African origins. Eastern Algeria and Tunisia were densely urbanized and Romanized in every way; Morocco, by this time the province of Mauritania Tingitana, was Romanized far less, in effect in a small triangle from Lixus to Volubilis to the Tangier Peninsula. Mauritania was reduced in size even further following a retreat ordered by Rome in 285.

JAMES A. MILLER

See also: **Carthage; North Africa: Roman Occupation, Empire.**

Further Reading

Abun-Nasr, J. *A History of the Maghrib*. Cambridge: Cambridge University Press, 1971.

Cherry, D. *Frontier and Society in Roman North Africa*. Oxford: Clarendon Press, 1998.

Clover, F. M. *The Late Roman West and the Vandals*. Aldershot, England: Variorum, 1993.

Frend, W. H. C. "The Christian Period in Mediterranean Africa, c. AD200 to 700." In *The Cambridge History of Africa*, vol. 2, *From 500BC to AD1050*, edited by J. D. Fage. Cambridge: Cambridge University Press, 1975.

Law, R. C. C. "North Africa in the Hellenistic and Roman Periods, 323BC to AD305." In *The Cambridge History of Africa*, vol. 2, *From 500BC to AD1050*, edited by J. D. Fage. Cambridge: Cambridge University Press, 1975.

———. "North Africa in the Period of Phoenician and Greek colonization, c.800 to 323BC." In *The Cambridge History of Africa*, vol. 2, *From c.500BC to AD1050*, edited by J. D. Fage. Cambridge: Cambridge University Press, 1975.

Raven, S. *Rome in Africa*. 3rd rev. ed. New York: Routledge, 1993.

Shaw, B. D. *Environment and Society in Roman North Africa: Studies in History and Archaeology*. Aldershot, England: Variorum, 1995.

———. *Rulers, Nomads, and Christians in Roman North Africa*. Aldershot, England: Variorum, 1995.

Berlin West Africa Conference, 1884–1885

The International Conference held in Berlin between November 1884 and February 1885 was convened because relationships between the great powers of Europe seemed, for the first time, likely to be seriously affected by the activities of their representatives on the

West African coast. As competition for access to possible export markets intensified, governors of British and French colonies were making treaties with African rulers that granted political rights over increasing lengths of the coastline, and covering their administrative costs by imposing customs duties. The British claimed that, provided such duties were not discriminatory, they did not infringe the principle of free trade; others did not agree.

Three areas became problematic during 1884. The British feared that France might aspire to monopolize the trade and navigation of the Congo River, recently explored; on February 26 they made a treaty with Portugal, recognizing old territorial claims covering the mouth of the Congo in return for guarantees of complete free transit and trade. France in turn feared a British monopoly of navigation on the Niger, where Goldie's National African Company was in process of buying out its French competitors. And in Namibia, where the German trader Lüderitz wished to establish a settlement, German chancellor Otto von Bismarck was greatly irritated by Britain's reluctance either to guarantee him the protection of the Cape Colony government or to authorize Germany to impose its own protectorate.

In October 1884, the French and German governments issued formal invitations to a conference in Berlin. There was a crucial diplomatic subtext; both governments were tentatively exploring a possible rapprochement in their European policies. The agenda of the conference was more limited:

i. Freedom of commerce in the basin and mouths of the Congo.
ii. Application to the Congo and the Niger of the principle [based on the Vienna treaty of 1815] of free navigation on international rivers.
iii. The definition of formalities to be observed in order that occupation on the coasts of Africa shall be effective.

Twelve European governments were represented, together with the United States and the Ottoman Empire. Liberia, the only West African state with diplomatic credentials, was not invited. But the interests of Leopold II's International Association of the Congo, shortly to become the Congo Free State, were closely watched by both Belgian and American delegates.

The General Act that the participants agreed to on February 26, 1885, did not partition Africa, nor did they intend it to do so. Their common aim was to find a legal framework that might allow the capitalist world to pursue the development of African resources with a minimum of international friction over tariffs or territory. Free trade in the Congo (which Britain's contentious treaty had been intended to secure) was

defined in precise and binding terms. Within a vast area defined as the Conventional Basin of the Congo (extending from the watershed of the Nile to that of the Zambesi, and toward the Indian Ocean) it was agreed that imports of any origin should be free of taxation. There might be exceptions for duties to compensate for "expenditure in the interests of trade," but these were to be nondifferential. These provisions served the interests of leading exporters—notably, Britain, Germany, and eventually the United States—in securing the "Open Door," and were to restrict the future fiscal policies of a dozen colonial governments: the British, French, German, Portuguese, and Belgian.

They did not, however, prove effective in preventing restrictive monopolies over natural resources. Perhaps the most fateful decision at Berlin was made outside the formal sessions of the conference; here Leopold II of Belgium so skillfully manipulated his diplomatic relationships as to secure recognition of his International Association as a political entity with sovereign rights over much of the Congo Basin. Each of the powers was persuaded that Leopold's personal rule would guarantee its future commercial interests more securely than any of the other contenders. But his Congo Free State did not effectively serve other professed aims of the delegates: to promote civilization, combat the slave trade, and protect African interests.

There was general acceptance of the principle that navigation on the Congo and its tributaries should be open to ships of all nations on equal terms, though France and Portugal offered some resistance to the proposal that this regulation should be supervised by an international commission. Britain undertook to apply similar principles to the navigation of the Lower Niger; but since the nation could claim by 1884 that no foreign governments of companies held rights on that part of the river navigable from the sea, no commission was established to enforce this.

Having agreed to these patchy and imperfect safeguards against the extension of protectionism in Africa, the conference tried to define procedures which might minimize future diplomatic squabbles over territory. Article 34 stipulated that any power taking possession of land, or establishing a protectorate, on the African coastline should give notice to the other signatories; Article 35 declared that the occupation of territory (though not, at Britain's insistence, the establishment of a protectorate) implied an obligation to establish an authority to protect existing rights and freedom of trade. Since most of the coastline was already subject to such claims, the direct effect of these provisions was very limited.

The conference can perhaps best be understood as a largely abortive attempt to impose some sort of international law on what—it was already possible to predict—would be a rather lawless "scramble" to appropriate African resources. For a few more years European governments remained reluctant to assume the costs of extending their control to the hinterland of their coastal possessions; but once they did, Articles 34 and 35 did not prove easy to apply to their relations with one another. On relations with Africans the Berlin Act said nothing concrete, and its statements of humanitarian intent, however sincerely intended, had negligible immediate effect. The most that can be said is that a few Europeans continued to believe that African development might be most effectively and economically undertaken by cooperation among themselves and that some sense of their responsibility as international trustees remained on the agenda of the antislavery movement, of the Mandates Commission of the League of Nations, and of the United Nations Trusteeship Council.

JOHN D. HARGREAVES

Further Reading

Anstey, R. *Britain and the Congo in the Nineteenth Century*. Oxford: Clarendon Press, 1962.

Brunschwig, H. *Le partage de l'Afrique noire*. Paris: Flammarion, 1971.

Crowe, S. E. *The Berlin West African Conference 1884–1885*. London: Longmans Green, 1942.

Forster, S., W. J. Mommsen, and R. Robinson (eds.). *Bismarck, Europe and Africa: The Berlin African Conference 1884–1885 and the Onset of Partition*. London: German Historical Institute and Oxford University Press, 1988.

Hargreaves, J. D. *Prelude to the Partition of West Africa*. London: Macmillan, 1963.

Bhambatha Rebellion, 1906

The Bhambatha—or Poll Tax—Rebellion was an uprising by Zulu-speaking Africans against the colonial government in the British colony of Natal in 1906. It was significant for southern African history in two main respects: It was the last major uprising—by the Zulu or any other southern African peoples—organized within the vestiges of precolonial African political structures, and it helped persuade whites in Natal and in Great Britain's three other southern African colonies to form the Union of South Africa. For the Zulu themselves, the rebellion indicated that Zulu ethnic identity was spreading, as many people who had hitherto been opposed to the Zulu king now rallied around him.

The main proximate cause of the Bhambatha Rebellion was the decision in 1905 by Natal's settler-dominated government to impose a £1 poll tax on all adult males except those who paid "hut tax" or were under terms of indenture. In practice, this meant that all adult male Natalians paid the tax except married,

non-Christian Africans and Indian indentured servants. As the tax was not indexed according to income, it was severely regressive and hit the poorest households hardest.

It was not just the imposition of the tax that caused Africans to rebel, however, but the fact that the tax was introduced at a moment of economic crisis for most Africans. Several factors contributed to this. First, an increasing number of European landowners were evicting their African tenants and choosing to farm the land themselves. Second, these evictions led to serious overcrowding on the small areas of land reserved for Natal's African majority. Third, the 1880s and 1890s brought a series of ecological disasters to Natal, including droughts, locust plagues, and, worst of all, an 1896–1897 epidemic of the cattle disease rinderpest that wiped out more than 90 per cent of the colony's cattle. Fourth, the South African, or Anglo-Boer, War of 1899–1902, which created economic boom conditions within Natal, was immediately followed by a severe economic slump. Finally, in 1904 Natal's government opened more than two and a half million acres of African-occupied land to white settlement, exacerbating overcrowding on the African reserves. All these factors dealt a serious blow to the Africans' ability to pay the new tax in addition to the old ones.

While these material stressors were perhaps necessary preconditions for the rebellion, they were in and of themselves the cause. In fact, right up to the eve of the rebellion the same factors had succeeded only in pitting Africans against one another, leading to endemic feuding in rural Natal. What the rebellion also needed was a motivating and unifying ideology, which came in the form of loyalty to the deposed Zulu king Dinuzulu. When the British released Dinuzulu from government custody in 1898, millenarian rumors about him began to circulate among Africans throughout Natal. According to the rumors, Dinuzulu, in league with other prominent Africans, was conspiring to launch a rebellion that would overthrow the colonial government and expel the white settlers. The rumors spoke of the supernatural forces that Dinuzulu would use to accomplish these ends, but they also called on Natal's Africans to unite and prepare to participate in the rebellion. There was some irony in this, for many of the same communities that rebelled in Dinuzulu's name in 1906 had fought for the British against the Zulu king in 1879, thereby contributing to the British conquest and dismemberment of the Zulu kingdom.

The imposition of the poll tax provided an ideal focus for this emerging ideology of unity through loyalty to a rebellious Zulu king. Immediately following the promulgation of the tax, and especially once tax collection commenced, young men throughout the colony engaged in spontaneous demonstrations replete with aural and visual allusions to the Zulu king. In most places chiefs and other elders tried to rein in their young men. In the Thukela Valley and the Natal Midlands, on the other hand, there was no shortage of African patriarchs willing to lead the young men into rebellion.

The rebellion proceeded in several stages. From January to March 1906, there were frequent demonstrations at poll tax collection assemblies, culminating in the deaths of two white constables in the Natal Midlands on February 8 and the declaration of martial law the following day. Just when it seemed the rebellion was over, Chief Bhambatha and his followers in the upper Thukela Valley initiated a small guerrilla war with colonial forces from April 3 onward. Bhambatha's rebellion only ended with his death and the routing of his followers at the Battle of Mhome Gorge on June 10. This was followed by another rebellion led by Chief Meseni in the lower Thukela Valley from June 19 to July 11. Finally, colonial forces spent the rest of 1906 rooting out small pockets of perceived resistance on a "shoot first, ask questions later" basis. In terms of African casualties, this last stage was the bloodiest of the war, leaving 3,000 to 4,000 African rebels dead, versus 24 whites and 6 Africans fighting on the colonial side. Ironically, in 1908 a special colonial court cleared the Zulu king Dinuzulu of any role in inciting, planning, leading, or fighting in the rebellion.

Although Natal's white settlers managed to crush the rebellion and to inflict far more damage than they suffered, the rebellion nevertheless convinced many whites throughout South Africa that they would have to unite in order to maintain white supremacy. Each of South Africa's four settler-dominated colonies (Natal, the Cape of Good Hope, the Orange River Colony, and the Transvaal) was too small and weak for whites to have much confidence in their chances against future African uprisings. Neither did most South African whites feel they could rely on the British government to bail them out, for they considered British attitudes toward South African blacks to be too liberal. South Africa's white legislators thus decided to pool their resources by uniting to form the Union of South Africa in 1910.

MICHAEL MAHONEY

See also: **South Africa: Peace, Reconstruction, Union: 1902–1910.**

Further Reading

Lambert, J. *Betrayed Trust: Africans and the State in Colonial Natal.* Durban: University of Natal Press, 1995.

Marks, S. "Class, Ideology, and the Bambatha Rebellion." In *Banditry, Rebellion, and Social Protest in Africa*, edited by Donald Crummey. London: James Currey, 1986.

———. *Reluctant Rebellion: The 1906–8 Disturbances in Natal.* Oxford: Clarendon Press, 1970.

Biafran Secession: *See* Nigeria: Biafran Secession and Civil War, 1967–1970.

Bigo: *See* Great Lakes Region: Ntusi, Kibiro, and Bigo.

Blantyre

With a population of about half a million, Blantyre, Malawi's largest city and commercial capital, is named after David Livingstone's birthplace near Glasgow, Scotland. Nestled in the Michiru, Ndirande, and Soche Hills, the city is also traversed by the Mudi River, which for a long time was its main source of water. Being in the Shire Highlands, Blantyre has a mild climate and, though today large-scale cultivation within the city is not practiced, its soils are fertile and rainfall adequate. It is a recipient of the cool and moist chiperoni winds that between May and August blow from Mozambique into southern Malawi, bringing with them rains during the dry season.

It is not surprising therefore that this was the home of the industrious Mang'anja under their ruler, Kankomba, conquered in the late 1860s by the Yao from Mozambique, who were in the process of establishing themselves all along the eastern side of the upper Shire region. Kankomba's authority was replaced by that of the Yao chief, Kapeni, who in 1876 was to host Henry Henderson and his guide and interpreter Tom Bokwito. Henderson was a member of a party of Scottish missionaries who had arrived in the Lake Malawi area to set up operations in memory of David Livingstone. Shortly afterward, Henderson was joined by other Scottish missionaries, clergymen, and laymen. Africans, mostly workers and students, also came to live near the mission, and descendants of early employees such as Lewis Bandawe and Joseph Bismark, both originally from Mozambique, still live in Blantyre. As more permanent buildings were constructed, the character of the place changed, and the mission station became a major center of activity in the Shire Highlands.

In 1878, a Glasgow-based firm, the African Lakes Company (ALC), established a base two miles from the Blantyre mission, just across the Mudi River; it was jointly managed by brothers Fred and John Moir. As the ALC's operations spread the length and breadth of the Lake Malawi region, their headquarters—which, like the company itself, came to be popularly known as Mandala—became a hive of activity. Mandala became a major employer of mission-trained and unskilled

Africans, and of former lay missionaries who had served their contracts. Among the latter were John Buchanan and R. S. Hynde, of the Blantyre and East Africa Company and also founding editor of the first newspaper, the *Central African Planter* and, later, the *Nyasaland Times,* which would become the voice of the European settler community.

After the country became a British protectorate in 1891, Europeans arrived to join the colonial service and, though most of them went to Zomba, the administrative capital, Blantyre remained the commercial and social center. In 1894, the ALC started banking services. At the invitation of the European community, the Standard Bank of South Africa had established a branch in the town in 1901; hotels also opened and, in 1894, Blantyre was declared a town, with a Council of Advice and a town clerk. Informal segregation became a feature of the town, with different races mixing little except in work situations. European residential areas were different from African ones and, as Asians from the Indian subcontinent settled in the town (originally as government employees and later mainly as retail traders), they lived in their separate areas. Even as the number of "coloureds" (people of mixed race) increased, they, too, lived in their own communities.

Five miles west of Blantyre, a small urban center was developing at Limbe. Although firms such as the British Central Africa Company (BSAC) were active in Limbe, which became a town in 1905, its growth greatly benefited from three principal factors: it was the main operating base of the Imperial Tobacco Company; the headquarters of the railways; and a predominantly Asian retail commercial center. Like Blantyre, Limbe had electricity and piped water systems, mainly in the European areas, by the end of World War I. Most Africans lived in villages around Blantyre but, as space became a problem with the arrival of more Africans, new informal settlements, such as Ndirande, began to develop. In the 1920s and 1930s, the two town councils had recommended that more African residential sites be identified, but only in the 1940s and early 1950s were they built. Among these were Soche, Kanjedza, and Naperi.

The Great Depression of the 1930s adversely affected all business in Blantyre, but with more overheads and cash investment, African businessmen faced particular hardship. Many people lost their livelihoods. Some recovered by the beginning of World War II, whereas others did not recover until after the war.

Blantyre was greatly affected by the 1949 famine, which devastated most of Malawi. The people managed to survive because African traders bought food from farmers far from the town.

In 1956, Blantyre and Limbe amalgamated under one mayor and, three years later, the Blantyre-Limbe Council became a municipality.

During the months leading to the declaration of the state of emergency on March 2, 1959, Blantyre was politically tense, primarily because it had become a pivotal point of advocates of decolonization; it was the headquarters of the main African political organization, the Nyasaland African Congress, and Dr. Banda returned to Malawi to live there. It was also the territorial base of the mainly European procolonial and the pro–Central African Federation movement, the United Federal Party. Hundreds of Africans detained under the emergency regulations were housed at a center at Kanjedza, Limbe.

The constitutional changes leading to the general elections of 1961, which ushered in an African-dominated government, were also reflected in the municipal government of Blantyre. In 1963, an eminent Asian lawyer, Sattar Sacranie, was elected the first non-European mayor; two years later, John Kamwendo became the first African mayor.

As more development aid came in and as Blantyre's prosperity beckoned investors, more buildings were constructed, greatly changing the landscape of the city. Roads were widened and extended; the national stadium, site of major celebrations, was enlarged to accommodate an additional 10,000 people. The University of Malawi opened in Blantyre in 1965. One of its constituent colleges, the Polytechnic, was a major structure on the Blantyre-Limbe road. On a hill in the Mitsidi area, the government built the Nsanjika Palace, which became the main residence of the country's president. Although government departments were in the capital in Zomba, they also had branch offices in Blantyre.

Throughout the 1990s, Blantyre continued to attract people who sought employment and a better life and, by the end of the decade, its population was 500,000, causing much pressure on services such as water and electricity. Another major problem for the city's social services was the increasing number of orphans, who had lost their parents to AIDS. In spite of these problems, Blantyre has remained a vibrant and friendly city.

OWEN J. M. KALINGA

See also: **Malawi.**

Further Reading

Emtage, J. E. R. "Reminiscences—Nyasaland 1925–1939." *Malawi Journal* 37, no. 2 (1984): pp.12–23.

Pachai, B. *Land and Politics in Malawi, 1875–1975.* Kingston, Limestone Press, 1978.

———. *Malawi: the History of the Nation.* London: Longman, 1973.

Power, J. "Individual Enterprise and Enterprsing Individuals: Afrian Entrepreneurship in Blantyre and Limbe, 1907–1953." Ph.D. diss., Dalhousie University, 1990.

Ross, A. C. *Blantyre Mission and the Making of Modern Malawi*. Blantyre: CLAIM, 1996.

Blyden, E. W. (1832–1912)
Educator, Scholar, Diplomat, Politician

Edward Wilmot Blyden became a leading figure in the fields of academia, politics, and black nationalism in Liberia and Sierra Leone from the 1850s to his death in 1912. Blyden's scholarly themes and his brand of black nationalism were fundamentally influenced by his experiences with the Western world.

Although they lived in a slave society, Blyden's parents were free and professional. His mother, Judith, taught in a primary school, and his father, Romeo, served as a tailor. The Blydens were accepted by their Jewish and English neighbors in Charlott-Amalie, the capital of the Virgin Islands. They worshiped in an integrated Dutch Reformed Church in St. Thomas. It is there that Edward also began his primary education. The family left for Porto Bello, Venezuela, in 1842, which contributed to Edward's fluency in Spanish. His acquaintance with the fact that menial tasks in Porto Bello were mostly done by blacks helped to give rise to his black nationalism.

After the family returned to St. Thomas in 1845, Edward Blyden attended school, but received subsequent training as a tailor from his father. His considerable intellectual ability was recognized by Reverend John P. Knox, a white American who served as a pastor of the Dutch Reformed Church in St. Thomas. Against this background, young Blyden was encouraged by the pastor to study oratory, literature, or theology in the United States, and he left St. Thomas for America in 1850. This was followed by his attempt to enroll at Rutgers Theological College, where Reverend Knox had received his training; Blyden was denied admission because he was black, and this too would contribute to his black nationalistic stance. His departure from America on the vessel *Liberia* on December 21, 1850, for Liberia, a country that had been established in 1822 by the American Colonization Society (ACS) for African Americans, was a manifestation of Blyden's nationalism. It was further bolstered by the fact that he now lived in a black-led country that was independent, at least in theory.

Such black nationalism, like that of nearly all Westernized blacks in the nineteenth century, is best described as a synthesis of opposites. Although Blyden praised African civilizations like the ancient empires of Ghana, Mali, Songhai, Abyssinia, Egypt, and others, he accepted the description "dark continent" that was employed by white officials of the ACS and Europeans to justify their "civilizing mission" in Africa. He also held the view that the enlightenment of Africa should be carried out by Westernized blacks. Against this backdrop he maintained that Liberia should be extended to include the area that became part of modern Ghana and Dahomey. Further, while Blyden condemned the settler elites of Liberia for their superior attitudes toward the indigenous people, he participated in the military actions taken against the Via and Kru ethnic groups of that country in the 1850s. Indeed, he later portrayed the defeats of the two ethnic groups as part of God's divine plan.

Blyden disliked the Liberian mulattoes because he felt they disliked dark-skinned blacks, yet he married Sarah Yates, a very light-skinned settler Liberian, in 1856. Blyden also wanted the settlers to interact with Muslims and other nonsettler Liberians. Nevertheless, he did not view such interaction as a means of bringing about a pluralistic Liberian society; rather, he saw it as a vehicle of assimilating the nonsettlers to the ACS-introduced American values in Liberia. Although he admired attributes of Islam and indigenous African values such as polygamy and communal modes of production and ownership, Blyden continued to be strongly committed to his acquired Western values throughout his life in Liberia and Sierra Leone. His black nationalism and concepts of building a powerful black country were greatly informed by European scholars such as J. G. von Herder, Giuseppe Mazzini, Count A. de Gobineau, James Hunt, and G. W. F. Hegel. His black nationalist sentiments were also contradicted by his strong support of the ACS, which was evidently racist and paternalistic. Mary Kingsley, who believed that blacks were inferior to whites, was portrayed by Blyden as among Europe's leading philosophers. Although he frequently condemned the Liberian settlers for behaving like white Americans, Blyden continued to be a great admirer of Britain throughout his life. In fact, he became a strong supporter of British imperialism in Africa, for he felt that such imperialism would enlighten Africa.

Evidently, Blyden was one of the leading champions of black people in the nineteenth century. Black pride and the rights of black people to determine their own destiny were among the dominant themes of his many publications and speeches from 1851 to 1912. His black nationalism and Pan-Africanism were, however, fundamentally informed by his favorable and unfavorable experiences with the Western world. It is no wonder that his activities in and worldviews on Liberia and Sierra Leone, like those of other Westernized black nationalists and Pan-Africanists, were contradictory.

AMOS J. BEYAN

See also: **Liberia.**

Biography

Born August 3, 1832 in St. Thomas, Virgin Islands. Family lived in Porto Bello, Venezuela from 1842 to

1844. Visited the United States in 1850, and attempted (unsuccessfully) to enroll at a theological college there; left the for Liberia that same year. Following his graduation from Alexander High School in Monrovia, Liberia, became editor of the *Liberia Herald*. Published his first major pamphlet, *A Voice from Bleeding Africa*, in 1856. Was ordained as a Presbyterian clergyman in 1858, and appointed principal of Alexander High School twice between 1858 and 1877. Represented Liberia in Britain, in the United States at the Court of St. James, and in France. Taught at and served as president of Liberia College and as Liberian secretary of State. Ran an unsuccessful attempt for the presidency of Liberia in 1885. Visited Freetown, Sierra Leone and Lagos, Nigeria several times between 1885 and 1905; Pan-Africanism and black nationalism were the dominant themes of his many publications and speeches from 1855 to 1906. From 1906 to 1912, lived mostly in Sierra Leone. Died in Freetown on February 7, 1912.

Further Reading

Adeleke, T. *UnAfrican Americans: Nineteenth-Century Black Nationalists and the Civilizing Mission.* Lexington: University Press of Kentucky, 1998.

Beyan, A. J. "The American Background of Recurrent Themes in the Political History of Liberia." *Liberian Studies Journal* 19, no. 1 (1994): 20–40.

———. *The American Colonization Society and the Creation of the Liberian State: A Historical Perspective, 1822–1900.* Lanham, Md.: University Press of America, 1991.

Lynch, H. R. *Edward Wilmot Blyden: Pan-Negro Patriot, 1832–1912.* London: Oxford University Press, 1970.

Moses, W. J. (ed.). *Classical Black Nationalism: From American Revolution to Marcus Garvey.* New York: New York University Press, 1996.

West, R. *Back to Africa: A History of Sierra Leone and Liberia.* New York: Holt, Rinehart, and Winston, 1970.

Boer Expansion: Interior of South Africa

By the time British colonial authority became entrenched at the Cape of Good Hope in 1806, a cordon of Boer settlement stretched eastward, about 200 kilometers wide, as far as the Great Fish River. According to the 1797 census there were only about 22,000 free white farmers in the entire colony. Although the word *Boer* is a Dutch term for farmer, the basis of the Boers' economy was the raising of cattle and short-haired fat-tailed sheep. The typical Boer farm was more than just a family affair. It was a little community headed by the patriarchal head of household, his wife, their children, and perhaps a few relatives. It often included as well some *by-wohners*, whose principal responsibility was the supervision of a workforce composed of a slave or two, and servants, many of whom had grown up on the property. The language of this little community had, by the nineteenth century, evolved from Dutch into a specialized dialect that came to be known as Afrikaans.

The expansion of this population was largely the result of private initiative. The former Dutch East India Company's governors had, on many occasions, tried to confine the Boers within prescribed frontiers. The government had contributed little or nothing to their well-being or defense. Boers on the frontier had evolved their own system of offensive warfare based on formations of horsemen. They would advance on their enemy, fire their muskets, then gallop away to a safe distance in order to reload before advancing again. They called this system of military action the "commando system" because it originated in a command to assemble. By the early nineteenth century, the commando system had become an institutionalized method of warfare. It was employed not only as a means of defense but also as a terrifying method of assault. It was also the means by which children could be captured to work on Boer farms. When the British took the Cape, they seized upon the commando system as a cheap way of consolidating their hold on the frontier districts. British governors always needed the Boers more than the Boers needed their governors.

When the advancing line of Boer settlement reached the realm of the Xhosa people, it ground to a halt. Further settlement east was effectively blocked. Expansion to the north was likewise halted for some time by the resistance of the San people, or "bushmen," who compelled Boer settlers to retreat from the lands they had claimed in the Sneuwberg Mountains. By the 1820s, however, some Boers were discovering new pastures for their animals north of the Orange River near the lower end of the Caledon River. The way for their entry into this territory had been paved by people very like themselves, the so-called Griqua, who though they were of mixed racial descent spoke Dutch. They relied on herding for their livelihood, and used their horses and guns to attack and rob the people they met. Like the Boers, they had waged wars of extermination against the San; like the Boers they captured children. Their disruptive entrance into the lands north of the Orange River created a wave of terror among Sotho and Tswana people of the Highveld regions, thus opening a way for others to follow.

At first, the Boers were a transient presence in those lands, using the pastures but establishing few permanent dwellings. The Cape government forbade their settlement north of the Orange but tolerated the occasional back-and-forth movement of these *trekboers* and their herds. (*Trek*, meaning "pull," was the word wagon masters shouted to their oxen at the beginning of a journey.) In the 1830s a series of events multiplied their numbers. First there were reports of rich lands lying vacant in Natal. Boers who accompanied Andrew Smith's expedition to Zulu territory in 1832 marveled at the vast grasslands they saw. Further private expeditions confirmed that new realms of settlement might be opened by negotiation or determined commandos. The abolition of slavery in 1883–1884 created resentment among slaveholders, who complained at the amount of compensation paid to them and the method used to pay it. More resentment was caused by the frontier war of 1834–1835. The government raised Boer commandos to fight the Xhosa, taking them away from their farms and families for a long period of time without pay. When Governor D'Urban announced the annexation of a large tract of Xhosa lands, many Boers looked to him for compensation for their forced military service. When the annexation was disallowed by the British government, a torrent of shrill criticism poured out from both Boers and British settlers in the eastern districts. Many Boers were determined to leave the colony, with or without permission, and to find new lands to colonize on the Highveld and in Natal. They sold their farms, fitted out their wagons, and trekked across the Orange with their retinues of relatives, ex-slaves, children, and servants.

The British government lacked the will to stop what they called "the movement of the emigrant farmers." The movement into the interior was almost entirely a movement of the eastern districts of the Cape. Very few middle-class or wealthy Boers joined the trek. No ordained minister could be persuaded to go with them. Many British officials privately let it be known that they condoned the emigration. British colonists in the eastern districts frankly cheered the movement on, hoping for fresh annexations of territory.

African rulers, of course, knew the trekkers were coming. Chiefs in the Caledon River Valley greeted them warily, but allowed them to pass through their territories without a challenge. However, Mzilikazi, king of the Ndebele, sent a party south to attack a trekker encampment and seize its cattle. The Boers retaliated with a vicious raid against the Ndebele settlement of Mosega, where many women and children died. More calamities marked the progress of the trekkers into Natal. The Zulu king, Dingane, prepared a trap for trek leader Piet Retief in February 1838 and dispatched soldiers to attack the Boer encampments and steal their cattle. The trekkers fought back in the battle they called Blood River (December 16, 1838), where 3000 Zulu died. Eventual victory in the war against the Zulu came after the defection of King Dingane's brother, Mpande, and many Zulu regiments in September 1839. After Mpande's forces routed Dingane, he and the Boers agreed that the boundary between their respective domains should be drawn at the Tukhela River. The trekkers now constituted themselves the independent Republic of Natalia.

By this time, however, the Cape government had become alarmed that the mayhem that had accompanied the great emigration would adversely impact on their own position on the eastern frontier. They also feared that an independent government in charge of the potentially important harbor at Port Natal could threaten their customs revenues as well as their strategic maritime interests on the route to India. In 1843 they annexed Natal.

Meanwhile, the friendly relations initially established between the trekkers and the African chiefs of the Caledon River Valley had soured. Instead of merely moving through the territory en route to other destinations, many Boers began to claim land for themselves. They also tried to exploit existing rivalries among chiefs in the area, such as Moshoeshoe of the Basotho and Sekonyela of the Tlokwa. As tensions mounted, the British again intervened. They first concluded a treaty with Moshoeshoe (1843), then attempted to define an incontestable boundary between the trekkers and African domains. When these measures failed to end tit-for-tat skirmishes and commandos, a new Cape governor, Sir Harry Smith, led a military expedition into the territory in 1848 and declared all the lands occupied by the Boer trekkers to be annexed to the crown as the Orange River Sovereignty. For Smith, who had served in the war of 1834–1835, the annexation was the vindication of D'Urban's policies.

Once again the British government stepped in to revoke annexations. The Sand River Convention of 1852 conceded sovereignty to Boers north of the Vaal, and by the time of the Bloemfontein Convention of 1854 the same rights were extended to settlers between the Vaal and Caledon rivers. Eventually these two territories were recast as the South African Republic and the Orange Free State; they became important building blocks of the system of apartheid which dominated South Africa in the twentieth century.

At the time of these agreements, most of the Boer settlements were in the Free State, where the introduction of thick-fleeced merino sheep laid the foundations of a new economy. North of the Vaal the trekkers were concentrated in a handful of widely scattered tiny villages, leaving much of the territory they claimed still effectively in the hands of African governments.

Toward the end of the nineteenth century, the growth of ethnic community sentiment among the white, Afrikaans-speaking population of South Africa caused the movement into the interior to be reinterpreted as the "Great Trek." The trekkers were celebrated as the *Voortrekkers*: nationalist patriots who had cleared a path for their countrymen to follow.

NORMAN A. ETHERINGTON

See also: **Difaqane on the Highveld; Mfecane; Natal, Nineteenth Century; Pedi Kingdom, and Transvaal, 1822–1879; Lesotho: Treaties and Conflict on the Highveld, 1843–1868.**

Further Reading

Du Toit, A. "No Chosen People: The Myth of the Calvinist Origins of Afrikaner Nationalism and Racial Ideology." *American Historical Review*, no. 88 (1983): 920–952.

Eldredge, E. A., and F. Morton. *Slavery in South Africa: Captive Labor on the Dutch Frontier.* Pietermaritzburg: University of Natal Press, 1994.

Marks, S., and A. Atmore (eds.). *Economy and Society in Pre-industrial South Africa.* London: Longmans, 1980.

Parsons, N. "The Boer Trek, or Afrikaner Difaqane." In *A New History of Southern Africa.* London: Macmillan, 1993.

Thompson, L. M. *Survival in Two Worlds: Moshoeshoe of Lesotho 1786–1870.* Oxford: Clarendon Press, 1975.

Van Jaarsveld, F. A. *The Awakening of Afrikaner Nationalism.* Cape Town: Simondium, 1964.

Walker, E. A. *The Great Trek*, 4th ed. London: A. and C. Black, 1960.

Wilson, M., and Leonard Thompson (eds.). *The Oxford History of South Africa*, vol. 1, *South Africa to 1870.* Oxford: Clarendon Press, 1969.

Boer War: *See* **South African War.**

Boganda, Barthélemy (1910–1959)
Founder, Central African Republic

Barthélemy Boganda is best known as the founding father of the Central African Republic and as an advocate of equatorial African unity, but he was also the first African priest from the colony of Ubangi-Shari, the first Ubangian to serve as a deputy in the French National Assembly, and the last president of the Grand Council of French Equatorial Africa.

Boganda was born in about 1910 in Bobangui, a village in the Lobaye River Basin of what was then the French colony of Moyen Congo. For administrative purposes, the date of his birth was later registered as April 4, 1910. Very little is known about Boganda's early years except that his father was murdered at about the time of his birth, and his mother was beaten to death by the agents of a concessionary company for not collecting enough rubber.

In about 1920, a French colonial officer took Boganda and some other orphans into his custody. Boganda was sent to a Catholic mission school and then a primary school at the St. Paul's Mission in Bangui, the capital of the French colony of Ubangi-Shari. It was at St. Paul's, in 1922, that Boganda was baptized and given the Christian name Barthélemy.

In 1931, his Catholic mentors decided to send him to Saint Laurent de Mvolve seminary in Cameroon.

Boganda studied theology and philosophy in Cameroon between 1931 and 1937 and then returned to Bangui where, on March 27, 1938, he was ordained, becoming the first Ubangian priest. For the next eight years, from 1938 to 1946, Boganda served as priest in Ubangi-Shari. During this period he became more outspoken and controversial; he argued with his superiors about the need to initiate more social work programs, and he led personal campaigns against the forced marriage of women, polygamy, and various other "un-Christian" customs.

During World War II, tension between Boganda and his superiors became more pronounced, but in 1946, when Ubangi-Shari held its first elections for deputies to the French National Assembly, Boganda's apostolic prefect, Monsignor Grandin, encouraged him to present himself as a candidate of the Second College, which included only a small number of Ubangians. Father Grandin wanted to prevent the election of a communist or socialist deputy. Boganda won the election and thus became the first Ubangian deputy in the French National Assembly. The First College, including the French citizens living in the colony, elected René Malbrant, a colonial veterinarian who soon became Boganda's most outspoken critic.

As a deputy in Paris, Boganda initially associated himself with the Mouvement Républicain Populaire (MRP), a new Catholic centrist party that posed a serious challenge to the strong socialist and communist parties of the postwar era. It soon became apparent, however, that the MRP was not really supportive of Boganda's efforts to end the abuses of the colonial regimes in Central Africa, and so Boganda turned his attention to the promotion of cooperatives and the establishment of a new political party in Ubangi-Shari. In 1948 he started the Cooperative Society of Ubangi-Lobaye-Lessé (Socoulolé), and in 1949 he launched the Movement for the Social Evolution of Black Africa (MESAN), the goal of which was "the complete development of the black race and its liberation by means of progressive and peaceful evolution."

Boganda's persistent exposure of the mistreatment of Central Africans and his active promotion of local cooperatives in Ubangi-Shari so annoyed his opponents that they attempted to end his career by having him convicted of breaking the law. Efforts to depict Boganda as a criminal and to have his parliamentary immunity removed increased in the period leading up to new elections in 1951, but these attempts made Boganda even more popular with the Ubangian voters. Thus, in spite of strong opposition by colonial businessmen, administrators, and missionaries, in 1951 Boganda was reelected to serve as a deputy in the French National Assembly. Then, in 1952, the MESAN gained control of the new Territorial Assembly of Ubangi-Shari, which chose Boganda to serve as one of its three representatives to the new Grand Council of French Equatorial Africa in Brazzaville.

In 1955, some members of the expatriate business community in Ubangi-Shari established the Ubangi Liberal Intergroup (ILO), which allied itself with Boganda's MESAN. One of the ILO's leaders, Roger Guérriot, formerly one of Boganda's fiercest opponents, concluded a pact with the deputy, according to which one-half of Ubangi's seats in the French National Assembly and one-fourth of its seats in the local Territorial Assembly would be reserved for European members of the ILO.

In 1956, Boganda was reelected to serve in the French National Assembly; he was also elected mayor of Bangui and president of the Grand Council of French Equatorial Africa in Brazzaville. As president of the council, Boganda became more vocal in his criticism of the French colonial administration. By this point, Roger Guérriot and his colleagues appear to have convinced Boganda that businessmen could play a critical role in the economic development of the territory, while colonial administrators would continue to impede progress. In other words, capitalism would bring economic development if it was released from government control.

In 1957, French Equatorial Africa was administratively reorganized to include a French high commissioner in Brazzaville, territorial heads of governments, government councils composed of ministers, and territorial assemblies with expanded powers. In March of 1957, Boganda's MESAN party won every seat in Ubangi's new territorial assembly, and every electoral district elected at least one European chosen by Guérriot and his ILO colleagues. Boganda stayed out of the new government but handpicked its ministers, who served on a council whose president was still the French governor of the territory.

Boganda chose two members of his own Ngbaka ethnic group, David Dacko and Joseph Mamadou, to serve as ministers, and he chose Abel Goumba, who belonged to the closely related Gbanziri ethnic group, to serve as vice president of the council. However, Guérriot was put in charge of both administrative and economic affairs, and soon gained Boganda's support for an "economic salvation" plan that envisioned dramatic increases in the production of export crops. Several members of the MESAN who voiced opposition to Guérriot's impractical schemes were accused of being communists and had their names removed from the party's membership list. These politicians published a pamphlet that accused Boganda of being "the toy of Guérriot and the other whites of the ILO."

Boganda's intolerance of political opposition became more evident in 1958, when he stated that "any political campaign would be considered a provocation to disorder and must be severely punished." He spoke ominously of using a machete to "get rid of the proponents of all political activities which are not in the interest of our country," and he toured the country making passionate speeches about the need for farmers to work harder in order to increase the new nation's production of cash crops. New animators were sent out to "encourage" greater production of cotton, though *enforce* would be a term more accurate for describing their actions.

Also in 1958, French president Charles de Gaulle announced that all French colonies would vote on whether to join the French Community or obtain complete independence without any further ties to France. Ubangi-Shari voted to join the French Community, membership in which Boganda described as "independence within interdependence." Interdependence meant, in part, that France should provide substantial assistance to the territory because the former colonial power was, in Boganda's words, "responsible for the harm she has done here and she must make amends."

By this time, Boganda was becoming increasingly aware that Guérriot's plans to attract private capital were attracting ridicule instead, and so he transferred responsibility for administrative affairs to Dacko and asked Goumba to take over management of the government. Boganda then turned his attention to promoting the idea of a unified Central African state "with French language, inspiration and culture." He argued that Central African unity was needed to prevent the establishment of small states with high administrative costs, and because of the growing threats of communism, Pan-Arabism, and the so-called Yellow Peril.

Boganda's effort to establish a united state in equatorial Africa was undermined by French opposition, by African politicians determined to retain their power, and by the opposition of richer territories unwilling to subsidize the poorer ones. Boganda accused his opponents of being "traitors to the African family" who gave a yes to joining the French Community but a no to African unity.

On November 28, 1958, the territorial assemblies of the French Congo, Gabon, and Chad voted to become separate member states of the French Community. On December 1, 1958, Boganda proclaimed the establishment of the Central African Republic and became its first head of government. His new French-style parliamentary regime announced that elections would be held on April 5, 1959.

On Easter Sunday (March 29, 1959), while Boganda was returning to Bangui from a campaign trip to Berberati, his plane exploded and everyone on board was killed. Investigators found clear evidence that a bomb had caused the explosion, and other evidence also suggests that Boganda was assassinated, but no definite proof has ever been found to link his death to any specific suspects.

Boganda's death transformed him into a martyr and national icon whose ideas are often treated with reverence, particularly by politicians who claim to be his heirs. Thus, the controversial nature of his leadership has been largely ignored. As a deputy in the French National Assembly, Boganda was an eloquent and relentless critic of the mistreatment of Central Africans by colonial officials and businessmen, and he overcame the opposition of many powerful interest groups to become the leader of Ubangi-Shari's independence movement. He also made a heroic effort to prevent the "Balkanization" of Central Africa. However, Boganda eventually became intolerant of political opposition, formed an alliance with opportunists in the local business community, backed unpopular and impractical economic development schemes, and, as an ardent assimilationist, shared many of the cultural prejudices of Europeans of his era.

RICHARD BRADSHAW

See also: **Central African Republic: Colonial Period: Oubangui-Chari.**

Biography

Born in about 1910 in Bobangui, a village in the Lobaye River Basin of what was then the French colony of Moyen Congo. In about 1920, was taken with some other orphans into the custody of a French colonial officer, and was subsequently sent to a Catholic mission school and then a primary school at the St. Paul's Mission in Bangui. From 1924 to 1931, attended seminaries. Ordained on March 27, 1938, and served as a priest in Ubangi-Shari from 1938 to 1946. Won election to the French National Assembly in 1946. In 1948, started the Cooperative Society of Ubangi-Lobaye-Lessé (Socoulolé) in 1948, and in 1949 launched the Movement for the Social Evolution of Black Africa. In 1956 was reelected to serve in the French National Assembly, and was also elected mayor of Bangui and president of the Grand Council of French Equatorial Africa in Brazzaville. On December 1, 1958, proclaimed the establishment of the Central African Republic and became its first head of government. On Easter Sunday (March 29 1959), while returning to Bangui from a campaign trip to Berberati, the plane exploded, resulting in his death and the deaths of everyone else on board.

Further Reading

N'Dimina-Mougala, A.-D. "Une Personalité de l'Afrique Centrale: Barthélémy Boganda (1910–1959)." *Guerres Mondiales et conflits contemporains*, no. 181 (1996): 27–51.
Pénel, J.-D. *Barthélémy Boganda, ecrits et discours 1946-1951: la lutte décisive*, Paris: l'Harmattan, 1995.

Bongo, Omar: *See* **Gabon: Bongo, Omar, and the One-Party State, 1967 to the Present.**

Bono: *See* **Akan States: Bono, Dankyira, Wassa, Akyem, Akwamu, Fante, Fifteenth to Seventeenth Centuries.**

Borno (Bornu), Sultanate of: Origins and Rise, Fifteenth Century

The establishment of the Borno sultanate was carried out in the fifteenth century by the ruling Sayfawa dynasty. It was preceded by the arrival of the Kanem court, under Mai Dunama Dibalami (about 1210–1248), in that area. From that point, Borno served as the central province of the Sayfawa polity in spite of the fact that several Mais continued to reside in the Kanem capital of Djimi.

The great instability in their original homelands, caused by threats from the Bulala warrior aristocracy of that region, caused the last decisive shift of the Sayfawa from the Kanem area to Borno. The movement of the dynasty to this well-developed province (generally portrayed in literature of the time as a monumental event), had occurred during the reign of the *mai* (sultan) 'Umar bin Idris, who settled in the town of Kagha (Kaka or Kawa), which appears to have been the first capital of Borno. This territorial loss did not affect the future development of the empire to a serious extent, since losses in the east were largely compensated for by earlier gains in the west.

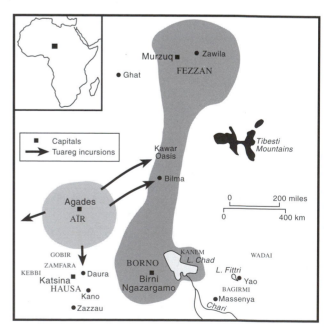

Borno, fifteenth–eighteenth centuries.

In the fifteenth century, the Sayfawa dynasty wandered up the banks of the Komadugu Yobe River. On its banks they built a series of temporary capitals such as Wudi, Birni Kime, and Yamia (Muniyo). Rulers of the Sayfawa dynasty were provided from the Magomi. The Magomi are believed to have been the most numerous Kanuri-speaking people, of those who migrated into Borno after the collapse of the Kanem polity.

Throughout the fifteenth century and beyond, the various Magomi settlements were distributed from Zinder and Munio in the northwest to the Gamergu area in the southeast, and from the Komadugu Yobe Valley in the north to Deia and Mabani in the south. Also with Magomi came various clans, such as the Ngalma Dukku, the Kai, the Tura, various sections of the Kanembu and other smaller groups.

The first mai to reign in the fifteenth century was Bir bin Idris, who was known by the name of 'Uthman. We know from al-Qalqashandi that this Mai had a friendly relationship with a Mamluk sultan of Egypt; at least, there was a letter sent from the Borno court to the Egyptian sultan Zahir Barquq.

During the reigns of the further 13 mais, stretching from about 1421 until 1465, there were constant feuds between the Dawud and the Idris dynasties. The interdynastic rivalry seems to have been associated with the problem of tracing lineage and descent caused by the fact that sons of Dawud were kindred to Bulala tribes on the mother's side, rather than sons of Idris. This caused lingering dynastic conflicts, although the later Borno chroniclers reinterpreted it as the Bulala wars. It was the continuity of "the Dark Ages" for the Sayfawa dynasty. Sometimes mais had not reigned more than a year before being killed by their rivals. Concurrent with these wars were encounters with the Kwararafa (Jukun), Kebbi, Songhai, and the continual rebellions of the so-called Sao tribes in the south.

By the end of the fifteenth century the situation had changed. The Sayfawa and their clan, Magumi, had obtained sovereignty to the southwest of Lake Chad, and under a series of able monarchs established their kingdom of Borno as a great power in the Sudan. The first of these rulers to organize and establish a powerful state was Ali Ghajedeni, the 48th sultan of the Sayfawa dynasty. He built a new capital called Birni Ngazargamo ("the walled fortress") at the north end of Bornu, and united this new kingdom under his control. Ali is supposed to have reconquered Kanem and reestablished control over the Saharan trade, while making war against Songhai to the west over the east-west trade routes across the Sudan. His reign was followed by a series of others no less notable; these subsequent mais maintained Borno at an apogee of greatness.

The last mai to reign in the fifteenth century was Idris Katagarmabe. By that time, Borno had secured its trading contacts along the Kawar-Fazzan route. For example, in the late fifteenth century, the mais of Bornu were in touch with the local Banu Makki and Banu Ghurab shaykhs of Tripoli.

Late in the century, the institution of a coruling senior female (gumsu), who had been in former times an essential factor in the designation of royal power, had changed. The real power of the gumsu was lessened under the influence of the emphasis of patrilinial ideology proliferating among the Muslim Sayfawa. Furthermore, the isolation of the Magomi from other clans must have led to a new system of mai legitimation. This resulted in the change of significance attached to the title of Gumsu, and in the appearance of a new female title of Magira.

Granted initially to an elder female relative of the mai, the title of gumsu was eventually simply given to his wife. Once the new title of magira had appeared, the title of gumsu shifted to the senior wife of the mai. Both titles were essentially honorific; neither the gumsu nor the magira took part in formal government activities.

During that time, there had been a steady migration of learned Muslims to the area following the fall of Baghdad to the Mongols. The late fifteenth century is distinguished by the first mahrams (charters of privilege) granted by the Sayfawa to a group of ulama (scholars). The mahrams as written documents confirmed the granting of hurma (inviolability) to an 'alim (scholar) in return for his promise to pray for the mai and provide him baraka (blessings). It was the starting point for further state and ulama relations that, in the process of the following ages, resulted in substantial independence for the ulama from the mai.

DMITRY BONDAREV

Further Reading

Bobboyi, H. "Relations Borno 'Ulama' with the Sayawa Rulers: The Role of the Mahrams." *Sudanic Africa: A Journal of Historical Sources*, no. 4 (1993): 175–204.

Cohen, R. *The Kanuri of Bornu*. New York: Holt, Rinehart, and Winston, 1967.

Hodgkin, T. *Nigerian Perspectives: An Historical Anthology*, 2nd ed. London: Oxford University Press, 1975.

Hogben, S. J., and A. H. M. Kirk-Greene. *The Emirates of Northen Nigeria: A Preliminary Survey of Their Historical Traditions*. London: Oxford University Press, 1966.

Borno (Bornu), Sultanate of: Mai Idris Alooma (1571–1603)

Kanuri Ruler of Borno

The greatest and most famous of all the Kanuri rulers of Borno, under whose rule the empire reached the peak of its glory, Mai Idris Alooma came to power after a period of about 25 years when feeble and incompetent rulers sat on the Kanuri throne. He ascended to the throne after a short period during which the reins of government were held by the queen mother, Magira Aisha, a forceful and influential woman. It was she who saved the young Idris from threats to his life and who, during her regency, instilled into her son the princely qualities of warlike courage and vigor—coupled with justice—that were to prepare him for his work as ruler in later years.

Records indicate that Idris Alooma was active at home as a soldier, administrator, and proponent of Islam, while in foreign affairs he was a skilled diplomat and negotiator, corresponding with the major Islamic powers of his days. Much of Borno's success under Idris was achieved by his army, the efficiency of which was greatly enhanced by numerous innovations in the spheres of transportation, supply, armaments, and leadership. Although he was well served by able commanders, it was Idris himself who was the leader and architect of Kanuri victories. Shortly after his ascension, he established diplomatic relations with the rulers of North Africa, especially Tripoli, and from them he was able to obtain muskets and a band of expert Turkish musketeers who helped him train his men and decide the issues of some of his most serious battles. Taking advantage of the numerous caravans who came from North Africa with many Arab horses and camels for sale, he built a large and well-equipped cavalry. As a good tactician and soldier himself, he equipped his troops with arms and saw to their efficient training by the Turks.

With a skillful deployment of his forces, Idris Alooma embarked on numerous campaigns of subjugation and empire building in and around the Lake Chad area. Within his kingdom, he subdued the So (or Sao), a warlike people, who had constantly threatened Borno since the reign of Mai Ali Ghaji, one of his predecessors, and captured their stronghold of Damasak. Similarly, he directed his military attention against the troublesome Tetala and Kotoko, whose power and threat he curtailed. He then turned west against northern Hausaland, especially the province of Kano, although his army failed to take Kano city. To the northwest he repulsed the Taureg, whose province of Ahir he successfully dismantled. With these and related military campaigns, he was able to destroy all resistance to Kanuri rule in the Lake Chad area, embark on the unification of Borno, and consolidate his authority in the region.

In the realm of religion, Idris Alooma saw the spread of Islam as a duty and a political necessity. He made Islam a state religion for all the notables of Borno as well as his subjects. His own pious conduct set an example for his subjects and encouraged strict adherence to the tenets of Islam. In the ninth year of his reign, Idris Alooma undertook a pilgrimage to Mecca, and there he built a hostel in the holy city for the use of Borno pilgrims. His numerous contacts with the Islamic world, including Turkey, earned him great respect throughout that world and helped to increase the prestige of his empire.

Judicial affairs in Borno under Mai Idris Alooma were organized in line with the Shari'a, the Islamic code of law. Numerous Muslim scholars from North Africa were attracted to the court, which took on a cosmopolitan character. Partly under their influence, coupled with the sights and experiences of his pilgrimage, Idris introduced a number of reforms that attempted to bring his empire increasingly in line with other Islamic lands. The Shari'a was substituted for customary law in several matters, while the adjudication of cases was transferred from the traditional rulers to the Muslim magistrates, the *qadi*, who also served as legal advisers to the local leaders. Under Idris Alooma, learning flourished, as the learned class, or *ulama*, received constant encouragement from him.

Idris Alooma built brick mosques that superseded those of reeds, especially in his headquarters at Ngazagarmu. Similarly, the process of urbanization received a boost as Gambaru, a town about three miles east of Ngazagarmu, is believed to have been built during his reign.

On the whole, Idris Alooma increased the prosperity of Borno and the wealth of the citizenry. Trade was boosted as the Kanuri empire maintained an effective control of trans-Saharan trade. His conquest of the Tuareg, in particular, ensured Kanem Borno's control of the important trade route to Tripoli. He brought the second Borno empire to the apogee of its greatness, securing for it the greatest territorial extent and its highest prestige in the entire central and western Sudan. His achievement was more striking as it coincided with the overthrow of Songhai, the counterpart and rival of Borno to the west, which was conquered by the Moroccans at the battle of Tondibi in 1591. It is significant that when the Songhai forces were defeated by the Moroccans, the fugitive Askia Ishaq sought refuge in Borno territory.

After a successful tenure spanning about 32 years, an aging Idris Alooma was assassinated when on an expedition in a marsh called Aloo, near Maiduguri, in the northwestern part of present-day Nigeria, during one of his many military campaigns. Much that is known about him today is derived from the detailed records of his chronicler, Ahmad ibn Fartuwa.

S. ADEMOLA AJAYI

See also: **Borno (Bornu), Sultanate of: Origins and Rise, Fifteenth Century; Religion, History of.**

Further Reading

Bawuro, B. "Early States of the Central Sudan: Kanem, Borno and Some of Their Neighbours to c.1500 A.D." In *History of West Africa*, 3rd ed., vol. 1, edited by J. F. Ade Ajayi and Michael Crowder. London: Longman, 1985.
Ifemesia, C. C. "States of the Central Sudan." In *A Thousand Years of West African History*, edited by J. F. Ade Ajayi and Ian Espie. Ibadan, Nigeria: Ibadan University Press/Nelson, 1965.

Lavers, J. E. "Kanem and Borno to 1808." In *Groundwork of Nigerian History*, edited by Obaro Ikime. Ibadan, Nigeria: Heinemann, 1980.

Palmer, H. R. *A History of the First Twelve years of the Reign of Mai Idris Alooma of Bornu*. Lagos, 1926.

Usman, B., and A. Nur (eds.). Studies in the History of Pre-colonial Borno. Zaria, Nigeria: Northern Nigeria Publishing, 1993.

Borno (Bornu), Sultanate of: Saifawa Dynasty: Horses, Slaves, Warfare

The Saifawa dynasty (claiming descent from the Yemenite culture hero Saif bin Dhi Yazan of Himyar) first came to prominence in Kanem, the area to the northeast of Lake Chad, between the tenth and eleventh centuries. After consolidating its position in the lake area by about the twelfth century, the influence of the dynasty expanded as far north as Traghan in the Fezzan (present-day Libya) by the thirteenth century. This was a remarkable feat in that Traghan is about 1,380 kilometers from Njimi, the capital of Kanem under the Saifawa.

However, the fortunes of the dynasty gradually began to wane so much that Kanem had to be abandoned for Borno, the area to the southwest of Lake Chad, in the fourteenth century. Situated in the Lake Chad Basin, Borno has been inhabited by pastoral and agricultural peoples since the beginning of the common era. Following the establishment of Gazargamo as a capital (in the confluence of the Yobe and Gana rivers) along the boundary of the present-day republics of Niger and Nigeria in the second half of the fifteenth century CE, the Saifawa dynasty witnessed a rebirth under Idris Alauma (c.1564–1576). For instance, under him, Borno's influence reached as far as Kano in Hausaland, as far north as Dirku and Agram in the central Sahara, as far east as the Shari River, and as far south as the Gongola River Valley.

This expansionist phase in the history of Borno, characterized by extensive military campaigns, was followed by what might be termed as a period of consolidation under the immediate successors of Idris Alauma. But decline set in from the mid-eighteenth century, culminating in the invasion of Borno by Fulani jihadists in the first decade of the nineteenth century. This event subsequently paved the way for a dynastic change, with the Borno rulers inviting a Muslim cleric, Muhammad al-Amin al-Kanemi, to assist them in ridding their territory of the Fulani menace. Having reigned for nearly 900 years, first in Kanem and later in Borno, the Saifawa dynasty was one of the longest ruling dynasties in the world.

Since its establishment by Ali bin Dunoma (also known as Ali Gaji) in the fifteenth century, the Borno sultanate relied upon the use of conquest and diplomacy to bring new groups within its fold. Militarism, especially during the Idris Alauma period, was revolutionized with the inclusion of Turkish musketeers, camel corps, and the use of canoes. The adoption of the scorched-earth policy incapacitated the enemy to the extent that surrender to the mighty Borno army was eventually ensured.

Given the crossroads position of Borno in terms of both trans-Saharan and trans-Sudanic trade, the acquisition of horses strengthened its cavalry, thus increasing the potency of the sultanate to engage in further warfare. Apart from locally bred ponies, Borno was well situated to replenish its stock with supplies from North Africa and from the Bahr al-Ghazal area, to the southeast of Lake Chad. Besides serving as an important status symbol, horses were needed by large states such as Borno for military purposes. Indeed, Borno's horsemanship was cultivated using similar methods to those of the Mamluk sultans of Egypt. The popularity of Borno in horsemanship is usually attested to by the common Hausa saying, "An kara wa Barno dawaki" (meaning, literally, "taking horses to Borno for commerce is synonymous with taking coal to Newcastle for sale").

Notably, there seems to have been a close relationship between the slave and horse trades and warfare in the sultanate. The demand for slaves, especially from the Muslim countries of North Africa and beyond, encouraged warfare for procuring this human merchandise. Though not every military campaign had the demand for slaves as its main aim, most encounters ended up in the acquisition of slaves as booty. The demand for slaves for export and for domestic use was further increased in a region like Borno, with limited items for foreign markets in the precolonial period. Leather, ostrich feathers, and ivory were important trans-Saharan exports from Borno. But slaves surpassed all other items throughout much of the precolonial period. And apart from their significance in the domestic, political, military, social, and economic life of the state, slaves were almost always crucial in trans-Sudanic trade between Borno and other neighboring states. It is perhaps worth noting that enslavement of non-Muslims was justified by Islam, and virtually all military campaigns against members of the other faiths were regarded as holy wars (jihad) in the cause of expanding the Islamic domain. Therefore, in analyzing warfare in the Borno sultanate under the Saifawa, one cannot help but see a corresponding close interconnection between the trade in horses and the trade in slaves, with all three converging at one level. The connection between the horse and slave trades lay in their relation to war. Horses were valued principally for their use in warfare, and were possibly especially useful in the pursuit and capture of fleeing enemies—that is, in securing slaves. Slaves, on the other hand, were most readily obtained through capture in warfare. The exchange of horses for slaves therefore tended to become a circular or reinforcing process: horses were purchased with slaves, and could then be used in military campaigns that yielded further slaves and financed further purchases of horses. Thus, trade and war reinforced one another in a self-sustaining process that in turn sustained the domination of the warrior aristocracies.

YAKUBU MUKHTAR

See also: **Borno (Bornu), Sultanate of: Seventeenth and Eighteenth Centuries; Borno (Bornu), Sultanate of: Mai Idris Alooma; Borno (Bornu), Sultanate of: Origins and Rise, Fifteenth Century.**

Further Reading

Adeleye, R. A. "Hausaland and Borno, 1600–1800." In *History of West Africa*, 2nd ed., vol. 1, edited by J. F. A. Ajayi and Michael Crowder. London: Longman, 1985.

Hunwick, J. O. "Songhay, Borno and the Hausa States, 1450–1600." In *History of West Africa*, 2nd ed., vol. 1, edited by J. F. A. Ajayi and Michael Crowder. London: Longman, 1985.

Lange, D. *A Sudanic Chronicle: The Borno Expeditions of Idris Alauma (1564–1576).* Wiesbaden: Franz Steiner Verlag, 1987.

Law, R. *The Horse in West African History: The Role of the Horse in the Societies of Pre-colonial West Africa.* Oxford: Oxford University Press, 1980.

Borno (Bornu), Sultanate of, Seventeenth and Eighteenth Centuries

The dynastic list, *Diwan of the Mais of Borno*, indicates eleven *mais* who reigned during these two centuries. Borno traditions claim that the seventeenth and eighteenth centuries witnessed a decline of the power of the sultanate. It is said that the state was becoming weak and overburdened with pomp and rituals celebrating the mai. However, this may have been a reinterpretation of Borno history by the new dynasty and their followers, who would naturally have played up the failures of the previous Sayfawa regime when they took over in the nineteenth century.

There is certainly evidence of many successful military campaigns during this period. At the time, Borno retained a widespread reputation as a great kingdom. Evidently, Borno had sustained contact with various other civilizations. For example, communication between Borno and Turkey was sustained for two centuries.

This is not to imply that Borno enjoyed friendly relations with all its acquaintances and neighbors. The northern trade route was increasingly threatened, as Tuareg and Tubu raiders attacked the northern boundaries of Borno and harassed the caravans with greater intensity than before. Under Mai Ali ibn Hajj 'Umar there were troubling developments in relations with both the Kwararafa (Jukun) and the Tuareg; both enemies were simultaneously besieging Birni Ngazargamu. At the same time, the Borno army suffered several defeats at the hands of the Mandara. They were also severely attacked by the growing numbers of Fulbe and Shuwa Arabs settled in the Dikwa area. There were long famines under various mais throughout the seventeenth and eighteenth centuries. It was also recorded that in the middle of the eighteenth century Borno attacked Kano, Katsina, Gobir, and Zamfara.

During this period Borno was actively involved in trade with the surrounding south regions. The main products were cotton, Manga salt, ivory, and Islamic books. Beginning in the late seventeenth century, Borno traders gradually replaced other merchants on alternate routes linking Borno to the south and the east. By the eighteenth century, elephant hunters from Borno had founded settlements north of the Benue Valley, to begin the ivory trade. Borno cotton weavers settled in the Adamawa region. From there they produced and traded woven strips, the latter being necessary among the local tribes for use as ritual items.

The power of the mai became strongly centralized and newly symbolic during this period. The ruling mai appeared in public in a cage, which only his most trusted servants could approach. He rarely led military expeditions himself. Turkish author Evliya Celebi relates that while traveling, the ruler of Borno covered his face and eyes in front of strangers. All this, while resembling the practices of non-Muslim Sudanic rulers, easily coexisted with Islam and its practitioners, which was increasingly influential given the rise of Muslim education. The mai of Borno was considered the *amir al-mu'minin* (commander of the faithful) or even *khalifa* (caliph).

By the end of the eighteenth century, the granting of *mahrams* (charters of privilege) closely resembled a juridical practice meant to distribute *hurma* (inviolability) and other privileges among the Muslim community. In this context a special status of *mallemtis* (settlements established by mahram holders) should be outlined: mallemtis afforded mahram holders a large degree of autonomy in the social system of Borno.

The increase of mallemties and augmentation of the Muslim community in Borno resulted in the appearance of a large and powerful social group that soon (early in the nineteenth century) would play a crucial role in the decline and the end of the Sayfawa dynasty.

In an educational context, "the inviolability of the mallemtis apparently attracted a large number of students and provided a stable basis for the conduct of educational activities during the Sayfawa period and beyond" (Bobboyi 1993, p.198). The high degree of deeply rooted Muslim education among Borno society can be confirmed by a copy of the Qu'ran written in Arabic, found in Borno and dating to 1669.

The mahram institution was open to individuals regardless of race or ethnicity; thus, it afforded Muslim scholars (and their relatives and ethnic group) a means of integrating into the mainstream Borno society. The population of the region was increasing rapidly at this time, and many were eager to reap the benefits of membership in greater Borno society. Various peoples were moving into Borno; simultaneously, residents of Borno were expanding into the neighboring regions. The Borno people (the future Kanuri) were spreading west, east, and south with a consequent sociocultural influence on the indigenous people of those regions, which encouraged the emergence of new peoples including the Babur, Gude, and Mandara.

Throughout the seventeenth and eighteenth centuries, Borno's expansion and integration into the surrounding areas was so considerable that some patterns of Borno's administrative system, warfare patterns, official titles, and Islamic tradition were adopted by the very different polities situated throughout the Mega-Chad region.

DMITRY BONDAREV

Further Reading

Bobboyi, H. "Relations of Borno 'Ulama' with the Sayawa Rulers: The Role of the Mahrams." *Sudanic Africa: A Journal of Historical Sources*, no. 4 (1993): 175–204.

Cohen, R. *The Kanuri of Bornu*. New York: Holt, Rinehart, and Winston, 1967.

Hodgkin, T. *Nigerian Perspectives: An Historical Anthology*, 2nd ed. London: Oxford University Press, 1975.

Hogben, S. J. and A. H. M. Kirk-Greene. *The Emirates of Northen Nigeria: A Preliminary Survey of Their Historical Traditions*. London: Oxford University Press, 1966.

Mohammadou, E. "Kanuri Imprint on Adamawa Fulbe and Fulfulde." In *Advances in Knuri Scholarship*, edited by N. Cyffer and Th. Geider. Cologne: Ruediger Koeppe Verlag, 1997.

Botswana: Nineteenth Century: Precolonial

Precolonial Botswana was populated by several ethnic groups scattered throughout the country. In the south were the so-called First People of Botswana, otherwise known as the Basarwa (Khoisan), the Bakgalagadi, and the Batswana. While these groups were initially close, they later became stratified, with the Batswana being the dominant group, followed by the Bakgalagadi and the Basarwa. The Basarwa were *malata* (servants) of the Bakgalagadi while the latter were under the Batswana, who enjoyed the privileged position of controlling both groups. However, not all the subjugated groups were under the Batswana. A substantial number fled to the remote areas of the Kgalagadi desert to maintain their independence. By 1820, most of what is now southern Botswana was controlled by the militarily strong Batswana groups of the Bakwena and the Bangwaketse.

Like the Basarwa, the Bakgalagadi are composed of various groups and have lived in southern Botswana for many years. These groups include the Bakgwatlheng,

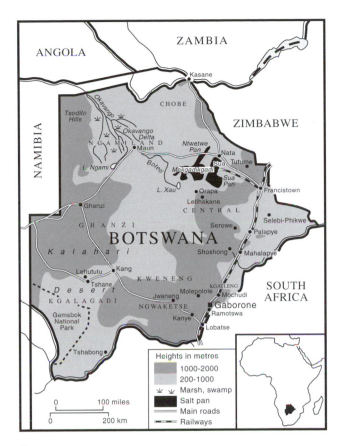

Botswana.

Babolaongwe, Bangologa, and Bashaga. The Baphaleng, another group of the Bakgalagadi, could be found in the northern part of the country, having broken away from the Bakgwatlheng in the seventeenth and eighteenth centuries.

By the seventeenth century, the Bakgwatlheng were firmly established at the Dithejwane Hills near Molepolole, where they were found and eventually defeated by a Batswana group of the Bakwena. The Bakwena not only made them *malata* but also made them pay tribute. Some ran away to Hukuntsi, farther toward the desert, where they earned a reputation for their trading and work in skins.

By 1790, the Bangwato and Bangwaketse had consolidated themselves, subjugating many other groups in the process. The Bangwaketse, under Kgosi (Chief) Makaba II, had built their capital at Kanye, while the Bangwato, under Kgosi Mathiba, settled near the Shoshong Hills. Meanwhile, the original Bakwena remained around the area of Molepolole under their despotic leader, Motswasele, who was later executed by his own people. By 1820, the Batswana were fairly established in the southern part of the country, raising cattle and farming. They also traded with other groups in the north in copper and grain.

The northern part of what is now Botswana was distinct from the south in terms of population by virtue of its population being non-Tswana. Among the people inhabiting this northern region were the Bakalanga, Basarwa, Bakgalagadi, Bayeyi (Wayeyi), Hambukushu, Babirwa, and Batswapong. The few Batswana lived in the present Central District of Botswana and included such groups as the Bangwato, Bakaa, Batswana, and Bakhurutshe.

By 1817, the Bangwato under Kgosi Kgari emerged as a strong *morafe* (nation) because it incorporated most other conquered groups. The Basarwa were, like those in the south, made malata.

The Bakalanga, one of the largest non-Tswana group of Shona descent, lived in the northern region of present Botswana for more than 1,500 years. By 1450, the Bakalanga had formed a powerful kingdom called Butwa under their king, Mambo, and they traded with the Portuguese in the east coast. The Bakalanga are really a conglomeration of different peoples; those linked to the Butwa Kingdom before 1680 are Balilima, while the immigrants are Banyayi. The Butwa kingdom attracted immigrants of the likes of the Bapedi and Babirwa, who later adopted the Bakalanga culture. By 1840, the Bakalanga were dominated by the Amandebele of Mzilikazi and later by the Bangwato.

Other groups in the north included the Batalaote, who were originally Bakalanga after they had split from Banyayi. Their leader, Dalaunde, had moved with his followers and sought refuge from the Bangwato in Shoshong, where they adopted the Setswana language and became an integral part of the Bangwato. The Batswapong are another group found in the north, around the Tswapong Hills. Originating from South Africa, some were Bapedi, while others were Transvaal Ndebele. Although they lived in scattered villages, each with its own leader, they fell under Kgosi Malete, a Ndebele leader. Sometimes they were called Bamalete, but they are not related to the Balete of Ramotswa. They were skilled ironworkers; they also traded iron goods.

Another large group found in the north were the Wayeyi (Bayeyi) who migrated to Ngamiland area from Zambia. Wayeyi were "fish people," and they traveled around the Okavango Delta in their *mekoro* (canoes). Although they had an overall ruler, he did not conduct much power. They avoided war, and lived peacefully with their neighbors. They cultivated grain on the river banks and specialized in trapping hippopotamuses; they traded in fish and grain with the Basarwa but also traded with the people of Angola.

The Hambukushu also lived in the Okavango area. They kept cattle, farmed, and traded in all kinds of goods. By 1800 they were living along the Okavango River, stretching to Angola. Some Bakgalagadi—notably the Bangologa—were found in Ngamiland. The Batswana made them malata, but most sought

independence by running away. They later became the neighboring Hambukushu.

In the 1830s, the Bakololo and the Amandebele invaded the Batswana *merafe* (nations). As a result of the invasion, some communities were completely ruined, others were weakened and scattered, and still others, facing starvation, turned on one another for survival.

The Amandebele also terrorized the Batswana, after being routed by the Boers of the "Great Trek" when they had moved west and northward. The Amandebele leader, Mzilikazi, not only captured and incorporated the Batswana into his group, but made them pay tribute in the form of grain and cattle. Many Batswana merafe lost their lives.

For a time, peace and prosperity returned to the Batswana. The peace was short-lived, however, as the Batswana faced another foreign threat: the Boers. Prosperity was still possible due to trade between the Batswana and European traders from the coast. The Batswana sold game products such as ivory in return for guns. The Batswana needed and used the guns to defend themselves against the Boers, the Amandebele, and the Bakololo. The missionaries—notably Dr. David Livingstone—encouraged the Batswana to trade not only in guns but also in European goods such as cloth and plows.

The Batswana employed the guns they acquired from the Europeans at the battle of Dimawe, which was fought against the Boers in 1852–1853. The Boers were intent on expanding and acquiring Batswana lands, using the Batswana as free laborers on their farms, and above all, taking away the Batswanas' guns. Sechele of the Bakwena was the hero of the Batswana as he not only withstood the onslaught of the Boers but also repelled their attacks at the Battle of Dimawe. The missionary Livingstone was accused by the Boers of arming Sechele and the Bakwena; the accusation may not have been unfounded.

After the Boer threat subsided, the Bakwena and the Bangwaketse emerged as powerful kingdoms due to their control of the trade in local game. They also took in refugees who escaped Boer domination. These included the Bakgatla-ba-ga-Kgafela, the Batlokwa, and the Balete, though all three groups later asserted their independence. Although there were intermerafe wars, by the 1880s the groups had established cordial relations in the face of European threats to the region.

In the northwest, the Batswana emerged as a powerful kingdom under their various leaders, Mogalakwe, Letsholathebe, and Moremi II. They expanded their territory by conquering other peoples in the area, including the Wayeyi, Habukushu, Khoe, Bakgalagadi, Ovaherero, and Basubia (Bekuhane). Like their southern counterparts, they controlled the ivory trade, which brought them guns, in turn making them more powerful. The

Batswana also established the *kgamelo* (bucket) system, which was based on lending herds of cattle to various headmen who in turn became servants of the *kgosi*. A system of *bolata* (servitude) was also instituted whereby conquered groups worked for the Batswana without pay.

The Bangwato emerged a powerful group between 1840 and 1885. The Bangwato exerted dominance over various other peoples in the area, including the Bakalanga, Batswapong, Babirwa, Bakaa, Bakhurutse, Bakgalagadi and Basarwa. The Bangwato also used the *kgamelo* system and conquered groups such as the Basarwa, who were subjected to slavery under a system of *bolata* (serfdom).

The Bangwato, having survived the attacks of the Amandebele and Bakololo, were, by 1840, involved in ivory trade with traders from the coast. Their capital, Shoshong, became an important commercial center linking the north with the south. Sekgoma I, then kgosi of the Bangwato, not only controlled his neighbors, but dominated the trade route. In the 1870s his son Khama III was baptized by the missionaries; he thereafter introduced Christian ideals among his people before he became kgosi in 1875.

P. T. MGADLA

Further Reading

Mackenzie, J. *Ten Years North of the Orange River* (1871). Reprint, Edinburgh: Edmonston and Douglass, 1971.

Morton, B. *Pre-Colonial Botswana: An Annotated Bibliography and Guide to Sources.* Gaborone: Botswana Society, 1994.

Morton, F., A. Murray, and J. Ramsay. *Historical Dictionary of Botswana.* London: Scarecrow Press Inc. 1989.

Tlou, T., and A. Campbell. *History of Botswana.* Gaborone, Botswana: Macmillan, 1997.

Botswana: Missionaries, Nineteenth Century

Protestant evangelical revivals spread across Europe in the late eighteenth century, resulting in the formation of mission societies dedicated to spreading Christianity to non-Christian lands. In Southern Africa, mission societies began proselytizing at the Cape from roughly 1800 onward, gradually extending their way ahead of formal imperial control into the interior. By the 1820s, the London Missionary Society (LMS) and the Wesleyan Methodist Missionary Society were working near the Orange River among the Thlaping and the Rolong, more southerly settled Tswana groups. Robert Moffat began work among the Thlaping in 1821. Missionaries from these societies forayed forth into what is today Botswana. Mission work there was disrupted by the *difaqane*, the internal skirmishes and fights that had origin in the chaos caused by European and Griqua slave-raiding as well as the northerly movement of Mzilikazi's Ndebele, fleeing from incorporation into the expanding Zulu state.

By the 1850s, the LMS had settled among the Ngwato, the Kwena, the Ngwaketse, and the Kgatla. Tswana chiefs invited missionaries to live with them with the intention of using missionaries as unpaid diplomatic aids (to negotiate for guns with the Cape and the Boer republics), but the result of such encounters was often very different from what these chiefs anticipated.

One of the first Tswana chiefdoms in Botswana to display an interest in missionaries was the Kwena, under their chief Sechele. Sechele had welcomed the LMS missionary David Livingstone's settlement near the Kwena capital in the 1840s, and through this connection had built up the Kwena supply of firearms to the extent that they were able to repel a Boer invasion from the Transvaal in 1852. In a bid to stave off further attacks from the Boer Republic to his east, Sechele acquired the services of five Hermannsburg Society missionaries in 1857, whom he hoped to use as diplomatic aids and as aids in the purchase of guns. However, the association of these missionaries with the Boers made them unpopular, and they left soon after.

Before leaving, the missionaries came into contact with some of the Ngwato royal family, in exile as a result of an internal coup during the late 1850s. Khama and his brother Kgamane, sons of the Ngwato chief Sekgoma, gained further exposure to Christianity during this period. When Sekgoma reasserted his control of the Ngwato chiefdom and returned to his capital city, Shoshong, he requested his own missionaries. In 1859 Heinrich Schulenburg, a German from the British colony of Natal, came to work among the Ngwato. In 1860 Khama was baptized, and in 1862 he and Gobitsamang Tshukudu were joined in first Christian marriage ceremony among the Ngwato, rejecting the bride chosen as part of Khama's previously arranged traditional marriage (Landau 1995, 12). In 1862 the Price and MacKenzie families arrived to become the first permanent LMS missionaries among the Ngwato. Under Khama, who promoted Christianity probably as much for material as spiritual reasons, the missionaries prospered and Christianity became more widespread, as greater numbers of people became adherents. Converts rejected Tswana customs and practices, causing rifts within the chiefdoms. In particular these occurred between Khama and his father, the former ultimately assuming rule over the Ngwato in 1875. This rule, which included Khama's promotion of Christianity, was to last until 1925. By this point Christianity, first brought by the missionaries, was well-established in Botswana.

Christianity and the missionaries brought the Ngwato into preeminence within Botswana. On the basis of a union forged between missionaries and the Ngwato, the latter established themselves as legitimate representatives of the Tswana to the British government when Botswana was annexed as the Bechuanaland Protectorate in 1885. Support for Ngwato policies and the promotion of Christianity came particularly from women.

This account of missionary influence in modern Botswana glosses over the cultural and ideological implications of missionary work. Missionaries to Africa have been described as agents of imperialism, encouraging the destabilization of African societies and their loss of independence to colonizing powers. More recently it has been suggested that this subordination was not only political, but cultural. According to John and Jean Comaroff (1991), exposure to missionaries and Western culture brought about the conversion of the Tswana in ways much more powerful than the extension of political overlordship. Africans were incorporated into a hegemonic European worldview, which ensured their collaboration with the project of modernity. This is believed to have resulted from the outlook and aims of missionaries, who believed not only in the necessity of Christianity but the superiority of European civilization, which they promoted assiduously.

The missionaries who settled among the Tswana believed that Africans were lost without the word of God and that it was their duty to bring Africans to an enlightened state. This was to be achieved through proselytizing and education. However, because they believed that African custom and social practice were detrimental to Christianity, that continual exposure to African ways of life would cause converts to regress, the missionaries were convinced that they would have to reeducate the Tswana in order for the seed of Christianity to flourish. This meant abandoning traditional rites and practices, social habits, and fundamental social renewal practices like those centered around marriage. In their place the Tswana were taught how to make European clothing, to practice agriculture instead of herding, and to build square houses. Moreover, they were introduced to a cash economy in which they could use agricultural surplus to buy the accoutrements of European life. This brought about the destruction of much of precolonial African society and its subordinate incorporation into a European system.

Africans, as is shown in the case of the Ngwato, adopted Christianity for what they could wrest from it spiritually and materially. Missionaries may have been deliberate or unwitting agents of imperialism, but some Tswana were able to shape the terms of their long conversation with missionaries, to ensure that they retained power even as colonialism was extended over the area.

NATASHA ERLANK

Further Reading

Comaroff, Jean and John. *Of Revelation and Revolution: Christianity, Colonialism and Consciousness in South Africa*, vol. 1. Chicago: University of Chicago Press, 1991.

Landau, Paul Stuart. *The Realm of the Word: Language, Gender and Christianity in a Southern African Kingdom*. Portsmouth, N.H.: Heinemann/London: James Currey, 1995.

Lye, William, and Colin Murray. *Transformations on the Highveld: The Tswana and the Southern Sotho*. Cape Town: David Philip, 1980.

Shillington, Kevin. *The Colonisation of the Southern Tswana 1870–1900*. Johannesburg: Ravan, 1985.

Wilmsen, Edwin, and James Denbow. "Paradigmatic History of San-speaking Peoples and Current Attempts at Revision." *Current Anthropology* 31, no. 5 (1990): 489–524.

Botswana: Bechuanaland Protectorate, Founding of: 1885–1899

The state of Botswana, as it is today defined territorially, originated as the Bechuanaland Protectorate, established in 1885. At the time of its founding, the protectorate was occupied by eight main Tswana chiefdoms: the Kgatla, Kwena, Lete, Ngwaketse, Ngwato, Tshidi-Rolong, Tawana, and Tlokwa. The establishment of the protectorate has to be seen in the context of the late-nineteenth-century European "Scramble" for Africa. In this case, four main external forces came to bear on Tswana territory at that time: British imperialism, Boer expansionism, German imperialism, and the expansionist drive of Cecil Rhodes.

From the late 1870s on there had been a period of instability in Tswana territory south of the Molopo River, which was to become the southern boundary of the protectorate. Divisions between Tswana chiefs were exploited and fueled by Boer freebooters from the Transvaal in search of new land. These freebooters formed alliances with particular chiefs and established two minirepublics in southern Tswana territory. The British government became alarmed in 1884 when Germany's declaration of a protectorate over southern Namibia presented the threatening prospect of German territory linking up with the Transvaal across Bechuanaland. The British intervened; in 1884 they declared a protectorate over Tswana territory south of the Molopo, and early in 1885 they dispatched a military expedition under General Charles Warren to drive away the Boer freebooters. In September 1885, the British extended the protectorate across a large area north of the Molopo, bounded by the Limpopo River in the east, the German protectorate in the west. In 1890, in agreement with Germany, Britain further extended the protectorate as far as the Chobe River in the north. Two Tswana chiefs, Khama of the Ngwato and Gaseitsiwe of the Ngwaketse, initially welcomed the establishment of the Bechuanaland Protectorate, seeing the British presence as protection against external threats from Transvaal Boers and from the Ndebele to the northeast.

After the gold discoveries on the Rand in 1886, the protectorate became a focus of attention for mineral prospectors. The search for a "second Rand" brought to the protectorate adventurers who believed that the Johannesburg gold reef might stretch westward and northward. From 1887 on, all the main Tswana chiefs in the protectorate sold mineral, land, and trading concessions to a number of these adventurers. These concessions mostly turned out to be worthless. Some concessionaires would be bought out by Cecil Rhodes and the British South Africa Company (BSAC), while other concessions were eventually disallowed by the British imperial government.

In this context of imperial expansion and increasing mineral exploitation in southern Africa, the status and future of the protectorate became a matter for discussion and contestation in the late 1880s and early 1890s. There were those like the missionary, John Mackenzie, and the British high commissioner, Sir Henry Loch, who wanted the protectorate to become a full-fledged British colony. (Protectorate status stopped short of this, allowing local chiefdoms a fair degree of autonomy.) For Rhodes the protectorate also held an important place in his expansionist ambitions. He saw the territory as an important artery: "the Suez Canal into the interior," he called it. In Rhodes's grandiose Cape-to-Cairo vision the protectorate was the gateway to the north, but in the shorter term the protectorate was also to serve as a stepping-stone for Rhodes. The BSAC's pioneer column (an expedition of white settlers that moved into Mashonaland in 1890) used Ngwato territory as a starting point. Three years later the company launched an aggressive, but risky, invasion of Lobengula's Ndebele kingdom. A supporting invasion by an imperial force from the protectorate created a second front, weakening the defensive capacity of the Ndebele.

In the meantime, the future status of the protectorate remained a matter of dispute in the early 1890s. Loch continued to push for imperial annexation. Rhodes demanded that the territory be transferred to the BSAC. The Tswana chiefs, however, were implacably opposed to a takeover by the company. In 1895 three chiefs, Khama, Sebele (the Kwena chief), and Bathoen (the Ngwaketse chief), went to Britain to voice their opposition to such a takeover. A deal was struck in November 1895: Khama, Sebele, and Bathoen would retain a large degree of autonomy under continuing imperial protection, but would also give up to the BSAC a narrow strip of territory on their eastern border as well as a vast swath of territory in the western and northern regions of the protectorate. The eastern strip was handed over for the ostensible purpose of railway construction. The real, immediate reason for the transfer was to provide Rhodes with a base for an invasion of the Transvaal. Within two months of the transfer, Leander Starr Jameson embarked upon his ignominious raid into Kruger's Transvaal republic

from his base at Pitsane in the protectorate, only to suffer a humiliating defeat at the hands of the Boers on January 2, 1896. The Jameson Raid wrecked Rhodes's political career, but ironically also spared the northern Tswana from the fate that had befallen the Shona and Ndebele. After the raid the British government abandoned the transfer of a large area of the protectorate to the company, so the Tswana were not to be swallowed up in a Rhodesian-type colony of white settlement.

Colonialism brought virtually no benefits to the northern Tswana in the last 15 years of the nineteenth century. Protectorate status was supposed to preserve the autonomy of the eight Tswana chiefdoms in the protectorate. In practice, though, the small British administration in the protectorate constantly interfered in the chiefdoms' internal affairs. The head of that administration from 1885 to 1895, Sir Sidney Shippard, was an authoritarian figure who expected the chiefs "to obey the Government in all things lawful." So the British administration intervened in dynastic disputes, limited the jurisdiction of Tswana courts, and overrode the right of chiefs to sell concessions to prospectors and other entrepreneurs. In 1899 the imperial administration arbitrarily demarcated reserves for the eight chiefdoms, and imposed a 10-shilling "hut tax" on all homesteads in the protectorate.

The administration was also concerned to keep colonial expenditure in the protectorate to a minimum. There was therefore no provision for expenditure on welfare or development during these years. Education and health were not deemed to be government responsibilities. The BSAC did oversee the extension of the railway from Vryburg to Bulawayo during the years 1896–1897, but this had the effect of undermining the local carrying trade. The last four years of the century were particularly difficult for the protectorate's inhabitants: about 90 per cent of cattle herds were lost in the rinderpest epidemic of the 1890s; this was followed by three years of drought and locust invasions.

Between 1885 and 1899, the protectorate was treated essentially as a kind of imperial appendage. It was viewed as an important artery for imperial expansion to the north. It was used as a launchpad for aggressive, expansionist colonial ventures. Imperial "protection" brought little to the northern Tswana except for irksome interference in their internal affairs and neglect of their economic interests

PAUL MAYLAM

See also: **Khama III; Rinderpest and Smallpox: East and Southern Africa.**

Further Reading

Maylam, P. *Rhodes, the Tswana, and the British*. Westport, Conn.: Greenwood Press, 1980.

Morton, F., Andrew Murray, and Jeff Ramsay. *Historical Dictionary of Botswana*. Metuchen, N.J.: Scarecrow Press, 1989.

Sillery, A. *Botswana: A Short Political History*. London: Methuen, 1974.

———. *Founding a Protectorate*. Paris: Mouton, 1965.

Tlou, T., and A. Campbell. *History of Botswana*. Gaborone, Botswana: Macmillan, 1984.

Botswana (Bechuanaland Protectorate): Colonial Period

Before the 1885 imposition of colonial rule, three types of Europeans had a major impact on Botswana: traders, missionaries, and Boers. Trade had existed with the Boers at the Cape and the Portuguese stations of coastal Angola and Mozambique since the early eighteenth century. Game products, including ivory, ostrich feathers, and skins, were traded over long distances and sold for guns and other goods from Asia, the Americas, and Europe. The London Missionary Society (LMS) sent missionaries as early as 1816 to work among the southern Batswana, but it wasn't until 1822 that Robert Moffat visited Kgosi Makaba II of the Bangwaketse to establish the first permanent mission. The famous explorer and missionary David Livingstone started the first church and school in Botswana at Kolobeng in 1845.

European contacts remained infrequent except for those of the South African Boers, who seized land from the Batswana for grazing cattle. The Batswana peoples traded for guns and combined their military strength to resist Boer incursions into their lands. Under the excellent leadership of Kgosi Sechele I, the Botswana were repeatedly able to drive the Boers back to the South African Republics in 1852 and 1853. In January 1853, a peace agreement was signed between the Batswana and the Boers.

Relations between the two groups remained tense for many years, due to border disputes and cattle raiding. Between 1882 and 1884 there were conflicts among the southern Batswana and Transvaal mercenaries; but the British administrators at Cape Town were not prepared to militarily intervene, following their withdrawal from the Transvaal in 1881. In 1885, the British unilaterally proclaimed the Bechuanaland Protectorate to counter Germany's occupation of Namibia and the growing infiltration of German soldiers, traders, and missionaries into Ngamiland. Ngamiland's wildlife resources, especially elephants, were abundant due to the Okavango River that flows into the region and forms a large delta. The Batswana peoples had conquered the region and consolidated their military power by selling ivory for guns and horses. Kgosi Moremi signed two mining concessions with British traders in the late 1880s, which led to Britain's successful bid for the region in 1890.

The British colonization of southern Batswana began with the 1871 annexation of territory containing the newly discovered diamond fields in and around Kimberly, South Africa. Recognizing that the mineral discoveries would lead to greater white settlement near the border, the Batswana formed another confederation to counter Boer raids on cattleposts inside Botswana. When Kgosi Khama of the Bangwato peoples asked for British support in keeping the Boers out of his territory, the British led an expedition to the region under the leadership of Charles Warren. Warren's main task was the enforcement of land promises made by Cecil Rhodes to the Boers, not the protection of Batswana interests. By May 1886 a British land commission, chaired by Rhodes's close associate Sidney Shippard, had robbed the Batswana living south of the Molopo of 92 per cent of their land. Shippard, who became known as *morena maaka* (lord of lies), was then appointed as Bechuanaland's administrator.

Meanwhile, the British government decided to end any possibility of a link between German Namibia and the Transvaal by extending the Bechuanaland Protectorate north of the Molopo River to include the southern half of Botswana. In March 1885, Warren was instructed to communicate this development to the Batswana leadership. Most Batswana *dikgosi* (chiefs) objected to colonial rule, especially Sechele and his son Sebele of the Bakwena. Khama had been convinced by the LMS missionary, John Mackenzie, that the British presence was a good thing and, despite Bangwato opposition, offered extensive lands for British settlement.

Fortunately, the British government accepted its South African high commissioner's conclusion that "as to the country north of the Molopo River. . . . it appears to me that we have no interest in it, except as a road to the interior." Subsequently, the British government refused the offer of settler land and ordered that the chiefs should rule over their own peoples. The British presence north of the Molopo would be limited to occasional police patrols and very limited settlement and administration. The Molopo River was the administrative dividing line; the lands south of the river became part of the colony of British Bechuanaland, which was later incorporated into South Africa. The Bechuanaland Protectorate north of the Molopo survived to become Botswana.

Before 1890, the British interfered little in the rule of the dikgosi. Thereafter they gradually began to introduce a system of indirect rule. Under this system, colonial officials ruled through the dikgosi, who were no longer free to run their own affairs without interference. The reason for the change was that Botswana became a base from which British imperialism could expand northward into central Africa. In October 1889 Queen Victoria issued Rhodes's British South African Company (BSAC) a royal charter to administer Botswana and Central Africa in the name of the British crown. In 1890 despite overriding local objections, the British granted themselves the right to exercise colonial control over Botswana through the Foreign Jurisdictions Act. The protectorate was also extended to Ngamiland and the Chobe River region in the north.

Meanwhile the growing power of the BSAC began to threaten the independence of the Batswana rulers and their ability to manage their own affairs under crown protection. Rhodes wanted to control all of southern Africa to exploit its rich mineral wealth in diamonds and gold. In order to accomplish his dream of complete dominance in the region, he needed to acquire administrative control of Botswana. In July 1895 the Batswana sent petitions to London against BSAC rule.

Three paramount chiefs, Bathoen, Khama and Sebele, decided to take their merafe's cases directly to the British government and people. They traveled to Britain, speaking in 40 English towns and cities. Queen Victoria granted them an audience and promised them continued protection against BSAC capitalist exploitation. The dikgosi left Britain with the belief that their territories were safe from Rhodes. However, important friends of Rhodes were strategically placed in the Colonial Office, and they plotted to take over Bathoen and Sebele's domains. The colonial secretary had also given Rhodes permission to go ahead and invade the Transvaal, because Paul Kruger was becoming a threat to Great Britain's control of gold mining in southern Africa.

Rhodes hired a mercenary by the name of Dr. L. S. Jameson to organize an armed force to overthrow Kruger's Transvaal Republic. Jameson invaded on the night of December 29, 1895, from Botswana, while British expatriates in Johannesburg were supposed to lead an uprising there. The rebellion was disorganized and failed due to poor leadership and planning. The Jameson Raid resulted in a huge international scandal and dashed Rhodes's plans for a takeover in Botswana. Four years after the Jameson Raid, war broke out between the British and Boer Republics in South Africa. The protectorate played a small but key role in the Anglo-Boer War by guarding the railway and border positions and working in British army camps.

The leaders of the Boers and the British met from 1908 until 1909 to discuss the formation of a new united state. In 1910 the Union of South Africa was formed as a self-governing state under the British monarch. The result of the formation of the Union for Africans was the loss of all their political rights, a development watched closely by fearful eyes in Botswana. The dikgosi knew that the South Africa Act, establishing the union, provided for the eventual incorporation of the three High Commission Territories of Bechuanaland, Swaziland, and Lesotho.

Over time, British administrative reforms in the protectorate reduced the powers of the dikgosi. The resident commissioners interfered in local politics and rarely listened to the African Advisory council's recommendations. In 1943, new proclamations restored some of the powers that the dikgosi had lost in 1934. The Botswana rulers were given limited jurisdiction in their own areas. Britain neglected the development of Bechuanaland for fifty years.

Such development that took place, whether political, economic, or social, occurred after World War II, with grants-in-aid from the Colonial Development and Welfare Fund. The war had an enormous impact on the protectorate in many ways. The dikgosi supported the British war effort with 10,000 men, food and money. After the conflict, growing nationalism in Africa encouraged the Batswana to unite for their freedom.

The Bechuanaland's People's Party (BPP) was formed in 1960 by Motsami Mpho and K. T. Motsete at the time when Britain was introducing constitutional changes through the Legislative Council. The BPP spoke out against white rule and demanded immediate independence. The Bechuanaland Democratic Party (BDP) was formed in 1961 by Seretse Khama and other educated leaders who stressed multiracialism for a better Botswana. Elections were held in March 1965, on the basis of the new constitution of 1963. The BDP, which had become a very strong, well-organized party, won the election with a large majority, taking 28 of the 31 seats in the National Assembly. Seretse Khama became the prime minister of the country's first African government.

DEBORAH SCHMITT

See also: **Jameson Raid, Origins of South African War: 1895–1899.**

Further Reading

Morton, Fred, and Jeff Ramsay (eds.). *The Birth of Botswana: A History of the Bechuanaland Protectorate from 1910 to 1966.* Gaborone, Botswana: Longman, 1987.

Parsons, Neil. *King Khama Emperor Joe and the Great White Queen.* Chicago: University of Chicago Press, 1998.

Ramsay, Jeff, Barry Morton, and T. Mgadla. *Building a Nation: A History of Botswana from 1800 to 1910.* Gaborone, Botswana: Longman, 1996.

Tlou, Thomas, and Alec Campbell. *History of Botswana.* Gaborone, Botswana: Macmillan, 1999.

Botswana: Independence: Economic Development, Politics

Prior to independence in 1966, Botswana was neglected to a degree unusual even in colonial Africa. The Act of Union of 1909 said that the three High Commission Territories (Basutoland, Bechuanaland, and Swaziland) would eventually be incorporated into the Union of South Africa. Britain therefore did very little for Bechuanaland; and South Africa did nothing because Bechuanaland was considered British. Britain did, however, refuse to allow incorporation, despite considerable pressure from the government of South Africa.

Botswana therefore inherited almost nothing in 1966 and was then one of the poorest countries in the world. Until just before independence the country had no capital city, having been governed from Mafeking in South Africa; there were just a few kilometers of tarred road; and in 1965, only 27 students had graduated from five years of secondary education.

The country was entirely surrounded until 1980 by hostile white-ruled states, apart from a theoretical pinpoint boundary with Zambia that was not acknowledged by the governments of Rhodesia or South Africa. The new government was dependent on British aid for half of the recurrent budget. On the other hand, ethnically and linguistically the population was relatively homogeneous, and the first president, Seretse Khama, was well-educated, having studied at Oxford and in London. A tradition of pragmatic diplomacy, to which the country owed its existence, was carried forward after independence into both foreign and economic policy.

The discovery of mineral deposits (copper and nickel at Selebi-Phikwe and diamonds at Orapa) made rapid economic growth possible. In addition, beef exports gained access to Europe at prices above those from other parts of the world, Botswana's sources of aid were diversified, and renegotiation of the Southern Africa Customs Union (SACU) increased Botswana's customs revenue. The copper and nickel mine was never profitable, but the government's share of large diamond profits, from the three mines eventually developed, generated a surplus on the recurrent budget in 1973 and on the development budget in 1984. By the 1990s, Botswana was the world's largest producer by value of gem diamonds. Financial surpluses continued in most years thereafter. As a consequence, the government accumulated balances equivalent to two years' spending, and foreign exchange reserves equivalent to three years' imports.

Botswana avoided the problems of other mineral boom economies. Government expenditure took account of the scarcity of skilled manpower and the government's own capacity to manage public spending. The result was not only rapid economic growth (Botswana's economy was bound to grow rapidly), but rapid growth of employment and considerable diversification of the economy. Employment growth did stop in the first half of the 1990s but resumed thereafter.

From the time of independence, the Botswana government handled relations with its white-ruled neighbors in a pragmatic way. Permission was sought and granted from the United Nations for Botswana not to apply sanctions to Rhodesia, although despite this there were security problems until the Rhodesian war for independence ended in 1980. Botswana offered sanctuary to refugees, but did not allow military training or military bases to be established. Again, this was not sufficient to prevent a number of military raids across the border from South Africa during the 1980s. Trade, however, was not seriously affected.

Botswana has been a multiparty democracy throughout the postindependence period, with elections every five years. For many years, the ruling Botswana Democratic Party held all but 3 or 4 seats out of approximately 30 in the country's parliament. The opposition achieved majorities in the main town councils, and came to hold most of the urban parliamentary seats, winning 14 out of 40 seats in the enlarged parliament in the 1994 election. As the country had moved from being 4 per cent to 50 per cent urban, it would appear that the opposition might have done even better and for the future to be on its side. However, it split badly between 1994 and 1999, when the election was contested by some 14 parties.

Although there was no change of ruling party arising from elections, there have to date been three peaceful changes of president. Sir Seretse Khama was succeeded on his death in 1980 by his vice president, Sir Ketumile Masire, who chose to retire in 1998. He was succeeded by the then vice president, Festus Mogae; Mogae's vice president is Ian Khama, who was formerly head of the Botswana Defense Force (BDF), and is the eldest son of Seretse Khama.

Botswana played a leading part in the creation of the Southern African Development Community (SADC). In the 1990s, SADC members were divided on a number of political issues, and attempts to establish a SADC free-trade area were subject to delays. Nevertheless, the SADC continued to be active in settling regional political issues, in which Botswana played a part, for example, contributing to troops brought into Lesotho by the SADC in 1998. The BDF also contributed to peacekeeping forces elsewhere in Africa.

Most of Botswana's other international trading agreements were in a state of uncertainty in the late 1990s. The SACU was in the process of renegotiation; South Africa had agreed to free trade with the European Union, which would result in reductions in customs union revenue and in the level of protection of SACU producers; the Lomé agreement was due for renegotiation and was not expected to continue substantially unchanged as previously; and a further global round of World Trade Organization negotiations was imminent. On the other hand, all of Botswana's neighbors were ruled by democratically elected governments, with which Botswana had normal diplomatic relations.

Both the economic and the strategic position of Botswana had therefore been transformed for the better since 1966. However, the period of diamond-led growth was coming to an end, and the economy could not depend indefinitely on further rapid growth of government spending. Future economic growth, and growth of employment, depended therefore on Botswana being able to attract foreign investment in such sectors as manufacturing, financial services, and tourism. Unusually, Botswana did not necessarily need the inflow of income, but did need scarce skilled management resources and access to foreign markets.

CHARLES HARVEY

Further Reading

Brothers, S., J. Hermans, and D. Nteta (eds.). *Botswana in the 21st Century*. Gaborone, Botswana: Botswana Society, 1994.

Colclough, C., and S. McCarthy. *The Political Economy of Botswana*. Oxford: Oxford University Press, 1980.

Edge, W. A. and M. H. Lekorwe (eds.). *Botswana: Politics and Society*. Pretoria: J. L. van Schaik, 1998.

Government of Botswana. *National Development Plans 1968, 1970, 1973, 1976, 1979, 1985, 1991*, and *1997*. Gaborone, Botswana: Government Printer, various years.

Government of Botswana, *Transitional Plan for Social and Economic Development*. Gaborone, Botswana: Government Printer, 1966.

Harvey, C., and S. R. Lewis Jr. *Policy Choice and Development Performance in Botswana*. Basingstoke, England: Macmillan, 1990.

Salkin, J. S., D. Mpabanga, D. Cowan, J. Selwe, and M. Wright (eds.). *Aspects of the Botswana Economy: Selected Papers*. Gaborone, Botswana: Lentswe La Lesedi/ Oxford: James Currey, 1997.

Boundaries, Colonial

During the nineteenth century, Europeans who had established colonies on the African coast found it increasingly necessary to define territorial boundaries. These would justify their claims to exercise jurisdiction over property rights in the territories of African neighbors and, more particularly, to collect customs duties from persons trading on neighboring coasts. Though many such claims were asserted unilaterally, more often they were based upon treaties with African rulers—who may or may not have understood the implications of the claims to which they assented. But beyond the coastline, boundaries were rarely defined. For example, one British Sherbro treaty of 1861 referred to territory extending "about thirty miles inland."

Since treaties with Africans did not automatically receive international recognition, European governments also increasingly made treaties among themselves. In the European peace treaties of 1783 and 1815, France and Britain attempted to allocate broad spheres of territorial and commercial interests in Senegambia; and as international rivalry intensified during the nineteenth century they made unsuccessful moves toward a comprehensive partition of the wider West African region. But increasingly there were bitter local disputes over points of commercial access, which could only be resolved by detailed bilateral agreements. By the time the Berlin Act of 1885 attempted to regulate such procedures, almost all the West African coast was already allocated by such treaties.

From about 1889 imperialist pressures in Europe led colonial governments to extend their ambitions from the coasts to the interior of Africa. During the 1890s, disputes over African territory became increasingly frequent and bitter; nevertheless, all were eventually resolved by bilateral agreements. The British Foreign Office collected and published these in an authoritative compendium entitled *Map of Africa by Treaty*.

The new boundary lines were drawn by negotiators meeting in Europe, remote from African realities. They did take advice from their colonial colleagues, and sometimes tried to respect the territorial integrity of African polities with which treaties of protection had been signed. More often the diplomats were concerned with making some rough allocation of territory and resources that the colonial lobbies in each country would find acceptable. Working with limited knowledge of African topography, and still less of human geography, they sometimes decided on the line of a river, or alternatively a watershed. Convenient though such identifiable features might seem, they did not always respect existing trade routes or settlement patterns. Many boundaries were drawn, with thick pencils, along lines of latitude or longitude, in hope that these would prove capable of objective survey. For diplomats, even such arbitrary lines were preferable to uncertainty. There was a tiny safeguard for rationality in the subsequent demarcation commissions, where surveyors laying down boundary posts were authorized to recommend minor deviations in accordance with "ethnological divisions." But even these proved politically contentious; substantive revisions of the initial boundaries, as in the Anglo-French Entente of 1904, were extremely rare. The major exception was the repartition of the German colonial empire, under mandate, in 1919.

Other colonial boundaries were unilaterally defined, and sometimes redefined, within a single recognized sphere of colonial influence. As the British empire in South Africa expanded and was reordered, three countries where British authority rested on treaties of protection—Basutoland, Bechuanaland, and Swaziland—retained their own identities, within historic boundaries. By orders in council, the British government also fixed the borders between the two Rhodesias and Nyasaland, and those with their South African neighbors. Similarly, French statutory instruments, motivated largely by administrative convenience, defined boundaries between the eight constituent colonies of Afrique Occidentale Française, and the four colonies of Afrique Equatoriale Française. In the case of Upper Volta (now Burkina Faso), France successively created, dissolved, and reconstituted an entire colonial entity. Regional and provincial boundaries of significance were also redefined within such colonies as Nigeria.

The impact on African populations of the colonial boundaries that were thus more or less arbitrarily imposed upon them varied considerably. The negative effects were at first most obvious. Virtually every borderline cut across some bonds of kinship, culture, and language, or threatened to impede the movement of persons and commodities along established routes. Colonial states incorporated diverse communities that might previously have had little in common, and imposed on them new laws, new taxes, and an alien language of government. Historically, few African boundaries could be represented by lines on maps, even mental ones; rather, they had identified populations as members or dependents of the same political authority, and legitimized obligations and payments which visiting strangers might be required to incur at points of entry to their territory. Colonial frontiers imposed territorial divisions unprecedented in their precision and rigidity, reducing communities that had formerly been accommodated as strangers to the new and vulnerable status of political minorities.

With time, however, colonial boundaries might come to seem more tolerable. Most of them proved easily permeable, too long and difficult for effective policing. The differences in tariff regime and fiscal policy which they were intended to enforce offered new opportunities to African entrepreneurs (or smugglers, in the eye of the authorities). Except where intimate relationships with close kinsfolk or traditional trading partners had been impeded, local communities often remained indifferent to political attempts to revive or construct wider tribal identities across the borders. Whether out of self-interest or habit, even African patriots gradually acquired new attachments to their own colonial masters. Although Pan-African idealists spoke of reversing the partition and redrawing boundaries after independence, this did not happen to any significant degree. Too many interests were now involved in maintaining new state identities. In 1963 the Organization of African Unity judged it prudent to guarantee the sovereignty and territorial integrity of each member-state. Since then the management of boundary disputes and cross-border relationships has been a major concern of African diplomacy.

JOHN D. HARGREAVES

See also: **Colonial European Administrations: Comparative Survey; Colonialism: Ideology of Empire: Colonialism: Impact on African Societies.**

Further Reading

Anene, J. C. *The International Boundaries of Nigeria*. London: Longman, 1970.

Asiwaju, A. I. *Artificial Boundaries. New York*: Civiletis International, 1990.

———. (ed.). *Partitioned Africans: Ethnic Relations across Africa's International Boundaries 1884–1984*. London: C. Hurst, 1985.

Brownlie, I., with I. R. Burns (eds.). *African Boundaries: A Legal and Diplomatic Encyclopaedia*. London: C. Hurst, 1979.

Hertalet, E. *Map of Africa by Treaty*, 3rd ed., three vols. (1909). Reprint, London: Frank Cass, 1967.

McEwen, A. C. *International Boundaries of East Africa*. Oxford: Clarendon Press, 1971.

Bourbon, Ile de France, Seychelles: Eighteenth Century

These Indian Ocean islands were known to Arab, Portuguese, British, and Dutch seamen of the sixteenth and early seventeenth centuries, but they were unpopulated until the 1640s, when a handful of Frenchmen from India and their slaves occupied Bourbon (Réunion). From here in the early eighteenth century French families, settling on the heels of the departed Dutch (1638–1710) from their Mauritius, turned Bourbon's companion island into Ile de France. Seychelles, which was explored in the 1740s, had to wait until 1770 to receive its own small complement of French settlers and slaves.

For Bourbon, coffee was the major agricultural export staple of the eighteenth century when aristocratic or *soi-disant* aristocratic families like those of the Bourbon-born poets Antoine de Bertin and Evariste-Desire de Forge de Parny built Indian-inspired mansions in timber or stone; the coffee dried on the flat roofs of the verandas. Cotton served Ile de de France and Seychelles, with Ile de France's stone-built Le Reduit reckoned a miniature tropical Versailles, though it was built inland between two ravines for defense against the British.

Ile de France and Seychelles, with their fine harbors so much safer for shipping than Bourbon's exposed roads, were directly attuned to world trade in peace and war, as calling points first for the Compagnie des Indes, which administered Ile de France and Bourbon, and then for the king's ships when the company retreated, and always for privateers. At the same time, a considerable proportion of ships were likely to be slavers from Mozambique, Zanzibar, and Madagascar, because these islands' worlds paralleled the Antillean slave-based world, under local interpretation of the Code Noire set out in letters patent of 1685 and 1723. The use of whips, iron collars, and heavy chains was in vogue as a matter of law and course. And equally as a matter of course, slaves were running away from the time of the beginning of the islands' settlement. In one early case on Bourbon, the cause was ascribed to quarrels between Frenchmen and slaves over a particularly beautiful Malagasy slave woman, which serves as a pointer to the appearance of populations of color. These were discriminated against in all islands, despite often being slaveowners themselves.

Human frailty was reckoned particularly visible among slaves who, if Malagasy, always seemed to be pining for their lost homeland. "They are very fond of nocturnal excursions, either to gratify their gallantry, or to pilfer from their neighbours," which necessarily meant that "I frequently rise in the night to see if they are in their huts," explained Charles Grant de Vaux, a 1740s soldier-settler in Ile de France from Normandy. And on the eve of the revolution itself, the virtuous lovers in Jacques-Henri Bernardin de St. Pierre's popular romance *Paul et Virginie* lived in Ile de France, outside its corrupted white society, but were nonetheless expected to have many slaves of their own.

The dodo was hunted to extinction in Ile de France, and timber in all the islands was being rapidly removed by fire and axe by 1800, even though it was remembered how Madeira had burned disastrously for seven years and conservation laws had been passed to prevent it here. Cinnamon, which the famous botanist Pierre Poivre had sent for planting on the Seychelles' main island of Mahé, eventually covered the mountain slopes after timber was cut there when the first settlers set a pattern of despoiling the place. Here an attempt at more tightly regulated colonization broke down, with settlers immediately requiring all the privileges assumed by Creole (meaning locally born) French people on these islands. A fruitless attempt was made to keep the free Indian Ramalinga family out of Seychelles. If Seychelles in the end became more relaxed than Ile de France and Bourbon, this was no fault of the major *grand blanc* families; and if one of the first signs appeared as early as 1785 when a Breton married a part-Malagasy girl, the reason was that she was heiress to land and slaves acquired more by despoiling the environment than by planting.

While Seychelles refreshed slave ships and Bourbon became a spice garden worked laboriously by the hoe, Ile de France, with its own expanding sugar plantations, still looked very much to the sea in the 1790s with its overseas merchants reckoned to have run into the hundreds, and its privateers legendary. Robert Surcouf, most famous of privateers, and unlike his brother and many others never captured by the Royal Navy, had started here in the slave trade. Under British blockade the island was kept alive by neutral Danes and Americans carrying off British prized goods.

All the time, from the outbreak of the revolution, Ile de France and Bourbon, too, with their relatively crowded port towns, were desperate to keep out overseas news like that of the Saint Domingue slave revolt and the National Convention's abolition of slavery; they were also efficient in hunting down any individual, whether free man or slave, whose language or demeanor indicated willingness to take revolutionary tenets about the rights of humankind seriously. Avowed Jacobins hunted down maroons even while the Colonial Assembly of Ile de France attempted to reduce the severity with which maroons might be treated. The threat of abolition in 1794—said the Assembly of Bourbon—meant that "everyone saw escaping fro his hands the feeble bonds still controlling the stupid and ferocious Africans." Colonial institutions involving those—in fact very strong—bonds actually survived revolutionary fervor as Paris attempted to impose it in the 1790s, were strengthened under the Empire, and, in Bourbon's case, were reckoned to have been vindicated (during that period of 1810–1815 when Bourbon was occupied by a British garrison that was determined to put down the slave trade) by the St. Leu slave revolt of 1811.

DERYCK SCARR

See also: **Mascarene Islands Prior to the French; Mauritius.**

Further Reading

De Vaux, C. G. *The History of Mauritius, or the Isle of France*. London, 1801.
———. *Slaving and Slavery in the Indian Ocean*. Basingstoke, England: Macmillan/New York: St. Martin's Press, 1998.
Scarr, D. *Seychelles since 1770: A Slave and Post-slavery Society*. London: C. Hurst, 1999.

Bourguiba: *See* **Tunisia: Bourguiba, Presidency of: Economic and Social Change; Tunisia: Bourguiba, Presidency of: Government and Opposition.**

Brazzaville

The site where Brazzaville emerged as the capital of French Equatorial Africa in 1910 was long held by the Teke as a trade center. Ncouna, as it came to be known when it was ceded in 1880 by the Teke *makoko* (king) to French explorer Pierre Savorgnan de Brazza, was only one of many thriving villages on the two banks of the River Congo. Its location was highly strategic for the Teke, as well as for the French, who evicted the Teke soon after the French post of Ncouna was established.

After its long course of almost 1,000 miles from its source in southeastern Zaïre, the Congo River curves westward across the equator for some 700 miles, then bends again southward across the equator and flows toward the Atlantic. Before rushing to the sea in a succession of cascades and rapids, through rock gorges that compress the water into fast-moving chutes of white foam, the powerful river bulges out to make Pool Malebo, an expanse so huge that it contains dozens of islands, including the island M'Bamou, 20 kilometers long and 10 kilometers across. Pool Malebo had been a prosperous and bustling region before the French and the Belgian presence. Sources point to the economic, political, and demographic importance of the area centuries before the colonial penetration and the founding of Brazzaville and its Belgian counterpart, Leopoldville, on the left bank.

In 1884, the Italian-born French explorer Savorgtnan de Brazza was honored for his efforts to give France a foothold in the region when the Geographical Society of Paris decided to name the French post at Pool Malebo after the Italian-born explorer. From then on, Brazzaville grew out mostly as an administrative center with little economic vocation, especially when compared to its twin, Kinshasa, across the river. Indeed, colonial Brazzaville, sometimes referred to as Brazza la verte, developed in the shadow of its rival twin, which the Belgians promoted as the most prosperous and bustling city in central Africa. Brazzavillians who flocked across the river either to work, to visit relatives, or to attend cultural events were amazed at the modern look of Kinshasa and the enviable social status of its African elite. In December 1903, Brazzaville became capital of the French Congo and, in 1910, capital of French Equatorial Africa (FEA). Its growing political vocation had General Charles de Gaulle name Brazzaville the capital of La France Libre (Free France), on October 27, 1940, after the Germans had occupied France.

Under French colonization, Brazzaville added to its administrative role to become a center of cultural creativity. There, in 1944, in the multiethnic neighborhood of Poto-Poto, was established the first "bar dancing," Chez Backer, which catered to the growing population of young blue-collar workers. At least 50 more such "bar-dancings" would proliferate in Brazzaville alone before independence, the most famous being Chez Faignon (founded in 1948), located also in Poto-Poto. Young male (mostly the urban educated elite) and female patrons used these strategic spaces not only for entertainment centered around dancing, eating, drinking, and socialization but also for subversion. In the 1950s, these "bar-dancings" housed the first political meetings and served as informal headquarters for several political parties.

During the 1930s, a variety of sports (soccer, basketball, volleyball and track and field) developed in Brazzaville under the aegis of the Catholic missionaries and the colonial government. The growing interest of Brazzaville's youth in sports prompted the French to build, in 1946, one the largest stadiums ever built in French colonial Africa, next to the Sainte-Anne Cathedral of Poto-Poto. The stadium was named after Felix Eboué, a black French native of Guyana who assumed the governorship of FEA in 1940 after he rallied de Gaulle's Free France.

In 1951 an art school was also founded—the Poto-Poto School of African Art—under the auspices of French painter Pierre Lods. Aspiring artists worked freely, producing both romanticized and traditional paintings, which became very popular in the major cities of FEA, catering mostly to the tourist market.

Up until the early 1990s, a substantial proportion of Congolese lived in Brazzaville: around 110,000 at independence and an estimated 937,000 in 1992, which represented more than one-third of the Congolese population. The end of the one-state party regime that held the country in a tight grip under the banner of scientific socialism heralded a new era of prosperity in Congo's largest city, with an influx of Congolese repatriated businessmen, artists, and college graduates who came back from abroad (mostly from France) with fresh ideas and capital. However, starting in 1993, the country was plunged into recurrent violent political conflicts between ethnopolitical factions that created militia groups to serve as private armies to the country's three main leaders. In the 1990s, an entrenched militia culture developed in the country's capital, fueled by widespread unemployment and a sense of hopelessness among the city's large youth population that played in the hands of power-driven political leaders. Brazzaville was the site of the latest conflict when, in June 1997, government forces attempted to disarm former president Denis Sassou-Nguesso's militia before the presidential elections. The five-month civil war that ensued, opposing Sassou's militia (the Cobras) against president Pascal Lissouba's and his prime minister Bernard Kolélas's forces (known respectively as the Cocoyes and the Ninjas), was marked by the use of heavy artillery that left Brazzaville totally destroyed. Over 10,000 people (mostly civilians) were reported dead, and hundreds of thousands fled Brazzaville to seek refuge in the villages in the interior or across the river to neighboring Kinshasa, reducing the population to less than 200,000. Ironically, the only building in Brazzaville spared by the bombing was the French embassy, which only sustained a single hit and was later looted by Sassou's militiamen when they entered Brazzaville, triumphant, in October 1997.

Today, Brazzaville resembles more a ghost town than the bustling and attractive metropolis it once was.

Insecurity linked to the ravages by militiamen; food shortages; and massive destruction and looting of private homes and public infrastructures still prevent people who have fled from returning. Most of Brazzaville's wards, especially the southern neighborhoods of Bacongo and Makelekele (where most southerners used to reside), have yet to recover from heavy damage before normal social activities can resume.

CHARLES DIDIER GONDOLA

See also: **Congo (Brazzaville), Republic of.**

Further Reading

Balandier, G. *Sociologie des Brazzavilles noires*. Paris: Presses de la Fondation Nationale des Sciences Politiques, 1955.

Gondola, Ch. D., *Villes miroirs. Migrations et identités urbaines à Brazzaville et Kinshasa, 1930–1970*. Paris: L'Harmattan, 1997.

Martin, P., *Leisure and Society in Colonial Brazzaville*. Cambridge: Cambridge University Press, 1995.

British Central Africa: *See* Colonial Federations: British Central Africa.

British Togoland

British Togoland was a region in Western Africa, bordering the Gulf of Guinea in the south. The western section of Togoland, the former British Togoland, is now part of Ghana. A German protectorate over Southern Togoland was recognized by the Conference of Berlin (1884–1885). The boundaries of Togoland were delimited in treaties with France (1897) and Great Britain (1904). In August 1914, British and French forces took Togoland from the Germans. In 1922, the League of Nations divided the region into two mandates, one French and the other British. In 1946, the mandates became trust territories of the United Nations. The area placed under British control amounted to 13,041 square miles (33,776 square kilometers). The northern part was placed under the administration of the Northern Territories of the Gold Coast (the colonial name of Ghana), and the southern section was made a district of the eastern province of the colony. The southern section held a plebiscite in May 1956 over the topic of joining Ghana when independence came. In 1957, British Togoland became part of the independent state of Ghana.

The League of Nations defined, in its treaty from July 1922, the task of the mandatory as being "responsible for the peace, order and good government of the territory, and for the promotion to the utmost of the material and moral well-being and the social progress of its inhabitants." The northern part of British Togoland contained ethnic groups who also lived in the protectorate. This was the reason why the mandate gave the Gold Coast government the right to administer them as a unit. In 1946, the population of the trust territory was about 400,000. The northern portion included in 1932 the districts of Kete-Krachi, Dagomba, Eastern Mamprussi, and Kumassi. In Eastern Dagomba, cattle raising and agriculture, as in most of this area, were the principal occupations of its people, along with crafts such as weaving, ropemaking, leather tanning, and pottery making. Yet British Togoland had neither the mineral resources nor the large plantings of cocoa as had the Gold Coast. Because of the fact that the future of the region was uncertain, the British hesitated to invest in a territory under international control.

During the period 1890–1930, a decentralization of native authority took place. After 1930, the numerous small divisions of the Northern Territories and north Togoland were reunited into several large states such as Mamprussi and Dagomba. In 1933, three ordinances relating to the executive, judicial, and financial reorganization were promulgated. The chiefs were able to use these new powers to carry out economic and social reforms. The Native Tribunal Ordinance permitted the chief commissioner to establish tribunals to define the extent of its civil and criminal jurisdiction. Moreover, the government passed in 1932 a Native Treasuries Ordinance that gave the chief commissioner the right to establish treasuries, to define the sources of revenue, to provide for specified forms of taxation, and so forth. The revenue was applied to roads, dispensaries, sanitary conveniences, and regular salaries for chiefs and tribunal members. The economic growth of the area was steadily improving, and a slow increase of interest in education, health care, and religion was occurring. In 1946, a Northern Territory council, representative of all the chiefs, was established.

South Togoland was much smaller, at 5,845 square miles. The ordinances of the Gold Coast Colony were applied to Southern Togoland, while those for the Northern Territories were promulgated in Northern Togoland. The five districts of the mandate were managed by district commissioners. As in the Northern Territories, from 1930 on the government aimed to amalgamate small ethnic groups. By 1939, all but 15 of the 68 divisions had amalgamated into 4 large states. After this, the local institutions were strengthened: the governor had the right to declare local authorities. Divisional and state councils were recognized and allowed to investigate political and constitutional disputes. The governor had the power to establish tribunals in each native authority area. An ordinance of

1932 granted the divisions the right to set up stool treasuries and collect taxes. In the mandate, education was in the hands of missionaries, assisted by government funds. Economic development resulted from an increased production of cocoa.

After 1951, the constitutional changes taking place in the Gold Coast began to affect conditions in Togoland. The government had taken measures to ensure that the people of Togoland participated in every level of government under the increased representation provided by the 1951 and 1954 constitutions. In June 1954, the British government informed the United Nations that it would not be in a position to administer the Togoland trusteeship separately after the Gold Coast became independent. At first, a majority of the members of the United Nations were opposed to the establishment of British Togoland as an independent state, but they soon recognized that this meant the rule of British Togoland as an independent African government and not a colonial annexation. In December 1955, the General Assembly of the United Nations agreed to a British Togoland plebiscite to determine whether the population preferred an integration with the Gold Coast after independence or its own independence as a separate entity. When the plebiscite was held on May 9, 1956, the majority, aware of the imminent independence of its neighbor, voted for the integration of Togoland with the Gold Coast. The UN General Assembly thus agreed to the reunification of British Togoland and the Gold Coast after the independence of this last territory.

The last constitution before independence was published in February 1957. The date of independence was fixed for March 6, 1957. On this date, the unified Gold Coast and British Togoland became an independent state within the British Commonwealth with the name of Ghana.

ULRIKE SCHUERKENS

See also: **Ghana (Republic of): Nationalism, Rise of, and the Politics of Independence.**

Further Reading

Bourret, F. M. *Ghana: The Road to Independence, 1919–1957*, 3rd ed. Stanford, Calif.: Stanford University Press, 1969.

Colman, J. S. *Togoland.* New York: Carnegie Endowment for International Peace, 1956.

Colonial Office of Great Britain. *Report by His Majesty's Government in the United Kingdom of Great Britain and Northern Ireland to the Council of the League of Nations on the Administration of Togoland under British Mandate,* for the years 1920–1938. London: His Majesty's Stationery Office, 1921–1939.

———. *Report by His Majesty's Government in the United Kingdom to the General Assembly of the United Nations on the Administration of Togoland under United Kingdom Trusteeship,* for the Years 1949–1955. London: His Majesty's Stationery Office, 1950–1956.

Metcalfe, G. E. *Great Britain and Ghana: Documents of Ghana History, 1807–1957.* London: T. Nelson, 1964.

Broederbond: *See* South Africa: Afrikaner Nationalism, Broederbond and National Party, 1902–1948.

Brussels Conference and Act, 1890

The first general treaty for the suppression of the African slave trade was negotiated at the Brussels Conference of 1889–1890. By this time the Atlantic slave trade had ended, but slave raiding and trading were widespread in Africa and slaves were still exported to the Muslim world or sent to European colonies disguised as contract labor. After the British outlawed their own slave trade, they had built up a network of separate treaties with the colonial and maritime powers, and with Asian and African rulers and peoples, granting rights to search and laying down rules for the arrest and trial of slavers. Although often mutual in theory, only the British exercised these rights continuously, and rival powers suspected that the British were trying to hinder their commerce and colonial development.

By the 1880s, with the "Scramble" for Africa in full swing, these treaties were out of date, and there was no treaty with France. The colonial advance, spearheaded by missionaries, traders, prospectors, and adventurers, provoked resistance. British settlers on the shores of Lake Malawi, French missionaries around Lake Tanganyika, and the posts of King Leopold II of Belgium's Congo Independent State in the far interior were threatened by Swahili/Arab traders and their African allies, who were importing quantities of arms and ravaging large areas in which slaving and raiding were endemic. To impose their rule, the imperial powers needed to disarm them.

The antislavery movement was now used to rally hitherto lukewarm domestic support for colonial ventures. The British public had been galvanized by David Livingstone's earlier appeals to end the trade, and, in 1888, Cardinal Lavigerie, the French founder of the missionary order of the Society of Our Lady of Africa, or White Fathers, toured European capitals calling for volunteers to fight the slavers. The British, anxious to retain leadership of the antislavery movement, and fearful of the havoc that might be created by the cardinal's "crusaders," asked King Leopold to call a conference of the European colonial powers to negotiate a new treaty against the export of slaves. The idea was popular in Britain, and an invitation from Brussels was less likely to arouse suspicion than one from London. The British initially merely wanted to prevent rival powers, particularly the French, from attracting trade to their colonies by allowing slavers to sail under their flags. Similarly powers could attract trade in the interior to the detriment of more scrupulous neighbors, by countenancing the slave traffic and the lucrative arms trade that supported it. King Leopold determined to extend the proposed treaty to further the interests of his nascent state. To achieve these aims, all the African colonial powers (Britain, France, Germany, Portugal, the Congo, Italy, and Spain) together with the other signatories of the Berlin Act (Holland, Belgium, Russia, Austria, Sweden, Denmark, and the United States) had to be invited. The Ottoman Empire, which had territories in Africa and Asia and imported slaves, was included to avoid appearing to launch a Christian "crusade." Zanzibar was asked in order to please its sultan, and Persia was added as it was a Muslim power believed to be cooperating against the slave trade.

The treaty that was hammered out, the General Act for the Repression of the African Slave Trade of 1890, known as the Brussels Act, declared that the colonial powers could best attack the slave trade by establishing their administrations, developing communications, protecting missionaries and trading companies, and initiating Africans into agricultural labor and the "industrial arts." Having thus established the exploitation of Africa as an antislavery measure, the signatories undertook to prevent wars, end slave trading and raiding, stop the castration of males, and repatriate or resettle freed and fugitive slaves. They agreed to restrict the arms traffic between 20° north latitude and 22° south latitude. The Ottoman Empire, Zanzibar, and Persia undertook the outlawing of the import and export of slaves, and the mutilation of males, as well as the freeing, repatriating, or caring for illegally imported slaves.

To maintain the right to search, the British agreed to restrict their existing rights to vessels of less than 500 tons and to search only in a designated "slave trade zone" that included part of the Indian Ocean, Madagascar, the Red Sea, and the Persian Gulf. In this zone signatories were to exercise strict control over the granting of flags to native vessels and over the movements of passengers. To minimize disputes, rules were laid down for the search and arrest of suspects. The French refused to ratify the clauses on the right to search or verify the flag, but they introduced regulations that virtually implemented them.

A bureau was to be established in Zanzibar to disseminate information that might lead to the arrest of slavers, and one in Brussels was to collect information on the measures taken to carry out the treaty, and produce statistics on the slave, arms, and liquor traffics.

Two modifications were made in the Berlin Act. To please British temperance and missionary societies, and help the Royal Niger Company keep control of trade on the Niger, the liquor traffic, between 20° north latitude and 22° south latitude, was to be subject to duties where it already existed, and to be banned altogether in still "uncontaminated" areas. Similarly, to assist King Leopold against rival traders, a declaration was appended to the treaty allowing import duties to be imposed in the conventional basin of the Congo.

The Brussels Act came into force in 1892. In 1919 it was abrogated together with the Berlin Act, by the victorious allies Britain, France, Belgium (now ruling the Congo), Portugal, Italy, the United States, and Japan. Theoretically it remained in force for the other signatories, but in practice it ceased to exist. The two acts were replaced by three conventions signed at St. Germain-en-Laye in 1919, embodying some of the arms, spirits, and commercial clauses. The slave trade, considered moribund, figured into only one article. This bound signatories to preserve the well-being of native peoples and secure the complete suppression of the slave trade and—a new departure—of slavery in all its forms.

The Brussels Act was only one factor in reducing the slave traffic. It contained no mechanism for enforcement, and it did not cover the various devices, including forced and contract labor, by which the European powers exploited Africans. However, it was in the interests of the colonial rulers to suppress slave raiding, large-scale slave trading, and the export of slaves, and these ended as their administrations were established. Slavery itself, not covered by the act, was tolerated for many years, and petty slave dealing, together with a small export traffic, continued in some areas until the end of colonial rule.

The Brussels conference brought the evils of the slave trade forcefully to public attention, and the act, while serving the interests of the colonial powers, bound them to suppress it. Humanitarians regarded it as a triumph, an important step in the doctrine of trusteeship. The principles embodied in it were passed on to the League of Nations and ultimately to the United Nations.

SUZANNE MIERS

See also: **Anti-Slavery Movement; Slavery, Colonial Rule, and.**

Further Reading

Documents relations a la repression de la traite des esclaves publijs en execution des articles et suivants de l'acte generale de Bruxelles, *1893–1913. English translations are included.*

Miers, S. *Britain and the Ending of the Slave Trade.* London: Longman/New York: Africana Publishing, 1975.

Protocols and General Act of the Slave Trade Conference Held at Brussels 1889–90, with Annexed Declaration. *Africa no. 8 (1890) L 1890 C–6049, British Parliamentary Papers,* London.

British South Africa Company: *See* **Lewanika I, the Lozi, and the BSA Company.**

Bu Hmara: *See* **Morocco: Resistance and Collaboration, Bu Hmara to Abdelkrim (Ibn 'Abd El-Krim).**

Buganda Agreement: *See* **Uganda: Buganda Agreement, Political Parties, Independence.**

Buganda: To Nineteenth Century

Popular oral traditions in Buganda, one of the ancient kingdoms in the East African interlacustrine region, center the origin of the kingdom around the figure of Kintu, the first king. Kintu, who is claimed to have arrived in Buganda from the northeasterly direction of Mt. Elgon leading a number of clans, did not find the country empty. There were a number of Baganda clans describing themselves as *banansangwawo* (or, simply, indigenous clans), claiming to have been ruled by at least 30 kings before the arrival of Kintul. It was their last king, Bemba Musota, who was defeated by Kintu. The little archaeological evidence that is available seems to indicate that these lakeshores had been settled by a Bantu-speaking population a long time ago, perhaps as early as the sixth century. These were the makers of the early Iron Age pottery now classified as Urewe pottery, which dates from the sixth to the twelfth centuries. By this time Buganda is said to have been a very small kingdom made up of just the three central counties of Kyadondo, Busiro, and Mawokota.

Numerous other clans moved in later, mainly coming in from the east and across Lake Victoria, to join other clans then settling down under Kintu's leadership. These traditions, which paint a larger-than-life graphic picture of Kintu at the time of settlement, also claim that Kintu simply disappeared without trace after laying the foundations of the kingdom.

The other important king besides Kintu was Kimera, who may have come into Buganda from neighboring Bunyoro, to the west. He is said to have led a number of clans that moved eastward at the time of the collapse of the Bachwezi hegemony in Bunyoro. It is now widely believed that Kimera may have founded a new dynasty in Buganda. The popular tradition, however, cites 36 kings of Buganda in an unbroken line of descent from Kintu to the present king, Ronald Muwenda Mutebi II. Among these past kings was Muteesa I, who invited Christian missionaries to Uganda; Daniel Mwanga, who had early Christian converts—now saints—executed for

rebellion; and Sir Edward Muteesa II, who was deported to Britain in 1953 for defying the colonial government and who in 1963 became the first president of Uganda before he was finally deposed and exiled to England by Milton Obote in 1966.

Buganda started territorial expansion during the sixteenth century after Bunyoro-Kitara had reached its peak and was declining. Buganda's expansion continued right into the nineteenth century, but this was not all at the territorial expense of Bunyoro, as it has often been claimed. There are several areas and semiautonomous chiefdoms that were conquered by or annexed into Buganda, such as Budu (Bwera), Kkoki, the Ssese and Buvuma islands, and parts of Kyagwe, as well as various principalities of Busoga that never belonged to Bunyoro of Babito, though some of these areas may have been under some influence of the earlier Bachwezi hegemony to which Bunyoro Kitara was the successor state.

Over a period of four centuries, Buganda increased its territory to at least 20 counties as compared to only 3 in the twelfth century. Most of this expansion occurred between the seventeenth and eighteenth centuries, particularly during the reign of three eminent Buganda kings: Kimbugwe, Katerega, and Mutebi. After them, kings Mawanda, Semakokiro, and Suna, in the last half of the eighteenth century and early nineteenth century, put the final touches on the boundaries of Buganda, which the Europeans found in place in the nineteenth century.

At the beginning of the nineteenth century, the Kabaka was ruling with three chief ministers including a prime minister (*katikiro*). Below them was a council of county chiefs who administered the districts of the kingdom. Buganda kings of the nineteenth century appeared despotic, but this was a development over the later years. In the early centuries, the Kabaka held his position at the mercy of the clan heads. Over the centuries these heads gradually lost their political power and hold over their clansmen to the kings, as clans gradually became more social, rather than residential, groupings. Buganda's residential pattern had gradually become socially heterogeneous as the kingdom expanded its territory, rendering kinship bonds and relations inept in dealing with political control.

One of the key elements that turned Buganda into the powerful and cohesive kingdom it had become in the nineteenth century was the evolution of the home-grown institution of kingship. This was a gradual process that saw the development of kingship as a focus of all the Baganda's loyalty to the kingdom. Each and every Muganda was linked to the kingship as an institution through his or her clan by a dint of constitutional genius and social engineering wherein the king took the clan of his mother in a strictly patrilineal society. This meant that since Baganda clans were exogamous, it became relatively rare for one clan to provide kings in any two successive reigns. As such, no exclusive royal clan ever developed in Buganda, unlike in Bunyoro, where the Babiito were distinct from their non-Bahima subjects.

Over time, Buganda was able to develop a very effective military organization, which it put to very good use in its wars of expansion. Many of the kings took active part in these military operations themselves, and indeed a number of them lost lives on the battlefield. Explorer H. M. Stanley was witness to and a participant in one such war, this time on the Buvuma Islands, where the Buganda king deployed his navy on Lake Victoria, and the battle was decisively won.

Buganda's political system also had a number of weaknesses, which sometimes negated development and political cohesion. Primary among these was the absence of a proper system of succession to the throne. In the beginning of the kingdom, it appears that succession to the throne was passed on from brother to brother rather than from father to son. This meant that all the surviving princes had equal right to claim the throne. Since all the brothers were not necessarily of the same mother, they each obviously had the backing of their mother's clansmen, who were all eager to provide the next king. By about the eighteenth century, many kings were coming to power after complete annihilation of their brothers. This had the disadvantage of dividing up the population into militant factions as wars of succession ravaged the kingdom soon after the death of a king. Many of these wars usually ended with the dispersion of people through clan persecutions as the victors and their nephew king installed themselves into power and positions of influence after the war.

DAVID KIYAGA-MULINDWA

See also: **Great Lakes Region.**

Further Reading

Cohen, D. "Peoples and States of the Great Lakes Region." In *General History of Africa*, vol. 6, edited by J. F. Ade Ajayi. London: Heinemann and UNESCO.
Kiwanuka, S. *History of Buganda: From the Foundation of the Kingdom to 1900.* London: Longman, 1972.
Ogot, B. A. "The Great Lakes Region." In *General History of Africa*, vol. 4, edited by D. T. Niane. London: Heinemann and UNESCO.
Wright, M. *Buganda in the Heroic Age.*

Buhaya: *See* **Great Lakes Region: Karagwe, Nkore, and Buhaya.**

Bulawayo

Bulawayo is the second largest city in Zimbabwe (formerly Southern Rhodesia), situated in the southwest, 111 kilometers from the Botswana border on the main rail and road links between southern Africa and the interior. The establishment of Bulawayo is related to Cecil Rhodes's efforts to open up the central African interior for European settlement. Inspired by the gold discoveries in South Africa, in the 1880s Rhodes (and others) hoped to find more gold in the interior. In order to gain a foothold there, Rhodes sent emissaries to GuBulawayo, capital of the Ndebele king Lobengula. Offshoots of the Zulu people of South Africa, at that time the Ndebele controlled a large part of what was to become Southern Rhodesia, including many of the indigenous Mashona inhabitants. They had a large, well-disciplined army and had to be carefully courted. Working with British missionary Helm, who lived in Lobengula's court, Rhodes's emissaries managed to trick Lobengula into signing away complete territorial rights, when he believed he was only granting access to limited mineral rights. Ignoring Lobengula's renunciation of the "concession," in 1890 Rhodes sent a pioneer column into the country. To appease Lobengula, the column passed around and to the south of his kingdom and settled in the Mashona area to the northeast.

The presence of European settlers and adventurers quickly upset the political and social balance of the region. Tension mounted, and in December 1893 Rhodes's agent, L. S. Jameson, led a punitive raid against the Ndebele capital. As Lobengula abandoned his capital in the face of the better-armed invading force, Jameson's men sacked and burned Bulawayo to the ground. The Ndebele defeat and Lobengula's death provided an opening for the settlers, and the modern town of Bulawayo was formally established in 1894, backed by Rhodes's British South Africa Company. A town plan established a central core, streets wide enough for an ox cart to turn, and a number of housing areas, carefully laid out in the rectangular grid pattern popular in North America at the time. The residential area for Europeans provided spacious gardens and wide streets. Parks were demarcated. An African location provided small, poorly built houses for Africans who were regarded as temporary members of the urban community.

Bulawayo soon became a busy hub for communications and business; the telegraph line reached there in July 1894. That year, Bulawayo boasted over 100 general stores, 3 banks, 12 hotels, 3 newspapers, 26 share brokers, and 9 solicitors. Cecil Rhodes built an elegant home on the foundations of Lobengula's former *kraal.* By 1895, over 1,500 Europeans lived in Bulawayo, including a few hundred women. Social clubs soon developed, along with hospitals, schools and churches. An uprising by the Ndebele in 1896 threatened the town and set back plans for expansion. However, once peace had been established, Bulawayo resumed its growth. It was declared a municipality in 1897, the same year the railroad arrived to link Bulawayo with major South African centers. The railroad would provide the economic backbone for Bulawayo's expansion in the twentieth century. Although mining in the area disappointed the hopes of the early settlers, Bulawayo soon became a hub for transporting goods, including minerals and agricultural products from the region. A dam provided more secure water, which would always be a problem in Bulawayo. Businesses flourished and the population grew. By 1904 the town had approximately 6,000 European residents and about the same number of African servants living within the township boundary. More Africans lived on the periphery, where they enjoyed greater freedom from European control. The population remained relatively stable until the 1920s. Cultural life flourished. By 1899 the Empire Theatre of Varieties was providing regular opera performances and musical concerts. In 1898 a choir performed George Frideric Handel's *Messiah*. In 1901 the Musical and Dramatic Society embarked on a long record of fine musical productions.

The African community in Bulawayo grew as well, contributing to the city's economic and cultural prosperity. Housing for Africans, however, lagged abysmally behind the needs of the population, and poor living conditions fueled African discontent. Tensions exploded in 1929, when riots broke out in the municipal location. The fighting raged for two days, encompassing the railway compound as well. The riots brought little immediate improvement to housing but put African urban living conditions on the government agenda. The most notable improvement for Africans in Bulawayo came with the government's construction in the late 1930s of Luveve, a township for African civil servants. For most Africans, crowding in the municipal housing areas continued to be the rule, with as many as five or more people sharing a single room. Employers' compounds and squatter camps were often much worse.

World War II fueled the Bulawayo economy and attracted large numbers of Europeans and Africans of both sexes. The hub of the colony's industrialization until the 1950s, when it was overtaken by Salisbury (Harare), Bulawayo was the epicenter of the widespread and partially successful railway workers' strike of 1945. By 1951 the European population had grown to 32,000, twice the figure for 1941, while the African population was above 60,000, with a marked increase in the number of women. Declared a municipality in 1943, the municipal council gradually improved housing for Africans, even introducing a home ownership scheme in 1952. Hugh Ashton, town clerk from the 1950s on, played a key role in Bulawayo's housing policies. Despite the government's Unilateral Declaration of

Independence in 1954, with its commitment to white supremacy, Ashton managed to maintain Bulawayo's earlier progressive record for housing and amenities with the support of key Europeans and Africans. However, housing continued to be demarcated along racial lines and the quality of African housing and amenities were, for the most part, well below European standards.

Since independence in 1980, Bulawayo has continued to expand, reporting a population of 621,742 in 1992. Access to housing is no longer based on race but on the ability to pay, and many middle-class Africans have moved into the former low-density (European) suburbs. During the 1980s and early 1990s, schools, housing, and hospitals improved for poorer Africans as well. The Bulawayo City Council continues to play a crucial role in city policies and practices under the leadership of African civil servants such as Ndubiwa (former town clerk) and Magagula, director of housing and community services. However, the efforts to maintain and expand Bulawayo's progressive urban policies have been hampered by a growing economic crisis that shows no sign of abating.

JANE L. PARPART

See also: **Rhodes, Jameson, and the Seizure of Rhodesia; World War II: Sub-Saharan Africa; Economic Impact; Zimbabwe: Nineteenth Century, Early; Zimbabwe (Southern Rhodesia): African Political and Trades Union Movements, 1920s and 1930s; Zimbabwe: Incursions from the South, Ngoni and Ndebele.**

Further Reading

Gussman, B. S. *African Life in an Urban Area: A Study of the African Population of Bulawayo.* 2 vols. Bulawayo: Federation of African Welfare Societies in Southern Rhodesia, 1953.

Phimister, I. *An Economic and Social History of Zimbabwe, 1890–1948: Capital Accumulation and Class Struggle.* London: Longman, 1988.

Raftopolous, B., and Ian Phimister. *Keep on Knocking; A History of the Labour Movement in Zimbabwe, 1900–97.* Harare: Boabab Books, 1997.

Ranger, Terence. *Voices from the Rocks.* Oxford: James Currey, 1999.

Rotberg, Robert. *The Founder: Cecil Rhodes and the Pursuit of Power.* Oxford: Oxford University Press, 1988.

Bunyoro

Iron Age communities probably moved into Bunyoro around 2,000 years ago, gradually moving inland from early riverine and lakeshore settlements. Very little archaeological work has been done on Nyoro iron-production sites, but Nyoro iron hoes were considered the best in the Great Lakes Region in historical times, and Bunyoro enjoyed an abundance of iron ore and wood for making charcoal. An economy based on cattle, grain, and plantains probably developed more than 1,000 years ago. Sites such as Ntusi and Bigo indicate that, in the first half of this millennium, cattle played a large part in the regional economy and there existed a relatively large degree of authority over labor. It is certainly likely that holders of political authority relied on Bunyoro's sources of wealth, iron products, cattle and later salt, to maintain themselves in power.

Buchanan's work on clan histories (1978) indicates that Bunyoro has received immigrants from all directions, but primarily from the north and west. The Songa, Gahi, Ranzi, Yaga, Rungu, Gabu and Yanga clans are held to be the oldest in Bunyoro, but are believed to have originated elsewhere, mostly to the west of Lake Albert. While these clans are assumed to have always been Bantu-speaking, Buchanan found that the traditions of twelve now completely Bantu-ized clans trace their origins to Luo-speaking areas north of the Nile. By 1800 most Nyoro were Bantu speaking, but northern and eastern Bunyoro was predominantly Luo speaking. These linguistic and cultural connections facilitated Bunyoro's attempts to exert influence over northern and eastern Uganda and to dominate the trade of the entire region.

Bunyoro's ancient political history has been the subject of some controversy. Nyoro have long claimed that their kingdom is the true heir to an immense empire called Kitara. Nyakatura (1973) asserts that Kitara, in its heyday, encompassed most of Uganda, parts of western Kenya, eastern Congo, northern Tanzania and Rwanda, and the southern Sudan. Court-related historians have detailed the divine origins of the empire: how it was inherited from the godly Batembuzi dynasty by the semidivine Bacwezi, who ruled for a short time before transferring power to the Babito clan, Luo immigrants from the northeast, who still rule today. Revisionist historians, such as Henige (1974) and Wrigley (1996), have argued that Nyoro historians' primary concern was with emphasizing the former importance and influence of Bunyoro, and they have questioned the lengths of Nyoro king lineages, the existence of an ancient empire, and the reality of a Bacwezi dynasty. Tantala (1989) has recently suggested that Babito, upon taking power in Bunyoro, synthesized numerous ancient traditions, including those relating to Bazwezi spirits, in order to legitimize their rule.

It is clear from traditions and linguistic evidence that kingship predated the arrival of the Babito. While many Babito personal names are Luo, there are only two Luo words in Bunyoro's political terminology. The predominance of Bantu political terms indicates that kingship preceded Babito rule. All precolonial kings in Uganda claimed to be the true heirs to Kitara, which suggests that such a state did preexist Bunyoro and its neighboring kingdoms. It is not inconceivable that Bacwezi did once possess political as well as sacred authority. The link between Kitara and Bacwezi was first reported by Emin Pasha as long ago as 1881. Bunyoro has as strong a claim as any to be the heir to Kitara. The Babito kingdom included the area regarded as the core of the Kitara state, while the dynastic histories of the region support the view that Bunyoro was preeminent in the Great Lakes until the eighteenth century.

It is impossible to know what form the pre-Babito state took, but its influence is likely to have been much greater than its actual area of sovereignty. Many sources confirm the existence of powerful Bantu clans in pre-Babito times, and it is likely that kingship in this period was heavily concerned with the building of alliances with the country's great clans. That this process took on a new form with the arrival of the Babito is suggested by Tantala's interpretation of certain legends about the Bacwezi spirits. Tantala believes that when the Babito took over Bunyoro, they respected the power and autonomy of Bacwezi ritual centers. It is certainly likely that Bunyoro's religious centers preexisted Babito rule, and that Babito acceptance of indigenous religion involved recognition of the position of the clans that were guardians of the Bacwezi shrines.

The Babito probably took power in Bunyoro around the late sixteenth century. Early kings appear to have secured some kind of regional dominance. Traditions in Rwanda, Nkore, and Karagwe describe a devastating invasion by Nyoro forces in this period, which, after great initial successes, ended in disaster. Evidence of Bunyoro's supremacy over ancient Buganda is ample. Babito princes established themselves in Kiziba, Busoga, and beyond Rwenzori. By 1800, however, Bunyoro had taken on the character of the "sick man" of the lakes region, suffering successive violent reversals of fortune. Through a series of military victories and alliances with rebellious princes and chiefs, Buganda had dispossessed Bunyoro of much of its territory. Nkore took advantage of Bunyoro's concern with Buganda to achieve dominance south of the Katonga River.

The classic interpretation of Bunyoro's decline portrays an ancient, loosely organized, pastoralist-dominated empire challenged by a younger, compact, and highly centralized agricultural neighbor, Buganda. This analysis may rely too heavily on a backward extrapolation from the mid-nineteenth century situation. The contribution of powerful clans to Bunyoro's problems has been overshadowed by the historiographical concentration on rebellious Babito on the borders. Bunyoro's decline was perhaps not one of an imperial structure falling apart, but rather resulted from localized, often clan-related, resistance to a newly centralizing and aggressive government in the eighteenth century. Buganda was quick to extend its influence in areas such as Bwera, where Bamooli clan guardians of a Cwezi shrine, on being persecuted by King Olimi (r. c.1710–1730) of Bunyoro, turned to Buganda for support. Bunyoro's greatest military defeats, moreover, occurred after it launched ill-considered invasions of its southern neighbors. Thus the weakness of Bunyoro by 1800 was the result of royal overambition, the desire of clans and princes for local autonomy, and the rising power of Buganda.

SHANE DOYLE

See also: **Great Lakes Region.**

Further Reading

Beattie, J. *The Nyoro State.* Oxford: Oxford University Press, 1971.

Berger, I. "The Kubandwa Religious Complex of Interlacustrine East Africa: An Historical Study c.1500–1900." Ph.D. diss., University of Wisconsin, Madison, 1973.

Buchanan, C. "Perceptions of Ethnic Interaction in the East African Interior: The Kitara Complex," *International Journal of African Historical Studies* 11, no. 3 (1978): 410–428.

Connah, G. *Kibiro: The Salt of Bunyoro, Past and Present.* London: British Institute in Eastern Africa, 1996.

Fisher, R. *Twilight Tales of the Black Baganda.* London: Marshall Brothers, 1911.

Gray, J. (ed.). "The Diaries of Emin Pasha—Extracts IV." *Uganda Journal* 26, no. 2 (1962): 121–139.

Henige, D. *The Chronology of Oral Tradition: Quest for a Chimera.* Oxford: Oxford University Press, 1974.

Karubanga, H. K. *As the Sun Rises and Sets,* translated by Rev. A. Katuramu. Kampala, Uganda: Eagle Press, 1969.

Nyakatura, J. *Anatomy of an African Kingdom: A History of Bunyoro-Kitara,* edited by G. N. Uzoigwe. New York: NOK, 1973.

Roscoe, J. *The Bakitara or Banyoro: The First Part of the Report of the Mackie Ethnological Expedition to Central Africa.* Cambridge: Cambridge University Press, 1923.

Schoenbrun, D. L. "Early History in Eastern Africa's Great Lakes Region: Linguistic, Ecological, and Archaeological Approaches." Ph.D. diss., University of California, Los Angeles, 1990.

Steinhart, E. "Vassal and Fief in Three Lacustrine Kingdoms," *Cahiers D'Études Africaines,* 7, no. 4 (1967): 606–623.

Tantala, R. "The Early History of Kitara in Western Uganda: Process Models of Political and Religious Change." Ph.D. diss., University of Wisconsin, Madison, 1989.

Wrigley, C. *Kingship and State: The Buganda Dynasty.* Cambridge: Cambridge University Press, 1996.

Burkina Faso (Upper Volta): Nineteenth Century

During the nineteenth century, the dense network of trade routes between the Sahel and the forest (as mapped by the explorer Heinrich Barth in 1853) provided links among the valleys of the Upper Volta (Mouhoun, Nazinon, and Nakambe in contemporary Burkina Faso). Cola nuts, livestock, salt, and slaves were the main commodities traded.

In the eastern half of this territory two relatively homogeneous concentrations of peoples, known as the Mossi and the Gulmaba, each formed a group of about 20 kingdoms. In several of these kingdoms the chiefs were effectively independent of the central government. As pretenders frequently competed for power, conflict continued among these kingdoms, but the relatively dispersed pattern of settlement undoubtedly allowed for a degree of security. Islam was present throughout the territory, from the courts of the rulers to the networks of merchants arriving from the Mande country (mainly Yarse, from the land of the Moaga) over preceding centuries.

The western half of the territory was a mosaic of peoples, mostly lacking centralized structures or hierarchies, who recognized the authority of hereditary chiefs and of the holders of religious offices linked to the worship of the land, rain, the creator deity, masks, and so on. There were village communities (Bwa, Bobo, Marka, San) and "clans" (Lobi, Birifor, Dagara), while in the eighteenth century the Wattara regiment of the reigning dynasty of Kong (modern Côte d'Ivoire) had begun to develop embryonic kingdoms around Sya (Bobo-Dioulasso). However, their authority had been considerably reduced, and some of their descendants no longer ruled anything more than their own villages along the caravan routes.

To the North, the Fulbe (or Peul), moving from the West in successive waves over centuries, had begun to form a stable society. At Dori, in about 1810, the Ferobe established the emirate of Liptako, pushing the Gulma kingdom of Coalla farther south. Finally,

Burkina Faso.

certain communities of livestock farmers (Dokuy, Barani) had carved out an area on the middle reaches of the Black Volta for themselves.

The Muslim resurgence in the early years of the eighteenth century, spreading from the Hausa lands to the Macina, had sparked off holy wars in certain areas. The jihad launched by Mamadou Karantao, a Marka of Ouhabou, along the middle reaches of the Black Volta during the first half of the nineteenth century was repeated in the 1880s by another Marka, Amadou Deme (Ali Kari), from Boussé in the San country (Tougan); the latter's confrontation with the French in 1894 ended with his death. From 1860 onward, the mounted Muslim Zabermabe, arriving from the left bank of the Niger by way of the Dagomba country, invaded the Gourounga country to the Southwest of the Mossi kingdoms. Their repeated raids have left indelible traces in the traditions of the Nuna, the Kassena, and the Lyele. One of their leaders, Babato, even led a victorious expedition into the Moaga country.

To the west and south of Bobo-Dioulasso, Tieba Traore, King of Kenedougou (in modern Mali), launched numerous expeditions against the villages of the Toussian, the Turka, the Samogo, and others. The Bobo, the Dioula, and the Tiefo formed an alliance against him and defeated him at Bama in 1893, but his brother Babemba continued his policy of expansion. It was the arrival of Samori in what is now Côte d'Ivoire that shifted the balance of power in the region: the impact that his armies made along the cliff, from Banfora to Toussiana, was devastating, resulting in the destruction of Noumoudara.

The 1890s sounded the death knell of independence for the whole of this region, which, following the Berlin Conference in 1885, became a bone of contention for three European powers—France, Britain, and Germany—each seeking to overtake its rivals in the Moaga country, known for the density of its population and the solidity of its political organization. A German captain, von François, left Togoland in 1888 on a mission to secure the maximum possible number of treaties. Having reached the borders of the Mossi kingdoms he had to turn back, however. Meanwhile, a French captain, Binger, took up residence at Ouagadougou, from June 15 to July 10, 1888, but all his attempts to arrange a treaty of "protection" were rejected. Neither Dr. Crozat, in 1890, nor Captain P. L. Monteil, in 1891, had any more success with successive local leaders. Finally, one Ferguson, acting on behalf of the British, who were seeking to preserve their trading interests in the hinterland of their colony of the Gold Coast, signed, on July 2, 1894, the first treaty of "friendship and free trade" at Ouagadougou. The chief, Wobogo, was undoubtedly convinced of the wisdom of signing by the Yarse and Haousa merchants engaged in business with Salaga. He agreed not to accept any protectorate, nor to conclude any agreement with any other foreign power, without the consent of the British.

At the beginning of 1895, the French enjoyed a diplomatic success in the Gulma country. Commandant Decoeur arrived there from Dahomey (Benin) and signed a treaty of "protection" with Bantchandé, a Nunbado, on January 20. The Germans had also conducted negotiations, but with chiefs whose advisers acknowledged shortly afterward that they were dependent on Nungu. In the same year a French mission, led by Commandant Destenave, reached the Yatenga. Baogo, the Yatenga *naaba,* had been in power for ten years by then, but had not yet succeeded in disarming his opponents. He therefore accepted a "complete treaty," providing for a French resident and escort, on May 18, 1895. His successor, the Yatenga naaba Bulli, renewed this treaty on November first of that year.

In 1896 Lieutenant Voulet, commanding 500 men, was ordered to overtake the British at Ouagadougou, and at Sati, the capital of the Gourounsi. The ruler's capital at Ouagadougou was attacked on September 1 of that year. Several clashes occurred, but by late afternoon the French flag was flying over the palace in the capital. A counterattack was repelled on September 7, 1896.

The French then went on to take control of the Gourounga country, where Babato, a Zaberma, was grappling with the rebellion of a Gourounga chief, Hamaria, in the region of Sati and Leo. Samori, who supplied himself with horses in the Moaga country, had imposed his good offices on him. On September 19, Hamaria, who had to be paid a tribute of horses, accepted a treaty of "protection" from Voulet.

For the French conquest of the Upper Volta, 1897 was the pivotal year. At Ouagadougou the French designated a candidate to succeed the leader Wobogo and, after signing a treaty of protection on January 20, 1897, the new leader Sigiri was duly invested in the customary manner. French rights over the Gulma country were enshrined in a Franco-German convention of July 23, and on September 11, Commandant Caudrelier signed a treaty of protection with Barkatou Wattara, the chief of Koubo and Lokhosso, at Lokhosso. Bobo-Dioulasso was taken over on September 25, despite the reistance of the Bobo-Dioula chief, Zelelou Sanon, and an army post was set up there on November 23. British interests, meanwhile, were secured via diplomacy in 1898. In June of that year a company of 200 soldiers, commanded by a Colonel Northcott, marched on Ouagadougou to enforce recognition of the treaty signed by Ferguson, but then the news of the conclusions of the Conference of Paris, on June 14, compelled him to turn back. The frontier between the French and British territories was fixed on the 11th parallel, north latitude.

To the north, the French resident at Dori, Captain Minvielle, still had to face the resistance of the Fulbe and the Tuareg. The response of one Tuareg chief to the French advance, in August 1898, reveals the prevailing attutude of a large number of the region's inhabitants: "My ancestors never surrendered, I shall never surrender. The French are not doing wrong, but they are not doing right either. If they want peace let them stay where they are. . . . The land belongs to God, and God shall decide what must become of it."

Nevertheless, one may regard this date as the beginning of the colonial era in what was to be the French colony of Upper Volta.

ANNE-MARIE DUPERRAY

Further Reading

Duperray, A.-M. *Les Gourounsi de Haute-Volta, conquête et colonisation, 1896–1933.* Stuttgart: Steiner, 1985.

Echenberg, M. *African Reaction to French Conquest: Upper Volta in the Late 19th Century.* Madison: University of Wisconsin Press, 1971.

Kambou-Ferrand, J.-M. *Peuples voltaïques et conquête coloniale, 1885–1914.* 44 Burkina Faso: ACCT/Paris: L'Harmattan, 1993.

Madiéga, Y. Georges, and Nao Oumarou (eds.). *Burkina Faso, cent ans d'histoire, 1895–1995.* 2 vols. Ouagadougou, Burkina Faso: Karthala/PUO, 1999.

Burkina Faso (Upper Volta): Colonial Period

In 1899 the lands on the Upper Volta had been absorbed into the first and second military territories, but between 1904 and 1919 they formed part of the vast colony of Haut-Sénégal-Niger. Taxes, initially in kind or in cowrie but later in French currency, were imposed on rubber, on cotton, and, above all, on trade with the British colony of the Gold Coast (now Ghana), to which the region sent livestock, shea butter, and cotton cloth in exchange for cola nuts. The Franco-British agreement of 1898 had established a zone of free trade from the coast to Ouagadougou.

In December 1915 the uncovering of a "Muslim conspiracy" resulted in trials and punishments along the middle reaches of the Black Volta, where numerous villages had joined in the rebellion. In 1916 heavily armed military units crisscrossed the region, and in June and July of that year the resistance was crushed.

The revolt led to the partition of Haut-Sénégal-Niger after World War I. The new colony of Upper Volta (Haute-Volta) was created on May 20, 1919, with its administration based in Ouagadougou, the capital of the Mossi. The French relied on the labor force drawn from these densely populated regions toward the centers of development in Côte d'Ivoire and Sudan. Hesling, the first governor of the new colony, remained

Moro Naba, the king of Upper Volta, visiting the French governor of the region. © SVT Bild/Das Fotoarchiv.

in post until 1927. The colony was initially divided into seven districts (Bobo-Dioulasso, Dédougou, Ouagadougou, Dori, Gaoua, Fada N'Gourma, and Say), but changes soon followed. The district of Ouagadougou was reduced in size with the formation of Ouahigouya, in 1921, and of Tenkodogo and Kaya, in 1922; a district of Boromo was created by dividing Dédougou; and Say was transferred to the colony of Niger in 1927.

The program of colonization was centered on the forced cultivation of cotton that was imposed throughout the colony, but this turned out to be a fiasco. In practice, the colonial system embodied numerous contradictions. In order to pay their taxes, many Voltaïques moved every year into the Asante country to sell livestock, shea butter, and *soumbala* (fermented *néré*). In the course of these movements some would work for a few months in the gold mines, on the cocoa plantations, or on the construction sites that had begun to be developed from the end of the nineteenth century. These migrations were also aimed at avoiding having to take part in maintaining roads inside the colony or recruitment for work outside it, whether on the railways between Thiès and Kayes, Kayes and Bamako, or Abidjan and Bobo-Dioulasso, or in private enterprises in Côte d'Ivoire, Sudan, or Senegal. The working conditions of such forced laborers were often appalling.

The crisis of 1930 revealed the disastrous consequences of these levies of workers. The drought of 1932 made an endemic state of famine even worse. A decree issued on September 5, 1932, divided the colony among its three neighbors, Côte d'Ivoire, Sudan, and Niger. Côte d'Ivoire took the largest share (with Ouagadougou and Bobo-Dioulasso), while Yatenga went to Sudan, and Niger absorbed the Gulmu and Liptako areas.

Thus, the main export product of what had been Upper Volta became its labor force, moving into the developing zones that bordered upon the territory.

Some went in response to calls for workers on infrastructure projects, such as canals or the Markala Dam, issued by the Office du Niger au Soudan from 1932 onward. However, the recruitment of workers for Côte d'Ivoire was on a larger scale, whether for building work in the port of Abidjan, or for the cocoa, coffee, and banana plantations. The *inspection du travail* (labor inspectorate) established for French West Africa in 1932 was supposed to protect the workers, but it often limited itself to helping employers in the south gain easier access to the workers of the north. The workers themselves, meanwhile, preferred to head off for the Gold Coast, where they were paid more and treated better.

Paradoxically, it was during this period that an embryonic sense of nationhood gained strength among the inhabitants of what had been Upper Volta, pushing the traditional chiefs as well as members of the intellectual elite to call for the recreation of the colony. In 1937 they secured the creation of a new administrative entity, Haute (Upper) Côte d'Ivoire, taking in Ouagadougou and Bobo-Dioulasso, and governed by an official based in Abidjan.

At the time of the elections organized within the Union française (French Union) from 1945 onward, in line with the decisions of the Brazzaville Conference, the Voltaïques were still divided among Côte d'Ivoire, Sudan, and Niger. Felix Houphouët-Boigny was elected to represent Haute Côte d'Ivoire; as leader of the Rassemblement démocratique africain (RDA, or African Democratic Rally) and the man responsible for the law that put an end to forced labor, Houphouët-Boigny came to play a decisive role in re-creating Upper Volta. He negotiated with the traditional ruler, known as the Moog-naaba, the supply of Mossi laborers to the plantations of Côte d'Ivoire in return for his assistance in reconstituting the colony. However, its resurrection, in 1947, was used against the members of his own party, the RDA, who were accused of collaborating with the Parti communiste (Communist Party) and abused by the colonial authorities.

The economy of Upper Volta was transformed by the construction of a railway line from Bobo-Dioulasso to Ouagadougou that was completed in 1954. This created a new migration route in the direction of the coast, with the result that workers heading for Côte d'Ivoire soon came to outnumber those setting off for the Gold Coast.

The French Four-Year Plans (for 1950–1954 and 1954–1958) contained proposals for developing both subsistence farming and cash crops, largely through investments in dams, silos, schools, and other projects by the Fonds d'Investissement pour le Développement Economique et Social (Investment Funds for Economic and Social Development) and the Fonds d'équipement rural et de développement économique et social (Funds for Rural Infrastructure and Economic and Social Development). The existing *sociétés de prévoyance* (literally, "foresight societies") became *sociétés mutuelles de production rurale* ("mutual societies for rural production"), with a reserve fund to support subsistence. However, annual exports of groundnuts remained below 10,000 tons, rather than reaching the 15,000 tons that had been hoped for, while exports of cotton stagnated at 3,000–4,000 tons, those of shea at 5,000–10,000 tons, and those of sisal and sesame at less than 500 tons. The only positive developments came with the cultivation of rice and the increase in livestock farming, with exports to the Gold Coast and Côte d'Ivoire. There was virtually no manufacturing in Upper Volta once the shea-processing factory near Boromo closed down in 1954, and the output of gold from Poura amounted to just a few kilograms. By 1960 exports accounted for 75 per cent of tax revenues, yet they were equivalent to just 4 per cent of gross domestic product, so customs dues and remittances from migrant workers were crucial. The budget for 1958, for example, within which 17 per cent of spending was earmarked for investment, was balanced only because the French government provided a subsidy of 5 billion francs.

The expansion in the number of salaried workers, in both the public and the private sectors, to about 20,000; the development of labor unions; the first experiment in democratic institution building, with the Assemblée territoriale (Territorial Assembly) and the Conseil de gouvernement (Council of Government) established in 1957—these formed the main legacy of the last few years before independence. After the death of Ouezzin Coulibaly, vice president of the council (or deputy prime minister) in 1958, leadership passed to Maurice Yaméogo, who became the first president of independent Upper Volta in 1960.

ANNE-MARIE DUPERRAY

Further Reading

Duperray, A.-M. "La Haute-Volta (Burkina-Faso)." In *L'Afrique occidentale au temps des Français: colonisateurs et colonisés, 1860–1960*, edited by C. Coquery-Vidrovitch. Paris: La Découverte, 1992.

Madiega, Y. Georges, and Nao Oumarou (eds.). *Burkina Faso, cent ans d'histoire, 1895–1995*. 2 vols. Ouagadougou, Burkina Faso: Karthala/PUO, 1999.

Burkina Faso (Upper Volta): Independence to the Present

Since achieving independence from the French on August 5, 1960, the history of Burkina Faso has been marked by a short-lived, democratically elected administration and a succession of military coups. Upon independence, the country's first president and leader of the Rassemblement démocratique africain (African Democratic Assembly), Maurice Yaméogo, promised great economic strides for the fledgling state; these were promises upon which he soon found it impossible to deliver.

A failing economy, combined with rigged elections, brought nationwide demonstrations that led the army to intervene and take control of the country in January 1966. General Sangoulé Lamizana was installed as the president and ruled for the next 15 years, gradually offering degrees of limited power to the people. Trade union–organized unrest led to a bloodless coup in November 1980, the reins of power going to Colonel Saye Zerbo, who lasted two years, being removed from office by a group of army officers in November 1982 amid corruption allegations.

Major Jean-Baptiste Ouedraogo was declared president by the officers who seized power, and Captain Thomas Sankara was appointed prime minister. Serious divisions within the new regime soon came to light, however, with Ouedraogo ordering the arrest of Sankara in May 1983. Unfortunately for the president, Sankara was very popular among the general population and army officers alike, as he was able to keep the ramshackle coalition government of radicals and conservatives together. Efforts to remove him from office led to riots among students, workers, and officers alike. Almost inevitably, given Burkina Faso's recent history, Ouedraogo was deposed in a military coup.

The disgruntled officers, who were responsible for Sankara being in power, now took control of the country, forming the Conseil national de la révolution (CNR), with Sankara as its president. Sankara managed to hold the council—another peculiar mix of left-wing civilians and army officers—together only with strong support from those allies who were responsible for removing Ouedraogo from power, among them Captain Blaise Compaoré, Captain Henri Zongo, and Major Jean-Baptiste Boukary Lingani.

Peasants building a stone wall near Kongoussie, Burkina Faso, to reduce erosion. © Knut Mueller/Das Fotoarchiv.

Sankara's popularity increased when he ordered all politicians, including himself, to make details of their personal bank accounts a matter of public scrutiny. And in 1984 he ordered the country's name, Upper Volta, changed to Burkina Faso—"land of righteous people"—in the hope of instilling some national pride and perhaps a sense of civic duty. The government headed by Sankara was also responsible for great strides in public health, through immunization programs, public housing, and women's rights.

Policy disagreements and growing personal animosities among different wings within the CNR led to Sankara's assassination in October 1987. The killers were Compaoré loyalists, and Compaoré lost no time in declaring himself president. The popularity of Sankara, alongside the violence of the takeover, led to swift condemnation from the international community and nationwide dissatisfaction at home. Compaoré moved to consolidate his position by replacing the CNR with the new Front populaire (FP). Further tightening his grip on the country, he had former allies Zongo and Lingani arrested in September 1989. They were charged with plotting to overthrow the government, summarily tried, and executed on the same night. In the subsequent government reorganization, Compaoré made himself head of both departments of defense and security.

A new constitution was drafted and approved by referendum in June 1991. Among the provisions of the new constitution were a commitment to multiparty democracy and the denial of legitimacy to any future government that came to power as the result of a coup. Compaoré attempted to show some relaxation of his rule, when the government that was formed in June 1991, under the banner of the Fourth Republic, contained some members of opposition parties, and the minister of defense was, for the first time, a civilian.

Presidential elections were held in December 1991, as Compaoré continued his attempts to appear conciliatory, but they were boycotted by opposition parties. Compaoré ran unopposed, being elected by a voter turnout of just 25 per cent. In legislative elections the following year, opposition groups managed to take only 23 seats out of a possible 107 for the National Assembly, largely as a result of their own disunity. The opposition fared no better five years later, when the ruling party took 101 seats out of the 111 available. The 1998 presidential election saw Compaoré reelected with a more realistic margin than he had eight years earlier. With a turnout of 56 per cent, the incumbent won 87 per cent of votes cast.

In December 1998, a prominent independent journalist and newspaper editor, Norbert Zongo, and three of his colleagues were found murdered, allegedly by members of the presidential guard. These deaths resulted in nationwide strikes and demonstrations, with a coalition of opposition and human-rights groups—the Collectif d'organisations démocratiques de masse et de partis politiques—demanding that a complete and transparent investigation be held. Surprised by the continuing strength of the protests, the government eventually agreed to hand Zongo's case over to the courts and compensate the families of the murdered men. It wasn't until 2001 that anyone was charged with the murder of Zongo, including certain individuals already in prison for other murders.

Further constitutional changes relating to the office of the president were introduced by the parliament in 2000. A minimum candidacy age of 35 was introduced, as well as a two-term limit, a reduction of the term length from seven to five years, and a stipulation that only civilians were permitted to run for election. However, as these changes were to be implemented after the 2002 elections, Compaoré, who resigned his army commission, would be eligible to run for office again in 2005 and 2010.

The May 2002 elections saw a more organized opposition, with the ruling Congrès pour la democratie et le progrès (CDP; a replacement of the FP after 1996) majority being significantly reduced. Polling half a percentage point less than 50 per cent of votes cast, the party managed to take just 57 seats out of 111 in the National Assembly. A cabinet reshuffle in June saw a reversal of an earlier policy of including opposition members in government, with the new 31-member cabinet containing only CDP ministers.

Despite holding onto power since 1987, Compaoré has never had the popular support of his predecessor, Sankara, and periodic rumors of planned coups allow him to maintain fairly draconian security measures. The latest reported plot, in October 2003, resulted in the arrest of 16 individuals, including a prominent opposition leader and one-time Sankara ally, Norbert Tiendrebeogo, head of the Social Forces Front.

EAMONN GEARON

Further Reading

Deschamps, A. *Burkina faso (1987–1992). Le pays des hommes integres.* Paris: L'Harmattan, 2001.

Englebert, P. *Burkina Faso: Unsteady Statehood in West Africa.* Boulder, Colo.: Westview Press, 1996.

Guion, J. R. *Blaise Compaore, Realism and Integrity: Portrait of the Man behind Rectification in Burkina Faso.* Paris: Berger-Levrault, 1991.

McFarland, D. M., and Lawrence A. Rupley. *Historical Dictionary of Burkina Faso,* 2nd ed. Lanham, Md.: Scarecrow Press, 1998.

Sankara, T., and S. Anderson. *Thomas Sankara Speaks: The Burkina Faso Revolution, 1983–1987.* New York: Pathfinder Press, 1989.

Burundi to *c*.1800

Small against the backdrop of the immensity of the African continent—it is one of Africa's smallest countries,

approximately 10,746 square miles (6,448 square kilometers) in area—Burundi promises to have considerable depth in antiquity of human and protohuman experience as its past becomes known.

Burundi's Western Rift Valley location places it squarely in the midst of the nexus of ancient human, and even protohuman, habitation in Africa. Although the tiny country remains largely unsurveyed by archaeologists, surface surveys and chance finds have turned up the cultural remnants of long and continuous occupation. For example, Acheulean biface hand axes characteristic of the early Stone Age (approximately 500,000–100,000BCE) have been uncovered at two Burundian sites. Middle Stone Age artifacts, including stone points for arrows and spears found in seven Burundian sites, demonstrate that prehistoric craftsmen of the region worked in the Sangoan-Lupembian style (dating from 100,000BCE). Microliths and other artifacts of the late Stone Age found throughout Burundi reflect a variety of techniques and tool-making cultures (or "industries"), including the Magosian, Upper Lupembian, Lupembo-Tshitolien, and Wilton-Tshitolien industries. These finds suggest an occupation of considerable time depth, and possibly of considerable diversity as well.

Situated in the fertile corridor of the Great Lakes Region (also called the interlacustrine region), ancient Burundi was home to many different groups of people who dwelled along its marshy waterways and forested hills. Its known history reaches back to beyond 1000BCE, when its densely vegetated hills and valleys (at that time part of the Congo Basin rain

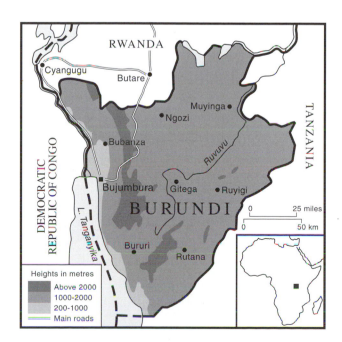

Burundi.

forest) supported small communities of foragers, hunters, and fishers. Aspects of these early lifeways have been preserved by rural Burundians, many of whom make active use of a vast reservoir of knowledge of plants and forest animals that has accumulated over millennia of human experience. The Burundian subcommunity that has preserved these ways of life most actively and completely is that identified collectively as the Batwa, some of whom live today in forest or riverine settings and incorporate foraging, hunting, and fishing techniques into their daily economic activities.

Food production emerged in Burundi around 1000BCE, and with it came changes in the relationship between people and their environment. Burundi became a patchwork of fishers, foragers, and farmers living side-by-side in particular microenvironments nestled among the valleys and hills. Environmental and social changes accelerated some time after 500BCE with the advent of ironworking. With stronger and sharper digging tools and axes, iron tool–using farmers felled the forests to make way for fields and homesteads. As forests thinned and gradually receded, forest-dwelling people became less proximate, and hence increasingly "remote" and "different" from the farmers, leaving a mark on their social dynamics. In addition, forest-dwelling predators, including the tsetse fly, receded from the farmers' zones. This opened up a new ecological corridor that could support new kinds of activities, including much denser agricultural settlement and the raising of livestock. These varied economic activities developed, over time, into more specialized lifestyles—including those that emphasized pastoralism (practiced by many of the forebears of the modern Tutsi and Hima identity groups) and those that emphasized farming (practiced by some of the forebears of the modern Hutu group). These specialized lifestyles developed in relation to each other and were interconnected through social relationships and trade.

The ecological particularities of Burundi's various subregions fostered a certain degree of regional variation in economic, cultural, and social patterns, and even in strategies for human organization. Small local and regional dynasties developed, as did various kinds of claims to authority, such as descent from an "original" family that had cleared away the wilderness, or ancestry from magical newcomers who had brought peace and order to residents whom they had found living in discord. By the second millennium of the present era, many such dynasties existed within the space of modern-day Burundi. They have left their traces upon Burundi's physical and cultural environment in many forms, from spirit shrines, toponyms, and tomb sites to family names, chanted expressions, and oral traditions.

Midway through the second millennium, certain local dynasties began to expand and coalesce, particularly in a political center remembered as Burundi of Nyaburunga in the south and a region associated with a leader named Ntare Karemera in the north. These two centers were unified, oral traditions recount, by a king named Ntare Rushatsi (whose name translates literally as "Shaggy-haired Lion"). Although many of the tales that center on Ntare Rushatsi are mythical in tone, Burundian scholars see him as an actual historical figure. Historical information about his successors, however, is somewhat sketchy and limited, until the beginning of the nineteenth century when Ntare Rugamba (literally, the "Battle Lion") reinforced and further expanded the kingdom. Ntare Rugamba (who is believed to have governed *c*.1800–1850) is remembered as an intrepid warrior who, with the help of his elder sons, significantly expanded Burundi's eighteenth-century boundaries. He followed up on his territorial gains by establishing a firm politicoadministrative structure: he is remembered as the founder of the Baganwa system of territorial governance, whereby his royal sons (the Baganwa), as well as his wives and men of confidence moved out to far-flung regions to build their own "courts." There, they represented the king's interest by working to erode the authority of local families or dynasties. And by obliging local families to give "gifts" or tribute as an expression of political support, they enriched themselves as well.

Ntare Rugamba's Baganwa system reached its apogee during the rule of his son, Mwezi Gisabo (*c*.1857–1906). Backed by a strong group of Baganwa as well as a skillful standing army and a shrewd and influential entourage of sorcerers, ritualists, and advisors, Mwezi Gisabo withstood numerous challenges to his authority and threats to his kingdom's security. These challenges included Arab-Swahili slave traders who tried to penetrate Burundi from the west and south; the militarized and expansionist Wanyamwezi who attacked from the east; long-standing rival Rwanda, with which he maintained an uneasy border to the north; would-be usurpers; and ecological and epidemiological disturbances.

MICHELE WAGNER

Further Reading

Chrétien, J.-P. *Burundi: L'histoire retrouvée*. Paris: Karthala, 1993.

Guillet, C. et Pascal Ndayishinguje. *Légendes historiques du Burundi*. Paris: Karthala, 1987.

Mworoha, É. *Peuples et rois de l'Afrique des lacs*. Dakar: Les nouvelles éditions Africaines, 1977.

Mworoha, É., et al. *Histoire du Burundi des origines à la fin du XIXème siècle*. Paris: Hatier, 1987.

Schoenbrun, D. *A Green Place, A Good Place: Agrarian Change, Gender, and Social Identity in the Great Lakes Region to the 15th Century*. Portsmouth, N.H.: Heinemann, 1998.

Burundi: Nineteenth Century: Precolonial

Located in fertile highlands overlooking the northeastern shore of Lake Tanganyika, the precolonial kingdom of Burundi developed during the course of the nineteenth century from a relatively small dynasty tucked between two politically more powerful and expansive regions, Rwanda and Buha, into a formidable political force of its own. By century's end, Burundi prevailed not only as an important regional power among the kingdoms of the Great Lakes corridor, but also as an African kingdom capable of staving off foreign penetration, keeping slave traders, missionaries, and colonial soldiers at bay.

Burundi's emergence in the nineteenth century was made possible by two long-ruling and adept kings, Ntare Rugamba (c.1800–1850) and Mwezi Gisabo (c.1857–1908). Ntare Rugamba, an intrepid warrior, expanded the kingdom's boundaries through conquest; he established a new territorial framework for the kingdom that his son and successor, Mwezi Gisabo, worked to consolidate politically. Mwezi's reign is considered to be the apogee of the Burundian monarchy.

It was military strategy and father-son cooperation that marked Burundi's nineteenth-century ascendance. Ntare Rugamba's carefully trained personal guard, the Abatezi ("attackers"), recruited from the sons of aristocrats, court advisors, and regional leaders, formed the nucleus of an army that could grow to several thousands in time of war. At their peak in the 1840s, the Abatezi were led by Ntare's son, Prince Rwasha, whose strategy relied on attacking with a main body archers while encircling the enemy from the flanks. These tactics brought the Abatezi success in campaigns against small regional dynasties as well as against the larger armies of Rwanda and Buha-Buyungu. In victory, Rwasha's warriors concentrated on seizing cattle, not generating casualties. If they captured the opposing leader, however, they were likely to behead him and burn his residence to the ground.

To bring newly conquered regions under his rule, Ntare Rugamba established a politicoadministrative structure known as the Baganwa system of territorial governance whereby he granted governing rights to his royal sons (the Baganwa), as well as to his wives, ritualists, clients, and confidantes. Thus armed with a royal mandate to claim territory, these potential governors moved out to far-flung regions to seek to build up their own "courts." There, if they managed to establish themselves, they represented the king's interest by working to erode the authority of preexisting local leaders or dynasties. Concurrently, they fulfilled their own interests as well by obliging local families to give gifts or tribute as an expression of political support. Under this system, a favorite client who had performed services for the king over the course of many years could hold governing rights to several noncontiguous territories, each territory representing a "reward." During Ntare Rugamba's reign, the largest landowners were his older offspring—particularly his sons Rwasha, Ndivyariye, Birori, and Busumano.

Although he bestowed territories on loyal supporters, Ntare directly controlled numerous domains, many of them in prime locations in the heartland. From these he drew wealth—for example, livestock, foods, beverages (such a honey wine), and beautifully crafted products (such as bark cloth)—that he could redistribute at court or bestow on loyal subjects. He also received these products as tribute.

Although military conquest and material wealth attested to the king's strength, the basis of his power was spiritual. The king's title, *mwami*, derives from the verb *kwama*, which means "to be fertile," and the king himself was seen by his people as the human embodiment of fertility. The mwami was a living charm from which derived the well-being of the Burundian people. Linked to this mystical aspect of the king's power was a constellation of images and rituals meant to express his mystical qualities and to augment them. This included a special vocabulary for aspects of the king's physical being; a complex set of charms—such as a royal bull, a royal python, sacred drums—protected by a broad network of ritualists; and an annual ritual, *umuganuro* (the first fruits or sorghum festival held in December), which blessed the king and reinvigorated his sacred aspect. The handling of a deceased king's body and the identification of a successor also came under the supervision of ritualists. The rituals of the court are best known for the reign of Mwezi Gisabo, the last king to maintain these rituals before the pressures of Christianity and colonialism led to their interdiction.

Great controversy and secrecy surround the circumstances of Mwezi Gisabo's birth and accession to *ubwami* (the office of the mwami that is represented by the drum, the Burundian symbol of royal power). One of the youngest of the royal offspring, Mwezi Gisabo was pushed into ubwami at the expense of the designated heir, his brother Twarereye. This move led supporters for each brother to take up arms on the battlefield, and ultimately to Twarereye's death. Throughout these skirmishes Mwezi, too young to rule, lived at court under the guardianship of his mother Vyano and his eldest brother Ndivyariye, who governed on his behalf. When Mwezi Gisabo grew into adulthood, he himself took up arms to force his reluctant guardian Ndivyariye to surrender power. This fraternal conflict, which took place in the late 1860s, generated a vendetta between their descendants (the Batare and the Bezi) that continued to influence Burundian politics 100 years later.

These initial challenges to Mwezi Gisabo's authority, which came from within the ranks of his own family, set the tone for his long and difficult reign. But backed by a strong faction at court, as well as by a skillful royal guard and a shrewd and influential entourage of sorcerers, ritualists, and advisors, Mwezi Gisabo withstood numerous challenges to his authority and threats to his kingdom's security. These challenges included militarized and expansionist Wanyamwezi who attacked from the east (1884); Arab-Swahili slave traders who tried to penetrate Burundi from the west and south (from the 1850s on); long-standing rival Rwanda, with which he maintained an uneasy border to the north (1880s–1890s); would-be usurpers; and ecological and epidemiological disturbances (1870s–1890s). Mwezi met each of these challenges and remained in power.

Despite the number of external threats that Mwezi confronted during his long reign, the greatest threats came from inside his kingdom, from his own relatives. The Baganwa system of territorial governance established by Ntare Rugamba had served the warrior-king well, but generated all manner of obstacles for his son. It had the flaw that once the recipients of Ntare Rugamba's mandate to govern actually established themselves in relatively remote regions, after the death of their patron, they and their offspring had little incentive to pursue active and loyal relations with his successor Mwezi Gisabo. It therefore behooved Mwezi Gisabo to dislodge these untrustworthy kinsmen and reallocate their lands to those loyal to him, such as his own sons. These conflicts among the Baganwa created an environment of internal instability and political intrigue which external challengers sought to exploit. It was internal dissent that brought success to the German conquest in the early years of the twentieth century.

MICHELE WAGNER

Further Reading

Chrétien, J.-P. *Burundi: L'histoire retrouvée.* Paris: Karthala, 1993.

Guillet, C., and P. Ndayishinguje. *Légendes historiques du Burundi.* Paris: Karthala, 1987.

Mworoha, É. *Peuples et rois de l'Afrique des lacs.* Dakar: Les nouvelles éditions Africaines, 1977.

Mworoha, É., et al. *Histoire du Burundi des origines à la fin du XIXème siècle.* Paris: Hatier, 1987.

Vansina, J. *La légende du passé.* Tervuren, Belgium: Musée Royal de l'Afrique Centrale, 1972.

Burundi: Colonial Period: German and Belgian

The precolonial kingdom of Burundi, which had expanded rapidly through military conquest in the early nineteenth century under king Ntare Rugamba (c.1800–1850), was engaged in the process of stabilizing and consolidating these gains under king Mwezi Gisabo (c.1850–1908), when the region found itself on the newest frontline of European imperial expansion.

This expansion made its presence felt in 1879 when a group of Catholic missionaries of the Société des Missionaires d'Afrique, known as the White Fathers, established a mission station on the Lake Tanganyika coast in the vicinity of the modern-day town Rumonge. This region, although not directly under Burundian control, was nevertheless within the orbit of the kingdom's political interest. The mission station was short-lived, however, when conflict with the local leader, Bikari, over the priests' attempt to "rescue" one of his retainers from what they perceived as slavery, brought the fledgling mission to a violent end in 1881. Despite this loss, the White Fathers persisted in their efforts to establish themselves in or near the densely populated kingdom.

As King Mwezi Gisabo monitored and thwarted the progress of the missionaries, in 1896 he confronted a new form of European encroachment on the edges of his kingdom: a military post established by Germans at the northern end of the lake. Unbeknownst to Mwezi Gisabo, his kingdom had been claimed by Germany, and was known on European maps as the Urundi district on the western frontier of German East Africa. Early communications between the king and the German officer in charge, in 1899, passed between emissaries in a diplomatic, even friendly, tone. But continued German presence under subsequent, more belligerent officers, led to a breakdown of diplomacy.

In 1902, the German officer in charge led a brutal and destructive campaign against Mwezi to force him to submit. This campaign, which relied on the assistance of several of Mwezi's personal enemies, deteriorated into a hunt across Burundi's heavily populated hillsides. In 1903, with his kingdom plundered and numerous of his subjects engaged in open revolt, Mwezi Gisabo presented himself to his pursuers. But far from suffering humiliation and political defeat, the king found his authority bolstered.

The German officer who had ravaged his kingdom and forced Mwezi Gisabo to surrender had done so in direct violation of the orders of the colony's governor, in faraway Dar es Salaam, whose political strategy centered on establishing cooperative relations with African leaders. Within months, Mwezi's vanquisher was recalled, and the officer sent to replace him worked to reaffirm Mwezi's authority.

The Germans who had sought to ruin Mwezi now protected him. Indeed, the king could influence the decision to send German military expeditions to target uncooperative regional leaders. With German help, Mwezi reestablished his hold over his father's kingdom and even expanded into regions that had not previously fallen under his control. By 1906, when German occupation shifted from military to civilian rule, the king and the German Residents at Usumbura were building a fragile collaboration. It lasted until 1908, when the elderly king died.

With Mwezi's death, and the coronation of the adolescent king Mutaga, 1908–1915), collaboration collapsed. Mutaga's enthronement had occurred only after much manipulation, and he was king in name only. In reality, his mother Ririkumutima, and his paternal uncle Ntarugera, both avaricious and shrewd, divided control of the kingdom. Many regional leaders, even princes, found their positions jeopardized by shifting favoritism at court, and appealed to the Germans for support. On the basis of their vigorous criticism and political information, the German Residents divided Urundi district into three political zones indicated by degree of loyalty to, or autonomy from, the central kingdom.

In this unstable political context, a rapid succession of German Residents sought to integrate Urundi district into the developing structure of the larger colony. They built a set of outposts in order to administer through local ties rather than by military expeditions, and relocated the district headquarters to geographically central Gitega. To prepare the population for a peasant-based economic program, they introduced money and taxes. To connect Urundi, with its enormous labor and agricultural potential, to the rest of the colony, they built a railway from Dar es Salaam out to the Lake Tanganyika port of Kigoma, and began a spur up to Urundi. These efforts were cut short, however, with the outbreak of World War I.

German East Africa's western boundary became the launching point for German assaults against the Belgian Congo. These operations engaged the administrators and soldiers of Urundi. Amid this destabilization, King Mutaga died under mysterious circumstances in November 1915. With the royal court wracked by conflict surrounding the succession of a young child, Mwambutsa, and with Belgian troops from the Congo set to invade, Urundi's German administrators fled in the spring of 1916.

Belgian military occupation of Urundi lasted from mid-1916 until 1924, when the League of Nations granted Belgium a formal mandate to rule. As Urundi's internationally recognized trustee, Belgium set about dismantling and reorganizing Urundi's politicoadministrative system along more convenient lines. The reorganization, which took place during the 1930s, reinforced the authority of members of select branches of the royal family, and their allies, while systematically disempowering a broad range of others who had previously wielded regional governing authority, including royal ritualists, women, advisers, and clients, and autonomous leaders from powerful local families. Although some of the disempowered leaders resisted vigorously—particularly in regions that had previously experienced relative autonomy or had been under the authority of respected ritualists—their resistance was subdued with force. Once opposition was eliminated, the territories were seized and incorporated into a streamlined and authoritarian three-tiered system of *territoires* (headed by a Belgian, staffed by Burundians), *chefferies* (governed by Belgian-appointed chiefs), and *sous-chefferies* (under Belgian-appointed subchiefs).

As the colonial government worked to reorganize the regional administrative system, the White Fathers, who had maintained a presence throughout the war and into the period of Belgian administration, worked to convert and educate those upon whom the new system would rely. Early mission schools targeted almost exclusively the sons of princes and prominent Tutsi pastoralists, with the goal of concentrating education upon the next generation of leaders. Their female counterparts—and intended wives—were young Christianized women from royal or prominent Tutsi families who were trained by nuns to uphold the norms of Western-style morality and domesticity. At the nexus of this effort to mold a Burundian colonial elite was the King Mwambutsa and his wife, Thérèse Kanyonga (they married in 1930). This young couple represented the epitome of Belgian ambition—and manipulation.

By the 1940s, the colonial system of indirect rule, that is, governance by a broad, regional network of Burundian administrators under the leadership of a relatively small group of Belgian officials, functioned very effectively. The vast majority of the population was comprised of peasant producers who grew cash crops—such as coffee or tea—for the state, and survived mostly on subsistence crops such as beans, cassava, corn, and peas. These peasant producers were legally categorized as being of Hutu ethnicity. *Hutu* was a word that had meant "servant"; it was also a label assigned to anyone who was of ordinary social status and hence a candidate for servitude. By contrast, Urundi's elites identified as Tutsi, a label that had once referred to pastoralists, and by extension to the wealthy, since livestock were a major form of wealth. Prior to colonialism, the labels *Hutu* and *Tutsi* denoted social reference points, and as such they were relative, flexible, and subject to correspond with new social realities, and hence subject to change. Under the Belgian colonial system, however, terms were transformed into fixed ethnic categories. By the prevailing social "rule of thumb," they denoted one ethnic group that the system empowered, the Tutsi, and the other which the system had explicitly or more structurally and passively disempowered, the Hutu.

The Belgian colonial system had created a small privileged elite, nearly all of whom were Tutsi (including members of the royal family who had been legally subsumed into the category) and a large underclass, the majority of whom were classified as Hutu. When the winds of change and independence swept through the colonial world in the 1950s, Urundi's modern political foundation was now built upon dangerously elitist and undemocratic principles.

MICHELE WAGNER

Further Reading

Gahama, J. *Le Burundi sous administration belge*. Paris: Karthala, 1983.

Louis, W. M. Roger. *Ruanda-Urundi, 1884–1919*. Westport, Conn.: Greenwood Press, 1963.

Burundi: Independence to 1988

Political conflict, as complex as it was intense, characterized Burundi's first generation of independence from 1962, when multiple power struggles, including the remnants of century-old antagonisms, converged.

Burundi's strong and optimistic beginning collapsed just months before the official transition to independence when in October 1961 the king's eldest son, Crown Prince Rwagasore, one of the organizers of the political party Union pour le progrès national (UPRONA) was assassinated. The prince had been the lynchpin of the massive UPRONA coalition. He had personified, and with his royal prestige had guaranteed the viability of, a middle ground. Without him the UPRONA, and the impetus to work in a broad-based coalition, disintegrated.

Burundi gained its political independence and separated from Rwanda in 1962, a year characterized by political floundering and violence. Inquiry into the prince's death uncovered a conspiracy led by two Batare of the Parti démocrate chrétien, the other dominant political party. The Batare were one of two conflicting branches of the royal family (the other being the Bezi); they had used colonialism to their advantage and wanted to retain their power. The discovery of their involvement in the prince's death, in combination with the political devastation caused by the inability to fill Rwagasore's void, taught newly independent Burundians the cynical lesson that, regardless of the courage and effort expended to develop a broad-based democratic movement, one well-placed assassination could bring democracy to its knees and reestablish the status quo for those not inclined to share power. It was a lesson to which future politicians would adhere. But in 1962, the immediate lesson that political extremists drew from Rwagasore's murder was the efficacy of political violence. The example was followed by others throughout the country who engaged in acts of arson, intimidation, and assassination.

As the UPRONA split into factions by multiple claimants to the mantle of Rwagasore, the prince's father tried to use his personal influence, and the notion of the monarchy as above and outside ordinary social groups, to maintain a political common ground. But with the spread of the notion that intimidation was the "easy" path to political victory, that common ground eroded and the *mwami*'s (king's) approach shifted toward the heavy-handed. Between 1963 and 1965, he became increasingly autocratic, in open violation of Burundi's constitution. The pattern of the mwami's interventions suggests an awkward balancing game, which he initially played through the office of the prime minister, but later played directly himself. From 1963 to 1965, Burundi saw a succession of five prime ministers, including Baganwa (members of the royal family) from each of the rival factions, a Tutsi, and two Hutus, the most popular of whom was assassinated. As the political balance was threatened, the mwami seized control of the army, and the national police, placing them under his exclusive jurisdiction, took over the national radio network and refused to recoognize newly elected parliamentarians. He even invested his own personal secretary as prime minister in a bid for direct political control.

These bold moves on the part of the mwami constituted his response to a growing trend of polarization between Hutus, who were rapidly gaining political skill and a sense of their potential for power in democratic politics, and a developing coalition of Baganwa and Tutsi who responded defensively to the threat of a Hutu-centric democracy. Although demographically inferior, the developing Tutsi lobby met the Hutus' straightforward numerical dominance with carefully crafted strategy. The prevailing Cold War political environment, and intense international interest in Burundi as a stepping-stone to resource-rich Zaïre (Democratic Republic of Congo), provided politicians such as Tutsi prime minister Albin Nyamoya the opportunity to make clandestine pacts with world powers. In one shrewdly orchestrated move, he manipulated the mwami into recognizing China, which distanced the king from his Western backers. Such moves represented not only clever gamesmanship in the Burundian political arena, but also a bid for non-Western support by those who perceived Western democracy as the source of their political destruction.

By 1965, tension, ambition, and polarization had reached such a pitch of intensity that in July the mwami took the desperate step of declaring an absolute monarchy. This move only increased the agitation on all sides; it ignited, in October of that year, a political explosion that has been alternately described as an uprising, a coup, or a set of coups carried out by Tutsi, then Hutu, instigators. The net effect of the October upheaval was to unleash two successive waves of political violence that concentrated in Muramvya, the center of royal politics, and in Bujumbura, the center of modern politics. The initial wave of violence was directed against Tutsi victims and led to the deaths of several hundred persons, including ordinary Tutsis living in rural communities in Muramvya who were killed not because of their politics but because of their misfortune in becoming targets of opportunity. With many of the Baganwa and Tutsi from traditionally powerful Muramvya families left shocked and devastated, the group with the greatest potential to move to the political fore appeared to be the Hutu political elite. This, therefore, was the group targeted for the second wave of violence.

This second wave centered on Bujumbura, where the inability of the mwami and the wounded prime minister to muster an effective response created a power void, into which stepped the army, commanded by Captain Michel Micombero, a young officer who had been handpicked and promoted by the mwami. Micombero was a political outsider, a Tutsi from a minor regional faction that came from outside the kingdom's heartland and that had not wielded influence at the royal court. Micombero seized the opportunity, using his outsider status to appear neutral and his military authority to appear dynamic. Within days, under Micombero's command, army units had killed the majority of the Hutu political elite, including labor and political leaders, and nearly all of the Hutu deputies recently elected to the parliament. Thousands of ordinary Hutus were killed as well, particularly in and around Muramvya—a move that helped to placate Baganwa and Tutsi families. In the aftermath of the killings, the mwami fled to Europe, key Hutu politicians were dead, detained or in exile, Baganwa and Muramvya Tutsi families were temporarily sidelined, and Captain Micombero remained the de facto strongman.

A year later, in two shrewdly executed moves, Micombero formalized his political dominance. First he assisted 19-year-old Crown Prince Charles Ndizeye, on a tour of Burundi from Europe where the royal family had remained, to depose his father, crown himself, and appoint Micombero as his prime minister. Then, in November 1966, when the young monarch departed on a state visit to a neighboring country, Micombero seized command, deposed him, and declared a republic.

With this declaration, Micombero brought about an important shift in Burundian politics. With Burundi now a republic, the long-standing Batare-Bezi aristocratic rivalry was diminished in significance and the Baganwa gradually coalesced into "Tutsi" politics. The October 1965 massacre of Hutu politicians had eliminated them from the political arena as well. Hence, in the politics of the new republic, what mattered was the particular Tutsi faction from which

a political aspirant hailed. Micombero's previously politically inconsequential group, from the southern province of Bururi, now moved into major cabinet positions and into key economic and judicial posts. Micombero narrowed the pipeline for political ascent by outlawing all political parties but one, the UPRONA, which he controlled. And in a sense, he superseded government by running the country through a national revolutionary council, his primarily military inner circle.

By 1968, much of the country was in the hands of Micombero's inner circle, including his relatives, coregionalists, and close associates. Monarchists and Hutus, now outside "the system," occasionally challenged it with what became the conventional tools of the disempowered, anonymous tracts and rumors. Micombero met these threats with his own increasingly conventional techniques: mass arrests, charges of treason, and death sentences. But while his government exerted tight control of the political climate, it failed to exert similar control economically. In 1968–1969, Burundi experienced an economic downturn that quickly became a political weapon for "nonsouthern" Tutsi factions to use against Micombero's group. This intra-Tutsi rivalry was expressed in the language of an anticorruption campaign. In 1971, Micombero's group arrested several prominent nonsouthern Tutsi politicians, charging them with treason and sentencing them to death. The sentences were commuted, however, for fear of backlash.

Into this simmering antagonism, in late March 1972, stepped ousted King Ntare Charles Ndizeye. Within hours of his arrival he was detained and placed under house arrest in Gitega, a town in the heartland of the old kingdom and adjacent to Muramvya Province. One month later, the political repercussions of the mwami's presence became clear. On April 29, 1972, Micombero dismissed his government, as well as the UPRONA's executive secretary, and announced on the radio that "monarchists" (a nomenclature often applied to nonsouthern Tutsis) had attempted to overthrow the government. As events unfolded, first in Bujumbura and in the vicinity of Gitega and then in southern Burundi, it was announced that the king had died while being "rescued," and that the true culprits behind the coup were "Hutu intellectuals." To "restore order," Micombero mobilized the army, which focused its retaliation on Hutus, and in particular those who had distinguished themselves by studying beyond the primary school level, or by their involvement in local-level commerce. The organized killing carried out by the army in April 1972 left between 100,000 and 200,000 persons dead and about 200,000 others seeking refuge in neighboring countries.

The massacre of 1972, or what Hutus have described as a genocide, effectively silenced not only Hutu voices, but even many of the nonsouthern Tutsi.

It provoked only muffled criticism from the international community, which preferred to describe it as "tribal slaughter" rather than political violence. Nevertheless, a certain uneasiness between Burundi and international donors festered, making Micombero a political liability to his country. In 1976, his coregionalist and fellow officer, Jean-Baptiste Bagaza, overthrew him and declared a "second republic."

Presented in the guise of democratic reform, Bagaza's program initially promised to be even-handed and inclusive. Bagaza spoke of national reconciliation and social integration. He emphasized the importance of elections and implemented universal adult suffrage, promoted land reform and outlawed an archaic system of overlordship and forced labor, and built roads and made other infrastructural improvements. Counterbalancing these progressive steps, Bagaza continued to ban all parties except the UPRONA, ran unchallenged in national elections, arrested and tortured accused critics (including members of the clergy), and in response to the resultant outcry, expelled large numbers of foreign clergy. He banned certain kinds of public gatherings and restricted religious and cultural celebrations. With governmental, political, and security structures that penetrated all the way down to the grassroots, Bagaza held Burundian society in a choke hold, allowing little room for individual autonomy or initiative. By 1986–1987, the tension had mounted to such a degree that it seemed that only a coup could alleviate it. In September 1987, that coup came from yet another military officer touting reconciliation and reform, once again a "southern" Tutsi from the Bururi region: Pierre Buyoya.

MICHELE WAGNER

See also: **Rwanda: 1962–1990.**

Further Reading

Eggers, E. K. *Historical Dictionary of Burundi*, 2nd ed. Lanham, Md.: Scarecrow Press, 1997.

Lemarchand, R. *Burundi: Ethnocide as Discourse and Practice.* Cambridge: Cambridge University Press, 1994.

———. *Rwanda and Burundi.* London: Pall Mall, 1970.

———. *Selective Genocide in Burundi.* London: Minority Rights Group, 1973.

Melady, T. P. *Burundi: The Tragic Years.* New York: Maryknoll, 1974.

Weinstein, W. *Historical Dictionary of Burundi*, 1st ed. Metuchen, N.J.: Scarecrow Press, 1976.

Weinstein, W., and R. Schrire. *Political Conflict and Ethnic Strategies: A Case Study of Burundi.* Syracuse, N.Y.: Maxwell School of Citizenship, Foreign and Comparative Studies/Eastern Africa, 1976.

Burundi: 1988 to Present

In August 1988, hundreds of Tutsi living in the north of Burundi were slaughtered by armed Hutu who explained their actions by claiming Tutsi provocation. In restoring order, forces of President Jean-Baptiste Buyoya's Union pour le progrès national (UPRONA) government, which had taken power eleven moths earlier, killed an estimated 20,000 Hutus and created in excess of 60,000 refugees, most of whom fled to Rwanda. In October, Buyoya both appointed a Hutu, Adrien Sibomana, as prime minister of the Council of Ministers and established a Commission for National Unity that had the task of examining the most recent massacres and suggesting ways to foster national unity. Significantly, both the council and the commission had equal numbers of Hutu and Tutsi, despite a national bias of more than five to one in favor of the Hutu.

Following the April 1989 publication of the commission's report, the government announced new legislation to fight all forms of discrimination and to create equal opportunities for Hutus in all walks of life, including the armed forces. Tensions remained high, however, and several unsuccessful coup attempts by supporters of former president Jean-Baptiste Bagaza and hard-line Tutsi followed. In April 1992, after the adoption of a new constitution and a cabinet reshuffle that gave 15 out of 25 ministerial positions to Hutus, violent clashes along the border with Rwanda continued to increase. The violence was blamed by the government on the Parti de libération du people Hutu, which it said had been trained in and armed by Rwanda. An agreement between the two countries on the repatriation of refugees and increases in border security did nothing to stop the violence.

Elections held in June 1993 for president and legislature both saw sizable victories for the Front pour la démocratie au Burundi (FRODEBU) and its presidential candidate, Melchior Ndadaye, who was sworn in in July. On October 21, members of the majority Tutsi armed forces staged a coup, taking control of the presidential palace and other key buildings before killing a number of Hutu politicians and the president and declaring a state of emergency. The scale of the ethnic massacres that ensued, along with internal and international protests, led to the ultimate failure of the coup (though it has been called the "creeping coup," leaving as it did the government in such a weak position as to be almost powerless).

Some 50,000 people were killed in a matter of weeks. Additionally, 700,000 individuals became refugees, while 600,000 were made "internally displaced persons." Clashes between ethnically based militia groups escalated in early 1994, partly disguised as "disarmament operations" and partly provoked by the government's request for an Organization for African Unity force to be sent to the country to protect its ministers. Hundreds more were killed during this period, and, again, thousands more were made refugees or internally displaced.

On April 6, 1994, President Cyprien Ntaryamira (elected by the national assembly in January that year) was killed when the plane he was traveling in with President Juvénal Habyarimana of Rwanda was shot down. Ethnic killings followed—though on nothing like the scale of those in Rwanda—as calls for peace by the interim president were largely heeded. Unable to stop Hutu rebel attacks against government forces, the June elections were suspended. Tensions increased, however, as more than 200,000 Rwandan refugees (almost exclusively Hutu) flooded into the country, away from the advancing Tutsi-dominated Front Patriotique Rwandais (Rwandan Patriotic Front).

In June, certain Hutu rebels formed together as the Front for the Defense of Democracy (FDD) and displayed a greater military capability than before. Interethnic killings and ethnic cleansing continued throughout 1995 and gathered speed from early 1996. Localized interethnic massacres continued throughout 1995 and 1996 while numerous power sharing and coalition agreements were tried and failed, even as the government and Tutsi opposition persuaded the United Nations not to intervene, as a negotiated settlement was possible.

Another coup was staged by the army in July 1996, forcing the remaining FRODEBU politicians to either flee or seek refuge with foreign missions in the capital while Buyoya was restored as interim president. A nationwide curfew was imposed, national borders sealed, and the forced repatriation of Rwandan refugees halted, while Burundi's neighbors reacted by imposing an embargo. This was relaxed somewhat in April 1997 in order to allow deliveries of food and medicine to resume. Fighting between the army and Hutu militia continued across large parts of the country throughout the year, as did the government's violent regroupment policy and institution of camps, causing further displacement of the civilian population.

Peace talks properly began in Arusha, Tanzania, in 1998. Progress was slow, and at various points during the proceedings certain key parties and rebel groups, both Tutsi and Hutu, refused to take part. An agreement for pretransition and transition periods to be followed by democratic elections was eventually signed in August 2000, an achievement due in no small part to the efforts of the former South African president Nelson Mandela. In October, Mandela also announced that a 700-member-strong force of South African troops, to be joined by troops from other African nations after a period, would be sent to Burundi to ensure the safety of returning politicians. The presence

of the head of the FDD at another summit suggested that they, too—who had so far refused to endorse the Arusha accords—might now agree to a ceasefire. However, the party split, with the breakaway group seemingly having the greater support.

In November 2001, under the terms of the August 2000 agreement, a transitional government was installed, with Buyoya to remain in power as president for a further 18 months, when he was to hand over power to a Hutu for the next 18 months, which would mark the end of the transition phase, with elections to follow. In May 2003 Buyoya did indeed hand over power to his Hutu counterpart, Domitien Ndayizeye, who had been the vice president for the preceding year and a half. Since then fighting has increased, steadily encroaching on the capital, and a lasting peace still appears to be some way off, a feeling widely shared by the 500,000 refugees who remain in Tanzania.

EAMONN GEARON

See also: **Rwanda: Genocide, 1994.**

Further Reading

Drumta, J. *From Coup to Coup: Thirty Years of Death, Fear and Displacement in Burundi.* Washington, D.C.: U.S. Committee for Refugees, 1996.

Eggers, E. K. *Historical Dictionary of Burundi,* 2nd ed. Lanham, Md.: Scarecrow Press, 1997.

Lemarchand, R. *Burundi: Ethnocide as Discourse and Practice.* New York and Cambridge: Woodrow Wilson Center Press and Cambridge University Press, 1994.

Longman, T. *Proxy Targets: Civilians in the War in Burundi.* New York: Human Rights Watch, 1998.

Reyntjens, F. *Burundi: Prospects for Peace.* London: Minority Rights Group, 1995.

Ruiz, H. A. *Burundi's Uprooted People: Caught in the Spiral of Violence.* Washington, D.C.: U.S. Committee for Refugees, 1995.

Scherrer, C. P. *Genocide and Crisis in Central Africa: Conflict Roots, Mass Violence, and Regional War.* Westport, Conn.: Praeger, 2002.

BuSaidi Sultanate: *See* **Zanzibar: Busaidi Sultanate in East Africa.**

Buthelezi and Inkatha Freedom Party

Mangosuthu Gatsha Buthelezi is the leader of the dominant political party in the South African province of KwaZulu Natal, the Inkatha Freedom Party. He has been a major actor in the late-twentieth-century history of South Africa, in a variety of capacities. Buthelezi was born August 27, 1928, in KwaZulu to Chief Mathole Buthelezi and Princess Magogo ka Dinuzulu, and into the upper levels of the Zulu aristocracy; on his mother's side he is a descendant of the Zulu king Cetshwayo, and on his father's side he is descended from Chief Mathole Buthelezi, prime minister to the Zulu king Solomon kaDinzulu.

Buthelezi received his education in the African school system, culminating in a B.A. from the University of Fort Hare in 1950. In 1952 he married, and shortly thereafter he began a career in the Zulu political system. The early 1950s were a major transitional period in South Africa. The National Party, which won the elections of 1948, was firmly in power and beginning the process of implementing its policy of apartheid.

Like many black South Africans of his generation, Buthelezi responded to these changes by becoming a member of the African National Congress (ANC). He joined the ANC Youth League while at Fort Hare, in 1949. The ANC would engage in a number of highly publicized struggles against the South African government; it was ultimately banned by the government on April 8, 1960, in the wake of the negative publicity it received after the police initiated the Sharpeville massacre of ANC and Pan-Africanist Congress (PAC) activists.

Buthelezi's greatest impact would be in the homelands government of his native KwaZulu. Starting in 1954, Buthelezi became the acting chief of the Buthelezi tribe, or division, of the Zulu. Later, during the 1970s, he would become the chief executive officer and chief executive counselor of the KwaZulu legislature.

The position from which he would make his greatest impact, though, was that of chief minister of KwaZulu (1975–1994). As chief minister, Buthelezi was essentially the head of government for the KwaZulu homeland. It was in this position of leadership that Buthelezi founded what was then the Inkatha liberation movement. Inkatha was a political organization based on the cultural traditions of the Zulu people. According to official Inkatha literature, the purpose of Inkatha was to "fill the vacuum caused by the banning of the ANC and PAC." Inkatha notes that its founding was roughly contemporary to that of the black consciousness movement founded by Steve Biko.

The differences among Inkatha, the black consciousness movement, and the banned organizations were quite profound. Whereas the black consciousness movement, the ANC, and the PAC all tried to make connections between the various communities that suffered from apartheid, Inkatha, though open to all, was founded firmly on a basis of Zulu culture, which had the effect of functionally limiting its appeal to members of the Zulu community. In particular, Inkatha tended to gain membership among men either in the rural homeland or among those workers who found themselves living in single-sex hostels in Johannesburg. These men were often unfamiliar with urban life, and Inkatha provided them with a sense of identity and importance. Many antiapartheid activists, however, regarded political organizations based on ethnic or tribal lines as playing into the preconceptions of the proponents of the apartheid system.

Throughout the period of struggle against apartheid, a majority of black South Africans were skeptical of Buthelezi and Inkatha, because Buthelezi retained his position in the homeland government despite a general agreement that the homelands were, at best, puppet regimes, and at worst, warehouses of potential labor for South African mining and industry. Although Buthelezi refused to accept "independence" for his homeland as part of the South African government's separate development strategy, many of his critics felt that this was not enough and that any participation in the homeland system invalidated his criticisms of the South African government.

Buthelezi and Inkatha disagreed significantly with other groups on the issue of economic sanctions against South Africa. While the ANC and PAC leadership strongly argued in favor of sanctions and increasing pressure on the apartheid state, Buthelezi argued that such actions were counter to the interests of poor, black workers. Buthelezi's stance against sanctions, along with the ethnic foundation of Inkatha, were his strongest sources of support in the period of the antiapartheid struggle.

For a period of time, some South African business and political leaders in the white communities saw Buthelezi as a leader who could offer an alternative to the ANC leadership, which was seen as too strongly allied to the Radical Left. For instance, in 1981 Buthelezi arranged a meeting with white business leaders during which he urged them to work toward dismantling the apartheid system. However, as the 1980s continued, it became clear that Buthelezi had a limited appeal, and that only the ANC would be able to provide the kind of legitimacy that would allow for a binding settlement between South Africa's communities.

In 1990 the South African president, F. W. de Klerk, released ANC leader Nelson Mandela from prison. From that point forward, it became clear that Mandela would be the key to any new political arrangement in South Africa. During the early 1990s Buthelezi began to search for political allies, to ensure a major role for himself and Inkatha in the transition process. At times, Inkatha engaged in talks with conservative groups such as the Afrikaner Volksfront, who sought to secure white homelands for themselves. Also of great significance were the clashes that regularly occurred between members of Inkatha and the ANC, especially in KwaZulu and Natal. (It later became clear that the South African security forces supported Inkatha in these violent clashes). In the years leading up to the election of the country's first nonracially determined government in 1994, these clashes came close to civil war and killed many thousands of people.

Buthelezi, along with former president de Klerk, would serve as vice presidents in the coalition government headed by newly elected president Mandela; Buthelezi also served as home affairs minister. The Inkatha Freedom Party is still active in South Africa as a political party, and still dominates politics in the province of KwaZulu Natal in the curent administration of President Thabo Mbeki.

ANTHONY CHEESEBORO

See also: **South Africa: Antiapartheid Struggle; South Africa: Transition, 1990–1994.**

Further Reading

Kane-Berman, J. "Inkatha, the Paradox of South African Politics." *Optima*, no. 30 (1982): 3.

Lodge, T., and B. Nasson (eds). *All, Here and Now: Black Politics in South Africa in the 1980s.* Cape Town: David Philip, 1991.

Mané, G., and G. Hamilton. *An Appetite for Power: Buthelezi's Inkatha and South Africa.* Bloomington: Indiana University Press, 1987.

Saphine, H. "Politics and Protest in Shack Settlements of the Pretoria-Witwatersrand-Vereeniging Region, South Africa, 1980–1990." *Journal of Southern African Studies*, no. 18 (1992): 670–697.

Southall, R. "Bthelezi, Inkatha and the Politics of Compromise." *African Affairs*, no. 80 (1981): 321.

Byzantine Africa, 533–710

Byzantine imperial control of North Africa, which lasted from 533 to about 700, will forever be associated with Justinian the Great (r.527–565) and his acclaimed military commander, Belisarius, whose conquest of the earlier Vandal Empire in 533–534 was chronicled by the historian Procopius. The task of defeating the Vandals was formidable, but the weakening of Vandal resistance had been prepared by the defection of Roman Christians in the North African cities (owing to their religious hostility to Vandal Aryanism) and especially by the independence of the indigenes, dubbed by the Romans as the Mauri (i.e., Moors; later known as the "Berbers").

Though both archaeological and literary evidence is sparse, there appears to have been considerable continuity in municipal administration between the Roman, subsequent Vandal, and later Byzantine governments, at the capital city of Carthage and at such well-known towns as Cillium, Casae Calanae, Apisa Maius, Calama, Hippo Regius, Bagai, and Lepcis Magna. But we know little about the ethnolinguistic composition of the settler populations or the administration of these towns during the Byzantine period. Virtually all the Byzantine farmers spoke Punic or Latin, while the Berbers were mostly herdsmen. The immigrant Greek population was probably limited to a few thousand soldiers, a few hundred officials, and several dozen merchants. At the height of its territorial power, the Byzantine Empire was organized systematically into the four praetorian prefectures of Italy, Illyricum, the East, and, significantly, "Africa." We know that Byzantine "Africa" centered on the territories that today comprise Tunisia, the eastern part of Algeria, and western Libya; and that it was subdivided into six provinces, each under a governor (or *dux*), including Mauretania Caesariensis, Mauretania Stitifensis, Zeugitana, Byzacena, Tripolitania, and Numidia.

At this time Byzantine Carthage, with a population of perhaps 10,000, was probably the largest city in the whole of Africa. Viewed in its totality, Justinian's reassertion of Roman (the Byzantines always called themselves "Roman") Mediterranean supremacy required a substantial bureaucratic and military establishment, which was extremely expensive. This imposed a heavy tax burden, including a ground tax or "tribute," and the *annona* (a land tax), on all subjects of the empire, including those of North Africa. Indeed, the burden of local taxes is cited as one of the causes for continued Berber intransigence against Byzantine rule in North Africa.

Recent archaeological excavations of Byzantine fortifications suggest that the Byzantine political presence extended inland from the Mediterranean to the great Dorsal of Tripolitania, including the Mountains of Tebessa, the Aures Plateau, and Hodna, but it scarcely touched the Berbers of the deep interior or the Atlas region (present-day Morocco). Beyond the coastal plain, Byzantine power depended on precarious alliances and delegated administrative powers with the leaders of friendly Berber tribes, who in return for cash payments intermittently undertook the collection of taxes and assistance in maintaining a frontier zone of relative order. The ability of the Byzantines to defend against hostile Berber attack depended less on their forts (which were, indeed, stronger than in Roman times) than on the ability of their soldiers (*comitatenses* and *limitanei*) to resist the Berbers in the field. Still, the outer limits of the African Prefecture remained in the hands of independent and resistant tribal chieftains; and there were violent insurrections in 539, from 544 to 548, and again in 563, all suppressed by the Byzantines—but only after great effort and cost in money and lives. Deepening the contemporary sense of turbulence and crisis were the terrible effects of the Bubonic Plague in 542–543. During the latter part of Justinian's reign and under succeeding emperors, the Byzantine military garrison depended increasingly on diplomacy and the playing off of one Berber subgroup against another.

Throughout the Byzantine period a substantial commerce between North Africa and other parts of the empire, including Asia Minor, continued to be based in part on the export of wheat, which accounted for a significant part of the prefecture's taxes to the imperial government at Constantinople. Another famous product was African "Red Slip" pottery, which found ready markets in many parts of the Mediterranean. Carthage, in turn, imported silks, spices, and oils from the Near East. In fact, the desire to gain control over the eastern spice and silk trades at the expense of the Persians had been one of the motivations behind the famous Red Sea expedition by Emperor Justin (Justinian's uncle) to assist the kingdom of Axum in Ethiopia in its invasion of Himyar in southwest Arabia in 524–525; and there were further diplomatic and commercial contacts with Axum during the reign of Justinian. Despite the fact that the Ethiopian Church followed the Monophysite doctrine while the Byzantines adhered to Orthodoxy, the emperors of the House of Justin always viewed Axum as a brother Christian kingdom and ally. Modern historians have begun to reassess the extent of Byzantine cultural influence in Africa wielded through the Greek language—frequently in conjunction with Latin—and through the priests and bishops of the Orthodox Church. Recent research reveals that there was an interesting and fluctuating interplay between the North African Church and both Rome and Constantinople. It further suggests that the Christianization of Nubia (especially the Novidae people) of the Nile Valley in the sixth century was accomplished mainly by Byzantine missionaries under the control of Constantinople, rather than by priests of the Coptic church of Egypt.

Though Byzantium ultimately failed in its efforts to displace the Persians in the Near Eastern/Asian trade, until the mid-seventh century the Byzantine Empire still held the Mediterranean Basin, including Egypt; most of the northwest African coast; Dalmatia; northwest Italy; Crete; Corsica; Malta; Sardinia; and the Balearics under its political and naval sway. And though there continued to be raiding by the Berber tribes, the impression gained from the chronicles is that the period from 564 to the 640s was one of relative stability and prosperity for Byzantine North Africa.

One indicator of the growing strains on the frontiers of the empire during the reigns of the Emperors Maurice (582–602) and Heraclius (610–641) was the subordination of Byzantine civil administrators at the two vital strategic prefectures of Italy and Africa to military control under governors general called exarchs. These exarchates set the tone for the further militarization of provincial administration under themes in the centuries ahead. But these changes were not enough to stem the erosion of territorial power under external assault—by the Persians in Asia, by the Lombards in northern Italy, and by the rising force of Islam in North Africa. The first invasion by Arabs on the eastern flank of the African Exarchate was reported in 647, when a small marauding party from Egypt defeated an army under the exarch Gregory at Sufetula in Numidia. Neither this, nor the landing of an Arab force by sea in 660, ended the Byzantine presence in North Africa. Byzantine "Africa," partly with the aid of Berber military support, continued to exist as a semi-independent kingdom against repeated Arab assault until the fall of Carthage in 698. Its presence was not finally extinguished until the Muslim march on the port of Ceuta, en route across the Straits to Spain, in 709–710.

RAYMOND E. DUMETT

See also: **Berbers: Ancient North Africa; Carthage; Monophysitism, Coptic Church, 379–640; Vandals and North Africa, 429–533.**

Further Reading

Cameron, A. *Changing Cultures in Early Byzantium.* Aldershot, England: Variorum, 1996.

Diehl, C. *L'Afrique byzantine.* Paris, 1896.

Papadopoullos, T. *Africano-Byzantina: Byzantine Influences on Negro-Sudanese Cultures.* Athens, 1966.

Procopius. *The Anecdota or Secret History,* edited and translated by E. H. Dewing. London: LCL, 1935.

Pringle, D. *The Defence of Byzantine Africa from Justinian to the Arab Conquest.* 2 vols. Oxford: BAR, 1981.

Treadgold, D. *A History of the Byzantine State and Society.* Stanford, Calif, 1997.

Vasiliev, A. A. *History of the Byzantine Empire.* 2 vols. Madison: University of Wisconsin Press, 1952, 1964.

Whittow, M. "Ruling the Late Roman and Early Byzantine City." *Past and Present,* no. 129 (1990): 3–29.

C

Cabinda

With the cessation of conflict between the Angolan government and UNITA militias in April 2002, attention turned to the ongoing separatist conflict in Cabinda. An oil-rich enclave separated from the rest of Angola by a slender strip of territory of the Democratic Republic of Congo (DRC), Cabinda has been the site of a decades-long war of independence between the Angolan government and various separatist factions, a struggle that has been called "Africa's forgotten war." Approximately 30,000 people have lost their lives in almost 30 years of struggles for independence. Despite the severe humanitarian crisis, access to the enclave has been largely closed to all but those who work in the oil industry.

Cabinda's massive oil wealth has made the enclave an essential contributor to Angola's national economy as well as a much contested site. Cabinda's oil fields generate approximately 60 per cent of Angola's oil. The province accounts for the majority of Angolan oil revenues, which contribute 42 per cent of the gross domestic product and 90 per cent of the state budget.

Cabinda's offshore deposit, Block Zero, is among the world's most lucrative oil fields and the cornerstone of Angola's petroleum industry. Concession rights to Block Zero were initially granted in 1957, and exploration began shortly thereafter. Since production started in 1968, Block Zero has produced more than two billion barrels of oil. By 1983 Gulf had invested $1.3 billion in the Cabindan operation, accounting for 90 per cent of Angola's foreign exchange.

The 1980s and 1990s saw substantial new investments in development and increased production. Oil exports from the enclave stood at $2.5 billion in 1997. By 2000, Angola's production was almost 800,000 barrels per day, almost six times 1980s levels. This placed Angola behind only Nigeria as the largest oil producer in Sub-Saharan Africa.

Chevron Texaco has dominated the province's development from its near-colonial operational base at Malongo. The company's complex, including oil storage depots, a residential area for Chevron employees, and a small refinery, is set apart from the rest of Cabinda and guarded by private security companies. Local staff do not live within the settlement, and there is much resentment over disparities in living standards. This has fueled local resentment regarding exploitation of the area's vast resources by outsiders.

Cabindans have been deeply critical of the role of oil companies in the region. In 1999 an oil spill near the Malonga base severely damaged fish stocks. Cabindan fishers have sought compensation for destruction caused by oil spills but have only received US$2000 in compensation from Chevron Texaco and this was paid to only 10 per cent of fishers. In addition to spills, ongoing pollution from regular prduction has also been identified as contributing to reduced fish stocks.

Cabinda's relationship with Angola has been a point of great conflict since the time of colonial rule. The territory was linked politically to Angola in the Treaty of Simulambuco of 1885, which acknowledged Cabinda's distinct status as an enclave. Cabinda was governed by Portugal as a separate colony until 1956, when it was incorporated into Angola and brought under direct authority of the Portuguese governor general of Angola. Despite its administrative connection to Angola, Cabinda has remained geographically, linguistically, and ethnically linked with what are now Congo-Brazzavile and the Democratic Republic of Congo. Many Cabindans have long maintained that theirs is an autonomous territory, and separatists insist that Cabinda should have been granted its own independence following the end of Portuguese colonial rule.

The first independence movement, the Movement for the Liberation of the Enclave of Cabinda was founded in 1960, the year of emergence of armed struggle against Portuguese rule in Angola. Two other groups, the Committee for Action and Union of Cabinda and the Maiombe Alliance, emerged around the same time. In 1963 the three movements combined to form the Frente para a Libertação do Enclave de Cabinda (FLEC).

The FLEC was excluded from participation in the April 1974 Alvor talks between the Portuguese colonial authorities and three Angolan nationalist groups, the MPLA, the FNLA, and the UNITA, which set the stage for Angolan independence. Article 3 of the Alvor Accord, signed in January 1975, maintained that Cabinda would remain an integral part of Angola. FLEC appealed to the Organization of African Unity and the United Nations, but, receiving no satisfactory assistance from those organizations, took up armed struggle against the MPLA government of Angola. The ensuing guerrilla war saw attacks on government troops stationed in Angola and the occasional kidnapping of Chevron employees.

During the 1980s, FLEC split over strategic differences to form FLEC-FAC, the main armed faction of FLEC, and FLEC-Renovada. FLEC-FAC has maintained some armed activities, but was severely weakened by the overthrow of their patron, Zaïre's president Mobutu Sese Seko, in 1996.

The talks between the Angolan government and the UNITA during 1991–1992 that culminated in the signing of the Bicesse Accords also excluded the Cabindan separatists. Left out of the peace agreement, they continued the war in the enclave. Once again, in 1994, a new peace agreement, the Lusaka Protocol, failed to include the Cabindan separatists, meaning that fighting continued unabated. FLEC-FAC did not participate in a 2002 conference on the constitutional future of Angola that was held in Angola and that discussed such matters of importance to Cabindans as local autonomy, decentralization, and constitutional reform.

Meetings throughout the 1990s among the various Cabindan independence groups and the Angolan government brought no resolution to the conflict. The Angolan government's involvement in the civil wars in the civil wars in the DRC and the Republic of Congo rendered those countries unavailable as bases of operation for the Cabindan rebels.

Since the 1990s the Angolan government has begun to address Cabindan grievances concerning the lack of infrastructure and development in the province. To this day only 10 per cent of oil revenues are returned to the province. Cabinda's oil wealth has ensured that the Angolan government, like the Portuguese government before it, would never willingly grant independence to the enclave.

A massive sweep of the enclave by Angolan forces in October 2002, targeted at driving secessionists out of Cabinda, destroyed FLEC-FAC's main base and forced many independence fighters to abandon the guerrilla struggle. By the end of the year the army had also captured the main base of FLEC-Renovada, causing the group to cease operations. The 2002 offensive that militarily defeated FLEC left its leaders in exile and renewed government hopes for an end to the lengthy conflict. A meeting in July 2003 between Angolan authorities and Ranque Franque, FLEC cofounder and leader, further raised hopes that a negotiated settlement was on the horizon.

While the military defeat left FLEC leaders willing to negotiate a settlement, any successful outcome of peace talks will depend in part on whether civil society groups, rather than only the FLEC leaders, take part in the process. Civil society groups have demanded a cease-fire, the end of human rights violations by the Angolan Army (which carried out atrocities against civilian population), and improved rights and conditions for local oil workers.

Calls by the separatists for Portugal to intervene and establish a transitional government have been rejected by the Portuguese government, which views the conflict as an internal Angolan issue. Similarly, FLEC calls for a referendum on independence, similar to the one held in East Timor and supervised by the United Nations, in which only Cabindans would vote, have been rejected by the government which argues that all Angolans should vote on an issue of national importance. While Cabindans still desire independence, many would now settle for autonomy, some form of which the Angolan government has claimed it would be willing to negotiate.

JEFF SHANTZ

Further Reading

Dos Santos, D. "The Politics of Oil in Angola's Enclave." In *African Islands and Enclaves*, edited by R. Cohen. Beverly Hills: Sage, 1983.

Hodges, T. *Angola: From Afro-Stalinism to Petro-Diamond Capitalism.* Oxford: James Currey/Bloomington: Indiana University Press, 2001.

Martin, P. "The Cabinda Connection: An Historical Perspective." *African Affairs* 76, no. 302 (1977): 47–59.

———. *Historical Dictionary of Angola.* Metuchen, N.J.: Scarecrow Press, 1980.

Porto, J. G. "Cabinda: Notes on a Soon to Be Forgotten War." African Security Analysis Oçassional Paper.

Wright, G. *The Destruction of a Nation: United States Policy toward Angola since 1945.* London: Pluto Press, 1997.

Cabral, Amílcar: *See* **Guinea-Bissau: Cabral, Amílcar, PAICG, Independence, 1961–1973.**

Cairo

Although the city of Cairo was not founded until the medieval era, the approximate geographical site has a much longer history. The city of Memphis, one of the capitals of ancient Egypt, was originally established on land currently part of the modern city of Cairo. After conquering Egypt, the Romans then established a nearby city they called Babylon (now located in the Misr al-Qadimah portion of the city of Cairo). Next came the city of al-Fustat, founded by the Arab conqueror of Egypt, 'Amr ibn al-'As, who was also responsible for bringing Islam to Egypt. The modern city of Cairo (in Arabic, *al-Qahirah*, "the victorious"), however, owes its establishment to the Fatimid caliph al-Mu'izz.

From its establishment in 969 and its adoption as the Fatimid capital a few years later, Cairo has remained the seat of political and economic power in Egypt and a city of major strategic importance. The Mamluk Sultanate (1260–1516) made Cairo its capital, and under Mamluk rule the city prospered. By about 1340, not only had Cairo's population swelled to half a million inhabitants (making it the largest city on three continents), but, as the home of al-Azhar University, it had also become the main seat of learning in the Islamic world. It was also well-positioned to profit from the spice trade from Asia to the Mediterranean. The later years of Mamluk rule were not so kind to Cairo, however. The bubonic plague swept through Cairo in 1348, resulting in severe human losses. Economic losses soon followed, as Portuguese adventurer Vasco da Gama successfully sailed from Europe to India, establishing a sea route to the east and thus allowing the spice trade to bypass Cairo.

The arrival of Ottoman rule in Egypt in 1517 did not help Cairo's fortunes either, as the city became one of many provincial capitals in the larger Ottoman Empire, ruled from Istanbul. The city remained relatively unimportant for several centuries; by the time Napoleon's armies invaded Egypt in 1798, Cairo's population had declined to fewer than 300,000.

The city began a period of renaissance, however, in the 1830s, due to the modernizing efforts of Muhammad 'Ali, who served as Ottoman governor of Egypt from 1805 until his death in 1849. Muhammad 'Ali's modernization program included improvements in irrigation, roads, agriculture, education, and the military, all of which had a positive effect on Cairo's economy and population. However, it was during the reign of the *khedive* Isma'il (1863–1879) that Cairo

David Roberts (1796–1864), *Cairo from the West* (CT25870). Victoria and Albert Museum, London. © Victoria and Albert Museum, London/Art Resource, New York.

became a truly modern city. Embarking on a lavish spending program that Egypt could not afford (and which was a major contributor to the huge foreign debt that provided Britain with an excuse to occupy the country in 1882), Isma'il set out to make Cairo a European city. He ordered the construction of a new city next to medieval Cairo, to be planned by French engineers. The districts of Abdin, al-Isma'iliyyah, and al-Ezbekiyyah (located in the center of present-day Cairo) were the fruits of his labors. These new districts became the heart of colonial Cairo after the British entry into Egypt in 1882.

The twentieth and twenty-first centuries have witnessed more changes for the city, chief among them massive growth in population as a result of migration from rural regions as well as higher overall population growth rates. This influx of people has crowded the city beyond its capacity, resulting simultaneously in the development of shantytowns on the outskirts of the city, the establishment of residences in the vast northern and southern cemetery complexes (known as the City of the Dead), and the development of new suburbs (such as Heliopolis and al-Ma'adi), satellite towns (such as Tenth of Ramadan City and Sixth of October City) and planned communities (such as al-Mohandessin and Medinat Nasr).

Nonetheless, Cairo, known for centuries as *Umm al-Dunya* (mother of the world) remains the heart of Egypt. To Egyptians, *Misr* (Egypt) means both Egypt and Cairo, further illustrating the importance of the capital city. In 1919, Cairo was the location of the short-lived 1919 revolution against British control; three years later Egypt gained formal independence (though Britain retained certain rights in Egypt, including the stationing of troops). The city also played a key role in further revolts against British domination (which continued until after the 1952 revolution) after

World War II. In January 1952, riots erupted in Cairo directed against centers of "foreign" influence, including targets such as the British Turf Club, the Shepherd's Hotel (long a center of European social life in Cairo), cinemas that showed foreign films, nightclubs, bars, and many Jewish-owned commercial establishments. Later that year, on July 23, the revolution (really a military coup) occurred, toppling the corrupt and widely despised King Faruq from power and installing in his place the kindly figure of General Muhammad Naguib (though real power was retained by the coup's mastermind, Gamal Abdel Nasser, who shortly took sole control of the government). Nasser's policies of sequestration and "Egyptianization" (particularly after the 1956 Suez War) affected Cairo as they did Alexandria: many of the city's foreign and minority residents opted to leave the country. Though Egypt benefited from a cessation of its state of war with Israel after the signing of the Camp David Accords in 1979, Cairo's status among Arab capitals suffered. Many Arab nations cut diplomatic ties with Egypt, and the League of Arab States moved its headquarters from Cairo to Tunis, leading to a mass exodus of Arab diplomats from the city. (Relations have been restored since, however.) An earthquake in Cairo in 1992 resulted in the deaths of approximately 1,000 people, when poorly constructed high-rise buildings and hastily built dwellings collapsed.

Today Cairo's population is approaching 20 million. As the year-round seat of government (the use of Alexandria as Egypt's summer capital having been halted after the 1952 revolution), the center of commerce and industry, the home of foreign embassies, once more the headquarters of the League of Arab States, and an eternally popular tourist destination, Cairo remains—as it has been since medieval times—the political, strategic, diplomatic, economic, and cultural key to Egypt.

AMY J. JOHNSON

See also: **Egypt: Fatimid Caliphate; Egypt: Muhammad Ali, 1805–1849: State and Economy; Egypt: Ottoman, 1517–1798: Napoleon and the French in Egypt (1798–1801)**

Further Reading

Abu-Lughod, J. L. *Cairo: 1001 Years of the City Victorious*. Princeton, N.J.: Princeton University Press, 1971.

Lane-Poole, S. *The Story of Cairo*. London: Dent, 1924.

Mostyn, T. *Egypt's Belle Epoque: Cairo 1869–1952*. London: Quartet, 1989.

Peccinotti, H. *Cairo: The Site and the History*. London: Stacey, 1988.

Rodenbeck, M. *Cairo: The City Victorious*. New York: Alfred A. Knopf, 1999.

Saad el-Din, M., et al. *Cairo: The Site and the History*. Baton Rouge: Louisiana State University Press, 1988.

Sanders, P. *Ritual, Politics, and the City in Fatimid Cairo*. Albany: State University of New York Press, 1994.

Stewart, D. *Cairo: 5500 Years*. New York: Crowell, 1968.

Wiet, G. *Cairo, City of Art and Commerce*, translated by Seymour Feiler. Westport, Conn.: Greenwood Press, 1983.

Cameroon: Nineteenth Century

During the nineteenth century, the history of what is now the Republic of Cameroon was characterized by extreme diversity and considerable change. This brief entry cannot do justice to the variety of societies and historical experiences key to that era, but will concentrate on a few examples. On the coast, the Duala had been involved in overseas commerce since the mid-eighteenth century, acting as middlemen between European traders and peoples of the interior. The Duala engaged in fishing and agriculture, the latter mostly carried out by slaves and women. However, their most lucrative activity was bartering goods (slaves, and in the nineteenth century, mainly palm oil and ivory) obtained through inland canoe expeditions and exchanged for important commodities brought to them by European trading vessels. In the nineteenth century, Duala *roi-marchands* (merchant kings) succeeded in bringing the littoral river network under their control. The influence of the Duala went beyond purely economic aspects, but could never be transformed into a stable political system. On the contrary, during this period the Duala split into rival lineages. Trading zones in the hinterland were divided up among Duala groups, but without coming under the political control of the various clans and lineages involved. *Big men* is probably the best label to describe the principal actors in a political system of this kind; they were successful operators of local enterprises, centered around trading canoes with large numbers of personal retainers including kinsmen, unrelated Duala, and slaves. Within nineteenth-century Duala society, slaves were the key element in constructing an effective commercial organization, as well as the exploited victims of such an enterprise. For centuries the Bamiléké highlands and the neighboring grasslands in what is now Western Cameroon had served as an important slave and labor reservoir not only for the Duala, but for the coastal and southern parts of Cameroon and Nigeria in general.

The term *Bamiléké* is a twentieth-century construction. For a long time most Bamiléké had no conception of themselves as such, but rather identified with the particular chiefdoms from which they originated. There were more than 100 of these entities, differing greatly in size, spread across the Bamiléké homelands. By the second half of the nineteenth century, various population movements, wars, and currents of commercial and cultural exchange had given rise throughout the grasslands to highly complex

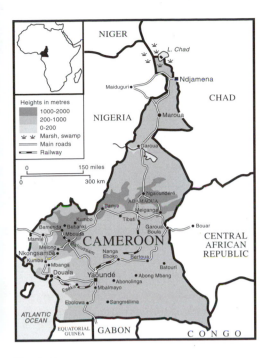

Cameroon.

political formations. Chieftaincies old and new (the very first—a polity called Baleng—existed in the sixteenth century) were coming into their own, developing increasingly centralized governments and systems of socioeconomic organization. By the 1880s, the Bamiléké social structure as it is described in the accounts of colonial observers was well in place. At the heart of this structure, in each chieftaincy, stood one central figure: the *fo*, an all-powerful, semidivine ruler. Each polity's citizens could be divided into four categories: notables and their heirs, chiefly retainers and their heirs, untitled folk, and slaves. Titles were available to men only, as were positions in the chief's employment. Though in many respects profoundly rigid, the system did allow for social mobility. Central to a notable's status was participation in at least one of the numerous associations charged with overseeing key aspects of the community's day-to-day life. The population of the grasslands grew more or less continuously from around 1700. In the nineteenth century, for instance, entire communities fled before the onslaught of Fulbe slave raiders hailing from the Muslim north; the attacks pushed thousands of men, women, and children across the Noun River to the Bamiléké Plateau.

By 1850, in the north of Cameroon, long-distance slave raids were a large-scale phenomenon. In Adamawa, with its center Ngaoundere, slavery took on major proportions. The Adamawa jihad, an extension of Usman dan Fodio's conquest of the Hausa states of Nigeria, was undertaken in the early nineteenth century by small groups of Fulbe who established a Muslim emirate and a number of lamidates. The Fulbe, however, were substantially outnumbered by the local "pagan" groups of the region. Ngaoundere was no exception in this regard, and the rapid integration of conquered Mbum and other peoples into the Fulbe state, which transformed large numbers of former enemies into effective elements of the state political and economic apparatus, is remarkable. In addition to locally conquered "pagan" peoples, the size of the servile population at Ngaoundere was further enlarged by slaves captured at distances of 200 to 500 kilometers from Ngaoundere town itself. European observers at the end of the nineteenth century estimated that as many as 8,000 to 10,000 slaves were taken on these raids annually. Those captives who were not settled at Ngaoundere were sold to Hausa or Kanuri traders, and Adamawa soon gained a reputation as a "slave traders' Eldorado." The structure of slavery in Adamawa in the nineteenth century was determined primarily by military and commercial factors. The involvement of slaves in production, while undoubtedly the source of much of the food on which the Fulbe states subsisted, was of relatively minor structural importance. The Fulbe conquest did not go beyond what is now northern Cameroon. However, the ruling aristocracy of the kingdom of Bamum in the grasslands was converted to Islam in the nineteenth century, following contact with Fulbe invaders and Hausa traders.

ANDREAS ECKERT

Further Reading

Austen, R. A., and Jonathan Derrick. *Middlemen of the Cameroon Rivers. The Duala and Their Hinterland, c.1600–c.1960.* Cambridge: Cambridge University Press, 1999.

Burnham, P. "Raiders and Traders in Adamawa: Slavery as a Regional System." *Paideuma*, no. 41 (1995): 153–176.

Geary, C. M. *Things of the Palace: A Catalogue of the Bamum Palace Museum in Foumban.* Wiesbaden: Franz Steiner, 1983.

Cameroon (Kamerun): Colonial Period: German Rule

The establishment of a German protectorate in Kamerun (English "Cameroon," French "Cameroun") in July 1884 came as a surprise to the British, who were slow to accept the requests from the Duala kings to annex their territory. The area that was called Kamerun was limited to the coast and the principal town was Douala, its inhabitants known as the Duala. King Akwa (Ngando Mpondo) and King Bell (Ndoumb'a Lobe) were the two principal kings in Douala.

After the 1840s, the British successfully established their trading and missionary activities in Douala and the Duala abandoned the inhumane trade in slaves in favor of trade in items such as palm oil and kernels, cocoa, and rubber. After 1869, however, British traders experienced stiff competition from the Germans. The British activities in Douala so impressed the Duala that their kings later requested the British to annex their territory.

Despite these appeals, the British government failed to act promptly because, among other reasons, it felt that the territory was not viable enough to finance without an additional tax burden on the British taxpayers; the "unhealthy" West African climate, "the whiteman's grave," did not help the Duala request. Meanwhile, the German government of Chancellor Otto von Bismarck encouraged the establishment of a German protectorate in Cameroon.

In February 1884, Bismarck instructed Gustave Nachtigal to go to Africa and safeguard the interests of German traders; the British Foreign Office was informed accordingly. However, in a secret dispatch to Nachtigal, Bismarck commissioned him to annex the coast between Bimbia and Cape St. John, hoist the German flag, and declare that German firms had signed treaties with the local chiefs. In Douala, Eduard Schmidt, of the Woermann Firm, was instructed to secretly convince the Duala kings to accept a German annexation of their territory. Through intrigues and gifts, the kings were persuaded to sign a treaty with the representatives of the German firms in Douala on July 12, 1884.

According to the terms of the treaty, the Duala kings and their subordinates ceded their rights of sovereignty, legislation, and administration over their people and land to the private German firms. However, the land of the towns and villages remained the private property of the indigents, and the kings were allowed to continue to levy their dues and retain their customs and usages. The Duala also retained their middleman commercial role. Although the treaty was between some German private firms and the Duala kings, the German government later took over the administration of the territory and expanded into the hinterland, through the subjugation of unwilling ethnic groups and active collaboration from others. This treaty was one of the 95 treaties that the Germans signed with various ethnic groups in Kamerun between 1884 and 1916 in which the indigenous kings or chiefs surrendered their rights of sovereignty, legislation, and administration.

In Kamerun, the colonial authorities used what the British later called the indirect rule system, though with certain modifications, to suit the given circumstance and environment. This system was used alongside the divide-and-rule principle. The colonial authorities also collaborated with prominent local chiefs. In Muslim northern Kamerun, the colonial administrators used the traditional rulers, the *lamibe*, though they did not hesitate to punish and/or depose recalcitrant rulers, as was done elsewhere in the territory.

Kamerun was, for administrative purposes, divided into divisions that were controlled by divisional officers. There were two distinct judicial systems for the maintenance of law and order, and the execution of justice: one for Europeans and another for Africans. The most common form of penalty was whipping, but women were, generally, exempted from this type of penalty. Offenses by African employees were punished by disciplinary sanction, which was either flogging or confinement in irons. These offences included desertion, laziness, theft, disobedience, and carelessness. The most severe sanction was the death penalty, and this was passed only after the approval of the governor. The police force assured public security, and in 1895 a regular colonial troop was created.

In order to foster German economic interests, the colonial authorities, traders, and agricultural agents ran into problems with the indigenous population, who resisted the German intrusion. The causes of the resistances included the forceful use of indigents as laborers for either the plantations or road and railway construction companies, the disappearance of the middleman monopoly of trade that several ethnic groups enjoyed, the reluctance and/or refusal to pay taxes by the local population, and the expropriation of indigenous land by the colonial administration. The resistances came mainly from the Duala, the Bakweri, the Beti, the Bangwa, the Banyang, and the Nso. The most celebrated resistance was the Duala resistance of 1910–1913, led by King Rudolf Duala Manga Bell.

Despite these resistances, the German colonial administration and economic interest groups wanted to establish a commercial colony in Cameroon. Several German companies subsequently established plantations, the most prominent of which was the West African Plantation Company, Victoria. In order to ease the transportation of goods, the authorities built roads and railways. Apart from economic interests, various German missionary bodies were involved in evangelization. These missionary bodies were the German Basel Mission, the German Baptist Mission, and the Roman Catholic Church, led by the Pallotin Fathers. J. Deibol was ordained in 1901 as the first indigenous Basel Mission pastor, and Lotin Same was consecrated in 1908 as the first indigenous German Baptist Mission pastor. The missionaries also established health centers and schools.

In the field of education, the first German teacher, Theodor Christaller, arrived in Cameroon in 1887. In 1910, the colonial authorities enacted an education law, and Article 2 stipulated that no other language, except German, could be taught or used as a medium of instruction. Article 3 of the law, however, defined the areas where the Duala language could be used as a medium of instruction. This law provided a school program for the mission schools and a primary cycle of five years. The administration, in an attempt to educate its future indigenous administrators, sent several Kamerunians to Germany for further studies. Incidentally, some of these German-educated Cameroonians returned home and became the flag bearers of the opposition force against German colonial rule, as was demonstrated by Rudolf Duala Manga Bell and Martin-Paul Samba on the eve of the outbreak of World War I. Others, like Charles Atangana, became fervent supporters of the Germans.

In August 1914, World War I was transported to Kamerun as Germany tried unsuccessfully to get Britain and France to respect the neutrality clauses (Articles 10 and 11) of the Berlin Act of 1885. A joint Anglo-French force, led by Major General Charles Dobell, and a Franco-Belgian force headed by General Joseph Aymerich invaded German Kamerun, but a French-proposed joint Anglo-French administration of Kamerun failed to materialize. The combined allied forces, nonetheless, eventually defeated the German forces in Kamerun and in February 1916 Britain and France provisionally partitioned Kamerun between themselves along the Picot Provisional Partition Line; Britain occupied one-fifth of the territory while France occupied four-fifths. With this, the German administration of Kamerun ended.

The Germans, in promoting their economic interests in Kamerun, introduced the people to the world market economy. Politically, despite the resistances, the Germans set in motion the steam to unite the coastal, southern, central, and northern peoples into a single cohesive Kamerunian unit and provided the foundation for a modern state. German rule enabled the politically conscious Kamerunians to regard the 1916 partition as ad interim because it reminded them of a period when, according to them, Kamerun was a single entity.

VICTOR JULIUS NGOH

See also: **Colonialism: Impact on African Societies; World War I, Survey.**

Further Reading

Ardener, S. *Eye-Witnesses to the Annexation of Cameroon 1883–1887*. Buea, Cameroon: Government Press, 1968.
Elango, L. Z. *The Anglo-French Condominium in Cameroon 1914–1916: History of a Misunderstanding*. Limbe, Malawi: Navi-Group, 1987.
Ngoh, V. J. *History of Cameroon Since 1800*, Limbe, Malawi: Presbook, 1996.

Cameroon: Colonial Period: British and French Rule

Cameroon has a checkered colonial history. Unlike most African states that experienced a single colonial administration, Cameroon came under three colonial administrators: the Germans, the French and the British. The legacies of colonialism have been a mixed blessing, but for the most part they have left the country with huge problems, the most prominent being the distinct British and French cultures that were nurtured simultaneously in the territory during 1916 to around 1961. These divergent cultures have made meaningful national integration in independent Cameroon elusive.

During World War I, the Allied forces, consisting of British and French troops, defeated the Germans (with some help from the Belgians) in Kamerun. The capitulation of the last German garrison at Mora in February 1916 brought about the end of the German Kamerun Protectorate. The victors established an Anglo-French protectorate that, for all intents and purposes, was financed and manned by the British, with the French playing only a passive role. The Anglo-French protectorate was short-lived: on March 14, 1916, the two powers, by mutual agreement, delineated their zones of influence. The division of German Kamerun between Britain and France was surprisingly lopsided. Five-sixths of the territory came under French rule, while the remainder went to Britain. This arrangement has engendered intractable problems in the politics of reunification up to the present.

Unlike the French mandate, which was administered as a distinct administrative unit, the British Cameroons was, for administrative expediency, managed as an integral part of Nigeria. Thus, the indirect rule system adopted by the British in Nigeria and other administrative structures were extended to British Cameroons. Some have justified this arrangement on the ground that British Cameroons was too small to warrant a separate administration.

Opinions are divided on the wisdom of administering British Cameroon from Nigeria. One school of thought holds that the British Cameroons did not receive adequate British attention, remaining a rural backwater. Another school of thought argues that British Cameroon benefited immensely from its association with Nigeria in political, economic, social, technical, and educational terms.

Regardless, Cameroonian politicians felt overshadowed by the more experienced Nigerian politicians in the Eastern House of Assembly. This nurtured among Cameroonian politicians feelings of animosity toward the Igbo people, and later on provided the platform for reunification with French Cameroon following the plebiscite of 1961.

Colonial developments in French Cameroon can be studied under two broad periods: pre-World War II and post-World War II. Until the 1944 Brazzaville Conference, France lived under the illusion that French colonies and France would one day fuse into a single integrated political and economic unit. Therefore, unlike Britain, the French at the time did little to prepare their colonies for self-government. Assimilation was the guiding policy.

Though retaining its autonomy as a mandate territory of the League of Nations, French Cameroon was governed as part of the French colonial empire. French rule was characterized by forced labor, the deposition of chiefs, and the creation of artificial chieftaincies and despotism.

At the apex of the administrative pyramid was the French high commissioner, who was the only link between the mandated territory and the French Colonial Ministry. The commissioner set up a series of *conseils* (councils) that had advisory but not legislative functions. The commissioner was, therefore, the kingpin in the power equation.

The much-discussed assimilation in Cameroon was basically a facade, for in reality only a negligible number of "black Frenchmen" (*évolués*) were created. Assimilation existed only insofar as it created a tiny elite of évolués who were set off from the vast majority of the population (the *indigénes*). In 1922, a modified version of association that involved some measure of indirect rule and accorded recognition to some indigenous institutions was put in place by Colonial minister Albert Sarrant.

From 1944, French colonies witnessed significant reforms. The Brazzaville Conference recommended administrative decentralization while retaining political assimilation as a goal. Thus, the idea of the colonies evolving outside the framework of the French Empire was dismissed. However, the defeat of the French in Indochina, the gaining of independence by Morocco and Tunisia, the Algerian revolution, and the radicalization of the independence struggle by Cameroonian political parties like the Union de Populations du Cameroun forced France to introduce sweeping reforms in the colony. These reforms, collectively called the *loi cadre*, made substantial concessions for African local autonomy.

A direct result of the loi cadre was the dissolution of the Territorial Assembly elected in 1952 to make way for fresh elections in 1956. On May 9, 1957, the assembly took the name of l'Assemble legislative du Cameron, and, on May 15, 1957, Andre-Marie Mbida became the first prime minister of French Cameroon.

However, his government, which was short-lived, paved the way for the regime of Ahmadu Ahidjo.

Through the "carrot and stick" approach, Ahidjo gradually peripheralized all political opposition. The United Nations approved the termination of the trusteeship, and French Cameroon became independent under Ahmadu Ahidjo on January 1, 1960.

The next item on the political agenda was reunification. In 1960 both Nigeria and French Cameroon gained their independence, thus leaving the British Cameroons in the cold. On both sides of the trust territories, the Anglo-French partition of Kamerun had been viewed as an act of brazen imperialism which had to be redressed. This goal was easily achieved, thanks to the joint efforts of both Dr. John Ngu Foncha, the premier of Southern Cameroons, and Ahmadu Ahidjo, the president of French Cameroun. Following the 1961 plebiscite, Southern Cameroons voted overwhelmingly to reunite with French Cameroun, while their northern counterpart voted in favor of remaining part of Nigeria.

CANUTE A. NGWA

See also: **Cameroon (Kamerun): Colonial Period: German Rule; Cameroon: Rebellion, Independence, Unification, 1960–1961.**

Further Reading

Chem-Langhee, B. "The Road to the Unitary State of Cameroon, 1959–1972." *Annals of the Faculty of Arts, Letters and Social Sciences* 7, nos. 1–2 (1990).

Kale, P. M. *Political Evolutions in the Cameroons.* Buea, Cameroon: Government Printing Press, 1967.

Le Vine, V. T. *The Cameroons from Mandate to Independence.* Berkeley and Los Angeles: University of California Press, 1967.

Ngoh, V. J. *Cameroon 1884–1985: A Hundred Years of History.* Yaounde, Cameroon: Navi-Group, 1988.

Tambi, E., and R. Brain. *A History of the Cameroon.* London: Longman, 1974.

Cameroon: Rebellion, Independence, Unification, 1960–1961

The processes of rebellion, independence, and reunification are closely linked and culminated in the birth of modern bilingual Cameroon. Rebellion broke out in the French Cameroon in 1955. The rebellion was championed by the Union des Populations du Cameroun (UPC), and it ultimately degenerated into a bloody guerrilla war that spilled over into the postcolonial era. Instead of implementing the provisions of the trusteeship system in Cameroon, France preferred to treat Cameroon like an ordinary overseas colony. Article 76(b) of the United Nations (UN) Charter set forth the political objectives of the trusteeship system, which was to promote the evolution of trust territories like Cameroon and Togo toward self-government and independence. France ignored this procedure and proceeded to integrate Cameroon into the French Union in line with its colonial policy of creating a "Greater France."

The UPC was formed on April 10, 1948, and under the leadership of its secretary general, Reuben Um Nyobe, the party adopted a radical nationalist program that envisaged immediate independence and reunification with the British Cameroons. Such a program aroused the wrath of the French because it ran contrary to their postwar integrationist colonial policy. The UPC further infuriated the French by establishing ties with the Rassemblement Démocratique Africain, an affiliate of the French Communist Party. The stage for a tug-of-war between France and the UPC was set. The UPC was therefore subjected to systematic harassment and discrimination ranging from the arrest and intimidation of its leaders to the obstruction of its members from winning any election organized in the territory.

The UPC responded in May 1955 by starting a series of violent demonstrations in a bid to oust the French from Cameroon. By the end of the month, when the colonial authorities had restored order, 26 people had lost their lives and 176 had been wounded. On July 13, 1955, the French government outlawed the UPC. This triggered a long-festering rebellion (1955–1971) that was initially concentrated in Basaland but finally spent itself in Bamileke country.

The independence of the French Cameroons was made inevitable by changing local and international circumstances. The UPC nationalist ideals were gradually espoused by moderate Cameroon nationalists, and France came under increasing international pressure, particularly from the anticolonial bloc in the UN to introduce political reforms in Cameroon. Furthermore, the defeat of France in Indochina forced the French to grant independence to the Associated States of Laos, Cambodia, and Vietnam in 1954 and to Morocco and Tunisia in 1956. These concessions signaled the possibility of an explosion in French Sub-Saharan Africa if constitutional reforms were not quickly introduced. So the French parliament enacted the *Loi-cadre* (Enabling Act) on June 23, 1956, which provided the introduction of internal self-government. The Loi-cadre dictated the holding of fresh elections in Cameroon on December 23, 1956. The UPC nationalists did not participate in the elections, which turned out to be the last before independence, because the ban on their party was still in force. The logical outcome of such an election, without the UPC, was the emergence of an overwhelmingly moderate and pro-French assembly.

Andre-Marie Mbida, the leader of the Démocrates Camerounais, was appointed premier by the French high commissioner and endorsed by the assembly on May 15, 1957. Owing to his firm opposition to independence and reunification, Mbida suffered from parliamentary sanctions and fell from office on February 17, 1958. His successor, Ahmadou Ahidjo, was wise to conform to the mode of the time by openly subscribing to the nationalist goals of independence and reunification, and France conceded.

On January 1, 1960, the French government proclaimed the independence of the French Cameroons in the presence of UN Secretary General Dag Hammerskjold, and Ahidjo became the first premier. Thus, by an ironic twist of events, the UPC that fought and shed their blood for independence failed to be its beneficiaries.

After the independence of the French Cameroons in 1960, reunification with the British Southern Cameroons followed in 1961. Reunification was the dream and struggle for, and the attempt at re-creating, German Cameroon within its original 1884–1916 boundaries. The sentiments of reuniting the British and the French Cameroons were nurtured by memories of a common colonial experience under the Germans. The Anglo-French partition painfully separated frontier ethnic groups and families, and subsequent attempts by Britain and France to impose boundary restrictions only worsened matters. During the interwar years, petitions from Cameroon's educated elite against the partition of their homeland were registered.

It was, however, in the post–World War II period that the reunification ideology was popularized and vigorously pursued. The UPC forcefully pursued reunification and implanted the idea in the British Cameroon through French Cameroonian émigrés. The UPC was sensitive to French colonial despotism and the reluctance of France to ensure the evolution of the territory toward self-government. By inserting reunification as part of their political program, the UPC hoped to locate the legal battle field for the advancement of the French Cameroons in the UN.

The first prominent British Cameroonian reunificationist was Dr. E. M. L. Endeley. When in December 1949, Endeley's Cameroon National Federation met with the UN Visiting Mission for the first time, it denounced the British colonial arrangement of administering the British Cameroons as an appendage of Nigeria, and requested the reunification of the two Cameroons. In 1953 Endeley formed the Cameroon National Congress to struggle for the achievement of independence.

Britain granted a quasi-autonomous regional status exclusively to the Southern Cameroons in the Nigerian federation in 1954, and Endeley started retreating from reunification. Reunificationist converts under the leadership of John Ngu Foncha abandoned Endeley and formed the Kamerun National Democratic Party in

1955, with secession from Nigeria and reunification as its avowed objectives.

The UN finally resolved the issue of the political future of the British Cameroons by organizing plebiscites in the Southern Cameroons on February 11, 1961 and in the North Cameroons on February 12, 1961. The Southern Cameroons overwhelmingly voted for reunification, with 235,571 votes against 97,741, while the Northern Cameroons opted to remain in Nigeria. On October 1, 1961 the Southern Cameroons obtained independence by reunifying with the independent Republic of Cameroon.

NICODEMUS FRU AWASOM

See also: **Ahidjo, Ahmadou; Cameroon: Colonial Period: British and French Rule; Colonial Federations: French Equatorial Africa.**

Further Reading

Chem-Langhee, B. "The Road to the Unitary State of Cameroon, 1959–1972." *Annals of the Faculty of Arts, Letters and Social Sciences* 4, nos. 1–2 (1990): 3–22.

Gaillard, P. *Ahmadou Ahidjo.* Paris: Jeune Afrique, 1994.

Joseph, R. A. *Radical Nationalism in Cameroon: Social Origins of the U.P.C. Rebellion.* London: Oxford University Press, 1977.

Martin, A. R. "French Capitalism and Nationalism in Cameroon." *African Affairs Review* 40, no. 1 (1997): 83–111.

Cameroon: Independence to the Present

By reputation one of Africa's stable nation-states, Cameroon enters the twenty-first century less than comfortably. Four decades after the reunification of French and British trust territories, the early years' achievements and search for symmetry are waning. Living standards decline, political disputes flare and linger, and sections of the borders are insecure. There are three distinct contours, corresponding roughly to three formal designations for Cameroon: the Federal Republic (1961–1972), the United Republic (1972–1984), and, simply, the Republic (1984–).

Two presidencies also mark contrasts. Until 1982, Ahmadou Ahidjo consolidated governance and, though contested, used an authoritarian yet skillfully balanced statecraft to advance Cameroon materially. The regime of Paul Biya, his successor, lacks Ahidjo's inclusiveness and endures economic crisis, so that questions now arise about his legitimacy and the nation-state's viability during his disputed constitutional mandate until 2010 and beyond.

The Union des Populations de Cameroun (UPC) insurgency challenged the terms of independence until 1970. But the constitutional bargain struck between the federated states of East and West Cameroon at

Foumban in 1961, and de facto one-party rule from 1966, with the Cameroon National Union (CNU) bringing the politicians under Ahidjo's control, harmonized elites from the francophone 75 per cent majority and Anglophone 25 per cent minority populations. Familiar African nation-building projects went ahead. Franc zone trade, investment, domestic food and export cash crops from naturally abundant or newly irrigated and fertilized soils, processing and refining agroindustries, an aluminum smelter with hydroelectric capacity, and then Cameroon's early oil boom brought macroeconomic growth and some microeconomic distribution. A bilingual language policy, a respected multicultural journal (*Abbia*), and a promising university at Yaounde made Cameroon appear progressive. Ahidjo's appointments and patronage ably managed the imbalances Cameroon shares with its neighbors, between a largely Muslim North with customary rulers and a more formally educated, commercially active, urban and transient Christian South, as well as the legacies of its own two colonial languages and 250 cultures. A "baronial alliance" politics emerged, and the armed forces kept to the barracks.

The system's first jolt was Ahidjo's hastily called referendum, which a vast majority approved, ending federalism in 1972. This now "United Republic" alerted Anglophones to the erosion, real or incipient, of "Anglo-Saxon" minority safeguards, values, and institutions in law, public service, education, and projects like Douala's harbor, with its silt preferred to deep-sea Limbe's; they smacked of unilateral decisions and development budget choices favoring francophones. Constitutional protest, muted then, began to feed other grievances that Biya would face a quarter century later. But the 1970s, as oil revenues rose, produced few open dissenters at home, and studies by UPC exiles like Mongo Beti and Abel Eyinga about domestic tyranny and French complicity were banned. Jean-François Bayart and Pierre Flambeau Ngayap record the mature Ahidjo years' hegemony, using 1,000 well-disciplined, mostly francophone appointees to various offices. The legislature and judiciary atrophied in a presidentially ruled Cameroon that Richard Joseph labeled "Gaullist Africa."

Ahidjo's abrupt 1982 resignation from the presidency (though not CNU leadership) brought Biya to power. He withstood Cameroon's one serious military coup threat in 1984, attributed to Ahidjo's northern supporters; it ended quickly and bloodily. Ahidjo was exiled, Biya's prime minister fled, and a fundamental realignment of state power from the northern to the southern pole of the CNU's ruling axis followed, as did a decree abolishing the "United Republic" and any formal trace of the federation. Biya's Beti ethnic coalition gained dominance as the Cameroon People's Democratic Movement

(CPDM) in 1985. Its governance and style, and the opposition it engenders, have defined public life ever since. A "communal liberalism" phase introduced policy and voting reforms in state and party, but any firm commitments to reform or lasting benefits fell prey to foreign debt and export price declines. Betis commandeered high political offices, the security apparatus, and scarcer state resources. By 1988 structural adjustment from global fiscal institutions, then by 1990 domestic democratization forces, following European and southern African leads but fully indigenous, sought to discipline a now parasitic and unwieldy regime, ushering in a most contentious decade.

It began when lawyer Yondo Black and nine associates called for human rights reforms and a multiparty political layout. A military court tried them, convicting some and acquitting others, and this provoked intense conflict on the street level throughout the country. Simultaneously, picking up threads of Anglophone hostility since federalism was gutted in 1972 and 1984, John Fru Ndi organized the Social Democratic Front (SDF) in Bamenda, Northwest Province. Massive state security challenged its peaceful founding rally, held on May 26, 1990. Six young people were shot dead, and a period of intense crisis began. The regime legalized multiple parties and liberalized press laws but the opposition demanded more—namely, an end to "presidential monarchy." A test of the new laws, Célestin Monga's open letter to Biya in Pius Njawe's *Le Messager*, led to a defamation trial, and street and then campus casualties. Protracted struggle began in mid-1991. All foreign interests except France urged regime concessions; internal debate weakened the CPDM, big cities in four of ten provinces took up a general strike call by a SDF-led coalition in support of a Sovereign National Conference, and an undeclared state of emergency enforced by a military Operational Command ruled seven of ten provinces.

A resolution could not be reached. The opposition peaked in 1991's strike, then declined as the regime stretched its resources and incumbency powers to detach resistance leaders, curb the press, and dodge demands for electoral code and constitutional reforms. Monetary and moral support, denied by others but given by France, helped Biya to "stabilize" Cameroon. Legislative elections in March 1992 reduced the CPDM's monopoly to a plurality and a coalition pact, for much of the north and the urban south (even in the capital Yaounde) defected, but Biya kept Fru Ndi from the presidency in the October 1992 election, broadly understood as rigged beforehand and fraudulently counted. A two-month-long state of emergency in Northwest Province enforced Biya's "victory" but intensified Anglophone hostility. A war of attrition set in for the rest of the decade, as local elections in 1996

mirrored 1992's patterns, and the SDF in 1997 entered the legislature as a minority party but pulled out of the presidential ballot, claiming misconduct. Biya won, in a setting his foes among intellectuals now stigmatize as no longer "Gaullist" but "Vichist."

In perceived "popular support" terms but never confirmed by valid elections, the CPDM in 2000 held the Center, South, and East Provinces; the SDF dominated the Northwest, West, and Littoral Provinces, and the National Union for Development and Progress party maintained Fulbe-Muslim hegemony in three northern provinces, claiming Ahidjo's legacy against the region's 1984 losses but allying with Biya in return for ministry posts in 1997. The tenth province, Southwest, sways in patronage winds, and the capital Yaounde remains volatile. In reality, Beti domination of key civilian and military offices, the nullification of Biya's electoral losses, and France sustain the regime while the SDF maintains a popular following that the CPDM frustrates but cannot subdue. A familiar patronage politics of ethnic and business lobbies continues, with many enclaves not easily satisfied in a stagnant economy. The mix since 1993 includes the SDF's "return to federalism" call and a militant anglophone Southern Cameroon National Conference lobbying the United Nations to return Cameroon to status quo 1960–1961 and to require francophones of "la république" to negotiate a constitution between equals—failing which, it advocates secession.

The past thus contested, the future may be problematic. World Bank studies disclose 14 million people compositely worse off in the year 2000 than in 1980. With reserves subject to depletion, oil and timber earnings will drop, further antagonizing 4 million anglophones, since France is the major beneficiary. Many Bamilekes—the richest, most migratory, and thus resented ethnicity as business and land use competition intensifies—leave the CPDM, join the SDF, or want their own party, a group all the more unsettled since a CPDM 1996 constitutional clause, risky for them or any Africans, favors autochthone rights over migrants. The "oil border" with Nigeria is disputed with arms and in the World Court. Other borders are porous, so people, loot, and grudges from central Africa's wars enter Cameroon, edging the once calm hub of the region toward its vortex.

The CPDM claims *une démocratie avancée* and enjoys French support. The SDF denies the regime's legitimacy and seeks anglophone and socialist international allies abroad. Paul Biya and John Fru Ndi have never met. Both in their 60s, they pose disruptive succession questions for their parties and not just the state. Absent a domestic resolution, perhaps brokered from outside, Cameroon could face difficult years ahead.

In April 2003, after delays and missed deadlines, a new stock exchange opened in the hopes that this will assist Cameroon's entrance into the modern world economy. As of this writing, no companies are yet quoted on the exchange; thus, shares cannot as of yet actually be traded.

MILTON KRIEGER

See also: **Ahidjo, Ahmadou.**

Further Reading

Joseph, R. (ed.). *Gaullist Africa: Cameroon under Ahmadu Ahidjo.* Enugu, Nigeria: Fourth Dimension Press, 1978.

Takougang, J., and M. Krieger. *African State and Society in the 1990s: Cameroon's Political Crossroads.* Boulder, Colo.: Westview Press, 1998.

World Bank. *Cameroon: Diversity, Growth, and Poverty Reduction.* Report No. 13167-CM. World Bank, 1995.

Campaoré: *See* Burkina Faso (Upper Volta): Independence to the Present.

Cape Colony: Origins, Settlement, Trade

The Cape Colony originated in 1652 as a settlement of the Dutch East India Company. With the development of its trading empire in Southeast Asia, the company sought to establish a refreshment station on the shipping route from Europe. Dutch failure in 1607–1608 to oust the Portuguese from Mozambique led to a search for other midway ports of call for supplies of water and fresh meat. They temporarily occupied Mauritius, but Table Bay, as the only known and sheltered source of fresh water along the southern African coast, was more regularly visited. In 1651, as a preemptive move against their English rivals, the company sent Jan van Riebeeck to the bay with instructions "to found a fort and garden there." They envisaged a dual role for the station: a defensive post against both European trading rivals and the local Khoi, as well as a source of fresh water and food for passing ships.

The early years were not easy. Although cattle and sheep were obtained from the Khoi, supplies were irregular and the post was dependent on rice imports from Madagascar. In order to achieve self-sufficiency as well as fulfill the need to supply produce, some company employees were released from their contracts in 1658 to become "free burgher" farmers. Despite the provision of slave labor and the ejection of Khoi herders from the land, this early farming was not successful, largely because the settlers used the intensive farming methods of the Netherlands in an unsuitable climate and soil. It was only with the adoption

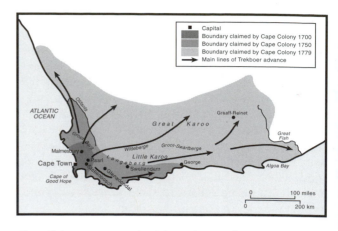

Cape Colony, seventeenth–eighteenth centuries.

of extensive methods of grain cultivation in the late 1670s, and with the successful growth of vines, that the settlement was able to find farming success. There were some later immigrants, including women brought from Dutch orphanages and 156 Huguenot refugees in 1688, but many Cape colonists were descended from ex-crewmen, a number of whom had only disembarked because of illness. Most became farmers, though a small burgher community also developed in Cape Town. In the seventeenth and early eighteenth centuries a few freed slaves also acquired farms, though most such "free blacks" lived in Cape Town.

The development of extensive agriculture led to geographical expansion of the settlement. From 1679 to the 1680s the company granted land to settler farmers, from which it had extruded Khoi pastoralists, initially in Stellenbosch and later in Paarl, Franschoek, and the Paardeberg regions. Although this system of freehold land grants was terminated in 1717, by the end of the eighteenth century colonial settlement had spread beyond the Drakenstein Mountains to the drier Bokkeveld, Roggeveld, and Namaqua regions of the north and along the coast to the east, reaching the Zuurveld and Great Fish River by the 1770s. New magistracies were established at Swellendam (1745) and Graaff-Reinet (1786). The farmers in these more arid frontier regions were sheep and cattle breeders, producing meat as well as tallow and hides.

There has been much debate about the causes of this geographical expansion. Neumark (1957) argued that it was encouraged by the potential profits of the Cape Town meat market, frontier suppliers replacing the uncertain bartering trade with the Khoi, who had been decimated by disease and colonial land encroachment. Later historians instead stressed factors that propelled settlers away from the southwestern arable regions. An exceptionally high birthrate and a system of inheritance led to a constant search for land by the sons of many burgher farmers who lacked sufficient capital to buy their way into the land market of the arable districts. The existence of slave labor preempted the possibilities of such men becoming a proletarian work-force. Such arguments have stressed the economic isolation and relative poverty of settler pastoralists on a remote frontier. More recently, Susan Newton-King (1999) has shown that frontier pastoralists required some capital, were certainly not removed from Cape markets, and were closely dependent on exchange of goods with Cape Town suppliers. At the same time she argues that many such farmers did live in relative poverty, vulnerable to market fluctuations and dependent on coercing local labor to work under indenture.

Certainly a high level of wealth disparity existed among the Cape colonists. Robert Ross (1983) has argued that during the eighteenth century there emerged a wealthy elite, or "Cape gentry," who owned the biggest farms and the largest number of slaves and dominated local politics. Yet the lack of a staple export crop meant that there were no large-scale plantations of the kind that existed in many other settler colonies at the time. Some wheat and wine was exported to Batavia, though in relatively small amounts. Access to lucrative contracts to supply the company with produce for the local garrison was therefore vital. Although the volume of company ships entering Table Bay stagnated, the number of foreign vessels greatly increased from the mid-eighteenth century on. Export of goods to outsiders by private individuals was forbidden by the company, though in practice a number of officials and colonists did undertake small-scale exchanges with foreign ships, and they also obtained imported goods for sale. The accumulation of private merchant capital was, however, limited. Only in the 1770s did some trading houses emerge, each headed by company officials. This angered those locals who were excluded from participation, and they voiced their complaints as "patriots" to the company directors in the Netherlands.

The internal market was more active. Exchange of produce among grain, wine, and stock farmers was constant, and Cape Town provided a ready market for rural produce. A particular boom took place in the 1780s when allied French and mercenary troops were stationed in Cape Town to defend the colony from the British. Supplies from rural areas poured into the town and inflation set in. After their departure there was a major slump, which was only overcome with the infusion of merchant capital and trading after the takeover of the Cape Colony by the British in 1795. There was also active barter in hides, tallow, iron goods, and livestock between settlers and the Xhosa in the eastern regions of the colony by the late eighteenth century, though this was disrupted by conflict over land and grazing in the 1790s. It was not until the

development of merino wool production in the nineteenth century that major mercantile activity transformed settler agriculture in the central and eastern Cape.

NIGEL WORDEN

See also: **Cape Colony: Khoi-Dutch Wars.**

Further Reading

Elphick, R., and H. Giliomee (eds.). *The Shaping of South African Society, 1652–1840*, 2nd ed. Cape Town: Maskew Miller Longman, 1989.
Newton-King, S. *Masters and Servants on the Cape Eastern Frontier, 1760–1803*. Cambridge: Cambridge University Press, 1999.
Ross, R., *Beyond the Pale: Essays on the History of Colonial South Africa*. Hanover, N.H.: Wesleyan University Press/ Johannesburg: Witwatersrand University Press, 1993.
———. "The Rise of the Cape Gentry." *Journal of Southern African Studies* 9, no. 2 (1983): 193–217.
Van Duin, P., and R. Ross, *The Economy of the Cape Colony in the Eighteenth Century*. Intercontinental no. 7. Leiden: Centre for the History of European Expansion, 1987.

Cape Colony: Khoi-Dutch Wars

The Dutch East India Company settlement at the Cape was established on land which had been occupied by Khoikhoi herders and pastoralists for well over a thousand years. They, in turn, had been preceded by San hunter-gatherers, many of whom had retreated to remoter mountainous sites by the seventeenth century. Since the sixteenth century, European ships calling at Table Bay obtained cattle and sheep from the Khoi in return for copper and iron, though there are signs that this local market for metals was becoming saturated by the early seventeenth century.

The building of a "fort and garden" on the shores of Table Bay, and the subsequent establishment of arable farming by the Dutch in 1658, encroached on the seasonal pastorage of Khoi herders. The Khoi refused to accept this and insisted on continuing to graze their livestock as before, breaking down the hedges built to exclude them. In 1659–1660 open conflict broke out; the free burghers formed a militia company and sent their families to the greater security of the fort. Despite a subsequent uneasy truce, conflicts continued. In the 1670s the Khoikhoi of the Saldanha Bay and Boland regions were defeated in a series of Dutch raids, lost their cattle, and were reduced to tributary status. The Dutch East India Company subsequently claimed this land by right of conquest and parceled it out for settler farms. From then on some Khoikhoi began to work alongside imported slaves as laborers on the farms, a clear sign of their loss of economic independence. The Khoi were further devastated by the smallpox epidemic of 1713, but it was the earlier loss of grazing land that had been decisive in their collapse. Although they were not formally enslaved, they were increasingly brought under company control and reduced to dependence on settlers for pasturage and employment.

As some Dutch settlers turned to pastoralism and expanded their activities farther inland, this pattern of conflict continued. To the north, the Khoikhoi were denied access to grazing and water resources and in some cases were robbed of cattle by settler commandos. There is clear evidence that by the early eighteenth century some Khoi were reduced to the hunter-gatherer existence of the San retreating to the mountains of the Cederberg or to the remoter and more arid lands of the Roggeveld. In the late 1730s there was a protracted period of guerrilla resistance by the Khoikhoi and San against white settler farmers beyond the Piketberg. This was intensified in 1739, after settlers on an illegal trading expedition to Little Namaqualand seized Namaqua cattle. It appears that some of the Khoi who had accompanied them were dissatisfied with their share of the loot and instead joined the Namaqua and raided Dutch herds and farms in the Bokkeveld. The company was only able to reestablish control over the region by sending a major commando to the area, killing a number of the Khoi "rebels" and thus also condoning settler theft of Namaqua cattle. As a result, settlers established control over the grazing lands of the Onder Bokkeveld, though guerrilla-type resistance continued in the mountains of the Bokkeveld and Roggeveld until the end of the century.

From the 1770s to around 1800, as settler pastoralists encroached still farther north, conflict over environmental resources again broke out. As a result the armed *trekboer* commando became more firmly established, both to combat Khoikhoi and San opposition and to capture women and children who were to be used as indentured laborers. Settler control was also extended over indigenous laborers by such devices as the enforced carrying of passes by "Bastaard Hottentots" (the offspring of Khoikhoi and slaves, or Khoikhoi and colonists).

As a result of these conflicts and controls, numerous Khoikhoi, San, and escaped slaves fled to Namaqualand and the Orange (Gariep) River region by the late eighteenth century, where they formed independent Oorlam captaincies (later known as the Griqua). For example, in the 1790s the notable Oorlam leader Jager Afrikaner killed a white settler in the Hantam region, with whom he had entered a clientship relationship, after a dispute over grazing rights, and fled with his kin to the islands of the Gariep River. From here he led raids on the surrounding areas, including both Nama and Dutch grazing lands, and attracted other Khoi and San refugees as followers. He was outlawed from the Cape and migrated in 1806 to Namibia, where he was converted by missionaries and turned to hunting and trading.

Meanwhile, settlers were also expanding eastward, parallel to the south Cape coast, controlling water and grazing lands. In the process they pushed back Khoikhoi pastoralists—already weakened by the influx of Khoi refugees from the west—toward the Karoo and Camdeboo regions, as well as shooting out much of the game upon which San hunters were dependent. By the 1770s, settlers had penetrated into the rich grazing lands between the Gamtoos and Fish rivers, which were also being used by Xhosa herders and cultivators. In 1786 the company formally extended the colony to this region with the establishment of a *landdrost* (magistracy) at Graaff-Reinet. This led to a protracted period of conflict in the 1770s–1790s.

Historian Susan Newton-King (1999) has demonstrated that the heightened violence of this period was at least in part the result of settler need to obtain war captives. Lacking sufficient capital to employ waged labor, settler commandos regularly captured Khoi and San women and children, as well as some men, to use as indentured *inboekseling* labor. Other Khoi and San were reduced to working for the trekkers as herders because they had lost access to cattle and pasturage. But this was not without retaliation. By the mid-1790s Khoisan resistance, both in the form of stock theft and direct attacks on settlers and their slaves, seriously disrupted the frontier meat trade. In 1799 a major rebellion broke out when Khoikhoi and San inboekselings deserted the farms, grouped themselves into captaincies (modeled on precolonial social structures), and began a four-year war aiming to reclaim the "country of which our fathers have been despoiled."

In several ways the 1799–1803 rebellion differed significantly from earlier Khoikhoi and San resistance. First, it was an uprising by those who had already lost the means of an independent existence, worked for the trekboers and aimed to overthrow settler society from within rather than simply to stem its territorial expansion. Moreover, the rebels made common cause with the Zuurveld Xhosa chiefs who were resisting colonial advances in the region with considerable success. They defeated a settler commando and raided the Graaff-Reinet and Swellendam districts, forcing many farms to be abandoned. The threat that this posed to the colonial order led to decisive intervention by the new colonial rulers who had taken over control of the Cape from the Dutch East India Company: the British and, for a brief interlude, the Dutch Batavian administration. Divisions among the Khoi and between them and the Xhosa eventually led to a truce in 1803. The rebellion marked the last consistent stand of the Khoisan against settler occupation.

By the early nineteenth century, few Khoi or San had retained independent access to land. Legislation introduced by the British, such as the Caledon Code (1809), attempted to lock them into farm labor. These restrictions were removed by Ordinance 50 (1828), and attempts were made to settle some Khoi groups at mission stations or on land at Kat River, though independent farming was discouraged. A number preferred to live among Xhosa farmers. In the northern Cape, further conflicts took place in the 1860s and 1870s against San who were displaced by the fencing of settler pastorage. In some places, this was tantamount to genocide.

NIGEL WORDEN

See also: **Cape Colony: Origins, Settlement, Trade.**

Further Reading

Elphick, R., and V. C. Malherbe. "The Khoisan to 1828." In *The Shaping of South African Society, 1652–1840,* 2nd ed., edited by Richard Elphick and Hermann Giliomee. Cape Town: Maskew Miller Longman, 1989.

Guelke, L., and R. Shell. "Landscape of Conquest: Frontier Water Alienation and Khoikhoi Strategies of Survival, 1652–1780." *Journal of Southern African Studies* 18, no. 4 (1992): 803–824.

Newton-King, S. *Masters and Servants on the Cape Eastern Frontier, 1760–1803.* Cambridge: Cambridge University Press, 1999.

Penn, N. "Land, Labour and Livestock in the Western Cape during the Eighteenth Century." In *The Angry Divide: Social and Economic History of the Western Cape,* edited by Wilmot James and Mary Simons. Cape Town: David Philip, 1989.

———. "The Orange River Frontier Zone, c.1700–1805." In *Einiqualand: Studies of the Orange River Frontier,* edited by Andrew Smith. Cape Town: University of Cape Town Press, 1995.

Cape Colony: Slavery

Chattel slaves were imported to the Cape Colony by the Dutch East India Company, which had long used slaves in its Asian settlements. The first company Cape commander, Jan van Riebeeck, had a few personal slaves in his household from the earliest years of the colony; he appealed to the company's directors in Batavia (Jakarta) for slave labor to support settler farming in the Cape Town hinterland in 1658. The first cargo of 228 slaves was imported from Dahomey, and the capture of a Portuguese slaving ship brought another 174 slaves from Angola. Thereafter the company traded for slaves in Madagascar and obtained others from its trading post at Rio de la Goa and along the Mozambique coast. Slaves were also brought to the Cape aboard ships returning to Europe from the company trading posts in South and Southeast Asia. They had been obtained in the extensive trading network of South and Southeast Asia and came mainly from Bengal; the Malabar and Coromandel coasts of India; Ceylon; and the Indonesian archipelago. After the British took over the Cape from the company in 1795, private merchants imported over 7,200 slaves to Cape Town from Mozambique and Madagascar before the trade was abolished in 1807. Although there are no complete extant records, it has been estimated that some 80,000 slaves were imported to the colony altogether. Children born to slave women at the Cape were automatically of slave status. In 1833, the last complete year of slavery, there were 38,343 slaves at the Cape.

Until the nineteenth century, the Cape Colony depended on imported slaves to maintain its labor force. The majority of these were male, and there was thus a major gender imbalance. There were four male slaves to one female slave in 1738. Even where family ties were forged, couples could be broken up and children sold. After the abolition of the slave trade, a higher proportion of slaves were Cape-born and the balance was redressed to a gender ratio of 1.18 males to 1 female in 1834. More extended slave kinship networks emerged in the nineteenth century. Families, however, were still often separated from each other among differing owners.

Slaves were used by the company on its cattle and defense posts as well as on public works in Cape Town. The majority of slaves worked for settlers on the grain and wine farms of the southwestern Cape. Almost all arable farmers owned slaves, though there were no large-scale plantations, and the number of slaves on each farm was usually less than 20. Some slaves were owned by pastoralist farmers, though the indigenous Khoi and San inhabitants were more often used as indentured or casual workers on frontier farms. Most Capetonians also had slaves as domestic servants and artisans. Together with the political exiles brought by the company from Asia, slaves formed the basis of a thriving Muslim community in Cape Town.

Recent historiography has shown that Cape slaves could be treated just as brutally as in other colonial slave societies. Some acquired small amounts of money or livestock from earnings permitted by their owners, but the majority lacked any resources of their own. Only a few acquired freedom, some 900 in the company period, though manumission rates increased in Cape Town in the early nineteenth century. Most freed slaves were urban women. A few ex-slaves obtained land or property, but the majority remained at the bottom of the social ladder.

Rebellion was difficult because slaves were physically separated in relatively small units on remote farms.

Arson was relatively common. Some slaves ran away, and a small community of escaped slaves existed at Cape Hangklip, opposite the Cape Peninsula, throughout most of the eighteenth century. A few runaways escaped from the colony altogether, becoming part of the mixed Oorlam and Griqua societies of the Orange River region and beyond or joining the Xhosa chiefdoms in the eastern Cape region. Not all slaves acted in such ways. Historian Robert Shell (1994) has argued that paternalism and deference, particularly of female household domestic slaves, inhibited open resistance.

After the British occupation of the Cape, changes took place in the slave system. The slave trade was abolished in 1807, cutting off external supplies, and high infant mortality levels made it difficult to maintain slave numbers from local births. The wine farms on which many slaves worked suffered a slump in the late 1820s, while wool production, the boom sector of the colony's economy, was less dependent on slave labor. As colonial settlement expanded in the eastern Cape, a more mobile labor force was needed. Hence, merchants and new commercial pastoral farmers began to oppose slavery and opt for cheap wage labor. The slaves themselves became more assertive and lodged complaints against their owners to the authorities. There were two rebellions: an uprising of over 300 slaves in the Cape Town hinterland in 1808 and a small revolt in the more remote Bokkeveld region of the northern Cape in 1825. Thus, when the British Parliament abolished slavery in 1834 (with a four-year period of apprenticeship until final emancipation in 1838), there was only muted opposition from the slaveowners.

Slave emancipation did not alter the social structure of the colony. As elsewhere in the British colonies, no land or capital was provided for the freed slaves, and though some moved to the towns and villages, and particularly to mission stations after 1838, many others remained on the farms as permanent or seasonal workers. Families were united and many women withdrew from farm work. But most freed slaves lacked the resources to obtain a truly equal position in Cape society.

Although indigenous South Africans were not formally enslaved, the existence of slavery in the Cape influenced other types of labor use. Many Khoi worked alongside slaves on settler farms in conditions that differed little from those of slaves, though they were not legally the property of their employers. Khoi and San captured in raids were used as indentured labor, especially in the eastern Cape from the 1770s. Most were women and children, though there were also some men. Slave raiding also took place in the Delagoa Bay region in the 1820s, and slaves were taken by the *trekboers* from the Cape into the interior in the 1830s. Slavery in the Transvaal was abolished by the Sand

River Convention in 1852, though indentured labor was still widely used.

NIGEL WORDEN

See also: **Slavery, Colonial Rule and.**

Further Reading

Reidy, M. "The Admission of Slaves and 'Prize Negroes' into the Cape Colony, 1797–1818." M.A. thesis, University of Cape Town, 1997.

Scully, P. *Liberating the Family? Gender and British Slave Emancipation in the Rural Western Cape, South Africa, 1823–1853.* Portsmouth, N.H.: Heinemann, 1997.

Shell, Robert C.-H. *Children of Bondage: A Social History of the Slave Society at the Cape of Good Hope, 1652–1838.* Hanover, N.H.: Wesleyan University Press/Johannesburg: Witwatersrand University Press, 1994.

Worden, N. *Slavery in Dutch South Africa.* Cambridge: Cambridge University Press, 1985.

Worden, N., and Clifton Crais (eds.). *Breaking the Chains: Slavery and Its Legacy in the Nineteenth-Century Cape Colony.* Johannesburg: Witwatersrand University Press, 1994.

Cape Colony: British Occupation, 1806–1872

During the first half of the nineteenth century, Cape society was radically altered in many respects by its integration within a British imperial system and a globalizing economy. But it was not necessarily transformed in the fundamentals of its racial structure. On the one hand, British administrations enforced "the replacement of slave-owner tyranny by a more powerful state regulation of labor," but on the other, they ensured the maintenance of "social hierarchy and inequality of race and class" (Worden and Crais 1994, p.13).

The Cape Colony first became a part of the British Empire on an indefinite basis during the Napoleonic War. It was seized from the Dutch Batavian Republic in 1806 due to its strategic location on the shipping route between Europe and the East Indies, but its retention was not confirmed until 1814. During the first two decades of British occupation, autocratic and predominantly military governors pursued conservative policies, similar to those adopted in Britain, which were intended to maintain an inherited social order. Thus, the 1809 Caledon Code, while it attempted to moderate physical abuse of the colony's Khoi workforce, nevertheless reinforced their subordination to colonists by imposing a pass system which restricted their movements. Close links were forged between the small number of British officials in the colony and the Dutch-speaking colonial elite, and British forces were used to secure the eastern colonial margins for frontier farmers by expelling Xhosa chiefdoms across the Fish River.

By the 1820s, however, the middle classes' ongoing struggle against aristocratic hegemony in industrializing Britain was undermining the status quo in the Cape as well as in the metropolis. In 1807, a campaign fought largely by middle-class evangelicals culminated in the abolition of the transatlantic slave trade for British ships, bringing labor shortages to many parts of the colony. Further British humanitarian intervention led to the amelioration of the Cape slaves' conditions during the 1820s. The colony's aristocratic governor, Lord Charles Somerset, was directly challenged by British settlers such as the journalists Thomas Pringle and John Fairbairn, who were advocates of reformist programs in Britain. Among the 4,000 "1820 settlers" located on the eastern frontier of the colony, the majority of the gentry, who had emigrated as leaders of group parties, joined in the pressure for an end to the governor's unmitigated powers. An official commission of inquiry appointed in 1823 recommended reforms that were the first step away from the old autocratic and mercantilist system and toward freer trade under an advisory legislative council.

Reformist pressure did not end with the assault on Somerset's ancien régime. The London Missionary Society director in the Cape, Dr. John Philip, represented the plight of the colony's Khoi as being akin to that of slaves. Metropolitan humanitarians took up his call for their freedom, and in 1828 Ordinance 50 abolished the pass laws and accorded Khoi equal rights to colonists under the law. Despite the vehement opposition of both established Dutch-speaking colonists and recent British settlers, Ordinance 50 was hailed by humanitarians as the Cape's own Charter of Freedom. In 1834, a British humanitarian campaign against the continuance of slavery in the West Indies culminated in the abolition of the institution of slavery throughout the British Empire, including the Cape.

While reform took precedence in the Cape under Somerset's successor, Lieutenant Governor Bourke, the humanitarian concept of freedom was nevertheless qualified. In Britain, humanitarian reformers held out the prospect of workers' freedom from arbitrary legal restraint, but advocated their docility, sobriety, and productivity within an unequal class system. In the Cape, freed slaves had four years of "apprenticeship" to their former masters in which to learn the traits of respectability and submission to "proper" authority. In case these lessons were not sufficient, the 1841 Masters and Servants Ordinance prescribed criminal sanctions for any laborer's breach of contract with a new employer. Although the legislation itself was nonracial, the vast majority of laborers were freed slaves or Khoi, by now known collectively as "colored," while the vast majority of employers were white. Only a tiny proportion of the Khoi freed under Ordinance 50 had

actually been allocated land along the Kat River on which they could attempt to acquire a living independent of colonial employers, and even this humanitarian "experiment" was part of a buffer strip defending the colony's eastern frontier from Xhosa raids.

British administration created favorable conditions for British merchants to operate from the Cape, especially once sterling had replaced the rixdollar as local currency and once British preference for Cape wine exporters had been removed, breaking the established Dutch elite's economic stranglehold. With their connections in London, British merchants were able to act as agents retrieving much of the compensation money offered to the Cape's slaveowners upon the "emancipation" of their workforce. Dutch-speaking merchants soon assimilated within this English-speaking elite and, from the 1830s, both helped to finance settler capitalist expansion, based on wool production, in the eastern Cape. These merchants were also behind the complex of scientific, literary, and artistic institutions centered on the company gardens in Cape Town—institutions that did much to bolster a sense of respectability and pride in a Cape colonial identity.

It was partly the "respectable" colonists' desire for metropolitan recognition that led to the "Convict Crisis." In 1848, the British government ordered that the Cape be used as a penal colony in order to appease Australian settlers, who had repeatedly complained about the "export" of British convicts to their territories. Dutch- and English-speaking commercial interests forged an alliance of classes in Cape Town to protest at this challenge to the Cape's status as a colony of free settlement. Governor Harry Smith, despite securing the support of eastern Cape settlers, whose expansion onto Xhosa lands he had facilitated, found that he could not govern effectively as long as the Cape Town elite boycotted the legislative council. He was forced to order the first and only convict ship to arrive in Table Bay on to Tasmania, saving the Cape from degradation in the eyes of its bourgeois elite. Victory in this struggle with metropolitan authority gave the colonial elite the confidence and the determination to follow Canada in securing greater powers of self-government.

When representative government was granted to the Cape in 1853, it came in the form of a compromise. Eastern Cape British settlers, many of whom supported a separatist movement which aimed to bring governmental authority under more direct settler expansionist influence, had generally argued for a franchise qualification that would include only wealthier capitalists such as themselves. But western Cape commercial and Afrikaner farming interests were generally in favor of a more inclusive franchise that would empower the entire white population (as well as wealthier "coloreds" and land-owning Africans). The constitution finally adopted contained the relatively low franchise qualification of £25 worth of property, regardless of race. It has been argued that the inclusion of a small minority of blacks within the enfranchised classes acted as a kind of "safety valve" for black grievances in the wake of the "colored" and Xhosa eastern Cape uprising of 1850–1852. The nonracial constitution served as a counter to the destabilizing effects of settler expansionism which had caused the rebellion, giving blacks the aspiration to join the governing elite rather than overthrow it.

With representative government, the Cape's authorities managed relatively successfully to contain the tensions within colonial society for the next 20 years while consolidating colonial control over Xhosa territory in British Kaffraria. Under the governorship of Sir George Grey (1854–1862), Xhosa resistance was overcome in the wake of the cattle-killing movement, and expenditure increased on roads, prisons, hospitals, and schools in both the east and the west of the colony. This created a budget deficit, which in turn contributed to an economic downturn in the 1860s, but it meant that by 1870 there was surplus capital in the Cape ready for speculation and investment in the mineral discoveries to the north. Ultimately, the success of black farmers occasioned by commercial expansion would threaten white dominance of the electoral roll under the Cape's nonracial franchise. But once the colony was granted responsible government in 1872, the white elite was in a better position to raise the franchise qualification and maintain white political privilege. There would be little protest from liberal merchants now that their economic interest had shifted from the agrarian enterprise of black farmers to the expansion of industrial activities.

ALAN LESTER

See also: **Boer Expansion: Interior of South Africa; South Africa: Missionaries: Nineteenth Century.**

Further Reading

Bickford-Smith, V. *Ethnic Pride and Racial Prejudice in Victorian Cape Town*. Johannesburg: Witwatersrand University Press, 1995.

Keegan, T. *Colonial South Africa and the Origins of the Racial Order*. London: Leicester University Press, 1996.

Legassick, M. "The State, Racism and the Rise of Capitalism in the Nineteenth Century Cape Colony." *South African Historical Journal*, no. 28 (1993): 329–368.

Macmillan, W. M. *The Cape Colour Question: A Historical Survey*. London: Faber and Gwyer, 1927.

Marks, S., and A. Atmore (eds.). *Economy and Society in Pre-Industrial South Africa*. London: Longman, 1980.

Peires, J. "The British and the Cape, 1814–1834." In *The Shaping of South African Society, 1652–1840*, edited by Richard Elphick and Herman Giliomee. Middletown, Conn.: Wesleyan University Press, 1988.

Trapido, S., "From Paternalism to Liberalism: The Cape Colony, 1800–1834." *International History Review*, no. 12 (1990): 76–104.

———. "The Origins of the Cape Franchise Qualifications of 1853." *Journal of African History*, no. 5 (1964): 37–54.

Worden, N. and C. Crais (eds.). *Breaking the Chains: Slavery and Its Legacy in the Nineteenth-Century Cape Colony*. Johannesburg: Witwatersrand University Press, 1994.

Cape Liberalism, Nineteenth Century

Liberalism has meant different things at different times in South Africa. Ideas relating to individual human rights—against the authoritarianism of big government—came to the Cape from the French Revolution in the late eighteenth century, reappeared with the advent of Batavian rule between 1803 and 1806, and then surfaced again in the 1820s, after the arrival of the British settlers. The challenge to the authoritarianism of early British rule at the Cape then mounted produced victory in the form of the establishment of freedom for the press in 1828, and then took the form of a campaign for colonial self-government, which was won in 1853.

A different, if related, meaning of liberalism concerned attitudes toward the oppressed, and in particular whites' attitudes toward blacks. In this meaning, liberalism involved a rejection of discrimination based on race, and a concern that people of color should be treated with equal justice. Such ideas were held in particular by missionaries—especially those of the London Missionary Society (LMS)—who pressed for the removal of restrictions imposed on the Khoikhoi and argued for liberating the slaves. Dr. John Philip, superintendent of the LMS, was the leading figure in this liberalism of the 1820s and 1830s, which won the passage of Ordinance 50 of 1828 and then saw the emancipation of the slaves in 1834. The 1836 House of Commons select committee on aborigines was a high water mark in humanitarian influence.

Such humanitarianism fell on hard times in the 1840s as liberal confidence faded in the face of settler assertiveness, but the British government insisted that in the representative government system granted to the Cape in 1853 the franchise should be color-blind. From this, the tradition emerged that all colonial legislation should be color-blind, and with very few exceptions this was the case at the Cape for the rest of the century. This set the Cape apart from other parts of South Africa, most strikingly from the tradition of "no equality in church or state" in the Boer republics of the Orange Free State and the Transvaal. The policies of Sir George Grey, Cape governor in the late 1850s, aimed at the assimilation of those Africans incorporated into the colony, and contrasted with the segregationist policies of Theophilus Shepstone in Natal. While the Cape tradition was one of identity, a uniform legal system for all, the other white-ruled states insisted on separation for blacks—both territorial and legal.

But Cape liberalism was not merely an imperialist imposition, or limited to missionaries who came to South Africa to work. It took root in the Cape Colony and became the ideology of local interest groups. It was William Porter, the Cape attorney general from 1839 to 1872, who was the prime advocate of a relatively low qualified franchise in the early 1850s, and his liberalism was shared by others who were colonial born. Merchants on the Eastern Cape frontier sought the formation of a prosperous black peasantry with whom they could trade, and promoted ideas of the incorporation of such a class. Local missionaries advocated liberal policies in the interests of conversion and, particularly in the eastern Cape, some white politicians appealed to black voters for support, and sometimes won thanks to their support. Individuals such as Saul Solomon, member of parliament for Cape Town, and, at the end of the century, Olive Schreiner, the novelist, stood up for the rights of oppressed peoples and expressed liberal values.

There were, of course, limits to the enlightened paternalism of such whites. Cape Town itself, the seat of government, was a long way from a large African population, and a cynical view is that whites there could afford to adopt liberal positions. There was no question of extending nonracialism to social relations, and nonracialism was not incorporated into the political parties that emerged from the 1880s. Nevertheless, there were real and substantial differences between the Cape tradition, which Cecil Rhodes summed up in the 1890s in the dictum "Equal rights for every civilized man," and the ideologies and policies of the other states of nineteenth-century South Africa.

As the mineral revolution gathered pace, mining interests (and those of Rhodes among them) sought to draw labor from the Cape's African reserves, and so took steps that undermined the African peasantry. With the incorporation of a large African population as the Transkei was annexed, at a time when social Darwinist ideas became popular, racial distinctions in social relations were drawn ever more distinctly, and the new educated African elite found that barriers rose on lines of race. The nonracial franchise remained, but the qualifications were raised in 1892, effectively excluding large numbers of blacks. Nevertheless, liberal values survived both in a small segment of the white community and among the black elite. Though Phyllis Lewsen (1971) has argued that liberalism was in a "terminal" phase by the end of the century, its continuing strength was to be seen at the National Convention in 1908–1909, when the Cape delegates strongly and largely successfully defended the Cape nonracial franchise. By the late twentieth century the Cape liberal tradition had been largely forgotten, and *liberal* had become a term of abuse, but many of the values of Cape liberalism of the nineteenth century were to be embodied in the constitutions of 1993 and 1996.

CHRISTOPHER SAUNDERS

See also: **Afrikaans and Afrikaner Nationalism, Nineteenth Century.**

Further Reading

Butler, J., R. Elphick, and D. Welsh (eds.). *Democratic Liberalism in South Africa*. Middletown, Conn.: Wesleyan University Press, 1987.

Keegan, T. *Colonial South Africa and the Origins of the Racial Order*. Cape Town: David Philip, 1996.

Legassick, M. "The Rise of Modern South African Liberalism: Its Social Base." Collected Seminar Papers, Institute of Commonwealth Studies, University of London, 1972.

Lewsen, P. "The Cape Liberal Tradition: Myth or Reality." *Race*, no. 13 (1971).

Trapido, S. "The Emergence of Liberalism and the Making of Hottentot Nationalism, 1815–34." Collected Seminar Papers, Institute of Commonwealth Studies, University of London, 1992.

———. "The Friends of the Natives: Merchants, Peasants and the Political and Ideological Structure of Liberalism in the Cape 1884–1910." In *Economy and Society in Preindustrial South Africa*, edited by S. Marks and A. Atmore. London: Longman, 1980.

———. "From Paternalism to Liberalism: The Cape Colony, 1820–1824." *International Review of History*, no. 12 (1990).

Cape Town

Cape Town was founded on the shores of Table Bay, the site of Khoi grazing lands, by Jan van Riebeeck of the Dutch East India Company in 1652. As one of the few sheltered harbors with supplies of fresh water on the southern African coast, it had been frequently visited by European trading vessels on their way to the Indian Ocean, and the company occupation was a preemptive move against English rivals—the first structure to be built was a defensive fort. Cattle and sheep were also bartered with the Khoi, and the company established a garden to grow fresh vegetables with which to supply its ships. After the establishment of settler farming, Cape Town became a market center for local produce. By 1775 a distinctive urban community had emerged of some 7,000 people, the majority of whom were slaves and company employees. There were about 2,500 free burghers, employed in a range of craft and boarding house occupations which served the needs of the port and of up-country traders.

The takeover of Cape Town by the British in the early nineteenth century brought about major transformations. British immigration and an influx of merchant capital led to the establishment of a commercial exchange, banks, and insurance companies, while shipping links with other parts of the British Empire—notably, India and Australasia—greatly increased. Yet Cape Town lacked a solid economic base and stagnated in the 1840s when the eastern Cape's wool boom instead benefited Port Elizabeth. This changed with the development of the Kimberley diamond fields in the 1870s–1880s, which brought a new influx of capital and immigrants into Cape Town and firmly established it as the prime city of the Cape Colony. A new harbor was completed in 1870 and extended in 1905. The flow of migrants was further intensified during the South African War (1899–1902). Cape Town's population more than doubled, from 80,000 in 1880 to 171,000 in 1904. Although economic power by then centered on the gold mines of the Rand, Cape Town's significance was confirmed when it became the seat of the new Union of South Africa Parliament in 1910.

Cape Town's nineteenth-century population was one of the most cosmopolitan of the British Empire. Descendants of Dutch and German settlers were joined by immigrants from Britain and, in the later nineteenth century, Eastern Europe. Slaves and exiles had been brought to Cape Town from a range of Indian, Southeast Asian, Malagasy, and Southeast African societies. After final slave emancipation in 1838 many worked as fishers, artisans, and in crafts. These, together with Indian traders and storekeepers who arrived from the 1870s, formed the basis of a sizable Muslim community in the city. The indigenous Khoisan had been driven into the interior, but black African migrants were an important component of the population, providing the mainstay of dock labor.

Yet Cape Town was a divided city. While the wealthy mercantile elite built houses on the slopes of Table Mountain and in the new southern suburbs, overcrowding was a serious problem in the many landlord-owned slum properties that existed in the center of the town. Disease was the inevitable outcome. Municipal politics in the 1870s–1880s were dominated by conflicts between mercantile interests advocating sanitary and housing reforms and landlords who resisted them. A regular water supply was only established by 1904.

Although there was a greater degree of interracial social interaction among the lower classes of nineteenth-century Cape Town than in other South African towns, social segregation markedly increased from the 1880s. This was largely the result of concern by the city's dominant English elite at what they perceived as lower class disorder and the need to protect the white "deserving poor," at a time when growing numbers of immigrants were arriving from Europe. An outbreak of plague at the docks in 1901 provided the municipality with the pretext for forcibly moving black African workers to a segregated location at Ndabeni on the outskirts of the town. In 1927 Africans were again relocated to the new township of Langa.

The docks continued to be the mainstay of the city's economy in the early twentieth century, though the growth of light manufacturing, food processing, and clothing industries also became significant by the 1920s. Many factory workers were colored women, though by the 1930s Afrikaner migrants added to their number. Afrikaner, African, and European (especially Mediterranean) migration into Cape Town increased its total population to 369,410 by 1945. These decades also saw the rise of trade unions (notably the precursor to Industrial and Commercial Workers' Union, founded by Clements Kadalie at the Cape Town dockyards in 1919) and organizations established to advocate colored people's political rights, such as the African People's Organization founded in 1902 by Cape Town's first colored city councilor, Abdullah Abdurahman, and the more radical National Liberation League, formed in 1935 by his daughter Cissie Gool. The latter was a predecessor of the Non-European Unity Movement, founded in 1943. Great disparities of wealth continued to exist, with informal squatter settlements emerging at the city's outskirts on the sandy Cape Flats.

The decades after World War II were ones of massive social engineering. In part this was the result of modernist city planning, which sought to demolish inner-city working-class slums. But it was given particular force by the implementation of apartheid. Black African migrants were barred from the city by influx control policies, and under the Group Areas Act (1950) over 150,000 people, most of them colored, had been forcibly moved from inner city areas such as District Six and the southern suburbs by the 1970s. They were relocated to low quality housing estates on the Cape Flats, far removed from places of employment. By the 1980s influx control was breaking down and large squatter settlements such as Crossroads emerged on the Cape Flats, despite constant state harassment. Acceptance of the status quo was finally marked by the building in 1983–1984 of a new township for black Africans at Khayelitsha, some 40 kilometers from the city center.

Opposition to apartheid policies intensified. During the Sharpeville crisis (1960), thousands of residents marched from Langa into the city center under PAC leader Philip Kgosana, and protests took place in Langa and other Cape Town townships after the 1976 Soweto uprising. But it was not until the 1980s, with the founding of the United Democratic Front, that extensive resistance took place in the black African and "colored" townships of the Cape Flats, leading to army suppression and occupation.

Postapartheid Cape Town faced numerous challenges. Migration had increased its population to over three million by 2000. But it lacked a strong industrial base, its traditional textile manufacturing suffered from foreign competition and unemployment levels soared to over 40 per cent. The burgeoning tourism industry offered some hope, attracted by the region's natural beauty, though this was threatened by urban terrorism in the late 1990s, apparently caused by conflicts of rival gang and drug-dealing interests.

NIGEL WORDEN

See also: **Cape Colony.**

Further Reading

Bank, A., and G. Minkley (eds.). *Kronos: Journal of Cape History* 25, no. 9 (1998). Special issue, "Space and Identity in Cape Town."

Bickford-Smith, V. *Ethnic Pride and Racial Prejudice in Victorian Cape Town: Group Identity and Social Practice, 1875–1902.* Cambridge: Cambridge University Press/Johannesburg: Witwatersrand University Press, 1995.

———. "South African Urban History, Racial Segregation and the 'Unique' Case of Cape Town?" *Journal of Southern African Studies* 21, no. 1 (1995): 63–78.

Bickford-Smith, V., E. van Heyningen, and Nigel Worden. *Cape Town in the Twentieth Century.* Cape Town: David Philip, 1999.

Worden, N., E. van Heyningen, and Vivian Bickford-Smith, *Cape Town: The Making of a City.* Cape Town: David Philip/Hilversum, Netherlands: Verloren, 1998.

Cape Verde, History of

The Republic of Cape Verde (in Portuguese, Republica de Cabo Verde) is a small West African country consisting of ten volcanic islands and five islets 300 miles due west of the westernmost point of Africa. The archipelago features two island groups. The Barlevento group on the north includes Santo Antão, São Vincento, Santa Luzia (uninhabited), São Nicolau, Sal, and Boa Vista, along with the islets Raso and Branco. The Sotavento group on the south includes Maio, São Tiago, Fogo, and Brava, and the islets of Grande, Luís, Carneiro, and Cima. Praia on São Tiago is the capital and main town of the Sotavento islands, while Mindelo on São Vincente is the main town in the north.

The majority of the population is *Crioulo* (Creole) or *mestiço*, the result of early relationships between slave owners and their female slaves. The people of Cape Verde descended from both European and African ancestry, developing a Luso-African culture.

The official language of Cape Verde is Portuguese. However, it is Crioulo that is the mother tongue and national language. Crioulo expresses the *saudade* (soul) of Cape Verde and is the defining linguistic feature of cultural identity. Crioulo, consisting of

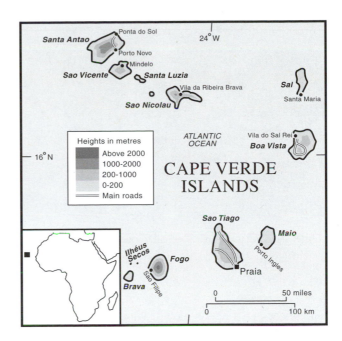

Cape Verde.

antiquated Portuguese modified through contact with various African languages, emerged in the sixteenth century. It initially served as the lingua franca for Portuguese and African slave traders, a hybrid language of commerce.

Although evidence is not conclusive, the Cape Verde Islands may have been visited, but not occupied, prior to the arrival of the Portuguese. It is possible that Phoenicians, Moors (Arab-Berbers), and West Africans visited the islands. Phoenician traders may have sailed there in the fifth and fourth centuries BCE, and the Moors may have arrived in the tenth and eleventh centuries. However, it was not until Portuguese and Italian navigators sailing for Prince Henry "The Navigator" of Portugal that the islands were colonized. It was between 1455 and 1462 that the islands were reached by navigators such as Ca da Mosta, Diogo Gomes, Diogo Afonso, and António and Bartolemeu da Noli. In 1462, early settlers (including Portuguese Jews) arrived at São Tiago and founded Riberia Grande (today known as Cidade Velha), the first European settlement and church in the tropics. The early intentions of the Portuguese were to use the islands as an entrepôt and site for producing cotton and sugar. In 1495, the islands were declared a crown possession of Portugal, which subsequently began importing slaves from the West African coast to cultivate the land.

Aside from importing slaves, the Portuguese imported criminals, exiles, social outcasts, and a feudal (*companhia*) system to Cape Verde. At this time, Portuguese slave masters began to initiate sexual relations with African slaves, developing a heterogeneous Crioulo society. The

Women carrying water in a little village near Tarrafal, Santiago, Cape Verde, 2003. © Wolfgang Schmidt/Das Fotoarchiv.

feudal social structure included *capitãos* (captains), *fidalgos* (noblemen), *cavaleiro-fidalgos* (noble knights), *almoxarites* (tax collectors), *degradados* (convicts), *exterminados* (exiles), and *lançados* (outcasts). Slaves occupied the bottom of the feudal social structure and were classified as *escravos novos* or *boçales* (raw slaves), *escravos naturais* (Cape Verde-born slaves), and *ladinos* (baptized or "civilized" slaves). Slaves often were used to clear land, labor in the salt flats of Sal, gather indigo, orchil, and urzella (plant dyes), and work on the cotton, sugar, and coffee plantations. In addition, runaway slaves called *badius* cultivated land in the interior and retained a degree of African authenticity (that is, they were less assimilated to Portuguese culture). Eventually, the companhia system was abandoned for the *morgado* or *capela* system of land ownership. *Morgados* were large tracts of privately owned land transmitted under the principle of primogeniture. In 1863 the morgado system gave way to land reforms and was abolished.

With the expansion of the slave trade in the sixteenth century, the Cape Verde Islands became a key interface among Africa, Europe, and America. The archipelago was soon at the center of a triangular trade, sending regular shipments of slaves, ivory, and gold to the Americas and Europe in exchange for cheap manufactured goods, cloth, firearms, horses, and rum. Due to the wealth accumulated from the transatlantic slave trade, the islands became attractive to Spanish, English, Dutch, and French pirates. These pirates and foreign raiders (William Hawkins in the 1540s, Francis Drake in 1585, and the French in 1712) repeatedly attacked the islands, especially the city of Riberia Grande during the following centuries. The islands were also attractive to smugglers, who would use *panos* (trade cloths) as currency (two panos were equal to one iron bar), thus undermining the Portuguese Crown trading monopoly. Wolof spinners and weavers made panos from cotton, which was then dyed using both orchil and urzella. Efforts, though unsuccessful, were made to control the corruption and smuggling. For example, the sale of panos was prohibited and punishable by death during the 1680s.

As the transatlantic slave trade was reluctantly abandoned in 1876, the Cape Verde Islands once again became an important commercial center during the late nineteenth century. With the advent of steam-powered ocean vessels, the islands served as a refueling stop (at Mindelo) on the transatlantic passage. Submarine cable stations also attracted many ships until World War II. Despite renewed interest in the islands, the people of Cape Verde still suffered from drought, famine, and poor administration. Most Cape Verdeans worked as tenant farmers and sharecroppers. Others sought employment in São Tomé and Príncipe as agricultural laborers, while many signed onto whaling and sealing ships. Between the late 1800s and early 1900s, tens of thousands of Cape Verdeans voluntarily migrated to the United States (mainly to southeastern New England) to work as longshoremen or in cranberry bogs and factories.

In the early twentieth century, opposition to the Portuguese crown was growing in both Cape Verde and Guinea-Bissau. In 1926, the fascists took control of the Portuguese government and later added a colonial policy into the constitution. Consequently, anticolonialist movements grew in Cape Verde and Guinea-Bissau. Prison camps, which were known for their brutality, were established at Tarrafal, São Tiago (known as Chão Bom), to house dissidents and nationalists from Guinea-Bissau, Cape Verde, Angola, and Portugal. Initial nationalist sentiments were expressed in the literary *claridade* (calrity) movement, founded by Baltazar Lopes, Jorge Barbosa, and Manuel Lopes in 1936. The claridade movement spoke out against racism, fascism, and Portuguese colonialism.

In 1951, Portugal changed Cape Verde's status to that of an overseas province, in an attempt to avert growing nationalism. Despite this action, nationalists responded by founding the clandestine Partido Africano da Independência da Guiné e Cabo Verde (PAIGC), a party founded (in Guinea-Bissau) by Amilcar Cabral and several others in 1956. The PAIGC's goal was to liberate both Guinea-Bissau and Cape Verde from Portuguese colonialism. In 1958 the PAIGC initiated a series of general strikes. In 1959 a strike at Pijiguiti, Guinea-Bissau, turned into a massacre. Still, the PAIGC concluded that the violence practiced by the colonial state could only be defeated by counter-violence and armed-struggle. The PAIGC thus abandoned peaceful means of protest for a war of national liberation. In 1963 the armed struggle began, with fighting concentrated in rural Guinea-Bissau. Due to logistical reasons, the PAIGC withheld from attacks in the Cape Verde Islands. With the PAIGC making steady military progress, the Portuguese responded with bombing attacks, using white phosphorous and napalm provided by the United States and North Atlantic Treaty Organization.

By 1972, the PAIGC controlled much of Guinea-Bissau despite the presence of Portuguese troops in fortified towns. On January 20, 1973, Amilcar Cabral was assassinated, but the PAIGC quickly intensified its attacks against the weakened Portuguese military and by September 24, 1973, independence was declared. Following this declaration, the fascist Portuguese government was toppled on April 25, 1974, thus prompting the new Portuguese government to negotiate a process of decolonization with the PAIGC.

In December 1974, Portugal and the PAIGC agreed to a transitional government. Full independence was achieved in Guinea-Bissau by September 24, 1974, and in Cape Verde by July 5, 1975. Aristides Pereira became the first president of the Republic of Cape Verde, and Pedro Pires became the first prime minister. Although the original constitution envisioned political unification with Guinea-Bissau, a coup in November 1980 strained the relations between the two countries. Shortly thereafter, Pedro Pires founded the Partido Africano da Independência de Cabo Verde (PAICV) abandoning the hope for unity with Guinea-Bissau. The PAICV established a one-party system and ruled Cape Verde from independence until 1990.

In 1991, the first multiparty elections took place. The PAICV leaders were replaced by the Movimento para Democracia (MPD). António Mascarenas Monteiro replaced Pereira, and Carlos Veiga replaced Pires. A new constitution was adopted in 1992 instituting multiparty democracy. The MPD won the majority of the votes in the 1995 elections, which were judged to be both free and fair by domestic and international observers.

The 2001 elections once again saw a changing of the guard, as Pedro Pires and Jóse Marie Neves, both members of the PAICV, became president and prime minister, respectively. Cape Verde is a member of the Organization of African Unity, the United Nations, and PALOP (African Countries with Portuguese as the Official Language). With assistance from the World Bank, Cape Verde has undertaken several infrastructure improvement projects, in such areas as urban development, water management, and education.

PAUL KHALIL SAUCIER

Further Reading

Foy, C. *Cape Verde: Politics, Economics and Society*. London: Pinter, 1988.

Halter, M. *Between Race and Ethnicity: Cape Verdean American Immigrants*. Urbana: University of Illinois Press, 1993.

Lobban, R. *Cape Verde: Crioulo Colony to Independent Nation*. Boulder, Colo.: Westview Press, 1995.

Lobban, R., and M. Lopes. *Historical Dictionary of the Republic of Cape Verde*, 3rd ed. Lanham, Md.: Scarecrow Press, 1995.

Carthage

The civilization of Carthage (now modern Tunisia), one of the great civilizations to be established in Africa, was situated at the great crossroads where Africa and the world of the Mediterranean met. Carthage began as a colony of the Phoenicians about 800BCE. It emerged in a location regarded as the most sizable single area of fertile agricultural land in northwestern Africa. As Phoenician power and influence suffered due to the depredations of Assyrians and the Persians, Carthage began to act more independently. By the sixth century, Carthage had emerged as an independent power and expanded along the African and Mediterranean shores and into the Balearic Islands, Sardinia, and the western part of Sicily.

It was ruled by a commercial oligarchy. Before long, Carthage had grown in wealth and importance to become a major city with an estimated population of about 400,000. In the fourth century it extended its control over the Tunisian plain to ensure a steady supply of food and of Berber elements for its army. By the beginning of the third century BCE, it had monopolized the trade not only of African territory, which reached almost to the Sahara Desert, but also that of the coasts of almost all of the area of the western Mediterranean, both of Africa and Spain, the islands of Sardinia and Corsica, and parts of Sicily.

As Carthage became more prosperous, it began to require considerable military and naval forces to protect itself from invaders drawn by its wealth. A formidable fighting force under great commanders was established. The army consisted almost entirely of mercenaries, of different tongues and races. An important feature of the army was the Numidian cavalry, which was made up of riders carrying shields of elephant's hide and wearing a lion's skin over their shoulder. They used no saddles or bridles, and were fearless riders and warriors.

Carthage did everything possible to extend the frontiers of commerce; this policy eventually brought it in conflict with Rome. Soon after the establishment of the Roman republic, both powers entered into an agreement in which the greater part of the western Mediterranean was recognized as Carthaginian, and only the coast of western Sicily was open to all. In fact, so completely did the Carthaginians control the western Mediterranean region that they declared the Mediterranean Sea a Carthaginian lake, in which nobody could even wash his hands without Carthaginian permission.

When the Carthaginians began to seize the Greek cities in eastern Sicily, the trouble with Rome began. The conquest of Magna Graecia (a Greek area in southern Italy) had made Rome a near neighbor of the Carthaginian state. Thus, when Sicilian Greeks appealed to Rome for help, the Romans welcomed an opportunity to cut Carthage down to size. The struggle between Rome and Carthage culminated in the First Punic (from the Latin word "Phoenician") War, 264–241BCE. In that war, the Roman fleet defeated the Carthaginians at sea. They then forced Carthage to give up all claim to eastern Sicily and to cede western Sicily as well.

To compensate for the losses, Carthage expanded its holdings into Spain, in order to partake of the latter's rich minerals and manpower. A military expedition under the great general Hannibal was dispatched to Spain.

In 218BCE, when the Second Punic War (218–201BCE) started, Hannibal took his troops across southern Gaul and then over the Alps into Italy. In that expedition, he lost in the snow half of his men, great quantities of baggage, and many of the elephants he used as pack animals. In spite of that, he won a string of victories as he marched southward. The Roman general Fabius Cunctator "the Delayer" tried to exhaust the Carthaginian forces by adopting his "Fabian" tactics: refraining from full battle, and instead merely attacking Carthaginian supply trains and patrols with the hopes of lowering their morale. But when this strategy was reversed in favor of an all-out battle at Cannae (216BCE), the Romans suffered a crushing defeat. Hannibal was able to achieve such a feat through his skill and daring, his genius for command, his concern for the welfare of his soldiers, and his good judgment.

It was not until several years later that another Roman general, Scipio, emerged to defeat Carthage. This was in 202BCE at Zama, a few miles south of Carthage. It was the last battle in a long and bitter war. For the first time in his career, Hannibal was defeated in war. The defeat was so devastating that Carthage had no option but to surrender. The terms of the peace treaty were extremely harsh: Carthage was to give up Spain and all of the islands between Africa and Italy, the king of Numidia was to be recognized as an ally of Rome, and Carthage was to pay to Rome an annual tribute of 200 talents for 50 years and relinquish its elephants and warships. However, Carthage was left as a free and independent nation. While Hannibal fled in shame to the court of the king of Syria, his adversary Scipio, in honor of his great victory over Carthage, was given the surname Africanus. He thus became the first commander in chief to whom the Romans bestowed the name of the people he had defeated.

Although Carthage had been humiliated, Rome watched its growing prosperity with increasing anxiety and jealousy. The speedy recovery alarmed the Roman ruling class and soldiers who thereafter agitated for its complete destruction. Cato the censor and senator would end each of his speeches with the words *Delenda est Carthago* (Carthage must be destroyed).

Thus, 52 years after the defeat of Hannibal, the Third Punic War (149–146BCE) began. War was declared against Carthage with the excuse that it had violated a treaty that made it mandatory for it to receive Rome's consent before engaging in war. (Carthage had made preparations to defend itself against constant raids by the king of Numidia.) In a war in which Rome showed neither mercy nor pity and in which Carthage was besieged for two years, the cruel order was finally given in 146BCE that Carthage must be utterly destroyed. The inhabitants were massacred, and the city plundered and burned. After leveling the city, the whole site was ploughed, salt was sprinkled on the earth, and a solemn curse was pronounced upon whomever would attempt to rebuild the city. The other territories that belonged to Carthage were then annexed as the Roman province of Africa.

OLUTAYO ADESINA

See also: **North Africa: Roman Occupation, Empire.**

Further Reading

Crane, B., J. B. Christopher, and Robert Lee Wolff. *A History of Civilization: Prehistory to 1715*, 4th ed. Englewood Cliffs, N.J.: Prentice Hall, 1971.

Fage, J. D. *A History of Africa.* New York: Alfred A. Knopf, 1978.

Warmington, B. H. *The North African Provinces from Diocletian to the Vandal Conquest.* Cambridge: Cambridge University Press, 1954.

Carvajal, Luis del Mármol (c.1520–c.1600)
Spanish Soldier, Geographer, and Historian

Along with the *Delle descrittione dell' Africa* by Leo Africanus, another popular sixteenth-century source for the geography of Africa was the *Descripcion general de Affrica*, written in Spanish by Luis del Mármol Carvajal. The first two volumes were printed in Granada in 1573; they were followed much later by a third volume printed in Málaga in 1599. While Spanish authors had published extensive accounts of the New World earlier in the century, it is somewhat surprising that the first comprehensive European description of Africa was written by a Spaniard—especially since Spain's connection with the continent was limited to the Barbary Coast. A French translation appeared in 1667. An Arabic translation, based on the French version, was published in Morocco in 1989.

English, Dutch, and German extracts were included in most of the popular seventeenth- and eighteenth-century encyclopedic works dealing with African geography and the history of European discoveries.

Little is known of the life of Carvajal except what he tells of himself in his preface, and what can be gleaned from the few surviving documents on his military career. Carvajal was born in Granada to a Castilian family around 1520. It has been suggested that Carvajal's family had Moorish ancestry, which could explain his knowledge of Arabic and interest in northern Africa.

After the Spanish conquest of Tunis in 1535 (in which he took part), Carvajal pursued his military career in Northern Africa for ten years until he was taken prisoner in a battle near Oran, probably in 1545. According to his own words, he spent the following seven years and eight months in captivity. During this period, he was transported as a slave into various parts of Morocco, Algeria, and Libya. The Christian captives, most of whom were Spaniards, played a vital role in the economies and societies of the North African states. They were important both as slave labor and for the substantial sums paid to rescue them. Carvajal was ransomed by an unidentified redemptionist order around 1554, but he carried on exploring the African continent as a free man, probably visiting Egypt and Ethiopia. He even went as far as the borders of the Sudanic zone. Having spent 22 years in Africa, he finally returned to Spain in 1557.

Thereafter Carvajal fought in the Spanish army in Italy, returning to Granada in time to witness the *Morisco* revolt in 1568–1572. At the end of the revolt, he settled near Málaga where he began to write his *Descripcion general de Affrica*. It was certainly during his long stay on the Barbary Coast that he learned to read and speak Arabic fluently. On the grounds of this knowledge, he was in 1579 on the point of being named Spanish ambassador to Morocco. At the last moment King Philip II rejected him, only because he was not a nobleman by birth. Nothing is known of the rest of his life. Carvajal died in Granada, probably in 1600.

Carvajal has been regarded for a long time as a mere copyist of Leo Africanus, and hence his work has largely been neglected by modern historians of Africa. He was criticized particularly by contemporary scholarly readers because he did not acknowledge Leo Africanus at all, despite incorporating large sections of his *Descrittione* in his own work. This accusation is not exactly accurate, as Carvajal does refer to his famous predecessor (whom he called Iuan de Leon) twice. Moreover, quoting earlier texts without any acknowledgment was not considered to be a mark of egregious scholarship, or a violation of copyright, as it is presently.

Carvajal nowhere reveals when and in what circumstances he became aware of the work of Leo Africanus, or his impetus for writing the *Descripcion general de Affrica*. He certainly relied on Ramusio's Italian edition of Africanus, rather than the French or Latin translations of 1556. It is tempting to speculate that Carvajal obtained a copy of Ramusio's *Delle navigatione et viaggi* while fighting in Italy. Perhaps he was commissioned, based on his experiences in northern Africa, to produce an updated, Spanish edition of Leo's text by Spanish military authorities. This would at least explain the contents and structure of Carvajal's work, and the fact that the second part was published at the author's expense more than 20 years after the first part. (The second part focuses on the Sahara, Egypt, Ethiopia, Sudanic Africa, and the Guinea Coast—all areas of little interest to the Spaniards, who were fighting against the Moorish corsairs in the western Mediterranean.)

Carvajal's work is not a mere regurgitation of that of Leo Africanus. He was able to supplement the latter's text with many new details and corrections on the grounds of what he had learned during his stay in northern Africa. It contains a lengthy exposition of the history of Islam up to the year 1571. The focus is understandably on the events in Islamic Spain and Northern Africa. This history, however, proves that Carvajal must have known some of the chronicles written by the Muslim historians in Granada and Morocco. During the long reign of King Philip II (1556–1598), a large quantity of Arabic manuscripts were acquired by the Escorial library from all of the Spanish cities where Muslim culture had flourished. Furthermore, Carvajal described areas which had been unfamiliar to Leo, such as the Guinea Coast, the kingdoms of Congo and Monomotapa, Zanzibar, and Madagascar. Carvajal, who was at Lisbon in 1579, seems to have had access to some unpublished Portuguese and Spanish sources; he also probably interviewed persons who had been to western Africa.

Besides his *Descripcion general de Affrica*, Carvajal wrote a history of the Moorish revolt in Granada, entitled *Historia del rebelión y castigo de los moriscos del reino de Granada*, which was published in Málaga in 1600. Moreover, there exists in the Escorial library a manuscript written by Carvajal, describing a Turkish standard that had been captured in the naval battle of Lepanto in 1571. (Carvajal himself did not participate in this battle.)

PEKKA MASONEN

See also: **Africanus, Leo.**

Biography

Born in Granada, Spain, around 1520. Participated in the Spanish conquest of Tunis in 1535. Pursued a military career in Northern Africa for ten years, until taken prisoner in a battle near Oran, probably in 1545. Held in captivity for seven years and eight months; ransomed by an unidentified redemptionist order, around 1554. Returned to Spain in 1557. Settled near Málaga, and there began to write the *Descripcion general de Affrica*. Died in Granada, probably in 1600.

Further Reading

Carvajal, Luis del Mármol. *Descripción general de Africa por Luis Marmol Carvajal (1573–99)*. Madrid: Instituto de Estudios Africanos, 1953.

Hair, P. E. H. "Sources on Early Sierra Leone (15): Marmol 1573." *Africana Research Bulletin* 9, no. 3 (1979): 70–84.

Masonen, P. *The Negroland Revisited: Discovery and Invention of the Sudanese Middle Ages*. Helsinki: Finnish Academy of Science and Letters, 1999.

Monroe, J. T. *Islam and the Arabs in Spanish Scholarship (Sixteenth Century to the Present)*. Leiden: E. J. Brill, 1970.

Casablanca

Casablanca, Morocco's largest city, with a population over 3 million (2.94 million in the 1994 census) was a construction of the French colonial occupation. It is the economic and cultural capital of contemporary Morocco. The city, organized into five separate prefectures since the early 1980s, holds 10 per cent of the Moroccan population. In the regional context of North Africa it is not only a demographic giant but a manufacturing powerhouse. In any given year, one-third of Morocco's industrial investments are made in Casablanca, which has yielded the city nearly 60 per cent of the country's factories and industrial employment.

"Casa," as it is commonly called by Arabic and French speakers alike, was a town of 20,000 in 1912 when the French arrived as colonizers. By 1952, it had become a major French metropolis of 682,000 inhabitants. Today, Casablanca spreads north and south of its central points (the Old Medina and the French-inspired central business district) to encompass a city remarkably differentiated in its quarters and neighborhoods. Casablanca is the southern anchor of the Rabat-Casablanca urban corridor. The city is growing inland and northward along the coast quite rapidly, and the distinction between Casablanca and the beginning of the oil-refinery port of Mohammedia has become blurred. Casablanca is 50 miles from Rabat, the political capital, a distance connected by rapid rail and four-lane expressway.

Atlantic Morocco has few natural harbors and no large bays or inlets. Casablanca's rapid growth is traceable to the decision by Lyautey, first resident general of the French Protectorate (as the colony was officially known) to build the port for French Morocco at Casablanca. The port is thus entirely artificial, and has undergone several significant enlargements, including that going on from the year 2000 to the present.

Casablanca was first so named by the Portuguese after a white house overlooking the ruins of the city in the same location, Anfa, which they had destroyed ff. 1486–1489 in their quest to quell corsair activity ("Casa Branca"). The Spanish renamed it Casablanca and the name was translated literally into Arabic as Dar al-Beida, which is used interchangeably with Casablanca in both French and Arabic today. Anfa is retained as the name of an elite residential neighborhood.

Sultan Muhammad III (*r*.1757–1790) rebuilt the city as a defensive coastal bastion (*skala*) between Rabat and El Jadida (then Mazagan), filling it with loyal Berber subjects from the Haha Plain (Essaouira region) and Arabs from Meknès. Once the city was rebuilt, wheat was exported to Spain from 1782 to 1794, when the governor revolted. The port was closed to commerce until 1830. European traders multiplied in Casablanca after 1840 (the first were French, in search of wool to replace British supplies), and the first diplomatic representative was named to the city in 1857. By the first decade of the 1900s, Casablanca was a scheduled port in maritime trade and the largest port in Morocco, exceeding the traffic of Tangier. Following the Conference of Algeciras in 1906, which internationalized the economic life of Morocco and prepared the way for full-scale colonization, French customs agents and construction managers took over the port of Casablanca. This provoked anger in the Chaouia (the outlying rural district), and on July 30, 1907, peasants attacked and killed nine Europeans and blocked the entrance to the French consulate. In retaliation, the French bombarded the very port they had coveted; looting, especially of the *mellah* (Jewish quarter), broke out; in August, more than 2000 French (and some Spanish) troops landed. The French created a security perimeter around the Chaouia, effectively creating the toe-hold that five years later culminated in the official establishment of the French and Spanish protectorates over Morocco.

Casablanca attracted over one million immigrants during the twentieth century, reaching a peak of over 56,000 new residents per year in the 1970s. The city quadrupled in population between 1907 and 1921, when the rate of growth was greatest, and added 622,000 people in the period from 1971 to 1982, when growth in absolute numbers was strongest. The positive additions to the city's population have taken place despite the subtraction of virtually the city's entire Jewish community, which numbered 75,000 in 1952 (more than one-third of Morocco's Jews) and most of the European population as well, which amounted to nearly 133,000 at the same time (near its highpoint). One should note, however, that Casablanca's contemporary Jewish population (variously estimated between 3,000 and 8,000) is the largest in North Africa, and that its French population (25,000) forms the largest single French expatriate community in Africa.

Much of Casablanca's population lives in poor urban conditions. The United Nations Development Program noted in 1993 that an average wage in Casablanca was 1400 DH (US$155) per month, while a typical three-room apartment rented for 2500 DH (US$278) per month. Since the 1930s, the problem of substandard housing (*bidonville*, to use the French term for shantytown; the term may even have been invented here) has been endemic in Casablanca, especially in the Ben Msik and Carrières Centrales neighborhoods. Casablanca largely consists of undifferentiated, bland apartment buildings three to five stories high. On the other hand, the city's central business district is a storehouse of art deco buildings from the 1930s to the 1950s, and includes several important examples of the Franco-Moorish style in its public buildings (the courthouse and city hall) and cathedral. The French architect Ecochard, imported to develop a new urban plan after World War II, was responsible for the development of several urban innovations, most important of which was the Nouvelle Medina, an attempt to synthesize traditional urban form with modern economic, administrative, and residential needs. The French often referred to Casablanca as "our Los Angeles," and the city truly reflects the style and flair of the new. The city houses many notable examples of the modern Moroccan architectural style, especially along the Corniche, in elite residential areas such as Anfa, and in the burgeoning central city, where the beginnings of a vertically oriented city were apparent by the 1980s. Casablanca is the location of Morocco's stock exchange. The skyline of the city was transformed by the construction, completed in 1993, of the enormous Hassan II Mosque along the coast on the southern edge of the central business district. Casablanca's University Hassan II, established in the 1970s, contains one of two medical schools in Morocco, a law school, and six other faculties, and enrolls approximately 35,000 students.

JAMES A. MILLER

See also: **Marrakech.**

Further Reading

Adam, A. *Casablanca; Essai sur la transformation de la société maroicaine au contact de l'Occident.* 2 vols. Paris: CNRS, 1968.
————. "(Al-)Dar al-Bayda." In *The Encyclopedia of Islam*, new ed., vol. 2. Leiden: E. J. Brill, 1985.

Hoisington, W. A., Jr. *The Casablanca Connection: French Colonial Policy, 1936–1943*. Chapel Hill: University of North Carolina Press, 1984.

Casamance: *See* Senegal: Casamance Province, Conflict in.

Casely Hayford, Joseph Ephraim (1866–1930)
Lawyer, Journalist, and Politician

Joseph Ephraim Casely Hayford was born on September 29, 1866, in Cape Coast. His father, Reverend Joseph de Graft Hayford, was a Wesleyan Methodist minister, and his son attended the Wesleyan Boys' High School in Cape Coast and later Fourah Bay College in Sierra Leone. On his return to the Gold Coast, Casely Hayford taught at the Accra Wesleyan High School and then became its principal. He lost this position on account of his journalistic activity as the subeditor of his uncle James Hutton Brew's weekly newspaper, the *Gold Coast Echo*; after this paper collapsed he was the editor of two other short-lived local newspapers. He also served as an articled clerk for a European lawyer in Cape Coast and eventually went to England, where he graduated from St. Peter's College, Cambridge. He then entered the Inner Temple, London, to study law. In 1896 he passed the bar exam and returned to the Gold Coast to practice law.

His return coincided with the Gold Coast Aborigines' Rights Protection Society's (GCARPS) opposition to the Lands Bill of 1894. Casely Hayford helped prepare the society's brief against this legislation, which was designed to regulate the administration of land in the Gold Coast. He collected a great deal of information on indigenous institutions and published his first book, *Gold Coast Native Institutions* (1903), on this subject. He felt that Africans had to preserve their own culture. His second work, *Ethiopia Unbound* (1911), took up this theme as its hero, Kwamankra, (in many respects Casely Hayford's stand-in in this hybrid of novel and "intellectual autobiography" [July 1967, p.433]), urges his countrymen to "emancipate [themselves] from the thralldom of foreign ideas inimical to racial development." Like much of Casely Hayford's thought, this work was deeply influenced by Wilmot Edward Blyden's "Ethiopianism," which had profoundly inspired the young man when he was a student in Sierra Leone. *Ethiopia Unbound* criticizes the blunders of colonial policy and the hypocrisy of materialistic Europe in contrast to the "simple idealism of unspoiled, persecuted Africa." The "gin trade" had undermined native chiefs. Christian churches preached brotherhood but practiced racial segregation among their congregations, and officials denied Africans representative government.

Protest against the Forestry Bill of 1911 inspired Casely Hayford to publish *The Truth about the West African Land Question* (1913), in which he sought to link this new attempt to "manage reserved lands" with the defeated Lands Bill of 1894. As an indication of his status in the colony, he went as a one-man delegation to London in 1911, and as part of a four-man delegation in 1912 to protest against this legislation. These delegations had little influence on the committee that the British government established to review land policies in West Africa, but the measure eventually died under the weight of deliberations in committee. Colonial policy was shifting in favor of an active role for the chiefs in the administration. Encroaching on their control of land seemed likely to undermine this policy.

The regional approach that the British government had taken to the question of land stimulated Casely Hayford to think of a more West African organization than the GCARPS, which his generation felt had become too parochial. To give himself more editorial freedom, in 1902 he had established his own newspaper, the Cape Coast weekly *Gold Coast Leader.* He used the paper to raise the idea of a conference of leading men from the four British West African colonies. However, World War I intervened, and it was not until 1919 that Casely Hayford, along with other Gold Coast professionals, was able to organize the Gold Coast Section of the Projected West African Conference. Allied war aims and the Versailles Peace Conference had popularized the idea of self-determination. Casely Hayford also felt that it was time for the "educated natives" to establish themselves as the "natural leaders" of their country, and he antagonized the leadership of the GCARPS and the colony's most prominent chief, Nana Ofori Atta of Akyem Abuakwa.

In 1920 the first meeting of what was to be known as the Congress of British West Africa took place in Accra, and Casely Hayford was elected its vice president. The congress passed 83 resolutions that dealt with such diverse issues as elected representative government, the creation of a British West African university and more opportunities for Africans in the upper ranks of the civil service. At first the administration of Governor Guggisberg was mildly sympathetic, but when the congress hastily organized a deputation to London to press for reforms this sentiment evaporated. The chiefs under the leadership of Nana Ofori Atta also attacked the idea that the educated elite were the natural rulers and undermined whatever chances Casely Hayford and his fellow deputation members might have had in influencing the Colonial Office in London.

The conflict between the chiefs and the educated elite allowed the government in the Gold Coast to dismiss the congress as unrepresentative. To challenge this perception the congress captured control of the GCARPS and Casely Hayford became vice president. In the Legislative Council, where he had been an unofficial member since 1916, he "impeached" Nana Ofori Atta and his supporters as "traitors to the cause of British West Africa." The damage had been done, however, and though there were a number of joint sessions (at Freetown, 1923; Bathhurst, 1925–1926; and Lagos, 1929) it was only at these times that the movement actually came alive.

In addition, Governor Guggisberg's new constitution of 1925 rapidly shifted the political focus. It heightened the conflict between the chiefs and the educated elite by giving the former more representation in the expanded Legislative Council. Casely Hayford bitterly attacked this legislation.

In 1926 he went as a one-man delegation to London, but in keeping with his pragmatic approach to politics, when he realized that further opposition was pointless, in 1927 he ran for election and became the municipal representative for Sekondi. This action split the ranks of the educated elite. A predominantly Cape Coast faction led by the lawyer Kobina Sekyi took control of the GCARPS and assailed Casely Hayford and those members of the educated elite who had gone along with him as "defective leaders." As a member of the Legislative Council in 1929 Casely Hayford effected a reconciliation with Nana Sir Ofori Atta, who had been knighted in 1927. Casely Hayford had been awarded the MBE in 1919. Shortly after this reconciliation he died in Accra on August 11, 1930.

ROGER GOCKING

See also: **Ghana.**

Biography

Born September 29, 1866 in Cape Coast. Attended the Wesleyan Boys' High School and Fourah Bay College in Sierra Leone. Taught at the Accra Wesleyan High School, also served as the school's principal, and then became its principal in Cape Coast.

Graduated from St. Peter's College, University of Cambridge. Studied law at the Inner Temple, London. Passed the bar and returned to the Gold Coast to practice law in 1896. Established a newspaper, the *Gold Coast Lead*, in 1902. Published first book, *Gold Coast Native Institutions,* in 1903. Published *Ethiopia Unbound* in 1911. Published *The Truth About the West African Land Question* in 1913. Elected municipal representative for Sekondi in 1927. Awarded the MBE in 1919. Died in Accra on August 11, 1930.

Further Reading

Cromwell, A. M. *An African Victorian Feminist: The Life and Times of Adelaide Smith Casely Hayford 1868–1960.* London: Frank Cass, 1986.

Ephson, I. S. *Gallery of Gold Coast Celebrities 1632–1958.* Accra: Ilen, 1969.

Kimble, D. *A Political History of Ghana 1850–1928.* London: Oxford University Press, 1963.

July, R. W. *The Origins of Modern African Thought.* New York: Frederick Praeger, 1967.

Sampson, M. *Makers of Modern Ghana: Phillip Quarcoo to Aggrey,* vol. 1. Accra: Anowuo Educational, 1969.

Catholic Church: *See* Augustine, Catholic Church: North Africa.

Cattle: *See* Great Lakes Region: Growth of Cattle Herding; Iron Age (Later): East Africa: Cattle, Wealth, Power.

Central Africa, Northern: Slave Raiding

It is now widely accepted that the institution of slavery, in one form or another, had deep roots in Africa long before Islam became a significant social influence. The first accounts of the early Arab penetration of the central Sahara to the frontiers of the Sudan (in its widest geographical sense) in the seventh century confirm that slavery, if not active slave trading, were already established there. The Arab conquerors were able to exact tributes in slaves from several of the places they conquered in Fezzan and even, according to one account, as far south as the oases of Kawar, two-thirds of the way to Lake Chad. Such accounts do not confirm that there was a regular or even an active slave trade in the Sahara at the time, either in Saharan peoples or in black slaves drawn from farther south. It is possible that in order to meet Arab demands for tributes of slaves, the conquered communities of Fezzan and Kawar had to draw on long-established sources of slaves from the central desert itself, or from the southern desert fringes around Lake Chad, or even farther south. It has been suggested that once the Arab demand for slaves had been established as a result of specific tributes levied by conquest, it evolved into a regular and larger traffic, conducted notably by Ibadi Berbers, based on the oasis of Zawila in Fezzan, from the eighth century onward.

Early Arab writers remarked how easily the black peoples of the Sudan were enslaved: "Blacks are caught with dates," was an old Arab adage. In the first instance, slaves were not usually made by outsiders, but by slaves' own rulers; by kidnapping; as punishment for crime; or in raids by stronger neighbors. Al-Yaqubi wrote, in the ninth century, "I have been informed that the Kings of Sudan will sell their people without any pretext or war." Al-Idrisi, in the twelfth century, told how the people of Lamlam in the western Sudan were constantly being seized by neighbors "using various tricks," and sold in Morocco. But, as medieval Arab sources confirm, slaves were more usually made during the course of wars, or as a result of organized slave raids into the lands of weaker and more vulnerable peoples. Thus the twelfth-century geographer, Al-Zuhri, reported that the Muslims of ancient Ghana made yearly (but not always successful) slave raids into the lands of the pagans whose ebony-wood clubs were no match for the iron weapons of the Ghanaians. Here are clearly established what were for centuries the common slavemaking practices of inner Africa, with more "advanced" organized and partly Islamized states, their armies equipped with superior (often imported) weapons, mounting regular slave raids against more "primitive" pagan neighbors.

Under Shari'a (Islamic law), Muslims were forbidden to enslave fellow Muslims; but as the enslavement of pagans was legal, and their conversion meritorious, slave raiding into heathen lands acquired some of the character of religious war (jihad), with nonbelief held to justify enslavement. Thus in the Sudan, the elusive and shifting borders between the Islamic world, the Dar-al-Islam, and the as-yet unconverted Dar-al-Harb (literally, "House of War") for centuries marked off these lands where slavemaking was considered a licit activity. And the many residual pockets of paganism within the boundaries of the Sudanese Dar-al-Islam were always equally vulnerable to slave raiding. There is indeed evidence that some pagan peoples (notably the Sara communities south of Lake Chad) were deliberately not converted to Islam simply to sustain their eligibility for enslavement.

Raiding campaigns usually took place during the dry season (October–April) after much of the agricultural work had been done and when travel was easier. Raiders' success depended on a combination of surprise, organization, numbers, and the use of horses and (before the more widespread use of firearms in the nineteenth century) superior iron weapons.

Most slaves were made for use in the raiders' own communities; only limited numbers were selected by successive markets for eventual export northward across the Sahara in exchange for the imported horses and weapons needed for further slave raiding. About two-thirds of those exported were women and young girls intended to meet the demands of Islamic domestic slavery. While it has been suggested that most of these exported slaves were the rejects of the Sudanese markets, some valued slaves, including eunuchs as the most valuable of all, were part of the northbound trade system.

There is evidence from nineteenth-century European travelers of raiders killing all surplus male slaves on capture, but it is not clear whether this was common practice in earlier times, before the use of firearms made slave raiding more widespread, bloody, and destructive. Again, nineteenth-century evidence that up to three-fourths of captured slaves died from mistreatment, starvation, and disease between first capture and points of final sale cannot be safely projected back to earlier times. What is clear is that the medieval Arab world regarded the Sudanese as numerous and prolific, a constantly replenished reservoir of slaves. According to modern estimates, at least 5,000 slaves were exported across the Sahara at its widest extent every year in the Middle Ages. But the slave raiders' initial annual booty must have been at least ten times greater, taking into account deaths after capture and retention of most slaves in the Sudan itself. It is also clear that despite these regular depredations, the countries beyond the Islamic slaving frontier remained prolific sources of more or less constant supply for many successive centuries.

JOHN WRIGHT

See also: **Bagirmi, Wadai, and Darfur; "Legitimate Commerce" and Export Trade in the Nineteenth Century.**

Further Reading

Fage, J. D. "Slavery and the Slave Trade in the Context of West African History." *Journal of African History* 10, no. 3 (1969): 393–404.

Fisher, A. G. B., and H. J. Fisher. *Slavery and Muslim Society in Africa: The Institution in Saharan and Sudanic Africa and Trans-Saharan Trade.* London: C. Hurst, 1970.

Miers, S., and I. Kopytoff. *Slavery in Africa: Historical and Anthropological Perspectives.* Madison: University of Wisconsin Press, 1977.

Levtzion, N., and J. F. P. Hopkins. (eds.). *Corpus of Early Arabic Sources for West African History.* Cambridge: Cambridge University Press, 1981.

Lovejoy, P. E. *Transformations in Slavery: A History of Slavery in Africa.* Cambridge: Cambridge University Press, 1983.

Wright, J. *Libya, Chad and the Central Sahara.* London: C. Hurst/Totowa, N.J.: Barnes and Noble, 1989.

Central Africa, Northern: Central Sudanic Peoples

Central Sudanic peoples belong to a subgroup of the Nilo-Saharan language group, one of the four major language groups found in Africa (along with the Niger-Congo, Afro-Asiatic, and Khoisan). The geographical distribution of these peoples is extremely large, running east to west from the southern Sudanese regions of Equatoria and the Bahr el-Ghazal and northernmost Uganda, through eastern parts of the Democratic Republic of Congo (DRC), across the Central African Republic, and into Cameroon. Although definite distinctions between ethnic and linguistic differences are even now not always possible, among those that are clearly belonging to the Central Sudanic subgroup are the Bongo, Kresh, Lendu, Lugbara, Mangbetu-Efe, and Sara-Bagirmi.

The Nilo-Saharan group of languages does not contain the same numbers as other African language families but the diversity of the Nilo-Saharan languages is, far greater than that of most other groups. Added to this, the geographical range of occurrence makes the study and classification among the most controversial of all. In general there is agreement on the six branches of the Nilo-Saharan group, which are Songhay, Saharan, Maban, Fur (Furian), Koman, and Chari-Nile. Under Chari-Nile we find the further distinction between Central and Eastern Sudanic (the Eastern, Western and Southern Nilotics) and Nubian. There are estimated to be anywhere between 20 and 30 million Nilo-Saharan speakers, while the numbers for speakers of Central Sudanic languages (of which there are estimated to be a total of 65 million) do not exceed 6 million.

The Nilo-Saharan shares many similarities with the Niger-Congo language family, enough to lead many scholars to suggest that there may have once been a common ancestor between the two. A majority of languages in both groups have adopted the same use of tones to make meaning clear, and both were essentially oral languages (Nubian excepted) until modern attempts used the Arabic and Roman alphabets to transliterate them. The earliest Nilo-Saharans lived between 15,000 and 11,000 BCE. At the same time that the Central and Northern Sudanic divergence occurred (c.8000 BCE) in southwestern parts of the Nile Basin, two other dramatic occurrences took place: the birth of pottery and the domestication of cattle. As a result, the various ethnolinguistic groups enjoyed a period of strong divergence and the growth of those elements that provide distinguishing features among them.

The Lendu people can trace their origins back to the western and southern shores of Lake Albert, with their greatest concentrations remaining in the northeastern part of the DRC and neighboring Uganda. Early on they developed the dual skills of farming and fishing, which allowed them to prosper and support a higher than usual density among people in the region as a whole. The Mangbetu (Manbetu) of the northwestern part of the DRC long ago stood out among the peoples of Central Africa for having created a centralized political system with a strong class system in place, thus allowing them to expand their territories and in the process assimilate other ethnic groups in the vicinity. Their language, basically Mangbetu or Kere, like that of the Lendu and the Madi of northwestern Uganda, is a part of the Ugandan-based Lugbara cluster of languages, which all fall into the

Central Sudanic group. The assimilation of other ethnic groups has, however, meant that there were some variations in the language, with the Chadic and Adamawa languages also being present among a number of their subgroups.

Chad's largest ethnic grouping is the Sara who, despite the fact that the name is often used to refer to a single ethnic entity, represent a large number of smaller, distinct ethnic groups that share similar languages. Among the Sara's many ethnic groups are the Gulay, Kaba, Mbay, Nar, Ngambay (the largest single group), and Sar. The Sara are non-Muslim, settled farmers. Also living largely in Chad are the Barma (Bagirmi) who were the sixteenth-century founders of the eponymous empire. Despite their adoption of Islam in the seventeenth century, large numbers retained their original languages, so that the Arab Barma spoke Arabic while the indigenous Barma spoke Tar Barma, a close relative of the language spoken by the Sara.

Among the Central Sudanic group of peoples are a number of pygmy groups of the so-called Eastern Cluster (one of the four major subgroups of pygmies). The Mbutis (Bambuti) contain the subgroups of the Aka (there is another, unrelated ethnic group called the Aka in the Western Cluster) and Efe, which are both pygmy. The Ituri forest in the northeastern part of the DRC is the traditional homeland for the Mbuti, while the Aka live to the northwest and the Efe to the east and north of them. The Bongo is a subgroup of the Mbenga, one of the largest remaining groups of hunter-gatherers inhabiting the tropical forests of Central Africa. The land over which they formerly ranged was gradually reduced in size as agriculturalist cultures grew in number and cleared their traditional lands.

One final Central Sudanic group of note is the Kresh (Kreich), who trace their origins back to the Nile Basin before their migration to the Ubangian Plateau in the east of what is today the Central African Republic. There they lived among, and increasingly became assimilated with, the Banda, members of the Niger-Congo language group, and thereby losing much that set them apart as being of the Central Sudanic family.

EAMONN GEARON

Further Reading

Heine, B., and D. Nurse (eds.). *African Languages: An Introduction*. Cambridge: Cambridge University Press, 2000.

Lobban, R. A., Robert S. Kramer, and Carolyn Fluehr-Lobban. *Historical Dictionary of the Sudan*, 3rd ed. Lanham, Md.: Scarecrow Press, 2002.

Olson, J. S. *The Peoples of Africa: An Ethnohistorical Dictionary*. Westport, Conn.: Greenwood Press, 1996.

Yakan, M. Z. *Almanac of African Peoples and Nations*. New Brunswick, N.J.: Transaction, 1999.

Central Africa, Northern: Chadic Peoples

The large number of ethnic groups present in Chad through the centuries makes the task of disentangling their separate strands challenging. As a result of its geographical position, combined with the presence of such favorable geographical features as Lake Chad, migrations to and through Chad from every direction and point of the African continent and beyond have gone on since at least 5000BCE. Consequently, this area has been the site of a great number of empires, all of which have left something of their culture, ethnicity or language in their wake.

The most powerful empires in the Lake Chad region during this period were those of Kanem and its neighbor for a time, Bornu. Their histories, however, became so close that they are often referred to as the single entity of Kanem-Bornu. Established in the ninth century (and lasting, in reduced form, until the nineteenth), it was initially peopled by an amalgam of nomadic tribes without urban centers. The location of the kingdom, across a great swathe of the Sahara, allowed it to prosper through exploitation of the trans-Saharan trade routes. Over time the tribes became more homogeneous, particularly with the influx of increasing numbers of Muslim Kanuri from the eleventh century on. This process was completed when their eponymous language supplanted the various preexisting Teda-Daza languages of the area.

The Fula (Fulani, Fulbe) were originally a pastoral nomadic people whose influence and size grew to such an extent that they became both the world's largest group of pastoral nomads and one of the largest Muslim groups in Africa. Early converts to Islam, they were instrumental in its spreading across the continent, while at the same time increasing their own range of influence. Following a series of religious wars the Fula controlled an empire that stretched from Lake Chad to the Niger Bend and back to their original Lower Senegal homeland. The empire declined not long after the start of the nineteenth century.

The Bagirmi (Barma) belonged to a state that was founded in the area southeast of Lake Chad by their fist king, Dala Birni, in 1522. By the start of the seventeenth century, it had adopted Islam and acted as a buffer to its two larger neighbors, Bornu to the northwest and Wadai in the northeast. Forced to pay tribute to both, it was eventually taken over by Bornu at the start of the seventeenth century and remained a vassal until the start of the nineteenth century. Over the years there has also been a large degree of assimilation between the Bagirmi and other local tribes—notably, the Fula, Kanemba, Sara, and Massa.

The first Hausa settlements were established in the eleventh century before the emergence of city-states in the late thirteenth century. With the mid-fourteenth-century introduction of Islam, which began among the prosperous walled cities of the region, notably Kano and Katsina, their numbers grew significantly and they moved into more of the Kanem-Bornu empire and, in the sixteenth century, the Songhai empire. The last effort gave rise to the Fula empire and the unification of the two groups initially under the spiritual leadership of Usman dan Folio.

The history of the Kanemba (Kanembu, Kanuri, Borno, Bornu) can be traced back to the ninth century, when they established the kingdom of Kanem. Of Arabic origin, the royal family adopted Islam in the late eleventh century, while also expanding their sphere of influence to cover from Kano to the Western Sudan. In the mid-thirteenth century they expanded farther out of Chad, into Bornu, where they moved their capital in the fourteenth century. At the end of the fifteenth century there was a further revival in the kingdom's power when it was transformed as the Kanem-Bornu empire. It reached its peak by the end of the seventeenth century before remaining stationary for a further hundred years before starting to decline in the eighteenth century.

Kotoko tradition claims ethnic descent from the Sao (Sau), a race of giants that used to inhabit the area to the south of Lake Chad, between the northern regions of both Nigeria and Cameroon. The Sao civilization, which dates back to 3000BCE, was first present in the Lake Chad region around the year 800CE. The Kotoko achieved preeminence in the fifteenth century when they moved out from their homeland, down the Rivers Logone and Chari, to rule large parts of northern Nigeria and Cameroon. Their conversion to Islam was relatively late, and they retained significant elements of their pre-Islamic beliefs.

The Maba (speakers of the Nilo-Saharan language of Bora Mabang) are another almost wholly Muslim ethnic group who were formerly the main power behind the Wadai kingdom. Perhaps as a result of this former glory, the Maba always refused to do manual work, viewing themselves as an aristocratic class. Their social framework was like that of the Fula, and they were closely related to the Moussei (Moussey) from the north and center of the country.

The Sara (Kirdi), found primarily in the south of the country, are a Nilotic race that are assumed to have arrived in the sixteenth century. From that early date they were subjected to violent slave raids from their northern neighbors—notably, the Fula—and as a result they moved progressively farther south. In spite of heavy losses to the slavers, they remained the single largest ethnic group present in Chad.

The Teda (Tebu, Tibbou, Toubbou) are made up of some 40 or so clans and have always enjoyed a nomadic or seminomadic lifestyle. Early converts to Islam, the Teda were known through the centuries as raiders of livestock when they weren't making money by charging a protection fee to travelers that happened across the extensive desert tracks they patrolled. Following the arrival of Ottoman authorities in the region, their activities were curtailed, forcing them into small-scale farming of dates in the Tibesti region.

One last group that should be mentioned is the Bilala (Bulala), whose cultural background is Arabic, and who claim descent from a common ancestor, Bilal (Balal). From the time of their conversion to Islam on they held onto a number of their former beliefs and partial nomadism alongside farming.

EAMONN GEARON

See also: **Fulbe/Fulani/Peul: Origins; Kanem: Decline, and Merge with Borno (*c.*1400).**

Further Reading

Azevedo, M. J., and Emmanuel U. Nnadozie. *Chad: A Nation in Search of Its History.* Boulder, Colo.: Westview Press, 1998.

Decalo, S. *Historical Dictionary of Chad*, 3rd ed. Lanham, Md.: Scarecrow Press, 1997.

Yakan, M. Z. *Almanac of African Peoples and Nations.* New Brunswick, N.J.: Transaction, 1999.

Central Africa, Northern: Islam, Pilgrimage

The identity of Islam in north-central Africa was peculiar to the region as a result of its growing out of a particular set of circumstances. To begin with, the spread of Islam was far slower in this region in part because it was not initially spread, as in other parts of the continent (and indeed the world), along major trade routes. The populations here, especially in Saharan areas, were also less in number and density than those of western Sudan and North Africa, which made the impact of the newly arrived faith less evident. Another feature particular to this region is that when Islam did take root, contact with the greater Muslim world was somewhat limited, resulting in its presence being nominal for a number of centuries. The lack of reputable religious schools and other centers of learning also hindered the growth of a strong religious sentiment among the population.

The relative remoteness of north-central African Islam meant that the undertaking of the pilgrimage to Mecca (*hajj*) required of all Muslims at least once in their lifetime (if they are able) was, to begin with, less well observed than among other Muslim populations.

Initially, the small number of local pilgrims would hope to meet up with caravans made up of their West African counterparts and travel to the *hijaz* along the latter's favored routes: north across the Sahara and via Cairo. One reason for this was that these routes, along which Islam had arrived to the west of the continent, were well-established, thriving trade routes, and both pilgrims and traders would have been familiar sights along their length. The new pilgrims were happy to follow these familiar paths and to travel in company, thereby reducing the risk of attack.

For many in the Muslim world the pilgrimage season had often as much to do with trade and diplomacy as it did with religion. It was the one time in the year that merchants would have ready access to large caravans to travel with, and the opportunity to trade over an area that might cover thousands of miles. The need to resupply distant customers, at least on an annual basis, and the chance of establishing new markets made the hajj a boon time for trade. And in an age when the hardships of travel should not be underestimated, there would be a substantial appeal in traveling in company where those hardships could be shared.

The primacy of trade was especially true for the kingdom of Kanem-Bornu, which had adopted Islam in the late eleventh century and began to rely on trade rather than warfare as its means of expansion. The influence of Islam on the kingdom was limited, however, with many pre-Islamic features being kept long after their supposed conversion, such as the divine status that was accorded to the king. The later use of warfare, including war in the name of Islam, saw the kingdom's influence expand as far as the River Niger by the mid-thirteenth century. Despite having the enormous advantage of controlling much of the Sahara through which traders wished to travel, a series of internal disputes saw its slow decline from the late fourteenth century onward.

Apart from the fact that the most well-established routes ran south to north through Kanem-Bornu, another reason for pilgrims and merchants not using the more southerly routes earlier was that these southern or savanna routes, which led directly to the Red Sea coast, were not common trade routes at that time. Once these trans-Sudanese routes became established in the fourteenth century they too proved to have trading opportunities of their own. Following the Muslim conquest of the kingdom of Makkura in 1317, this route to Mecca—which ran from northern Nigeria, through Chad to Darfur in western Sudan, and on to the Suakin on the Red Sea coast—became a practical possibility, though the numbers using it initially were very small. Not until the Fulani holy war in the early nineteenth century and the emergence of a more radical form of Islam did the numbers of ordinary citizens making this southern journey increase significantly.

Another result of the late adoption of the savanna route was that Islam was not as firmly entrenched along its path, even if it was nominally present. And while the local rulers may have adopted Islam following limited contacts with the Muslim world, there was less protection for pilgrims, traveling through what remained largely pagan areas. Coupled with this, there were far fewer opportunities for traveling in the company of holy men and receiving religious instruction along the way, a sought-after benefit of the pilgrimage.

Conversion of the Nubians started in the early fourteenth century, and by the end of the sixteenth century they were known to be most fervent and Christianity had disappeared from their ranks. They too, however, maintained significant portions of their original culture, such as an unwillingness to adopt the Arabic language. The conversion of the Funj, which began in the fifteenth century, met with similar success and, providentially for the spread of Islam, coincided with the Funj making large territorial gains to the south and west of their heartland; thus, another prominent central African dynasty was within the Islamic fold.

By the time of the conversion of the Fur in the seventeenth century, Islam was very secure across the region. Territorial gains made by the Fur in the following century also assisted the spread of Islam and significantly impacted pilgrimage routes in the area, though for at least a century after their conversion the rulers of Darfur continued to travel via Cairo. Poverty, too, combined with increased religious fervor, persuaded the growing numbers of ordinary citizens, who wished to make the hajj but were too poor to take the Cairo route, to accept the risks of the savanna route.

The execution of the pilgrimage journey across the region no doubt was a major reason for the continuing practice of Islam across territorial boundaries. Making such diverse groups of people aware of Islam's wider context provided a degree of unity between Muslim societies everywhere. They were also kept informed of such religious developments that might have come out of the Hijaz, which was especially true for the large numbers of holy men and rulers who went on pilgrimage, bringing their newfound knowledge home to their followers and subjects.

EAMONN GEARON

See also: **Kanem: Slavery and Trans-Saharan Trade.**

Further Reading

Eickelman, D. F., and J. Piscatori (eds.). *Muslim Travellers: Pilgrimage, Migration, and the Religious Imagination.* London: Routledge, 1990.

Hiskett, M. *The Course of Islam in Africa*. Edinburgh: Edinburgh University Press, 1994.

Levtzion, N., and R. L. Pouwels (eds.). *The History of Islam in Africa*. Athens, Ohio: Ohio University Press/Oxford: James Currey, 2000.

McHugh, N. *Holymen of the Blue Nile: The Making of an Arab-Islamic Community in the Nilotic Sudan 1500–1800*. Evanston, Ill.: Northwestern University Press, 1994.

Peters, F. E. *The Hajj: The Muslim Pilgrimage to Mecca and the Holy Places*. Princeton, N.J.: Princeton University Press, 1994.

Trimingham, J. S. *Islam in the Sudan*. London: Oxford University Press, 1949.

Central Africa, Northern: Arab Penetration, Rise of Cavalry States

The arrival of Islam in north-central Africa was synonymous with the arrival of the Arab world. Religion and trade came as a package, and the single imported item that was to have the longest lasting effect, altering and directing the course of regional history for the next 500 years, was the horse. Although horses had been seen in Egypt, perhaps as early as the seventeenth century BCE, they did not travel far and it was not until the first century BCE that they were widely traded as a most valuable item across the Maghreb and into Nubia.

One of the reasons for the late widespread introduction of the horse in Sub-Saharan Africa was the initial logistical difficulty of moving the animals through areas where there would be a guaranteed water supply at all times. While they were not well suited to life in the desert, horses proved to be ideally matched to conditions in the savanna lands to the south of the Sahara. Farther south, too, and in the tropics west of Ghana, they also failed to prosper, being susceptible to the diseases in those parts. Once transportation routes were established, they spread fairly quickly, at least among those peoples who were wealthy enough to pay or trade for them. When proper knowledge permitted, sometime toward the end of the twelfth century, breeding took place on a local level, in areas along the River Niger.

From its first appearance in north-central Africa, the horse was utilized in a military role, playing a major part in the rise or fall of a number of states there. The cavalry units that were established locally tended to be elite divisions, often only having members of the aristocracy or ruling classes among their number, as was the case in the empires of both Songhai and Mali. The main reason for such exclusions to otherwise perfectly competent foot soldiers was the cost of horses, which gave them a status that would have been unseemly if bestowed on the common man; there were, after all, limited numbers of horses and a far more disposable supply of men.

The kingdoms of Kanem-Bornu, Mali, Songhai, and Ghana all depended, to a greater or lesser extent, on both trade and conquest for their success. The arrival of Islam from the north, along with the markets that it opened, played a leading role in this growth. Unsurprisingly, history shows that it tended to be the ruling and or merchant classes that were keenest to adopt the new religion when it appeared. This was certainly true in Kanem-Bornu (founded *c.*800), the growth of which was significant following the tenth-century arrival of Islam from central Sudan. The kingdom was ruled from about 1085 to 1097 by Mai (King) Umme, who upon his conversion to Islam opened his kingdom to the Arab world. Unpopular with the general population, Islam was slow to gain acceptance in spite of the kingdom's expansion under its newfound religion. The growth continued under the rule of Umme's son and heir, Dunama (Dibbalemi), with N'jimi being established as the capital and the northward and westward expansion gathered momentum, and conquests often being carried out under the clarion of jihad, or holy war, in the name of Islam.

By the reign of Dunama II, the army boasted an enormous cavalry of more than 30,000 as well as a mounted camel force for desert fighting. These innovations made the conquest of the Fezzan and subsequent control of trans-Saharan routes a possibility for the first time. Newly conquered lands were also patrolled by a cavalry force, thereby ensuring the stability of their newly acquired and extremely precious trade routes. Islam also benefited from the devout nature of Dunama II, who insisted on conversion to Islam for the ruling class of all lands he conquered.

Islam was introduced to the capital of Ghana, Kumbi Saleh, in the middle of the eleventh century before the city was overrun by the Almoravids in 1076. While it is apparent that many did leave the city at this time, it is far less certain that the city's inhabitants were offered the choice between death or conversion as once commonly believed; again, it is more likely that Islam was simply adopted by the ruling class and merchants as was the case elsewhere. The Almoravids held sway for only a short time before it regained its independence while remaining Muslim.

In Ghana, the early discovery of how to work with iron, thereby allowing soldiers to fight with metal spears and iron-tipped arrows, gave them a powerful advantage over iron-technology-free enemies. This fact, combined with a standing army and cavalry numbering 200,000 in the eleventh century, made it the most powerful empire in the region until 1200. The immense gold supply available in Ghana was, obviously, a major factor in allowing the country to develop such a sizable force.

Kangaba, the earlier foundation of Mali inhabited by the Mandingo, was invaded by the neighboring

Kaniaga under their ruler, Sumanguru, who had all but one of the royal princes murdered to prevent their rising against him in the future; the sole survivor was allowed to live because he was unable to walk, weak, and not expected to live. However, this prince, Sundiata, eventually grew strong and led a cavalry force back to Kangaba, successfully winning back the throne that was rightfully his. Sundiata continued to use these forces to unite and expand the empire, taking advantage of the declining power of Ghana, which by 1240 had been completely absorbed within Mali's territory. In its turn the empire of Mali was destined to go into decline partly due to dynastic infighting and partly due to extravagant spending on the part of its rulers.

Once again it was cavalry that tipped the balance in the battlefield, and allowed the region's next ascendant power, the Songhai (who had been rivals for some time), to defeat the ailing Mali. The enormous advantages that these so-called cavalry states had over their infantry-based or cavalry-deficient neighbors ceased to matter from the fifteenth century on, superceded by the growing availability of the latest technological advancement to reach the battlefield—guns—and the slow replacement of the bow and arrow and spear and horse.

EAMONN GEARON

See also: **Central Africa, Northern: Islam, Pilgrimage; Yusuf ibn Tashfin: Almoravid Empire: Maghrib, 1070–1147.**

Further Reading

Bovill, E. W. *The Golden Trade of the Moors.* London: Oxford University Press, 1968.

Bulliet, Richard W. *The Camel and the Wheel.* Cambridge, Mass.: Harvard University Press, 1975.

Fage, J. D., and Roland Oliver (eds.). *The Cambridge History of Africa.* London: Cambridge University Press, 1977.

Law, Robin. *The Horse in West African History: The Role of the Horse in the Societies of Pre-Colonial West Africa.* Oxford: Oxford University Press for the International African Institute, 1980.

Smith, Robert S. *Warfare and Diplomacy in Pre-Colonial West Africa.* Madison: University of Wisconsin Press, 1989.

Central African Empire: *See* **Central African Republic: Nationalism, Independence.**

Central African Federation: *See* **Welensky, Roy; Zambia (Northern Rhodesia): Federation, 1953–1963: Zimbabwe (Southern Rhodesia): Federation.**

Central African Protectorate: *See* **Malawi: Colonization and Wars of Resistance, 1889–1904.**

Bahr el-Ghazal: *See* **Rabih ibn Fadl Allah.**

Central African Republic: Nineteenth Century: Gbaya, Banda, and Zande

The terms *Gbaya, Banda,* and *Zande* are ethnolinguistic labels for the largest groups of people who speak Ubangi languages belonging to the Niger-Congo family and reside in the savannas north of the Congo forest. These groups were little affected by external forces until the nineteenth century, when African slave traders, and then European colonialists, introduced unprecedented violence and economic exploitation into their lives.

The Gbaya lived in small, scattered hamlets in the western half of the Central African Republic (CAR) and adjacent areas of Cameroon in the early nineteenth century, when traders from Hausaland and Borno began to penetrate this region. Then, from the mid-nineteenth century on, the Fulbe state of Ngaoundere on the Adamawa Plateau began to send slave-raiding expeditions into Gbaya territory. Some Gbaya clans accepted Fulbe hegemony and began to raid their neighbors for slaves to sell to Muslim merchants who settled in their territories. Other Gbaya clans united under a leader named Bafio to resist the Fulbe slave raiders.

In the last decade of the nineteenth century, French missions from the south moved up the Sangha River into Gbaya territory. Pierre Savorgnan de Brazza, commissioner general of the French Congo, dreamed of

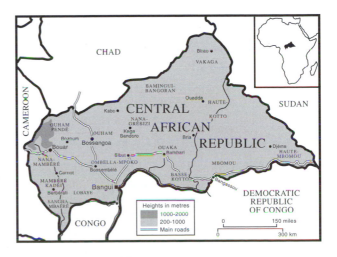

Central African Republic

establishing a French-supported Fulbe protectorate over this area, and so the French initially assisted the Fulbe in fighting Bafio's alliance. In 1894, however, a boundary between the French Congo and German Kamerun was drawn through Gbaya territory and left Ngaoundere to the Germans, after which the French helped Bafio's Gbaya defeat Fulbe slave raiders.

In 1899, the French granted private European companies the right to exploit all of the resources of huge concessions in the Gbaya region, and brutal European and African employees of these concessionary companies began to force the Gbaya to collect wild rubber. The territory inhabited by the easternmost Gbaya group, the Manja, was not granted to concessionary companies because the French wanted to use the Manja as porters for their missions to Chad. The Manja suffered terribly as a result.

The Banda were concentrated in the northeastern part of the CAR and adjacent areas of Chad and the Sudan at the turn of the nineteenth century, when African traders from the north began to establish small commercial centers in Banda territory. Then slave raiders from Wadai and Darfur began to penetrate Bandaland with increasing frequency, leading some Banda groups to migrate southward toward the Ubangi River. The decision of the Egyptian government to curtail the slave trade on the Nile in the 1860s encouraged Khartoumers such as al-Zubayr and his lieutenant Rabih to shift their operations westward into Banda territory. This led Banda groups to migrate westward. During the 1880s Rabih sent so many slave raiders into Banda territory that the depopulation of the eastern CAR began. Before Rabih moved north into Chad, he set up a client, al-Sanusi, as sultan of the state of Dar al-Kuti in northern CAR. Al-Sanusi procured a large number of firearms by ambushing a French mission in 1891 and signing a treaty with the French in 1897. Dar al-Kuti was thus able to send very well-armed slave raiders throughout Banda territory during the 1890s and to defeat Banda leaders who had become rival slave traders in the northeastern region of the CAR.

The Banda were also raided from the south in the late nineteenth century by slave traders from Zande states. The Zande people lived just north of the Congo forest in what is today the southeastern region of the CAR and adjacent parts of the Sudan and the Republic of the Congo (formerly Zaïre). Unlike the majority of Ubangians who lived in stateless societies, the Zande were ruled by members of a Zande clan, the Vongara, which had established its dominance over most Zande and many non-Zande neighbors over the past century. By the mid-nineteenth century, the number of people calling themselves Zande had increased sharply as a result of "Zandeization," but the Zande were not united politically because competing members of the Vongara

clan established numerous small states which captured men and women in order to transform them into Zande laborers, soldiers, and wives.

The arrival of slave raiders from Sudan in the mid-nineteenth century led Zande rulers to focus their efforts on the capture of slaves rather than on the conquest and assimilation of their neighbors. Some Zande rulers allied themselves with Sudanese slave traders while others fought them and attacked their caravans. The Zande had to contend with growing European influence in their region by the late nineteenth century as well. The defeat of British troops by the Mahdists in the Sudan in the 1880s encouraged Belgian king Leopold II and French expansionists to set their sites on the Nile Valley. Belgian and French agents thus moved up the Ubangi River toward the Nile and signed treaties with Zande leaders, and this initially enabled these rulers to procure more arms and thus to expand their slave-raiding activities.

In 1894 Leopold II and the French agreed that the Mbomu River running through Zandeland would serve as the border between their colonies, and so the Zande north and south of the river found themselves under different colonial administrations. When the French sent the Marchand mission up the Ubangi and to Fashoda in the Sudan at the end of the century, Zande rulers helped to provide porters and paddlers. After the British asserted their control over the southern Sudan, the eastern Zande found themselves under British administration.

Thus, Zandeland became a neglected cul-de-sac of three different European colonies. In the French colony, Zande territory was granted to a huge concessionary company that both collaborated and competed with the Zande rulers, who continued to capture Banda slaves.

The arrival of African slave raiders and European colonialists and businessmen clearly had a very negative and often fatal impact on the lives of many Gbaya, Banda, and Zande individuals during the nineteenth century, but the flexible social structures and subsistence economies of the Ubangians who survived this violent period were not destroyed but rather have continued to exist in modified form until the present.

RICHARD A. BRADSHAW

See also: **Concessionary Companies; Fulbe/Fulani/ Peul: Origins; Libya: Muhammad Al-Sanusi (c.1787– 1859) and the Sanusiyya.**

Central African Republic: Colonial Period: Occupation, Resistance, Baya Revolt, 1928

The French colony of Oubangi-Shari (renamed at independence the Central African Republic) was slowly occupied by France in the 1890s and 1900s. It had an indigenous population of several ethnic groups including the Azande (who had an important kingdom partly occupied by the Congo Free State), the Banda, and the Gbaya (or Baya). There was considerable resistance to the French occupation and especially to the harsh impositions it meant for the Africans. Oubangi-Shari formed part of a large area called at first French Congo and then, from 1910, French Equatorial Africa. To occupy this area inexpensively the French government, following the example of Leopold II in the Congo, allocated huge areas of it to concessionary companies in 1899.

These companies were subject to French sovereignty, but in fact had almost unlimited control over the Africans in their areas, whom they were allowed to exploit ruthlessly to produce wild rubber and other goods. Rubber was the main product demanded in Oubangi-Shari as in the Congo Free State; Africans were forced to collect it by all sorts of means, including the taking of families as hostages until the rubber was brought in. The French administration and its troops helped enforce the regime of extortion, and officials supplemented the terror imposed by the company staff. One murder of an African by the officials Gaud and Toqué in 1903 led to a public outcry in France and to the dispatch of a commission of inquiry into French Congo under Pierre Savorgnan de Brazza, the original colonizer of the area (1905). Little improvement resulted, and the companies lost only some of their territories and rights. Wild rubber collection was largely abandoned a few years later, but in the 1920s the government imposed forced cotton cultivation in Oubangi-Shari, while from 1921 to 1934 its men were conscripted in large numbers for work on building the railway from Pointe-Noire to Brazzaville (the Congo-Ocean Railway), which led to the death of thousands of workers.

African resistance was persistent, but scattered and sporadic, and defeated quite easily, though slowly, as the administration and troops were thin on the ground. There were uprisings in 1903–1905, especially among the Mandjias, a Baya subsection subjected to conscription of porters for the French route to Chad. In 1907 revolts hit the Mobaye region in the southwest and many areas in the center and east of the colony, where the leader, Baramgbakié, was captured in 1909. In 1914 there was a revolt of the Langbassis, a Banda-speaking people in central Oubangi-Shari, refusing to collect rubber and ivory to pay taxes; their leader Amba was captured in late 1915.

In 1911 a considerable area of western Oubangi-Shari was added to the German colony of Cameroon, but in World War I it was retaken by the French in operations for which Africans were forced to endure new impositions. New uprisings followed: the Dji and Mangana uprisings in 1915, the 1916 insurrection led by Mopoi Inguizimo (heir to the former Zande rulers), and the Bongbou and Mobaye insurrections in 1918. In fact there was for years an almost regular cycle of risings, "police operations" involving great brutality and more uprisings. This was admitted by the French governor general himself in a circular in 1921, saying that after repressive actions, "The idea of revenge, perfectly excusable, filled the minds of the natives; an ambush threatened every agent of the government, an African or French soldier was felled by some arrow." The Bongbou leader Ajou led a new revolt in 1926. The greatest rising of all was to come later, in 1928. The Baya people played a major role in this revolt, which is often called the "Baya revolt," but others also joined, over a large area of contiguous portions of Oubangi-Shari, Chad, French Cameroon and Middle Congo.

This rising is called the Kongo-Wara War (*kongo-wara* meaning "hoe handle," a symbol of the insurgent peasants). It initially had a leader, a Messianic Baya "native doctor" named Karinou or Karnu, invoking supernatural powers and considered by some as an ancestor returning to earth, but showing great organizing skill. Originally named Ngainoumbey Barka, he adopted the name Karinou (meaning "he who can change the world") and spread the message of rejection of European rule from 1927 without the French knowing for months. He preached nonviolence at first, but people who had been oppressed for years, and now were suffering even more from the Congo-Ocean Railway conscription, took up arms in mid-1928. Fighting began with a clash between Bayas and Fulanis; but then French traders, and chiefs and soldiers working for the French, were attacked, as were French government posts, for example at Bouar (which was occupied and burned down). For months the insurgents, though very poorly armed, continued advancing. Then came a French counterattack with reinforced troops, and Karinou was killed in action on December 11, 1928. But others fought on, continuing even to spread the revolt, and French forces did not succeed in defeating them until 1931; two of Karinou's lieutenants, Bissi and Yandjere, were captured only in 1935. Echoes of the revolt reached Europe and led to condemnations of French rule in the area by communists and others. (French suspicions of communist instigation of the rising, however, were absurd.) After the revolt there was tighter administrative control, with forcible movement of Bayas into new villages, but for long there was little change for the better in the treatment of Africans. Further resistance, however, waited until the era of modern nationalism, after World War II.

JONATHAN DERRICK

233

See also: **Concessionary Companies.**

Further Reading

Birmingham, D., and P. Martin (eds.). *History of Central Africa,* vol. 2. London, 1983.
Kalck, P. *The Central African Republic.* New York, 1971.
Suret-Canale, J. *French Colonialism in Tropical Africa, 1900–1945,* New York and London, 1971.

Central African Republic: Colonial Period: Oubangui-Chari

Although an administration had been set up at Bangui, the future capital, in 1889, Oubangui-Chari was at that time, to quote Pierre Kalck (1971), "not more than a great white blank on the map." It took another 20 years for its boundaries to be finalized, its indigenous rulers subdued, and an effective colony-wide administration set up. In the meantime, France had turned to the concession company as an instrument to develop the colony and provide revenue for its maintenance. From the turn of the century onward, over 20 of these companies, such as the Compagnie des Sultanats, commenced operations in Oubangui-Chari, imposing quotas on chiefs for the collection of rubber and ivory, and punishing those who failed to meet them.

However, little had been achieved by the outbreak of war in 1914. Few companies had made any substantial return, and Oubangui-Chari remained an isolated backwater. Following the collapse of rubber prices in 1920–1921, the colonial authorities took a direct hand in development and introduced cotton as a cash crop, again setting quotas but giving bonuses to chiefs with good production records. The cultivation of cotton increased substantially, and it became Oubangui-Chari's main export crop, though returns to peasant producers were small, once high transportation and other overhead costs had been deducted by the government.

Despite its success in ending the precolonial slave trade and creating a stable administrative system, early French colonial rule had a negative impact on Oubangui-Chari's people. A sleeping-sickness epidemic in the first decade of the twentieth century caused severe loss of life, but the continuing extraction of labor was probably more deleterious to traditional life and economy. The production of subsistence crops suffered, with cultivators being obliged, through a shortage of available labor resulting from the impressing of able-bodied men into work, to switch to easily grown (but less nutritious) staples such as manioc, with consequent widespread malnutrition. This forced labor regime continued, in spite of the revelation in 1906 of concession company abuses and André Gide's later exposé *Voyage au Congo* (written after his October 1925 visit), which attacked the use of compulsory labor

recruited from the colony for the construction of the Pointe Noire–Brazzaville railway in the neighboring (French) Congo. A prominent victim of this abuse was the future leader Bokassa's father, a local chief who was beaten to death in November 1927 after refusing to provide labor supplies. The state added further burdens, imposing taxation on the colony's peasants (one of the causes of the Baya revolt against the authorities in the later 1920s). Obligatory labor thus remained a feature of life in Oubangui-Chari until after World War II, when it was abolished, along with the *indigénat,* which had allowed administrative officials on their own authority to sentence "indigenous" people to short periods of imprisonment.

World War II witnessed the beginnings of some improvement in Oubangui-Chari. The region's accession to the Free French cause, proclaimed by the black governor general of French Equatorial Africa, Felix Éboué (1884–1944), a former district official in the colony, led to the development of internal communications to meet the demands of the Allies' war effort, such as the construction of airfields and roads, bringing the colony more into contact with the outside world. After the war ended, France embarked on a new political structure for its empire, setting up a *conseil représentatif* (representative council) for the colony, with a limited franchise that favored local settlers and black *évolués.* The young charismatic nationalist and former priest Barthélémy Boganda was elected to the National Assembly in Paris the same year (1946), and launched the Mouvement d'Evolution Sociale d'Afrique Noire (MESAN) as a mass nationalist organization in September 1949.

However, the 1950s saw some faltering in the colony's economic development. Cotton fields showed growing evidence of overcropping and environmental degradation, with lowered yields, and efforts to set up a textile industry on the basis of this production failed. Attempts to diversify black agriculture were blocked by local white farmers, who were determined to safeguard their monopoly of production. Although diamond production had steadily increased in importance from the mid-1930s to become a significant contributor to the economy, it failed to fill the gap between revenue and expenditure. Even in the late 1950s, two-thirds of the colony's revenue was supplied by Paris, and the average annual per capita income at independence was only 3,000 French community francs, one of the lowest in the world.

The 1950s nevertheless witnessed speedy political evolution, especially after the 1956 *loi cadre* (enabling law) approved by the French National Assembly. The franchise had been progressively widened since 1946, until the first election on a one-person, one-vote basis was held in March 1957. Boganda's

MESAN won this election with an overwhelming majority and dominated the new *Conseil de gouvernement* (council of government), nominating its ministers.

Thereafter, France accelerated the pace of decolonization. In 1958, Oubangui-Chari voted to accept autonomy within the French Community in the Charles de Gaulle referendum, and on August 13, 1960, it became independent. Boganda and his successor David Dacko had reservations about the speed of the process, believing that the underdevelopment of the economy, institutions of state, and infrastructure left the new state unprepared for the burdens of self-rule and thus still dependent on the outgoing colonial power. These concerns increased after their failure to persuade the other territories of the outgoing French Equatorial African federation to form a united Central African Republic, a title that was eventually assumed by Oubangui-Chari itself at independence. The course of events after independence certainly upheld many of their reservations about the political and economic viability of the new state.

MURRAY STEELE

See also: **Boganda, Barthélemy; Concessionary Companies.**

Further Reading

Kalck, P. *Central African Republic: A Failure in De-colonisation.* London: Pall Mall Press, 1971.

Manning, P. *Francophone Sub-Saharan Africa, 1880–1985.* Cambridge: Cambridge University Press, 1988.

O'Toole, T. *The Central African Republic: The Continent's Hidden Heart.* Boulder, Colo: Westview Press/London: Gower, 1986.

Roberts, S. *The History of French Colonial Policy, 1870–1925* (1929). Reprint, London: Frank Cass, 1963.

Suret-Canale, J. *French Colonialism in Tropical Africa, 1900–1945.* London: C. Hurst, 1971.

Weinstein, B. *Éboué.* London: Oxford University Press, 1972.

Central African Republic: Nationalism, Independence

Black nationalism developed slowly in the colonial Central African Republic (CAR), delayed by the exploitative nature of French rule, the paucity of educational facilities, and the area's geographical isolation. This legacy of underdevelopment has continued to disfigure its political progress since independence, creating a palpable French neocolonialist presence that persisted into the late 1990s and facilitating the emergence of one of the most brutal military regimes in Africa in the 1970s.

Prodded into life by World War II and the creation of the French Union in 1946, black politics evolved steadily under the leadership of the charismatic Barthélémy Boganda, who set up the Mouvement d'Evolution Sociale d'Afrique Noire (MESAN) in September 1949, in which his Mbaka ethnic group, who lived in the most developed, southern part of the colony, were to play a dominant role. Under his inspirational leadership, MESAN won all of the seats in the first fully democratic election held after the 1956 *loi cadre* (enabling law), which authorized French jurisdiction over its African colonies). The momentum toward independence quickened with the 1958 referendum, which transformed the colony into an autonomous republic within the French community. Sensing that the balkanization implicit in the devolution process would weaken his scarcely viable country, Boganda attempted to preserve the unity of the old French Equatorial Africa entity by pressing for its transformation into the Central African Republic, but failed to win the support of his neighbors. His death the following year in a plane crash (still shrouded in mystery) robbed his country of the one leader who might have coped with the sudden thrusting of independent status upon it, as the Central African Republic, on August 13, 1960. At that stage, it was one of the poorest countries in the world, with an educational system staffed by, and a budget largely subsidized by, the departing colonial power.

David Dacko, a relative of Boganda, succeeded to the leadership of MESAN and took office as president of the CAR with French support. Described by many authorities as lackluster and vacillating, Dacko soon attracted criticism, which he met by imprisoning his chief rival Abel Goumba and delaying elections until he had built up MESAN into a mass party that could safely secure a popular mandate, a goal achieved at the end of 1963 when Dacko was elected unopposed for a seven-year term with 99 per cent of the vote, followed soon afterward by a clean sweep in the parliamentary elections. The Dacko administration rewarded its supporters with patronage, including civil service posts, while opportunities were taken to lease out for personal profit housing built with public funds. Despite increasing French aid and an increase in diamond production, the CAR's economy came under increasing strain. By late 1965, profligate expenditure resulted in a payments crisis, at which point Dacko opportunistically turned to Beijing for an interest-free loan. Alarmed, Paris looked to other figures in the CAR who might be counted upon to protect French interests. However, the installation of their main hopeful, head of the police force Jean Izamo, was forestalled by Colonel Jean-Bedel Bokassa, commander in chief of the army, who seized power on New Year's Day 1966, placed Dacko under house arrest, and disposed of Izamo after charging him (ironically) with planning a pro-Chinese coup.

Bokassa invoked the spirit of Boganda, claimed as a relative, to legitimize his takeover, and embarked on a program of austerity and reform. This proved to be short-lived. He was swept along by the same forces that had undermined his predecessor, and expenditure on the civil service and army continued to rise, reinforcing the CAR's dependence on France. Bokassa added personal vices of his own: an intolerance of criticism, an arbitrary cruelty, an extreme vanity, and a growing venality. The first vice is exemplified in his treatment of his finance minister Alexandre Banza, reputedly the only person in his cabinet who stood up to him. In April 1969, Banza was executed for allegedly plotting a coup, and several of his male relatives were imprisoned. Bokassa's 1972 decree, laying down the penalty of mutilation for theft, is an example of the second vice: an international outcry forced him to rescind it.

Bokassa's vanity is epitomized in his declaration of himself as Emperor Bokassa I, ruling over the "Central African Empire," in December 1976. He was strongly influenced by Napoleonic precedent; as a young man, he had served overseas in the French army and had achieved commissioned rank; and as head of state, he had gathered together an extensive library on Napoleon. The French president Valéry Giscard d'Estaing supported the imperial project, providing most of the US$22 million required for Bokassa's coronation, and is alleged to have received presents of diamonds on his various visits to the country.

The "emperor's" generosity to his guest is indicative of the wealth he managed to obtain through his various business interests. One of these contributed indirectly to his eventual downfall. In January 1979, he ordered that high school students should buy uniforms, available only from a business owned by his wife. Students staged a protest, in which several were killed, and then mounted a bigger demonstration in April, after which over a hundred young people were beaten to death in prison. Following protests by Amnesty International, a commission of inquiry from other francophone African countries investigated and sustained these charges. Meanwhile, Bokassa had traveled to Libya (then in dispute with France) to seek financial support. This gave France the opportunity for military intervention in September 1979, and the installation of Dacko as president of the restored republic.

Bokassa's already woeful reputation has been further vilified by stories of ritual cannibalism, of prisoners being thrown into crocodile pools, and the claim that he personally killed several young people after the April 1979 student demonstration. While not denying his cruelty, vanity, and venality, a recent study by Brian Titley suggests that the veracity of these lurid stories is questionable.

MURRAY STEELE

See also: **Boganda, Barthélemy.**

Further Reading

Decalo, S. *Psychoses of Power: African Personal Dictatorships* (1989). Reprint, Gainesville, Fla.: Florida State University Press, 1998.

Kalck, P. *Central African Republic: A Failure in De-colonisation.* London: Pall Mall Press/New York: Praeger, 1971.

O'Toole, T. *The Central African Republic: The Continent's Hidden Heart.* Boulder, Colo.: Westview Press/London: Gower, 1986.

Titley, B. *Dark Age: The Political Odyssey of the Emperor Bokassa.* Montreal: McGill-Queen's University Press, 1997.

Central African Republic: 1980s and 1990s

The French military intervention of September 1979 resulted in the restoration of the republic, the reinstatement of David Dacko as president, and the renewal of the French military and economic presence. Dacko attempted to restore the political system of his first term of office, setting up the Union Démocratique Centraficaine as a successor to the old Mouvement d'Evolution Sociale d'Afrique Noire of the early 1960s. A new constitution, giving the head of state a six-year term of office, a maximum of two terms, and powers to appoint a prime minister, was introduced in January 1981. In the subsequent election, Dacko was returned as president amid allegations of ballot rigging. The popularity of his government soon waned; an economic downturn sparked off urban unrest, which he attempted to curb using repressive measures, as he had done in the early 1960s.

On September 1, 1981, Dacko's army chief of staff André Kolingba seized power from the local French military detachment, claiming that the country was drifting toward civil war. His regime embarked upon an austerity and anticorruption campaign, which included the detention of opponents but avoided the worst excesses of the Bokassa period (1965–1979). However, Kolingba lacked either the will or the authority to sustain his campaign of reform, and within a year the bureaucratic class was back in control and able to protect its privileges. By the mid-1980s the civil service was absorbing some 80 per cent of the republic's budget, thus sustaining its continuing dependence upon Paris. Attempts to raise further revenue via an export tax on diamonds, the Central African Republic's (CAR) chief source of wealth, merely stimulated widespread smuggling. Meanwhile, Kolingba had followed the example of brother military leaders in Africa, civilianizing his regime, and declaring himself "chief of the nation" in 1986. The other major event of his period of government was the trial of Bokassa, who returned voluntarily to Bangui in the autumn of 1986. After a protracted show trial, the former "emperor" was sentenced to death, but that sentence was commuted to life imprisonment in February 1988.

Under considerable pressure from France and other Western countries, Kolingba restored multiparty democracy in 1991, but elections were delayed until August 1994, when a former Bokassa minister, the northerner Ange-Félix Patassé, was elected president. The resulting eclipse of Kolingba's southern Yakoma group, well represented in the armed forces, led to a growing military disaffection, aggravated by a government freeze of salary levels. Three army mutinies occurred, in April, May, and November 1996. The first was over pay, the second saw a mob attack on the French cultural center in Bangui, and the third was inspired by a government decision to relocate the soldiery to a safe distance from the capital. On each occasion, Patassé's reliance on French military protection was further underlined.

In January 1997, the Patassé government and its opponents attempted to resolve their differences with the signing of the Bangui Accords. A Government of National Unity was to be set up, and it was agreed that a supervisory force drawn from other African francophone states, the Inter-African Mission to Monitor the Bangui Accords (MISAB), should be created to oversee the process of political reconciliation, and to replace the increasingly unpopular French military presence. Over the next year, the issue of logistical and financial support for the MISAB was discussed, alongside arrangements for a withdrawal of French combat troops, with negotiations conducted by the administration clearly anxious about its future security. Further violence, this time directed against the MISAB, led to renewed discussions between CAR politicians and the signing of the National Reconciliation Pact of March 1998, which set out arrangements for legislative elections later that year. Several African states, concerned with what they perceived to be a threat to the security of the CAR's neighbors, prevailed upon the United Nations to intervene. A Security Council resolution (No. 1155) established MINURCA (the UN Mission in Central Africa), comprising MISAB and military detachments from Canada and France, all wearing the UN blue beret and charged with the responsibility of monitoring the election arrangements. Eventually held in November 1998, the election gave Patassé's Central African People's Liberation Movement a narrow victory (by just one legislative seat), created when an opposition deputy in Dacko's coalition, the Movement for Democracy and Development, defected to the government's side after the results were announced. However, after a short boycott, the opposition took up the portfolios that had earlier been offered by the new administration in accordance with the March 1998 pact. Similarly, in September 1999, Patassé was reelected by a narrow margin (51.63 per cent of votes cast in the first ballot), again triggering accusations of fraud.

Although the mid- to late 1990s was a period of extreme political crisis during which the government became progressively dependent on outsiders for its very survival, the essential structure of the CAR's ruling elite, the Gallicized political and bureaucratic class based in Bangui, remained substantially intact: it is significant that Kolingba, Dacko, and Dacko's old rival from the early 1960s, Abel Goumba, took part (albeit unsuccessfully) in the 1999 presidential elections. Meanwhile, the CAR's dependence on its former colonial master, reliance on a single major item of production (diamonds), and its geographical isolation continue to hinder its economic development.

The early twenty-first century has seen a continuation and deepening of the political crisis, with the CAR's neighbors playing an increasing role in its affairs. Two major coups occurred: the first (unsuccessful), in May 2001, led to its alleged instigator Kolingba being sentenced to death in absentia and resulted in the displacement of many Yakoma from Bangui; the second (successful), in March 2003, brought to power Patassé's erstwhile ally and fellow northerner, General François Bozize, who for the time being suspended the CAR constitution.

MURRAY STEELE

Further Reading

Decalo, S. *Psychoses of Power: African Personal Dictatorships.* Gainesville, Fla: Florida State University Press, 1998.

O'Toole, T. *The Central African Republic: The Continent's Hidden Heart.* Boulder, Colo: Westview Press/London: Gower, 1986.

Titley, B. *Dark Age: The Political Odyssey of Emperor Bokassa.* Montreal: McGill-Queen's University Press, 1997.

Central and Southern Africa: *See* Stone Age (Later): Central and Southern Africa.

Cetshwayo (c. 1826–1884)
Zulu King

Cetshwayo, oldest son of Mpande and Ngqumbazi of the Zungu chiefly house, was born near present-day Eshowe. Nephew of the founder Zulu kings Shaka and Dingane, he was to live through all but a decade of Zululand's independent history.

Like all of the Zulu kings, Cetshwayo lived through turbulent times. He witnessed the first battles between Zulu armies and European invaders in his childhood,

CETSHWAYO (c.1826–1884)

Zulu king Cetshwayo, sketched in the 1880s. © Das Fotoarchiv.

secretary for native affairs, Theophilus Shepstone, to mediate. In 1861 Shepstone traveled to Zululand and, for his own motives, endorsed Cetshwayo as heir. The kingdom was now effectively in Cetshwayo's hands. Boer encroachment persuaded Cetshwayo and Mpande to unite, yet the dynastic disputes had given both Natal and the Boers an entry into Zulu politics which had serious repercussions for Zulu independence.

In 1872, Mpande died and Cetshwayo inherited a still formidable polity, numbering some 300,000 people. Nevertheless, he faced serious internal and external problems. Hoping for Natal's support against the Boers and an end to the threat from Natal-based pretenders, Cetshwayo began accumulating firearms and invited Shepstone to preside over his installation as king in 1873. Cetshwayo's alleged noncompliance with Shepstone's coronation "guidelines" was later justification for war.

It was, however, the changes wrought in southern Africa by the diamond discoveries in Griqualand West in the late 1860s that overwhelmed Cetshwayo's kingdom and ended its independence. Accelerated capitalist development and the greatly intensified encroachment on African land and labor in the scramble for mineral rights, coupled with the proliferation of firearms in African hands, heightened black-versus-white conflict all over southern Africa. Everywhere white settlers believed Cetshwayo was conspiring against them with local chiefs, a view sustained by his communication network all over southern Africa.

Lord Carnarvon, secretary of state for the colonies (1874–1878), became convinced that the complexity of affairs in southern Africa could only be dealt with by confederating its assortment of British colonies, Afrikaner republics, and independent African chiefdoms. The humiliation of the South African Republic at the hands of the Pedi, widely believed to be colluding with Cetshwayo, gave Carnarvon his opportunity, and at the end of 1876 Shepstone was instructed to annex the republic. With this the Zulu struggle with the Boers was transformed, as Shepstone, hitherto a Zulu supporter, changed sides and persuaded the new British high commissioner, Sir Bartle Frere, that Cetshwayo was the chief obstacle to peace in the region.

Anxious to avoid war, Cetshwayo approached the Natal governor to appoint a commission of inquiry into the disputed territory. Although it fully supported Zulu claims, Frere used the commission's report to demand the surrender of Zulu accused of border incursions, the payment of a huge fine, and the disbanding of the Zulu military system, which effectively meant the dismantling of the Zulu state. Compliance was impossible, and on January 11, 1879, British troops entered Zululand.

was present at the negotiations between Mpande and the Boers that led to their alliance, and saw his father attack Dingane in January 1840 and become Zulu king with Boer assistance in exchange for the cession of the land south of the Tugela River that became the Afrikaner Republic of Natalia. As a young man he observed its annexation by the British in 1843 and the coming of British settlers.

Allegedly introduced to the Boers in 1840 as Mpande's heir, Cetshwayo's actual succession remained far from certain. Mpande's apparent acquiescence in Boer importunities, inability to reward his soldiers as raiding declined in the face of settler expansion, and deferment of regimental demobilization all led to disaffection in the army. When in the last major Zulu campaign against the Swazi (1852–1853) Cetshwayo revealed his military prowess and young men flocked to join him, Mpande felt his authority challenged.

Nor did Cetshwayo's popularity escape his half-brother, Mbuyazi. At the end of 1856, rivalry between the brothers, perhaps deliberately fomented by Mpande, culminated in civil war between their followers. Despite the support of Mpande and the white trader and gun runner John Dunn, Mbuyazi was overconfident and outnumbered, and at Ndondakusuka, near the mouth of the Tugela, his army was annihilated. Mbuyazi and five of Mpande's sons were slain, as were thousands of his supporters.

Cetshwayo's ascendancy was now assured, and Mpande was forced to share power with him. When, despite this, the king began to favor a younger son by a junior wife as his heir, the wife was murdered by Cetshwayo's followers, the Usuthu. Her sons fled, first to Natal, then to the Boers on the northwestern borders of Zululand. To secure their return, Cetshwayo negotiated with the Boers while Mpande called on Natal's

Well aware of the superior firepower and overseas reserves of the British army, Cetshwayo adopted a defensive strategy, hoping to negotiate a settlement, but in vain. After initial spectacular success at Isandhlwana, the Zulu soon suffered severe setbacks, and after the battle of Ulundi on July 4, Cetshwayo's exhausted followers acknowledged defeat. Two weeks later, Sir Garnet Wolseley, now in command of the British forces, announced the end of the Zulu kingdom, promising the people their land and cattle, if they laid down arms and surrendered the king. After six weeks of torture and terror, Cetshwayo was betrayed, and sent into exile in Cape Town.

Wolseley promptly dismantled the Zulu regiments and installed 13 appointed chiefs, subject to the authority of a British resident, over the kingdom. Cetshwayo's immediate family and supporters, known as the Usuthu, were placed under Zibhebhu and Uhamu, who had been the first chiefs to defect, and who were most closely allied to the British authorities and the colonial economy. Violence erupted almost immediately as they seized Usuthu cattle and built up their own political and economic power.

In exile, Cetshwayo displayed extraordinary diplomatic skill, attracting influential supporters, including Bishop Colenso of Natal, who helped publicize Cetshwayo's case in South Africa and Britain. In 1882 the new colonial secretary, privately acknowledging the injustice of the war, finally allowed Cetshwayo to put his case in person in Britain. His dignity and royal bearing made a deep impression on a British public long fed tales of his "bloodthirsty" tyranny, and faced with widespread disorder in Zululand the British government decided to restore Cetshwayo.

In his return to South Africa in January 1883, Cetshwayo found, that, despite his objections, his kingdom had been severely truncated. A large tranche of country in the north was allocated to his chief enemies, Uhamu and Zibhebhu, while in the south a sanctuary was reserved for those who rejected his rule. The true destruction of the Zulu kingdom now followed. Usuthu protests against their loss of territory went unheeded, and their unsuccessful attacks on Zibhebhu simply invited retaliation. The ensuing civil wars culminated in Zibhebhu's attack on Ulundi on July 23, 1883, in which Cetshwayo's most trusted and experienced councilors were killed. Once more forced to flee, Cetshwayo attempted in vain to rally his supporters from the Nkandhla forests, and on October 17 he surrendered to the British Resident commissioner at Eshowe. He died there suddenly on February 8, 1884; many Zulu were convinced he had been poisoned. He was succeeded by his son Dinuzulu, an inexperienced boy of 16. The independence of the Zulu kingdom was over.

SHULA MARKS

See also: **Natal, Nineteenth Century; South Africa: Confederation, Disarmament, and the First Anglo-Boer War, 1871–1881.**

Biography

Born about 1826 near present-day Eshowe. Embroiled in civil war with half brother for rule of the kingdom in 1856. In 1872, inherited rule of the kingdom upon half-brother's death. On January 11, 1879, British troops entered Zululand. Surrendered to the British after the battle of Ulundi on July 4, 1879, and was sent into exile in Cape Town. Restored to power by the British government and returned to South Africa in January 1883. Surrendered to the British resident commissioner at Eshowe on October 17, 1883. Died there on February 8, 1884.

Further Reading

Binns, C. T. *The Last Zulu King: The Life and Death of Cetshwayo.* London: Longmans, Green, 1963.

Duminy, A, and C. Ballard (eds.). *The Anglo-Zulu War: New Perspectives.* Pietermaritzburg, South Africa: University of Natal Press, 1881.

Guy, J. *The Destruction of the Zulu Kingdom: The Civil War in Zululand, 1879–1884.* London: Longman, 1979.

Laband, J. *Rope of Sand: The Rise and Fall of the Zulu Kingdom in the Nineteenth Century.* Johannesburg: Jonathan Ball, 1995.

Webb, C. de B., and J. B. Wright (eds.). *A Zulu King Speaks: Statements Made by Cetshwayo kaMpande on the History and Customs of His People.* Pietermaritzburg, South Africa: University of Natal Press, 1978.

CFA: *See* Communaute Financière Africaine.

Chad, Nineteenth Century: Kanem/Borno (Bornu) and Wadai

Kanem-Borno, a former Muslim kingdom located northeast of Lake Chad, was created by a branch of the Zagawa people called the Beni Sefi, with the likely collaboration of the Tubu, around the year 800. While Kanem is part of Chad today, Bornu, located in Kanem's southernmost part and west of Lake Chad, is part of Nigeria, a result of the imperial territorial divisions that occurred between the French and the British during the 1880s and 1890s. The first Beni Sefi dynasty seems to have taken power around 1075, under the Sefuwa dynasty, which was headed by *Mai* (King) Hummay (1075–1180). A mythical mai named Idris Sayf Ibn Dhi Yezan is said to have converted to Islam during the second half of the eleventh century and exerted pressure on the rest of

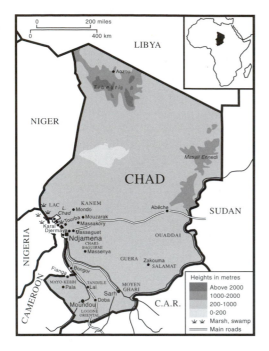

Chad.

the kingdom to embrace Islam as the state's religion. During the thirteenth century, the Sefuwa were able to designate a specific capital for the kingdom, Njimi.

As the mais solidified their power, Kanem expanded considerably during the thirteenth century, controlling the Bornu principality and virtually all that constitutes northwest Chad today, particularly during the reign of Mai Dunama Dabbalemi (1221–1259). Under his rule, the sultanate encompassed Wadai and the Adamawa Plateau in northern Cameroon. Parts of Nigeria, Niger, and Sudan were also incorporated into the sultanate. The greatness of Kanem was predicated upon two major factors. First was Kanem's ability to control the trans-Saharan trade route, resulting from its location at an important trade crossroads. During the first zenith of its power during the thirteenth century, Kanem's markets exchanged, sold, and bought such items as salt, horses, ostrich feathers, camels, hides, cotton, cloth, perfumes, copper objects, kola nuts, ivory, jewelry, and, evidently, slaves.

The second source of power was Kanem's extensive intercourse with North Africa via the Sahara Desert from Tripoli, down to the oases of Fezzan, and to south of Kawar on to Lake Chad. Contact with North Africa not only resulted in active commerce but also in cosmopolitan contacts and influences, as well as the infusion of intellectual and religious trends that enlightened the new kingdom and its people. Firm control of the trade routes and the safety created by the Sefuwa state was such that there was a common saying that even "a lone

woman clad in gold might walk with none to fear but God."

Imperial expansion notwithstanding, the Sefuwa dynasty was plagued with inherent royal conflict, as virtually no sultan or mai was totally secure on his throne. Fratricidal incidents were common, as well as overthrows, poisonings, blindings, vicious assassinations, and intrigues. Militating also against the rulers were the intermittent uprisings of the Bulala (classified variously as farmers or nomads) and the constant incursions of the desert Berbers and the Tuaregs. A major revolt by the Bulala forced the weakened dynasty to leave the kingdom during Mai Umar Ibn Idris (1384–1388) and seek refuge at Bornu, most likely a Kanem principality then, establishing a new capital at Ngazargamu, in present Niger, around 1484. Obviously, the new mais would attempt at various times to reconquer Kanem, but to no avail, until Mai Idris Katakarnabi (1504–1526) partially succeeded in the effort. However, only Mai Idris Alooma (1580–1619) completed the protracted task of recovering the old kingdom. Yet the sultans or mais continued to reside in Borno or Bornu, inaugurating the kingdom's second zenith, characterized by renewed and purified Islam, new brick mosques, and the introduction of new military tactics and weaponry, including "fixed military camps, armored horses, Berber cavalry, iron-helmet musketeers, and scorched earth tactics" that frightened the neighboring states and principalities. Despite the reconquest of Kanem by the old dynasty, for several reasons Bornu was maintained as the capital. First was the fact that the Tubu in Kanem seem to have been very hostile to the dynasty. Second, the Tuareg incursions never subsided. Third, agriculturally, Bornu was more productive than Kanem. Thus, for reasons of security and resources, the mais preferred Bornu, which sometimes was interchangeably called Kanem.

The year 1804 presaged the decline and eventual demise of Kanem-Bornu as a kingdom. Islamic warrior and leader 'Uthman dan Fodio sacked the capital with his Hausa-Fulani crusaders, and in 1814, Shehu Mohammad el-Amin el-Kanemi, a scholar-warrior, virtually replaced the ruling mai and assumed total control of the kingdom in 1837. He ruled unhindered until 1853, but could not maintain the kingdom as a cohesive whole. Meanwhile, the displaced mai was forced to move the capital to Kukawa, in Bornu. To the Sefuwa dynasty's chagrin, Rabih ibn Fadl Allah, a former slave from Sudan, turned into a formidable potential conqueror of all of Central Africa, and dislodged the mais from Kukawa, a city he sacked in 1893. Kanem-Bornu was finally conquered by the French and the British who had appeared in the area during the 1880s and 1890s and divided the imperial spoils once Rabih had been killed at Kuseri (present

Cameroon) in 1900. The Tubu, assisted by the Turkish or Ottoman Empire and the Senoussyia Muslim order, resisted the French for a time but, by 1920, the latter had prevailed and Kanem became part of the military colony of Chad. Today, it is one of Chad's 14 prefectures, and, with support from Nigeria, Kanem has at times been a source of several rebel movements against the central government. Bornu is an emirate in northeastern Nigeria.

The history of Kanem-Bornu endured for more than a thousand years. During much of its existence, Kanem-Bornu became not only a hegemonic state at several stages in North Central Africa but also an Islamic entrepôt encompassing several learning centers that drew scholars from several parts of western, northern, and northeastern Africa. Kanembu society was hierarchic, and the king was assisted by a council. The existence of the council has caused a debate among scholars as to whether or not the mai was an absolute monarch. Apart from the consistent raids by the Berbers and the Tuaregs, Kanem's greatest weakness was internal strife, of which citizens or subjects, such as the Bulala, took advantage. Caught up in the turmoil that beset Chad during the nineteenth century, reflected in the rivalries between Wadai and Baguirmi, Kanem-Bornu was doomed to failure even prior to the French conquest. Rabih had dealt it a deadly blow in 1893.

Located in eastern Chad, Wadai became one of the most powerful states in Central Sudan during the mid-nineteenth century. Its existence as a state dates back to some point between the fourteenth and sixteenth centuries. According to the scanty records available, the Tunjur may have been the founders of the sultanate, which turned to Islam during the seventeenth century from the conversion of Sultan Abdel el Kerim following an uprising of the Maba. Notwithstanding its imposing presence, up until the eighteenth century Wadai paid tribute to Bornu (part of Kanem) and Darfur (in Sudan), but it subsequently freed itself from the tribute and expanded its territory to include the small sultanates of Dar Sila, Dar Kuti, and Salamat. Wadai was a typical predatory state, spending most of its time in battle against other states in the region, including Bagirmi, which it sacked on numerous occasions (e.g., in 1805 and the 1870s), eventually annexing it during the reign of Kolak (King) Abdel el Kerim II. However, victory against Bagirmi was tempered by a defeat under the weight of Darfur troops. Wadai's defeat resulted in the crowning of a puppet kolak, Mohammad Shariff (r. 1825–1858). In 1850, Shariff transferred the capital from Wara to Abeche, the present capital of the prefecture. During Shariff's reign and thereafter, the influence of the Senoussyia brotherhood became paramount.

Wadai managed to put up a fierce resistance against the French for a time. Several inconclusive battles ensued between the two following declaration of a holy war against the French by Sultan Doud Murra from 1904 to 1908. After a series of battles between 1909 and 1913, the French eventually prevailed and Wadai became a de facto part of Chad in 1913, even though a 1900 Franco-British treaty had already designated it as such. Yet, Wadai continued to pose a threat to the French presence, thereby forcing the colonial government to install a military administration in the area.

Undoubtedly, during its zenith, the state of Wadai achieved high stature in the affairs of central Sudan. Indeed, just prior to the French arrival, Wadai commanded the largest and strongest army in the area. Unfortunately, just as in Kanem-Borno, dynastic infighting in the sultanate was rampant, and the state coffers relied on violent slave raids carried out among the non-Muslim societies in the south and southwest. Early explorers estimated that Wadai received a minimum of 4,000 slaves a year from tributary states and from its yearly and seasonal raids, or *gazawas*, over which the state, at least in theory, had the sole monopoly. Therefore, Wadai's resistance to France's presence was a means not just of preserving its sovereignty, but also of maintaining its economic lifestyle, which was heavily dependent upon the capture, employment, and sale or exchange of slaves, along with the region's trans-Saharan trade items such as horses, salt, and ostrich feathers.

MARIO J. AZEVEDO

Further Reading

Azevedo, M. *Roots of Violence: A History of War in Chad*. Langhorn, Penn.: Gordon and Breach, 1998.

Azevedo, M., and E. Nnadozie. *Chad: A Nation in Search of Its Future*. Boulder, Colo.: Westview Press, 1998.

Chapelle, J. *Le peuple tchadien*. Paris: Harmattan, 1980.

Cohen, R. *The Kanuri of Bornu*. New York: Holt, Rinehart, and Winston, 1967.

Collelo, T. (ed.). *Chad: A Country Study*. Washington, D.C.: Government Printing Office, 1990.

Decalo, S. *Historical Dictionary of Chad*. Metuchen, N.J.: Scarecrow Press, 1987.

Reyna, S. P. *Wars without End: The Political Economy of a Pre-Colonial African State*. Hanover, N.H.: University Press of New England, 1990.

United Nations Educational, Scientific and Cultural Organization. *A General History of Africa*. Paris: United Nations, 1989.

Chad: Colonial Period: French Rule

Chad was one of the last territories to be added to the French colonial empire. Its conquest by France occurred in several stages. The French appeared in southern Chad with imperial designs for the first time in 1892. The native population was friendly to the

Kitoko woman pounding grain, Chad, French Equatorial Africa, 1950s, wearing a skirt showing the British queen. © SVT Bild/Das Fotoarchiv.

French, as it saw them as liberators from the enslavement they suffered under the Islamic northern states, including Kanem-Bornu, Baguirmi, and Wadai. By 1899, the French had built a permanent post at Fort-Archambault in the present-day Moyen-Chari Prefecture and had secured several agreements with the southern traditional authorities, as was the case at Moissala and Bediondo. By 1912, the French had imposed their authority, to the extent that, notwithstanding sporadic resistance from some ethnic groups and traditional authorities, one could say that, for all practical purposes, they had secured what later became Southern Chad.

The conquest of the north, by contrast, was a different story. The sultans and the Muslim religious brotherhoods, such as the Senoussyia, fiercely resisted French intrusion and did not give up until they were overpowered militarily, but only after many French lives had been lost. Costly French military successes started around 1900, when Rabbah Fadlallah was defeated and killed at Kusseri by a combined contingent of three French expeditionary forces. In 1905, Kanem was subdued, followed by Abeche (Waddai's capital) in 1909 and 1912, Fada in 1914, Bardai in 1915, and Zouar in 1917; finally, the Tubu resistance was quelled in 1920. Until then, Chad had been under a colonial military government. A civilian government was subsequently installed, and Tibesti, detached from Niger, was made part of the new colony in 1929. Chad itself had been administered as one entity with the colony of Oubangui-Chari, now the Central African Republic.

Once conquest had been completed, the problem was how to administer this huge but poor colony to tap into its scarce natural resources. Few civil servants wished to be posted to Chad, as such an appointment was considered to be a demotion. As a result, Chad became replete with unmotivated officers, military adventurers, and poorly educated personnel. Up to 20 per cent of the government positions remained vacant from the 1920s to the 1940s.

To maintain a semblance of peace and progress, the French pursued a policy of appeasing the north and developing the south, called *Le Tchad utile* ("useful Chad"), at the expense of the southern populations. Whereas in the north the sultanates were left politically intact as long as they paid taxes and allowed free access to the colonial authorities, southerners, especially the Sara (who for decades have constituted a third of the Chadian population), turned into a reservoir of forced labor (*corvée*), porterage, military conscription, and the enforcement of compulsory cotton cultivation initiated around 1928. Concessionaire companies, such as the Societe Cotonniere Franco-Tchadienne, founded in 1925, were granted a monopoly over cotton cultivation, rubber collection, and timber harvesting. The task of developing Chad, however, was difficult.

Thousands of military conscripts from the south were used as part of the intercolonial mobile army. Up to 20,000 southern Chadians were forcibly recruited to participate in the completion of hundreds of government and private projects in the colony and elsewhere in the French African empire. Thousands of others were employed as porters, traveling with and outside Chad, and carrying heavy loads on their backs and heads, with an attending mortality rate of 15 per cent, according to explorer Pierre Savorgnan de Brazza. In this context, the worst French project was the construction of the Congo-Ocean Railway in 1924–1934, which required 120,000 forced laborers, most of whom were Sara. While about 50,000 of them died in the *chantiers*, an additional 50,000 never returned home.

The south was also burdened with irregular and abusive tax collection by both the French *commandants de cercle* and subdued African authorities. This resulted in violence that subsided only during the 1950s, when the French took measures to put a halt to colonial abuses. As a consequence of the violent reaction by the Africans, Chad's jails were full of "criminals," at times encompassing over 2 per cent of the able population in some areas. The absence of able-bodied males, who had been siphoned from the villages to serve in the administration projects, resulted in famines, migrations, and revolts against both the administration and the traditional authorities on whom the French relied throughout the colonial period, especially in the countryside.

Ever since the beginning of their empire, the French believed in the gradual assimilation of some of their colonial subjects as a guiding policy. Thus, they created what was called *le systeme de l'indigenat*, which divided the African population into the assimilated and the indigenous (or "noncivilized"). While the former, by law, had to be treated like French citizens, with political representation (along with the expatriates) in the metropolis, the indigenous were subjected to forced labor, had to follow traditional customs, and could lose their property at any time through confiscation.

Political and social reforms were finally enacted immediately following World War II, partly as a way of showing gratitude to the Africans for their heroic participation in the war. Chad, in particular, under black governor Felix Eboue (who later, in 1941–1944, became governor general of French Equatorial Africa), was the first African colony to join the French resistance led by General Charles de Gaulle against the Germans.

Thus, in 1946, following a conference presided over by de Gaulle himself at Brazzaville, the systeme de l'indigenat was abolished and all Africans were declared French citizens of a multiracial French empire. Political parties were allowed in the colonies, though the hope was that they would be affiliated with the French political parties in the metropole. Yet, voting was still separate: there was a dual college, with one side for white and educated voters and the other for the Africans. This racialist practice was, however, eliminated in 1956, by the so-called *loi cadre* (enabling act), the result of which was the overwhelming number of the Chadian population at the polls, almost invariably voting for black candidates.

By 1959 dozens of parties, some based on religion and some based along ethnicity and region lines, emerged and disappeared, leaving only a few to endure and form territorial governments prior to independence. Included among these were the Union Democratique du Tchad, based in the North, and the Parti Progressiste Tchadien (PPT), founded in 1946 by Gabriel Lisette of the Antilles. Southern-based but with northern appeal as well, at least during its early existence, the PPT came to be dominated by the southerners, especially the Sara, under the leadership of a former teacher and labor union organizer, François Tombalbaye. The PPT trounced its rivals by securing a landslide victory at the polls on March 31, 1958, when it captured 57 of the 85 seats in the Territorial Assembly. It was allowed to form a new government. Eventually, on June 16, 1959, Tombalbaye formed a permanent government, which propelled him to the country's presidency following

ascension to independence from France on August 11, 1960. France remained the protector of Chadian sovereignty through treaties signed with the new government, agreements subsequently invoked by every Chadian government since the early 1970s. Indeed, until 1965 French influence was marked by the presence of its military forces in the BET Province in the north, in an attempt to suppress any potential revolt in that part of the country.

There is no doubt that, in Chad, France lost more of its soldiers and officers than anywhere else in its drive to create a vast empire for itself. At the heart of Africa, Chad, notwithstanding its shifting sands and its lack of abundant natural resources, was considered to be of a strategic importance for France in its dogged effort to control West and Central Africa, and as a springboard to its colonies and outposts on the Indian Ocean. In Chad, France followed a policy of exploiting the south at the expense of its inhabitants whom it regarded primarily as a reservoir of labor and military conscription, while the north, considered more civilized and hard to govern, was given a virtual free rein. What followed was a split of the colony along religious, regional, and ethnic lines, exacerbated by the precolonial slaving activities of the north over the southern populations. Although slavery ended during the 1920s, the French had little time to prepare the colony for independence.

The promulgation of the loi cadre and the acceptance of Western education by the south allowed this region to come out of the colonial experience united under the banner of the PPT, forcing the French to reverse themselves, as they ended up handing over power to southerners rather than their northern proteges. What resulted were bitter social, political, and economic cleavages, fueled by unforgettable recriminations predating the colonial period, a concoction ripe for civil strife that has endured up to the present. The role of France both prior to and following independence appears to have been more detrimental than helpful to Chad's future as an aspiring nation-state.

MARIO J. AZEVEDO

See also: **Colonial Federations: French Equatorial Africa.**

Further Reading

Azevedo, M., *Chad: A Nation in Search of Its Future*. Boulder, Colo.: Westview Press, 1998.

———. *Roots of Violence: A History of War in Chad*. Langhorn, Penn: Gordon and Breach, 1998.

Collelo, T. (ed.). *Chad: A Country Study*. Washington, D.C.: Government Printing Office, 1990.

Grey, R., and D. Birmingham (eds.). *Precolonial African Trade: Essays on Trade in Central and Eastern Africa*. New York: Oxford University Press, 1980.

Lemarchand, R. "The Politics of Sara Ethnicity: A Note on the Origins of the Civil War in Chad." *Cahiers d'Etudes Africaines*, no. 20 (1988): 449–472.

Chad: Independence to the Present

For the most part, Chad's postcolonial history has seen unremitting civil strife, interspersed with cyclical external interventions. Reasons for the conflict overlap in a complex web of ethnic, religious, economic, and political motivation.

On an elemental level, an animus between the Goranes Muslim ethnic groups—especially the Toubou—of northern Chad and the Christian Sara people of the south was exacerbated and entrenched by a negligent French colonial administration. On August 11, 1960, Chad became an independent republic. The first president, François (later renamed Ngarta) Tombalbaye, consolidated his rule using all possible means. In 1963, his Parti Progressiste Tchadien (PPT) was declared the country's only authorized party. Tombalbaye's prime motivation was the retention of power. Politicians, civil servants, and eventually the military, whether from the north or south, were subject to arrest and imprisonment. However, after 1963 many in the north perceived themselves to be the target of a calculated strategy of domination by a southern elite. Tax excesses and ill-conceived economic and cultural policies ensured continued resentment. In April 1975 Tombalbaye was killed in a coup d'état and replaced by a political prisoner, General Félix Malloum.

Digging a well, Gredaya, Chad. © Frank Kroenke/Das Fotoarchiv.

As early as 1966, a rebellion had coalesced behind the Front de Libération Nationale de Tchad (FROLINAT). Foreign involvement in the Chadian conflict was already evident. Various elements within the FROLINAT, itself established in Sudan, received support from Libya or Nigeria. Between 1969 and 1972, Tombalbaye accepted French military intervention to contain the increasingly successful rebellion. However, Tombalbaye's ouster intensified pressures toward fragmentation and factionalism within the rebellion. In the absence of an integrating ideology, the FROLINAT had depended on the battle against the oppressive regime for its cohesion. The movement was ideologically multifaceted. Moreover, the sociology of the conflict had always extended beyond the crude dimensions of a north/south or Christian/Muslim dichotomy. Around a hundred distinct language groups, frequently split into several subgroups, exist among a population of only five million people. Furthermore, intragroup relations, especially in the bellicose north, were highly prone to segmentation. The factionalism of the civil war underscored this inclination to find allies among neighboring subgroups, rather than among inclusive ethnic, religious, or linguistic groups. In this respect, the Chadian conflict fits the "warlord" model, with its stress on regional centers of power based on personalized rule and military force, and the consequent prevalence of a politics of conflict and war.

Malloum's new administration pursued a policy of national reconciliation. At the same time, Libyan leader Moammar Gaddafi's continued incursion from the contested Aouzou Strip in the far north and his meddling in factional politics led to a pivotal schism within the FROLINAT and increased concern in the West. Anti-Libyan elements under Hissène Habré, retaining the name Forces Armées du Nord (FAN), joined a short-lived coalition government with Malloum's military council under a "fundamental charter." The remaining majority of the FAN under Goukouni Oueddei, having regrouped as the Forces Armées Populaires (FAP), maintained a strong territorial and military position. In mid-1978, French military reinforcements were needed to halt the advance of Goukouni's troops on the capital. As the Habré-Malloum coalition began to collapse, a process of recurring disintegration occurred. The result was a proliferation of factions. Together with the FAN and FAP, two groups proved to be especially significant: the remnants of the national army regrouped as the Forces Armées Tchadiennes under Colonel Wadal Kamagoué in the south and Ahmet Acyl's New Vulcan Army in the north and center of the country.

The resignation of Malloum in April 1979 was followed by a series of reconciliation conferences. As a result, a broad-based Gouvernement d'union nationale de transition (GUNT) was formed with Goukouni as president, Habré as minister of defense, and Kamougué as vice president. These were to prove essentially fictitious positions in a government that existed in name only. Civil war resumed. An inter-African peacekeeping force sponsored by the Organization of African Unity met with intractable obstacles of mandate and resources. Actions by external powers were more pertinent. While Gaddafi chose a temporary tactical withdrawal, French diplomatic manoeuvres and American covert aid promoted Habré's FAN. Following an offensive launched from the Biltine, home of the FAN's operational commander, Idriss Deby, Habré entered the capital on June 7, 1982.

Factionalism endured. The south fragmented between a number of private militias, dubbed "codos." In the north, Goukouni successfully reformed the GUNT with Libyan support. Only intervention by French paratroops in 1983 stopped the GUNT from taking N'Djaména. Habré realized that if he was to maintain power he had to extend control both beyond the capital and his own core constituency. That he was largely successful was a consequence of iron rule and pragmatic policy. Beyond military superiority and repression, Habré relied on the twin props of the United States and France—especially the latter. Throughout the 1980s, French president François Mitterrand's support had been contingent on Chad maintaining a bulwark against Libyan incursion, while remaining compliant to French influence. In 1986 and 1987 Chad inflicted costly military defeats on Libya. As a result, Gaddafi accepted the arbitration of the International Court of Justice (ICJ) in the Hague to settle the Aouzou Strip dispute. In 1994, the ICJ found in Chad's favor.

At the Franco-African Summit in 1990, President Mitterrand sought to publicly realign French policy to African democratization, endorsing pluralism and liberal democracy. Despite voicing objections to the new line from Paris, Habré had already instigated preemptive constitutional reform. A referendum on December 10, 1989, both adopted a new constitution and elected Habré as president for a seven-year term— by a reported 99.94 per cent of votes cast. In reality, freedoms and rights enshrined in the constitution were not actionable in law. Regardless of the credibility of the proposed nonparty National Assembly, Habré and his ministers would remain above censure.

Throughout 1989, ethnic tension among government troops serving in the south led to insecurity that was mirrored by disaffection in N'Djaména. Leading members of Habré's subclan, the Anakaza, sought to prevent other groups within the alliance from profiting from the sale of Libyan arms captured during the 1986–1987 campaign. Isolated groups, especially the Bideyat and Zaghawa, found champions in war heroes Deby and Hassan Djamous, together with the influential minister of interior, Mahamat Itno. After a failed coup, only Deby survived to flee to Darfur in western Sudan in order to regroup. The Mouvement Patriotique du Salut (MPS) was constructed, with Libyan support, mainly from alienated Hadjerai and Zaghawa, including substantial Zaghawa elements from Sudan. Following Habré's outspoken reaction to Mitterrand's initiative at La Baule, France executed an about-face, effectively withdrawing support from Habré. On December 2, 1990 Deby, at the head of the MPS, entered N'Djaména.

The transition to democracy, promised by Deby on his assumption of power, developed into a long and difficult process. In early 1993, a Sovereign National Conference was held to formulate a draft constitution. It would be a further three years before the recommendations of the conference would be put to a referendum. Two-thirds of the electorate voted for the new constitution based on that of the French Fifth Republic, with a strong presidency. The result cleared the way for presidential and legislative elections. A two-round election in June and July of 1996 saw Deby defeat Kamougué for the presidency. Legislative elections held in January and February 1997 saw Deby's MPS win an outright majority over nine other parties in a new National Assembly. The outcomes of the three polls were generally held by both domestic and foreign observers to have fulfilled the wishes of the majority of the electorate. However, it became apparent that there was evidence of malpractice in each poll. While manipulation of the process and result was slight in the referendum, it was more visible in the legislative elections and manifest in the presidential ballot.

The Deby era has seen a decline in the level of civil violence. Negotiated peace accords have resulted in several politico-military groups abandoning rebellion to amalgamate with the government and national army. Nonetheless, conflict endures. In January 1999, rebel forces launched an offensive in the north and east of the country. Moreover, the government has been accused by human rights associations of employing repressive tactics, including extrajudicial execution and torture, against opponents. The most salient determinant of Chad's immediate future is the potential wealth from the oil fields in the southern subprefecture of Doba. This controversial project, while having the capacity to transform the Chadian economy, might also result in environmental degradation and provoke a return to civil war.

SIMON MASSEY

See also: **Chad: Libya, Aozou Strip, Civil War; Tombalbaye, F. Ngarta.**

Further Reading

Decalo, S. *Historical Dictionary of Chad.* 3rd ed. Lanham, Md.: Scarecrow Press, 1997.

Foltz, W. "Reconstructing the State of Chad." In *Collapsed States: The Disintegration and Restoration of Legitimate Authority*, edited by I. William Zartman. Boulder, Colo.: Lynne Rienner, 1995.

Lanne, B. "Chad: Regime Change, Increased Insecurity and Blockage of Further Reforms." In *Political Reform in Francophone Africa*, edited by J. F. Clark and D. E. Gardinier. Boulder, Colo.: Westview Press, 1997.

May, R., and S. Massey. "Chad." In *Peacekeeping in Africa*, edited by Oliver Furley and Roy May. Aldershot, England: Ashgate, 1998.

Nolutshungu, S. C. *Limits of Anarchy: Intervention and State Formation in Chad*. Charlottesville: University Press of Virginia, 1996.

Chad: Libya, Aozou Strip, Civil War

In 1853 Muhammad ibn al-Sanusi established his *zawiya* (place of learning) at Giarabub (Jaghbub) in eastern Libya. Born in Algeria, educated in Islamic Sufism at Fez and orthodoxy at Mecca, *al-Sanusi al-Kabir,* the Grand Sanusi, became famous for his teachings that attracted *talibes* (students) from everywhere in North Africa and Arabia. After his death in 1859, the Sanusiyya evolved from a religious brotherhood into a political and commercial organization by the spiritual confidence and military support of the Bedouins in the interior that was accepted by the ruling Ottoman Turks of the coast. His son, Muhammad al-Mahdi al-Sanusi, increased the number of Sanusi lodges throughout southern Libya and northern Chad from which they imposed their authority over the merchants and the faithful. This symbiotic relationship could not survive the advance of the French between 1902 and 1914 from the south at the time the Sanusiyya were confronted by Italians in the north.

Italy had become a unified nation in the nineteenth century and a frustrated imperial state at the beginning of the twentieth. Its leaders were determined to convert the Mediterranean into an "Italian Strait" by the conquest of Libya. On September 29, 1911, Italy declared war against the Ottoman Turks to revive the glories of ancient Rome by new conquests in Africa. The Ottoman Turks made peace in 1912, leaving Libya to the Italians and the Sanusiyya, whose Bedouin waged guerrilla warfare from their desert sanctuary for another 30 years. The Italo-Sanusi wars were a contest between advanced military technology and organization, and the Sanusiyya, who knew the territory, possessed the faith, and were led by the charismatic military leadership of Sidi Umar al-Mukhtar. Half the Bedouins lost their lives in battle and concentration camps, and when Umar, the "Lion of the Desert," was hanged on September 18, 1931, the Sanusi insurgency collapsed. The imposed *pax Romana* was brief, for British and French forces conquered Libya in 1943 during the North African campaigns of World War II. Libya survived the war impoverished

and governed by an Anglo-French military administration until the Sanusiyya were restored when Idris Muhammad al-Sanusi was acknowledged king of the United Kingdom of Libya on December 24, 1951.

The discovery of oil in 1965, Arab nationalism, and the paternal mismanagement of Idris led Libyan captain Muammar Gaddafi and his fellow officers to seize the government on September 1, 1969. He terminated the British and American military presence, expelled the Italian colonists, and used the abundant revenues from new oil resources to seek the unity of the Arab world. His efforts to forge a united Arab state were compromised by theology, terrorism, and imperialism. His political and religious philosophy was published in the *Green Book* of 1976, which was unacceptable to many Muslims. His hostility to the West and disputes with his Arab neighbors gave sanctuary, encouragement, and resources to terrorists willing to undertake missions against the West and the Libyan opposition—particularly the Sanusiyya. His pursuit of a unified Arab *Dar al-Islam* committed Gaddafi to an imperial war against Chad for the Aozou Strip.

The Aozou Strip lies on the border between Libya and Chad. Italian dictator Benito Mussolini had claimed this wasteland as an essential link with the Italian East African empire. In Rome on January 7, 1935, the French recognized Italian ownership of Aozou, but after the Italian invasion of Ethiopia in October of that year the Laval-Mussolini treaty was never consummated. Despite attempts by France and the kingdom of Libya to define their ambiguous frontier between Chad and Libya, Gaddafi's revolutionary government was determined to lead his Arab revolution down the ancient trans-Saharan caravan routes that passed through the Strip to Africa south of the Sahara. In November 1972 the Libyan army occupied Aozou that precipitated 20 years of conflict with Chad.

The war for Aozou was sustained by Gaddafi's determination to expand his revolution and Islam south of the Sahara, rumors of rich uranium in Aozou, and the personal ambitions of traditional leaders threatened by the elite in Ndjamena and Tripoli. His political and religious imperialism was made possible by oil revenues to purchase sophisticated armaments from the Soviet Union that proved of limited success in the Sahara. Two decades of futile warfare on a barren frontier resulted in many thousands of casualties and refugees, political instability in Chad, and the anxiety by African states and those in the West to deny Gaddafi's obsession to acquire the Aozou Strip. On December 2, 1990, Idriss Deby seized control of the government of Chad in yet another coup. In February 1991 he announced during a state visit to Tripoli that Aozou belonged to Chad. The combatants, exhausted by 20 years of war, were no longer prepared to fight for a wasteland. In February 1994 the World Court ruled, 16 to 1, that Aozou belonged to Chad. In May the last Libyan troops left the Aozou Strip. In June of that year Deby and Gaddafi signed a Treaty of Friendship that ended a half-century of struggle for these wastelands on a barren frontier.

ROBERT O. COLLINS

See also: **Libya: Gaddafi (Qadhdhafi) and Jamahiriyya (Libyan Revolution); Libya: Italian Invasion and Resistance, 1911–1931.**

Further Reading

Burr, J. M., and R. O. Collins. *Africa's Thirty Years War: Libya, Chad, and the Sudan 1963–1993.* Boulder, Colo.: Westview Press, 1999.

Evans-Pritchard, E. E. *The Sanusi of Cyrenaica.* Oxford: Clarendon Press, 1949.

Lanne, B. *Tchad-Libye: La querelle des frontières.* Paris: Karthala, 1982.

Wright, J. *Libya.* New York: Praeger, 1969.

———. *Libya, Chad and the Central Sahara.* London: C. Hurst, 1989.

Changamire Dombo: *See* Torwa, Changamire Dombo, and the Rovzi.

Chilembe Rising: *See* Malawi (Nyasaland): Colonial Period: Chilembwe Rising, 1915.

Chimurenga: *See* Zimbabwe: Second Chimurenga 1966–1979.

Chissano: *See* Mozambique: Chissano and, 1986 to the Present.

Chokwe: *See* Angola: Chokwe, Ovimbundu, Nineteenth Century.

Christian Conversion: *See* Medical Factor in Christian Conversion.

Christianity: *See* Alexandria and Early Christianity: Egypt; Angola: New Colonial Period: Christianity, Missionaries, Independent Churches; Augustine, Catholic Church: North Africa; Kongo Kingdom: Afonso I, Christianity, and Kingship; Lalibela and Ethiopian Christianity.

Chwezi Dynasty: *See* Great Lakes Region: Kitara and the Chwezi Dynasty.

Civil War: Postcolonial Africa

Since 1945, Africa has witnessed a range of wars, beginning with independence struggles against the colonial powers that often merged into postcolonial power struggles and civil wars, while after 1960 there have also been a number of wars between African states. Civil wars in postcolonial Africa from 1960 onward fall into three broad categories: racial or ethnic wars; ideological wars; and power struggles. As a rule these causes overlap and are often indistinguishable from one another.

Most of Africa's civil wars have been deeply affected by the colonial legacy and the divisions that the colonial powers left behind them. For example, the tribal or ethnic basis of many African civil wars poses questions about the nature of the divisions which the colonial powers created and encouraged, and a number of wars broke out as a direct result of the end of colonialism. The centralizing tendencies of the European colonizers created artificial states, with the principal unifying factor being the colonial presence itself (as with the British in Nigeria, the French in Chad, or the Portuguese in Angola).

The end of an empire always leaves in its wake a series of power vacuums. In Africa four European empires came to an end during the 1960s and 1970s: those of Britain, Belgium, France, and Portugal. In the circumstances of the abrupt disappearance of imperial power over a period of 25 years it is not surprising that

In Lueshe, eastern Congo, close to the Virunga National Park, the German company Somikivu is mining the rare metal niobium, which is used in space research as well as in the production of mobile phones. The plant was closed for several years because of the civil war; it reopened in the summer of 2000. © Sebastian Bolesch/Das Fotoarchiv.

a series of power implosions followed. The subsequent search for power, clashing ideologies, and ethnic divisions lent themselves to civil confrontations and conflicts, and these duly occurred.

African leaders were acutely aware of the dangers of ethnic divisions, and in such countries as Kenya, Tanzania, and Zambia, for example, the postindependence leaders worked hard to persuade their people that they were Kenyans, Tanzanians, and Zambians first rather than members of competing ethnic groups, while Julius Nyerere of Tanzania justified the one-party state, in part, on the grounds that a multiparty system would inevitably lead to particular ethnic groups associating themselves with opposed political parties. Ethnic divisions and rivalries were not to be disposed of that simply, however, and they have been at the root of many African conflicts. In the years since 1960, civil wars have occurred in Algeria, Angola, Burundi, Chad, Congo (Brazzaville), the Democratic Republic of Congo, Ethiopia, Liberia, Mozambique, Nigeria, Rwanda, Sierra Leone, Somalia, Sudan, and Zimbabwe, and ethnic divisions have always played a part and sometimes the dominant part in these conflicts.

The genocidal massacres of Hutus by Tutsis and Tutsis by Hutus that have been a regular feature of life in Burundi and Rwanda since before independence in 1962 have deep historical causes, yet in colonial times divisions that could have been played down were in fact highlighted first by the Germans, and then by the Belgians, who emphasized the dominant role of the Tutsi minority in both countries by using them as their principal instruments of control. The introduction of European-style democracy on the eve of independence in two countries where the Hutus enjoyed a majority 85 per cent of the population while the Tutsis represented only 14 per cent meant the permanent domination of the minority group; the ugly civil conflicts that have periodically exploded in both countries since 1960 were fueled by Tutsi fears of such domination. These particular conflicts raise issues about the kind of democracy that makes sense for such societies.

The drawn-out civil war in Sudan between north and south (1957–1972, and then 1985–present) embraces a number of divisions that reinforce each other. First, ethnic divisions between north and south also coincide with religious differences. The northern peoples, the majority, are Arab or Arabicized and Muslim, while the minority southern peoples are from a number of Nilotic ethnic groups and are Christian or follow African animist religions. Second, for centuries the northerners saw the south as a source of slaves and regarded its people as inferior, a racist attitude that continued after independence. Third, in the postindependence era after 1956, political power and control of economic decisions lay with the north, so that southerners saw themselves being both exploited and treated as second-class citizens, a perception that was increased when northern Muslim politicians tried to impose the Shari'a (Islamic law) upon the non-Muslim south. The result has been one of the longest, most bitter civil wars in postcolonial Africa. This war, moreover, has raised a question that African political leaders have determinedly avoided ever since independence: whether intransigent conflicts based upon irreconcilable differences should be solved by partitioning the state rather than clinging to an inherited boundary that makes little sense and ensures continuing conflict. A strong case could be made for dividing north and south Sudan into separate states, despite the early Organization of African Unity resolution that Africa's new states should all accept their inherited colonial boundaries.

The Nigerian civil war illustrates how the colonial legacy can lead to breakdown. During the nineteenth century the British created several colonial structures in what later became Nigeria, which they only brought together to form a single, centralized colony on the eve of World War I. Subsequently, British colonial administrators became fierce rivals as they safeguarded (as they saw it) the interests of their different regions—the north, west, and east. These rivalries were to be carried on after independence in 1960 in a power struggle to see which ethnic group could control the political center. Moreover, the discovery of major oil wealth centered in the eastern region made an Ibo secession an attractive and practical possibility. When Nigeria did descend into civil war in 1968, the British role in supporting the federal government was dominated by its oil interests; the Soviet readiness to support the federal government followed from its desire to obtain hitherto nonexistent influence in West Africa's largest state; and the French concern to support breakaway Biafra (through support provided by proxy African states) reflected its determination to lessen British influence in the region. As a result, by the end of the war the Nigerians had acquired a healthy suspicion of, and disrespect for, the motives of the major powers in Africa.

In Angola, following the departure of the Portuguese in 1975, the three principal causes of civil wars became intertwined. At first, when the Portuguese left, the war that at once erupted between the three liberation movements—the Movimento Popular de Libertaçao de Angola (MPLA), which became the government, and the Frente Nacional de Libertaçao de Angola (FNLA) and the Uniao Nacional para la Independencia Total de Angola (UNITA)—was fiercely ideological, with the MPLA fighting to establish a Marxist state and its rivals claiming to stand for a Western-style capitalist system. Not surprisingly, in the years that followed, since the Cold War was then at its height, the

MPLA received massive assistance from both the USSR and Cuba, while its opponents obtained U.S. and South African assistance. Later, though ethnic loyalties became increasingly important, the war developed into a blatant power struggle: this was clearly demonstrated after Jonas Savimbi and his UNITA party lost the United Nations-brokered elections of 1992 and promptly returned to the bush to continue the war.

Most of Africa's civil wars have been both complicated and prolonged by foreign interventions of two kinds: those of major powers from outside Africa "safeguarding" their interests, and those of African neighbors. The general weakness of African states, their dependence upon international aid, and continuing Western pressures for influence (neocolonialism) have ensured that outside interventions have constantly taken place. Sometimes these interventions have been in the form of peacekeeping operations; at others they have been in support of a regime or contender for power that suited the outside power as was the case in the 1997 civil war in Congo (Brazzaville), when France was determined to see former President Sassou-Nguesso replace Pascal Lissouba as the Congo head of state.

In the neighboring Democratic Republic of Congo, five African states intervened when that country collapsed into civil war in 1998, a year after Laurent Kabila had ousted Mobutu Sese Sheko from power. Rwanda and Uganda sent forces to support the Tutsi-led rebels against Kabila, while Angola, Namibia, and Zimbabwe sent troops to support his government. The motives of these intervening states were mixed but appear to have been more concerned with looting the wealth of the DRC than anything else.

The complexities of Africa's wars sometimes defy easy analysis. Somalia possesses one of the most homogeneous populations in Africa, yet it collapsed into fratricidal clan warfare at the end of the 1980s, a disaster made worse by UN and U.S. interventions in the early 1990s. The long-lasting war in Ethiopia from 1962 to 1991 included the ultimately successful bid by Eritrea to break away and become an independent state; the Tigrayan revolt which was more about power than secession; and the Oromo revolts, which represented the dissatisfaction of an ethnic group that had long been oppressed by the Amharic ethnic center.

Other civil wars have been ignited by religious extremism (Algeria), or ethnic-based power struggles (Liberia and Sierra Leone) in the 1990s.

GUY ARNOLD

See also: **Algeria: Islamic Salvation Front, Military Rule, Civil War, 1990s ; Angola: Cold War Politics, Civil War, 1975–1994; Angola: Independence and Civil War, 1974–1976; Congo (Brazzaville), Republic of: Independence, Revolution, 1958–1979;** **Ethiopia: Civil War and Liberation (to 1933); Liberia: Civil War, ECOMOG, and the Return to Civilian Rule; Nigeria: Federalism, Corruption, Popular Discontent: 1960–1966; Rwanda: Civil Unrest and Independence: 1959–1962; Somalia: Independence, Conflict, and Revolution.**

Further Reading

Africa Watch. *Arms Trade and Violation of the Laws of War since the 1992 Elections.* New York: Africa Watch, 1994.

———. *Civilian Devastation: Abuses by All Parties in the War in Southern Sudan.* New York: Africa Watch, 1995.

Alao, A. *Peace-Keeping in Sub-Saharan Africa: The Liberian Civil War.* London: Brassey's, 1993.

Arnold, G. *Wars in the Third World since 1945*, 2nd ed. London: Cassell, 1995.

———. *Historical Dictionary of Civil Wars in Africa.* Lanham, Md.: Scarecrow Press, 1999.

Baynham, S. *Military Power and Politics in Black Africa.* London: Croom Helm, 1986.

Beri, H. M. L. "Civil War in Chad." *Strategic Analysis* 10, no. 1 (1986): 40–49.

Destexhe, A. Rwanda, *Essai sur le Genocide.* Brussels: Editions Complexe, 1994.

Finnegan, W. *A Complicated War: The Harrowing of Mozambique.* Berkeley and Los Angeles: University of California Press, 1992.

First, R. *The Barrel of a Gun: Political Power in Africa and the Coup d'Etat.* London: Allen Lane, 1970.

Gershoni, Y. "War without End and an End to War: The Prolonged Wars in Liberia and Sierra Leone." *African Studies Review* 40, no. 3 (1997): 55–76.

Lee, J. M. *African Armies and Civil Order.* London: Chatto and Windus, 1968.

Middle East Watch. *Human Rights Abuses in Algeria: No One Is Spared.* New York: Middle East Watch, 1994.

St. Jorre, J. de. *The Nigerian Civil War.* London: Hodder and Stoughton, 1972.

Climate and Vegetational Change in Africa

Climate is a major factor that has affected vegetation, human settlement, and subsistence patterns in Africa. Regional differences in vegetation can best be explained in terms of variation in the amount and seasonal distribution of rainfall.

Two prevailing wind systems have a dominant influence on the climate of equatorial Africa. These are the Atlantic moisture-laden southerly monsoon and the continental, dry northeast trade winds. The former predominate in summer, bringing rain, while the latter predominate in winter, bringing the harmattan winds (dry, dusty winds that blow along the northwest coast) from the Sahara. It is believed that at least the southerly monsoon wind system probably has blown from the southwest since the Palaeocene period (approximately 65 million years ago). Periodic variations in the vigor of these two wind systems and relative latitudinal positions of the intertropical discontinuity (where the two winds meet) contribute to climatic changes in the region.

Climatic fluctuations are historically characterized by alternating wet and dry phases, resulting in general atmospheric circulation. During the wet phases, which lasted from a few to several thousand years, the southwesterly monsoons were invigorated, causing a northward shift in the intertropical discontinuity far above its present-day July position. Then during the dry phases, the northeast trade winds pushed down the intertropical discontinuity below its present-day January position.

It is believed that up to about 70 million years ago, the equator was situated around northern Nigeria. Most of Africa at this period was in a wet phase. It was after this period that the equator started a southward shift to its present position, the wet phase therefore giving way to a dry one. There were, however, fluctuations in between. The change from a wet to a dry phase was caused by the reinforcement of the northeast trade winds, thus bringing about the establishment of desert conditions in the Sahara.

Geomorphologic and paleological evidence also suggests that there was a climatic change from a predominantly wet equatorial condition to a tropical seasonally dry one in north-central and northwestern Nigeria 26 million years ago.

The effect of these climatic changes on the vegetation of Africa was enormous. There is evidence to show that at the beginning of the Tertiary period (approximately 70 million years ago) there existed a tropical savanna in the present-day Sahara belt, which was due largely to regular supply of summer rain. Furthermore, there is presently no fossil botanical evidence of the occurrence of grasses in the tropics as a whole during this period. This therefore suggests that the tropics at this period were thickly forested. It was, however, only from about 26 million years ago that savanna in the form of an open grassland became established in Nigeria.

During the Late Paleocene and Early Eocene periods (approximately 70 million years ago) equatorial conditions prevailed in the present-day southern Sahara, especially in Mali and Niger. These conditions prevailed until there was a significant change in climate to a drier, tropical, seasonal one approximately 26 to 36 million years ago.

Some of the main plant families as represented by their pollen were *Euphobiaceae*, *Combretaceae*, *Caesalpinaceae*, *Papilionaceae*, *Palmae*, *Sapindaceae*, and *Annonaceae*. In the northern Sahara region, including Egypt, a savanna with abundant grass cover and presumably woody species of *Sapotaceae* and *Bombacaceae* was present at about the same period.

In West Africa, plant species seem to have retained their basic character over the last 26 million years, even though paleological evidence indicates that subsequent to the Miocene period (approximately 26 million years ago) there were some cases of extinction.

Generally, the major tropical vegetation belts stretching across West, central, and East Africa have many species in common. Compared to the present day, there had been a series of changes in the characteristic features of the savanna during its evolution about 26 million years ago. These changes involved the appearances of a new species as well as intermittent significant shifts in the climatic fluctuations. Human factors only became evident within the last 3,000 years.

It is believed that the most dramatic climatic and vegetational changes in Africa took place during the Quaternary period, which is the latest geological period, spanning the last 1.8 million years (it is often referred to as the Ice Age). It is characterized as the geological interval during which the climate of the earth witnessed spectacular alternations of cold dry phases and warm wet phases. These changes were more varied and widespread in Africa. While desert sands, soils, alluvia, lacustrine deposits, cave earth, and mountain glacial sediments accumulated in different parts of the African continent, peat beds, deltaic, shelf and shoreline sands, deep-sea fans, and carbonates were laid down on the continental margin and deep-sea floor. Sea levels rose and fell as ice caps melted. Rivers rapidly filled their valleys, only to dry up at the next abrupt change of base level; lake levels rose and fell, and some lakes even vanished completely. Subsequently, forests turned into deserts. Plant and animal groups responded to these sharp climatic changes primarily by migrating frequently.

Fairly recent climatic changes in Africa are those of the last 40,000 years. From 40,000 to 20,000 years ago, lakes in North Africa were high as it was relatively wet, though a dry episode in Lake Chad had set in by about 30,000 years ago. From 20,000 to 12,000 years ago, lakes within the same area were low as a result of a dry cold period. From 7,000 to 5,000 years ago, lakes in the same area again rose. Then from about 5,000 to 3,000 years ago, there set in a drier condition heralding the fairly rapid evolution of the African climate to the conditions which prevail today. This evolution, however, was punctuated by minor fluctuations with higher precipitation setting in the last 1,000 years.

JOSEPH MANGUT

Further Reading

Kogbe, C. A., and M. A. Sowunmi. "The Age of the Gwandu Formation (Continental Terminal) in North-Western Nigeria." *Annales des Mines et de la Geologie* 28, no. 3 (1980).

Medus, J., M. Popoff, E. Fourtanier, and M. A. Sowunmi. "Sedimentology, Pollen, Spores and Diatoms of a 148 m Deep Miocene Drill Hole from Oku Lake, East Central Nigeria." *Palaeogeography, Palaeoclimatology, Palaeoecology*, no. 68 (1988). 79–94.

Sowunmi, M. A. "Change of Vegetation with Time." In *Plant Ecology in West Africa Systems and Processes*, edited by G. W. Lawson. New York: John Wiley and Sons, 1986.

———. "Late Quaternary Environmental Changes in Nigeria." *Pollen et Spores* 23, no. 1 (1981): 125–145.

Clothing and Cultural Change

It is revealing to analyze prevailing fashion and clothing trends, especially in periods when a traditional system has been subjected to sudden upheavals, as was the case in Africa during the colonial period. From the late nineteenth century on, fundamental social, economic, and political changes occurred in most parts of the continent that strongly influenced and shaped its socio-cultural history. These changes were manifested in shifting fashion trends and clothing styles. Fashion became a form of symbolic language, or a code that assisted in the comprehension and explication of the entire colonial period. Besides this, clothing styles became an instrument for examining the mannerisms and daily habits of social groups in that era. An indicative but extremely significant illustration of this phenomenon is the lifestyle of the Creoles of Sierra Leone, the Saros of Lagos, and the Gold Coast elite in the nineteenth century; and the Asante elite in the twentieth century. Elite groups, as distinct and self-conscious social entities, set trends in various aspects of everyday life and in particular modes of dressing, and their trendsetting was not limited to a particular gender or generation. The elite group was composed of affluent individuals who had acquired their wealth through commerce or were prominent members of the teacher/clerk group that has been described as "professional culture bearers." As an entity, the colonial elite set trends in fashionable behavior. Therefore, emulating them enhanced one's prestige. Thus, other people in society attempted to mold their lifestyles after trends set by these groups.

The agencies through which social change was transmitted included Christianity, Western education, European colonial rule, industrialization, and increased inclusion in the global economy. Individuals who either converted to Christianity or were educated felt the need to set themselves apart. Such groups included the Assimilés in francophone Africa and the Evolués in Portuguese Africa.

This period was characterized by the transformation of subsistence economies into ones in which cash transactions increased. By the beginning of the twentieth century, indigenous Africans in most parts of the continent had reasonable access to cash as a result of the expansion of the cash economy. Cash in most African societies was not uniformly distributed. The more affluent members of colonial elite society were therefore in a better cash position, and sometimes even felt the need to demonstrate their affluence by subscribing to a lifestyle that visibly set them apart from others of their own group. A typical example was the Kumase *akonkofuo* (merchants) in the Gold Coast. The elite there cherished their right to participate in wealth accumulation within the cash economy. They endeavored to accumulate and to store wealth in forms that could be publicly displayed to emphasize affluence.

Clothing was an aspect of popular culture that revealed different areas of the cultural conflict between tradition and modernity in Africa. From the earliest period European clothes were presented as gifts to traditional rulers. Such presents included laced hats, shirts, coats, walking sticks, and ties. They were almost exclusively for important individuals, and their possession therefore helped to reinforce their unique status within society. These exotic presents were accepted and worn out of a sense of decorum, and a desire to preserve good diplomatic relations.

There were mass conversions to Christianity during the colonial period. This was part of an attempt to be accepted as part of the new regime. The Christian missions were also prominent in the provision of formal education. Through the schools and the churches, Africans were encouraged to adopt European culture. Although Africans sometimes reacted against European discrimination and racism by forming syncretist movements, they still maintained perceived trappings of (European) "civilization." Among these was clothing. Thus, though the Kimbaguists in the Congo and members of the Watchtower movement in Nyasaland rejected orthodox Christianity, they continued to wear European clothes. A reconstruction of the changes in clothing styles that were caused by shifts and deep-seated influences in fashion over the period therefore reveals conceptions of social mobility. Thus, these developments can be discussed as historical phenomena. European clothes became a mark of distinction among certain social strata such as the educated and Christianized groups. The kinds of clothes that the colonial elite wore inform us about culture and hegemony, as well as their influence. They were linked to the "superior" European culture.

In the colonial period, there was also a great desire for imported European goods that stemmed from the fact that they were still a novelty, but one to which access was now beginning to broaden for the very first time to incorporate a general public. New practices such as the use of mail order eliminated the role of the middleman. This made it more attractive and enabled individuals to order up items that suited their own particular desires and tastes. Thus, it satisfied individualism and augmented the desires of the fashion conscious.

The basic disruptions that occurred in colonial African society increased the scope for individual acquisition of wealth. Consequently, the changes contributed to the emergence of new elite groupings. However, since incomes were not evenly distributed it became necessary to establish the relative marks and indicators of a superior status. Thus, individuals who had acquired substantial independent incomes and those who had new Western education sought to set themselves apart by simulating a lifestyle that was reminiscent of the perceived behavior of great men. Increasingly, it became fashionable to adopt and to adapt new trends in clothing. These changes were relentlessly enhanced by external stimuli, such as mail order from overseas that made available endlessly new sources and types of commodities.

WILHELMINA JOSELINE DONKOH

See also: **Colonial Imports versus Indigenous Crafts; Colonialism: Impact on African Societies.**

Further Reading

Agbodeka, F. *Ghana in the Twentieth Century.* Accra: Ghana Universities Press, 1972.

Arhin, K. "Rank and Class among the Asante and Fante in the Nineteenth Century." *Africa* 53, no. 1 (1983): 1–22.

Barber, K., and P. F. de Moraes Farias (eds.). *Self-Assertion and Brokerage: Early Colonial Nationalism in West Africa.* Birmingham: Centre of West African Studies, University of Birmingham, 1990.

Daniel, E. *Ghanaians: A Sovereign People in Profile.* Accra: Asempa, 1993.

Donkoh, W. J. "Colonialism and Cultural Change: Some Aspects of the Impact of Modernity upon Asante." Ph.D. diss., University of Birmingham, 1994.

Etienne, M. "Women and Men, Cloth and Cultivation: Transformation of Production-Distribution Relations among the Baule." *Cahiers d'Etudes Africaines*, no. 17 (1977). Reprinted in *Women and Colonization: Anthropological Perspectives*, edited by M. Etienne and E. Leacock. New York: J. F. Bergen/Praeger, 1980.

Freund, B. *The Making of Contemporary Africa: The Development of African Society since 1800* (1984). Reprint, London: Macmillan, 1987.

Guyer, J. (ed.). *Money Matters: Instability, Values and Social Payments in the Modern History of West African Communities.* London: James Currey, 1995.

Jeffries, R. *Class, Power and Ideology in Ghana: The Railway Men of Sekondi.* Cambridge: Cambridge University Press, 1978.

Konig, R. *The Restless Image: A Sociology of Fashion.* London: Allen and Unwin, 1973.

McCaskie, T. C. "A Pictorial Resource for Asante History: A Preliminary Description." *Asantesem: Asante Biographical Project Bulletin*, no. 8 (1978): 41–43.

Roach, M. E., and J. B. Eicher. *Dress, Adornment and the Social Order.* New York: John Wiley and Sons, 1965.

Cold War, Africa and the

In Africa, the Cold War served above all to impede the socioeconomic development of African states and peoples from the hour of independence through the end of the 1980s. The United States and the Soviet Union competed with one another on the continent by providing aid and ideological reinforcement to favored clients or insurgent groups. In so doing they increased the scale of fighting in many conflicts whose roots were essentially indigenous. African leaders of ethno-regional constituencies often found that the adoption of a particular ideological label brought increases in military aid from the corresponding superpower. The main positive ramification of the Cold War for African peoples was that the two superpowers also sometimes competed in the provision of economic aid. Since the end of the Cold War, Soviet/Russian aid has largely evaporated, while aid from the United States has declined.

Surprisingly, neither superpower benefited substantially from the Cold War competition in Africa. The most important perceived measure of success in the competition was the establishment and maintenance of "client regimes," yet such regimes did not act reliably in the interest of their superpower patrons. Moreover, neither those regimes identifying themselves as market capitalists nor those considering themselves Marxist-Leninist in orientation were able to devise practical development programs based on their putative ideologies. Meanwhile, many moderate African leaders were alienated from both superpowers by the patterns of intervention and counterintervention that characterized the competition. As a result most chose to be formally nonaligned, even if they received aid from one superpower or the other. In economic terms, most superpower investment on the continent yielded meager financial returns. Several Marxist-Leninist states, notably Angola, continued to carry on a mutually beneficial trade with the West, to the chagrin of the Soviets. The maintenance of client regimes in power often required substantial subsidies to keep them financially afloat while they proved to be ideological failures and political embarrassments. This was the case in the United States–Congo/Zaïre relationship, for instance. Thus, the only benefit of client regimes was often to deny a "strategic space" to the competing superpower.

The rise of the superpower competition in Africa coincided with the rise of nationalist movements for independence across the continent. Until the moment of independence, the United States mostly deferred to its European (colonial) allies on questions of African politics and development and remained largely absent from the continent. Meanwhile, in the Soviet Union, Stalin took a dim view of the potential contribution that "bourgeois nationalists" might make to the global socialist struggle, and demurred from meaningful support for African nationalist movements. After Joseph Stalin's death in 1953 and Nikita Khrushchev's consolidation of power in the Soviet Union over the ensuing years, however, Soviet policy began to change. Khrushchev reinterpreted Marxist-Leninist ideology in a way that allowed for vigorous Soviet support for nationalist, "anti-imperialist" movements in the developing world.

The Soviets were soon providing both rhetorical and material support to African nationalists like Algeria's Ben Bella and Egypt's Gamal Abdel Nasser. Soviet political support was especially important in 1956, when Nasser nationalized the Suez Canal and was subsequently attacked by Britain, France, and Israel. Despite a lack of deep ideological affinity, the anti-imperialist rhetoric and intentions of African nationalist and Soviet leaders resonated closely during this period. The intensely bitter war against France for national liberation in Algeria further estranged African nationalists from the West.

The United States lost a position of primacy in Africa to the Soviets in this period through its ambivalent attitude toward national liberation movements and its constant fretting about the communist ties of African nationalists. The United States rarely put any pressure on its European allies to hasten the pace of decolonization in Africa, while it generally gave tacit support to the apartheid regime in South Africa. The U.S. Central Intelligence Agency (CIA) even cooperated with South African security in monitoring and undermining the activities of the African National Congress.

The Cold War competition in Africa escalated dramatically with the onset of the Congo (Kinshasa) crisis in July 1960. While both superpowers supported the United Nations peacekeeping mission to Congo, each had a different interpretation of the UN's mandate. Accordingly, each put pressure on UN secretary general Dag Hammarskjold to carry out the mission in keeping with its own preferred vision. The United States saw it as a neutral effort, designed to keep peace among warring factions; the Soviets saw it a mission to support the elected government of Patrice Lumumba in the face of foreign intervention and internal secession (of the Katanga province). When the United States prevailed in this competition, the Soviets ceased cooperation with the UN effort and called for Hammarskjold's dismissal. Meanwhile, each superpower engaged in its own unilateral, clandestine interventions, which sought to promote local favorites. Ultimately the United States was the more determined intervenor. Congo's radical, charismatic prime minister Lumumba was murdered in January 1961 with the encouragement and support of the CIA. Likewise, American operatives encouraged Joseph D. Mobutu to seize power on two occasions, in 1960, and later, permanently, in November 1965.

Beginning in the late 1950s, the superpower competition was complicated by the advent of an independent and vigorous Chinese policy on the continent. China provided some modest economic assistance and somewhat successfully presented itself as the natural leader of nonindustrialized, revolutionary regimes in Africa. China's impressive aid to Tanzania and Zambia in the construction of the TanZam Railway in the late 1960s pleased many nonaligned African leaders and indirectly challenged both superpowers. While Chinese rhetoric in Africa was initially more anti-Western, it became more balanced in its condemnation of both superpowers after the early 1970s.

In the period between 1975 and 1980 the Soviet Union was the more determined intervenor in African conflicts, as evidenced by the Angola and Ethiopia cases. In the Angolan case, three local parties were contesting control of the country at its independence in 1975. A struggle for power among them that had started several years earlier had begun to escalate, with each superpower providing clandestine aid to its preferred local client. African opinion on the legitimacy of the various parties was sharply divided until South Africa launched an invasion of the country in October 1975. This quickly swayed African opinion in favor of the Marxist MPLA party, which then controlled Luanda. Politically, it also allowed the Soviet Union to launch a major, overt military intervention in support of the MPLA, partly at the initiative of its Cuban ally. The Soviet-Cuban intervention soon resolved the conflict in the MPLA's favor, though it also marked the beginning of a 25-year civil war in Angola. In the Ethiopia-Somalia war of 1977, the Soviets had international law as well as African opinion on their side when they intervened on behalf of Ethiopian president Mengistu Haile Mariam. While the Soviets lost favor in Somalia as a result of their dispatch of Cuban troops to Ethiopia, they gained a more populous, regionally important ally.

The Cold War began to wind down in Africa in the late 1980s, and its decline is marked particularly by the promulgation of the Angola-Namibia Peace Accords in December 1989. These accords, negotiated with the full participation of the superpowers, led to a phased withdrawal of Cuban troops from Angola, and independence (from South Africa) for Namibia in 1990. These accords also facilitated an end to the apartheid regime in South Africa, given that anticommunism had been a legitimating tool of the National Party of South Africa among the white community. Several other regimes in Africa whose existence depended heavily on superpower support, including those in Liberia, Ethiopia, and Somalia, also collapsed within two years of the Angola-Namibia Peace Accords.

JOHN F. CLARK

See also: **Socialism in Postcolonial Africa; Soviet Union and Africa.**

Further Reading

Laïdi, Z. *The Superpowers and Africa: The Constraints of a Rivalry, 1960–1990,* translated by Patricia Boudoin. Chicago: University of Chicago Press, 1990.

Ogunsanwo, A. *China's Policy in Africa, 1958–71.* Cambridge: Cambridge University Press, 1974.

Ottaway, M. *Soviet and American Influence in the Horn of Africa.* New York: Praeger, 1982.

Porter, B. D. *The USSR in Third World Conflicts: Soviet Arms and Diplomacy in Local Wars, 1945–1980.* Cambridge: Cambridge University Press, 1984.

Schraeder, P. J. *United States Foreign Policy toward Africa: Incrementalism, Crisis and Change.* Cambridge: Cambridge University Press, 1994.

Collaboration as Resistance

Even though very limited areas of Africa were under European domination by 1880, during the period of the "new imperialism" that followed, virtually the whole continent came under European domination. However, African reactions and responses to European imperialist conquest and occupation were not indifferent or passive. Various leaders resorted to different devices and measures designed to maintain their independence. Different types of motivation and calculations went into assessing the interests and probable consequences of collaboration, resistance, or compromise. Whereas some African chiefs vehemently opposed the change in their political fortunes, others chose to ally with the Europeans in the hope that they would maintain their sovereignty rather than lose it through war. In fact, almost all states, and most of the rulers recognized as resisters (such as Samori Touré in Guinea and Menelik II in Ethiopia), attempted in some way to come to terms with the European powers, and even manipulate them when possible, so that they would not have to fight against them. The African leaders who resorted to this type of delaying action have been referred to as collaborators. But more often than not, they were the same people at the center of all policies, both those centered on resistance and those focused on collaboration.

Collaboration was a means by which African leaders responded to imperialism using an active policy of cooperation and compromise rather than submission. Collaboration, in this case, was a method of resistance. It was adopted by those African rulers who felt that the best way to recover territory lost to enemies or rivals was to cooperate with the Europeans. Thus, collaboration and resistance are different sides of the same coin. The focal point in either case was how best to deal with European invasion of the African continent. Short-term advantages from treaties or collaboration with Europeans included access to firearms, consumer goods, and opportunities to enlist powerful allies in internal and external conflicts. Any distinction between collaborators and resisters is, therefore, mechanistic.

Faced with the option of surrendering, retaining, or regaining sovereignty and independence or going to war, many African rulers opted to defend their sovereignty; but they differed in their tactics. Touré of the Mandinka empire and Kabarega of Bunyoro adopted the strategy of both diplomacy and military means. Touré, aptly called the "Napoleon of the Sudan," resisted the French conquest of the Western Sudan with remarkable tenacity between 1891 and 1898. Yet, in the initial phase of European contact, Touré was ready to negotiate bases for genuine cooperation with the European powers (France and Britain) on condition that they recognized his sovereignty and independence. On the other hand, the French seemingly accepted Touré's overtures while they built up their military force in the Niger Valley and invaded Boure in early 1885. When Touré realized the extent of French hostility, he contacted the British in Freetown and tried to secure their support to ward off the French. The British response to Touré's overtures was cool. The latter's diplomacy was doomed to failure by the incompatibility in objectives and the hostility of the French.

In much the same way, Wobogo, the Mogho *naba,* first received Captain Binger cordially to the Mossi Kingdom. Over time, however, his cordiality and cooperation were replaced by cautious awareness and suspicions of French activities as a threat to his independence. In 1891, Wobogo refused to receive P. L. Monteil at all, and in 1894 signed a treaty of friendship with George Ekem Ferguson for British protection. But the remoteness of British troops reduced the practical value of the treaty. In July 1895, when French lieutenant Voulet set out to occupy Ouagadougou, Wobogo raised an army of horsemen in defense of his state.

Like Touré and Wobogo, the *damel* of Cayor in modern Senegal accepted the French. Later, when General Louis Faidherbe tried to replace him, the damel resisted forcefully. He outlived Faidherbe and cooperated with succeeding French governors, but the construction of a railway through his territory convinced him that the French were out to take his land, and he died in war against them in 1886.

Similarly, the Dahomean government of Porto Novo collaborated with the French to combat the expansion of British Lagos. In the end, French merchants secured a duty-free entry for their trade. The checkered course of French fortunes in Porto Nov was a direct result of the activities of the Dahomean government.

Thus, rather than see examples of African resistance as gallant anachronisms and collaborators as farsighted rulers who sought to ensure the survival of their kingdoms and regimes, scholars have increasingly come to see resistance and collaboration as two sides of the same coin. African reaction and responses to European invasion in the nineteenth century were conditioned by a multitude of ethnocultural, political, and economic factors. The introduction of European norms and power was resisted everywhere. In the end, different groups were concerned with how best to maintain their sovereignty and independence. Collaboration became the means by which some African leaders preserved this independence and even where some signed away their territories, others were remarkably successful in harnessing European support for their aims, namely, maintenance of independence, retention of power in their dominions, and elimination of rivals.

EDMUND ABAKA

See also: **Ethiopia: Menelik II, Era of; Senegal: Faidherbe, Louis and Expansion of French Senegal, 1854–1865; Touré, Samori (c.1830–1900) and His Empire.**

Further Reading

Boahen, A. A. *General History of Africa*, vol. 7, *Africa - under Colonial Domination 1880–1935*. Paris: UNESCO, 1985.

Collins, R. O. Burns, James McDonald. Ching, Erik Kristofer (eds.). *Historical Problems of Imperial Africa*. Princeton, N.J.: Markus Wiener, 1996.

Hargreaves, J. D. "West African States and the European Conquest." In *Colonialism in Africa 1870–1914*, vol. 1, edited by L. H. Gann and Peter Duignan. Cambridge: Cambridge University Press, 1969.

Isaacman, A., and B. Isaacman. "Resistance and Collaboration in Southern and Central Africa, c. 1850–1920." *International Journal of African Historical Studies* 10, no. 1 (1977): pp.31–62.

Owen, R., and B. Sutcliffe (eds.). *Studies in the Theory of Imperialism*. London: 1975. See especially pp.117–142.

Ranger, T. O. "African Reactions to the Imposition of Colonial Rule in East and Central Africa." In *Colonialism in Africa 1870–1914*, vol. 1, edited by L. H. Gann and Peter Duignan. Cambridge: Cambridge University Press, 1969.

Colonial Administrations, Africans in

According to Max Weber, the great sociologist and theoretician of modernity, the modern state can be compared with a factory. It is he who insisted that "the real power, the power which has an impact on daily life, inevitably is in the hands of the bureaucracy." The importance of those Africans—the overall majority of them male—who staffed the colonial bureaucracy primarily hails from the fact that they inherited power at the end of colonial rule. Many of the first generation of independent Africa's political elite had previously worked—at least for a certain period—for the colonial administration. In Tanzania, for instance, nearly all African members of Julius Nyerere's first cabinet were former members of the colonial administrative staff. But in colonial times they played a pivotal role, because the colonial state was first of all an administrative state, with markedly despotic features. Hence it was the administrators who to a large extent made up the state. Or at least they were perceived as the true representatives of state power. This has not changed very much with independence. Now, as then, the state in Africa is in many places synonymous with the government, and the government is synonymous with government services—that is, the administration.

Sure enough, in colonial times the government was by definition European, as were the higher ranks of the administration. But due to their very weak number—"the thin white line" (Kirk-Greene 1980)—from early on the Europeans had to rely on a number of local people in order to administer their African territories. Most of these locals were employed in auxiliary services; a few of them, however, were put in charge of local affairs in faraway places. Some, such as the ubiquitous government interpreters working with the European district officers, were even at the very center of things. Although they had no position of official authority, they had great influence simply due to their language skills.

All colonial powers were faced with a dilemma which centered on how to create an effective administrative structure with inadequate local revenues. Local administrations were run through those Africans that were perceived by the Europeans as "traditional rulers" or "natural rulers," which they called "chiefs" or sometimes "kings" or "princes." This solution was essentially a pragmatic one; it was not perceived as optimally efficient, but it was felt to be the best system that the limited resources allowed. In colonial Africa, *chiefs* stands for a bewildering variety of rulers, some very powerful; others with extremely limited access to material, coercive, and other resources; some more or less "invented" by the European administrators. Colonial government often used chiefs as a shield to be held between their unpopular measures and popular critique. In any case, for the vast majority of Africans throughout the colonial period, their most immediate contact with government was to be at the hands of these "traditional authorities."

In the early twentieth century, at least, many chiefs were preliterate. Other Africans had to have a Western-style education in order to obtain even low positions in the colonial administration. Colonial governments might try to limit the content of that education—as the Belgian Congo did, emphasizing literacy and vocational training under missionary management but until the mid-1950s systematically curbing any form of postsecondary schooling for Africans (apart from seminary training for the clergy). But such limitations rarely worked. In between the two world wars, educated Africans, or *évolués*, many of them former pupils of mission schools and now working for the colonial government, started to organize themselves into political parties, trade unions, and other voluntary associations. After World War II the new development ideology of Britain and France allocated to the "clerk class" a more important role in administration and politics. However, the local administrative power of chiefs only rarely was cut back. Moreover, access to higher administrative posts was given to Africans only at the very end of the colonial period. In Kenya as late as 1960 there were only five Africans holding senior posts; in Malawi, the first four Africans were not appointed to the Administrative Service until 1959; their number increased to 40 by 1964, the year of independence. The situation was slightly better in Ghana, where African numbers in the administration rose from 550 in 1952 to 1,950 in 1958, the year after independence.

Even a cursory look at contemporary source materials shows that the European colonizers found it hard to come to terms intellectually with their African administrative staff. In general, they depicted the Africans in very derogatory terms, which boiled down to the stereotype that almost all Africans were at best half-educated and corrupt to the bone, and at worst arrogant cheats and indolent idlers. What little admiration and respect there was was reserved for chiefs and peasants, not the "African bureaucrats" (Feierman 1990): the further they were removed from colonial culture, the better they were perceived. These stereotypes are undoubtedly mainly due to the very hybrid position of African government clerks as pupils, collaborators, and competitors of the Europeans. However, little is known about the ways in which the Africans who worked for the colonial government machinery managed their lives, and there is scant information about their professional

ethos, concepts of authority and power, behavior in public, and treatment of their fellow citizens.

Africans in colonial administrations formed a rather heterogeneous group with many different goals and conflicting interests. One could think of the conflict between bureaucratic ideals, with its stress on achievement, division of labor, and impersonality on the one hand, and the loyalty to local political culture on the other—not to mention the influence of chiefly politics with their stress on accumulation, generosity, and personal loyalty. But for all of their differences, the African bureaucrats had one thing in common: their position in the middle, between the local and the global, between the old and the new. As a consequence, one of their main tasks was to mediate between different worlds, to act as cultural brokers. No doubt, this intermediate position was cause of many new conflicts, but it also resulted in a peculiar understanding of power and authority developed from a mix of local cultural repertoires and quite specific forms of social interaction, neither traditional nor modern.

ANDREAS ECKERT

See also: **Colonial European Administrations: Comparative Survey; Colonialism: Ideology of Empire: Supremacist, Paternalist; Colonialism: Impact on African Societies.**

Further Reading

Baker, C. A. "Africanization of the Administrative Service." In *The Transfer of Power: The Colonial Administration in the Age of Decolonisation*, edited by Anthony Kirk-Greene. Oxford: Inter-Faculty Committee for African Studies, Oxford University, 1979.

Feierman, S. *Peasant Intellectuals: History and Anthropology in Tanzania*. Madison: University of Wisconsin Press, 1990.

Kirk-Greene, A. "The Thin White Line: The Size of the Colonial Service in Africa." *African Affairs* 79, no. 314 (1980): 25–44.

Mang'enya, E. A. M. *Discipline and Tears: Reminiscences of an African Civil Servant on Colonial Tanganyika*. Dar es Salaam: Dar es Salaam University Press, 1984.

Rathbone, R. *Nkrumah and the Chiefs: The Politics of Chieftaincy in Ghana 1951–60*. Oxford: James Currey, 2000.

Colonial European Administrations: Comparative Survey

In spite of their rivalry, a collective cultural arrogance shared by Great Britain, France, Germany, Belgium, and Portugal asserted itself at the time of the colonial conquest. At the Berlin Africa Conference of 1884–1885, and later at the Brussels Conference of 1889–1890, the European powers set out rules for colonization, agreeing on the duties necessary to bring order to an African continent considered disorderly. However, the colonial powers lacked clear concepts of how to administer and exploit their African territories. Thus, colonial rule was marked by a great variety of administrative expedients, which in turn reflected the highly different situations on the ground, as well as changes over time.

None of the European powers had at their disposal all-conquering forces of superior strength when they established colonial rule in Africa. In the beginning, the colonizers usually concealed their numerical inferiority by pursuing a policy of selective terror. The practice of massacre seemed to be the best means for the colonizer to achieve maximum intimidation with minimum use of resources, most notoriously in King Leopold's Congo and Portuguese Angola.

It was only during the post-conquest period that the power of the colonizers could be strengthened into colonial domination. For this to be possible, power needed to be firmly secured; this was provided by establishing district officers or *commandants de cercle*, civil servants who operated at the local level. They were in charge of all aspects of district administration, from judicial appeals to tax collection, road construction to education, usually with a few assistants, plus specialized personnel for engineering, medicine, agriculture, or education. With the help of such people, the colonial state built itself up. Colonial rule was thereby bureaucratic rule, though it admittedly always had the despotic instrument of violent repression at its disposal. Its bureaucratic character ripened during a third period of rule, when the colonial state gained growing control over knowledge. A continuously raised bureaucratic tax became a central feature. Educational institutions, literacy, and statistics were introduced, and the capabilities of the colonial headquarters were strengthened by technical innovations such as the telegraph.

However, the bureaucratic colonial state always remained "incomplete," its power limited. In any case, it did not produce the social or economic forms it sought. The everyday life of colonial rule, characterized by violence, indicates the organizational impotence of the administration. Moreover, colonial rule never was true territorial rule. Its laws and decrees often were no more than unrealized academic plans and hopes. The routinization of colonial power and the establishment of a colonial administrative structure very soon demanded alliances and collaboration with local figures—first with persons who were perceived as "traditional" or "natural rulers," and later, though often hesitatingly, with educated "commoners." Although it was above all the British administrative philosophy of indirect rule that explicitly implied the incorporation of chiefs into the bureaucratic state apparatus, the French system of more direct rule, too, in its daily administrative routine, heavily relied on local African collaborators. Whether in this context the difference stressed by some historians between ruling *through* chiefs

(British) and ruling *over* chiefs (French) was always relevant to the colonial practice seems doubtful. All other colonial powers relied on Africans (mostly on "traditional authorities") as well in order to administer their territories. At the high noon of colonial rule in Africa between the wars, there were astonishingly few European administrators for the extent of territory they governed. The whole of French Equatorial Africa in the mid-1930s was run by only 206 administrative officers, assisted by 400 specialists and technical officers. In the same period the whole of British Africa (except Egypt, the Sudan, and southern Africa) was governed by around 1,000 general administrative officers, plus another 4,000 or 5,000 European specialists, while the Belgians ruled the Congo in 1936 with 728 officers. In Rwanda and Burundi, they ruled with an administrative staff of less than 50 Europeans. Within British Africa, the ratio of colonial administrators to local population considerably differed, running in the 1930s from 1:19,000 in Kenya to 1:54,000 in Nigeria. In any event, most day-to-day governing had to be done by African intermediaries. In the administrative sphere, Africans always had a critical role in shaping encounters between Europe and Africa.

Colonial government was remarkably uniform, regardless of the European power in charge. The key administrative unit of a colony was a district. Above this level, the larger colonies had an intermediary level of provinces, grouping several districts. At the center sat the governor, assisted by his staff and usually sharing power with some form of administrative or legislative council. These councils might consist only of the heads of government departments, sitting as a kind of advisory cabinet, but they often included important nonofficial interests such as a few "traditional rulers," the chambers of commerce or agriculture, or key trading firms. Sometimes European missionaries represented African interests. British governors enjoyed considerable freedom of action in their territories, while their French counterparts more often had to obey an order from Paris. The British regarded each colonial territory in Africa as an autonomous administrative unit. Projects of a close cooperation among neighboring colonies (the East African Closer Union; the Central African Federation) in the end never went beyond initial stages. In contrast, France united several colonies in Federations (French West Africa, or FWA; French Equatorial Africa, or FEA) and by this created long-term structures. The French insisted firmly on the spreading of the French language, while in British territories some local languages (Ewe, Haussa, Swahili) played an important role in the administrative realm. Still, the famous distinction between British indirect rule and French association was less significant than the political realities on the ground. These realities were characterized frequently by newly defined struggles between colonizers and colonized as well as within these groups. The parameters of these struggles in turn depended upon the conditions of the respective colony: the existence of mineral resources, the condition of the soil, the climate, the density and structure of the population, local political cultures, and forms of division of labor. Administrative models could never be applied consistently for one colony, let alone for all African territories of one European power.

Never before was Africa so important for the European colonial powers than in the 15 years after World War II. In a strictly economic sense this is especially true for Africa's oldest colonial power, Portugal. But it was mainly France and Britain that launched a "development colonialism" characterized by considerable public investments that were supposed to grant the centers direct economic benefits and Africans the "maturity" necessary for future independence. Throughout British Africa, there was a great intensification of government activity; in contrast to earlier years, and to the recent war period when territories were drained of staff, this access of official energy amounted to a "second colonial occupation."

Africans were drawn into more direct contact with agents of the colonial state than ever before. Young British graduates and ex-servicemen were recruited by the hundreds, with every expectation of a lifetime career in colonial administration, and instructed in the new doctrines of good government in a series of university summer schools. Specialists were recruited to implement new policies for agricultural production and marketing, to provide new social and medical services, to work in fisheries or education.

However, the overall success of these projects was fairly limited due to financial restraints but also to British ignorance and paternalism. Moreover, the "Africanization" of public services, though an important part of the new development rhetoric, proceeded only sluggishly, especially concerning higher ranks. Numerous local government reforms suffered from permanent experiments. The growing number of educated Africans was integrated into local politics only hesitatingly. The French territories experienced a great political restructuring. Africans gained rights to electoral politics, trade-union organization, and steps toward citizenship. Administrative expansion paralleled the growth of electoral politics. The governments general in Dakar (FWA) and Brazzaville (FEA), spurred on by the new politics of development and social responsibility, sought to expand port facilities, schools, and hospitals. They were encouraged further by the demands of elected officials and their constituents, and they were funded in part by money raised through FIDES. By the mid-1950s, however, France

and Britain recognized Africa's irrelevance to the reinvigorated European and global economies: the possibility of negotiating a disengagement and a positive postcolonial relationship with African elites began to seem more attractive than continuing colonial rule, which carried immense political risks and socioeconomic uncertainties.

ANDREAS ECKERT

Further Reading

Berman, B. *Control and Crisis in Colonial Kenya: The Dialectics of Domination.* London: James Currey, 1990.

Clarence-Smith, W. G. *The Third Portuguese Empire 1825–1975: A Study in Economic Imperialism.* Manchester: Manchester University Press, 1985.

Cooper, F. *Decolonization and African Society: The Labor Question in British and French Africa.* Cambridge: Cambridge University Press, 1996.

Cooper, F., and A. L. Stoler (eds.). *Tensions of Empire: Colonial Cultures in a Bourgeois World.* Berkeley and Los Angeles: University of California Press, 1997.

Curtin, P., et al. *African History: From Earliest Times to Independence,* 2nd ed. London: Longman, 1995.

Hargreaves, J. D. *Decolonization in Africa,* 2nd ed. London: Longman, 1996.

Kirk-Greene, A. *Britain's Imperial Administrators 1858–1966.* New York: St. Martin's Press, 2000.

Osterhammel, J. *Colonialism.* Princeton, N.J.: Marcus Wiener, 1997.

Phillips, A. *The Enigma of Colonialism: British Policy in West Africa.* London: James Currey, 1989.

Smith, W. D. *The German Colonial Empire.* Chapel Hill: University of North Carolina Press, 1978.

Spittler, G. *Verwaltung in einem afrikanischen Bauernstaat. Das koloniale Französisch-Westafrika 1919–1939.* Wiesbaden: Franz Steiner, 1981.

Colonial Federations: British Central Africa

A federation is defined as a union of states that delegate certain powers to the central government and retain others for local administration. Generally, federations are formed to make common goals achievable. Federations are generally established for sociopolitical and economic expediency.

The British East African Federation exemplifies the concept. Kenya, seen as the would-be site of the central government, would harness the economic potentials of the other two sister countries of the federation, Uganda and Tanganyika (now Tanzania) for the benefit of all in the region.

The British Central African Federation of 1953–1963 was formed along similar lines. It was initiated by the settlers of Southern Rhodesia (now Zimbabwe), a territory that was named after, and administered on behalf of, the British government by the diamond magnate and imperialist Cecil John Rhodes. He ruled it through a chartered company granted by the British government called the British South Africa Company.

Following the death of Rhodes in 1902, the end of company rule, and the attainment by the settlers of responsible government in 1923, the settlers agitated for some kind of amalgamation with the territories of Northern Rhodesia (now Zambia) and Nyasaland (now Malawi). The two were British protectorates (as opposed to British colonies like Southern Rhodesia and Kenya). For such an amalgamation of a protectorate and a colony to come to fruition, it was understood by British government officials that it had to have the support of the African inhabitants.

In 1929, the British government set up the Hilton-Young Commission ostensibly to conduct feasibility studies on the proposed Federation of Central Africa; the results affirmed the possibility of such a venture, but with an emphatic proviso that African interests had to be taken into account. Sir Godfrey Huggins, prime minister of Southern Rhodesia from 1933 to 1953, pursued the federation scheme vigorously. Following the 1935 Victoria Falls conference between Southern and Northern Rhodesia, another commission was requested to look at the possibility of a federation. The 1939 British Bledisloe Commission accepted the federation in principle, but deferred taking any action on the matter until after the end of the war.

Many reasons were advanced for the formation of the federation. Closer political ties of the federated territories would help in the development of their respective resources; individual territories were thought to be too vulnerable because their economies were not balanced. Copper deposits in Northern Rhodesia, agricultural products and labor from Nyasaland, and the budding industrial and agricultural sectors of Southern Rhodesia could all be harnessed to make a sound Central African economy; railways could be built, rivers dammed, power developed to supply the growing industry, and farming improved to feed the ever-growing population. The federation was also supposed to attract foreign investments that would contribute to a stronger economy, and the standard of living would be raised as the federation generated more employment opportunities. More subtly, the federation was intended to halt the onslaught of the rise of African nationalism emanating from the Gold Coast (Ghana), which sought self-government and eventual independence. The settlers feared that African nationalism would end their colonial program.

The federation came into existence in 1953 with the support of almost two-thirds of the settler electorate in all three territories. Its government was headquartered in Salisbury, then the capital of Southern Rhodesia. The federal constitution was designed in such a way that the settlers dominated the electoral roll, quite contrary to notions of multiracialism and equality, the premises upon which the federation was ostensibly built. Africans were initially only allowed paltry representation in the federal parliament by two members from each federated territory. In the subsequent years of the federation, the settlers increased African representation to 15 seats out of a total of 65, in a bid to appease mounting African discontent.

The key concept of the federation, pursued by the successive federation prime ministers Garfield Todd, Sir Roy Welensky, and Sir Edgar Whitehead, was *partnership*. It was a subtle term designed to convince the British government and the Africans that the federation was color-blind, and that the Africans and the settlers were partners in championing the region's future.

The vagueness of the term *partnership*, and continued race-based policies, sparked African opposition that eventually led to the federation's demise. The federation was increasingly seen as a settler ploy intended to dominate all aspects of African life. The franchise was restrictive, allowing only a selected number of Africans to vote. The salaries and working conditions of the Africans were not comparable to those of settlers. Land continued to be owned by Europeans and racial discrimination was rife.

Nationalists then opposed the federation. They formed political movements, designed to achieve self-determination for the Africans. The northern territories of Northern Rhodesia and Nyasaland, in particular, wanted secession from the federation. They argued that they were protectorates and not colonies like Southern Rhodesia. The British prime minister Harold Macmillan's 1960 speech on the "winds of change blowing across the continent of Africa" strengthened African opposition to the federation. Ghana had become independent in 1957, and other countries of Africa were about to follow suit, territories of the federation included.

Southern Rhodesia had a larger settler community and was not prepared to change the constitution of the federation; therefore it opted to secede from the federation and perpetuate settler domination. With the independence of Northern Rhodesia and Nyasaland looming, the federation was headed for a demise. Southern Rhodesia, however, was adamant that it was not going to follow the example of its northern neighbors. Instead, it was intent on negotiating with and if need be wrenching power from Britain in a determined effort to secure independence for the minority settlers. In 1963, after ten years of existence, the federation collapsed as Northern Rhodesia and Nyasaland were just about to become independent, while Southern Rhodesia agitated for a unilateral declaration of independence, which came into being in 1965.

P. T. MGADLA

259

Further Reading

Cliffe, L. *Zimbabwe: Politics, Economics and Society.* London: Pinter, 1989.

Hancock, I. *White Liberals, Moderates and Radicals in Rhodesia 1953–1980.* London: Groot Helm/New York: St. Martin's Press, 1984.

Mlambo, E. *Rhodesia: The Struggle for a Birthright.* London: C. Hurst, 1972.

O'Meara, P. *Rhodesia: Racial Conflict or Co-existence.* Ithaca, N.Y.: Cornell University Press, 1975.

Windrich, E. *The Rhodesian Problem: A Documentary Record, 1923–1973.* London: Routledge and Kegan Paul, 1975.

Colonial Federations: French Equatorial Africa

French Equatorial Africa (FEA) was a vast region of central Africa ranging from tropical rain forest to arid desert. Its constituent parts became the modern states of the Central African Republic, Chad, the People's Republic of the Congo, and Gabon. Although one of the largest territories of colonial Africa, it was very sparsely populated (an estimated 3.2 million people in 1930) and had one of the least developed infrastructures of the colonial era.

French interest began with coastal trade to Gabon and the establishment of a settlement for freed slaves at Libreville in 1849. The explorer and adventurer Pierre Savorgnan de Brazza was the first European to penetrate the dense interior in the 1870s and 1880s and explore the tributaries of the Congo River. The establishment of the Congo Free State by King Leopold of Belgium and concurrent French expansion south from Algeria and east from Senegal created a strong interest among French imperialists in an empire converging on the remote Lake Chad. The Comité de l'Afrique Française was founded in 1890 to encourage public interest in Africa and the support of new missions. By 1900 the French claimed all of the territory between the Congo Free State frontier on the Ubangi and the central Sahara. Resistance was considerable, especially from the kingdom of Wadai and the sultanate of Dar Kuti, but these were reduced by 1911.

The administrative structure of FEA was patterned on the recently established French West Africa, with a division into four territories (Gabon, Moyen-Congo, Oubangui-Chari, and Tchad) governed as a federation from Brazzaville, on the Congo River. African sovereignty was legally suspended in a series of decrees in 1899, which annulled all existing treaties and vested sovereignty in the French state. However, effective administration was almost impossible given the paucity of financial and human resources, and in 1908 only 26 per cent of the territory was governed by colonial officials. The lack of revenue produced by this huge area, especially compared to the Congo Free State, led the French government to grant commercial monopolies to concessionary companies in return for rent and 15 per cent of the profits. The companies operated virtually free from government oversight and paid low prices for products such as ivory that could be resold for huge profits. Company agents conscripted African labor and extracted quotas for productivity that rivaled the abuses widely reported in the neighboring Congo Free State (after 1908, Belgian Congo). Despite the protests of liberal opinion in France, the system remained largely unchanged through the interwar period. A reported 17,000 African laborers reportedly died building 100 miles of railroad from Brazzaville to Pointe Noire. Government revenues, derived primarily from a poll tax, were used to support the (small) colonial administration and police force, and very little was left for education or other services that would directly benefit the inhabitants. In 1960, on the eve of independence, the entire territory had only five university graduates.

The poverty and brutality of French rule, the sparse population, and poor education made FEA difficult ground for nationalist movements. Nevertheless, a Christian messianic movement founded by André Matswa Grenard in the 1920s had elements of a modern political character. A product of mission schools and the customs service, Grenard founded a kind of self-help movement in 1928 that collected funds in Brazzaville and enjoyed wide support among the Bakongo people. Official suspicion led to his imprisonment for fraud, touching off violent protests in Brazzaville. The movement survived, avoiding all contact with Europeans, but played no role in the future political development of the colony.

Events in metropolitan France had the greatest effect on the political evolution of French Equatorial Africa. Colonial administration in Africa was largely unaffected by Germany's defeat of France in June 1940 and the replacement of the Third Republic by a collaborationist regime at Vichy. Under the terms of the June 22, 1940, armistice, France retained administrative responsibility for its empire until a final peace was negotiated. There was much support for the Vichy regime among French colonial personnel, with the exception of the Guianese-born governor of Chad, Félix Éboué, who in September 1940 announced his switch of allegiance from Vichy to the Gaullist Free French movement based in London. Encouraged by this support for his fledgling movement, Charles de Gaulle traveled to Brazzaville in October 1940 to announce the formation of an Empire Defense Council and to invite all French possessions loyal to Vichy to join it and continue the war against Germany; within two years most did.

In January 1944, de Gaulle returned to Brazzaville for a meeting of France's African governors to discuss the postwar administration of the empire. Autonomy or self-government was ruled out in favor of territorial assemblies and the election of two representatives from each territory to France's Constituent Assembly. The Fourth Republic constitution of 1946 allowed each African territory to send representatives to Paris. French Equatorial Africa's small uneducated population ensured that the political process was dominated by the French colonial administration and by events in Paris. In contrast to French West Africa, no political party or nationalist movement of any importance emerged in French Equatorial Africa. Parties were organized on a territorial basis in the 1950s among the colonial elite and were loyal to the French state. This changed in 1956, when the *loi cadre* (enabling law) reforms dramatically widened the franchise. Parties then became more populist and ethnically based. Nevertheless, events elsewhere propelled French Equatorial Africa toward independence; de Gaulle's French Community proposals of 1958 (which replaced the 1946 French Union) granted greater territorial autonomy but retained the preeminence of French sovereignty, and finally France's willingness to grant independence to French West Africa in 1960. In August 1960, the four territories of French Equatorial Africa became independent, but remained closely tied to France economically and fiscally.

DAVID R. DEVEREUX

See also: **Central African Republic: Nationalism, Independence; Chad: Colonial Period: French Rule; Congo (Brazzaville), Republic of: De Brazza and French Colonization; Gabon: Colonial Period: Administration, Labor and Economy; Gabon: Colonial Period: Social Transformation; Gabon: Decolonization and the Politics of Independence, 1945–1967.**

Further Reading

Betts, R. R. *Assimilation and Association in French Colonial Theory, 1890–1911.* New York: Columbia University Press, 1961.

Coquery-Vidrovitch, C. "French Colonization in Africa to 1920: Administration and Economic Development." In *Colonialism in Africa 1870–1960*, vol. 1, edited by L. H. Gann and Peter Duignan. New York: Cambridge University Press, 1969.

Hargreaves, J. *Decolonization in Africa.* London: Longman, 1988.

Marseille, J. *Empire colonial et capitalisme français: Histoire d'une divorce.* Paris: Albin Michel, 1984.

Suret-Canale, J. *French Colonialism in Tropical Africa, 1900–1945.* New York: Pica Press, 1971.

Thompson, V., and R. Adloff. *The Emerging States of French Equatorial Africa.* Palo Alto, Calif.: Stanford University Press, 1960.

Colonial Federations: French West Africa

The administrative federation of French West Africa comprised the modern states of Benin, Burkina Faso, Guinea, Côte d'Ivoire, Mali, Mauritania, Niger, Senegal, and Togo. It was the largest administrative unit in Africa, with a total area of 1.8 million square miles. Until 1891, the largely desert region (generally known as the Western Sudan) was under the control of army officers largely independent of the nominal governor at the coast in Saint-Louis. As French expansion proceeded eastward from Senegal and southward from Algeria, a greater level of administrative efficiency was required. The post of governor general of French West Africa was created in 1895, but was held by the governor of Senegal, who enjoyed only modest powers over the interior regions. In 1904 a separate administration was formally created, with a governor general based in Dakar who was responsible for agriculture, health, communications, and public works. Interior boundaries were constantly redrawn through the 1920s as military "pacification" gave way to civilian administrators. Eventually all of the French West African territories were brought under a federal structure (including the mandated territory of French Togoland). The governor general in Dakar in turn supervised the governors of the separate colonies within the federation. Each was advised by an administrative council made up of officials and business representatives.

The French tendency toward centralization was evident in 1902 when the governor general was vested with the full powers of the French Republic to promulgate laws and issue decrees. Article 33 of the Financial Law of April 1900 required all administrative costs to be charged to the colony, with the exception of military expenditure. The latter was particularly important because large portions of French West Africa remained unpacified until well into the 1920s. Although various African rulers maintained a successful resistance to French rule, even those who had submitted to treaty relationships or protectorate status saw this reversed in 1904 when the theoretical sovereignty of the African chiefs was abolished and replaced by the sovereignty of the French state. The chiefs did not disappear, but they were wholly subordinate to French administrators and functioned at the bottom of the colonial apparatus, at the canton and village levels. Their duties were often onerous and unrewarding, and included tax collection, labor requisition, compulsory crop cultivation, and the provision of military recruits.

French West Africa's relative economic poverty, when compared to its British neighbors (in 1924, all of French West Africa could afford £9 million in imports, compared to £23 million for Nigeria and the Gold Coast), meant that the French territory relied more heavily on direct taxation instead of customs duties. A *capitation* (head tax) was collected from people as young as ten, and a *prestation* (labor tax) was necessary for various public works. French West Africa provided 180,000 recruits for the French Army in World War I, and after 1919 French Africans were liable for military service or work in labor battalions. French administrative practices were derived primarily from metropolitan France or Algeria. Apart from the four communes of Senegal, where *les citoyens* elected a member to the French parliament, French West Africa was unrepresented in the metropolitan government. Education remained at a minimal level; in 1945 an estimated 95 per cent of the population was illiterate. The sparse and often dispersed population (apart from Senegal) and economic poverty ensured a minimum of political or nationalist activity until after World War II.

The fall of the Third Republic in the wake of military defeat by Germany in June 1940, and its replacement by the Vichy regime, had no effect on the administration of French West Africa, many of whose bureaucrats and soldiers were in sympathy with the political Right during the 1930s. A Gaullist-British attack on Dakar in September 1940 was a failure. The November 1942 Allied landings in North Africa, however, brought a change of allegiance to the Free French, who soon established their headquarters in Algiers. At Brazzaville in January–February 1944, Charles de Gaulle and the senior administrators of French Africa discussed the future of the empire but did not effect a fundamental political reappraisal: "The aims of the civilizing work accomplished by France in the colonies exclude any thought of autonomy." Nevertheless, in 1945 the provisional French government headed by de Gaulle invited each of the French African territories to elect two representatives to the Constituent Assembly. Representation of the African territories was incorporated into the Fourth Republic's constitution of 1946, of which French West Africa had 67 members (20 senators, 20 deputies, and 27 counselors of the French Union; of these, 45 were of black or mixed descent). This had the effect of removing French West Africa's evolving political class to Paris, where most associated with the Socialist or Communist party. Among the leading figures were Léopold Senghor of Senegal and Félix Houphouët-Boigny of Côte d'Ivoire. The elimination of the communists from the French coalition government in 1947 led to political upheaval in Côte d'Ivoire and eventually forced a divide between the French communists and their African allies, the *Rassemblement Democratique Africain* (RDA). Led by Houphouët-Boigny, the RDA skillfully played the factional French politics of the 1950s to extract concessions for French West Africa.

The *loi cadre* (enabling act) of 1956 granted some internal self-government to French West Africa. Universal suffrage was introduced, and African representation in the territorial assemblies increased. Executive power, however, was still concentrated in the hands of the high commissioner (formerly governor general) in Dakar. Independence on the model of Ghana in 1957 still seemed out of the question. The collapse of the Fourth Republic in May 1958 and the reaccession of Charles de Gaulle to French leadership signaled yet further change. In proposing a French Community as part of the Fifth Republic, de Gaulle envisioned a federal arrangement in which African territorial autonomy was increased but Paris still held substantial reserve powers. A referendum in September 1958 offered a choice between the French Community or independence; the latter implied a termination of all French assistance. Only the anti-Gaullist Sekou Touré of Guinea urged his supporters to reject the French proposals, and Guinea was promptly propelled to independence.

Guinea's example nevertheless heralded the collapse of federal French West Africa. In 1959 Senegal and Sudan formed a smaller federation called Mali, which in 1960 requested independence from France. When this was granted, the other territories also demanded independence, so that by the end of September 1960, French West Africa had become nine independent states, though still with close ties to France.

DAVID R. DEVEREUX

See also: **Burkina Faso (Upper Volta): Colonial Period; Côte d'Ivoire (Ivory Coast): Colonial Period: Administration and Economy; Côte d'Ivoire: (Ivory Coast): Colonization and Resistance; Guinea: Colonial Period; Mauritania: Colonical Period: Nineteenth Century; Niger: Colonial Period to Independence; French Occupation and Resistance; Senegal: Colonial Period: Administration and "Assimilation"; Senegal: Colonial Period: Economy; Togo: Colonial Period: Dual Mandate, 1919–1957.**

Further Reading

Crowder, M. *West Africa under Colonial Rule*, Evanston, Ill.: Northwestern University Press, 1968.

Foltz, W. *From French West Africa to the Mali Federation,* New Haven, Conn.: Yale University Press, 1965.

Gifford, P., and W. R. Louis (eds.). *The Transfer of Power in Africa: Decolonization, 1940–60*. New Haven, Conn.: Yale University Press, 1982.

Hargreaves, J. *Decolonization in Africa*, London: Longman, 1988.

Kanya-Fostner, A. S. *The Conquest of the Western Sudan: A Study in French Military Imperialism*. London: Cambridge University Press, 1969.

Manning, P. *Francophone Sub-Saharan Africa, 1880–1985*. Cambridge: Cambridge University Press, 1988.

Suret-Canale, J. *French Colonialism in Tropical Africa 1900–1945*. New York: Pica Press, 1971.

White, D. S. *Black Africa and De Gaulle, from the French Empire to Independence*. University Park: Pennsylvania State University Press, 1979.

Colonial Imports versus Indigenous Crafts

Before European rule was formally established in the nineteenth century, a vibrant indigenous manufacturing sector existed in many parts of Sub-Saharan Africa. The production of cotton textiles was the most important industry; next, in order of importance, were ironworking, leather crafts, and pottery. Locally grown cotton was ginned, spun, woven, dyed, and made into garments. Major cloth-making centers were found in Côte d'Ivoire, Ghana, the Republic of Benin, and Nigeria. In Kano in northern Nigeria, textile production was deemed to be the "national industry," and contemporary observers claim that the city's cloth was unrivaled in Africa for its beauty and excellence.

Iron mining and manufacturing was generally done on a small scale throughout Sub-Saharan Africa. However, there were large centers in Oume in southern Côte d'Ivoire and Oyo in southwest Nigeria. Metalworking was done by blacksmiths and metalworkers who either traveled to mining centers with portable tools or purchased pig iron from traders. Hoes, spearheads, knives, blades, and swords were the main items produced for local consumption. Leather goods were manufactured from hides and skins; production was concentrated in the savanna lands of Sub-Saharan Africa, where animals were reared. Pottery making was widespread, and was done mainly by women; the industry provided most of the containers that were used to store liquids and foodstuffs.

The industrial sector in Sub-Saharan Africa underwent a profound transformation after Portuguese explorers opened up the African continent more fully to trade with Europe and Asia. Between 1500 and about 1850 European traders made a conscious attempt to replace indigenous products with cheaper imports from Europe. Their efforts were enhanced by the economies of scale accruing to them because of the Industrial Revolution. The increase in European imports provided a disincentive for the improvement of technology in the cotton manufacturing and ironworking industries of Sub-Saharan Africa. Cheap imported yarn was more attractive to weavers than yarn produced by the much slower weaving process, and cotton

Weaving in Africa: traditional methods on an industrial scale, Cameroon, 1920s. © SVT Bild/Das Fotoarchiv.

could also be purchased in a greater variety of colors than was available locally. Imported iron bars allowed metalworkers to overcome some of the deficiencies in the African manufacturing process. By the 1820s, for example, cotton textiles from Europe were West Africa's most important import. Significant quantities of iron bars, metal vessels, blades, and tools were also imported. Prior to the onset of colonial rule, the high costs of internal transportation in Sub-Saharan Africa and the quality and intricacy of locally manufactured garments enabled textile industries in the interior to remain competitive. On the other hand, ironworkers survived by using imported iron bars to manufacture blades, hoes, and woodworking instruments.

Formal European colonization in Sub-Saharan Africa began in the second half of the nineteenth century, and by the beginning of the twentieth century most states in the region were under either French, British, Portuguese, German or Belgian rule. Colonization led to the dismantling of many of the physical barriers that had permitted indigenous manufacturers to withstand the competition from European imports. Critically factoring in this process were the roads and railways that were constructed to facilitate the exploitation of the resources of the interior. In addition, the pressure exerted on traditional industries during colonial rule increased because colonial administrators sought to retain the advantages of market control by opposing industrialization. As the cost of moving manufactured goods and raw material between Europe and Sub-Saharan Africa declined, there was no reason for large overseas firms to invest in industrialization. Worse still, technological and capital constraints did not allow African producers and merchants to promote the development of internationally competitive indigenous industries.

During the colonial era a concerted effort was made to expand cotton production for export in the hope that this would have lead to increased African demand for imported cotton. In French and Belgian colonies in Equatorial Africa, local chiefs in cotton-growing areas were forced to sell given quotas to merchant firms and/or government officials. Cotton imports also increased significantly throughout Sub-Saharan Africa. In West Africa, for example, imported cotton yarn from England increased from an estimated 200,000 pounds in the 1890s to about 1,000,000 pounds by 1914. In Nigeria colonial administrators were confident that local textile production would have declined as the industry was exposed to foreign competition. However, as in many parts of Sub-Saharan Africa, their expectations were not fulfilled.

The local cotton industry survived in part because there was a guaranteed market among the elite and status-conscious Africans for local textiles such as those manufactured at Iseyin in western Nigeria and Kente cloth in Ghana. Also, in parts of Nigeria, for example, weavers usually belonged to households that produced their basic needs of food as well as other necessities. Often they were farmers, merchants, or Muslim clerics for whom textile production was a part-time activity or off-season occupation. For them the marginal cost of production was virtually nonexistent. Therefore, they were able to produce cloth that could compete in price with imported cloth.

The nature of the organization of production also enabled the pottery industry to survive. Leather craft, on the other hand, retained its importance primarily as a result of the growth in the livestock industry in Sub-Saharan Africa during the colonial period. The traditional industry most affected by colonial imports was iron mining and manufacturing. It declined significantly during the colonial era because even though the capital outlay for traditional smelting was negligible, the iron output of furnaces was small and inferior to the European import. By 1939 cheap colonial imports had virtually eliminated the markets for locally smelted iron and its byproducts, in all but the very remote areas of Sub-Saharan Africa.

ALLISTER HINDS

See also: **Colonial European Administrations: Comparative Survey; Colonialism: Impact on African Societies.**

Further Reading

Austen, R. *African Economic History*. London: James Currey, 1987.

Birmingham, D., and P. Martin. *History of Central Africa*, vol. 2. London: Longman, 1983.

Callaway, A. "From Traditional Crafts to Modern Industries." *Odu*, no. 2 (1965): 28–51.

Hogendorn, J. S. *Nigerian Groundnuts Exports*. Oxford: Oxford University Press, 1978.

Dewey, C., and A. G. Hopkins (eds.). *The Imperial Impact: Studies in the Economic History of Africa and Asia*. London: Athlone Press, 1978.

Hopkins A. G. *An Economic History of West Africa*. London: Longman, 1977.

Manning, P. *Francophone Sub-Saharan Africa 1880–1995*, 2nd ed. Cambridge: Cambridge University Press, 1998.

Colonialism: Ideology of Empire: Supremacist, Paternalist

The nineteenth century saw a dramatic change in Africa's contact with Europe, as European powers sent their armies to initiate and implement their plans of colonization. The gradual European penetration into the African hinterland escalated in the 1870s, so that by the 1890s the entire map of Africa was altered, with large tracts of land nevertheless still unconquered. Numerous European exploratory and missionary expeditions were made into the African interior, with clear motives. For example, the International Geographical Conference held in Brussels in 1884 had the theme of bringing civilization to Africa and an end to the transatlantic slave trade. European nations initiated and maintained the trade, making huge profits from the barbaric conditions of the transatlantic passage and the enslavement of Africans in the Americas. Thus, the supremacist and paternalistic underpinnings of colonialism were etched in the motives of European exploratory and missionary expeditions that were precursors of invading armies. By 1914, when World War I broke out, all of Africa, except for Ethiopia and Liberia, was under European colonial rule.

In Africa, European expansionism and empire building manifested themselves in the forceful acquisition of territories and colonization. Europe's relationship with Africa was marked by domination; fundamental decisions that affected the lives of everyone within the carved colonies were made and implemented by European colonial rulers (governors, their supporting administrative officers and armies) in pursuit of the interests of the colonial powers. European colonialism in Africa meant rejection of political, economic, and cultural compromises with Africans based on the conviction of European superiority and a belief in a divine mandate to rule and to civilize Africa.

Europe had interest in Africa for three reasons that were mutually inclusive, all of which were supported by the notion of European superiority. The first was to gather scientific knowledge of Africa, the "Dark Continent." Exploratory expeditions were, therefore, made to "discover" the unknown for Europe. The second was to proselytize and convert Africans to Christianity; so scientific research and geographical investigations were combined with missionary work. Evangelical activities often accompanied military campaigns that killed hundreds of thousands of Africans in order to save the heathen and lost Africans who survived the massacres. The third was imperialistic. European patriots augmented national pride, political and economic grandeur of their nations, by invading Africa and laying claim to vast territories.

The rationale for European imperialism in Africa was political, cultural, and economic. The European ideological stance of the period equated colonial expansion with prestige and status. Overseas colonial possessions also brought geopolitical advantages. African colonies provided European powers with strategic advantage in their global imperialistic expansion and competition. They were provided cheap sources of labor and natural resources. European intellectuals found moral and philosophical justification for colonialism in ethnocentric arguments that Africans were physiologically, intellectually, and culturally inferior. These arguments were buttressed by military victories of colonial armies overrunning indigenous armies of African kingdoms and states. African armies equipped with old-fashioned rifles, spears, and bows and arrows were no match for cannon and machine-gun wielding colonial armies. Technological advancements in Europe were, therefore, presented as evidence of European superiority at all levels of human endeavor. Racism was an integral component of colonialism in Africa. Skin color, physiology, and a notion of the African being "the white man's burden" (expressed by Rudyard Kipling in a poem with the same title as well as his description of African people as "half-devil and half-child") captured the racism and paternalism that characterized European colonial presence throughout Africa. It was argued that to "uplift" and to "civilize" Africans was a duty divinely sanctioned, so the colonization of these peoples was right for the European "civilizing mission."

While each European colonial power approached the "civilizing mission" with a peculiar national trait, they all established colonial systems that were inherently paternalistic. The French introduced "the assimilation policy" with the goal of transforming Africans into French people. Africans and African cultures were considered primitive, and though race seemed not to matter, in reality "Frenchness" in the African colonial experience was racist, supremacist, and paternalistic because it negated "Africanness." Colonial rule was administered through *direct rule*, which took political power away from indigenous rulers and put every aspect of polity under the control of the French government.

The Portuguese and the Germans used direct rule as well. Portuguese ruled the colonies as overseas provinces inseparable from Portugal. The German system was also highly centralized. Traditional African rulers were completely disregarded, and any resistance was quickly and violently suppressed by German military officers and private entrepreneurs, who were given power and responsibility to rule the colonies by the German chancellery in Berlin.

The Belgians operated the most brutal colonial system in Africa, that of company rule. King Leopold II of Belgium, the ultimate paternalist, made the Congo Free State his personal property. Despite its name it was in no way free, and Belgium businessmen were allowed to exploit its natural resources using forced labor. The colonized were virtually slaves enduring the most severe deprivations and were mutilated or killed if they resisted. The administrative system was controlled by a coalition of Belgian businessmen, administrators, and the clergy of the Catholic Church.

The British administered their colonies through *indirect rule*, in which the colonial administration identified the local power structure, especially the chiefs and elders, and incorporated them into the colonial hierarchy. The chiefs were at the bottom of the hierarchy and passed down to the citizenry demands for taxes and forced conscription into the colonial army or for labor. The colonial army and police force were always at hand to enforce demands and decrees should the chiefs and elders refuse to carry them out.

In every case of the European colonial system, Africans were not allowed to exercise political or economic will. Colonial administrators acted as if they understood the needs of the colonized and argued that colonization was good for them. Colonialism was presented as order that would rectify African "chaos." African languages were termed dialects or "vernacular," and all, especially students, were taught and forced to speak "cultured" European languages. Colonial pedagogy showed disdain for African cultures, and education was employed as a vehicle for establishing cultural imperialism and maintaining European hegemony.

The European colonizers of Africa were not only armies of occupation, but also economic exploiters, cultural chauvinists, usurpers of power, and disrupters of political growth in Africa. Supremacist ideology informed the European understanding of Africans and their cultures; thus home government policies and colonial administrations forced European cultural norms on Africans. European paternalism in the colonies was underlined by racist and ethnocentric trends of the era that were ingrained in the oppressive political, economic, and social practices.

LEONARD GADZEKPO

See also: **Colonialism: Impact on African Societies.**

Further Reading

Ayittey, G. B. N. *Indigenous African Institutions*. Ardsley-on-Hudson, N.Y.: Transnational, 1991.

Baumgart, W. *Imperialism: The Idea and Reality of British and French Colonial Expansion, 1880–1914*. Oxford: Oxford University Press, 1982.

Boahen, A. A. *African Perspectives on Colonialism*. Baltimore: Johns Hopkins University Press, 1987.

Count, E. W. *This Is Race: An Anthology Selected from the International Literature on the Race of Man*. New York: Shuman, 1950.

Khapoya, V. B. *The African Experience: An Introduction*. Upper Saddle River, N.J.: Prentice Hall, 1998.

Memmi, A. *The Colonizer and the Colonized*. Boston: Beacon Press, 1991.

Morel, E. D. *The Black Man's Burden: The White Man in Africa from the Fifteenth Century to World War I*. London: Monthly Review Press, 1969.

Osterhammel, J. *Colonialism: A Theoretical Overview*. Kingston, Ian Randle, 1997.

Wesseling, H. L. *Imperialism and Colonialism: Essays on the History of European Expansion*. Westport, Conn.: Greenwood Press, 1997.

Colonialism, Overthrow of: Nationalism and Anticolonialism

The anticolonial struggle in Africa began as soon as the European colonial powers sought to establish their control of African states and territories. What has been called "primary" resistance was waged throughout the nineteenth century by rulers and states such as the Mandinka empire of Samori in West Africa; Moshoeshoe in Lesotho; and Emperor Menelik II, the Ethiopian conqueror of the Italians at Adwa in 1896.

Other early forms of anticolonial resistance, which had a more popular character, were in response to the economic demands made by the colonial authorities or European settlers and include the 1898 "hut tax" rebellion in Sierra Leone and the Bambatha rebellion in Natal in 1906. Other anticolonial economic protests used religion as a unifying ideology such as the Maji Maji rebellion in German Tanganiyka in 1905–1907 and the Chimurenga revolt of the Shona people in 1896–1897. In some instances the adaptation of Christianity provided the ideological basis for anticolonialism, as in the Ethiopian and Independent African Churches in different parts of the continent, the Kitawala movement in Central Africa, and the 1915 rebellion associated with John Chilembwe in Nyasaland. Islam provided a unifying force for the anticolonial struggles of the Sanusiyya in Libya, and the resistance of Sayyid Muhammad Abdille Hassan in Somalia. In 1929–1930 in Nigeria, gender played a significant role when Igbo women organized anticolonial resistance to

British rule, in a revolt that became known as the Aba Women's War. The rebellion, which may have been precipitated by opposition to the perceived threat of taxation, led to the destruction of native courts, looting of local stores owned by British firms, and opposition to the "warrant" chiefs imposed by the colonial authorities and to the authority of the colonial regime itself.

As early as the late nineteenth century, there were the beginnings of various "secondary" forms of anticolonialism, waged by those new social classes and strata that were formed partly as a consequence of European imperialism in Africa. In the Gold Coast, the Aborigines' Rights Protection Society (ARPS), formed in 1897, was an early example of the role of the Western-educated elite in anticolonial politics. The ARPS forced the colonial administration to withdraw legislation that threatened African property rights and proposed to alienate land to the crown. In the twentieth century, anticolonial resistance waged and led by the new educated African elite increasingly assumed the form of nationalism. At first African nationalism was based on the demand for reforms to the colonial system and subsequently, especially after World War II, for African political sovereignty or political independence in the new states created by colonial rule. Anticolonial nationalism eventually had the aim of uniting all sections of the population in a colony, irrespective of national origins, against colonial rule. Often anticolonial nationalism took advantage of increasing literacy, and newspapers such as *al-Liwa* in Egypt and Azikiwe's *West African Pilot* became important means of anticolonial agitation and propaganda. Also of importance were the ideologies of anticolonialism that developed within the continent, often influenced by political trends in the African diaspora. These were sometimes fueled by the need to vindicate the "African race" and to demand "Africa for the Africans," as in the Pan-Africanist ideas of Edward Wilmot Blyden, Marcus Garvey, and others and the *Négritude* movement that was influential throughout francophone and much of lusophone Africa. Africans living abroad, especially students in the United States and Europe, often played an important part in developing the nationalist movements and transmitting anticolonial ideologies and formed influential anticolonial organizations such as the West African Students Union in London and La Ligue de Defense de la Race Negre in Paris. Increasingly, often as a result of the activities of Africans abroad, anticolonialism was not only influenced by Pan-Africanism, or notions of European nationalism, but also by the internationalism of socialism and communism.

In North Africa several nationalist political parties, based on elites that had existed in precolonial times, emerged after World War I. These included the Wafd Party in Egypt and the Neo-Destour Party, founded in Tunisia in 1934, which is sometimes seen as the continent's first true nationalist party. Nationalist organizations were formed throughout the continent; one of the earliest in Sub-Saharan Africa was the African National Congress, founded in South Africa in 1912. In West Africa the political and commercial elite of all four British colonies joined together to form the National Congress of British West Africa in 1920. In East Africa in the early 1920s, Harry Thuku's East African Association not only united Africans of many nationalities but also began to establish African and Indian unity and agitated against the political and economic consequences of colonial rule. In many colonies, however, there was little organized political activity of this kind before World War II.

Colonial rule continued to provoke widespread economic protests that necessarily assumed an anticolonial character, especially during the era of the Great Depression. There were armed rebellions in French Equatorial Africa during the 1920s in response to taxation demands, the collapse in international rubber prices, and French demands for forced labor on the Congo-Ocean Railway. In the 1930s farmers in the Gold Coast, with general popular support, organized two cocoa "holdups." The most successful boycott in 1937 kept most of the crop off the market, until the major European trading companies agreed to raise the price paid to the producers and the government was forced to intervene to reform the monopolistic practices of the trading companies. Protests by workers also sometimes assumed a political or anticolonial character, such as those associated with Clement Kadalie's Industrial and Commercial Workers' Union in Southern Africa. But actions by workers were seldom effective, at least until the 1940s, when the general strikes in Nigeria and Tanganyika showed the political potential of concerted trade union activity.

World War II, which for Africa can be said to have begun with the Italian invasion of Ethiopia in 1935, ushered in a new period of anticolonial struggle. African involvement in the war, which was ostensibly fought by the Allied powers against racism and for the right to self-determination, raised expectations that at its conclusion Africa and Africans would reap their just rewards. The war considerably weakened the European colonial powers, both economically and politically, and led to the world dominance of two anticolonial superpowers, the United States and the Soviet Union. The declarations in the Atlantic Charter and at the Brazzaville Conference, the founding of the United Nations, and the postwar success of anticolonial struggles in Asia heralded the beginning of the end of colonial rule for millions of Africans. Perhaps most important, the war led to significant economic changes, increasing urbanization and the emergence of the masses of African people onto the political stage. Anticolonial nationalism entered the era of mass support for nationalist movements and of the demand for independence. This demand, the need to mobilize the masses in the anticolonial struggle, and the threatened use of force if necessary were in evidence in the resolutions of the delegates at the Manchester Pan-African Congress held in 1945.

In the postwar period urban and rural workers began to play an increasingly significant part in anticolonial politics and new and more radical nationalist parties were formed, such as the interterritorial Rassemblement Democratique Africain (RDA) in French West Africa and the Convention Peoples' Party (CPP) in the Gold Coast. Nevertheless, in much of Sub-Saharan Africa—especially in those colonies without European settlers—African nationalism was generally channeled along constitutional lines by the colonial governments. For most African nationalists the goal was political control of the colonial state, with more or less Africanization of the economic and political institutions handed down by the colonial rulers. Such aims were ultimately not in contradiction with the need for continued economic domination by the major world powers.

It was the CPP that became the preeminent nationalist party of the postwar period, adept at utilizing popular support for electoral success and mass actions such as economic boycotts and strikes. It paved the way to Ghana's independence in 1957 and constitutional independence in most of Britain's other Sub-Saharan colonies throughout the following decade. In the French African colonies and especially in Cameroon, the RDA and other nationalist parties, even with mass popular support, had a more difficult and complex path to political independence, which for the majority occurred in 1960. With the exception of Sekou Touré's Guinea, the French government was often able to retain considerable economic and political control of its former colonies with the connivance of the local nationalist elite.

The violence that characterized the anticolonial struggle in Cameroon, where there were significant numbers of French settlers, was repeated, sometimes on a much larger scale, in most other colonies with substantial numbers of European settlers. Armed "national liberation" struggles broke out in Madagascar, Tunisia, Morocco, Algeria, Kenya, Rhodesia, and in the Portuguese colonies of Guinea Cape Verde, Mozambique, and Angola. In the Portuguese colonies independence was only achieved in the 1970s. Independence only came to Namibia after a lengthy guerrilla war in 1990, while the nationalist struggle against settler control in South Africa, which included guerrilla actions as well as other forms of political struggle and concerted international pressure, led to majority rule only in 1994.

HAKIM ADI

See also: **Colonialism, Overthrow of: Women and the Nationalist Struggle; Ethiopia: Menelik II, Era of; Libya: Muhammad Al-Sanusi (*c.*1787–1859) and the Sanusiyya; Moshoeshoe I and the Founding of the Basotho Kingdom; Tanganyika (Tanzania): Maji Maji Rebellion, 1905–1907; Touré, Samori (*c.*1830–1900) and His Empire.**

Further Reading

Boahen, A. Adu (ed.). *UNESCO General History of Africa*, vol. 7, *Africa under Colonial Domination*. Paris: UNESCO/ Heinemann, 1985.

Davidson, B. *Let Freedom Come: Africa in Modern History*. London: Little, Brown, 1978.

Fanon, F. *The Wretched of the Earth*. Harmondsworth, England: Penguin, 1961.

Hargreaves, J. D. *Decolonization in Africa*. London: Longman, 1988.

Hodgkin, T. *African Political Parties*. Harmondsworth, England: Penguin, 1961.

———. *Nationalism in Colonial Africa*. London: Muller/New York: New York University Press, 1956.

Maddox, G. (ed.). *Colonialism and Nationalism in Africa*, vol. 4, *African Nationalism and Revolution*. London: Garland, 1993.

Welliver, T. (ed.). *Colonialism and Nationalism in Africa*, vol. 3, *African Nationalism and Independence*. London: Garland, 1993.

Colonialism, Overthrow of: Northern Africa

The overthrow of colonialism depended upon the development of nationalism, which marked a break with primary forms of resistance to colonialism in nineteenth- and early-twentieth-century northern Africa. Initial resistance was based on regional and Muslim solidarity, like the resistance of 'Abd al-Qadir to the French in Algeria between 1830 and 1847. Meanwhile, in Tunisia and Egypt, there was a renewal of ideological leadership through the development of nationalist ideologies and the reform of Islamic thought. Nationalist and Islamist ideologies were formulated by those exposed to modern European thought and appealed to new social categories created by the modernizing programs of African state builders such as Tunisia's Ahmed Bey and Egypt's Muhammad 'Ali. Educated in Western languages and political concepts, administrators, professionals, and entrepreneurs identified their interests within the nation-state. They provided the personnel of the colonial state system after the French occupation of Tunisia in 1881 and the British occupation of Egypt in 1882. In Algeria the colonial state enabled the formation of similar social groups by the early twentieth century, as it did in Morocco after the French occupation in 1911. Muslim clerics, heads of religious brotherhoods, and lineage groups of the traditional type also played a role in the overthrow of colonialism. For instance, the Sanusiyya

brotherhood in Libya led the resistance against the Italian occupation until 1932 and thereby won the recognition of the British after the Allied occupation in 1943. As a result, when Libya became independent in 1951 the leader of the Sanusiyya founded a new, ruling dynasty. In Morocco, the Rif rebellion in the early 1920s was led by 'Abd al-Karim, who combined the ideology of Islamic reformism with a social base among Berber lineages. This movement was unsuccessful, though it did topple the French resident, General Lyautey, who had attempted to win the support of the Berbers for the French colonial state.

While the old elites resisted social and economic change, the new professional elites were exposed to pressures that made them more in favor of change. For instance, the nationalists in Tunisia did not reject economic change; rather they protested the increasing marginalization of Tunisian investors and liberals in the period after 1907, when the French adopted more reactionary politics and a prosettler economic policy. A Muslim reformist, 'Abd al-'Aziz Tha'alibi, formed the Constitutional (Destour) Party in 1919 to demand the restoration of the constitution written by the nineteenth-century reformer Khayr al-Din. However, Tha'alibi's constitutionalism was superseded by a more radical, working-class movement in the 1920s and 1930s, resulting in a split in the Destour and the formation of the Neo-Destour under Habib Bourguiba in 1934. After riots in Tunisia in 1938, Bourguiba was arrested and radical activism suppressed, thus favoring the liberal moderation of the old Destour Party. Similar developments occurred in Egypt. Entrepreneurs profited from the colonial administration's reform of Egypt's finances, yet free-market fluctuations and dislocations in production caused by the war economy adversely affected landholders, peasants, and professionals alike, prompting the national rising against the British in 1919. The revolt was initiated by lawyers, civil servants, and students, and led by the politician Sa'd Zaghlul, who formed a Delegation (Wafd) to petition the European powers at the Paris Peace Conference in 1919. The British adopted a policy of treaty negotiations with the more moderate, Liberal-Constitutional Party and reformed the colonial system in 1923. However, elections in that year brought Zaghlul's ultranationalist Wafd Party to power in 1924, which legitimated the nationalist demand for complete independence.

In Tunisia and Egypt the reforms that followed the conclusion of World War I fell short of independence and therefore failed to satisfy nationalist demands. In Algeria, on the other hand, the Young Algerians did not demand independence in 1919, but only equal rights for the Algerian majority as French citizens in colonial Algeria. Assimilationists, such as Ferhat Abbas, appealed to the republican and democratic traditions of France, yet the inability of French governments to override settler resistance to the assimilation of Algerian Muslims meant that the representatives of the Algerian population adopted an increasingly nationalist stance. In the elections of 1919–1920 the grandson of 'Abd al-Qadir, Emir Khalid, rejected assimilation by demanding equal rights for Algerians without any loss of their Muslim status or Arab cultural identity. Nascent nationalism developed a popular base with the absorption of the trade unionists, led by Messali Hadj after 1927, and the formation of an organization for Islamic reform, led by Ben Badis from 1931. An occasion to reform the colonial system was lost in 1937, when representatives of the settlers in the French National Assembly blocked discussion of the Violette Reform Bill; likewise, Charles de Gaulle failed to provide a workable framework for a settlement after World War II. Consequently, the followers of Messali Hadj turned to open confrontation, forming the Secret Organization (OS) in 1947, which served as the nucleus for the later National Liberation Front (FLN).

Colonialism in northern Africa increased the amount of land and minerals exploited for colonial development, causing dislocations in the traditional agrarian sector and swelling the size of the modernizing, urban sector of colonized societies. Consequently, northern Africans were included in modern European economic and social realities, yet excluded from participation in political systems of the modern type. This fundamental contradiction within the colonial system provided the nationalists with a massive constituency among the lower and middle classes. In French North Africa the colonial economy divided the indigenous population from the settler minority, which controlled the best arable lands and the profitable export economy. In Egypt, similar social divisions existed between a landholding aristocracy, who were often culturally Westernized, and the mass of the urban poor and peasant population. As a result, the struggle against colonialism took on the character of a social and cultural revolution. From the late 1930s on, the Egyptian Islamist organization the Muslim Brothers organized demonstrations against social injustice, Western cultural influence, and the British military presence in Egypt and Palestine. After clashes between British forces and Egyptians in the Canal Zone in January 1952, rioters burned the colonial sectors of Cairo. The monarchy and the Wafd government, bereft of popular support, were brought down in the July Revolution, which was led by Colonel Gamel Abdel Nasser. The social revolution was begun with a land reform that dispossessed the aristocracy, but colonialism was overthrown only after the nationalization of the Suez Canal, which provoked the invasion of Egypt by Britain, France, and Israel in 1956. The Egyptian victory, more diplomatic than military, finally destroyed Britain's colonial ambitions in Egypt.

In North Africa, the defeat of France in 1940 and the Allied occupation had a profound impact on the nationalist movements. In Morocco, the nationalist parties of the prewar period united into the Independence (Istiqlal) Party in December 1943. After the war, the French attempted to pit a Muslim brotherhood, led by al-Khittani and a southern feudal lord, Thami al-Glaoui, against the sultan and the urban nationalists. But when the French exiled the sultan in 1953, the national movement burst into full-scale armed struggle. After his restoration, the sultan was able to outmaneuver the Istiqlal in the negotiations for independence, which came in 1956. Likewise, in Tunisia the ruler Bey Moncef petitioned the French for reform during World War II, while Bourguiba was liberated by the Germans and restored to the leadership of the Neo-Destour. However, the death of Moncef in 1948 secured Bourguiba's leadership of the national movement, which had a popular base among the trade unions as well as a guerrilla army, formed in 1950. Bourguiba's arrest in 1952 intensified resistance; as a consequence the French freed Bourguiba for negotiations between 1954 and 1956, rather than wage a war against the guerrillas.

In Algeria, the French crushed the OS in 1950, but the militants formed the Revolutionary Committee and the Liberation Army in 1953. In 1954, the defeat of French forces by the Vietnamese at Dien Bien Phu convinced the militants to mobilize for immediate guerrilla war. The FLN was formed and the campaign against France began on November 1, 1954. Although the French captured Ahmed Ben Bella and other FLN leaders in 1956, the guerrilla war within Algeria had the support of the Algerian population and was supplied by Egypt (and thus the Eastern Bloc) through Tunisia and Morocco. As a result, a massive French military occupation was required to defeat the guerrillas in the field, which further alienated the Algerian population. While the French could claim to have won a military victory by 1958, the war undermined the Fourth Republic. A coup d'état with military support brought Charles de Gaulle to power with greater presidential powers, enabling him to negotiate with the FLN in the teeth of settler and French military opposition. The FLN itself reorganized in 1958 with the formation of a provisional government in Cairo, which immediately demanded self-determination for the Algerian nation. Negotiations in 1960 were answered by a French terrorist group, which targeted the French government and FLN supporters in Algeria. France nevertheless conceded to FLN demands for complete sovereignty in 1961 and an agreement was signed in

March 1962. After the flight of the settler population and clashes between guerrilla groups within Algeria, the FLN leadership occupied Algiers in September 1962 to proclaim an Algerian republic under Ben Bella.

Colonialism spurred the growth of nationalist and revolutionary movements in northern Africa. In Algeria, the determination of France to hold onto the colony meant that a long, violent struggle was necessary to overthrow French rule. Tunisia and Morocco, on the other hand, were protectorates whose settler population did not elect deputies to the French assembly; therefore, negotiated settlements were less problematic. However, even in those cases armed insurrection was required to compel France to negotiate independence on African terms. This was also true of Egypt, which remained under colonial domination until Nasser forced the issue between 1952 and 1956.

JAMES WHIDDEN

See also: **'Abd al-Qadir; Egypt: Muhammad Ali; 1805–1849; Tunisia: Ahmad Bey and Army Reform; Tunisia: Bourguiba, Presidency of: Government and Opposition.**

Further Reading

Beinin, J., and Z. Lockman. *Workers on the Nile: Nationalism, Communism, and the Egyptian Working Class*, 1882–1954. Princeton, N.J.: Princeton University Press, 1987.

Bennoune, M. *The Making of Contemporary Algeria 1830–1987*. Cambridge: Cambridge University Press, 1988.

Berque, J. *French North Africa: The Maghrib between Two World Wars*. London: Faber and Faber, 1967.

Berque, J. *Egypt: Imperialism and Revolution*. London: Faber and Faber, 1972.

Cannon, B. J. "The Beylical Habus Council and Suburban Development: Tunis 1881–1914." *Maghreb Review* 1–2, no. 7 (1982): 32–40.

Green, A. *The Tunisian Ulama, 1873–1915: Social Structure and Response to Ideological Currents*. Leiden: E. J. Brill, 1978.

Hermassi, E. *Leadership and National Development in North Africa: A Comparative Essay*. Berkeley and Los Angeles: University of California Press, 1973.

Laroui, A. *The History of the Maghrib: An Interpretative Essay*. Princeton, N.J.: Princeton University Press, 1977.

Morsy, M. "Maghribi Unity in the Context of the Nation-State: A Historian's Point of View." *Maghreb Review* 3–4, no. 8 (1983): 70–76.

Colonialism, Overthrow of: Sub-Saharan Africa

After World War II, nationalists in Africa and Asia overthrew European colonial rule and regained their peoples' independence in one of the world's great revolutionary movements. In Sub-Saharan Africa, this political revolution stretched from the birth of Ghana in 1957 to the first democratically elected government of South Africa in 1994. The character and pace of decolonization varied from relatively peaceful constitutional transfers of power to protracted liberation struggles, but everywhere it eventually reflected the irresistible nationalist demands of self-determination and democracy.

The confluence of African initiatives and a receptive international setting provided the preconditions for successful liberation struggles. The resistance of traditional African leaders to European imperialism in the late nineteenth century offered an indigenous base for this movement. Colonial rule itself had produced a new class of Western-educated Africans and independent Christian churches that increasingly challenged colonial authorities with their own ideals. As African leaders escalated their demands, they frequently won mass support from those who attributed their economic hardships to the colonial systems, such as young people, peasant farmers, and urban workers. Black struggles against racism in the Americas and the Pan-African visions of Edward Wilmot Blyden, Marcus Garvey, W. E. B. Du Bois, and George Padmore also influenced and energized African intellectuals.

World War II, and to a lesser extent the Italo-Ethiopian War that preceded it, aroused African nationalism and undermined colonial rule. Fascist Italy's invasion of Ethiopia in 1935 angered African intellectuals on the continent and throughout the black diaspora. This anger expanded into a growing disillusionment with the other colonial powers when they failed to effectively assist Ethiopia, long a symbol of African freedom.

During World War II, early Allied defeats and the military experiences of thousands of African soldiers cracked the image of invincible European colonial rulers. At the same time, Allied leaders appealed in the name of democracy for a crusade against Nazi tyranny. African intellectuals generally supported this appeal while recognizing the obvious, if unintended, logic that it must lead to African self-determination after the war. Further, the significant contributions made to the Allied cause by soldiers and raw materials from Africa created a belief that some form of political and economic compensation was due.

After the war, African independence movements formed part of the global revolt against Western imperialism. In 1945 African activists, meeting in Manchester for the Fifth Pan-African Congress, shifted their efforts from colonial reform to ending colonial rule. Two years later, India's independence offered an example of successful tactics and achievement. Continued European colonial rule also encountered pressures from the Cold War policies of the United States and the Soviet Union, the world's newly dominant superpowers.

At the United Nations (UN), the advocates of African liberation grew as former colonies gained their independence and admission. The UN trusteeship system, which provided international oversight in the former German colonies, sent visiting missions to Africa and provided a global forum for African nationalists such as Julius Nyerere of Tanzania.

In West Africa the end of colonial rule was relatively rapid and peaceful. Kwame Nkrumah's remarkable success in Ghana set the pace and then resonated across the continent. Accurately sensing popular opinion, Nkrumah demanded immediate self-government and established the mass-based Convention People's Party. In 1951 the party won a landslide victory at the polls that convinced British officials to release Nkrumah from prison and offer him the position of leader of government business. Over the next six years, Nkrumah won repeated electoral victories and negotiated the constitutional transfer of power that reached a climax with Ghana's independence in 1957. The following year African nationalists from across the continent gathered in Accra for the All-African Peoples' Conference. Tom Mboya of Kenya captured the delegates' intentions and determination when he pointedly told European imperialists that "Africa must be free. Scram from Africa."

Throughout western and central Africa this is just what happened in the spectacular outburst of 1960. In that year Nigeria, Africa's most populous state, gained its independence. Nigeria followed the Ghanaian pattern of a negotiated settlement with Britain, though this was complicated by efforts to reconcile the competing objectives of the nation's ethnic groups.

Most of France's African territories gained independence at the same time, but after traveling along a different political road. The French had attempted to accommodate the growing postwar African demands for liberty by conceding increasing equality within a framework of Franco-African cooperation. West African leaders, such as Léopold Senghor of Senegal and Félix Houphouët-Boigny of Côte d'Ivoire, were elected as deputies to the French National Assembly where they joined together in a federation of parties known as the Rassemblement Démocratique Africain and achieved influential bargaining positions in Paris.

In 1958, Charles de Gaulle returned to power in a France weary of colonial wars. Hoping to preempt further colonial conflict in Africa, he proposed a Franco-African Community in which the African states would have autonomy but not independence. De Gaulle used his personal charisma and the pressure of French economic assistance to win support for his plan in a referendum held throughout the French territories of western and central Africa. Although some African leaders were reluctant to abandon the goal of independence, only Guinea voted against the proposal. There, the popular Sékou Touré led opposition to

France's continued dominance of African affairs. Despite French attempts to isolate and punish Guinea, Touré received foreign aid and recognition.

The attraction of independence soon proved too powerful for the French-educated African elite in the other states, and in 1960 the remaining French territories became independent. Yet in spite of formal African independence, France maintained strong economic, cultural, political, and military influence in many of its former colonies.

Elsewhere in Africa, the winds of change sweeping the continent encountered entrenched colonial opposition. Until the eve of independence in the Belgian Congo, paternalistic colonial authorities banned political parties and provided few opportunities for higher education. Confronted with growing Congolese unrest, Brussels suddenly reversed its policies in 1959. Although politics in the enormous territory fractured along ethnic lines, Patrice Lumumba emerged as a champion of national unity and a rapid end to colonial rule. The precipitous independence that followed in 1960 was quickly marred by Lumumba's murder, chaotic ethnic and political conflict, Belgian intervention, and the need for intervention by UN peacekeeping forces.

Portugal, even more recalcitrant than Belgium, refused any significant concessions to African nationalism. Free of democratic pressures, the dictatorial regime in Lisbon brutally suppressed independence movements in its African colonies, leading to protracted liberation struggles in Guinea-Bissau, Angola, and Mozambique. Independence came only after discontented Portuguese soldiers overthrew their country's dictatorship in 1974. Ironically, these African liberation struggles indirectly brought democracy to Portugal but left an unfortunate legacy of continued instability in Africa.

Colonies with significant European settler communities also resisted the growing African demands for democracy and independence. In Kenya, the exploitation of African labor by white settlers, along with other factors, provoked the uprising of the Land Freedom Army (or Mau Mau Rebellion) in 1952. Although Britain defeated the rebellion after a major military campaign and the imprisonment of Jomo Kenyatta, the country's most prominent nationalist leader, the effort failed to preserve colonial rule and settler privileges. Disillusioned with the military effort, the British eventually released Kenyatta and negotiated Kenya's independence in 1963. Failing to learn a lesson from Kenya's example, British settlers in Rhodesia attempted to maintain white rule by declaring unilateral independence in 1965. Britain and the United Nations imposed sanctions, but only after a protracted armed struggle did freedom fighters win majority rule in 1980.

In the Republic of South Africa the National Party, with the overwhelming support of Afrikaner voters, won control of the white-minority government in the crucial election of 1948. The Afrikaners, primarily the descendants of long-established Dutch settlers, had struggled both to secure control of the land from its African inhabitants and to overthrow British colonial rule dating from the early nineteenth century. To maintain white power and privileges, the National Party imposed the system of rigid segregation and brutal exploitation of the African population known as apartheid.

The African National Congress, advancing an alternate vision of racial equality, led the opposition to apartheid through decades of struggle. After demonstrations, civil disobedience, boycotts, an armed struggle and international sanctions, the South African government finally was compelled to abandon apartheid. In the process Namibia, sometimes called Africa's last colony, gained its independence from South African rule in 1990. When South Africa finally held its first democratic election, the African National Congress won a convincing victory in 1994, and its leader, Nelson Mandela, became president.

For both the country and Sub-Saharan Africa as a whole, this election marked the end of the long struggle for political emancipation from colonial rule. Although South Africa's complicated conflicts among Africans, Afrikaners, and Anglo-Saxons could tempt some historians to portray the creation of the Union of South Africa in 1910 or the establishment of the Republic in 1961 as the overthrow of colonialism, these developments were designed to perpetuate white minority rule. It was the democratic election of 1994 that brought majority rule.

The political overthrow of colonial rule in Africa left much unfinished business. The partition of the continent in the nineteenth century compelled African nationalists in the twentieth century to operate within established colonies and to wrest power from differing European political systems. As a consequence, the independence struggles often served to reinforce colonial borders despite the Pan-African ideals of many African leaders. Discontented African nationalists soon levied charges of neocolonialism, where the former colonial powers protected their economic interests and sometimes maintained their political influence despite the formal independence of African states. In many countries the rise of new African elites meant that the majority of the population exchanged one group of exploiters for another.

The transfer of power was frequently accompanied by elections and the creation of democratic constitutions, but these generally proved fragile foreign instruments. The formal structures of newly independent African governments often lacked strong foundations in either their African societies or the colonial experience. Frequently the unifying force of the nationalist struggles was replaced by ethnic conflict after independence. Soon the continent also was rocked by military coups d'état, as colonial armies proved a more durable inheritance from imperialism than constitutions.

In spite of these limitations, the recovery of African independence, with its promises of liberty and equality regardless of race, remains a momentous achievement of African nationalists and a dramatic chapter in the continent's history.

BRIAN DIGRE

See also: **Colonialism, Overthrow of: Nationalism and Anticolonialism; Colonialism, Overthrow of: Women and the Nationalist Struggle; Ghana (Republic of): Nationalism, Rise of, and the Politics of Independence; Nkrumah, Kwame; South Africa: 1994 to the Present; South Africa: Transition, 1990–1994; World War II: Sub-Saharan Africa: Economic Impact.**

Further Reading

Birmingham, D. *The Decolonization of Africa*. Athens, Ohio: Ohio University Press, 1995.

Gifford, P., and W.M. Roger Louis, *Decolonization and African Independence: The Transfers of Power 1960–1980*, New Haven, Conn.: Yale University Press, 1988.

———. *The Transfer of Power: Decolonization, 1940–1960*. New Haven, Conn.: Yale University Press, 1982.

Hargreaves, John. *Decolonization in Africa*. London: Longman, 1988.

Mazrui, A. A., and M. Tidy. *Nationalism and New States in Africa*. London: Heinemann, 1984.

Meredith, M. *The First Dance of Freedom: Black Africa in the Postwar Era*. New York: Harper and Row, 1984.

Nkrumah, K. *Ghana: The Autobiography of Kwame Nkrumah*. London: T. H. Nelson, 1957.

Young, C. *The African Colonial State in Comparative Perspective*. New Haven, Conn: Yale University Press, 1994.

———. *Politics in the Congo: Decolonization and Independence*. Princeton, N.J.: Princeton University Press, 1965.

Colonialism, Overthrow of: Thirty Years War for Southern African Liberation

The decolonization process that unfolded across Africa in the 1950s and 1960s as the British, French, and Belgians felt constrained (albeit from continued bargaining positions of relative economic strength) when entering into negotiations with rising nationalist elites in their several colonies came to a halt when African aspirations confronted the established power of intransigent white minorities in southern Africa. Portugal remained in colonial occupation of Angola and Mozambique, and the white settlers would soon consolidate their own control over Southern Rhodesia (Zimbabwe) through the 1965 Unilateral Declaration of Independence from Britain. Most centrally, South Africa's apartheid government stood firm in its illegal possession of Southwest Africa (Namibia) and confident of the sustainability of its own racist premises and practices inside South Africa itself. Such regimes were not prepared to yield to the nationalist and democratic claims of the majority in any of these territories. As had happened only infrequently in Africa north of the Zambezi—and as was not to be required in the British-controlled High Commission Territories within the region, independent from the mid-1960s onward as Botswana, Lesotho, and Swaziland—revolutionary violence and ever more effective forms of mass action would be necessary to defeat white minority rule, both colonial and quasi-colonial, across most of southern Africa. In consequence, the "overthrow of colonialism" that ultimately did occur in this region has come to stand as one of the most dramatic and heroic moments in all of African history.

Between 1960 and 1990, southern Africa became a theater of war. This was a period bounded, in its beginnings, by the 1960 banning of the African National Congress (ANC) and Pan-Africanist Congress, which precipitated attempts by these movements to launch armed struggles in South Africa, by a further build-up in Angola of the pressures that erupted into violent confrontation there in 1961, and by Dar es Salaam's emergence as the central staging ground for liberation movements dedicated to struggles farther south in Angola, Mozambique, Zimbabwe, Namibia, and South Africa. The period spanned the ensuing conflicts that brought independence to both Angola and Mozambique in 1975 and the establishment of majority rule in Zimbabwe in 1980. And it closed, in 1990, with the liberation of Africa's last colony, Namibia, and with the release in South Africa of Nelson Mandela and the lift of the ban on the ANC that set the stage for a period of negotiations (1990–1994) toward establishment of a democratic constitution there and the holding of the "freedom elections" of 1994 that brought the ANC to power.

This regional war of liberation can be seen as having significance on three levels. First, there was W. E. B. Du Bois's remarkable assertion, in 1902, that the chief issue facing the twentieth century would be "the color bar," the "world movement of freedom for colored races." In this respect, the Thirty Years War in southern Africa had produced, by the turn of the century, the overthrow of the last (and most intransigent) expression of institutionalized and unapologetic racist rule in the world. Second, in continental terms, the liberation of southern Africa was the final act in the continent-wide drama of nationalist-driven decolonization that was at the center of African history in the post–World War II period. Finally, the nationalist assertions in

southern Africa in the 1960s and 1970s also partook in the anti-imperialist radicalization of the time that seemed to promise, at least momentarily, a socialist advance in many parts of the developing world. On this front, however, and for a variety of reasons (perhaps above all the growing hegemony of global neoliberalism by the end of the period), neither the guerrilla-based "people's wars" nor (in South Africa) a genuine mass mobilization produced sustainable socialist projects or even, in many cases, markedly democratic ones. Moreover, given the importance of Eastern military support for the liberation wars, southern African nationalism intersected with Cold War rivalries (the American preoccupation with Cuban assistance to the MPLA regime in Angola offering one especially negative case in point) and with Sino-Soviet tensions that also compromised radical outcomes.

The various territorial theaters of war (Angola, Mozambique, Zimbabwe, Namibia, South Africa) had their own concrete histories and dynamics, each considered elsewhere in this volume. Here it is important to underscore the distinctly regional dimensions of the war of liberation carried out across the subcontinent. Military relations established between liberation movements ranged from the abortive joint military campaign of the ANC and Zimbabwean African People's Union (ZAPU) in Rhodesia in the 1960s to the far more effective links forged between the Front for the Liberation of Mozambique (Frelimo) and the Zimbabwean African National Union (ZANU) in northern Mozambique and eastern Zimbabwe during the 1970s. Political ties also developed, with Frelimo, Angola's MPLA, and the PAIGC in Portugal's West African colony of Guinea-Bissau cooperating to establish an alternative international voice to Portugal's own posturing, for example. Indeed, the liberation movements more broadly shared in the work of projecting the importance of the southern African struggle in Africa; in international forums; in the "socialist" countries; and, together with their supporters from nongovernmental organizations, churches, trade unions, and even some governments (notably in Scandinavia), in Western countries. Nor should the pan-regional symbolism of shared struggle be underestimated; the successes of Frelimo and the MPLA were potent and oft-cited points of reference for activists inside South Africa as the popular movement revived there in the 1970s and 1980s.

The various liberation movements were also forced to take cognizance of the regional nature of the resistance to their claims. Economic, political, and military links established among Portugal, Rhodesia, and the apartheid regime in South Africa in defense of white minority rule were significant. Equally so was the fact that victories in the region did not occur simultaneously. This meant, for example, that Mozambique and

Angola, coming to independence in the mid-1970s a full fifteen years before Mandela's release, became targets of ruthless wars of destabilization waged by a South Africa anxious to retain a protected perimeter against the precedent of liberation and the establishment of ANC rear bases. Hence South Africa's invasion of independent Angola, and its creation of and/or support for such markedly destructive counterrevolutionary forces as UNITA in Angola and Renamo in Mozambique (Renamo itself having first been created by the Rhodesian regime). Such aggression also was backed, both tacitly and overtly, by various Western interests, notably by the United States under President Ronald Reagan, who was both well-disposed toward apartheid South Africa and, driven by countersocialist and Cold War considerations, quite willing to target countries like Angola and Mozambique for "roll back," and to delay Namibian independence.

Against this, the extent to which the liberation of southern Africa became a focus of continental political endeavor bears noting. Despite differences among themselves in terms of concrete political priorities and the levels of commitment of resources each was prepared to offer, the already independent African states did assume, through the Organization of African Unity (OAU), a significant responsibility for the waging of the struggle. Central in this regard was the OAU's Liberation Committee, itself successor to the Pan-African Freedom Movement of East, Central, and Southern Africa. Moreover, the part played by the front-line states—notably, Tanzania and Zambia, and, once they had achieved their own freedom from Portuguese rule, Angola and Mozambique—in advancing the struggle farther south was notable. The establishment of the Southern African Development Coordination Conference (SADCC) was also noteworthy as a move, however modest, to provide countries within the region with an institutional counterweight to South Africa's overbearing economic power. Indeed, despite very real shortcomings, the role of Africa in contributing to the struggle for liberation of southern Africa stands as the most significant expression of Pan-Africanism in practice yet witnessed on the continent.

The outcome of the Thirty Years War remains contradictory. Certainly, the overthrow of white minority rule was an achievement of world-historical consequence. At the same time, the devastation inflicted across the region during the war, and especially upon Mozambique and Angola (where, indeed, violent confrontation continued after 1990), was vast both in material and human terms. And, as noted, the broader goals that emerged in the course of these struggles—for the transformation of the impoverished state of the mass of the population of the region—have proven difficult to realize. Even the sense of a common regional

identity that might have been expected to surface from shared region-wide struggle has been offset, if not entirely effaced, by many of the same kinds of xenophobia and interstate rivalries that mark the rest of the continent. The transformation of SADCC into a new Southern African Development Community that now includes South Africa may hold some greater promise, though it is, at present, a regional project driven more by elite than popular interests, and one rooted in neoliberal premises.

JOHN S. SAUL

See also: **Angola: Independence and Civil War, 1974–1976; Angola: Civil War: Impact of, Economic and Social; Angola: MPLA, FNLA, UNITA and the War of Liberation, 1961–1974; Angola: Peace Betrayed, 1994 to the Present; Angola: Revolts, 1961; Cold War, Africa and; Mozambique: Frelimo and the War of Liberation, 1962–1975; Namibia: Struggle for Independence, 1970–1990; Namibia: SWAPO and the Freedom Struggle; South Africa: African National Congress; South Africa: Antiapartheid Struggle: Townships, the 1980s; South Africa: Antiapartheid Struggle, International; Zimbabwe (Rhodesia): Unilateral Declaration of Independence and the Smith Regime, 1964–1979.**

Further Reading

Birmingham, D. *The Decolonization of Africa.* London: UCL Press/Athens, Ohio: Ohio University Press, 1995.

Cox, R. *Pan-Africanism in Practice: PAFMECSA 1958–1964.* London: Oxford University Press, 1964.

Davidson, B., J. Slovo, and A. R. Wilkinson. *Southern Africa: The New Politics of Revolution.* Harmondsworth, England: Penguin, 1976.

Harding, J. *The Fate of Africa: Trial by Fire.* New York: Simon and Schuster, 1993.

Minter, W. *King Solomon's Mines Revisited: Western Interests and the Burdened History of Southern Africa.* New York: Basic, 1986.

Moorcroft, P. *African Nemesis: War and Revolution in Southern Africa (1945–2010).* London: Brassey's, 1994.

Saul, J. S. *Recolonization and Resistance: Southern Africa in the 1990s.* Trenton, N.J.: Africa World Press, 1993.

Colonialism, Overthrow of: Women and the Nationalist Struggle

African women played a crucial role in post–World War II national liberation movements. Their contributions, many and varied, demonstrated their courage and devotion to national liberation. Their participation in these wars also introduced the complex interrelationship between national liberation and women's emancipation.

In the settler colonies in which these wars of national liberation took place, colonial capitalism introduced and institutionalized migrant labor and alienation of African land for white settlers or foreign economic enterprises. The majority of the migrant laborers were male. As a result, women came to shoulder increased responsibilities and to discharge some tasks that, in precolonial Africa, would have been considered male duties. To facilitate the flow of African labor, the African family's economic viability as a relatively self-sufficient unit had to be thoroughly compromised. This involved reduction of land available to Africans and imposition of colonial taxes that had to be paid in colonial cash. In Kenya there was alienation of land in Central Province and also the introduction of cash crops. These two factors restricted women's access to land. Together with constant colonial labor needs, there was economic desperation among African families (especially among those in Central Province, the Rift Valley squatters, and the slum residents of Nairobi) in the period after World War II. In Algeria, forcible expropriation of land for the white settlers, *pied noir*, undermined the indigenous local domestic economy and led to massive unemployment, poverty, and desperation. African women in settler colonies were rarely spared from compulsory labor. In Mozambique, this entailed the forcible "cultivation of cotton and rice."

Women's duties and roles varied from one liberation movement to another. In all of the liberation movements (in Algeria, Guinea-Bissau, Kenya, Mozambique, Angola, Zimbabwe, South Africa, and Namibia), the majority of the women activists were peasants. In Algeria, those women who volunteered were generally excluded from combat roles. During the course of the liberation war some of the women came to bear arms to perform specialized duties like strategic assassinations or delivery of bombs. The majority of the women performed noncombat roles specified by the FLN; these included roles traditionally associated with women, such as nursing or cooking. In the Mau Mau revolt in Kenya, women procured food and transported it to the edge of the forests or sometimes into the interior of the forests where guerrillas resided. They also gathered information and, like women in the other movements, spied on behalf of the national liberation movement. This information involved movement of government troops with the purpose of gaining the colonial government's secrets about the prosecution of the war. A significant degree of trust had to exist and be actively maintained between the guerrillas and the women who rendered this courier service. Those women who accompanied the Mau Mau guerrillas to the forests rarely engaged in combat. Most of them performed noncombat duties: cooking, keeping camps clean, caring for the sick, and singing.

In the Mozambican revolutionary war under (Frelimo), women were initially assigned to perform traditional female roles. They transported war material from Tanzania to internal bases in Northern Mozambique and also from one base to another. They cultivated food to feed the guerrillas and washed clothes. Men in Frelimo were initially very reluctant to cede any power to women. In 1967, a women's detachment was formed. Subject to the same training as men, this unit was deployed to defend liberated areas and also to engage in combat. Women of Namibia whose activities were coordinated by the SWAPO Women's Council also trained and fought as guerrillas alongside men. As in Mozambique, male fighters (and some leaders) in SWAPO were initially very reluctant to accept women as comrades in arms. Other women participated as teachers and nurses in the refugee camps, while some were engaged in the production and preparation of food for the guerrillas.

Women's traditional familial roles determined their roles in the liberation war (Chimurenga) in Zimbabwe. Mothers stayed in Zimbabwe and became crucial in the "passive wing." They cultivated food that fed the guerrillas, made cash contributions, and attended clandestine meetings called by the guerrillas to "spread the word." There were those young women, or daughters, who went out of Zimbabwe to join the liberation movements in neighboring countries (Zambia, Mozambique) and those who remained at home. Those young who joined the liberation movements outside Zimbabwe trained in several capacities, including guerrilla warfare. It has been estimated that, by 1977, up to one third of the guerrillas in ZANLA (Zimbabwe African National Liberation Army) were women. At home, the young women known as *chimbwidos* prepared food and carried it to the bush for the guerrillas while evading police detection. They did laundry and obtained supplies; their services were crucial in the rural support network for the guerrillas. In all of the liberation movements, women were effective mobilizers and recruiters for the nationalist struggle.

These women activists who participated in national liberation struggles were, above all, nationalists. In almost every settler colony, the demands of women and those of the nationalist activists came to converge on the need to uproot colonialism from Africa. As well, no sizable African women's movement devoted exclusively to women's emancipation existed in any territory under colonial rule; it would have been difficult to have one. There was also the question of the definition of women's emancipation embraced by even the most radical of these national liberation movements, which tended to differ from the definitions associated with liberal Western feminism.

In Mozambique, the Organization of Mozambican Women (OMM) was subsumed under Frelimo. At its first conference in 1973, Machel stated that "The liberation of women is the fundamental necessity of the liberation, a guarantee of its continuity, and a precondition for victory." This conference was at pains to warn Mozambican women against the danger of identifying men as the enemy. Gender warfare was seen as counterproductive to the revolutionary cause. It was the result of "inaccurate analysis." In Angola, the Organization of Angolan Women (OMA) operated under the MPLA. Since its formation in 1962, the OMA had always seen its activities as complementary to those of the MPLA. The OMA's definition of emancipation continued to embrace the legal, political, economic and social aspects of a woman's life. The emancipation of women in Angola was seen both by the MPLA and the OMA as a long-term process. Overcoming colonial legacies and parts of traditional cultures not receptive to gender equality required structural changes, economic development, stability, and political education. Legal equality alone would not guarantee emancipation and liberation. In South Africa, the African women organized under the African National Congress Women's League (ANCWL) saw apartheid as the fount of misery, oppression, and exploitation. There could be no progress or freedom as long as apartheid remained in place.

The linkage—indeed, the close affiliation—between women's movements like the OMA, OMM, ANCWL, and their male-dominated national liberation movements has been criticized by several Western academic feminists and also increasingly by some African feminists. These feminists have argued that the integrity of these women's movements was compromised and that their focus shifted away from critical gender problems and issues because of male domination of the discourse.

The success of these nationalist struggles as champions of women's emancipation was dependent on several factors, including how fervently each nationalist struggle embraced gender equality as a precondition for victory. There were movements like the Mau Mau that failed to address themselves to gender questions, either during the revolt or in a possible liberated society. There were others that advocated for a radical transformation of the postliberated society. These included the Frelimo, the MPLA, and the PAIGC. Others opted for a more cautious, even contradictory, position. This was true of the FLN in Algeria. To avoid alienating its male supporters, the FLN chose to be vague and ambiguous when dealing with gender issues. Its dual strategy of a possible socialist transformation of society and "cultural restoration" underlined this ambiguity.

The radical liberation movements that embraced gender equality had to undertake this and other social problems within the context of almost collapsed economies, a desperate lack of amenities, and massive poverty. In the case of Angola and Mozambique, there would also be the fateful external aggression that aimed to destroy the revolutions.

Wunyabari O. Maloba

See also: **Angola: MPLA, FNLA, UNITA, and the War of Liberation, 1961–1974; Kenya: Mau Mau Revolt; Mozambique: Frelimo and the War of Liberation, 1962–1975; Women: History and Historiography.**

Further Reading

Armstrong, A., and J. Stewart (eds.). *The Legal Situation of Women in Southern Africa*. Harare: University of Zimbabwe, 1990.

Knauss, P. *The Persistence of Patriarchy: Class, Gender and Ideology in 20th Century Algeria*. New York: Praeger, 1987.

Lazreg, M. *The Eloquence of Silence: Algerian Women in Question*. New York: Routledge, 1994.

Likimani, M. *Passbook No.l F 47927: Women and Mau Mau in Kenya*. London: Macmillan, 1985.

Meena, R. (ed.). *Gender in Southern Africa*. Harare: Sapes, 1992.

Organization of Angolan Women. *Angolan Women Building the Future*. London: Zed, 1984.

Presley, C. A. *Kikuyu Women, the Mau Mau Rebellion and Social Change in Kenya*. Boulder, Colo.: Westview Press, 1992.

Tetreault, M. A. (ed.). *Women and Revolution in Africa, Asia, and the New World*. Columbia: University of South Carolina Press, 1994.

Urdang, S. *Fighting Two Colonialisms: Women in Guinea-Bissau*. New York: Monthly Review Press, 1979.

———. *And Still They Dance: Women, War and the Struggle for Change in Mozambique*. New York: Monthly Review Press, 1989.

Walker, C. *Women and Resistance in South Africa*. London: Onyx Press, 1982.

Colonialism, Inheritance of: Postcolonial Africa

Three hundred years of foreign domination and a century of formal colonial rule in Africa left political, economic, and social scars that are still conspicuously evident in contemporary African society. The colonization of Africa resulted in the territorial ordering of the hitherto disparate communities into defined specific territories under the ambit of the colonial powers. The territories were administered as nation-states, a development that had gained wide currency in the Europe of the late nineteenth century as the premier form of political organization. But the ordering of the African societies into the artificial construct of nation-states was so arbitrary that some communities, clans, and even lineages were torn apart and placed under different nation-states. In the same vein, many and varied societies, with little in common, were lumped together into nation-states whose construction and boundary drawing was not reflexive of African cultural interests.

The interterritorial boundaries drawn by the colonial powers in the pursuit of nation-states disregarded preexisting cultural bonds among the various communities. One of the major challenges to the postcolonial state has been how to reconcile the arbitrariness of the boundaries and its offspring, the nation-state, with the obtaining cultural realities existing in the continent. While at its formation in 1963, the Organization of African Unity (OAU) upheld as sacrosanct and inviolable boundaries as they were at independence, postcolonial conflict—such as the search for a greater Somalia, which has led to wars between Somalia and most of its neighbors—is a manifestation of the persistent plague of colonial boundary drawing in postcolonial Africa. So too are the conflicts in the Great Lakes Region, which have claimed millions of lives over the last four decades, as well as the Western Sahara conflict of the 1980s. The travails of colonial boundary demarcation and the constructed nation-state are persistent themes in the discourses on African political stability.

Colonial governance thrived on the strategy of divide and rule. It emphasized differences in culture, economy, and politics among the various communities. Under the colonial order, terms that were hitherto merely expressive of ethnic identity became transformed into stereotypical prisms of ethnic differences. By nurturing and privileging myths in which some communities were adulated as superior and enlightened while others were made to seem inferior as indolent and permanent subjects, the colonial state instituted and charted a course of unholy competition, rivalry, hatred, and destruction. Indeed, the uneven nature of economic development during the colonial period and the nature of administration—direct or indirect—privileged certain groups over others. While these characterizations were kept in control by the authoritarian colonial state and its coercive apparatus, the end of colonial rule unleashed these forces of cultural, ethnic, economic, and national intolerance with untold suffering to the citizenry.

Africa stills finds itself battling with the legacy of its colonial past in the attempts to institutionalize liberal democracy. The colonial state was not a democratic state; it was the very antithesis of liberal democracy. Thus, nationwide political parties were not encouraged. Political organization was domesticated at the ethnic or regional levels. This development, coupled with the fact that the strategy of divide and rule fostered difference and rivalry over compromise and unity, has complicated Africa's experiment with multiparty politics and majority rule.

Most of the African countries were allowed less than five years to exercise open, competitive multiparty politics leading to decolonization. This was an extremely brief period of time considering the scars of difference and division that had been nurtured and carried to frightening extremes by the colonial order. It is also instructive that, in the case of the former Portuguese colonies of Angola and Mozambique, the colonial power had an impractical time table for readying the country for independence. Their abrupt departure at a time when the Cold War was at its high noon exacerbated the interparty rivalry in these two countries, whose lands were reduced to "Cold War playgrounds." Indeed, Angola has yet to stabilize its polity since independence; the same is also true of the Democratic Republic of Congo, a former colony of Belgium. The Nigerian Civil War of the 1960s, the ethnic genocide within Rwanda in the 1990s, and the turmoil in Uganda between 1971 and 1985 are all expressive of the challenges facing the postcolonial African state as a result of its colonial legacy.

But African leadership has been equally responsible for some of the political and economic problems that plague the continent. Even though the majority of European powers bequeathed to their former colonies constitutions that were meant to encourage liberal democracy, most of the African countries ended up with either de facto or de jure one-party systems or military dictatorships within the first decade of independence. The democratization of the state as well as the establishment of supportive structures for civil society became quite elusive. With pressures from ethnic constituencies, economic challenges, and external politics of the bipolar world of the Cold War era, the postcolonial African state became not only overdeveloped but also quite authoritarian in protecting local clients as well as external patrons. Indeed, the majority of the African leadership turned the coercive instruments of the state against their own citizenry.

Postcolonial African economies are replete with the scars of the uneven and exploitative nature of colonialism. African countries are among the least developed and industrialized nations in the world. While three decades or more in the life of a nation is not short and African countries must share the blame for their economic predicament, it cannot be denied that the postcolonial African economies are, by and large, a function of their colonial past. Industrialization of the colonies was hardly accorded a pride of place by the colonial powers. At independence, no African country, except South Africa, had its share of manufacturing more than 20 per cent of its gross domestic product. The continent was reduced to the role of provider of primary products such as coffee, cocoa, tea, palm oil, rubber, and cotton, whose prices were determined by the importing countries. In addition, the farm inputs as well as machinery had to be imported from those very colonial powers that imported the raw materials, processed them, and determined the prices.

The colonial economies were directly linked to the economies of their respective metropolitan powers through an array of policies ranging from control of currency, trade policies, and infrastructure. The development of colonial economy and attendant infrastructure was not meant to promote trade within the continent. The colonial rail and road networks in Africa speak to the intent of their planners. The infrastructure invariably linked "economic areas of interest" in the hinterland to the ports at the coast, where the primary products were shipped abroad to the metropolitan countries for processing before being exported back to the country. This deliberate underindustrialization, coupled with slanting infrastructure, manipulation of currency, and trade policies through price fixing and monopolistic tendencies has adversely impacted Africa's postcolonial economies.

Out of the gloom of the past there is, however, a guarded optimism as Africa, like most parts of the world, is grappling with the transition to liberal democracy by instituting various reforms in support of that goal. Although most African countries have embraced competitive multiparty politics, this is only one step on the long road to liberal democracy. Africa has not been oblivious to the adverse economic scars of its past. African countries have instituted a number of correctives with a view to taming the wild economic excesses of its colonial legacy. The formation of regional economic blocks, namely the Economic Organization of West African States (ECOWAS), East African Community, and Southern African Development Coordinating Conference, was aimed at reducing tariffs among the member states with a view to promoting trade within the continent. Industrialization is also a topical theme in the development plans of African governments.

Despite these positive moves to redress the economic shortcomings of the past, African countries have to contend with a whole array of external economic actors dictating the nature, course, and speed of economic reforms in their countries. Both the World Bank and International Monetary Fund exercise unparalleled economic influence over Africa. The African state in the era of structural adjustment programs is being forced to cut costs by implementing prescribed measures such as debureaucratization, import liberalization, and cost-sharing in the provision of basic needs such as education and health care under the threat of otherwise losing economic aid. While it is too early to assess the extent to which the policies will catapult Africa from its economic quagmire, it is a point of fact that Africa has never overcome the setbacks put in place during the colonial era.

GEORGE ODUOR NDEGE

See also: **Angola: Independence and Civil War, 1974–1976; Congo (Kinshasa), Democratic Republic of/Zaire: Evolués, Politics, Independence; East African Community, the, 1967–1977; Economic Community of West African States (ECOWAS); Mozambique: Frelimo and the War of Liberation, 1962–1975; Nigeria: Colonial Period: Intelligentsia, Nationalism, Independence; Polisario and the Western Sahara; Rwanda: Civil Unrest, and Independence: 1959–1962; Somalia: Independence, Conflict, and Revolution; Southern African Development Community; Uganda: Independence and Obote's First Regime, 1962–1971; World Bank, International Monetary Fund, and Structural Adjustment.**

Further Reading

Anyang', P. Nyong'o, and P. Coughlin (eds.). *Industrialization at Bay: African Experiences.* Nairobi: African Academy of Sciences, 1991.

Boahen, A. A. *African Perspectives on Colonialism.* Baltimore: Johns Hopkins University Press, 1987.

Clapham, C. *Africa and the International System: The Politics of State Survival.* Cambridge: Cambridge University Press, 1996.

Davidson, B. *The Black Man's Burden: Africa and Curse of the Nation State.* New York: Random House, 1992.

Mamdani, M. *Citizen and Subject: Contemporary Africa and the Legacy of Late Colonialism.* Princeton, N.J.: Princeton University Press, 1996.

Ogot, B. A., and W. R. Ochieng' (eds.). *Decolonization and Independence in Kenya, 1940–93.* Athens, Ohio: Ohio University Press/London: James Currey, 1995.

Ottaway, M. *Africa's New Leaders: Democracy or State Reconstruction.* Washington, D.C.: Carnegie Endowment for International Peace, 1999.

Preston, P. W. *Development Theory: An Introduction.* Oxford: Blackwell, 1966.

Colonialism: Impact on African Societies

Although the European colonial intrusion into Africa had roots that stretched back to the Portuguese enclaves of the sixteenth century and the Dutch East India Company's South African colony in the seventeenth century, the colonization of the continent as a whole could be said to have begun with the French invasion of Algeria in 1830; it lasted until Namibian independence in 1990. Within this 160-year time span, European governments both consciously and unconsciously caused massive changes in African politics, economies, societies, cultures, and religions.

In keeping with nineteenth–century ideas about the role of government, European powers in Africa set up administrations whose main focus was the maintenance of order rather than any type of economic or social development. At the same time, there was a notion that the colonies should be made to pay for themselves; European powers wanted the colonies but did not want them to become economic burdens. As a result, during the early years of colonialism European governments either kept relatively small colonial staffs or contracted out the duties of governance to chartered companies (as with the British Royal Niger Company in northern Nigeria). In either case, the European administrations needed to make alliances with elite groups in the colonial population to ensure effective governance (e.g., the Barotse in Northern Rhodesia, the Baganda in Uganda, the Fulbe in northern Nigeria, and the coastal Swahili peoples in German East Africa). These types of alliances had the effect of favoring certain groups over others, often creating or exacerbating ethnic and tribal divisions (e.g., Belgian support of the Tutsi vis-à-vis the Hutu in Rwanda and Burundi). They also resulted, in many instances, in the creation of a privileged class from which the colonial governments drew their indigenous administrators, police, interpreters, and clerks.

While a small minority of peoples were privileged by colonial rule, a vast majority suffered. Groups that refused to cooperate with the colonial regime, as well as traditional enemies of the now-privileged groups, quickly found themselves frozen out of the power structure in the colonies. Examples of groups who resisted, rather than cooperated with, colonial rule are numerous. The Ndebele and Mashona in Southern Rhodesia revolted against the white colonizers several times in the late nineteenth century; these groups lost their lands and were forced onto reservations, often deprived of their livestock, where they lived in new circumstances in societies broken up as a result of war and forced migration. In Uganda, British favoritism toward the Baganda met with resistance from the latter's traditional enemies, the Bunyoro; British rule included giving Bunyoro lands to the Baganda, deposing the Bunyoro ruler, and insisting upon the Bunyoro appointing Baganda administrators. In German Southwest Africa (Namibia), the Herero revolt resulted in two-thirds of the Herero population being killed, all their lands seized by the colonial state, and the government forbidding survivors to own livestock.

In some instances colonies were used as settlements for relatively large numbers of Europeans (e.g., German eastern and southwest Africa, Cameroun, and Togo; French Algeria; Portuguese Angola and Mozambique; the British South Africa Company's encouragement of settlement in Southern and Northern Rhodesia; and, most obviously, South Africa). In most cases, governments (or companies) encouraged European settlement by providing economic incentives, some of which included free land, provision of agricultural supplies, transportation and relocation costs, and favorable trade terms with the home country. In some areas (such as the Portuguese colonies), settlers operated like feudal states; settlers had the right to tax, administer justice, recruit laborers, and raise private police forces on their own estates. In other cases (e.g., Algeria), settlers comprised a powerful lobbying group in the home country and were able to significantly affect colonial policy.

In the economic sphere, colonialism also brought major changes to the continent. Before the colonial era, most African regions did not have any system of wage labor. For colonial administrations, this presented a difficulty: how to mobilize people to do the labor of the government, such as constructing roads, canals, and bridges. The answer in many cases was simply to force Africans to labor for the colonial regimes; colonial administrations worked with local chieftains, who supplied the governments with slaves and tribute labor. The Congo Free State under the Belgian King Leopold (and from 1908 ruled by Belgium as the Belgian Congo) is the classic example of the abuses of colonialism. In exploiting the region's wild rubber, ivory, and palm oil resources, the government not only used forced labor but also introduced bodily mutilation and lashings as punishments for a variety of offenses and often used hostage taking as a way of ensuring villages met their rubber quotas.

Despite such abuses, colonial governments did succeed in many instances in improving infrastructure; by World War I, the road system in central Africa had opened up most of the interior of the continent for transportation. Though development per se was generally not a priority for colonial regimes, construction of roads, railways, canals, and the like was important, as these were needed for moving troops, supplies, and trade goods through the continent. Many historians argue that the diminution of conflict between African peoples and the construction of this sort of infrastructure led to a period of "colonial peace" that in turn resulted in more attention being paid to development and to social, cultural, and religious issues. Others, however, stress the dislocation of African societies and the disruption of indigenous laws and authority and argue that the colonial peace was instead a type of cultural warfare.

In West Africa, colonial governments entered into an economy that already included the production of cash crops used for trade with Europe (though most agriculture was still for subsistence). Colonial administrators thus could simply tax already existing trade and agriculture and encourage further developments in peasant production in order to raise revenue (as the French did in Senegal). In central and eastern Africa, Africans were also required to pay tax to colonial governments; the result was that Africans were in effect forced to work for Europeans (usually as migrant laborers on agricultural estates) in order to raise the money needed to pay their taxes. Economic reorganization of this type, coupled with the use of coins and notes, helped expand trade and bring parts of Africa into a cash-based market economy. Yet it did so at terrible cost to the people. As Africans were forced into wage labor in order to pay colonial costs, they tended to work in nonagricultural sectors; not only did this disrupt rural life, increase rural poverty, and contribute to rural-to-urban migration, but it was also ultimately to contribute to the postcolonial famines of the 1970s.

African societies and cultures also experienced significant dislocations and alterations during the colonial era. As colonies were established on the continent, borders were drawn that in many cases bore no relationship to indigenous and political realities. Colonial borders thus served to group together traditional enemies and to divide communities that had previously been united, the worst example of the latter being the division of the Somali people among British, Italian, French, and Ethiopian authorities.

Though primarily a European conflict, World War I affected Africa profoundly. The European colonial powers used their African colonies as sources of men for battle and resources and wealth to finance the war and supply their troops. Initially, African men joined the war as part of already established colonial militaries (e.g., the British West African Frontier Force, the Belgian Force Publique, the French Tirailleurs, and the German Schütztruppen). These regiments were enlarged when the war began, and African men joined them either out of obedience to their traditional leaders or in hopes of earning wages. However, as the war continued and loss of life mounted, colonial powers began to require greater military service of the mass of their subjects. French forces during the war included over half a million Africans, some 200,000 of whom died in the war. The British conscripted over a million men as combatants and support personnel; German, Belgian, and Portuguese forces also included large African contingents. While there is no agreement on the total number of African lives lost in the conflict, a conservative estimate puts the figure at 300,000. Not only did Africans lose their lives, but African societies were further disrupted as men fled and hid to avoid conscription or staged protests that turned violent.

As European authority began to replace traditional authority, crimes began to be tried in colonial courts, and local chieftains began to be forced or enticed to work (in a subordinate position) with the European administrators, traditional leaders began to lose their legitimacy. Since most traditional leaders relied on religious sanction for their rule, as they lost legitimacy and were increasingly seen as unimportant, religious questions began to be raised as well.

Since colonial governments tended to focus on political and economic matters, education and social work were left largely to European missionary societies; in most parts of Africa, missionary work preceded the formal establishment of colonies. Colonialism gave new energy to these missions, as European men and women were increasingly attracted to the idea of converting the indigenous populations of the colonies. Mission work was most often done through the establishment of village schools, where children would be taught basic reading, writing, and mathematics and given religious instruction. Conversions to various denominations of Christianity were quite successful almost everywhere in Africa where Islam was not the predominant religion. The result was the formation of a new class of mission-educated Africans who often became not only the driving force behind further education and mission work, but also a rival center of power challenging the traditional elites. Those educated in the mission schools were able to deal with colonial administrators more easily and as a result often gained positions in the colonial administration.

While missionary education might have been initially beneficial for the colonial powers, it gradually became a source of opposition to European rule. Mission-educated leaders began to demand the Africanization of the religious and political institutions implanted by the West; it is from this group in society that many of the first generation of African nationalists came. These African Christians not only began to criticize colonial government, but also to criticize the churches in the colonies, emphasizing the contradictions between the Christian doctrines they were taught in the mission schools and the actual practices of colonial government. One result of this was the formation of independent African Christian churches in the early twentieth century. Yet not all depictions of mission work in Africa are positive. Many historians argue that it was mission work that set the stage for colonialism by bringing Africa to European attention, portraying its indigenous peoples as weak, divided, and uncivilized.

Colonialism thus had both positive and negative effects on African societies, but in general the balance was not in favor of Africa. Colonial systems were founded for the benefit of Europe. Economies were reorganized to benefit the administration, the home country, and the European merchants, industrialists, and traders in the colonies. Political systems aimed at keeping African populations obedient and docile, rather than at providing Africans with tangible benefits. Although railways were introduced, they were to facilitate trade for the benefit of Europe. Although education was spread, it was education via mission schools that served to break down African societies and traditional patterns of social organization. Although European administration resulted in greater resource extraction, its profits were not used to develop the colonies. And although Europe introduced modern technologies to Africa, it did not train Africans in their uses. The roots of many of the political, economic, social, and cultural problems of several modern African states can be traced back to the colonial era.

AMY J. JOHNSON

Further Reading

Chidester, D. *Savage Systems: Colonialism and Comparative Religion in Southern Africa.* Charlottesville: University Press of Virginia, 1996.

Cooper, F. *Decolonization and African Society: the Labor Question in French and British Africa.* Cambridge: Cambridge University Press, 1996.

Coquery-Vidrovitch, C. *African Women: A Modern History,* translated by Beth Gillian Raps. Boulder, Colo.: Westview Press, 1997.

Friedrichsmeyer, S., et al. (eds.). *The Imperialist Imagination: German Colonialism and Its Legacy.* Ann Arbor: University of Michigan Press, 1998.

Mamdani, M. *Citizen and Subject: Contemporary Africa and the Legacy of Late Colonialism.* Princeton, N.J.: Princeton University Press, 1996.

Miers, S., and M. Klein (eds.). *Slavery and Colonial Rule in Africa.* London: Frank Cass, 1999.

Prakash, G. (ed.). *After Colonialism: Imperial Histories and Postcolonial Displacements.* Princeton, N.J.: Princeton University Press, 1995.

Colored Identity: *See* South Africa: Colored Identity.

Commonwealth, Africa and the

Growing organically out of the British Empire, the British Commonwealth generally attempts to work by consensus. For a time, as a new commonwealth emerged after World War II, the suspicion persisted that it represented no more than an easy let-down for Britain as its empire diminished, but this perception died away during the 1970s and 1980s when issues such as apartheid in South Africa or the Unilateral Declaration of Independence (UDI) in Rhodesia placed Britain in opposition to most of the new commonwealth. The principal value of the commonwealth association is a membership that bridges the gap between two regions (in this case, north and south) and provides its members with an additional international forum through which to express their views and needs. There are a range of commonwealth organizations dealing with many aspects of development; for example, its finance ministers meet every year. The Commonwealth Secretariat is situated in London.

From the Act of Union of 1910, which created it, until 1948, South Africa was treated as one of Britain's white dominions (with Australia, Canada, and New Zealand), but when the National Party came to power in the latter year and began to implement apartheid, this policy set South Africa upon a path that would lead to its isolation within the commonwealth.

The decision of newly independent India to remain in the commonwealth, and the new formula devised by Britain under which the British monarch became head of the commonwealth association, allowed India to join as a republic. This naturally made it possible later for fiercely nationalist African ex-colonies also to join as republics. Led by Ghana in 1957, almost every British African colony joined the commonwealth at independence. There were two exceptions: Sudan did not become a member of the commonwealth, while British Somaliland was united with former Italian Somalia to form the Somali Republic.

The Suez Crisis of 1956, though an African commonwealth problem, just preceded the era of African independence and only South Africa took part in the heads of government debates, supporting British military action against Gamal Abdel Nasser's Egypt.

Two major long-running crises defined African attitudes toward the commonwealth and Britain: apartheid in South Africa, and the UDI in Rhodesia. The subject of South Africa's race policies was raised at the 1960 commonwealth meeting in London but was shelved. The issue was again raised at the 1961 meeting (the South African white electorate had meanwhile voted in a referendum to become a republic), and the South African prime minister Hendrik Verwoerd did not seek readmission for South Africa to the commonwealth as a republic.

Over the years, Commonwealth Heads of Government Meetings (CHOGMs) regularly discussed the South African issue. This dominated the 1985 meeting in Nassau, Bahamas, which established the Eminent Persons Group (EPG) to make recommendations for change in South Africa, though the EPG was rebuffed in Pretoria. South Africa also dominated the CHOGMs of 1987 (Vancouver) and 1989 (Kuala Lumpur), while in 1990 a group of commonwealth leaders met Nelson Mandela, the leader of the African National Congress (ANC), in Lusaka. The 1991 CHOGM in Harare proposed a three-stage lifting of sanctions as South Africa dismantled apartheid. Following the all-race elections of 1994 that brought Nelson Mandela to power as the country's first black president, South Africa was invited to rejoin the commonwealth, which it did in May 1994.

Rhodesia, whose white minority government under Ian Smith made the UDI in 1965, was to be central to commonwealth discussions for 15 years, and it has been argued, without the pressures exerted upon it by the African commonwealth members, Britain might have allowed Rhodesia to go its own way under a white minority government. A special commonwealth meeting was held in Lagos, Nigeria, during January 1966 when the formula "no independence before majority rule" was adopted. At the 1979 CHOGM in Lusaka, Britain's prime minister Margaret Thatcher agreed to accept a process that involved months of negotiations in London and led to elections in March 1980 and independence for Rhodesia (as Zimbabwe) on April 18 of that year.

The Harare Declaration, arising from the 1991 Harare CHOGM, set forth commonwealth principles in relation to democracy and human rights. Newly independent Namibia was welcomed as the 51st member of the commonwealth. The 1995 CHOGM at Auckland was especially concerned with African affairs. On the eve of the conference, in defiance of many pleas from around the world, the Nigerian government of General Sani Abacha had the Ogoni leader, Ken Saro-Wiwa, and eight other environmental activists hanged. The CHOGM then suspended Nigeria's membership for human rights abuses. The same CHOGM welcomed two new members to the commonwealth: Cameroon, which had been created out of the British and French mandates of the former German Cameroon, and Mozambique, which was the first country with no previous connection with the British Empire to join the commonwealth.

One of the principal subjects at the 1997 CHOGM at Edinburgh concerned the civil war in Sierra Leone. The death of General Sani Abacha of Nigeria in June 1998 opened the way for Nigeria to resume its membership in the commonwealth.

Seventeen African countries are also members of the commonwealth, and though over the years several members have threatened to leave the association (always in reaction to a disagreement with its most powerful member, Britain) none have done so. The reentry of South Africa into the commonwealth in 1994 gave the association a new sense of primacy and purpose, while the successful applications to join made by Cameroon and Mozambique illustrated that the commonwealth was valued for reasons beyond links with the former imperial power.

The 17 African members of the commonwealth (in 1999) were Botswana, Cameroon, Gambia, Ghana, Kenya, Lesotho, Malawi, Mauritius, Mozambique, Namibia, Nigeria, Sierra Leone, Swaziland, Tanzania, Uganda, Zambia, and Zimbabwe.

GUY ARNOLD

See also: **Colonial Federations: British Central Africa; Colonialism, Overthrow of: Sub-Saharan Africa; South Africa: Peace, Reconstruction, Union: 1902–1910.**

Further Reading

Arnold, G. *The Third World Handbook*, 2nd ed. London: Cassell, 1994.
Brockway, F. *The Colonial Revolution.* London: Hart-Davis, MacGibbon, 1973.
Charlton, M. *The Last Colony in Africa: Diplomacy and the Independence of Rhodesia.* Oxford: Basil Blackwell, 1990.
Lewis, R., and Y. Foy. *The British in Africa.* London: Weidenfeld and Nicolson, 1971.
Royle, T. *Winds of Change: The End of Empire in Africa.* London: John Murray, 1996.

Communaute Financière Africaine

At independence, the former French colonies and territories under French mandate entered into a series of agreements with France on a wide range of political, military, economic, and cultural issues. Regarding financial matters, the countries agreed to continue the monetary union they had with France when they were colonies by remaining within the French franc zone. This led to the organization of the former colonies (except Guinea and Mali) into a common currency zone called the Communaute Financière Africaine (CFA; African Financial Community). In 1984, Mali abandoned its own version of the franc that it had used since 1962 and joined the CFA zone. The former Spanish colony of Equatorial Guinea also joined the CFA area in 1985, and in so doing dispelled the image of the CFA as an exclusive club of former French colonies.

The CFA's activities are regulated by two central banks—one for the West African countries, known as Banque des Etats de l'Afrique de l'Ouest (BEAO) and the other for the Central African countries, called Banque des Etats de l'Afrique Centrale (BEAC). The BEAO is headquartered in Dakar, Senegal, and the BEAC in Yaounde, Cameroon. The two banks issue the currency in use in member countries, with *CFA* inscribed on the currency. Each member country also has a national unit of the bank that acts to regulate the activities of commercial banks, develop national banking laws, and deal with monetary policies (interest rates, inflation, etc.).

The French treasury guaranteed the convertibility of the CFA at a fixed parity rate of 50 CFA francs to one French franc. CFA members who had financial difficulties were allowed to borrow from the French treasury at the low interest of 1 per cent for amounts not exceeding five million French francs. The French treasury also provided security for commercial transactions made between or among members of the community. In return, members of the community were obligated to hold a portion of their foreign reserves in the French treasury. Further, France was equally represented on the board of directors of the Central Banks, where monetary decisions and regulations were made.

In 1994, France devalued the CFA, raising its parity rate against the French franc by 50 per cent. France also insisted that future aid to countries in the CFA monetary area would henceforth be tied to the World Bank and International Monetary Fund conditions.

The adoption of a common European currency, the Euro, in 1999 led to speculations that France would devalue the CFA again. France, however, dismissed such speculations as unfounded. As a member of the European Union, France does not itself have complete control over its own monetary policy, which is regulated now by the European Central Bank. For that reason, it may not continue to back up the CFA in international currency matters and markets, when that may weaken its own monetary situation within the European Union.

Since the CFA is connected to the French franc and enjoys the backing of the French treasury, it has enjoyed greater stability in currency markets and the confidence of those engaged in business transactions with the region than the currencies of other African countries (except for South Africa). However, the arrangement also raises the issue of the independence of the CFA countries. Because the arrangements virtually give France a veto power over what the countries can and cannot do, many analysts consider such a veto power to be too high a price for the benefits of currency stability and convertibility.

MOSES K. TESI

See also: **World Bank, International Monetary Fund, and Structural Adjustment.**

Further Reading

Ake, C. *A Political Economy of Africa.* New York: Longman, 1981.

International Monetary Fund (IMF). *Surveys of African Economies*, vol. 1. Washington, D.C.: IMF, 1968.

M'Bet, A., and N. A. Madeleine. "European Economic Integration and the Franc Zone: The Future of the CFA Franc after 1999, Part II." Nairobi, Kenya: African Economic Research Consortium, 1998.

Communications

As the global economy increasingly revolves around an emerging global information infrastructure (GII), Africa will find it more difficult to compete in the twenty-first century. Since independence, most of Africa has steadily lost ground in communications development. With the exception of those of a handful of states, most African national transportation and communications networks are badly deteriorated, outdated, and grossly insufficient for the large and growing urban populations who depend upon them, let alone rural citizens (who have rarely enjoyed such services). Africa's information infrastructure is by far the least developed,

least accessible, and most restrictive in the world. Privatization of telecommunications and broadcasting has led to some improvement in a few countries, however, such as Uganda and Botswana.

In setting priorities for communications development, all African governments face painful dilemmas. Never before have African states been presented with such an array of choices in telecommunications services and providers. Dependence on expensive, increasingly sophisticated imported communications technologies is near total. At the same time, the communications infrastructure in most places is so rudimentary that one must rank road construction and rural electrification far ahead of even extension of telephone service, newspapers, and television to rural areas. Only far into the future might one realistically put in a claim for meaningful expenditure on development of computer networks, microwave links, and satellite access despite the fact that these have already become the "basics" of the global communications infrastructure.

Former Tanzanian President Julius Nyerere once remarked that "while you (the United States) are trying to reach the moon we are still trying to reach the village." In the past, and continuing to a certain extent today, extension and development of communications in Africa was based primarily on the interests of the Western colonial and global economic powers. Historically, this meant linking African colonial cities with European capitals via oceanic cables and the laying out of national transportation and communication infrastructures from coastal capital cities to regional administrative centers, with very little effort to connect colonies with each other. It has always been easier to phone Paris or London than to communicate with fellow citizens up-country, and even today there are few interstate highways linking African states.

Until the 1970s, railways built by the departing colonial powers constituted the principal commercial lifelines for many new African states. Most lines suffered declines in quality of rolling stock and track, were put under parastatal management, and cut back service as debt forced deferred repairs and maintenance. Few passenger lines remain. Freight lines are significantly better off, at least within and between some countries, particularly in the South African Development Community subregion.

Following independence, paved, all-weather roads built by colonial governments fell progressively into disrepair, particularly in areas where climate conditions break down pavement rapidly, as in tropical West Africa. A few states, like Botswana, maintained, expanded, and modernized road networks with significant external financial assistance.

Most African countries set up national airlines, as parastatals, after independence. Escalating costs, inefficiency, and growing competition from global carriers forced many into debt, resulting in deteriorating service and fewer destinations. Indebtedness plagues even those airlines which have been well managed, forcing cutbacks.

There are more personal telephone lines in New York City's borough of Manhattan than in all of Sub-Saharan Africa, where the number of main lines is lower than one per 100 persons. Nigeria, Africa's most populous state, at over 111 million, has fewer than 500,000 main lines. South Africa and Botswana maintain and are extending modern, dependable telephone and telecommunications systems, including telex, telegraph, fax, and radio communications services. Until very recently, these were managed by government parastatals. Botswana's 40,000 telephones are connected internationally through satellite stations and microwave relays.

Video technology has enjoyed a limited educational and developmental impact but made a deeper entertainment impact in Africa. Videocassette recorders (VCRs) have been employed by religious groups in evangelization and social work. Some countries have employed the technology (audiovisual education) to teach literacy and to educate women on issues of child care, nutrition, health, and income-generating activities. Most VCR technology in Africa is used in private homes for entertainment. Videocassette recorders and players are generally owned by middle- and upper-income urban dwellers, supplanting boring, single-channel state-run television services and movie theaters. Most African cities today have several large video rental shops with a wide selection of popular movies from the United States, Europe, and India.

African access to satellite communications technologies significantly increased in the 1990s. The most common applications were to extend national telephone and telex communication networks. Only in the mid-1990s did satellite distribution of national television and radio broadcasts become an option for some state networks who could afford the high costs involved. Some of the larger countries have domestic satellite systems with transponders leased from INTELSAT for purposes of receiving foreign news via satellite. By the close of the decade, considerable progress had been made in establishing regional satellite systems for common carrier telecommunication and for broadcasting.

Significant inter-African communications cooperation is now occurring via such organizations as the Union of National Radio and Television Organizations in Africa, the Regional African Satellite Communications System, and the Pan-African Telecommunications Network. Despite the creation of the Pan-African News Agency in 1983, most African countries continue to depend upon Western, transnational news agencies, even for news about Africa. These organizations continue to suffer from severe shortages in finance, equipment, and personnel. The United Nations Educational, Scientific, and Cultural Organization, the World Bank, the German government, and the United States Agency for International Development have provided significant assistance.

By late 1995, well over half of all African countries (33 of 54) had developed some form of low-cost dial-up service to the Internet. Fourteen had achieved live Internet public access service, and full Internet access had been achieved by South Africa, Botswana, Namibia and Lesotho, with at least as many countries soon to follow.

A number of Western-based communications interests have begun to undertake special efforts to promote and underwrite development of African telecommunications infrastructures, including Teledesic, Iridium, American Telephone and Telegraph (AT&T) and the Internet Society. Cellular telephones feature prominently in these plans, as do satellite links. AT&T's Africa One plan calls for an undersea fiber-optic cable system that will ring the entire continent.

The Internet Society proposes an "Internetworking" facility, installing new Internet nodes and improving upon existing national and regional African networking links. One of the key elements of this plan involves training African network service providers so that systems are rapidly owned and operated by Africans and financially self-sustaining, and networks are open, accessible, and able to serve education as well as commerce.

The most serious obstacle to telecommunications development in Africa is lack of financial resources. For example, Iridium in 1997 estimated it would cost US$28 billion to increase telephone availability in Sub-Saharan Africa to one line per 100 people.

Africa must find ways to transform its communications infrastructures to levels where the continent can smoothly connect with the rest of the world. Whole economies will soon be either fast or slow, with economic information and global commerce operating at near real-time speeds. Without radical, rapid telecommunications growth, economic growth prospects for Africa over the medium term are not promising.

JAMES J. ZAFFIRO

See also: **Journalism; Media; Press.**

Further Reading

Internet Society, "Facilitating Internetworking in Africa"; online at http://www.undp.org/sdnp/aif/isocprop.html.

Iridium. *Iridium Today* 3, no. 3 (1997).

Jensen, M. "Governments Back Info-Highway." *Computers in Africa*, March–April 1996.

M' Bayo, R.. "Africa and the Global Information Infrastructure." *Gazette* 59, nos. 4–5 (1997): 345–364.

Morris, M. L., and S. E. Stavrou. "Telecommunication Needs and Provision to Underdeveloped Black Areas in South Africa." *Telecommunications Policy* 17, no. 5 (1993): 529–539.

Mustafa, M. A., B. Laidlaw, and M. Brand (eds.). *Telecommunications Policies for Sub-Saharan Africa*. Washington, D.C.: World Bank, 1997.

Schwartz, R. E. *Wireless Communication in Developing Countries: Cellular and Satellite Systems*. Norwood, Mass.: Artech House, 1996.

Teledesic. "Global Network to Help Africa Achieve Broadband Connectivity" (1996); online at http://www.teledesic.com/overview/pr/blaise.html.

Thapisa, A., and E. Birabwa. "Mapping Africa's Initiative at Building and Information and Communications Infrastructure." *Internet Research* 8, no. 1 (1998): 49–58.

United Nations Educational, Scientific, and Cultural Organization (UNESCO). "Intergovernmental Conference on Communications Policies in Africa." Yaonde, Cameroon: UNESCO, 1980.

United States Agency for International Development. "Leland Initiative: Africa GII Gateway Project" (1996); online at http://www.info.usaid.gov/regions/afr/leland/project.htm.

World Bank. "Telecommunications" (1997); online at http://www.worldbank.org/html/af4co/book/8.htm.

Community in African Society

Introduction

In spite of the continent's great size and diversity, many African states and communities interacted with one another on an ongoing basis during the lengthy period preceding colonial rule. Such interactions produced certain tangible commonalities among various African societies regarding belief systems and cultural characteristics and practices. At the same time, specific kin lineages, communities, and ethnic groups also bear, to one degree or another, marks of distinction by means of those same qualities, which also include language and heritage, among other traits. Historically speaking, a separate lineage often emerged within a community in Africa when the membership of a kin group had grown beyond one generation.

Kinship

African history began as, and largely remains, a tale of family interdependence and connectedness. Kinship is a set of relationships linking a number of people who may or may not be connected through biology. The institution of kinship, in which social and biological conventions are filtered through distinctly designed value systems, has long been used to establish formal relationships with members of outside communities through birth, marriage, or other family-based rituals. In precolonial Africa, the institution of kinship was often the most embraced and privileged mode of social relationship. In order to identify such networks, each African society selected specific genealogical links, while ignoring others. The history of each lineage was grounded in common ancestry, and this became the glue that held communities together. Kinship as a primary social institution was also at the core of the labor force, with the nuclear family at the helm. The emergence of advanced agriculture introduced a differentiated and more complex kind of human organization and recognized inventory of rights and obligations.

The institution of kinship enabled communities in both centralized and decentralized societies to facilitate social, political, and economic activities. Centralized states such as the Oyo, Zulu, and the Luba-Lunda, which had a strong political structure usually headed by a king or queen, emphasized the sacred nature of kinship rule that covered peripheral fishing, farming, and pastoral communities. Royal families often had a designated male or female kin member who behaved toward the king in an informal manner, enhancing formal events by praise-singing or lampooning festivals in the evaluation and appreciation of the ruler's social and political activities. Decentralized societies like the Tallensi, Igbo, Luo, Logoli, and Nuer had no single authority enjoying a concentration of political, judicial, or military power or governance and were organized primarily by a hierarchy of kinship relations.

Kinship ideology assigned roles among kin members, which served as guides for appropriate social actions and cultural behavior. It also determined the allocation of resources and validated the outcome of physical residency among various communities. With the aid of oral traditions such as proverbs, folklore, and songs, African communities expressed the importance of the connection between kin networks and individual actions. Other activities that promoted kinship obligations included visitations, such as frequent social or home calls during designated market days; festivals or social activities, like child-naming ceremonies, weddings, and funerals; the obligation to help a kin in times of physical need, as with agricultural and construction undertakings; and the obligation to fulfill emotional needs, especially in times of distress or calamity. Important social and familial functions such as the disposal of property, wills, claims, and duties all depended on the institution of kinship. Practices like scarification, the bearing of distinct tattoos or hairstyles, and even dress codes often identified the connections between the individual, the extended family and their community. As an article of social organization, kinship gave the individual full personhood. This is visible in the Yoruba proverb *Ebi eni l'aso eni* ("your extended family members act as your closet apparel"). Hence, cultural markers like scarification, tattoos, or brands served as physical representations of kinship protection and social currency.

Traditional social education in African communities focused on an individual's obligations to family and community. Different ethnic groups emphasized their own unique historical experiences to define related kinship requirements. In this sense, though kinship was based largely on biological connections, it was a social convention that was equally reinforced through specific values and social usage. Other forms of social networking combined to coordinate the activities of a community, including the function of age grade societies, secret rituals, and occupational societies and guilds. The relevance of the institution of kinship does not minimize the fact that other social networks were also very influential in providing supplemental support for the survival of African communities.

Family

The functional value of education in African communities cannot be overemphasized. Kin groups devised means to pass down their store of accumulated knowledge across generations in what became a succession of cultural activities. Parents and adults in both the nuclear and extended family had the responsibility of educating children about the cultural obligations tied to kinship and ethnicity. The primary functions of education in indigenous African communities thus included the acquisition of knowledge, the preservation of culture and the transformation of intellectual traditions. As a micropolitical and economic organ in precolonial Africa, kinship functioned to stress relationships of consanguinity and affinity (i.e., blood or marriage). It also emphasized ancestry and the historical developments in a society, which influence differentiation between one group and another. In addition, the role of elders in preserving the centrality of the institution of kinship was a form of political contract.

The nuclear family (i.e., a family incorporating the father, mother or mothers, and their children) was the building block for kinship systems and, by extension, communities. As a rule, Africans believed that the extended family reflected the continuity that bound various generations and nuclear families through lineal or horizontal networks of affinity. In addition to providing the core of labor force for agricultural production, the extended family offered a network of security. It also imposed the burden of extensive obligations that called for reciprocal actions, moral sanctions, and codes that could not be violated without the threat of sanctions. The function and value of the extended family was dependent on certain resources and territorial bases, power, status, and prestige in African social thought. Large families, which were particularly prevalent in precolonial Africa, were highly valued for economic and social reasons. As previously noted, the extended family served as the main labor force in an agricultural setting. Children were raised by their parents, but also belonged by extension to the community

of relatives, who were closely united by a bond interlocking functions and reciprocities.

Associated with the development of agriculture was the increased value and significance of land, which was regarded as a symbol of wealth and prestige. The agricultural system was closely linked with the position of authority from which, in principle, every member of the community derived his or her right to land cultivation. Villages, towns, and markets also emerged as a result of agricultural development. As related economic units, they all relied on the corporate ownership of land, which united all members of a community as a cohesive force. Every African society had laws and regulations on access to and distribution of its land, as well as on how to settle disputes over its allocation. Though these laws varied from one community to another, there were some underlying features they all had in common. Elders administered communal land, with group consent being paramount over individual decisions. Like the agriculturists, pastoralists were also connected to particular pieces of land through perennial use for grazing. On the other hand, hunting bands and food collectors had less need for rigid rules about land ownership and use because they moved frequently in search of food over large areas. Land was thus useful as a key item in the economic system of individual communities, and it was also used as a political tool since political power and organization takes effect over particular territories.

Various indigenous concepts of citizenship were utilized to establish people's rights to settle and exploit land. In many African communities, there were religious beliefs and sanctions behind the land tenure system. Land was often deified, and it was considered sacrilegious to sell it. Among the Igbo and several other communities, the earth deity or spirit force of the land was the guardian of the people's morality. It was also considered a special abode of the gods, buried ancestors, and their shrines, thus creating a bond between living individuals, comprising descent and lineage groups, and the dead. The nature of this connection was a major factor in nineteenth- and early-twentieth-century African communities' resistance to European colonizers, who demanded the choicest land.

The relationship of communities to their land was highly altered by colonial political, economic and social policies. The Kikuyu system of landholding had been based upon the *githaka*, an assemblage of not necessarily contiguous land, owned by a subclan or small lineage called *mbari*. Traditionally, each male mbari member was entitled to a portion of his clan's githaka, thus providing him with economic support and securing his personal position within his section of the Kikuyu nation. Since the entire Kikuyu society was built upon the mbari system, loss of githaka with the advent of colonial land policies was more than an economic disaster; it involved the loss of the very identity of the individual or group and, therefore, the cohesion of the Kikuyu people.

Gender

The principle of kinship can be subdivided into two descent groups, patrilineal and matrilineal. The majority of precolonial African societies recognized descent through the male or patrilineal line, while fewer recognized relationships through the female or matrilineal line. Examples of the latter group included the Asante, Bemba, Tonga, and some Tuareg groups. In a handful of other cases, such as with the Yoruba, a combination of both matrilineal and patrilineal descent practices was adopted. Lineage membership affected the residence of bride and groom after marital vows; whereas in the case of matrilineal descent the couple moved in with a male member of the bride's maternal family, with a patrilineal system the bride was expected to join the household of the groom's relatives.

The hierarchy and distribution of power in the kinship structure usually favored male offspring. In most nuclear families, the eldest son assumed control of the family's contractual arrangements and economic welfare in the society. He was expected to provide structure, permanence, and continuity in family social life. Generally, the oldest male figure in a patrilineal setting guided the family toward conforming to customs, law, and traditions of the kin group. He controlled the means of production and access to political power (a king, however, could overrule an elder's decision). As the transmitter of kinship solidarity, he was also usually well-versed in folklore and ancestral theology, and family relics.

The institution of marriage was often used to build meaningful and enduring ties between families and kin groups. Marriage, in this sense, increased the social capital of the joined lineage. In African parlance, it created networks with social linkages and implied societal responsibilities. The payment of a dowry for the wife was seen as a reflection of the honor, beauty, and righteousness of the bride, as well as the reputation of her family. Payment and collection of the dowry was a collective responsibility that helped maintain interrelationships among lineage members. Dowries were also a form of compensation to the bride's kin groups for the "loss" of a daughter and her productive capabilities.

Although the hierarchy dominating most kin groups favored men, in many circumstances women wielded enormous power as well. Senior wives often helped facilitate the growth and development of African communities. The senior wives in Yoruba communities were addressed as "mothers of the house," and the Swazi of southern Africa recognized the title of "mother" of the kingdom, while the Lozi have a title for the king's sister. Among the Ankole, the king's maternal uncle collects tributes and the royal ladies have the authority to demand cattle from community members. In communities such as that of the Dahomey, women participated in politics, and in ancient Egypt, as among the Baganda, Ankole, and Shilluk, significant political responsibilities were also given to the queen mother.

Ethnicity

Africa is a very large and diverse continent in terms of physical and human geography. It is difficult to place an exact number on how many ethnic groups exist in Africa, though by rough estimations there may be eight to twelve hundred, depending on how the lines are drawn between closely related people. Precolonial ethnic boundaries are often very difficult to decipher, as constant population expansion and sociocultural contacts often frustrate such attempts. The relationship between people and their physical environment plays an important role in determining regional characteristics and patterns of population distribution and economic activities. For example, among the people who had geographical advantages were those in the highlands of Ethiopia, the equatorial regions of East Africa, and most parts of West Africa. In contrast, communities in Central Africa or those situated along the northern parts of the Nile River were constrained by their physical environment. Ethnic groups have culturally acquired characteristics, such as languages or beliefs. Where there is an absence of written records, linguistic relationships provide the most dependable evidence of historical connections between groups.

Varying historical experiences and sociopolitical structures triggered a wide range of forms of identity politics and ethnicity. Distinctive ways of life, shared values and meanings, and exchanges of labor and goods within and between groups were also highly important in defining social life and ethnicity. Multiple adaptation has also developed based on environmental niches. The open savanna country supports both sedentary agriculture and nomadic or seminomadic pastoralism. In addition, lakes and rivers support fishers. Such multiple adaptations are often utilized unequally by groups within the same area so that diverse ecology supports different or differentiating units. In many precolonial east African communities, the sense of day-to-day life focused on localized and autonomous kinship and territorial associations. Acephalous, or decentralized, political structures such as that of the Turkana mean that relation to the environment, occupation or military conquests often defines identity. Natural dichotomies are important in defining the boundaries between groups such as the Shambaai, a people named after their mountainous abode, and the Nyika of the lowland areas. Over time, the Maasa became known as the archetypal pastoralists. There was cooperation in the organization of regional trade that the moved through the west African forest, connecting it to the savanna and, ultimately, to the traffic across the Sahara to North Africa. Thus, in addition to the exchange of ideas and commodities, there was also the movement of people and interethnic relationships.

Ethnic identification could also be very fluid in nature. In Kenya, the emergence of ethnic groups such as the Kikuyu, Kamba, Embu, Mbeere, and Meru owed more to shifts in social formation in the transition to the modern era than to culturally inherent characteristics. Commerce became the specialty of certain groups, such as for the Dyula of west Africa, who had their representatives located strategically along trade routes. The marketplace featured a wide range of goods from various communities or ethnic groups. These included gold dust, fabrics, kola nuts, shea butter, and other food products and consumer goods. In each community, these marketplaces were more than centers of economic exchange. They were also zones for leisure and the exchange of information and ideas.

The transatlantic slave trade and the ongoing warfare that accompanied it disrupted the African institution of kinship with regard to familial, ethnic, and gender relations. The emergence of European colonial administration between 1890 and 1914 led to a redefinition of African administrative bureaucracy and ethnic identity. European colonialism witnessed the external creation of nation-states that were held together by mostly new coercive and legal instruments of governance. The strategic logic of political control in the colonial state rested on the application of a policy of "divide and rule." This fragmented and isolated African political activity within the confines of local administrative subdivisions, thereby inhibiting the spread of opposition and resistance. The creation of new "tribes," chiefs, and identities meant, in most cases, that ethnicity became a zero-sum game in which the winner took all in the competition for resources. The policy of ruling indirectly through existing structures introduced a new form of patron-client relationship. In addition, though households retained an independent productive base through access to land, the relationship between the state and its various communities was imposed by political force rather than being based on mutual economic development. The emergence of new cities as centers of administration also engendered the dissolution of family and community-based civic structures.

In Sub-Saharan African, the failure of the decolonization process and the postcolonial state has resulted in competitive elections and the ethnicization of the modern bureaucracy. "Tribal" unions emerged, later developing into political parties, which did not augur well for the nation-state models birthed at the departure of European colonialism. Western education also helped facilitate the use of literature like books and newspapers to help advance the cause of one ethnic group over the other. This weakness, which amounted to multinations within one nation, was subsequently exposed and the colonial legacy of bureaucratic authoritarianism, pervasive patron-client relations, and a complex ethnic dyslectic of assimilation, fragmentation, and competition continued in the postcolonial era. Patronage networks have often been extended to include links between state officials, local middlemen, military officers, and international capital.

Conclusion

In precolonial African society, the institution of kinship was the ideological platform that held African communities together. The learning process was also a cultural activity that enhanced the continuity of communities. Communities devised ways to pass down their store of accumulated wealth and wisdom from one generation to another. The task of socializing the child was a community affair. As a result, the African child was deeply aware of the debt owed to the family, the extended family, kinship groups, and, in modern parlance, ethnic communities. These institutions enhanced the survivability of groups in physical residence and during various historical periods of social transition. The father, mother, chiefs, queens, and kings all had functional roles dedicated to carrying out these activities that represented the core values of civil society in Africa.

Although African states have remained conscious of the use of education as a tool for community and nation building, economic problems and competition for scarce resources continue to prove a major obstacle. The transition to modernity in many African societies was imposed by a combination of external forces and international capital. In many instances, particularly in urban cities of colonial legacy, individuality has replaced collectivity, and communities have been fraught with unstable political atmospheres and economic hardships. In this climate, there has repeatedly been a lack of fiscal and material investment in societal infrastructures, even when the will to nurture civic institutions and organizations has been present. Nevertheless, cultural standards and traditions have continued to play out their functions. In this resilience lies the enormous potential African communities possess both commercially and culturally in relationship to the rest of the world.

SAHEED A. ADEJUMOBI

See also: **Identity, Political.**

Further Reading

Ali, Zacheus, J. A. Ayoade, and A. Agbaje. *African Traditional Political Thought and Institutions.* Lagos: Civiletis International, 1989.

Cohen, R., and J. Middleton. *From Tribe to Nation: Studies in Incorporation Process.* Scranton, Pa.: Chandler, 1970.

Goody, J. (ed.). *The Character of Kinship.* Cambridge: Cambridge University Press, 1973.

Moore, H. L., and Megan Vaughan, *Cutting Down Trees: Gender, Nutrition, and Agricultural Change in the Northern Province of Zambia, 1890–1990.* Portsmouth, N.H.: Heinemann, 1993.

Vansina, J. *Paths in the Rain forest: Toward a History of Political Transition in Equatorial Africa.* Madison: University of Wisconsin Press, 1990.

Waller, R. "Ecology, Migration and Expansion in East Africa." *African Affairs,* no. 23 (1985).

Comoros: Before 1800

The geographical position of the Comoros Islands—Ngazidja (Grande Comore), Nzuani (Anjouan), Mwali (Mohéli), and Maoto (Mayotte)—is one of the main determinants of their history. The islands act like stepping stones from northern Madagascar to northern Mozambique, and they have been the main route by which human migrations and cultural influences have moved between Africa and Madagascar. It is likely that Indonesian migrants used this route when settling in Madagascar; migrations from central Africa to Madagascar have taken place continually over the centuries. With the arrival of Islam in the tenth century, Islamic migrants also used this route, bringing the cultures of the Swahili coast of eastern Africa to northern Madagascar. The population of the Comoros Islands was continuously added to by new arrivals and always reflected the threefold influence of Madagascar, Bantu central Africa, and the Islamic culture of the Swahili cities.

Early town and burial sites in the islands suggest an active commercial civilization as early as the tenth century, but it is from the fifteenth century that written evidence of trading towns like Domoni survives. The traditional histories of the different towns, though recorded at a much later date, nevertheless make it clear that the ruling families of the islands had close ties with Kilwa and, like the rulers of Kilwa itself, laid claims to a Shirazi origin.

In the sixteenth century the island merchants traded both with the East African coast and with the towns of northern Madagascar. The main products of the islands were foodstuffs, but there was also a boat-building industry and almost certainly a trade in slaves as well. In spite of persistent traditions to the contrary, there is no

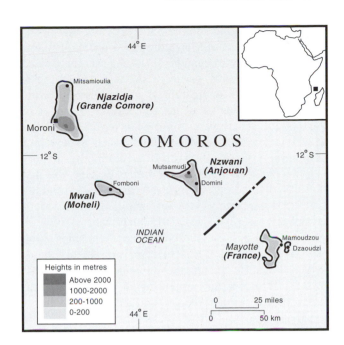

Comoros.

record of the Portuguese ever having conquered or settled the islands, though boats from Mozambique Island regularly made the short crossing to buy provisions. Early in the seventeenth century, Portuguese was widely known as a trading language, Spanish currency circulated, and traders from as far as the Red Sea and the Gulf came to the islands in search of slaves.

With the arrival of Dutch, English, and French traders, the Comoros Islands suddenly assumed a considerable importance in international affairs. The Portuguese control of the East African coast forced the newcomers to look for ports of call elsewhere, and from the later sixteenth century on the Comoros Islands became the focus of their attention. Dutch ships used the Mayotte lagoon as a base for their attacks on Mozambique Island in 1607 and 1608, and French traders stopped to repair their boats and take on provisions. It was the British East India Company, however, that made the most regular use of the islands to restock their ships, as a place to leave the sick to recover and as a post office.

Not all of the islands were equally favored by the visiting ships. Wheras Anjouan and Mohéli supplied fresh water, had relatively protected anchorages and a population anxious to do business, Grande Comore acquired a reputation for the hostility shown by its inhabitants to foreigners which complemented the rugged, inhospitable coastline and the almost total lack of fresh water. Mayotte, on the other hand, was difficult to reach, as it was surrounded by coral reefs with narrow entrances into its lagoon.

The regular visits of European ships to Mohéli and Anjouan probably had the effect of increasing the wealth of the ruling families, in particular that of the main Anjouan port of Mutsammudu, whose ruler came to claim primacy in island affairs and was recognized by the Europeans as sultan of the whole island. The constant demand for fresh food and provisions for the fleets helped to develop the agricultural resources of the islands. Slaves were imported as agricultural labor as well as for resale, and the islands began to develop a plantation economy. As a result, a cultural division developed between the Islamic families of the towns that traditionally had ties with East Africa, Arabia, and the Gulf, and the largely African inhabitants of the countryside who were only partially Islamized.

An increase in the number of merchant ships using the islands, and the prosperity of the islands themselves, began to attract the unwelcome attention of pirates. With corsairs operating along the shipping lanes of the Indian Ocean and establishing bases for their operation in northeastern Madagascar, the Comoros Islands found themselves increasingly involved in their activities. Pirate ships visited Anjoan and Mohéli to dispose of captured plunder or slaves, and they used the Mayotte lagoon to waylay British East India Company vessels. It was in the waters off the Comoros Islands that many of the naval actions between company vessels and pirates took place.

By the 1730s, most of the pirates had been captured or had abandoned their trade; until the 1790s, the islands were relatively free from external threats. British East India Company ships continued to visit Anjouan and Mohéli. In these islands, the Sultan of Mutsammudu emerged as the dominant political figure and was recognized by the British as sultan of the whole island. Mohéli, with two ancient trading towns, Fomboni and Numa Choa, also came increasingly under the influence of the Sultan of Anjouan. Grande Comore was seldom visited by Europeans, but by the eighteenth century the rivalry between the 20 towns on the island was already well established. Each of these towns had its own sultan, one among them being recognized as Sultan Thibé, a sort of ceremonial, paramount sultan. However, Sultan Thibé had no real power, and the ruling families of the towns, some of them only a few miles apart, continued with their often violent and bloody feuds.

In the second half of the eighteenth century the French began to develop a slave trade route rom Madagascar and eastern Africa to their sugar plantations in Ile-de-France and Ile de Bourbon. Once again the Comoros Islands became an important slave market. However, the slave trade was to backfire on the islanders, when in the 1790s Sakalava and Betsimisaraka raiders from northern Madagascar found the islands to be an easy target for their raids.

MALYN NEWITT

See also: **Comoros/Mayotte: Nineteenth Century to 1975; Comoros/Mayotte: Independence to the Present; Slavery, Colonial Rule and; Slavery: Mediterranean, Red Sea, Indian Ocean.**

Further Reading

Chagnoux, H., and A. Haribou. *Les Comores*. Paris: Presses Universitaires de France, 1980.

Flobert, T. *Les Comores*. Travaux et Mémoires de la Faculté de Droit et de Sciences Politiques d'Aix-Marseilles no. 24, Marseilles, 1974.

Gohin, O., and P. Maurice. *Mayotte*. Réunion: Université de la Réunion, 1992.

Newitt, M. *The Comoro Islands: Struggle against Dependency in the Indian Ocean*. Boulder Colo.: Westview Press, 1984.

Ottenheimer, M., and H. Ottenheimer. *Historical Dictionary of the Comoro Islands*. London: Scarecrow Press, 1994.

Comoros/Mayotte: Nineteenth Century to 1975

At the beginning of the nineteenth century, the Comoros Islands—Ngazidja (Grande Comore), Nzuani (Anjouan), Mwali (Mohéli), and Maoto (Mayotte)—were repeatedly raided by slave-hunting Sakalava and Betsimisaraka pirates from northern Madagascar. The raids led to depopulation, destabilization of the agricultural and commercial economy, and the construction of defensive walls around the main island towns. The British East India Company offered some protection to Anjouan, with which it had the closest relations, and the British diplomats encouraged Merina conquests of the Sakalava coast. By 1820, the pirate raids had come to an end, but one of the Sakalava princes, Andrian Souli, fled the Merina conquest and settled on Mayotte with his followers. At the same time one of the Merina generals, Ramanetaka, fearing arrest and execution, seized control of Mohéli.

The arrival of these chiefs linked the fortunes of the islands closely with the struggle unfolding in Madagascar. At the same time, the islands were affected by the growth of the commercial power of Zanzibar. In particular the islands became important entrepôts in the east African slave trade, and many slaving dhows used the islands as a staging post for journeys to the south and for the shipment of slaves to Madagascar itself.

During the 1840s, rivalry increased between Britain and France in the western Indian Ocean. While Britain concentrated on suppressing the slave trade and on protecting the interests of British Indian traders, the French were seeking opportunities to expand the plantation economy of Réunion and to continue the supply of slave or *engagés* laborers to the sugar fields.

In 1841 the French occupied Nossi Bé off the coast of northwest Madagascar and in 1843 negotiated a treaty of protection with Andrian Souli in Mayotte. According to this treaty, the French were allowed to build a naval base on the small island of Dzaoudzi as well as rent lands for sugar production. The French presence in Mayotte stimulated the British to establish a consul in Anjouan in 1846. The man appointed, William Sunley, owned a sugar plantation and used slave labor.

During the 1850s, Mohéli came under the influence of Zanzibar. Ramanetaka died in 1841, and his seven-year-old daughter was married to a Zanzibari prince. However, in 1860 pro-French factions on the island expelled the Zanzibaris and called in the aid of a French adventurer, Joseph Lambert, who obtained vast land concessions as the price of his support. A final attempt by the Zanzibari party to expel Lambert failed when French warships intervened, and from 1871 French influence dominated the island. A formal protectorate was declared in 1886 at the height of the "Scramble" for Africa. In 1901 the last queen of Mohéli eloped with a French gendarme, and in 1912 the island was formally annexed.

Grande Comore remained divided between the 20 nominally separate sultanates, but after 1843 the French from Mayotte consistently backed the claims of the Sultan of Bambao, whose capital was Moroni, to be the paramount sultan, or Sultan Thibé. When Sultan Thibé, Said Achmet, died in 1875, the French hastened to back the claims of the French-educated Said Ali. In 1883 Said Ali, desperate for more active French support, signed a huge land concession with a French naturalist and entre-preneur, Léon Humblot. Said Ali's rivals tried to obtain German support, but this only precipitated the French declaration of a protectorate over the island. Said Ali eventually went into exile in 1893, leaving Humblot as virtual ruler of the island. Humblot's Société de Grande Comore established a kind of feudal regime over the island which the various French residents never success-fully challenged. Humblot died in 1914, and the island was then annexed as a colony.

Anjouan remained firmly under the influence of the British consuls, who introduced sugar as a crop and plantation agriculture. However, British attempts to force an unpopular treaty outlawing slavery on the sultan in 1882 led to the latter seeking French aid. A protectorate treaty was signed with France in 1886. In 1889 widespread rebellion among the slave population broke out in Anjouan. This gave the French an excuse to intervene and conquer the island and to distribute the lands of the former sultans to French companies.

In 1908 the French began the process of consolidat-ing the islands with Madagascar. The families of the sultans were forced to give up their claims, and in 1914 the four islands were finally incorporated into the colony of Madagascar.

For the next 40 years the islands remained a colo-nial backwater in which the plantation companies dominated, producing vanilla, sugar, cloves and scent-bearing plants (principally ylang ylang). The population of the islands tried to survive on noncompany land but was increasingly driven abroad to Zanzibar, Majunga, and South Africa. The islands became increasingly dependent on remittances from emigrant workers.

The government of Madagascar sided with the Vichy regime in 1940, and in 1942 the British and South Africans captured the port of Diego Suarez, sending a small force to take Mayotte and restore the Comoros Islands to France. Many of the leading island families became strongly Gaullist and in 1946 the Comoros were declared a *territoire d'outremer* and allowed to elect a *conseil général* (general council). More autonomy was granted to the islands in 1947 and 1952, and formal ties with Madagascar came to an end in 1960. From 1947 on, the islands sent deputies to the French Assembly. The period up to 1970 was dominated by the cautiously conservative Said Mohammed Chaik, who remained loyal to France and negotiated a series of development loans and grants from the French gov-ernment. Chaik made no moves to claim independence during the 1960s, and it was only with his death in 1970 that the rival political groupings in the islands began to demand independence from France. This had the effect of splitting the islands as Mayotte, which had been un-der French rule the longest and was dominated by a strongly Gaullist party, the MPM, wanted to retain the links with France. In 1975 three of the islands declared their independence, while Mayotte voted in a referendum to remain French.

MALYN NEWITT

See also: **Comoros: Before 1800; Comoros/Mayotte: Independence to the Present; Madagascar: Colonial Period: French Rule.**

Further Reading

Chagnoux, H., and A. Haribou. *Les Comores*. Paris: Presses Universitaires de France, 1980.

Flobert, T. *Les Comores*. Travaux et Mémoires de la Faculté de Droit et de Sciences Politiques d'Aix-Marseilles no. 24. Marseilles, 1974.

Gohin, O., and P. Maurice. *Mayotte*. Réunion: Université de la Réunion, 1992.

Newitt, M. *The Comoro Islands: Struggle against Dependency in the Indian Ocean*. Boulder, Colo.: Westview Press, 1984.

Ottenheimer, M., and H. Ottenheimer. *Historical Dictionary of the Comoro Islands*. London: Scarecrow Press, 1994.

Comoros/Mayotte: Independence to the Present

The four islands of the Comoros archipelago are Ngazidja (Grande Comore), Nzuani (Anjouan), Mwali (Mohéli), and Maoto (Mayotte). Until July 1975 the four islands had collectively had the status of *territoire d'outremer*, which gave them local autonomy under the overall control of France. Various nationalist parties, notably MOLINACO and PASOCO, had campaigned for total independence with the support of the Organization of African Unity (OAU), and it was largely to preempt further gains by these parties that the islands' elected head of government, Ahmed Abdullah, a member of a leading family from Anjouan, declared independence from France on July 15, 1975.

The move was at once denounced by the MPM, the ruling party in Mayotte, which was firmly pro-French. France recognized the independence of three of the islands, while a referendum was held in Mayotte which voted to stay with France as a *collectivité territoriale* (territorial collective). From that time, the Comoros Islands have been divided; one island has remained French, while the other three have established an independent Islamic Republic. This division of the islands is not recognized by the OAU, which continues to press for the unification of the archipelago.

Within a month of his declaration of independence, Ahmed Abdullah was overthrown by a coup carried out by French mercenaries under Bob Denard. Abdullah was replaced by the conservative prince Said Hussein, but he was rapidly replaced in his turn by a group of radical politicians led by Ali Soilih, a French-trained economist. Ali Soilih ruled the three islands for just over two and a half years. During this time he attempted a fundamental reorganization of the economy and social structure, addressing many of the issues which had been identified as problems for the islands. He broke up and distributed some of the large landed estates; he nationalized vanilla marketing, and in a sweeping move abolished the central bureaucracy (the idea being to return decision making to the local level). He also attacked many of the religious customs and in particular abolished the *grand mariage*, the expense of which had bankrupted many families and used up capital accumulated by overseas migrant workers.

Soilih's government was rapidly overtaken by economic, human, and natural disasters. Under the chaos of the changes he introduced, the economy collapsed, revenue was not collected, and schools and hospitals closed down. On top of this, Madagascar expelled large numbers of Comorians from Majunga after serious rioting and the Karthala volcano on Grande Comore erupted, causing devastation on the eastern part of the island.

Ali Soilih's government was overthrown, and Soilih himself was killed in another mercenary coup in July 1978. This time the mercenaries worked closely with the French DGS, with the objective of returning Ahmed Abdullah to power.

Abdullah introduced a new constitution, and signed a bilateral defense agreement with France and an agreement linking the Comorian franc to the French franc. Abdullah ruled the islands without serious opposition for 11 years. His rule was supported by a presidential guard made up of Denard's mercenaries, who were partly supported by France and partly by the South African Ministry of Defense. South Africa emerged as one of Abdullah's strongest backers, as it needed to use the islands to import arms and to provide a base for supplying Renamo guerrillas operating in Mozambique. South African businessmen also began to invest in tourist infrastructure in the islands.

Abdullah's internal power base was his Ufumu Party and the strong backing he received from his native island of Anjouan. His opponents could not unite behind any one leader, and some of them went into exile as Abdullah took a strong hand against the activities of dissident politicians. Abdullah himself was one of the leading vanilla traders in the islands, and his regime was backed by a number of business syndicates which made large profits from the concessions he allowed them.

Mayotte, meanwhile, remained firmly under the control of the MPM. The islanders voted Gaullist and received pledges from Debré, and later from Jacques Chirac, that the question of their future would be put to them in a referendum. The MPM has campaigned for full departmental status like that of Réunion, but no French government has actually proposed this solution, partly because of the international opposition that it would arouse and partly because of the huge financial cost of raising living standards and services in Mayotte to the level of metropolitan France.

Abdullah's rule left many of the islands' problems unresolved. The government ran a huge deficit and had to be propped up by French aid. The population grew, and the crude subsistence agriculture led to a rapid degradation of the environment. Services and the infrastructure were neglected, while Abdullah practiced a shameless patrimonial politics, rewarding his supporters with government jobs, many of which were mere sinecures.

Abdullah's increasing reliance on South Africa lost him support in the rest of Africa and in France. On November 26, 1989, in circumstances that have never been fully explained, mercenaries of his guard murdered the president and took control of the country. France mobilized its forces in Mayotte and, after two weeks, the mercenaries agreed to hand over power, according to the constitution, to Said Mohammed Djohar, the president of the Supreme Court. In 1990 Djohar was voted in as president, his main rival being Said Mohamed Taki Abdulkarim. Djohar had the backing of France and was able to negotiate a structural adjustment policy with the International Monetary Fund in 1991.

Djohar remained president until 1996, but during this time Comorian politics became increasingly chaotic. Over 20 political parties contested elections, forming a veritable kaleidoscope of alliances and coalitions. Djohar was not able to establish a strong party of government, as Abdullah had done, and came increasingly to depend on his son-in-law, Mohamed Mchangama, who became the power behind the throne. During this period there were frequent attempts to stage coups, with allegations of mercenary involvement. One of these, in 1993, led to the arrest and imprisonment of Abdullah's two sons. During this period Djohar's various governments tried to grapple with the demands of structural adjustment, in particular the reform of the civil service and revenue collection. In December 1993 the coalition of Djohar's supporters barely managed to win a majority in the elections, and it became clear that the president lived on borrowed time. More seriously, he began to lose the support of France. In 1994 the structural adjustment program came to an end and, smothered by mounting debts and an unbalanced budget, Djohar was toppled by a successful coup in October 1995—led, once again, by Denard, with the backing of the French.

Djohar was removed to Réunion, ostensibly for medical reasons, but he refused to resign and the OAU continued to support him as the legitimate president. In any case, he had to be restored to office, if not power, pending presidential elections in March 1996. These brought a clear victory for Mohammed Taki Abdulkarim. Taki at once began to decisively shape Comorian politics, merging most of the political parties into one or two groupings and adopting a range of Islamic policies that proved highly popular with the heads of the traditional families.

Mayotte remained in its political limbo as a collectivity. The French made no moves to hold a referendum on departmental status, while the MPM retained its hold on power and demanded full integration with France. The weakness of the island's economy led to huge French subsidies, which in turn attracted economic migrants from the poverty-stricken neighboring islands and to demands from dissidents in Anjouan that they return to direct rule by France as well, so that they could enjoy the same economic benefits.

MALYN NEWITT

Further Reading

Chagnoux, H., and A. Haribou. *Les Comores.* Paris: Presses Universitaires de France, 1980.
Gohin, O., and P. Maurice. *Mayotte.* Réunion: Université de la Réunion, 1992.
Newitt, M. *The Comoro Islands: Struggle against Dependency in the Indian Ocean.* Boulder Colo.: Westview Press, 1984.
Ostheimer, J. "The Politics of Comorian Independence." In *The Politics of the Western Indian Ocean*, edited by John Ostheimer. New York: Praeger, 1975.
Vérin, P. "Les Comore indépendantes sous Ahmed Abdullah." *Mondes et Cultures*, no. 50 (1990): 217–223.

Conakry

Conakry, the capital city of the Republic of Guinea, had an estimated population of over one million people in the late 1990s, only a century after its official founding by the French colonial authority. The location for the new city was chosen both because there was a political vacuum on the coast, and because of the region's potential as an international harbor. It formed the outermost extremity of the Kaloum region, a small and flat peninsula (or island) previously known as the Tumbo Peninsula. Some villages on the peninsula predated the French conquest, totaling about 300 inhabitants in the 1880s. One of them, Conakry, gave its name to the new city. These villages, possibly founded in the late eighteenth century, were inhabited by the Susu and Baga peoples, who had migrated from the hinterland; they were joined later by the Fula.

In 1885, it was decided that the French resident of the new administrative district (the "cercle de Dubréka") would be established there. After a military confrontation in 1887, the French took over and proclaimed themselves the sole landowners. This enabled them to plan the city according to their will. In a few years, under Governor Ballay, the city was laid out as an example of French colonial urbanism. Conakry soon became known as "the pearl of West Africa."

The plan of the town, conceived in 1890, was simple, consisting of a grid of 14 avenues crossing 12 boulevards. It was efficient and forward looking at a time when the island was almost empty. The monumental architecture of its official buildings and the scale of the streets made it into a showcase for French power. A segregationist policy divided the town into quarters, according to social status. The result was a dual city, made up of the European quarter, and a native quarter (*zone indigène*) where public facilities were less developed; there was almost no electricity in private housing in the native quarter, for example, and the sewage system was insufficient.

The administrative and commercial functions of Conakry attracted many newcomers and, by the end of the nineteenth century, the population had grown to approximately 10 to 15,000 habitants, mainly Susu and Fula.

Subsequently, however, Conakry entered a financial slump because of the end of the wild rubber boom and attendant economic problems that afflicted the colony of Guinea. In the late 1940s urban growth began to accelerate, the town spread onto the mainland, and the suburbs were integrated into the city. A new town-planning scheme was adopted in 1947, but its implementation was not possible due to the rapidity of urban growth. The post–World War II period also saw the building of new public facilities, financed by a public investment program, including a new market, a hospital, and a secondary school. From around 30,000 people in 1948, the population rose to 100,000 ten years later.

Conakry had been granted municipal status in 1904, but its mayor was an administrator and the African population had only a consultative and politically marginal role. In 1955, the municipal law was drastically changed, as local elections were declared. The first elected mayor, in 1956, was Sekou Touré, the leader of the Parti Démocratique de Guinée (PDG) and future first president of Guinea. Conakry became, increasingly, a center of political activities and the location of demonstrations and active opposition to colonial power.

Today, Conakry stretches beyond the peninsula along approximately 22 miles (35 kilometers). This long and narrow space is the source of many traffic problems, due also to the prevalence of spontaneous growth and the absence of public planning. Only recently have new roads been opened, while at the same time, some neighborhoods have been demolished with the intent of replacing them with areas marked for better construction and planning. The city is administratively divided into four communes, united under the supervision of a nominated governor.

Due to limited financial means, only a few new significant buildings were built under Sekou Touré. These include the Palais du Peuple, which was built by the Chinese as the site for large cultural and political events, and the villas and meeting house constructed for the 1984 meeting of the Organization of African Unity (OAU). The city underwent accelerated changes after Touré's death in 1984, including significant construction, and the subsequent opening up of the country, both economically and politically. Some fine colonial buildings were destroyed, while others, such as the old customs house, were carefully renovated. As in many other African cities, the large population (about 60 per cent of the urban population of Guinea and 20 per cent of the total population) has led to high density, overconstruction, and a lack of facilities, especially as most of the new neighborhoods grew without any real planning. Attempts to correct the chaos were made recently, as Conakry continues to attract a rapidly growing population. As the center of the railway system and the main international harbor, it is the outlet for the exports of the main products (bauxite and iron ores and agricultural products such as bananas). It also has plentiful administrative jobs and light industries.

Conakry's cultural life is active, with many famous bands, dating from Sekou Touré's time and revived recently. (The most famous is the Bembeya Jazz Band.) Conakry is also a focal point for the press, the broadcasting system, and higher education facilities.

ODILE GOERG

See also: **Guinea.**

Further Reading

Dollfus, O. "Conakry en 1951-52, étude humaine et économique." *Recherches africaines/Etudes guinéennes*, nos. 10–11 (1952): 3–111.

Goerg, O. "From Hill Station (Freetown) to Downtown Conakry (1st Ward): Comparing French and British Approaches to Segregation in Colonial Cities." *Canadian Journal of African Studies/Revue Canadienne des Etudes Africaines* 32, no. 1 (1998): 1–30.

———. *Pouvoir colonial, municipalités et espaces urbains. Conakry et Freetown, des années 1880 à 1914.* 2 vols. Paris: L'Harmattan, 1997.

Richard, A., E. Tombapa, and M. A. Bah. *Conakry. Porte de la Guinée.* Paris: Ganndal/EDICEF, 1998.

Concessionary Companies

Concessionary companies were an important component of economic development in much of colonial Africa, particularly during the early consolidation phase from 1885 to 1920. Most typically, these were private European businesses lured to make investments of capital and manpower in Africa in return for a grant (or concession) of land, over which it gained privileged rights of exploitation. While specific features varied from colony to colony, as well as over time, the widespread use of this policy highlights two crucial features of African colonialism. First, it reflects the prevailing philosophy that economic development should be led by private enterprise, much as it had been done in European history. As a consequence, most colonial administrations lacked the financial resources and the personnel to undertake development alone. Second, the concessionary policy embodied a pervasively negative European perception of Africans and their culture. The promotion of European enterprise in Africa was in part based on the belief that Africans were too backward and lazy to make a meaningful contribution beyond the role of common laborer. Together, these constraints and beliefs forged a colonial policy that favored European interests over those of Africans, and helped to lay the foundations for African economic underdevelopment.

The concessionary policy in colonial Africa evolved out of the European tradition of chartered companies, which had successfully enlarged imperial possessions and trade in Asia and North America in the sixteenth and seventeenth centuries. When Europeans became interested in Africa in the mid-nineteenth century, private companies again expanded the territorial and commercial domain of European powers. The United African Company (later renamed the Royal Niger Company), the Imperial British East Africa Company, and Cecil Rhodes's British South Africa Company, for example, secured for Britain future colonies in eastern, western, and southern Africa. Following the partition of Africa at the Berlin Conference of 1884–1885, concessionary companies played a crucial role in consolidating European rule. In many colonies, companies took the lead in expanding Western influence, improving transportation, and introducing Africans to export-commodity production. To attract private investment, colonial administrations commonly offered large land concessions and varying amounts of administrative power. A general exception was found in the colonies of West Africa, where a longer tradition of European-African trade encouraged the colonists to rely more heavily on African household production.

From 1885 to 1920 in some areas of colonial Africa, concessionary companies dwarfed all other forms of economic activity. In King Leopold's Congo Free State, one large mining consortium, the Katanga Company, gained administrative and commercial control over a huge tract covering more than 100 million acres. In the neighboring French Congo, forty companies were granted concessions totaling nearly 70 per cent of the entire colony. Additional huge portions of equatorial forest were ceded to businesses interested in the ivory and rubber trade. In return, colonial administrations frequently took a substantial share of the profits, as well as company commitments for investments in railways and other expensive projects. As a result, the success and well-being of many colonial governments became firmly intertwined with company profits, resulting in a close collusion of interests, policies, and personnel.

The early reign of concessionary companies was generally abusive, unprofitable, and ultimately untenable. Granted sweeping administrative powers, private companies ruled their territories absolutely, erecting economies oriented toward short-term profits over long-term investment. In the forest regions of central Africa, the rubber and ivory trade quickly degenerated into a brutal and violent system. Company agents and administrative personnel were typically rewarded or promoted in proportion to the amount of exportable commodities produced in their territories, resulting in widespread atrocities and a reign of terror. African workers who failed to meet their ever-increasing quotas of rubber or ivory were beaten, whipped, and tortured. In some regions, forced labor dramatically undermined normal subsistence activities, causing famine, illness, and early death. But such wholesale exploitation of people and resources ultimately proved counterproductive. African armed resistance required costly military interventions and diminished production, causing several companies to declare bankruptcy. Excessive harvesting of rubber and ivory also destroyed natural resources, causing a steady decline in production and profits by 1900. Finally, when missionary reports of the atrocities reached Europe, an outraged public demanded reform. In the most dramatic case, King Leopold was forced to cede his Congo Free State to Belgium in 1908.

By 1920, the concessionary policy in much of colonial Africa was significantly reduced or revised. European private enterprise was still widely encouraged, but under stricter supervision and tighter control. An illustrative example is seen in the Belgian Congo's agreement with Lever Brothers, the British soapmaker. In 1919, the company received five concessionary zones (much smaller than those awarded earlier by the Congo Free State), in which to establish palm plantations and processing facilities. In addition, Lever Brothers was required to improve and invest in the welfare of its workers by instituting labor contracts and by building schools and clinics. In the Belgian Congo, as in other colonies, such reforms were heralded as promoting long-term economic development for the benefit of Europeans and Africans alike. But in reality, the basic Eurocentric structure and orientation of the colonial economy remain unchanged. While the concessions were smaller, they were often more numerous, resulting in even greater European control of the economy. Company investments in African welfare were generally minimal and rarely enforced. Instead, the state actively ensured the success of private European capital, enacting taxation and other policies to create a large, compliant, and cheap labor force. To protect company interests, African economic competition was stifled or prohibited, under the pretext that such production would yield inferior quality exports. Lacking viable alternatives, African participation in the colonial economy remained largely limited to the role of unskilled laborer. Despite the reforms, the enduring concessionary policy shows that European profits and interests remained preeminent over African needs and concerns.

Colonial concessionary companies have left a lasting legacy to postcolonial Africa. At independence, African governments inherited economies dominated by European capital and oriented toward European markets. Prohibitions placed on African competition had successfully hindered the rise of an African entrepreneurial class, which might have served as the catalyst for new economic growth and opportunities. Instead, the vast majority of the population remained underskilled and underfinanced. In some former colonies, the lingering economic power of European companies has promoted neocolonialism, whereby foreign interests have exerted considerable influence over the policy decisions of African leaders, often at the expense of its citizens. Moreover, lacking the capital and resources to restructure their economies, many African nations have been forced to maintain the same cash crop, export-oriented economies created by the concessionary companies, reinforcing a continuous cycle of underdevelopment that has proved exceedingly difficult to overcome.

SAMUEL NELSON

See also: **Colonial European Administrations: Comparative Survey; Colonialism: Impact on African Societies.**

Further Reading

Boahen, A. Adu (ed.). *Africa under Colonial Domination, 1880–1935.* London: John Curry, 1990.

Coquery-Vidrovitch, C. *Le Congo au temps des grandes compagnies concessionnaires, 1898–1930.* Paris: Mouton, 1972.

Depelchin, J. *From the Congo Free State to Zaire: How Belgium Privatized the Economy. A History of Belgian Stock Companies in Congo-Zaire from 1885 to 1974.* Oxford: Codresria, 1992.

Duignan, P., and L. H. Gann (eds.). *Colonialism in Africa, 1870–1960,* vol. 4, *The Economics of Colonialism.* Cambridge: Cambridge University Press, 1975.

Fieldhouse, D. K. *Unilever Overseas: The Anatomy of a Multinational, 1895–1965.* London: Croom Helm/Stanford, Calif.: Hoover Institute Press, 1978.

Harms, R. "The World ABIR Made: The Maringa-Lopari Basin, 1885–1903." *African Economic History,* no. 22 (1983): 125–139.

Hopkins, A. G. *An Economic History of West Africa.* New York: Columbia University Press, 1973.

Nelson, S. *Colonialism in the Congo Basin, 1880–1940.* Athens, Ohio: Ohio University Center for International Studies, 1994.

Confederation: *See* South Africa: Confederation, Disarmament, and the First Anglo-Boer War, 1871–1881.

Congo (Brazzaville), Republic of: Nineteenth Century: Precolonial

As with most African countries, Congo is a recent colonial creation, the result of late-nineteenth-century European imperialism and violent conquest. Before the onset of colonialism, two kingdoms and several chiefdoms populated the area. In the early 1300s, the Bakongo, the largest ethnic group, established one of the most powerful early kingdoms in central Africa. The Kingdom of Kongo, as it was known, extended south of present-day Congo and through the western region of the present-day Democratic Republic of

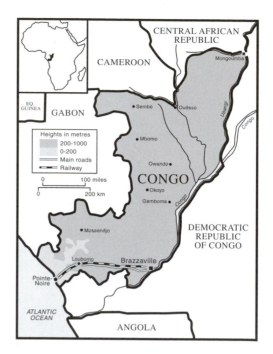

Congo.

Congo; its capital, Mbanza Kongo, was located in the northern part of present-day Angola. The kingdom was well organized, with a centralized administration. Trade was the most important economic activity of the kingdom, using palm cloth and cowrie shells (called *nzimbu*) as currencies. When in 1484 the Portuguese arrived at the mouth of the Congo River, the Mani Kongo (king of Kongo) had managed to assert his authority south of the Lower Congo River by establishing several vassal states. The Mani Kongo exerted power across his vast kingdom through appointed provincial governors who were responsible for collecting taxes and monitoring trade. Portuguese presence and involvement within the kingdom stimulated a dynastic dispute between those in favor of greater foreign contacts and those opposed. Aided by the Portuguese, the former emerged victorious, and in 1506 a Kongolese Christian convert became the Mani Kongo under the title of Affonso I (1506–1543). Under the influence of the Portuguese, Christianity was introduced to the Kongolese elite. Mbanza Kongo, where most of them resided, took the name of São Salvador. The most important change instigated by the Portuguese, and which led to the decline of Kongo, was slavery and the slave trade. During the course of the seventeenth century, the authority of the Mani Kongo collapsed and the kingdom disintegrated into rival factions battling each other in order to get prisoners of war that would be sold in slavery.

Another important kingdom that developed in Congo was the Tio or Teke kingdom, arising in the fourteenth century west of the Lower Congo River region through the fusion of former smaller kingdoms. The Tio kingdom was less centralized than the Kongo, for the king only received tribute from vassal groups and did not maintain a military presence outside of his capital.

In the early nineteenth century, on the eve of the European takeover, the Teke people found themselves in a very strategic position, serving as middlemen in the trading system between the Kongo in the south and the Mbochi and Boubangi in the north. These latter groups were mostly hunters and gatherers organized in various chieftaincies in the rain forest of northern Congo. The trading system used the Congo River as a means of transportation to exchange products as varied as copper, ceramics, ivory, tobacco, groundnuts, cattle, goats, yams, textiles, mats, nets, and boats.

This economic activity along the Congo River reached its climax in the nineteenth century as the Teke asserted their authority in the Malebo Pool region, halfway between the northern savanna and the coastal areas. Their strategic presence in the Malebo Pool region, the area where Brazzaville and Kinshasa are located, allowed them to control the economy of the whole region by serving as middlemen between the people of the forest in the north and the Kongo in the south. Before colonial penetration, the Malebo Pool region was a thriving hub where products from the forest and the coast were exchanged among various groups. Teke chiefs monopolized the trade, used slave labor, and directed market activities on the two banks of the Congo River. Their most important trading strongholds were Mpila and Mfwa on the north bank. On the south bank the major settlements controlled by the Teke were Kintambo, Kinshasa, Kingabwa, Ndolo, and Lemba. The Congo River did not demarcate two different economic and political domains, as it came to be known after the onset of colonialism. It was, on the contrary, used as a "highway" to accelerate the flow of products, ideas, and people. Sometime in the eighteenth century, the Teke imposed upon their trading partners the *ngele* (copper bar), which replaced the Kongolese nzimbu as the most indispensable currency in the region.

Although economically nineteenth-century Congo appeared to be thriving, with a well-built commercial network linking the rain forest to the Loango coast, it was a politically fragmented region. In the north, political power was even more diluted than in previous centuries as individuals strove to connect themselves with the trading networks commanded by the Teke from the Malebo Pool region. The Teke society itself resembled only remotely the powerful centralized kingdom that reached its climax in the seventeenth century. Major chiefs in the northern region of the Teke kingdom had grown wealthy and autonomous through

trade. They now claimed political and spiritual independence as well. This situation led to a series of wars between the Teke and their northern neighbors, especially the Boubangi and the Mbochi, that were not settled until the 1840s. By the nineteenth century the Teke *makoko* (king) ceased to be regarded by his former vassals as a lord but more as a primus inter pares. In the south, the territorial cohesiveness of the Teke kingdom was also encroached by the arrival of the Kongo after their kingdom dismantled in the late 1600s. The Kongo occupied strategic positions (previously held by the Teke) around Mindouli, Boko, and Kinkala, and gradually drove the Teke back beyond the Djoue River, upstream from the Malebo Pool. At the end of the nineteenth century, this lack of centralized territorial polities accounted for the somewhat easy colonial conquest by the French.

CHARLES DIDIER GONDOLA

Further Reading

Balandier, G. *Daily Life in the Kingdom of the Kongo from the Sixteenth to the Eighteenth Century*, translated by Helen Weaver. New York: Pantheon Books, 1968.

Fegley, R. *The Congo*. World Bibliographical Series, vol. 162. Oxford: Clio Press, 1993.

Gondola, Ch. Didier, *Villes miroirs. Migrations et identités urbaines à Brazzaville et Kinshasa, 1930–1970*. Paris: L'Harmattan, 1997.

Guiral, L. *Le Congo français du Gabon à Brazzaville*. Paris, 1889.

Hilton, A. *The Kingdom of the Kongo*. Oxford: Clarendon Press, 1985.

McDonald, G. C., et al. *Area Handbook for the People's Republic of the Congo (Congo Brazzaville)*. Washington, D.C.: U.S. Department of the Army, 1971.

Thornton, J. K. *The Kingdom of Kongo*. Madison: University of Wisconsin Press, 1983.

Vansina, J. *Paths in the Rain Forests: Toward a History of Political Tradition in Equatorial Africa*. Madison: University of Wisconsin Press, 1990.

———. *The Tio Kingdom of the Middle Congo: 1880–1892*. London: Oxford University Press, 1973.

West, R. *Congo*. New York: Holt, Rinehart, and Winston, 1972.

Congo (Brazzaville), Republic of: De Brazza and French Colonization

In the 1830s, the French were already present on the fringes of western equatorial Africa through several trading stations and missionary centers on the Gabon coast. This period corresponds to the beginning of European penetration of Africa. The Atlantic slave trade had become unprofitable for European countries, and many countries (especially Britain and France) began to view Africa no longer as a reservoir of slaves but as a source of raw materials (ivory, rubber, nuts, and gold) and a market for the manufactured products of the growing industrial economies of Europe. Africa was also regarded, as in the case of America and Australia, as a virgin land where Europe could export its troubled minorities and social groups. In 1830, France conquered Algeria and began relocating criminals and religious minorities there.

When the French abolished the slave trade and founded in 1849 the coastal settlement of Libreville (Gabon) as a haven for freed slaves, the interior of western equatorial Africa still remained a terra incognita to them. In 1875, the French government decided to dispatch Pierre Savorgnan de Brazza (1852–1905), a French explorer of Italian origin, on a first mission to establish French influence over the Central African Basin. On his first journey, Brazza left from Lambaréné on January 11, 1876, and traveled up the Ogooué River and into the Congo River Basin. During his second mission (1879–1882), accompanied by Malamine, a sergeant and interpreter from Senegal, Brazza traveled up the Congo River, crossed the Teke plateaus, reached the Lefini and Congo Rivers, and came in contact with the by now declining Teke kingdom. By the time Brazza arrived at Malebo Pool, another European explorer, Henry Morton Stanley, was roaming the land in search of a colony to satisfy the gargantuan appetite of his employer, Belgian king Leopold II, who had hired him to carve out a piece of Africa. In order to prevent Leopold II's control of the northwest bank of the Congo River, Brazza signed a dubious treaty with Makoko, the Teke king, allowing a permanent French settlement in central Africa. This treaty, ratified by the French parliament in November 1881, ceded to France the site of N'couna, where the city of Brazzaville is now located. This soon led to a French colony on the northwest bank of the Congo River. It is likely that Makoko had given Brazza ownership of the land on behalf of France, but only the usage since according to Teke's laws land belonged to the ancestors and could be only ceded in usufruct. Further treaties were to be made with several chiefs of the lower Ubangi during Brazza's third expedition, when he joined forces with his lieutenant, Albert Dolisie. This third expedition took Brazza and Dolisie as far as the west coast, where Brazza made another questionable protectorate treaty with Ma Loango, the Vili chief, who ceded outright to France the area known as Pointe Indienne.

By 1885, Brazza had carved out for France the whole region west of the Congo River, preventing the king of the Belgians, who had already claimed the east bank of the river through the work of Stanley, from spreading his claims eastward. A year before, in November 1884, the European powers had met at the Berlin Conference, called by German Chancellor Otto von Bismarck to thwart British colonial ambitions in Africa. The resultant Berlin Act formalized the colonial claims made by European nations. This on-paper division of the region was followed by a series of bilateral treaties that delineated the boundaries between the Congo and the neighboring colonies. In 1885, the boundary between the Congo and Cabinda was established via a treaty with Portugal, and the border with Cameroon was demarcated via an agreement with Germany. In 1887, two other treaties recognized the Oubangui and Congo Rivers as the frontier between the French Congo and Leopold II's État Indépendant du Congo (Congo Free State). In the bargain, France lost direct access to the mouth of the Congo River but retained possession of the Niari Basin and the areas explored by Brazza.

In 1886, the "Scramble" for Africa was underway, and more territories, regardless of whatever African population inhabited them, remained to be acquired and claimed in the Congo Basin. Brazza, now commissioner general of the Congo, set out on a fourth mission in the Upper Sangha River, an area coveted by the Germans. Under Brazza's leadership, all of the French Equatorial African territories (Congo, Gabon, and Oubangui-Chari-Tchad) were grouped into one administrative unit known as Congo-Gabon. Three years later, in 1891, Congo-Gabon became known as the French Congo, and in 1903 Congo was detached from Gabon and renamed Moyen-Congo (Middle Congo).

Unwilling to be directly involved in the colonization of the Congo, France decided to divide up the colony among large concessionary companies. These companies were granted, for a period of 30 years, exclusive economic and political rights over the areas conceded. They had right over all agricultural, forest, and industrial exploitation. After 30 years of exploitation, they retained ownership of any land they had developed. In exchange, they were required to exploit the wealth of the concessions for the benefit of the French economy. They paid the state a quitrent depending on the size of their concession and 15 per cent of their annual profits. In addition, they were to build roads, enforce justice, and safeguard natives' rights by creating reserves for them and respecting their customary use of land and forests. In 1893–1894, Théophile Delacassé, then French minister of colonies, signed decrees granting two individual entrepreneurs 30-year concessions covering nearly 150,000 square kilometers. More decrees were to follow, conferring to 40 concessionary companies monopolies over 650,000 square kilometers, a little more than the whole area of France. All of the land from the coast to the Oubangui Bend, except for small areas around Libreville and Brazzaville, were claimed in this way. In effect, the whole Congo was handed over to large companies with a registered capital of 59 million francs. The government in practice abdicated its functions and limited itself to the imposition of taxes and the collection of quitrents.

In 1898 several decrees transferred ownership of the land and waterways from the Africans to the French State, thus laying the groundwork for the establishment of the concessionary regime. That same year Brazza, who opposed these decrees in favor of a more humanitarian colonial approach and who was increasingly branded a "negrophile" by the French government and the French press alike, was dismissed from his position and recalled to France. A commission of colonial concessions was created in Paris and paved the road for the adoption of the concessionary system, which was notorious for its abuses and cruelties as it caused depopulation and misery in regions that were once populated and prosperous. Natives were forced to work as porters and rubber collectors in order to pay taxes. They received low wages and were severely punished when they attempted to avoid compulsory labor. Punitive expeditions conducted by both officials and company agents resulted in the destruction of farms, the burning of habitations, and the massacre of women and children. In the early 1900s charges of cruelty and abuses of Africans by French settlers surfaced, and the French government dispatched Brazza to investigate the charges. On his return from Moyen-Congo, Brazza died at Dakar (Senegal) on September 14, 1905. Although Brazza's conquering methods could be considered pacifist, especially when contrasted to those of Stanley, they led to a brutal colonial rule in Congo.

CHARLES DIDIER GONDOLA

See also: **Concessionary Companies; Stanley, Leopold II, "Scramble."**

Further Reading

Decalo, S., Virginia Thompson, and Richard Adloff. *Historical Dictionary of Congo.* Lanham, Md.: Scarecrow Press, 1996.

Fegley, R. *The Congo.* World Bibliographical Series, vol. 162. Oxford: Clio Press, 1993.

McDonald, G. C., et al. *Area Handbook for the People's Republic of the Congo (Congo Brazzaville).* Washington, D.C.: U.S. Department of the Army, 1971.

Roberts, Sir Stephen. *The History of French Colonial Policy (1870–1925).* London: P. S. King and Son, 1929.

West, R. *Congo.* New York: Holt, Rinehart, and Winston, 1972.

Congo (Brazzaville), Republic of: Colonial Period: Moyen-Congo

In 1910, the French decided to reorganize their possessions in Equatorial Africa, as they had done in West Africa in 1904, by uniting Moyen-Congo, Gabon, and Oubangui-Chari (the future Central African Republic, which was then coupled with the military territory of Tchad) into one federal territory. French Equatorial Africa (FEA), as it came to be known, was headed by a governor general appointed directly by the French minister of colonies in Paris. Brazzaville, the capital of Moyen-Congo, was then promoted to be the federal capital of FEA.

Due to its administrative importance, Moyen-Congo received preferential treatment. In 1934, Brazzaville was connected to Pointe Noire by the Congo-Ocean Railway, the only railway in the entire federation. Brazzaville was provided better public buildings, schools, telecommunications, trading houses, and health facilities than the other three colonies of FEA.

During colonization, Moyen-Congo experienced economic and social upheavals caused by two offshoots of the Berlin Act of 1884–1885, which formalized European colonial claims: missionary enterprises of all denominations could carry their venture with the help of the colonial state, and concessionary companies were encouraged to exploit the natural wealth of the colony. Education was first provided by Catholic missionaries, who sought not only to evangelize the Congolese but also to organize their social and cultural life. This cultural colonization referred to by the French as a *mission civilisatrice* (civilizing mission) soon sparked different forms of sociopolitical protest that culminated in the 1930s and the 1940s when messianic cults spread throughout the south of the colony. The concessionary companies' regime in Moyen-Congo, under whose terms some 40 companies were granted 30-year monopolies on the economic production and administration of huge portions of territory, turned out to be disastrous in financial as well as human terms. Ivory and rubber disappeared from the conceded territories, which also experienced dramatic demographic losses. Compulsory labor, colonial discipline, and diseases imported by Europeans took their high toll.

In the early 1900s, portage from the interior to the coast took such a toll on the local populations of FEA and gave such meager returns that it became obsolete. The French then started to build a railroad to evacuate raw materials to the coast (Pointe Noire) and from there to Europe. The project started in 1921 using forced labor from all over the federation. It was open to traffic on July 10, 1934, and cost France 231 million gold francs. In all, at least 30,000 African workers perished during the construction of the 511 kilometers of this railroad. In 1925–1926, French writer André Gide (1869–1951) set off for FEA in order to fulfill his childhood longing to see the Congo. Gide was to witness the dramatic effects of French colonization in the Congo. In his travel account, published in 1927 under the title *Voyage au Congo*, he wrote, "I did not foresee that the agonizing social questions raised by our relations with the natives would soon preoccupy me and become the *raison d'être* of my journey."

It is against the backdrop of this colonial exploitation that the most important anticolonial movement developed against the French. It was led by André Matswa, a former Catholic catechist, who in the early 1920s had left Moyen-Congo to settle in Paris. In 1926, Matswa founded a movement in Paris called the Association of Natives of French Equatorial Africa. The movement catered to natives of FEA living in France and stressed education, mutual aid, and the promotion of Africans to equal status with French citizens. The movement spread to Moyen-Congo and gained enough support among the Lari and Sundi populations of Brazzaville and the Malebo Pool region to alarm the colonial government.

When Matswa returned to Brazzaville in 1930 to campaign for his movement, he was immediately arrested along with three other leaders, Constant Balou, Jacques Mayassi, and Pierre Nganga. The three were tried and deported to Chad. This decision sparked a series of riots, and workers in Brazzaville went on strike. Throughout the 1930s and 1940s the movement took roots in the rural communities of the Malebo Pool region and fostered an atmosphere of indiscipline among the Lari peasants. At first undecided about an appropriate repression, the colonial government took advantage of the restrictive climate of World War II to crack down on the movement. In 1940, several Matswanist activists were executed and Matswa fled to France, where he volunteered to serve in the French army. After being wounded in battle in April, he was arrested and sent back to Moyen-Congo to be jailed in Mayama, where he died under mysterious conditions. Matswa's death not only reinforced the basic anticolonial undertones of the movement, but it placed him at the center of a new religious syncretist and messianic cult among the Lari and Sundi. Many of them believed that Matswa was not dead but in exile in Paris and would return as a savior to liberate Congo from French colonial rule.

After World War II, political reforms were introduced in French colonial Africa and prompted the development of political parties. In 1946, Jean-Félix Tchicaya founded the first political party in Moyen-Congo, the Congolese Progressive Party (Parti Progressiste Congolais), an ethnic-based party with a large Vili constituency. Two more major parties were to be created along similar ethnic lines: the African Socialist Movement (Mouvement Socialiste Africain) of Jacques Opangault from the Mbochi group; and the Democratic Union for the Protection of African Interest (Union Démocratique pour la Défense des Intérêts Africains) of Fulbert Youlou, a former Catholic priest who claimed the mantle of Matswa and catered to the Lari people.

In November 1956, after a rough political campaign that opposed these three parties, Youlou was elected mayor of Brazzaville and became the first African to be elected mayor in FEA. In 1958, General Charles de Gaulle's return to power in France prompted further reforms that would eventually lead to the proclamation of the autonomous Congo Republic as part of the French community. De Gaulle took this reform a step further, granting "full independence" to France's former African colonies. After a successful campaign, Youlou became the first president of an independent Republic of Congo on August 15, 1960.

CHARLES DIDIER GONDOLA

See also: **Berlin West Africa Conference, 1884–1885; Concessionary Companies; Congo (Brazzaville), Republic of: Independence, Revolution, 1958–1979.**

Further Reading

Balandier, G. *The Sociology of Black Africa: Social Dynamics in Central Africa*, translated by Douglas Garman. New York: Praeger, 1970.

Decalo, S., V. Thompson, and R. Adloff. *Historical Dictionary of Congo*. Lanham, Md: Scarecrow Press, 1996.

Fegley, R. *The Congo*. World Bibliographical Series, vol. 162. Oxford: Clio Press, 1993.

Gauze, R. *The Politics of Congo-Brazzaville*, Stanford, Calif.: Hoover Institution Press, 1973.

Sinda, M. *Le messianisme congolais et ses incidences politiques*. Paris: Payot, 1972.

Thompson, V., and R. Adloff. *The Emerging States of French Equatorial Africa*. Stanford, Calif.: Stanford University Press, 1960.

West, R. *Congo*. New York: Holt, Rinehart, and Winston, 1972.

Congo (Brazzaville), Republic of: Independence, Revolution, 1958–1979

By the eve of Congo's independence in 1958, three notable politicians had taken center stage in the country's fascinating political drama. One, Félix Tchicaya, had been a fixture on the Congolese scene since 1945, when he was elected to the French National Assembly. His local party, the Parti Progressiste Congolais (PPC), was at that time affiliated with Houphouet-Boigny's Rassemblement Démocratique Africain (RDA) political movement. Tchicaya had support among the coastal Vili people, as well as among many intellectuals.

Jacques Opangault, with an ethnic base among the northern Mbochi, was a second important leader of the era. Opangault led the local affiliate of the French socialist party, which became the Mouvement Socialist Africain (MSA) in August 1957. Tchicaya and Opangault had been long rivals in the postwar period, but joined in coalition with one another in 1957 against Congo's third important political figure of the era, Fulbert Youlou.

Although he was a Catholic priest, Youlou began his political career by mobilizing the Lari people, many of whom had been previously devoted to a martyred, messianic hero, André Matsoua (also spelled Matswa); the Lari had essentially disenfranchised themselves after Matsoua's death. Youlou created the Union Démocratique de Défense des Intérêts Africains (UDDIA) in May 1956 and was elected mayor of Brazzaville in November.

Following the implementation of the *loi cadre* (enabling act) and the elections of March 1957, the territorial assembly was divided nearly evenly between deputies of the MSA-PPC coalition (25 seats) and the UDDIA (24 seats). As a result, the colonial governor insisted upon a coalition government, headed by Opangault. In September, however, one MSA delegate defected, giving the UDDIA a bare majority. Afterward, there was a sharp increase in intragovernmental tension, but no change of regime. In August 1958, Charles de Gaulle appeared in Brazzaville in support of the French Community referendum, which Congo duly approved the following month with 79 per cent in favor. In November of that year, after the defection of another MSA delegate, the UDDIA party forced through a new constitution and formed a new, provisional government with Youlou as the prime minister. In February 1959 ethnic violence between Lari UDDIA partisans and Mbochi MSA loyalists erupted in Brazzaville, and Opangault was briefly arrested. Youlou was able to consolidate his power when his UDDIA won an overwhelming majority in new elections for the assembly. On August 15, 1960 Congo became a fully independent republic. Later that year Youlou brought Opangault back into the government as vice president.

During his short period of rule, Youlou managed to alienate all of the major political forces in Congo. His "natural" Matsouanists constituents renounced him when he pursued national goals, while he never reconciled other ethnic groups to his rule. Meanwhile, the youth, unions, and educated classes recoiled at his conservative foreign policies and lackluster development efforts. Finally, the country's few pluralists were put off by his intention, announced in August 1962, to create a one-party state. Youlou's opponents coalesced in three days of mass demonstrations (*les trois glorieuses*) between August 13 and 15, 1963, leading to his resignation. A Conseil National de la Révolution (CNR), including union, army, and youth elements, took control of the country. In December, the speaker of the assembly, Alphonse Massemba-Débat, was elected president, and a constitution based on "scientific socialism" was adopted.

In 1964, the country's new leaders instituted a single, national party, the Mouvement National de la Révolution (MNR), as well as mass organizations for youth (JMNR), women, civil defense, and labor; education was nationalized. In 1965, Congo established relations with the Soviet Union, China, North Korea, and Vietnam while severing relations with the United States. The CNR remained the locus of real power, though the army exercised considerable influence behind the scenes. Meanwhile, JMNR leaders perpetually tried to push Massemba-Débat further to the left, causing a serious rivalry between that organization and the army. Unable to reconcile the various institutional and ideological factions in his own regime, Massemba-Débat finally succumbed to a coup d'état led by Captain Marien Ngouabi in July 1968. Thus ended Congo's second republic.

Ngouabi soon made Congo's commitment to Marxism-Leninism even more unequivocal. At the end of 1969, the country was renamed the People's Republic of Congo, and a more rigorously Leninist constitution was adopted, launching the third republic. The Parti Congolais du Travail (PCT) replaced the MNR. Despite this rhetoric, the real politics of the country centered on competing ethnoregional barons and various army factions. The most important factional leader to contest Ngouabi was Ange Diawara, an ardent Maoist, who attempted a coup on February 22, 1972; Diawara remained an important clandestine opponent of the regime until he was killed by the army in April 1973. Ngouabi frequently purged the PCT and senior army ranks of those he suspected of disloyalty or independent ambition. On the economic front, rising oil production and prices allowed Ngouabi to nationalize many foreign firms and create state-owned enterprises as well as expand the civil service and army.

Ngouabi was assassinated on March 18, 1977, by a group of soldiers who were themselves then quickly killed by loyal army troops. Officially, the assassination was the work of Barthélemy Kikadidi, a former chief of military intelligence under Massemba-Débat, but the real origins of the assassination remain a matter of highly contentious debate in Congo. A number of southern politicians, including Massemba-Débat, were subsequently executed by the regime, and a prominent Catholic cardinal, Emile Biayenda, was murdered by unknown assassins. Many PCT figures, including President Denis Sassou-Nguesso, have also frequently been implicated in the death of Ngouabi, who is now widely remembered as Congo's least corrupt and most devoted leader.

Ngouabi was succeeded as president by Joachim Yhombi-Opango, another prominent Kouyou army officer, but one far less committed to socialism. Yhombi began a process of reconciliation with the United States that was finally concluded in 1979. Yhombi never managed to consolidate his grip on power, however, and was himself displaced in a bloodless coup by Sassou, a Mbochi, in February 1979. Sassou soon returned the country to a more "revolutionary" path in principle, but in practice he proved himself pragmatic in foreign relations and his development strategy.

JOHN F. CLARK

See also: **Congo (Brazzaville), Republic of: Liberalization, Rebellion, 1980s and 1990s; Sassou-Nguesso, Denis.**

Further Reading

Decalo, S. "Ideological Rhetoric and Scientific Socialism in Benin and Congo." In *Socialism in Sub-Saharan Africa*, edited by Carl Rosberg and Thomas Callaghy. Berkeley and Los Angeles: University of California Press, 1979.

Levine, V. T. "Military Rule in the People's Republic of Congo." In *The Military in African Politics*, edited by John W. Harbeson. New York: Praeger, 1987.

Racine, A. "The People's Republic of Congo." in *The New Communist Third World* by Peter Wiles (ed.). New York: St. Martin's Press, 1982.

Congo (Brazzaville), Republic of: Liberalization, Rebellion, 1980s and 1990s

Both Congo's economy and its political fate were tied to the value of its petroleum revenues during the 1980s. Following the oil price shock of 1979 and production increases, Congo was flush with official funds during the first half of the decade. While some of these funds were diverted for patronage and conspicuous consumption by regime barons, much was recirculated to the population through civil-service staff salaries, parastatal support, educational stipends, and other public subsidies. An ambitious Five-Year Development Plan for 1982–1986 was adopted by the Congolese Worker's Party (PCT) in December 1981. In these favorable circumstances, President Denis Sassou-Nguesso was able to consolidate his power with little public protest. In foreign relations, Sassou signed a Treaty of Friendship and Cooperation with the Soviets in 1981, but he also allowed the French Elf-Aquitaine company to take the lead in developing Congolese oil and improved relations with the United States.

The oil price collapse of 1985 led to a rapid rise in public discontent during the second half of the decade. In June of that year, the PCT Central Committee canceled the costly 1982–1986 Development Plan. Meanwhile, the government began negotiations with the International Monetary Fund for a debt-relief plan that would lead to a standby agreement in July 1986. Sassou reshuffled his cabinet in December 1985, and

began to speak of the need for liberalizing economic reforms, but these were instituted only halfheartedly. Under the resulting austerity economy, both public protests and attempted coups d'état increased over the following years. Sassou was forced to rely more on repression and less on patronage to remain in power as the decade wore on.

Following the National Conference in Benin (another francophone, Afro-Marxist state), as well as the end of the Cold War in Europe, public pressure on the Sassou regime to liberalize escalated sharply in 1990. Under this pressure, Sassou announced in July 1990 that Congo would take steps to become a multiparty state. The opposition, however, demanded the immediate convening of a sovereign national conference. Students, unionized workers, and religious groups organized public demonstrations to rally support for such a conference during the final months of the year. At year's end Sassou finally bowed to this demand, and the conference was allowed to convene on February 25, 1991. Once the opposition gained control over the conference, it proceeded to expose the sins of the Sassou regime, dismantle the one-party state, organize a transitional government, and set up a constitution drafting committee.

The new constitution was approved in March 1992 and legislative elections were held in June and July. Three important parties emerged in these elections. Finishing first was the Pan-African Union for Social Democracy (UPADs) led by Pascal Lissouba and regionally based in the Niari, Bouenza, and Lékoumou regions (the Nibolek); second was the Congolese Movement for Democracy and Comprehensive Development (MCDDI) led by Bernard Kolélas, and supported chiefly by the Lari people of the Malebo Pool region; third was the reformed PCT led by Sassou, which drew most of its support from the North. In August 1992 Sassou was defeated in the first round of the presidential elections, after which he endorsed Lissouba. The latter then defeated Kolélas in the second round by a margin of 61 per cent to 39 per cent.

When Lissouba named his first cabinet, however, it contained few PCT members, and the UPADS-PCT alliance quickly broke apart, depriving Lissouba of a majority in the parliament. Instead of naming an opposition prime minister, though, Lissouba illegally dissolved the parliament and ordered new elections. This led to a wave of civil unrest that was only ended by the appointment of a neutral cabinet in December 1992. When the legislative elections were rerun in May 1993, the opposition rejected the results and boycotted the second round. Serious military confrontations between the militias of Lissouba and Kolélas followed, continuing through early August. In that month, intensive foreign mediation achieved an agreement to rerun the elections for contested seats. Nonetheless, serious fighting resumed during the November 1993–January 1994 period. When all of the final elections results were in, Lissouba had regained a parliamentary majority through a coalition excluding both the MCDDI and the PCT. Approximately 2,000 or 3,000 Congolese were killed between December 1992 and February 1994.

Although an uneasy peace prevailed over Congo from mid-1994 until May 1997, Lissouba's record was undistinguished. Reforms of the parastatal sector and civil service were perpetually delayed, and Congo remained as oil dependent as ever. Meanwhile, the level of corruption and the diversion of petroleum revenues increased. Lissouba relied heavily in his administration on staff from the Nibolek, and particularly on Bembe partisans.

As the elections scheduled for July 1997 approached, the population perceived that Lissouba was not seriously preparing for free elections. Meanwhile, Sassou returned from a long exile in France and began readying his militia as well as his electoral campaign. In May 1997 violence broke out during one of Sassou's campaign swings through the northern town of Owando, home of former president Yhombi, then serving as Lissouba's campaign director. Despite an apparent settlement of the resulting dispute, Lissouba sent a military detachment to arrest "certain associates" of Sassou at his home on June 5, 1997. Sassou's militia's successfully resisted this attempt, and a full-scale civil war soon commenced. As in the first civil war, ethnic cleansing accompanied the fighting. In late August, Kolélas foreswore his previous neutrality and ordered his militia into battle against Sassou. In early October, however, a large contingent of Angolan troops joined the fray on behalf of Sassou, allowing his forces to seize power. Some 10,000 Congolese died in this round of fighting.

Throughout 1998 Sassou followed a dual strategy of coopting some opposition politicians, while assassinating or jailing others. Yet his regime remained dependent on military support from Angola, and financial support from friendly French commercial interests. Lissouba, Kolélas, Yhombi and other important figures had escaped into exile, whence they launched campaigns to undermine the Sassou government. In December 1998 the militia based in the Malebo Pool region and in Nibolek began serious efforts to seize power. Again, hundreds were killed and many thousands displaced. While Sassou's army and militia forces were able to rebut these assaults, some parts of the country fell into rebel hands. As the fighting continued in 1999, Sassou's grip on power remained uncertain.

JOHN F. CLARK

See also: **Congo (Brazzaville), Republic of: Independence, 1958–1979; Sassou-Nguesso, Denis.**

Further Reading

Bazenguissa-Ganga, R. "The Spread of Political Violence in Congo-Brazzaville." *African Affairs*, no. 98 (1999): 37–54.

Clark, J. F. "Congo: Transition and the Struggle to Consolidate." In *Political Reform in Francophone Africa*, edited by John F. Clark and David E. Gardinier. Bolder, Colo.: Westview Press, 1997.

———. "Democracy Dismantled in the Congo Republic." *Current History* 97, no. 619 (1998): 234–237.

Decalo, S., V. Thompson, and R. Adloff. *Historical Dictionary of Congo*, rev. 3rd ed. Lanham, Md.: Scarecrow Press, 1996.

Congo (Kinshasa), Democratic Republic of/Zaire: Nineteenth Century: Precolonial

Although the nineteenth century was an epoch of great changes for the Congo, many of the critical historical transformations began well before external influences became decisive. The first half of the century witnessed the expansion of two great savanna kingdoms, the Lunda and the Luba, as well as of other related states such as the Kanyok, the Yaka of Kiamfu, and the Lunda of Kazembe. Along the southern limits of the great equatorial forest, the Teke (Tio) and Kuba kingdoms continued to exercise their control over large territories. New political configurations emerged on the savanna north of the forest edge as well. Generally less powerful than the kingdoms of the southern savanna, these included the Mangbetu, Zande, and Ngbandi chiefdoms. On the northern savanna, armed Sudanic peoples exerted pressure that resulted in the militarization and gradual southward displacement of many groups. This ultimately explains why the conquests of the Ngombe affected the distant Mongo living in the heart of the forest.

The nineteenth century witnessed a dramatic growth of long-distance commerce. For centuries, central Africa had been linked both to the Atlantic and the Indian oceans. But these links were achieved by a multitude of relays, and trade goods circulated as by capillary action. In the nineteenth century, commerce was increasingly organized into well-structured networks. Large caravans, sometimes composed of thousands of people, spread out across the continent along established itineraries controlled by groups linked to trade. As in preceding centuries, the slave trade remained the principal form of commerce. The European ban on the slave trade progressively redirected commercial interests toward ivory and other

Democratic Republic of Congo.

products such as rubber, palm oil, or beeswax. But because commerce in those products required porters and because European prohibitions had little effect on the internal African slave markets (Zanzibar and Angola especially), the slave trade survived until about 1910. Slaves continued to be exchanged for cloth, weapons, beads, and other manufactured goods.

Four great commercial networks dominated the nineteenth century. The oldest linked the Angolan coast with the southern savanna. The primary actors in this network came from the Portuguese colony of Angola and the African states of the Kasanje, Matamba, Ovimbundu, and Lunda. In addition, between 1850 and 1870, the Chokwe and the Luluwa entered and expanded this commercial sphere. The second network began in the Lower Congo and its hinterland, and reached the Malebo Pool, where the great Pumbu market was located. From there it continued up the Congo River and its tributaries for several hundred kilometers. Many groups were part of this system. The most important were the Teke, the Bobangi, and the Bangala. The third great network linked the Congo to the Indian Ocean. Although it was very old, and even though Kazambe's kingdom had attracted coastal merchants several decades earlier, this eastern system had not substantially extended into the Congo until after the 1850s. But by the 1880s and 1890s it had affected most of the eastern part of the region. Finally, beginning in the 1860s, a fourth circuit developed. More modest, it was established by merchants from modern-day Sudan who traded with people in northeastern Congo, principally in the Uele Basin.

The establishment of these extensive economic domains led to the diffusion of great trade languages. This was the case with Kikongo (in the Lower Congo region), Lingala (in the area above the Malebo Pool), and Swahili (in the east). These economic developments also led to the creation of markets, some of which became the first colonial posts that later evolved into modern cities.

The expansion of the commercial networks advanced in conjunction with an enormous movement of people and firearms that led to an unprecedented political upheaval. Therefore, in a matter of several decades, the Chokwe, seminomadic hunters from northern Angola who were little known before 1850, established their ascendancy over dozens of southern savanna groups. Even though they acted in small groups without any centralized political structure, they defeated all of the Lunda chiefdoms of the region and overran Musumb, the royal capital in 1885. Thanks to the support of their Luluwa allies, their commercial sphere reached well into the interior of Kasai. Only the Kuba kingdom remained relatively intact during the upheavals that spread through this region.

To the east, the sphere oriented toward the Indian Ocean also experienced radical transformations. About 1850, under the impetus of their leader M'siri, the Yeke, a group originating in Tanzania, settled in southern Katanga, where they seized the strategic location at the intersection of the trade routes leading to the two oceans. From 1870 to 1890, after being deeply integrated into the social fabric of the region, they undertook several wars of conquest against their Lunda and Luba neighbors. The Swahili Arabs linked to the Sultanate of Muscat-Zanzibar would eventually constitute the greatest challenge to European occupation. Starting from bases in the regions around Lakes Tanganyika and Mweru, they settled in the Maniema beginning in the 1860s. There they created two towns, Nyangwe and Kasongo, containing 30,000 and 60,000 inhabitants, respectively; even today these two remain important Muslim centers in the Congo. In 1874, Tippu Tip, the most famous of all of the Swahili Arab merchants, asserted control and unified the area into a nascent state. Under his influence, the Swahili Arab commercial domain penetrated deep into the interior to include the Aruwimi Basin, the lands far to the west of the Lower Lomami, and northern Katanga. His territory even reached eastern Kasai where he was assisted by his allies Ngongo Luteta and Lumpungu, and where he tapped into the active southern savanna Atlantic trade. For a long time, the Kivu frontier zone, along with the great interlacustrine kingdoms, remained outside this commercial sphere. But they did not escape the cultural influence imposed by the Swahili Arabs on the entire eastern part of the Congo.

Throughout the first half of the nineteenth century, the Congo was, with the exception of the area near the mouth of the Congo River, a territory unknown to Europeans. Between 1870 and 1885 the first great wave of explorations filled in this lacuna. The most notable voyages were those of Schweinfurth and Junker in the north, of Cameron in Maniema and Katanga, of Pogge and Wissman in the Kasai Basin, and of Henry Morton Stanley, who descended most of the Congo River in 1876–1877. Then, beginning in the 1880s, Catholic and Protestant missions followed the paths of the explorers, especially along the Congo River and in Katanga.

Throughout this period of exploration, the Belgian King Leopold II sponsored a series of ostensibly philanthropic or scientific associations. As a result, the Congo Free State was recognized during the Berlin Conference in 1885. Although theoretically this was a free-trade area, in actuality Leopold's intent was to transform the region into a Belgian colony. Increasingly, from 1880 onward, Europeans made treaties with indigenous chiefs and founded new posts legitimizing the ambitions of the king. Now all that remained for Leopold was to conquer the African powers in the region. This goal was realized by subduing the Madhist state in modern Sudan that threatened the northeastern part of the Congo Free State (just before and after 1890); by the conquest of the Yeke state (1891); and by the campaign against the Swahili Arabs (1892–1895). The great Luba and Lunda kingdoms, greatly destabilized by the slave trade, offered only weak resistance. Elsewhere, the Force Publique (the Free State's militia) engaged in campaigns against lesser states such as the Yaka (1889–1893) or the Kuba (1888–1889, and again in 1900) or against the armed resistance of groups not organized in states. The Congo Free State even had to contend with several rebellions of the Force Publique's African soldiers, who had turned against their European officers. For the most part, 1900 marked the end of extensive military operations.

The end of the nineteenth century was a crucial period for the creation and stabilization of the ethnic identities that exist in the Congo today. Up to this time ethnic identities were fluid and (except in the large kingdoms) often only referred to small groups. The political and economic upheavals and the European explorations of the nineteenth century led to the attribution of new identities to groups that earlier had not been known by the same ethnic name. Thus, the Bangala and the Mongo emerged in the forest. Two enormous groups, their names and identities were the convenient constructs of the period of exploration and early colonial rule. Elsewhere, ancient names became crystallized in a way that bore almost no relation to their more subtle and limited earlier usage.

PIERRE PETIT

Further Reading

Harms, R. *River of Wealth, River of Sorrow: The Central Zaire Basin in the Era of the Slave and Ivory Trade, 1500–1891.* New Haven, Conn.: Yale University Press, 1981.

Miller, J. C. *Way of Death: Merchant Capitalism and the Angolan Slave Trade, 1730–1830.* Madison: University of Wisconsin Press, 1988.

Vansina, J. *The Children of Woot: A History of the Kuba Peoples.* Madison: University of Wisconson Press, 1978.

———. *Kingdoms of the Savanna.* Madison: University of Wisconsin Press, 1966.

———. *Paths in the Rain Forests: Toward a History of Political Tradition in Equatorial Africa.* Madison: University of Wisconsin Press, 1990.

Congo (Kinshasa), Democratic Republic of/Zaire: Congo Free State, 1885–1908

The Congo Free State, or the Congo Independent State (État Indépendant du Congo), has earned an infamous place in the history of colonial Africa. Established during the Berlin Conference of 1884–1885, it was a colony without a metropolis, governed in an absolute fashion by King Leopold II of Belgium. The primary goal of Leopold and his European agents was profit maximization, and they soon turned the Congo into a veritable "heart of darkness." Using fear and terror to compel Africans to collect wild rubber and other exportable commodities, the Congo Free State's economy became dependent on an ever-increasing spiral of violence. When news of the atrocities eventually reached Europe, Leopold was forced to cede his private empire to Belgium in 1908, initiating a new phase of Belgian colonialism that lasted until 1960.

The origins of the Congo Free State can be traced to voyages of the American explorer Henry Morton Stanley. During his unprecedented trip across central Africa in the mid-1870s, Stanley discovered tremendous commercial potential in the Congo Basin. The land seemed rich in natural resources, and along the river he encountered large African trading expeditions, in canoes filled with valuable ivory tusks and other goods. Stanley's well-publicized trip caught the attention of King Leopold II who, having failed to win a colony in Asia, now turned his attention to Africa. In 1876, Leopold created the Comité d'études du haut Congo (Committee for the Study of the Upper Congo, later renamed the International Association of the Congo), an ostensibly scientific organization that masked his true imperialistic motives. He secretly hired Stanley to return to the Congo to collect treaties from African leaders and to establish preliminary stations. Leopold's strategy ultimately proved successful: European delegates at the Berlin Conference recognized his territorial claims and endorsed the creation of the Congo Free State, to be headed by Leopold himself. According to its charter, the Free State was to embody four basic principles: freedom of trade and navigation by all; neutrality in the event of war; suppression of the slave trade; and an improvement in the well-being of Africans. Under King Leopold's direction, however, these principles were soon ignored.

At the conclusion of the Berlin Conference, European traders from various nations wasted little time in launching their steamboats up the Zaire River and its tributaries in search of exportable commodities. Ivory quickly became the principal export, for it was plentiful, cheap, and highly prized in Europe. Although some African river traders attempted to block the advance of foreigners into their territories, many others contracted mutually beneficial commercial partnerships with the Europeans. Vast quantities of ivory were obtained from African traders in exchange for cloth, metal bars, beads, and other manufactured goods. Free trade in the Congo proved remarkably lucrative: between 1888 and 1890, European traders exported approximately 140 tons of ivory from the Free State, worth nearly seven million Belgian francs.

One individual not profiting from the Congo was King Leopold himself. On the contrary, he saw his personal fortune decline from 1885 to 1890, a direct result of the expenses incurred from early exploration, pioneering, and the numerous military campaigns required to exert control over the territory. Unsuccessful in his efforts to acquire assistance from private investors or the Belgian government, he became increasingly possessive of what he considered to be his personal colonial enterprise. In 1892 Leopold abandoned the original colonial charter and created a new economic order that would secure him the profits that he felt he so rightfully deserved. Claiming that all vacant land belonged to the state, he divided his colony into distinct commercial zones, each defined by monopolistic rights of exploitation. Huge territorial concessions were awarded to private commercial interests in return for capital investments and a significant share of the profits. To ensure his own success, Leopold created a large "crown domain" (*domain de la couronne*) as his own personal fiefdom. By the mid-1890s, nearly three-quarters of the Free State had been assigned to special interests, leaving only a small territory still open to free trade. Once the concessionary zones were established, Leopold initiated new policies to force large numbers of Africans into the production of exports, principally rubber latex tapped from the wild vines of the equatorial forest. In 1892, a rubber tax was instituted that left quotas and enforcement to company employees or government officials. To ensure maximum production and profits, European rubber agents and their African auxiliaries were rewarded and promoted in proportion to the amount of rubber collected. Inevitably, the new system encouraged widespread abuses and horrific violence against Africans. Individuals who did not meet their assigned quotas were beaten, whipped, and tortured. Mutilations became a common punishment to heighten fear and to set an example for others. Recalcitrant villages were burned, and women were taken as hostages until rubber or other goods were procured. In addition to the shock and terror caused by such brutality, the demands for ever-increasing amounts of rubber and other goods disrupted normal subsistence activities, causing famine, illness, and depopulation in many regions. Although African resistance was common and extensive, it never succeeded in eliminating the Europeans or their unceasing demands.

For Leopold and his allies, the savage economic system paid handsomely. Rubber exports rose from 135 tons in 1890 to over 5,800 tons by 1900, a more than 40-fold increase. The crown domain earned the king an additional profit of approximately 70 million Belgian francs. But this success was short-lived, for the system proved self-destructive. Rubber production began a slow but steady decline after 1900, a result of the excessive exploitation and deliberate sabotage of wild vines by African workers. Moreover, missionary reports chronicling the ruthless system created an international outcry, resulting in the formation of the Congo Reform Association in 1904. After a series of investigative reports, King Leopold was compelled to relinquish his empire to Belgium in 1908.

The Congo Free State bequeathed a harsh and lasting legacy to the newly created Belgian Congo. For Africans, the severe deprivations associated with forced labor caused widespread social disruption, sickness, and, for many, a lasting suspicion of and hostility toward Europeans. For the colonizers, annexation produced no real departure in policy. While the most drastic features of Leopold's system were terminated, colonial profit making remained the preeminent concern. To this end the new administration reformed its policy of land concessions, took on the role of labor recruiter, and passed a series of laws that hindered African economic activity that might compete with European interests. As was the case in the Congo Free State, the economic and social welfare of Africans was largely neglected or ignored.

SAMUEL NELSON

See also: **Colonialism: Impact on African Societies; Concessionary Companies; Congo (Kinshasa), Democratic Republic of/Zaire: Belgian Congo: Colonial Economy, 1908–1960.**

Further Reading

Anstey, R. "The Congo Rubber Atrocities: A Case Study." *African Historical Studies*, no. 4 (1971): 61–74.

Ascherson, N. *The King Incorporated: Leopold II in the Age of Trusts*. New York: Doubleday, 1964.

Cattier, F. *Étude sur la situation de l'État Indépendant du Congo*. Brussels: F. Larçier, 1906.

Gann, L. H. and P. Duignan. *Rulers of Belgian Africa, 1884–1914*. Princeton, N.J.: Princeton University Press, 1979.

Morel, E. D. *Red Rubber: The Story of the Rubber Slave Trade Flourishing on the Congo in the Year of Grace 1906*. London: T. F. Unwin, 1906.

Nelson, S. *Colonialism in the Congo Basin, 1880–1940*. Athens, Ohio: Ohio University Center for International Studies, 1994.

Slade, R. *King Leopold's Congo: Aspects of the Development of Race Relations in the Congo Independent State*. London: Oxford University Press, for the Institute of Race Relations, 1962.

Stengers, J. "The Congo Free State and the Belgian Congo before 1914." In *Colonialism in Africa, 1870–1960*, vol. 4, *The History and Politics of Colonialism, 1870–1914*, edited by Peter Duignan and L. H. Gann. Cambridge: Cambridge University Press, 1969.

Congo (Kinshasa), Democratic Republic of/Zaire: Belgian Congo: Administration and Society, 1908–1960

The administration of the Congo changed little after it was handed over by Leopold II to Belgium. The Belgians' concerns with the Congo did not differ much from what Leopold II envisioned or, more generally speaking, what Europeans deemed necessary to take into consideration with respect to their African domains. A Belgian version of Lord Lugard's dual mandate was implemented, including one overriding concern which recognized that the colony had to generate profit for the metropolis. The riches of the Congo had been, after all, one of the major factors in persuading the Belgians to go along with the annexation. Another principle that presided over the takeover was the notion that Europeans had a *mission civilisatrice* (civilizing mission) of both Christianization and education to perform in Africa. Hence the colony was governed according to a colonial charter drafted in 1908 that allowed the king to retain a great deal of authority and influence over affairs in the Congo by appointing high-ranked officials and signing laws. On the local level, in most rural areas the people were ruled indirectly through the native chiefs, many of whom were put in place by the local colonial administrator. However, what best describes Belgian administration in the Congo is what many authors have termed the "colonial trinity." Three forces—the state, missions, and big companies—collaborated in the Belgian Congo to rule a territory 80 times larger than Belgium. Concessionary companies, such as Huileries du Congo Belge (palm oil), an extension of Unilever, La Forminière

(diamonds), Kilo Moto (gold), and L'Union Minière du Haut Katanga (copper) were not only capitalistic ventures but had a mandate from the colonial state to erect schools and hospitals, to build roads and railways, and to police the Congolese natives.

In 1911, Huileries du Congo belge (HCB) alone had been granted an area one-fourth the size of Belgium to create five concessions of wild palm trees. In the operation, HCB displaced thousands of peasants and stripped them of their plantations of cultivated palm trees. The conditions given by the colonial government amounted to a total development of the areas conceded. HCB had to create a network of paved roads and railroads and a postal and telegraph service that could be used and even expropriated by the colonial state in exchange for compensations. Furthermore, HCB was mandated to build health and education infrastructures for its workers and families. In 1926, these social achievements included 15 hospitals and 5 schools for 23,000 African workers and families as well as for 335 Europeans. On the transportation front the balance sheet seemed impressive as well: 650 miles of paved roads and 50 miles of railroad. What these figures did not reflect is that in order to create such infrastructures and still be able to pay the colonial government its annual dividend, HCB literally pauperized thousands of Congolese living and working within the concessions and established a tight social control system that deprived people of their freedom and humanity.

The missionary presence in the Congo also played an important role in creating an administrative network that facilitated political control and repression. In 1935, the Catholic and Protestant denominations held, respectively, 261 and 168 posts with 2,326 and 718 white clergymen dedicated to a purported population of 1,048,511 and 233,673 African believers. Of all of the denominations granted privileges in the Congo, the Catholic Church espoused the colonial civilizing mission ideology with such conviction that it played into the hands of the colonial state as an agent for pacification and civilization. Most other denominations, especially Protestant foreign missions, were held in suspicion and regarded as agents of whatever European country they emanated from. This allowed the Catholic Church to stretch a network of nearly 600 parishes serving more than 24,400 villages and small towns. In 1946, the Catholic Church could boast of 18,000 schools serving the needs of 800,000 pupils, 561 hospitals and medical centers, 19 printing houses, 24 newspapers, and 1,432 European priests.

Although instrumental in asserting the authority of the Europeans in Congo, the role of the concessionary companies and the religious missions was superseded by the activity of the colonial state agents. Public indifference to colonial affairs paved the way to a colonial policy governed by bureaucratic conservatism, a blatant paternalism toward the Africans, and the interests of a minority. The vast majority of the population, whether Europeans or Africans, were not permitted political organization and representation in the colony until after World War II, when demands were heard and reforms made to gradually integrate Africans into the affairs of the colony.

African resistance to the Belgian colonial system took many forms. Africans perceived the imposition of European administration, business, and religion on their lives and customs according to their own interests. Responses varied from collaboration to open resistance, especially in areas where heavy taxation coupled with compulsory recruitment and low wages colluded into driving the population below poverty level. Armed resistance occurred among the Azande in the northeastern Congo, the Yaka and Pende in the southwest, the Luba in the southeast, and the Lele between the Lulua and the Loango Rivers. In a few cases religious movements took on overtones of political protests. Historians pay less attention to the use of popular cultures by Africans in many of the urban centers of the Belgian Congo to circumvent colonial prescriptions and voice their frustrations with the colonial system. Such domains include popular music, fashion, the use and abuse of alcohol, illegal migrations, and so on, which until the 1950s were perhaps the only means Africans could use both as a recreative outlet and a political tribune.

The 1950s constituted a major turning point, in that the Belgians had to rethink their ways of dealing with the Africans. For many years the Belgians had ruled the Congolese as though they were children, but as the gulf was narrowed by African education and what some have termed the political awakening of the Congolese, this policy was bound to change. Under the pressure of the *évolués*, the Congolese social and intellectual elite, "native councils" were set up at the territorial level on which Africans acquainted themselves, albeit remotely, with the colonial affairs. Some évolués were also invited to sit on various advisory boards such as the Fonds du Bien-Être Indigène, a social welfare organization, and the Office des Cités Africaines, concerned with native housing. These cosmetic changes, however, were far from satisfactory to the évolués.

CHARLES DIDIER GONDOLA

See also: **Concessionary Companies; Congo (Kinshasa), Democratic Republic of/Zaire: Belgian Congo: Colonial Economy, 1908–1960; Congo (Kinshasa), Democratic Republic of/Zaire: Evolués, Politics, Independence.**

Further Reading

Fetter, B. *Colonial Rule and Regional Imbalance in Central Africa*. Boulder: University of Colorado Press, 1983.

Kaplan, I. (ed.). *Zaïre: A Country Study*. Area Handbook Series. Washington, D.C.: American University Press, 1979.

Lemarchand, R. *Political Awakening in the Belgian Congo*. Berkeley and Los Angeles: University of California Press, 1964.

Martelli, G. *Leopold to Lumumba: A History of the Belgian Congo, 1877–1960*. London: Chapman and Hall, 1962.

Young, C. *Politics in the Congo: Decolonization and Independence*. Princeton, N.J.: Princeton University Press, 1965.

Congo (Kinshasa), Democratic Republic of/Zaire: Belgian Congo: Colonial Economy, 1908–1960

When in 1908 King Leopold II relinquished his private domain of the Congo to a somewhat reluctant Belgian government, the economy of the area was already becoming a brutal system of exploitation—one of the distinctive features of Belgian colonization. This system of economic exploitation was based on compulsory labor. The colonial administration that took over after Leopold II brought about a few changes but furthered the exploitation of the Congolese population by introducing a new method of forcing people to work: taxes. The imposition of a heavy head tax forced able-bodied men to migrate to the working areas: plantations, mines, railway roads, ports, and white residential regions.

Although this economic activity triggered substantial development and modernization in major cities, it bore little direct relationship to the needs of the Congolese people. It benefited mostly foreign companies and shareholders as well as the Belgian state itself which had holdings in many of the companies.

During the period between the two world wars, the colonial government's major economic policy was aimed at encouraging private foreign investment for the development of agricultural commodities for export. The Belgian government did also implement, as had the French in the neighboring French Congo, an open concessionary system by allowing large companies to exploit portions of the colony in return for promises to create infrastructures. Needless to say, the Belgian colonial government concerned itself very little with social infrastructure and the well-being of the Congolese population. Instead it granted the religious missions and the large concessionary companies permission to provide health and education to the population.

In order to curtail labor shortage and ensure adequate supplies of labor at low wages to private and state-owned companies, the colonial administration, known to the population as *bula matari* ("rock breaker"), resorted to compulsory recruitment that was reminiscent of the brutal forced labor of the Leopoldian Congo. Restrictions were also placed on the establishment of foreign commercial activities that would have stimulated the farmers to produce surpluses that would have been turned into cash rather than take low-paying jobs on plantations and mines.

The extroversion of the economy of the Belgian Congo is best noted with reference to the transportation system, which was established for the sole purpose of extracting and evacuating goods out of the colony. Katanga was linked to Rhodesia by a railway from Sakania to Elizabethville. Another line was constructed from Katanga to Dilolo and connected at the Angolan frontier with the Portuguese railway from Lobito Bay. By the 1930s, over 2,500 miles of rivers and an equivalent mileage of railway and paved roads eased the evacuation of Congo's goods to Europe.

Congo's increasingly dependent economy suffered greatly during the turmoil caused by the Great Depression of the 1930s. In some places economic activities came to a standstill, and this resulted in huge layoffs of skilled and semiskilled workers.

The years after World War II witnessed the growth of the copper, gold, and tin industries, which had picked up during the war as part of the Belgian Congo's war effort in favor of the Allied forces. American and British armies demanded ever more rubber for the tires of hundreds of thousands of military vehicles, uranium (80 per cent of the uranium for the Hiroshima and Nagasaki atomic bombs came from the Congo mine of Shinkolobwe), and cotton for army uniforms. As before, the profits flowed out of the colony and coercive measures were customarily used to force workers to mine (*chicotte*, or flogging, was applied unmercifully to discipline the Congolese). Needless to say, working conditions in the mines were abysmal. Scores of workers died each year of brutality, disease, and despair to the extent that methods of recruitment differed little from those employed in Leopold's time. These conditions, as one would suspect, attracted few migrants even though male heads of households were hard-pressed to get cash to pay taxes. Recruiters from the mines ventured to remote villages accompanied by soldiers and used bribery on village chiefs as well as force whenever necessary to coerce people into migrating to the mines. Often local government administrators assisted company agents in recruiting and holding villagers through the imposition of penalties. Those who resisted were rounded up, chained, and taken by force to the mines. For every recruit who fled, a member of his family was imprisoned until he turned himself in to the recruiting agents. Fines and imprisonment were imposed upon workers for breach of contract.

World War II not only stimulated Belgian Congo's economy, but also resulted in a shift in foreign trade. Since ties with Belgium had been severed by the German occupation, new markets were found abroad and new industries were set up to supply the colony with consumer goods (clothing, tobacco, beer, furniture, radio sets, bicycles, sewing machines, etc.) previously imported, largely from Belgium. These new industries catered to the rising African middle class that consisted of Europeans' servants, teachers, qualified artisans, and foremen who had acquired their skills in the big mining and industrial companies. Also included were the Africans who had set up businesses on their own, operating bars or selling goods and crafts in small shops. The colonial government luckily recognized this growing group of relatively prosperous Africans and supported wage increases and steps toward the development of an African middle class.

At independence, many observers looked at Congo as one of the most thriving colonial domains. Behind this facade of a *colonie modèle* (model colony) there was an entirely different picture: Africans were confined to the most menial and unskilled tasks while more than 90 per cent of the high-skilled positions, managerial posts, and economic wealth continued to be monopolized by foreigners and expatriates. One can therefore argue that the roots of Zairian economic dependency and weakness are to be found in the colonial period that transformed, in a matter of 70 years, a territory of more than ten million inhabitants into a class-divided society and a fragile economic giant.

CHARLES DIDIER GONDOLA

See also: **Concessionary Companies; Congo (Kinshasa), Democratic Republic of/Zaire: Belgian Congo: Administration and Society, 1908–1960.**

Further Reading

Hochschild, A. *King Leopold's Ghost: A Story of Greed, Terror, and Heroism in Colonial Africa.* New York: Houghton Mifflin, 1998.

Kaplan, I. (ed.). *Zaïre: A Country Study.* Area Handbook Series. Washington, D.C.: American University Press, 1979.

Martelli, G. *Leopold to Lumumba: A History of the Belgian Congo, 1877–1960.* London: Chapman and Hall, 1962.

Northrup, D. *Beyond the Bend in the River: African Labor in Eastern Zaire, 1865–1940.* Athens, Ohio: Ohio University Center for International Studies, 1988.

Congo (Kinshasa), Democratic Republic of/Zaire: Evolués, Politics, Independence

The Belgian colonial project in the Congo was constructed around a policy of paternalism. Paternalism, with its overt emphasis in this case on the white man as father and the African as child, became the philosophical framework (and justification) of the Belgian occupation of the Congo. This policy was articulated in governor general Pierre Ryckman's 1948 treatise *Dominer Pour Servir* (*Dominate to Serve*). One of the products of paternalism was the emergence of an elite social class. Called *évolués*, these were Congolese who had relatively advanced education and/or civil service jobs. The évolués were regarded as symbols of the "civilizing" mission. They were defined by the colonial government as those blacks in the midst of the transition from "traditional" tribal customs to Western "developed" culture, usually because of education or training at European firms. After a 1948 colonial decree, the évolués were awarded the *carte du mérite civique* (card of civic merit), which was granted to Africans who could prove that they were "living in a state of civilization." Many Africans declined to apply for the card and, by 1958, the colonial state recognized only 1,557 Africans as "civilized."

By mid-century, the évolués actively pressed for a greater voice in the colony's future. The changes Brussels begrudgingly instituted were relatively small and slow in coming. Still suffering from socioeconomic constraints, Congolese achieved limited access to higher education in the 1950s and promotion within a tightly regulated civil service. Furthermore, *La Voix du Congolais*, a nation-wide publication that became a forum for indigenous ideas and art, was established. Yet, most of these changes were largely reserved for the évolués, and not the masses. Moreover, because the colonial state only permitted "cultural" or "mutual self-help" indigenous associations, most of the political movements that emerged, such as the Alliance des Bakongo (ABAKO), were firmly rooted in ethnic or regional identities.

Throughout the late 1950s, pressure for independence mounted and Belgian resolve weakened. The first tentative steps toward decolonization occurred under the 1954–1958 Belgian coalition government of socialists and liberals, who had succeeded in temporarily breaking the social Christians' hold on power. Yet, the changes that the Belgian colonial state allowed were frustratingly meager to the Africans when compared to the decolonization practices of England and France. The situation came to a head in January 1959, when anticolonial riots broke out in Leopoldville. In their wake, a more pronounced nationalist/proindependence discourse emerged in the Congo. The most popular articulator of these discourses was Patrice Emery Lumumba, a young politician from Stanleyville who attempted to make the Mouvement National Congolais (MNC) a national party.

The Leopoldville riots shocked a sleepy Belgian populace, who had assumed that the nationalist movements sweeping across Africa would somehow bypass their colony. In the wake of the 1959 riots, the Belgian

government moved quickly to decolonize. In his annual New Year's address, King Baudouin (the grandson of Leopold II's nephew and successor, Albert I), announced that Belgium would give its colony the "gift" of independence "without undue haste." The Belgian government organized a series of roundtable meetings in Brussels with prominent Congolese leaders and eventually established a timetable for independence. The political structures put in place were similar to the Belgian parliamentary system, and national elections were held in May 1960. Lumumba emerged as the most popular of the numerous Congolese politicians, with his MNC winning the most votes but not an outright majority. In a gesture of national unity, Lumumba formed a coalition government, accepting the positions of prime minister and defense minister for himself, with his chief rival, Joseph Kasavubu of ABAKO, as president. Following independence, évolués quickly moved into positions of leadership.

On June 30, 1960, King Baudouin presided over the independence ceremony that transformed the Belgian Congo into the Republic of the Congo. The independence of the Congo was soon marred when, on July 5, 1960, several units in the Force Publique (the Congolese army) mutinied, demanding promotions, pay raises, and the removal of white officers. Belgian troops stationed in the Congo intervened and actively engaged the Congolese army and civilians. On July 9, 1960, the Belgian Council of Ministers dispatched additional paracommandos to the Congo, against the wishes of the Congo government. As a result, more Congolese troops mutinied and violence intensified. On July 11, Moise Tshombe, the regional leader of the southern province of Katanga, announced his region's secession and asked for Belgian support. At Lumumba and Kasavubu's request, the United Nations (UN) responded by sending a multinational force to the Congo in order to "restore law and order." Sensing Western discontentment with Lumumba and with strong encouragement from his European advisers, President Kasavubu fired Prime Minister Lumumba on September 5, 1960. Lumumba responded the same day by firing Kasavubu, creating a standoff that had both leaders claiming legitimacy. The internal political situation was further muddled on September 14, when Joseph Mobutu announced a military coup and created yet another national government. Despite being under UN protection/house arrest, Lumumba managed to escape from Leopoldville and flee toward Stanleyville. However, he was captured en route by Congolese armed forces and imprisoned at Camp Hardy in Thysville, then flown to Elisabethville in Katanga, where he was handed over to the secessionist forces. Lumumba was beaten, tortured, and eventually murdered.

KEVIN C. DUNN

See also: **Congo (Kinshasa), Democratic Republic of/Zaïre: Mobutu, Zaire, and Mobutuism; Lumumba, Patrice.**

Further Reading

Brausch, G. *Belgian Administration in the Congo.* London: Oxford University Press, 1961.

De Witte, L. *The Assassination of Lumumba.* New York: Verso, 2001.

Merriam, A. *Congo: Background of Conflict.* Evanston, Ill.: Northwestern University Press, 1961.

Ryckmans, P. *Dominer Pour Servir.* Brussels: L'Edition Universelle, 1948.

Slade, R. *The Belgian Congo: Some Recent Changes.* London: Oxford University Press, 1960.

Willame, J.-C. *Patrimonialism and Political Change in the Congo.* Stanford, Calif.: Stanford University Press, 1972.

Young, C. *Politics in the Congo: Decolonization and Independence.* Princeton, N.J.: Princeton University Press, 1965.

Congo (Kinshasa), Democratic Republic of/Zaïre: Mobutu, Zaire, and Mobutuism

Born on October 14, 1930, Joseph-Désiré Mobutu spent his early years as a journalist and as a student in Brussels. In 1958, he joined Patrice Lumumba's Mouvement National Congolais (MNC) and was appointed state secretary when Lumumba became prime minister at independence. After the mutiny of Force Publique (the Congolese army) units on July 5, 1960, Mobutu was named army chief of staff at the level of colonel. On September 14, 1960, Mobutu announced he was "neutralizing" the country's political leaders and establishing a college of commissioners to run the country. The college returned power to the constitutional government in February 1961, after the assassination of Lumumba.

On November 25, 1965, Joseph Mobutu announced that he and his military supporters had overthrown the beleaguered government of President Joseph Kasavubu and Prime Minister Moïse Tshombe. Though ostensibly a military coup, Mobutu's government quickly took on civilian trappings, organizing a one-party state around the Mouvement Populaire de Révolution (MPR), which he formed in 1966.

In May 1966, the Mobutu government began the policy of renaming many of the country's major cities, replacing their colonial names with African ones (e.g., Leopoldville became Kinshasa). On October 27, 1971, he announced that the Congo would henceforth be known as Zaire. Mobutu proclaimed that all citizens of Zaire were required to change their names by adopting more "African" ones; those who refused to do so ran the risk of losing their citizenship. On January 12, 1972, Joseph-Désiré Mobutu changed his own name to Mobutu Sese Seko Kuku Ngbedu Waza Banga.

These name changes were justified on the grounds of overcoming the colonial legacy, making the country more authentically African, and fostering a national identity. Mobutu's construction of a national identity for Zaire was further articulated in his *authenticité* campaign, which sought to move away from borrowed or imposed ideas toward an increased awareness and privileging of indigenous cultural beliefs and values. The most explicit goal of authenticité was to restore to the Zairian people a sense of pride in their own traditional culture that had been taken away by colonialism. Much of this entailed synthesizing different cultural traditions and beliefs into a single Zairian identity. In their invention of common Zairian traditions, the regime defined tradition as undemocratic, helping to establish Mobutu as an authoritarian ruler.

Mobutu's authenticité project was followed by introduction of *Zairianization*, or the "radicalization of the revolution." Announced on December 30, 1974, Zairianization was aimed at addressing the "scourges" eating away at Zairian society, such as excessive liberty and social injustice. Zairianization involved the nationalization of the economy, basically entailing the transfer of ownership of most foreign-owned small and medium-sized businesses to a small Zairian elite (usually close allies of Mobutu) who, often lacking managerial experience or interest, used these businesses for their own personal enrichment.

By the late 1970s, *Mobutism* was proclaimed the official ideology of the MPR and Zaire. Defined as the "thought and vision of Mobutu Sese Seko," Mobutism encompassed all policies and ideological thoughts of Mobutu, and represented a clear shift toward a cult of personality. One of the effects of this shift was a rise in anti-Mobutu sentiment among the dispossessed. Mobutu's regime was threatened twice when armed rebels invaded the southern province of Shaba (formerly Katanga) in 1977, and again in 1978. Mobutu was quick to claim that the governments of Angola, Cuba, and the Soviet Union were behind the invasions. He succeeded in acquiring material support from the governments of the United States, Belgium, France, China, and Morocco by playing on Cold War fears and economic concerns.

By the 1980s, Mobutu had constructed a political aristocracy that was less interested in providing security to its citizens than in extracting resources for its own enrichment. Mobutu's rule in Zaire became increasingly symbolic of what many observers labeled "kleptocracy" and the "criminalization of the state." The late 1980s were characterized by rising inflation, increased foreign debt, falling standards of living among the populace, and Mobutu's reliance on support from France, Belgium, and the United States. By the 1990s, Zaire was officially in shambles. Its formal economy shrank more than 40 per cent between 1988 and 1995. Its foreign debt by 1997 was around $14 billion. At $117, its 1993 per capita gross domestic product was 65 per cent lower than its 1958 preindependence level. It has been estimated that Mobutu and his close friends pillaged between $4 billion and $10 billion of the country's wealth, siphoning off up to 20 per cent of the government's operating budget, 30 per cent of its mineral export revenues, and 50 per cent of its capital budget. Physically, Mobutu's control effectively ended a few hundred kilometers outside of Kinshasa, while the rest of the country operated through a web of complex power relations featuring regional "Big Men" with tentative ties to Mobutu's central government.

Responding to internal and external pressures, Mobutu announced the end of his own regime on April 24, 1990, and inaugurated a system of political pluralism. A National Conference was convened, but Mobutu retained control, artfully exploiting divisions in the opposition, co-opting dissidents, and occasionally unleashing the army. By the mid-1990s, however, Mobutu was dying from prostate cancer and he was spending more time in France and Switzerland, undergoing treatment, than he was in Zaire.

In the wake of the 1994 Rwandan genocide, over 2 million Rwandans fled to refugee camps inside Zaire. These refugees were a mix of civilians, Interhamwe (the militia largely held responsible for the genocide), and members of the defeated Rwandan army (Forces Armées Rwandaises, or FAR). The refugee camps quickly became controlled by the Interhamwe and the FAR. Over the next two years, these groups (with the blessing of Mobutu's central government) reorganized and rearmed. Soon they began launching attacks from the camps into neighboring Rwanda. In response, the Rwandan government fostered a rebellion in eastern Zaire in August and September 1996. The rebels attacked the refugee camps, the Interhamwe, and the Forces Armées Zaïroises (Zairian army). Orchestrated and assisted by the RPF regime in Kigali, the rebels quickly swept across the country.

Mobutu returned to Kinshasa on December 17, 1996, and tried to organize a counteroffensive in early 1997. As the rebels moved westward, they were joined by other anti-Mobutists. Their external supporters included the regimes in Rwanda, Uganda and Burundi. Mobutu's counteroffensive collapsed as Kisangani fell to the rebels on March 15. By April, the rebels gained control of the mineral-rich provinces of Kasai and Shaba, thus robbing Mobutu and his power elite of a major economic lifeline. By May 17, 1997, Kinshasa had fallen and Mobutu and his entourage had fled. Soon afterward, Laurent-Désiré Kabila proclaimed himself the new president and renamed the country the

Democratic Republic of the Congo. On September 7, 1997, Mobutu died from the cancer while in exile in Morocco.

KEVIN C. DUNN

See also: **Cold War, Africa and the; Congo (Kinshasa): Post-Mobutu Era; Lumumba, Patrice.**

Further Reading

Braeckman, C. *Le Dinosaur: Le Zaïre de Mobutu.* Paris: Fayard, 1992.

Callaghy, T. M. *The State-Society Struggle: Zaïre in Comparative Perspective.* New York: Columbia University Press, 1984.

Kelly, S. *America's Tyrant: The CIA and Mobutu of Zaire.* Washington, D.C.: American University Press, 1993.

MacGaffey, J. *Entrepreneurs and Parasites: The Struggle for Indigenous Capitalism in Zaïre.* Cambridge: Cambridge University Press, 1987.

Mobutu Sese Seko, *Discours, Allocutions et Messages, 1965–1975.* 2 vols. Paris: Éditions J.A., 1975.

Schatzberg, M. G. *The Dialectics of Oppression in Zaïre.* Bloomington: Indiana University Press, 1988.

Young, C., and T. Turner, *The Rise and Decline of the Zaïrian State,* Madison: University of Wisconsin Press, 1985.

Congo (Kinshasa), Democratic Republic of/Zaire: Mineral Factor

Minerals have played a central role in the politics and economy of Congo/Zaire from its inception as the Congo Free State. Even earlier, copper from Katanga (renamed Shaba after independence) had been smelted and worked by Africans and fed into the continent's overlapping trading networks. The distinctive Katanga copper crosses found their way as far afield as China. Msiri, the last African ruler of Katanga, owed his political position at least in part to his control of the copper reserves. Europeans were more interested in gold. Prior to the Berlin West Africa Conference of 1884–1885, Belgian king Leopold II had made a series of bilateral treaties with various European powers, setting the boundaries of the area he intended to control. In the aftermath of the conference, however, when required to specify the area in which he would guarantee neutrality, he moved the southern border of the Congo Free State several hundred miles south, to the Congo-Zambesi watershed, where he hoped to find gold.

Rumors of gold in Katanga also attracted the attention of Cecil Rhodes, who wanted to incorporate the region into British South Africa Company territory. In 1890 the two men sent rival expeditions to claim the territory; the Rhodes expedition lost its way. Shortly thereafter, the Belgian geologist Jules Cornet investigated the region's minerals, found little gold, and decided that the extensive copper deposits could not be worked profitably. Despite the fact that Katanga's high-grade copper ores were very close to the surface and were highly oxidized and therefore relatively easy to smelt, this conclusion was by no means unjustified. Substantial investment was required not only to work the mines, but also for the construction of a railway to the coast, without which no significant mining activity could be successful. Leopold turned his attention back to trade in rubber, ivory, and palm oil, which paid well but required little or no capital investment on his part.

In 1895, George Grey, an Englishman with aristocratic connections, began exploring on the Northern Rhodesian side of the watershed in an effort to find a profitable investment opportunity for the Countess of Warwick, one of the Prince of Wales's mistresses. He made an illicit foray over the border and concluded that Cornet could have been wrong. Grey's employer, Robert Williams, a friend of Rhodes, began negotiating with Leopold and, once the dust of the Jameson Raid had settled, reached an agreement in 1900 to develop the region's copper resources. Leopold's continued reluctance to take the heavy risks involved in mineral development were reflected in the arrangement for the Comité Speciale du Katanga (CSK), the region's administrative body, to invest a maximum of £3 million annually only after Williams and his company, Tanganyika Concessions, had spent UK£5 million. The financing of deposits considered viable was to be shared equally, but the CSK would get 60 per cent of the profits, leaving Tanganyika Concessions the remaining 40 per cent.

With some evidence that the deposits could indeed be commercially viable, and as part of a wider scheme to ensure Belgian control over the Congo's resources, the Union Minière du Haut-Katanga was formed in 1906 to take over the enterprise. To provide the essential rail link to the coast Williams had in 1902 secured a Portuguese concession to build the Benguela Railway across Angola, while, as part of its wider plans, the Congo Free State in 1906 also formed the Compagnie du Chemin de Fer du Bas-Congo au Katanga (BCK) to link the mine area to the navigable portions of the Kasai and Congo Rivers. To serve the purpose more immediately, after protracted negotiations, agreement was reached to connect the Rhodesian rail system to the Katanga border, then to the mines via the Chemin de Fer du Katanga. Katanga traffic came to provide Rhodesian railways with a major source of revenue not only from the importing of equipment from Europe and the export of smelted copper but also from the carriage of large amounts of coal from the Wankie colliery to Katanga, which had no sources of coal suitable for smelting the copper ores.

Technical difficulties and some personal tensions meant that sustained copper production only became possible in 1912, but from then on the metal became increasingly important for the Congo's economy. Between the two world wars, facing lower prices forced in part by new producers—one of which was Northern Rhodesia—coming into world markets, Union Minière refused to cooperate with cartel attempts to sustain prices by limiting output and substantially increased production. It was also in this period that they began to experiment with the use of longer-term stabilized labor, as opposed to short-term migrant labor, as most of their workers had previously come from Northern Rhodesia but were increasingly needed on the Copperbelt. From then on, with periodic difficulties arising out of changing world markets, Union Minière and its Belgian parent, the Société Générale de Belgique, grew increasingly wealthy.

It was a source of great disappointment to Robert Williams that the Benguela Railway, despite being the most direct route from Katanga to the coast, never fulfilled his initial expectations as the major outlet for Katanga copper. War and politics joined with financial difficulties to delay construction, and the line only reached the mines in 1928. By that time the BCK had also been completed and the Belgians preferred to use that route as much as possible, notwithstanding the added costs of transshipment from rail to river and then again to rail at Léopoldville. Although the Rhodesian rail network took the copper to the east coast and a longer sea route to Europe, that line also continued to be used, in part to ensure continued supplies of Wankie coal.

Katanga's copper became so significant for both the Belgian and Congolese economies that when the Congo became independent in 1960 the region seceded and formed a separate government under Moise Tshombe, with support from Belgium and other Western countries. There was a strong expectation that Katanga's control over the copper supplies would give it the necessary economic base to maintain its independence. After the secession was brought to an end in 1963, Union Minière gave way to the state-owned Générale des Carrières et des Mines. Copper continued to provide nearly 40 per cent of the country's export earnings well into the 1980s, but world demand for copper has fallen in the face of competition from plastics and glass fibers in recent years.

Some gold was found at Ruwe, but the precious metal never met Rhodes's and Leopold's expectations. Other minerals found in Katanga have included mica, tin, and uranium, which was first identified in 1913. The first atomic pile built under the Stagg Fields Stadium in Chicago used uranium from Katanga, which also provided a substantial portion of the Western world's supplies of cobalt during the Cold War. After copper, however, the most economically and politically significant mineral found in the Congo has been the diamonds of Kasai, part of the Congo that was also brought firmly into Leopold's Congo State ambit with the southward shift of his borders.

It was to exploit Kasai's extensive diamond deposits that the third major 1906 company, the Société Internationale Forestière et Minière du Congo was formed, though, as the company's name implies, there was also hope for the development of other economic resources. The major financial backing for this company came through the British financier Sir (Alfred) Chester Beatty. The proximity of the navigable section of the Kasai River, feeding into the navigable Congo, facilitated transportation and made it unnecessary to build a railway line to serve the mines. Diamond mining also required substantially less initial capital investment, and there was a much shorter delay between initial investment and first returns.

Kasai's diamonds are generally of industrial rather than gem quality, but they nonetheless quickly became and remained a major source of revenue for the Congo State and the Belgian Congo. For the independent Republic of the Congo/Zaire, diamonds were important not only for their direct export value but also because of the advantages accruing from smuggling them. In the early 1960s diamond smuggling was rampant, but the authorities did little to prevent it because that smuggling was considered a means of limiting the rise in value of the Congolese franc on the parallel money market. By late 1963, Congolese francs traded at more than 400 to the U.S. dollar on the free market as against an official rate of 65. Smuggled diamonds also helped finance the Kasai secession. This was more short-lived than that of Katanga, but Kasai continued to be a center of rebellion. Diamonds, legitimately exported and smuggled, have more recently played a major role in the civil strife surrounding Laurent's and Joseph Kabila's governments and the involvement in that conflict of foreign governments such as Angola and Zimbabwe.

SIMON KATZENELLENBOGEN

See also: **Jameson Raid, Origins of South African War: 1895–1899; Stanley, Leopold II, "Scramble."**

Further Reading

Anstey, R. *King Leopold's Legacy*. Oxford: Clarendon Press, 1962.

Gérard-Libois, J. *Sécession au Katanga*. Bruxelles: Institut National d'Etudes Politiques, 1963.

Gibbs, D. N. *The Political Economy of Third World Intervention: Mines, Money, and U.S. Policy in the Congo Crisis*. Chicago: University of Chicago Press, 1991.

Katzenellenbogen, S. E. *Railways and the Copper Mines of Katanga*. Oxford: Clarendon Press, 1973.

Katzenellenbogen, S. "It Didn't Happen at Berlin: Politics, Economics and Ignorance in the Setting of Africa's colonial Boundaries." In *African Boundaries: Barriesers, Conduits and Opportunities*, edited by Paul Nugent and A. I. Asiwaju. London: Pinter, 1996.

Lunn, J. *Capital and Labour on the Rhodesian Railway System, 1888–1947*. Basingstoke, England: Macmillan, in association with St Antony's College, 1997.

Congo (Kinshasa), Democratic Republic of/Zaire: National Conference and Politics of Opposition, 1990–1996

Following the end of the Cold War, Zaire lost both its strategic importance and the crucial international assistance that went with it. Due to a poor human rights record and generally bad governance, the country's leader, President Mobutu Sese Seko, bowed to both internal and external pressure and abolished the country's one-party state on April 24, 1990. The incumbent secretary general of the Economic Community of Central African States, Lunda Bululu, was appointed head of a restructured transitional government that was installed on May 4 of that year. Over the next year, the constitution was revised to permit the formation of trade unions and at least two additional political parties.

However, the euphoria generated by the prospect of a new political social order quickly evaporated as a result of Mobutu's continuing repression of opposition political activity. In particular, Mobutu's announcement that a limited multiparty system would not come into effect for at least two years led to a bloody confrontation at the University of Lubumbashi on May 11, 1990. It was reported that security forces killed more than 50 student demonstrators. Eventually Mobutu was persuaded by opposition pressure to announce, on December 31, both presidential and legislative elections. They were scheduled to be held in 1991, as was a referendum on another new constitution.

In 1991 a fragmented party system of over 100 parties emerged, with three main groups. First among these was the pro-Mobutu bloc, led by the Popular Movement for Renewal (Mouvement Populaire Renouveau, or MPR). It comprised, in addition, dozens of parties headed by Mobutu supporters. Second, there was the main anti-Mobutu bloc, led by three opposition parties: the Union for Democracy and Social Progress (Union pour la Démocratie et le Progrès Social, or UDPS), the Union of Federalists and Independent Republicans (Union des Fédéralists et Républicains Indépendents, or UFERI), and the National Christian Social Democratic Party (Parti Démocratie et Social Chrétien, or PDSC). Finally, there was a large number of what are best described as "pseudo-parties," often consisting of not much more than a handful of individuals with a lack of clear or consistent political orientations.

With broad popular support, the anti-Mobutu coalition insisted successfully on the formation of a National Conference. The conference was an indigenously generated contribution to the country's political institution building and regime transition, which convened for the first time on August 7, 1991. Its proclaimed purpose was to provide a transition mode, whereby both government and opposition forces, along with representatives of civil society groups, could meet in order to thrash out a consensual political way forward. Within the Conference, the UDPS, UFERI, PDSC, and groups from civil society formed the so-called Union Sacrée in July 1991, designed to be a democratic opposition platform. Headed by Archbishop Laurent Monsengwo, the conference quickly became the main forum for the power struggle between the Mobutu camp and the opposition. It was, however, characterized by prevarication, principally from Mobutu and his government, and this led to a prolonged stalemate between the latter and the opposition.

At the end of September 1991, under pressure from the opposition, Mobutu not only appointed as prime minister Etienne Tshisekedi, a leading opposition politician, but also agreed to the formation of an opposition-dominated cabinet and diminished presidential powers. In addition, the conference adopted a transitional constitution that reinstalled the separation of powers, and strengthened human and civil rights. It also drafted a new federalist constitution to be subject to a referendum.

President Mobutu dismissed Tshisekedi and his government illegally in December 1992. Still retaining the loyalty of the security forces, Mobutu managed to remain in power by a complex strategy that involved seemingly to agree to reforms but without implementing them, repression of the opposition, instigation of mutinies in the armed forces, the fueling of ethnic grievances, and co-optation of prominent opposition leaders, such as UFERI leader Karl-i-Bond. In 1993, such was the conflict between pro- and anti-Mobutu forces that there resulted a duplication of political institutions: two governments, two parliaments, and two currencies. The political deadlock was finally overcome at the end of the year when the two legislatures merged into the transitional High Council of the Republic (Haut Conseil de la République, or HCR). Unlike the National Conference, pro-Mobutu forces dominated the HCR.

In April 1994 the transitional Parliament passed an interim constitution which not only recognized the principle of separation of powers and guaranteed basic human and civil rights but also permitted Mobutu to remain in power. Supported by France, a compromise candidate for prime minister, Kengo wa Dondo, was elected in June. In mid-December Kengo announced that long overdue presidential and parliamentary elections, as well as a constitutional referendum, would be held in July 1995; they were, however, postponed in May. As a result, a two-year extension of the political transition period was announced.

In February 1996 Kengo ousted 23 cabinet ministers, including all remaining opposition sympathizers, and filled their posts with his supporters. Meanwhile, the National Elections Commission was charged with preparing for a constitutional referendum in December 1996, presidential and parliamentary elections in May 1997, and local balloting in June and July 1997. However, before the elections and referendum could take place, Laurent Kabila, a veteran in the fight against Mobutu for over 30 years, formed a four-party military alliance, the Alliance for the Liberation of Congo-Zaïre (Alliance des forces pour la Démocratie et la Liberation du Congo-Zaïre, or AFDL). The AFDL was supported by Zaïre's neighboring countries, Rwanda, Uganda and Burundi, as well as by the United States.

On October 29, 1996, Kinshasa declared a state of emergency in North and South Kivu as previously sporadic fighting between Rwandan and Zairean regular forces escalated into intense cross-border shelling. Kinshasa accused the Rwandan and Ugandan governments of attempting to take advantage of President Mobutu's absence. (Mobutu was convalescing in France following surgery for cancer.) Over the next few months, the AFDL forces made steady progress before eventually controlling the entire country. The victorious AFDL entered the capital, Kinshasa, on May 17, 1997.

JEFF HAYNES

See also: **Congo (Kinshasa): Post-Mobutu Era; Congo (Kinshasa), Democratic Republic of/Zaire: Mobutu, Zaire, and Mobutuism.**

Further Reading

Aronson, D. "The Dead Help No One Living." *World Policy Journal* 14, no. 4 (1998): 81–96.

Brittain, V. "The Congo Quagmire." *World Press Review,* November 1998, 14–15.

Gondola, Ch. Didier, "Dreams and Drama." *African Studies Review* 42, no. 1 (1999): 23–48.

Leslie, W. *Zaire: Continuity and Change in an Oppressive State.* Boulder, Colo.: Westview Press (1993).

Tanner, Henry. "A Congo Reporters' Nightmare." *Nieman Reports,* nos. 53–54 (1999–2000): 187–189.

Wamba-dia-Wamba, E. "Democracy, Multipartyism and Emancipative Politics in Africa: The Case of Zaire." *Africa Development* 18, no. 4 (1993): 95–118.

Congo (Kinshasa): Post-Mobutu Era

Commander of the army Major General Joseph-Désiré Mobutu (later, Mobutu Sese Seko Kuku Ngbendu wa

Dress rehearsal of the swearing-in of the new president Joseph Kabila, Congo, January 26, 2001. © Ludger Schadomsky/Das Fotoarchi.

za Banga) achieved power in 1965, following 75 years of Belgian colonialism and 5 years of civil war in Congo (Kinshasa). He promptly dissolved the civilian regime and proclaimed himself president of the second republic. Mobutu stayed in power for 23 years, until May 1997, when he fled the country for Togo, and eventually Morocco, where he died on September 7 of that year.

During his time in power, Mobutu laid the framework for the current form of government. He established what has been called a "kleptocratic" dictatorship, in which the constitution and separate executive, legislative, and judicial branches of government existed on paper only. The primary role of the government was to extract money from the land and people. On paper, Mobutu and his successors, Laurent-Désiré Kabila and his son Joseph Kabila, answered to a bicameral parliament including a senate, chamber of representatives, and independent judiciary.

Laurent-Désiré Kabila, who seized power on May 17, 1997, cited civil war as a deterrent to democratic rule. He managed to operate the entire country with the help of only 12 men, comprising his interim assembly. Kabila, originally from the Katanga province, was the leader of anti-Mobutu rebels who marched across the country, capturing urban centers and eventually entering the capital, Kinshasa, in May 1997. In January 1999, Kabila dissolved his own party, the Alliance of Democratic Forces for the Liberation of Congo-Zaire (AFDL), and subsequently engaged in fighting several armed factions opposed to his rule. Until his assassination by one of his bodyguards on January 16, 2001, Kabila's rhetoric included the goal of transferring power to the people through the use of People's Power Committees, which were scheduled to begin operations in each province at some time in the future.

The late president's son, Joseph Kabila, was sworn in as the country's new president on January 26, 2001. The younger Kabila promised that free and fair elections would take place in the near future. However, by the end of 2001 elections had not occurred, explicable in large measure by the continuing civil war. Initial celebrations at Mobutu's ousting in 1997 had been followed by a civil war that involved five other African nations and led to over a million deaths by late 2001.

Laurent-Désiré Kabila announced war against the Tutsi in early 1998, despite the fact that they were the ethnic group that most supported his campaign against Mobutu and his regime. Because of the lack of civil rights and equality in the country, the Tutsi were not granted citizenship even if they could prove they were born there. The Tutsi goal was to overthrow Kabila and replace his government by a more democratic regime that would recognize their rights. However, the continuing conflict is about more than ethnic rivalries in the post-Mobutu era. It is also informed by decades of colonialism, Mobutu's policy of divide and rule, and the push of Western multinational corporations to control the country's natural resources, estimated to be worth billions of U.S. dollars.

The complex set of factors informing the conflict brought in neighboring countries: Rwanda, Zimbabwe, Namibia, Angola, and Uganda. Each took sides, creating what some observers have called "Africa's World War I." After more than a year of often intense fighting, the Lusaka Peace Accords, designed to deliver a cease-fire, were signed in July 1999. However, this did not lead to a cessation of the conflict. The active engagement of neighboring Rwanda in the war continued to be provoked by the presence in Congo (Kinshasa) of armed Interahamwe militiamen and former members of the Rwandan armed forces, who had been responsible for the Rwandan genocide of 1994. Uganda also sought to protect its interests not only by occupying eastern areas of Congo (Kinshasa) in order to protect its borders from rebel encroachment but also by aiding opponents of the regime in Kinshasa. The nature of the war as a regional conflict, rather than a civil war confined to Congo (Kinshasa) was further made clear by extensive military support for the Kabila regime from Zimbabwe, Angola and, to a limited extent, Namibia.

Another attempt at a cease-fire was made in April 2000. The combatants agreed to stop fighting and, the following month, the then U.S. representative to the United Nations (UN), Richard Holbrooke, visited Kinshasa to prepare the way for UN observers and support troops. However, the introduction of peace-keepers was held up as opposing forces refused to withdraw from established positions in a way that would enable UN forces to be deployed. Later, in mid-August, the Southern African Development Community held an emergency summit in Kinshasa that tried, unsuccessfully, to try to break the deadlock. The failure of the summit led Kabila officially to suspend the Lusaka accords, to call for direct negotiations with Rwanda, Uganda, and Burundi, and to reject the deployment of UN peacekeepers.

The war seemed to be going Kabila's way during the first months of 2000. Encouraged by his opponents' divisions, Kabila appeared to reject a negotiated settlement when in July he launched a partly successful offensive in Equateur Province against Uganda's allies in the Congolese Liberation Movement (MLC). Buoyed by what he saw as progress, Kabila established a transitional parliament in Kinshasa that effectively excluded any form of political opposition since Kabila himself nominated all 300 members. But when, in August and September, government troops suffered a series of reverses at the hands of the MLC and the new parliament ruled out any political solution to the conflict, Kabila's intractable position became a major problem for both allies and opponents.

The key event in 2001 was Laurent Kabila's assassination in January. Surprising many observers, his son assumed power but was unable either to build a firm regime or to make sustained progress in the war. The year was marked by a continuing stalemate between the combatants, pronounced war-weariness among the country's inhabitants, and the failure of international attempts to reach a solution to the conflict.

JEFF HAYNES

Further Reading

Aronson, D. "The Dead Help No One Living." *World Policy Journal* 14, no. 4 (1998): 81–96.

Brittain, V. "The Congo Quagmire." *World Press Review*, November 1998, pp.14–15.

"Congo's Hidden War." *Economist*, June 17, 2000, 45–46.

Emizet, K. "The Massacre of Refugees in Congo." *Journal of Modern African Studies* 38, no. 2 (2000): 162–174.

Tanner, H. "A Congo Reporters' Nightmare." *Nieman Reports*, nos. 53–54 (1999–2000): 187–189.

Coptic Church: *See* Monophysitism, Coptic Church, 379–640.

Corruption and the Criminalization of the Postcolonial State

Corruption and the criminalization of the state in postcolonial Africa have posed numerous economic and political difficulties that still dog the continent today. *Corruption* is defined as the deliberate combination of public office positions with the process of accumulation of wealth. The *criminalization* of the state, on the other hand, is the use and institutionalization of the political or government apparatuses as instruments of graft and as conduits of individuals' accumulation of wealth. In reality, corruption and criminalization presuppose that there is a correlation between political power sharing and the distribution of wealth in society. Perceived in the above context, the interaction of power with political practice has produced a crisis in governance of states where dominant social groups or the ruling elites have been engaged in activities of criminal nature. These activities include the generation of rents by those groups wielding political power in the international economic mode of dependency in which Africa is engaged.

Almost all countries of Africa have suffered corruption and witnessed the criminalization of the state in varying degrees since attainment of independence of most countries in the 1960s. A culture of institutional neglect and the systematic plunder of national economies and uncontrolled privatization of the state in Congo, Chad, Ghana, Egypt, Algeria, Morocco, Kenya, Cameroon, Guinea, Togo, São Tomé, and Madagascar, among others, bear testimony to the criminal nature of the postcolonial state in Africa. Leaders have been engaged in outright violations of constitutional laws, which are the cornerstone of good governance and economic management. The ruling elites have undermined judicial rules, thus effectively transforming the legal process into a permanent state of illegality. Such systems have concentrated power in the hands of a few personalities who have obliterated dissent opting for political unanimity.

The abundant literature on corruption and malpractices in the corridors of government indicate something is wrong with the process of governance if government officials are not constrained by countervailing forces or by legal institutions. There are incidents where legitimate organs of the state have been used to terrorize people into supporting criminal activities. There are also close interactions among power, war, an insatiable drive for accumulation of wealth, and illicit activities in political practice. This has given rise to illegal economic transactions in the governments of most African countries. Leaders in political positions have used violence as instruments and as strategies of wealth acquisition. The leaders have employed brutal torture and murder as techniques of power and mechanisms of domination; notable examples are Idi Amin Dada of Uganda, Jean-Bedel Bokasa of central Africa, and Said Barre of Somalia.

Certain countries stand out as examples of how power has been abused in postcolonial Africa, including Sierra Leone, Liberia, and Somalia. In these countries warlords have employed warfare as both instrument of political domination and avenue to wealth and riches. They have received arms from the international community, and they have used them to control power and the nations' wealth. They have used such power to establish parallel economies (black markets and widespread smuggling, for instance).

The international community has indirectly supported the activities of warlords involved in conflicts in Africa because of the business relations they have with some of these warlords. Thus, the criminalization of the postcolonial state has been a result of a whole series of relationships and actions generated by the continent's insertion in the international economy of dependence. Diplomatic and military alliances and the control of exports of agricultural goods, oil, and external donor financing and aid are key themes. For example, diamonds, gold, and other mineral and natural resources from Sierra Leone have found ready markets in Western metropolises in exchange for small arms. The dominant social groups in the various countries of Africa have also readily participated in the political economy of dependence.

Some African political leaders have helped to construct and maintain economies of dependence because of the profits derived from relationships with Western nations. While it is true that the ideologies of democracy and humanitarianism dominated Africa in the 1990s, the same ideologies have also been used for material gain. For instance, in the Democractic Republic of Congo/Zaire, the main opposition party, the Union pour la Democratic et le Progres Social (UDPS), helped itself to a share of available profit in the diamond business. The Kenyan main opposition was accused of receiving money from one leading money-laundering organization, Goldenberg International. The president of Kenya set up a commission of inquiry to investigate Goldenberg's activities; it became clear that the company was involved in cases of corruption at the state level. In Madagascar, Congo, and the Central African Republic, newly elected presidents in the 1990s sought parallel financing from organizations that clearly front for international money-laundering networks.

Postcolonial African leaders in single-party-dominated states equated the state with ruling political parties and sought to monopolize national resources. Notable cases in which one-party systems of government have been accomplices to state-instigated crimes are those of Algeria, Angola, Cameroon, Chad, the Central African Republic, the Democratic Republic of Congo, Egypt, Ghana, Guinea, Kenya, Morocco, Tanzania, Uganda, and Zambia. In these countries, political monopolies have fostered patron-client relations and neopatrimonial networks, effectively institutionalizing corruption and nepotism.

Party functionaries have used state apparatuses and the positions they held in government to build vast business empires. In some cases they have created economies based on kinship and ethnic alliances. Such economic conditions have produced self-made ethnic heroes out of plundered state wealth. Given the institutionalization of corruption and the criminalization of the state, the private sector has also been compelled over time to engage in corrupt activities rather than competitive activities in order to maximize commercial profits.

The relationship of powerful individuals to the state has largely enabled them to gain great wealth and exert significant influence over political affairs. Studies have shown (in Nigeria, for instance) that there has been more exploitation from contracts, licenses, and public jobs provided by state officials than in the labor market. Elsewhere in Africa, the family of the first president of Kenya, Jomo Kenyatta, emerged as head of the most powerful and widespread private business in East Africa in the 1960s. Kenyatta's successor, Daniel arap Moi, followed suit by allowing his close associates to use their position in government to accumulate wealth. Corruption and the criminalization of the state led the third president of Kenya, Mwai Kibaki, to set up several commissions of inquiry to investigate corrupt activities in all aspects of social and economic life.

There is evidence that at the peak of his autocratic rule, President Mobutu Sese Seko of Zaire controlled between 17 and 22 per cent of the national budget as his personal funds. It was estimated that in 1982, while Zaire had a debt of about US$5 billion dollars, Mobutu had US$4 billion dollars tucked away in foreign bank accounts. In Egypt, the former finance minister Mohieddin El-Gharibu appeared in court in the early 2000s to answer charges related to tax evasion.

The difficulties caused by corruption and the criminalization of the state have become more acute with time, constituting a serious problem in postcolonial Africa.

HANNINGTON OCHWADA

Further Reading

Bayart, J.-F. *The State in Africa: The Politics of the Belly.* London: Longman, 1993.

Bayart, J.-F., Stephen Ellis, and Beatrice Hibou. *The Criminalization of the State in Africa.* Bloomington: Indiana University Press, 1999.

Hope, K. R., Sr., and B. C. Chikulo (eds.). *Corruption and Development in Africa: Lessons from Country Case Studies.* London: Martin Press, 2000.

Chabal, P., and J.-P. Daloz. *Africa Works: Disorder as Political Instrument.* Bloomington: Indiana University Press, 1999.

Fatton, R., Jr. *Predatory Rule: State and civil Society in Africa.* Boulder, Colo.: Lynne Rienner, 1992.

Côte d'Ivoire (Ivory Coast): Colonization and Resistance

French policies toward Côte d'Ivoire were characterized by more than 200 years of hesitation and ambivalence.

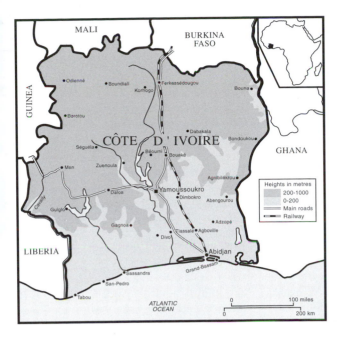

Côte d'Ivoire (Ivory Coast).

Although first contacts had been established with the local population of Assinie in 1637 (the first missionary attempt), trade relations with this part of the West African coast had been rather casual after the destruction of a French fort in 1704. However, from 1840 onward, France became interested again in the littoral of Côte d'Ivoire and resumed contact in a search for new markets and out of fear of the dominance of English merchants. The initiative was sustained by French traders from Bordeaux who acted with the support of the French navy. Thus, in 1842, Captain Bouet-Willaumëz signed a treaty with the King of Sanwi, and in the same year de Kerhaller and Fleuriot de Langle reached an agreement with Roi Peter of Grand-Bassam. Both rulers were paid an annual tribute and in return offered exclusive rights for French settlements and commerce. Similar contracts with chiefs of the other trading stations along the Ivorian coast followed in the next 25 years.

The French encountered a population familiar with European traders due to their longtime involvement in transatlantic trade. Assinie, Grand-Bassam, and Grand Lahou were important coastal trading stations that were linked with producers in the hinterlands through a relay system along the main rivers Cavally, Bandama, and Comoé leading to the northern markets of the trans-Sahara trade. This inner-African relay system was controlled by different ethnic groups with distinct economies, most of them belonging to decentralized acephalous societies, except for the various small-scale kingdoms of the Agni and Abron. The trade network was controlled by local chiefs in the hinterland and

along the littoral by groups of wealthy middlemen of Afro-European origin. Inland producers as well as coastal traders and middlemen were determined to safeguard their interests against French intrusion into the hinterland. When Bouet-Willaumëz tried to move up the Bandama with a gunboat, conflict erupted. An army of 1200 Ebrie and Nzima soldiers attacked the French post in 1852; it took the French over six months to regain control. But despite their gaining the upper hand, Victor Regis, who had opened a trading company in Grand-Bassam, withdrew from the area as he realized that French products could not compete with English goods, which were favored due to their better quality and adaptation to African tastes.

This economic setback was a serious blow for future French engagement. In 1863, the minister of commerce decided to offer Britain Assinie and Grand-Bassam in exchange for Gambia. After Britain's refusal, it took the French government almost 20 years to formulate a new policy for its West African possession. The intention was to unify the French forts along the coasts and their territorial conquests in the Western Sudan, Chad, and Cameroon. This plan was very much in tune with the beginning of the "Scramble" that was already underway long before the Berlin Conference of 1884–1885 officially recognized it. Taking a chance on the favorable circumstances, France declared "L'établissement Français de la Côte d'Or" on August first, 1889. It was annexed in 1893.

The new colony was placed under the leadership of the governor general in Senegal, who appointed a local resident to consolidate the new territory. Despite the treaties that Binger and Treich-Laplène had concluded with chiefs in the northern and eastern areas during the course of their explorations, France possessed isolated pieces of territory, which had to be joined together into a coherent colony. This became the task of the French military, which played an important role in the process of colonization.

Treich-Laplène, the first head of the colony, pursued a primary objective of political consolidation in the form of territorial conquest. The exploration and conquest of the hinterland was a main project. The easiest way to accomplish this was seemingly by moving along the main rivers as the (natural) gateway into the Western Sudan. The main obstacle was the powerful chief of Tiassale, Etienne Komlan, who controlled the main trade routes. Although the chief had accepted an unfavorable treaty in 1892, despite an earlier military success against the French army, he barred the way for Captain Marchand, who intended to regain the Western Sudan by traversing the Baule country. After Marchand had forced him to flee (after heavy resistance), he traversed the Baule country without any problems and founded colonial posts in Toumodi, Gbuekro (Bouaké), and Kotiakoffikro.

Of all of the African leaders that the French had dealt with, Samori Touré provided the strongest resistance. He had defeated the French several times with his well-organized army and was equally skillful in diplomacy.

In order to finance his imports of arms, including some of the most modern weaponry, he enslaved the weaker ethnic groups, like the Djimini and Tagbana, and sold them on the flourishing slave market in Tiegbo (near Bouaké) and Kotiakoffikro, enabling the Baule and Agni populations to the south and along the Comoé to buy slaves. It was therefore not at all in the interests of the Baule chiefs to support Marchand in his plan to attack Samori. The precarious situation became explosive when the Colonne Monteil, predominantly composed of Senegalese troops and sent as reinforcement, continued with the liberation of slaves and the looting of Baule villages. The Colonne was attacked from all sides and defeated by Samori.

French policy of an intended peaceful penetration had failed even before it had begun. At the end of the century, after eight years of intensive fighting, the colonial government was still in the initial stage of conquest. It took the government fourteen more years to suppress the last military resistance; over the course of that time the campaigns became ever more brutal, destroying whole villages. The failure of French politics to rapidly conquer their new colony implicated military as well as civilian governments, which were often at odds with each other. Another reason for its failure to come to terms with the local population was the decentralized structures of most Ivorian societies, whose web of strategic alliances they were unable to understand, being used to the hierarchically organized kingdoms in the Western Sudan.

For the African societies, the long-term resistance incurred heavy losses and a radical change in structure. Although their fluid political relationships helped them survive and continue the fight for nearly three decades, many chiefs altered their policies, changing from resistance to cooperation or vice versa. In the beginning of the struggle, the French had just been a single entity in a series of complex power plays. However, when it became clear that the French intended to stay, the political situation had to be redefined. Former enmities among groups were given up, and new alliances had to be defined in order to safeguard their economic interests, their military strength, and their sovereignty. Internal conflicts deepened as liberated slaves and discontented women sought to cooperate with the French colonizers. Although the French were successful in the end, that success was accompanied by economic devastation, social strife, and human loss.

UTE LUIG

Further Reading

Atger, P. *La France en Côte d'Ivoire de 1843 à 1893: Cinquante ans d'hésitations politiques et commerciales.* Dakar: Publications de l'université de Dakar, 1962.

Crowder, M. *West African Resistance: The Military Response to Colonial Occupation.* London, 1971.

Schnapper, B. *La politique et le commerce française dans le golfe de Guinée, 1838–1871.* Paris, 1961.

Weiskel, T. *French Colonial Rule and the Baule Peoples: Resistance and Collaboration 1889–1911.* Oxford: Clarendon Press, 1980.

Côte d'Ivoire (Ivory Coast): Colonial Period: Administration and Economy

Côte d'Ivoire became a French colony on March 10, 1893, and was subsequently also made part of the Fédération de l'Afrique Occidentale (West African Federation). An administration was put in place under a lieutenant governor, and the colony was divided into *cercles* (circuits). Following the military conquest, the burden of colonization made itself felt through various obligations, including a poll tax, compulsory service, porterage, and military conscription. The creation of the Front populaire (Popular Front) government led to some improvements. During the 1930s, a communal movement struggled against the colonial regime, but the Vichy government put a stop to it.

After 1945, the colonial regime underwent a degree of evolution. The first Constituent Assembly, which included elected African deputies, enacted an important body of laws, among which the one known as the Loi Houphouët-Boigny (April 11, 1946) abolished forced labor. Nationalist parties made use of the local assemblies, and two "study groups" played decisive roles: the Comité d'études francoafricain (French-African Study Committee) and the Groupes d'études communistes (Communist Study Groups). Several labor unions were also established, including the Syndicat agricole africain (African Farmers Union), which gave birth to the Parti Démocratique de Côte d'Ivoire (PDCI; Democratic Party of Côte d'Ivoire) in 1946.

Of all of the political parties, the PDCI achieved the strongest position, and Félix Houphouët-Boigny became its uncontested leader. However, relations between the PDCI and the administration deteriorated in 1949–1950, and there was severe repression. Within the Rassemblement démocratique africain (African Democratic Rally), it apparently came to be thought that its connections with the Partie communiste français (French Communist Party) had served as the pretext for the repression. The breaking of the link was announced on October 18, 1950.

Development required an infrastructure. External trade was secured through the construction of wharfs, the most important being the one at Grand Bassam

Côte d'Ivoire: a house from the colonial period in Grand Bassam. © Melters/missio/Das Fotoarchiv.

(1901). The first attempts to create a port ended in failure, and the port was not opened until July 23, 1950. The prosperity of the colony increased rapidly from this moment on. The second element in the development of the economy was the railway (from 1904 on); by 1940 it was carrying 7,444,760 passengers and 263,753 tons of freight, and by 1948 the network had a total length of 10,850 kilometers. An airport was opened to traffic at Port-Bouët on April 26, 1952.

From the outset, the French concentrated on exploiting natural resources. There was a crisis in the rubber industry in 1913, and exports ceased, while the exploitation of the oil palm led to exports of palms amounting to 10,400 tons in 1938. Forestry developed in response to mechanization and the opening of the port, and exports reached 214,000 tons in 1956. Development was focused above all on cocoa and coffee. The first cacao plants were introduced in 1904; they were successfully cultivated, and by 1959 exports of cocoa had reached 63,300 tons. The cultivation of coffee had been introduced in 1881, but little progress was made until after 1945; by 1960, however, coffee exports had reached 144,000 tons. Bananas and pineapples appeared later: by 1958, the output of bananas was 46,000 tons, and the output of pineapples was 15,000 tons. Industrial fisheries developed after the opening of the port, reaching an output of 3,217 tons in 1960. The needs of the metropolis stimulated a rise in commercial traffic from 1945 onward, and territorial specialization was such that between 1940 and 1960 coffee and cocoa accounted for the bulk of exports.

The first rudimentary health service was created at Assinie in 1843, but a genuine service did not come into existence until after the decree of June 11, 1901. The Assistance Médicale Indigène (Native Medical Assistance) service was created on July 24, 1906, and the Sociétés Indigènes de Prévoyance Médicale (Native Societies for Medical Provision), allowing popular participation, were established on May 16, 1939. A Treichville satellite of the hospital at Abidjan became a hospital in its own right on December 31, 1953; similarly, the Bouaké ambulance service became independent in 1956. By 1957, the colony had 3 hospitals, 48 medical centers, and a total hospital capacity of 6,470 beds. The health service was particularly active in the battle against yellow fever, both along the entire coast and in the city of Bassam: the 1899 epidemic remains famous. The discovery of a vaccine led to the curbing of yellow fever from 1934 onward, but smallpox continued to appear every year. In addition to these two diseases, we should also mention trypanosomiasis (sleeping sickness), leprosy, and malaria. On January 30, 1939, the federal Service Général Autonome de la Maladie du Sommeil (SGAMS; General Autonomous Sleeping Sickness Service) conducted an exemplary struggle in the colony, in which the disease was prevalent at Man, Danané, Daloa, and Adzopé. Leprosy raged mainly in the north. From 1945, the struggle against disease was the responsibility of the Service Général d'Hygiène Mobile et de Prophylaxie (General Mobile Hygiene and Prophylaxis Service), following in the footsteps of the SGAMS. The European population suffered a great deal from malaria, while up to 1934 the medical community believed that Africans were incapable of contracting it. The distribution of quinine and the struggle against mosquitos began at that point, and the general health of the population started to improve.

Education was provided by missionaries from the early days of the colony. Secular education was introduced into the Fédération de l'Afrique Occidentale in 1903, but it did not reach Côte d'Ivoire until after the reorganization of July 6, 1911. The authorities decided that its purpose was to provide practical instruction that would help to promote economic development. More schools were opened between 1924 and 1944, and the number of pupils rose from 10,018 in 1937 to 24,961 in 1945. The higher elementary schools were transformed into modern colleges in 1947, the professional school in Abidjan became a technical college on November 12, 1947, and the teacher-training school at Dabou became a federal institution. The secondary classes in Abidjan were made into a *lycée* in 1953. Between 1954 and 1958, there was significant growth in the numbers of students enrolled, from 29,772 to 172,466. By the time that Côte d'Ivoire became independent, it had a relatively small elite, along with basic facilities that could have been more advanced, given that the territory was reputed to be a wealthy one.

The Framework Law of June 23, 1956, gave the territory a genuine executive government. The crisis of 1958 brought about a new relationship with the

Communauté, which Côte d'Ivoire joined on December 4, 1958. Its first government was formed on April 30, 1959, with Félix Houphouët-Boigny as prime minister, and on August 7, 1960, Côte d'Ivoire became independent.

DANIELLE DOMERGUE-CLOAREC

See also: **Côte d'Ivoire: Parti Dèmocratique de la Côte d'Ivoire; Houphouët-Boigny, Félix.**

Further Reading

Désalemand, P. *Histoire de l'Education en Côte d'Ivoire. Des Origines à la Conférence de Brazzaville.* Abidjan: CEDA, 1983.

Loucou, J.-N. *La Vie Politique en Côte d'Ivoire de 1932 à 1952.* 2 vols. Aix-en-Provence: Université de Provence, 1976.

Mundt, R. J. *Historical Dictionary of Ivory Coast (Côte d'Ivoire)*, 2nd ed. Lanham, Md., 1995.

Côte d'Ivoire (Ivory Coast): Independence to the Present

Côte d'Ivoire acquired its independence from France reluctantly. Under Félix Houphouët-Boigny's leadership, Côte d'Ivoire attempted to push for a unitary community structure with ultimate sovereignty resting with France. Other French-speaking African leaders did not share Houphouët-Boigny's vision. For that matter, many Ivorians did not share it. The United Nations recognized Côte d'Ivoire as an independent republic on December 7, 1960. Houphouët-Boigny was elected president, and he remained the country's dominant political figure until his death in November of 1993.

The main objective of the framers of the Ivorian constitution was to endow the country with a set of legal institutions that would ensure national unity in an ethnically and regionally diverse nation. In this respect, the constitution of 1959 was designed to limit what the framers viewed as the inherent divisiveness of a parliamentarian form of government. Thus, the emphasis was placed on a strong executive form of government.

Following the French Fifth Republic constitution, the framers of the Ivorian constitution sought to limit the range of legislative powers by clearly defining the areas of legislative authority. In addition to this, even within the limited legislative domain defined by the constitution, the National Assembly could set forth broad guidelines, leaving specific proposals to the executive branch in many areas. The National Assembly consisted of 147 deputies who nominally represented the districts from which they were elected. Since the legislative process was actually in the hands of the executive branch, the National Assembly was more of an echo chamber for presidential wishes than an autonomous legislative body.

The most important institution in Côte d'Ivoire is the presidency. The constitution that was finally adopted in 1960 gave the president preeminence over the legislative and judiciary. The president is elected for five years by direct universal suffrage and is able to renew his term an unlimited number of times. After Houphouët-Boigny's first election in 1960, he was repeatedly reelected, with more than 90 per cent of the popular vote.

While the initial objective of the framers of the constitution was to give Côte d'Ivoire a strong executive branch, the institution became less important than the occupant. Houphouët-Boigny came to dominate the country's political system; he was able to utilize the broad powers provided him by the constitution to push through legislation without any significant opposition. Thus, there was no real separation of powers between the various branches of government. Power and decision making were in the hands of the president and the ministers whom he personally selected.

Considering the limited legislative role of the Ivorian National Assembly and the fact that its members all belonged to the same party until 1990, it would not be an exaggeration to say that its institutional and political role was limited. The situation of the National Assembly changed somewhat following the 1985 elections; 175 deputies, instead of 147, were elected to the assembly under new electoral rules. Before the elections the government had introduced a degree of competition in the selection of party leaders. The members elected in 1980 were more interested in servicing their constituency than had been the case with the handpicked deputies of past. While the National Assembly has not become a powerful legislative body, it now plays a much more important role in reviewing legislation submitted to it by the government than had previously been the case.

Until the reintroduction of multiparty competition in 1990, the Parti Démocratique de Côte d'Ivoire served as the political guardian for Houphouët-Boigny's regime. No other parties were permitted, and the country's major socioprofessional groups were obligated to associate themselves with the party. Nevertheless, in the postcolonial period, the party quickly lost its function as a mass mobilization machine. Rarely did it mobilize Ivorians for ideological purposes; its primary task was to ensure that opposition forces did not take root in Ivorian society.

More than 60 ethnic groups inhabit the country. They form six main divisions: the Akan, mainly in the southeast; the Kru, in the southwest; the Lagoon or Kwa, along the littoral; the Mande, nuclear and peripheral, and the Senufo throughout the north; and the Lobi in the central regions. Also, because of the country's economic expansion in the 1960s and 1970s, a large number of non-Ivorian Africans live in the country, particularly immigrants from Burkina Faso, Mali, and Guinea, as well as smaller numbers of French and Lebanese.

Cocoa, coffee, and timber are the underpinnings of the Ivorian economy and postcolonial state. For cocoa and coffee exports, the state absorbed into its budget the differences between the price paid to rural producers and the price the crop was finally sold for on the international market. For the peasantry, the price was fixed in the early 1960s at 400 CFA, with little variation. Much of the surplus acquired by the state was used in the development of the country's infrastructure and the proliferation of state-owned industries.

After two decades of rapid economic expansion, the economy entered a prolonged crisis in the 1980s. As the economic crisis deepened, the International Monetary Fund, the World Bank, and popular forces demanded economic and political reforms. Reluctantly, President Houphouët-Boigny introduced a number of changes in the early 1990s. First, as mentioned above, there was the introduction of new electoral rules. Second, the government attempted to decentralize decision making by creating municipal governments. Before 1980, there were only two municipalities, Abidjan and Bouaké. Afterward there were over 100 municipal governments. Finally, in 1990, Houphouët-Boigny appointed a prime minister, Alassane Ouattara, to manage the day-to-day affairs of the country.

Despite the efforts on the part of the Houphouët-Boigny regime to shore up its legitimacy by introducing institutional reforms, the economic situation in the country continued to deteriorate. In the early part of the 1990s, the government was forced by the international donor community to take drastic steps. In the spring of 1990, the government announced a series of draconian economic measures. First, the price paid to cocoa and cocoa producers would be reduced from 400 F CFA (8 FF) to 100 F CFA (2 FF); thus, for the first time in 20 years the price paid to rural producers had been changed. Second, a major reform of the public sector would begin, with the main objective of reducing its bloated numbers. Third, the process of privatization of the public sector firms would be accelerated. Finally, public and private sector employees would be required to take a cut in pay.

Faced with a social crisis that was increasingly bordering on open rebellion, Houphouët-Boigny made a number of concessions to the protesters. The austerity program would not be fully implemented. Multiparty elections would be permitted during the upcoming presidential election in the fall of 1990 and the government recognized the principle of freedom of association.

Houphouët-Boigny won reelection. By this time, however, he was nearly 90 years old; he would survive in office for only three years. Following his death, Henri Konan Bédié, the president of the National Assembly, succeeded him. The succession process had been prepared with a revision of the constitution in 1990, which stipulated that in case of death of the president, the president of the National Assembly would assume his office until the next scheduled presidential elections.

As successor, Konan Bédié faced the dual task of continuing the changes introduced under Houphouët-Boigny and establishing his own political authority. In accomplishing these tasks he adopted a strategy of regulated openness. At the political level, his strategy of regulated openness was similar to the limited political changes allowed by Houphouët-Boigny before his death. Konan Bédié sought to maintain control of the political process and limit the influence of opposition forces in the political process. His government alternated between co-optation and repression. Konan Bédié's strategy of regulated openness, however, did not work.

During Konan Bédié's presidency, ethnic tensions rose sharply. His government tried to define who was an Ivorian and who was not. The term *Ivoirité* (meaning the purported characteristics of an indigenous Ivorian) entered the political and social lexicon of the country, further exacerbating ethnic and regional divisions. These divisions manifested themselves in growing attacks on foreign migrant workers from neighboring Muslim states and increasingly strident efforts to block Houphouët-Boigny's successor from competing in national elections by claiming that he was not an Ivoirian by birth. Attacks on Ouattara, a Muslim from the north, contributed to a widening rift between the country's predominantly Muslim north and mainly Christian south.

On December 24, 1999, the military took power from a civilian-elected government for the first time. Over the next two years, Côte d'Ivoire experienced a succession of crises: the ousting of the military leader of the December 1999 coup, Robert Guei; the election of Laurent Gbagbo as president; and acts of ethnic cleansing by the military against northerners and a failed attempt at national reconciliation. In September 2002 a bloody mutiny within the military resulted in the death of the former military ruler Guei and hundreds of other Ivorians, precipitating a civil war.

Once viewed as a beacon of stability in a region bedeviled by ethnic conflicts and civil wars, Côte d'Ivoire has entered a cycle of economic decline, ethnic conflict, and civil war similar to that of other countries in West Africa. Current president Gbgabo presides over a divided country that is desperately searching for a way out of the stalemated civil war. Neither the predominately Muslim north nor the predominantly Christian south has the means to win the civil war outright; however, violence and the collapse of trust between different ethnic and religious communities have made reconciliation very difficult.

DWAYNE WOODS

See also: **Houphouët-Boigny, Félix.**

Further Reading

Cohen, M. *Urban Policy and Political Conflict in Africa: A Study of the Côte d'Ivoire.* Chicago: University of Chicago Press, 1974.

Toungara, J.-M. "The Apotheosis of Côte d'Ivoire's Nana Houphouët-Boigny." *Journal of Modern African Studies* 28, no. 1 (1990).

Woods, D. "Ethno-Regional Demands, Symbolic and Redistributive Politics: Sugar Complexes in the North of the Côte d'Ivoire." *Journal of Ethnic and Racial Studies*, no. 12 (1990): pp.470–488.

———. "The Politicization of Teachers' Associations in the Côte d'Ivoire." *African Studies Review*, no. 39 (1996): pp.113–129.

Zolberg, A. *One-Party Government in the Côte d'Ivoire.* Princeton, N.J.: Princeton University Press, 1964.

Côte d'Ivoire (Ivory Coast): Parti Démocratique de la Cote d'Ivoire

At the time of his election as a deputy in the Assemblée constituante (French Constituent Assembly), Félix Houphouët (later Houphouët-Boigny), understood that he would have to have the support of an established political party. The first meeting of the Parti démocratique de Côte d'Ivoire (PDCI; Democratic Party of Côte d'Ivoire) took place at Treichville on April 6, 1946. By 1949 the party had 350,000 members. Its organization was modeled on that of the Parti communiste français (PCF; French Communist Party); its highest organ was the party congress, which met three times, in 1947, 1949, and 1959. It was this congress that determined the orientation of the PDCI and chose both its executive committee and its officials.

The PDCI was thus well established before the Congress of Bamako, which created the Rassemblement démocratique africain (RDA; African Democratic Rally) and elected Houphouët-Boigny as its president. He had envisaged a single party for each colony: accordingly, the PDCI became the official section of the RDA in Côte d'Ivoire. The history of the PDCI thus came to be merged with the history of the RDA and the career of Houphouët-Boigny, who encouraged Africans elected to the assembly to divide themselves among the three parties in power. This was the origin of the RDA's affiliation to the PCF.

The Assemblée constituante achieved a great deal, and it was in this context that Houphouët-Boigny proposed the abolition of forced labor. The law to that effect was passed on April 11, 1946. The new French constitution did not meet the expectations of Africans, however, the sole concession to them being the creation of a territorial assembly, known as the Conseil général (General Council).

The political climate in the colony deteriorated. The second congress of the RDA was held June 2 through June 6, 1949, at Treichville, in the presence of several parliamentarians and journalists with links to the PCF, which had been in opposition since 1947. Following a series of incidents, 30 RDA militants, including 8 members of the executive committee, were arrested and imprisoned at Grand-Bassam. On July 24, 1949, Houphouët-Boigny denounced the repression. The PDCI-RDA launched a consumer boycott, and on December 22 of that year there was a women's march to Grand-Bassam. This action had profound repercussions: the colony reached the boiling point. Serious incidents occurred at Bouaflé on January 22, 1950, at Dimbokro on January 30, and at Séguéla on February 2, and during the night of January 27–28 Senator Biaka Boda was assassinated. The repression caused nearly 50 deaths and left 5,000 injured.

Only two alternatives remained: either to continue the struggle or to collaborate. Houphouët-Boigny understood that his communist connection gave the authorities their pretext; he therefore committed himself to breaking the connection. The first contacts were made by R. Saller, who met the governor, Paul Henri Siriex. After informing the leaders of the PCF, Houphouët-Boigny announced the breaking of his link with them on October 17, 1950, causing a degree of turmoil within the RDA and in Côte d'Ivoire.

On October 6, 1951, at the Géo André Stadium, Houphouët-Boigny launched his appeal for a "union of all men of good will," a union that became a reality at the time of the elections to the Territorial Assembly on March 30, 1952. The PDCI-RDA took control both of the assembly and of the leading municipalities, while in France the RDA's parliamentary group had announced, on February 6, 1952, its affiliation to François Mitterand's Union démocratique et socialiste de la Résistance (Democratic and Socialist Union of the Resistance). By the end of 1952, Houphouët-Boigny had apparently succeeded in convincing even the most reluctant to follow his new policy. Thus, 1952 marked a turning point: the PDCI-RDA had been transformed from a party of anticolonial struggle into a party of government.

The PDCI scored a crushing success in the legislative elections of January 2, 1956, though there were two islands of resistance, in the Bété country (Gagnoa) and in the Agni country (Abengourou). It was as members of this newly elected legislature that several RDA deputies, including Houphouët-Boigny, joined the French government. Houphouët-Boigny enjoyed his greatest influence as a junior minister in Guy Mollet's government (February 1956), and as a minister of state, in charge of implementing the Framework Law, in Bourgés-Maunoury's government (June 1957). The PDCI won the majority of mayoralties in the municipal elections of November 18, 1956.

Union became a recurrent theme. As in 1951, on May 21, 1956, Houphouët-Boigny launched another appeal for union at the Géo André Stadium. This led to the absorption of the opposition into the PDCI-RDA. In the territorial elections of March 31, 1957, the PDCI won every seat, and, given its hegemonic position, it formed the first Council of Ministers of Côte d'Ivoire on May 15 of that year. Houphouët-Boigny had brought about the triumph of his ideas. Nevertheless, there was some turbulence within the party. There had been no party congress since 1949, and the leading positions had been filled by a simple process of cooptation. By 1957, Houphouët-Boigny combined the offices of president of the RDA, president of the PDCI, deputy of the French National Assembly, mayor of Abidjan, speaker of the Territorial Assembly, and chairman of the Grand Conseil (Great Council) of the Fédération de l'Afrique Occidentale (FAO; West African Federation), and minister in the French government. Within the PDCI, his position was that of supreme arbiter, to such an extent that nothing could be decided without his agreement.

At the beginning of 1958, the RDA demanded constitutional reform to reflect the political development of France's African territories. In the referendum held in September 1958, the PDCI called for a yes vote, and on December 4 of that year Côte d'Ivoire became a republic. The Territorial Assembly became a constituent assembly, and on March 26, 1959, it adopted a new constitution. On this occasion, Houphouët-Boigny defined his conception of opposition within very narrow limits. The PDCI congress had met beforehand, for the third time, from March 19 to 23; it had transformed the political bureau into the supreme organ and replaced A. Denise with J. B. Mockey as secretary general. This was the first sign of a crisis.

After the elections of April 1959, the new legislative assembly called on Houphouët-Boigny to take office as prime minister. He went on to form the first government of the republic. Through measures of both attraction and coercion, the PDCI was able to impose itself rapidly as a single party, despite the crisis of 1963.

DANIELLE DOMERGUE-CLOAREC

See also: **Houphouët-Boigny, Félix.**

Further Reading

Loucou, J.-N. *Le Multipartisme en Côte d'Ivoire.* Abidjan: Neter, 1992.

Mundt, R. J. *Historical Dictionary of Ivory Coast (Côte d'Ivoire),* 2nd ed. Lanham, Md., 1995.

Siriex, P.-H. *Félix Houphouët-Boigny, Homme de la paix.* Paris: Seghers, 1975.

Zolberg, A. *One-Party Government in the Côte d'Ivoire.* Princeton, N.J.: Princeton University Press, 1964.

Cotton: *See* Sudan: Cotton, Irrigation, and Oil, 1970s.

Coups d'État and Military Rule: Postcolonial Africa

Coups d'état is a French phrase that means, literally, a "strike at the state." Such a strike takes place when force is used to bring about leadership change without regard to legitimate constitutional processes for accomplishing such change; they are, in that respect, unconstitutional. The military is usually behind coups d'état in Africa. Although military governments are generally unconstitutional, they have sometimes acquired legitimacy because of their success in dealing with problems facing the state.

Coups in postcolonial Africa date back to 1952, when Colonel Gamel Abdel Nasser and the Free Officers Movement overthrew King Farouk of Egypt and established military rule. This was followed in 1958 by the coup of General Ibrahim Aboud in Sudan. The military increasingly became involved in state administrative affairs in the postcolonial era. In one country after another—in Benin in 1963 and 1965, Congo (Zaire) in 1965, Algeria in 1965, Ghana in 1966, Nigeria in 1966, and Sierra Leone in 1967, among others—the military overthrew the postindependence civilian governments and either installed themselves, or their preferred candidate, in power. The army mutiny in the Democratic Republic of Congo (Zaire), or DRC, in 1960 and the capture and handover of Prime Minister Lumumba to his enemies in 1961 are examples of the military becoming involved in politics without assuming full, formal control.

By the 1970s and 1980s, over half of the countries in Africa were either under military rule or had at one point been ruled by the military. For some countries (Nigeria, Ghana, and Burkina Faso), the number of coups exceeded five. Coup-installed regimes had varied colonial experiences and ideological leanings. Burkina Faso under Thomas Sankara, Ethiopia under Mengisto Haile Miriam, and the DRC under Sassou

Nguesso sought to transform their societies through a socialist-Marxist ideology. Others, among them Zaïre under Mobutu Sese Seko and Somalia under Siad Barre, were staunchly capitalist in their orientation, and sought a capitalist revolution as the basis for bringing change. A third category of countries—Uganda under Idi Amin Dada and the Central African Republic (renamed the Central African Empire) under Jean Bedel Bokassa—were distinguishable mainly by the level of brutality that was associated with their rule.

The factors that explain the frequency of coups d'état and military rule in Africa are many and varied. They include the weakness of the postindependent state in Africa, the economic, political, and social problems that African states inherited from colonial rule, and their inability to successfully resolve such problems. Economic mismanagement and corruption by civilian governments and the personal ambitions of military leaders are other factors. The military was, and remains, one of the most organized institutions in Africa. In addition, the military is well equipped and has an important weapon that civilian governments do not have—namely, arms. These elements give the military an advantage over a civilian government when it comes to mobilizing people and resources to deal with a particular problem in a country.

Despite the rationalization of coups d'état and military rule as discussed above, military governments in Africa were not, generally speaking, any more successful than civilian governments in dealing with Africa's economic and social problems. Issues of poverty, unemployment, low incomes, weak communication infrastructures, poor educational systems, inadequate and poorly equipped health care systems, and ethnic conflicts were as rampant under military rule as under civilian rule. In many cases, the policies and behavior of military governments were similar to those of their civilian predecessors. Corruption and mismanagement did not go away; rather, they increased in some cases.

The military governments adopted the same tactics that their civilian counterparts used to maintain political control. Upon seizing power, most sought legitimacy for their leadership by adopting civilian institutions. Most adopted titles such as *president* rather than *general*. Most also turned the state into a one-party system, with their party as the sole party. Other instruments for political manipulation under civilian rule, such as the establishment of a patronage system of reward for supporters and punishment for opponents, noncompetitive elections, the suppression of dissent, and censorship to preempt perceived threats to their power were also used to institutionalize the military leaders' control.

In the early 1990s, most of Africa's military regimes were forced by worsening economic and social problems, political unrest, and external pressure to liberalize the political system. Beginning with Benin in 1990, and continuing with Mali, the DRC, and Niger, many succumbed to pressure and introduced democratic reforms that brought about new constitutions and governments. Others (Ghana, Togo, and Guinea) were able to manipulate the electoral process and remain in power. By the late 1990s, coups and armed insurgency had again become a problem. New waves of coups overthrew governments in Sierra Leone, Gambia, and Niger.

Coups d'état are not a thing of the past in Africa. To the extent that genuine economic and political change remains illusive Africa's militaries may exploit the situation to stage a comeback to politics.

MOSES K. TESI

Further Reading

Decalo, S. *Coups and Army Rule in Africa*. New Haven, Conn.: Yale University Press, 1976.

Gutteridge, W. "Undoing Military Coups in Africa." *Third World Quarterly* 7, no. 1 (1985).

Liebenow, G. J. *African Politics: Crises and Challenges*. Bloomington: Indiana University Press, 1986.

Owusu, M. "Customs and Coups: A Juridical Interpretation of Civil Order and Disorder." *Journal of Modern African Studies* 24, no. 1 (1986).

Welch, C. E., Jr. *Soldier and State in Africa*. Evanston, Ill.: Northwestern University Press, 1970.

Cromer: *See* Egypt: Cromer Administration, 1883–1907: Irrigation, Agriculture, and Industry.

Crop Cultivation: The Evidence

The most direct evidence for crop cultivation in the past comes from archaeobotany, the study of plant remains preserved on archaeological sites. Such remains are normally preserved in carbonized form, by ancient contact with fire, though desiccated remains are preserved due to the extreme desert conditions of more recent millennia. Archaeobotanical remains are often overlooked unless excavations have undertaken systematic recovery through water flotation and sieving. The evidence consists primarily of wood charcoal, derived primarily from fuel gathered from local trees and shrubs, and seeds from wild gathered food plants, harvested crops, and the weeds of cultivated land. Identification of these seed remains may be challenging due to incomplete preservation of distinctive features and the lack of established collections of modern botanical reference material. Ancient plant use can also be identified on the basis of impressions preserved in pottery, when plant materials have been used as ceramic temper. At present, available archaeological evidence in Africa is still limited to relatively few sites over such a vast continent, but recent research efforts have provided a basis for inferring certain larger patterns of early cultivation.

Important additional evidence, and essential background information, comes from modern botanical studies, including genetics and biogeography. Through comparative botanical studies, with important potential contributions from modern genetic techniques, the wild progenitors of crops can be identified. As genetic techniques are applied, it becomes possible to narrow down modern wild populations most closely related to domesticated forms. The geographical and ecological distribution of these wild progenitors provides important clues as to where initial domestication is likely to have occurred. Modern distributions, however, are unlikely to indicate precisely where species first domesticated due to the effects of past climatic change which would have forced changes in the distributions of many species. Thus modern wild distributions must be adjusted based on inferences of how climate has changed. Thus in the early and middle Holocene periods, savanna environments were shifted much farther north into what is today the Sahara. The emergence of plant cultivation appears to have occurred after 3000BCE, as these distributions contracted southward toward those under modern conditions.

In the study of early agriculture, a distinction needs to be made between cultivation and domestication. Cultivation is a human activity, the planting of seeds from previous harvests normally on prepared ground, while domestication is an evolutionary state of the plant, morphologically altered from the wild form, usually to become more dependent upon human dispersal. A complete history of the beginnings of cultivation would therefore need to include evidence for the transition from wild gathering to cultivation and subsequent domestication. Evidence relating to wild plant-gathering traditions that are probably ancestral to plant cultivation comes from a number of sites in the Sahara desert, dating to 7000–4000BCE. During this early to mid-Holocene era, rainfall was higher, and much of the Sahara had savanna or sahelian vegetation. Archaeobotanical evidence indicates widespread traditions of wild grain harvesting, including a fairly diverse range of grass species. Sites in the western desert of Egypt (Nabta Playa, Dakleh Oasis, Farafra, and Abu Ballas) all include evidence that wild sorghum was among the grasses utilized. Sites in southwest Libya, in the Tadart Acacus (Uan Tabu, Uan Afuda, Uan Muhuggiag, and Ti-n-Torha) indicate a range of wild grasses but lack evidence of sorghum use. Of interest from the Acacus is evidence for

domesticated watermelons, probably used for oily seeds, by about 4000BCE. Similar grass-harvesting is suggested by identifiable impressions on ceramics of the Shaheinab Neolithic tradition in the Sudanese Middle Nile region from the fifth to fourth millennia BCE. There is no evidence yet to tie these traditions of wild grass use to the beginnings of cultivation and subsequent domestication of these species.

The earliest evidence for cultivated crops in Africa comes from nonnative species, while the earliest archaeological finds of native Africa crops yet found are from India. In the Egyptian Nile Valley wheat, barley, lentils, and peas, all of which had spread from southwest Asia, were known by 4500BCE. These Near Eastern crops were the basis of agriculture in the Nile Valley at least as far south as the Third Cataract region by 3000BCE, and probably also in Mediterranean North Africa. Crops that must have been domesticated from Africa where their wild forms occur—including sorghum, pearl millet, cowpea, and hyacinth bean—occur archaeologically in India by 1800BCE and perhaps as early as 2200BCE, while finger millet of east African origin occurs by 1000BCE. These finds indicate that cultivation must have begun even earlier within Africa. The most important domesticate of the East African savanna, sorghum, is still poorly documented in terms of the beginnings of cultivation and domestication. Finds include the early Kushite/Napatan site of Kawa in Nubia from before 500BCE, and several in greater Nubia from the last centuries BCE and the first centuries CE. Thus evidence to link early wild sorghum use with the domesticated form that had spread to India in later prehistory remains elusive.

Within Africa, early evidence for the spread of pearl millet cultivation across West Africa dates to the first half of the second millennium BCE. Fully domesticated pearl millet has been identified from pottery impressions from Tichitt tradition sites in southwest Mauritania and Karkarichinkat, northeast of the Niger River Bend in Mali, while grains have been recovered from Winde Kiroji on the Middle Niger and Birimi in northern Ghana of the Kintampo culture. At another Kintampo site in central Ghana comes the earliest evidence for cowpea. Kintampo sites also indicate widespread exploitation of the oil palm. Both cowpea and oil palm represent a forest margin complex of crops that may have distinct origins from the savanna cereals. Early evidence for other Savanna grains, African rice, and fonio, both date to the first millennium BCE, though wild rice use is documented from Gajiganna, Nigeria, by 1200BCE.

More difficult to document are those species reproduced vegetatively, such as tuber crops and many important fruits. Tuber foods (such as yams or the ensete of Ethiopian forest zones) are cultivated and utilized in such a way so as to not bring seeds into contact with preserving fire. Bananas and plantains, introduced to Africa in prehistory from lands across the Indian Ocean, are sterile hybrids with seedless fruits. For these species different approaches to identification are necessary, such as through phytoliths (microscopic silica bodies from within plant tissues) or through the anatomical identification of charred tissue (parenchyma) fragments. Phytoliths of banana and ensete leaves are highly distinctive, and banana phytoliths have been identified from an archaeological pit fill dating to the later first millennium BCE in Cameroon (Nkang). The anatomical identification of parenchyma tissues from tubers shows promise from studies of European, Pacific, and palaeolithic Egyptian material but has yet to be applied to tropical African materials. In the absence of archaeological evidence, historical linguistics has also provided inferences about past agriculture.

DORIAN Q. FULLER

Further Reading

D'Andrea, A. C., and J. Casey. "Pearl Millet and Kintampo Subsistence." *African Archaeological Review*, no. 19 (2002): 147–173.

Harlan, J., J. M. J. de Wet, and Ann B. L. Stemler (eds.). *Origins of African Plant Domestication*. The Hague: Mouton, 1976.

Marshall, F., and E. Hildebrand. "Cattle before Crops: The Beginnings of Food Production in Africa." *Journal of World Prehistory*, no. 16 (2002): 99–143.

Neumann, K., A. Butler, and S. Kahlheber (eds.). *Food, Fuel and Fields: Progress in African Archaeobotany*. Köln: Heinrich-Barth-Institute, 2003.

Van der Veen, M. (ed.). *The Exploitation of Plant Resources in Ancient Africa*. New York: Kluwer Academic/Plenum, 1999.

Crowther, Reverend Samuel Ajayi and the Niger Mission

Samuel Ajayi Crowther (*c.*1806–1891) was a nineteenth-century Anglican bishop and missionary. As one of the founders of the Niger Mission, the first Church Missionary Society (CMS) post in Nigeria, Crowther was instrumental in the development of Anglicanism in the country.

The Yoruba Wars of the early nineteenth century fed the Atlantic slave trade at the very time that Britain sought to eradicate it. Consistent with practices of the era, captives taken during the wars were sold to slave dealers. Ajayi had been such a victim. He was taken prisoner in early 1821, at approximately age 15, when the Muslims invaded Oshogun, his hometown. After being bought and sold numerous times, he was on the Portuguese slave carrier, the *Esperanza Felix*, off Lagos, when it was captured and impounded on April 7, 1822, by British naval forces on an antislavery patrol off the West African coast. The British liberated the slaves that they discovered in impounded or interdicted ships. For most such captives however, liberation included being transported to Sierra Leone. Thus was the case for the young Ajayi.

Sierra Leone was a colony in transition in the 1820s. Fueled in large part by the depositing of liberated Africans there and by the immigration of former slaves from the Americas, especially the United States, it had a multiethnic population. A variety of economic opportunities were available in construction, commerce, and agriculture. Missionary groups, particularly the Church Missionary Society, actively sought to convert the indigenous people as well as liberated Africans—those rescued from slavery. On their arrival in the colony younger liberated Africans were enrolled in schools to be educated and "civilized." Some received skilled training to be artisans.

Ajayi was trained to be a carpenter at the CMS mission school. His quick mastery of his vocational and religious instructions impressed his tutors and induced them to select him for more extensive educational instruction than was made available to most students. On Ajayi's baptism in 1825 the Reverend J. C. Raban gave him the name of an eminent patron of the CMS, Samuel Crowther, Vicar of Christ Church, Newgate. The following year, a Reverend Davy took him to England and enrolled him in Islington Parish School. He returned to Freetown in 1827 and became one of the first students to enroll in the institution that later became Fourah Bay College. He went on to teach at missionary and government schools.

Crowther was teaching at a mission school when CMS officials in Sierra Leone urged him to join the Niger Expedition being organized by Thomas F. Buxton. His account of the venture, published as the *Journal of the 1841 Expedition*, so enthralled CMS officials in England that they directed missionary officials in Freetown to send him to the CMS Training College in London. He was ordained in 1843 and immediately returned to Sierra Leone, where he was persuaded to join a party preparing to create a mission in Nigeria. Crowther was chosen in part because of his fluency in Yoruba. The CMS intended to establish its Nigerian headquarters at Abeokuta in the Yoruba heartland for more than evangelical reasons. It also wanted to contest the Wesleyan Methodist Society, the initiator of missionary enterprise in Nigeria with the opening of its first station on September 24, 1842, and Southern Baptists from the United States who alleged that Yoruba leaders had invited them to the area. The officials expected Crowther to immigrate to Nigeria, not merely to participate as a member of the expedition as before. Reluctant to uproot his family, he demurred at first, but eventually elected to go.

The initial party comprised teachers, artisans, interpreters, and three clerics: the Reverend C. A. Gollmer, Reverend Henry Townsend, and Crowther. It arrived in Nigeria in January 1845. While the mission party was in transit, Sodeke, the ruler at Abeokuta, died. The Yoruba custom of not conducting any major venture during an interregnum meant that Crowther and his associates could not relocate in Abeokuta until a new ruler was chosen. They therefore settled at Badagri instead. Even after the new ruler was chosen, an entire year passed before the first Abeokuta station was opened. In the meantime, Gollmer was selected to teach school while Townsend, the effective head of the mission, and Crowther embarked on "true" missionary work, seeking converts through evangelization. Growth was slow; the missionaries held that novices had to be thoroughly prepared before they could be fully accepted into the Church. Crowther conducted the mission's first baptism, on February 5, 1848, for three converts, one of whom was his own mother. He later converted other relatives, including one of his sisters.

Crowther was active on a number of fronts. In 1851, during the height of the discussion over whether Britain should annex Lagos, Reverend Henry Venn, the CMS secretary, invited him to England and used him as a prime exhibit of African potential. To the likes of Lord Palmerston, the lords of the admiralty, and leaders of the House of Commons, African potential under British authority was writ large in the former slave captive. Crowther was a member of the 1854 expedition up the Niger in which Dr. William B. Baikie demonstrated the efficacy of quinine against malaria. Crowther also directed an antismallpox campaign. He became a linguist, producing significant works of grammar for the Igbo, Nupe, and Yoruba. His groundbreaking translation of the Bible into Yoruba established the standard followed by other speakers of English in translating scripture into other African languages. He did not hesitate to involve himself in factional conflicts if he perceived a possibility to advance Christianity. He supervised the mission's expansion throughout much of Yorubaland, into areas to the south, and laid the foundation for its movement into the Hausa region to the north.

Crowther was consecrated bishop of the Niger Mission in June 1864. His advance up the ladder of authority and position brought conflicts between European and African missionaries of the Niger Mission into the open even before his nomination to the bishopric. A number of the Europeans firmly believed that only Europeans should hold leadership positions in the mission and in the Church. Townsend, the senior member of the mission, not only held that view but actively campaigned against any elevation of Crowther.

Although he was aware of the anti-African campaign, Crowther usually refrained from participating in efforts to rebut it even to the extent of not defending himself unless pointedly asked to do so by his superiors. That quality and his intellect contributed to the continued high esteem in which he was held by Henry Venn and other officials at the London headquarters of the society. Those officials could not ignore their European agents totally. Thus when made bishop, Crowther's authority did not include any European missionaries or their territories. Later, management of financial matters and in such personnel areas as the appointing, transferring, and disciplining of African agents was withdrawn and given to young Europeans, some of whom were without any African experience and who made no effort to hide their anti-African racism. He died on December 31, 1891, following a stroke.

ASHTON WESLEY WELCH

See also: **Anti-Slavery Movement; Religion, Colonial Africa: Missionaries.**

Further Reading

Ajayi, J. F. A. *Christian Missions in Nigeria 1841–1891: The Making of a New Elite.* Evanston, Ill.: Northwestern University Press, 1965.
———. *A Patriot to the Core: Samuel Ajayi Crowther.* Ibadan: Anglican Diocese of Ibadan, 1992.
Ayandele, E. A. *The Missionary Impact on Modern Nigeria 1842–1914: A Political and Social Analysis.* New York: Humanities Press, 1967.
Crowther, S. A. *Journal of an Expedition up the Niger in 1841,* 2nd ed. London: Frank Cass, 1970.
Crowther, Samuel A. *Journal of an Expedition up the Niger and Tschadda Rivers,* 2nd ed. London: Frank Cass, 1970.
Crowther, S. A., and J. C. Taylor. *Journal of the Niger Expedition of 1857 and Missionary Notices.* London: Dawsons, 1968.
Decorvet, J. *Samuel ajayi Crowther: un père de l'Église en Afrique noire.* Paris: Distribution Cerf, 1992.
Dike, K. O. *Origins of the Niger Mission 1841–1891,* Ibadan, 1962.
Groves, C. P. *The Planting of Christianity in Africa.* London, 1958.
Hastins, A. *Church and Mission in Modern Africa.* London, 1967.
Page, J. *Samuel Crowther: The Slave Boy Who Became Bishop of the Niger.* London: S. W. Partridge, 1889.

Currencies and Banking

The formal imposition of colonial rule over most of Africa after 1900 was preceded by centuries of commercial relations between the continent and the West. As the colonial powers began to occupy the continent from the late nineteenth century on, economic infrastructure such as banks and currencies had to be installed not only for commercial transactions but also to ensure a smooth administration. This essay illustrates the development of colonial banking and currency systems in Africa with the example of West Africa.

The first commercial bank in British West Africa, the Bank of British West Africa (BBWA), was established in 1894 by a group of British businessmen led by the shipping magnate A. L. Jones. It operated in the British colonies of Nigeria, Gold Coast, Sierra Leone, and Gambia, and later in Liberia. In French West Africa, the first commercial bank was the Banque du Senegal, established at St. Louis in 1854. It later gave way to the Banque de l'Afrique Occidentale (BAO), founded in 1901. These banks held a virtual monopoly of banking in the respective colonial territories; it was only in 1926 that the Barclay's Bank was founded as a rival to the BBWA in the British colonies. This did not, however, threaten the BBWA's entrenched position in the banking business, as it handled the bulk of government and commercial accounts.

The BBWA and BAO played crucial roles as banks of issue in the respective colonial territories. While the former had a brief tenure from 1894 to 1911 (being superseded in 1912 by the West African Currency Board), the latter maintained its monopoly over French West African colonial monetary systems from 1901 to 1955. The two banks' commercial practices were, however, broadly similar. First, they aided capital flight from the colonies by investing colonial reserves in the metropolitan economies, apparently because the colonial economies did not provide as many favorable investment opportunities. Second, their primary interest, as reflected in their lending policy, was in fostering the growth of expatriate commercial interests. While they gave credit to the big expatriate firms, they discriminated against indigenous ones, which could not satisfy their deliberately stiff collateral conditions.

The attitude of these banks toward indigenous enterprise contributed to the rise of economic nationalism in colonial West Africa. Attempts were made by African nationalists to establish banks sympathetic to the aspirations of African businessmen. Although the celebrated attempt by W. Tete-Ansa and Herbert Macaulay to run the nationalist Industrial and Commercial Bank had failed by 1931, subsequent efforts bore fruit. In Nigeria, the National Bank of Nigeria, founded in 1933, was the first of the indigenous banks that were to thrive from the 1950s onward. But these only managed to secure a small share of the market in the colonies. The expatriate banks thus maintained their dominance of the colonial banking systems throughout the colonial period.

Commercial banking did not operate in a vacuum: it had been necessitated by the increasing volume of European currencies in circulation. These currencies,

too, antedated the formal establishment of colonial rule. By the middle of the nineteenth century, British and French coins had come to coexist with traditional currencies in the commercial systems of West Africa. As soon as formal colonial rule was imposed from 1900 onward, colonial governments sought to displace the precolonial traditional currencies and to replace them with those issued by themselves. This was achieved by prohibiting the use of traditional currencies, paying the staff of colonial establishments in the colonial coinage, and insisting on the payment of tax in the official legal tender.

Coinage of various denominations was issued. Coins were made of silver, aluminum, and alloy. Currency notes were later introduced, but they faced popular antipathy partly because the material was too flimsy and also because the notes, unlike coinage, did not have any intrinsic value. The colonial currency systems were generally characterized by the shortage of coins, especially silver, owing partly to the practice of the colonial subjects of hoarding or smelting them into ornaments, and partly because of the cost of minting arising from the worldwide shortage of silver. In any case, there was never a consistent supply of small-denomination alloy coins which were in high demand in retail transactions. One response to the perennial crisis in the colonial currency systems was the practice of counterfeiting by the colonial subjects, but this was ultimately suppressed by the individual and cooperative action of the British and French colonial administrations in West Africa. Be that as it may, traditional currencies remained popular in certain areas, such as Eastern Nigeria, where 30 million *manillas* (open bracelets, cast from copper, brass, or iron) were still in circulation up to 1949, about a decade before independence.

The colonial currency systems were tied to those of the metropolitan countries. This was in spite of the creation of separate currencies for the colonies: in 1912 the WACB began issuing a separate currency for British West Africa while in 1945 the Colonies Francaise d'Afrique franc was introduced with the formation of a currency board, Caisse Centrale de la France d'Outre-Mer. Until then the colonial currencies were freely convertible with the metropolitan ones.

The introduction of colonial banking and currency systems in West Africa from the nineteenth century resulted in the expansion of the economy. They eased commercial exchange between the colonies and the metropolis, and also within and across colonial territories. Modern currencies also facilitated colonial administration, as they made tax collection and the transfer of money within and across colonies much easier. These colonial economic infrastructures enabled expatriate banks and currency boards to transfer capital from the colonies to the metropolis, particularly by investing colonial reserves, including currency board earnings from seigniorage, in the mother countries.

AYODWI OLUKOJU

See also: **Colonial Federations: French West Africa; Communaute Financière Africaine.**

Further Reading

Austen, R. *African Economic History: Internal Development and External Dependency.* London: James Currey/Portsmouth, N.H.: Heinemann, 1987.

Hogendorn, J., and H. A. Gemery. "Continuity in West African Monetary History? An Outline of Monetary Development." *African Economic History*, no. 17 (1988): 127–146.

Hopkins, A. G. "The Creation of a Colonial Monetary System: The Origins of the West African Currency Board." *African Historical Studies*, no. 3 (1970): 101–132.

———. *An Economic History of West Africa.* Harlow, England: Longman, 1973.

Ofonagoro, W. I. "From Traditional to British Currency in Southern Nigeria: Analysis of a Currency Revolution, 1880–1948." *Journal of Economic History*, 39, no. 3 (1979): 623–654.

Webb, J. L. A., Jr. "Toward the Comparative Study of Money: A Reconsideration of West African Currencies and NeoClassical Monetary Concepts." *International Journal of African Historical Studies* 15, no. 3 (1982): 455–466.

Cushites: Northeastern Africa: Stone Age Origins to Iron Age

Paleontological research has placed humanity's earliest known ancestor, *Australopithecus Afarensis* (popularly known as "Lucy"), in the Horn of Africa more than a million years ago. Thus, the region of Northeast Africa, which includes the Horn of Africa, may have been the earliest cradle of humanity (Brandt 1992).

Early *Homo sapiens* are thought to have replaced hominids about 125,000 years ago in the Horn of Africa. Considerably later, at 25,000 years ago, a particular type of Stone Age industry with characteristic blades and flint tools developed in northern Somalia around the city of Hargeisa (Brandt 1992, p.29), but nothing is known about who made those artifacts. Likewise, there is no information on the identity of the Stone Age inhabitants of the Horn even during the later Stone Age, some 12,000 years ago. Thus, early archaeology does not offer us any information that is ethnic group specific in its early stages. In short, we cannot speak of Cushitic groups or Semitic groups in the region yet, but only of early human groups.

In the north, data "ranging from Acheulian sites to Neolithic rock art" was found in the twentieth century by a few searches. Some of the sites indicated successive occupations with radiocarbon dates between 18,000 and 40,000 years ago (Brandt, Brook, and Gresham 1983, pp.7, 14–15). However, search in that

area still lags behind that done in parts of the continent, especially the Nile Valley and West Africa. In the midst of the hills and valleys of the north, between Erigavo in the mountains and Las Koreh on the Gulf of Aden, an archaeological survey of limited scope in 1980 revealed "a series of caves and rock-shelters, many of which revealed surface scatters of Middle to Later Stone Age artifacts and fossilized bone" (Brandt, Brook, and Gresham 1983, p.8).

Rock shelters at Karin Hagin, a natural mountain pass approximately 70 kilometers southwest of Bosaso, contain extensive rock paintings (Brandt, Brook, and Gresham 1983, p.16); the important feature is a type of cattle, today extinct in the Somalian areas, but found in Egypt, called jamuusa. The paintings also depict goats. These paintings bear interesting stylistic similarities the rock art of Ethiopia and northeastern Africa in general.

The Cushites, in the past mostly called Hamites, are an indigenous people of Northeast Africa, who are found today as far south as past the Equator in East Africa proper. Both the terms *Cushite* and *Hamite* have been drawn from the Christian Bible; however, the latter term has been mostly abandoned. European anthropologists, in their attempts to devise a multitude of races and subraces in Africa, have long argued about the provenance of Cushites and have sometimes treated them as a mongrel race born out of Caucasoid or white immigrants from outside Africa and dark-skinned or Negroid Africans. Thus, unluckily, we have seen Cushites called Black Caucasoids or Europoids (Seligman 1930). The fact is that divisions on the human spectrum are not clear, and choosing any number of features to establish human typologies means ignoring some other features. Furthermore, such definitions reflect nothing more than the biases of those doing the classifications and run counter to the fact that all human groups have always been mixing first with the immediate neighbors and then with groups farther afield through intermediate groups. In other words, all human groups are mixed groups. Additionally, such classifications do little to advance our knowledge of human dispersal in general, and in particular have led to erroneous assumptions about the provenance of the Cushitic peoples of Africa, as well as the greatest ancient civilization that sprang in Northeast Africa, ancient Egypt.

For as long as recorded history is available for the region (perhaps as far back as 7,000 years ago, during the late Stone Age), the Cushites have been an indigenous people of Northeast Africa. Yet little is known about their ancient past. Perhaps one of the reasons lies in the fact that researchers and archaeologists have mostly concentrated their efforts on ancient Egypt and the Nile Valley in isolation, and to the detriment of a holistic picture of the whole region and its people.

Linguistics explains what other languages may be related to those spoken by today's Cushites. Thus, we know that the languages of the Cushites are part of a larger family of languages currently known as the Afroasiatic "superfamily" of languages, which includes Ancient Egyptian, Semitic, Chadic, and Berber. Of these, the only group whose native speakers partly extend to Asia (through migration from the African side of the Red Sea) is the Semitic group. Thus, it is likely that the ancestors of the speakers of Afroasiatic languages originally inhabited northeastern Africa, especially on the Red Sea coasts, before spreading, with the Chadic group crossing into Western Sudan, while some Semitic groups crossed over the Bab el Mandab straihts into the Arabian Peninsula.

After the Stone Age, and starting about 6,000 years ago, herding of domesticating animals became the main economic activity of the inhabitants of the lowland areas of the Horn along the Red Sea and the Gulf of Aden. In those early times, the mountains and coastal areas had a wetter climate, which facilitated animal husbandry (Brandt, Brook, and Gresham 1983, p.10).

According to recent, limited research in northeastern and eastern Africa, domesticated cattle, wheat, and barley were being grown and raised in southern Egypt more than 8,000 years ago, while sheep and goats became domesticated about 7,500 years ago (Brandt 1992, p.30). The different peoples of the region learned from one another, with those dwelling in the Nile Valley becoming agriculturalists and cattle herders-while those in the drier areas took up domestication of small stock such as goats and sheep. Groups in the highlands or plateau country, such as found in Ethiopia, adopted agriculture at about the same time. By the age of the Egyptian civilization, the populations of northeastern Africa were fairly well established along the Red Sea coast up to Egypt and down to Cape Guardui, in what is now Somalia.

While early Cushites have usually been described as essentially pastoralists, it is more likely that their activities depended on their environment; if the area was well watered, they practiced agriculture, whereas when the area was mostly dry they were pastoralists breeding sheep and goats. Early Cushites were also

societies where certain trades were practiced by caste groups; for example, metallurgy and leatherworking were practiced by only certain groups. Likewise, the practice of war was the domain of the warrior class, while the practice of religion was the domain of the priests. This same division of trades has survived up to our times.

Early Cushites left behind materials that await further research and study; among those are monumental shrines in the Horn of Africa. The best known of these is a series of monumental graves and raised cairns situated in northern Somalia, which extend to southern Ethiopia up to the Dawa River, where the ancestors of the Oromo settled. These monumental graves are unknown in the areas not associated with early Cushitic settlement.

The building of these monumental graves points to a highly organized and ritualized religion. This is more so because we know that pre-Islamic and pre-Christain Cushites were fairly monotheistic and believed in one sky god, Waaq. The *ahan*, or ceremony of grave building and burial, demanded that considerable efforts be put into it; it is still practiced among Somalis today.

MOHAMED DIRIYE ABDULLAHI

See also: **Stone Age (Later): Sahara and North Africa.**

Further Reading

Brandt, A. S. "The Importance of Somalia for Understanding African and World History." In *Proceedings of the First International Congress of Somali Studies*, edited by Adam M. Hussein and Charles L. Geshekter. Atlanta: Scholars Press, 1992.

Brandt, A. S., G. A. Brook, and T. H. Gresham. "Quaternary Paleoenvironments and Prehistoric Human Occupation of Northern Somalia." In *Proceedings of the Second International Congress of Somali Studies*, edited by Thomas Labahn. Hamburg: Buske, 1983.

Chittick, H. Neville. "Cairns and Other Drystone Monuments in Somali Regions." In *Proceedings of the First International Congress of Somali Studies*, edited by Adam M. Hussein and Charles L. Geshekter. Atlanta: Scholars Press, 1992.

Clark, J. D. *The Prehistoric Cultures of the Horn of Africa.* Cambridge: Cambridge University Press, 1954.

Seligman, C. G. *The Races of Africa.* New York, 1930.

D

Dadog: *See* Nilotes, Eastern Africa: Southern Nilotes: Kalenjin, Dadog, Pokot.

Dahomey: Eighteenth Century

The Aja are believed to have originally migrated to southern present-day Benin from Tado (Togo) in the twelfth or thirteenth century and to have founded the town of Allada. According to oral tradition, a dispute in 1625 between three brothers over the throne caused further migrations. One brother, Kokpon, took over Allada; another, Te-Agbanlin, founded the coastal town of Ajatche, renamed Porto-Novo by Portugese merchants; and the third brother, Do-Aklin, moved inland and founded the town of Abomey. Here, the Aja gradually mixed with the local population to form the Fon ethnic group.

By the end of the seventeenth century, Do-Aklin's grandson Wegbaja (*r. c.*1645–1685) and his successor Akaba (*r.*1685–1708) had made Abomey the capital of a powerful state, Dahomey. The kingdom was an absolute monarchy, quite unlike the surrounding traditional kingdoms. Its king's divine powers were hereditary. It was central to his role to honor former monarchs and establish the omnipotence of the royal line unequivocally. Hence the national day of celebration, the Annual Customs, included numerous human sacrifices to inspire the proper degree of fear in his subjects and provide a communication path with ancestors.

At Annual Customs, kings assembled the entire population, offered sacrifices, conducted Vodun ceremonies, gave gifts, reviewed the previous year, and planned future activities. "Messengers," previously condemned to death, were dispatched to the council of former kings in the otherworld to consult them. Answers to the questions delivered by the messengers were received through divination or possession. At the height of Dahomey's power, the king's palace was decorated with human skulls, as was his throne; human sacrifices occurred regularly.

The king was the unchallenged head of a rigidly stratified society. He granted and withdrew chieftancies at will. He governed through a centralized bureaucracy staffed by commoners who could not challenge his authority. Succession to the throne was by primogeniture. By 1708, under King Agaja, every Dahomean citizen knew that his life must be devoted to the service of his king.

Dahomey was organized for war not only to expand its territory, but also to take captives as slaves. At first, in the sparsely populated land, these were kept to work the royal plantations. Later, they were sold to Europeans in exchange for weapons. The army consisted largely of regulars renowned for their marksmanship. It included the famous Amazon corps, probably originally a palace guard.

While Dahomey flourished, the coastal kingdoms of Allada and Ouidah were prey to succession struggles, disrupted by competition between European traders who played one chief against another, and vulnerable to Dahomey's intention to expand toward the coast to claim its share of the slave trade.

When in 1724 Soso, the king of Allada, died, two brothers vied to succeed him. The loser asked Agaja for help. Agaja marched south with his army, but instead of restoring his ally on the throne occupied Allada and exiled both contenders. By this unexpected action, Agaja destroyed the traditional ties that had bound the peoples together. He asserted that force alone would henceforth determine the survival of kingdoms in the region. Yet Hufon, king of nearby Ouidah, still trusting the validity of traditional ties, took no preventive measures. In 1727, on a pretext, Agaja invaded. He met with little resistance and easily conquered and occupied Ouidah. His expansion caused the powerful Oyo empire, whose tributary Allada had become at the beginning of the

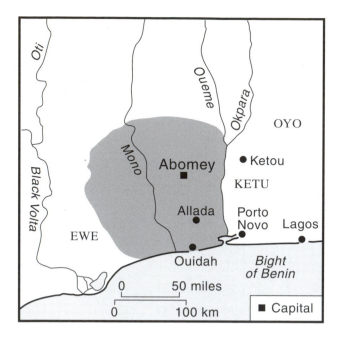

Dahomey, eighteenth century.

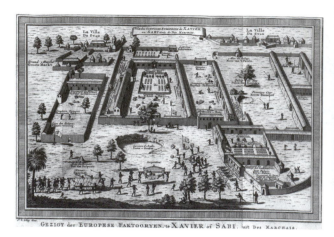

Engraving of a general view of the European trading forts and the royal palace in Xavier of Sabi in Dahomey (Benin). © Das Fotoarchiv.

eighteenth century, to intervene and invade Dahomey. The war continued from 1726 until 1730.

Agaja resorted to all available tactics; he even burned down his capital and dispersed his subjects. But in the long run Oyo cavalry triumphed over Dahomey's guns. Agaja had to sign a peace agreement, accept Oyo's sovereignty, agree to pay an annual tribute, and move his capital from Abomey to Allada, the ancient Aja capital. In return, he was allowed to keep all of Ouidah, a substantial part of Allada, overall control of his internal affairs, and his army.

Agaja then concentrated on reestablishing relations with the Europeans. He wanted the slave trade to be a royal monopoly, because his sales were guided only by his need for guns; but the Europeans forced him to negotiate with them. They recognized him as head of the land; in return he took responsibility for the safety of Europeans and promised to cooperate with their traders. However, the Oyo invaded again because Dahomey failed to pay the proper tribute. Agaja fled, and died in 1740.

After a contentious succession, his son Tegbesu (r.1732–1774) became king. He found his treasury empty and concluded that it was preferable to trade than to make war. By 1750 the slave trade was efficiently organized, and it looked as if it would solve Dahomey's problems. While the other parts of the Oyo empire were disintegrating, Dahomey stood firm. Nonetheless, the end of the eighteenth century marked a decline. Slaves from Oyo were being diverted from Dahomey's ports, and Fon raids were unable to capture sufficient numbers of slaves in the depleted northern regions. At the same time European demand was

dwindling, first as a result of the chaos created by the wars, and then in response to the abolition of the slave trade by Britain (1808). Dahomey's situation improved only after 1818, under King Guezo.

Dahomey has been denounced because of its human sacrifices and its large sales of slaves Recently, however, historians have attempted to explain rather than judge. They point out that while Dahomean culture found human sacrifices acceptable, Dahomey also offered its citizens order and protection. It developed a complex system of government not without constitutional checks and balances; it had an effective bureaucracy, courts of law, professional fighting units; it guaranteed its citizens fulfillment of their spiritual needs, and access to means of livelihood. Historians also underscore that Dahomean culture legitimized the enslavement of conquered people as field hands and servants, and found it easy to move from there to selling a few "undesirables." This led to growing European demands. Fon leaders seem to have gone into the trade reluctantly, but they became dependent on it to obtain weapons. The inescapable alternative they saw was to enslave others or be enslaved.

NATALIE SANDOMIRSKY

See also: **Allada and Slave Trade.**

Further Reading

Akinjogbin, I. A. "The Expansion of Oyo and the Rise of Dahomey 1600–1800." In *History of West Africa*, vol. 1, 2nd ed., edited by J. F. A. Ajayi and Michael Crowder. London: Longman, 1976.

Bay, E. G. *Wives of the Leopard: Gender, Politics and Culture in the Kingdom of Dahomey*. Charlottesville: University of Virginia Press, 1998.

Cornevin, R. *Le Dahomey*. Paris: PUF, 1970.

Davidson, B. *The African Slave Trade*. Rev. and expanded ed. Boston: Little, Brown, 1980.

Fage, J. D. *A History of West Africa: An Introductory Survey*, 4th ed. Cambridge: Cambridge University Press, 1970.

Herskovits, M. J. *Dahomey, an Ancient West African Kingdom*. 2 vols. London, 1958.

Manning, P. *Slavery, Colonialism, and Economic Growth in Dahomey, 1640–1960*. Cambridge: Cambridge University Press, 1982.

Meillassoux, C. (ed.). *L'Esclavage en Afrique précoloniale*. Paris: Maspéro, 1975.

Oliver, R. (ed.). *The Cambridge History of Africa, from c.1600 to c.1790*, vol. 4. Cambridge: Cambridge University Press, 1977.

Thomas, H. *The Slave Trade*. New York: Simon and Schuster, 1997.

Dakar

Dakar, the capital of Senegal, is the westernmost city on the African mainland. It is located at the tip of the Cape Verde Peninsula, roughly midway between the mouths of the Senegal and Gambia Rivers. The rocky coast and steep drop-off along the eastern side of the peninsula provide a sheltered deepwater harbor, and as the closest point in Africa to South America, Dakar is the logical departure point for voyages across the South Atlantic.

Dakar was founded in the mid-nineteenth century after more than four centuries of European activity in the area. The original inhabitants were Lébou fishing people who lived in villages at Yoff, Ouakam, Ngor, and Hann on Cape Verde. After the Portuguese arrived in 1444, a succession of European traders occupied Gorée Island, located two kilometers to the east. In 1815, Gorée was restored to France by the Congress of Vienna, and in the early 1820s it provided a base for several failed attempts by private firms to settle the mainland.

Napoleon Bonaparte's 1851 accession to power launched a new stage in French imperialism. In 1857, the governor of Senegal, Louis Faidherbe, ordered the occupation of the promontory opposite Gorée Island, and on May 25 of that year a group of marines began to build a fort. Several residents of Gorée joined them by building homes and planting gardens to supply food to the garrison and the island. The Messageries Impériales chose Dakar as a regular stop on its route from Bordeaux to Rio de Janeiro and purchased land near the waterfront to stockpile coal. To accomodate the company's large ships, the French administration launched a program of port improvements from 1862 to 1866 that added two jetties and navigation lights at Cape Dakar and on two offshore islands.

During the next two decades, French imperial interest waned as the German threat grew. Dakar was poorly placed to serve the Senegalese interior, so commercial traffic shifted to the port of Rufisque, 9 miles (15 kilometers) farther east. Dakar stagnated until 1885, when the French connected it by rail to Saint-Louis, near the mouth of the Senegal River. Although large ships used the Senegal River during the flood season, a sand bar limited access to the harbor at Saint-Louis, and once the railroad was completed, Dakar became the principal port for trade between Senegal and Europe. From 1885 to 1888, Dakar's population more than doubled, and it had nearly doubled again by 1891.

The French government financed a new round of improvements between 1892 and 1899. At first they simply extended one of the existing jetties and added more space for ships to dock. From 1899 to 1902, the administration constructed a naval base at the north end of the harbor, added a dry dock, and designated Dakar as the capital of French West Africa. Further construction from 1903 to 1910 increased the capacity of the commercial port to accommodate materials for railroad construction and increased exports of peanuts.

In 1902 the French selected Dakar as the capital of French West Africa. The governor general's palace and other administration buildings were completed by the end of the decade, including the École Pinet-Laprade, which provided technical training. The outbreak of World War I halted government investment, but private commerce flourished despite the war, and Dakar's population rose from roughly 24,000 inhabitants in 1914 to 32,000 by 1921.

Dakar's rapid growth provided an opportunity for French planners to test their theories about health in the tropics. In 1916, the authorities established a separate African neighborhood called Medina in an effort to reduce the effect of yellow fever epidemics. The French also opened a medical school in Dakar for "native doctors" and midwives in 1918, and schools for pharmacists and veterinarians in 1919.

After the war, the government united Dakar, Gorée, and the surrounding communities under a separate municipal authority. In 1924 harbor dredging resumed, and the refuse was used to create a zone for loading peanut shipments at the north end of the harbor. With the completion of the railway to the Niger Valley in 1923, the port of Dakar entered another period of rapid growth. Dakar's population reached 40,000 by 1924 and exceeded 92,000 by 1936.

As tensions in Europe increased, the administration improved the submarine base at Dakar, added concealed oil storage tanks, and constructed a floating dry dock in 1938. After France's defeat in 1940, Dakar's governor general Boisson remained loyal to the Vichy government and repelled an invasion by troops under the command of Charles DeGaulle on September 23 through 25. However, the Allies controlled the seas, making communication with Vichy France difficult, and Dakar's port became nearly idle as a result of the war. Despite attempts to restore trade by means of a road across the Sahara Desert, the local economy stagnated, and Dakar eventually yielded to the Free French in November 1942 following the Allied invasion of North Africa.

As the largest urban center in French West Africa, Dakar was a focal point for labor unrest following the end of World War II. A strike by workers on the Dakar coal dock in November 1945 was the first in a series that culminated in the Senegalese general strike of January 1946. Dakar's workers, both European and African, became the most thoroughly unionized in French West Africa, and in 1947, African railroad workers in Dakar led a five-month railway strike that spread to the rest of the colonies. Dakar also became a center of political activity that propeled men like Mahmadou Lamine-Guèye, Leopold Senghor, and Mahmadou Dia into office.

Dakar expanded again after the war, as a large influx of rural migrants raised its population to more than 250,000 by 1952. New housing developments included Grand-Dakar and the SICAP neighborhoods north and northwest of Medina, while other African neighborhoods filled in the peninsula around Dakar. In June 1960, Dakar became the capital of the Mali Federation, and remained the capital of Senegal after the federation dissolved. The city is also home to the University of Dakar, the Institute Fondamental d'Afrique Noire, a major research facility on African history and culture, and Gorée Island, a United Nations Educational, Scientific, and Cultural Organization World Heritage Site.

JAMES A. JONES

See also: **Senegal: Colonial Period: Four Communes: Dakar, Saint-Louis, Gorée, and Rufisque.**

Further Reading

Betts, R. F. "Imperial Designs: French Colonial Architecture and Urban Planning in Sub-Saharan Africa." In *Africa and the West: Intellectual Responses to European Culture*, edited by Philip Curtin. Madison: University of Wisconsin Press, 1972.

———. "The Problems of the Medina in the Urban Planning of Dakar, Senegal." *African Urban Notes* 4, no. 3 (1969): pp.5–15.

Charpy, J. (ed.). *Fondation du Dakar (1845–1857–1869): documents récueillis et publiés.* Paris: Larose, 1958.

Seck, A. "Dakar." *Cahiers d'Outre-Mer*, no. 14 (1961): pp.372–392.

Whittlesey, D. "Dakar and the other Cape Verde Settlements." *Geographical Review* 31, no. 4 (1941): pp.609–638.

Dar es Salaam

Tanzania's largest city, main industrial center, and former capital, Dar es Salaam has over the past century acted as the principal link between African peoples of the territory and the wider world. Its historical importance as an economic and cultural entrepot has resulted in the emergence of a cosmopolitan modern city whose population contains substantial South Asian, Middle Eastern, and European minorities as well as a diverse African population drawn from throughout East and Central Africa.

Located on a fine natural harbor, the site was selected by Seyyid Majid, Sultan of Zanzibar, in 1862 as a base to consolidate his hold on the East African coast and the caravan trade with the interior. After an initial burst of building, the settlement became known as Dar es Salaam or Dar Salaam (Haven of Peace, Abode of Peace). After the death of Majid in 1870, however, it was neglected by his successor, Seyyid Barghash. Nevertheless, fueled by an expanding trade in agricultural products with the predominantly Zaramo hinterland, Dar es Salaam continued to grow. By the mid-1880s the population numbered several thousand, including the indigenous Shomvi Swahili, whose village at Mzizima was soon to be engulfed by the town, alongside numerous Zaramo, Arab officials, soldiers and traders, and Indian merchants.

After a period of local resistance in the late 1880s, Dar es Salaam was subordinated to German and later British colonial rule, becoming in 1891 the capital of German East Africa (after 1920, Tanganyika). In subsequent years the kernel of the modern town was developed. A port was constructed on the western side of the creek on which the town is situated, and official and European residential buildings were erected to the north. Lutheran and Catholic churches were built on the creek front, and two urban hospitals were established. Adjacent to the port an Indian commercial and residential area emerged. It has constituted the principal business center ever since. In the colonial period, the town was divided into three zones that represented the principal residential areas for Africans, Indians, and Europeans. In the 1920s an open space (Mnazi Mmoja) was established between the predominantly African and the predominantly Indian and European zones. The heart of the African town grew up around Kariakoo (a corruption of "Carrier Corps," the British Army division that had camped there after World War I), to the west of the business center. After an initial burst during German rule, the African population grew relatively slowly, having reached about 18,000 by 1900 (it was only around 23,500 by 1937). It contained urbanized communities of Manyema freed slaves and Sudanese and Shangaan ex-soldiers alongside the more numerous, though less permanent, African migrants from upcountry (most notably the Zaramo from the immediate hinterland). Migrants to the town predominantly worked as temporary blue-collar laborers, though there was also a small, educated minority employed as clerks and petty officials. By contrast, the Indian community grew rapidly after the British assumed control, doubling between 1919 and 1939 from around 4,500 to around 9,000.

Dar es Salaam's political importance was reflected in the construction of numerous government buildings along the creekfront, many of which are still in us—most notably, the governor's residence. Meanwhile, its development as a major commercial center was confirmed by the construction of a central railway line that by 1914 connected it with Lake Tanganyika and all points in between, and after World War I with Lake Victoria. In the areas surrounding the town sisal and coconut plantations were established, but Dar es Salaam's main economic role was as an entrepôt for the rest of the territory.

From the late-1930s the African population began to grow at an ever-escalating rate, thus exerting considerable strain on the urban infrastructure. By 1957 the African population had reached almost 100,000. The town's physical expansion was prodigious, incorporating former villages on the urban periphery such as Buguruni and Kinondoni, as well as officially planned European (Oyster Bay), Indian (Upanga; Chang'ombe), and African (Ilala; Magomeni; Temeke) suburbs. While housing construction boomed, however, the scale of rural-to-urban migration was also resulting in the emergence of shanties such as Mikoroshoni and Manzese, which exist up to the present.

The flow to the town was fueled by an upturn in the territorial and urban economies, which began in the mid-1940s and lasted for about a decade. Improved cash-crop prices, along with the extension of the docks, resulted in unprecedented levels of trade passing through the port. This prosperity was reflected in the commercial area, which in the years following the war was transformed in a construction boom. At the same time, secondary industries such as bottling and meat processing emerged for the first time. All of these developments, as well as an expansion of government employment (partly thanks to Dar es Salaam's elevation to municipal status in 1949), resulted in a growing demand for labor. Increasingly migrants, particularly from within the Eastern Province, were attracted by the opportunities offered by the town for earning money. Despite general prosperity, however, unemployment remained a persistent feature among the urban African population, and with the end of the boom in the early 1950s the position was dramatically exacerbated. While urban employment was actually contracting by the late colonial period, the rural-to-urban flow continued unabated and the symptoms of urban poverty became ever more apparent.

With the achievement of independence in 1961 the contraction in the urban labor market was reversed. Dar es Salaam's regional importance as a port grew, partly thanks to the completion of the Tazara Railway in 1975, which linked it to the Zambian Copperbelt. By the 1970s trade from as far afield as Zaire passed through the port. Meanwhile, there was a considerable expansion in industry—mostly import substitution—in the town, and the new government increased public-sector employment. As a source of income within the territory (which, as Tanzania, included Zanzibar after 1964), employment in the capital grew ever more important. By 1979 it provided 29 per cent of employment and 40 per cent of wages earned in Tanzania. Dar es Salaam continued to attract large numbers of immigrants from the rural areas. The population mushroomed, continually exceeding expert projections; by 1988 it exceeded 1.6 million. Urban resources were stretched to the limit. While the number in employment grew, it was outpaced by rates of urban unemployment. By the mid-1980s, with the Tanzanian economy in crisis, the majority of urban households were reliant in one form or another on the informal sector to get by. Meanwhile, although Dar es Salaam expanded dramatically after independence, the bulk of this occurred unplanned. The scarcity of surveyed plots encouraged squatting by homeowners from all income levels. As a result, the city now sprawls out beyond Ubungo to the west, Mbezi to the north, and Mbagala to the south. A dramatic increase in the numbers living in unserviced communities, along with the shortage of waged employment, has resulted in the corresponding growth of urban poverty and its associated problems.

Dar es Salaam in recent years has remained Tanzania's most important urban center (though no longer its capital, which was switched to the centrally located Dodoma in 1975). Its large population (around three million in 2000) provides an important market for domestically produced agricultural and industrial products. Its formal and informal economies provide the opportunity for millions to earn anything from a bare subsistence to substantial wealth. As the main transportation hub, commercial and cultural center, the home of numerous newspapers, radio and television stations, and the main university, it is the principle arbiter between Tanzania and the wider world. It continues to exert a disproportionate influence on Tanzanian society as a whole.

ANDREW BURTON

See also: **Tanzania.**

Further Reading

Armstrong, A. "Colonial Planning and Neocolonial Urban Planning: Three Generations of Master Plans for Dar es Salaam, Tanzania." *Utafiti*, no. 8 (1986): pp.44–53.

Banyikwa, W. F. "The Making of a Hybrid Millionaire City in Dar es Salaam, Tanzania." *Africa Urban Quarterly* 4, no. 3 (1989).

Bryceson, D. F. "A Century of Food Supply in Dar es Salaam." In *Feeding African Cities*, edited by Jane I. Guyer. Manchester: Manchester University Press, 1987.

Burton, A. "Urchins, Loafers and the Cult of the Cowboy: Urbanisation and Delinquency in Dar es Salaam, 1919–1961." *Journal of African History*, no. 42 (2001): pp.199–216.

Gilman, C. "Dar es Salaam, 1860 to 1940: A Story of Growth and Change." *Tanganyika Notes and Records*, no. 20 (1945): pp.1–23.

Iliffe, J. *A Modern History of Tanganyika.* Cambridge: Cambridge University Press, 1979.

Leslie, J. A. K. *A Survey of Dar es Salaam.* Oxford: Oxford University Press, 1963.

Leue, A. *Dar es Salaam: Bilder aus dem Kolonialleben.* Berlin: 1903.

Lugalla, J. *Crisis, Urbanization, and Urban Poverty in Tanzania: A Study of Urban Poverty and Survival Politics.* Lanham, Md.: University Press of America, 1995.

Sutton, J. E. G. (ed.). *Tanzania Notes and Records*, no. 71 (1970). Special edition, "Dar es Salaam: City, Port and Region."

Tripp, A. M. *Changing the Rules: The Politics of Liberalisation and the Urban Informal Economy in Tanzania.* Berkeley and Los Angeles: University of California Press, 1997.

Darfur: *See* Bagirmi, Wadai, and Darfur.

Daworo: *See* Ethiopia: Muslim States, Awash Valley: Shoa, Ifat, Fatagar, Hadya, Dawaro, Adal, Ninth to Sixteenth Centuries.

De Brazza: *See* Congo (Brazzaville), Republic of: De Brazza and French Colonization.

Debt, International, Development and Dependency

A debt crisis afflicted Africa through the 1980s and 1990s. Debt to northern governments and banks and to multilateral institutions like the World Bank and the International Monetary Fund (IMF) rose from $9 billion in 1970 to $109 billion in 1980, $270 billion in 1990, and $321 billion in 1997.

The debt crisis has its roots in the 1970s, when there was a surplus of investment capital and international banks made ever-riskier loans. In the mid-1970s, real interest rates were negative and developing country finance ministers were chased by bankers who urged that they take out what were effectively free loans; many did.

The election of Ronald Reagan as president of the United States in 1981 marked a dramatic change. Between 1979 and 1982, international interest rates rose 12 per cent. Suddenly, free loans were so expensive they could not be repaid; governments had to borrow more just to repay old loans.

At the same time, commodity prices fell sharply, and terms of trade fell dramatically. By 1988, African exports only bought 64 per cent of the manufactured goods that they would have in 1980; by 1993 this figure had fallen to 60 per cent. If African earnings had remained at 1980 levels, the extra earnings between 1980 and 1995 would have paid the entire debt twice over.

As Africa provided the basic resources for an economic boom in the north, the crisis grew in the south. Per-capita African gross domestic product (GDP) fell from $770 in 1980 to $639 in 1994, according to the World Bank; government revenues were also hit. The result was an economic crisis across Africa. The industrialized countries responded with slow increases in aid—from $10 billion a year in 1980 to $17 billion in 1989 and $21 billion in 1993. But more than one-third of that was food aid, loans, or technical assistance determined by donor governments. In the 1990s, grants averaged $12 billion a year, according to the World Bank. While these grants have eased the debt crisis, they have not compensated for falling commodity prices. With a huge debt burden, spiraling interest rates, and falling commodity prices, African countries used a mix of three measures: diverting money from social expenditure to debt service; simply not paying loans as they fell due; and "rolling over" the loans by taking out new loans to repay old loans.

Of the $321 billion in debt in 1997, $57 billion was arrears that had not been paid. Indeed, half the increase in debt between 1988 and 1998 was simply the piling up of unpaid arrears. Several African countries were expected to pay more than one-fifth of the entire GDP in debt service but, not surprisingly, they failed to do so.

The result was a net flow of wealth from south to north, which has continued since 1980. Each year in the 1990s, African countries borrowed $21 billion but paid back $25 billion in interest and principal repayments—a net transfer of $4 billion a year from Africa to the industrialized world. Each year unpaid debts grew larger and were added on to existing debts: total debt grew by nearly $8 billion a year. In other words, the cost of the debt burden was $12 billion a year—$4 billion in payments and $8 billion in increased debt. This is exactly what Africa received in grants, so aid really only filled the gap caused by the debt crisis.

Governments became increasingly dependent on aid to pay for social services, and that gave increasing power to the donor community, which began to impose political and economic policies. In the 1980s, the socialist bloc was an alternative provider of loans and policies, but with the end of the Cold War the victorious West was able to step up its demands for free market, neoliberal policies. This included a reduction in the role of government, privatization, and an increase in the role of the market. Water, health care, and education were commodities to be paid for; government spending fell sharply; primary school enrollment rates fell between 1980 and 1990. Cuts in spending were demanded both on political grounds and in order to release money for debt service.

As the crisis deepened and debt grew, donors and creditors could impose further conditions. By 1990, all aid was conditional on countries having IMF and World Bank programs, and if the IMF ruled that a government was not following the program, aid stopped. Governments were forced to cut spending and keep up debt service payments under IMF structural adjustment programs (SAPs).

The Cold War also had a direct impact on the African debt crisis, with both sides giving loans to its allies. But the West was much more extravagant in its lending. Nearly $19 billion was lent to prop up the apartheid regime, $13 billion to Mobutu Sese Seko in Zaire, $13 billion to military dictators in Nigeria, and $2 billion to Hastings Banda in Malawi. The majority-rule government of Nelson Mandela in South Africa was asked to repay the loans given to the apartheid state—in effect, Mandela was asked to pay the cost of his own previous imprisonment.

This caused a backlash in Africa, where there are growing calls to refuse to repay what under international law are known as odious debts. That is, if an oppressive regime borrows money and uses it against the interests of the people, then the debt should not be fall to a successor government. In 1982, early in the sanctions campaigns, U.S. banks were warned by the own lawyers that loans to apartheid South Africa might be ruled as odious and not be repaid, and lending did stop three years later. In 1999, the British House of Common International Development Committee used the term *odious debt* and called for cancellation of loans that had been made in the early 1990s to the genocidal government in Rwanda.

Recognition of the debt crisis and of the political nature of debt has grown since the crisis started in 1980. At first, each country had to negotiate each year with its creditors to roll over the loans it could not pay, or to obtain World Bank loans to repay commercial banks. In 1988, the Group of Seven (G7) meeting in Toronto, Canada, agreed that bilateral debt—that is, aid loans and unpaid export credits owed to governments—could be rescheduled on concessional terms, and 1991 and 1994 G7 meetings agreed to actually cancel some bilateral debt. However, the only large debt cancellation was explicitly political. In 1990 the United States wrote off $10 billion of Egypt's debt in exchange for its support of the first Gulf War.

By the mid-1990s the end of the Cold War had slowed the economic decline, and in some countries there was a small per-capita increase in GDP (the IMF claimed this was due to adjustment policies, but this was disputed within Africa). But total debt was still growing much faster. Most African countries were only paying part of the debt service that was due, but still spending more on debt service than on education or health. Debt was proving a block to development; since debt service had the first call on export earnings, the debt overhang was also discouraging foreign investment.

The realization that there was no chance of this debt ever being repaid finally led the World Bank and IMF to propose, in 1996, the Heavily Indebted Poor Countries Initiative (HIPCI) to cancel some of the debt of up to 41 countries, 33 of them in Africa. This gained substantial publicity as an "exit" from the debt crisis, and was significant because it was the first time that the World Bank and IMF had agreed to cancel some of their own loans. But the HIPCI was soon shown to be ineffective. It was very slow, granting debt relief to only two or three countries a year, and it proved to only cancel the debt that countries were not paying in any case. Mozambique and Uganda, the first countries in Africa to be promised debt relief, ended up paying almost as much as they did before the HIPCI—and still spent more on debt service than health care.

In 1999 the G7 met in Cologne and promised further debt cancellation under the HIPCI. But the proposals were widely rejected, both in Africa and by the international Jubilee 2000 movement, which was campaigning for cancellation of the unpayable debts of the poorest countries by the year 2000. They said Cologne did not go far enough, and that the poorest countries would still have heavy debt burdens; that too many deeply indebted countries, including Nigeria and Morocco, were excluded from the HIPCI; and that HIPCI debt cancellation remained conditional on even stricter structural adjustment programs, which were seen to be increasing poverty and restricting growth. Thus, the African debt crisis continues into the twenty-first century.

JOSEPH HANLON

See also: **World Bank, International Monetary Fund, and Structural Adjustment.**

Further Reading

Adams, P. *Odious Debts: Loose Lending, Corruption and the Third World's Environmental Legacy*. London: Earthscan, 1991.

George, S. *A Fate Worse than Debt*, rev. ed. London: Penguin, 1989.

Hanson, I., and A. Travis. *Breaking the Chains: The New Jubilee 2000 Debt Cutter's Handbook*. London: Jubilee 2000, 1999.

Payer, C. *Lent and Lost: Foreign Credit and Third World Development*. London: Zed, 1991.

World Bank. *African Development Indicators 1998/99*. Washington, D.C.: World Bank, 1998.

Defiance Campaign: *See* **South Africa: Defiance Campaign, Freedom Charter, Treason Trials: 1952–1960.**

Delta States, Nineteenth Century

By the beginning of the nineteenth century, the political economy of the Niger Delta was dominated by the more prosperous middleman trading states of Bonny (Ibani), New Calabar (Kalabari), Nembe-Brass, Okrika, and Itsekiri. These states are key to an understanding of the consequences of Euro-African connections in the nineteenth and twentieth centuries; they therefore captured the attention of Nigeria's pioneer historians in the middle of the twentieth century.

These pioneering scholars—K.O. Dike (1956) and G. I. Jones (1963) in particular—initiated discussions revolving around two overlapping themes in the history of the nineteenth-century Niger Delta. The first theme was the nature of the economic transition from the slave trade to "legitimate commerce" in palm produce, and the implications of that transition for the political stability of the Delta states. The second theme was the role of the British Consul, including the British Navy, in subverting the indigenous economic and political organizations before "formal" colonial rule was imposed in 1885. As a 1995 work edited by R. Law indicates, these themes are still generating considerable debate among historians of economic change in West Africa.

Furthermore, though these pioneering studies were primarily concerned with the economic and political forces of change in the Niger Delta, they also drew attention to another very potent aspect of change during the nineteenth century—the missionary factor. An extensive study of the implications of the missionary factor for the indigenous sociocultural and religious heritage of these Delta states was subsequently undertaken by two scholars in quick succession: Ayayi (1965) and Ayandele (1966). As with the study of commerce and politics, the need for a more in-depth understanding of the missionary factor in the Niger Delta has given rise to further case studies, including those authored by G. O. M. Tasie (1978) and W. E. Wariboko (1998).

In the centuries leading up to the economic transition (1600–1800), the middleman trading states in the Niger Delta had heavily relied on the foreign exchange accruing from the overseas slave trade to sustain their sociopolitical, cultural, and military institutions. This being so, the leaders of these states initially perceived the antislave trade movement of Great Britain, as translated through the British Consul to the Niger Delta, including the anti–slave

trade Naval Squadron in West Africa, as inimical to their immediate economic and political interests. However, their fear that ending the slave trade would be economically disastrous was unfounded for three reasons.

The prevailing high prices of palm oil, which made possible the huge profits between 1830 and 1850, provided adequate assurance that the "new" trade was equally a viable source of foreign exchange. It was also soon realized that the palm oil trade did not threaten to upset the existing production relations between the ruling merchant chiefs and the exploited servile members of their trading houses. Finally (and this is related to the above points) there was the realization that both forms of trade could be simultaneously pursued to maximize revenue. Hence the middleman states, notwithstanding the presence of the British Consul and Navy, tried to participate in both forms of transtlantic commerce between 1800 and 1850. As M. Lynn (1995) has argued, everything considered, the middleman states made a smooth transition with very little or no financial dislocation.

But what was the political relationship between those states that engaged in the slave trade beyond 1807 and the abolitionists in the Niger Delta during this phase of transition? Between 1848 and 1854, antislave trade treaties were signed between consul John Beecroft and the trading states. Thereafter, in all cases of treaty violation, one or all of the following sanctions were imposed on disobedient states and their potentates: naval bombardment of the city-state; and the denial or suspension of mutually agreed anti–slave trade compensation to the offending king. These actions to exterminate the slave trade marked the beginning of the agonizing chain of events that undermined the political sovereignty of the Delta states. Hence this period has been referred to as the "empire of informal sway" in the Niger Delta.

The second half of the century witnessed the advent of the Church Missionary Society in Akassa (1860), Bonny (1864), Nembe-Brass (1868), New Calabar (1874), and Okrika (1882). For the Niger Delta, this completed the coming together of the extraterritorial forces of change that worked concertedly to transform society. The missionary propaganda intended to culturally transform society was directed principally at the lineage or house institution (the basic socioeconomic unit of production and political organization in the Delta states). Because of the strategic relevance of the house to the overall survival of the trading states, the ruling traditional elite tried, unsuccessfully, to curb the influence of the missionaries. The success of planting the church, however perceived, was in part due to the active support given to the exercise by the British Consul and the European merchants trading in the Niger Delta.

This period of intense missionary propaganda coincided with the protracted economic depression of the nineteenth century; but it was the latter that intensified competition between the trading states for greater shares in the palm oil export market. Between 1863 and 1882, for instance, New Calabar had to protect its interior palm-oil producing markets by fighting against interlopers from the competing rival states of Bonny, Nembe-Brass, and Okrika. The social and commercial relationship between the Itsekiri and Urhobo communities also reached its lowest level as the economic crisis fostered disputes over prices to be asked and given in the trans-Atlantic trade.

The second half of the century also witnessed the resurgence of mutual feuding between trading houses vying for economic and political supremacy in their respective states. For example, S. J. S. Cookey (1974) has shown that the renewed internecine struggles at Bonny between the two most dominant groups of houses led to the founding of Opobo in 1870 by Jaja of Opopo. Between 1881 and 1883, similar internecine conflicts also led to the breaking up of New Calabar. These feuds provided needed excuses for the consuls to interfere incessantly in the internal affairs of the affected states before "formal" colonialism was imposed at the end of the Berlin Conference in 1884–1885.

The 1885 British declaration of the Oil Rivers Protectorate in the Niger Delta notwithstanding, no proper administration was put in place; for this reason, the period before 1891 has been referred to as the era of the "paper protectorate." However, with the establishment of the first full-fledged administration headed by Major (later Sir) Claude MacDonald in 1891, the coercive capacity of the evolving colonial state was strengthened to pursue the goals of the British "civilizing mission" to Africa. Shortly after the foundation of this maiden administration, the Niger Delta was politically renamed the Niger Coast Protectorate.

As defender of the civilizing mission the invigorated colonial state began to relentlessly denounce the kings of the middleman trading states as obstructionists to the attainment of the economic, sociocultural, and political goals of Britain in the Niger Delta. Among other things, obstruction to the civilizing mission meant resisting the planting of Christianity, with its alien spiritual and secular values, and—most important—resisting European trading companies seeking to establish themselves in the interior primary producing communities of Southern Nigeria.

The last point above was the greatest source of conflict in Anglo-African relations between 1885 and 1900. At close intervals during this period, the following Niger Delta potentates and middlemen were denounced as obstructionists to the civilizing mission before being dethroned and exiled from their communities: Jaja of Opobo in 1887; Nana of Ebrohimi-Itsekiri in 1894; Koko of Nembe-Brass in 1895; and Banu Suku of Okrika in 1896. J. C. Anene (1966), among other historians, has shown that the manner in which these men were removed marked the zenith of the "gunboat diplomacy" introduced by the British Naval Squadron in the years leading up to "formal" colonialism. In 1900, shortly after the removal of these strongmen, the political map of the Niger Delta was redrawn by subsuming it as a part of the new protectorate of Southern Nigeria under Ralph Moor.

WAIBINTE ELEKIMA WARIBOKO

See also: **Anti-Slavery Squadron, Decline of Export Slave Trade, Nineteenth Century; Berlin West Africa Conference; 1884–1885; "Legitimate Commerce" and the Export Trade in the Nineteenth Century; Religion, Colonial Africa: Missionaries.**

Further Reading

Anene, J. C. *Southern Nigeria in Transition, 1885–1906.* Cambridge: Cambridge University Press, 1966.

Ayayi, J. A. *Christian Missions in Nigeria, 1841–1891.* London: Longmans, 1965.

Ayandele, E. A. *The Missionary Impact on Modern Nigeria, 1842–1914.* London: Longmans, 1966.

Cookey, S. J. S. *King Jaja of the Niger Delta: His Life and Times, 1821–1891.* New York: Nok, 1974.

Dike, K. O. *Trade and Politics in the Niger Delta, 1830–1885.* Oxford: Oxford University Press, 1956.

Ikime, O. *The Fall of Nigeria: The British Conquest.* London: Heinemann, 1977.

Ifemesia, C. C. *Southern Nigeria In the Nineteenth Century: An Introductory Analysis.* London: Nok, 1978.

Jones, G. I. *The Trading States of the Oil Rivers: A Study of Political Development in Eastern Nigeria.* London: Oxford University Press, 1963.

Law, R. (ed.). *From Slave to "Legitimate" Commerce: The Commercial Transition in Nineteenth Century West Africa.* Cambridge: Cambridge University Press, 1995.

Lynn, M. *Commerce and Economic Change In West Africa: The Palm Oil Trade in the Nineteenth Century.* Cambridge: Cambridge University Press, 1997.

———. "The West African Palm Oil Trade in the Nineteenth Century and the 'Crisis of Adaptation.'" In *From Slave to 'Legitimate' Commerce: The Commercial Transition in the Nineteenth Century West Africa*, edited by Robin Law. Cambridge: Cambridge University Press, 1995.

Mbaeyi, P. M. *British Military and Naval Forces in West African History, 1807–1874.* London: Nok, 1978.

Ofonagoro, W. I. *Trade and Imperialism in Southern Nigeria 1881–1929.* London: Nok, 1979.

Tasie, G. O. M. *Christian Missionary Enterprise in the Niger Delta, 1864–1918.* Leiden: E. J. Brill, 1978.

Wariboko, W. E. *Planting Church-Culture at New Calabar: Some Neglected Aspects of Missionary Enterprise in the Eastern Niger Delta, 1865–1918.* Bethesda, Md.: International Scholars, 1998.

Democracy: Postcolonial

The political frameworks bequeathed to the African continent at the beginning of the postcolonial era embodied an authoritarian-democratic paradox in which African leaders educated in authoritarianism during the colonial era were expected to perform like seasoned experts in democracy. Despite their almost complete disregard for the promotion of democratic values during the colonial era, departing colonial administrators hastily constructed multiparty political arrangements that purported to embody Western democratic ideals—such as systems of checks and balances—in which offices of the president, legislatures, and judiciaries would balance each other's power and check the emergence of authoritarianism. The relatively decentralized Westminster model of parliamentary governance was grafted onto the authoritarian structures of colonial rule in the former British colonies, and the more centralized Elysée model was similarly introduced into France's former colonies. For the most part, however, the so-called democracies left behind by the departing colonial powers represented largely untested and ill-suited political practices and procedures that in any case were not grounded in African traditions or political cultures.

Except in the unique case of Botswana, the first generation of African leadership resolved this paradox of independence by replacing the political systems left behind by the former colonial powers with more authoritarian forms of governance based on a centralization of power and personal rule. Even the most principled of African leaders invariably turned to a variety of authoritarian measures to enhance their political power and ensure political survival at the expense of competing political interests. Those actions taken included the staffing of administrations, militaries, and police forces with members of the leader's ethnic or clan groups, as well as with those of their principal ethnic or clan allies, and the rejection of "federalist" arrangements, such as constitutional amendments, that allowed for the political autonomy of groups or regions based on ethnic, linguistic, or religious claims. Another trend was the marginalization, or even disbanding, of independent parliaments and judiciaries that at best became "rubber stamp" organizations incapable of serving as a check on the powers of the executive. The imprisonment or exile of vocal critics from civil society, including labor unions, student organizations, and religious groups; and the outlawing of rival political parties was another representative action.

During the last decade of the twentieth century, however, dozens of countries in Africa, Asia, Latin America, and Eastern and Southern Europe made transitions from authoritarian to democratic forms of governance, prompting proponents of democracy to speak of the third wave of democratization in world history, the first two waves having occured in the 1820s and 1940s. In the case of Africa, this third wave was sparked by the fall of the Berlin Wall in 1989. The collapse of single-party regimes throughout Eastern Europe and the former Soviet Union set powerful precedents for African prodemocracy activists who already had begun organizing against human rights abuses and political repression. Severe economic stagnation and decline in most African economies served as the internal spark for political discontent. The most notable outcome of this historic turning point, often referred to as Africa's "second independence" or "second liberation," was the discrediting of more than 30 years of experimentation with single-party political systems in favor of more democratic forms of governance based on multiparty politics and the protection of human rights.

The third wave of African democratization has fostered both optimism and pessimism. Optimism was initially generated by a host of early successes, such as the national conference experiment in Benin. This third wave culminated in what numerous observers have referred to as the South African "miracle": the emergence of Nelson Mandela as the first democratically elected leader of South Africa. Pessimism increasingly has been generated by the simple reality that several transitions to democracy have resulted in democratic decay, often ending in military coups d'état and a return to authoritarianism. In the case of Niger, for example, Colonel Ibrahim Maïnassara Baré achieved the dubious honor of leading the first successful coup d'état against a democratically elected government in francophone West Africa since the beginning of the third wave of democratization. In a throwback to an earlier era of authoritarian rule and highly questionable democratic practices, Colonel Baré announced that there would be multiparty elections in 1996, presented himself as the "civilian" candidate of the ruling party, and subsequently won what international observers agreed to be a grossly flawed electoral contest. Less than three years later, Baré was assassinated in a military coup and replaced by Commander Daouda Malam Wanke. Needless to say, Wanke's promise of holding free and fair democratic elections in 1999 was greeted warily by the general population.

Even in those cases marked by a successful transition to more democratic forms of governance, newly elected leaders are confronted with the long-term challenge of ensuring the consolidation (institutionalization) of democratic practices in political systems still marked by democratic fragility. "The frequency of democratic breakdowns in this century—and the difficulties of consolidating new democracies—must give serious pause to those who would argue . . . for the inevitability of global democracy," explains Larry Diamond, a senior research fellow at the Hoover Institution. "As a result, those concerned about how countries can move 'beyond authoritarianism and totalitarianism' must also ponder the conditions that permit such movement to endure. . . . To rid a country of an authoritarian regime or dictator is not necessarily to move it fundamentally beyond authoritarianism" (Diamond).

One means for assessing the consolidation of democracy is to examine the evolution of political rights enjoyed by African populations, including the ability to form political organizations free from government intrusion; the meaningful representation of ethnic, racial, religious and other minority groups in the political process; and the right to choose national and local political leaders through free and fair competitive elections. Although individual countries will obviously vary, the African continent as a whole has benefited from the steadily rising protection of political rights since 1989. It is important to note, however, that the establishment of a multiparty political system (most often cited by Western observers as the lynchpin of democratic practice) can actually undermine the process of democratic consolidation, especially when electoral arrangements make it difficult, if not impossible, for the opposition party to emerge victorious in national elections. In the case of Botswana, for example, the ruling Botswana Democratic Party has controlled the reins of power since independence in large part due to a political system that heavily favors the incumbent president and his ruling party.

It is precisely for this reason that some proponents of democratization argue that the true test of Africa's newly established democratic systems is their ability to foster and survive the alternation of power between rival political parties. Benin stands out as a model of a newly established, multiparty democracy that has successfully weathered an alternation of power through the ballot box. The net political outcome of the 1990 national conference was the 1991 holding of "founding elections," in which a technocrat, Nicéphore Soglo, was elected president. Mathieu Kérékou, the former Marxist dictator, graciously accepted defeat and retired from the political system, only to return five years later as the leading opposition candidate in the 1996 presidential elections. With Soglo's reelection campaign severely hampered by the poor performance of the national economy and public perceptions of his disregard for the average citizen, Kérékou overcame the political odds and emerged victorious in the presidential elections. Dubbed the "chameleon" by friends and enemies alike, Kérékou returned to office serving as a powerful example of the further consolidation of democratic practices on the African continent.

A second means for assessing the consolidation of democracy is to determine the nature and depth of civil liberties enjoyed by African populations, including the right to freedom of speech and assembly; access to vigorous, independent media; constitutional guarantees of due process by independent judiciaries; freedom of religion and worship; and the general protection of individual rights regardless of one's ethnicity, race, religious creed, or gender. Although individual cases will obviously vary, the African continent as a whole has also benefited from the steadily rising protection of civil liberties since 1989. It is precisely for this reason, argue optimists of Africa's democratic prospects, that one can speak of the gradual strengthening of a democratic culture that increasingly will become self-sustaining.

The caution one must nonetheless exert when assessing the consolidation of newly formed democracies is clearly demonstrated by events in Zambia, a country that in 1991 made a successful transition from a single-party system headed by President Kenneth Kaunda to a multiparty political system under the leadership of President Frederick Chiluba of the Movement for Multiparty Democracy (MMD). Eighteen months after achieving victory, Chiluba reinstated a "state of emergency" that had existed throughout Kaunda's rule, and arrested and detained without charges at least 14 members of the official opposition, the United National Independence Party. Critics of the government's actions drew parallels between Kaunda's use of states of emergency during the 1970s and the 1980s to silence political opponents and Chiluba's desire to curb rising criticism of his regime's inability to resolve Zambia's pressing economic problems. Most important, critics noted that the domination of Zambia's parliament by Chiluba's ruling MMD party (125 out of 150 seats) called into question the independence of the legislature from the executive, especially after Chiluba was successful in acquiring legislative approval for his harsh measures. Indeed, prior to the presidential elections of 1996, Chiluba oversaw the ratification of two constitutional amendments that harkened back to the authoritarian excesses of his predecessor and threatened to undermine the very democratic political system he sought to create. The first required that the parents of any presidential candidate be Zambians by birth; the second limited any presidential candidate to two terms of office. Since Kaunda's parents were born in neighboring Malawi, and he had ruled Zambia for a total of 27 years (1964–1991), he was forced to withdraw from the race. Chiluba's political maneuvering removed the only serious challenge to his rule and ensured his reelection.

Whether Africa's third wave of democratization will result in further democratic consolidation or democratic decay will largely depend on how the new generation of democratically elected elites respond to the authoritarian-democratic paradox. Will they graciously accept defeat and join the ranks of the loyal opposition, as was the case in Soglo's defeat in the 1996 Benin presidential elections, or will they increasingly turn to a variety of authoritarian tactics to maintain themselves in power at any cost, as Chiluba's manipulation of the 1996 Zambian presidential elections illustrates? Indeed, the response of the first generation of African leaders to this authoritarian-democratic paradox in the 1950s ushered in nearly four decades of single-party rule. The ways in which Africa's newly elected democratic leaders resolve these paradoxes during the decade of the 1990s and beyond potentially portend the creation of new forms of political rule destined to last well into the beginning of the twenty-first century.

PETER J. SCHRAEDER

See also: **Political Systems.**

Further Reading

Ake, C. *Democracy and Development in Africa.* Washington, D.C.: Brookings Institution, 1996.

Bratton, M., and N. van de Walle. *Democratic Transitions in Africa: Regime Transitions in Comparative Perspective.* Cambridge: Cambridge University Press, 1997.

Buijtenhuijs, R., and C. Thiriot. *Democratization in Sub-Saharan Africa, 1992–1995: An Overview of the Literature.* Leiden: African Studies Centre, 1995.

Clark, J. F. and D. Gardinier (eds.). *Political Reform in Francophone Africa.* Boulder, Colo.: Westview Press, 1997.

Ottaway, M. (ed.). *Africa's New Leaders: Democracy or State Reconstruction?* Washington, D.C.: Carnegie Endowment for International Peace, 1999.

Schaffer, F. C. *Democracy in Transition: Understanding Politics in an Unfamiliar Culture.* Ithaca, N.Y.: Cornell University Press, 1998.

Demography: *See* Population and Demography.

Denkirya: *See* Akan States: Bono, Denkyira, Wassa, Akyem, Akwamu, Fante, Fifteenth to Seventeenth Centuries:

Development, Postcolonial: Central Planning, Private Enterprise, Investment

The underlying basis for public planning in Africa is development. Almost all African states have as their primary objective the goal of raising the quality of life of their citizens. This goal—variously referred to as development, modernization, or economic growth—has dominated discussions on Africa since the 1950s, when nationalist leaders in the various territories that make up the modern countries of Africa challenged colonial rule for independence. During the early years of independence, in the 1960s and 1970s, development remained the single most important goal of African countries. Now, in the twenty-first century and in the wake of independence, the various countries have continued to struggle to achieve a better quality of life.

African countries' approach to development was conditioned by the particular circumstances in which the countries found themselves at independence. In almost all countries the governments faced mounting expectations from a restless populace that saw in independence the only hope they had of transforming their impoverished conditions. People looked up to the government to satisfy their aspirations for a higher quality of life through the provision of better economic opportunities such as higher-paying jobs, social services, education, health care, and a reliable infrastructure. Despite their promises of improved economic and social conditions, most of the nationalist leaders soon realized that the new states did not have adequate resources for them to work with in satisfying the expectations and aspirations of their citizens. With its low earnings, tedious working conditions, and long hours, agriculture continued to be the principal source of income for most people. Because industries were few, most countries were deprived not only of the high wages found in the industrial sector but also of the economies of scale that industry generates. Due to such weaknesses in the postcolonial economies, taxes and export earnings, two principal sources of revenue for any state, were much too low to enable African states to meet the development needs of their citizens. In addition to public resource deficiencies, the private sector was either too weak or virtually insignificant because of the low level of private savings. This situation led most African governments to define their responsibility at independence not only in terms of protection, regulation, and the provision of basic social services but also in terms of resource mobilization and production. To perform such tasks required careful planning. Consequently, postcolonial African governments devised long range, five-year development plans that served as the mechanism through which they sought to plan and hasten the development of their societies.

Even though there was hardly a country in Africa that did not devise a five-year development plan as the basis of economic strategy, there were enormous differences in both content and style among the plans of the various countries. The basic component of a five-year plan is a broad statement of economic and social goals, the mechanisms through which to realize such goals, and the list of activities and projects to be undertaken so as to accomplish the goals. Five-year plans included mechanisms through which the activities would be financed, and details of the amount of financing that would come from the government, the private sector, and/or from loans. Each five-year plan was usually divided into short-range annual plans. The five-year and annual plans were further divided into sectoral components—that is, activities in various specialized areas such as health, education, roads, agriculture, and telecommunications. The appeal of such plans for African nations was that they enabled the nations to mobilize resources despite a lack of capital, and to organize the use of such resources in an efficient manner.

Although all African states were involved in planning, they did not all adopt the same ideological approach to guide their respective societies toward economic and social development. One can identify three different ideological perspectives that were employed at one point or another by different countries in their planning processes. Some countries adopted an orthodox Marxist approach—that is, the state played an activist role by deciding, directing, and regulating economic policies, as well as engaging in the production and distribution of goods and services. Among countries in this category were Ethiopia (1976), the Democratic Republic of Congo-Brazzaville (1969), Somalia (1970), and Benin (1974). These countries' strategy was to bring about a complete transformation from what they saw as the corruption and ills of capitalism to a classless egalitarian system. Other countries, including Côte d'Ivoire (Ivory Coast), Malawi, and Kenya, adopted a more capitalistic approach toward development. The state's role in the economies of these countries was theoretically detached and limited to regulatory activities. In practice, however, it still was very involved, although not nearly as much as the Marxist-socialist states. The third ideological orientation that guided economic planning in Africa was a variant of socialist ideologies. These ranged from the humanist socialism of Kenneth Kaunda in Zambia to the communal socialism model (ujama) of Julius Nyerere of Tanzania. Many countries did not often profess a rigorous ideological orientation as a guiding principle. But even in such countries, such as Nigeria and Cameroon, the state often played a significant role in mobilizing and organizing production.

Through the process of planning, African governments became deeply involved in economic production, creating state-owned companies known as parastatals. Many nations also sought to eliminate foreign competition, through import substitution and high external tariffs for imports. Others took over some foreign-owned companies through a process known as nationalization, while others reserved certain sectors of the economies mainly for nationals. African governments also became involved in providing subsidies to their nationals, to enable them to defray the cost of items ranging from grain to fertilizers or insecticides.

Despite the efforts at public planning for development in Africa, the economic situation in most countries in the region during the 1980s became worse. A fall in global demand for Africa's predominantly agricultural products due to the economic recession in most developed countries lowered prices and led to an economic slump in Africa. Because most countries had borrowed substantial amounts during the 1970s to finance their development, or to pay for oil during the global oil crisis of the 1970s, the stagnant economy led to a heightened debt problem. Interest on the debt itself took up sizable shares of most countries' export earnings. For some countries in the Sahel and in southern Africa, drought and wars exacerbated an already serious situation by further decreasing agricultural production, especially food crops. The overall consequence of the situation was a revenue shortfall of unprecedented magnitude. Meanwhile, expenditures kept on mounting, leading to massive deficit in most countries. In an attempt to focus global attention to the situation, the United Nations (UN) convened a special conference in 1986 on what became known as the African Economic Crisis.

Despite efforts on the part of the UN; other multilateral, bilateral, and nongovernmental groups; and African governments and nongovernmental organizations, the economic and social problems in Africa remained unresolved.

The African economic crisis that started in the late 1970s and early 1980s has continued into the new millennium. It has led many to question the wisdom of various aspects of public planning in Africa, especially those involving the state's engagement in various productive activities through parastatals. Other aspects of public planning such as subsidies, inefficient revenue collection, overvalued currencies, trade restrictions, poor governance, a bloated civil service, ill-informed economic priorities, and poor project choices have also been singled out for criticism. The World Bank and the International Monetary Fund (IMF) required African countries to undertake reforms laid out in structural adjustments programs before they could receive funds from these two organizations. The adjustments required by the World Bank and IMF in Africa call for a restructuring and a complete restoration of a market economy with little government involvement to correct the imbalance between demand and supply.

By the early 1990s over 30 countries had accepted the World Bank's conditions. In all the countries, five-year plans were virtually derailed. Although some form of planning continues to be performed in Africa at the beginning of the twenty-first century, the plans are reactive, short range, and market driven rather than comprehensive or far reaching.

MOSES K. TESI

See also: **Cameroon: Independence to the Present; Ethiopia: Famine, Revolution, Mengistu Dictatorship, 1974–1991; Côte d' Ivoire (Ivory Coast): Independence to the Present; Kenya: Independence to the Present; Malawi: Independence to the Present; Nigeria: Agriculture, Irrigation, Rural Development; Nigeria: Industry, Oil, Economy; Tanzania (Tanganyika): Democracy and Capitalism: 1990 to the Present; World Bank, International Monetary Fund, and Structural Adjustment.**

Further Reading

Ake, C. *A Political Economy of Africa*. New York: Longman, 1981.

Berman, B. J. J., and Collin T. Leys (eds.). *African Capitalists in African Development*. Boulder, Colo.: Lynne Rienner, 1993.

Gordon, A. A., and D. L. Gordon. *Understanding Contemporary Africa*. Boulder, Colo.: Lynne Rienner, 1992.

Hyden, G. *No Shortcuts to Progress: African Development Management in Perspective*. Berkeley and Los Angeles: University of California Press, 1983.

Keller, E. J., and Donald Rothchild (eds.). *Afromarxist Regimes: Ideology and Public Policy*. Boulder, Colo.: Lynne Rienner, 1987.

Kennedy, P. *African Capitalism: The Struggle for Ascendacy*. Cambridge: Cambridge University Press, 1988. Nyang'oro, Julius E., and Timothy M. Shaw (eds.). *Beyond Structural Adjustment in Africa: The Political Economy of Sustainable and Democratic Development*. New York: Praeger, 1992.

Nyerere, J. K. *Uhuru Na Ujamaa: Freedom and Socialism*. Oxford: Oxford University Press, 1968.

Sandbrook, R. *The Politics of Africa's Economic Stagnation*. Cambridge: Cambridge University Press, 1985.

Schraeder, P. J. *African Politics and Society*. Bedford St. Martins, Boston, 2000.

World Bank, *Adjustment in Africa: Reforms, Results and the Road Ahead*. Oxford: Oxford University Press, 1994.

Young, C. *Ideology and Development in Africa*. New Haven, Conn.: Yale University Press, 1982.

Diagne, Gueye, and Politics of Senegal, 1920s and 1930s

Senegal was exceptional among the French colonies in Africa because in a small part of it—the Four Communes of Dakar, Rufisque, Saint-Louis and Gorée—French rule was already established by he early nineteenth century, and their African and half-African inhabitants, as well as French ones, had privileges, including the vote, from 1833 on. Under the Third French Republic, there was a free and lively political arena in this multi-ethnic community called the Originaires. The communes (created in 1872 in Saint-Louis and Gorée, 1880 in Rufisque, and 1887 in Dakar) had their local councils, a general council for them was established in 1879, and there was a deputy in the French parliament, usually a European, until 1902 when the (partly African) Creole François Carpot was elected. Further inland, when French rule was extended (mainly from the 1880s) the Africans were treated as "subjects" without the rights of the Originaires, whose position was exceptional in twentieth-century French Africa. In fact, the French authorities became hostile to the Four Communes' privileges in the early twentieth century, some court judgments cast doubt on some of the privileges, and 2,000 of the 10,000 voters were removed from the register in 1906. However, with virtually complete freedom of the press and of political activity, Africans could respond to the feared threat to their position.

Galandou Diouf (1874–1941) was the first prominent African leader in the Four Communes, becoming a member of the General Council in 1909 with backing from the Lebous, who had a special grievance as the original inhabitants and owners of land in Dakar. In 1912 a mainly African party, the Jeunes Sénégalais, was founded in Saint-Louis (which had for a long time been the seat of the French administration of Senegal) by clerks, teachers, and others (Originaires held such posts all over French-ruled Africa). This party, which continued until 1921, called for better pay, more education, and other changes but—typical of such elite groups in Africa at that time—professed complete loyalty to the colonial power.

In 1914 Blaise Diagne (1872–1934), a Customs officer from Gorée, returned to the Four Communes and stood for election to Senegal's seat in the French National Assembly. He won in the second round and became the first man of pure African descent to serve as the deputy for Senegal. He promised to have the Originaires' position regularized, and found an opportunity to do so in World War I. The Originaires had been barred from joining the armed forces, besides being excluded from the compulsory military service imposed on France's African "subjects" in 1912. In 1915 Diagne persuaded the assembly to allow their enlistment. Then, in 1916, Diagne—who had become a deputy without being a French citizen—introduced a law passed unanimously by the assembly to declare that the Originaires were French citizens subject to the military service obligations of French citizens. Later Diagne was appointed by Prime Minister Clemenceau as a special commissioner for recruitment of more

Africans for the French Army in 1917–1918, and about 63,000 were recruited in French West Africa and 14,000 in French Equatorial Africa. Some Africans criticized Diagne for this, but he was reelected several times and remained a generally respected figure; Senegal's deputy for 20 years, he was even considered by some Africans of other French territories as an unofficial representative. He ran his own newspaper, called first *La Démocratie* and then *L'Ouest Africain Français*.

Having encountered considerable French hostility at first, Diagne signed an agreement in 1923 with the Bordeaux firms dominant in business in Senegal, under which he agreed to defend their interests in return for their support. Diouf, who served as mayor of Rufisque in 1921–1923, was for several years Diagne's close colleague, but later he disagreed with Diagne's policies and in 1928 stood against him in the candidacy for Senegal's deputy. Diagne won narrowly, amid allegations of rigging; soon afterward he served in the French government as deputy minister of the colonies, and went so far as to defend France's colonial forced labor policies before the ILO. Opposition, supported by the newspaper *Périscope Africain*, centered around Diouf, who was nonetheless beaten by Diagne again in 1932.

Diagne died in 1934 and Diouf was elected his successor. In the elections of 1936, which brought the Popular Front to power in France, Diouf was opposed by Amadou Lamine Guèye (1891–1968), a lawyer prominent in the Four Communes' politics, having been mayor of Saint-Louis in 1927; he had founded the Parti Socialiste Sénégalais (PSS), separate from the French Socialists of the SFIO, in 1934, and had an impressive party organization like none seen before in Senegal, but he lost the election to Diouf. Later a new Senegal "federation" of the SFIO was formed but the PSS remained in existence. The Popular Front government, and Marcel de Coppet, who was appointed by it as governor general of French West Africa, did not challenge the continuation of the French Empire, but only started limited reforms of which one was the legalization of trade unions. Politics in Senegal, as before, remained within the framework of French rule. Change was to come after World War II, when Guèye's political career continued and he won particular fame as the author of the law of May 7, 1946, declaring all inhabitants of all the French colonies to be full French citizens.

JONATHAN DERRICK

See also: **Colonial Federations: French West Africa; Senegal: Colonial Period: Four Communes: Dakar, St Louis, Gorée, and Rufisque.**

Further Reading

Johnson, G. Wesley, Jr. *The Emergence of Black Politics in Senegal: The Struggle for Power in the Four Communes, 1900–1920.* Stanford, Calif.: Stanford University Press, 1971.

Diamonds

Diamonds are a mineral resource of great value to a number of African countries; they have also featured prominently in several African conflicts—in Angola, the Democratic Republic of Congo, and Sierra Leone—where control of the diamond industry has been a primary military objective and a means of financing a continuing war effort.

The main African diamond producers are Angola, Botswana, the Central African Republic, the Democratic Republic of Congo (formerly Zaire), Ghana, Guinea, Namibia, Sierra Leone, South Africa, and Zimbabwe. Botswana, the Democratic Republic of Congo, and South Africa are producers on a major scale, though South Africa's diamond resources were in a steep decline by 2000. Namibia, with a relatively small output in terms of carats, is a lead country in the quality of its stones, of which more than 90 per cent are top-quality gems. Approximately half the world's diamond output (and a majority of gemstones) comes from the African continent.

South Africa, long seen as the world's leading diamond producer, has witnessed a steady decline in output since 1987 and by 1995 production had fallen below ten million carats a year, though gemstones still accounted for 9.8 per cent of exports for the year, and South Africa was then the world's fifth largest producer. The discovery of diamonds near Kimberley in 1867 transformed the economic outlook of the region and led to the influx of *uitlanders* whose numbers swelled dramatically when gold was discovered on the Rand in the 1880s. Diamonds and gold provided the wealth that would allow South Africa to begin its industrialization. The development of the diamond mines and the construction of the railways to service them led to the use of migrant labor on a large scale, which was to become a major feature of the South African economy thereafter, creating a number of political and social problems. One result was to be the extension of white control over African lands that were turned into labor reserves to serve the mines and so became the structural basis for the later apartheid system.

Only after achieving independence in 1966 did Botswana discover and develop its huge diamond resources, which became the lead export, thereafter providing up to 35 per cent of government revenues and helping fund a remarkably steady economic performance, one of the best in Africa.

Namibia's diamonds were developed by De Beers, the Anglo-American conglomerate, in the period after World War I, and control remained with the South African company until independence in 1990. Although Namibia's output is relatively small, at about two million carats a year (it is the world's eighth largest producer by volume), output consists mainly of high quality gemstones and these, variably, may account for as much as 80 per cent of the country's export earnings by value.

Approximately 90 per cent of diamond production in the Democratic Republic of Congo (DRC) is alluvial, centered upon Eastern Kasai, and almost all the output consists of industrial diamonds. In 1995 diamonds accounted for 17.2 per cent of Zaire's exports. Until 1986, when it was overtaken by Australia, Zaire (now the DRC) was the world's leading producer of industrial diamonds (it also produced some gemstones) and in 1993 Zaire passed Botswana in total output. However, precise figures for the country's output are difficult to assess since diamond smuggling is carried out on an elaborate scale. Estimates for 1993, for example, pointed to US$300 million worth of diamonds being smuggled out of the country every year. The country's one large-scale diamond producer, Societé Minierè de Bakwanga (MIBA) produced in excess of eight million carats a year in the 1980s and early 1990s before production declined, due to both smuggling and political problems. In 1993 diamonds became Zaire's principal source of foreign exchange while in 1994 output exceeded 18 million carats, although in real terms it was higher, the difference being accounted for by smuggling. At that time De Beers marketed all of MIBA's output, then valued at US$400 million.

During the conflicts of the 1990s, diamonds exported through Uganda became the principal source of finance for the rebels. Apart from MIBA, the balance of production comes from artisan diggers whose output steadily increased during the 1990s as chaos engulfed much of the country.

In 1973 Angola's diamond output exceeded two million carats a year, but thereafter output declined sharply as a result of the postindependence civil war. It recovered in the 1990s, even though the production area was fought over by government forces and União Nacional para a Independencia Total de Moçambique (UNITA). As in Namibia, a high proportion of Angola's diamonds (about 90 per cent) are gemstones. The main diamond producing area is Lunda Norte, and this was under UNITA control for much of the 1990s when the civil war continued to devastate much of the country. Diamonds then provided UNITA with an estimated income of US$600 million a year; these were smuggled out through Zaire (DRC) and were sufficient to finance the UNITA's war effort.

Sierra Leone normally produces about 0.3 million carats of diamonds per year, apart from those that are extracted and exported illegally, but during the 1990s diamonds played a major part in that country's civil war. For example, during Valentine Strasser's term of office the South African mercenary organization Executive Outcomes was hired, originally in 1995 after the bauxite, rutile, and diamond mining areas had been overrun by the Revolutionary United Front, to guard the diamond producing areas. And one of the diamond companies, Diamond Works, whose employees were rescued by Executive Outcomes, had in turn hired Lifeguard (an affiliate of Executive Outcomes) to guard its exploration properties in Sierra Leone at a fee of US$60,000 per month. In 1996 Executive Outcomes was found operating in both Sierra Leone and Angola guarding diamond mines.

The selling of diamonds has always been tightly controlled. In 1930 the major producers, led by De Beers, formed the Diamond Corporation to market the bulk of the world's rough diamond production. The corporation became known as the Central Selling Organization (CSO) and handled approximately 75 per cent of world output. In 1990 De Beers Centenary of South Africa and the Soviet (subsequently Russian) diamond monopoly Glavalmazzoloto agreed that 95 per cent of their rough gem diamonds for export would be handled by the CSO. The agreement was maintained after the breakup of the USSR. The CSO provides a guaranteed market for producers and stockpiles diamonds during recession periods so as to stabilize the market—that is, keep prices high.

De Beers of South Africa is the world's leading diamond producer; outside of South Africa it has formed Debswana Diamond Company in partnership with the Botswana government, while in Namibia Consolidated Diamond Mining (CDM) was a subsidiary of De Beers until 1994, when the Namibian government and De Beers formed Namdeb Diamond Corporation on a 50–50 ownership basis.

GUY ARNOLD

See also: **Angola: Peace Betrayed, 1994 to the present; Congo (Brazzaville), Republic of: Liberalization, Rebellion, 1980s and 1990s; Congo (Kinshasa): Post-Mobutu Era; South Africa: Gold on the Witwatersrand, 1886–1899.**

Further Reading

Bhagavan, M. R. *Angola's Political Economy: 1975–1985.* Uppsala, Sweden: Scandinavian Institute of African Studies, 1986.

Greenhaugh, P. *West African Diamonds: An Economic History 1919–83.* Manchester: Manchester University Press, 1985.

Harvey, C., and S. R. Lewis. *Policy Choice and Development Performance in Botswana*. Basingstoke, EWngland: Macmillan, 1990.

Hodges, T. *Angola to the 1990s: The Potential for Recovery*. London: Economist Intelligence Unit, 1987.

Sparks, D. L., and R. Murray. *Namibia's Future: The Nation after Independence*. London: Economist Intelligence Unit, 1985.

Weeks, J. *Development Strategy and the Economy of Sierra Leone*. Basingstoke, England: Macmillan, 1992.

Wilson, M., and L. Thompson (eds.). *The Oxford History of South Africa*, vol. 2, *1870–1966*. Oxford: Clarendon Press, 1971.

Diaspora: Colonial Era

Before the colonial subjugation of the continent, millions of black Africans found themselves in other parts of the globe, due chiefly to the trans-Saharan and the Atlantic slave trades. Virtually everywhere the diaspora encountered color and political disabilities. These were extended to Africa during the colonial era that began with the Berlin Conference of 1884–1885 and ended by 1960.

From 1885 to 1912, the European nations shared Africa, with the exception of Abyssinia and Liberia. South Africa and Algeria were occupied much earlier. In spite of a compelling need for a permanent remedy, the diaspora in the Asiatic and Arab worlds hardly showed any concern on account of their absorption into the local culture after emancipation and conversion to Islam. Elsewhere the story was different.

Even before the colonial conquest was accomplished, the exiles in America summoned a congress in Chicago in 1893. Racism and the future of Africa dominated the discussion. Bishop Henry Turner, founder of the African Methodist Episcopal Churches in Sierra Leone and Liberia, urged the diaspora to return and regenerate the homeland.

In 1897 the African Association emerged in London through the initiative of an Afro-Caribbean barrister, Henry Sylvester Williams, with the goal of drawing members of the race closer together. A Pan-African conference convened by the association three years later was attended by 32 representatives, including W. E. B. DuBois. After the London congress, many a colonial African working or studying abroad continued to join forces with the diaspora to combat discriminatory practices and the excesses of imperial regimes. An early exemplar was Bandele Omoniyi (1884–1913), a Nigerian enrolled at Edinburgh University. Although aware that private gain lay behind Europe's interference, he welcomed the ideas, techniques, and institutions being introduced by the adventurers, for these innovations were bridging the wide gap between backward Africa and preeminent Europe. It was no wonder then that he emphasized humane government, not immediate self-rule. Omoniyi's moderation not withstanding, the British overlords felt outraged by his links with socialist circles and articles in Scottish and West African newspapers.

Duse Mohammed Ali, an Egyptian educated at King's College, London, also resented the color bar. To refute wrong opinions about his country, he wrote *In the Land of the Pharaohs* (1968). Next, in collaboration with the Gold Coast lawyer and nationalist, Joseph E. Casely-Hayford, he started and edited *The African Times and Orient Review*. Short-lived, it enjoyed worldwide circulation. Among its staff in 1912 was Marcus Garvey, then sojourning in England. The Jamaican used the opportunity to read extensively about Africa and to interact with colonial Africans.

About the same time, the Negro history movement, with roots in the nineteenth century, was revived in the United States by the Jamaican publicist John E. Bruce and the Afro–Puerto Rican Arthur Schomburg; they inaugurated the Negro Society for Historical Research.

These developments firmly engraved in the mind of Garvey the idea of a respectable "Negro national state." Returning to Jamaica in 1914, he launched the Universal Negro Improvement Association (UNIA) and African Communities League. Two years later he moved to Harlem in New York City, where he brought out the organization's mouthpiece, *The Negro World*. The fact that it appeared in English, French, and Spanish with contributions by such mature writers as Duse Mohammed, John E. Bruce, and the Jamaica poet Claude Mckay ensured penetration of the entire black world. The colonial masters in Africa felt the impact of Garvey's loud voice and hastened to silence it.

To *The Negro World* was added, among other enterprises, the Black Star Steamship Company and the African Orthodox Church, headed by Bishop George Alexander McGuire of Antigua. Garvey's church exercised enormous influence upon African separatist churches in southern and central Africa—notably, Simon Kimbangui's messianic movement, which spread from the Belgian Congo to neighboring French Congo and Angola.

From the UNIA'S branches bestriding three continents, delegates came to a convention held in Harlem in August 1920. Since the auditorium accommodated only 25,000 representatives the rest, numbering several thousands, overflowed into the surounding streets. Garvey told the gathering that the 400 million black people in the world were determined to suffer no longer; if Europeans controlled Europe, Africa must be for Africans and their dispersed brethren. The time had come for black men to liberate and repossess their native land. After appointing Garvey provisional president of the African Republic, the convention adopted a Declaration of the Rights of the Negro Peoples of the World, embodying a comprehensive plan of action. Similar conventions took place between 1920 and

1925. Thus, though the colonial authorities prevented Garvey from visiting Africa, he aroused a very strong feeling of black solidarity among the masses there.

It was under the shadow of the assertive Garvey, whom he dismissed as either "a lunatic or a traitor," that DuBios summoned Pan-African meetings in London, Paris, Brussels, and Lisbon in 1919–1923. Garvey proved bold beyond his strength. His very threats united the "great powers" against him. They forced Liberia, which had agreed to be a nucleus of the proposed Negro national state, to renounce Garveyism. With the agitator's deportation to Jamaica in 1927 for alleged mail abuse, the UNIA sank into obscurity.

New associations surfaced. Of these the most militant in France was the *Ligue de la Defense de la Race Negre* (LDRN), led by a Guinean left-wing intellectual, Tiemoho Garan-Kouyate. The French government suppressed it because of its links with L'Etoile Nord Africaine, an anticolonial pressure group organized by Messali Hadj. It subsequently became the Algerian People's Party. Far less radical than the LDRN was the *Negritude* movement initiated by Aimé Cesairé of Martinique and Leopold Sedar Senghor of Senegal. They ran a journal (*L'Etudiant Noir*) and derived pride from the fact that, despite modern Africa's failure to produce sophisticated technology, the continent developed relatively peaceful, contented, and humane societies. In Britain the West African Students' Union and the League of Coloured People helped to keep the flag flying. Their leaders were, respectively, Ladipo Solanke, a Nigerian lawyer, and Harold Moody, a Jamaican medical practitioner.

Meanwhile, Italy's fascist ruler, Benito Mussolini, was itching to avenge his country's defeat at Adowa (Abyssinia) in 1896. In anticipation of the attack, the diaspora in Britain established the International African Friends of Abyssinia (IAFA) under the chairmanship of C. L. R James, an Afro–West Indian writer. Throughout the black world, Italy's unprovoked invasion in 1935 was seen as another rape of the continent. The failure of the League of Nations, of which Abyssinia was a member, to impose sanctions on the aggressor brought colonial Africans and the diaspora still closer together. In France the LDRN and L'Etoile Nord Africaine held joint meetings. Statements expressing solidarity with beleaguered Abyssinia were issued by them as well as by black workers in Holland and the French Caribbean.

Loss of confidence in the league also led to the transformation of the IAFA into the International African Service Bureau (IASB). George Padmore, a Trinidadian ex-communist, became chairman, while James now edited the Bureau's *International African Opinion*. Other prominent members included Amy Jacques Garvey, ex-wife of the provisional president; I. T. A. Wallace-Johnson of Sierra Leone, and founder of the West African Youth League; Jomo Kenyatta, who would lead the Mau Mau Revolt in the 1950s; and Nnamdi Azikiwe, future president of Nigeria. The IASB vigorously opposed proposals to transfer the British protectorates of Swaziland, Bechuanaland (Botswana), and Basutoland (Botswana) to white-dominated South Africa.

Further impetus flowed from the Atlantic Charter of August 1941. Since its principle of self-determination implied a repudiation of imperialism, dark-skinned patriots applied it to the homeland—contrary to the intentions of the charter's signatories. Thus the Pan-African Federation (PAF) was founded in Manchester in 1944 with two Guyanese, Dr. Peter Milliard and T. Ras Makonnen, as president and secretary general, respectively; when Kwame Nkrumah arrived from the United States, he was made regional secretary. (He was soon to become president of the Gold Coast [Ghana].)

The next year, in keeping with its aim coordinating the scattered exertions of black peoples, the PAF called a Pan-African congress at Manchester, the most famous in the series. Trade unions, political parties, and cultural associations in Africa sent delegates. DuBois, and Padmore were also among the 200 participants. After the congress, freedom fighters in Africa maintained contact with the PAF, resulting in the overthrow of the imperialists.

The conclusion that can be drawn here is that the diaspora offered an effective challenge to racism and foreign domination the open quarrel between Garvey and DuBois and the hostile contemporary environment notwithstanding. Not only did the exiles' numerous pressure groups serve as training grounds for budding nationalists; they also demonstrated the practicability of continental cooperation in Africa after the colonial era.

PETER OLISANWUCHE ESEDEBE

See also: **Commonwealth, Africa and the; Diaspora: Historiographical Debates.**

Further Reading

Chinweizu, Madubuike. *The West and the Rest of Us*. London: Nok, 1978.

Cronon, E. D. *Black Moses: The Story of Marcus Garvey and the Universal Negro Improvement Association*, Madison: University of Wisconsin Press, 1972.

Davidson, B. *Africa in Modern History: The Search for a New Society*. Middlesex, England: Penguin Books, 1978.

DuBois, W. E. Burghardt. *The Negro*. Oxford: Oxford University Press, 1970.

Esedebe, P. Olisanwuche. *Pan-Africanism: The Idea and Movement, 1776–1991*. Washington, D.C.: Howard University Press, 1994.

Garvey, A. J. *Garvey and Garveyism*. London: Collier-Macmillan, 1970.

Morel, E. D. *The Black Man's Burden: The White Man in Africa from the Fifteenth Century to World War I*. New York: Monthly Review Press, 1969.

Shepperson, G. "Notes on Negro American Influences on the Emergence of African Nationalism." *Journal of African History* 1, no. 2 (1960): pp.299–312.

Weisbord, R. G. *Ebony Kinship: Africa, Africans, and the Afro-American*. Westport, Conn.: Greenwood Press, 1974.

Diaspora: Historiographical Debates

The term *African diaspora* refers to the dispersal of people of African descent throughout the world, especially in those regions of the New World and Asia that were major destinations of the slave trade. In later times the definition of the diaspora has been expanded to include the voluntary movements of Africans and their descendants to Europe and the major metropolitan areas of North America. The term *diaspora* itself is a Greek word that was first used to describe the dispersal of the Jews after their defeat at the hands of the Babylonians. African and African American scholars adopted the term because of the obvious parallels between the two groups.

Although intellectuals concerned with Africans and people of African descent have observed the dispersal of Africans throughout the world as far back as the early nineteenth century, the actual term *African diaspora* was not used until the 1960s. Early predecessors to diaspora studies are numerous. They include scholars such as Robert B. Lewis (*Light and Truth: Collected from the Bible and Ancient and Modern History, Containing the Universal History of the Colored and Indian Race, from the Creation of the World to the Present Time*, 1844) and William Wells Brown (*The Rising Son; or the Antecedents and Advancement of the Colored Race*, 1876). These men were self-trained scholars who used the Bible and popular and classical historical references as the source of much of their information; they primarily sought to counteract the widespread prejudice and negative imagery directed against people of African origin. By the turn of the twentieth century, African descended scholars with formal academic training began to produce literature that dealt with the African diaspora in subject, if not by name. The most famous of these scholars was W. E. B. DuBois, who published *The Negro* in 1915; also significant was Carter G. Woodson, who wrote *The African Background Outlined* (1936). Both DuBois and Woodson were interested in questions of uplift, and DuBois in particular would be quite active in raising the consciousness that would eventually lead to the formal adoption of the concept of the African diaspora through his participation in the Pan-African conferences beginning in 1900.

In addition to African and African American scholars, a number of white scholars also began to work in the area of diaspora studies in the early twentieth century. One of the most significant of these scholars was Melville J. Herskovits. Herskovits was a student of the pioneering anthropologist Franz Boas, a man who had produced a significant body of work on the African diaspora himself; Herskovits's most important work was *The Myth of the Negro Past* (1941). The major thesis that he put forth was that African-descended people retained palpable "survivals" or customs, modes of expression, language, and artistic expression that are directly descended from their African ancestors. In reality, Herskovits's thesis was not materially different from conclusions that had been reached by earlier scholars, but his status as a prominent white scholar at a major university gave his ideas a level of exposure that black scholars could not attain. Although some scholars, especially the African American sociologist E. Franklin Frazier, were uncomfortable with Herskovits's conclusions, his ideas (with some modification) have become accepted as a basic conceptual framework in diaspora studies.

After World War II, the political situation in the world changed in such a way as to allow for a more open assertion of black identity, Pan-Africanism, and African nationalism. The first signal of this change was DuBois' reconvening of the Pan-African Congress after a hiatus of over 20 years. Unlike the congresses that had been held a generation earlier, which were held together by blacks from the diaspora, these meetings were soon dominated by Africans like Nnamdi Azikiwe and Kwame Nkrumah who would lead their respective countries to independence within the next two decades. By the 1950s, the civil rights movement in the United States and the granting of independence to Ghana created an atmosphere in which people of African extraction developed a keen awareness of the problems that they shared throughout the world.

It was in this environment that the term *African diaspora* was first used. According to the historian George Shepperson, the term first srose at the International Conference of African Historians in Tanzania in 1965 by historian Joseph Harris, in a speech entitled "Introduction to the African Diaspora." The first book to use the term was *The African Diaspora*, edited by Martin Kilson and Robert Rotberg (1976). The actual use of the term represented a turning point in the field in that it signified an overt political consciousness that had been previously missing from much of the work in the field.

Specifically, some scholars, especially those from European backgrounds, had been taken on the aura of scientific disinterest in their study of African people around the world. This disinterest was generally demonstrated by the avoidance of making any statements about their subjects that could be deemed overtly political. This approach was a source of tension between scholars. Those researchers who actively used their work to promote political and social change found themselves objects of derision by "neutral" scholars. St. Clair Drake gives the example of Herskovits, who despite being a hugely influential figure in diaspora studies, was quite hesitant to advise black students and was known to make disparaging remarks about the research of political scholars.

Also according to Drake, the formal recognition of the political implications of diaspora studies was not the only major change that developed in the 1960s. Drake argued that the 1960s also saw the end of what he termed "traditional" Pan-African interest in the diaspora. By "traditional," Drake meant the tendency of diasporan blacks to look at Africa as a unit and to focus primarily on the struggle of Africa against foreign domination. This came about due to African nations gaining independence and then often suffering coups and bitter political rivalries in which blacks outside of those nations were often unable to clearly differentiate heroes and villains. Another significant drift in focus developed between those researchers who had a continental definition of Africa and those African scholars and politicians who developed a continental definition of Africa that allowed Africans to develop common ground between the states of Sub-Saharan and northern Africa. Obviously such a definition was problematic, for diasporan Africans have almost universally been identified by "racial" characteristics.

Although there are limits to the utility of the African diaspora as a category of study, the concept still has the ability to explain many otherwise unclear differences. One of the most readily apparent contributions of diaspora studies has been a clearer understanding of the nature of racism and discrimination in different societies. Western researchers who studied societies such as Latin America and the Islamic world often assumed that these cultural regions lacked the racism that is endemic in Northern Europe and English-speaking North America. The reason for this belief was due to the fact that these countries tended to lack the prohibitions on interracial sexual relations and social intercourse that were common in Anglophone regions.

A major scholar who has worked in the area of Africans in the diaspora is Bernard Lewis, whose major works are *Race and Color in Islam* (1971) and *Race and Slavery in the Middle East* (1990). Lewis notes in his work that Islam traditionally cites several injunctions made by Muhammad and Islamic scholars that insist on the equality of people before God. Lewis, however, shows that even these injunctions of equality suggest that often in Middle Eastern culture there was the perception of Africans as different, and at least unattractive if not inferior. For instance, in the article "The African Diaspora and the Civilization of Islam," Lewis mentions a saying that claims a man should value piety above beauty and wealth, even to the extent of marrying a blunt-nosed African woman. Similarly, Lewis quotes the Prophet Muhammad, who once said that authority should always be respected, even when coming from a black Ethiopian. What these sayings show, according to Lewis, is the recognition that many within Middle Eastern culture perceive Africans as unattractive and inferior even if their religion clearly states that such beliefs are improper.

Lewis also demonstrates that though Arab culture allowed interracial marriage, these marriages most commonly involved Arab men marrying African women, not African men being allowed to gain access to Arab women. This fits within the patriarchal pattern of Arab society in which the most important factor is male Arab ancestry and the perpetuation of bloodlines. Although not as explicitly racist as the practices of Western societies, the result was often quite discriminatory.

In the area of work on the social roles of Africans in Middle Eastern and Asian society, there has been considerable research done not only by Lewis but also by another notable scholar, Joseph Harris, whose most notable work is *The African Presence in Asia* (1971), which is primarily concerned with settlements of Africans in Iran and the Indian subcontinent, most of whom had been slaves or slave soldiers. The most interesting of these groups were the Sidis, the ruling caste on the island of Janjira, which is located in the Indian Ocean not far from Mumbai. The island of Janjira was quite important because of its strategic location on the trade route between India and other areas to the west. The Sidis were apparently the descendants of military soldiers who gained control of the island and held it until 1879 when it came under the control of Great Britain. During the period of their power, they were allied with the Mughul dynasty of India, which, like the Sidis, was Muslim. Another example of military slaves cited by Harris are warrior slaves of Gujarat who gained control of the government of that region during the sixteenth century.

Diaspora specialists in Latin America have also produced a significant body of work that demonstrates the great variety of experiences that Africans have participated in throughout the world. Most notable from the diasporan point of view are comparative works dealing with the experience of slavery in Latin America and North America. A noteworthy book in this field is Carl Degler's *Neither Black Nor White* (1971), which compared the slave experience in Brazil and the United States. In this study, Degler makes many observations that have since become standard when comparing the racial traditions of Brazil with those of the United States. Specifically, Degler notes that although Brazilian culture readily accepted the idea interracial mating and did not develop the rigid social distance that characterizes white and black interaction in the United States, the society is not without racial problems. Degler notes that Afro-Brazilians have never had equal access to economic or political power, and have therefore never been able to compete effectively with Brazils' white population. In addition to the work of Degler, another major scholar of the Latin American portion of the diaspora is Leslie Rout, whose most notable work is *The African Experience in Spanish America* (1976). Rout's work covers much of the same ground as Degler's, but deals with the entirety of Spanish-speaking people in America. The work is notable in that unlike many earlier historians, Rout demonstrates that racial discrimination against Afro-Hispanics was and is a major fact of their lives. Rout cites policies in Chile and Argentina that had the affect of reducing the African population to insignificance, and he also records instances of active oppression in tropical South America.

One of the most significant areas of recent diaspora research has been that of women's studies. Most studies of the diaspora have focused on men, either consciously or not. Although some studies, like Robert Farris Thompson's *Flash of the Spirit* (1983) and Joseph Holloway's *Africanisms in American Culture* (1990), were concerned with topics that were practiced and affected by women (such as quilting, clothing design, and religious expression), the books were not expressly focused on women of the diaspora. Recent studies like *More than Chattel* (1996), edited by David Gaspar and Darlene Clark Hine, have moved to correct what had been a long-standing oversight. This collection of essays expressly focuses on women of the African diaspora during slavery. One essay of particular significance in this collection is "Africa into the Americas," by Clare Robertson, which surveys the literature on slavery in Africa with a special attention to matirfocality or social formations within which women take a dominant role in economic and food production within the household. Robertson is concerned with this question because scholars concerned with the African American experience have often cited African matrifocality as the reason behind female headed households in the United States. Another important section of this collection deals with the role diasporan women in rebellion and the culture of resistance.

Although the study of slavery is central to diaspora studies, scholars of the African diaspora rightly point out that slavery should not be seen as the sole focus of the diaspora. In this vein, works dealing with more recent social and political phenomena should also be mentioned. An important work of diasporan political and social history is Wilson Jeremiah Moses's *The Golden Age of Black Nationalism, 1850–1925* (1978), This book is concerned with the development of conservative nationalism which primarily sought to bring about "racial uplift," which is usually defined as attempts to improve the moral and cultural standards of black people in addition to improving their material well-being. In the context of nineteenth-century African American intellectuals, this meant largely emulating the values of the dominant white culture while still fostering a pride in blackness and sense of historic pride in the accomplishments of the African race. Although most of the figures in this book are African Americans, they are figures like W. E. B. Du Bois, Booker T. Washington, and Alexander Crummel—those who had a huge intellectual impact among people of African origin outside of America. At a certain level, one could make the argument that Moses's book really shows the origins of what became Pan-Africanism and by extension shows the foundations of the African diaspora concept. The connections that Moses makes between African American intellectuals and the diaspora are especially important for George Fredrickson's *Black Liberation* (1995), which compares the liberation ideologies of African Americans and black South Africans and is a sequel to Frederickson's earlier *White Supremacy: A Comparative Study in American and South African History* (1981), a work that was concerned with the development of white domination in both countries. *Black Liberation* focuses on the efforts of black South Africans and African Americans to overcome the inequities of the systems in which they found themselves. Fredrickson notes that despite the obvious demographic differences of the both black populations relative to their white antagonists, the strategic and ideological questions that were raised by both groups of leaders tended to be quite similar. Obviously, as Fredrickson notes, the end result of the South African struggle has been profoundly different from the conclusion of the civil rights struggles of the 1960s, but the parallels of mutual influence remain.

A scholar who has looked to the diaspora for political influence in anther direction is Manning Marable, whose *African and Caribbean Politics From Kwame Nkrumah to Maurice Bishop* (1987) examines attempts to establish Marxist/Leninist regimes in both the Caribbean and Africa, with a particular emphasis on the efforts of Kwame Nkrumah in Ghana and Maurice Bishop in Grenada. Marable focuses on the difficulty of translating Marxism, which was envisioned as a mass-based ideology, into a working reality in countries where there had been little or no tradition of organized labor. Generally speaking, Marable sees Ghana under Nkrumah as less mass-based in its politicization that Grenada. Grenada, however, had the misfortune of being a small country with an political economy despised by its powerful neighbor, the United States.

Throughout most of the twentieth century, students of the diaspora have tended to be centered culturally in the West. Most of the writers, whether black or non-black, African American, Afro-Caribbean, or African, all tended to examine the diaspora from a Western perspective, especially that of the United States. One of the truly refreshing changes in the study of the diaspora has been the emergence of scholars who instead examine the diaspora from the vantage point of Africa or Europe. St. Clair Drake's *Black Folk Here and There* (1987) was an important precursor to this trend. In this massive, two-volume work, Drake attempts to trace some of the fundamental issues of western perceptions of blackness within the diaspora to their roots in ancient and medieval civilizations. In moving to historical periods long before the rise of the Atlantic plantation economy, Drake manages to substantially broaden the scope of intellectual inquiry for diaspora scholars.

A seminal work among Africa-centered diaspora scholars was Kwame Anthony Appiah's *In My Father's House* (1992), which is noteworthy in that one of its central ideas is an attack on unity based on blackness, a central tenant of Pan-Africanism. Appiah argues that for people coming out of an African tradition, blackness in itself had no intrinsic value. Instead, the unity of blackness was essentially a defensive response based on the discrimination that members of the African diaspora felt in their dealings with whites. Appiah spends much of the rest of the book examining other sources of identity. Whether or not he finds something as powerful as the idea of race is debatable, but his willingness to confront long held assumptions is noteworthy.

Paul Gilroy, a sociologist of black Britain, is also noteworthy in his efforts to broaden the scope of the diaspora. *The Black Atlantic* (1993) is significant in that he brings several new levels of understanding to traditional issues within the concept of the diaspora. Specifically, Gilroy is interested in applying the concepts of postmodernism to black culture. He is also interested in demonstrating the interconnectedness of contemporary black British culture to African American, Caribbean, and African cultures. Like many within the postmodern tradition, Gilroy looks to unconventional "texts" to demonstrate the ties between the regions of the diaspora. Specifically, he examines contemporary popular culture and music to show how the various regions of the diaspora have learned from each other.

Of all of the new generation of diaspora scholars, the one who may be coming closest to fully establishing all links among people of African origin is Manthia Diawara. Although Diawara's *In Search of Africa* (1998) is more of a memoir than a formal academic monograph, it brilliantly demonstrates contemporary consciousness of the complexity of the diaspora. Diawara's method is to mix his own personal experiences with greater issues involving Africa and the diaspora. For instance, in the open chapter, he speaks of his class's reaction to Jean-Paul Sartre's "Black Orpheus," an essay that sees the *Négritude* movement as potentially a catalyst for a worldwide liberation movement instead of a narrowly black doctrine of consciousness raising. In later chapters, Diawara recounts his return to Guinea, the country in which he was born, and to Mali, the nation in which he grew to adulthood. In these chapters, he looks at the reality of Sekou Touré's legacy versus the lofty goals that Toure (Guinea's first president) had originally announced. He also examines questions like the impact of Western economic demands on the traditional production of art in Africa. As for the diaspora, Diawara examines African American writer Richard Wright's reaction to Africa in his book *Black Power* (1956), in which Wright demonstrates the seeming contradictory tendencies of black pride and a certain uneasiness with African culture. In later chapters Diawara examines other diasporan topics, from Malcolm X to hip-hop culture, for their impact on black people and the world.

Clearly the study of the African diaspora has continued to advance and expand since black writers first attempted to explain the history and role of African people in the world during the nineteenth century. The formal recognition of the diaspora concept itself in the 1960s was a major development, and the multiplying diversity of topics and perspectives from which the diaspora is being studied will guarantee the health of this discipline for the foreseeable future.

ANTHONY Q. CHEESEBORO

See also: **Du Bois, W. E. B. and Pan-Africanism; Ghana (Republic of): Nationalism, Rise of, and the Politics of Independence; Guinea: Touré, Ahmed Sekou, Era of; Négritude; Women's History and Historiography in Africa.**

Further Reading

Diawara, M. *In Search of Africa*. Cambridge, Mass.: Harvard University Press; 1998.

Drake, St. Clair. *Black Folk Here and There*. 2 vols. Berkeley and Los Angeles: University of California Press, 1987, 1990.

Harris, J. (ed.). *Global Dimensions of the African Diaspora*, Washington: Howard, 1982.

Gaspar, D. B., and D. Clark Hine (eds.), *More Than Chattel: Black Women and Slavery in the Americas*. Bloomington: Indiana University Press, 1996.

Gilroy, P. *The Black Atlantic: Modernity and Double Consciousness*. Cambridge, Mass.: Harvard University Press, 1993.

Difaqane on the Highveld

Difaqane is the plural form of the SeSotho word *lifaqane*. Used in the 1820s to designate raiding parties moving south across the Orange River into Xhosa and Thembu territory, the word gradually shifted in meaning. The plural form came to be used by historians to denote an historical era: the entire period of turbulence and warfare that swept various parts of the South African Highveld in the 1820s and early 1830s. The Xhosa word *imfecane* evolved in the same way into *mfecane*. Most twentieth-century historians treated the words *mfecane* and *difaqane* as interchangeable. Some historians have claimed, on slight evidence, that the words meant "the crushing" or "the uprooting."

Among the central events usually grouped under the heading of *difaqane* are:

- the migration, beginning in 1822, of Hlubi and Ngwane groups from Natal into the Caledon Valley, where they clashed with the Tlokwa, Sia, and other Sotho chieftaincies;
- the formation of the BaSotho nation under Moshoeshoe I, based at his stronghold of Thaba Bosiu in the Caledon Valley after 1824, from which grew the modern nation of Lesotho;
- the migration from Natal of the warrior chief Mzilikazi and a group of armed followers who engaged in large-scale cattle raiding and warfare in the central and northwestern areas of the Highveld. After a period of residence on the Vaal River, Mzilikazi moved his capital first to the Apies River not far from modern Pretoria, and then pushed into territory northwest of modern Rustenburg formerly dominated by the Hurutshe people. Although Mzilikazi preferred to call his nation the *Zulu*, the name that eventually stuck with them was the word applied to them by their Sotho enemies: *Ndebele*;
- the formation by the warrior chief Sebetwane of a similar armed following, known as Kololo, composed of diverse Sotho/Tswana groups, who raided widely in the western and northwestern regions before moving north across the Zambezi into modern Zambia, where he founded the Barotse kingdom;
- warfare among Tswana groups in the western and northwestern Highveld regions, chief among them the Hurutshe, Ngwaketse, Rolong, Fokeng, Ngwaketse, and Tlhaping;
- the consolidation of defeated sections of the Rolong and their eventual great migration to the Thaba Nchu area.

Historians once believed these events were causally linked in the following sequence: The rise of the Zulu kingdom under Shaka drove the Ngwane and Hlubi onto the Highveld. This caused the Tlokwa under the Queen Regent 'MaNthatisi to flee west, where they made war on the Sotho, the Rolong, and other groups. A vast miscellaneous horde of remnant peoples then raided in the northwest before attacking the Tlhaping capital, Dithakong, in June 1823, where they were defeated in thanks to timely assistance from Griqua riflemen. Taking advantage of these disruptions, Mzilikazi's Ndebele imposed their rule across the entire central, northwestern and northeastern Highveld until they were driven north by the Voortrekkers in 1836–1837.

This version of the difaqane was subjected to intense scrutiny by historians in the 1980s and 1990s. A revisionist polemic launched by Julian Cobbing insisted that the entire concept of the difaqane/mfecane had been flawed from the start by the systematic exclusion of disruptive influences stemming from European activities on the eastern Cape frontier and the Delagoa Bay region. The gradual infiltration of mounted raiders with firearms after 1780 could be shown to have created waves of dislocation in the western regions, well before the arrival of Nguni regiments in 1822.

The idea of the difaqane as a purely African affair collapsed in the face of the revisionist assault. It proved impossible to disentangle the intrusion of Griqua and Voortrekker groups from discussions of warfare on the Highveld. The idea of Shaka as a first cause was discredited by research revealing that warfare in the hinterland of Delagoa Bay in the eighteenth century was probably related to the militarization of Ndwandwe, Ngwane, Qwabe, and Mthethwa groups. Shaka's Zulu kingdom began to look like the result of these struggles rather than their instigator. Neither could eighteenth-century warfare in the northwestern interior be attributed to influences emanating from faraway Natal. Mzilikazi's kingdom was shown to have been much smaller than earlier historians had imagined, and his conquests confined to a much smaller area.

Doubt has been cast as well on the loss of life that may have resulted from the wars of the 1820s. The common nineteenth-century estimate of one million dead has been comprehensively discredited. It justified European conquest by suggesting that Africans had practically exterminated themselves on the eve of the "Great Trek" of 1836, thus leaving the land empty and available for colonization. Prior to the arrival of guns, African warfare on the Highveld and surrounding territories was aimed at the capture of cattle rather than the destruction of opposing forces. Early European travelers who found deserted towns and homesteads failed to realize that Africans had been living there, tilling fields and keeping cattle for upward of a thousand years. Many ruins they attributed to warfare were actually part of the long history of settlement.

The most important consequence of the wars of the 1820s and 1830s was the relocation, not the extermination, of people. Scattered and defeated populations gathered around effective military leaders. New nations arose, many of whom proved able to defy the power of white colonists for decades. The most important of these were the Basotho under Moshoeshoe; the Zulu under Shaka and his successors; Mzilikazi's Ndebele; the Swazi under Mswati and Sobhuza; and the Pedi under Sekwati. The emergence of these kingdoms permanently altered the face of Southern Africa.

It seems likely that future historians will drop the concept of the difaqane as a useful way of thinking about early-nineteenth-century South Africa. As more is learned about conflict in the eighteenth century it becomes difficult to set the 1820s off as a special era. African warfare on the Highveld forms a part of a larger story including colonial wars against the Xhosa and the arrival of the Voortrekkers.

NORMAN A. ETHERINGTON

See also: **Boer Expansion: Interior of South Africa; Mfecane; Moshoeshoe I, and the Founding of the Basotho Kingdom.**

Further Reading

Cobbing, J. "'The Mfecane as Alibi': Thoughts on Dithakong and Mbolompo." *Journal of African History*, no. 29 (1988): pp.487–519.

Hamilton, C. (ed.). *The Mfecane Aftermath: Reconstructive Debates in Southern African History*. Johannesburg: Witwatersrand University Press, 1995.

Lye, W. F., and C. Murray. *Transformations on the Highveld: The Tswana and Southern Sotho*. Cape Town: David Philip, 1980.

Omer-Cooper, J. D. *The Zulu Aftermath: A Nineteenth-Century Revolution in Bantu Africa*. London: Longman, 1966.

Parsons, N., *A New History of Southern Africa*. London: Macmillan, 1993.

Shillington, K. *History of Southern Africa*. London: Longman,1987.

Dinka: *See* Nilotes, Eastern Africa: Western Nilotes: Shilluk, Nuer, Dinka, Anyuak.

Diop, Cheikh Anta (1923–1986)
Historian

Accomplished archaeologist, historian, Egyptologist, writer and distinguished Pan-Africanist political thinker and leader, Anta Cheikh Diop emerged in the twentieth century as a cultural nationalist whose contribution to ideological debate helped to galvanize the struggle for independence in Africa. His emergence coincided with a time when the desire to locate Africa in its rightful place in history needed a solid cultural basis. Diop's classical work on African cultural history, as well as his exposition of ancient Egyptian civilization as purely African, has earned him an esteemed reputation in African and international scholarship.

His educational career at the Sorbonne in Paris—an institution then noted for its radical intellectualism—left a decisive impact on the budding Africanist historian. From 1946 on, Anta Diop became actively involved in the growing African students anticolonial and Pan-African movements for independence in Paris. He was a founding member, and later secretary general (1950–1953) of the student wing of the Rassemblement Democratique Africain, the first French-speaking Pan-African political movement launched in 1946 at the Bamako Congress to agitate for independence from France. He was one of the organizers of the first Pan-African Students Political Congress in Paris in 1951. And in 1956 and 1959, he participated in the First and Second World Congresses of Black Writers and Artists, in Paris and Rome, respectively. These international congresses and movements were influential in the development of the African liberation movement.

With his deep insight into the vitality of traditional African culture, Diop commenced painstaking research into the history of African civilizations. This work was an important part of the growing intellectual debate on colonialism and racism. Diop's framework provided—and still provides—African studies with some general hypotheses for research and several epistemologies in which to locate intellectual discourse.

Diop concluded a doctoral dissertation in which he made a breakthrough in reclaiming Egypt for Africa from an uncompromising African perspective. He postulated that ancient Egypt was a black African civilization in origin, people, and character, and that from pharaonic Egypt, part of the African civilization spread to Europe via ancient Greece and Rome. According to this thesis, scholars from Europe were informed by the Greeks and Romans, who had themselves borrowed from pharaonic Egypt. Black Africa, as stressed by Diop, is therefore the intellectual and scientific principal source from which Europe studied arts, law philosophy, mathematics, and science. Diop further argued in his thesis that black Africa set the pace in several other fields of civilization. Presented at a time when the prevailing atmosphere in Europe maintained European cultural superiority over Africans, Diop's revolutionary thesis was rejected by the authorities at the Sorbonne. His work (published in 1974 as *The African Origin of Civilization: Myth or Reality*) nevertheless garnered worldwide attention, establishing Diop as a distinguished scholar. Ever since, he has been associated with the reconstruction of the African past and the continent's place in world history.

In 1960, Diop was eventually awarded his doctorate by the Sorbonne, after a successful defense before a panel of multidisciplinary scholars. He returned to Senegal that same year, when his country became independent. In 1961, Anta Diop was appointed a research fellow at the Institut Fondamental d' Afrique Noire (IFAN) where he later set up a radiocarbon dating laboratory. At IFAN, he continued establishing his theory of ancient Egypt being the precursor of modern civilization. By 1980, Diop had become famous for his free-carbon-dating work for African scholars from whom he received archaeological specimens for identification and analysis. His own research culminated in the production of several books that were originally published in French, but are now available in English. These include *The Cultural Unity of Black Africa: The Domains of Patriarchy and Matriarchy in Classical Antiquity* (1978); *Black Africa: The Economic and Cultural Basis for a Federated State* (1978); *Pre-Colonial Black Africa: A Comparative Study of the political and Social System of Europe and Black Africa, from Antiquity to the Formation of Modern States* (1987); and *Civilization or Barbarism: An Authentic Anthropology* (1991). In all of these works Diop's commitment to, and search for, African dignity and self-empowerment through a reconstruction of the colonially fragmented African identity comes into clear focus. He was therefore not only making his historical research serve the politics of decolonization and nation-building, but was actually shaking the foundation of the Eurocentric historiography of Africa, which had for long dominated the academic world.

Meanwhile, in 1961 and 1963 respectively, Diop cofounded political opposition parties in Senegal as well as the Front National Du Senegal. With these he spearheaded opposition against the pro-French policies of the government of President Lepold Senghor. Following the dissolution the Front National *and* other opposition parties in 1965, Diop and his intellectual and socialist colleague regrouped and formed the Rassemblement National Democratique (RND) in 1976. The RND established a Wolof-language journal, *Siggi* (and later renamed *Taxaw*, which means "rise up" in Wolof), of which Diop became editor. The journal became a platform for articulating the aspirations of the Senegalese. In 1979 the RND was banned while Diop was charged for breaches of law prohibiting his running of an unregistered political organization. The proscription order was lifted in 1981 by President Abdou Diouf, who succeeded Senghor.

Dedication and service of the type associated with Diop were bound to bring with them recognition, honors and distinction. In 1966, at the First World Festival of Black Arts held in Dakar, he was honored as an African scholar who had exerted the most profound influence in Africa and international history in the twentieth century. He was subsequently involved in the organization of the 1977 Second World Festival of Black and African Arts and Culture in Lagos. Diop's struggle for an African school of history was realized in the 1970s with his invitation to join the committee responsible for writing *The General History of Africa*, sponsored bt the United Nations Educational, Scientific, and Cultural Organization. In 1980, he was appointed professor at the University of Dakar, where he taught ancient history. In 1982, he received the highest award for scientific research from the Institut Cultural Africain. In 1985 Diop was invited to Atlanta by Mayor Andrew Young, who proclaimed April 4 "Dr. Cheikh Anta Diop Day." Diop died in Dakar on February 7, 1986.

S. ADEMOLA AJAYI

See also: **Egypt, Ancient; Négritude.**

Biography

Born in Diourbel, in west-central Senegal, on December 23, 1933; elementary education in Senegal. On completing a bachelor's degree in Senegal, went to France to do graduate work at the Sorbonne in 1946, successfully defending dissertation in 1960. In 1961, appointed a research fellow at the Institut Fondamental d' Afrique Noire. In 1980, appointed professor at the University of Dakar, teaching ancient history. In 1982, he received the highest award for scientific research from the Institut Cultural Africain. Died in Dakar on February 7, 1986.

Further Reading

Amadiume, I. "Cheikh Anta Diop's Theory of Matriarchal Values as the Basis for African Cultural Unity." Introduction to *The Domains of Patriarchy and of Matriarchy in Classical Antiquity,* by Cheikh Anta Diop. London, 1989.

Diop, Cheik Anta. *Nations negres et culture.* 2 vols. (1954). Reprint, Paris, 1979.

———. *Towards the African Renaissance: Essays in African Culture and Development 1946–1960.* London, 1996.

Gray, C. *Conceptions of History: Cheikh Anta Diop and Theophile Obenga.* London, 1989.

Legum, C. *Pan Africanism: A Short Political Guide.* New York, 1965.

Sall, B. "History and Historical Consciousness in the Philosophy of History in Cheikh Anta Diop's Works." *Africa Development* 13, no. 3 (1988).

Van Sertima, I. (ed.). *Great African Thinkers: Cheikh Anta Diop.* New Brunswick, N.J., 1989.

Diouf, Abdou (1932–)

President of Senegal, 1980–2000

Abdou Diouf, the second president of the West African nation of Senegal, came to power in 1981 after the resignation of Leopold Sedar Senghor, and served as president until 2000. He was one of the few democratically elected leaders in Africa and maintained Senegal's tradition of civilian democracy.

A native of Louga, in northern Senegal, and of joint Wolof-Serer heritage, Diouf was educated at the University of Dakar and received a law degree from the University of Paris. Upon his return to Senegal, he held increasingly important government positions and became a protégé of Senghor, the country's first president since 1960. In 1964, Diouf was named secretary general to the presidency, and a key figure in the ruling Parti Socialiste (PS). In 1970, when Senghor reintroduced the office of prime minister, previously abolished during a constitutional crisis in 1962, he chose the little-known Diouf, then only 38 years old, above many senior civil service leaders and established politicians. The new prime minister was viewed by many as the embodiment of Senghor's attempt to establish a technocratically oriented administration with a low profile subordinate in the new office. Diouf quickly extended his rule into all facets of government through many changes in the cabinet. He was praised as an extraordinarily able and efficient administrator.

On December 31, 1980, Senghor, approaching his 75 year, stepped down from the presidency in favor of Diouf, who immediately lifted many of his predecessor's restrictions on political opposition parties. He also restructured his administration in ways that were generally credited with making it less corrupt and more efficient. Some reform-minded opposition leaders claimed that Diouf's reforms never went far enough, while others insisted that Diouf had to struggle against his party's old guard and entrenched interests. (Diouf, a Muslim, kept the critical support of the country's religious leadership, especially the Murids.)

In the 1980s, the opposition party, the Parti Democratique Senegalais, initially saw its support steadily eroded and some of its members arrested on suspicion of having received money from Libya. Diouf launched an anticorruption campaign and reshuffled his cabinet in July 1981. The next month Diouf responded to a plea from Gambian president Dawda Jawara for assistance against an attempted overthrow. Senegal's intervention restored Jawara, and by the end of the year the two countries agreed to form the Confederation of Senegambia, which stressed military coordination in foreign affairs and economic and financial matters. Diouf was named president of the confederation and Jawara was designated vice president. The promises of confederation were not realized, however, and the project was abandoned in September 1989.

In 1983, Diouf was elected president in his own right, with 82 per cent of the vote. After the election, Diouf took steps to replace the old-line politicians with younger men, and abolished the position of prime minister. Many labeled the country a quasi- or semi-democracy because of the dominance of the PS and the lack of a viable opposition to Diouf. In 1985, Diouf was elected head of the Organization of African Unity. A deteriorating economy, a growing separatist movement in the southern Casamance province, and the failure of the Senegambian confederation posed the main problems. Protests and strikes by university students and the police in 1987 caused the government to crack down on opposition forces. In the 1988 elections, Diouf won with 73 per cent of the vote, but evidence of vote rigging and ballot box tampering sparked serious disturbances in Dakar. A state of emergency was declared and some opposition leaders were arrested. Diouf made some changes in his cabinet and reestablished the post of prime minister. Critics called for radical changes to make Senegal a genuine democracy whereas Diouf proceeded with incremental constitutional and electoral reforms.

Senegal continued to face serious economic problems in the late 1980s and early 1990s, and the rebellion in the Casamance periodically flared up. In the 1993 elections, Diouf won with almost 60 per cent of the popular vote, and the PS again dominated the legislative elections. The 1993 elections, most likely the fairest and most monitored elections in Senegal's history, were not marred by violence but turnout was low.

Within a year, Diouf faced a serious crisis with the devaluation of the CFA franc by the French, which caused the most serious uprisings in Senegal since independence. Hundreds were arrested, including urban youth and many radical Muslims who called for an Islamic state in Senegal.

A serious issue that faced Diouf from the mid-1990s on was the separatist movement in the Casamance. Diouf refused to negotiate independence or even autonomy for the province, which is situated south of Gambia. The Diouf regime vacillated between negotiations with moderate leaders and harsh repression of suspected rebels. Senegalese intervention in neighboring Guinea-Bissau in 1998–1999 provided Diouf with an opportunity to weaken the rebels in the Casamance, many of whom received arms through Guinea-Bissau and took refuge there. However, while the crisis was resolved in Bissau, the situation in the Casamance began to worsen in late 1999.

Diouf lost the next presidential election, in 2000, to current president Abdoulaye Wade. Diouf now lives in France. In October 2002, he was elected secretary general of the International Francophonie Organization.

ANDREW F. CLARK

Biography

Born in Louga, in northern Senegal, in 1932. Educated at the University of Dakar, received a law degree from the University of Paris. Named secretary general to the president, and became a key figure in the ruling Parti Socialiste (PS) in 1964. Named prime minister in 1970. Named president when Senghor stepped down from the office on December 31, 1980. Reelected president in 1982. Elected head of the Organization of African Unity in 1985. Reelected president in 1993. Lost the presidential election in 2000. Elected secretary general of the International Francophonie Organization in 2002.

See also: **Senegal: Casamance Province, Conflict in; Senegal: Independence to the Present.**

Further Reading

Clark, A. F., and L. C. Phillips. *Historical Dictionary of Senegal*, Metuchen, NJ: Scarecrow Press, 1994.

Gellar, S. *Senegal: An African Nation Between Islam and the West*. Boulder, Colo.: Westview Press, 1995.

Vengroff, R., and L. Creevey, "Senegal: The Evolution of a Quasi Democracy." In *Political Reform in Francophone Africa*, edited by John F. Clark and David E. Gardiner. Boulder, Colo.: Westview Press, 1997.

Villalon, L., and O. Kane. "Senegal: The Crisis of Democracy and the Emergence of an Islamic Opposition." In *The African State at a Critical Juncture*, edited by Leonardo Villalon and Philip Huxtable. Boulder, Colo.: Lynne Rienner, 1998.

Disarmament: *See* South Africa: Confederation, Disarmament, and the First Anglo-Boer War, 1871–1881.

Djibouti: Nineteenth Century to the Present: Survey

The Republic of Djibouti, with a territory of 23,200 square kilometers, lies between the Horn of Africa and the Arabian Peninsula on the strait of Bab el-Mandeb, which links the Red Sea with the Gulf of Aden. To the north and west of the Gulf of Tadjourah live the Afars; to the south are the Issas, who belong to one of the six Somali confederations, the Dir. In contrast to the Issas, the Afars have a tradition of state building, and since the fourteenth century four sultanates—Tadjourah, Rahaïta, Awsa, and Gobaad—have emerged among them.

The opening of the Suez Canal in 1869 transformed the Horn of Africa into a highly strategic region. The British, who already controlled the strait, had occupied Aden since 1839, and also occupied the islands of Perim and Socotora. In response, France had sought a port of call on the way to the Indian Ocean that would bring it into closer relations with Ethiopia. In 1857, Henri Lambert, who owned sugar plantations on Mauritius, opened relations with the Afars. After Lambert

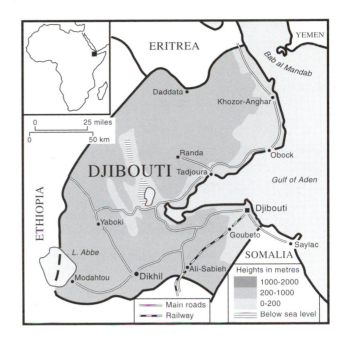

Djibouti.

was assassinated in 1859, Napoleon III gave Commander Fleuriot de Langle the mission of punishing the assassins and making official contact with the sultans. This was the origin of the Treaty of Paris of March 1862, signed by an Afar representative and the French minister of foreign affairs, which recognized a French coastal zone to the north of Obock in exchange for a payment of 10,000 thalers. The French, particularly after their defeat by Germany in 1870, neglected Obock, where several Europeans attracted from Ethiopia established themselves. Their settlement, however, faced powerful military resistance from local Afar and Issa.

In 1883 the government of the French Third Republic decided to occupy Obock in order to end its dependence on Aden, where its fleet, mobilized for the conquest of Tonkin (northern Vietnam), had not been able to take on coal. From 1884 to 1888, the French governor, Léonce Lagarde, conducted a policy of active diplomacy, intended to establish French sovereignty over the perimeter of the Gulf of Tadjourah while maintaining good relations with the King of Shoa, Menelik II, who was the emperor of Ethiopia from 1889 on. Obock, which was neither a safe anchorage nor a terminus for the caravan routes, was displaced in 1896 by Djibouti, the new capital of a colony known, inaccurately, as the Côte française des Somalis (CFS; French Somali Coast).

By the end of the nineteenth century, the whole of the Horn of Africa, apart from Ethiopia, had been colonized. The territorial division carried out by France, Italy, and Britain imposed fixed frontiers on an area characterized by the mobility of pastoralists, cutting

Referendum about independence in Djibouti: anti-French graffiti, 1967. The French rigged the result in their favor by expelling thousands of Somalis before the referendum was brought to the polls. © SVT Bild/Das Fotoarchiv.

off the Issas from the Somali confederations, which were now controlled by the British and the Italians, and separating the Afars from their kinsmen in the Ethiopian Awsa and Italian Eritrea.

Between 1896 and 1977, colonial France developed Djibouti as a commercial port and stopover on the routes of empire. It was also a terminus for a railway line built by the Ethiopian Imperial Railway Company, which was founded in 1896 by Ilg of Switzerland, Chefneux of France, and Menelik II. The section, 311 kilometers long, that linked Djibouti with Dirre-Daoua began service in 1903. In 1917, it was extended to Addis Ababa by the Compagnie du chemin de fer franco-éthiopien (Franco-Ethiopian Railroad Company), which was owned by French investors.

Djibouti thus became the principal outlet for Ethiopia, which was then landlocked, and handled both its imports and its exports (coffee, hides, cereals, and the like). The CFS also exported sea-salt produced by the Salines de Djibouti, a company created in 1912. Revenue also came from the provisioning of vessels with water, ice, and fuel—coal at first, and then, after 1939, hydrocarbons. The contrast between the emptiness of the territory left to the nomads and the unique focus of development that attracted all the investment was thus reinforced.

World War II, which may be said to have started with the Italian conquest of Ethiopia (1935–1936), also affected the CFS; in 1938, Italy sought to paralyze it by opening up a route between Addis Ababa and Assab. Then, Mussolini threatened to annex it. The colony's governor, Nouailhetas, appointed in September 1940 by Marshal Pétain, made the CFS into a bastion of Vichy France. The British, supported by a handful of Free French, imposed a blockade on the CFS from 1941 to December 1942, and then liberated it.

After the war, the colony, along with the rest of the French empire, entered a new era, prefigured at the Brazzaville Conference of 1944. In 1949, France, hoping to make Djibouti into the "Hong Kong of the Red Sea," introduced the Djibouti franc, a currency convertible into U.S. dollars; established a free port; and, using funds from the FIDES, completed deepwater port facilities. Despite these reforms, the port of Djibouti suffered from the competition of a rival port, Assab, as well as from the Arab–Israeli conflicts, which brought its operations to a halt in 1956, and then again from 1967 to 1975. Djibouti sank into a long-lasting recession, aggravated in 1960 by the closing of the salt works, its sole industrial activity.

The population increased, through both natural growth and immigration, from 45,000 inhabitants in 1945 to 250,000 in 1975. Young people demanded better educational facilities, since the schools were all inadequate: there were 600 school students in 1947, 6,500 in 1966, and 10,000 in 1973. The pastoralists, confronted with the vast and uninhabitable deserts, took refuge in the capital, a cosmopolitan city that had 20,000 inhabitants in 1947, 60,000 in 1967, and 110,000 in 1975. The labor market could not absorb them, so the colonial administration continued to be the main employer. By 1969, officials constituted 37.6 per cent of the active population and absorbed 57 per cent of the budget. Economic difficulties exacerbated intercommunal tensions.

While most of France's African territories gained their independence in 1960, the CFS developed along a different path. In 1946, within the framework of the Union française (French Union) and the Fourth Republic, voters in the CFS chose members of a local *conseil representatif* (representative council), as well as representatives to join the legislature in France. Then, the framework law of 1956 relaunched political life by establishing, alongside the governor, a *conseil de gouvernement* (governing council), the members of which were nominated by those elected to the *assemblée territoriale* (territorial assembly). The vice presidency of this conseil went to Mahmoud Harbi, a member of the party Mouvement pour l'Union republicaine (Movement for a Republican Union).

When the referendum on the proposed Communauté française (French Community) was held in 1958, Harbi, a supporter of the notion of a Greater Somalia, campaigned for immediate independence. Faced with this challenge from the nationalist minority, the French authorities modified their attitudes, and began supporting the Afars, who were hostile to Pan-Somali ideas, as well as moderate Somalis. Harbi went into exile, and new political leaders appeared: Hassan Gouled, who was elected as a deputy to the French Assemblée nationale (National Assembly) in April 1959; Ahmed Dini, an

Afar who became Vice-president of the Conseil; and Ali Aref Bourham, who replaced Dini in June 1960.

From around the end of 1960, the antagonism between Aref, who wanted to maintain the link with France, and Gouled, who preferred to seek internal self-government, widened the gulf between the Afars and the Somalis. While Gouled, in Paris as a deputy, defended his cause, the Assemblée territoriale in the CFS declared in favor of the status quo, arousing strong protests from the Parti du Mouvement Populaire (PMP; Party of the Popular Movement), the heir to the nationalist ideas of Harbi, who had died in an airplane accident in September 1960. Members of the PMP suspected of being in league with the Republic of Somalia were arrested—notably, in 1964, when Mogadishu launched a powerful campaign, claiming the CFS as Somalian territory, within both the United Nations (UN) and the Organization of African Unity (OAU). Ethiopia responded by seeking to annex the territory, invoking its historic rights.

As the Somali opposition within the CFS had been muzzled, the leadership of those opposed to the colonial authorities passed to Ahmed Dini and Abdallah Mohamed Kamil of the Union démocratique afar (UDA; Afar Democratic Union). Just before an official visit by the French president, Charles de Gaulle, the PMP and the UDA forged a strategic alliance based on two ideas: the removal of Ali Aref, and independence. On August 25, 1966, de Gaulle was met by demonstrators demanding independence. Opposition was transformed into violent conflict.

On September 26, 1966, France, hostile to the notion of independence by stages, announced that the voters would be consulted about whether or not to keep the CFS as part of the republic. This revived the nationalist opposition. Against this explosive background the army was mobilized to confront the Somalian and Ethiopian troops massing on the frontiers of the CFS. The referendum held on March 19, 1967, showed 22,555 voting yes and 14,666 voting no—that is, *in favor of* independence. This division corresponded to the ethnic makeup of the voters: Somalis agitated for independence, while the Afars agitated in favor of the link with France. The announcement of the results was followed by an outbreak of serious unrest, which led to the cordoning off of Somali districts, the expulsion of foreigners, and the building of a barricade around the capital, intended to control immigration by Somalia. France was strongly criticized by the UN and the OAU. In July 1967, the "territoire français des Afars et des Issas" (TFAI; French Territory of the Afars and the Issas) obtained internal self-government. Ali Aref remained president of the conseil, despite some opposition.

In December 1975 French president Valéry Giscard d'Estaing distanced himself from Gaullist policy by recognizing the right of the TFAI to independence. The TFAI set out on the road to independence just as the Horn of Africa was aflame with the "socialist" revolution in Ethiopia and the Ogaden War. Aref, still strictly cooperating with France, rallied to the idea of independence somewhat late, which did not please his critics, including Ahmed Dini and Hassan Gouled. It was these two men who founded the Ligue populaire africaine pour l'Indépendance (Popular African League for Independence). Aref, abandoned by Paris, left his post in July 1976.

On February 28, 1977, France convoked a round-table conference in Paris, at which the nationalists—both those from inside the TFAI and those who had fought for independence while residing in Ethiopia and Somalia—studied the modalities for achieving independence. The last remaining obstacles were removed at a meeting in Accra, sponsored by the OAU, from March 28 to April 1, 1977. Once African endorsement had been obtained, the Arab League provided a guarantee of the integrity of the future state.

A referendum held on May 8, 1977, produced an overwhelming majority in favor of independence. Legislative elections, held the same day, were won by the list of candidates of the Rassemblement populaire pour l'indépendance (Popular Rally for Independence). On June 24, the 65 deputies—33 Somalis, 30 Afars, and two Arabs—elected Hassan Gouled as president. The Republic of Djibouti, recognized within its colonial frontiers, was born on June 27, 1977. On July 2, the new state became the 45th member of the OAU; it also joined the Arab League (August 9), the UN (September 22), and the Organization of the Islamic Conference (April 28, 1978). Djibouti, where Islam is the state religion, faced several challenges: it would have to enhance its shipping and commercial activities, based on the Djibouti franc, maintain its unity, and reduced the imbalance between the capital and the interior.

In November 1991, fighters from the Front pour la Restauration de l'Unité et de la Démocratie (Front for the Restoration of Unity and Democracy) confronted government troops, inaugurating a civil war. National reconciliation got under way from December 26, 1994, when Afars joined the government.

At the age of 83, President Gouled, the "father of the nation," retired from politics. He was replaced by Ismaïl Omar Guelleh, who was elected in April 1999 with 74 per cent of the votes. Djibouti, a haven of peace in an unstable Horn of Africa, moved toward an economic revival as the war between Eritrea and Ethiopia (1998–2001) meant that Ethiopia's trade was redirected through Djibouti. Since September 11, 2001, Djibouti, which counts Yemen and Somalia among its neighbors, has participated in the struggle against international terrorism: within the framework of bilateral agreements, formerly with France alone but now with the United States and Germany as well.

Nevertheless, there are still some problems. Djibouti is deeply in debt, and the International Monetary Fund is demanding economic reform and budgetary stabilization. Development is hampered by a lack of energy resources, and by a demographic explosion, as the population grows by 6 per cent a year and Djibouti plays host to 120,000 refugees.

President Guelleh has launched some reforms that have had uneven results: they include the democratization of politics, the liberalization of the economy, and the creation of a free trade zone. Djibouti, which has now been independent for more than 25 years, seeks to play a diplomatic role. Since the Arta Conference in 2001, for example, the president has been active in the search for peace and reconciliation in Somalia.

COLETTE DUBOIS

See also: **Ethiopia: Early Nineteenth Century; Somalia: Independence, Conflict, and Revolution.**

Further Reading

Aden, M. Ourrou. Djibouti 1991–1994. Du maquis Afar à la paix des braves. Paris: L'Harmattan, 2002.

———. Sombloloho. Djibouti La chute du président Ali Aref (1975–1976). Paris: L'Harmattan, 1999.

Coubba, A. Ahmed Dini et la politique à Djibouti. Paris: L'Harmattan, 1998.

———. Le mal djiboutien, rivalités ethniques et enjeux politiques. Paris: L'Harmattan, 1996.

Dubois, C. Djibouti 1888–1967. Héritage ou frustration ? Paris: L'Harmattan, 1997.

———. L'or blanc de Djibouti (XIXe-XXe siècles). Salines et sauniers. Paris: Karthala, 2002.

Oberle, Philippe, and Pierre Hugot. Histoire de Djibouti, des origines à la République. Paris: Présence africaine, 1995.

Doe, Samuel K: *See* Liberia: Doe, Samuel K., Life and Era of.

Domestication, Plant and Animal, History of

The advent of the domestication of plants and animals in Africa had significant social and economic ramifications for the continent's people, regardless of whether they became food producers themselves, or still retained their foraging lifestyle. Domestication for food production often leads to inequalities in access, since surpluses can be produced that can be controlled by individuals (chiefs) or corporate bodies (lineages), and used as a social and economic lever to increase authority over labor/production, and to gain status.

Since the eastern Mediterranean, including North Africa, could possibly be considered as a single biome (Smith 1998a), the two areas had many species in common. Considerable debate continues regarding the earliest appearance of domestic cattle in the Sahara. Wendorf (1994) argues on environmental grounds that the cattle bones found at Nabta Playa in the western desert of Egypt some 100 kilometers west of the Nile Valley and dated to around 9300 years ago, were domesticated. This would make them the oldest domestic cattle anywhere.

Contemporary with the sites at Nabta Playa, a number of caves in the Acacus Mountains of southwest Libya were occupied by hunter-foragers. In one of these caves, Uan Afuda, there is a thick dung layer, which could only have been accumulated from keeping wild Barbary sheep penned up (Di Lernia 1998). The large number of bones of this animal, as well as their depiction on the walls of several caves, suggests that the sheep were more than a meat source, and may have been used ritually. Thus, there were attempts to control wild animals by early Holocene hunters of the Sahara.

An alternative argument to indigenous domestication of African cattle relies more heavily on the earliest appearance of small stock in North Africa (Smith 1986), again at Nabta Playa, around 7500 years ago. Since the Barbary sheep are the only ovicaprids found in Africa, and they contributed no genetic material to the domestic sheep and goats found in the continent, all small stock found in Africa must have originated in the Near East. At this time the animals were entering an ameliorated environment in North Africa, and the grasslands of the Sahara opened up a niche that was filled by pastoral people. The diffusionist argument would say that this was also the time when domestic cattle, which had already been domesticated in the Near East, entered Africa.

Regarding plant domestication in Sub-Saharan Africa, there is little reason to doubt that the process was developed independent of outside influences, since many of the plants are completely different from the dominant grains of the circum-Mediterranean basin, such as wheat and barley, and required specialized propagation and harvesting strategies. The range of African plant domesticates is huge (Purseglove 1976), which reflects both the immense richness of Africa's flora, as well as the traditional knowledge of plant foods and pharmacopeia.

On the basis of the distribution of the wild forms of African domesticates, three areas of independent domestication can be suggested: the savanna grassland zone (including the Sahel and the Central Niger Delta); the savanna/forest ecotone; and highland Ethiopia. The first zone is a belt that stretches across Africa at its widest point, from the Sudan to Mauretania. It is where major cereals would have originated, such as *Sorghum bicolor*, *Pennisetum glaucum* (pearl millet) and *Oryza glaberrima* (African rice). The second zone was probably the original source of many domesticates presently found farther south in the forests, such as the large yam, *Dioscorea rotundata*, the oil palm, *Elaeis guineensis*, and watermelon, *Citrullus lanatus*. The Ethiopian highlands are a unique ecosystem, and most of the domesticates are still only found there, such as *Eragrostis tef* and *Ensete ventricosa*.

The history of domestication of these plants is not well known, due to the poor preservation of plants in the archaeological sites of tropical environments. The earliest *Sorghum* found at Nabta Playa, dated to c.8000 years ago, is part of a floral "package" that includes a number of wild plant foods, such as *Ziziphus* and other grasses: *Panicum*, *Echinochloa*, *Setaria*, *Digitaria* and *Urochloa/Brachiaria*. This suggests that sorghum was also still "wild" (Wasylikowa et al. 1993). Although grain domestication may have been tied in with African herding societies, there is reason to believe that this was a late occurrence (Marshall and Hildebrand 2002). Even today herders harvest wild grains for domestic use (Smith 1980; Tubiana and Tubiana 1977).

Surprisingly, the earliest dates for domestic sorghum come not from Africa, but India, around 4000 years ago (Harlan 1993). This means that the grain would have been domesticated in Africa before this date. Domesticated pearl millet, while it may have the same time depth as sorghum, is only recognized after 3000 years ago at Dhar Tichitt in Mauretania from grain impressions in pottery (Munson 1976).

Of the forest domesticates, since yams are propagated by tuber cuttings, there are no seeds to preserve on archaeological sites (Coursey 1976). The antiquity of their origins as domesticates may be tied in with other plants, such as the oil palm, whose carbonized seeds have been found at a number of sites in West Africa associated with pottery. At one such site, Bosumpra, in Ghana, the oil-bearing fruit *Canarium schweinfurthii* gave way to *E. guineensis* around 5000 years ago (Smith 1975), so may be an indication of the age of this domesticate.

The age of the earliest Ethiopian domesticates still eludes us. All the radiocarbon dates for both plants and animals are late, with cattle bones producing the oldest dates of the last millennium BCE (Phillipson 1993). As Ethiopia is considered an early source of cattle into the rift valley of East Africa, possibly as early as 4000 years ago (Ambrose 1982), it would seem that there is still a great deal we do not know about early farming societies in the highlands.

The spread of bovines into the rest of Africa occurred as the Sahara dried up, around 4500 years ago. Since the rainfall belt of the intertropical convergence zone was moving farther south, this aridification opened up the Sahel and parts of the savanna to pastoralists who hitherto had been excluded from these areas due to tsetse fly infestation (Smith 1979). Some of the West African breeds, such as the N'Dama and the West African shorthorn, show tolerance to Trypanosomias, the fatal disease transmitted by the tsetse, indicating a long period of association. These animals do not have humps, and would be directly descended from the *taurine* species of cattle. Cattle also entered East Africa, where they may have encountered other epizootic diseases transmitted via wild animals (Gifford-Gonzalez 2000), which delayed their southward movement to the rest of the Rift Valley by as much as 1,000 years. Small stock, which accompanied the spread of cattle southward, were probably less susceptible to these epizootic effects, so were able to move into the rest of southern Africa by the turn of the Christian era, reaching the Cape around 1900 years ago (Henshilwood 1996). Eventually cattle were also adapted to the southern lands (Smith 1998b).

Many of Africa's cattle today are of the humped variety. These are descended from *Bos indicus*, the Indian zebu, which were introduced to Africa, possibly via Arabia, before 1000CE (Blench 1993). Crosses of zebu and taurine cattle have produced two of southern Africa's most prominent breeds: Sanga and Afrikander.

It is not known when camels first entered Africa. In fact, their early domestication is still a matter of conjecture. It is possible that they came initially during the early dynastic period of Egypt (Clutton-Brock 1993), but only in significant economically viable numbers during the Roman period in North Africa in the last centuries BCE. By this time, North Africa had attained the present degree of aridity, and these desert-adapted animals allowed communication throughout most of the Sahara by nomads. Introduction of the camel to East Africa probably was the result of contact between the Horn of Africa and Arabia within the last 2000 years.

Equids are common throughout Africa. No known domestication of zebras occurred, so all the donkeys of Africa are descended from the wild ass, *Equus africanus*. The earliest dated domestic donkey comes from Egypt c.4400 years ago (Clutton-Brock 1993). Domestic horses and war chariots are reputed to have been introduced to dynastic Egypt by the Hyksos between 1640–1530BCE, and later spread to West Africa where cavalry became important in military conquest and state formation (Blench 1993). Archaeological evidence for domestic equids south of the Sahara is sparse, and often confounded by the difficulty in separating the skeletal remains of zebras from domestic horses and donkeys.

ANDREW B. SMITH

Further Reading

Ambrose, S. H. "Archaeology and Linguistic Reconstructions of History in East Africa." In *The Archaeological and Linguistic Reconstruction of African History*, edited by C. Ehret and M. Posnansky. Berkeley and Los Angeles: University of California Press, 1982.

Blench, R. "Ethnographic and Linguistic Evidence for the Prehistory of African Ruminant Livestock, Horses and Ponies." In *The Archaeology of Africa: Food, Metals and Towns*, edited by T. Shaw, P. Sinclair, B. Andah, and A. Okpoko. London: Routledge, 1993.

Clutton-Brock, J. "The Spread of Domestic Animals in Africa." In *The Archaeology of Africa: Food, Metals and Towns*, edited by T. Shaw, P. Sinclair, B. Andah, and A. Okpoko. London: Routledge, 1993.

Coursey, D. G. "The Origins and Domestication of Yams in Africa." In *Origins of African Plant Domestication*, edited by J. R. Harlan, J. M. J. de Wet, and A. B. L. Stemler. The Hague: Mouton, 1976.

Di Lernia, S. "Cultural Control over Wild Animals during the Early Holocene: The Case of Barbary Sheep in Central Sahara." In *Before Food Production in North Africa*, edited by S. di Lernia and G. Manzi. Forli, Italy: A.B.A.C.O. Edizioni, 1998.

Gifford-Gonzalez, G. G. "Animal Disease Challenges to the Emergence of Pastoral Economies in Sub-Saharan Africa." *African Archaeological Review* 17, no. 3 (2000): pp.95–139.

Harlan, J. R. 1993. "The Tropical African Cereals." In *The Archaeology of Africa: Food, Metals and Towns*, edited by T. Shaw, P. Sinclair, B. Andah, and A. Okpoko. London: Routledge, 1993.

Henshilwood, C. 1996. "A Revised Chronology for Pastoralism in Southernmost Africa: New Evidence of Sheep at C.2000 B.P. from Blombos Cave, South Africa." *Antiquity*, no. 70 (1996): pp.945–949.

Marshall, F., and E. Hildebrand. "Cattle before Crops: The Beginnings of Food Production in Africa." *Journal of World Prehistory* 16, no. 2 (2002): pp.99–143.

Munson, P. J. "Archaeological Data on the Origins of Cultivation in the Southwestern Sahara and Their Implications for West Africa." In *Origins of African Plant Domestication*, edited by J. R. Harlan, J. M. J. de Wet, and A. B. L. Stemler. The Hague: Mouton, 1976.

Phillipson, D. W. "The Antiquity of Cultivation and Herding in Ethiopia." In *The Archaeology of Africa: Food, Metals and Towns*, edited by T. Shaw, P. Sinclair, B. Andah, and A. Okpoko. London: Routledge, 1993.

Purseglove, J. W. "The Origins and Migrations of Crops in Tropical Africa." In *Origins of African Plant Domestication*, edited by J. R. Harlan, J. M. J. de Wet, and A. B. L. Stemler. The Hague: Mouton, 1976.

Smith, A. B. "Biogeographical Considerations of Colonisation of the Lower Tilemsi Valley in the 2nd Millenium B.C." *Journal of Arid Environments* 2 (1979): pp.355–361.

———. "Early Domestic Stock in Southern Africa: A Commentary." *African Archaeological Review* 15, no. 2 (1998a): pp.151–156.

———. "The Environmental Adaptation of Nomads in the West African Sahel: A Key to Understanding Prehistoric Pastoralists. In *The Sahara and the Nile*, edited by M. A. J. Williams and H. Faure. Rotterdam: Balkema, 1980.

———. "Intensification and Transformation Processes towards Food Production in Africa." In *Before Food Production in Africa*, edited by S. di Lernia and G. Manzi. Forli, Italy: ABACO Edizioni, 1998b.

———. "Radiocarbon Dates from Bosumpra Cave, Abetifi, Ghana." *Proceedings of the Prehistoric Society*, no. 41 (1975): pp.179–182.

———. "Review Article: Cattle Domestication in North Africa." *African Archaeological Review*, no. 4 (1986): pp.197–203.

Tubiana, M-J., and J. Tubiana. *The Zaghawa from an Ecological Perspective*. Rotterdam: Balkema, 1977.

Wasylikowa, K., J. R. Harlan, J. Evans, F. Wendorf, R. Schild, A. E. Close, H. Hrolik, and R. A. Housley, R.A. "Examination of Botanical Remains from Early Neolithic Houses at Nabta Playa, Western Desert, Egypt, with Special Reference to Sorghum Grains." In *The Archaeology of Africa: Food, Metals and Towns*, edited by T. Shaw, P. Sinclair, B. Andah, and A. Okpoko. London: Routledge, 1993.

Wendorf, F. "Are the Early Holocene Cattle in the Eastern Sahara Domestic or Wild?" *Evolutionary Anthropology* 3, no. 4 (1994): pp.118–128.

Donatist Church: North Africa

Persecution of the early Christians often elicited differing, and even rival, responses, exposing deeper tensions within the Christian community. Such was the case in Carthage, the chief city of Roman North Africa (near modern Tunis), during the Great Persecution initiated by emperor Diocletian in 303. The specific bone of contention was Caecilian's fitness to be bishop of Carthage, for some believed that one of his consecrators in 311–312, Felix, Bishop of Apthungi, had during the persecution committed the spiritually fatal offence of *traditio*, the "handing over" or "betrayal" of the Holy Scriptures on demand. Such surrender, as an act of compliance with an idolatrous pagan state, disqualified not only the *traditor* himself, Felix, but all who associated with him, from any Christian ministry. It was tantamount to apostasy. The gravity of the act no doubt owed something to African Christians' reverence for the sacred text itself, which was a more rare commodity in a manuscript age.

Underlying the opposition to Caecilian were deep-seated suspicions about the Carthaginian Church leadership's collusion with the persecuting authorities, or at least its distaste for intense devotion to the martyrs. Personal grievances and frustrated ambitions played their part, as did the Numidian bishops' affront at the exclusion of their senior bishop from Caecilian's hasty consecration. The anti-Caecilianists elected one Majorinus as counterbishop. He was succeeded in 313 by Donatus from Casae Nigrae (Négrine) in Numidia, and the schismatic movement had its name. Donatus led the movement with impressive vigor. Its growth was such that by approximately 336 he could preside over a council of 270 bishops, the largest number ever assembled for a Christian synod.

With the end of persecution, Emperor Constantine disbursed funds to help repair its damage. When these were given to Caecilian's party in Carthage, the dissenters appealed to the emperor for adjudication of their claim to be the true church. Ecclesiastical and imperial enquiries vindicated Caecilian (and cleared Felix), and Constantine vainly attempted to coerce the Donatists toward unity (316–321). This policy simply confirmed the Donatists' conviction of the righteousness of their cause, for the saints of God had ever been persecuted by the church's enemies. Constantine's son and successor, Constans, again attempted bribery and repression in 347, in what became known as the Macarian persecution (from the name of the imperial official involved). It also evoked from Donatus the classic utterance, "What has the emperor to do with the church?" Donatus and other leaders were exiled, and relaxation of the anti-Donatist ban had to await the accession of Julian as emperor in 361.

Donatus died in exile in approximately 355, succeeded by another able leader, Parmenian, who served as (Donatist) bishop of Carthage until 391 or 392. He also provided intellectual weight for the movement. His (lost) work on Donatist ecclesiology merited a response from Optatus, Bishop of Milevis (Milev), which is a major source for the beginnings of Donatism (367; revised with an addition c.385). In the nonconformist layman, Tyconius, who flourished around 370–380, Donatism produced the ablest Christian mind in Africa since Tertullian and Cyprian. His *Book of Rules* was an early essay in Christian hermeneutics, which was incorporated by Augustine into his guide *Christian Teaching*. Tyconius's commentary on the Apocalypse of John can be partly reconstructed from the succession of later commentaries that it influenced. But his critique of some basic Donatist convictions resulted in his excommunication, though he never became a Catholic. He could be called a representative of Afro-Catholicism.

A number of different factors in the late fourth century conspired to undermine Donatism's ascendancy in North Africa. Parmenian's successor, Primian, was not his equal. His high-handedness contributed to internal Donatist divisions (especially with the Maximianists), which were not always dealt with consistently and in terms of Donatist principles. Support given by some Donatists to local revolts against Roman rule led by Firmus (372–375) and more seriously by Gildo (397–398) strengthened the hand of opponents who viewed Donatism as a threat to law and order. The emergence of the Circumcellions in the late 340s had encouraged this view. Although still not beyond scholarly debate, they were self-styled "warriors of Christ," given to violence as a means of redressing economic and social injustice. At once rootless peasants and devotees of martyrs' shrines (*cellae*), they were at least in part associated with Donatism and engaged in anti-Catholic thuggery.

It was finally the combined skills of Aurelius of Carthage and Augustine of Hippo in the early fifth century that precipitated Donatism's decline. Augustine's massive historical and theological refutation of Donatist claims was allied to state repression in the Edict of Unity of 405 (which declared Donatism heresy) and after the huge conference of the rival episcopates under an imperial commissioner, Marcellinus, at Carthage in 411. Greatly diminished through forcible reunification, Donatists nevertheless lived on, perhaps in some areas finding a common cause with Catholics under Vandal persecution. After the Byzantine conquest of North Africa (c.600), Pope Gregory I urged Catholic bishops to deal more energetically with Donatists, but only Islam finally ensured its demise.

Donatism is best understood in religious terms, not primarily as a nationalist or liberation movement fired by political or socioeconomic motives. It claimed the authority of the great martyr-bishop, Cyprian of Carthage, in refusing to recognize baptism given outside the church (which it restricted to its own ranks). Hence it rebaptized Catholics in pursuit of its pure community. In its rigorousness, glorification of martyrdom, apocalyptic rejection of an idolatrous state, and obsession with ritual holiness Donatism recalled the distinctive African Christian heritage from Tertullian's age.

The Donatist Church undoubtedly provided a vehicle for expressions of African particularism and social discontents. Yet there is little evidence of its special interest in Berber or Punic language and culture, and its demographic concentration in rural Numidia (a region north of the Sahara, generally correlating to the boundaries of modern-day Algeria) probably reflected more effective repressive measures in the cities. Certainly the campaign against Donatism provoked Catholicism into a somewhat un-African alignment with the Roman church and state.

DAVID WRIGHT

See also: **Carthage; North Africa: Roman Occupation, Empire; Religion, History of.**

Further Reading

Brown, P. *Religion and Society in the Age of Saint Augustine.* London: Faber, 1972.

Edwards, M. (trans. and ed.). *Optatus: Against the Donatists.* Liverpool: Liverpool University Press, 1997.

Frend, W. H. C. *The Donatist Church.* Oxford: Clarendon Press, 1952.

Greenslade, S. L. *Schism in the Early Church*, 2nd ed. London: SCM Press, 1964.

Maier, J.-L. *Le Dossier du Donatisme.* 2 vols. Texte und Untersuchungen 134–135. Berlin: Akademie-Verlag, 1987, 1989.

Markus, R. A. *From Augustine to Gregory the Great.* London: Variorum, 1983. See especially chapters 6–9.

Tilley, M. A. *The Bible in Christian North Africa: The Donatist World*. Minneapolis: Fortress, 1997. Willis, Geoffrey G. St Augustine and the Donatist Controversy. London: SPCK, 1952.

Tilley, M. A. (trans. and ed.). *Donatist Martyr Stories: The Church in Conflict in Roman North Africa*. Liverpool: Liverpool University Press, 1996.

Dongola: *See* Soba and Dongola.

Douala

Douala, the largest city and a major seaport of Cameroon, is situated on the tidal Wouri Estuary, a good natural harbor used for centuries for trade with the West. The Duala people, after whom the city they founded is named, traded in slaves and then in palm produce with Europeans from the seventeenth through the nineteenth centuries; the Wouri Estuary was then called the Cameroons River after the crayfish (*camarões* in Portuguese) that swarmed there regularly The Duala chiefs signed a treaty with Germany in 1884 that led to German colonization of the whole territory, which took the name of the Duala settlement, Cameroon (Kamerun). By then the Duala were divided into four main sections: the Bonadoo (also called Bell), Bonambela (also called Akwa), and Bonebela (also called Deido) on the south bank, and the Bonaberi on the north bank.

At first called Kamerunstadt by the Germans, the town was then called Douala after the name of the indigenous inhabitants (normally the French spelling is used for the city). Under the Germans the town was a center of missionary work, education, and some modern development. The Duala became a typical West Coast elite people, acquiring Western education, serving the Europeans in subordinate posts, but also feeling the weight of colonial rule and protesting against it. In the case of Duala the most famous protests were against a plan for segregation in which the Duala living along the southern bank of the estuary would be moved to new sites slightly inland. In 1914 the first phase of the plan was carried out; the Bonadoo were largely moved out of their homes, and their ruler, Paramount Chief Rudolf Duala Manga Bell, was executed. But then, after the outbreak of World War I, Douala was quickly captured by a largely British expeditionary force. After a short spell under mainly British administration (September 1914–April 1916) it then passed to French rule, along with most of Kamerun, and became the first capital of the French–mandated Territory of Cameroun.

The partial expropriation of the southern bank of the estuary was not reversed by the French, despite years of continued Duala protests accompanied by petitions for self-government. The seized Bonadoo territory, especially the area named Bonanjo, was used for European offices. Some Duala still had homes there and many did in Akwa, Deido and Bonaberi, where many more privileged people (clerks, teachers, etc.) built masonry houses. Close to Bonanjo the expropriated Bell Duala built such houses in Bali in the 1930s. The area originally set aside for them, a little further inland, retained the name New-Bell, but though its land was under nominal Duala ownership it came, from the 1920s, to be peopled mainly by Africans from other parts of Cameroon. Douala was the main seaport of French Cameroon and the center of economic activity, though the capital was moved to Yaoundé in 1921. Business offices were established in Akwa in particular, where Africans unable to build modern houses were forced to move out (without loss of land rights) in 1937.

The population in 1939 was officially 34,002, including 17,871 Duala and 13,847 other Africans. In fact other Africans may have been a majority before then. There was a continual influx of other Cameroonians (Bassas, Betis, and especially Bamilekes) from the 1920s. This continued and amplified after World War II (when French Cameroon was taken over by the Free French in 1940 and Douala then became the capital again for a few years). Economic development, including extension of the port installations, caused the city to grow rapidly in the 1940s and 1950s. The Bamilekes became then, and have remained, the largest immigrant element in the city, soon far outnumbering the Duala and now the main ethnic group in the urban area. The expanding urban population of Douala was much involved in the nationalist politics of the 1940s and 50s, and in political unrest at times, as in 1955 and 1960. This happened again after multiparty politics returned, in 1991, when Douala was—as before—a main center of opposition to the regime in power.

A bridge over the Wouri, linking the main (southern) part of the city with Bonaberi, was completed in 1955. Since the German period, Douala has been the terminus of the country's two railways, one starting from Bonaberi. The airport, developed from small beginnings in the 1930s, became Cameroon's main international airport and remains so today.

In independent Cameroon, Douala has remained by far the most important port for overseas trade, handling over 90 per cent of the country's trade, as well as some trade with the Central African Republic and Chad. The port has been expanded and is still a major West Coast port although it now has problems (silting up of the estuary, and high charges). The economic capital of Cameroon, Douala is a hive of business activity of all sorts, including many industries whose main location is in the Douala-Bassa area east of the historic city center. The built-up area now extends to that district and to the airport, covering former rural districts in between. The city has continually expanded and increased in population, with a regular influx of immigrants. For decades there have been immigrants from other African countries and now there are large communities of these, especially Nigerians. Most numerous however are the Bamilekes, who run most of the city's small and medium-sized businesses (taxi services, cinemas, bars, hotels, import enterprises, shops of all sorts) and who, in 1976, were estimated to number 215,460 out of a total Douala urban population of 458,426. The Duala are now a small minority, though they still own considerable amounts of land and their language is widely spoken. There are affluent areas like Bonanjo where a minority—farther enriched since the oil boom began in the 1970s (some oil being pumped in the Douala region)—live in comfortable conditions. The multiethnic general population lives crowded over other districts, served by several markets, shops, and services everywhere, and places of worship; there are numerous Muslims but the city's population is mainly Christian, the Catholic cathedral in Bonanjo (1934) being an important landmark.

A crowded, noisy and lively city, Douala has for long been well known for its relaxations and night life. However, the city has numerous social problems such as inadequate drainage (the land being flat and the rainfall heavy) and inadequate and expensive housing for large numbers. The present population of the city is well over a million.

JONATHAN DERRICK

See also: **Cameroon.**

Further Reading

Austen, R., and J. Derrick. *Middlemen of the Cameroons Rivers.* Cambridge University Press, 1999.

Derrick, J. "Colonial Élitism in Cameroon: The Case of the Duala in the 1930s." In *Introduction to the History of Cameroon in the Nineteenth and Twentieth Centuries*, edited by M. Njeuma. Macmillan, 1989.

Gouellain, R. *Douala: Ville et Histoire.* Paris: Institut d'Ethnologie, 1975.

Joseph, R. *Radical Nationalism in Cameroon.* Oxford University Press, 1977.

Drama, Film: Postcolonial

African drama and film are driven and defined by the language, culture, and ethnic group of the individual artists. It is, however, at times these artists' protests of poor conditions and failed promises of independence that bring them national and international attention—not only as, for example, an Amharic writer, a Yoruban writer, or an Akan writer, but as one born out of the neocolonial realities of Ethiopia, Nigeria, or Ghana.

The salient question that artists pose throughout their work is how traditionalism and modernism should be balanced against the everyday dire realities of people as they struggle to survive the chaos caused by the historical trajectory of colonialism and postcolonialism.

In addressing this question, a canonical group of playwrights exists that seeks to reaffirm the greatness of Africa while demonizing the white man whose colonial imposition tempered this greatness. The plays *Chaka* by Leopold Sedar Senghor of Senegal and *Kurunmi* by Yoruban writer Ola Rotimi are representative of this canon. Ebrahim Hussein of Tanzania also demonstrates the themes of this canon in his play *Kinjeketile*, which revises the history of the 1904 Maji Maji Uprising for dramatic effect.

In attempting to address postcolonial political issues in their work, many authors come into conflict with their governments. The clash between the individual artist and state authority can be seen in the lives of Wole Soyinka in Nigeria; the Gikuyu (now exiled) Ngugi wa Thiong'o from Kenya; and Amadu Maddy in Sierra Leone. The imprisonment, exile, and, at times, execution of artists demonstrate that aesthetic expressions carry with them great risks. Wole Soyinka, "the great protester," who has been recognized as the most prominent African playwright, is an example. His plays have been produced in Nigeria, London, and in the United States on Broadway. Soyinka and his contemporaries—most notably, Dexter Lyndersay and Ola Rotimi—have successfully worked to establish a viable Nigerian theater. But Soyinka's "protest drama," revealing the contradictions of modernism, has brought the ire and wrath of the Nigerian government upon him. Using satire and parody, his plays reveal how power corrupts absolutely and, thus, is the basis of chaotic society. Both his *Madmen and Specialists* and *The Man Died,* written in the context of the chaotic Nigerian civil war, and the abuse he received while imprisoned, clearly demonstrate the difficulty of artists using drama to clarify the many issues within postcolonial state formation.

On another level, these artists, as do most others, address the contradictions of using European dramatic forms by developing theatrical plays that have a peculiarly indigenous orientation, sensibility, language, theme, context, spirit, and values. In Nigeria, for example, university drama students, using the indigenous Hausa language and working with village actors, dramatized the annual Kalankuwa festival, which satirized the transitional process of military to civilian rule.

Even when the English language is used, these playwrights have done "great violence to standard English," according to the South African playwright Ezekiel Mphahlele. They have sought to contour the language to indigenous semantic forms, opening up their dramatic work to audiences on the world stage. All African playwrights seek to create viable and legitimate works of dramatic art that will stand the scrutiny of critics of the West. The criticism that these plays and playwrights have received broaches various dimensions. Critics have examined the "functionality" of drama as it does or does not express real social structures within the collective African ethos. Does drama that addresses a social malaise restrict the writer to such "political questions"? Critics pose the question of whether such questions as *Négritude* should be a driving force that defines drama; as Soyinka sarcastically observes, "A tiger does not have to proclaim his tigritude." In the context of the problematics of postcolonialism, is there such a thing as art for art's sake?

Responding to the criticism from within and without, the Arab Theatre Conference was held in Casablanca in November 1966. Conferees from Algeria, Libya, Tunisia, Morocco, Syria, Lebanon, and the United Arab Republic attempted to address various critical questions, problems, and issues in developing institutional drama. The growth of Arab drama can be seen in the work of Egyptian playwright Tewfik Al-Hakim, whose *The Tree Climber* was published by Oxford University Press; in Algerian playwright Mouloud Mammeir's *Le Foehn* and Emmanuel Robles's work, which have received international praise; and in the numerous works of Amharic playwright Tsegaye Gabre-Medhin.

Receiving critical praise in Francophone Africa are Bernard Dadie's plays *Beatrice du Congo* and *Monsieur Thogo-Gnini*, which have continued presence in African theater today even though they were first performed in the early 1970s. In Cameroon, Guillaume Oyono-Mbia defined its national theater with his social comedy *Trois Pretendants . . . un mari*. South Africa's Athol Fugard's plays, which have been produced internationally, reveal the problems and issues that existed under the now collapsed system of apartheid. Kenya produced the promising female playwright Rebecca Njau, whose play *Scar* has been widely noted. In Ghana, two women, Efua Sutherland and Ama Ata Aidoo, established their works as creative revelations. Sutherland's Ghana Experimental Theatre has worked to establish theater among the traditional masses through the Kodzidan ("story house") in Ekumfi-Atwia.

Arguably, drama and film were transitioned through the works of the Yoruban/Nigerian playwright Hubert Ogunde, whose works were produced on film in the 1970s and early 1980s. But it was Ousmane Sembene's 1963 film *Borom Sarret* that defined African cinema in the postcolonial period.

However, the rise of African film was first a struggle by Africans to extricate their film from the European neocolonialists who controlled production, distribution, and exhibition. Unlike the later dramatists who often clashed with the state, some early filmmakers thought that the state could help in alleviating foreign domination. Francophone filmmakers took the lead by organizing the Federation of Panafricaine des Cineastes (FEPACI) in Algiers in 1969. The FEPACI as a dialogic film festival sought to use film as a tool to mold mass revolutionary consciousness. By the 1960s, both Tunisian and Algerian filmmakers, with the support of state cinematic offices, had produced such classics as *L'aube des dammes* by Ahmed Rachedi, *Vent des aures* by Mohamed Lakdhar-Hamina, and *La voix* by Slim Riad. In Mozambique, the National Film Institute was established in 1975; it created the monthly film series Kuxa Kenema ("Birth of the Image"), which sought to mold a mass social consciousness. Film as political art was introduced in Nigeria by Ola Balogun with *Ija Ominira* (1977) and *Cry Freedom* (1981).

A turning point in independent African film occurred when young filmmakers met at the Quagadougou Festival in 1981 and established the oppositional Le Collectif L'Oeil Vert, which criticized the FEPACI for not doing enough to support and help develop a truly independent African film industry. Responding to this challenge, the FEPACI met in 1982 and produced "Le Manifeste de Niamey," which restated their commitment to their first principles.

The tensions within African filmmakers combined with their creative energies to produce internationally recognized films. In 1967, Cannes awarded Lakhdar Hamina's *Vent des Aures* a prize. This achievement was followed in 1969 with the prize-winning *Le Mandat*, by Ousmane Sembene, at the Festival of Venice. The ultimate legitimation of African cinema occurred at Cannes in 1975 when Hamina's *Chronique des Annees de Braise* was honored with a major prize. Other prize-winning films during this period were Sembene's *Xala*, Mahama Traore's *N'Diangane*, and the Mauritanian filmmaker Med Hondo's *Les Bicots Negres Vos Voisins*. Africa's own acclaimed film festival at Ouagadougou conveyed prizes for the excellent *Djeli*, by Fadika Kramo Lancine of the Ivory Coast; and *Finye*, by Soulemane Cisse of Mali.

The Guadeloupean Sarah Maldoror established herself with the only fictionalized view of the Angolan liberation struggle in *Sambizanga*, while in the same year the Senegalese woman filmmaker Safi Faye addressed sexism of both the French man and the African man in her short Parisian based-film, *La passante*. The South African film *You Have Struck A Rock*, by Debbie

May, chronicled the resistance of black women to the pass system, and the Burkina Faso filmmaker Idrissa Ouedrago has won prizes for her work, including the noted *Tilai*. Cheick Oumar Sissoko's *Finzan* reveals how women are socially and sexually oppressed, but also how they gain their dignity via collective struggle. Kenya's Anne Mungai's *Saikati* (1992) explores the dichotomous world of rural and urban women.

All the African liberation movements produced documentary film to highlight and dramatize their struggle. The African-American filmmaker Robert Van Lierop, and other foreign directors produced films that chronicled ongoing wars of liberation. Sarah Maldoror's short film *Monangambee* illustrates the conflict between Portuguese colonialism and African revolutionary struggle. Glauber Rocha's *The Lion Has Seven Heads* constructed a Pan-African format of struggle by filming a story by which Che Guevara is "magically resurrected in Zumbi-the spirit of Amilcar Carbral."

Even greater international critical acclaim for African film came in 1987 when Souleymane Cisse's *Yeelen* won a prize at Cannes by exploring the interpersonal dynamics of father and son within the Bambara people of Mali. In 1992, the Ethiopian-born Haile Gerima's *Sanfoka* became a commercial success by advocating a Pan-Africanist connection between slavery in the Americas and the African return by those of the diaspora.

African postcolonial drama and film continues to develop and address broad issues and topics, and will tell complex stories that will clarify the past, elucidate the present, and give direction for the future.

MALIK SIMBA

See also: **Art and Architecture, History of African; Art, Postcolonial; Négritude.**

Further Reading

Bakari, I., and M. Cham (eds.). *African Experiences of Cinema.* London: British Film Institute, 1996.

Basrber, K., J. Collins, and A. Ricard (eds.). *West African Popular Theatre.* Bloomington: Indiana University Press, 1997.

Bjornson, R. *The African Quest for Freedom and Identity: Cameroonian Writing and the National Experience*, Bloomington: Indiana University Press, 1991

Diawara, M. *African Cinema: Politics and Culture.* Bloomington: Indiana University Press, 1992.

Etherton, M. *The Development of African Drama.* London: University Library for Africa, 1982.

Harrow, K. W. *With Open Eyes: Women and African Cinema,* Amsterdam: Rodopi, 1997.

Martin, M. T. (ed.). *Cinemas of the Black Diaspora.* Detroit: Wayne State University Press, 1995.

Tomaselli, K. *The Cinema of Apartheid: Race and Class in South African Film.* London: Routledge, 1989.

Drought, Famine, Displacement

Drought was the main cause of famine in Africa until the early 1980s. Since 1972, the continent has had to cope with a repetitive phase of climatic change that, as historians have demonstrated, is far from being exceptional in the light of Africa's long history. Nevertheless, during the past 30 years the role played by drought in its crises of subsistence has continuously become less important.

The memory of the major famines of the colonial era is preserved both in colonial archives and in memoirs. The earliest such famine authentically within living memory resulted from the catastrophic cycle of droughts in the closing years of the nineteenth century, which unfortunately coincided with the harshest phase of colonial conquest. One-third, or even half, of the population of tropical Africa was wiped out between 1880 and 1920. The main cycles of drought and famine occurred in West Africa during the twentieth century

- between 1900 and 1903 on the loop of the Niger;
- in 1913–1914, at the start of World War I; this was probably the greatest famine of the century, since the colonial administration still had neither the means nor the will to act against it;
- the drought and famine of 1931–1932, which coincided with the worldwide economic depression;
- the famine of 1941–1942, the effects of which were accentuated by the impact of war;
- the famines of 1954 and 1967, known as the *bandabari* ("turning the back," or "turning away") since, in a sign of the times, customary solidarities began to break down;
- the famine of 1973–1975, known among the Songhay as the *dabari-ban* ("nothing more to be done");
- the famine of 1984–1985, known as the *Ce-taafa*, which, according to residents of Timbuktu, was "comparable to that of 1913" (see Gado 1992).

Some famines directly linked to drought have occurred relatively recently, the result not of a single bad season but of a series of successive years of shortage that, by obstructing potential recovery year upon year, have eventually culminated in catastrophe. This is what happened in Ethiopia in 1979–1980, and again in Ethiopia and Sudan in 1984–1985.

There has been considerable progress in forecasting the hazards of climate, both on the national level and among the providers of international aid, since the long phase of drought in the years 1972–1975 and the period that followed it up to the early 1990s. Policies for prevention have been applied, for example, in Niger, which is far from exceptional in arranging for the systematic cultivation of rice. It has been supported by substantial aid from China and the centralized warehousing of harvest surpluses in anticipation of bad years, which remain a possibility. Such arrangements have proved to be relatively effective. Hence, it is possible to observe a breaking of what used to be an inevitable linkage between drought and famine as long as other factors, such as warfare or an aberrant political regime, do not intervene.

Detailed study has shown that this change was heralded, around the end of the colonial period, by the famine that occurred in 1949 in Malawi (then known as Nyasaland). This famine undoubtedly began after a severe drought, but the way in which the catastrophe developed from that point on differed significantly from the way in which famines, caused by shortages and negligence, developed during the early years of colonization. The famine of 1949 resulted from a new agrarian structure and a new means of organizing labor, in the context of an accelerated growth in population. The farmers exported a significant proportion of their output, both of subsistence crops (in this case, sorghum) and of nonedible crops (cotton and tobacco), and were thus increasingly dependent on the market for their own subsistence. After the famine, many of them set out to plant manioc, a crop that matures relatively quickly, as a provision against the risk of future shortages. This famine was, then, no longer the result of the abandonment of subsistence cultivation in favor of cultivation for export. It represented instead a new division of labor. As the men departed for construction sites, mines, cities, and foreign countries, the women, left at home, took on the burden of rural labor. The victims of famine were no longer the same as before: the old, the infirm, the sick, and children were given aid by the authorities just as much as those earning their livings were. In short, from this time onward the colonial state took on the role formerly played by customary systems of solidarity. Yet it neglected the women who now formed the main agricultural labor force, forcing them to turn to older social structures that were no longer capable of meeting their needs. The welfare state undoubtedly alleviated suffering, but it did so more unevenly, in response to the degree of integration of individuals into the market economy. Thus it was that later famines came to differ from the "crises of subsistence" of earlier times (Vaughan 1987).

According to international statistics, in any "normal" year 100 million Africans (out of a total population estimated at around 800 million) are suffering from hunger or malnutrition. In addition, almost all famines are aggravated by human intervention, whether in the form of massive, authoritarian displacements of populations or in the form of warfare (often at the same time), which has the same effect.

Two types of migration have a more or less direct relationship with this desperately low level of nutrition: forced migration and migration to the cities. The displacements of population that are often the most lethal are directly linked to war—which means, mainly, civil war. The appearance of organized refugee camps should not allow us to forget either the masses of people whose fates are unknown, or the fact that massive transfers of population, generating famine, malnutrition, and massacre, always result in enormous numbers of fatalities: half a million in the war over Biafra, perhaps a million in Ethiopia, and certainly as many as that in Sudan, Mozambique, Rwanda, and Congo. These forced displacements are not necessarily due to military operations in the strict sense, but may be induced by authoritarian politics, as in Sudan. As a result, there are many different types of refugee (Salih 1999).

The most paradoxical of famines are those caused in the name of "development," by "villagization" or by the construction of large dams, or even for the sake of protecting the environment, as in the case of national parks. Famines no longer result—at least not directly—from drought, but from the clumsy authoritarian measures taken to supposedly remedy drought. This was the case with the campaigns of authoritarian "villagization" undertaken in the postcolonial era by "socialist" regimes (Tanzania in the late 1970s, Ethiopia from 1981, Mozambique between 1977 and 1983, Somalia in 1988). In itself, the idea was not a bad one. In countries where settlements were utterly dispersed and there was a very low level of technology, the modernization of agriculture seemed to require the creation of cooperatives, bringing people together on terrain that was, sometimes, less dry; hence the forced removal of Ethiopians from the north to the south of their country. However, these projects were implemented in an authoritarian, precipitous, and unplanned manner, with hordes of starving farmers being sent off without having time even to gather provisions for the coming year. The results were catastrophic, as millions died.

As for migration to the cities, this followed a pattern similar to what had occurred during the colonial era. Life in the cities might be difficult, yet it seemed more likely to provide employment, however informal, as well as security (through education, health care, and so on). Since the attainment of independence, the exodus from the countryside has taken on unprecedented proportions all over the continent, as people depart to the cities of South Africa, the diamond mines of the Central African Republic and Zimbabwe, or the port cities of the Ivory Coast, where 36 per cent of the population consists of foreigners. Even a relatively small crisis of subsistence can aggravate this tendency, given the rapid growth of populations and the increasing exhaustion of the land. Accordingly, movement toward the cities has accelerated ever since the long phase of drought in the 1970s, and on into the 1980s and 1990s. In Zimbabwe, for example, the drought of 1991–1992 had a drastic impact on an agricultural sector that had been developed mainly on the basis of maize and yet had been presented by many observers as a "success story." Faced with a harvest of around one-fifth of normal output, 4.5 million people soon came to require aid merely to survive, and more than 2,000 tons of grain had to be imported as a matter of urgency. The agricultural crisis in certain countries, such as Lesotho, the Central African Republic, Zambia, or the countries of the Sahel, has been so extensive as to make a profound impact on the whole of the rural system of production, as well as on education. Imbalances have therefore been accentuated even further in favor of the cities, notably in Congo or Côte d'Ivoire. We find ourselves with this new paradox: drought and subsistence crises have increased the influx of poor people into the cities, and it is the cities that are expected to deal with the poverty that results from the fragility of the countryside. Given the relative lack of education among workers, the cities disintegrate under the swarms of illiterate laborers coming straight from the country, while rural area often find themselves short of workers. In such cities as Dakar or Lagos, where the growth of the so-called informal sector prevents the resolution of the structural problem of underemployment, the situation is becoming explosive. It appears that certain factors that used to be considered separately are now irretrievably interconnected: ecological hazards, demography, politics, and the cities.

CATHERINE COQUERY-VIDROVITCH

Further Reading

Braun, J. von, Tesfaye Teklu, and Patrick Webb. *Famine in Africa: Causes, Responses, and Prevention*. Baltimore: Johns Hopkins University Press, 1999.

Dalby, D. (ed.). *Drought in Africa*. London: International African Institute, 1975.

Gado, Alpha Boureima. *Crises alimentaires et stratégies de subsistance en Afrique sahélienne*. Paris: L'Harmattan, 1992.

Hjort af Ornäs, Anders, and M. A. Mohamed Salih. *Ecology and Politics: Environmental Stress and Security in Africa*. Uppsala, Sweden: Scandinavian Institute of African Studies, 1989.

Sahn, D. E., P. A. Dorosh, and Stephen D. Youger. *Structural Adjustment Reconsidered: Economic Policy and Poverty in Africa*. Cambridge: Cambridge University Press, 1997.

Salih, M.A. M. *Environmental Politics and Liberation in Contemporary Africa*. Dordrecht, Netherlands: Kluwer Academic, 1999.

Tarver, J. D. *The Demography of Africa*. London: Praeger, 1996.

Touré, M., and T. O. Fayodami (eds.). *Migrations, Development and Urbanization Policies in Sub-Saharan Africa*. Oxford: CODESRIA Books, 1992.

Vaughan, M. *The Story of an African Famine: Gender and Famine in Twentieth-Century Malawi*. Cambridge: Cambridge University Press, 1987.

Watts, M. *Silent Violence: Food, Famine, and Peasantry in Northern Nigeria*. Berkeley and Los Angeles: University of California Press, 1983.

Dual Mandate: *See* Togo: Colonial Period: Dual Mandate, 1919–1957.

Du Bois, W. E. B. and Pan-Africanism

The life of William Edward Burghardt DuBois (1868–1963), the distinguished African American intellectual, partly mirrors the story of Pan-Africanism. Du Bois was born in Massachusetts in 1868 and died a citizen of the independent West African state of Ghana in 1963. By 1900, Du Bois had studied in the United States and Germany and written books on the history of the U.S. slave trade and a sociological study, *The Philadelphia Negro* (1899). He taught in various black colleges, but increasingly became disenchanted with scholarship. In his book of influential essays, *The Souls of Black Folk* (1903), DuBois described the "double consciousness" experienced by African Americans living in a white-dominated society. He also challenged Booker T. Washington's conservative ideas on race and black education through artisanal skills. As a member of the Niagara Movement (1905), DuBois argued that racial discrimination should be confronted and that African American interests could best be promoted by the activities of an educated elite, what he called the "talented tenth." Du Bois became actively involved in the struggle for African American civil rights. In 1910 he joined the National Association for the Advancement of Colored People (NAACP), becoming editor of its critical journal, *The Crisis*, which became an outlet for his radicalism and literary ideas, and earned him the title of "spokesman of the race."

DuBois was also deeply interested in the African diaspora and Pan-Africanism, an interest reflected in his study *The Negro* (1915). In 1900 he had taken part in the Pan-African Conference that met in London. After World War I, DuBois helped to organize four Pan-African Congresses: in Paris (1919); London, Brussels, and Paris (1921); London and Lisbon (1922–1923); and New York (1927). These small gatherings, composed mainly of African Americans from the United States and the Caribbean along with white sympathizers, passed resolutions demanding an end to racial discrimination and the extension of democracy to the colonial empires. In late 1923 DuBois visited Africa for the first time.

Pan-Africanism had its origins in the late eighteenth century and arose out of the experience of enslavement and the black diaspora. It resulted in demands for repatriation to Africa and the cultural idea of a black world, and of one unified African people. Africa was often symbolically identified as Ethiopia, and "Ethiopianism" has a long legacy running through African American Christian organizations, Marcus Garvey's "Back to Africa" movement, and Rastafarianism, which claimed the emperor of Ethiopia as a divine figure. For most of its history Pan-Africanism has been an idea espoused by black people outside Africa. As such, it contains strong elements of racial romanticism. In the late 1890s DuBois had spoken of "Pan-Negroism," while Henry Sylvester Williams, from Trinidad, planned the Pan-African Conference of 1900 to represent members of the "African race from all parts of the world."

Small "Back to Africa" movements existed in the Americas in the nineteenth century but the idea was given new life by Marcus Garvey, the Jamaican populist, who emigrated to the United States. In 1914 Garvey had founded the black nationalist United Negro Improvement Association (UNIA). The UNIA expanded rapidly in North America from 1918 to 1921, with its appeal as an international organization which encouraged racial pride and self-improvement, and a radical program denouncing colonialism in Africa and advocating black repatriation to the continent. Garvey bitterly denounced DuBois and the NAACP. The UNIA had a small following in Africa but its newspaper, *The Negro World*, was banned in most colonies as subversive.

In the interwar years Pan-Africanism was shaped principally from three directions; first, by Garveyism, which was also influential in the Harlem Renaissance, an African American literary and artistic movement focused on New York during the 1920s; second, by cultural ideas emanating from the Caribbean in the 1920s–1930s and generally known as *Négritude*, which argued that black people must regain their African culture; and third, by international failure to act against the Italian fascist invasion of Ethiopia in 1935, which served as a political catalyst for black people both within Africa and throughout the diaspora.

World War I helped stimulate political consciousness in both Africa and the black diaspora. World War II had a much more profound impact, especially on Africa. A fifth Pan-African Congress met in Manchester, England, in 1945 and, as before, DuBois played a major part in organizing and presiding over its proceedings. However, unlike previous congresses which had been run by African Americans, the meeting was dominated by Africans, including nationalists such as Jomo Kenyatta, Obafemi Awolowo, Hastings Banda, and Kwame Nkrumah, all of whom were all later to become political leaders in their own countries. The Manchester congress passed resolutions calling for the end of racial discrimination and for independence for the colonies. Some of the declarations denounced capitalist imperialism, one concluding with a rallying cry mirroring the Communist Manifesto: "Colonial and Subject Peoples of the World—Unite." The fifth congress indicated a revived interest in Pan-Africanism, but perhaps more important, it marked a new and vital phase in the struggle against colonial rule that resulted in the large-scale transfer of power in Africa during the next two decades.

DuBois's contribution to Pan-Africanist ideas was considerable. At Manchester he was honored as a founding father by the younger African and Caribbean nationalists. But after 1945 his influence began to wane as he was superseded by younger, more radical voices. DuBois was not always an easy man to work with. His career within the NAACP had been punctuated by often vigorous political controversy with fellow African Americans, a tension increased by DuBois's growing interest in communism and his denunciation of colleagues' conservatism over matters of race. In 1934 he resigned from the NAACP only to rejoin ten years later. Tensions continued as DuBois moved further to the left and in 1948 he was dismissed from the NAACP. DuBois then formed, with Paul Robeson and others, the Council of African Affairs, a socialist anticolonial organization. The growing hostility to communism in the United States in the early 1950s led to the now avowedly communist DuBois clashing with the courts and having his passport seized. In 1959 he emigrated to Ghana, where at the invitation of President Kwame Nkrumah, he became a citizen and also started work on editing an abortive *Encyclopedia Africana*.

Pan-African ideas had a strong appeal to some of the nationalist leaders in colonial Africa. The most outspoken advocate was Nkrumah, who led Ghana to independence in 1957. His thinking was partly influenced by George Padmore, originally from Trinidad and a former Stalinist, who argued in *Pan-Africanism or Communism* (1956) that the coming struggle for Africa depended on nationalist leaders resolving their communal and ethnic differences and embracing Pan-Africanism. Socialism was central to the Pan-Africanism of both Padmore and Nkrumah. Nkrumah's book, *Africa Must Unite* (1963) was dedicated to Padmore and "to the African Nation that must be."

This kind of idealism was based more on rhetoric than realistic politics. Good reasons could be advanced for African unity: only political unity would lead to economic strength and enable the continent to be truly free of colonial influence; the artificial frontiers imposed on Africa by colonial rule would be ended;

and a united Africa would wield influence along with other noncommitted powers in a world divided between East and West. But attempts to create even binational federations failed, as African leaders were divided by political and economic ideologies. At independence, the fragile unity of many new African states was threatened by internal ethnic, political, and religious rivalries, and there were also tensions with neighboring states. In 1963 the Organization of African Unity was created in Addis Ababa. Its founding members agreed to promote unity "by establishing and strengthening common institutions"; at the same time they pledged to uphold each state's sovereignty and maintain the integrity of the inherited colonial frontiers. Lip service continued to be given to the ideal of African unity, though increasingly this was interpreted in terms of history and cultural heritage and not as a realistic short-term political ambition. A sixth Pan-African Congress, meeting in Dar es Salaam in 1974, revealed many of these divisions. A number of Pan-African organizations were created, but these mainly represent sectional (e.g. trade union) or regional interests within the continent. Closer economic cooperation is a sought-after goal, the Abuja conference in 1991 declared that it aimed to create a Pan-African Economic Community by 2025.

By the end of the twentieth century Pan-Africanism had little significance within Africa other than as rhetoric. The main proponents of Pan-Africanism were within the black diaspora communities, mainly in the United States. Such ideas were strengthened by the Black Power movement of the 1960s–1970s, with its strong political agenda and stress on cultural and artistic identification with Africa.

DAVID KILLINGRAY

See also: **Négritude; Nkrumah, Kwame.**

Further Reading

DuBois, W. E. B. *The Negro.* New York (1915). Reprint, London: Oxford University Press, 1970.
———. *The Souls of Black Folk* (1903). Reprint, New York: Dover, 1994.
Esedebe, P. Olisanwuche. *Pan-Africanism: The Idea and the Movement 1776–1963.* Washington, D.C.: Howard University Press, 1982.
Geiss, I. *The Pan-African Movement* (1968). London: Methuen, 1974.
Lewis, D. Levering. *W. E. B. DuBois: Biography of a Race 1868–1919.* New York: Henry Holt, 1993.
Moses, W. J. *The Golden Age of Black Nationalism, 1850–1925* (1978). Reprint, New York: Oxford University Press, 1988.
Nkrumah, K. *Africa Must Unite.* London: Heinemann, 1963.
Padmore, G. *Pan-Africanism or Communism?* London: Dennis Dobson, 1956.
Rudwick, E. M. *W. E. B. DuBois: Propagandist of the Negro Protest.* Philadelphia: University of Pennsylvania Press, 1960.

Dube, John Langalibalele (1871–1946)
First President of the South African Native National Congress

John Langalibalele Dube, often called the Booker T. Washington of South Africa, was an educator, minister, newspaper editor, and the first president of the South African Native National Congress (SANNC), the forerunner of the African National Congress.

In the 1900s, all over South Africa, *kholwa* (Christian converts, ardent exponents of the Protestant work ethic and the value of private property) were hampered in their quest for accumulation and acceptance. In response, they created a network of political associations, among them the Natal Native Congress, which John Dube helped found in 1901. It aimed to secure a nonracial franchise and freehold land tenure for Africans. Dube's many activities led most white Natalians to regard him as a dangerous agitator in these years, and he was detained for alleged sedition during the South African War and was reprimanded for his articles during the 1906 Poll Tax rebellion in Natal. When, in 1907–1908, the Zulu king Dinuzulu was arrested and tried for allegedly inciting the rebellion, Dube's *Ilanga lase Natal*, an English- and Zulu-language newspaper, defended him passionately.

The impending unification of the South African colonies spurred more unified black action, and Dube used the columns of *Ilanga* to urge British intervention against a union in which Africans would not be citizens. In 1909, he helped convene the South African Native Convention to oppose the color bar in the Act of Union, and accompanied a deputation to Britain to lobby against the legislation. Known at this time as Mafukuzela, "the one who struggles against obstacles," Dube was elected first president general of the newly formed SANNC in 1912.

In 1913, the Natives Land Act, which restricted African landholding, and transformed rent-paying and sharecropping tenants into laborers, enabled the SANNC to mobilize a far wider constituency. In 1913–1914, Dube denounced the act, and led a SANNC delegation to Britain in an unsuccessful attempt to get it reversed. Nevertheless, by 1917 he had been ousted from the organization's presidency, ostensibly because of his preparedness to accept the principle of segregation embedded in the act.

In the interwar years, Dube was part of a conservative establishment of wealthier *kholwa* landowners and professionals who felt increasingly threatened by rising radicalism among African workers, and what he termed the "socialistic" principles espoused by Africans on the Rand. In 1927 he refused to cooperate with the African National Congress under the left-wing Josiah Gumede, and in 1930 threw his weight behind the conservative Pixley Seme as president, joining his executive administration. They soon fell out, however, and Dube retreated to his Natal base. Successive attempts to bring Dube and Natal back into the national fold failed, and by the 1940s Dube was too ill to remain active. In 1945 his designated successor, Abner Mtimkulu, was defeated in the elections for presidency of the Natal Congress by A.W.G. Champion, Dube's longtime rival and former leader of the Industrial and Commercial Workers' Union in Natal. Champion now returned Natal to the national fold.

During the 1920s Dube attended the second Pan-African Conference in London called by W. E. B. DuBois and was clearly influenced by the latter's call for race pride and purity. These ideas affected Dube's thinking on his return to South Africa, and he now sought popular support through strengthening his links with the Zulu royal family. In 1924 Dube became deeply involved in the restructuring of the first Inkatha movement, which aimed to gain state recognition for the Zulu monarchy as the "mouthpiece of the Zulu nation."

At the same time, Dube participated in government-created native conferences and with white liberals in the Joint Council of Europeans and Non-Europeans in Durban. In 1935, despite his membership in the executive committee of the All-Africa Convention (which was formed to fight legislation designed to remove Cape Africans from the voters' roll), Dube supported the legislation, persuaded that it would secure extra reserved land for Africans. In 1937 and again in 1942 he was elected by rural Natal to the Native Represetative Council created by this legislation, but when he retired in 1945, his seat was won by the then unknown Chief Albert Luthuli.

For all his ambiguities, Dube was one of the pioneers of African nationalism in South Africa and a man of considerable educational and literary achievement. In addition to his journalism for *Ilanga lase Natal*, he published *Isita Somuntu Nguye* (*The Enemy of the African is Himself*, 1922), *Insila ka Shaka* (*Jeqe, the Bodyservant of King Tshaka*, 1933), and *Ushembe* (1935), a biography of the independent leader and prophet who founded the independent Israelite Church in Natal. In 1936 he was the first African to be awarded an honorary degree by the University of South Africa, for his contribution to African education. He died of a stroke in 1946.

SHULA MARKS

See also: **Plaatje, Sol T.; South Africa: African National Congress; South Africa: Peace, Reconstruction, Union: 1902–1910.**

Biography

Bornn 1871 at the American Zulu mission of Inanda. Educated at Inanda and Amanzimtoti Training Institute (later Adams). Sailed for the United States in 1887, and subsequently attended Oberlin College. Returning to Natal, married Nokutela Mdina, and together they began mission work among the Qadi. Returned to study at a theological seminary in the United States in 1896; ordained, and used the opportunity to collect money for a school planned to for the Ohlange in the Inanda district. Returned to Natal in 1899 and was appointed pastor there at Inanda (until 1908). Opened Ohlange in 1901, the first industrial school founded and run by an African, and in 1903 launched *Ilanga lase Natal*, remaining its editor until 1915. In 1936 was the first African to be awarded an honorary degree by the University of South Africa, for contributions to African education. Died of a stroke in 1946.

Further Reading

Cope, N., *To Bind the Nation: Solomon kaDinuzulu and Zulu Nationalism, 1913–1933*. Pietermaritzburg, South Africa: University of Natal Press, 1993.

Davis, R. Hunt, Jr. "John L. Dube: A South African Exponent of Booker T. Washington." *Journal of African Studies* 2, no. 4 (1975–1976).

"John L. Dube." In *From Protest to Challenge: A Documentary History of African Politics in South Africa, 1882–1964*, vol. 4, edited by Gail M. Gerhart and Thomas Karis. Stanford, Calif.: Hoover Institution Press, 1977.

Marks, S. *The Ambiguities of Dependence: Class, Nationalism and the State in Twentieth-Century Natal*. Baltimore: John Hokins University Press/Johannesburg: Ravan Press, 1986.

Walshe, P. *The Rise of African Nationalism in South Africa: the African National Congress, 1912–1952*. London: C. Hurst, 1970.

Durban

The coastal city of Durban (Zulu name, Tekweni) originated as the British trading settlement of Port Natal in 1824 and developed in the twentieth century into one of southern Africa's most important commercial ports, manufacturing centers, and holiday resorts. Until the latter half of the nineteenth century, the surrounding region was dominated by the Natal Nguni-speaking peoples and the Zulu kingdom that lay to the north. After Portuguese explorer Vasco De Gama noted, in 1497, that it afforded an ideal natural harbor and elevated bluff, European merchants arrived at the site to trade with African communities for skins and ivory. Thereafter, the white presence in Durban and its environs increased, culminating in the establishment of an urban society deeply divided by race and class.

Durban's early history was characterized by the ebb and flow of frontier relations among Boer Voortrekkers, English traders, and the majority Nguni. In the first half of the nineteenth century, the fledgling trading settlement, established by ex-Cape Colonists Francis Farewell and Henry Fynn, was dominated by African society and overshadowed by the emerging Zulu kingdom. Initially, the founder of the Zulu state, Shaka kaSenzangakhona, granted the white settlers permission to occupy the site and trade in the area subject to Zulu authority. In the early 1820s, African custom and law prevailed in Port Natal society as white settlers adapted to the local context and the majority African population, to the extent that they acted as "client" Zulu chiefs. As Shaka consolidated his control over the region through a process referred to as the *mfecane*, Nguni chiefdoms which were not subordinated to the Zulu dispersed, sending waves of refugees toward Port Natal. Tensions rose between the settlement and the Zulu state as the Zulu king perceived the burgeoning refugee population as a potential threat. Following Shaka's assassination in 1828, his successor, Dingane, faced two fronts of white expansion; one from Port Natal, and one from Boer Trekkers, who had recently fled the British-dominated Cape, and settled in the region.

Over the course of the next 20 years, Cape colonial and British imperial intervention supported the settlement's expansion. In 1835 an uneasy peace between the Port Natal settlers and the Zulu was established by the British missionary, Allen Gardiner, who laid the foundations for an organized permanent urban settlement and named it after the then governor of the Cape, Sir Benjamin D'Urban. An initial alliance between the Trekkers and Durban traders against the Zulu led to military conflict as the Boers and traders sought to push the Zulu back. The Boers, however, asserted their hegemony over the region by establishing the Republic of Natalia after their victory over the Zulu at the Ncome River in 1838. In response, British troops occupied Durban in 1842. The early settler, Dick King, then saved Durban from Boer retaliation at the battle of Congella by making a now legendary ride to Grahamstown for relief. After the repulse of Boer forces, the Cape governor, Sir George Napier, annexed Natal on May 31, 1844, because of British concern over intensified Boer conflict with Africans which threatened to spill over into the Cape and the potential for the strategic port to fall into the hands of a foreign power.

In the second half of the nineteenth century, Durban developed into a white-dominated city as the forces of settler capitalism transformed the urban space and the region. In 1846, Sir Theophilus Shepstone, diplomatic agent to the native tribes, implemented a system of segregation that limited African ownership of land to a series of fragmented reserves. Thereafter, white settlement proceeded apace as land with the potential for sugar-cane cultivation came available. Demands for cheap labor grew as the port and merchant sectors of Durban expanded with the development of rail links to mining centers in the interior. These demands were filled with Indian immigrants, who later established themselves as market gardeners and merchants, and migrant African workers who established niches as dockworkers and domestic servants. Despite the upheaval of violent conflict in the region during the Anglo-Zulu War of 1879 and the Anglo-Boer War of 1899–1902, Durban flourished. Indeed, these conflicts only served to stimulate the local economy and to galvanize white racist attitudes. A combination of a burgeoning white settler population and economic development culminated in Britain granting Natal, and its principle city, responsible government in 1893.

After the turn of the century, Durban became increasingly ordered and segregated along racial lines. Municipal authorities instituted the notorious Durban System, a pernicious structure of racist administration for urban Africans founded on the local government's monopoly over beer brewing and sales to African workers. Revenue from the monopoly paid for the intensified control of African lives in cramped barrack accommodations. Nevertheless, Africans and Indians established a vibrant presence in the city and it was home to some of South Africa's leading opposition politicians, including John Dube, A. W. G. Champion, and Mohandas Gandhi. During the 1920s and early 1930s, African society took advantage of a small legislative window of opportunity, prior to implementation of the Natives Law Amendment Act (1937), to purchase land on the fringes of the city. There, Africans established informal townships which grew into significant communities such as the Chateau and Good Hope estates.

By the end of the 1920s, however, racial tensions and oppression led to increased African resistance and opposition to the local white state. Africans responded to low wages, harsh working conditions, and egregious pass laws with a series of strikes that climaxed in the 1929 dockworkers' municipal beer hall boycott and a pass-burning demonstration in 1930. Both were brutally suppressed by the white authorities. During the later 1930s, the Durban government tightened control of Africans in the city, proclaimed the municipality a whites-only area and relegated Africans to a series of planned townships such as KwaMashu, Umlazi, and Chesterville. Thus, the city government segregated completely and made invisible the African presence outside the workplace.

In the apartheid years (1948–1991) African worker tensions intensified as the city's economy and population grew rapidly, rising from 162,000 people (over half African) in 1950 to 395,000 in 1970 and topping 2.5 million today. Increased urbanization and industrialization in the 1940s heightened tensions not only between whites and Africans, but also between Africans and the minority Indian population. In 1949, unable to make an effective attack on dominant white society, impoverished Africans struck at the Indian merchants they believed were taking advantage of them and plunged the city into riots. This was a turning point for Durban society, as each ethnic group sought to define itself in opposition to the others during the height of the Apartheid era. During the 1970s, the city was the focus of national attention as widespread strikes presaged the "Durban Moment," a period when local opposition groups set the pace for political change in South Africa. The catalyst for this united opposition to apartheid was the forced removal of informal African communities, such as Cato Manor, from the city and their "consolidation" into adjoining areas of the KwaZulu homeland. By 1984–1985 the tide was turning against the white minority government. African strike action intensified and African workers launched the Congress of South African Trade Unions in Durban's King's Park rugby stadium. Thereafter, Durban was often at the forefront of the struggle against apartheid.

ARAN S. MACKINNON

See also: **Natal, Nineteenth Century.**

Further Reading

Brookes, E. H., and C. de B. Webb. *A History of Natal*. Pietermaritzburg, South Africa: University of Natal Press, 1965.

Bryant, A. T. *Olden Times in Zululand and Natal, Containing Earlier Political History of the Eastern-Nguni Clans*. London: Longman, 1929.

Cooper, F. (ed.). *Struggle for the City: Migrant Labour, Capital and the State in Urban Africa*. Berkeley and Los Angeles: University of California Press, 1983.

Duminy, A., and B. Guest (eds.). *Natal and Zululand from Earliest Times to 1910*, Pietermaritzburg, South Africa: University of Natal Press, 1989.

Edwards, I. "Swing the Assegai Peacefully? 'New Africa,' Mkhumbane, the Co-operative Movement and Attempts to Transform Durban Society in the Late 1940s." In *Holding Their Ground: Class, Locality and Conflict in Nineteenth Century South Africa*, edited by P. Bonner, P. Delius, and D. Posel. Johannesburg: Zed Press, 1989.

Hattersley, A. *The British Settlement of Natal*. Cambridge: Cambridge University Press, 1950.

Hemson, D. "Class Consciousness and Migrant Workers: Dockworkers of Durban. "Ph.D. diss., University of Warwick, 1979.

Hindson, D. *Pass Controls and the Urban African Proletariat*. Johannesburg: Raven Press, 1987.

La Hausse, P. "The Message of the Warriors: The ICU, the Labouring Poor and the Making of a Popular Political Culture in Durban, 1925–1930." In *Holding Their Ground. Class, Locality and Conflict in Nineteenth Century South Africa*, edited by P. Bonner, P. Delius and D. Posel. Johannesburg: Zed Press, 1989.

Marks, S. *The Ambiguities of Dependence in South Africa*. Johannesburg: Raven Press, 1986.

Marks, S., and R. Rathbone (eds.). *Industrialisation and Social Change in South Africa: African Class Formation, Culture and Consciousness, 1870–1930*. London: Longman, 1982.

Maylam, P. "Aspects of African Urbanization in the Durban Area before 1940." In R. Haines and G. Buijs (eds.). *The Struggle for Social and Economic Space: Urbanization in Twentieth Century South Africa*. Durban: University of Natal Press, 1985.

Maylam, P., and I. Edwards (eds.). *The People's City: African Life in Twentieth Century Durban*, Portsmouth, N.H.: Heinemann, 1996.

Posel, R. "The Durban Ricksha Pullers' Strikes of 1918 and 1930." *Journal of Natal and Zulu History*, no. 8 (1985).

Swanson, M. "The Rise of Multiracial Durban: Urban History and Race Policy in South Africa, 1830–1930." Ph.D. diss., Harvard University, 1965.

———. "'The Durban System': Roots of Urban Apartheid in Colonial Natal." *African Studies*, no. 35 (1976).

Welsh, D. *The Roots Of Segregation: Native Policy In Colonial Natal, 1845–1910*. Cape Town: Oxford University Press, 1971.

Dyula: *See* Juula/Dyula.

E

East African Community, the, 1967–1977

The East African Community, which formally came into existence on December 1, 1967, was largely a reorganization of an already existing customs union (also providing other services) between Kenya, Tanzania and Uganda, which shared a joint British colonial heritage.

This customs union had come under increasing strain since the three nations had achieved independence. The East African Treaty of Cooperation sought to make their association more amenable to all involved parties. The three countries were associated by means of a common market that included a uniform external tariff and free trade on imported goods, a common currency, and a number of shared services such as railways, ports, and airways which had been brought together under the former East African Common Services Organization (EACSO). The main problem that needed to be rectified, as seen by Tanzania and Uganda, was that both the common market and services operated to the advantage of Kenya rather than the other two members, and sometimes to their actual disadvantage. In essence, because Kenya was more developed, it attracted the most investment while also maintaining the majority of employment opportunities, as the headquarters of most were located in Kenya.

Attempts at reform during the early 1960s had not worked, and by 1965 the common market was in danger of collapse. A commission under an independent chairman, the Danish economist Professor K. Philip, drew up a new treaty of East African cooperation (EAC), which came into force in December 1967. Its most important features were a transfer tax, an East African development bank, and the decentralization of the various common services headquarters. The object of the transfer tax (an import duty) that the three could impose on each other was to protect new manufacturing industries from existing ones in Kenya; in effect, the measure was deigned to encourage the growth of new industries in the two weaker partners. Under the treaty each member had to appoint a minister responsible for community activities.

A factor that worked against the success of the community was the clear divergence, in both character and political beliefs, of the three heads of state. Kenya's Jomo Kenyatta was a generation older than both Tanzania's Julius Nyerere and Uganda's Milton Obote. While Kenyatta was a conservative pragmatist, Nyerere was a dedicated socialist and something of an ideologue; meanwhile Obote was also in the process of moving to the political left. By 1970 a growing gap had developed between the moderate pro-Western policies of Kenya and the increasingly left-wing policies of the other two. One result of the 1967 Arusha Declaration in Tanzania, for example, was to persuade a number of Tanzanian civil servants to leave government service to go into the private sector, or seek jobs in the civil service.

The coup of January 1971, which ousted Obote and brought the unpredictable Idi Amin to power in Uganda, posed a potentially disastrous threat to the EAC. Tanzania refused to recognize the new government, and Nyerere declined to meet with Amin while giving political asylum to Obote. For most of 1971 the EAC was in crisis while the continuing (and growing) disparity in economic development between Kenya and the other two partners led to more or less permanent tensions between them. At that stage, the three determined to keep the EAC alive, as each considered dissolving the organization to be against their best interests. A row between Tanzania and Uganda centered on Amin's unilateral appointment of a new minister to the EAC without consultation as required under the treaty. Kenya attempted to mediate between the two nations.

The uneasy relations between the three led Zambia, which had opened formal negotiations in 1969 to join the EAC, to suspend its application. Kenya, meanwhile, complained that generous Chinese aid to Tanzania to help finance the TANZAM (Tanzania/Zambia) railway was undermining the demand for competitive goods (that is, Kenyan products) elsewhere in the community. Heavy losses by the East African Airways Corporation were another cause for concern.

By 1973 the situation had demonstrably worsened. Amin's erratic policies were wreaking havoc with the EAC, disrupting community trade and damaging tourism, which was vital to all three members. At the same time, both Tanzania and Uganda were imposing restrictions on Kenyan manufactured goods. In Kenya's parliament a call was made to revise the treaty. Amin called for an East African Federation. Meanwhile, most of the joint services or corporations ran into trouble, and the East African Income Tax Department was dismantled. In 1974 Kenya refused to remit Harbour Corporation funds to the head office in Dar es Salaam. Tanzania accused Kenya of depositing funds in a secret railway account to avoid sharing the money with its partners. Relations between Kenya and Tanzania deteriorated to the point that in December 1974 Kenya closed all but one border post with its neighbor, accusing Tanzania of trying to ruin its trade with Zambia.

The crisis in the community came to a head in 1975. In August a treaty review commission was set up to alleviate the growing tension. However, the EAC finally collapsed at the end of 1976, after a seminar attended by community specialists and the review commission both failed to produce any acceptable remedy.

Instead, the primary issue became how to disentangle the various joint services. This was made no easier by the fact that some services, most notably East African Railways, had been woefully mismanaged. Kenya favored a free trade common market and the retention of the East African Development Bank. Uganda was most troubled by the collapse of the EAC because it had no access to the sea. Under Nyerere, Tanzania was always suspicious of the capitalist path pursued by Kenya.

The end came in December 1977, when President Nyerere attacked Kenya for trying to alter the structures of the EAC in its favor and for behaving as though the community was primarily Kenya's, while treating Tanzania and Uganda as poor relations. There was no precisely negotiated end to the community; rather, it disintegrated gradually, although in January 1978 a Swiss diplomat, Victor Umbricht, was selected to preside over the liquidation of the community's assets.

Perhaps the differences between the three countries, and the different political paths they pursued, were always bound to bring an end to such an association. The principal reasons for the growing disunity could be summarized under four headings: political deadlock and mistrust, the disparities in gains and losses, the operation of the various joint corporations, and the imbalance in trade (trade restrictions between members had been increased through 1974).

GUY ARNOLD

Further Reading

Arnold, G. *Kenyatta and the Politics of Kenya*. London: J. M. Dent and Sons, 1974.

Bevan, D., et al. *East African Lessons on Economic Liberalization*. Brookfield, Vt.: Gower Publishing Co., 1987.

Hazlewood, A., ed. *African Integration and Disintegration*. Oxford: Oxford University Press, 1967.

———. *Economic Integration: The East African Experience*. London: Heinemann Educational Books, 1975.

Hughes, A. J. *East Africa: The Search for Unity*. Harmondsworth: Penguin Books, 1963.

East African Protectorate: *See* Kenya: East African Protectorate and the Uganda Railway.

Eastern Africa: Regional Survey
Introduction

Eastern Africa, including northeastern Africa, is a region of considerable diversity in terms of physical geography, climate, ethnicity, and culture. It is also the cradle of humankind itself. While it is no straightforward matter to enclose the history of such a vast region within a single encyclopedic entry, the purpose of the present essay is to describe the key political, economic, and social themes that have defined the region's historical development. Geographical as well as chronological cut-off points are so often arbitrary, and sometimes misleading; but they are, for the sake of convenience and clarity, usually necessary. In the context of eastern Africa, it will be shown that, while there are discernible historical links between north-east and central-eastern Africa—most notably in the migration of Cushites and Nilotes from the Horn southward—the two areas are in many ways quite distinct in terms of patterns of change, and in particular in terms of political organization, population, and culture. Yet thematically they have much in common.

Perhaps the most important theme shared by polities and communities from the Red Sea coast to the more southerly shoreline of the Indian Ocean is the fact that the entire region has historically always had close links with the Middle East, and in particular the Arabian peninsula and the Persian Gulf. These links were strengthened with the rise of Islam, following which the Indian Ocean, with the Red Sea as a vital appendage, formed a vast arena of commercial and cultural interaction. This region of Africa has, therefore, always looked to the east in terms of cultural and material exchange, just as Eastern Africa has historically been a natural area of interest to western and central Asians, both before and after Muhammad, and the socioeconomic consequences of the external relations thus developed have been significant and on-going. This basic historical fact has scarcely been altered by the opening of the Suez Canal in the late nineteenth century, or the European colonial experience in the twentieth.

Geography helps to explain patterns of human history across this vast region. The Ethiopian highlands, including parts of Eritrea, consist largely of volcanic material that breaks down to give a rich, deep soil; in general, rain falls abundantly and the cool uplands offer a favorable climate. This fertile highland area is a natural center of civilization, and for much of its history the region's rugged terrain engendered a certain degree of isolation from other parts of northeastern and eastern Africa, facilitating the growth of some of the continent's most distinctive cultures and polities. Between the highland area and the sea is the plain of Somalia, also linking up with Djibouti and coastal Eritrea, which is generally dry and torrid and incapable of sustaining a large settled population, instead being home predominantly to nomadic societies. Further south lies the vast plateau of central East Africa, which has its highest point in the Ruwenzori Mountains, sometimes described as the "spine" of Africa. To the east and south of the Ruwenzori ranges lies the Great Lakes region of eastern Africa: the main lakes are Victoria, Tanganyika, and Malawi, but there are many others. Much of the great plateau land of central East Africa is hot and dry, representing a challenge to cultivators, but there are important exceptions. The cool and fertile Kenyan highlands contain excellent farming country; the slopes of Kilimanjaro on the Kenyan-Tanzanian border and the Shire highlands south of Lake Malawi have similar advantages. The region between lakes Victoria, Kyoga and Kivu (the area of present-day Uganda, Rwanda, and Burundi) has abundant rainfall and the resulting fertility has made it another natural center of civilization.

Northeastern Africa to the Late Nineteenth Century

The movement of Semitic peoples across the Red Sea from the Arabian peninsula into the highlands of modern Eritrea and northern Ethiopia, sometime around the middle of the first millennium BCE, was a major stimulus to state-formation in the region. Intermingling with indigenous peoples, they developed Ge'ez, the ancestor of modern Tigrinya and Amharic, as a written language and created a centralized state in the northern highland area whose capital was soon fixed at Axum in Tigray. Taking advantage of Red Sea trade through their port at Adulis, Axum had, by the third and fourth centuries CE, become the dominant state in the region, boasting effective military organization, remarkable stone architecture and considerable commercial wealth. It was also, from the mid-fourth century, that King Ezana (c.320–350), a Christian, is credited with the adoption of Christianity in what appears to have been the culmination of a long period of contact with Greek traders. Axum remained powerful until the seventh century, when its trading power was weakened by both Persia and, more significantly, the rise of Islam, while environmental degradation may also have occurred in the northern Ethiopian highlands. As Axum disintegrated, its agricultural peoples found themselves increasingly isolated from the Eurasian core of Christianity, with profound consequences for the region.

Axum declined, but Christianity and Semitic culture continued to flourish. In the centuries that followed the eclipse of the Axumite state, the Christian polity incorporated the Agaw-speaking Cushites, particularly those in the area of Lasta, into Christian and Semitic culture. Evolving as part of the political and military elite, the Agaw-speakers of Lasta seized control of the kingdom in the middle of the twelfth century, establishing what has become known as the Zagwe dynasty. The Zagwes were responsible for continued Christian expansion southward into Gojjam and Shoa, and for some of Ethiopia's most remarkable architecture, in the form of rock-hewn churches; they also presided over considerable commercial and religious interaction with Egypt and the Holy Land. Nonetheless, they were derided as usurpers, both by contemporary and subsequent chroniclers. They were overthrown in 1270 by a ruler claiming descent from King Solomon and Makeda, the queen of Saba. Thus established, or "restored," as the dynasty would have it, the so-called Solomonic line would continue to claim political and spiritual legitimacy through imaginative use of the Old Testament down to the twentieth century. Elaborate myths were subsequently developed around the idea of a continuous historic "Ethiopian" state with biblical connections.

The Christian kingdom of the central Ethiopian highlands enjoyed a period of military expansion through much of the fourteenth and fifteenth centuries, particularly during the reigns of Amda Sion (1314–1344) and Zara Yaqob (1434–1468), who must count among the region's most successful rulers. Yet even during the fifteenth century, resurgent Islam represented a new threat. Islam, of course, had increasingly enclosed the Ethiopian highlands for the past several centuries, but relations between Christians and Muslims in northeast Africa had been largely peaceful for much of the period between the seventh and fifteenth centuries, notwithstanding periodic clashes mostly on the eastern Ethiopian plateau. Commerce had thrived between the Christians of the highlands and the Muslim merchants of the coast; relations with Egypt from the eleventh century onward had been good enough to allow highland Christians to make the pilgrimage to Jerusalem in safety. But conflict escalated in the fifteenth century, probably in large part related to commercial rivalry, and stemming from the growing hold of Islam over the pastoral Somali peoples in the eastern Horn.

In the early sixteenth century, the Muslim polity around Harar under the leadership of Ahmed ibn Ibrahim launched a full-scale invasion of the Christian highlands in the name of a jihad that came close to destroying the Christian church in the region. The latter ultimately survived, with the assistance of the Portuguese who had lent military aid and introduced the first European missionaries to the area; but so too did Islam, which continued to expand through the region. This occurred at least partly as the result of Oromo movement into the Ethiopian highlands from the southern plains, a fairly rapid migration that was made possible by the religious wars of the mid-sixteenth century.

The Ethiopian church, meanwhile, had developed some quite distinctive characteristics, based on the notion that the Christians of the region, surrounded by Muslim and pagan enemies, constituted a second Israel, chosen by God. This was closely intertwined with the Solomonic myth upheld by the ruling elite. Through the seventeenth century, meanwhile, the Christian kingdom steadily shifted its center of gravity northward, with a permanent capital established at Gondar and Tigray more fully incorporated into the state; in part this shift was occasioned by the expansion of trade through Massawa on the coast, under Ottoman suzerainty.

While the Red Sea, including much of the Eritrean coastline, remained under Ottoman control, centralized authority in the Ethiopian highlands had collapsed by the middle of the eighteenth century. The Solomonic rulers were reduced to mere figureheads, the idea of a great and unified Christian empire being merely part of the region's historic imagination. In some senses this may be seen as the culmination of a process stretching back several centuries. While central government had undergone periods of expansion and contraction since the collapse of Axum, the basis of political power had always been locally or provincially rooted, with autonomous districts and even small individual "kingdoms" paying periodic military, diplomatic, and material tribute as much to an idea (the Solomonic myth) as to an actual physical center of power.

From the mid-eighteenth century, provincial rulers became wholly independent and the ensuing century, known as the "Zemene Mesafint," or "era of the princes," witnessed regional conflict between them. Only with the rise of Tewodros (1855–1868), who claimed the Solomonic inheritance, was some degree of unity achieved in northern and central Ethiopia, although even this was accomplished through sheer force, while much of Tewodros's reign was spent suppressing insurrection. Tewodros himself committed suicide in 1868 in the face of a British expedition to rescue a number of European hostages; but the unification process begun by him was taken up by Yohannes (1872–1889), the first Tigrayan ruler of the Christian state for several centuries, and was completed by the Shoan king Menelik (1889–1913). Menelik created modern Ethiopia: not only did he defeat an Italian army invading from Eritrea in 1896, thus saving his state from the colonial experience endured by the rest of the region, but he actively participated in the carving up of vast tracts of land to the south and east, demarcating his new empire with the agreement of the European colonial authorities in the territories adjacent to it.

Central East Africa: Interior and Coast

The early history of the central eastern African interior is to a very large extent the history of migrations and population movements that occurred over three millennia or more. Throughout this period, it is possible to discern a gradual and complex evolutionary process in which people adopted new technologies, techniques and economic forms, always adding the innovations introduced by immigrants to the corpus of past knowledge and experience. Integration, both cultural and economic, was continuous, while at the same time economic specialization gave rise to a flourishing regional commercial network. The first discernible movement into the region occurred around 2000BCE, when domesticated cattle were introduced by Cushitic-speakers into the area of central Kenya. Over the next millennium, a new kind of economy emerged in which livestock were becoming increasingly important. Next came the Bantu-speakers, who moved into the area from the west and southwest over the ensuing centuries: these ironworking farmers spread through and beyond the Great Lakes region, developing diversified economic systems based on agriculture and pastoralism. Their successful spread through the region was directly linked to their ability to adapt to new environments, borrowing and utilizing the knowledge of indigenous peoples.

Major changes continued to take place in the middle centuries of the second millennium CE. Further migrations between the eleventh and fifteenth centuries, suggested by increased cattle keeping and changes in pottery styles, seem to have had some bearing on the growth of a large number of small chiefdoms throughout the lacustrine region, among which a thriving commercial network developed. By around the middle of the fifteenth century, some of these chiefdoms had merged to form the state of Kitara, in southwest Uganda, which was initially ruled by a dynasty known as the Chwezi from their capital at Bigo. Between the fifteenth and the seventeenth centuries, a series of Nilotic migrations (so called because of their original use of Nilo-Saharan languages) entered the area from southern Ethiopia and Sudan. These had a major impact on state building and on the creation of new societies and cultures in the area, usually interacting with Bantu-speakers and adopting Bantu languages. The "western" Nilotes carved the new state of Bunyoro out of the former Kitara and appear to have been instrumental in the founding and growth of the kingdom of Buganda; they also probably originated the pastoralists groups of Ankole and of Rwanda and Burundi, areas in which they were known as Hima and Tutsi, respectively. The "southern" Nilotes, whose movement probably began rather earlier, moved into the highlands east of Lake Victoria, absorbing the Cushites and laying the foundations for the emergence of the Kalenjin and Dadog groups, while the "eastern" Nilotes, unusual in that they retained their own language and culture, originated the Karamojong and Maasai.

Through the seventeenth and eighteenth centuries, Buganda, with an economy based very largely on the banana plantation, became the dominant state in the lacustrine region, developing an effective and highly hierarchical administrative system, and articulating a developed sense of identity, expressed most effectively in the military context. It supplanted Bunyoro as the main regional power and expanded to control, directly or indirectly, a large area of modern southern, central, and western Uganda. Further south, in equally fertile climes, were the states of Rwanda and Burundi, in which the agricultural majority came to be increasingly dominated by a pastoral minority. These ruling elites were well established by the eighteenth century. The Tutsi of the highlands interacted with the local Hutu, at first trading cattle for food with the agricultural population; in time, however, the Tutsi clans developed a commercial relationship into a position of domination, lending cattle to farmers who offered herding services in return.

Political leadership in both Rwanda and Burundi came to be associated with ownership of cattle; livestock owners became an aristocratic warrior elite, offering protection to their subjects from raids by rival clans. Elsewhere, largely decentralized but no less successful or dynamic, the pastoral Maasai expanded across central Kenya and northern Tanzania, their age-set social structure and ideology of pastoral purity providing them with both the means to, and justification for, such expansionism. Yet they also interacted peacefully with the many smaller agricultural communities which were scattered across the Tanzanian plateau. Overall, central eastern Africa had, by the nineteenth century, developed remarkable economic and political, as well as cultural, diversity, which lent itself to both cooperation and conflict.

Meanwhile, the Indian Ocean coast was witnessing the rise of one eastern Africa's most remarkable and successful civilizations, the result of dynamic interaction between coastal African culture and Islamic civilization. The east African coast had been known to Greek and Roman traders in the early centuries CE, but the expansion of Islam from the seventh and eighth centuries brought the region into a vast commercial network linked with Arabia, the Persian Gulf, and India. Both political refugees and merchants from the Islamic world began settling along the northern coast, their presence easing trading relations between the regions; Arab traders used the patterns of the oceanic monsoon winds to travel down to Mogadishu, Barawa, and the Lamu islands.

As trade expanded, larger numbers of Arabs settled in coastal towns, often located on off-shore islands, where they intermarried with local elites, and by the ninth century a number of market towns had been established, such as those at Lamu, Zanzibar and Kilwa. Trading links, moreover, existed between coastal settlements along the entire stretch of coast from Mogadishu to Mozambique. These were essentially African settlements linked to a thriving long-distance trade network that carried ivory, wood, slaves, and gold out of eastern Africa and brought glassware, pottery, textiles, and Islamic luxury goods into the region. The most important import of all, however, was Islam itself, which would become deeply rooted in coastal society.

From this vibrant commercial environment emerged Swahili coastal civilization. The term "Swahili" itself denotes both a language (basically Bantu, with Arabic influence) and a distinctive culture, describing a series of commercial city-states along the coasts of modern Somalia, Kenya, Tanzania, and Mozambique. It can be discerned as having begun to emerge around the area of the Lamu islands between the tenth and fourteenth centuries. Its expansion was occasioned by increasing demand for eastern African gold and ivory as well as increased Arab settlement along the coast, particularly from the direction of Oman and the Persian Gulf. Islam was adopted by local ruling elites, into which Muslim settlers married, and a number of towns built mosques; Arab immigrants were drawn ever further south to the expanding settlements of Zanzibar, Mafia, Pemba, and Kilwa. Kilwa was particularly successful, controlling the gold trade from the Zimbabwe plateau through its southerly settlement at Sofala. Other Swahili city-states (there were approximately forty of them of varying sizes by the thirteenth century) generated considerable wealth and functioned as self-governing political units ruled by prosperous African-Islamic dynasties, which accurately or otherwise usually traced their ancestry to the Persian Gulf area.

This "golden era" of Swahili civilization, however, was violently interrupted by the arrival of the Portuguese in the Indian Ocean at the end of the fifteenth century. Searching for a new route to the commerce of the east, they stumbled on the thriving coastal trade, which they now sought to control, attacking one city-state after the other with characteristic brutality. Having seized control of the southern coast, the Portuguese built stone fortresses at Kilwa, Sofala, and Mozambique, providing bases for journeys to India and giving them control of the interior gold trade. Swahili resistance, however, continued in the north, centered around Mombasa, which was attacked repeatedly through the sixteenth century. The Portuguese finally overcame this resistance, building an imposing fortress, Fort Jesus, at Mombasa at the end of the sixteenth century. Fort Jesus became the center and symbol of Portuguese control in eastern Africa, a period of commercial dominance maintained by violence. This was also the period which witnessed, further north, the Portuguese moving into the Red Sea and opening relations with the Ethiopian highlands.

At the close of the seventeenth century, a fleet from Oman drove the Portuguese from most of their coastal settlements, apart from their southernmost colony of Mozambique, initiating a gradual recovery of Swahili commercial culture. Through much of the eighteenth century, Omani control of the Swahili coast was weak and decentralized, but toward the end of the century the Omani sultan began to strengthen his hold over the city-states and the trade networks which connected them. The main focus of Omani expansion and the center of their increasing authority was the island of Zanzibar, and it was to here that the energetic Sultan Seyyid Said moved his permanent capital in the 1830s. Seyyid Said presided over a substantial increase in the Omani Zanzibari sphere of influence, as well as the penetration of Zanzibari merchants into the interior: trading caravans had reached the Great Lakes region by the end of the 1840s. The nineteenth century thus saw intense commercial activity throughout central eastern Africa, with the states and societies of the interior becoming linked to the Indian Ocean commercial system; the system itself was dominated by Zanzibar until the partition of the region in the 1880s.

This had major consequences for vast areas of the interior. Omani-Swahili merchants had established permanent trading posts at Unyanyembe, in northern central Tanzania, and at Ujiji, on Lake Tanganyika, by the 1840s. These functioned as entrepôts drawing the region into long-distance commerce. Some traders penetrated beyond the lakes, such as Tippu Tip, who carved out a vast trading-raiding empire in the forests of the eastern Congo basin. These aggressive adventurers sought to take advantage of decentralized or acephalous societies; but further north, Buganda kept coastal traders under their control, notwithstanding the growing influence of Islam within the society itself, while commercial impulses gave rise to new and equally aggressive states. Mirambo among the Nyamwezi created a new state in northwest Tanzania in the 1870s that was highly militaristic and that aimed at breaking Arab domination of interior commerce and controlling Lake Victoria trade routes.

Slaves were the main export from the region: the East African slave trade had been escalating since the late eighteenth century, as demand for labor on Zanzibar, Pemba, and French-controlled islands in the Indian Ocean rose, and as the expansion of the Russian Empire closed off traditional sources of slaves to the Islamic world. Ivory was also important, with demand for African tusks increasing through the nineteenth century.

The overall impact on the interior was a rise in violence, the increasing militarization of African society, and considerable dislocation of people. The Yao, for example, became actively involved in slave raiding across southern Tanzania, northern Mozambique, Malawi, and eastern Zambia; the ravages of the slave trade later provided the British with an excuse, albeit largely disingenuous, for colonial intervention in this area. Buganda also responded aggressively to long-distance commerce, becoming the largest exporter of slaves in the northern lacustrine region and developing a fleet of canoes with the aim of controlling Lake Victoria; the Nyamwezi, finally, became famous initially as porters, and later as highly successful traders, adventurers, and entrepreneurs themselves.

Eastern African trade received a further boost following the opening of the Suez Canal in 1869. Yet the commercial system was inimical to the region's long-term economic development: the slave trade was doomed, especially as Europeans sought to crush the slave traders in East Africa, both African and Arab. The commerce in ivory was also heading for disaster: too many elephants were being destroyed, and ivory resources were disappearing deep into the central African interior. On a fundamental level, these two trades were based on war and violence, with little hope of progress, and certainly involving no significant agricultural development. Colonial occupation changed this pattern dramatically, establishing cash crops for export as the basis for the East African economy.

The Modern Era

Like every other region across the continent, eastern Africa was subjected to colonial invasion in the last two decades of the nineteenth century. The advent of colonialism was preceded in many areas by the presence of missionaries (for example, those in Buganda and south of Lake Victoria), explorers, and consular officials. By the 1880s, Britain and Germany, by mutual agreement, had divided central eastern Africa: Britain took Kenya and Uganda, surrendering its traditional sphere of influence over the central Zanzibari coast to Germany, which acquired Tanganyika, Rwanda, and Burundi. Further north, the pastoral and agricultural peoples of the Horn, including Somalis, found themselves partitioned between Britain, France, and Italy; the last, a newcomer to the "Scramble," also acquired Eritrea on the Red Sea coast. Menelik's new empire-state (popularly referred to as Abyssinia, later Ethiopia) was an additional participant in the "Scramble" for this region, as already noted. Ethiopia's independent status awarded it a unique role in the region's modern history, particularly during the reign of Haile Selassie (1930–1974), serving as an inspiration to African nationalists across and beyond the continent, presenting itself as the guardian of ancient African civilization, and being regarded somewhat romantically (and, in general, sympathetically) by the West.

Responses to the European invasion varied from society to society. In some areas, resistance was more or less immediate. The Germans, for example, were confronted with stiff resistance from the peoples of southern and central Tanzania from the mid-1880s, while the kingdom of Bunyoro fought against the British almost as soon as the latter had established a permanent presence north of Lake Victoria. There was also strong resistance from Zanzibari-Arab coastal communities. Other societies sought to turn the European presence to their advantage; perhaps the most dramatic example of such "collaboration" was Buganda, which acted as the agent of British imperialism in southern and central Uganda through much of the 1890s, and later gave its name to the territory. In some areas, "primary" resistance—the initial attempt to defend sovereignty against colonial invasion—was followed by a phase of "secondary" resistance, involving spontaneous and popular revolt against the established colonial state. The most notable example of this is probably the "Maji Maji" uprising in southern Tanzania, lasting from 1905 to early 1907. At the same time, however, it should be borne in mind that across huge swathes of eastern Africa, cumulative environmental crises had undermined the ability of many states and societies to offer effective resistance to colonial invasion. Large areas of central eastern Africa had, through the nineteenth century, witnessed changing patterns of human settlement as a result of the slave trade, leading to a dramatic expansion of sleeping sickness. Then, at the end of the 1880s, a rinderpest epidemic swept from Eritrea down through Ethiopia, Somalia, Kenya, Uganda, and Tanzania, indeed continuing all the way to the Cape Colony by 1897. This great cattle disease devastated pastoral communities throughout the region, leaving them destitute and vulnerable at a time of foreign incursion.

The colonial experience differed from territory to territory. Kenya was singled out early on as a colony for white settlement, which had profound consequences for the territory's subsequent development: massive land alienation would produce a mounting social crisis on overcrowded reserves and in the burgeoning slums of cities, while deep social divisions among Africans themselves, particularly the Kikuyu, would further complicate the struggle for economic and political representation. Uganda was more typical in that the cash-crop production of cotton was in the hands of African peasant producers, but the latter were still discriminated against by a marketing system controlled by foreigners, in this case predominantly Asians.

The key theme of Uganda's colonial experience, however, was the favored treatment given by the British to Buganda, which dominated the territory at the expense of several other significant ethnic groupings. A similar situation arose in Rwanda and Burundi, where the Germans, followed after 1919 by the Belgians, deepened social divisions between Hutu and Tutsi by awarding the latter special political status. Tanganyika, under British control after 1919 through a League of Nations mandate, enjoyed rather greater unity through the further promotion and growth of Swahili as a territorial language. To the north, while modern Eritrean identity was to a substantial degree forged by its colonial experience, through the development of a light manufacturing economy and the emergence of discernible working and middle classes, Ethiopia continued to function very much along the feudal lines of the past. It found itself in a considerably weaker position in 1935 than in 1896, both diplomatically and militarily, and the Italian invasion ordered by Mussolini was this time successful, even if the triumph was short-lived.

In 1940–1941, British forces swept through Eritrea, Ethiopia, and Italian Somaliland, ending the Italian East African empire, while Ethiopia regained its independence. With United States and British backing, and with the acquiescence of a largely indifferent United Nations, Haile Selassie laid claim to and ultimately acquired Eritrea, first through a spurious "federation"

(1952–1962) and thereafter through direct occupation and administration. Eritreans responded with a war of liberation, and by the time Eritrea won independence in 1991 its armed struggle had the dubious honor of being the longest in Africa's modern history.

While Eritreans took up arms to end their peculiar form of "black-on-black" colonialism, much of the rest of eastern Africa ultimately achieved independence relatively peacefully, although nationalists in Eritrea, Uganda, and Kenya had much in common. In Uganda and Kenya in the 1940s and 1950s, deep social, ethnic, and geographical divisions were reflected in the nationalist movements, just as in Eritrea in the same period the nationalist movement was unable to achieve a coherent unity. The nations of eastern Africa experienced the same problems in this period as their counterparts in other parts of the continent: the dilemma facing would-be nationalist leaders was the fact that while anticolonialism was the unifying factor for African independence movements, and independence the common goal behind which disparate groups might align themselves, colonialism itself had created states wholly artificial in composition and form, in which "nationalism" was often an abstract term introduced by essentially external circumstances. Ethnicity, regionalism, and, in some cases, religion were the defining elements in the expression of "nationalism." This meant that in the years preceding formal decolonization, there was in many territories as much concern among competing nationalist parties about the postcolonial balance of internal power as about the actual achievement of sovereign status.

Ugandan independence finally came about in 1962 through a compromise between the Buganda kingdom's monarchist party and the predominant party in the north, led by Milton Obote; but such deals proved temporary, and within a decade Uganda had succumbed to the brutal military rule of Idi Amin. Only after several years of bloodshed and civil strife has political tension eased to some degree. Tanganyika was able to more effectively unite under the leadership of the charismatic Julius Nyerere, who self-consciously played down the significance of ethnicity, while the territory also benefited from the linguistic unity provided by Swahili. Tanganyika achieved independence in 1961, uniting with Zanzibar in 1964 to form Tanzania. Kenya's mounting social tensions erupted in the "Mau Mau" revolt of the early 1950s, which witnessed deep anger directed at both white settlers and members of the African elite. The British crushed the uprising with considerable brutality, at the same time imprisoning leading Kenyan nationalists such as Jomo Kenyatta, despite the fact that the latter was a largely moderate politician who had little in common with the "Mau Mau" radicals. The revolt itself did not succeed; but it

ultimately created a new political environment in which the British were no longer prepared to back the white minority and instead made way for African majority rule. Kenyatta led the country to independence in 1963.

While coups d'état and ethnic tensions have been common enough in Uganda, Kenya and Tanzania have achieved relative, if uneasy, political stability. The worst instances of ethnic violence have occurred in Rwanda and Burundi, where colonialism, exaggerating precolonial divisions, has left a bitter legacy of ethnic mistrust and hatred between Hutu and Tutsi. Further north, Ethiopia and Somalia are among those African states that have experienced varying degrees of ideological revolution, rather more dramatic than Nyerere's failed socialist program in Tanzania in the 1960s and 1970s. Somalia, the united former Italian and British colonies that achieved independence in 1960, enjoyed Soviet support after the advent to power of Siad Barre in 1969 and the emergence of a military-socialist state. But the Soviet Union soon switched its attention to Ethiopia, where a group of Marxist army officers overthrew the *ancien regime* of Haile Selassie in 1974 and proclaimed a Marxist revolution. Massive Soviet military aid was used to fight Eritrean and Tigrayan uprisings in the north and in Somalia in the south, the latter seeking the incorporation of the Somali peoples of the Ogaden. Ethiopia kept the Ogaden, but it lost Eritrea. The Marxist state of Mengistu Haile Mariam collapsed in 1991, leaving a new balance of regional power whose potential fragility was exposed by the outbreak of war between Eritrea and Ethiopia in 1998.

RICHARD REID

Further Reading

Abir, M. "Ethiopia and the Horn of Africa." In *The Cambridge History of Africa*. Vol. 4, *From c.1600 to c.1790, edited by Richard Gray*. London: Cambridge University Press, 1975.

Bennett, N. *Arab versus European: Diplomacy and War in Nineteenth-Century East Central Africa*. New York: Africana Publishing Company, 1986.

Beattie, J. *The Nyoro State*. London: Oxford University Press, 1971.

Chittick, H. Neville. "The East Coast, Madagascar and the Indian Ocean." In *The Cambridge History of Africa*. Vol. 3, *From c.1050 to c.1600*, edited by R. Oliver. London: Cambridge University Press, 1977.

Connah, G. *African Civilisations: Precolonial Cities and States in Tropical Africa: An Archaeological Perspective*. Cambridge: Cambridge University Press, 1987.

Ehret, C. *Ethiopians and East Africans: The Problem of Contacts*. Nairobi: East African Publishing House, 1974.

Lewis, I. M. *A Modern History of Somalia*. London: Longman, 1980.

Marcus, H. *A History of Ethiopia*. Berkeley: University of California Press, 1994.

Nurse, D., and T. Spear. *The Swahili: Reconstructing the History and Language of an African Society 800–1500*. Philadelphia: Philadelphia University Press, 1985.

Reid, R. *Political Power in Pre-Colonial Buganda: Economy, Society and Warfare in the Nineteenth Century.* London: James Currey, 2001.

Eastern Nilotes: *See* **Nilotes, Eastern Africa: Eastern Nilotes: Ateker (Karimojong); Nilotes, Eastern Africa: Maasai.**

Eastern Savanna, Political Authority in

Between 1600 and 1800, the savanna areas of East Africa experienced diverse, often dynamic political development, and a gradual expansion of political systems linking wider networks of communities than ever before. These changes were often responses to increased social complexity spurred by a combination of factors, including the control of iron technology, increasing agricultural sophistication, and the growth of interregional trade. In some areas, increased complexity led to more hierarchical forms of authority, while in others it produced political segmentation into small chiefdoms. In many areas, people strove to maintain decentralized forms of organization, while at the same time incorporating more communities into a shared social and political framework. For the purposes of this entry, the eastern savanna can be roughly seen as two overlapping zones: a northern area of independent decentralized communities, stretching from Lake Turkana to the Maasai Steppe; and a southern area that included both decentralized villages and complex chiefdoms, occupying most of present-day Tanzania.

In the northern zone, a diverse array of languages, cultures, forms of subsistence, and micro-environments, gave rise to a highly decentralized and fluid arena of politics. At the beginning of the seventeenth century, the area was occupied by a mosaic of communities, including early hunting-gathering peoples, Cushitic and Nilotic-speaking pastoralists, and Bantu-speaking agriculturalists. Political activity generally focused on localized institutions: the village, lineage, or age-set. Councils of elders made decisions instead of kings, chiefs, or bureaucrats, and many societies also sought guidance from ritual diviners and prophets. Individuals usually were not allowed to lay claim to land or other productive resources, so political influence accrued only to those who skillfully built up networks of allies and followers through manipulation of the structures of kinship, residence, and age. Kamba settlements, for example, were scattered across eastern Kenya and northeastern Tanzania and developed a range of subsistence strategies, from intensive agriculture to pastoralism and hunting, as each community learned to exploit its own micro-environment. In such a diffuse setting, politics retained a localized character,

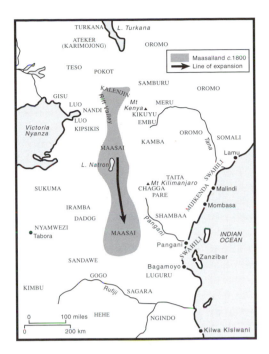

East African savanna, *c.*1800

and individuals gained authority and leadership by distributing their wealth to attract followers and demonstrating exceptional character. It is important to note that technology, trade, and social organization were highly dynamic in the north, just as they were in the south, but that smaller political units rather than increased centralization were often the more appropriate way to deal with increasing complexity.

The northern zone was deeply influenced by the cultural outlook of migratory pastoralists, who moved into the area in waves over the course of several centuries. In the sixteenth century, Cushitic-speaking Oromo pastoralists began to expand from their Ethiopian homeland into the central highlands of Kenya. They brought a form of social organization rooted in small, scattered homesteads, linked by the ritual leadership of a prophet (*qallu*), as well as generation-sets and age-sets, which gave all Oromo males a common bond. It is likely that Oromo introduced many of these now-familiar institutions to the eastern savanna. But by the seventeenth century, another wave of pastoralists, Nilotic-speakers from the lands northwest of Lake Turkana, began to challenge Oromo for dominance in the central highlands. These newcomers, led by Maa-speaking communities as well as Kalenjin and Turkana, would eventually filter southward as far south as the Maasai Steppe, but they too adhered to a decentralized political ideology, with age-set organizations and prophetic ritual leaders. Many agricultural communities adopted forms of social organization from pastoralists as a means of facilitating relationships.

Kikuyu agriculturalists, for example, who settled along the highland ridges of central Kenya during the seventeenth and eighteenth centuries, had territorial councils (*kiama*) of their own, but also initiated young men into age-sets parallel to those of the neighboring Maa-speaking peoples, with whom they also traded and intermarried.

The southern zone, in contrast to the north, was characterized by Bantu-speaking agricultural societies. Many of these, such as the Gogo, Hehe, and Fipa, remained decentralized until the nineteenth century, but others were organized under hierarchical systems of chiefship much earlier. In the northeastern mountains of Tanzania, these hierarchies became the most fully developed in all of the eastern savanna, with despotic kings, subchiefs, and classes of bureaucratic officials. Before 1500, these societies had been dominated by the families of blacksmiths, who gained prominence through their control of the production of tools and weapons. The blacksmiths performed ritual duties, but administrative authority remained in the hands of elders appointed by commoners.

During the course of the next three centuries, however, the region's population grew steadily, the result of a favorable climate with good rainfall and soil, combined with increasing mastery of iron technology. New systems of authority emerged to cope with this emerging social complexity. In the Pare Mountains, for example, the Washana clan of blacksmiths was overthrown at the beginning of the sixteenth century by the Wasuga clan. The founding ruler, Angovi, followed by his son Mranga and grandson Shimbo, established the centralized state of Ugweno, which functioned through an elaborate hierarchy with a paramount chief (*mangi mrwe*), governing councils (*chila*), ministers (*wanjama*), and district chiefs (*wamangi*). The Ugweno kingdom expanded to control all of the North Pare plateau and lasted until the nineteenth century. In the Usambara Mountains, a similar process of centralization took place in the eighteenth century, when Mbega consolidated his power, possibly by offering an organized defense against Maa-speaking pastoralists. The Kilindi dynasty continued to consolidate power under Mbega's son, Shebughe, and then his successor Kimweri, who ruled until the 1860s.

These highly centralized state systems, however, were exceptional cases among the agricultural societies of the southern zone. Most of these areas were much drier than the northeastern highlands and could not support as many inhabitants. A common form of chiefship in the southern zone was the institution of the *ntemi*. This broad term refers to the leaders of perhaps three hundred small chiefdoms stretched across the broad savanna of present-day western, central,

and southern Tanzania. The *ntemi* chiefdoms were generally independent but linked together through networks of kinship or clientship. These communities incorporated a steady stream of immigrants as people moved away from the crowded kingdoms of the northeast. While increasing complexity had produced centralization in Pare and Usambara, in the "*ntemi* region" political development often produced different results. Among the Nyamwezi of western Tanzania, the trend until the nineteenth century was toward segmentation, with chiefdoms splitting apart into ever smaller political units. In Ufipa differing factions contested the very notion of political legitimacy throughout the eighteenth century, as invading pastoralists advanced their style of leadership based upon personal effort at the expense of the existing dynasty based upon kinship relations. In general, the *ntemi* chiefships can be seen as dynamic, flexible institutions that responded in diverse ways to local and regional circumstances.

By 1800 the eastern savanna was home to an array of strikingly varied political systems, the result of steady demographic, technological, and agricultural change during the previous centuries. Throughout the region, political links had been forged that encompassed wide social and cultural networks. During the nineteenth century, however, economic and demographic changes would reach an unprecedented level, and these institutions would face entirely new and often overwhelming challenges. The penetration of Arab caravan trade and the rise of European colonial power brought slavery, guns, and a new commercial mindset to the region. In many cases these new ideas and tools would strengthen the institutions that had developed in the eastern savannah during the previous centuries, but just as often they would serve as catalysts for revolutionary change in local and regional political systems.

CHRISTIAN JENNINGS

Further Reading

Feierman, S. *The Shambaa Kingdom: A History*. Madison: University of Wisconsin Press, 1974.

Kimambo, I. N. *A Political History of the Pare of Tanzania, c.1500–1900*. Nairobi: East African Publishing House, 1969.

Ochieng, W. R. "The Interior of East Africa: The Peoples of Kenya and Tanzania, 1500–1800." In *General History of Africa*. Vol. 5, *Africa from the Sixteenth Century to the Eighteenth Century*, edited by B. A. Ogot. Berkeley: University of California Press, 1992.

Ogot, B. A., ed. *Zamani: A Survey of East African History*. Nairobi: East African Publishing House, 1973.

Roberts, A., ed. *Tanzania Before 1900*. Nairobi: East African Publishing House, 1968.

Spear, T. *Kenya's Past*. London: Longman, 1981.

ECOMOG: *See* **Liberia: Civil War, ECOMOG and the Return to Civilian Rule.**

Economic Community of West African States (ECOWAS)

A major aftermath of World War II was the reconceptualization and redefinition of economic development strategies in Sub-Saharan Africa. The immediate postindependence era witnessed the burgeoning of a more decisive economic nationalism, which questioned the existing dependent economic relationship of unequal partnership. For independence to be meaningful and development oriented, emphasis had to be on how best to strengthen the objective bases of national economies. It was against this background that attention shifted to regional integration as an alternative development strategy. Theoretical support for economic integration developed from the theory of "custom union" as practiced in the developed economics of the West. In a custom union, members enjoy a preferential tax on the intra-union trade, expanded trade creation prospects, and interactive trade diversion.

Economic planning on a state-by-state basis started in West Africa after World War II in 1945. The British Colonial Office requested that its colonial dependencies produce a Ten-Year Development Program that would be funded by the Colonial Development and Welfare Fund. The Nigerian (1960–1962) and Ghanaian (1963) plans fell short of expected achievements. The failure of similar planning exercises undertaken in the Francophone West African States under the auspices of Investment Fund for Social Development (FIDES) led to a search for a more viable development program. In 1959 France wanted to unify French territories in West Africa (UDAO) into a loose economic bloc. The Custom French Union for Africa did not succeed because of the rivalry between Côte d'Ivoire and Senegal. By introducing value-added tax, Côte d'Ivoire destroyed the competitiveness of Senegalese manufactured goods in the trade area. The succeeding Union of French West African States (UDEAO) was an economic arrangement united by a council of ministers and a committee of experts.

The Mano River Union (MRU) marked the consummation of diplomatic collaboration between Liberia and Sierra Leone, dating back to the 1960s. Both countries had a relatively lengthy period of political stability, and share ethnic and cultural affinity, a common border, and similar economic potentials. The MRU was designed to be a custom union established to expand trade through the elimination of all forms of trade barriers and the creation of conducive climate for setting up joint industrial capacity for the common market.

The Economic Community of West African States (ECOWAS) is the biggest economic bloc in contemporary West Africa. The arrangement encompasses all sixteen countries along the West African Coast, stretching from Mauritania to Nigeria, including of course the landlocked states of Mali, Upper Volta, and Niger as well as the islands of Cape Verde. From this geographical spread, ECOWAS is inclusive of the MRU. In 1967 twelve countries signed an agreement establishing ECOWAS, and an interim council of ministers that was to prepare a treaty embodying the principles of a common West African market and identifying priority areas for immediate implementation was set up. At the signing of a protocol creating the West African Regional Group in 1968, heads of state meeting in Monrovia were delegated in Nigeria and Guinea to prepare studies on the first set of priority areas. Liberia and Senegal were to study the specific requirements for a custom union. After 1968 there was a lull in the activities of the Union following the outbreak and intensification of the Nigerian civil war. However, there was a renewal of interest on the part of all stakeholders from 1975. By the beginning of 1975, arrangements for the summit of heads of states, at which the treaty creating ECOWAS would be signed, were finalized.

The aim of ECOWAS was set out in Article 2 of the treaty: it shall be the aim of the community to promote cooperation and development in all fields of economic activity particularly in all fields of industry, transport and telecommunications, energy, agriculture, natural sciences, commerce, monetary and financial issues and in social and cultural matters for the purpose of raising the standard of living of its peoples, of increasing and maintaining economic stability, of fostering close relations among the members and of contributing to progress and development of the African continent. To achieve these lofty aims, the following steps and sequence were adopted:

(a) elimination of custom duties and other charges of equivalent effect on imports and exports.
(b) elimination of quantitative and administrative restrictions on trade among members;
(c) establishment of a common tariff structure and commercial policy toward nonmember states;
(d) elimination of obstacles restricting the free movement of persons, services and capital among member states;
(e) harmonization of the agricultural polices and the promotion of common projects in the member states, notably in the fields of marketing, research, and agroindustrial enterprises;
(f) evolution of common policy in, and joint development of transport, communication, energy, and other infrastructural facilities;

(g) harmonization of economic, industrial, and monetary policies of members and the elimination of disparities in the level of development of members; and

(h) establishment of a fund for cooperation, compensation, and development.

Certain institutions were created to give effect to the goals of ECOWAS. Article 4 of the treaty established the authority of heads of ECOWAS member states as the supreme and final authority in the community. This organ meets once a year to approve and authorize decisions and policies recommended to it by the council of ministers. The Council of Ministers holds one of the biennial meetings just before the meeting of the heads of states to prepare the ground and formulate the agenda. Two ministers from each member state form the Council of Ministers, which is charged with the responsibility of directing the operations of the community in pursuance of the set goals as set out in the enabling treaty. There are four technical commissions:

(i) Industrial, Agricultural, and Natural Resources Commission;
(ii) Transport, Telecommunication, and Energy Commission;
(iii) Trade, Customs, Immigration, Monetary and Payments Commission; and
(iv) Social and Cultural Affairs Commission.

They were created to assist the Council of Ministers in the discharge of duties to the community. The chief function of the technical commissions involves policy formulation and recommendations for implementation in the specialized and respective fields.

The ECOWAS secretariat is headed by the executive secretary who is assisted by two deputy secretaries, one for administration and economic matters, and the other who is the controller of finance. To promote even development, capacity building, industrial integration, treaty building, and industrial integration, treaty of Lagos provides for compensation losses arising from preferential tariffs as a result of intra-ECOWAS trade and location of ECOWAS enterprises. The fund for compensation, cooperation, and development was created to meet the financial demands of poor member states embarking on industrial projects. The sources of funding for the Lomé-based body include capital budgets of the community as well as foreign and interest payments on loans granted or attracted by the fund. Judicial resolution of disputes arising from conflicting interpretations of the treaty lay in the hands of the Community Tribunal.

AKIN ALAO

See also: **Colonial Federations: French West Africa.**

Further Reading

Adedeji A. *The Evolution of a West African Economic Community.* Lagos: Federal Government Press, 1974.

Amin, S. *Neo-Colonialism in West Africa.* Middlesex: Pengiun Books, 1973.

Krauss, M., ed. *The Economics of Integration: A Book of Readings.* London: George Allen and Unwin, 1973.

Okwuosa, E. *New Direction for Economic Development in Africa.* London: Africa Books, 1976.

Onwuka, R. I. *Development and Integration in West Africa: The Case of the Economic Community of West African States.* Ile Ife: University of Ife Press, 1986.

Education in Colonial Sub-Saharan Africa

Education in colonial Sub-Saharan Africa varied over the course of the colonial period and by the nature of different colonizing cultures. The colonial period in Sub-Saharan Africa lasted about seventy-five years for most countries, with the colonizing powers including France, Portugal, Britain, Belgium, Italy, and Spain.

Within each colonial power, opinions diverged as to the role that formal education in African contexts had performed, could perform, or should perform in the future. Sharp contrasts in views often occurred within the Christian missions, between missions and the colonial offices, between the metropole and officials in the field, and within colonial political parties. Some of the debate centered on whether education should follow the Western model or should be adapted to the realities of African societies and cultures.

In general, the object of education in colonial Africa shifted from the spreading of European civilization (assimilation of Western ideas) to Africanization of education (or "development from within"). Most colonial powers in Sub-Saharan Africa attempted to "Africanize" schools after World War I (Sivonen, 1995). Teachers introduced subjects into the school curriculum which reflected the child's natural environment and their own community, stories and folklore, tribal and traditional dances, and instruction in local handicrafts. These attempts were largely unsuccessful for various reasons: lack of desire to effect this transformation, limitations in resources, well-based African opposition, and social changes outside the schools. The period from 1918 to 1930 was marked by confusion regarding the aims of African education and government disinterest.

Overall, the pattern of educational provision during the colonial period was very uneven. Colonial education in Sub-Saharan Africa was elitist. The vast majority of

African people did not attend school at all, and most of those who did attend had only a few years of primary schooling. They were very unevenly distributed in terms of regions, sex, locality, ethnic, and social background.

Foreign missions (Christian and Islamic) with interests in Africa pioneered and dominated the educational sector for many years. Islamic religion had considerable influence on African education in western Africa, and some countries in eastern and central Africa. Islamic schools and universities flourished centuries before the arrival of Christian evangelism and colonialism. By the early 1950s, Sub-Saharan Africa held as many Christians of all denominations as Muslims.

The vast majority of schools and colleges opened during the colonial period were run (and mostly financed by) European or American missionary societies. The first schools resulted from coastal trading contacts in the fifteenth century, but most were established in the eighteenth and nineteenth centuries. In the 1790s numerous Christian organizations formed themselves into missionary societies including the Baptist Missionary Society, the Edinburgh and Glasgow Missionary Society, the London Missionary Society, and the Church Missionary Society. Others followed in the early nineteenth century, including the Wesleyan Missionary Society, the American Bible Society, and the Church of Scotland Missionary Committee. Throughout the colonial period, the development of missionary education was spatially uneven.

Bringing Christianity to the non-Christian world was the central objective of mission education in colonial Africa. The language of the Europeans was used as the medium of instruction. Schools inculcated students with Christian beliefs and attitudes on marriage (monogamy), lifestyle (a rejection of traditional beliefs and practices), and work (discipline). The missionary dominance of educational objectives limited the curriculum of most mission schools to the essentials of the Christian or Muslim life, while other schools followed a basic academic curriculum similar to those used in European schools at the time. Overall, the nature (as well as quality) of education offered by mission schools varied greatly, with different emphases placed on vocational training, literacy, obedience, and religious instruction.

The educational activities of these missionary societies had a profound effect on the long-term development of many African societies, particularly those not already under the influence of Islam. The value of missionary influences on education is highly contentious. Some researchers depict missionaries as noble altruists bringing enlightenment, literacy, useful new skills, and superior health care. Other writers portray them as agents of an oppressive and exploitative foreign presence, alienating Africans from their traditional culture and beliefs by imposing inappropriate values, school curricula, ambitions, and expectations on unwilling and powerless colonial subjects.

In general, for most of the nineteenth century, mission education operated without much government intervention; then missionaries cooperated with colonial governments (to varying degrees) after 1900, and particularly after World War I. This mirrored a curriculum change from a purely religious education to a diluted semi-secular education, though the curriculum remained relatively narrow.

Missionaries and colonial governments did not always share the same aims. Colonial rulers tended not to give education a high priority. Education was viewed as a way of training people to meet colonial expectations rather than a way of bringing about social change or getting greater social equality and justice. Governments needed some local people to read and write in the European language, do numerical calculations, know European practices and traditions, and be trained in particular skills. Graduates assumed lower-ranking positions within the colony, trained as mechanics, nurses, teachers, tradespeople, and administrative assistants. Education was based on racial segregation. For example, in Kenya and Tanzania, different schools were established for Europeans, Asians, Arabs, and Africans.

The colonial rulers officially neglected education at the tertiary level. Only a few universities existed in colonial Africa, including the Lovedale Institution (South Africa), Gordon Memorial College (Khartoum), Makerere Government College (Kampala), Yaba Higher College (Lagos), and the Prince of Wales School and College, Achimota (Ghana). These university colleges have been criticized for a narrow curriculum, training an elite to occupy government positions, and exacerbating class differences.

The colonial approach to education varied by nationality. For example, the Portuguese and French systems aimed to create a very small class of officially "assimilated" Africans who were given an elite education (sometimes including a study period in Europe). The British developed secondary and higher education much earlier than the French, and were relatively more supportive of missionary education. Enrollment rates were generally much higher in British than in French territories, partly because missionary activities began earlier in the former, partly because most of the French territories in West Africa were highly Islamicized. British colonial administrations prohibited the expansion of missionary activities into Muslim areas, mainly to avoid conflict with the traditional rulers of these areas. The French pursued a more aggressive policy against Islam which resulted in much bloodshed and the closing of many Quranic schools.

As the colonial period progressed, the various European administrations became more and more involved in education, both as builders of schools in their own right and as supervisors and subsidizers of mission schools. The main impetus behind this increasing involvement was not the desire to expand educational facilities for Africans, but the desire to restrict the expansion of schools, particularly of academic secondary schooling, which was deemed to be inappropriate to African needs.

Mungazi (1983) argues that the quest for education has influenced the struggle for independence in southern Africa. Prior to 1965 (when almost all countries in Sub-Saharan Africa had obtained their independence), Africans began to ask for more education, particularly for higher education, and for a redefinition of the goals and purposes of education. There was general discontent expressed against colonial education, especially in British Africa. They demanded an educational system that reflected African conditions. After independence, Sub-Saharan African governments began to transform education to promote national awareness, economic productivity and political consciousness. Some countries, such as Tanzania, Kenya, and Nigeria, embarked upon free compulsory primary education.

Education in colonial Africa remains a contested subject. One approach holds colonial power responsible for an unthinking transfer of Western formal educational institutions into Africa, resulting in the destruction of the cultural inheritance of African peoples. For instance, Taiwo (1995, p.891) argues that indigenous modes of knowledge production were "profoundly altered for the worse," if not "utterly destroyed" by "Islam, Slavery, Christianity, Colonialism, and Capitalism." Certainly, indigenous African education was relevant and closely linked to the spiritual and material aspects of social life before colonization by European imperial powers. This educational process reflected the realities of African society and produced people with an education that equipped them to meet the material, spiritual, and social needs of the society.

The "modernization" approach, according to Kuster (1994), views education as a precious gift of civilization, benevolently bestowed on colonial subjects. For instance, Summers (1994) argues that in Southern Rhodesia "civilization" was a social ideal first developed by the missionaries, which then became the ideology of the ruling race as a whole.

The "underdevelopment" approach (according to Kuster [1994]) sees colonial education as an instrument of European cultural imperialism. Mugomba and Nyaggah (1980, p.1) argue that the colonial system of education "both subordinated and relegated to a peripheral role the African educational systems and the existing political, economic, and social orders." The newcomers introduced alternative theories of education and imposed a new set of educational institutions that either partly or completely replaced previous forms of learning. Colonial schools aimed to instill deference to the foreign authority, unquestioned acceptance of hierarchy, the full embrace of Christianity, and emphasized the "superiority" of everything European and the "inferiority" of everything African. African culture was synonymous with superstition and backwardness and uncivilized. The colonizer's culture, history, religion, and way of life were thus promoted in the curriculum as well as in the discipline itself.

Some researchers argue further that education in colonial Africa was an effective means of achieving social control. Ajayi et al. (1996, p.28) argue further that education policies were "the most effective instrument for the colonial administrations to try to control the pace and direction of social change." Yet others question the influence of education as a tool of social control and point to the small proportion of the population with access to schools.

CAMILLA COCKERTON

Further Reading

Ajayi, F. F. Ade, Lameck K. H. Goma, and G. Ampah Johnson. *The African Experience with Higher Education*. Accra-North, Ghana: The Association of African Universities, 1996.

Kuster, S. *Neither Cultural Imperialism nor Precious Gift of Civilization: African Education in Colonial Zimbabwe, 1890–1962*. Munster: Lit., 1994.

Mugomba, A. T., and Mougo Nyaggah, eds. *Independence without Freedom: The Political Economy of Education in Southern Africa*. Santa Barbara, Calif.: ABC-Clio, 1980.

Mungazi, D. A. *To Honor the Sacred Trust of Civilization: History, Politics, and Education in Southern Africa*. Cambridge, Mass.: Schenkman Publication Company, 1983.

Sivonen, S. *White-Collar or Hoe Handle? African Education under British Colonial Policy, 1920–1945*. Helsinkei: Suomen Historiallinen Seura, 1995.

Summers, C. *Civilization to Segregation: Social Ideals and Social Control in Southern Rhodesia*, 1890–1934. Athens, Ohio: Ohio University Press, 1994.

Taiwo, Olufemi. "Colonialism and Its Aftermath: The Crisis of Knowledge Production." *Callaloo* 16, no. 4 (1993): 891–909.

Education in Postcolonial Sub-Saharan Africa

Education, cultural change, and development are closely entwined in postcolonial Sub-Saharan Africa. The view that education is critical in developing Africa is pervasive. Since attaining independence, Sub-Saharan African countries have paid considerable attention to the role of education in national development. They have viewed expenditure on education as the best possible investment for the future. Rather than perpetuating the colonial practice of educating an elite minority, African governments aimed to increase educational opportunities for as many people as possible. After achieving independence, governments gave very high priority to the expansion of education at primary, secondary, and tertiary levels.

Enrollments in primary schools grew more than six-fold between 1960 and 2000, and secondary and college education expanded even more rapidly. Between 1960 and 1989 the number of children in primary schools increased from 12 million to almost 61 million in Africa south of the Sahara (excluding South Africa). Secondary enrolment jumped from almost 800,000 to 12 million. The numbers enrolled in postsecondary courses rose from 21,000 to 600,000. Prior to independence, most countries in Sub-Saharan Africa had no universities, and today every country has at least one university.

To make these gains possible, African countries have heavily invested in education. They have dispensed vast sums both in physical infrastructures (e.g., buildings, books, and supplies) and in human capital (e.g., teachers). While substantial amounts of foreign assistance were received for educational development, the bulk of resources has come from within.

With the expansion of educational facilities at all levels and the corresponding financial commitment, African countries have also reexamined the goals of education in relation to individuals' and their nation's needs and aspirations. Sub-Saharan African countries since independence have placed increasing emphasis on "education for development," particularly at the secondary and postsecondary level. This implies the orientation of the content and objective of education and training toward realizing the goal of economic and social advancement. Despite substantial progress to reform educational systems, post-colonial education in Sub-Saharan Africa continues some links to the colonial period in terms of curriculum and language of instruction.

The 1960s and 1970s witnessed rapid educational expansion and expenditure in Sub-Saharan Africa. Governments made particular efforts to improve school enrollment for girls. In the 1960s the percentage of girls aged six to eleven years enrolled in primary schools doubled (from 17 to 35 per cent) compared with an increase from 46 to 63 per cent for boys. The figures rose to 44 per cent for girls and 74 per cent for boys in the 1970s. In the 1980s, at the secondary level, only 11 per cent of girls and 20 per cent of boys aged twelve to seventeen years were enrolled in school.

Educational development across the various countries in Sub-Saharan Africa is markedly uneven. For example, the adult literacy rate in 1990 ranged from 26 per cent in Lesotho to 82 per cent in Burkina Faso. Primary school enrollment rates range from 15 per cent of the primary school-aged population in Somalia to 100 per cent in Lesotho. In 1987 public expenditures on education (as a per cent of total public spending) ranged from 3 per cent in Nigeria to 25 per cent in Swaziland.

Educational development also varies enormously within each Sub-Saharan African country. Significant spatial variations in access to education first emerged during colonial times and still persist. Generally, urban areas have received proportionally more investment in education than rural areas, particularly at the secondary and tertiary levels. For example, in Botswana, most schools are situated in the more heavily populated southeastern region, occupied primarily by Batswana. And, within this region, most schools are located in or near the larger towns along the main transportation route. The one university is located in the capital city, Gaborone. The desert peoples have historically had far less access to education than BaTswana, until at least the 1990s. Few schools existed within central and northwestern Botswana, where desert peoples continued to reside.

Particular issues surrounding education, cultural change, and development have intensified since the mid-1980s. Sub-Saharan African countries have been plagued by declining enrollment rates, reduced public expenditure on education, quality erosion, management inefficiencies, growing regional and gender biases, and low literacy rates.

Although Africa currently spends about 5 per cent of its gross domestic product (GDP) on education, which is more than in any other developing region, the slow economic development combined with rapid population growth has hampered educational policies. In the 1990s, several Sub-Saharan African countries with weakened economies and debt undertook structural adjustment policies implemented by the International Monetary Fund (IMF) and the World Bank. These countries reduced their per capita spending on education by 0.7 per cent a year in the decade up to 1996. The Organization of African Unity (OAU) declared the period 1997 to 2006 the Decade of Education. The Conference of African Ministers of Education, held in Zimbabwe in March 1999, approved a program of action with three objectives: access to primary education for all and a reduction in gender and urban/rural discrepancies, emphasis on the quality and relevance of education and vocational training, and a highly efficient staff through capacity building.

Despite the great improvements in education over the postcolonial period and the considerable efforts to introduce universal primary education, very few Sub-Saharan African countries have attained primary education for all. In 1990, 71 per cent of the primary school-aged population was enrolled in primary school, 20 per cent in secondary school, and 2.4 per cent in a university.

For the region as a whole, the adult literacy rate in 1990 was 42 per cent. Adult illiteracy rates in Sub-Saharan Africa remain higher than in any other region of the world. The rural-urban and gender gap are still significantly wide in most countries, with rural girls being the most disadvantaged. One-third of adult males and one-half of females are illiterate. Female illiteracy rates remain significantly higher than those for males in every country of Africa south of the Sahara.

Opportunities for education at any level still remain limited, and educational opportunities for girls continue to lag behind those for boys. Although females make up more than half of the school-age population in most Sub-Saharan African countries, recent trends show that women account for only 44 per cent of primary school enrollments, 34 per cent of secondary school enrollments, and 21 per cent of university level enrollments (World Bank, 1988). When compared with their male counterparts, African women students also have higher attrition and repetition rates, and lower levels of attainment. It is commonly asserted that gender disparities in education in Sub-Saharan Africa are the direct result of economic difficulties. Logan and Beoku-Betts (1996) argue that they result from a complex interaction between economic factors, cultural and societal norms, and stereotypes of gender roles.

CAMILLA COCKERTON

Further Reading

Logan, B. I., and J. A. Beoku-Betts. "Women and Education in Africa: An Analysis of Economic and Sociocultural Factors Influencing Observed Trends." *Journal of Asian and African Studies* 31 (1996): 3–4, 217–240.

Marope, P. T. M., and S. G. Weeks, eds. *Education and National Development in Southern Africa.* Gaborone: Comparative Education Interest Group and Botswana Educational Research Association for Southern African Comparative and History of Education Society (SACHES), 1994.

Mungazi, D. A. *The Challenge of Educational Innovation and National Development in Southern Africa.* New York: Peter Lang, 1991.

Mungazi, D. A., and L. K. Walker. *Educational Reform and the Transformation of Southern Africa.* Westport, Conn.: Praeger Publishers, 1997.

World Bank. *Education in Sub-Saharan Africa: Policies for Adjustment, Revitalization and Expansion.* Washington, D.C.: World Bank, 1988.

Education, Higher, in Postcolonial Africa

Education in Africa during the colonial era was closely linked to religion and missionary activity. Belgian, British, French, and Portuguese colonial education systems were almost all initiated and run by Christian missionary societies and churches. Major expansion of educational institutions only took place after World War II, when many colonial administrations introduced development and welfare programs in the colonies. Education featured prominently in some of these welfare programs.

Colonial governments increased both financial support and physical presence in the education system. For the first time, for instance, the Ugandan government appointed a special education officer charged with overseeing the development of girls' education. The missionaries became receding, supporting partners in education. In South Africa, the Extension of Universities Act (1959) led to the founding of open universities vis-à-vis the racially segregated ones. Out of these measures emerged University of Cape Town, University of Witwatersrand, and the University of South Africa. The five nonwhite universities of Zululand, Western Cape, Turfloop, Fort Hare, and Durban also came into being at this time. The University of South Africa in 1946 started outreach programs serving people of all races both within and outside South Africa.

The postwar period also witnessed an increase in universities and colleges in Africa. Among these were the University of Gold Coast (1947), College of Technology at Kumasi (1951) in Gold Coast, University College of Ibadan (1948), and Makerere University College. All these were colleges associated with the University of London system, as was the Royal Technical College of Nairobi in Kenya. There were also University Colleges founded in Dakar (Senegal) and in Antananarivo (Madagascar) in 1950, and the University College of Rhodesia and Nyasaland in Salisbury in 1953. In the Belgian Congo, Lovanium University was established in 1954 in Leopoldville (Kinshasa), and then the State University of Elizabethville was started in Katanga.

The focus of university education in many of these institutions, with the exception of a few such as Makerere Medical School and Royal Technical College in Nairobi, was generally the arts and humanities, with little emphasis on sciences, medicine, or vocational studies.

At the time of independence in the early 1960s, education in Africa had already been taken on board as a state responsibility, and with this, there was a corresponding decline in missionary control over the education sector. Many institutions of higher education, especially university colleges, started cutting links with the mother institutions overseas. Whereas in the preindependence period, Western universities tended to provide academic inspiration and control, in the postindependence period, many African universities sought independence as well and looked elsewhere (to the USSR and the United States, for example) for academic links and inspiration, as they became established as full national universities. With this new measure of autonomy, there was noticeable change in administration, internal structures, and curricula. African universities became more dependent on the government for financial support. Increased government control in the daily administration of the university brought with it a corresponding decline in university autonomy. With increased government interference in university administration, student unrest was reported at several African universities, resulting in the death, at government hands, of scores of students on campuses in Zaire/Congo, Ethiopia, and Uganda.

The economic crisis which has hindered African countries since the 1980s has greatly affected both capital and academic developments at most African universities. While government funding appears to have increased tremendously (for example, assistance to the University of Ghana rose from 64 million cedes in 1980 to 2,465 million cedes in 1991, an increase of 5,000%), in real terms of the local currency value against the dollar, government funding had actually shrunk to incredibly low levels.

The 1960s and 1970s had reported very positive quantitative change in most African universities. Government budgets in the education sector had appreciably increased in most countries. Large investment in secondary education at independence had resulted in a phenomenal increased intake by the thousands at universities. For instance, Zaire/Democratic Republic of Congo, which had only 30 graduates at independence in 1960, admitted 10,000 university students in 1973.

In spite of increased intake, there were still more qualified candidates for university entry than what universities could manage to admit, especially in view of capital development stagnation. No additional lecture halls, laboratories, or student residences had been built since the early 1970s, but the demand for university education has kept rising annually. This demand has led to the founding of privately funded universities. From the 30 universities in 1960, there are now well over 100 universities in Africa, many of them private. Maintaining quality university education in the face of all these pressures is a struggle for most African universities.

Female student enrollment has remained low for a long time. A number of African universities are only now waking up to this gender imbalance, sometimes by slightly lowering entry requirements for girls. Changes are already observable, although gradual. In 1975 female university students totaled about 26 per cent; in 1985 the percentage rose to 28 and then to 31 in 1991.

After independence east, central and southern African countries experimented with regional university systems: University of East Africa (Kenya, Uganda, and Tanzania); University of Lesotho, Botswana, and Swaziland, and the University of Rhodesia and Nyasaland. These were commendable attempts at regional cooperation in this vital development sector basically intended to avoid duplication of costly university education programs. Unfortunately, these systems collapsed as nationalist passions in the participating countries flared up and factious tendencies tore these regional university systems apart. The East African Joint University Council in Kampala is the only remnant of this worthy system in existence today, still checking on academic and other standards within the East African public universities.

On the continentwide level, the heads of African universities founded the Association of African Universities in 1967 to promote and strengthen regional cooporation in research and university education, with its headquarters in Accra, Ghana.

With the break from mother universities in the West, many African countries began to question the Western-based university curricula. There has been extensive soul-searching about the role and identity of the "African University." Nonacademic and nonformal education programs, offered through extramural extension services, adult education, and short courses became quite popular in many African universities. Vocational and specialized professional courses were also offered at vocational and teacher training colleges. Kwame Nkrumah and Julius Nyerere led the call for the indigenization of education in Africa. University education, according to Nyerere, should "foster the social goals of living together, and working together, for the common good." This sense of commitment to community would counter university graduates' attitudes of "elitism, intellectual snobbery, and intense individualism" which were rather common among African graduates soon after independence.

Many African governments have, since the 1970s, shifted the overall focus of higher education to national economic and social development goals. There is now greater emphasis on science and technology programs at universities, although the greater enrollment is still in humanities and social sciences. The aim is to achieve a sixty to forty ratio in favor of science enrollment, so that a professional class, so badly needed in servicing development programs, which demand science and technological skills, can be available. It is, however, surprising that science graduates are affected by unemployment in the same way as their arts and social science counterparts. The question is whether African university programs are being designed to satisfy economic demands, or are simply giving theoretical training. Generally, higher education figures have been on the rise in most African countries since the early 1990s. Sub-Saharan African enrollment for 1995 was

1,750,684 (3.3 per 1,000 inhabitants), and public expenditure on education, as a percentage of total public expenditure for that region, was 16.7 per cent but represented 42 per cent per student as a percentage of GDP.

With the economic squeeze of the 1980s, the research function at African universities was one of the major casualties. Allocations for research in most universities are meager or nonexistent. Research output in African universities has therefore remained very low: in 1995 only 5,839 research papers were recorded as published from the region, and perhaps not necessarily all were presented by academics who were permanent residents of Africa. While there is no doubt about research potential among African academics, there are simply too many pressures, both social and economic, that mitigate against research. Those African scholars who have moved to universities abroad have managed to keep abreast of the "publish or perish" expectations affecting Western academics.

However, there has been a move to shift from fully government-funded higher education to a system where cost sharing will eventually become the norm. There are now more self-sponsored students than those on government scholarships, for instance at Makerere University in Kampala, Uganda, one of the African universities that has embraced this bold shift to private sponsorship with a great measure of success. A new development of private universities is now taking root in Africa, and many governments are putting in place legal frameworks for the control and checking of standards of these new private institutions of higher education.

D. KIYAGA-MULINDWA

Further Reading

Bengu, S. M. E. "The Role of Universities in Training for Employment." Paper read at HSRC Seminar, February 1993.
ESAURP. *University Capacity Utilization in Eastern and Southern Africa: Resume of the Report Overview, Conclusions and Policy Recommendations.* Dar-es-Salaam, 1992.
Ngara, E. *The African University and Its Mission.* Rome: Institute of Southern Africa Studies, 1995.
Nmah Gapeh, D. "Higher Education in Africa: Challenges of the Future." *Whydah* 3, no. 10 (December 1994).
World Bank. *Higher Education in Developing Countries: Peril and Promise,* Washington, D.C.: World Bank, 2000.

Education: French West Africa

The first government school in French West Africa was opened by Jean Dard at Saint-Louis in 1816, but with the end of French settlement plans, the school closed and education was largely handed over to the missions for the rest of the century. The one exception to this was the creation by Governor Faidherbe (governor of Senegal from 1854 to 1861 and 1863 to 1865) of a secular government school for the sons of chiefs and other

A Catholic school in Cameroon in the 1930s. © Das Fotoarchiv.

notables in Saint-Louis in 1855, in the belief that education was a means of extending French influence and that a secular school was more likely to attract Muslims than missionary schools. However, it was only with the establishment of the Government-General of French West Africa that a concerted official attempt was made to organize education in the colony.

A series of decrees establishing a network of secular government schools was issued in November 1903, and at the same time the control of education was wrested from the missions, who were accused of providing an education that was too "bookish" in nature and insufficiently geared to the Administration's perception of the colony's needs. Official subsidies were withdrawn from mission schools, although they continued to operate in those parts of French West Africa, notably Côte d'Ivoire and Dahomey, where they were able to fund themselves.

The education system was designed to meet two objectives. The system was pyramidal in shape. First, there was "mass" education, which took place in the village schools. The curriculum was rudimentary (basic French, hygiene, and arithmetic), but its primary aim was to extend French influence among Africans in order to prepare them for work in the cash economy. Above them, situated in the main population centers, were the regional schools, which selected those Africans considered suitable for continuing their education beyond the first two years of primary school. In those urban centers where there were sufficient Europeans to justify their creation, urban schools following a metropolitan syllabus were opened. Second, there was "elite" education, which took place in the upper primary schools and for which those Africans considered suitable for further training were selected. Their aim was to select and train suitable Africans to meet the personnel needs of European firms and the colonial administration for lower level staff such as clerks, primary school teachers, and medical assistants. The intention was that each territory would ultimately have one of these schools, although initially the only one to be created was the École Faidherbe in Saint-Louis. In addition, two other schools were created in Saint-Louis, which in theory recruited students from throughout the federation: the École Pinet-Laprade, which trained technicians, and the École Normale, which trained primary teachers and was subsequently transferred to Gorée Island, where it became the École William-Ponty. No provision was made for secondary or higher education for Africans.

The 1903 decrees remained little more than declarations of intent, however, until the arrival in Dakar of Georges Hardy, who was the energetic director of the education service from 1912 to 1919. It was during his period of office that the colony's public education system was truly put in place. He pursued a policy of adapted education. This meant that the education provided to Africans had to be practical in nature, as one of its key objectives was to make the African more productive by "teaching him to work"; the intellectual content of education had to be reduced, so as to put it within reach of "primitive" pupils; and great importance was attached to education remaining in close contact with indigenous society, so that it did not become an agent of social dislocation by producing rootless individuals who might then become a source of social or political unrest.

There has been an enduring belief that France was, fundamentally, assimilationist in its approach to education in West Africa. The use of the French language; the fact that education was under government, rather than church, control; the fact that French Black Africans appeared more *francisé* than their British African counterparts; and the widespread use of French teachers in schools, all these have been taken as signs that French colonial education policy was basically assimilationist. Other factors have contributed to this impression. Official republican colonial discourse, which accorded pride of place to the French "civilizing mission," lent support to the notion that France sought to export its metropolitan education system to Africa in the hope of creating "Black Frenchmen," and the achievements of French Black Africa's best-known *assimilé*, Léopold Sédar Senghor, who gained the highest French education qualification, the *agrégation*, in French grammar, have also lent credence to this view. In addition, this general impression was reinforced in the English-speaking world by the work of two British colonial experts, W. B. Mumford and Major G. St. J. Orde-Brown. The thrust of their study, published under the title *Africans Learn to Be French*, was that the objective of French education policy in West Africa was to create "Black Frenchmen." By World War I, however, the emphasis had in practice moved away from assimilation toward a policy of adapted education.

By the 1930s the colonial authorities felt that further measures to adapt education to the African situation were necessary. The education provided was still considered too bookish in nature. Moreover, with only some 40,000 pupils in French schools throughout French West Africa, plus approximately a further 6,000 in mission schools, which taken together represented less than 5 per cent of the school-age population of the colony, it was felt that the schools had not done enough to advance the education of the peasant masses. A further corrective to the "assimilationist drift" within the system was thus introduced, and the rural schools initiative was launched. This initiative, which lasted until 1946, was intended to increase the number of pupils passing through the French school system while reducing the amount of time individual pupils spent at school. All rural schools were to have a "school garden," and the curriculum emphasis was very much on rudimentary skills and on "teaching Africans to work." The rural schools were widely resented by African families and teachers, however, and their abolition was one of the early demands of the new political movements established in French West Africa after World War II, since they were seen by African *assimilés* and *évolués* as a way of maintaining Africans in a position of permanent inferiority to Europeans.

The emerging nationalist movement in French West Africa made the introduction of full metropolitan-style education for Africans, including secondary and higher education following a metropolitan curriculum, a key demand after the war. African students were also given grants to study in France. It was largely as a result of these post-war developments that the former colonies of French West Africa emerged at independence in 1960 with education systems which were closely modeled on the French metropolitan system.

TONY CHAFER

Further Reading

Chafer, T. "*Decolonisation and the Politics of Education in French West Africa, 1944–58.*" PhD Diss., University of London, 1993.
———. "Education Policy in French West Africa 1903–44: French Culture Not for Export?" In *Popular Culture and Mass Communication in Twentieth Century France*, edited by R. Chapman and N. Hewitt. Lampeter: Edwin Mellen Press, 1992.
Gardinier, D. E. "The French Impact on Education in Africa, 1817–1960." In *Double Impact: France and Africa in the Age of Imperialism*, edited by G. W. Johnson. Westport Conn.: Greenwood Press, 1985.
Gifford, P., and T. C. Weiskel. "African Education in a Colonial Context: French and British Styles." In *France and Britain in Africa: Imperial Rivalry and Colonial Rule*, edited by P. Gifford and W. R. Louis. New Haven, Conn.: Yale University Press, 1971.
Moumouni, A. *L'Education en Afrique*. Paris: Maspero, 1964.

Mumford, W. B., and G. St. J. Orde-Brown, *Africans Learn to Be French*. London: Evans Brothers, n.d.[c.1935].

Education: North Africa (Colonial and Postcolonial)

Colonial educational systems in North Africa were designed to carry out a "civilizing mission," which was a justification for European political domination, and to establish a modern basis for collaboration between Europeans and North Africans. Colonial educational policy created a cadre of North Africans educated in European languages and technical subjects, who then carried out many of the administrative duties in the colonies. Yet, the European system of education also nurtured among the North Africans the principles of constitutional government and civil rights, which colonial governments denied North Africans. Educational policy thus displayed fundamental contradictions within the colonial systems and was an important cause of nationalism.

Prior to the colonial period, education in North Africa was religious, based upon rote learning of the Qur'an at the primary level, as well as textual commentaries and legal precedents at the institutions of higher education, such as al-Azhar in Cairo (the longest-running continuous educational institution in the world), al-Zaytuna in Tunis, and al-Qarawiyin in Fez. Learning within the Muslim institutions was distinct from a new, European model of schooling designed to instruct students in practical subjects for more mundane applications in business, government, and industrial or engineering projects. Beginning in the 1860s and 1870s, new schools organized on the modern principles were established by reformers such as Khayr al-Din in Tunisia and 'Ali Mubarak in Egypt. The former established the Sadiqi College in Tunis, which offered courses in Arabic and Islamic studies, as well as Western languages and technical subjects.

A colonial educational system was established after the French occupation of Tunisia in 1881. It was completely French in its design (except for some courses in the history and geography of North Africa), and all courses were conducted in the French language. Since most of the indigenous population did not meet the French language requirements, the new schools mainly serviced the needs of Europeans. Graduates of Sadiqi College—known as the "Young Tunisians"—led a campaign for the expansion of the colonial school system, as the basis for a truly national system of education. Indeed, colonial regimes reversed some of the educational reforms begun by North Africans. In colonial Egypt, regulations ensured that only those Egyptians who graduated from schools of the European type were eligible for positions in the colonial administration. The policy was designed to restrict modern education to a small minority of the population. Nevertheless, by the early twentieth century an entire generation of Egyptians imbued with Western ideas of social and political development studied in European-type schools and learned English and French rather than Arabic.

Educational policies in the other colonies of North Africa were similar in kind, if different in degree of impact. The Italian school system in Libya was designed to teach Italian language and culture, to the exclusion of Arabic and Muslim culture. The Sanusiyya, however, fostered a separate educational system that developed national resistance to the Italian occupation. In Algeria the colonial educational system was taught entirely in French, the curriculum was French, and the vast majority of those taught were Europeans. Among a population of 10 million, only 7,000 Algerians attended secondary schools in 1954. Nevertheless, the nationalist leadership emerged among those educated in secondary schools, notably Ait Ahmad Hocine, who was one of the founding members of the Algerian National Liberation Front. In Morocco the French Protectorate created one system for the European population and a separate system for the Moroccans, which was taught in Arabic in the primary cycle but strictly in French in the secondary cycle. The Moroccan nationalists were highly critical of this system, opening schools "free" of colonial restrictions in 1938. French in model, the free schools were also militantly anticolonial and therefore were suppressed by the French during the World War II. In general, Arab and Berber children were either excluded or segregated from the European-type schools during the colonial period; however, the small minority that entered these schools emerged as a nationalist leadership.

Men and women educated in European-type schools were highly critical of Muslim culture, notably on the issue of women's emancipation. The campaigns of Egypt's Feminist Union led to the admission of girls from middle-class families to secondary schools in 1925 and to Cairo University, which was chartered as a public institution in 1925. After the revolution of 1952 all Egyptians, male and female, were guaranteed a free education in primary and secondary schools, as well as the universities. Women particularly valued these reforms, since a university education meant that women could find regular employment outside the home.

The September Revolution of 1969 in Libya brought about a new educational policy that increased the obligatory period of education to nine years, which had some impact upon the customary seclusion of girls from public education. The Libyan reforms meant that literacy rates increased from 21 per cent in 1952 to 51 per cent by 1977. Similar advances were achieved in other North African countries. For instance, the Tunisian educational system was made universally available in 1958, regardless of race, sex, or religion. In 1960 the new University of Tunisia absorbed the Zaytuna University, which had been a redoubt of conservatives during the colonial period. The brutal character of the Algerian war for independence meant that the educational system had collapsed by 1962; however, the percentage of the eligible population enrolled in primary schools doubled between 1960 and 1980, reaching approximately 90 per cent in 1980. The Algerian government also invested heavily in secondary education and a new university system. Such reforms indicated the concern of nationalists to overcome a colonial legacy of dependence upon European technical expertise. Curricula were remodeled to foster an "authentic" Arab and Islamic national identity to counter the effect of the "civilizing mission," which had made the language of government, business, and education English or French, rather than Arabic.

Given the legacy of the "civilizing mission," postcolonial educational reforms in Morocco, Algeria, Tunisia, Libya, and Egypt represented a dramatic development of North Africa's human resources. Yet, the expansion of the educational systems had the unintended result of creating a surplus number of highly trained personnel, which, when coupled with the economic crises of the 1980s and 1990s, resulted in a culture of disappointment and resentment. In spite of reforms, families continued to sacrifice the education of their daughters to ensure the education of their sons. On average only 40 per cent of North African women advanced to secondary schools in the last quarter of the twentieth century. Economic crises at the end of the century meant that educational services were strained, so that methods of instruction in primary schools were often not far removed from the rote learning of the traditional religious schools. At the same time, Muslim charitable institutions were revived to provide an alternative educational system at the primary level, which emphasized Muslim values and fed into the disenchantment with the postcolonial governments. Within the universities this phenomenon was most apparent, where Islamist groups organized associations that opposed some of the basic premises of the postcolonial political and social systems, including education, which had been rebuilt upon colonial and therefore Western foundations. Another result of economic crisis was that, in spite of the best efforts of national governments to create universal educational systems, parallel systems developed for the wealthier classes. Finally, the percentage of North Africans literate and educated at the end of the twentieth century was low in relation to other developing countries. Moreover, government investment in primary and secondary schools in North Africa was relatively low, in spite of the fact that improvements in education were essential to engage in global communications and economic systems.

JAMES WHIDDEN

See also: **Algeria: War of Independence, 1954–1962; Morocco: Education since Independence; Tunisia: Khayr al-Din and Constitutional and Administrative Reform, 1855–1878.**

Further Reading

Anderson, L. *The State and Social Transformation in Tunisia and Libya. 1830–1980.* Princeton: Princeton University Press, 1986.

Bennoune, M. *The Making of Contemporary Algeria 1830–1987.* Cambridge: Cambridge University Press, 1988.

El-Nasif, H. *Basic Education and Female Literacy in Egypt.* Cairo: Third World Forum, 1994.

Henry, C. M., and Robert Springborg. *Globalization and the Politics of Development in the Middle East.* Cambridge: Cambridge University Press, 2001.

Joffe, E. G.H., and K. S. McLachlan, eds. *Social and Economic Development in Libya.* Cambridgeshire: Middle East and North African Studies Press, 1982.

Kerr, M. H. "Egypt." In *Education and Political Development*, edited by James Coleman. Princeton: Princeton University Press, 1965.

Richards, Alan, and John Waterbury. *A Political Economy of the Middle East: State, Class, and Economic Development.* Boulder, Colo.: Westview Press, 1990.

United Nations Children's Fund (UNICEF). *The State of the World's Children 1999.* New York: Oxford University Press, 1999.

United Nations Education, Scientific, and Cultural Organizations (UNESCO). *Correspondence on Cross Enrollment Ratios.* Paris: UNESCO, November 1997.

Egypt, Ancient: Chronology

The relative chronology of ancient Egypt is centered on a structure of dynasties, or royal houses, akin to the European Windsors, Hohenzollerns, Bourbons, or Habsburgs. These dynasties are taken from a history of Egypt, the *Aegyptiaka*, written in Greek by the Egyptian priest, Manetho, for the Macedonian king of Egypt, Ptolemy III, around 300BCE. This work is now lost, but excerpts survive in the works of later antique authors. Manetho divided the royal succession into thirty dynasties, and although there are numerous problems with his system, it is retained by Egyptologists to this day as the most straightforward way of delineating the progress of ancient Egyptian civilization.

These dynasties are usually grouped into periods and kingdoms corresponding to distinct phases in the country's political or cultural evolution. Thus, the Old Kingdom embraces the third through sixth dynasties, the time occupied by the great pyramid builders, while the Middle Kingdom, comprising the eleventh, twelfth, and thirteenth dynasties, represents a reunification of

Egypt.

the country, consolidation and cultural development, and its decline. The New Kingdom (the eighteenth through the twentieth dynasties) is the era of Egypt's imperial power in Asia, seeing the construction of an empire that extended from the Sudan to the Euphrates. The three Intermediate Periods, following each of the Kingdoms' periods, highlight centuries during which central authority was eroded, accompanied in some cases by foreign rule of parts of the country.

In addition to the Manethonic framework, we have a number of earlier, and thus far more reliable, king lists that help to confirm the ordering of rulers. These lists all date to the New Kingdom and comprise an administrative listing, giving full reign lengths as well as royal names (the badly damaged papyrus known as the Turin Canon), and four monumental offering lists, three of which place their contents in historical order. Of the latter, by far the best is that from the temple of Sethy I at Abydos; all of them, however, are incomplete and omit rulers for political and other reasons. Nevertheless, the lists combine with contemporary monuments and documents to permit the construction of our modern framework of Egyptian history.

The Egyptians did not employ an era-dating system such as BCE/CE (BC/AD), or AH, instead determining time by reference to the regnal years, months, and days of the reigning king. Thus, to ascertain the time between two events, the exact length of the reigns of all kings ruling between the events must be known. This information is only rarely available in a consistent manner, but in general a roughly reliable relative chronology can be formulated for most periods.

Putting absolute dates BCE to the dynasties thus reconstructed is often difficult and the subject of intense scholarly debate. Some astronomical events, recorded in monumental inscriptions and papyri, can be of some help, but all dates prior to 664BCE must be regarded as approximations only. The key is to identify events that can be dated with reference to an astronomical phenomenon, or by reference to another culture with an absolute and secure chronology. Unfortunately, both kinds of link are frequently more or less equivocal and dangerously subject to circular reasoning: there are examples where a Mesopotamian "fixed" date is actually based on an Egyptian "fixed" date, which is based on the original Mesopotamian "fixed" date, in turn based on an Egyptian "fixed" date.

Two main astronomical phenomena have been used to identify absolute dates; one is the new moon, the other the rising of Sirius, or Sothis. The former is used for refining dates where the basic time period has been pinpointed by other means, since it places an event within a cycle that repeats approximately every dozen years. Sothic dating is based on the fact that the Egyptian civil year had 365 days, and thus the "natural" year lost a quarter day each year, only coming back into synchronization every 1,460 years. Sothis was supposed to rise on New Year's Day, but gradually drifted away, and so any record of the rising of Sothis dated to a specific day, month, and year can be placed accurately within a 1,460-year cycle. Unfortunately, the result varies depending on where the rising was observed within Egypt, the accuracy of the observation; it also depends on the assumption that the calendar was never reformed to bring the Sothic and civil year into synchronism artificially. There is, however, no evidence for such a reform.

The main pegs used to establish an absolute chronology for ancient Egypt begin at 664BCE, when the beginning of the Twenty-sixth Dynasty can be fixed with reference to unimpeachable Assyrian data and is, in fact, the earliest absolutely fixed date in Egyptian history. All earlier dates are more or less problematic.

These begin with the biblical record (1 Kings 14: 26–35; 2 Chronicles 12: 3–4) of the plundering of Jerusalem by Shishak, dated to around 925BCE via Assyrian connections. Although objections have been raised (e.g., James 1991, pp.229–231), Shishak is almost certainly to be identified with Shoshenq I, founder of the Twenty-second Dynasty; depending on where the campaign is to be placed in his reign, the beginning of this dynasty can be fixed within the range 948/929BCE. On this basis, a lunar date under Rameses II can be used to place the latter's accession in the range 1304/1254BCE, with probability favoring 1279/1254BCE. Moving earlier, a dendrochronological date from the Uluburun shipwreck, containing an

Dodson, A. "Towards a Minimum Chronology of the New Kingdom and Third Intermediate Period." *Bulletin of the Egyptian Seminar* 14 (2000): 7–18.

James, P., in collaboration with I.J. Thorpe, Nikos Kokkinos, Robert Morkot and John Frankish. *Centuries of Darkness: A Challenge to the Conventional Chronology of Old World Chronology.* London: Jonathan Cape, 1991.

Ward, W. A. "Dating, Pharaonic." In *Encyclopedia of the Archaeology of Ancient Egypt*, edited by K. A. Bard. London: Routledge, 1999.

One of the sources for the Egyptian chronology are lists of kings to whom offerings are being made. Here, in Sethy I's temple at Abydos, Prince Ramses (later King Ramses II) reads a prayer, some of whose beneficiaries' names are seen in front of him. These are arranged in chronological order and begin with Menes, unifier of Egypt, in the top line. The list runs all the way down to the time of Rameses' father, Sethy I, but omits the whole Second Intermediate Period and certain "undesirable" kings such as Akhenaten and Tutankhamun. Photo © Aidan Dodson.

object of the wife of Akhenaten places the end of his reign before 1300BCE; a Sothic date for Amenhotpe I has many problems, and may (or may not) place his accession at 1553/1526BCE. Before this we have but one dating peg, a Sothic date under Senwosret III, that places his accession around 1880BCE. All other absolute Egyptian dates are derived from these pegs, and are thus wholly dependent on dead reckoning.

Radiocarbon dating has thus far played little role in historic Egyptian dating, since its error range generally exceeds that of other techniques. However, determinations from the beginning of the First Dynasty place its foundation in the range 3350/3000BCE, comparing with the around 3150/3050BCE arrived at by means of dead-reckoning back from the accession of Senwosret III.

The chronology of ancient Egypt is broadly well-founded, but it must be emphasized that there remain considerable difficulties, and for the New Kingdom at least, dates may have to be lowered by up to half a century compared with the current consensus figures given in this encyclopedia.

AIDAN DODSON

Further Reading

Balmuth, M. S., and R. H. Tykot, eds. *Sardinian and Aegean Chronology: Towards the Resolution of Relative and Absolute Dating in the Mediterranean.* Oxford: Oxbow Books, 1998.

Beckerath, Jürgen von. *Chronologie des Pharaonischen Ägypten* [Chronology of Pharaonic Egypt]. Mainz: Philipp von Zabern, 1997.

Egypt, Ancient: Predynastic Egypt and Nubia: Historical Outline

Early cultural and historical development in the Nile Valley is strongly dictated by its immediate environment. Natural landscape changes also marked basic cultural divisions. From north to south, these are Lower Egypt (the Nile Delta), Upper Egypt (between the Delta and Aswan/First Cataract), Lower Nubia (First to Second Cataract, spanning the modern Egyptian/Sudanese border), and Upper Nubia (Second Cataract to modern Khartoum and beyond to an ill-defined point along the White Nile). Lower Nubia and Upper Egypt are more thoroughly investigated, but work now has intensified farther north and south and into the present deserts. The Upper Nubian Nile intermittently has shifted course over time, chiefly westward to its present position although earlier positions remain only partially traced. Strictly speaking, the term "Predynastic" is applicable only to Egypt, but this section also considers Nubia up to the equivalent date. Absolute dates, invariably based on radiocarbon results and usually given as BP (i.e., before 1950), have varied considerably in the literature although now are much clarified by Hassan (1986). This section begins with the Neolithic "Revolution," following a short but intense arid period around the 6500 BP calibrated C14 date, when much of the Sahara essentially still was a cultivable grasslands; comparable conditions are some 500 kilometers or more farther south today. This arid phase caused some of the population to shift to the Nile floodplain, with whom the remaining desert peoples continued to interact. Saharan rock art also changes emphasis from hunting to farming scenes about this time, reflecting a change in their lifestyle.

It has only been recently realized that the main characteristic features of Predynastic Nilotic culture generally were assimilated from peoples outside it, in Egypt both from southwestern Asia and what is now the Sahara desert and in Nubia only from the latter. These features include cattle herding, farming, long-distance trade and communication, and perhaps even the beginnings of true sedentarism. Nonetheless, it was along the Nile that these activities precipitated the increasingly rapid developments that culminated in various distinctive Nilotic cultures, aided by the one stabilizing feature these desert peoples did not possess: the annual Nile inundation. Politically, all four basic Nile regions progressed without abrupt change but at differing times from numerous small organizational units into larger "statelets" governed by increasingly powerful leaders, producing relationship dynamics that ultimately can be traced down even to modern times. We progress here, with the Nile, from south to north.

Upper Nubia in this period is becoming more understood but remains little known except for the Khartoum/Sixth Cataract region. Some differences are apparent in the few sites investigated beyond this area that suggest groups of related cultures. Pottery has been found in the Khartoum area at an earlier date than in Egypt, and even earlier farther south around Lake Turkana (northern Kenya), suggesting an expansion of this technology northward into Egypt rather than the reverse. The same is indicated for bone harpoon technology. The then-fertile Sahara grasslands were cultivated, although we are only now beginning to investigate beyond the Nile itself especially where its "palaeo-channels" (dried-up river branches) had then existed. Steady development toward sedentarism and an agrarian economy are indicated by domesticated barley and other crops, with large numbers of grinding stones and domesticated animals (cattle, goats, sheep, dogs) coming from beyond the Nile Valley. While settlements generally appear egalitarian, cemetery analysis shows an escalating population growth and developing social hierarchy, with a small elite class having inherited wealth and status. Stone tools and weapons became increasingly sophisticated, some being socially significant such as mace heads. Jewelry became more common, and brilliantly handmade pottery was elaborately decorated, suggesting both specialist production and technological innovation. Trading connections were widespread in all directions, with stones from the Tibeste region (modern Chad) and elsewhere, and shells from the Red Sea coast found in some, mainly elite, graves. The most extensively investigated Neolithic sites are Kadero and El-Geili near Khartoum, and El-Kadada near the Sixth Cataract. Investigation of peripheral areas has revealed other, related, sites such as Rabak (Early Neolithic) south of Khartoum and Kassala (Late Neolithic) farther into the desert from the present river, indicating a much larger population and cultural spread than had previously been recognized.

At the northern end of Upper Nubia, above (south of) the Third Cataract, investigations in the Wadi el-Khowi and especially at Kadruka have revealed numerous Mesolithic to Neolithic cemeteries and related poorly preserved settlements in what had been an extremely fertile floodplain abandoned when the course of the river shifted west. These show again an increasing social stratification within agriculturally based sedentary communities having animal domestication, culturally related to the "Early Khartoum Neolithic" culture. A similar pattern of development is seen in the Wadi el-Howar leading westward to modern Chad, but with a seasonal seminomadic lifestyle and direct connections to both the Nile and those regions farther west. Survey along the Nile floodplain is beginning to indicate the development of formalized "statelets" that eventually became the Kerma culture.

Lower Nubia, spanning the modern border of Egypt and the Sudan, has only a very narrow and fragmented strip of cultivable land, resulting in a smaller population capacity having much greater reliance on fishing and hunting than farming or animal husbandry, and overwhelmingly on their middlemen role in the trade between Upper Nubia and Egypt. Despite intensive surveys before the successive Aswan Dam constructions flooded this entire region, neither settlement nor cemetery of the period was found, suggesting a far more nomadic lifestyle than elsewhere along the river. Three related but distinct cultures were identified by their lithic assemblages, the locally developed Abkan, and two others related to, and possibly belonging to immigrants from, those of Early Khartoum Neolithic farther south and "Naqada" in Upper Egypt. All span the Late Neolithic period, although Abkan does begin earlier. Not until nearly the end of the Egyptian Predynastic, with the early (Early and Classic) phases of A-Group culture in "Naqada II" times (see below), does occupational evidence become apparent. This also marks the beginnings of formalized political grouping(s) or even loosely organized "statelets" with increasing social hierarchy, ultimately based on trade wealth, culminating with the "royal" tombs at Qustul Cemetery.

The Egyptian, like the Nubian, deserts continued to be inhabited by peoples who apparently remained powerful and influential, and with whom the Nile Valley communities continued to interact. Nabta Playa, some 100 kilometers west of the Nile near Egypt's southern border, provides overwhelming evidence of hierarchical social complexity and early public architecture by Late Neolithic times, before its occurrence along the Nile.

The wide cultivable floodplain along the entire length of the Upper Egyptian Nile assured the most favorable conditions for agricultural development and the introduction of initially semipermanent and later permanent settlements of rectangular buildings along its length. The lack of impedimenta in the river favored both considerable cultural unity and political development, with a social hierarchy already apparent in the Early Neolithic "Badarian" period (after the type-site of Badari) in communities of varying size and some status graves. The "Naqada" period (after the type-site of Naqada, from where it also originated) is divided into three main phases: Naqada I ("Amratian"), II ("Gerzean"), and III (the period of Egyptian unification). Each phase follows its predecessor without abrupt cultural change; each is defined (and further refined) on the basis of its ceramics. Naqada I is essentially a technologically developed relative of the late Badarian culture, located farther south and with relatively little external contact beyond the deserts. It expanded south to Hierakonpolis and northward to Assyut, supplanting the Badarian culture. Naqada II penetrated farther, by its conclusion reaching north into the Delta and south at least to Aswan. Three apparently autonomous political states can now be distinguished, centered at Hierakonpolis, Naqada, and This (near Abydos). The Gebel Sheikh Sulieman rock inscription, dating to Naqada II, records a military incursion into Lower Nubia, probably by the Hierakonpolis ruler(s).

Steady social development, craft specialization, technological sophistication, and status-related unequal distribution of wealth are present already in Naqada I. All intensify dramatically in Naqada II, concurrent with a strong influx of foreign goods and influences from beyond the deserts (mainly southern Palestine and Mesopotamia), probably through increased contact with Lower Egypt and the Red Sea through the Eastern Desert. The famous "Painted Tomb" 100 at Hierakonpolis, undoubtedly a royal burial, dates to this period.

Lower Egypt has a similar riverine landscape although, instead of one long floodplain, the Delta's numerous branches form an essentially triangular shape. Recent surveys have shown it to have been densely populated. Unsurprisingly, it was a sedentary agricultural society with domesticated animals, supported by fishing and limited hunting and, more importantly, considerable trade connections with Palestine and elsewhere. Its culture was quite egalitarian initially and for most of the predynastic era, to judge from excavated cemeteries and (mainly) settlement sites with oval, Palestinian-influenced underground housing. Major sites include Merimde (Early Neolithic, spanning the arid phase and early Naqada I), El-Omari (EN, about late Naqada I–early II) and Ma'adi (Late Neolithic, about Naqada II), and in the related Fayum B (earlier than Merimde) and subsequent Fayum A (EN) cultures. Lower Egypt is culturally distinct from, and technologically inferior to, Upper Egypt until near the end of the Predynastic when late Naqada II cultural material begins to appear in Delta graves and occupation strata, before actual political annexation in Naqada III.

JACKE PHILLIPS

Further Reading

Bard, K. A. *From Farmers to Pharaohs: Mortuary Evidence for the Rise of Complex Society in Egypt.* Sheffield: Sheffield Academic Press, 1994.

Hassan, F. A. "Chronology of the Khartoum Mesolithic and Neolithic and Related Sites in the Sudan: Statistical Analysis and Comparisons with Egypt." *African Archaeological Review* 4 (1986): 83–102.

Keding, B. "The Yellow Nile: New Data on Settlement and the Environment in the Sudanese Eastern Sahara." *Sudan & Nubia* 2 (1998): 2–12.

Krzyzaniak, L., K. Kroeper, and M. Kobusiewicz, eds. *Interregional Contacts in the Later Prehistory of Northeastern Africa.* Poznan: Poznan Archaeological Museum, 1996.

Reinhold, J., and L. Krzyzaniak, "6,000 Years Ago: Remarks on the Prehistory of the Sudan." In *Sudan. Ancient Kingdoms of the Nile*, edited by Dietrich Wildung. Paris and New York: Flammarion, 1997: 9–36.

Wilkinson, T. *State Formation in Egypt: Chronology and Society.* Oxford: Tempus Reparatum, 1996.

Egypt, Ancient: Unification of Upper and Lower: Historical Outline

Throughout the nearly 3,000 years of their dynastic history, the ancient Egyptians themselves viewed their homeland as "Two Lands," the unification of which was the beginning of that history—and indeed the foundation for it. Kings and (later) pharaohs always bore the title of "King of Upper and Lower Egypt" and wore a "double crown" combining the originally separate "White Crown" of Upper Egypt (the Nile River Valley, south from modern Cairo) and "Red Crown" of Lower Egypt (the Nile Delta, to its north).

Both royal and "national" insignia combined symbolic representations of these two distinct geographical entities, and only rarely (and then for specific reasons) was one used without the other. Such dualistic motifs abound throughout ancient times, the most common pairs being the sedge plant (Upper Egypt) and bee (Lower Egypt), the lotus (UE) and papyrus (LE), and the vulture (UE) and cobra (LE) who represent the "Two Ladies," the goddesses Nekhbet (UE) and Wadjet (LE) of the royal titulary. The combination of "black land" (agriculturally rich land alongside the river) and "red land" (the red-sand desert beyond it on either side) carried quite different connotations: Egypt (both valley and delta) was the "black land" inundated by the annual Nile flood, while the desert borderlands both flanking and protecting it from outsiders was not. Even during the three "Intermediate" periods of Egyptian history, when instability and loss of central authority divided Egypt into multiple smaller political units (some ruled by foreigners), the concept of Egypt as a unification of the "Two Lands" remained unshakeable and pervasive.

The process of unification is partly recorded in the ancient texts and artifacts, and partly reconstructed from archaeological research. Ancient Egyptian tradition credits a king named "Menes" with actually uniting the two lands under a single ruler, and in the process becoming its founder king. He also founded the city of Memphis, just south of modern Cairo at the apex of the Delta and therefore at the natural junction of the Two Lands, which remained the administrative capital of the united Egypt even after the political capital had been transferred elsewhere. He did so by damming and diverting the Nile, in order to reclaim "virgin" land on which to build his capital. This tradition, recorded by Herodotus (II.4, p.99), can be traced back at least to the New Kingdom, by which time the political capital was firmly settled at Thebes far to the south.

Archaeological research, while not confirming the tradition in that no contemporary record of a king named Menes has ever been recovered, does provide a more complete picture of the unification and in some respects does not disagree with it. The ancient Egyptians themselves always mention Upper Egypt first, strongly suggesting it was from here that unification was initiated and that it ultimately conquered the Delta region. While far less excavation has been conducted in the Delta than along the river valley, reconstruction of the historical and political circumstances of the unification period has confirmed this suggestion. It is, however, far more complicated than tradition implies.

By the period we now call Naqada III, the multiple small "statelets" of the Naqada II period appear to have been consolidated and absorbed—by domination of one over another, or more peaceful political unification—into a smaller number of larger units along the Nile and in the Delta. Three "statelets" can be distinguished in Upper Egypt by Naqada II, centered at This (near Abydos), Naqada, and Hierakonpolis. The last, extensively excavated, site has revealed a major temple, large city, and several large cemeteries. Although the southern cultural sequence initially was developed at Naqada, it is from the stratified excavations at Hierakonpolis that its details are now defined. There may have been other smaller entities, the whole extending south at least to around the First Cataract and possibly beyond. Naqada III also is characterized by rapid administrative development, actually initiated in Naqada II with the earliest recognizable hieroglyphic writing. Large-scale public architecture such as mudbrick temples and royal tombs, achievable only through organized labor, becomes evident throughout the Nile Valley.

Cultural and probably economic dominance by the south preceded actual political control of Lower Egypt, as successive occupation layers of stratified Delta sites such as Minshat Abu Omar have revealed an escalating percentage of "southern" cultural material from late Naqada II into Naqada III equivalent-levels,

including the names of several southern predynastic rulers mostly inscribed on imported pottery. Native "northern" features are discarded, indicating a developing unified culture and interaction originating in, and dominated by, the south. A continuing escalation of social hierarchy is now found in the cemeteries, ranging from simple burials almost entirely lacking in grave goods to extremely wealthy élite and even "royal" tombs of elaborate construction and contents. In contrast, little if any northern material has been recovered from Upper Egyptian sites. This process probably took about two centuries to achieve, and concluded with political annexation of the Delta, at which point the ancient Egyptians considered the Two Lands united and Manetho's dynastic period begins. The exact sequence of events, however, remains obscure.

The archaeologically attested individual usually credited as the "unifier" of the Two Lands is Nar(mer), who apparently was a dynastic ruler of This at the end of the fourth millennium, and the first of eight Dynasty I kings listed in regnal order on a sealing excavated in the Abydos royal cemetery where all chose to be buried. Nothing related to Nar(mer)'s reign has been found at Memphis, however, although he is widely attested in both Upper Egypt and the Delta, as well as the northern Negev. It was his successor, (Hor-)Aha, who transferred the political capital to Memphis (which already existed in the time of Ka, Nar(mer)'s immediate predecessor at This). (Hor-)Aha also campaigned into Lower Nubia, probably against the Qustul kings. The "royal tomb" at Naqada, originally associated with Menes, is now generally accepted as belonging to a woman named Neith-hotep, who probably was Nar(mer)'s wife (perhaps in a political alliance between the ruling families of Naqada and This) and the mother of (Hor-)Aha. Thus "Menes" probably is a conflation of the first two kings of the Two Lands. However, the names of other rulers before Nar(mer), who probably exercised only regional authority, also are known and are grouped generally as "Dynasty 0." They may have played a substantial role in unifying some of the regional "states," but we are unsure of events. Some southern "statelets" may have been later additions *after* annexation of Lower Egypt by Nar(mer). We also have virtually no knowledge of political divisions within Predynastic Lower Egypt, although several sites were extensive and presumably regional centers. Following its annexation, the agricultural "breadbasket" of the Delta seems to have become little more than a border buffer against the desert peoples and, in the northeast, a pipeline for trade goods from southern Palestine. When trade routes shifted at the end of Dynasty I, its large communities died out.

One of the most important discoveries at Hierakonpolis is a cache of objects uncovered in the temple in the earliest excavations, many associated with the kings who span the unification period. One is a commemorative stone palette, where Nar(mer) is named and depicted on one side wearing what is recognizably the White Crown of Upper Egypt while bashing the head of a fallen enemy thought to represent Lower Egypt. On the opposite side, he wears the Red Crown of Lower Egypt viewing the decapitated bodies of his enemies, complete with standard-bearing entourage. Previously thought to commemorate the unification itself, reconsideration has suggested the initial directly historical interpretations of this palette and other evidence were somewhat simplistic; they are now seen more as visual statements of aspects of royal authority, rather than of specific historical events.

Although the Two Lands were unified, the iconography of this event (or series of events) developed over several generations. The titular "Two Ladies" name of the king does not appear before Den, the fifth king of Dynasty I, nor is the double-crown itself found before his immediate predecessor Djet, although both crowns appear separately on the Nar(mer) palette. Although the Red Crown is later symbolic of Lower Egypt throughout the remaining dynastic period, during Naqada times it belonged to the Upper Egyptian Naqada "statelet" rulers. The earliest instances of the White Crown appear even farther south, at Qustul, Aswan and Hierakonpolis, and it is associated with the Hierakonpolis rulers. A ceremonial stone mace-head depicts a Predynastic king, known to us as "Scorpion," wearing the White Crown; he is not attested in the Thinite area and probably was a ruler of Hierakonpolis near-contemporary with Nar(mer).

JACKE PHILLIPS

Further Reading

Adams, B. *Prehistoric Egypt* (Shire Egyptology 7). Aylesbury: Shire Publications, 1988.

Adams, B., and R. Friedman, eds. *The Followers of Horus: Studies Dedicated to Michael Allan Hoffman 1944–1990.* Egyptian Studies Association Publication 2 and Oxbow Monographs 20. Oxford: Oxbow Books, 1992.

van den Brink, E. C. M., ed. *The Nile Delta in Transition: 4th–3rd Millennium B. C.* Tel Aviv: R. Pinkhaus, 1992.

Herodotus. *The Histories*, translated by Robert Waterfield, with introduction and notes by Carolyn Dewald. Books II–III. Oxford: Oxford University Press, 1998.

Hoffman, M. A. *Egypt Before the Pharaohs: The Prehistoric Foundations of Egyptian Civilization.* Chap. 19. London: Routledge and Kegan Paul, 1980.

Hoffman, M. A., ed. *The Predynastic of Hierakonpolis: An Interim Report.* Egyptian Studies Association Publication 1. Giza and Malcomb Ill.: Cairo University Herbarium, 1982.

Millet, N. B. "The Narmer Macehead and Related Objects." *Journal of the American Research Center in Egypt* 27 (1990): 53–59, and correction in vol. 28 (1991): 223–225.

Spencer, A. J. *Early Egypt: The Rise of Civilisation in the Nile Valley.* Chap. 3. London: British Museum Press, 1993.

Wilkinson, T. "A New King in the Western Desert." *Journal of Egyptian Archaeology* 81 (1995): 205–210.

———. *Early Dynastic Egypt.* London and New York: Routledge, 1999.

Egypt, Ancient: Old Kingdom and Its Contacts to the South: Historical Outline

The Old Kingdom is usually defined as embracing the Third, Fourth, Fifth, and Sixth Dynasties (*c.*2700–2200 BCE), although it has been suggested that the Third Dynasty is perhaps better bracketed with the preceding First and Second Dynasties in the Archaic/Early Dynastic Period. The Old Kingdom is often characterized as the "Pyramid Age," as it was during this period that the pyramid was developed and reached its apogees of size, craftsmanship, and sophistication.

The second half of the Second Dynasty seems to have seen civil war that was only ended by the last king, Khasekhemwy. His son and successor, Djoser, was regarded subsequently as beginning a new dynasty, and his reign seems to have marked a major step forward in the economic and technological development of the reunified country. He seems to have been the first monarch to exploit the turquoise mines of the

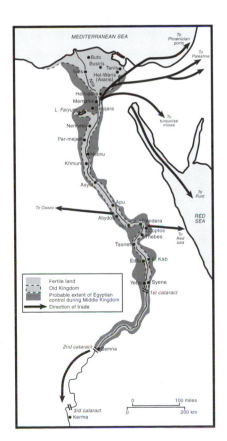

Ancient Egypt: Old and Middle Kingdoms.

Menkaure, penultimate king of the Fourth Dynasty and one of his wives, as shown in an unfinished statue from his pyramid complex at Giza. Now in the Museum of Fine Arts, Boston. Photo © Aidan Dodson.

Sinai peninsula, and built a chapel at Heliopolis, but the most striking manifestation of his activities is the Step Pyramid at Saqqara, his tomb, and the first monumental stone building in the world.

The succession after Djoser's reign is imperfectly known, and none of the immediately following kings were able to complete a pyramid. At the end of the dynasty, however, King Huni seems to have constructed a series of small ritual pyramid-shaped monuments around Egypt, together with a vast (and now all but vanished) brick pyramid at Abu Rowash. He was followed by Seneferu, founder of the Fourth Dynasty, and builder of no fewer than four pyramids, a small ritual structure and three more that were successively intended to be his burial place; he seems to have finally been interred in the Red Pyramid at Dahshur.

The reign of Seneferu marks a major upswing in the quantity of available historical data. Events recorded from Seneferu's reign include expeditions against Libya and Nubia, activity in the turquoise mines of the Sinai, and the import in a single year of forty shiploads of cedar. These seem to have come from the port of Byblos in the Lebanon, which was for centuries Egypt's principal trading partner in that area.

Seneferu seems to have been fondly remembered by posterity, but his son, Khufu, had a poor reputation in later tradition. This presumably centered on the sheer scale of his tomb, the Great Pyramid at Giza, the most massive free-standing monument ever built. On the other hand, the amount of material and effort contained within Seneferu's four pyramids far exceeded that expended at Giza, with an apparently diametrically opposite effect on posterity's opinion.

Little evidence survives concerning the events of Khufu's reign, other than that he sent expeditions to the Sinai, and worked the diorite quarries that lie deep in the Nubian desert, northwest of Abu Simbel. For much of his reign the Vizierate was in the hands of his nephew, Hemiun. Many other members of the royal family are known from the huge cemetery of mastabas (tombs with rectangular bases, sloping sides, and flat roofs) that was laid out around the royal pyramid.

Khufu was succeeded by two of his sons in turn, Djedefre and Khaefre, and then Khaefre's son, Menkaure. Following the reign of the latter's successor, Shepseskaf, there was a change of dynasty, the Fifth being begun by Userkaf, possibly a grandson of Djedefre. The pyramids built by the new royal house were far inferior to those of Seneferu and his immediate successors, being smaller and less well built, but with much larger, superbly decorated adjoining temples.

The second half of the Old Kingdom seems to have been a period of fairly extensive state-sponsored foreign enterprises, both peaceful and otherwise. Under Sahure, Userkaf's successor, we have depictions of the return of ships from a voyage to Byblos; we also have the first recorded expedition to the territory of Punt, which lay on the coast of the Red Sea, apparently comprising parts of modern Sudan, Eritrea, and Ethiopia.

During the Fourth Dynasty, the Vizierate had been largely in the hands of the royal princes; under the Fifth, this was no longer the case. Officials maintained royal links, occasionally marrying a daughter of the king, but no longer did kings' sons aspire to major posts in the administration, a situation that was to last until well into the New Kingdom.

A feature of the Fifth Dynasty kings is their building of a sun temple, as well as a pyramid. Most of these monuments lay in the area of Abusir, near the capital, Memphis. Sahure was succeeded by his brother Neferirkare, who was followed by his son, Neferefre, and then Niuserre. Of uncertain antecedents was Shepseskare, perhaps Neferefre's successor, who probably began a pyramid at Abusir that was barely begun. Their successors, Menkauhor, Isesi, and Unas, however, moved back to Saqqara, the last of them introducing religious texts to the walls of the royal burial chamber.

Exploitation of the minerals of the Sinai continued, as did other royal activities, but subtle changes are to be seen from the reign of Isesi onward. Most obvious is the end to sun-temple building, but there were also alterations in the system of ranking titles bestowed upon the nobility. Perhaps most significant was the recognition of the status of the provinces by the

The sculpted head of the wife of a noble of the late Fourth Dynasty. In contrast to her husband, the lady is shown with features that show clearly that she, or her ancestors, originated in Nubia or farther south. From tomb G4440A at Giza; now in the Museum of Fine Arts, Boston, 14.719. Photo © Aidan Dodson.

appointment of more than one vizier, one of whom was based in the southern part of the country.

The last part of the Old Kingdom, the Sixth Dynasty, is characterized by the increase in the number and quality of the tombs built at provincial centers by local dignitaries, in particular by the provincial governors. The first king of the new dynasty was Teti, who was ultimately followed on the throne by his son, Pepy I. His long tenure on the throne saw expeditions sent south and east, the latter both to the mines of Sinai and further afield, into southern Palestine.

Evidence of the king's building activities comes from a number of sites: the remains of a chapel survive at Bubastis, with other elements coming from Aswan (Elephantine) and Abydos. Pepy I was succeeded by his elder son, Nemtyemsaf I, who may have previously served as his father's co-regent for a number of years. His relatively short reign saw the first of a number of African expeditions by Harkhuf, the governor of Aswan. The interest now being shown by the pharaohs in the lands to the south is illustrated by Nemtyemsaf's visit to Aswan in his ninth regnal year to receive a group of southern chieftains.

Nemtyemsaf's sudden death, when still a young man, brought his brother Pepy II to the throne while yet a child. Power seems to have lain in the hands of his mother and his uncle, the Southern Vizier, Djar. Under their charge, the extensive foreign ventures of Harkhuf and other Aswan dignitaries continued apace, extending far into the African continent in search of trade items.

On three previous occasions, Harkhuf had visited the land of Yam, probably lying in the area to the south of modern Khartoum. His fourth journey took place not long after Pepy II's accession, and during it he acquired a dancing *deneg* (either a pygmy or a dwarf). This fact was included in the report sent ahead to the royal court while he undertook the northward journey back to Egypt. The idea of the *deneg* clearly delighted the boy pharaoh, who exhorted Harkhuf to return with his charge as quickly as possible. Harkhuf later reproduced the text of the king's letter on the facade of his tomb.

Other Aswan-based desert travelers included Sabni, who journeyed into Nubia to recover the body of his father, Mekhu, one of many who had found death while seeking the exotic products of the south. Tjetjy, Khui, and, one of the most important, Pepynakhte, also called Heqaib, can likewise be numbered among these early explorers. Heqaib made two military expeditions into Nubia, before being sent into the eastern desert to recover the body of a colleague who had been murdered while building a boat on the Red Sea coast in preparation for a trip to Punt. He succeeded in this task, as well as punishing those responsible for the killing. Of particular interest is the fact that in the years after his death, Heqaib became a god, worshipped in a chapel on the island of Elephantine, which drew royal patronage for many generations.

Having come to the throne young, Pepy II had a long reign, of either sixty-four or ninety-four years; if the latter is correct, it will have been the longest reign in human history. Pepy was, like his father and brother, buried at Saqqara, and was succeeded, by his son, Nemtyemsaf II. However, Nemtyemsaf II's short reign was followed by a series of rulers whose number and order are unclear.

It thus appears that within a short time of Pepy II's death, there was a major collapse in royal power, with a corresponding rise in provincial authority, leading ultimately to the effective breakup of the state. The following First Intermediate Period (7th to 10th Dynasties) was characterized by conflict, which was only resolved in the civil war that ended in the establishment of the Middle Kingdom around 2040 BCE, one and a half centuries after Pepy II's death.

AIDAN DODSON

See also: **Egypt, Ancient: Chronology; Egypt, Ancient: Middle Kingdom, Historical Outline.**

Further Reading

Aldred, C. *Egypt to the End of the Old Kingdom.* London: Thames and Hudson, 1965.

Edwards, S. *The Pyramids of Egypt.* Rev. ed. London: Penguin Books, 1993.

Kemp, B. J. "Old Kingdom, Middle Kingdom and Second Intermediate Period, *c.* 2686 BC." In *Ancient Egypt: A Social History*, by B. G. Trigger, B. J. Kemp, D. O'Connor, and A. B. Lloyd. Cambridge: Cambridge University Press, 1983.

Lehner, M. *The Complete Pyramids.* London and New York: Thames and Hudson, 1997.

Malek, J., and W. Forman. *In the Shadow of the Pyramids: Egypt During the Old Kingdom.* London: Orbis, 1986.

Manley, B. *The Penguin Historical Atlas of Ancient Egypt.* London: Penguin Books, 1996.

O'Connor, D. "The Locations of Yam and Kush and Their Historical Implications." *Journal of the American Research Center in Egypt* 23 (1986): 27–50.

Smith, W. S. "The Old Kingdom in Egypt and the Beginning of the First Intermediate Period." In *The Cambridge Ancient History.* Vol. 1, edited by I. E. S. Edwards, C. J. Gadd, and N. G. L. Hammond. Cambridge: Cambridge University Press, 1971.

Strudwick, N. *The Administration of Egypt in the Old Kingdom.* London: Kegan Paul International, 1985.

Wilkinson, T. A. H. *Early Dynastic Egypt.* New York: Routledge, 1999.

Statue of King Auibra Hor, with gilt collar and inlaid eyes. The figure is naked and bears on his head the *Ka* hieroglyph. The long beard indicated divine status. Egypt, Middle Kingdom, Thirteenth Dynasty, 1700–1650BCE. Egyptian Museum, Cairo. Anonymous. © Werner Forman/Art Resource, New York.

Egypt, Ancient: Middle Kingdom, Historical Outline

After the demise of the Old Kingdom, Egypt had split into two separate polities, one based on Herakleopolis (Ehnasiya el-Medina) and the other on Thebes (Luxor). Intermittent conflict occurred between the respective Ninth/Tenth and Eleventh Dynasty kings, which only ended around 2040BCE, when King Montjuhotpe II of Thebes gained control of the entire country, thus establishing the Middle Kingdom. The king then began to extend his influence beyond its borders, undertaking police actions in the surrounding deserts and penetrating southward into Nubia.

It seems that the preceding period had witnessed the appearance of a quasi-Egyptian polity centered around the area of Abu Simbel, as the names of a number of kings were found in this area, together with those of their followers. Montjuhotpe's forces moved against this southern state, and by regaining control over the area below the Second Cataract laid the foundations for the campaigns of the kings of the Twelfth Dynasty.

Montjuhotpe II built extensively, in particular in the area occupied by the original Theban kingdom. Fragments of his works survive at a number of sites, but his most impressive monument is the mortuary temple he erected at Deir el-Bahari at Western Thebes, where the tombs of his family and officials were also constructed.

After a reign of over half a century, the king was succeeded by his son and namesake, Montjuhotpe III. He continued the work of his father, before being followed by a fourth King Montjuhotpe. Apart from the reunification of the country, the period is important for raising the town of Thebes from a minor provincial center to the status of royal residence. It also marked the beginning of the ascent of the god Amun from local deity to all-powerful King of the gods, a process which was not to become complete for another four centuries.

Montjuhotpe IV was succeeded by his vizier (a high ranking official), Amenemhat, around 1994BCE; it is not known whether the transition was planned, or the result of a coup d'état. The latter option might be favored if a series of texts describing famine and other troubles have been correctly assigned to this point in time. In connection with this, it may also be noted that official propaganda rapidly cast Amenemhat in the role of the true reunifier of Egypt, thus carrying out a number of prophecies, allegedly made centuries before.

A key act of the new king was to transfer the royal seat from Thebes to a new site in the north, the city of Itjtawy. This remained the main residence of the king for the next four hundred years. Amenemhat I also founded a series of forts intended to protect the area north of Suez from incursions from Palestine.

In the king's twentieth regnal year, he appointed his son Senwosret I as his co-regent. Senwosret eventually became responsible for the leadership of military expeditions, in particular into Nubia, a region Egypt wished to bring back under its control. Other warlike activities extended into the Sinai and the Western Desert. Senwosret was returning from a campaign against the Libyans, ten years after his induction as co-regent, when Amenemhat I was assassinated while asleep in his bed.

Senwosret I interred his father in his pyramid at Lisht, near Itjtawy, where he was himself later also

Senwosret III was responsible for the full annexation of Lower Nubia to the Egyptian crown. Granite head from Karnak, now in the Luxor Museum, Luxor Egypt, J.34. Photo © Aidan Dodson.

buried. The long reign of Senwosret I saw Nubia occupied as far as the Second Cataract, with a presence extended further south. Extensive building took place, including the core of the temple of Amun at Karnak in Thebes, and various works at Heliopolis, in the north. Senwosret I's co-regent and successor, Amenemhat II, had led a Nubian expedition while yet a prince, and more expeditions are recorded on the great annalistic inscription produced during his lengthy occupation of the throne. Amenemhat II was buried at Dahshur, the principal necropolis of the dynasty.

Less is known about the next king, Senwosret II, but he seems to have been responsible for the large-scale development of the Fayoum, the oasis region, approximately 43 miles south of modern Cairo. There he also built his pyramid.

He was succeeded by his son, Senwosret III, who was to become one of the most important kings of the period, and worshipped as a god for many centuries after his death. Material dating to his reign is found at a number of locations, particularly in the southern part of Egypt. The king's statues are notable for their extremely naturalistic portrayal of features.

The reign of Senwosret III saw an increasing centralization of the administration, leading to a gradual withering away of the great courts of the local governors that had been a major feature of the preceding four centuries, as their leaders moved to work for the king at the national capital. There is relatively little evidence for Egyptian military activity in the direction of Palestine during the Middle Kingdom. Senwosret III's expeditions into Nubia were, however, far more extensive, and marked the full subjugation of the territory by the Egyptian crown.

The intention was to establish a clear southern boundary for Egypt, and regulate its intercourse with the peoples who lived below it. This frontier was set at Semna, where a complex of forts was built to house Egyptian governors and garrisons. They incorporated huge bastions and other defenses, and contained a great number of military and civil structures. These included very large grain storage containers, most probably intended to provide supplies for campaigning soldiers temporarily camped in the area, rather than the permanent personnel. No Nubians were allowed north of the forts, one of which acted as a trading post, through which all southern trade had to be carried out. Although setting the frontier at the Second Cataract, the Egyptians regularly penetrated into the territory further south.

The eldest son of Senwosret III was Amenemhat III. He appears to have served as co-regent for a considerable period before the elder king's death. Unlike his father, Amenemhat III has left few memorials of military activities. Reforms in the national administration were continued. At that point, the country was divided into three administrative regions, controlled by departments based at the national capital.

The Fayoum region had received the attention of Senwosret I and II, but it was only under Amenemhat III that more extensive works were apparently carried out there. In particular, a dam was constructed to regulate the flow of the water into the lake, thus reclaiming a large fertile area, which was then protected by an earthen embankment. Amenemhat III had the turquoise mines of the Sinai worked. Other regions which saw Egyptian expeditions for the extraction of raw materials were the Wadi Hammamat and the diorite quarries of the Nubian desert.

It appears that Amenemhat III may have contemplated making his daughter, Neferuptah, his successor. However, she died prematurely, and he appointed as his co-regent and successor a man of apparently nonroyal birth, Amenemhat IV. The latter's independent reign was short, and he was succeeded by a daughter of Amenemhat III, Sobkneferu, the first female king in Egyptian history whose reign is supported by firm evidence.

At the end of Sobkneferu's four-year reign, the throne passed to a son of Amenemhat IV, Sobkhotpe I. With him the Thirteenth Dynasty began, around 1780BCE. The transition between the dynasties seems to have been peaceful, but in contrast with the long, well-documented reigns of the Twelfth Dynasty, the Thirteenth is characterized by kings for whom few records were kept, and with brief tenures on the throne. Fragments of buildings erected by kings of the dynasty are known from a range of sites, in particular Thebes and Medamud, just to the north. The relatively small number of known royal tombs are concentrated in the area of Dahshur.

The Thirteenth Dynasty did not comprise a single family line, a number of monarchs having undoubtedly been born commoners. Coupled with the short reigns of many of them, this led to a theory that the real power was usually in the hands of a parallel dynasty of viziers. More recent work, however, has cast doubt on this interpretation (Ryholt 1997, 282–283).

The last fifty years of the Thirteenth Dynasty seem to represent a gradual decline. Although featuring some of the dynasty's longest reigns, a withdrawal from Levantine and Nubian commitments was accompanied by the establishment of independent or quasi-independent polities in the northeast Delta and a new state in Upper Nubia. Ultimately, the whole of northern Egypt fell under the control of an aggressive new line of Palestinian rulers, the Hyksos (Fifteenth Dynasty), ending the Middle Kingdom around 1650BCE, and beginning an era of conflict, the Second Intermediate Period, which would only end with the military victory of Egyptian forces, over a century later.

AIDAN DODSON

See also: **Egypt, Ancient: New Kingdom and the Colonization of Nubia.**

Further Reading

Bourriau, J. *Pharaohs and Mortals: Egyptian Art in the Middle Kingdom.* Cambridge: Cambridge University Press, 1988.

Edwards, I. E. S. *The Pyramids of Egypt.* Rev. ed. London: Penguin Books, 1993.

Hayes, W. C. "The Middle Kingdom in Egypt: Internal History from the Rise of the Heracleopolitans to the Death of Ammenemes III." In *The Cambridge Ancient History.* Vol. 1, edited by S. Edwards, C. J. Gadd, and N. G. L. Hammond, Cambridge: Cambridge University Press, 1971.

Kemp, B. J. "Old Kingdom, Middle Kingdom and Second Intermediate Period, c.2686BC." In *Ancient Egypt: A Social History,* by B. G. Trigger, B. J. Kemp, D. O'Connor, and A. B. Lloyd. Cambridge: Cambridge University Press, 1983.

Manley, B. *The Penguin Historical Atlas of Ancient Egypt.* London: Penguin Books, 1996.

Quirke, S., ed. *Middle Kingdom Studies.* New Malden: Sia Publications, 1991.

Ryholt, K. S. B. *The Political Situation in Egypt During the Second Intermediate Period, c.1800–1550BC.* Copenhagen: Museum Tusculanum Press, 1997.

Winlock, H. E. *Rise and Fall of the Middle Kingdom at Thebes.* New York: Macmillan, 1947.

Egypt, Ancient: New Kingdom and the Colonization of Nubia

While the Old Kingdom kings were content to trade with the inhabitants of Upper Nubia and the Middle Kingdom rulers ordered construction of massive

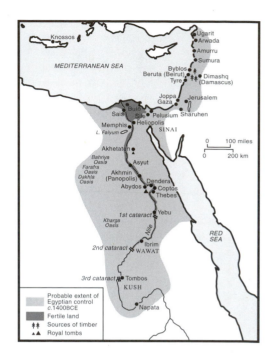

Ancient Egypt: New Kingdom.

fortresses along the Lower Nubian Nile in order to control access to the luxury trade goods from the Kerma peoples, the political events that gave rise to the New Kingdom in Egypt produced an entirely new policy to ensure the "Two Lands" would not be overrun by foreigners again: actual colonization and absolute control of Nubia as far south as possible. To this end, the New Kingdom pharaohs invaded the Nile corridor all the way at least to Kurgus between the Fourth and Fifth Cataracts, where several royal boundary inscriptions boast this achievement.

Self-laudatory royal monuments constructed after Egypt had taken control of the surrounding territory testify to the speed of this achievement. Initial royal policy apparently intended only to reconquer areas lost to the Kerma state at the end of the Middle Kingdom, which were considered Egyptian territory under foreign rule. Ahmose, founder of the Eighteenth Dynasty and of the New Kingdom, constructed a temple at Buhen and then appointed a governor-in-residence to administrate his regained estate. His successor Amenhotep I built another temple at Semna, the furthermost point of Middle Kingdom control, and then looked beyond it and revised official policy to that of invasion and colonization of Upper Nubia, which had never been part of Egypt before but posed a standing threat. He wanted a buffer zone.

It was, however, his successor Thutmose I who actually broke through the Kerma frontier to take Sai, penetrated the Third Cataract, and by his second regnal year was able to proclaim that he had reached Tombos

First pylon, pylon of Rameses II, Temple of Amun, Luxor, Egypt. In front of the pylon is a 25 m high obelisk (its twin stands on the Place de la Concorde, Paris) and two colossal seated statues (thirteenth century BCE) of Pharaoh Rameses II (1290–1224 BCE), Nineteenth Dynasty, New Kingdom. Temple of Amun, Luxor, Egypt. Anonymous. © Erich Lessing/Art Resource, New York.

(just north of Kerma itself) in a monumental rock inscription carved there. Sometime over the next decade, Thutmose again prominently carved his name on a boundary inscription at Hagar el-Merua near Kurgus (although the rest of the inscription remains problematic) that marks the farthest known point of actual Egyptian penetration. Egypt had conquered virtually all of Nubia in less than sixty years, and then held it all for another two and a half centuries, at least to the reign of Rameses II (19th Dynasty) whose name also is inscribed at Kurgus, before declining power at home again forced it to withdraw over the next century. The immediate effect of this invasion was virtual eradication of the native Kerma civilization and culture, which can be documented in the very short "Late" or "Post-Kerma" period of annexation. The city of Kerma was destroyed and apparently never regained its importance.

Following their conquest of Nubia, the Eighteenth Dynasty pharaohs began a massive program of construction, foundation, and suppression that continued for most of their occupation of the country. Amenhotep I first appointed a viceroy, titled the "King's Son of Kush," who ruled Nubia virtually as king but in the name of his pharaoh at Thebes. More than twenty-five successive viceroys held this title until the end of the Twentieth Dynasty with the aid of two deputies, one for Wawat

(Lower Nubia) based at Aneiba and the other for Kush (Upper Nubia) probably at Soleb. The first or second "King's Son," a man named Turi, already had been Ahmose's governor in Buhen; this was a promotion both in rank and in territorial control. The sons of elite Nubian families were taken to Egypt to be educated at court before returning home to Kush and (usually) a royal appointment, in a classic policy of ensuring the loyalty of both their relatives at home and of the succeeding generations.

The pharaohs initially restored and enlarged those Middle Kingdom forts still strategically important, transforming them into fortified towns. They also founded entirely new fortified towns throughout both Upper and Lower Nubia as far as Napata at the Fourth Cataract, and strongly encouraged Egyptians and their families to emigrate. These towns continued to expand in both size and population, eventually outside their original walls, being protected by the strength of Egyptian control of the native population. Predominantly soldiers, civil servants, merchants and priests, these colonists established an Egyptian social structure and administrative bureaucracy there, whose main purpose was to ensure the continued flow into Egypt of "tribute" (cattle, slaves, gold) and exotic goods from even further south. As a result, the Nubian elite who also became part of this bureaucracy adopted a strong veneer of Egyptian customs, including use of Egyptian language and writing and bestowing Egyptian names upon their children. Although some native Nubian beliefs and customs continued, an "Egyptianization" of ideas, attitudes, and iconography dominated and indeed even overwhelmed them.

Enough continuity exists between the previous Kerma and subsequent Napatan periods of native Nubian hegemony to confirm that both custom and belief must have survived through the period of Egyptian rule, but it is hardly visible in either the archaeological or contemporary historical record. Apart from the "Egyptianized" elite and bureaucracy, we know little of the native Nubians themselves at this time. It is usually presumed that they may have been driven into one of two possible main occupations, either as agricultural laborers on the estates created by the Egyptian administrative system, or as pastoralists either in the service of these estates or in the hinterland. In either case, they are not discussed in the texts (but see below) and are not distinguished archaeologically after about the mid-Eighteenth Dynasty.

The pharaohs also constructed vast stone temples at several key sites (Soleb, Sedinga, Kawa, Jebel Barkal) in Upper Nubia, and numerous smaller temples all along the Nubian river, usually but not always in conjunction with their new and expanded settlements. Beginning in earnest with Thutmose II, this program of temple foundation continued to a lesser extent under his successors and cumulated in the intensive building program of Rameses II (Dynasty XIX), the most memorable of whose seven temples is at Abu Simbel. Some glorified the pharaoh himself, his wife, or a predecessor. Official policy and the colonists themselves almost immediately imposed worship of the Egyptian gods on Nubia, to whom most of these temples were dedicated. They quickly dominated the older native pantheon, of which we know extremely little. Amun, supreme god of Thebes and of the empire, became the supreme god of Nubia in an adapted form, having some standard native Nubian features not found previously in Egypt, being represented as ram-headed with a sun-disc on his head. This policy of iconographical absorption, later used with equal effectiveness in the promulgation of Christianity worldwide, was so successful that Amun remained supreme (and others also introduced in the New Kingdom continued to be worshipped) in Nubia for more than a millennium after the Egyptians had departed.

All was not peaceful during their occupation, however. Numerous Egyptian inscriptions, records, and archaeological evidence survive as testimony to events. Unsurprisingly, the initial invasion was as bloody and repressive as we would expect. All New Kingdom pharaohs record the suppression of at least one and usually more native rebellions that continually opposed Egyptian rule and attempted to force withdrawal, especially from Upper Nubia. Nonetheless, these uprisings seem to have been viewed as comparatively minor annoyances, at least in Thebes. The pharaohs were far more interested in maintaining their Empire in the Near East against the greater threat posed by the Hittites and (later) the "Sea Peoples" and themselves against the Libyans. Egyptian forces heavily occupied both Nubia and the Near East, but it was the gold extracted from the eastern desert of Nubia that paid the majority of expenses required to maintain administrative and military control of the Levant as well as Kush. Nubia therefore was overwhelmingly important to Thebes, which continually sent out numerous exploratory missions into the eastern desert to find and quarry its gold; more than a hundred such mines are known to have been exploited in the New Kingdom. For this reason, the army rapidly and forcibly dealt with any hint of opposition to Egyptian rule by the archaeologically "silent" native population. In many ways, this period of Nubian history mirrors the policies and attitudes of Ottoman rule and European colonialism nearly three millennia later.

Following the reign of Rameses II, the pharaohs gradually experienced a lengthy decline in control of their empire, both internally against the increasingly powerful priesthood of Amun at Thebes, and externally against the "Sea Peoples" and Libyans who

steadily began to wear away at the northern and eastern borders of the empire. As more resources were required to combat these external enemies, Egypt began to withdraw again from Nubia as well as the rest of its conquered lands. The gold mines, no farther south than the Third Cataract, probably dictated the extent they were prepared to abandon, but eventually access to the mines became increasingly difficult to maintain in the Twentieth Dynasty and the "King's Son of Kush" even moved his residence to Thebes.

Final abandonment coincided with the fall of the Twentieth Dynasty and beginning of the Third Intermediate Period of Egyptian history, when the Twenty-first Dynasty kings ruled only Lower Egypt from Tanis, and the high priest of Amun effectively controlled Upper Egypt from Thebes. Virtually all of Lower Nubia seems to have been abandoned by both Egyptians and the native Nubian population, while Upper Nubian occupation also is not archaeologically attested for some 350 years until the rise of the Napatan royal dynasty that eventually conquered Egypt.

JACKE PHILLIPS

Further Reading

Adams, W. Y. *Nubia: Corridor to Africa*. Chap. 9. Reprint with new introduction, Princeton: Princeton University Press, 1984.

Davies, W. V. "New Fieldwork at Kurgus: The Pharaonic Inscriptions." *Sudan & Nubia* 2 (1998): 26–30.

Davies, W. V., ed. *Egypt and Africa: Nubia from Prehistory to Islam*. London: British Museum Press and Egypt Exploration Society, 1991.

Leclant, J. "The New Kingdom." In *Sudan. Ancient Kingdoms of the Nile*, edited by Dietrich Wildung. New York: Flammarion, 1997: 119–142.

Spencer, P. *Amara West*. Vol. 1, *The Architectural Report*. Egypt Exploration Society Memoir 63. London: Egypt Exploration Society, 1997.

Egypt, Ancient: Ptolemaic Dynasty: Historical Outline

For five hundred years, Persian rulers had used Egypt as a source of troops for invasions of Greece. When Alexander the Great arrived in 332 BCE, Egyptians welcomed him, as the Persian rulers had cruelly oppressed them. The general in charge of the invading force was Ptolemy I, a member of Alexander's inner circle of advisers. Egyptians called him *soter*, meaning "savior."

Although Alexander initiated the construction of Alexandria, he did not live to see its completion. He left Egypt in 331 BCE and died of malaria in Babylon in 323 BCE. His kingdom was so vast that the Greeks split it into three smaller kingdoms. Ptolemy became ruler of Egypt and Libya. He rebuilt holy temples at Luxor and throughout Egypt. He also restored and

Jean Adrien Guignet (1816–1854), *Cambyses and Psammetich.* Persian King Cambyses II conquered Egypt in 525BCE and overthrew the Pharaoh Psammetich III of the Twenty-sixth Dynasty. Louvre, Paris. © Erich Lessing/Art Resource, New York.

repaired walls destroyed by the Persians. On one temple relief, he offers gifts to Amun-Min, a phallic god. Ptolemy I made Alexandria his capital.

Ptolemy admired the wealth, luxury, industry, and intelligence of the Egyptian pharaohs. Rather than bury Alexander the Great at Vergina with the other great Macedonian kings, Ptolemy kidnapped Alexander's body and buried him in Alexandria. With Alexander's body under his control, Ptolemy consolidated his claim to rule and legitimated it. After defeating Antigonous at Gaza in 312BCE, he became satrap ("protector of the realm") of Egypt. Ptolemy added Palestine and lower Syria to his territory.

Ptolemy founded an Egyptian dynasty, known in his honor as the Ptolemaic pharaohs. They were efficient administrators and excellent businessmen. These rulers created a stable state and used the surplus agricultural products of Egypt as the basis of their wealth. They traded farm goods and mineral wealth, such as gold, to extend their influence beyond Egypt.

The Ptolemies founded a university, a museum, and two libraries at Alexandria, which attracted scholars throughout the ancient world. The Pharos lighthouse is one of the Seven Wonders of the ancient world. The Egyptian elite learned to speak and read Greek. Two-way cultural exchange took place. The Ptolemies admired Egypt's religion and culture and declared themselves pharaohs, or god-kings. They even adopted the Egyptian culture of royal incest and married their sisters so as to ensure the godliness of the royal line. They opened a canal to the Red Sea, and Greek sailors explored the east coast of Africa, trading with its population. The art of the time and region displayed a blend of Greek and Egyptian characteristics.

To maintain law, order, and stability the Ptolemies treated the Egyptian priesthood with respect (even if that respect rarely went beyond a superficial level), and they maintained an excellent civil service. Their faces appeared on coins and their names on traditional cartouches.

In 285BCE, Ptolemy I abdicated his throne in favor of his son, Ptolemy II. Ptolemy II Philadelphus (309–247BCE) extended trade and made the Greek ruling class adopt more aspects of the local Egyptian culture. Alexandria briefly became the center of Greek civilization. He sent expeditions deep into the heart of Africa, as Psammeticus and other Egyptian pharaohs had long before.

Upon his death, his son, Ptolemy III Euergetes I, assumed leadership. His armies invaded Syria, India, and parts of Greece. Under him, the Ptolemaic dynasty attained great wealth and power.

Ptolemy XII Auletes, father of Cleopatra, made a decision that would drastically affect the course of Egyptian history. He turned to Rome, beseeching the empire's assistance in maintaining power in Egypt. Rome became the major force in Mediterranean affairs. Ptolemy XII ruled Egypt by paying Julius Caesar and Gabinius, the Roman proconsul of Syria, to give him three Roman legions to enforce his decrees. Upon his death in 51BCE, his seventeen-year-old daughter Cleopatra VII inherited the throne. As custom demanded, Cleopatra married her brother Ptolemy XIII, to produce a royal heir. Her brother planned to murder her, but she discovered the plot and sought refuge in Syria. There she gathered an army and returned to claim the throne of Egypt.

Simultaneously, Julius Caesar was embroiled in combat against Pompey for control of Rome. Caesar defeated Pompey at Pharsalus in 48BCE. Pompey sought asylum with his Egyptian ally Ptolemy XIII. Ptolemy XIII feared Caesar; so when Pompey landed in Alexandria, Ptolemy had him arrested and beheaded. When Caesar arrived, Ptolemy presented Caesar with Pompey's head, thinking that this would please Caesar. Pompey, however, was Caesar's boyhood friend and son-in-law. Appalled at Ptolemey's murder of Pompey, Caesar executed Pothius, as he had advised Ptolemy to commit the act.

Caesar learned of the dispute between Cleopatra and Ptolemy XIII. He ordered both to appear before him, to settle the dispute. Ptolemy's troops controlled Alexandria and had orders to kill Cleopatra on sight. Cleverly, Cleopatra had herself rolled up inside of a large rug and delivered to Caesar's palace. When the rug was unrolled, out fell Cleopatra. She captivated Caesar with her wit, charm, and sensuality. When Ptolemy arrived for the scheduled meeting the next morning, he found Caesar and Cleopatra sharing the throne. Ptolemy was outraged and unsuccessfully laid siege to the Romans on Pharos Island. Ptolemy drowned during the attack. To prevent defeat, Caesar burned his fleet and the docks. However, he also accidentally burned down the great library at Alexandria, the greatest depository of knowledge in the ancient world.

To maintain her throne, Cleopatra married her brother Ptolmey XIV, but she remained Caesar's mistress. She bore Caesar a son named Ptolemy XV Caesarion. Caesar flaunted his affair with Cleopatra by moving her into one of his palaces in Rome where she lived for years. The Roman Senate grew concerned that Caesar had no male heirs by his Roman wife. They feared that Cleopatra would use this to encourage Caesarian to lay claim to Rome. In addition, Caesar captured Brutus, for he had served as Pompey's general in Egypt. Rather than kill him, Caesar chose to rehabilitate Brutus. Unknown to Caesar, Brutus sought revenge for Pompey's death and secretly opposed Caesar's rule. Brutus led a group of Roman senators in murdering Caesar. Cleopatra fled to Egypt, fearing for her life.

Anarchy gripped Rome following Caesar's assassination until Caesar's nephew Octavian Augustus, Marcus Lepidus, and Mark Antony divided Rome among them. Mark Antony ruled the Eastern Roman Empire, including Egypt. He called Cleopatra in to question her about Caesar's murder, and she seduced him, in an attempt to acquire power for herself and autonomous rule for Egypt.

Cleopatra and Mark Antony married and had three children, Cleopatra Selene, Alexander Helois, and Ptolemy Philadelphus. This outraged the Roman Senate. War broke out and Antony's forces were defeated in a sea battle at Actium, Greece. He retreated to Egypt with Cleopatra, pursued by Octavian Augustus and his army. Realizing defeat was imminent at Alexandria, Antony took his own life. Cleopatra allowed a poisonous snake, an asp, to bite her in 30BCE. In traditional Egyptian religion, the asp is the minister of the sun god and his bite confers divinity, as well as immortality. Cleopatra VII was the last pharaoh and the last member of the Ptolemaic dynasty to rule Egypt. When she died, the 3,000-year reign of the pharaohs ended. Egypt became a province of Rome and a pawn in a series of foreign empires for the next 1,900 years.

DALLAS L. BROWNE

See also: **Egypt, Ancient: Roman Conquest and Occupation: Historical Outline.**

Further Reading

Abbott, J. *History of Cleopatra, Queen of Egypt.* London: T. Allman, 1857.
Baines, J., and J. Malek. *Atlas of Ancient Egypt.* New York: Facts on File Publications, 1980.
Bevan, E. R. *The House of Ptolemy: A History of Egypt Under the Ptolemaic Dynasty.* Rev. ed. 1969.
Clayton, P. A. *Chronicle of the Pharaohs: The Reign-by-Reign Record of the Rulers and Dynasties of Ancient Egypt.* New York: Thames and Hudson, 1994.
Flamarion, E. *Cleopatra: The Life and Death of a Pharaoh.* New York: Harry Adams. 1997.
Foss, M. *The Search for Cleopatra.* New York: Arcade Publishing. 1997.
Fuller, J. F. C. *Julius Caesar: Man, Soldier, and Tyrant.* New Brunswick, N.J.: Rutgers University Press. 1965.
Ludwig, E. *Cleopatra: The Story of a Queen.* London: ECA Association. 1999.
Meir, C. *Julius Caesar.* London: Folio Society, 1998.
Payne, E. *The Pharaohs of Ancient Egypt.* New York: Landmark Books, Random House, 1964.
Silverman, D. P. *Ancient Egypt: Language and Writing.* New York: Carnegie Series on Egypt, 1990.
Warmington, E. H., ed. *Plutarch's Lives with an English Translation by Bernadotte Perrin in Eleven Volumes.* The Loeb Classical Library. London: William Heinemann, 1967.
White, J. E. Manchip. *Ancient Egypt: Its Culture and History.* New York: Dover Publications, 1970.

Egypt, Ancient: Roman Conquest and Occupation: Historical Outline

When Rome annexed Egypt in 30BCE, it was assuming control of an area with a coherent complex culture already 3,000 years old—far older than Rome itself. It was, however, an already occupied land; Egypt had been ruled by a series of Greek kings, the Ptolemies, ruling from a Greek city, Alexandria, since the conquest of the area by Alexander the Great in 332BCE. Rome itself had diplomatic ties to these Hellenistic rulers since 273BCE. Closer ties were established in the first century BCE when the dynasts Julius Caesar and Mark Antony interfered directly in Egyptian government through personal relationships with Cleopatra VII. Following his civil war with Antony and Cleopatra, Augustus, the first Roman emperor, annexed Egypt in 30BCE. In his own words "Aegyptum imperio populi Romani adieci" ("I added Egypt to the power of the Roman people").

Rome ruled a land with layers of culture already in place; three hundred years of Greek rule had not destroyed the traditions, customs, language, and lifeways of the Egyptians. It overlaid them with an overclass of Greek administrators and merchants. Beginning in the Ptolemaic and continuing into the Roman period, Egypt maintained its character as a dual state. The largest component was the Egyptian population living in villages and rural areas. For them, Greek or Roman rule did not change life significantly. Traditional ways of life continued as did Egyptian architecture, language, and religion. Roman emperors were conceived of as new pharoahs and depicted in temples in the traditional trappings of Egyptian royalty. Greek culture, including architecture, philosophy, urban planning, and language, was largely a phenomenon of the urban

Portrait mask of a young woman with long plaited hair. Probably of Greek ancestry, her attire is Roman, contrasting with the Egyptian images of the four sons of Horus and the *Ba* bird at the back of the head. Romano-Egyptian, early second century CE. H = 58 cm. Christie's, London. Anonymous. © Werner Forman/Art Resource, New York.

areas, notably of Alexandria. Rome adopted new governing systems to address the needs of this complex, multilingual, and multicultural land.

Augustus's policy preserved with minor modifications the administrative system of the Ptolemies, which had been in place for almost three hundred years, and created a unique governing system. To this he added Roman features including the census on a fourteen-year cycle, a new poll tax (*laographia*), and the establishment of a prefect (*praefectus Aegypti*) in place of the king. The Greek cities and inhabitants retained many of their rights of relief from taxes as well as local city councils. Local officials in Greek communities continued to be drawn from those of the highest level of Greek education and upbringing assuring a cultural, but not racial, hierarchy in favor of the Greeks over the native Egyptians. The relationship between Egypt and the remainder of the Roman world was also unique. Egypt, supplying as it did much of the grain consumed at Rome, was off limits to Roman senators and even prominent equestrians. The governor was himself an equestrian, keeping the rich prize of the province out of the hands of senators who might be potential rival emperors.

Egypt's vital role in maintaining Rome's stability led to much imperial attention, including extended visits including that of the emperor Hadrian in 130CE, when he founded Antinoopolis, the only new city of

Roman Egypt, which combined Roman political and economic advantages with Greek cultural institutions. Other visits were undertaken by Septimius Severus in 199–201 and his son Caracalla in 215. These were not sightseeing tours, but inspection trips connoting imperial concerns and attempts to oversee administration of the province.

Such close inspection by imperial authorities was precipitated by problems in the province. The intermixture of different cultures was not peaceful or entirely successful. The result of this contact between Egyptian, Greek, Jewish, and, eventually, Christian communities was a succession of civil, political, and military disturbances that plagued Egypt, especially Alexandria, from the first century to the third century. The earliest wave of violence under Roman rule occurred in the reigns of Caligula and Claudius, 38–41CE, when Alexandrine Greeks, offended by the visit to Alexandria of the Jewish King Agrippa I, rioted against the Jews, driving them into one quarter, sacking houses and shops and killing those they caught on the streets. The *praefectus* sided with the Greek population, declaring the Jews foreigners and arresting and executing many of the Jewish council of elders. Delegations of Greeks and Jews appealed to the emperor Claudius, who ordered both sides to keep the peace, not to interrupt each other's festivals or observances, and the Jews not to draw reinforcements from Syria or Egypt outside Alexandria. Further outbreaks of violence occurred in 66 when the Jews threatened to burn down the amphitheater. The *praefectus*, himself an Alexandrian Jew, called in the army and 50,000 people were killed.

The final violence occurred in a Jewish revolt of 115–117 spreading over the provinces of Egypt, Cyrene (Libya), and Cyprus. More of an attack against the Greeks than against Roman rule, it was nevertheless answered by Roman troops. The response from the emperor Trajan and the *praefectus* was conclusive; the Jewish community of Alexandria was wiped out. In contrast, Greek culture continued its privileged place in Egypt into the third century: a papyrus from the 260s from Hermopolis preserves the welcome by a town clerk to a fellow Roman citizen returning from an embassy to Rome by quoting a line from the *Ion* of Euripides.

The end of "Roman Egypt" and the origin of the Byzantine period in Egypt is traditionally dated to the reign of the emperor Diocletian (284–305). The history of this period is largely known through the ecclesiastical writers whose interest is largely doctrinal. Nevertheless, evidence from Alexandria shows the profound changes that occurred under the Byzantine emperors. One was a change in the tax base of Roman government. In Egypt the new system of taxes, no longer based on the poll tax, destroyed the privileged position of the Greeks and of other favored classes. Egyptians, Greeks, and Romans alike paid new property taxes. The effect on Alexandria was devastating. Greek institutions disappeared by the fourth century, and the cultural isolation of the Greeks ended in a merging of the Greek and Egyptian populations. Cities that once identified themselves as Greek communities became known as the seats of Christian bishoprics. Egypt remained a Byzantine province until 642, when it passed into Arab rule.

STEVEN L. TUCK

See also: **Egypt, Ancient: Ptolemaic Dynasty: Historical Outline; Egypt, Ancient: Religion; Egypt, Ancient: Social Organization; Egypt: Arab Conquest.**

Further Reading

Alston, R. *Soldier and Society in Roman Egypt: A Social History.* New York: Routledge, 1995.

Bagnall, R. S. *Egypt in Late Antiquity.* Princeton, N.J.: Princeton University Press, 1993.

Delia, D. "Roman Alexandria: Studies in Its Social History." PhD. Diss., Columbia University, 1983.

Frankfurter, D. *Religion in Roman Egypt: Assimilation and resistance.* Princeton, N.J.: Princeton University Press, 1998.

James, T. G. H. *A Short History of Ancient Egyp: From Predynastic to Roman Times.* Baltimore: Johns Hopkins University Press, 1998.

Johnson, J. H., ed. *Life in a Multi-cultural Society: Egypt from Cambyses to Constantine and Beyond.* Chicago: Oriental Institute of the University of Chicago, 1992.

Kasher, A. *The Jews in Hellenistic and Roman Egypt: The Struggle for Equal Rights.* Rev. Eng. ed. Tubingen: J. C. B. Mohr, 1985.

Lewis, N. *Life in Egypt under Roman Rule.* Oxford: Clarendon Press; New York: Oxford University Press, 1983.

———. *On Government and Law in Roman Egypt: Collected Papers of Naphtali Lewis*, edited by Ann Ellis Hanson. Atlanta, Ga.: Scholars Press, 1995.

Egypt, Ancient, and Africa

Egypt is obviously a part of Africa, and yet this simple fact has been denied by Western scholars, who wished to relate ancient Egyptian culture to Near Eastern civilizations for quite a long time. The relationship between Egypt and Africa was accordingly seen as a one-way flow, as the spreading of cultural traits or elements of an "advanced" or "higher" culture over an "uncivilized" continent. This view has to be seen within the context of Western scientific tradition and, it is hoped, a matter of the past.

The actual knowledge about the relationship between ancient Egypt and Africa (with the exception of Nubia) is, however, still limited. Most of those cultural achievements of African peoples south of the Sahara, which in the past were regarded as indicators of an advanced civilization—such as divine kingship, ironworking, inhumation rites, and the religious cult of the ram—have at times been attributed to an Egyptian origin. The basis of these hypotheses has usually been superficial comparisons between ancient Egyptian practices nearly five thousand years old and African cultural features of today. Over the decades quite a list of assumed correspondences has been compiled. Their scientific or methodological basis has to be regarded as shaky, and few of these diffusionist theories are currently accepted by Egyptologists or Africanists. Over the last few decades the debate on the relationship between ancient Egypt and Africa has become more and more controversial and ideologized. In the course of this development many of the above-mentioned ideas have been revived by Afrocentrists, who in some cases uncritically adopted what can be shown to be unscientific fantasies. Beyond possible common cultural traits the discussion on the relationship between ancient Egypt and Africa has focused on the question of the "racial" affiliation of the ancient Egyptians. Egyptologists and anthropologists of the late nineteenth and early twentieth centuries tried to prove that the Egyptians could not possibly have had black skin, nor could they have belonged to the "Negro race." With the same vehemence, the African response, under the leadership of Cheikh Anta Diop, was compelled to show that the ancient Egyptians had been black as evidence for the African origin of the ancient civilization. Especially in Afrocentric circles, the issue of the race of the ancient Egyptians is still of great importance, although now the whole concept of race has been challenged by geneticists.

The discussion on the relationship between Egypt and Africa is, up to this day, dominated by ideology and prejudice. This seems to have prevented serious investigations in many fields, and the scientific findings are still poor. Linguistically, the Old Egyptian language belongs to the so-called Afroasiatic phylum together with Semitic in Asia and Africa, the Berber languages in northern Africa, Cushitic in northeast Africa, Omotic in Ethiopia, and Chadic in present-day Chad. The homeland of this linguistic phylum can be located in northeast Africa, presumably in present-day Sudan, and the settling of Egypt was therefore the result of migrations of these African people into the Nile Valley. From earliest times on the Egyptians explored and penetrated the regions south of their homelands. Trade with the south was well established in pre dynastic times and included ivory, incense, ebony and animal skins. The famous funerary biography of Harkhuf of the Sixth Dynasty mentions the import of a pygmy or dwarf, whose designation can be traced back to a Cushitic linguistic origin. It is likely that the ancient Egyptians were also attracted by the Chad region, which could be reached via ancient valleys of the Nile and caravan routes that led to the west. However, no evidence for a westward exploration so far has been found.

Of periodic importance throughout the ancient Egyptian history was the country of Punt. As early as the fifth dynasty, the Egyptians referred to this African region where they obtained myrrh, electrum, aromatic herbs, ivory, and gold. The longest account of an expedition to Punt is found on the walls of Eighteenth Dynasty Queen Hatschepsut's temple at Deir al-Bahri, near Thebes. Here we find not only details of the expedition but also illustrations of the domestic life and the people in Punt. The name of Punt is recorded only in Egyptian sources, and nothing is known about the Puntites' names for themselves or their homelands. Accordingly, the debate on the geographical location of Punt, despite being over a century old, is still going on. There now seems to be some general agreement based on critical examination of the written and pictorial sources and supported by archaeological evidence that Punt can be located inland from the Red Sea coast. It is possibly related to the Gash delta cultures in eastern Sudan which show evidence of contact with the Ethiopian highlands and the Upper Nile valley. Early in the twelfth century BCE virtually all historical references to Punt cease and the trade seems to have died out.

Despite a fair amount of evidence for interrelations between ancient Egypt and Africa, it has only rarely been possible to tie African products, regions, or peoples mentioned in Egyptian sources with modern African designations. An intensification of linguistic and ethnoarchaeological research free from ideological bias might in the future close this unfortunate gap in our knowledge.

MARIANNE BECHHAUS-GERST

See also: **Diop, Cheikh Anta; Punt and Its Neighbors**

Further Reading

Bechhaus-Gerst, M. "Old Egyptian and Afroasiatic: The State of the Art." *Afrikanistische Arbeitspapiere* 56 (1998): 111–129.

Davies, W. V., ed. *Egypt and Africa. Nubia from Prehistory to Islam.* London: British Museum Press, 1991.

Diop, Cheikh Anta. *The African Origin of Civilization. Myth or Reality.* Chicago: Lawrence Hill Books, 1974.

Kitchen, K. A. "The Land of Punt." *The Archaeology of Africa: Food, Metals and Towns,* edited by Thurstan Shaw et al. New York: Routledge, 1993.

O'Connor, D. *Ancient Nubia: Egypt's Rival in Africa.* Philadelphia: University of Pennsylvania Museum, 1993.

Egypt, Ancient: Agriculture

The earliest evidence for agricultural practice in Egypt, in the form of crops and livestock remains, found at sites in the Fayum Depression and the Delta dates to approximately 5,000 BCE. Farming and animal husbandry evolved quickly and became well established throughout Egypt between around 4,000 and 3,800 BCE. Arable land was limited to the areas adjacent to and flooded by the Nile River and the oases. Additional cultivatable land was procured by basin irrigation and a loose system of canals, all dependent on the annual inundation of the Nile. The value of agricultural land, especially for taxation purposes, was based on its relationship to a water source. Thus, land that was directly on the riverbank and prone to flooding was of less value than land located at a slight distance from the river or near a canal. Land near the desert margin would, in turn, be of less value than land closer to the Nile and canals.

The Nile not only provided irrigation water but also washed out salts from the soil, and deposited rich silts at the approximate rate of 2.2 kilograms per square meter per year, providing an excellent soil composition for a rich variety of crops and virtually obviating the need for animal fertilizer. During the pharaonic period, basin irrigation with an accompanying canal system was augmented by water that was hand-carried in jars from the Nile to the fields. The *shadduf*, a simple water–raising device, is first visible in pictorial evidence from the New Kingdom (*c.*1450 BCE); the *sakkia*, an animal-powered water wheel, and the archimedian screw were not present in Egypt until the Greco-Roman period (4th BCE onward). These last two tools notably increased the cultivatable land available in Egypt.

In ancient Egypt the Nile's ebb and flow, and thus the cycle of agriculture, provided the basis for the Egyptian and Coptic calendars. The first season was that of inundation, or *akhet*, which lasted approximately from June to October. During these months, fields lay fallow or under water, while more floodwater was collected in basins and canals for use throughout the year. The next season was *peret*, meaning "coming forth," and was the time for cultivation after the flood waters had receded. This lasted from October to mid-February. During this time the fields were prepared using ploughs and hoes, the seed was scattered, and in some instances trampled into the ground by herds of sheep, goats, and pigs. The final season, *shemu*, meaning "drought," was when crops were harvested and lasted from mid-February to June, with much of the activity taking place in April. It is unclear when the Egyptians started to grow two cycles of crops, but in the Roman period two harvests of many crops were common. The second crop was manually watered with water carried from the Nile as by *shemu* the water in the canals and basins had already been emptied. It was this agricultural wealth that made Egypt an attractive prize for the Roman Empire, and once part of the empire, Egypt became its main grain producer.

The majority of agricultural land belonged to the pharaoh and the temples, with both keeping exact records of its productivity, taxation details, and lease agreements. Nobles and other wealthy individuals also owned land. Land was frequently rented out to tenant farmers, and details of these transactions have been found on papyri from most periods of Egyptian history.

The main crops produced were cereals. The Egyptians produced wheat, most commonly emmer (*Triticum dicoccum*), although some scholars have also identified cultivated and wild einkorn (*Triticum monococcum*, *Triticum boeoticum*) and barley (*Hordeum*). These were used to produce bread and beer, and were the staples of the Egyptian diet. The grain was grown on large fields; however, vegetables were grown in small square plots that were easy to water. The types of vegetables, fruits, and herbs cultivated in Egypt changed during the course of history with new plants being introduced by trading, conquest, and immigrant groups. The list of vegetables included onions, leeks, garlic, peas, lentils, chickpeas, various types of beans, radishes, cabbage, cucumbers, cress, a kos-type lettuce, and perhaps some form of marrow. Fruit included grapes grown on arbors for eating or wine production, dates of different varieties, sycamore figs, figs, pomegranates, dom-palm nuts, *nabk* berries, persea, and melons. Apples, pears, apricots, and peaches were cultivated in the Greco-Roman period, and possibly earlier. Although olives were cultivated, they were not successful enough to form a significant part of the oil industry, which was dominated by sesame, castor, and flax. Flax (*Linum usitatissimum*) was used not only for oil but was also the primary material used in textiles. Herbs included marjoram, purslane, fenugreek, coriander, celery, anise, fennel, mustard, basil, cumin, and rosemary. Papyrus was cultivated in the marshlands of the delta for making paper and boats, as well as for its edible tubers.

Vegetables and fruits were all harvested by hand, although there is a tomb scene at the site of Beni Hasan showing apes being used to help in the harvest of figs. In addition to being farmed on a large scale, fruits and vegetables were often produced in vegetable gardens on wealthier estates.

Agricultural tools pictured on tomb walls as well as those recovered from archaeological contexts include ploughs (powered by cattle as well as by humans), hoes, clod hammers, and mattocks for ground preparation and maintenance. Wooden sickles with flint blades were used to harvest grains, while flax was harvested by being hand-pulled. Grain was threshed on threshing floors with animals, generally cattle, walking over the grain to separate the seed from its covering, or by being beaten by thick sticks. Winnowing fans and sieves were used to separate the grain from the chaff. Grain was transported in baskets, and sacks were carried on donkeys and stored in mud-built granaries. Deities associated with agriculture include Nepri, the god of grain, Ernutet, the harvest goddess, and Sekhat-Hor, a cattle goddess.

SALIMA IKRAM

See also: **Herding, Farming, Origins of: Sahara and Nile Valley.**

Further Reading

Baer, K. "An Eleventh Dynasty Farmer's Letters to His Family." *Journal of Archaeology and Oriental Studies* 83 (1963): 1–19.

Bowman, A. K., and E. Rogan, eds. *Agriculture in Egypt from Pharaonic to Modern Times*. London: Oxford University, 1999.

Butzer, K. *Early Hydraulic Civilization*. Chicago: University of Chicago, 1976.

de Vartavan, C., and V. Amoros. *Codex of Ancient Egyptian Plant Remains*. London: Triade, 1997.

el-Hadidi, M. N. "A Historical Flora of Egypt, A Preliminary Survey." In *Biological Anthropology and the Study of Ancient Egypt*, edited by W. V. Davies and R. Walker. London: British Museum, 1993.

Hartmann, F. *L'Agriculture dans l'Ancienne Egypte*. Paris: Riunies.

Keimer, L. "Agriculture in Ancient Egypt." *American Journal of Semitic Languages and Literature* 42 (1926): 283–288.

Strouhal, E. *Life in Ancient Egypt* Cambridge: Cambridge University Press, 1992.

Wetterstrom, W. "Foraging and Farming in Egypt: The Transition From Hunting and Gathering to Horticulture in the Nile Valley." In *The Archaeology of Africa: Food, Metal and Towns*, edited by P. Sinclair et al. London: Routledge, 1993.

Zohary, D., and M. Hopf., *Domestication of Plants in the Old World*. Oxford: Clarendon, 1994.

Egypt, Ancient: Architecture

The basic building material of ancient Egypt was the alluvial mud of the river Nile. Mixed with some straw or other organic material, it could be shaped in moulds into bricks, which could be hardened in the heat of the sun. These could be used to produce anything from a shed to a temple or pyramid. In an arid climate such as Egypt's, mud brick can be incredibly durable, with walls from around 2700BCE still standing 10 meters tall at Abydos. Even after the adoption of stone as a monumental building material, mud brick still remained the principal material used, even for such structures as the royal palace. Stone only appeared as such things as doorjambs and column bases. This was because houses of whatever size were intended to last for a finite period; temples and tombs were meant to last forever.

Stone is first found around 3000BCE, when granite slabs were used to pave the tomb of King Den. Its use then increases until the beginning of the Third Dynasty,

The pylon of the temple of Luxor (late Eighteenth and early Nineteenth Dynasties), showing typical features of a New Kingdom temple, with a pylon gateway, fronted by obelisks and colossal statues, and an approach lined with sphinxes. The temple was built of sandstone, the normal building material for temples in southern Egypt from the time of the New Kingdom on. Photo © Aidan Dodson.

around 2700BCE, when the world's first large stone monument was built at Saqqara. This is the Step Pyramid complex, constructed as the tomb of King Djoser, by the architect Imhotep. In many ways, the stone architecture mimics earlier forms, with stone blocks the size of mud bricks, and many imitations of plant-material framing and roofing. However, over the next century, the full capability of stone was recognized, with the use of blocks weighing up to fifteen tons being used in the construction of the vast pyramids and temples at Giza.

The high-quality masonry seen at Giza rapidly declines in the latter part of the Old Kingdom, with more modest structures built with smaller, roughly shaped blocks used for core-work, relying on casings for stability. Of course the loss of such casings to stone robbers has resulted in later pyramids being in far poorer state than the earliest ones.

The extensive use of stone for nonmortuary temples comes rather later than its use for tombs, Old and Middle Kingdom temples relying heavily on mud brick. New Kingdom and later cult buildings tend to have their inner areas of stone, but their pylon gateways are sometimes still of brick. Foundations are generally poor and made worse by the burying of foundation deposits under many pillars. Such buildings are essentially held up by their sheer mass, and once decay has set in, collapse is often the result. Today, a number of ancient structures have had to be taken down and re-erected from scratch on modern foundations.

The Egyptian temple was typically approached through a gateway, flanked by obelisks and massive tapering pylons. A colonnaded court would be followed by a high, pillared (hypostyle) hall, lit by clerestory windows. Succeeding rooms would be less well-lit, with the floor rising and ceiling falling in level. The final sanctuary would be pitch black. The exception to this pattern were temples dedicated to the sun, which would be open to the sky.

Domestic structures vary considerably, from a peasant's hut, to the palace or mansion of an individual of the very highest status. The latter tend to center on a large, pillared, reception hall, out of which open the private apartments; many good examples are known from Tell el-Amarna, around 1350BCE. The focus on the reception room is also found in lesser, but still multi-room, dwellings; this reception room might house the shrine to the household gods, a platform that seems also to have been used by women who would squat on it to give birth.

Planned artisans' dwellings are known from Amarna, Deir el-Medina (New Kingdom), and Kahun (Middle Kingdom), while an ideal city layout may be inferred from Amarna, built from scratch by King Akhenaten as a new capital city. The latter featured a strong processional axis, onto which many of the public buildings faced. The latter were concentrated into the central part of the site, with mixed residential suburbs spreading north and south of the central city.

An integral part of any major settlement was its cemetery. Ideally, this should have lain to the west, the home of the dead, but this very much depended on the local topography. The latter would also largely determine whether the chapel element of tombs would be cut into a cliff face, or be a freestanding structure. In turn the latter could have the appearance of a miniature temple, or be a bench-shaped structure known as a mastaba, into the core of which the chapel might be

Sun-baked mud brick was the most ancient, and most widely used, building material in ancient Egypt. This is part of the funerary enclosure of Khasekhemwy, the last king of the Second Dynasty, at Abydos, and displays the characteristic paneled motif seen on many monuments of this period. Photo © Aidan Dodson.

built. The burial apartments (substructure) were almost always cut into the rock, approached either by a shaft or a stairway. They frequently lay below, or in proximity to, the chapel, but might lie a considerable distance away.

Kings' tombs follow the same basic pattern, the main differences being scale, and the fact that during the Old and Middle Kingdoms the tomb was surmounted by a pyramid, standing directly over the burial chamber, and immediately behind the tomb chapel (mortuary temple). The earliest pyramids are stepped, but from the beginning of the Fourth Dynasty become straight-sided, probably representing the sun's descending rays. Almost all are stone-built until the middle of the Twelfth Dynasty, when they adopt brick construction. In the New Kingdom, the mortuary temple, now devoid of an accompanying pyramid, was constructed over a kilometer from the substructure, which lay in a remote valley at Thebes, known as the Valley of the Kings.

Ancient Egyptian architecture remained in use for religious buildings well into the Roman period. In the nineteenth century there was a revival of the style in both Europe and the United States following the first major archaeological work in the country, with another revival in the 1920s, following the discovery of the tomb of Tutankhamun.

AIDAN DODSON

See also: **Egypt, Ancient: Funeral Practices and Mummification; Egypt, Ancient: Religion; Egypt, Ancient: Social Organization; Egypt, Ancient: Roman Conquest and Occupation: Historical Outline.**

Further Reading

Dieter A. *The Encyclopaedia of Ancient Egyptian Architecture.* London: I. B. Tauris, 2003.

Curl, J. S. *Egyptomania: The Egyptian Revival. A Recurring Theme in the History of Taste.* Manchester: Manchester University Press, 1994.

Dodson, A. *After the Pyramids: The Valley of the Kings and Beyond.* London: Rubicon Press, 1999.

Edwards, I. E. S. *The Pyramids of Egypt.* Rev. ed. London: Penguin Books, 1993.

Smith, W. S. *The Art and Architecture of Ancient Egypt.* 3rd ed. rev. New Haven, Conn.: Yale University Press, 1998.

Egypt, Ancient: Economy: Redistributive: Palace, Temple

The economy of ancient Egypt was based on agriculture. The ecology of the Nile, which every summer inundated the fields with silt-bearing water, ensured that farming was both simple and capable of producing considerable surpluses. It was upon the latter that ability to produce Egypt's stunning monumental civilization was predicated.

Men harvesting grapes. Detail of a wall painting in the tomb of Nakht, scribe and priest under Pharaoh Thutmosis IV (Eighteenth Dynasty, sixteenth–fourteenth centuries BCE). Tomb of Nakht, Shaykh Abd el-Qurna Cemetery, Tombs of the Nobles, Thebes, Egypt. Anonymous. © Erich Lessing/Art Resource, New York.

In theory, Egypt and all its resources were the property of the king, god's representative on earth. Thus, the palace (in essence, "the state") remained the ultimate economic center of the country. However, while the palace possessed estates, the vast majority of the land had, at some stage, been donated to individuals and institutions, the state benefiting through taxation.

Individuals would receive land initially as a grant from the crown in return for services rendered. It would then become the property of the family, being passed on through the generations, disposed of by sale, or incorporated into a funerary endowment. The latter involved the setting up of a kind of trust, the produce from the land being used to provide offerings for the mortuary cult of the person making the endowment, and to pay for a mortuary priest and the administration of the endowment. Such endowments formed an important part of the economy, akin to the chantries set up in medieval Europe.

Land held by individuals could be subject to complicated divisions and transfers, as shown by various surviving documents. Some long-running legal cases were felt to be so important that their outcome might be recorded in a tomb, for example in the tomb of Mose, who had been involved in wrangling that had stretched across several reigns during the late fourteenth and early thirteenth centuries BCE.

The major institutional landowners were, however, the temples. Kings wishing to show their religious devotion would allocate land to a temple, as well as manpower and other resources. The latter could include booty from war and tribute from subject peoples, particularly during the New Kingdom, when Egypt's international power and status were at their height. Private individuals also made donations, all ostentatiously celebrated by the giver to ensure that his or her piety was fully appreciated by the divinity.

Temples ranged greatly in size and economic ramifications. Most sanctuaries were strictly local affairs, with their land-holdings equally constrained. However, deities with "national" roles—such as Ptah of Memphis, Re of Heliopolis and, in particular, Amun of Thebes—had huge temples, with estates spread throughout Egypt and Nubia. These ensured that the temples had pivotal roles in the economy, both as landlords and as users of the surpluses generated.

Apart from supporting the clergy, and providing the goods that were offered daily to the deity, these surpluses enabled the maintenance of an extensive body of craft specialists. These were employed in the construction, decoration, and maintenance of the temple and its furnishings. In the process, they became centers of excellence in the broad spheres of craft, technology, and literacy, and seem to have thus also served as centers for technical and literary education for those outside the sacerdotal sphere.

The state's share of these surpluses, and those generated by other institutions and individuals took the form of taxation. In exceptional cases, the king might declare a given person or institution exempt from tax. It has been argued that overuse of this power may have played an important role in the economic decline of Egypt in the later New Kingdom.

The redistributive economy is particularly well illustrated by the New Kingdom community of Deir el-Medina at Thebes. This village housed the workmen who built the royal tombs in the Valley of the Kings, together with their families. It lay in a small desert valley and was entirely dependent on outside deliveries for food, drink and materials, provided by the state. Within the village, however, there was thriving trade, where goods and services were exchanged, as evidenced by many extant documents from the village.

Something that stands out from such material is that all trade was in the form of barter: coinage was not to appear until the very end of pharaonic times and was not common until the time of the Ptolemies. However, New Kingdom documents make it clear that there were by then notional units of account relating to metals that could allow the relative value of wholly dissimilar items to be reckoned. Back in the Middle Kingdom, (nominal) loaves of bread seem to have been used in a similar way.

Tax was levied by the state on all kinds of production. Texts relating to a biennial census of cattle, and later gold and land, date back to before the Old Kingdom.

Later depictions show officials measuring agricultural land to allow the calculation of tax liabilities. Collection was in the hands of local officials, much of the revenue taking the form of grain, which went to state granaries and formed the key medium for paying state employees of all kinds. Thus, the overseer of the granary of the Pharaoh held a pivotal role in the taxation process, although ultimate control lay with the vizier (prime minister).

AIDAN DODSON

See also: **Egypt, Ancient: Agriculture; Egypt, Ancient: Religion; Egypt, Ancient: Social Organization.**

Further Reading

Gaballa, G. A. *The Memphite Tomb-chapel of Mose*. Warminster: Aris and Phillips, 1977.

Gariner, A. H. *The Wilbour Papyrus*. 4 vols. Oxford: Oxford University Press, 1941–1952.

Haring, B. J. J. *Divine Households: Administrative and Economic Aspects of the New Kingdom Memorial Temples in Western Thebes*. Leiden: Nederlands Instituut voor het Nabije Oosten, 1997.

Janssen, J. J. *Commodity Prices from the Ramesside Period*. Leiden: E. J. Brill, 1975.

Katary, S. L. *Land Tenure in the Ramesside Period*. London: Kegan Paul International, 1989.

Warburton, D. *State and Economy in Ancient Egypt*. Fribourg: University Press/Göttingen: Vandenhoek und Rupprecht, 1997.

Egypt, Ancient: Funeral Practices and Mummification

The continued existence of the body on earth formed an important part of the ancient Egyptian view of the necessities for the afterlife, and seems to have been the dead person's link with earth. From this conception stemmed the requirement that the body be preserved from corruption and disintegration, which led to the development of the elaborate practices of mummification.

Early bodies, buried in the sand, often experienced natural mummification. After the introduction of burial chambers around 3200 BCE, artificial preservation was attempted by wrapping bodies in linen bandages, and sometimes additionally with plaster. This was supplemented during the Old Kingdom by the use of a mixture of salts known as natron, as well as the removal of the internal organs. The use of plaster was abandoned before the Middle Kingdom, a standard technique being developed for the highest status individuals by the New Kingdom. This began with the removal of the brain, lungs, and abdominal viscera (the latter two elements for separate preservation in "canopic" jars and chests); the body was then completely covered in natron for up to seventy days. Once fully desiccated, it

The Old Kingdom necropolis at Giza, showing a full range of tombs. In the background is the Great Pyramid of Khufu, and in the middle ground rows of *mastabas*. Finally, nearest the camera are the entrances to a number of rock-cut tombs. Photo © Aidan Dodson.

was entirely wrapped in linen, and equipped with a mask that fitted over the head; this would be placed inside the coffin. In some cases, the remains were enclosed in a rectangular sarcophagus of wood or stone, and placed in the burial chamber, along with the possessions of the deceased.

The designs of these mortuary containers changed considerably over time. The earliest coffins were rectangular, and very short, to reflect the early placement of the body in a fetal position. The coffins lengthened during the Old Kingdom, and gained a pair of eyes on one side; these were to allow the body, which lay on its left side, to "see" out. During the Middle Kingdom, mummy-shaped ("anthropoid") coffins began to develop out of the masks that some mummies then wore. By the early New Kingdom, these had all but replaced the old rectangular type; they were usually of wood, or occasionally, stone.

The detail and decoration of these items display a constant evolution. The color schemes of the coffins, in particular, show changes over time. Likewise, the four canopic jars initially had human-headed stoppers, but by the middle of the New Kingdom switched to depictions of different creatures' heads for each of the deities regarded as protecting the contained organs: Imseti—human (liver); Hapy—ape (lungs); Duamutef—dog (stomach); Qebehsenuef—falcon (intestines). These deities, along with the embalmer-god, Anubis, and the goddesses Isis, Nephthys, Neith, and Selqet, are also frequently found depicted upon coffins and sarcophagi.

The tomb ideally comprised two elements, the below-ground closed burial chamber (the substructure) and an above-ground offering place (the superstructure). The offering place might simply be the ground above the grave, an area in front of a simple stela, or a large freestanding or rock-cut complex; this could be either above the burial place, or some distance away. At the superstructure, the family, friends, or priests left foodstuffs, or communed with the departed on feast days (similar tomb visits, with family picnics, continue in Egypt today).

The forms of the elements of the tomb complex varied considerably with time and place, but at all times the fundamental concepts remained constant: the burial apartment(s) centered on the corpse itself, and the chapel centered on a "false door," the interface between the two worlds, through which the spirit could emerge.

Superstructure decoration usually focused on the earthly life of the deceased, including the individual's preferred recreation activities. In contrast, in the fairly rare cases where it was actually adorned, the substructure concentrated on such compositions as the *Book of the Dead*, or on providing lists of offerings to the dead.

Egyptian funerary ceremonies began when the prepared mummy was retrieved from the embalmers and was taken, in procession with the tomb goods, to the tomb. The procession included the family and friends of the deceased, priests, and, if the deceased had been wealthy, professional mourners.

The spirit of the deceased individual faced an arduous journey into the afterlife. The spirit first had to overcome the obstacles placed in its way by the guardians of the various gates that lay between it and its goal, the Hall of Judgment. Aid in doing so was provided by a series of guidebooks to the hereafter, such as the *Coffin Texts* and the *Book of the Dead*. These supplied spells intended to combat the threats that lay between the dead person and resurrection. The final

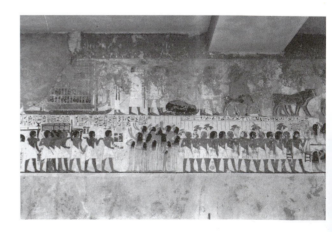

The funeral procession of the vizier Ramose (late Eighteenth Dynasty), shown in his tomb chapel (TT55) at Thebes. The large shrine at the left of the top register contained the dead man's body, before which a group of female mourners (bottom register) lament. Servants carry the furniture that formed an important part of the outfit of the burial chamber. Photo © Aidan Dodson.

part of the ordeal involved the weighing of the deceased's heart (regarded as the seat of intelligence and knowledge) against the feather of truth, order, and justice. If the scale balanced, the deceased went before Osiris and passed into eternal life in a realm essentially visualized as an idealized Egypt. If the heart proved heavier than the feather, it was fed to a monster called the Devourer, and the spirit of the deceased was cast into darkness. The guidebooks provided by the mourners contained spells designed to prevent such an outcome. These texts were generally written on papyrus and placed within the coffin, but they were occasionally written on the coffin itself or the walls of the tomb.

The spirit or soul was believed to have a number of aspects, including the *ka*, and the *ba*. The latter was depicted as a bird with a human head, which seems to have been the form in which the spirit traveled into the spiritual realm. The *ka* was conceived as having been created at the same time as the body, but surviving beyond the bodily death; it was to the *ka* that offerings were made during the burial rites.

AIDAN DODSON

See also: **Egypt, Ancient: Religion; Egypt, Ancient: Social Organization.**

Further Reading

Adams, B. *Egyptian Mummies.* Princes Risborough: Shire Publications, 1984.

D'Auria, S., P. Lacovara, and C. H. Roehrig. *Mummies & Magic: The Funerary Arts of Ancient Egypt.* Boston: Museum of Fine Arts, 1988.

Dodson, A. *Egyptian Rock-cut Tombs.* Princes Risborough: Shire Publications, 1991.

Ikram, S., and A. Dodson. *The Mummy in Ancient Egypt: Equipping the Dead for Eternity.* London and New York: Thames and Hudson, 1998.

Kanawati, N. *The Tomb and Its Significance in Ancient Egypt.* Cairo: Ministry of Culture, 1987.

Spencer, A. J. *Death in Ancient Egypt.* Harmondsworth: Penguin Books, 1982.

Taylor, J. H. *Egyptian Coffins.* Princes Risborough: Shire Publications, 1989.

Egypt, Ancient: Hieroglyphics and Origins of Alphabet

Egyptian is part of the Afroasiatic phylum of languages, covering large areas of the Levant and the northern part of Africa. Examples include Agaw, Akkadian, Bedja, Hausa, Hebrew, Kabyle, Somali, Tuareg, and Ugaritic, all of which have a number of features in common. Egyptian has been, for all intents and purposes, a dead language for some centuries; its latest form, Coptic, was replaced as a daily vernacular by Arabic by the Middle Ages. It is still to be found, however, in the liturgy of traditionalist Coptic Christian churches.

A typical use of hieroglyphs on a stela of the Twenty-second Dynasty. This one was dedicated at the funeral of a sacred Apis bull. It is interesting that its author, Pasenhor, uses it to recount his ancestry, which included many kings, and is thus useful for reconstructing the royal genealogy of the period. From the Serapeum at Saqqara; now in the Louvre, Paris, N481. Photo from A. Mariette, *Le Sérapeum de Memphis* (Paris: Gide, 1857), pl. 31.

Coptic is written in a modified version of the Greek alphabet; earlier forms were written in scripts based on hieroglyphs, which are first found around 3200BCE. Their first appearance is on individual pot markings from the prehistoric royal cemetery at Abydos, more coherent groupings being immediately following the unification of Egypt. Even then, however, the signs do not appear to write full sentences; rather they provide words to be read in the context of a central picture. The first "proper" hieroglyphic texts seem to date to the beginning of the Old Kingdom, after which progress seems to have been rapid. "Old Egyptian" is the term used to describe the first phase of the developed language. By the Middle Kingdom, it had evolved into Middle Egyptian, subsequent phases being known as Late Egyptian and Demotic. Middle Egyptian was regarded as the classic form of the tongue; it was still in use for some monumental inscription two thousand years after it had ceased to be the vernacular.

Almost all hieroglyphs represent an animate or inanimate object, and in their most elaborate inscribed form can be tiny works of art in themselves, and thus ideal for monumental and decorative purposes. However, they were less so for everyday purposes, and accordingly, from early on in Egyptian history, a distinct

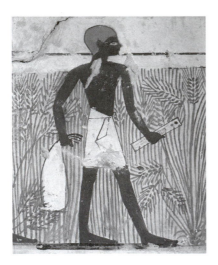

Scribe with reed pen box measuring grain. Detail of a wall painting in the tomb of Mennah, scribe of the fields and estate inspector under Pharaoh Thutmosis IV (Eighteenth Dynasty, sixteenth–fourteenth centuries BCE). Tomb of Mennah, Shaykh Abd el-Qurna Cemetery, Tombs of the Nobles, Thebes, Egypt. Anonymous. © Erich Lessing/Art Resource, New York.

handwritten version of the hieroglyphic script developed, known today as hieratic. In its early phases it is little more than a simplification of the underlying signs, but by the Middle and New Kingdoms hieratic has taken on various distinctive attributes. Hieratic script was used for a vast range of religious and domestic purposes, its principal media being papyri and ostraka (fragments of stone or pottery used for casual jottings).

Hieratic remained the principal script for religious purposes, in particular the funerary books such as the *Book of the Dead*, down to the latest parts of ancient Egyptian history. However, for domestic uses, the handwritten script had continued to develop, and around 700BCE a fully distinct variety, Demotic, came into use. Although fully developed hieratic is far removed from the traditional hieroglyphs, the origins of many signs are still more or less visible. In contrast, demotic script is almost unrecognizable as a derivative of hieroglyphs and has a number of its own linguistic peculiarities.

Although hieroglyphs and their developments are based on pictures, only certain signs function as pictures of the things to which they refer. The vast majority represent one, two, or three of the twenty-four consonants of the Egyptian alphabet. The latter does not include true vowels, which, in common with modern printed Arabic and Hebrew, were not written and had to be supplied by the reader from his own knowledge of the language. This leads to problems when one attempts to vocalize a set of Egyptian words, for example to produce versions of personal names that are acceptable to the nonspecialist reader. This is the explanation for the wide variety of spellings that are to be seen in print.

All ancient Egyptian words are made up of the sounds contained within the alphabet, and, indeed, there were signs that expressed every single one of them. Thus, in theory, any word could be written using purely alphabetic signs. However, in practice, this was not done, and there are over six hundred signs regularly used in writing. Nevertheless, it is possible that the Levantine development of a true alphabetic script was based on a knowledge of the alphabetic aspect of the hieroglyphic script. What may be the earliest alphabetic script, based on signs derived from hieroglyphs, Proto-Sinaitic, is known from the Egyptian-run mining settlements in the Sinai peninsula, dating to the Middle Kingdom/early New Kingdom. However, there are major difficulties with the interpretation of this script, and no definitive conclusions have been reached, even after some ninety years of study.

The hundreds of hieroglyphic signs fall into a number of categories. They include determinatives, needed to distinguish between words that, because they lack written vowels, are spelled in exactly the same way. Other important categories of sign are those that write two consonants, three consonants, or even a whole word (known as "bilateral," "trilateral," and "word" signs). The line between multiliterals and word signs is a fine one; indeed, some signs can fall under both headings, depending on the context within which they are used.

Knowledge of the ancient forms of the Egyptian language is now highly developed, and the majority of texts may be read with little difficulty. Research is therefore now directed toward understanding the underlying structures of the language, rather than basic meaning. However, until the 1820s, the hieroglyphic, hieratic, and demotic scripts were completely unreadable, knowledge having been lost since the middle of the fifth century, when the last known demotic text had been carved; the last dated hieroglyphic inscription was carved in 394.

During the intervening centuries, various more-or-less fantastic speculations were made, most based on the fundamental misunderstanding that saw hieroglyphs as pictures and not as phonetic signs. This misconception persisted even after an Egyptian-Greek bilingual text, the Rosetta Stone, was found in August 1799. It was not until the beginning of the 1820s that Thomas Young in the United Kingdom and Jean-François Champollion in France began to make real progress. It was the latter who finally was able to carry the task forward, producing the first grammar of the ancient Egyptian language, which appeared posthumously from 1836 to 1841.

AIDAN DODSON

See also: **Egypt, Ancient: Literacy.**

Further Reading

Baines, J. "Writing, Invention and Early Development." In *Encyclopedia of the Archaeology of Ancient Egypt*, edited by K. A. Bard. London: Routledge, 1999.

Collier, M., and B. Manley. *How to Read Egyptian Hieroglyphs*. London: British Museum Press, 1998.

Davies, W. V. *Egyptian Hieroglyphs*. London: British Museum Press, 1987.

Dodson, A. *The Hieroglyphs of Ancient Egypt*. London: New Holland, 2001.

Gardiner, Sir Alan. *Egyptian Grammar: Being an Introduction to the Study of Hieroglyphs*. 3rd ed. Oxford: Griffith Institute, 1957.

Griffith, F. L l. "The Decipherment of the Hieroglyphs." *Journal of Egyptian Archaeology* 37 (1951): 38–46.

Iversen, E. *The Myth of Egypt and Its Hieroglyphs in European Tradition*. Princeton, N. J.: Princeton University Press, 1993.

Loprieno, A. *Ancient Egyptian: A Linguistic Introduction*. Cambridge: Cambridge University Press, 1995.

Pardee, D. "Proto-Sinaitic." In *The Oxford Encyclopedia of Archaeology in the Near East*. Vol. 4. Edited by Eric M. Meyers. Oxford: Oxford University Press, 1997.

Parkinson, R. *Cracking Codes: The Rosetta Stone and Decipherment*. London: British Museum Press, 1999.

Egypt, Ancient: Literacy

Literacy was highly prized in ancient Egypt and was a sure guarantee of a significant position in the state administration. Given the vast number of inscribed temples, tombs, and statues that were a part of the landscape of ancient Egypt, it is surprising that literacy was relatively uncommon in ancient Egypt. Counting the occurrence of titles found in tombs associated with writing and extrapolating from these, it seems that a very low percentage of Egypt's population was literate.

The percentage of literate people in Egypt changed over time, with a presumed increase in literacy occurring from the Early Dynastic to the Late Period. However, when calculating basic literacy, one must remember that the degree of literacy varies: some people might have been more adept at reading than writing, or vice versa (although this is more unusual), and some could perhaps do both, but at a rudimentary level, while others could merely sign their names. The titles associated with literacy skills implied a higher level of literacy than the minimum level of competence (i.e., to sign or recognize one's name). A higher level of literacy was a prerequisite for those who wished to hold a significant position in the Egyptian bureaucracy. Titles—such as scribe, overseer, doctor, or priest, and so on—described those who were fluent in reading and writing, as well as numeracy.

There were possibly a significant number of individuals, such as itinerant professional letter writers, who were literate, but left little trace of their presence in the archaeological record. For example, the letters to the dead inscribed on papyri, or *ostraka*, and pottery vessels, might have been written by professional letter writers, such as are found in Africa and the Middle East today. Such people might have helped provide services for the illiterate, but might not have had the wherewithal to own rich inscribed tombs, and thus remain unmarked in the archaeological record. It has been suggested, however, that such services might have been rendered by low-level priests.

The site of Deir el-Medina, a Theban village, home of the New Kingdom workmen who carved and decorated the royal tombs in the Valley of the Kings, is a rich source of inscribed material. Evidence from the site indicates that many draughtsmen, quarrymen, and carpenters were literate. However, this village of artisans might have been the exception rather than the rule. At this point, evidence from other well-preserved workmen's villages, such as the one at Tell el-Amarna, or the Middle Kingdom village of Lahun, does not provide parallels in the literacy levels or the inscribed finds of Deir el-Medina.

An increase in literacy over the course of Egyptian history might, in part, be due to the evolution of the language, as well as the composition of the population. In earlier Egyptian history (Old Kingdom), literacy was rare. The formulaic manner in which standard inscriptions (especially funerary) were expressed may suggest that many texts are derived from the oral tradition and could have been, with an initial prompting, "read," or at least recognized by a large portion of the population. The discoveries of schoolchildren's practice texts seem to indicate an increase in scribal schools after the First Intermediate Period. As the number of people to whom education became accessible increased, the literacy level rose. In the later part of Egyptian history—when demotic, the common cursive script, was used—it is quite probable that more members of the population were literate. Certainly, the amount of graffiti from the later periods of Egyptian history would support this, as the earlier graffiti consists primarily of crude petroglyphs, or vignettes virtually unaccompanied by text, while from the Late Period onward there is an increase in verbal graffiti. In fact, the largest number of texts are written in demotic; however, this might be due to an accident of archaeological discovery and preservation rather than to any real reflection of the amount of written material present at any one time.

The number of literary genres increased and diversified with time. It is unusual, however, that virtually no inscribed papyri (other than religious works such as the *Book of the Dead*) have been found in tombs. Given our knowledge that intact Egyptian tombs contained all that the living presumed the dead might need in the afterlife, it seems reasonable to assume that tombs might have contained works of fiction for light relief, or examples of the improving didactic literature of which the Egyptians were so fond. The majority of literary texts that have been recovered from ancient Egypt come from fragments found in temple areas and at town sites.

Both men and women were literate, although the majority of literate individuals were men. Despite the fact that elite women were literate, few held high positions in the bureaucracy (with the notable exception of the priesthood, which did employ female priests). Royal women and many noble women and priestesses were, presumably, able to read and write. In Egyptian literature, some women are depicted as being literate, and a major divinity and the patroness of writing is a goddess, Seshat. In general, women's literacy might have been of a more rudimentary nature than that of men. However, the evidence gleaned from many demotic documents suggests that nonelite women who managed their own properties, as well as those of their male family members when they were absent, were literate. A significant amount of the evidence of female literacy, especially from the nonelite classes, comes from Deir el-Medina. However, there is little evidence of schools where women were commonly pupils; thus it is possible that women were taught literacy skills in temples.

SALIMA IKRAM

See also: **Egypt, Ancient: Hieroglyphics and Origins of Alphabet.**

Further Reading

Baines, J. "Literacy and Ancient Egyptian Society." *Man* n.s., 18 (1983): 572–599.

Baines, J. and C. J. Eyre. "Four Notes on Literacy." *Gottinger Miszellen*, 61 (1983): 65–96.

Bryan, B. "Evidence for Female Literacy from Theban Tombs of the New Kingdom." *Bulletin of the Egyptological Seminar*, 6 (1984): 17–32.

Eyre, C. and J. Baines. "Interactions betweeen Orality and Literacy in Ancient Egypt" in *Literacy and Society*, edited by K. Schousboe and M. Larsen. Copenhagen: Center for Research in the Humanities, 1989.

Janssen, J. "Literacy and Letters at Deir el-Medina" in *Village Voices: Proceedings of the Symposium 'Texts from Deir el-Medina and Their Interpretation': Leiden, May 31–June 1, 1991*, edited by R. Demaree and A. Egberts. Leiden, 1992.

Lesko, L. "Some Comments on Ancient Egyptian Literacy and Literati" in *Studies in Egyptology: Presented to Miriam Lichtheim*, edited by S. Israelit-Groll. Jerusalem, 1990.

Lesko, L. "Literature, Literacy, and Literati" in *Phawaoh's Workers: The Villagers of Deir el Meddina*, edited by L. Lesko. Ithaca, N.Y.: Cornell, 1994.

Velde, H. "Scribes and Literacy in Ancient Egypt" in *Scripta Signa Vocis: Studies about Scripts, Scriptures, Scribes and Languages in the Near East Presented to J. H. Hospers by His Pupils, Colleagues and Friends*, edited by H. Vanstiphout. Groningen, 1986.

Wente, E.F. "The Scribes of Ancient Egypt" in *Civilizations of the Ancient Near East*, edited by J.M. Sasson, vol. 4, New York: 1995.

Egypt, Ancient: Religion

In order to understand ancient Egyptian religion, it is important to take two points into account. The first is that ancient Egyptian religion was not separated from state affairs. Both religious and governmental fields were overseen by the king, who passed all matters onto his civil servants and the priests. The second is that the people in ancient Egypt were excellent observers of their environment. They watched the celestial bodies as well as significant factors of their surroundings, such as the annual inundation of the Nile, and they had profound knowledge about wild and domesticated animals. Therefore, every observation they made in this field was translated into a genuine mythological language.

Sources

Evidence of religion is mostly of funerary origin. Tombs and burial accessories of both common people and royal families exist. Besides the earliest and simple royal tombs at Saqqara and Abydos, there are monumental pyramids from 2630–1990BCE at Saqqara, Giza, Dahshur, Hawara, and Meidum, and for later periods the tombs in the Valley of the Kings on the west bank of the Nile near Luxor. The earliest collection of texts, the so-called Pyramid Texts, was written about 2340BCE directly on the walls in the interior of the pyramids. This corpus consists of a collection of different spells for the protection of the deceased king in the afterworld. During the New Kingdom (1550–1070 BCE) the royal tombs at Thebes convey diverse texts, which are called Books of the Netherworld, with comprehensive written material about ancient Egyptian ideas of the life after death. Those texts describe the nocturnal journey of the sun through the netherworld, the realm of the dead, from which he will rise in the next morning.

The private tombs are situated near the rim of the ancient sites at the borderline of the desert. They contain coffins made of wood, inscribed with another important and extensive collection of spells called the Coffin Texts (about 2100BCE) which are intended to protect the deceased against the risks of the hereafter. From the New Kingdom about 1500BCE onward the Book of the Dead, another collection of spells, takes the place of the Coffin Texts.

Another significant monument is the temple. Most temples are situated in Upper Egypt, while in Lower Egypt nearly all sites are destroyed. The earliest well-preserved temples with wall decorations are from the Middle Kingdom (2000BCE). For the New Kingdom the complex of Karnak, the Luxor temple, the mortuary temples on the west bank of Thebes, and the temples of Abydos are the primary sites. In a much better condition are the temples of the Greco-Roman era (300BCE–300CE) at Dendera, Esna, Edfu, Kom Ombo, and Philae. As a rule, every wall or column of an Egyptian temple is decorated with reliefs. Typically they include scenes of the king making offerings to different deities. These scenes are carefully composed following a decorative program that is called "grammar of the temple." All figures of a scene are inseparably connected with the integrated hieroglyphic inscriptions. Here the temples of the Greco-Roman time present more details in cult and other religious themes, because of the more extended inscriptions. The texts of the above-mentioned monuments and text-corpora include hymns, prayers, ritual texts and magical texts. But these texts may occur separate in other sources as well.

The Egyptian Pantheon

The genuine style of representing Egyptian deities and deified objects was developed very early and appears static during a history of nearly three thousand years. However, this does not mean that religious ideas and beliefs were unchanged and static throughout this period.

Only a few names and figures from deities and holy objects, so-called fetishes, are preserved from Predynastic and early dynastic times (3000–2500BCE), but the ideas people had concerning these objects are not transmitted.

The Pyramid Texts (about 2340BCE) show that Egyptian deities were divided into different categories. They worshiped cosmic or universal gods like the sun-god Ra or the moon-god Thoth. Other gods actually embodied space, like Nut, the goddess of the sky, the earth-god Geb or Shu, the air who filled the space between sky and earth.

In general, Egyptian deities are connected with a fixed place, where they were worshiped. Old Kingdom (2340BCE) texts show that the most important center of religion was Heliopolis; others were Memphis, Hermoupolis, and Abydos. Thebes, where the falcon-god Mont was first venerated, later became an important center, when Amun enriched the local pantheon in the beginning of the Middle Kingdom (2040BCE). Amun, who had a close connection to the kingship, became a universal deity, which means that there were also fluid transitions between universal and local deities. The majority of gods in Egypt are those with special tasks, like protection-gods, and their number was great

Over time, deity combinations became more important. In this way the name of the universal sun-god Ra was added to the name of another local-deity. Amun,

for example, became Amun-Ra, which meant that the local deity Amun acted as the universal sun-god Ra. Earlier scholars called such combinations syncretistic, but today this term is no longer used, since those deities did not actually meld together into a single being. The union could be loosened at any time. In a similar way different animals with their own characteristics are used to describe the quality of a god. Some gods had a close union with a specific animal.

Groups of deities were organized like structures in the society. Most of the cult places constituted during the New Kingdom a holy family, which consisted of a god, a goddess, and a divine child, but older and of greater significance was the father-son relationship, which played an important role in cosmological ideas as well as in the determination of the secular succession to the throne.

Egyptian Deities and Adjacent Cultures

Several near-eastern deities were worshiped in Egypt. Their names appear not only in Egyptian texts but also in texts of their home countries; thus it is not difficult to verify their sources. The situation with the gods of African neighbors was quite different. As far as is known at the time of this writing, gods of the Meroitic culture, like Sebiumeker, Apedemak, or the Lower Nubian god from Kalabsha Mandulis, were neither of Egyptian origin nor worshiped in Egypt. The source of Arensnuphis, who was worshiped in Philae and in the Nile Valley of Lower and Upper Nubia is still disputed, as are the origins of numerous local forms of Amun with their characteristic ram shape, which differs from the ram-icon in Egypt.

DANIELA MENDEL

Further Reading

Hornung, E. *Conceptions of God in Ancient Egypt: The One and the Many*, translated by John Baines. London: Routledge and Kegan Paul, 1983.

Quirke, S. *Ancient Egyptian Religion*. London: British Museum Press, 1992.

Shafer, B. E., ed. *Religion in Ancient Egypt, Gods Myths, and Personal Practice*. London: Routledge, 1991.

Egypt, Ancient: Social Organization

The social organization of ancient Egypt is best envisaged as a pyramid with the pharaoh at its apex. All temporal power, and much spiritual power, ultimately rested with the Pharaoh. In his official capacity the pharaoh was regarded as supreme ruler and commander, a god on earth, as well as high priest of all the gods. He had a divine contract with the gods whereby he had to honor them by building temples, making offerings and prayers; in return they would endorse his

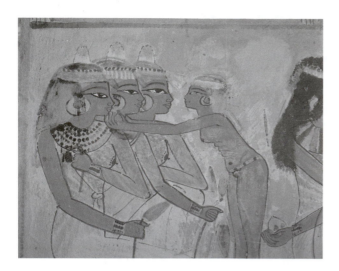

Slave girl dressing a lady for a feast. Detail of a wall painting in the tomb of Nakht, scribe and priest under Thutmosis IV (Eighteenth Dynasty, sixteenth–fourteenth centuries BCE). Tomb of Nakht, Shaykh Abd el-Qurna Cemetery, Tombs of the Nobles, Thebes, Egypt. Anonymous. © Erich Lessing/Art Resource, New York.

rulership and ensure the regularity of the Nile flood and the safety of Egypt, thereby maintaining cosmic order (*maat*). All branches of government including the military, the treasury, the priesthood, and the civil service were responsible to him. This view of the pharaoh and his court is well illustrated by the layout of the Giza necropolis with the pharaohs' pyramid located centrally, surrounded by the different-sized tombs of his family, courtiers, and officials. A separate Mortuary Temple was used to celebrate the cult of the pharaoh after his death, and in some instances during his lifetime. Only the Pharaoh's mother and his wives, obviously important in the hierarchy, also had pyramid tombs. The succession to the throne was patrilineal; generally the son of the chief wife was chosen as crown prince, although this was not an immutable rule. Although rare, female pharaohs existed at various periods in Egyptian history.

The vizier came below the pharaoh in the administrative hierarchy. In the earlier Old Kingdom (Third–Fifth Dynasties) most viziers were members of the royal family, either sons or brothers of the king, with one example of a female vizier. Toward the end of the Old Kingdom (Fifth–Sixth Dynasties) viziers came to be chosen from among nobles with fewer or no direct blood ties to the ruler. Like many courtiers and officials, viziers were often priests in addition to their other duties.

An understanding of the organization of the rest of society can best be gained from funerary contexts (size of tomb and title of owner), taxation and accounting records, and literary texts. Below the viziers came the highest officials who were nobles, many of whom were blood relations of the Pharaoh (especially in the Third–Fifth Dynasties), followed by courtiers, and the highest local officials, such as provincial governors (*nomarchs*). Below this tier of society came lesser courtiers and high local officials, followed by an even lower tier of courtiers and lesser local officials. Under these were minor functionaries, followed by the semi-official margin, and the peasantry. It was possible for people to change their social status through personal ability, special services rendered to the Pharaoh, by the acquisition of wealth, or by marriage. A basic criterion for being an official was being literate; all officials were scribes together with whatever other title they held.

Bureaucrats from all levels were engaged in different types of work related to government and religion, often holding more than one title, including different priestly titles. As the government was supposed to regulate agriculture, collect taxes, administer justice, and maintain order at home and abroad, officials worked in a variety of departments in the general bureaucracy, treasury, military, and in temples. Temples were second only to the pharaoh in wealth and, consequently, had large bureaucracies of their own and powerful priesthoods. Priests often had to serve both the temple bureaucracy and the pharaoh, depending on the god they served and the position they held.

The military, with the pharaoh as its supreme commander, played an important role in Egyptian society, not only in providing a police force and an army for protection and conquest, but as a source of manpower used for mining and quarrying expeditions.

For the most part the officials were men, but several women had titles suggesting responsibility as well as independent means. Certainly royal women owned significant amounts of land and held important religious and secular positions, most notably that of regent. Noblewomen held positions such as overseer of weavers, as well as high priestly rank, while women of lower positions would work as weavers, maids, laundresses, priestesses, singers, dancers, and tradespeople. Egypt was unusual in the fact that women, regardless of rank, could own and dispose of property, divorce and marry. For the most part Egyptian marriage, consisting of a civil contract and not a religious service, was monogamous, although concubines were common. Children were highly regarded and came to adulthood during the period now considered puberty.

While merchants, craftspeople, and tenant farmers were not always directly involved with the administration, they intersected with it at several points as the pharaoh (or the temples) had ultimate control over most of Egypt's wealth. Permission to trade on a significant scale in Egypt and certainly abroad came from the administration. Traders plying the Nile as well as traveling abroad no doubt supplied Egyptians with many of their luxury goods (in addition to what was brought into the country at different times as tribute or spoil of war). Foreigners frequently came and settled in Egypt, either as mercenaries, traders, or refugees. Most were Asiatics or Nubians, although Libyans and Bedouins have also made their mark in Egyptian society. The majority of immigrants adapted to Egyptian culture, taking Egyptian names and marrying into Egyptian families. Foreign divinities were frequently absorbed into the Egyptian pantheon, and foreign arts, motifs, and crafts assimilated and adapted by the Egyptians. There are occasional reports of tension between foreign and native groups, although for the most part the Egyptians were accepting of foreigners as long as they were peaceful and adaptable. Most slaves were foreign as well, and were often adopted and freed by their owners.

On the whole, Egyptian society was flexible, capable of assimilating people from a variety of backgrounds and providing scope for social mobility.

SALIMA IKRAM

Further Reading

Baer, K. *Rank and Title in the Old Kingdom*. Chicago: University Press, 1960.

Bakir, Abd el-Mohsen. *Slavery in Pharaonic Egypt*, Cairo: Government Press, 1952.

Bierbrier, M. *The Tomb Builders of the Pharaohs*. London: British Museum, 1982.

Donadoni, S. (editor), *The Egyptians*, Chicago: University of Chicago, 1997.

Fischer, H. G. "Four Provincial Administrators at the Memphite Cemetery." *Journal of Archaeology and Oriental Studies* 74 (1954): 26–34.

Gardiner, A. *Ramesside Administrative Documents*. London: Oxford University, 1948.

Hayes, W. C. "Notes on the Government of Egypt in the Late Middle Kingdom." *Journal of Near Eastern Studies* 12 (1953): 31–39.

James, T. G. H. *Pharaoh's People: Scenes from Life in Imperial Egypt*. London: 1984.

Kanawati, N. *Governmental Reforms in Old Kingdom Egypt*, Warminster: Aris and Phillips, 1980.

Janssen, J. and R. *Growing Up in Ancient Egypt*. London: Rubicon, 1990.

Janssen, J. and R. *Getting Old in Ancient Egypt*. London: Rubicon, 1996.

Kemp, B. J. *Ancient Egypt: Anatomy of a Civilization*. London: Routledge, 1989.

Martin, G. *Egyptian Administration and Private Name Seals*. Oxford: 1971.

Quirke, S. *The Administration of Egypt in the Late Middle Kingdom*. Kent (UK): Sia, 1990.

Robins, G. *Women in Ancient Egypt*. London: British Museum Press, 1993.

Strudwick, N. *The Administration of Egypt in the Old Kingdom*. London: Kegan Paul, 1985.

Trigger, B. G., B. J. Kemp, D. O'Connor, and A. B. Lloyd. *Ancient Egypt: A Social History*. Cambridge (UK): University Press, 1983.

Valbelle, D. *Les Ouvriers de la Tombe: Deir el-Medinih a l'Ipoque Ramesside*. Cairo: Institut Français d'Archiologie Orientale, 1985.

Van den Boorn, G. P. F. *The Duties of the Vizier*. London: Kegan Paul, 1988.

Ward, W. *Index of Egyptian Administrative and Religious Titles of the Middle Kingdom*. Beirut: American University of Beirut, 1982.

Wente, E. F. *Letters from Ancient Egypt*. Atlanta, (6): Scholars Press, 1990.

Egypt: Arab Conquest (639–645)

The Arab conquest of 639–645 introduced the Arabic language and Islam to Egypt, which united Egypt with the rest of the Islamic world from 639 until the present. Before the Arab conquest, Greek was the official language of the administration and all written documents. The Arab conquest shifted Egypt's cultural alignment away from Europe and toward the East, that is, with the Arabian Peninsula.

The Prophet Mohammed unified a formerly divided Arabian Peninsula by converting tribal Arabs who worshiped many different gods under the banner of Islam and its one god, Allah. Shortly after Mohammed's death Mohammed's relative, Abu Bakr, succeeded him as caliph, or deputy. Byzantine Christians and Persians to the north offered stiff resistance to Arab plunderers. To overcome this resistance, Abu Bakr decided to occupy Christian territory. Arab armies headed north in 635.

The Arabs defeated both the Persian armies to the northeast and the Byzantine Christian armies to the northwest, especially those in Syria. Conquest of Syria was vital because missionaries and soldiers departed for Africa and the Middle East from Syria. It had large cathedrals and fortresses and was a Christian stronghold. To secure Syria the Arabs needed to capture Christian Egypt. Arab generals feared that Egypt's large, sympathetic, Christian armies could launch a counteroffensive and drive the Arabs out of Syria. Beyond its strategic importance, the Arab general Amr ibn al-As had visited Egypt and knew that its Christian population was fragmented and easy to conquer. He also wanted to gain control of Egypt's vast wealth. Egypt's agricultural surplus could feed expanding Arab armies, and Amr ibn al-As could use its wealth to attract new followers to Islam. The Prophet Mohammed made him a military commander and had sent him to Oman to convert its rulers. He succeeded, thereby winning the friendship and praise of the Prophet. Abu Bakr sent him to conquer Palestine (modern Israel); he not only vanquished it but converted its majority Christian population to Islam. It is, however, his conquest of Egypt that earned him his reputation as a brilliant soldier, an able administrator, and an astute politician.

He organized the system of taxation and the justice system still in use in many parts of Egypt to this day. He also established garrison cities to defend Egypt. Most important, Amr ibn al-As converted Egypt from an overwhelmingly Christian country into a Muslim nation, with small Coptic Christian and Jewish minorities.

Amr ibn al-As had 4,000 cavalry, armed with lances, swords, and bows and arrows. He crossed into Egypt from Syria on December 12, 639, at Al Arish. His army's objective was to capture the fortress at Babylon (Bab al Yun), a suburb of modern Cairo. The important town of Pelusium (Farama) fell to the Arabs after one month. The army next attacked Bilbays (El-Kantara), the garrison town protecting Cairo, which also fell after a one-month siege. When Amr ibn al-As reached the outskirts of Babylon, he stopped at the edge of Misri (Cairo) near Old Memphis until the caliph sent reinforcements. His rejuvenated army crushed the Byzantine Christian army at Heliopolis in 640. Misri, or Cairo, fell soon after, but the Christian soldiers defending the fortress at Babylon fought on bravely until their emperor, Heraclius, died. After this their morale suffered and they abandoned the fortress without a fight, sailing upriver to Alexandria. Amr ibn al-As's army next marched against Fayyum and subdued Middle and Upper Egypt before laying siege to Alexandria.

The Arab army was able to take Alexandria with little resistance, despite its heavy fortifications. Egypt's morale was low, and Dometianus, entrusted with defending the city, was more interested in fighting the Christians in Upper Egypt than he was in fighting the Arabs. Moreover, constant riots rocked the city as Christian factions warred against each other. The emperor Cyrus was forced to sign a peace treaty surrendering Egypt to the Arabs. Under Islamic law, a treaty (*sulh*) secured Egypt; thus, it could not be divided among the conquering soldiers in Amr ibn al-As's army. They had to take other lands by force to earn compensation for battle. This forced them to drive across North Africa and eventually into Spain.

Since Egypt was gained through treaty arrangements, its people were considered *dhimma*, or clients, and thus entitled to the protection of the ruler. Accordingly, Egyptian land could be taxed by Arab rulers. Increasing such taxes did not violate Islamic law. Therefore, the Treaty of Alexandria protected the Arab rulers from land claims made by their own army. Moreover, it headed off internal power struggles by forcing the army to expand into neighboring territory to win booty. This deflected attention from the vast riches gained by Arab leaders.

Muslim conquerors offered those whom they vanquished the choice of converting to Islam or remaining Jews or Coptic Christians. Converts qualified for no-interest loans to start businesses and were given full citizenship rights. Those who remained Coptic Christians or Jews could continue to worship as they pleased, but they had to pay an additional tax. Many Copts converted, although others maintained their Christian faith and received fair treatment. Copts put up little resistance to the Arab invasion. The Coptic bishop of Alexandria was reinstated, exiled Coptic bishops were recalled home, and Copts were permitted to return to government posts held before the conquest. Amr ibn al-As then moved Egypt's capital from Alexandria to Al Fustat, today known as Old Cairo, to symbolize the uniqueness of his regime.

Arab governors appointed by caliphs who lived in eastern capitals ruled Egypt for centuries. Egypt's grain fed Arab urbanites and soldiers for generations and provided needed tax revenues. In time, most Egyptians accepted Arab colonialism. Most adopted the Muslim faith, often through intermarriage or trade. Arabic became the dominant language of the country. It was used in schools, government offices, and market transactions, and it replaced Greek as the national language. Continuous Arab immigration to Egypt facilitated the Arabization of Egypt, just as whites would later colonize South Africa. The Arab conquest of Egypt inseparably links its history with Arab world history.

DALLAS L. BROWNE

See also: **Arab and Islamic World, Africa in.**

Further Reading

Bell, H. I. *Egypt from Alexander the Great to the Arab Conquest*. Oxford. Claredon Press. 1948.

Bosworth, C.E. and E. Van Donzel, eds. "Misr." *The Encyclopedia of Islam*. New Edition. Leiden.: E.J. Brill. Volume 7, pp:146–186. 1991.

Butler, A. *The Arab Conquest of Egypt*. New York: AMS Press. 1973.

Holt, P. M., Ann K. S. Lambton and Bernard Lewis. *The Cambridge History of Islam: The Central Islamic Lands*. Cambridge: Cambridge University Press. Volume 1, 175–230. 1970.

Hourani, A. *A History of the Arab Peoples*. Cambridge: The Belknap Press of Harvard University Press, 1991.

Lapidus, I. M. *A History of Islamic Societies*. Cambridge: Cambridge University Press, 1988.

Lewis, B. "Egypt and Syria." In P.M. Holt, Ann K.S. Lambton, and Bernard Lewis (eds.), *The Cambridge History of Islam*. Cambridge: Cambridge University Press, pp:175–232. 1970.

Lewis, B. *The Arabs in History*. London: Hutchinson University Library, 1970.

Mahmud, S. F. *A Short History of Islam*. Karachi: Pakistan Branch, Oxford University Press, 1960.

Mansfield, P. *The Arab World: A Comprehensive History*. New York: Thomas Y. Crowell Company, 1976.

Mitchell, T. *Colonizing Egypt.* Cambridge: Cambridge University Press. 1988.

Murphy, E. Jefferson. *History of African Civilization.* New York: Dell Publishing Company, 1978.

Noshy, I. *The Coptic Church.* Washington, DC: Ruth Sloane Associates, 1975.

Shaban, M. A. *Islamic History A.D. 600–750 (A.H. 132): A New Interpretation.* Cambridge: Cambridge University Press, 1971.

Spuler, B. *The Age of the Caliphs: History of the Muslim World.* Princeton: Markus Wiener Publishers, 1995.

Watt, W. M. *Mohammed at Mecca.* Oxford: Clarendon Press, 1960.

Wissa Wassef, C. *Egypt.* New York: Scala Books, 1983.

Egypt: Arab Empire (640–850)

The Prophet Muhammad died in the year 632. Seven years later, with 'Umar ibn al-Khattab as the second caliph, the Arabs marched on Egypt, and in less than two years, the "cradle of civilization" had become a province under the Arab Empire (the caliphate).

Prior to the Arab invasion, Egypt had been ruled by foreigners for two millennium, and by 639, the granary of the Mediterranean was under the suzerainty and governorship of the then weak Byzantium Empire. 'Amr ibn al-'As was the initiator and instigator of the conquest.

For a long time, Arabs had been interested in Egypt; its land was fertile, in contrast with the aridity of the nearby Arabian desert. Newly galvanized by Islam, the conquest of Egypt was relatively easy for the Arabs. There was little sympathy between the rulers and the ruled, with religious cleavage and exorbitant taxes. The Arabs, seen as liberators, were determined, while the Egyptians in general were docile, passive, and indifferent.

The Byzantine garrison at the fortress of Babylon capitulated to the Arab army on April 9, 641, and in September 642 Alexandria was occupied. The Arab pacification of Egypt was complete. The next two centuries saw the rule of Egypt by Arab governors beginning with its conqueror, 'Amr ibn al-'As, and ending with 'Anbasa. This period of Arab hegemony in Egypt was to be followed by a period of Muslim dynastic rule, although few of the rulers were Arab.

The 210 years of Arab rule in Egypt also marked the era of Arab ascendancy in the nascent Muslim world; starting with the Prophet's *hejira* (emigration) from Mecca to Medina in 622, and the consolidation of the young Medinese community of Allah, followed by the rule of the caliphs, it saw the rise and fall of the Umayyad dynasty and ended with the founding of and the beginning of the decline of the Abbasid dynasty.

The empire was an Islamic historical and political phenomenon infused and imbued with the Arab idea and fueled by the message that they were determined, as commanded, to give to the world. However, by the mid-ninth century, the Arabs had lost their grip on the empire and were themselves to be ruled by those they had conquered and Islamized.

A total of ninety-eight governors ruled in Egypt from 'Amr ibn al-'As until the Turkish leader, Ahmad ibn Tulun, established an independent dynasty in 868. These governors served the caliphs first of Medina, the Classical Caliphate (632–661), and then of Damascus, the Umayyads (661–750), and then of Baghdad, the 'Abbasids (750–850). The 'Abbasid Caliphate was to retain its power precariously until the mid-thirteenth century. The average Umayyad governor ruled twice as long as the Abbasid counterpart. The latter were more frequently changed, a reflection of the instability in the caliphal capital.

The process of Arabization in Egypt started early. Most governors came escorted by thousands of Arab troops, who were highly privileged and settled in towns, thus frequently affecting Egypt demographically. The Arabs freely intermarried with the Copt women and thereby became increasingly indigenized.

Before his recall to Medina in 644, 'Amr had set up a local government system with the center in his capital, Fustat. He absorbed officials of the supplanted government. The central administration did not bother the local levels of government as long as taxes were paid regularly. Agriculture was the highest priority. A special department was set up to oversee irrigation. The governor, himself appointed by the caliph, chose the war secretary, the exchequer, and the *qadi*, or justice secretary. This system was more or less adopted by subsequent governors.

By the mid-seventh century, Egypt had been consolidated under Arab rule. Byzantine menace or any external threat was ruled out. The Arabs under the Umayyads developed their naval power. Insurrection, however, abounded, especially under the Abbasids. It was a time of intensive schism in Islam, marked by the Malikite-Shafiite difference and the Sunni-Shi'ite divide. The Copts often agitated over what they regarded as excessive taxes. The rivalry for the throne between al-Amin and al-Ma'mun also helped to divide the Egyptians in their allegiance.

Anbasa, the last governor (852–856), oversaw a period of political turmoil; there was the Roman insurgency (Damietta, 853) and the Nubian repudiation (854) of the annual tribute they had paid since the mid-seventh century. With the recall of 'Anbasa in 856, there followed the exasperating rule of Turkish governors until Ahmad ibn Tulun restored order and established his dynasty.

This period of Arab conquest and rule was important not only in Egypt's history but also in Islamic history. Egypt was imparted with more Arabic and Islamic characteristics. Egypt remained the food basket of the Mediterranean and was populated with an influx of Arabs. A distinct Egyptian Arabo-Islamic milieu developed that would serve as the foundation of the Islamic intellectual and cultural heritage, which was to make Egypt the bulwark of Islam, when other centers of political and cultural Islam were in decline.

JAMIU A. OLUWATOKI

Further Reading

Bennabi, M. *Islam in History and Society*. Translated by Asma Rashid. Islamabad: Islamic Research Institute, 1988.

Gabrieli, F. *Muhammad and the Conquest of Islam*. Translated from the Italian by V. Luling and R. Linell. London: World University Library, 1968.

Hitti, P. K. *History of the Arabs: From the Earliest Times to the Present*. 10th ed. London: Macmillan, 1970.

Lane Poole, S. *A History of Egypt in the Middle Ages*. London: Frank Cass and Co., 1968.

Lewis, B. *The Arabs in History*. London: Hutchinson and Co.

———. ed. *Islam: From the Prophet Muhammad to the Capture of Constantinople I*. New York: Oxford University Press, 1987.

Saunders, J. J. *A History of Medieval Islam*. London: Routledge and Kegan Paul, 1965.

Schacht, J. *The Legacy of Islam*. 2nd ed. Oxford: Clarendon Press, 1974.

Sydney, N. Fisher. *The Middle East: A History*. 2nd ed. New York: Alfred Knopf, 1968.

Egypt: Tulunids and Ikhshidids, 850–969

After being ruled as a colony of the early Islamic empires for the first two centuries after the Arab conquest, Egypt experienced brief periods of autonomy under the dynastic rule of the Tulunids and then the Ikhshidids. Although these regimes never formally renounced their allegiance to the Abbasid caliphs, they built up independent armies, established total control over the resources of this rich land, and instituted hereditary rule, all of which the caliphs were powerless to stop.

Ahmad ibn Tulun became the governor of Egypt in 868 during a period of considerable turmoil in Samarra, then the capital of the Abbasid Empire. He was of Turkish origin, his father having been a slave who worked his way up to be a commander of the caliph's guard. After becoming governor, Ibn Tulun had to struggle for several years with the power of Ibn al-Mudabbir, financial director of Egypt since 861 and answerable only to the caliph. A revolt that broke out in nearby Palestine and Syria, however, offered a pretext for building a new army in Egypt, composed primarily of Turkish, Nubian, and Greek slaves and mercenaries. To pay for this army, Ibn Tulun took control of the revenues of the country, arranging for Ibn al-Mudabbir's transfer to Syria in 871.

The revolt quickly fell apart, even before Ibn Tulun intervened, but he was now in complete control of Egypt and possessed a strong military force. His growing independence was facilitated by the fact that the caliph's brother al-Muwaffaq, the commander of the caliphal armies, was increasingly preoccupied with a massive revolt of East African slaves in southern Iraq, as well as continuing problems in the eastern provinces. Ibn Tulun never formally repudiated Abbasid authority, but with his new army and a distracted caliphate he was able to establish himself as virtually autonomous. In 877 al-Muwaffaq launched an abortive attempt to bring Egypt back under Abbasid control, but this only succeeded in convincing Ibn Tulun to strengthen his position. Claiming a desire to lead the jihad against the Byzantine Empire, Ibn Tulun occupied all of Syria up to the Byzantine frontier.

When Ibn Tulun died in 884, the succession of his son Khumarawayh was effected smoothly. Although al-Muwaffaq would once again attempt to forcibly reestablish Abbasid control, by 886 he had given up and a treaty was agreed upon that officially granted the governorship of Egypt to Khumarawayh and his descendants for a period of thirty years. His twelve years of rule saw peace and prosperity in Egypt, but the extravagance of his lifestyle and his lavish patronage of building projects, along with the expense of paying for a large standing army, overtaxed the state's resources. When Khumarawayh was murdered by one of his slaves in 896, the treasury was reportedly empty. He was succeeded by his sons Jaysh and then Harun, but they found it difficult to manage growing economic and political problems. The assassination of Harun afforded the caliph an opportunity to reassert control in 905, and Abbasid rule was reestablished for the next thirty years.

The new governors sent to Egypt continued to be Turkish generals, but their tenures were short. The one exception was Takin who served several terms as governor between 910 and 933, but he was repeatedly dismissed from that office with the changing fortunes of factional politics in Baghdad. Administrative continuity was instead provided by the al-Madhara'i family, financial officials in Fustat (Old Cairo) since the reign of Ibn Tulun. They would continue to play an important role in the country's administration well into the Ikhshidid period.

During this "Abbasid intermezzo," Egypt suffered from a series of internal disturbances and the near constant threat of Fatimid invasion. The Fatimids were an Isma'ili Shi'ite dynasty that had established itself in Ifriqiya (modern Tunisia) in 909, repudiating the authority of the Abbasid caliphs. They soon set their sights on Egypt and mounted major invasions in 913–915 and 919–921, though both failed after the intervention of Abbasid armies sent from the East.

A new period of autonomy began for Egypt in 935 with the appointment of Muhammad ibn Tughj, later known as the Ikhshid. After having served as an Abbasid governor in Syria, his connections in Baghdad secured for him the governorship of Egypt. Immediately upon entering the province, Muhammad ibn Tughj had to face the prospect of yet another Fatimid invasion, but after this was beaten off in 936 there was not to be another major attack until that which ended Ikhshidid rule in 969. The lingering Fatimid threat, however, once again justified building up a strong army in Egypt, and increasing disorder in Iraq left the caliph with little leverage over yet another governor establishing an independent power base for himself. In 939 the caliph even acceded to Muhammad ibn Tughj's demand to be given the title *al-Ikhshid*, held by rulers in the Farghana region of Central Asia whence his grandfather had come. Furthermore, a treaty was negotiated in which the caliph granted to the Ikhshid and his heirs governorship over Egypt and Syria for thirty years, virtually the same arrangement the Tulunids had.

When the Ikhshid died in 946 he was succeeded by his son Unujur (d.961), but real power was thereafter in the hands of the regent Kafur, a Nubian eunuch who now took control of administrative and military affairs. Only after Unujur's brother and successor 'Ali died in 966 did Kafur take over in his own name, but he was the real power in Egypt throughout their reigns. Most of the Kafur era was a period of security and stability, if not prosperity. In 963–968, however, there was a series of poor harvests and consequent famine, and in the last years of the dynasty these economic problems were compounded by increasing political disorder.

When Kafur died in 968, a child grandson of the Ikhshid was installed in Fustat, but squabbling between financial administrators, military commanders, and members of the Ikhshidid family produced circumstances quickly exploited by the Fatimid caliph al-Mu'izz. In July 969, after some heavy fighting, the Fatimid general Jawhar entered Fustat. For the next two hundred years the prayers in Fustat's mosques would be said in the name of al-Mu'izz and his successors. Nevertheless, the Fatimids soon transferred their capital to Cairo and it was upon the foundation laid by the Tulunid and Ikhshidid regimes that they built up their new Egypt-based empire.

LENNART SUNDELIN

See also: **Egypt: Arab Conquest; Egypt: Fatimid Caliphate.**

Further Reading

Bacharach, J. L. "The Career of Muhammad ibn Tughj al-Ikhshid: A Tenth-Century Governor of Egypt." *Speculum* 50 (1975): 586–612.
Bianquis, T. "Autonomous Egypt from Ibn Tulun to Kafur, 868–969." In *The Cambridge History of Egypt*. Vol. 1, edited by Carl F. Petry. Cambridge: Cambridge University Press, 1998.
Grabar, O. *The Coinage of the Tulunids*. New York: American Numismatic Society, 1957.
Hassan, Z. M. *Les Tulunides: Études de l'Égypte musulmane à la fin du IXe siècle, 868–905*. Paris: Établissements Busson, 1933.
Randa, E. W., Jr. "The Tulunid Dynasty in Egypt: Loyalty and State Formation during the Dissolution of the 'Abbasid Caliphate.'" Ph.D. diss., University of Utah, 1990.

Egypt: Fatimid Caliphate

The Fatimids (969–1073) were an Ismai'ili Shi'a dynasty that controlled Egypt and portions of North Africa and Syria in the tenth and eleventh centuries. The founder of the Fatimid dynasty, Ubayd Allah, claimed direct descent from Isma'il, whom the Isma'ilis regarded as the legitimate seventh imam in the line of Ali and his wife Fatima, daughter of the Prophet Muhammad. As the legatees of the spiritual authority handed down through this line of descent, Ubayd Allah and his successors claimed to be the rightful leaders of the entire Islamic world. They therefore rejected the legitimacy of the 'Abbasid caliphs of Baghdad, who belonged to the Sunni branch of Islam, and made a concerted effort to spread their influence by a combination of missionary activity and military conquest.

Isma'ili expansion was initiated in 902 when Ubayd Allah left his headquarters in Salamiyya, Syria, and moved to Ifriqiyya (present-day Tunisia), where Isma'ili missionaries had enlisted the support of the Kutama Berbers in advance of his arrival. Backed by

Cairo's Mosque al-Ahzar, the foremost center of theology in Islam and, with Moroccan Fez, the world's oldest university. Begun 970CE. The central court of the Fatimid period (969–1171). Anonymous. © Erich Lessing/Art Resource, New York.

the Kutama, Ubayd Allah created the first Fatimid State in 909. Al-Mu'izz, who was the fourth Fatimid caliph, expanded the Fatimid realm further. After several failed attempts by his predecessors, al-Mu'izz conquered Egypt in 969 from the Ikhshidids, a Sunni dynasty that was semi-independent of the 'Abbasids. Immediately following the campaign, al-Mu'izz's general Jawhar established a new Isma'ili capital "al-Qahira" (Cairo) near the city of Fustat. Al-Mu'izz relocated to the new capital in 973, leaving Ifiqiyya in the control of the Sanhaja Berber Zirids. Cairo thereafter functioned as the royal Isma'ili enclave. In 969–970 Mecca and Medina submitted to al-Mu'izz. Fatimid control over the Hijaz would last until the fall of the dynasty. Aided by Yaqub ibn Killis, a Jewish convert to Islam, al-Mu'izz centralized Egypt's system of tax collection and improved the functioning of the administrative departments (diwans), which dealt with the fiscal, military, and diplomatic affairs of the state. As was the case with previous Muslim dynasties in Egypt, Christians staffed many of these departments. In addition, al-Mu'izz withdrew the debased Ikhshidid coinage from circulation and replaced it with gold dinars of exceptional value. These coins, products of the gold mines of Upper Egypt, remained standard currency throughout the Mediterranean Basin for the duration of the Fatimid period.

During the reign of al-Mu'izz's successor al-'Aziz (ruled 975–996), the Fatimids expanded into Syria at the expense of the 'Abbasids and Byzantines. In an effort to enhance Fatimid military effectiveness, al-Aziz introduced highly skilled Turkish horse archers into his army. These soldiers were recruited as slaves and trained in accordance with the barrack system developed by the 'Abbasids in the tenth century. The presence of Turkish troops was resisted by the Kutama Berber contingents, which were the original mainstay of the dynasty. Ethnic tensions within the Fatimid military were further complicated by the recruitment of black African troops. Despite divisions within the military, Fatimid power reached its greatest extent during al-Aziz's reign, with Fatimid sovereignty recognized in North Africa, the Western Mediterranean, and the Red Sea.

Al-'Aziz was succeeded al-Hakim (r.996–1020) whose polices differed in many respects from those of his predecessors. In contrast to the religious tolerance of previous Fatimid caliphs, al-Hakim adopted persecutory measures against Christians, Jews, and Sunni Muslims, going so far as to destroy synagogues and churches, including the Church of the Holy Sepulcher in Jerusalem. This latter act angered both Eastern and Western Christendom and led to the First Crusade. Al-Hakim's reign was also marked by revolts on the part of Muslim subjects in North Africa and Palestine, which the Fatimids managed to suppress. A number of Egyptian Isma'ilis considered al-Hakim to be the incarnation of God and when he mysteriously disappeared in 1020 they believed that he had entered into a state of occultation and would return at a later time. The Fatimid establishment accused this group, called the Druze, of extremism and disbelief. Most probably, al-Hakim was murdered at the behest of his sister, Sitt al-Mulk, who desired that al-Hakim's son, al-Zahir, ascend to the throne in place of the official designate. Sitt al-Mulk acted for a time as regent for al-Zahir (r.1020–1035) whose reign was marred by rebellion in Syria and famine in Egypt.

Economic decline and unrest continued into the long reign of the next Fatimid leader, al-Mustansir (r.1035–1094) whose caliphate marks the end of the classical Fatimid period. During his reign a series of low Niles plagued Egypt. Additionally, fighting broke out between the Turkish and black African slave soldiers. In an effort to bring the situation under control, al-Mustansir appealed for help from a Fatimid general of Armenian origin in Syria, Badr al-Jamali. Badr succeeded in putting down the rebellious troops in 1073 and for his efforts was awarded the title "Commander of the Armies." Badr was the first of a series of military commanders who would be the real rulers of the Fatimid state until its collapse in 1171.

Throughout the period of the early Fatimid state, Isma'ilis remained a minority in Egypt. Although the Fatimids made little effort to impose Isma'ili ritual on the general population, Cairo functioned as the main center of Isma'ili doctrine and the spread of Isma'ili propaganda in other lands. The famous mosque-university of al-Azhar was founded in 969 in part as a teaching center for Isma'ili missionaries. Al-Mu'izz commissioned the scholar al-Qadi al-Nu'man to systematize a corpus of Isma'ili law. Many Persian Isma'ilis, including the famous Nasir-i Khusraw, made pilgrimages to Cairo. However, the appearance of the Seljuq Turks who were militaristic champions of Sunni Islam in Persia and Mesopotamia in the mid-eleventh century restricted the success of the Fatimid mission in eastern Muslim lands.

JOHN CALVERT

See also: **Egypt: Fatimids, Later.**

Further Reading

Farhad Daftary, F. *The Isma'ili: Their History and Doctrines.* Cambridge: Cambridge University Press, 1990.
Sanders, P. A. *Ritual, Politics, and the City in Fatimid Cairo.* Albany: SUNY Press, 1994.
———. "The Fatimid State, 969–1171." In *The Cambridge History of Egypt,* Vol. 1, edited by Carl F. Petry. Cambridge: Cambridge University Press, 1998.

Walker, P. E. *Exploring an Islamic Empire: Fatimid History and Its Sources*. London: I.B. Tauris in Association with the Institute of Ismaili Studies, 2002.

Egypt: Fatimids, Later: 1073–1171

Starting in 1062, Fatimid Egypt experienced a long period of economic and political decline accompanied by the breakdown of civil administration, chaos in the multiethnic army due to incessant factional rivalries, and exhaustion of the public treasury. Matters came to a head when open warfare broke out near Cairo between the Turkish faction of the army aided by the Berbers, and the black Sudanese troops. The Turks prevailed and their commander, Nāsir al-Dawla, became the effective authority in Egypt, wrestling all power from the Fatimid caliph al-Mustansir. Egypt's problems were worsened by a seven-year (1065–1072) period during which the Nile River reached extremely low levels, causing widespread famine and aggravating the economic crisis, while the Turkish troops ravaged the land and even pillaged the Fatimid palaces. During these years—known in the historical sources as the "Days of Trouble" (*ayyām al-fitna*)—rioting was widespread, and led to the complete breakdown of law and order. At the same time, after al-Yāzuri, (d. 1058) numerous ineffective viziers followed one another.

Finally, al-Mustansir appealed for help to an Armenian general, Badr al-Jamālí, who already had a distinguished career in Syria in the service of the Fatimids. Badr accepted the caliph's summon on the condition of taking his Armenian troops with him. He arrived in Cairo in 1073 and, after ending the menace of the Turks, speedily restored order to various parts of Egypt. Badr acquired the highest positions of the Fatimid state. He became not only the "commander of the armies" (*amír al-juyúsh*) but also the head of the centralized and hierarchical civil, judicial, and even religious administrations. He was also the first person to be designated as the "vizier of the pen and of the sword" with full delegated powers. In effect, Badr assumed the powers of a military dictator. Henceforth, with minor exceptions, real power in the Fatimid state remained in the hands of viziers who possessed military bases of power and acted independently, while the caliphs remained the nominal heads of state and as Ismaili imams also functioned as supreme leaders of the Ismaili *da'wa* or religious organization. A distinguishing feature of the Fatimid vizierate during its final century is that several viziers were Christians, notably Armenians.

As a result of Badr's policies, Egypt enjoyed peace and relative prosperity during his vizierate, coinciding with the remaining twenty years of al-Mustansir's reign. Meanwhile, the Fatimids, like other Muslim dynasties, faced the growing menace of the Saljūq Turks who were laying the foundations of a new empire. By the end of al-Mustansir's reign, of the former Fatimid possessions in Syria and Palestine, only Ascalon and a few coastal towns like Acre and Tyre still remained in Fatimid hands. In North Africa, the Fatimid dominions were practically reduced to Egypt itself. Badr died earlier in the same year 1094 as al-Mustansir, after having arranged for his son al-Afāal to succeed him as vizier with all his prerogatives. A few months later, in December 1094, the Fatimid caliph-imam al-Mustansir died. The dispute over his succession caused a major split in the Ismaili community. Al-Afāal deprived al-Mustansir's eldest son and heir-designate Nizār of his succession rights and proclaimed a much younger son as caliph and imam with the title of al-Musta'lī. Thus, al-Afāal guaranteed that al-Musta'lī, who was also his brother-in-law, would remain a puppet in his hands. Nizār rose in revolt to claim his rights, but was defeated and executed in 1095. Subsequently, the Ismailis of Iran and Syria upheld Nizār's rights and severed their relations with Cairo and the Fatimid regime; they became designated as Nizārí Ismailis in distinction to the Musta'lī Ismailis of Egypt and elsewhere who had acknowledged the Fatimid caliph al-Musta'lī as al-Mustansir's successor to the Ismaili imamate.

During al-Musta'lī's short reign, the Fatimids of Egypt faced the threat of the Crusaders, who had appeared in Syria in 1097. The Crusaders seized Jerusalem in 1099, after defeating a Fatimid army led by al-Afāal himself. In the midst of these entanglements al-Musta'lī died in 1101. Al-Afāal now proclaimed al-Musta'lī's five-year-old son as the new Fatimid caliph with the title of al-Āmir bi-Ahkām Allāh. During the first twenty years of al-Āmir's caliphate (1101–1121), al-Afāal remained the effective master of Egypt and concerned himself mainly with repelling the Crusaders. Nevertheless, Egypt was briefly invaded in 1117 by Baldwin I, king of the Latin Kingdom of Jerusalem. On the assassination of al-Afāal in 1121, al-Āmir asserted his authority and did not appoint any vizier after al-Afāal's immediate successor, al-Ma'mūn, preferring to run the affairs of the state personally. When al-Āmir himself was assassinated in 1130, another succession dispute ensued while the Fatimid state embarked on its final phase of rapid decline with numerous periods of crisis.

A son, named al-Tayyib, had been born to al-Āmir a few months before his death. However, power was now assumed by al-Āmir's cousin 'Abd al-Majīd, who ruled officially as regent, pending the delivery of another child by al-Āmir's pregnant wife. Nothing more was heard of al-Tayyib's fate. Soon afterward, al-Afāal's son Abū 'Alī Ahmad, nicknamed Kutayfāt, was raised to the vizierate by the army. Kutayfāt imprisoned 'Abd al-Majīd and declared the Fatimid dynasty deposed, proclaiming the sovereignty of the hidden twelfth imam of the Twelver Shi'ites whose reappearance as the eschatological Mahdi had been expected since 874. Kutayfāt ruled briefly as a dictator and adopted Twelver, instead of Ismaili, Shi'itsm as the state religion of Egypt. In December 1131, Kutayfāt was overthrown and killed in yet another coup d'état organized by an Armenian general, Yānis, and the Berber faction of the Fatimid army. 'Abd al-Majīd was restored to power and initially ruled once again as regent, but three months later, in February 1132, he was proclaimed caliph and imam with the title of al-Hāfiz li-Dīn Allāh; and Ismailism was reinstated as Egypt's state religion. The proclamation of al-Hāfiz as imam, even though he was not a direct descendant of the previous imam, was supported by the official *da'wa* organization and by the majority of the Ismailis of Egypt. These Musta'lī Ismailis recognized al-Hāfiz and the later Fatimid caliphs as their rightful imams, and they became known as Hāfizīs. However, many Musta'lī Ismaili groups in Egypt acknowledged the rights of al-Tayyib and his "hidden" descendants to the imamate; they became known as Tayyibīs.

From the 1130s, rivalries also broke out between individuals and commanders who occupied and those who aspired to the office of vizier, such as the prolonged conflict between the Armenian Bahrām (d.1140) and the Sunni Muslim Ridwān who became viziers under al-Hāfiz. Like al-Hāfiz, who died in 1149, the last three Fatimid caliphs, al-Zāfir (1149–1154), al-Fā'iz (1154–1160) and al-'Ādid (1160–1171) were also recognized as imams of the Hāfizī Ismailis, now located almost exclusively in Egypt. However, these Fatimids who died in their youths were no more than puppets in the hands of their scheming viziers. The Armenian Ibn Ruzzīk succeeded 'Abbās as the all-powerful vizier in 1154 and retained his position throughout the reign of al-Fā'iz, who was sickly and died at the age of eleven. Ibn Ruzzīk now placed a nine-year-old grandson of al-Hāfiz on the Fatimid throne with the title of al-'Ādid li-Dīn Allāh. When Ibn Ruzzīk was assassinated in 1161, al-'Ādid was obliged to confer the vizierate on Ibn Ruzzík's son, Ruzzīk, who soon afterward met a similar fate. In the final years of Fatimid rule, the internal problems of Egypt were aggravated by the struggle between Shāwar, who had assumed the vizierate upon killing Ruzzīk in 1163, and Dirghām, who drove Shāwar out of office a few months later. Meanwhile, the Zangids of Syria and the Crusaders were both entertaining the conquest of Egypt. The Franks had already entered Egypt in 1161 and forced Ibn Ruzzīk to pay them an annual tribute.

Shāwar fled to Syria where he sought the help of the Zangid ruler, Nūr al-Dīn, to regain the Fatimid vizierate. Nūr al-Dīn sent Shāwar back to Egypt with a force commanded by Asad al-Dīn Shīrkūh, who took with him his nephew, Saladin, the future founder of the Ayyūbid dynasty. This was the first of three separate Zangid expeditions to Egypt. Dirghām was defeated in 1164 and Shāwar restored to the vizierate. His second term as vizier lasted some five years, a most confusing period in the closing years of Fatimid history marked by more Frankish and Zangid invasions of Egypt and Shāwar's vacillating alliances with Amalric I and Nūr al-Dīn, whose forces fought several battles in Egypt.

In 1169 Shāwar was killed at the instigation of Shīrkūh, who had led the third Zangid expedition to Egypt, again in the company of Saladin. Thereupon, al-'Ādid appointed Shīrkūh to the vizierate; and when Shīrkūh died suddenly two months later, in March 1169, Saladin succeeded his uncle as the last of the Fatimid viziers. Saladin gradually prepared the ground for ending Fatimid rule in Egypt, an objective sought by the Sunni Nūr al-Dīn as well as the Abbasids. At the same time, he adopted anti-Ismaili policies. Saladin formally ended Fatimid rule in September 1171 when he had the *khuñba* or sermon at the Friday midday prayer read in Cairo in the name of the reigning Abbasid caliph. Egypt had now returned to the fold of Sunni Islam. A few days later, on September 13, 1171, al-'Ādid, the fourteenth and the last Fatimid caliph, died following a brief illness. The Fatimid caliphate, established in 909, thus came to a close after 262 years. On Nūr al-Dīn's death in 1174, Saladin acquired his independence from the Zangids and succeeded in founding the Ayyūbid dynasty.

FARHAD DAFTARY

See also: **Egypt: Salah al-Din/Saladin.**

Further Reading

Dadoyan, S. B. *The Fatimid Armenians.* Leiden: E. J. Brill, 1997.
Daftary, F. *The Ismā'īlīs: Their History and Doctrines.* Cambridge: Cambridge University Press, 1990.
Halm, H. *The Fatimids and Their Traditions of Learning.* London: I. B. Tauris in association with The Institute of Ismaili Studies, 1997.
Lev, Y. *State and Society in Fatimid Egypt.* Leiden: E. J. Brill, 1991.
Sanders, P. A. "The Fātimid State, 969–1171." In *The Cambridge History of Egypt.* Vol. 1, *Islamic Egypt, 640–1517,* edited by Carl F. Petry. Cambridge: Cambridge University Press, 1998.

Stern, S. M. "The Succession to the Fatimid Imam al-Āmir, the Claims of the Later Fatimids to the Imamate, and the Rise of Tayyibū Ismailism." *Oriens* 4 (1951): 193–255.

Egypt: Fatimids, Later (1073–1171): Army and Administration

During the middle of the eleventh century, the Fatimid empire endured an unprecedented crisis. Egypt faced a seven-year famine, disease, social unrest, and economic collapse, while military factions of Turks, Berbers, Arabs and Blacks struggled for power. In the hands of the ineffectual caliph al-Mustansir (r.1036–1094), it appeared that the Fatimid state was on the verge of disintegration. Some of the provinces of the empire gained independence—including Sicily (1036), Tunisia (1051), and the Hijaz (1088)—while others were conquered by rival states. The nominal and tenuous Fatimid suzerainty in Iraq was lost to the rising power of the Seljuk Turks after 1059, followed by the Seljuk conquest of Syria and most of Palestine (1064–1071), and an abortive Turkish invasion of Egypt itself (1077).

Complete collapse of the Fatimid state was averted by the rise to power of an Armenian mamluk (slave-soldier), Badr al-Jamali (r.1073–1094), who was summoned by al-Mustansir in 1073 to overthrow a Turkish warlord who had usurped power in Cairo. Badr al-Jamali defeated the Turks and restored order in Egypt. But, while retaining al-Mustansir as the nominal ruler of the country, he concentrated real power in his own hands as "Wazir [minister] of the Sword" and supreme "Commander of the Armies" (*Amir al-Juyush*).

In the century between the Fatimid conquest of Egypt (969) and the rise of Badr al-Jamali as wazir and warlord of Egypt (1074), the Fatimid caliphs directly controlled the administration of the Fatimid state, though day-to-day affairs were generally overseen by their ministers (*wazir*) and military commanders (*amir*). The Shi'ite Fatimid caliphs claimed descent from Fatima, the daughter of Muhammad, and thus proclaimed a divine mandate to rule the Muslim world as the Prophet's legitimate successors. The propagation of Shi'ite Fatimid religious ideology was a crucial element of state policy before the coup of Badr al-Jamali. Succession to the caliphate remained within the extended Fatimid family, though which specific son should succeed was determined through nomination (*nass*) by the current caliph: succession did not necessarily pass to the eldest son.

Although wazirs had always served as administrators for the Fatimid caliphs, after Badr al-Jamali's coup, the caliphs were frequently mere puppets of the warlord wazirs, who controlled the state and frequently manipulated succession, often raising child-caliphs to the throne whom they could more easily dominate. Fatimid wazirs were generally Muslims, though several were

A rider and four warriors. Panel of woven Coptic textile. Fatimid period, eleventh century. Museum of Islamic Art, Cairo, Egypt. Anonymous. © Erich Lessing/Art Resource, New York.

Christians and others nominal converts from Christianity or Judaism. Occasional power struggles between rival wazirs and generals, or between caliphs and wazirs continued throughout the twelfth century, resulting in numerous plots, assassinations, riots and armed conflicts, and creating an increasing problem of political stability in Egypt. Failed or disgraced wazirs could be imprisoned and tortured, have their property confiscated, or be executed or assassinated.

By medieval standards, the Fatimid administration was highly centralized and sophisticated with an extensive educated and (generally) efficient bureaucracy. The administration was divided into civil and military branches (the "Pen" and "Sword"), with organized hierarchies, ranks, pay scales, with special ritual, clothing, and insignia of power and authority. There were a number of different departments (*diwan*), including military, treasury, religious, missionary and judiciary. A hierarchical corps of eunuchs controlled the harem and personal life of the caliphs. Court etiquette and ritual included sophisticated and flamboyant pageantry, designed to enhance the state prestige and ideology. Agriculture, industry, and trade with the Middle East, India, Africa, and the Mediterranean flourished, and were encouraged by the state as important sources of revenue. In the periods of prosperity and stability cultural and intellectual life thrived under court patrons.

The rise of Badr al-Jamali (1073) and the domination of subsequent Fatimid caliphs by the military wazirs were accompanied by a transformation of the army. The Fatimid army was organized into ethnic regiments, including Berbers, Blacks, Arabs, Turks, Daylamis and Armenians. The relative significance of each regiment shifted through time; after Badr al-Jamali, Armenian, Arab, and Black regiments predominated. Some elite regiments like the Hujariya and Ustadhs were multiethnic. Black soldiers—largely mamluks recruited from the slave trade from the Sudan and Swahili coast—numbered up to 12,000 and tended to serve as infantry. Interregimental rivalry was one of the factors contributing to the political instability of the twelfth century.

The Fatimid army included a professional officer corps and many permanent regular and elite regiments stationed in Cairo or in garrisons throughout Egypt. The army was administered by the Army Ministry (*diwan al-jaysh*), which oversaw salaries and land grants (*iqta'*). Regular reviews and inspections insured that training and equipment met official standards. A number of arsenals existed for the manufacture, storage, and distribution of arms, including the full range of medieval military technology such as mail, scale armor, horse armor, helmets, shields, pikes, lances, spears, javelins, swords, two-handed maces, slings, bows, and crossbows. The total army size ranged from 20,000 to 30,000, with a roughly equal division between infantry and cavalry. Field armies generally ranged from 5,000 to 10,000, with larger armies mobilized in special circumstances.

By the mid-twelfth century the efficiency of the army had seriously declined, through ongoing factional feuding and corruption, degenerating into anarchy and leaving Egypt susceptible to outside invasions by the Crusaders and Nur al-Din of Syria in the 1160s. This culminated in the usurpation by Saladin (r.1169–1193) and his abolishment of the Fatimid caliphate through his assassination of the last caliph, al-Adid (1171).

WILLIAM J. HAMBLIN

See also: **Salah al-Din/Saladin.**

Further Reading

Beshir, B. J. "Fatimid Military Organization." *Islam* 55 (1978): 37–56.
Daly, M. W., and Carl F. Petry, eds. *The Cambridge History of Egypt.* Vol. 1, *Islamic Egypt, 640–1517.* Cambridge: Cambridge University Press, 1998.
Gibb, H. A. R., et al., eds. *The Encyclopedia of Islam.* 11 vols. Leiden: Brill, 1960–2002.
Hamblin, W. J. "The Fatimid Army during the Early Crusades." Ph.D. diss., University of Michigan, 1984.
Hamblin, W. J. "The Fatimid Navy during the Early Crusades, 1099–1124." *American Neptune* 46 (1986): 77–84.
Lev, Y. "The Fatimid Army, AH 358–427/968–1036 CE: Military and Social Aspects." *Asian and African Studies* 14 (1980): 165–192.
Lev, Y. *State and Society in Fatimid Egypt.* Leiden: Brill, 1991.
Lev, Y. "Regime, Army and Society in Medieval Egypt, 9th–12th Centuries." In *War and Society in the Eastern Mediterranean, 7th–15th Centuries,* edited by Y. Lev. Leiden: Brill, 1997.
Sanders, P. *Ritual, Politics, and the City in Fatimid Cairo.* Saratoga Springs, N.Y.: State University of New York Press, 1994.
Walker, E. P. *Exploring an Islamic Empire: Fatimid History and its Sources.* London: I. B. Tauris, 2002.

Egypt: Fatimids, Later: World Trade

Egypt had always played a key role in regional trade networks in the eastern Mediterranean, the Nile Valley, and North Africa. In the early Islamic period, however, only a trickle remained of the important commerce once carried between the Indian Ocean and the Mediterranean via the Red Sea and Roman Egypt, it being instead shipped through the Persian Gulf and Iraq. Nevertheless, by the tenth century these patterns of trade had begun to shift once again. In the Fatimid period (969–1171) a newly vibrant "international" trade network developed which was shipping goods to and from Egypt, directly reaching lands as far apart as Southern Europe, the Yemen, East Africa, and India, and then by further links Northern Europe, Southeast Asia, and even China. Geographers writing in the late tenth century could already see that Fustat (Old Cairo) was replacing Baghdad as the Islamic world's great mercantile hub. By the later Fatimid period, Egypt had become the crossroads of an extensive long-distance trade system that would endure for centuries.

The credit for this remarkable commercial prosperity has sometimes been given to Fatimid economic policies, and these did provide many of the essential ingredients for a flourishing trade. The security of merchants' lives and property was generally guaranteed, and the Fatimids established a gold coinage of such a consistently high degree of fineness that it was widely accepted as currency. The government did reserve the right to purchase certain goods by preemption, and for reasons of both security and revenue it was heavily involved in the trade of particular commodities (especially grain, war materials, flax, and alum). Moreover, government officials were often personally involved in trade. Indeed, the Fatimid imams themselves and their relatives appear as commercial investors, partners, even ship owners. Yet, there was otherwise little state interference in the market, and Fatimid trade policies have often been described as laissez-faire. While customs dues provided the Fatimids with considerable income, they were not usually excessive, and rates could be surprisingly flexible when the purpose was to encourage trade with particular states or in certain types of merchandise.

It was, however, primarily a set of longer-term political and economic trends which proved decisive in creating this flourishing commerce. First, Egypt benefited from a prolonged period of economic and demographic expansion in Christian Europe and the Mediterranean basin. The consequent growth in commercial activity, most dramatically seen in the Italian maritime states, produced early demand for Egyptian flax and alum for use in the textile industry. Likewise, there was increasing interest in other Egyptian products, like sugar, and in the luxury merchandise coming from the Indian Ocean world. In addition to considerable trade by land and sea with Spain, North Africa, Sicily, and Syria, by the late tenth century Egypt was also trading with Christian Europe via Ifriqiya (modern Tunisia), and there is already some evidence for Italian merchants from Amalfi active in Alexandria and Fustat-Cairo. Direct trade with Christian Europe intensified considerably in the eleventh century, and traders from Genoa, Pisa, and Venice gradually replaced the Amalfians. The Mediterranean trade brought to Egypt weapons and other war materials (iron, pitch, and especially timber), as well as silk, cotton, wool, finished textiles, furniture, cheese and honey and wine, olive oil and soap, coral for re-export to the Indian Ocean, hides and furs and leather, various metals, and slaves.

Meanwhile, Egypt's share in the Indian Ocean trade had been growing as the Persian Gulf routes were disrupted by political troubles and long-term economic decline in Iraq. This had begun as early as the ninth century, but by the eleventh century these routes had definitively shifted to the Red Sea. Trade went up and down the Nile to Qus or Aswan in Upper Egypt, and then across the desert to the Red Sea at Aydhab. This route had been operating on a regional scale since at least the ninth century, ferrying merchants and pilgrims across to Jedda and Mecca in Arabia. By the eleventh century, however, there was a burgeoning trade in merchandise from the Indian Ocean world coming via Aden in the Yemen, through the Red Sea and then Egypt, for transshipment to the Mediterranean. This commerce was dominated by spices, aromatics, perfumes, dyes, and gums, but also included pearls and gems, medicinal plants and drugs, metalwork, textiles, and ceramics. These were products coming from South Arabia, India, Southeast Asia, and even China, and there was also ivory, gold, and exotic wood from the East African coast. In exchange, merchants heading East carried Mediterranean and Egyptian products such as textiles, glass, metal vessels and ornaments, paper and books, coral, oils, silks, and even various foodstuffs, as well as copious amounts of gold and silver.

Fatimid Egypt's trade also continued or increased along other, less well-documented routes. Via the oases, caravan traffic connected Egypt with West Africa, particularly the kingdom of Ghana, which served as an important source for the gold used in Fatimid coinage. Likewise, soon after the Fatimids came to power, they sent an envoy to Nubia. Although he failed in his mission to convert the king to Islam, he did manage to reestablish the famous baqt tribute-barter treaty which sent ivory, ebony, exotic animals, and especially slaves to Egypt in exchange for various commodities. These slaves were of especial importance for the Fatimids who used them not only as domestic servants, but also in their army. And commerce with the Muslim East continued, too, even after the arrival of the Crusaders at the end of the eleventh century. Egyptian merchants went to Palestine and Syria, both by land and sea, and they traveled further east, reaching Iraq and as far as Central Asia. Similarly, Syrian and Iraqi merchants are well-attested in Egypt, many choosing to settle there permanently as economic fortunes and the political situation in their homelands worsened.

By the later Fatimid period, Egypt had come to play a central role in several long-distance trade networks moving goods from lands as far apart as Europe and India, Ghana and China. This position as a crossroads of world commerce would persist for centuries, long after the end of the Fatimid dynasty, enhancing the power, prosperity, and prestige of the successive medieval Islamic empires centered in Egypt.

LENNART SUNDELIN

See also: **Egypt: Fatimids, Later.**

Further Reading

Balard, M. "Notes sur le commerce entre l'Italie et l'Égypte sous les Fatimides." In *L'Égypte fatimide: Son art et son histoire*, edited by Marianne Barrucand. Paris: Presses de l'Université de Paris-Sorbonne, 1999. Beshir, Beshir Ibrahim, "New Light on Nubian-Fatimid Relations," *Arabica*, 22 (1975): 15–24.

Goitein, S.D. "From the Mediterranean to India: Documents on the Trade to India, South Arabia, and East Africa from the Eleventh and Twelfth Centuries." *Speculum*, 29 (1954): 181–197.

Goitein, S.D. "Letters and Documents on the India Trade in Medieval Times," *Islamic Culture*, 36 (1963): 188–205.

Goitein, S.D. *A Mediterranean Society: The Jewish Communities of the Arab World as Portrayed in the Documents of the Cairo Geniza, Volume I: Economic Foundations*. Berkeley and Los Angeles: University of California Press, 1967.

Goitein, S.D. "Mediterranean Trade in the Eleventh Century: Some Facts and Problems," in *Studies in the Economic History of the Middle East*, edited by M.A. Cook, London: Oxford University Press, 1970.

Jacoby, David. "The Supply of War Materials to Egypt in the Crusader Period." *Jerusalem Studies in Arabic and Islam*, 25 (2001): 102–132.

Udovitch, A.L. "Fatimid Cairo: Crossroads of World Trade—From Spain to India" in *L'Égypte fatimide: Son art et son histoire*, edited by Marianne Barrucand. Paris: Presses de l'Université de Paris-Sorbonne, 1999.

Udovitch, A.L. "International Commerce in Mid-Eleventh Century Egypt and North Africa" in *The Economic Dimensions of Middle Eastern History: Essays in Honor of Charles Issawi*, edited by Haleh Esfandiari and A. L. Udovitch. Princeton: Darwin Press, 1990.

Udovitch, A.L. "International Trade and the Medieval Egyptian Countryside," *Proceedings of the British Academy*, 96 (1999): 267–285.

Udovitch, A.L. "Merchants and Amirs: Government and Trade in Eleventh-Century Egypt." *Asian and African Studies*, 22 (1988): 53–72.

Egypt: Ayyubid Dynasty, 1169–1250

Ayyub, the eponymous ancestor of the Ayyubid dynasty, was a Kurdish mercenary, who in 1138 entered the service of the warlord Zengi (1127–1146) of northern Mesopotamia and was given command of the city of Baalbak in Syria. Ayyub and his son Saladin (Salah al-Din) continued their military service under Zengi's son and successor Nur al-Din (1146–1174). When Nur al-Din chose Ayyub's brother Shirkuh as commander of an expeditionary force designed to prevent Crusader dominance of an increasingly anarchical Egypt, Shirkuh enlisted his nephew Saladin as an officer under his command. In 1164, 1167, and 1168–1169, Shirkuh and Saladin intervened in Egypt, nominally to assist the Fatimid wazir and strongman Shawar against Crusader invaders and Fatimid rivals. Their first two campaigns ended in strategic stalemates, but in their third invasion Shirkuh and Saladin defeated the Crusaders; thereafter Shirkuh was installed as Fatimid wazir, or minister, to be succeeded after his death a few weeks later by his nephew Saladin (March 1169).

Saladin (1169–1193), the real founder of the Ayyubid dynasty, spent the next two years securing his own power base in Egypt, in part through the destruction of the Fatimid Sudani regiments of black mamluks in chaotic street fighting in Cairo; by 1171 he felt secure enough to overthrow al-Adid, the last of the moribund Shi'ite Fatimid caliphs, restoring the country to allegiance to the Sunni caliph of Baghdad. Although nominally still a vassal of Nur al-Din of Syria, Saladin undertook an increasingly independent foreign policy, becoming openly independent upon Nur al-Din's death in 1174. Over the course of the next decade, he consolidated his power in Egypt and defeated Nur al-Din's weak and divided successors, conquering Syria and northwestern Mesopotamia (1174–1183), while his generals conquered Libya and Yemen (1173). By 1183 Saladin was the strongest ruler in the Middle East, allowing him to turn all his attention toward jihad against the Crusaders. This struggle culminated in 1187 at his decisive victory at Hattin, followed by his reconquest of Jerusalem and most of the Crusader kingdom. The complete destruction of the Crusaders was forestalled by the arrival of the Third Crusade (1189–1192), which retook Acre and the coast of Palestine, but ended in stalemate outside Jerusalem, followed shortly thereafter by the death of Saladin (1193).

The Ayyubid state from 1193 to 1250 can best be understood as a confederation of rival principalities ruled by the extended Ayyubid family, generally under the hegemony of three sultans of Egypt: Saladin's brother al-Adil (1200–1218), his son al-Kamil (1218–1238), and the latter's son al-Salih (1240–1249). When faced with a serious outside threat—such as a Crusader invasion from Europe—most of the rival princes united, only to again fall into bickering when the threat was removed. Saladin himself laid the foundation for this instability when, true to contemporary Near Eastern concepts of succession, he divided his empire among kinsmen, with brothers, sons and other relatives receiving semi-autonomous fiefs and principalities. With the feuding and incompetence of Saladin's sons weakening the state, Saladin's brother al-Adil (1200–1218) organized a coup, declared himself Sultan of Egypt, and established hegemony over the rival Ayyubid princes. Thereafter, although there was some expansion of Ayyubid power in northwestern Mesopotamia, for the next half century the Ayyubids generally remained on the defensive, facing two major enemies: Crusaders and Mongols.

In general, Ayyubid policy toward the Crusaders in the thirteenth century was one of truce, negotiation and concession. However, Crusader aggression aimed at recovering Jerusalem brought three major invasions. The Fifth Crusade (1218–1221) attacked Egypt and temporarily conquered Damietta, but was defeated at Mansura in 1221. Under the emperor Frederick II the Sixth Crusade (1228–1229) capitalized on an ongoing Ayyubid civil war and succession crisis, in which the Ayyubid princes of Syria and Palestine were allied against al-Kamil of Egypt. To prevent a simultaneous war against these rebellious Ayyubid princes and Frederick's Crusaders, al-Kamil agreed to cede a demilitarized Jerusalem to the Crusaders (1229). This respite provided the opportunity to force his unruly Ayyubid rivals into submission and establish himself firmly on the throne of Egypt. The last Crusader invasion of Egypt, the Seventh Crusade under Louis IX of France (1249–1251), also invaded Egypt, culminating with a great Ayyubid victory over the Crusaders at Mansurah (1250). But the untimely death of the sultan al-Salih at the moment of his triumph created a succession crisis resulting in the usurpation of power by mamluk generals, founding the Mamluk dynasty of Egypt (1250–1517).

Following the Mamluk usurpation of Egypt, supporters of Ayyubid legitimacy rallied around al-Nasir Yusuf (1236–1260), the grandson of al-Adil and ruler of Damascus and Syria. His failed attempt to invade Egypt in 1251 was overshadowed by the threat of the

Mongols from the east, who destroyed Baghdad (1258), invaded Syria (1259), and captured and brutally sacked Aleppo, and conquered Damascus (1260). Al-Nasir was captured and put to death along with most surviving Ayyubid princes in Syria. The Mamluk victory over the Mongols at the battle of Ayn Jalut (1260) allowed them to add most of Palestine and Syria to their new sultanate.

WILLIAM J. HAMBLIN

See also: **Egypt: Fatimids, Later; Salah al-Din/Saladin.**

Further Reading

Daly, M. W., and Carl F. Petry, eds. *The Cambridge History of Egypt. Vol.1, Islamic Egypt,* 640–1517. Cambridge: Cambridge University Press, 1998.

Gibb, H. A. R., et al. eds. *The Encyclopedia of Islam.* 11 vols. Leiden: Brill, 1960–2002.

Humphreys, R. S. *From Saladin to the Mongols: The Ayyubids of Damascus.* Syracuse: State University of New York Press, 1977.

Ibn al-Furat. *Ayyubids, Mamlukes and Crusaders.* Translated By U. and M. C. Lyons. Cambridge: Heffer, 1971.

Lev, Y. *Saladin in Egypt.* Leiden: Brill, 1999.

Maqrizi. *A History of the Ayyubid Sultans of Egypt.* Translated by R. J. C. Broadhurst. Boston: Twayne Publishers, 1980.

Lyons, M. C., and D. E. P. Jackson. *Saladin: The Politics of the Holy War.* Cambridge: Cambridge University Press, 1982.

Setton, K. M., ed. *A History of the Crusades.* 6 vols. Madison: University of Wisconsin Press, 1969–1989.

Vermeulen, U., and D. de Smet, eds. *Egypt and Syria in the Fatimid, Ayyubid and Mamluk Eras.* 3 vols. Leuven: Uitgeverij Peeters, 1995–2001.

Egypt and Africa: 1000–1500

From Egypt, Islamic influence extended in three directions: Through the Red Sea to the eastern coastal areas, up the Nile Valley to the Sudan, and across the western desert to the Maghrib.

The Arab conquest, and the southward expansion of Islam from Egypt, were arrested by the resistance of the Christian kingdoms of Nubia. By the tenth century, however, a peaceful process of Arabization and Islamization was going on in northern Nubia as a result of the penetration of Arab nomads. Muslim merchants settled in the capitals of the central and southern Nubian kingdoms, al-Maqurra, and 'Alwa. They supplied slaves, ivory, and ostrich feathers to Egypt. From the eleventh century, a local Arab dynasty, Banu Kanz, ruled the Nubian-Egyptian border. For four centuries they served both as mediators between Egyptian and Nubian rulers and as proponents of Egyptian influence in Nubia. By the beginning of the fourteenth century, they assumed control of the throne of Nubia after they had married into the Nubian royal family.

Arab revolts in Upper Egypt were endemic during the Fatimid and Ayyubid periods. The trained Mamluk troops defeated the Arab tribes that were forced to move southward, thus intensifying the process of Arabization of Nubia. Since the second half of the thirteenth century the Mamluk sultans had frequently intervened in the internal affairs of the Nubian kingdoms, and gradually reduced them to the status of vassals. In 1315 the Mamluks installed as king a prince who had already converted to Islam. This was followed two years later by the conversion of the cathedral of Dongola into a mosque. The Christian kingdom became practically a Muslim state. Christianity lingered on until the beginning of the sixteenth century.

Once the barrier formed by the Nubian kingdoms had been broken, waves of Arab nomads coming from Upper Egypt pushed beyond the cataracts, and spread westward into the more open lands of Kordofan and Darfur, and as far as Lake Chad. In 1391 the king (mai) of Bornu, 'Uthman ibn Idris, wrote to Barquq, the Mamluk sultan of Egypt, concerning harassment by Arab nomads, who captured slaves including the king's own relatives. These slaves were sold to Egyptian merchants, and the king of Bornu asked the sultan to return the enslaved people.

With the decline of Christianity in Nubia, Ethiopia remained the only Christian power in Africa. There were close contacts between Ethiopia and Egypt throughout the Mamluk period. There was some awareness of the fact that the Ethiopians controlled the sources of the Blue Nile. The Ethiopians were concerned with the fate of the Christian Copts in Egypt, and when in the middle of the fourteenth century the Patriarch of Alexandria was arrested the Ethiopians retaliated by seizing all Muslims in their country and drove away all the Egyptian caravans. The Mamluks released the patriarch, and trade was resumed.

Beginning in the Fatimid period in the tenth century, Egypt developed trade with the Red Sea and the Indian Ocean. Muslim seamen from Egypt and Arabia established commercial centers along the Red Sea and Africa's east coast. Ivory and spices were exported via Egypt to the Mediterranean trading cities. Ethiopian slaves were in great demand in all Muslim countries. In the fourteenth century Egyptian economic influence was paramount in Zeila and other ports which were the starting points for trade routes to the interior. Muslim principalities emerged on the fringes of Christian Ethiopia, and the Egyptian rulers sought to be their protectors. Students from southern Ethiopia had their own hostel in al-Azhar. The Egyptians did not venture beyond Zeila, and there is no evidence for direct contacts between Egypt with the rest of the Horn of Africa and East Africa. Still, the role of Egypt in the development of Muslim trade all over the Indian Ocean must have indirectly influenced also the rise of Muslim trading towns on the East African coast. At the end of the period surveyed in this article the Portuguese entered the Indian Ocean and broke the monopoly of Egypt as the commercial intermediary between the Indian Ocean and the Mediterranean.

Between the tenth and the sixteenth centuries Egypt absorbed huge numbers of black slaves from various parts of Africa, mainly from Nubia and Ethiopia. During the Mamluk period there were also slaves from central and western Africa. Black eunuchs in the service of the Mamluks were exported to Egypt from West Africa. Nupe (in present-day Nigeria) might have been the site where eunuchs were castrated.

According to Ibn al-Faqih (writing shortly after 903), there was a busy route connecting the Egyptian oases of the Western Desert with Ghana. But, according to Ibn Hawqal (writing between 967 and 988), this route was abandoned during the reign of Ibn Tulun (868–884) "because of what happened to the caravans in several years when the winds overwhelmed them with sand and more than one caravan perished."

In the middle of the thirteenth century, a hostel was founded in Cairo for religious students from Kanem. In the second half of the thirteenth century, two kings of Mali visited Cairo on their way to Mecca. But the most famous pilgrim-king was Mansa Musa, whose visit to Cairo in 1324 left such an impression in Egypt that all Egyptian chronicles, as late as the middle of the fifteenth century, recorded the event. The huge quantities of gold that he spent affected the exchange rate between gold and silver.

After the exhaustion of the Nubian gold mines of al-'Allaqi, Mamluk coins were minted from West African gold. According to al-'Umari (writing in 1337), the route from Egypt to Mali once again "passed by way of the oases through desert country inhabited by Arab then by Berber communities." Early in the sixteenth century, Leo Africanus said that the people of the Egyptian oases were wealthy because of their trade with the Sudan. Another route passed through Takedda and Gao. Egyptian merchants visited the capital of Mali, and some of them bought from a profligate king of Mali, Mari Jata II (1360–1373), a boulder of gold weighing twenty qintars. In return for gold, Mali was a market for Egyptian goods, particularly fabrics. Mamluk brass vessels found in the Brong region, north of Asante, are silent witnesses to the trade with Egypt. The flow of gold to Egypt diminished somewhat in the fifteenth and sixteenth centuries because of competition by Italian merchants in the North African coast, who channeled the gold to the Italian cities that were hungry for gold.

In the second half of the fifteenth century, the growth and refinement of scholarship in Timbuktu may largely be explained by influence from Cairo, then the greatest Muslim metropolis. Scholars of Timbuktu, on

their way to Mecca, stayed for some time in Cairo, and studied with its distinguished scholars and Sufis. The Egyptian scholar who had the greatest influence in West Africa was Jalal al-Din al-Suyuti (1445–1505). In his autobiography al-Suyuti boasted about his fame in West Africa. Indeed, his *Tafsir* is still the most widespread Koranic exegesis in this part of the world. He corresponded with West African rulers and scholars.

In 1492 Askiya Muhammad led a religiopolitical revolution in Songhay that made Islam the cornerstone of the kingdom. Four year later, in 1496–1497, Askiya Muhammad visited Cairo on the way to Mecca. In Cairo he met Jalal al-Din al-Suyuti, from whom he learned "what is permitted and what is forbidden." It was probably al-Suyuti who introduced Askiya Muhammad to the 'Abbasid Caliph, who lived in Cairo under the patronage of the Mamluk sultans. The 'Abbasid Caliph delegated authority to Askiya Muhammad that gave legitimacy to his rule. Twelve years earlier, in 1484, al-Suyuti was instrumental in arranging a similar investiture by the 'Abbasid Caliph to the king of Bornu 'Ali Gaji (1465–1497).

Al-Suyuti's teaching mitigated the uncompromising zeal of the North African radical al-Maghili, who sought to become the mentor of Sudanic kings at that time. Al-Suyuti saw no harm in the manufacture of amulets and ruled that it was permissible to keep company with unbelievers when no *jizya* was imposed on them. Al-Suyuti's pragmatic approach, representing the conservative tendencies of the alliance of scholars, merchants, and officials in Mamluk Egypt, contributed to the elaboration of an accommodating brand of Islam in Timbuktu of the fifteenth and sixteenth centuries.

NEHEMIA LEVTZION

Further Reading

Hasan, Y. F. *The Arabs and the Sudan*. Edinburgh: 1967.

Hrbek, I. "Egypt, Nubia and the Eastern Deserts." *The Cambridge History of Africa*. Vol. 3 (1977): 10–97.

Levtzion, N., and J. F. P. Hopkins. *Corpus of Early Arabic sources for West African History*. Princeton, N.J. 2000.

Levtzion, N. "Mamluk Egypt and Takrur (West Africa)." In *Islam in West Africa*. Aldershot: 1994.

Sartain, E. M. "Jalal al-Din al-Suyuti's Relations with the People of Takrur." *Journal of Semitic Studies* (1971): 193–198.

Egypt: Mamluk Dynasty: Baybars, Qalawun, Mongols, 1250–1300

The Mamluk dynasty rose to power in Egypt through a series of crises forced upon the Ayyubid dynasty by exterior threats. The Mamluks themselves were slaves purchased in large quantities by Sultan al-Salih Ayyub (r.1240–1249), who were then trained as soldiers, converted to Islam, and then manumitted. The Mamluks

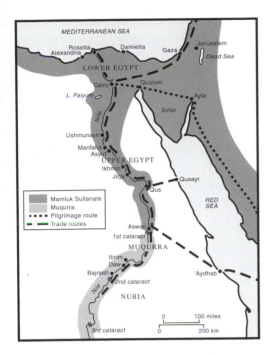

Egypt under the Mamluks, c.1250–1500.

formed an elite corps of soldiers with loyalty only to their former master. With the Mongol invasions of the Kipchak steppe, in what is now Russia, large numbers of Turks were readily available.

The first exterior threat that led to the rise of the Mamluks was the Seventh Crusade led by King Louis IX (1226–1270) of France in 1249. As the army of King Louis invaded Egypt, al-Salih Ayyub died. His son, al-Mu'azzam Turan-shah (r.1249–1250) was not immediately present, and the Ayyubids of Egypt were briefly without leadership. Meanwhile, King Louis's army had halted at the fortified city of Mansurah. His vanguard swept away all opposition and entered the city before becoming trapped and annihilated by the defenders led by the Bahriyya regiment of al-Salih's Mamluks. The Muslim forces led by the Mamluks soon surrounded the Crusaders and King Louis. Facing the potential annihilation of his disease-ridden army, King Louis surrendered.

Upon victory, Sultan Turan-shah arrived and became the ruler of Egypt in 1249. The Bahriyya Mamluks, along with other Mamluks desired more power in the government due to their efforts at Mansurah. Turan-shah, however, disagreed and only placed his own Mamluks in positions of powers, thus alienating his father's Mamluks. In retaliation, Rukn al-Din Baybars, who also led troops at Mansurah, and other Mamluk leaders staged a coup and assassinated Turan-shah in 1250, three weeks after the victory at Mansurah.

The Mamluks then elevated al-Mu'izz Aybak al-Turkmani (1250–1257) to the throne. During the reign

of Aybak, a power struggle between the Bahriyya and other regiments ensued, resulting in the flight of most of the Bahriyya to Syria and to Rum (modern Turkey). After Shajar al-Durr, Aybak's queen, assassinated him in 1257, the victorious faction, the Mu'izziyya led by Kutuz, elevated Aybak's son, al-Mansur 'Ali (1257–1259) to the throne though he was only fifteen. Nevertheless, he served as a figurehead while the Mamluk leaders waged their own power struggles behind the throne.

The second crisis that led to the firm establishment of the Mamluk dynasty was the invasion of the Mongols. After destroying the Abbasid Caliphate based in Baghdad in 1258, the Mongol armies led by Hulegu (d. 1265), a grandson of Chinggis Khan (1162–1227) marched into Syria, capturing Aleppo and Damascus with relative ease by 1260. There was little reason to think that the Mongols would not also invade Egypt after they consolidated their Syrian territories.

Their arrival prompted a change in policy among the Mamluks. Sultan al-Mansur 'Ali's reign came to an end as al-Muzaffar Kutuz (1259–1260) became the ruler under the rationale that it was better to have a seasoned warrior rather than a child. In addition, the Bahriyya regiment led by Baybars came back to Egypt to join the Mamluk army against the Mongols. After executing the Mongol envoys, Kutuz decided to go on the offensive rather than await the Mongol advance. His decision was well-timed as the bulk of Hulegu's army had withdrawn from Syria, and only a small force remained under the Mongol general Ket-Buqa, whom Kutuz and Baybars defeated at the battle of 'Ayn Jalut.

Kutuz's glory was short-lived, however, as Baybars staged a coup against him during their return to Syria. Rukn al-Din Baybars Bunduqari (1260–1277) thus was elevated to the Mamluk throne of a kingdom that now consisted of Egypt and Syria. Baybars immediately began to secure his throne by moving against the Ayyubid princes of Syria as well as dealing with any dissenting Mamluk factions. Furthermore, although the Mongol Empire dissolved into four separate empires and became embroiled in a civil war, the Mongol Il-Khanate of Iran and Iraq remained a very dangerous foe.

To counter this, Baybars arranged an alliance with the so-called Mongol Golden Horde, which dominated the Russian lands to the North, who also fought the Il-Khanate. In addition, Baybars focused his offensive campaigns against the Mongols allies in Cilicia or Lesser Armenia and against the Crusader lord, Bohemund of Antioch (1252–1275) and Tripoli. Baybars's invasions of their territories effectively neutralized them as a threat.

Not all of the Crusaders allied with the Mongols, as did Bohemund. Initially, Baybars left these in peace while he dealt with more urgent threats. He, however,

The Sultan Barquq complex was built in 1384 by the first tower or Burgi Mameluke sultan who ruled from 1382 until 1399. This complex includes a cruciform *medersa*; a *khanqa*, which offered living quarters for the Sufi mystics; and a tomb of one of the sultan's daughters. Cairo. © Mich. Schwerberger/Das Fotoarchiv.

was very active in ensuring their downfall. Through diplomatic efforts, he was able to divert another Crusade led by King Louis IX to Tunis with the help of Charles D'Anjou, the king's own brother. Charles D'Anjou enjoyed profitable commercial and diplomatic relations with Egypt and did not want to dampen them with an invasion. Without the assistance of another Crusade, those Crusaders who remained in Palestine could only defend their territories. Baybars quickly relieved them of a number of strongholds including Crac des Chevaliers, Antioch, Caesarea, Haifa, Arsuf, and Safad. He also crowned his military career with a second defeat of the Mongols at Elbistan in 1277.

Baybars died in 1277. His military success was due to not only generalship but also to his use of diplomacy to gain allies, which in turn prevented the Mongols of Iran from focusing their efforts on him. Much of Baybars' reign focused on securing Syria from the Mongols, which led to his efforts against the Crusader states, and Cilicia. Furthermore, in Egypt he solidified the power of the Mamluks, allowing their rule to continue after his death.

Baybars's son and successor, al-Malik al-Sa'id Muhammad Barka Khan (1277–1279), however, did not have the opportunity to equal his father's deeds. Although appointed as joint sultan in 1266, and secretly elevated to power on his father's deathbed, another coup soon developed in which another Mamluk emir named Qalawun committed regicide, as had the previous rulers, and soon rose to the throne in 1279.

To secure his power, Qalawun (1279–1290) purged the al-Zahirriya, or Baybars' own Mamluks. He then quelled any internal revolt. Qalawun, like Baybars, however, still had to contend with the Mongols. Abaqa (1265–1282), the ruler of the Il-Khanate of Persia sent another army into Syria in 1281. This force, however, met a similar fate as those before it. Qalawun's army emerged victorious and routed the Mongols.

This victory allowed Qalawun to turn his attention against the remaining Crusaders. Through diplomacy and force, Qalawun steadily reduced the Crusader castles one by one. By 1290 only Acre and few minor castles remained in the hands of the Crusaders. Though he laid siege to Acre, Qalawun would not see the fall of this remaining stronghold, as he died in 1290.

Qalawun, however, was somewhat more successful than Baybars at establishing a hereditary succession. His son, al-Ashraf Khalil (1290–1293) continued the siege and captured Acre in 1291. This victory allowed him to firmly establish himself on the throne. After this, al-Ashraf swept away the remaining Crusader footholds and ended their two hundred year presence in Palestine.

Regicide, however, was an ever-present threat in the Mamluk sultanate. When al-Ashraf attempted to replace the Turk–dominated Mamluk corps with Circassian recruits, the Mamluks rebelled again. Qalawun had actually initiated the introduction of Circassians, but al-Ashraf's continuation of it and arrogance prompted another rebellion. Though al-Ashraf Khalil died under the sword in 1293, his Mamluks, known as the Burjiyya, successfully gained control of Cairo and the sultanate allowing the Qalawunid dynasty to continue in name, if not in actual power.

The uncertainty of the Mamluks' legitimacy as rulers that surrounded the Mamluk kingdom and the threat of the Mongols in the Middle East hampered the Mamluks' interests in Africa. Trade with North and Sub-Saharan Africa remained a constant. Furthermore, the Mamluks did maintain and stabilize their rule in southern Egypt by quelling the Beduin tribes. As the threat from the Mongols and Crusaders diminished, the Mamluks began to become more involved with other powers to the south and west.

TIMOTHY MAY

Further Reading

Amitai-Preiss, R. "In the Aftermath of 'Ayn Jalūt: The Beginnings of the Mamlūk-Ilkhānid Cold War." *Al-Masāq* 3 (1990): 1–21.

Ayalon, D. *Outsiders in the Lands of Islam*. London: Variorum Reprints, 1988.

Holt, P. M. *The Age of the Crusades: The Near East from the Eleventh Century to 1517*. London: Longman, 1986.

——. *Early Mamluk Diplomacy (1260–1290): Treaties with Baybars and Qalâwûn with Christian Rulers*. Leiden: E. J. Brill, 1995.

Humphreys, R. Stephen. *From Saladin to the Mongols: The Ayyubids of Damascus, 1193 to 1260*. Albany: State University of New York Press, 1977.

Egypt: Mamluk Dynasty (1250–1517): Literature

Literary production during the Mamluk Sultanate was massive in scope. Authors from divers backgrounds produced works across the gamut of genres and in different languages, supported in part by the patronage of the Mamluk elite. While much of the literary output of any medieval Muslim society defies easy categorization into the genres or modern literary analysis, the Mamluk era is known today for its works of poetry, history, and for what may be called, popular entertainment.

Arabic poetry was produced in vast quantities, although the *diwan*s (collected verses) of many poets remain unedited. Thus our knowledge of this key aspect of Mamluk literary culture remains spotty and uneven in coverage. Classical poetical types such as *fakhr* (self-praise), *ghazal* (love poetry), *hamasah* (personal bravery), *hija'* (invective), *madih* (panegyric), *ritha'* (elegy), and *wasf* (descriptive) were all well represented as well as less traditional styles such as the highly rhetorical *badi'* and the colloquial verse known as *zajal*. Interest in Mamluk poetry, however, has often been affected by later aesthetic trends. Techniques such as *tawriyah* (forms of word-play resembling double entendre), for example, were quite common in Mamluk poetry.

The popularity of ornamentation and literary devices among Mamluk-era poets no doubt contributed to their being classified by earlier Western scholars as "merely elegant and accomplished artists, playing brilliantly with words and phrases, but doing little else" (Nicholson 1969, pp.448–450). Some modern Arab literary critics, meanwhile, dismiss this poetry as "decadent, pallid, worn out, and lacking authenticity" (Homerin 1997, p.71). These views, while still encountered, are under increasing challenge by recent scholars who approach the material on its own terms as well as viewing Mamluk poetry as a vast and rich source for the study of Mamluk-era life and culture.

Major poets include al-Ashraf al-Ansari (d.1264); Al-Afif al-Tilimsani (d.1291) and his son, known as al-Shabb al-Zarif (d.1289); al-Busiri (d.1295), well-known for his ode to the Prophet; Safi al-Din al-Hilli (d.1349);

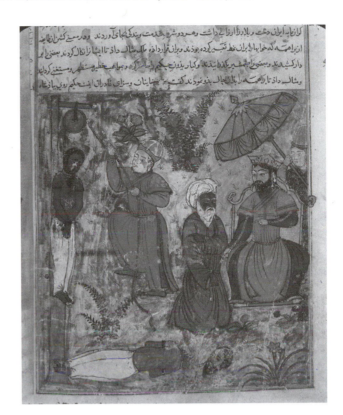

The sultan rendering justice. Miniature from *The Fables of Bidpai: The Book of Kalila and Dimna* (Arabic translation of the *Panca-Tantra*), fol. 100. Fourteenth century. National Library Cairo. Anonymous. © Giraudon/Art Resource, New York.

Ibn Nubatah al-Misri (d.1366), particularly well-known for his use of *tawriyah*; Ibn Abi Hajalah (d.1375); Ibn Makanis (d.1392); Ibn Malik al-Hamawi (d.1516); and the female poet 'A'ishah al-Ba'uniyah (d.1516). While technically an Ayyubid-era poet, the work of 'Umar Ibn al-Farid (d.1235) was well known and extensively cited after his death, and should be mentioned as representing the blending of poetry with mystical (*sufi*) concerns.

The Mamluk age is commonly celebrated for its prolific production of historical works. The major cities of the Mamluk sultanate were centers of learning and commerce, and in no small part the revenues of the latter supported the producers of the former. As a result, the Mamluk era is well recorded in many contemporary chronicles, regnal histories, celebrations of cities and other locales, biographical compilations, and other historically oriented texts. These works are in a variety of styles, ranging from ornate rhymed prose to straightforward narratives containing significant amounts of colloquial language. The authors of these texts were as varied as the texts themselves. Histories were written by Mamluk soldiers, government clerks, and the learned class of the *'ulama'* (those learned in the Islamic sciences). To cite a minimum of examples, Baybars al-Mansuri (d.1325) was a Mamluk officer who participated in many of the military events he later discussed in his writings. Al-Maqrizi (d.1442) was a jurist and disappointed civil servant who frequently poured vitriol and criticism on the ruling Mamluk elite in his many works. Ibn Taghri Birdi (d.1470), the son of a major Mamluk amir, wrote histories reflecting the sympathies and insights made possible by his close association with that same ruling elite. Polymaths such as Ibn Hajar al-Asqalani (d.1449) and al-Suyuti (d.1505) produced important historical works as but a small part of their vast *oeuvre* addressing many topics. Finally, in a similar situation to that of Mamluk poetry mentioned above, many important historical works, such as much of the chronicle of al-Ayni (d.1451), remain in manuscript form.

While often looked down upon by the literary elite past and present, the Mamluk period produced significant works of what may be termed popular entertainment. Apparently performed or recited in public spaces, these works are increasingly studied for what they tell us about the lives and attitudes of the lower social classes absent from the majority of the Mamluk historical works. In particular, the texts of three shadow plays by Ibn Danyal (d.1311), otherwise known as a serious poet, have survived. They are populated with a rogues' list of characters and while clearly works created for entertainment, give a glimpse of the seamier side of Mamluk Cairo as it was perceived by their author.

Much more well known are the tales known by the title *Alf Layla wa Layla*, commonly rendered as the "Thousand and One Nights," or "the Arabian Nights Entertainments" (or some combination thereof). These stories, ranging from a few paragraphs to hundreds of pages in length, are far from the collection of sanitized and selective children's stories with which many modern readers are familiar. They are a complex conglomeration of many tales that likely took an early shape among the professional storytellers of the Mamluk domains. As Muhsin Mahdi has shown, the earliest known manuscript of the *Nights* dates from late Mamluk Syria. It contains both the famous frame-story of the cuckolded and murderous King Shahriyar as well as the first thirty-five stories told by his latest wife and potential victim Sheherezade to postpone his deadly intentions. While some of the stories are clearly of earlier origin, and many are set in the golden past of the Abbasid Baghdad of Harun al-Rashid, descriptive details in many of these thirty-five tales and the later accretions reveal their Mamluk context. Their potential for providing insights into Mamluk-era life has been demonstrated by Robert Irwin.

WARREN C. SCHULTZ

Further Reading

Guo, L. "Mamluk Historiographic Studies: The State of the Art," *Mamluk Studies Review* 1 (1997): 15–43.

Homerin, Th. Emil, ed. *Mamluk Studies Review.*

Homerin, Th. Emil, ed., "Reflections on Poetry in the Mamluk Age," *Mamluk Studies Review* 1 (1997): 63–86.

———. *Mamluk Studies Review.* 8 (2003).

Irwin, R. *The Arabian Nights: A Companion.* London: Allen Lane/Penguin, 1994.

Kahle, P. *Three Shadow Plays by Muhammad Ibn Danyal.* E. J. W. Gibb Memorial, n.s. 32. Cambridge: Trustees of E. J. W. Gibb Memorial, 1992

Little, D. P. "Historiography of the Ayyubid and Mamluk epochs." In *The Cambridge History of Egypt.* Vol. 1. Edited by Carl F. Petry. Cambridge: Cambridge University Press, 1998.

Mahdi, M. *The Thousand and One Nights.* Leiden: E.J. Brill, 1995.

Meisami, J. S., and Paul Starkey, eds. *Encyclopedia of Arabic Literature.* New York: Routledge, 1998.

Nicholson, R. A. *A Literary History of the Arabs.* Reprint. Cambridge: Cambridge University Press, 1969.

Egypt: Mamluk Dynasty (1250–1517): Army and Iqta' System

Although the phenomenon of using slaves as soldiers had antecedents in pre-Islamic and early Islamic times, the formal institution of military slavery in the Islamic world had its origin in the Abbasid caliphate in the ninth century, when al-Mu'tasim (833–842), distrusting the loyalty of some regiments of his army, came increasingly to rely on his personal slaves for protection, eventually expanding his slave bodyguard to an alleged 20,000 men, garrisoned at Samarra. From the ninth through the eighteenth centuries the Mamluk soldier-slave corps formed an important part of the armies of many Islamic dynasties, including the famous Janissaries of the Ottoman sultans. It was in Egypt, however that the mamluk military system reached it apogee, under the Mamluk Sultanate (1250–1517), when Egypt was ruled for a quarter of a millennia by an aristocracy of slave-soldiers.

Mamluk is an Arabic term meaning "possessed" or "owned," and generally refers to military slavery. (Military slaves were also sometimes called 'abd or ghulam.) During the Mamluk dynasty the major source of recruitment was Turkish nomads from the steppes of Central Asia, who were viewed as exceptionally hardy, loyal and warlike, and who had learned basic skills of archery and horsemanship during their nomadic youth on the steppe. During the early Mamluk dynasty the majority of the mamluks came from Kipchak tribes; after the reign of Sultan Barquq (1382–1399), recruitment focused on Circassians. However, during different periods of the dynasty, smaller numbers of Mamluks were recruited from a number of additional ethnic groups, including Mongols, Tatars, Byzantines, Russians, Western Europeans, Africans, and Armenians.

Mamluks began their military careers as young nomad boys on the steppes of Central Asia, who were captured as slaves during military campaigns or raids. Slave merchants would select boys in their early teens with the proper physique and skills, transporting them to the slave markets of Syria or Egypt. There, agents of the sultan would purchase the most promising candidates, enrolling them in a rigorous training program. The new Mamluk recruits were taught Islam, and at least nominally converted, while engaging in multi-year military training focusing on horsemanship, archery, fencing, the use of the lance, mace and battle-axe, and many other aspects of military technology, tactics and strategy; several dozen military manuals survive detailing all aspects of Mamluk military science and training. Emphasis was placed on skill at mounted archery; Mamluk warriors represented an amalgamation of long-established Islamic military systems with a professionalized version of the warrior traditions of steppe nomads.

The displaced young teenagers soon became fiercely loyal to their new surrogate families, with the sultan as their new father and their barracks companions as their new brothers. They came to realize that, despite their technical slave-status, the Mamluk military system provided them a path to wealth, power, and honor, and, for the most fortunate and bold, even the sultanate itself. Upon completion of the training program, which lasted around half a dozen years, young Mamluk cadets were manumitted and began service in the army, the brightest prospects being enlisted in the *Khassikiyya*, the personal bodyguard of the sultan. Mamluks were distinguished from the rest of society by ranks, titles, wealth, dress, weapons, horse riding, special position in processions, and court ritual—they were renowned for their overweening pride in their Mamluk status. The Mamluks thus formed a military aristocracy, which, ironically, could only be entered through enslavement.

Armies were organized into regiments often named after the sultan who had recruited and trained them—for example, the Mamluks of the sultan al-Malik *al-Zahir* Baybars (1260–1277) were the *Zahiriyya*. Successful soldiers could be promoted from the ranks. The Mamluk officer corps was divided into three major ranks: Amir ("commander") of Ten (who commanded a squad of ten Mamluks), the Amir of Forty, and the highest rank, "Amir of One Hundred and Leader of One Thousand," who commanded one hundred personal Mamluks, and lead a 1000-man regiment in combat. There were traditionally twenty-four Amirs of One Hundred, the pinnacle of the Mamluk army, who formed an informal governing council for the sultanate; some eventually became sultan.

The Mamluks had a formal and highly organized system of payment based on rank and function, overseen by a sophisticated bureaucracy. Remuneration included monthly salaries, equipment and clothing, food and fodder supplies, and special combat pay. Many Mamluk officers and soldiers were given land grants known as *iqta'*, both for their own support and to pay for the maintenance of additional soldiers under their command. Such grants were carefully controlled and monitored by the bureaucracy, and amounted to regular payment of revenues and produce of the land rather than a permanent transfer of ownership; the grant of an *iqta'* could be withdrawn and redistributed.

At its height, the Mamluk military system was one of the finest in the world, with the Mamluks of Egypt simultaneously defeating both the Crusaders and the Mongols in the second half of the thirteenth century. During most of the fourteenth century, however, the Mamluks faced no serious outside military threat, and their military training and efficiency began to decline. During this period the major fighting the Mamluks engaged in was usually factional feuding and civil wars associated with internal power struggles and coups. When faced with the rising military threat of the Ottoman Turks in the late fifteenth century, the Mamluks initiated military reforms, which ultimately proved insufficient. The Mamluks were also unsuccessful at efficiently integrating new gunpowder weapons into a military system dominated by a haughty mounted military aristocracy. The Mamluks were decisively defeated in wars with the rising Ottomans (1485–1491, 1516–1517), who conquered Egypt in 1517, overthrowing the Mamluk sultanate.

WILLIAM J. HAMBLIN

Further Reading

Amitai-Preiss, R. *Mongols and Mamluks: The Mamluk-Ilkhanid War, 1260–1281.* Cambridge: Cambridge University Press, 1995.

Ayalon, D. *The Mamluk Military Society.* London: Variorum Reprints, 1979.

Ayalon, D. *Studies on the Mamluks of Egypt (1250–1517).* London: Variorum, 1977.

Ayalon, David. *Islam and the Abode of War: Military Slaves and Islamic Adversaries,* (Aldershot, Great Britain; Brookfield, Vt.: Variorum, 1994).

Ayalon, D. *Gunpowder and Firearms in the Mamluk Kingdom: A Challenge to Mediaeval Society,* 2nd ed. London and Totowa, N.J.: F. Cass, 1978.

Gibb, H. A. R., et al., eds. *The Encyclopedia of Islam,* 11 vols. Leiden: Brill, 1960–2002.

Har-El, S. *Struggle for Domination in the Middle East: The Ottoman-Mamluk War, 1485–1491.* Leiden: Brill, 1995.

Holt, P. M. *The Age of the Crusades: The Near East from the Eleventh Century to 1517.* New York: Longman, 1986.

Irwin, R. *The Middle East in the Middle Ages: The Early Mamluk Sultanate 1250–1382.* London: Croom Helm/Carbondale: Southern Illinois University Press, 1986.

Nicolle, D. *The Mamluks 1250–1517*. London: Osprey, 1993.

Petry, C. F. *Protectors or Praetorians?: The Last Mamluk Sultans and Egypt's Waning As a Great Power*. Albany: State University of New York Press, 1994.

Petry, C. F. *Twilight of Majesty: The Reigns of Mamluk Sultans Al-Ashraf Qaytbay and Qansuh al-Ghawri in Egypt*. Seattle: University of Washington Press, 1993.

Pipes D. *Slave Soldiers and Islam: The Genesis of a Military System*. New Haven: Yale University Press, 1981.

Daly, M. W. and C. F. Petry. eds. *The Cambridge History of Egypt, Vol. 1: Islamic Egypt, 640–1517*, Cambridge: Cambridge University Press, 1998.

Egypt: Mamluk Dynasty (1250–1517): Plague

In the middle of the fourteenth century a destructive plague swept through Asia, North Africa, and Europe, devastating nations and causing serious demographic decline. Cities and buildings were laid waste, roads and way signs were obliterated, settlements and mansions became empty, dynasties and tribes grew weak. The entire inhabited world changed.

Thus wrote Ibn Khaldun in his *Muqaddimah* (v.1, p.64). The famous North African scholar spent the last decades of his life in Mamluk Cairo and saw firsthand the effects the early occurrences of the plague had on the lands and people of the Mamluk Sultanate.

The phrase "Black Death" was not used in the medieval Islamic world. In the Mamluk sources, the devastating and recurring pandemics were usually referred to by the common Arabic nouns *ta'un* (plague) or *waba'* (pestilence). From the initial outbreak of 1347–1349 to the end of the Mamluk Sultanate in 1517, there were approximately twenty major epidemics that affected large areas of Mamluk Egypt, occurring about every eight to nine years. Mamluk Syria seemed to be slightly less afflicted, with only eighteen epidemics over the same period. Given the descriptions of symptoms and the general mortality reported, it seems clear that the disease was that linked to the plague bacilli *Pasteurella pestis* or an earlier variant thereof. Buboes, for example, were frequently referred to as "cucumbers" (*khiyar*) in the sources. Michael Dols has argued convincingly that during several of the outbreaks a total of three forms of the disease—the pneumonic, bubonic, and septicaemic—struck simultaneously. The outbreak of 1429–1430, for example, was especially severe and was called in some sources the "great extinction." The accompanying epizootics among animals frequently mentioned suggests a variant form, or perhaps an accompanying and as yet undetermined agent.

While demography for this period is inexact, it seems probable that the population of Egypt suffered a prolonged and aggregate decline of approximately one-third or so by the beginning of the fifteenth century.

Egypt's population remained at levels lower than its pre-plague years into the Ottoman period. The plague did not afflict all segments of society equally. Reflecting the bias of the sources, we know more about the impact on the cities of Egypt then we do on the rural areas. It is common to encounter statements like the following in the chronicles: "the plague caused death among the Mamluks, children, black slaves, slave-girls, and foreigners" (Ayalon, p.70). The evidence suggests that the Royal Mamluks were especially hard hit, perhaps due to their recent arrival in Egypt, and previous lack of exposure to the plague. The cost of replacing these expensive recruits no doubt contributed to the increasing economic strain on the Mamluk regime during the fifteenth century.

The recurrent nature of the pandemic had other negative repercussions on the regime. While there is no evidence for a complete breakdown of either government or religious administrations, we read of confusion and disruption in land-holding, tax-collecting, military endeavors, the processing of inheritances, and the filling of vacated offices, not to mention the looting of abandoned properties and other civil unrest. Economic ramifications took the shape of price disruptions, labor shortages, decreased agricultural production in both crops and livestock, and an overall decline in commerce. Many modern scholars argue that the demographic decline brought about by the plague is the main contributing factor to the economic difficulties of the fifteenth century, and that the policies adopted by the Mamluk regime in that century are best understood as reactions to, not causes of, that decline.

Normative societal reaction to the plague was shaped by the *'ulama'*, those learned in Islamic knowledge. The guidance provided by this communal leadership was shaped primarily by those *Hadiths* of the prophet Muhammad related to disease epidemics, and featured these main points. First, the plague was both a mercy and a martyrdom for the believer, but a punishment for the unbeliever. Second, a Muslim should neither flee nor enter a plague-stricken region. And third, there was no interhuman transmissibility of the disease; it came directly from God (medieval Arabic medical terminology did not distinguish between contagion and infection). Other reactions on the part of the populace were condemned as innovation. The recurrent stressing of these points in the numerous *pestschriften* that survive, along with contrary reports in the chronicles, would seem to indicate that these policies were not always followed to the letter.

Nevertheless, it is clear that religion shaped both the individual and communal response to the horror and unpredictability of the plague, as seen in the poignant passage by the Mamluk-era author Ibn al-Wardi, who died in 1349, during the latter stages of the first outbreak:

I take refuge in God from the yoke of the plague. Its high explosion has burst into all countries and was an examiner of astonishing things. Its sudden attacks perplex the people. The plague chases the screaming without pity and does not accept a treasure for ransom. Its engine is far-reaching. The plague enters into the house and swears it will not leave except with all of its inhabitants. "I have an order from the *qadi* (religious judge) to arrest all those in the house." Among the benefits of this order is the removal of one's hopes and the improvement of his earthly works. It awakens men from their indifference for the provisioning of their final journey. (Dols 1974, p.454)

WARREN C. SCHULT

See also: **Ibn Khaldun: Civilization of the Maghrib.**

Further Reading

Ayalon, D. "The Plague and Its Effects upon the Mamluk Army." *Journal of the Royal Asiatic Society* (1946): 67–73.

Dols, M. W. "Al-Manbiji's 'Report of the Plague': A Treatise on the Plague of 764–65/1362–64. In *The Black Death: The Impact of the Fourteenth-Century Plague*, edited by Daniel Williman. New York: Center for Medieval and Early Renaissance Studies, 1982.

Dols, M. W. *The Black Death in the Middle East.* Princeton: Princeton University Press, 1977.

Dols, M. W. "The Comparative Communal Responses to the Black Death in Muslim and Christian Societies." *Viator: Medieval and Renaissance Studies* 5 (1974): 269–287.

Dols, M. W. "The General Mortality of the Black Death in the Mamluk Empire." In *The Islamic Middle East, 700–1900*, edited by A. L. Udovitch. Princeton: Darwin, 1981.

Dols, M. W. "Ibn al-Wardi's *Risalah al-Naba' 'an al-Waba'*, A Translation of a Major Source for the History of the Black Death in the Middle East." In *Near Eastern Numismatics, Iconography, Epigraphy and History: Studies in Honor of George C. Miles*, edited by Dickran K. Kouymjian. Beirut: American University Press, 1974.

Dols, M. W. "The Second Plague Pandemic and Its Recurrances in the Middle East: 1347–1894." *Journal of the Economic and Social History of the Orient* 22 (1979): 162–189.

Ibn Khaldun. *The Muqaddimah.* Translated by Franz Rosenthal. 3 vols. London: 1958.

Egypt: Ottoman, 1517–1798: Historical Outline

In January 1517 the *mamluk* sultan of Egypt, Tumanbay, was defeated by the Ottoman sultan Selim I. The Ottoman conquest ended a sultanate that had ruled independent Egypt since 1250. The Ottomans were militarily superior, having cannon and arquebus in the hands of well-organized infantry troops, the Janissaries. The *mamluk* forces, mostly cavalry, had already been defeated in a battle in Syria. The occupation of Cairo by Selim reduced Egypt to a tributary of the Ottoman Empire, symbolized by the removal of the caliph, the spiritual head of the *mamluk* sultanate and of the Islamic world, to the imperial capital of Istanbul.

The Ottoman conquest capitalized on rivalries among the *mamluk*s, which had become evident during the Ottoman conquest of *mamluk* Syria in 1516. By supporting Khayr Bey of Aleppo against his rivals in Cairo, the Ottoman sultan ensured Ottoman supremacy, and in September of 1517 Khayr Bey was appointed the sultan's viceroy in Cairo. The viceroy initially was known by the traditional *mamluk* title of *malik al-umara'*, or commander of the princes, as well as residing in the Cairo citadel in a style very much like that of the previous *mamluk* sultans. Moreover, he reprieved the remaining *mamluk*s, who continued to hold land as a type of feudal assignment, or *iqta'*, in the twelve administrative districts of Egypt, each of which was headed by a *mamluk* bey.

Upon the death of Khayr Bey in 1522 the *mamluk*s revolted, resulting in a series of reforms decreed by the Grand Vizier, Ibrahim Pasha, according to the prescriptions of Sultan Sulayman al-Qanuni. Sulayman codified laws for imperial administration across the empire, designed in part to regularize land revenue. In Egypt the reforms ended the system of land assignments and replaced the *mamluk* assignees with salaried officials, *amins*. The laws of 1525 established a political constitution that gave Egypt some degree of self-government, specifically through the *diwan*, or assembly, which contained religious and military notables, such as the *agha*, or commander of the Janissary troops. The Janissaries were the most important of the seven imperial regiments stationed in Egypt, including another infantry regiment, the Azaban, and two troops of bodyguards or attendants of the viceroy. There were three cavalry units, one of which was composed of *mamluk*s. The *mamluk*s were also given high positions that carried the rank of bey, such as the office of commander of the pilgrimage (*amir al-hajj*), treasurer (*daftardar*), command of the annual tribute caravan (*hulwan*) to Istanbul, and military commands with the rank of *sirdar*. On the side of the imperial officials, the newly drawn fourteen districts of Egypt were placed under the authority of an Ottoman *kashif*, who stood above the *amins*. The formal constitutional structure of 1525 remained intact until the end of the eighteenth century, when Ottoman power in Egypt declined.

Ottoman rule in Egypt depended to a large extent upon maintaining the prestige of the imperial troops. The imperial troops and officers were paid salaries, but the introduction of American silver in the Mediterranean commercial system in the sixteenth century reduced the value of Ottoman currency. The imperial cavalry units revolted against an investigation by the viceroy into Egyptian finances in 1586. This was

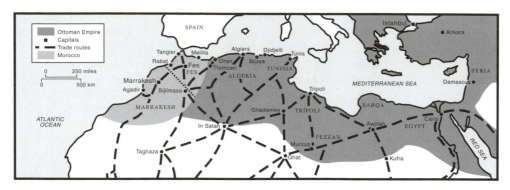

North Africa under the Ottomans, c.1650.

because the cavalry depended upon illegal taxes to supplement their reduced incomes. In this instance, the troops toppled the viceroy. A second revolt in 1589 resisted a proposed reorganization of the troops. These troubles were followed by an epidemic, and in 1605 the viceroy of Egypt, Ibrahim Pasha, was murdered by his troops. In 1607 the viceroy Muhammad Pasha investigated and suppressed an illegal tax levied by the cavalry. Finally, after a revolt of the imperial troops in 1609, the viceroys turned to the beys whose power was independent of the regiments. As a result, in the seventeenth century the power of the *mamluk* beys increased in relation to the seven imperial troops.

The foremost regiment, the Janissaries, established their power bases in the cities, particularly through influence over commercial wealth, while the *mamluk* beys invested in landholdings. Personal landholdings were revived with the development of the *iltizam* system, another form of land assignment that gave the *mamluk*s tax-collecting privileges. The revival of quasi-feudal landholdings undermined the authority of the kashifs, a position that in any case was often given to *mamluk*s beys. Consequently, the *mamluk*s were able to reassert their corporate strength when, in 1631, the beys removed the viceroy, Musa Pasha, and replaced him with a *mamluk* bey who acted as interim viceroy. This set a precedent recognized by the sultan.

By 1660 the distinction between the constitutional roles of the imperial troops and *mamluk* beys had become blurred, for instance, a conflict among the leading *mamluk* factions, the Faqariyya and the Qasimiyya, also involved the Janissary and Azaban troops. At that time the Faqariyya and Janissaries allied and established an ascendance not broken until the great insurrection of 1711. At this point, although the constitutional system remained intact in theory, real power passed to the leading member of the ascendant *mamluk* faction, the Qazdughliyya, who carried the unofficial title of *shaykh al-balad*. Through the eighteenth century, individual *mamluk*s built power bases independently of the Ottomans. 'Ali Bey ruled as *shaykh al-balad* from 1757 to 1772. He was said to have wanted to revive the *mamluk* sultanate in Egypt, and challenged the authority of the Ottoman sultan when he invaded Syria in 1770.

Although the viceroys were not effective arbiters of power in Egypt, the Ottoman troops in Egypt had some success in influencing Egyptian politics and economy. Evidently, the Janissaries were integrated into the leading *mamluk* families through their role as patrons of merchants and artisans. As a result, patronage, rather than formal constitutional procedure, became the usual method of raising revenue and consolidating political power. The decline in the power of the Janissaries in the first half of the eighteenth century is largely the result of their inability to control economic resources, particularly the essential spice and coffee markets. These were undermined by the development of European colonies specializing in their production. By the second half of the eighteenth century Egypt no longer paid an annual tribute to the Ottoman sultan, while ambitious *mamluk*s based their autonomous power on new forms of revenue collection that weighed heavily on the Egyptian population. As a result, at the end of the eighteenth century Egypt was practically independent from the Ottoman Empire, while in political, social, and economic tumult. The period of declining Ottoman power in Egypt, therefore, mirrored events in the rest of the Ottoman Empire, where regional warlords reasserted their autonomy from the middle of the seventeenth century, until Sultan Selim III began modernizing reforms at the end of the eighteenth century.

JAMES WHIDDEN

Further Reading

Ayalon, D. "Studies in al-Jabarti I. Notes on the Transformation of *Mamluk* Society in Egypt under the Ottomans." *Journal of the Economic and Social History of the Orient* 3, no. 1 (1960): 275–325.

Hathaway, J. *The Politics of Households in Ottoman Egypt: The Rise of the Qazdaglis.* New York: Cambridge University Press, 1997.

Holt, P. M. *Egypt and the Fertile Crescent, 1516–1922.* London: Longman, 1966.

Lane-Poole, S. *A History of Egypt in the Middle Ages.* London: Methuen, 1901.

Shaw, S. J. *The Financial and Administrative Organization and Development of Ottoman Egypt, 1517–1798*. Princeton: Princeton University Press, 1962.

Winter, M. "Ottoman Egypt." In *The Cambridge History of Egypt, Modern Egypt from 1517 to the End of the Twentieth Century*. Vol. 2, edited by M. W. Daly. Cambridge: Cambridge University Press, 1998.

Egypt: Ottoman, 1517–1798: Mamluk Beylicate (*c.*1600–1798)

The beylicate institution revolved around a number of prestigious appointments to the Ottoman government of Egypt. The holders of these appointments held the rank of *bey*. The most important appointments were command of the pilgrimage, *amir al-hajj*, and treasurer, *daftardar*, as well as the distinctive title of *shaykh al-balad*, which was applied to the *bey* who had established his political supremacy over his peers. The supremacy of the beylicate was enabled by the formation of *mamluk* households, led by men who won political power through the military, commerce, or landholding. The households were factions composed of officers, merchants, and other notables, as well as freed slaves (the meaning of the term *mamluk*). Politics involved contests to control households, the most important being the Faqari, Qasimi and Qazdughli households.

The political role of the households begins in the early seventeenth century, with the rise of the Faqariyya, led by Ridwan Bey al-Faqari. Ridwan Bey succeeded to the office of *amir al-hajj* when, in 1631, the *beys* deposed the Ottoman viceroy, Musa Pasha, because he executed one of the *bey* commanders. From 1640 Ridwan had the support of the Sultan Ibrahim. After 1649 Sultan Mehmed IV and his viceroy Ahmad Pasha attempted to reduce the growing power of the Faqariyya by blocking Ridwan's hold on the command of the pilgrimage. But factional strength was more enduring, and Ridwan held the post until 1656. Yet, upon Ridwan's death, the viceroy gave the command of the pilgrimage to Ahmad Bey, the head of the Qasimiyya household.

The Faqariyya had the support of the Janissaries, who profited from protection money taken from the Cairo merchants. As a result, the Janissary officers were resented by the other imperial troops, and in 1660 the Azaban infantry troop allied with the Qasimiyya against the Janissary officers. The Faqariyya *beys* fled, and the factional ascendancy passed to the Qasimiyya. Yet, Ahmad was not allowed to attain the autonomous power of Ridwan, and in 1662 he was assassinated by a supporter of the viceroy. Until 1692 the Qasimiyya *beys* ruled with the support of the Ottoman viceroys, who attempted to bring about some reform to the system of hereditary estates, or *iltizams*. However, Ottoman reform only tended to divide Egyptian society between urban factions dominated by imperial troops, particularly the

Janissaries, and rural society under the control of the *mamluks*. It was in this period that the *iltizam* system was firmly entrenched, with the *mamluks* converting state lands into private domains while the Janissaries converted their control of the custom houses into *iltizam* hereditary rights in 1671. Thus, in the seventeenth century there was increasing competition between factions for control of resources.

In 1692 the Faqariyya, led by Ibrahim Bey, increased their influence over the Janissaries by winning over the Janissary officer Kucuk Mehmed. But when Kucuk attempted to cancel the Janissary system of protection money in Cairo, he was assassinated by Mustafa Kahya Qazdughli, probably with the support of the Faqariyya faction within the Janissaries. The Faqariyya political and economic dominance lasted until 1711, when an imperial decree against military patronage of economic ventures resulted in another factional war. The "Great Insurrection," as it was called, pitted the Qasimiyya and the Azabans against the Faqariyya, who were divided. The defeat of the Faqari household also meant the end of Janissary dominance in the cities. Consequently, the authority of imperial troops declined and political power passed to the *beys*.

After 1711 the preeminence of the beylicate was recognized by the unofficial rank of *shaykh al-balad* ("lord of the country"). The Qasimiyya head, Isma'il Bey, ruled as *shaykh al-balad* until 1724 when he was assassinated, as were his two successors. However, during the long rule of Isma'il, the two *mamluk* households were reconciled. The outcome is evident in the formation of a new household, the followers of alQazdughli. This household rose to prominence by controlling appointments to the Janissaries and Azabans. With the imperial troops now controlled by one household, rivalry between the Azabans and Janissaries was no longer a feature of Egyptian politics. Meanwhile, the Qazdughliyya also placed its followers in the beylicate. As a result the political power of the beylicate became supreme, and the heads of the household alternated holding the posts of *amir al-hajj* and *shaykh al-balad*.

In 1754 an insurrection of the Janissaries resulted in the assassination of Ibrahim Kahya Bey, the head of the Qazdughliyya. 'Ali Bey, a *mamluk* follower of Ibrahim, became the *shaykh al-balad* in 1757 and began a period of innovation. He created a personal retinue by elevating his supporters to the beylicate and destroying his factional adversaries. According to the chronicler 'Abd al-Rahman al-Jabarti, 'Ali Bey wanted to make himself the sultan of Egypt. Therefore, he created an army of mercenaries with modern firearms. To raise revenue to pay for the army, he imposed extraordinary taxes on the Egyptian peasants, landlords, and merchants. He also confiscated the properties of his rivals. These innovations were accepted by the Ottoman authorities in return for a pledge to pay off the Egyptian deficit to the imperial treasury. Although challenged by opposition groups in Upper Egypt, 'Ali Bey held power long enough to meet his obligations to the sultan. After these were fulfilled in 1768, he deposed the viceroy and took the office of interim viceroy, *qa'im al-maqam*. Established as the absolute ruler of Egypt, he turned to conquest, defeating a local warlord in the Hijaz, where he appointed an Egyptian *bey* as viceroy. In 1771 'Ali Bey defeated the Ottoman troops defending Damascus, thus establishing the previous frontiers of the *mamluk* sultanate.

The innovations of 'Ali Bey were premature. He could not stand independently of both the Ottomans and the *mamluk* households. The Ottomans won over one of his closest supporters, Muhammad Bey Abu al-Dhahab. At the same time, his *mamluk* rivals who had sought refuge in Upper Egypt, particularly members of the Qasimi faction, allied with the Hawwara, a tribal group in Upper Egypt. Therefore, a combination of factors, but particularly the political rivalries of the beylicate itself, brought about a coalition of forces that defeated 'Ali Bey in the battle of 1773.

The period from 1773 to 1798 was a time of economic, social and political upheaval, occasioned to a degree by the innovations of 'Ali Bey. According to the chronicler 'Abd al-Rahman al-Jabarti, it was a period when the *beys* practiced expropriation and oppression, levying excessive taxes that ruined cultivation and forced the peasants to take flight. Similarly, merchants were extorted, which caused inflation and brought the markets to ruin. Three Quzdughliyya *beys*, Isma'il, Murad and Ibrahim, contested for power in this period. In 1778 Murad and Ibrahim, followers of Muhammad Bey, forced Isma'il to flee Egypt. Ibrahim, the *shaykh al-balad*, shared power with Murad. Murad employed Greek technicians to develop a navy and artillery. To raise the necessary revenues, Murad seized the customs and forced the merchants to sell their grain through his monopoly. This was an important innovation, indicating the development of mercantilist economies by the *mamluk beys*.

When the *beys* reneged on the obligation to organize the pilgrimage in 1784 and 1785, an Ottoman force under Hasan Pasha intervened and Ibrahim and Murad fled to Upper Egypt. Although an Ottoman restoration under Isma'il was promised, the two rebels profited from a severe epidemic in 1791 which claimed the life of Isma'il and weakened the Ottoman regime in Cairo. Murad and Ibrahim returned to Cairo, defeated the Ottoman forces, and signed an agreement with the Ottoman sultan in 1792. However, the innovations of the *beys* of the latter half of the eighteenth century shattered the structure of the beylicate and imperial authority. They also increased the involvement of foreigners in the Egyptian economy and society, particularly the French, who sought control of the Egyptian export economy. Therefore, Egypt was in a very much weakened state when Napoleon invaded in 1798.

JAMES WHIDDEN

Further Reading

Crecelius, D. *The Roots of Modern Egypt: A Study of the Regime of 'Ali Bey al-Kabir and Muhammad Bey Abu al-Dhahab, 1760–1775*. Minneapolis: Bibliotheca Islamica, 1981.

Gran, P. *Islamic Roots of Capitalism, 1760–1840*. Austin: University of Texas Press, 1979.

Hathaway, J. "The Military Households in Modern Egypt." *International Journal of Middle East Studies* 27, no. 2 (February 1995): 2943.

Hourani, A. "Ottoman Reform and the Politics of Notables." In *The Modern Middle East: A Reader*, edited by Albert Hourani, Philip S. Khoury, and Mary C. Wilson. Berkeley: University of California Press, 1993.

Jabarti, 'Abd al-Rahman al-. *'Abd al-Rahman al-Jabarti's History of Egypt*. Edited by Thomas Phillip and translated by Moshe Perlman. 4 vols. Stuttgart: Franz Steiner Verlag, 1994.

Raymond, A. *Artisans et commercants au Caire au 18e siecle*. 2 vols. Damascus: French Institute, 1973–1974.

Shaw, S. J. *Ottoman Egypt in the Eighteenth Century*. Cambridge, Mass.: Harvard University Press, 1962.

Egypt: Ottoman, 1517–1798: Napoleon and the French in Egypt (1798–1801)

The French expedition to Egypt initiated the modern period of European colonialism in Africa, because it was spurred by strategic, economic, and scientific interests. The strategic importance of Egypt lay in its position on the route to Asia. After 1798 Egypt would be the scene of continual competition by the European powers for influence and political control, particularly between Britain and France. Egypt was of economic importance to France as a source of grain. Moreover, French merchants had been able to market luxury goods in Egypt during the course of the eighteenth century. French and Egyptian commercial relations had suffered during the reign of Ibrahim, who forced the French merchants out of Egypt in 1794. As a result, a commercial lobby in France wanted French intervention in Egypt to secure free trade. The scientific objectives of the expedition were to study ancient and Islamic Egypt, probably to enable colonial occupation. Scientific expertise was certainly indispensable to the project of conquering, administering, and colonizing Egypt. Finally, the expedition exposed Egyptians to modern Europe, beginning a period of interaction that would transform Egyptian culture, society and politics in the nineteenth century.

Napoleon's strategy was to drive toward Britain's empire in India, instead of the proposed invasion of England. The French fleet landed Napoleon's army near Alexandria on July 1, 1798, and broke local resistance on the following day. Napoleon advanced toward Cairo against the *mamluk* commander, Murad Bey, who fell back and was defeated decisively at Imbaba on July 21, at the so-called Battle of the Pyramids. The *mamluk* commander, Ibrahim, retreated with the Ottoman viceroy to Syria. Shortly afterward, Nelson destroyed the French fleet at the Battle of the Nile. This victory won the British the support of the Ottoman Sultan, who formally declared war on France in September 1798.

The French conquest of Egypt required an occupation of the Delta and the pursuit of Murad, who adopted guerrilla tactics in Upper Egypt. Aswan was taken in February of 1799 and at the same time Napoleon began his campaign into Palestine. But in neither case were the *mamluk* forces entirely defeated, as Murad engaged in a continual resistance and Ibrahim joined Ottoman forces in Syria. The French conquest also relied on propaganda, with Napoleon's publicists using revolutionary dogma to attempt to win the support of the Egyptian middle classes against what was described as *mamluk* tyranny. Equally, it was hoped this would neutralize the Ottoman sultan, to whom the French declared their friendship. The propaganda was produced by specialists in Arabic and printed as bulletins from a press established at Bulaq. The Egyptians nevertheless regarded the expedition as an invasion, rejected the dogma of the revolution, and viewed the scientific works with interested suspicion. 'Abd al-Rahman al-Jabarti recorded his impressions in his chronicles. From his testimony it appears that the Egyptians resented the foreign presence, viewed Orientalist interest in Arabic texts as cultural interference, as they did the conversion of French officers to Islam, such as in the case of General Jacques Menou.

The expedition nonetheless marks the end of an era, as the *mamluk beys* never again established their political and social dominance. Having disbanded the old aristocracy, Napoleon turned to the Egyptian notables, marking the *ulama*, or religious elite, for special favor. The purpose was to rally support for the French regime, and so Egyptian notables were given high positions in the administration. A system of representative assemblies was organized for the localities, as well as the general assembly, *al-diwan al-'umumi*, which was convened in September 1798. Napoleon claimed that the natural leadership of Egyptian society was the *'ulama'* and that the creation of assemblies would accustom them to ideas of representative government. Yet, *'ulama'* and merchants were already established as a national leadership, having led several protest movements against the misrule of the *mamluk beys* in the last years of the eighteenth century. Similarly, there was a revolt in October 1798 against the French regime led by the *'ulama'* of Cairo. The French brutally suppressed the revolt, executing some members of the

'ulama' and dissolving the general assembly. Nevertheless, the French occupation seems to have consolidated the political role of the urban notables and strengthened the national leadership.

In spite of the political experiments initiated by Napoleon, the French regime in Egypt was principally concerned with the collection of tax. The economist Jean-Baptiste Poussielgue created the Bureau of National Domains to administer the former *iltizam* estates, which were declared state property after the flight of the defeated *mamluks*. The bureau was directed by French officials, *payeurs*, who conscripted Coptic tax collectors, *intendants*, and the heads of the villages, shaykhs, to collect tax at the local level. Under Napoleon's successor, General Kleber, even more radical reforms were begun as the French regime became more entrenched and adopted a defensive posture in late 1799. The provincial districts were reorganized into eight *arrondisements*, administered by the *payeurs*, *intendants*, and shaykhs. At the same time a multitude of existing taxes were abolished and replaced with a single, direct tax payed in cash. Finally, land registration was begun and peasants were given individual property rights. This amounted to an abolition of the Islamic and customary laws of Egypt, bringing to an end a quasi-feudal social order. At the same it began a process of modernization that prefigured much of the subsequent history of Egypt.

After the retreat of the French army from Syria in June 1799, the Ottoman and British armies advanced, landing in Abuqir, where Napoleon defeated them on July 15, 1799. Yet, Napoleon failed in his grand design to control the Middle East and the Mediterranean. He escaped to France the same month. Kleber attempted to negotiate an evacuation of Egypt, withdrawing his troops first from Upper Egypt. At the same time the *mamluks* infiltrated Cairo and organized another revolt with the support of Ottoman agents and the Egyptian notables. The revolt lasted a month, through March and April 1800. It was crushed only when Murad Bey gave his support to Kleber. On June 14, 1800, Kleber was assassinated and succeeded by General 'Abdullah Jacques Menou, who rejected negotiation in favor of strengthening the French position in Egypt. It was during this period that the more radical administrative reforms were carried through in Egypt. But Menou suffered a military defeat at the hands of a combined Ottoman and British force on March 8, 1801 at Abuqir. Under siege in Alexandria, he capitulated to the allied command in August 1801 and departed for Europe on British transports in September.

The man widely credited with founding the modern Egyptian nation-state, Muhammad 'Ali, was an officer in an Albanian regiment of the Ottoman army. His first lesson in politics began the last chapter of *mamluk*

Egypt, when the Ottomans attempted to destroy the *mamluk* commanders after the French departure in 1801. In this instance the British secured the amnesty of the *mamluks*. After he seized power in 1805, Muhammad 'Ali finally eliminated the *mamluks*. But his political ascent relied upon the support of the Egyptian notables. The French expedition strengthened the position of the notables, but it also provided the blueprints for future attempts to strengthen the state. These were taken up by Muhammad 'Ali, who adopted Napoleon as his exemplar and brought about the modernization of the system of landholding, the military, and the administration.

JAMES WHIDDEN

See also: **Egypt: Muhammad Ali, 1805–1849.**

Further Reading

Dykstra, D. "The French Occupation of Egypt, 1798–1801." In *The Cambridge History of Egypt: Modern Egypt from 1517 to the End of the Twentieth Century*. Vol. 2, edited by M. W. Daly. Cambridge: Cambridge University Press, 1998.

El Sayed, A. L. "The Role of the Ulama in Egypt During the Early Nineteenth Century." In *Political and Social Change in Modern Egypt, Historical Studies from the Ottoman Conquest to the United Arab Republic*, edited by P. M. Holt. London: Oxford University Press, 1968.

Girgis, S. *The Predominance of the Islamic Tradition of Leadership in Egypt During Bonaparte's Expedition.* Frankfurt: Herbert Lang Bern, 1975.

Herold, J. Christopher. *Bonaparte in Egypt.* New York and London: Harper and Row, 1962.

Jabarti, 'Abd al-Rahman al-. *Napoleon in Egypt, Al-Jabarti's Chronicle of the French Occupation, 1798.* Translated by J. S. Moreh. Princeton, N.J.: M. Weiner Publishing, 1993.

Shaw, S. J. *Ottoman Egypt in the Age of the French Revolution.* Cambridge Mass.: Harvard University Press, 1964.

Egypt: Ottoman, 1517–1798: Nubia, Red Sea

After waves of pastoral incursions between the thirteenth and sixteenth centuries, Nubian society was reduced to Lower Nubia, the area between Aswan and the third cataract. Upper Nubia adopted an Arab identity through Arabic and Islam; it also came under the sway of the Funj Sultanate of Sennar. Another result was that Nubia was no longer the important intermediary between African and Mediterranean commercial systems. The trade in gold, ivory, and slaves was in the hands of the Islamic sultanates of Dar Fur and Funj. Consequently, the economy of Nubia declined, as the pastoralists encroached upon the Nubian farmers of the Nile valley. When the Ottomans annexed Nubia in the sixteenth century, all trace of the prosperous societies of the Christian kingdoms had been erased.

Although Nubian traditions claim that Nubia was conquered during the reign of Selim I, it seems that the conquest took place between 1538 and 1557, during the rule of his successor, Sulayman the Magnificent. The conquest was staged from Upper Egypt in an expedition that might have come after an appeal made by the Gharbia, an Abdallabi or Ja'ali ruling group. The appeal was made to the Ottoman sultan by the Gharbia against their adversaries, the Jawabra. The campaign was led by Ozdemir Pasha, a *mamluk* officer, who was perhaps directed to engage in a campaign against Funj, which had expanded from the confluence of the White and Blue Nile to Lower Nubia. It is likely that a battle took place at Ibrim and the defeated Jawabra fled southward to Dongola. According to Abdallabi traditions, the Funj defeated the Ottoman troops in a subsequent battle. This reputedly took place at Hannik, near Kerma, probably in the early seventeenth century. In any event, Hannik became the southern boundary of Ottoman Nubia.

The Ottoman ruler of Nubia was given the rank of *kashif*, a *mamluk* term for the head of a province in Egypt. Therefore, Ottoman Nubia had a status similar to an Egyptian provincial district. The Ottoman tax system was imposed, but Ottoman *firmans*, or decree laws, exempted the cavalry from having to pay tax. So, just as the *kashifs* established a hereditary ruling house, the cavalry evolved into a privileged aristocracy, known as the Ghuzz. The *kashifs* and Ghuzz resided in several castles, notably those of Aswan, Ibrim and Say, although there were several others.

The *kashifs* were the appointees of the Ottoman authorities, nominally responsible to the Egyptian viceroy, who paid them a salary. Equally, the *kashifs* were obliged to pay an annual tribute to the viceroys. Tax was collected from the Nubians by a display of superior force, during regular tours of the Nubian villages. Therefore, the *kashifs* created their own private armies, composed of members of the ruling lineage and slaves. The Nubians paid their taxes not in cash but in sheep, grains, dates, and linen. This provided the *kashifs* with trade merchandise, enabling them to count their wealth in cash as well as in slaves. The European traveler Burckhardt observed at the beginning of the nineteenth century that Nubian subjects were victims of slave raids if their conversion to Islam could not be proven. The *kashif* ruling lineage also intermarried with the local, Nubian lineages, providing another means to increase the size of the ruling house, as well as its properties, which were extorted from the Nubian lineages.

By the eighteenth century, the Nubian *kashifs* ruled as independent monarchs of the Upper Nile Valley, much like the *mamluks* in Egypt. The annual tribute to the Ottomans was not paid, and emissaries of the sultan could not expect free passage through Nubian territory. The Ottoman connection remained only as a theoretical guarantor of the privileged position of the *kashifs* and the Ghuzz in Nubian society. As a consequence of the warlike nature of these elites, the Nile Valley above the first cataract was an insecure trade route and caravans were forced to take the arduous desert routes. The inclusion of Nubia in the Ottoman Empire did, however, enable Nubians to migrate to Egypt, which has since become a common feature of Nubian society. Nubians fled southward also, to escape the *kashifs* and to engage in trade. Some went on a seasonal basis to engage in caravan trade among Egypt, Funj, and Darfur, or found employment in Egyptian markets and industries on a permanent basis.

The Ottoman period in Nubia continued the process of Islamization in Nubian society. The Ottoman elite became integrated into the lineage systems established by the Arab nomads, resulting in social stratifications in which the Nubians were a subject peasantry. The *kashifs* and Ghuzz, meanwhile, lived in the quasi-feudal style of a military aristocracy, much like that established by the medieval Christian kings.

A similar process occurred in the Red Sea after the Ottomans occupied the *mamluk* port of Suez, where they built a fleet to control the lucrative Red Sea trade to India. Trade had already been intercepted by the Portuguese, who landed emissaries in the Red Sea, near Massawa, in May 1516 and April 1520. The first Ottoman expedition to the Red Sea brought the Ottomans to Yemen in 1538. Afterward, Ozdemir Pasha descended from Upper Egypt to the port of Suakin on the Red Sea to forestall the Portuguese advance. The port of Massawa was taken in 1557. By 1632 the Ottomans had shut the Red Sea ports to all Europeans, while the Portuguese contained the Ottoman fleet in the Red Sea. At the same time, Africa became a battleground between Christians and Muslims in the Horn. The Muslim Imam, Ahmad Gragn, was defeated by Christian Ethiopia with Portuguese assistance in 1543.

The Ottoman province of Abyssinia, or Habesh, was situated in the region between Suakin and Massawa. Ozdemir Pasha built fortifications and a customs house at Massawa and left the port under the command of the *agha* of a Janissary troop. Suakin became the center of Ottoman power in the Red Sea, with a garrison of Janissaries under a governor with the rank of *sandjak bey*. When the Red Sea lost its important commercial importance in the seventeenth and eighteenth centuries with the decline of the spice and coffee trade, Ottoman authority on the African coast evaporated. The ports fell under the nominal authority of the pasha of Jidda. By the mid-eighteenth century even this connection was severed when the *aghas* discontinued their nominal payment of tribute to Jidda.

The Red Sea ports were foreign enclaves on the coast of Africa, engaged exclusively in trade between the interior of Africa, India, and the Ottoman Middle East. The ports therefore coexisted with the surrounding societies, composed of mixed African and Arab populations. Several lineages of the Beja constituted the ruling groups in these predominantly pastoral societies. In 1671 the Beja besieged the port of Suakin, and in 1694 the caravan trade to the interior from Massawa was intercepted. Before long the Beja were exerting their political authority in the ports. The heads of a royal line of the Beja, the Bani Amir, became the rulers, *na'ibs*, of Massawa. The Bani Amir participated in the government of the port, controlled caravan traffic, and took a share of the customs duties collected by the *aghas*. By 1769 the *na'ibs* were the rulers of Massawa, sharing customs duties with Abyssinian rather than Ottoman authorities. In Suakin the Ottoman officials relied on the support of another Beja lineage group, the Hadariba, who enforced their right to a share in the customs duties of the port by controlling the movement of caravans to the interior. The head of the lineage became the ruler of Suakin, known as the *amir* (emir), while the *aghas* controlled the customs house. This arrangement lasted into the nineteenth century.

JAMES WHIDDEN

See also: **Egypt: Ottoman, 1517–1798: Trade with Africa; Funj Sultanate, Sixteenth to Eighteenth Centuries; Nubia: Relations with Egypt (Seventh–Fourteenth Centuries).**

Further Reading

Adams, W. Y. *Nubia—Corridor to Africa.* Princeton: Princeton University Press, 1977.
Burckhardt, J. L. *Travels in Nubia.* London: James Currey, 1918.
Bruce, J. *Travels to Discover the Source of the Nile in the Years 1768, 1769, 1770, 1771, 1772 and 1773.* 5 vols. Edinburgh: J. Ruthren, 1805.
Crawford, O. G. S. *The Fung Kingdom of Sennar.* Gloucester: John Bellows, 1951.
Holt, P. M. "Sultan Selim I and the Sudan." *Journal of African History* 8, no. 1 (1967): 19–23.
MacMichael, H. A. *A History of the Arabs in the Sudan.* Cambridge: Cambridge University Press, 1922.
Trimingham. *Islam in the Sudan.* Oxford: Clarendon Press, 1949.

Egypt under the Ottomans, 1517–1798: Trade with Africa

When the Ottomans took Egypt in 1517 they were placed at the crossroad of African, Indian, and Mediterranean commercial routes. In 1538 the Ottoman navy was launched from Suez to Aden by the Egyptian viceroy, Sulayman Pasha, to control trade in the Indian Ocean. However, the Portuguese defeated the Ottoman fleet in the Indian Ocean, and the Ottoman presence in the Red Sea became of importance principally for trade to Yemen and to Africa. The Red Sea port of Massawa placed the Ottomans in contact with the commercial sphere of the African state of Abyssinia (modern-day Ethiopia). When Nubia was taken sometime after 1538, the Ottomans established a frontier with Funj on the Nile.

By far the most important trade with Africa was through the states of Funj and Darfur. The ruling lineages of these states adopted Islam in the early seventeenth century, probably to enable better trade relations with Ottoman Egypt. The principal trade route to Egypt from the Sudan was along the Forty Days' Road, the Darb al-Arba'in, which by-passed the unsettled regions of Nubia. Darfur caravans followed this route from Qubayh to Asyut in Upper Egypt. Funj caravans followed several routes from Qarri or Shandi to Ibrim, where the caravans converged to form a caravan that went on to Isna in Upper Egypt. This line could also connect with the Darb al-Arba'in at Salima by crossing the Nile at al-Damir. At Asyut and Isna the caravans were taxed by the Egyptian authorities and some merchandise was sold, but the merchants moved onward to Cairo where the remainder of merchandise was again taxed and sold in the markets. The caravan merchants remained in Cairo for six to eight months, purchasing goods for shipment to Sudanic Africa. The circuit was completed when the next Sudanic caravans arrived. Another route to Egypt was by way of Cyrenaica, in Libya, which was also traversed by caravans coming from Darfur. There were also east-west routes, from the Funj town of Shandi to Suakin on the Red Sea, and from Shandi and Sennar westward to Darfur.

Caravan trade required a high degree of organization. As many as five thousand people made up the Darfur caravan, with at least as many camels. As a result, the Darfur caravan was organized on an annual basis as a state monopoly. This allowed the sultans to raise revenue through customs, accumulate slaves for their armies, and to reward their followers with luxury goods. The caravans of Sennar appear to have been less of a state-led concern because several caravans were organized independently; however, the Funj sultans also relied on customs duties for revenue and slaves for their armies.

The intermediaries between the sultans of the Sudan and the Egyptian viceroys were merchants. The Darfur caravan was accompanied by five hundred merchants who were known as the *jallaba*, an ethnically mixed group who were predominantly from the Upper Nile Valley region. Many came from Arab-Nubian lineage groups, such as the Ja'ali, the Juhayna, and Abdallabi. The *jallaba* were responsible for financing the caravans as well as paying the customs duties to the authorities. Many Sudanic cities were simply commercial crossroads, as was Sennar, the capital of Funj, where customs were collected and merchandise was exchanged.

The lesser towns of Qarri and Shandi were also commercial markets. The capital of Darfur, al-Fashir, was the seat of the sultans, whereas the *jallaba* were probably responsible for creating a city that specialized in commerce. This was the town of Qubayh, just north of the capital.

The trans-Saharan caravans also required the cooperation of the Saharan and Nile Valley nomads, who controlled the desert routes. The nomads demanded a customs duty for providing the caravans with protection and acting as guides and camel drivers. The Arab-Nubian lineage group, the 'Ababda, guarded the Funj caravans to Upper Egypt. In 1798 the 'Ababda collected three gold pieces for every slave and one and a half for every camel. The protection of caravans through nomadic territories was regarded as a prescriptive right. As a result, any caravan without its designated protectors was subject to plunder. Trade with Africa therefore required cooperation between the representatives of the states in the north and the south, merchants, and the pastoralists who lived on the peripheries of the states.

The slave trade was certainly the most important commerce. Perhaps as many as six thousand slaves passed along the Darfur routes annually, with Funj delivering approximately five hundred. The slave trade was legal. The capture of non-Muslim Africans, a practice sanctioned by Islam, provided the nomadic pastoralists with an important item of exchange and thus access to markets. Slaves were normally non-Muslims living on the southern borders of the Sudan. Darfur's source of slaves was in the Bar al-Ghazal region, in the Nuba mountains, or among the Shilluk and Dinka people. In the case of Funj, Abyssinia provided a number of slaves. The Abyssinian slaves were predominantly women. They sold for as much as sixty gold pieces in 1798. On average, slaves sold for thirty-five gold pieces in the Cairo markets in 1798, although eunuchs, aged between eight to ten years, sold for double or triple that amount. In the Darfur caravan approximately four-fifths of the slaves sold were women. Slaves were purchased by Cairo merchants or by slave merchants of Istanbul; however, many were purchased by the *mamluk* households of Cairo. The Egyptian governors at Isna and Asyut imposed a tax of four gold pieces for each slave imported. In Cairo there were further taxes amounting to one and a half gold pieces. As with Darfur and Funj, the slave trade was a significant source of income for Ottoman Egypt.

Besides slaves, the caravans supplied camels, gold, senna or cassia, tamarinds, gum, natron, alum, ebony, ostrich plumes, elephant tusks, tiger skins, and hippopotamus whips (*kurbaj*). As European demand increased in the eighteenth century, ivory and ostrich plumes became increasingly profitable. In 1798 the usual tax on a camel load by the Egyptian authorities was two gold pieces, but for camels carrying ostrich plumes the rate was five and a half gold pieces. In exchange the southbound caravans carried Indian muslins, Syrian and Egyptian silks and cottons, and in the later period, inexpensive European cottons. Luxury items included European firearms and swords, lead, gunpowder, copper, as well as rice, sugar, perfumes, spices, horses, glass, velvet, writing paper, and coffee.

Cairo was the primary market for African merchandise. The Janissaries controlled the Cairo customs houses of Old Cairo and Bulaq as tax farms, which enabled them to take two-thirds of the revenue as private income. Alexandria was the conduit for African and Egyptian merchandise to Europe. Rosseta and Damietta launched transports to Syria and Asia Minor. All of these ports were controlled by the Janissaries, who monopolized most of the revenues collected. Europe was a market for ivory, ostrich plumes, gum, tamarind, senna, and gold. Istanbul received animal skins, gum, tamarinds, senna, and African slaves. However, slaves, the most significant item of trade, were mainly traded in North Africa.

The Ottoman province of the Hijaz in the Arabian peninsula was another market for African products. In this case the trade was connected with the annual pilgrimage. The African sultans provided tribute to be delivered to Mecca annually. The Darfur tribute caravan joined with the great Egyptian convoy in Cairo. With the rise of the Sudanic Sultanates the flow of pilgrims also increased and, like those from the Maghrib and West Africa, the pilgrims engaged in trade along the way. Although pilgrim traffic followed the caravans to Egypt, Suakin also provided an alternate route, both for pilgrims from the Sudan and from West Africa. Ottoman trade with Africa therefore followed a pattern set during the Islamic conquest of Africa, when commercial contacts encouraged the Islamization of African societies.

JAMES WHIDDEN

See also: **Funj Sultanate, Sixteenth to Eighteenth Centuries; Sahara: Slavery: Trans-Saharan Trade.**

Further Reading

Burckhardt, J. L. *Travels in Nubia.* London: James Currey, 1918.

Holt, P. M. *A Modern History of the Sudan, from the Funj Sultanate to the Present Day.* London: Weidenfeld and Nicolson, 1961.

O'Fahey, R. S. "Slavery and the Slave Trade in Dar Fur." *Journal of African History* 14, no. 1 (1973): 29–43.

Shaw, S. J. *Ottoman Egypt in the Age of the French Revolution.* Cambridge, Mass.: Harvard University Press, 1964.

Trimingham, J. S. *Islam in the Sudan.* Oxford: Clarendon Press, 1949.

Walz, T. *The Trade between Egypt and Bilad al-Sudan.* Cairo: French Institute, 1978.

Egypt: Muhammad Ali, 1805–1849: Imperial Expansion

In 1805 the Ottoman sultan named Muhammad Ali (1769–1849) the pasha (governor) of Egypt. In 1811 the sultan sought Egyptian military assistance against the Wahhabi rebellion in Arabia. It was to Cairo that Istanbul again turned for assistance when the Greeks rose in revolt, in 1821, to back their demand for independence from the Ottoman Empire. Egypt was able to effectively respond to these requests because Muhammad Ali had, from the first, set a high premium on an efficient military establishment. This army enabled him to create his own empire and ultimately defy the sultan.

The campaign against the Wahhabis gave Muhammad Ali control of the Hijaz (the key Islamic holy cities, Mecca and Medina). This success gave impetus to Muhammad Ali's imperialist designs. His 1819 treaty with the imam of Yemen, along with his control of Arabia, ensured Egypt's dominance of the east coast of the Red Sea. A revolt by Yemen-based Albanian soldiers prompted an invasion of the territory in 1833. The Egyptian forces easily defeated the rebels and by 1838 controlled the entire Arabian coast.

Motivated by the need for conscripts for his military and the need for gold, Muhammad Ali invaded Sudan in 1820. Within a year, much of Sudan was under Egyptian jurisdiction and became the foundation of his empire. In 1822 Khartoum was founded as the headquarters of Egyptian operations; in 1830 the first Egyptian governor of the Sudan was installed there. The military success did not yield the 20,000 to 30,000 conscripts Muhammad Ali had anticipated. Many Sudanese died resisting the Egyptians; transportation difficulties resulted in the deaths of many thousands more before they reached Egypt; and of the 20,000 who reached Aswan, only 3,000 remained alive by 1824. The hopes for minerals were similarly disappointed. The Egyptians were more successful in improving agricultural productivity in Sudan, for Egypt's benefit. Not only did Egypt control all external trade, considerable quantities of Sudanese products were also sent there. There was also the high taxation on Sudan, again for Muhammad Ali's coffers.

From Sudan, Egyptian domination was extended to include Suakin and Massawa. This undertaking established Muhammad Ali's power over the entire Red Sea and linked his two colonies, Arabia and Sudan. In the operations against the Greeks, Muhammad Ali encountered serious complications. European countries supported the Greek demand for independence. To head off a confrontation with the Europeans, the pasha urged the sultan to accede to Greek self-determination; this was declined. In June 1827, the Egyptian forces took Athens, Crete, and the Morea, only to be defeated by a combined Anglo-French force. For his efforts, the sultan gave Muhammad Ali jurisdiction over Crete.

Muhammad Ali recovered quickly enough from the defeat in Greece to invade Syria in November 1831. There were several incentives for this adventure: conscripts for the Egyptian army; an additional and lucrative source of minerals and agricultural wealth, especially timber for military and non-military ships; control of two major Islamic cities, Damascus and Jerusalem; and simply, the incorporation of Syria into Egypt's steadily expanding empire. Muhammad Ali had previously invaded Ottoman territories at the behest of the sultan; in Syria he was fighting Ottoman forces and thus clearly defying the sultan for the first time. By May 1832 Egypt had overrun Syria; by 1833 they were in Konya, inside Anatolia, where the sultan's army was battered. With the way to Istanbul totally open, Muhammad Ali's soldiers advanced to Kutahia, a day's march from the capital.

After the Konya debacle, the sultan (Mahmud II) sought but failed to secure British military assistance; he then sought and received Russian assurances of support. Nonetheless, Britain favored the maintenance of the integrity of the Ottoman Empire. This and the realization that he was in no position to confront the Europeans influenced Muhammad Ali's decision to restrain his men from marching to Istanbul from Kutahia. The settlement that followed in May 1833 made Muhammad Ali the overlord of the Hijaz, Acre, Damascus, Tripoli, Aleppo, Syria, and the passes of the Taurus Mountains at the gates of Anatolia.

Britain, which had been using the Red Sea and its overland stretch at Suez for mails and passengers to and from India since 1820, was worried by Muhammad Ali's dominance of these regions. In 1839 Britain occupied Aden at the southwestern tip of the Arabian peninsula, driving a wedge between Muhammad Ali's Arabian and Sudanese possessions. This British move encouraged the sultan's attempt, in June 1839, to expel Muhammad Ali from Syria; an attempt that was easily repelled by Egyptian forces. Shortly thereafter, the sultan died, and the entire Ottoman fleet surrendered to Egypt. Egypt had become the strongest power in the Mediterranean and the Red Sea. Britain, meanwhile, coordinated the response of a jittery Europe.

Besides the European consensus that Muhammad Ali's ambitions threatened the Ottoman Empire, Britain was particularly concerned about the strategic importance of the Red Sea and the Mediterranean and surrounding countries, and Russia's growing influence in Istanbul. On July 27, 1839, Britain, France, Russia, Prussia, and Austria delivered a note to Istanbul. This

was intended to forestall direct Cairo-Istanbul negotiations that could further Muhammad Ali's imperial ambitions, a distinct possibility given Istanbul's very weak position. In July 1840 Britain convened a conference in London. The conference gave Muhammad Ali an ultimatum to withdraw from Syria, Adana, Crete, and Arabia. When he refused, a British force landed at Beirut in September, defeated the Egyptian army there, and forced them to withdraw to Egypt. Muhammad Ali was thus compelled to accept the conditions of the European coalition. By the Treaty of London, he lost his Syrian and Arabian colonies. On 1 June 1841, the sultan issued a *firman* (decree) that named Muhammad Ali governor of Egypt for life and granted his male descendants hereditary rights to office; retrenched the Egyptian army to 18,000 in peacetime; and stipulated that all treaties between the sultan and the European countries would apply to Egypt. These restraints curbed Muhammad Ali's imperial drive for the remainder of his reign.

EBERE NWAUBANI

Further Reading

Dodwell, H. *The Founder of Modern Egypt*. 1931. Reprint, Cambridge: Cambridge University Press, 1967.

Fahmy, K. *All The Pasha's Men: Mehmed Ali, His Army, and the Making of Modern Egypt*. New York: Cambridge University Press, 1997.

Ibrahim, H. "The Egyptian Empire, 1805–1885." In *the Cambridge History of Egypt*. Vol. 2, *Modern Egypt, From 1517 to the End of the Twentieth Century*, edited by M. W. Daly. New York: Cambridge University Press, 1998.

Lawson, F. H. *The Social Origin of Egyptian Expansion During the Muhammad Ali Period*. New York: Columbia University Press, 1992.

Marlowe, J. *Anglo-Egyptian Relations 1800–1953*. London: Cresset Press, 1971.

Marsot, Afaf Lutfi al-Sayyid. *Egypt in the Reign of Muhammad Ali*. New York: Cambridge University Press, 1984.

Egypt: Muhammad Ali, 1805–1849: State and Economy

Muhammad Ali (1769–1849) came to Egypt as part of the Ottoman force sent to expel the French who had occupied the country in 1798. With the French evacuation in 1801, the Albanian soldiers became one of the major power brokers in Egypt. It was against this background that Muhammad Ali emerged as a formidable political figure. In 1805 the Ottoman sultan had to name him the pasha (governor) of Egypt. The pasha's ferocious campaign against the Mamluks in 1811–1812 finally secured his position.

Muhammad Ali hoped to bring Egypt up to par with European countries. A strong army, trained, equipped, and organized along Western lines, he believed, was essential in this regard. This was to be the pivot of most

The Mohamed Ali Mosque in Cairo. Completed in 1830, it was built as a half-scale replica of Hagia Sophia in Istanbul. © Das Fotoarchiv.

of his policies. He invaded Sudan in 1820 to secure conscripts for his army. As this did not materialize, he turned to the Egyptian peasantry. To train their Turkish officers, a military school and a navy war college were respectively established at Aswan and Alexandria, both with European instructors.

Education, health services, agriculture, land ownership, and the tax system were all overhauled by Muhammad Ali. The educational system had previously operated along religious lines: Islamic, Coptic, and Judaic. Concerned with quickly producing the personnel needed for his programs, Muhammad Ali established state-run Western schools to train accountants, administrators, and for languages and translations. For the same reason, students were sent to Europe for advanced studies.

The Abu Za'bal, a military hospital, opened in 1827. Renamed the Qasr al-Aini hospital after it moved to Cairo in 1837, it served as a medical school. In 1837, it trained 420 medical students, many of whom went to France for specialization. In 1832 a school for midwives was opened in Cairo, to create a female medical corps. In 1837 a hospital was opened in Cairo for civilians. There were also free clinics in the major cities.

Egypt's agriculture had traditionally relied upon the annual flood of the Nile. Muhammad Ali improved on this by constructing new, deep canals and by regularly maintaining the old ones. This increased the cultivable land by 18 per cent between 1813 and 1830 and made all-year irrigation and farming possible, especially, in the Nile Delta. There was also the introduction (in 1821) and spectacular increase in the production of long-fibered cotton, which was highly valued in Europe's textile industries. These innovations resulted in higher agricultural output and a buoyant export commodity trade.

Muhammad Ali inherited a system of land ownership and taxation (iltizam, or tax-farming) system that benefited specific elites (the villages haykhs, religious leaders, and the Mamluks). In return for a fixed tax, they were granted tax rights over land. The tax was extorted from the peasants who cultivated the land; and the tax farmers were entitled to keep any excess beyond the set tax. This system and the tax exemption enjoyed by religious lands denied the state of considerable portions of the land tax and gave the tax-farmers a lot of leverage over the peasants. In 1816, tax farming was eliminated; taxes were now paid at the village level.

Under Muhammad Ali, the state controlled agricultural production as well as internal and external trade. The peasants were forced to grow crops sold only to the government at fixed prices, which were well below the market price. They then bought their foodstuffs at prices much higher than the original sale prices while the export commodities were sold abroad at substantially higher returns. Muhammad Ali himself controlled the bulk of Egyptian imports, and there was a state monopoly on grain exports.

Because of the agricultural, land, and tax reforms, higher taxes, state control of trade, and considerable expansion in international trade (notably with Europe), public revenues rose phenomenally and funded expansive military, social, and infrastructural (especially, communications and transport networks) projects. Intent on replicating Europe's industrial revolution, Muhammad Ali established a formidable military-industrial complex producing armaments, uniforms, footwear, and frigates as well as sugar refineries, rice mills, tanneries, and textile industries, all dependent on European machinery and technical expertise.

Through Muhammad Ali's reforms, Egypt became the most powerful and wealthiest of the Ottoman provinces. This outcome and his imperialist expansion, from Kordofan to the Red Sea and the Aegean Sea, troubled European countries. In 1838 London persuaded Istanbul to sign a treaty banning monopolies in the Ottoman Empire. This was important because taxes and profits from the sale of monopolized goods accounted for three-quarters of Egypt's revenue. Equally devastating was the 1841 Treaty of London that eliminated Muhammad Ali's empire in western Asia and also curtailed the size of the Egyptian army, the bedrock of his reforms. From then, the pasha lost the zeal and incentive for reform.

In the end, Muhammad Ali did not achieve an industrial revolution, nor did he bring Egypt to the same political and military status as the European powers. Even without British intervention, his policies were self-destructive. There was hardly any effort to win mass support for his policies. Instead, the confiscation of agricultural products, high taxation, and conscripting peasant labor for public works alienated the masses. Besides, Egypt lacked adequate financial resources (especially, after the 25 per cent decline in the export price of cotton in 1833) and skilled personnel to sustain the reforms; moreover, many of the Europeans in Muhammad Ali's service lacked the expertise they claimed, leading to bad management and the failure of many projects. And there was the endemic bickering between Turko-Circassian officials and their Arabic-speaking subordinates.

The peasantry paid a very high price for whatever counted for Ali's successes. It is also true that since the military and the civilian bureaucracy were dominated by Turko-Circassians, the indigenous Arabic-speaking Egyptians were very much marginalized by Muhammad Ali's rule. Indeed, to him, Egyptians were simply serfs, only useful for his ambitions. Nonetheless, he endowed Egypt with the structural foundation which transformed it into a "modern" state.

EBERE NWAUBANI

Further Reading

Cuno, K. *The Pasha's Peasants: Land, Society, and Economy in Lower Egypt, 1748–1858.* New York: Cambridge University Press, 1992.

Dodwell, H. *The Founder of Modern Egypt.* 1931. Reprint, Cambridge: Cambridge University Press, 1967.

Heyworth-Dunne, J. *An Introduction to the History of Education in Modern Egypt.* London: Frank Cass, 1968.

Fahmy, K. "The Era of Muhammad 'Ali Pasha, 1805–1848." In *The Cambridge History of Egypt.* Vol. 2, *Modern Egypt, From 1517 to the End of the Twentieth Century*, edited by M. W. Daly. New York: Cambridge University Press, 1998.

Fahmy, K. *All the Pasha's Men: Mehmed Ali, His Army, and the Making of Modern Egypt.* New York: Cambridge University Press, 1997.

Marsot, Afaf Lutfi al-Sayyid. *Egypt in the Reign of Muhammad Ali.* New York: Cambridge University Press, 1984.

Egypt, North Africa: Scramble

The "Scramble" for Africa south of the Sahara did not begin in North Africa. The Maghrib had been an integral part of the Mediterranean world for three millennia until suddenly disrupted in 1830 by the invasion of the French. No longer able to seek conquests in Europe after the Napoleonic wars, the restored monarchy under Charles X sought to revive the empire by invading Algeria in 1830. The Arabs and Berbers rallied under the leadership of 'Abd al-Qadir (Abd el Kader) to oppose the French. Born into a prominent family from western Algeria in 1807, he studied in Medina and after returning to Algeria mobilized the Sufi brotherhoods

and declared a jihad in 1832 against the Christian French. After fifteen years of unremitting resistance he was forced to surrender after 100,000 French troops of the *Armée d'Afrique* under General Thomas-Robert Bugeaud had laid waste to Algeria. The campaign exhausted French imperial ambitions, but it provided training for French officers, the *officiers soudanais*, who thirty years later seized vast amounts of sahel and savanna in western Sudan for imperial France when the British were occupying the fertile valley of the Nile.

British interests in Africa were transformed by Isma'il ibn Ibrahim Pasha (1830–1895), the khedive of Egypt from 1863 until his deposition in 1879. His determination to modernize Egypt by public works and personal palaces was symbolized by the opening of the Suez Canal in 1869. It reduced the long journey around Africa to a quick passage beside it. Profligate spending made possible by exaggerated cotton revenues during the American Civil War provided the resources for imperial adventures in Ethiopia and the Sudan. In 1875 and 1876 Isma'il sent two military expeditions to Ethiopia whose disastrous defeats confirmed his bankruptcy and left Massawa, the Ethiopian port of entry on the Red Sea, to the Italians.

Europe was not about to abandon its investments in Egypt whether cotton, railways, or the canal. In 1876 British and French advisers, the Caisse de la Dette Publique, were thrust upon Isma'il to restructure his debt that by 1878 could not be refinanced without reducing his autocratic powers. Isma'il refused, and in 1879 he was forced into exile leaving the government to European financial advisers. Led by Colonel Ahmad Urabi ('Arabi) Pasha and his Egyptian officers, the army intervened in September 1881 with the support of liberal nationalists, Muslim conservatives, and the great landlords to regain Egyptian control of the government. Anti-European riots in Alexandria were followed by the British naval bombardment on July 11, 1882. On July 19 Urabi announced he would seize the Suez Canal. On August 16 a British expeditionary force under General Sir Garnet Wolseley landed at Suez and on September 13 destroyed the Egyptian army at Tall al-Kabir to accelerate the "Scramble" for Africa.

The British were reluctant to occupy Egypt, but Suez could not be secured without an administration in Cairo that would protect the foreign investments and their nationals that could not be entrusted to the defeated Egyptian nationalists. The khediviate would be retained, but acting upon the advice of its consul-general, Sir Evelyn Baring (latter Lord Cromer), the British would remain to cleanse the government of corruption, release the *fallahin* (peasants) from injustice, and produce surplus revenue for the European bondholders and public works for the Egyptians. His program to regenerate Egypt for stability in Cairo and security at Suez was dependent, however, on the presence of British troops at the canal and British officials in the Egyptian administration that by 1889 had become more permanent than temporary.

In 1882 Egypt lost its independence to Great Britain. In 1885 Egypt lost its empire in Sudan to Muhammad Ahmad 'Abd Allah who had proclaimed himself the expected Mahdi in 1881 to relieve Sudan of religious and administrative corruption by the Turkish rulers from Egypt. His appeal united the disparate Sudanese ethnic groups into the *Ansar* (followers) who systematically annihilated every punitive expedition sent against them. Having occupied Egypt, the British also acquired responsibility for the defense of its empire in the Sudan against the Mahdists seeking freedom from the same oppression that the British used to justify their conquest of Egypt.

To resolve this dilemma the British government sent Charles George "Chinese" Gordon to Khartoum with ambiguous instructions that became irrelevant when the *Ansar* besieged the city. Gordon organized a tenacious defense, but at the approach of a British relief expedition the Mahdi ordered his *Ansar* to storm the city on 26 January 1885. Gordon was beheaded to become an instant English martyr that ignited the determination of his fellow officers, the British public, and its politicians to seek revenge for his death and the humiliation of a great power by savage Sudanese. Gordon became the moral motivation for the reconquest of Sudan in the "Scramble" for the Upper Nile.

The triumph of the Mahdi was short-lived. He died on June 22, 1885, but his legacy, an independent Mahdist state, was consolidated by his successor, the Khalifa 'Abd Allahi Muhammad Turshain. Four years later, in June 1889, Lord Salisbury, the British prime minister, reluctantly accepted the arguments of his proconsul in Cairo that the regeneration of Egypt to secure Suez would require a more permanent British presence that would be dependent upon control of the Nile waters. This decision determined the beginning of the "Scramble" in northeast Africa that reverberated far beyond the Nile basin. Thereafter Lord Salisbury assiduously pursued diplomacy in Europe to neutralize all competitors whose pursuit of African territory might jeopardize the Nile flow.

In 1890 Salisbury concluded the Anglo-German (Heligoland) treaty that transferred British sovereignty of a tiny but symbolic island off the North Sea coast to Germany in return for German claims to Lake Victoria. In 1891 he concluded the Anglo-Italian agreement by which Britain would ignore Italian pretensions to seize Ethiopia in return for a commitment not to interfere with the flow of the Blue Nile. The Nile waters, Cairo, and Suez appeared secure for Britain until January 20, 1893, when the new khedive, Abbas II, sought to assert his independence that was promptly frustrated by a demonstration of British military power. On the same day Victor Prompt, the distinguished French hydrologist, coincidentally delivered a lecture at the Egyptian Institute in Paris that inspired France to challenge Britain for control of the Nile waters and ultimately Cairo and Suez. The French advanced up the rivers of the Congo basin toward the Upper Nile at Fashoda and through the highlands of Ethiopia. The prospect of a French empire from the Atlantic to the Red Sea was irresistible.

During the beginnings of the "Scramble" for northeast Africa, Britain had encouraged Italian imperial ambitions as a potential ally in the Mediterranean and to frustrate French designs in Ethiopia. Emperor Menelik skillfully manipulated each, acquiring weapons from the French to defend Ethiopia against the Italians and neutrality from the British when they refused to accept his exorbitant claims to the Nile below his highlands. On March 1, 1896, Menelik had assembled at the village of Adua 100,000 men, 70,000 of whom were equipped with rifles accompanied by forty-six pieces of artillery and 20,000 spearmen. The Ethiopians decimated the Italian expeditionary force advancing through deep valleys under General Oreste Baratieri. The Ethiopians lost 17,000 killed and wounded. The Italians lost 7,000 killed, wounded, and captured and their dream of an African empire.

Four months later, on June 25, 1896, Captain Jean-Baptiste Marchand left France for Africa and Fashoda. Three other French expeditions were being assembled in Addis Ababa under the scrutiny of Menelik to march to the Nile. The "Race to Fashoda" was the end of the "Scramble" for Africa begun by the deposition of the Khedive Isma'il in 1879, but after thirty years Nile control for Suez and the empire could no longer be achieved by a naval demonstration in the harbor of Alexandria. To secure the Nile waters from the French, the British government approved a railway from Mombasa to Lake Victoria and when construction was delayed authorized a military expedition from Uganda that never reached Fashoda. The final solution was to send General H. H. Kitchener up the Nile to defeat the Khalifa and confront the French at Fashoda. On September 2, 1898, his Anglo-Egyptian army of 25,000 men defeated the 70,000 *Ansar* the Khalifa had mobilized on the plains of Karari outside Omdurman. Kitchener had completed the revenge for the martyrdom of Gordon in 1885 to the satisfaction of Queen Victoria and the British public. On September 19, Kitchener and his flotilla met Captain Marchand and his 125 *Tirailleurs Sénégalais*, beleaguered at Fashoda, to the satisfaction of Lord Salisbury and the security of the Nile waters and Suez. Marchand withdrew on instructions from a French government humiliated at the end of the "Scramble" for the Nile, if not all of Africa.

ROBERT O. COLLINS

Further Reading

Landes, D. S. *Bankers and Pashas*. London: Oxford, 1958.

Langer, W. L. *The Diplomacy of Imperialism*. New York: Knopf, 1951.

Robinson, R., and J. Gallagher with Alice Denny. *Africa and the Victorians: The Official Mind of Imperialism*. New York: St. Martin's Press, 1961.

Sanderson, G. N. *England, Europe, and the Upper Nile*. Edinburgh: Edinburgh University Press, 1965.

Pakenham, T. *The Scramble for Africa, 1876–1912*. New York: Random House, 1991.

Egypt: Urabi Pasha and British Occupation, 1879–1882

Urabi Pasha Ahmad (*c*.1842–1911) was an Egyptian soldier and nationalist politician who is regarded as the first hero of modern Egyptian nationalism. Leader of the anti-European nationalist movement in Egypt before the British occupation of the country in 1882, Urabi Pasha was one of the first Egyptians of indigenous descent to rise to officer rank in the foreign-dominated Egyptian army. He was himself the son of a peasant or *fellah* who, like other Egyptian *fellahin* (as the peasants were called), had suffered heavily under the foreigners before and after joining the Egyptian army. Apart from him and very few other Egyptian officers, all top positions in the Egyptian army were monopolized by the Turks, Albanians, and Circassians who enjoyed higher pay and rapid promotion.

Since the sixteenth century, Egypt had been subjected to various foreign influences, namely the Turks, the French, and the British. The Turkish conquest of 1517 had made Egypt a province of the Ottoman Empire. On the other hand, British interest in Egypt began to be prominent at the end of the eighteenth century when the French, under Napoleon, invaded and occupied the country. For commercial and strategic reasons the British did not want the French to dominate or administer Egypt, as French control was likely to become a springboard for an attack on conquest of British India and to threaten British trade in the Middle East and Far East. By the 1870s, when Urabi Pasha appeared on the scene as the embodiment of the growing spirit of Egyptian nationalism with the slogan "Egypt for the Egyptians," he was given solid support by every segment of Egyptian society.

Mounting Egyptian indebtedness to foreign financiers, emanating largely from projects initiated and executed by Khedive Ismail, coupled with his incompetent management of Egypt's finances, had virtually caused Egypt to lose its independence. At the peak of its financial crisis, representatives of Britain and France were sent to Egypt in 1878 to investigate and regulate the country's financial situation. When the representatives clashed with Ismail, he dismissed them, generating a reaction from the powers, who made use of their influence with the sultan of Turkey to depose the khedive, a request which the former granted. Following the removal of Ismail as ruler of Egypt, his son Tawfiq was immediately installed. Tawfiq could not ameliorate the situation and became a puppet of Britain and France, who manipulated him at will. The two powers acting together compelled Tawfiq to place Egyptian finances under joint Anglo-French control on the grounds that Egypt could not be relied upon to fulfill its obligations to its European creditors. This development provoked a powerful reaction that ended the joint control scheme or device, and set in motion a chain of events that culminated in outright British occupation of Egypt.

The Egyptian elite class began nationalist agitation through the press and the General Assembly for the removal from office of Tawfiq and a number of corrupt Turkish officeholders. These educated Egyptians denounced British and French interference with the domestic affairs of their country, and insisted that if allowed to control their country's financial affairs, they could fulfill Egypt's international obligations. However, since the British and French were unwilling to surrender their control of Egyptian finances, they remained resolute in preserving the power of the Khedive in order to continue to control the country through him. As the nationalist agitation increased, it spread to the army, whose senior officers were themselves disenchanted.

Urabi Pasha and his Egyptian officer colleagues spearheaded an opposition directed against the Europeans and Khedive Tawfiq, his autocratic government, and the Turko-Egyptians—people of Turkish descent—who monopolized the land, the wealth, the offices, and administration of the country by reducing Egyptians to servitude.

Urabi Pasha drew his support from the diverse elements of the Egyptian population, with the prevailing situation in the country reinforcing the support. His background as a *fellah* who suffered similar injustice as other *fellahin*, the sale of the Egyptian share of the Suez Canal to the British in 1875, the setting of a dual control or international commission to handle Egyptian finances, and the corrupt and oppressive foreign officeholders, all enhanced the nationalist cause. Petitions continued to pour in to Urabi Pasha from Egyptians who had suffered injustice and sought redress for their grievances.

On May 20, 1890, Colonel Urabi and his colleagues, Colonels Ali Bey Fehmi and Abdul-Al, presented a petition to Khedive Tawfiq on the subject of Egyptian grievances, for a redress of the lopsidedness regarding pay and promotion for the rank and file of the Egyptian army as well as the reinstatement of those earlier dismissed from the force. The khedive summoned his Council of Ministers, which decided that the three colonels should be arrested and tried by court martial. When the news reached Urabi and his colleagues, they defiantly offered themselves for arrest. Before the court martial could decide their fate, however, a regiment of their soldiers arrived and freed their popular officers. Strengthened by this triumph, and the increasing powerlessness of the khedive, Urabi presented more demands, including constitutional reforms, and the control of the national budget by Egyptians themselves, as against the Anglo-French control of the fiscal policy of Egypt. Britain and France objected in strong terms, jointly sending a stiff note in which they stated that the only authority they recognized was the Khedive. Tawfiq, however, had become powerless in the face of the immense popularity then being enjoyed by Urabi. Continued nationalist agitation compelled the dismissal of the minister of war, Osman Rifki and in his place Urabi Pasha was appointed, while another nationalist, Mahmud al-Barud, was appointed prime minister.

It became clear then that Urabi and his nationalist counterparts were in firm control. The British and the French were naturally alarmed at this unusual development and feared the nationalists were working toward overthrowing the khedive, declaring Egypt a republic, and refusing responsibility for the discharge of the debts that the khedives had incurred. Both powers, under pressure from their citizens with financial interests in Egypt, intervened and mounted a naval blockade outside the port of Alexandria. This action provoked Egyptian nationals in Alexandria, and during the violent disturbances in June 1882 the British consul was injured and about fifty Europeans were killed. This episode provided an excuse for armed intervention by Britain, which decided that a show of force was necessary if the collapse of European authority in Egypt was to be prevented. Meanwhile, Urabi had started fortifying Alexandria in preparation for the next show of power.

The British became anxious about the security of Europeans in Egypt. France had recalled its fleet from Alexandria to deal with a revolt in Tunisia, so Britain had to act alone. On July 11, 1882, the British navy bombarded Alexandria, but when they could not quell the nationalist riots, troops landed. On September 13, the British forces led by General Garnet Wolseley defeated Urabi's forces at the celebrated battle of al-Tal al-Kabir. Two days later, Urabi himself was captured in Cairo. He was exiled to Ceylon (now Sri Lanka) where he remained until 1901, when he was pardoned and allowed to return to Egypt. Urabi died on September 21, 1911. Meanwhile, from 1882 to 1922, Egypt became an integral part of the British Empire.

S. ADEMOLA AJAYI

See also: **Egypt: Nationalism, World War I and the Wafd, 1882–1922; Egypt: Ottoman, 1517–1798: Historical Outline; Suez Canal.**

Further Reading

Ahmed, J. M. *The Intellectual Origins of Egyptian Nationalism.* Oxford: Oxford University Press, 1960.

Al-hajj, M. A. "The Nile Valley: Egypt and the Sudan in the Nineteenth Century." In *Africa in the Nineteenth and Twentieth Centuries*, edited by J. C. Anene and G. Brown. Ibadan University Press and Nelson, 1966.

Collins, R. O., and R. L. Tignor. *Egypt and the Sudan.* Englewood Cliffs N.J.: Prentice Hall Inc., 1967.

Dodwell, H. H. *The Founder of Modern Egypt.* Cambridge, 1931.

Holt, P. M., ed. Political and Social Change in Modern Egypt. London, 1968.

Holt, P. M. *Egypt and the Fertile Crescent, 1516–1922.*

Issawi, C. *Egypt at Mid-Century.* London, 1854.

Marlove, J. *Anglo-Egyptian Relations, 1800–1953.* London, 1954.

Safran, N., *Egypt in Search of Political Community, 1804–1912.* Cambridge University Press, Harvard, 1961.

Egypt: Cromer Administration, 1883–1907: Irrigation, Agriculture, and Industry

In 1882 Britain invaded Egypt. British reasons for military intervention included the suppression of a nationalist revolt led by Colonel Ahmed Urabi, protection of the rights of Egypt's legitimate ruler, Tawfiq, protection of the Suez Canal (and hence the route to India), and, perhaps most important, protection of British financial interests in Egypt. Though the occupation of Egypt was the result of long-term developments (including a mounting external debt and gradual separation from the Ottoman Empire), the immediate effect was the establishment of British control over the Egyptian administration. From 1882 to 1907, British control of Egypt manifested itself in the person of British agent and consul general, Sir Evelyn Baring (made Lord Cromer in 1891).

Though the nominal head of Egypt were the khedives Tawfiq (until 1892) and Abbas II, Cromer remained the effective ruler of Egypt until his resignation in 1907. Cromer's rule was neither official nor direct; the Cromer administration is often referred to as the "veiled protectorate." Based on his own philosophy of colonial rule, developed in part during his service in India, Cromer placed primary emphasis on the need for a strong, sound financial system in Egypt. In his view, native rulers were tyrants; British rule, therefore, brought much-needed reforms and fair government. Since Cromer believed that the basis of successful reform must be economic, his administration in Egypt concerned itself with strengthening the Egyptian economy through the improvement of irrigation and agriculture and the building of industry.

Egypt's system of canals and irrigation had deteriorated markedly from Roman times until the French invasion in 1798, but during the nineteenth century Muhammad 'Ali and his successors revitalized irrigation and agriculture by deepening canals, building dams, and expanding the cultivation of cotton. According to British officials, however, the irrigation system had been expanded on a less than scientific basis: canals had the wrong slope or capacity and were closed at improper times, channels were filled with silt, drainage was inadequate and confused, and the much-touted Nile barrages, begun by French engineers, had fallen far short of expectations. In 1884 a group of Anglo-Indian engineers, led by Colin Scott-Montcrieff, began reorganizing Egypt's irrigation system. Dividing Egypt into five irrigation districts, Cromer's engineers unblocked old canals, separated drainage from irrigation channels, cut new canals, and repaired the barrages. The result of the first year's efforts was a 30,000 ton increase in the cotton crop. Further irrigation efforts followed: the eastern Delta Canal was dug, river banks in Upper Egypt were raised and canals there enlarged so as to ensure an adequate supply of river water for irrigation even in seasons of low Nile floods, and more barrages were built in the Delta and in Upper Egypt.

Irrigation policy was tied not only to finances but also to control over Sudan. Plans were afoot to build a dam at the first cataract of the Nile in 1894 at the time when Anglo-Egyptian forces were about to embark upon the reconquest of Sudan (following the Mahdist revolt and the death of General Charles George "Chinese" Gordon in 1885). In Cromer's view, the new dam would help generate the income needed to retake and administer Sudan. Although the British government was hesitant to provide the funds for the dam, loans made by financier Sir Ernest Cassel allowed the dam to be built; it was completed in 1902. The successful reconquest of Sudan in 1898 afforded further irrigation possibilities; by 1904 British administrators had decided that the White Nile would provide for Egypt's irrigation needs, while the Blue Nile would be geared toward providing for Sudanese agriculture (on the theory that whatever helped Egyptian agriculture generated further income that could be used to develop Sudan).

Although these changes in irrigation resulted in a dramatic increase in cultivated land, they came at a price. Soil quality diminished as soils were exhausted from continual use and perennial irrigation, pest problems increased, and a rising water table caused by continued inadequate drainage combined to reduce yields during Cromer's administration. Despite the emphasis placed on irrigation as a way of increasing agricultural yields and hence national income, general agricultural policy under Cromer was not well developed. Cromer discouraged the formation of a governmental ministry or department of agriculture (the Ministry of Agriculture was not founded until 1914), and few efforts to improve agricultural techniques were undertaken. Agriculture was increasingly funneled toward the production of Egypt's primary export crop—cotton—and away from cereal crops for domestic consumption. Overall, irrigation policy was well intended and designed to increase cultivatable land; its unfortunate effects on soils and the overall lack of a coherent supporting agricultural policy limited its long-term benefits.

As Egyptian agriculture was undergoing a transformation, industry was undergoing changes as well. Industry during the British occupation developed along two lines: industries related to agriculture and those producing luxury goods for the urban elite. Industries based on agriculture (e.g., the processing of cotton, sugar, and tobacco) flourished with a union of governmental and private firms dedicated to the creation of a modern export sector. With few exceptions, large-scale industry in Egypt during this period was owned and operated by Europeans, and the majority of debts and shares of industrial concerns were held outside Egypt. Despite the growth of such industries, most manufacturing in Egypt remained traditionally organized, labor-intensive, and Egyptian-owned. At the same time, guilds were being replaced with small-scale wage labor, as the government either officially abolished guilds or simply began referring in its regulations to occupations without recognizing any guild structures. During Cromer's time in Egypt, little attention was given to the development of heavy industry, and the government took steps to prevent the development of a modern textile industry. In short, industrial policy, like irrigation and agricultural policy, was formulated with an eye toward maximizing revenue for the British-led government and for foreign investors in Egypt.

Cromer retired from his post in 1907 following the "Dinshaway incident," in which a British officer was killed in the village of Dinshaway and brutal sentences were imposed on the villagers in consequence. Reaction against the sentences swept through Egypt and Britain; pressure mounted for a more accommodating British policy in Egypt. Though Cromer had been out of Egypt during the sentencing, he nonetheless astutely realized that change was in the air and retired to England, where he spent his remaining time writing, serving in the House of Lords, advocating free trade, and presiding over the 1916 Dardanelles Convention. He died in 1917, his Egyptian post having been taken over by Sir Eldon Gorst.

AMY J. JOHNSON

Further Reading

Collins, J. G. *The Egyptian Elite under Cromer, 1882–1907.* Berlin: K. Schwarz, 1983.

Marlowe, J. *Cromer in Egypt.* London: Elek, 1970.

Richards, A. *Egypt's Agricultural Development, 1800–1980.* Boulder, Colo.: Westview Press, 1982.

Zayn al-Din, Ismail Muhammad. *al-Ziraah al-Misriyah fi ahd al-ihtilal al-Baritani, 1882–1914.* Cairo: al-Hayah al-Misriyah al-Ammah lil-Kitab, 1995.

Egypt: Salafiyya, Muslim Brotherhood

In the late nineteenth century, and throughout the course of the twentieth century, Egypt was the scene of important developments in reformist and politicoactivist forms of Islam. These forms included the Salafiyya, a purely intellectual trend, which aimed at the renewal of Islam, and the Muslim Brotherhood, a social movement, which began as a religious and philanthropic organization but eventually adopted a distinctive political agenda.

Although the Muslim Brotherhood was influenced by the Salafiyya's intellectual orientation, especially its emphasis on the pious traditions of Islam's early generations, its focus on activism and social reconstruction has prompted many contemporary scholars to label it an Islamist group. Islamism, according to these scholars, is characterized by the efforts of concerned Muslims to establish the Shari'a, or code of Islamic law, within the secular nation-state. As elsewhere in the Islamic world, Islamism in Egypt has adopted both moderate and radical means to attain its primary goal of creating a polity governed by Quranic principles.

The origins of the Salafiyya are closely associated with Jamal al-Din al-Afghani (1839–1897), Muhammad Abduh (1849–1905), and Rashid Rida (1865–1935), whose efforts to reform Islam were prompted by the West's political and cultural domination of Egypt and other countries of the Islamic world. In order to once again make Islam a dynamic force in the world, these men sought to rid the Muslim community of intellectual stagnation, blind adherence to tradition, and non-Islamic elements, which had crept into Islam through the vehicle of Sufism. In their view, the key to reform was to be found in the practice of ijtihad, the individual effort to discern God's will directly through the investigation of Islam's two primary sources of guidance, the Quran and the Sunna (the normative custom of the Prophet Muhammad).

Although the Salafis upheld the principles enshrined in these two sources as valid for all times and places, they also believed that they should be applied in a manner consonant with the social and scientific requirements of modernity, for only thus could the general interest of the community be served. Thus, according to the Salafis, Islam emphasized the virtues of consultative government and encouraged the study of nature. The Salafiyya intended its program to bridge the growing gulf between the Westernizing and traditional sectors of Muslim society.

The teachings of the Salafiyya inspired the Muslim Brotherhood, which combined the message of Islamic reform with a willingness to mobilize the Egyptian population against the Western cultural influences favored by many within the ruling establishment. Founded in 1928 in the British-occupied Canal Zone by Hasan al-Banna, a primary school teacher, the brotherhood adopted a political strategy that was moderate and gradualist. Rather than take control of the state by direct political action, it sought to influence the direction of politics by "awakening" Egyptians to authentic Islam, which, its propagandists claimed, "lay dormant within their souls." In time, the Brothers hoped, the Quran would be adopted as Egypt's "constitution." During its heyday in the 1940s, the Muslim Brotherhood claimed one million members and sympathizers, who were organized, throughout the country, in some two thousand branches. However, in the mid- and late 1940s some members of the brotherhood adopted a radical stance in response to gains made by the Zionists in Palestine, and to the heightened mood of anti-regime sentiment in Egypt itself. In 1948 a Muslim Brother assassinated the Egyptian prime minister, Nuqrashi Pasha, an action that precipitated the retaliatory killing of al-Banna by security police a few months later.

With the encouragement of their new leader, Hasan al-Hudaybi, the Muslim Brothers supported the 1952 coup d'etat of Abd al-Nasser and the Free Officers, with whom they had forged close links in the previous decade. When it became clear, however, that the officers intended to establish a secular regime, rather than one governed by the Shari'a, they withdrew their support. In 1954, in response to an attempt on his life by a Brother, Nasser banned the movement and imprisoned its leading members.

In 1971 Anwar Sadat, Nasser's successor, released many of the prisoners and granted the Brotherhood a degree of official legitimacy. In so doing, he hoped to use the organization as a counterweight against Nasserists and leftists, whose political influence he was eager to diminish. Abandoning the confrontational politics of the 1940s and 1950s, the Brotherhood resumed the original, Salafi-inspired strategies of social conversion favored by its founder. In addition to publishing weekly journals and magazines, the Brotherhood has, since the 1980s especially, infiltrated labor syndicates and professional organizations, and has petitioned the government to grant it political party status, a request that has repeatedly been denied.

Some Muslim Brothers, however, were forever radicalized by the prison experience of the 1950s. Sayyid Qutb, a literary intellectual who joined the Brotherhood in 1953, articulated the Islamists' ill will toward the Nasser regime in a series of writings composed during the period of his incarceration. In these works he equated the moral universe of Nasser and his followers with that of the Jahiliyya, the condition of ignorance and cultural barbarism that existed among the peninsular Arabs prior to the advent of Islam. Released from prison in 1965, Qutb was immediately implicated in another alleged Islamist conspiracy against the government and hanged in August 1966. Although Qutb himself never explicitly called for armed action against Egypt's secular establishment, his writings nevertheless provided ideological inspiration for the underground Islamist cells, which since the 1970s have waged campaigns of violence and terror against the powers that be.

One such organization, the Jihad movement, assassinated Anwar Sadat in 1981 on account of his close relations with the West and Israel. In the 1990s, the Islamic Group attacked groups of foreign tourists, in addition to government officials. The Mubarak government struck out against this latter movement with extreme force, with the result that in 1998 its leadership called a halt to violence.

JOHN CALVERT

See also: **'Abouh, Muhammad**

Further Reading

Ayubi, N. *Political Islam: Religion and Politics in the Arab World*. London, New York: Routledge, 1991.
Esposito, J. *Islam and Politics*. 2nd rev. ed. New York: Syracuse University Press, 1987.
Heyworth-Dunne, J. *Religious and Political Trends in Modern Egypt*. Washington, D.C.: American Council of Learned Societies, 1950.
Kepel, G. *Muslim Extremism in Egypt*. Berkeley: University of California Press, 1984.
Mitchell, R. *The Society of the Muslim Brothers*. New York, Oxford: Oxford University Press, 1993.

Egypt: Nationalism, World War I and the Wafd, 1882–1922

In Egypt the term "nationalism" was first used to refer to the native officers' movement, led by Col. Ahmad 'Urâbî, against Egyptian government policies that favored officers of Turkish, Circassian (Caucasus region), or other foreign extraction. In 1881–1882,

Egyptians formed several societies, usually lumped together as the "National Party," that demanded constitutional rule, fought the Anglo-French Dual Control, and resisted Britain's invasion of Egypt to protect the Suez Canal and the rights of European creditors. The invasion triumphed, 'Urâbî was arrested and exiled, and the party was disbanded.

In the early years of Britain's military occupation, there was little overt resistance, because Egypt's viceroy, Khedive Tawfîq (r.1879–1892), suppressed it. Nationalism revived after the succession of his son, 'Abbâs Hilmî II (r.1892–1914). Various European and Near Eastern palace functionaries urged the young khedive to resist Britain's consul general in Cairo, Sir Evelyn Baring (Lord Cromer), who was Egypt's de facto ruler. Although Cromer's access to military reinforcements from Britain intimidated the khedive's backers, there arose in his place an informal opposition movement that also called itself the "National Party." Its leader was Mustafâ Kâmil, a French-trained lawyer who initially served as a liaison between 'Abbâs and potential European and Ottoman backers. As he became better known, Kâmil founded a daily newspaper, *al-Liwâ* ("The Banner"), a boys' school, and a political party open to all Egyptians seeking to end the British occupation. The revived National Party appealed to students, young professionals, and seekers of government jobs who felt their access was blocked by the influx of British subjects serving in Egyptian ministries. Most Egyptians were enraged by the 1906 Dinshawây Incident, in which several peasants were hanged, flogged, or jailed for assaulting British officers who entered the Delta village of Dinshawây to shoot pigeons, which Egyptians keep as barnyard fowl. The Nationalists also wanted Khedive 'Abbâs to grant them a constitution with an elected parliament to whom his ministers would be responsible, reducing the power of British advisers in the Egyptian government. Soon after Kâmil became president of the National Party, he died in 1908 at age thirty-three. The large-scale demonstrations of grief at his funeral testified to his support from the Egyptian people.

Soon after Kâmil's death, the Nationalists elected their party's vice president, Muhammad Farîd, as its new leader. Although less charismatic than his predecessor, Farîd was high-principled, financially independent, and determined to continue the independence struggle. In addition to organizing party branches throughout Egypt, he also set up workers' night schools and consumer cooperatives and lent support to the growing trade union movement. He continued to court European support but also strengthened ties with the Ottoman government and hired Shaykh 'Abd al-'Azîz Jâwîsh, an Islamist writer, to edit *al-Liwâ*. Jâwîsh soon antagonized both the Copts and the

British and, although popular with many Muslim students, moved the National Party toward extremism, terrorism, and pan-Islam. When a Nationalist murdered Egypt's prime minister, Butros Ghâlî, in 1910, the Egyptian government (abetted by its British advisers) curbed the Nationalists. Within two years, both Farîd and Jawîsh, having served prison terms, sought refuge in Istanbul. The National Party, with many of its newspapers banned, went into eclipse.

Concurrent with the Nationalists were two other self-styled Egyptian "parties": *Hizb al-Umma* ("Party of the People") and *Hizb al-Islâh al-Dustûrî* ("Constitutional Reform Party"). The *Umma* Party, composed of landowners and intellectuals, advocated a gradual winning of independence, to be achieved by cooperation with Britain in educating the Egyptian people and showing them the rights and duties of citizenship. It upheld Egyptian interests and denounced pan-Islam, shunning both Khedive 'Abbâs and the Ottoman Empire. The *Islâh* Party, however, upheld the khedive's rights and advocated Islamic unity. Neither was as popular as the National Party.

When World War I began, Britain severed Egypt's ties with the Ottoman Empire (which in November 1914 joined the Central Powers), deposed 'Abbâs, declared a British protectorate over Egypt, and barred all nationalist activity for the duration of the war. Although Egypt's cabinet ministers, legislative leaders, and people did not want these changes, Britain's military presence, augmented to protect the Suez Canal after an Ottoman-German attack in 1915, squelched all opposition. Wartime conditions led to price inflation, restrictions on the acreage allotted to growing cotton, martial law and tight controls on civil liberties, conscription of Egyptians for the campaign to take Palestine and Syria from the Ottomans, and requisition of draft animals and foodstuffs from the peasants.

During the war Egyptians hoped that the British would withdraw their troops as soon as it ended, or that they could persuade Britain's allies to back their cause. The idea of sending representatives to the postwar talks may have come from Sultan Fuâd (r. 1917–1936). The proposed delegation's charter members were Sa'd Zaghlûl, 'Alî Sha'râwî, 'Abd al-'Azîz Fahmî, Ahmad Lutfî al-Sayyid, 'Abd al-Latîf al-Makabbâtî, Muhammad 'Alî 'Allûba, Hamad al-Bâsil, and Sînût Hannâ, most of whom had belonged to the *Umma* Party. They opened their campaign with a visit by Zaghlûl, Fahmî, and Sha'râwî to Britain's high commissioner, Sir Reginald Wingate, in November 1918, two days after the armistice, stating their desire to go to London to negotiate with the Foreign Office for an end to the British Protectorate. A similar request was made the same day by Premier Husayn Rushdî and 'Adlî Yakan. The Foreign Office replied that it was too busy preparing

for the Paris Peace Conference to meet even an official Egyptian deputation, let alone Zaghlûl, who was convening Egyptian legislators, demanding complete independence, and proposing to head a delegation to the Peace Conference. When Britain challenged the credentials of Zaghlûl and his friends to represent Egypt, his followers set up a committee to gather contributions and circulate petitions, authorizing their *wafd* (delegation) to speak for the Egyptian people. Wingate banned political meetings, and the Interior Ministry seized some of the petitions, but Rushdî and 'Adlî resigned from the cabinet when the Foreign Office refused to see even them. Zaghlûl and his backers sent memoranda to the conference, President Wilson of the United States, the representatives of the Western powers in Egypt, and foreign residents.

Although the Wafd's main aim was to achieve Egypt's complete independence by peaceful means, Britain's failure to gauge the Wafd's popularity led to repressive measures in March, including the internment of Zaghlûl and three of his associates, sparking the nationwide 1919 revolution, in which all classes and religions joined in opposing the British; even women took part in demonstrations. London appointed General Allenby to replace Wingate as high commissioner and authorized him to take any measures necessary to restore order. Allenby suppressed the violence but also declared Zaghlûl free to go to Paris. The other Wafdists drew up a covenant, chose Zaghlûl as president of the Wafd, and bound themselves not to negotiate in its name with persons of political standing without his permission. Formally organized like a European political party, the Wafd delegated many powers to its leader. Once Zaghlûl was free to go to the Peace Conference, the other seventeen members of the Egyptian delegation met before their departure to form a central committee to gather funds and information on Egypt's situation. It became the nerve center of Egyptian resistance to British rule. When Britain dispatched the Milner Mission to Egypt, the Central Committee set up a boycott and demonstrations against it.

The Wafd's hopes of addressing the conference were dashed when the U.S. government formally recognized the British Protectorate. Unable to make its case directly, the Wafd's members issued manifestos and met other delegates, seeking supporters for independence. In 1920 Lord Milner and Zaghlûl held informal talks on the Egyptian question without reaching an agreement. New disturbances erupted in 1921, and the British again exiled Zaghlûl. Some of the men who had left the Wafd formed the Constitutional Liberal Party (similar to the *Umma* Party) and drafted Egypt's 1923 Constitution. Once it took effect, the Wafd reconstituted itself as a party to run candidates in the first parliamentary elections, but many Wafdists continued to see themselves as standard-bearers of Egyptian nationalism rather than as a partisan movement.

ARTHUR GOLDSCHMIDT JR.

See also: **World War I: North and Saharan Africa; World War I: Survey**

Further Reading

Cole, J. R. I. *Colonialism and Revolution in the Middle East: Social and Cultural Origins of Egypt's 'Urabi Movement.* Princeton, N.J.: Princeton University Press, 1993.

Gershoni, I., and J. P. Jankowski. *Egypt, Islam, and the Arabs: The Search for Egyptian Nationhood, 1900–1930.* New York: Oxford University Press, 1986.

Goldschmidt, A. "The Egyptian Nationalist Party, 1892–1919." In *Political and Social Change in Modern Egypt,* edited by P.M. Holt. London: Oxford University Press, 1968.

Landau, J. M. *Parliaments and Parties in Egypt.* Tel Aviv: Israel Oriental Society, 1953.

Schölch, A. *Egypt for the Egyptians! The Socio-Political Crisis in Egypt, 1878–1882.* London: Ithaca Press, 1981.

Zayid, M. Y. *Egypt's Struggle for Independence.* Beirut: Khayat's, 1965.

Egypt: Monarchy and Parliament, 1922–1939

On February 28, 1922, the British unilaterally declared Egypt an independent and sovereign state, after having failed to negotiate a treaty with the nationalist delegation (Wafd). The declaration also limited Egypt's sovereignty by reserving the issues of imperial communications, defense, foreign interests and minorities, and Sudan for further negotiations. The British declaration also initiated a new political constitution by establishing the Egyptian monarchy, while allowing the Egyptians to define the details of the new political system in a constitutional commission. The constitution was drafted as a compromise between conservative monarchists and liberal constitutionalists, who alternately held power between 1922 and 1923. A Liberal-Constitutional Party formed in 1922, with the support of the British high commissioner in Egypt, Edmond Allenby; however, the monarchists did not form a party until 1925. In the meantime, the Liberal-Constitutional Party was the main political opposition to the Wafd.

The Wafd rejected the declaration of 1922, as well as the liberal and monarchist governments that supervised the drafting of the constitution of 1923. The constitution defined civil and political rights and created a parliament that consisted of two chambers elected by a male suffrage. The chamber of deputies had the power to initiate legislation, which had not been the case in earlier assemblies, such as those formed in 1866, 1883, and 1913. In addition, the majority party in the chamber had the right to form a government. Therefore, the constitution was dubbed the liberal constitution. However, the final stages of the drafting of the constitution

secured special privileges for the monarchy. King Ahmad Fu'ad had the right to appoint two-fifths of the senate and enjoyed the right to dissolve parliament, write legislation in the absence of parliament, veto parliamentary legislation, and control appointments to the ministry of religious trusts and personnel at the national mosque, al-Azhar. Consequently the leader of the Wafd, Sa'd Zaghlul, declared the constitution a "feudal and medieval text."

Nevertheless, the constitution created the political arena in which monarchists and nationalists contested for power in the interwar years. The Wafd Party gained legitimacy as the leading national party at the polls, taking 90 per cent of the vote in the first elections of 1923. The Liberal-Constitutional Party was defeated and afterward served in numerous coalition governments, oscillating between the nationalist Wafd and monarchist parliamentary blocs. Political contests revolved around the issues of treaty negotiations with the British and the constitutional role of the king. When the premier, Sa'd Zaghlul, failed to reach an agreement with the British Labour government on treaty negotiations in 1924, a conservative faction within the Wafd Party seceded to the monarchists. As a result, Zaghlul moved to a more radical, nationalist position on treaty issues to rally support and confront the king. To do so involved a confrontation with the British also, who now depended upon the king as a counter to the nationalists. Dramatically, the Wafd failed in its contest with the king and the British after the assassination of the British commander of the Egyptian army in Sudan by unidentified assailants in November.

Blame fell on the nationalist government of Zaghlul, who was forced to resign. Afterward, the parliament was dissolved, and Allenby and the Conservative foreign secretary, Austen Chamberlain, worked with the king to organize a monarchist party, named the Unity (Ittihad) Party. The elections of March 1925 gave the Wafd 54 per cent of the vote, which showed that the monarchists could, by vote rigging and patronage, secure a significant section of the electorate. Yet, the first vote within the parliament defeated the monarchist government. Rather than bow to the deputies, the king exercised his constitutional right to dissolve the parliament and appoint a government that included Ittihad and Liberal-Constitutional ministers.

King Fu'ad was key to this coalition because only the king had sufficient powers of patronage to draw support away from the Wafd and neutralize the Liberals. For example, prominent Liberals aligned with the monarchy in 1925, including Isma'il Sidqi, who accepted the post of Minster of the Interior, while 'Adli Yakan and Husayn Rushdi accepted royal appointments to the senate. Royal patronage of this type resembled the style of politics practiced by the khedives of nineteenth-century Egypt. Consequently, the king could count upon the support of politicians bred in the culture of autocratic rule before 1922. Politicians such as Sidqi, 'Adli, and Rushdi were distrustful of the populist politics of the nationalists; therefore, the monarchy seemed to them, as it did to the British, as the last line of defense against a more radical nationalist alternative.

The split in the monarchist and liberal coalition in September 1925 was caused by a conflict of political principles between those in favor of royal autocracy and those defending the idea of constitutional monarchy. Fearing a reinvigorated monarchy, many Liberals allied with the Wafd against the monarchist Ittihad Party in preparation for the third round of elections in 1926. To win over the Liberals and disarm colonial interference, the Wafd leadership adopted a more moderate tactic based on constitutional precedent. Zaghlul published a declaration supporting a convention of the dissolved parliament on November 21, according to article 96 of the constitution. The parliamentarians met and condemned the dissolution of parliament in 1924, agreeing on the convention of a national congress on February 15, 1926. This forced the monarchist government to schedule elections, which were held in May. The Wafd took 70 per cent of the seats and the Liberals 13 per cent. However, a Liberal, 'Adli Yakan, led the coalition government instead of Zaghlul. When Yakan resigned in 1927 another Liberal, 'Abd al-Khaliq Tharwat, led the government from April 1927 until March 1928. In the meantime, the Wafd Party suffered the loss of its leader in 1927. While Zaghlul had taken an increasingly moderate position in his relations with the British and the monarchists after 1925, his successor, Mustafa al-Nahhas, adopted a confrontational stance when he briefly held office in 1928. The king dismissed Nahhas, dissolved parliament, and selected a Liberal, Muhammad Mahmud, to rule in the absence of parliament from June 1928 until October 1929, when 'Adli took the premiership and supervised elections that brought the Wafd back to power in 1929.

The political divide between monarchists and nationalists explains the shifting balance of power between king and parliament. The return of an elected Wafd government with 90 per cent of the seats in parliament in 1929 resulted in a renewed contest between the monarchy and the parliament. As in 1924, the major issue was the question of treaty negotiations and the constitutional powers of the king. The Wafd's negotiating tactics alienated the British, who therefore tolerated the king's dissolution of the parliament and suspension of constitutional government in 1930. The king's instrument in this experiment in autocratic rule was Isma'il Sidqi, who rewrote the constitution in 1930 to make the ministers responsible to the king. As well, the electoral law was redrafted to restrict the franchise to a few, particularly the provincial landholding notability.

Sidqi created a People's Party (Hizb al-Sha'b) to muster votes in the elections of 1931, which were boycotted by the opposition parties and marred by violence. The parliament of 1931 consolidated the monarchist bloc, but lacked legitimacy. Sidqi reacted to violent attacks against his regime with decrees that silenced the press and gave the police emergency powers. These measures resulted in some prominent monarchists, such as 'Ali Mahir, breaking with the government. By 1933 Sidqi had lost the king's confidence and therefore resigned the premiership in September. Parliament was dissolved and the 1930 constitution rescinded. Afterward, the king ruled supreme through the ministries of 'Abd al-Fattah Yahya and Tawfiq Nasim.

In 1935 the Wafd convened a congress of opposition parties that called for a return to constitutional rule. The king appointed 'Ali Mahir to the premiership and restored the constitution of 1923. In April 1936 King Ahmad Fu'ad died and was succeeded by his son, Faruq. Elections were held in May and the Wafd took a majority of the seats in parliament. The premier of the Wafd government, Nahhas, successfully negotiated a treaty with the British in 1936. Meanwhile, 'Ali Mahir moved from the premiership to the head of the royal cabinet, where he sustained the autocratic vision of monarchy by exerting royal patronage through the normal channels, such as al-Azhar and the senate, as well as patronizing the military and an extreme right-wing organization, Young Egypt (Misr al-Fatat).

The last contest between an elected Wafd government and the monarchy in the period before the World War II revolved around the question of royal patronage over the military officers. Consequently, the place of the officer corps in politics was debated, as was the question of whether the allegiance of the officers belonged first to the king or the elected government. This debate, provoked by the issue of whether ultimate authority belonged to the king or parliament, also involved debates on the form and setting of the official coronation ceremony in 1937. The monarchists wanted the coronation to take place in a religious setting and the oath to follow a religious rather than secular formula. The resulting controversy brought about the dismissal of Nahhas from the premiership in December 1937. During the election of 1938 the Wafd Party split again, and the new Sa'dist Party formed a coalition government with the Liberal-Constitutional Party. Indicating the continuing role of the monarchy in politics, Mahmud was dismissed by Faruq in August 1939, and the prominent monarchist, 'Ali Mahir, was appointed to the premiership.

To conclude, during the interwar period the monarchy adopted a policy that stressed the advantages of authoritarianism over the instabilities of parliamentary politics. But parliament was nevertheless the new arena of politics. Under these conditions, the monarchy could not establish its supremacy over the dominant parliamentary party. The king patronized prominent politicians, but their shifting coalitions undermined the formation of a cohesive political opposition to the Wafd. Isma'il Sidqi and 'Ali Mahir introduced new tactics through constitutional and electoral revisions, as well as patronage over extraparliamentary constituencies, such as religious and military personnel. However, the revolution of 1952 indicated that neither religious nor military organizations could provide the monarchy with a sound base upon which to secure the dynasty as the symbol of a sovereign Egypt. Indeed much of the rivalry of the Wafd-led parliaments and the monarchy in the interwar years revolved around this fundamental issue of what the symbols and bases of political authority should be in modern Egypt.

JAMES WHIDDEN

See also: **Egypt: Nationalism, World War I and the Wafd, 1882–1922.**

Further Reading

Berque, J. *Egypt: Imperialism and Revolution.* London: Faber and Faber, 1972.

Binder, L. *In a Moment of Enthusiasm: Political Power and the Second Stratum.* Chicago: University of Chicago Press, 1978.

Deeb, M. *Party Politics in Egypt: The Wafd and Its Rivals 1919–1939.* London: Ithaca Press, 1978.

Kedourie, E. *The Chatham House Version and Other Middle Eastern Studies.* London: Wiedenfeld and Nicolson, 1970.

Rafi'i, 'Abd al-Rahman. *Fi a'qab al-thawra al-misriyya [In the Era of the Egyptian Revolution].* Cairo: Maktaba al-nahda al-misriyya, 1947–1951.

Sayyid-Marsot, Afaf Lutfi al-. *Egypt's Liberal Experiment 1922–1936.* Berkeley: University of California Press, 1977.

Tripp, C. "'Ali Mahir and the politics of the Egyptian army, 1936–1942." In *Contemporary Egypt: Through Egyptian Eyes,* edited by Charles Tripp. London: Routledge, 1993.

Vatikiotis, P.J. *The History of Modern Egypt: From Muhammad Ali to Sadat.* 2nd ed. London: Weidenfeld and Nicolson. 1980.

Egypt, World War II and

In 1922 Great Britain officially recognized Egypt's independence. This granting of independence, however, was not total; Britain attached four reservations to Egyptian independence that year. Britain reserved for itself the rights of security of imperial communications, protection of religious minorities and foreigners, a continued role in Sudan, and, perhaps most significantly, defense of Egypt from outside attack. The 1936 Anglo-Egyptian treaty reduced some British rights in Egypt (e.g., it abolished the office of high commissioner, set a date for abolishing the capitulations and consular courts, and gave the Egyptian government jurisdiction over non-Egyptians), but the agreement did not address the issue of Sudan and it reaffirmed British rights to defend the Suez Canal and to station troops in Egypt in the event of war.

When war came in 1939, Britain, within its rights according to the 1936 treaty, used Egypt as its main base in the Middle East. The British also forced King Faruq to sever relations with Hitler's Germany, and censorship was imposed. The use of Egypt as a major Allied base did have some short-term economic benefits, however. Expansion of industry and increased opportunities for employment resulted in bank deposits in Egypt almost tripling from 1940 to 1943. Yet neither the immediate economic profits of the war nor the fact that Britain was within its treaty rights to station troops in Egypt resulted in much support for the Allied cause. The massive influx of foreign troops was disruptive to Egyptian society, and it reminded the people that the country was not truly free. In fact, many Egyptians sympathized with the Axis, and throughout the Middle East, Arabs began to see the Axis as potential liberators. In February 1942 the strength of British influence and the weakness of the king were brought to light in a way no Egyptian could forget.

Prior to 1942 a series of prime ministers had been appointed and dismissed by the king. Prime ministers were either mildly pro-Axis or carefully neutral, but none were pro-British. When Husayn Sirri showed signs of Allied sympathies by severing relations with Vichy France in 1941, the king dismissed him. At this point, the British decided to put an abrupt end to pro-Axis governments. Former Prime Minister Ali Maher, known for his Axis leanings, was arrested and charged with espionage. More seriously, in February 1942, the king was given a choice by British Ambassador Sir Miles Lampson (by then Lord Killearn): either appoint a pro-British prime minister (meaning a prime minister from the nationalist Wafd Party) who would uphold the 1936 treaty or give up the throne. To demonstrate the seriousness of the British position, Lampson ordered British tanks to be stationed outside Abdin Palace, where the king was deliberating his next move, and went armed into the palace to hear Faruq's decision. Faruq, a practical man in this instance, decided to save his throne, and the Wafd was brought back to power, just as German forces (under the command of Erwin Rommel) were preparing to invade.

Rommel had come to North Africa in 1941 as the commander of the German Afrika Korps. Initially sent to assist the weak and almost defeated Italian army in Libya, Rommel's successful attacks earned him the nickname the "Desert Fox" and a promotion to field marshal from Adolf Hitler. In 1942 Hitler, who had never seen North Africa as an important theater of war, nonetheless commanded Rommel to invade Egypt and take Cairo. Although Rommel had repeatedly requested rest for his troops and warned Hitler that supply lines were weak, the invasion began. Rommel's troops met with initial success but were defeated by the British at the battle of el-Alamein, about sixty miles outside the coastal city of Alexandria.

The British victory at el-Alamein did not generate much enthusiasm in Egypt, however. The incident at the Abdin Palace had aroused widespread contempt for the king, resentment against the Wafd, and further hatred of the British. Whereas the Wafd previously had been seen as the party of the nation, the incident discredited it in the eyes of many nationalists and it was seen increasingly as the party of the British. The economic benefits brought by the onset of the war began to dissipate, and this too resulted in widespread discontent. Though some Egyptians profited from the war, most (including the peasantry) suffered. Inflation was rampant, poverty rates rose, wheat shipments in Cairo in 1942 were attacked by starving mobs, and unemployment skyrocketed after the withdrawal of Allied forces after the war.

The poor economic conditions and unpleasant political situation during the war increased the popularity of the Muslim Brotherhood, a socioreligious group originally founded in 1928. The Brotherhood became increasingly political by the 1930s; by the 1940s it had transformed itself from a religious reformist movement to a militant opposition group. Wartime conditions also fostered the growth of two other alternative political movements: the communists and the Young Egypt Party (*Misr al-Fatat*). Until 1942 the communist movement in Egypt had been fairly weak, its popularity confined largely to non-Muslim intellectuals. The Soviet Union's entry into World War II, combined with Egypt's economic deterioration, gave the communists greater (though still relatively limited) prominence. The Young Egypt Party was founded by Ahmad Husayn before the war and was initially modeled on Italian and German fascist groups. Called by the nickname "the greenshirts," Husayn's organization gained adherents during the war. After the defeat of Nazi Germany, the organization changed ideologies, first becoming the Islamic Nationalist Party and then adopting socialism as its philosophy. Like the communists, though, Husayn's group in all its manifestations never succeeded in gaining enough support to pose a credible threat to the government.

Immediately after the war and in part as a result of its effects, more attention began to be paid to the idea of social and economic reform in Egypt. In the wake of massive unemployment, inflation, and greater awareness of the plight of the peasantry (some 1.2 million of

whom had had to file for tax exemption due to poverty in 1942), more debates were held, speeches made, projects and plans formulated, statistics kept, and studies conducted into social and economic conditions, particularly in the countryside. Urban workers' strikes became more commonplace, in part due to the efforts of the communist movement, and demonstrations frequently became violent. Even though various government agencies sought to address the social and economic crises of the nation that the war had highlighted and though some progress was made, significant changes did not come until several years after the war, when, in 1952, a military coup under the direction of Colonel Gamel Abdel Nasser overthrew the corrupt and ineffective government of King Faruq and began instituting a series of domestic social and economic reforms.

AMY J. JOHNSON

Further Reading

Beinin, J., and Z. Lockman. *Workers on the Nile: Nationalism, Communism, Islam and the Egyptian Working Class, 1882–1954*. Princeton: Princeton University Press, 1987.

Berque, J. *Imperialism and Revolution*. London: Faber and Faber, 1972.

Delaney, J. *Fighting the Desert Fox: Rommel's Campaigns in North Africa, April 1941 to August 1942*. London: Arms and Armour, 1998.

Gershoni, I., and J. P. Jankowski. *Redefining the Egyptian Nation, 1930–1945*. New York : Cambridge University Press, 1995.

Kriebel, R. *Inside the Afrika Korps: The Crusader Battles, 1941–1942*. London: Greenhill Books, 1999.

Egypt: Printing, Broadcasting

Egypt has had a periodical press since Napoleon founded *Le Courrier de l'Égypte* and *La Décade égyptienne* in 1798. The official journal, *al-Waqâi' al-misriyya*, began publication in 1828. The introduction of the telegraph and steamships into Egypt aided the dissemination of news. The first privately published Arabic newspaper was 'Abdallâh Abû al-Su'ûd's *Wâdî al-Nîl* (1866). Many daily, weekly, and monthly periodicals, both in Arabic and in European languages, followed, reaching an early peak during the 'Urâbî revolution of 1881–1882. The British occupation briefly halted the growth of the press, but by 1895 Arabic newspapers and magazines were burgeoning. Mustafâ Kâmil showed in publishing *al-Liwâ* that journalism could inspire nationalist resistance to British rule. Periodicals also appeared, such as *al-Hilâl* and *al-Muqtataf*, which promoted the spread of science. Others advocated feminism, moderate reform (e.g., *al-Jarîda*), and support for the khedive (e.g., *al-Muayyad*) and for the British (e.g., *al-Muqattam*). Martial law in World War I closed many newspapers and magazines, but in 1919 journalistic activity resumed, aided in part by the introduction of the linotype typesetter and wireless telegraphy. Political parties played a major role in the growth of newspapers, with *al-Akhbâr* and later *al-Misrî* serving as organs for the Wafd Party and *al-Siyâsa* for the Constitutional Liberals.

Fearing that journalistic license would threaten public order and its own control, the Egyptian government tried to limit what journalists could print. In its 1881 Press Law, the regime was permitted to suppress an Egyptian newspaper or periodical "in the interests of order, morality, and religion" on the interior minister's orders after two previous reprimands or on a decision by the cabinet without any prior warning, in which case the offending paper could also be fined £E5 to £E20. The law was rigorously enforced at first, but newspapers discovered that foreign owners or editors could claim immunity from the law under the Capitulations, and so the government stopped trying to enforce it in 1894. Its revival in 1909, directed against the excesses of the nationalist press, aroused protests by Egyptians and foreigners, who again used the Capitulations to impede its enforcement. The cabinet stiffened press laws as part of the its efforts to clamp down on opposition after Prime Minister Butros Ghâlî was murdered in 1910. Severe limitations on press freedom were imposed during World War I and lifted slightly after the 1919 revolution. The Press Law was reactivated by 'Abd al-Khâliq Tharwat in 1922, by Sa'd Zaghlûl in 1924, and by Muhammad Mahmûd in 1929, often to curb press criticism from rival parties.

The 1952 revolution, which brought Jamâl 'Abd al-Nâsir to power, led to ownership of the press by the government or by mobilizational parties controlled by the state, such as the National Union from 1958 to 1962 and the Arab Socialist Union from 1962 to 1978. The number of daily newspapers declined, but their circulation was greatly expanded, in part by keeping down the price of an issue. Their content became propagandistic and subject to state censorship, but the major dailies, especially *al-Ahrâm*, published works by leading short-story writers, poets, and scholars. Literary and academic journals also flourished during the Nâsir era, but fell into desuetude under Sâdât. Religious periodicals have grown in popularity, but the literary and political content of Egypt's periodical press has declined. Foreign-language publications decreased with the flight of foreigners from Egypt under Nâsir but revived during the presidency of Husnî Mubârak. Political and religious censorship still hobbles journalistic creativity in today's Egypt.

Radio transmission was introduced into Egypt by the British armed forces during World War I. By the late 1920s, some private citizens in Alexandria and Cairo owned radio receivers and even transmitters, but the government closed all private stations in 1931 and

in 1932 chartered its own system. In 1934 the Cairo studios of the Egyptian Broadcasting Service, built by the Marconi Company with BBC help, were formally opened. Because foreigners owned a large percentage of the radio receivers in Egypt, the initial formula of 70 per cent Arabic and 30 per cent foreign-language programs did not work well, and special stations were set aside for European broadcasts. The early Arabic broadcasting stressed Qurân reading and Arab music, European shows were mainly BBC relays, and all programs were kept free from politics and advertising. By 1937 Egyptian broadcasts could be heard in Palestine, Syria, and Iraq. The Egyptian government took over the ownership and management of the service in 1947. By 1950 Egyptian State Broadcasting was transmitting programs in Arabic, English, Greek, and Italian, and there were 260,000 radios in the country. This number would increase by 1975 to 4.9 million radio sets and to an estimated 16.4 million in 1990. In 1982 Egypt's home service was broadcasting in Arabic, English, French, Armenian, German, Greek, Italian, and Hebrew. Its foreign service included broadcasts in twenty-eight languages (many of them African); this figure reached thirty-two in 1991. Egyptian state radio was notorious during Nâsir's presidency for its tendentious broadcasts, inspiring Arabs in other countries to oppose their own governments. Since 1970, however, government stations broadcast mainly Arabic music, some situation comedies, informational programs, and hourly news. There are regional programs designed for specific areas of the country. A new commercial radio service, provided by the Société Égyptienne de Publicité, opened during the 1990s.

In 1960 Egypt became the third Arab country to begin television broadcasting. Nâsir used television as well as radio to reach the people, many of whom were illiterate. The culture ministry installed public television receivers in cities and villages, although Egyptians flocked to buy private sets as soon as they became available. It is estimated that 550,000 television receivers were in use in 1970, 1.1 million in 1978, and 5 million in 1990. In 1991, the Egyptian television organization had two main and three regional channels, presenting forty-two hours combined of daily programming. News, music, educational programs, and situation comedies (American as well as Egyptian) predominate, but religious programs are growing more popular. State-owned television faces competition from videocassettes and from rooftop dishes capable of receiving signals from satellites transmitting other countries' programs. A privately owned television channel, Nile TV, began broadcasting in the 1990s.

ARTHUR GOLDSCHMIDT JR.

See also: **Press: Northern Africa.**

Further Reading

Ayalon, A. *The Press in the Arab Middle East: A History.* New York: Oxford University Press, 1995.

Boyd, D. A. *Broadcasting in the Arab World: A Survey of the Electronic Media in the Middle East.* 2nd ed. Ames: Iowa State University Press, 1993.

Hartmann, M. *The Arabic Press of Egypt.* London: Luzac, 1899.

McFadden, T. J. *Daily Journalism in the Arab States.* Columbus: Ohio State University Press, 1953.

Nasir, M. *Press, Politics and Power: Egypt's Heikal and al-Ahram.* Ames: Iowa State University Press, 1979.

Egypt: Nasser: Foreign Policy: Suez Canal Crisis to Six Day War, 1952–1970

Gamal Abdel Nasser's tenure of power in Egypt, from the military coup d'état that he initiated in July 1952 until his death in 1970, was punctuated by both remarkable foreign policy triumphs and shattering failures. Many of them reverberated well beyond the Middle East, even involving Egypt in momentous Cold War confrontations. That the Nasser government would involve itself in foreign affairs was entirely predictable. Nationalist struggles to force the British army of occupation to evacuate Egypt and Egypt's military defeat in the war against Israel in 1948 had undermined the legitimacy of Egypt's parliamentary leadership and inspired the young military officers to seize power in 1952. Once in office, Nasser and his fellow officers made it obvious that their primary goal was the achievement of full-scale political independence. This desire exceeded even their well-publicized proposals to promote economic development and rid the country of its grinding poverty and lack of education. Achieving political independence meant, first and foremost, removing the large British army, numbering nearly 100,000 men, that was housed in a massive military base along the Suez Canal.

The British, often with the backing of the United States, were not eager to withdraw. From the outset of the British occupation of Egypt in 1882, they had turned the country into the strategic and military lynchpin of their empire. Withdrawal, in a very real sense, meant loss of imperial greatness. In addition, the British were anxious to press Egypt into a British-dominated Middle Eastern military alliance, designed to thwart the expansionist tendencies of the Soviet Union in an area of crucial importance to Europe and the rest of the Western world because of its large oil resources. Yet, on October 19, 1954, under constant threats of guerrilla attacks on their forces, the British agreed to evacuate their forces, thus securing for the Nasser regime its most cherished goal: political independence.

Within a matter of a mere four months from the date at which all British soldiers were to be withdrawn from Egypt, British troops, in league with French and Israeli forces, were on their way back into the country. The ostensible reason for the invasion of the country at the end of October and the beginning of November 1956 was Nasser's decision to nationalize the Suez Canal Company. Nasser's actions followed the British-American–World Bank announcement that the West would no longer be willing to finance one of Nasser's favorite projects: the construction of a huge hydroelectric and irrigation dam south of the already existing Aswan dam. In reality, other factors produced the invasion. A number of British officials in the Tory Party, including Prime Minister Anthony Eden, wanted to reassert imperial ambitions. They had come to regard Nasser as a threat to British interests throughout the Middle East. The French were enraged at Egypt's support of the Algerian war of independence while the Israelis feared Nasser's growing popularity in the Arab world and his agreement in 1955 to purchase arms from the Soviet bloc, which they feared that Egypt would use against them.

The tripartite invasion proved to be a military and political disaster for its initiators and a stunning success for Nasser. Condemned by the world community, including the leadership of the United States and the Soviet Union, the British and French governments had no choice but to call a halt to their military operations along the Suez Canal zone before they had been brought to a conclusion. The Israeli forces had swept through the Sinai virtually unchecked and reached the east bank of the Suez Canal, but like the British and French, they, too, had to abandon their military plans and to withdraw their forces from Egyptian soil. Without engaging in any sustained military action, Nasser and the Egyptians had achieved an incredible political triumph. They had repulsed once great European imperialist powers and foiled the Israeli plans to undermine the regime's legitimacy. Nasser basked in the region's praise as his reputation for astute political leadership and his championship of pan-Arabism gained numerous new followers.

Nasser's promotion of Pan-Arab goals was put to the test sooner than he anticipated and would have liked. In February 1958, as communist elements were becoming a more powerful force in the Syrian state, leading Pan-Arab politicians and military officers to approach the Egyptian leadership with a proposal for the unification of their two countries. While believing that the time was not yet ripe for a union of Egypt and Syria, in part because Egypt was preoccupied with its own internal development, Nasser agreed to the creation of the United Arab Republic because he feared that without such a union Syria could fall into a state of anarchy or drift into the Soviet camp.

Nasser's fears that a political unification of Arab countries was premature proved entirely correct. The

471

main reason for the dissolution of the United Arab Republic in September 1961, however, was the overbearing attitude of the Egyptian leaders to their Syrian counterparts. In what was meant to be a union of equals, Egypt dominated the Syrian leadership. Hence, when, in July 1961, the Egyptian government introduced a series of radical socialist laws into Syria, conservative, pro-capitalist elements in that country could tolerate Egyptian authority no longer. Supported by aggrieved civil servants and a discontented Syrian military leadership, they ousted the Egyptian civil and military leaders and reclaimed their country's autonomy. The break-up of the UAR did not, however, cause Nasser to abandon his Pan-Arab aspirations. In 1962, the Egyptian army intervened in a Yemeni civil war, sending upwards of 50,000 troops to support the new republican regime there against the monarchy that it had overthrown. The war dragged on for five years and the Egyptian forces suffered great loss of life.

Nasser's reputation, tarnished in Syria and Yemen, suffered a nearly fatal blow in the Six Day War in 1967. In 1956, when the Israeli forces withdrew from Sinai, the United Nations agreed to place military observers along the Israeli-Egyptian border as a way to defuse the tensions between the two countries. The presence of observers brought the desired reduction of tensions until 1967, when, under pressure from other Arab countries and provided misinformation by their Soviet allies about Israeli intentions to attack Syria, the Egyptians demanded the withdrawal of the UN observers, threatening to close off the Strait of Tiran at the mouth of the Gulf of Aqaba to Israeli shipping. The United Nations complied, and immediately the Middle East was thrust into a crisis. Unwilling to wait for diplomatic interventions or to expose their peoples to attacks from Arab military forces, the Israelis launched a preemptive military strike against Egypt on June 5, 1967, destroying virtually the whole of the Egyptian air force on the ground. In the few days of ground warfare that followed, Israeli armored and infantry divisions overran Sinai all the way to the east bank of the Suez Canal. The Israeli Defense Forces also seized the Golan Heights, and, when toward the end of the war Jordanian troops entered in support of their fellow Arab countries, the Israelis took East Jerusalem and the entire west bank of the Jordan River, previously in the hands of the government of Jordan.

It is hardly any wonder that the Six Day War has gone down in Arab history as the *nakba*, or the "catastrophe." The Arab armies were soundly defeated, and the governments of Egypt, Syria, and Jordan lost vital territories to the Israelis. The Egyptian military performance was so abysmal that President Nasser publicly offered his resignation. Even though the people of the country turned out in huge numbers to demand that

he withdraw the resignation and remain their leader, his reputation as a shrewd man of affairs, able to manipulate the major powers and enhance Egypt's place in the world, was never repaired. It was only his successor, Anwar al-Sadat, who won back Sinai from the Israelis.

ROBERT L. TIGNOR

Further Reading

Brands, H. W. *Into the Labyrinth: The United States and the Middle East, 1945–1993.* New York: McGraw-Hill, 1994.

Kerr, M. *The Arab Cold War: Gamal Abd al-Nasir and his Rivals, 1958–1970.* Oxford: Royal Institute of International Affairs by Oxford University Press, 1971.

Oren, M. B. *Six Days of War: June 1967 and the Making of the Modern Middle East.* Oxford and New York: Oxford University Press, 2002.

Seale, P. *The Struggle for Syria: A Study of Post-War Arab Politics, 1945–1958.* Oxford: Oxford University Press, 1965.

Waterbury, J. *The Egypt of Nasser and Sadat: The Political Economy of Two Regimes.* Princeton: Princeton University Press, 1983.

Egypt: Nasser: High Dam, Economic Development, 1952–1970

The Egyptian military leaders who seized power in 1952 were committed to promoting the economic development of the country. In their view (confirmed by numerous statistical indicators), the country had lagged badly behind economically. Countless Egyptians were living in a state of acute distress, and one of the reasons that the Free Officers—whose acknowledged leader was the young Colonel Gamal Abdel Nasser—had ousted the parliamentary regime and sent the much maligned King Faruq into exile was to provide new economic initiatives. The entire Egyptian elite, including those who were removed from power and those who now occupied the seats of authority, recognized that Egyptians would have to diversify their economy and make industry as vital a part of the country's production as agriculture.

The Egyptian economy has always depended upon the Nile waters, without which the country would be little more than the easternmost extension of the Sahara desert. Hence, not surprisingly, plans for the economic diversification and industrialization of the country were linked to a more efficient use of the Nile River. Prior to the nineteenth century, Egypt relied on the annual Nile flood for its agriculture, but beginning with the modernizing ruler Muhammad Ali (1805–1848), hydraulic engineers had begun to build dams across the Nile capable of carrying irrigation waters from run-off canals, so that cultivators would be able to harvest two and three crops per year where they had once grown only one. This system, called perennial irrigation, led to a large increase in cultivable lands during the nineteenth century and made it possible for Egypt to become the world's leading exporter of high-staple cotton. But it was clear by the end of World War II that Egypt needed to make even more efficient use of the Nile waters and to use any dam or dams that it constructed to generate cheap and large electrical supplies for industrialization. The country already had a large dam at Aswan, dating from the turn of the century, which had been heightened in the 1930s and equipped with electrical generating capacity. But with a rapidly expanding population, more irrigation water and more abundant electricity were desperately needed as the country entered the post–World War II period.

Of the many different plans laid before the government, the one that had the greatest appeal to the Egyptian rulers (civilian and military alike) was that put forward by a Greek engineer, Adrian Daninos, who proposed the construction of a massive dam just south of the one standing at Aswan that would be capable of holding back enough of the Nile waters to introduce perennial irrigation throughout the entire country, and even to reclaim land from the desert. The dam would also be equipped with a series of electricity-generating turbines, yielding abundant and cheap supplies of electricity to light the whole country and spur its industrial development. For many intensely nationalist Egyptians, the most attractive feature of the Aswan dam scheme was that it would be constructed inside Egypt. Hence, its water would be stored in Egypt, under Egyptian control, rendering Egypt independent of other Nile riverine powers for its economic well-being.

Egypt lacked the financial resources, estimated at more than $500 million and destined to grow, as well as the technical capabilities to construct the dam on its own. The leaders looked to the outside for help, and at first received a warm welcome from the United States and Great Britain. In July 1956, just as the Egyptians were preparing to sign an agreement with the United States, Britain, and the World Bank for the financing of the dam and for its construction by Western electrical and hydraulic firms, the American Secretary of State, John Foster Dulles, announced that the United States, Britain, and the World Bank had changed their minds and were no longer willing to finance the building of the dam. The official reason that he offered for the change of mind was that, given Egypt's record of financial profligacy, the country would not be able to handle such a big project with its attendant high level of indebtedness. In reality, Dulles had decided to punish the Egyptians for having purchased arms from Czechoslovakia in 1955, and to demonstrate to other countries that the United States would not tolerate overtures to its Cold War opponents. Nasser's riposte occurred on July 26, 1956, when he announced his decision to nationalize the Suez Canal Company and to use the receipts from the canal traffic to finance the building of the dam. Shortly thereafter, he signed agreements with the Soviet Union for the necessary financing and technical assistance for the dam.

The Soviet Union did oversee the construction of the Aswan dam, which was not finished until January 15, 1971, shortly after Nasser's death, at a total cost of close to $1 billion. As Nasser and the other Egyptian leaders had hoped, the dam spurred the industrialization and economic progress of the country, but in decidedly Soviet-influenced directions. The program of industrialization carried out during the Nasser years drew heavily on Soviet models rather than Western ones and involved state interventions in the country's economic activities. Following the British-French-Israeli invasion of 1956, the government nationalized those business companies that had been owned by British, French, and Egyptian Jewish citizens. In 1961 it took over Belgian-run firms, and then steadily throughout the 1960s, the state increased its control over all branches of the industrial sector. By the time of Nasser's death, virtually all of the country's large-scale business firms in industry, finance, and commerce were state-owned. The Nasser government also carried out substantial land reform schemes in the 1950s and l960s, resulting in the redistribution of large landed estates to small holders and setting the ceiling of any individual holding at fifty feddans (roughly 50 acres). By grouping nearly all Egyptian cultivators into state-dominated agricultural cooperatives, whose members were required to grow those commodities determined by the state and to sell their produce to state-owned purchasing and distributing firms, the state also became Egypt's primary economic agent in the agricultural sector. At the time of Nasser's death in 1970 the private sector had become so weakened that it operated only in small-scale business operations.

Nasser's economic programs did achieve many impressive goals. Income was substantially redistributed. From a country that had been characterized by gross disparities in wealth between a tiny landed and business elite and a large, impoverished peasantry and unemployed or partially employed urban population, the country now provided educational and occupation opportunities for an expanding middle class. Yet its state-run industries were highly inefficient. They failed to break into the international markets as the advocates of industrialization had hoped. The new Aswan dam had permitted the expansion of arable land, but a large segment of the Egyptian peasantry still lived at or even below the poverty line. In short, the Nasser years had enabled Egypt to keep pace economically with a population expanding at the high rate of close to 3 per cent per annum and even to provide better social services for more of its people, but they had not launched the country into the kind of sustained economic development that Nasser and the other young military officers who had seized power in 1952 had envisioned.

ROBERT TIGNOR

See also: **Egypt: Muhammad Ali, 1805–1849: State and Economy; Suez Canal.**

Further Reading

Brands, H. W. *Into the Labyrinth: The United State and the Middle East, 1945–1993.* New York: McGraw-Hill, 1994.

Collins, R. O. *The Waters of the Nile: Hydropolitics and the Jonglei Canal, 1900–1988.* Oxford: Oxford University Press, 1990.

Mabro, R. *The Egyptian Economy, 1952–1972.* Oxford: Clarendon Press, 1974.

Tignor, R. L. *Capitalism and Nationalism at the End of Empire: State and Business in Decolonizing Egypt, Nigeria, and Kenya, 1945–1963.* Princeton, N.J.: Princeton University Press, 1998.

Waterbury, J. *Hydropolitics of the Nile Valley.* Syracuse, N.Y.: Syracuse University Press, 1979.

Egypt: Sadat, Nationalism, 1970–1981

In the aftermath of the overthrow of the monarchy in Egypt in 1952 by the Free Officers, under the leadership of Gamal Abdel Nasser, Egypt reemerged as an important actor on the world stage. As one of the major figures in the post–World War II nonaligned movement, Nasser emerged as a spokesperson of the aspirations of millions in the Arab world and Africa by championing Pan-Arab and Pan-African anti-imperialist sentiments. Even when faced with problems of his country's exploding population and limited natural resources, Nasser refused to let his government become dependent on a single superpower. Instead, he implemented a policy of developmental socialism geared toward total self-sufficiency (*iktifaa dhaati*).

However, by the time of his death in 1970, many Egyptians had begun to question some aspects of Nasser's policies due to the country's mounting debts spurred by enormous military spending and increasing economic problems. Anwar al-Sadat, who had been one of the original Free Officers and had served as Nasser's vice-president from 1964 to 1967 and again from 1969 to 1970, assumed the reins of power in accordance with constitutional procedure.

Immediately upon taking office, a new phase in Egyptian politics was ushered in by Sadat. He introduced a "revolution of rectification," which involved new political, economic, and foreign policy initiatives Sadat believed were needed to correct the errors of his predecessor. A master of timing, Sadat took bold steps at unexpected times to advance Egypt's regional and international image.

Egypt had been renamed the United Arab Republic in 1958 when Egypt and Syria, inspired by radical Arab nationalism, formed their ill-fated union. Sadat, anxious to jettison the ideological and political baggage of radical Arab nationalism, created the compromise name, the Arab Republic of Egypt, in 1971.

The first major act by Sadat was the expulsion of 15,000 Soviet advisers in 1972, even though they were training his army and supplying all his military equipment. His objective was to reduce Egypt's dependency on a single foreign power. As he calculated, the United States was eager to come to his aid.

In October 1973 Sadat ordered his forces to cross the Suez Canal in a surprise attack that broke through Israeli defense lines in occupied Sinai. With Syrian forces invading Israel from the east, through the Golan Heights, the coordinated attacks drove the Israelis back with heavy casualties on both fronts. Even though the Israelis eventually regrouped and won back most of the lost ground, Sadat had shattered Israel's image of invincibility.

The October 1973 war did offset the legacies of the 1967 war. The October confrontation was seen by Egyptians as a conflict that was forced upon them in order to remind the international community that the Middle East problem needed urgent attention. It was not a war that Egypt fought for conquest. Instead, it was a war designed to change political perceptions. In the process, the Egyptians restored their national honor by regaining some of their territory and by avoiding defeat.

The sense that the 1973 war restored Egypt's honor had a powerful impact on Sadat's capacity to enter into negotiations with Israel. By declaring victory, Sadat was able to convince his fellow Egyptians that the next phase of the Arab-Israeli conflict must be fought on the diplomatic front. Relying on the United States to promote an honorable peace settlement with Israel, Sadat, over the next six years, became the leading champion of peace in Egypt and in the Arab world.

In November 1973, Sadat addressed a hushed meeting of the People's Assembly and declared his intention to visit Israel and launch his peace initiative. His successes in foreign policy, leading to the 1979 Camp David peace treaty between Egypt and Israel, boosted Sadat's prestige in the international community. Sadat's status as peacemaker was confirmed that same year when he and Menachem Begin of Israel were awarded the Nobel Peace Prize.

In 1974 Sadat launched a new program for postwar economic recovery he called *infitaah* ("opening"). It was an open-door policy designed to end Nasser's state-run socialist system. Foreign investors were encouraged with tax exemptions to invest in Egypt; foreign experts were enticed to bring their technological knowledge to help develop industries; and modest measures were implemented to relax official constraints imposed on management of the public sector and the small private sector, particularly in construction, finance, and tourism. For Sadat, *infitaah*, properly implemented, would be the economic miracle Egypt needed.

However, *infitaah* did not bring back the free market. Instead, it slowly prepared Egypt for such an eventuality. Rather than withdraw, the government continued to weigh heavily on the economy and the productive process in general. The private sector was kept out of large areas of industrial activities. In addition, government expanded rather than decline; government expenditure went up sharply, and public employment increased precipitously.

By the end of the 1970s, only a few foreign banks had opened overseas branches in Egypt. Consequently, foreign investors responded slowly and in a limited way. Afloat with cash from external sources, the consumer goods market boomed and conspicuous consumption sullied *infitaah*. Another major development was that the Egyptian economy rapidly moved toward a rentier system: that is, an increase in revenue from foreign aid, remittances from expatriates, Suez Canal fees, tourism, and oil royalties.

In 1976 Sadat launched what seemed to be an initiative for a multiparty system when he declared that three ideological "platforms" would be organized within the Arab Socialist Union (ASU). With Sadat's personal support, the centrist group, the Egyptian Arab Socialist Organization (EASO), won a vast majority of the seats in that year's parliamentary election. Nevertheless, Sadat refused to allow the formation of independent parties. As a consequence, the three organizations never took root as genuine vehicles of political participation. Violent clashes over increased prices of basic commodities in January 1977 forced Sadat to allow parties to be formed. As the opposition by these parties became too strong for Sadat, he clamped down on such groups as the New Wafd Party and the leftist National Progressive Unionist Party.

In July 1978 Sadat inaugurated the national Democratic Party (NDP) and later allowed a leftist party to organize as an official opposition. In April 1980, both the EASO and the ASU were abolished. The functions of the old ASU were now being carried out by the newly created Advisory Council. In the September 1980 elections, Sadat's new NDP won all 140 seats, with the 70 remaining posts being appointed directly by Sadat. Like his predecessor, Nasser, Sadat wanted to create a political organization but was unable to tolerate the loss of political power that would ensue if these parties were to become vehicles for mass participation.

Sadat's increasingly authoritarian rule, as well as his abandonment of socialism and foreign policy initiatives, made him a marked man for many opponents. And in 1981, he was assassinated at the age of sixty-three. Earlier that year, Sadat had had about 1,600 people arrested in what was dubbed a massive crackdown on religious unrest. However, in addition to religious leaders, many journalists, lawyers, intellectuals, provincial governors, and leaders of the country's small but growing political parties were also arrested. Since many of those arrested were not even connected with any fundamentalist Islamic movement, most Egyptians believed that Sadat had overreacted. At that point, he had lost the support of his people. In contrast to Nasser's funeral, Sadat's saw only few tears. Most of the people who attended Sadat's funeral were foreign dignitaries, as most of his fellow citizens opted to stay home.

ABDUL KARIM BANGURA

Biography

Anwar al-Sadat was born into a family of thirteen children in 1918 at Mit Abul Kom, a village in the River Nile delta forty miles to the north of Cairo. Graduated from the Egyptian Military Academy in 1938. Joined Gamal Abdel Nasser and other young military officers in the Free Officers, a secret organization that worked to overthrow the Egyptian monarch and rid the country of British influence. Imprisoned during the 1940s for his revolutionary activities. After the successful coup, held a series of important government positions, including serving as vice-president of Egypt from 1964 to 1967 and again from 1969 to 1970. On October 6, 1981, Sadat and government leaders were reviewing an armed forces parade in Cairo to mark the eighth anniversary of the Crossing (i.e., the October 1973 war) when a group of young military men belonging to *al takfir wal hijra* ("Repentance and Flight from Sin," a secret group that advocates the establishment of a pure Islamic society in Egypt—by violence, if necessary) assassinated him.

Further Reading

Baker, R. *Egypt's Uncertain Revolution under Nasser and Sadat*, Cambridge, Mass.: Harvard University Press, 1978.

Bangura, Abdul Karim *The Effects of American Foreign Aid to Egypt, 1957–1987*, Lewiston, N.Y.: Mellen Press, 1995.

Burrell, R. Michael and Kelider, Abbas. *Egypt: The Dilemmas of a Nation, 1970–1977* (The Washington Papers, #. 48), London: Sage Publications, 1977.

Cooper, M. N. *The Transformation of Egypt*. Baltimore: Johns Hopkins University Press, 1982.

Dawisha, A. *Egypt in the Arab World: The Elements of Foreign Policy*, London: MacMillan, 1976.

Harik, I. *Economic Policy Reform in Egypt*. Gainesville; University Press of Florida, 1997.

Hirst, D. and Beeson, I. *Sadat*. London: Faber and Faber, 1981.

Hopwood, D. *Egypt: Politics and Society 1945–1981*. London: George Allen and Unwin, 1982.

Sadat, A. *In Search of Identity*. New York: Harper and Row, 1977.

Shoukri, G. *Egypt: Portrait of a President*. London: Zed Press, 1981.

Egypt: Mubarak, Since 1981: Agriculture, Industry

Hosni Mubarak inherited the "Open-Door Economic Policy" from his predecessor, President Anwar al-Sadat. The economic opening was a measure intended to encourage the private sector of the economy, particularly foreign, Arab, and Western investment and export-led growth. When the Arab states withdrew financial aid after the peace with Israel in 1979, the United States became the main source of aid, amounting to $20 billion between 1979 and 1987. U.S. aid was negotiated through the World Bank and International Monetary Fund (IMF), which applied pressure on Egypt to induce economic liberalization; for instance, the system of state subsidies on domestic food prices was first targeted in 1977. The logic was to bring market forces to bear upon the prices of agricultural commodities, which would in theory stimulate the development of profitable agricultural development in Egypt. It also meant increasing the cost of food for the average Egyptian household. In 1977 this resulted in a popular revolt, the first of a series of warnings that Egyptian society would not accept a complete dismantling of the socialist inheritance. After the revolt, price controls were reintroduced. From 1981 Mubarak avoided disruptive economic reforms, but with an economic downturn in 1986 the IMF and the United States Agency for International Development made further aid conditional on liberal, economic reform. Begun in 1990, the "Economic Reform and Structural Adjustment Program" only became effective after the IMF halved the Egyptian debt to $20 billion in 1993.

Egyptian indebtedness was the result of state-led, public sector development, the armaments build-up from the Nasser through the Mubarak eras, and the inability of agricultural production to keep pace with the rise of population. In the 1980s and 1990s agricultural production increased at a rate of 2 per cent while population increased at a rate of 2.7 per cent annually. While the Aswan Dam increased the size of arable land from six to eight million feddans (a feddan is about an acre), Egyptians inhabited only 4 per cent of their overall territory. With a population of nearly 70 million at the end of the twentieth century, Egypt had one of the highest birth rates in the world, increasing at a rate of one million every ten months. It was necessary for Egypt to import 80 per cent of its food in the 1990s.

In 1994 structural adjustments to improve productivity in the rural sector began to reverse Nasser's land reforms, perhaps the most significant legacy of the socialist era. But the rural peasantry, which constituted three-quarters of the population in 1952, was a much smaller percentage of the population at the end of the century. Population increase, however, meant that overall greater numbers lived off the scarce land resource, approximately half the total population at the end of the century.

An important legacy of the Nasser era was a developmental strategy that favored the urban sector and heavy industry over the rural sector of the economy. This developmental bias had a negative impact upon Egypt's agricultural sector; as a result, there was a relative decline of the once lucrative cotton industry. By 1980 cotton accounted for only 14 per cent of Egypt's total export earnings, falling from 66 per cent in 1960. Oil replaced cotton as the major export from the 1960s, accounting for 58 per cent of Egypt's export earnings in 1980. The development of the oil refining industry had been a cornerstone of Nasser's development policies and provided Sadat and Mubarak with an important source of foreign currency. But the oil industry did not favor the development of an integrated domestic economy; hence the term rent was applied to income from oil, as it was to the revenues of the Suez Canal. By the 1980s these two types of rent provided Egypt with $4 billion annually, before the price of oil collapsed in 1986. The other important sources of foreign currency were tourism, remittance payments of migrant workers in the oil-rich Arab states, and foreign loans. Privatization was applied first of all to the tourist industry, which brought revenues of $1 to $2 billion before the tourist industry collapsed in 1997. Oil, tourism, and migrant labor indicated Egypt's growing dependence upon foreign markets in this period.

Egyptian dependency was compounded by the concentration of domestic, private sector development in industries of short-term returns, such as tourism and real estate development, as opposed to long-term industrial or agricultural development. Likewise, domestic savings were unproductive because private sector developers and investors preferred to invest profits safely overseas. The remittances of Egypt's migrant workers represent a different but no less unproductive economic trend, because their savings were invested in the Islamic investment companies, which eschewed "usurious" banking and financial institutions. Similarly, state revenue went into subsidies for agricultural commodities rather than more productive development. Therefore, the economy continued to be characterized by state-led redistribution of subsidized food, which strangled producers and importers on the "open," private sector market. But the Egyptian food processing industry flourished, profiting from the protected market created by the subsidy system. The armaments industries also profited from the expertise and assistance of the United States, Egypt's major strategic ally, as well as the market for arms created by the Iran-Iraq War in the 1980s.

One of the most heavily populated regions in the world, Egypt had a demography complicated by rural-to-urban migration, a signal feature of twentieth-century Egypt. Urbanization served as a release for impoverished, rural Egyptians. Moreover, educational policies favored urbanization, because industrial development was stressed at the expense of the traditional, rural sector. Cairo's expansion was phenomenal: a population increase of fifteenfold in the course of the twentieth century against a twofold increase in the rural sector. At the end of the twentieth century, half of Egypt's population was urban, and Cairo accounted for 70 per cent of that urban population. Rapid urbanization did not bring social improvement. Forty per cent of Cairo's population lived below the poverty line at the end of the 1980s. The Egyptian authorities invested in food subsidies and urban infrastructure to alleviate the problems of massive urbanization. Yet, even while consuming 45 per cent of Egypt's food supply, Cairo's food requirements in the mid-1990s could hardly be met. Likewise, Cairo's consumption of water exceeded the drainage capacity of the system. The incapacity of Egypt's infrastructure indicated that overpopulation and urbanization were the most pressing problems facing the Mubarak government at the end of the century.

Mubarak adopted structural adjustment policies in the 1990s to bring about economic liberalization, a policy favored by the international lending agencies. The reforms of the 1990s brought a new sales tax, the elimination of tariffs, a decrease in the size of the public sector economy, and the elimination of subsidies on some agricultural commodities. Structural adjustment certainly did not benefit the millions living in the urban slums. In general, the reforms decreased the real income of an average Egyptian household. Particularly among the middle classes tied to public-sector wage scales, there was a real decline in living standards. At the same time, a new generation of university graduates faced almost certain unemployment as structural adjustment decreased the size of the public sector. On the other hand, the new bourgeoisie that arose with the economic opening was a privileged minority, earning on average ten times the salary of an employee in the public sector. As a result, although debt reduction after the Gulf War provided Mubarak with some relief from these economic and social tensions, economic and demographic trends indicated that Egypt's ability to meet society's basic needs was greatly reduced.

JAMES WHIDDEN

See also: **Egypt: Sadat, Nationalism, 1970–1981; World Bank, International Monetary Fund, and Structural Adjustment.**

Further Reading

Adams, R. H. *Development and Social Change in Rural Egypt.* Syracuse: University of Syracuse Press, 1986.

Hansen, B. *The Political Economy of Poverty, Equity, and Growth: Egypt and Turkey.* New York: Oxford University Press, 1991.

Harik, I. *Economic Policy Reform in Egypt.* Gainesville: University of Florida Press, 1997.

Ibrahim, Saad Eddin. *Egypt, Islam, and Democracy: Twelve Critical Essays.* Cairo: The American University in Cairo Press, 1996.

Richards, A. "Ten Years of Infitah: Class, Rent, and Policy Stasis in Egypt." *Journal of Development Studies* 20, no. 4 (1984): 323–338.

Springborg, R. *Mubarak's Egypt: Fragmentation of the Political Order.* Boulder, Colo.: Westview Press, 1989.

Waterbury, J., and A. Richards. *A Political Economy of the Middle East: State, Class, and Economic Development.* Boulder, Colo.: Westview Press, 1990.

Egypt: Mubarak, Since 1981: Politics

Hosni Mubarak acceded to power after the assassination of President Anwar al-Sadat in 1981. Sadat's legacy to his successor was multifold. He created a "boss-state" in which the president had extensive executive powers and the remnants of a populist base in the Arab Socialist Union, the ruling party. But Sadat also initiated a policy of "democratization," reflected in the new name given to the ruling party in 1979, the National Democratic Party (NDP). Democratization resulted in the formation of an active opposition, including the New Wafd, Liberal, Socialist-Labor, and Communist parties, as well as the unofficial Islamic, political opposition. The opposition parties and Islamic groups rallied together against Sadat's foreign policy initiative, the negotiated peace with Israel in 1979, based on the Camp David Agreement of 1978. After Sadat's assassination by a radical Islamic group in 1981, Mubarak encouraged the political participation of the opposition parties while attempting to establish links with moderate Islamic organizations. The peace with Israel was a cold one, as Mubarak sought to appease domestic and foreign opponents and end Egypt's isolation in the Arab world.

The National Democratic Party (NDP) was an extension of the government and bureaucracy, which by the mid-1980s employed three million people. President Mubarak, who had been a military officer, maintained close links with the military and appointed officers to key positions in the bureaucracy, security, defense, and foreign affairs. But just as Mubarak lacked the charismatic style of Nasser or Sadat, his appointees to key positions were often faceless officials, giving his regime a lackluster reputation. Likewise, while the NDP was a controlling factor in Mubarak's authoritarian regime, it did not have a popular base. However, democratization did provide a means to implicate the upper and middle classes in Mubarak's authoritarianism. The reactivated New Wafd Party allowed a new bourgeois class, which developed with the economic opening to foreign investment, to participate in parliamentary politics alongside the NDP. Similarly, Mubarak allowed the Muslim Brothers, the largest Islamic organization in Egypt, to gain control of university associations, mosques, and professional associations. The Muslim Brothers infiltrated the medical association in the late 1970s, and afterward the engineering and legal associations. Control over the legal association was significant because it had formerly been a bastion of liberal opinion, as well as one of the bases of the NDP. But, by allowing the Muslim Brothers to operate within the associations, Mubarak hoped to integrate moderates into the authoritarian, political structure.

The Islamic movement had a popular base through educational and charitable programs. Although these had the tacit approval of the government until the 1990s, they tended to place the Islamic issue at the center of political discourse and therefore challenged the secular foundations of the government. Since it was illegal to form an Islamic political party, in the 1984 elections the Muslim Brothers ran candidates as members of the liberal and secular New Wafd Party. By 1986 the Muslim Brothers had split with the New Wafd, but dominated the membership of the Socialist-Labor Party. When the New Wafd and liberal critics of the regime challenged the constitutionality of Mubarak's electoral and parliamentary laws, new elections were held in 1987. Yet, the Muslim Brothers emerged as the largest opposition group in parliament. The 1987 election campaign also marked the revival of the radical Islamic groups, beginning with attacks on bars, video-rental shops, and members of the Coptic community.

Mubarak's absorption of the Islamic opposition through democratization was unsuccessful because the democratic process did not stimulate a real increase in political participation. A government emergency decree forbade public assemblies, except during elections, and electoral results were manipulated to ensure the election of the NDP. As a result, the important parties boycotted the elections of 1991. In 1992 a radical Islamic group assassinated a prominent, liberal critic of the Islamic movement, Faraj Fuda. When the security forces raided the headquarters of the Muslim Brothers, they claimed to have established links between the Muslim Brothers and the radical Islamic groups. Emergency powers and military tribunals provided Mubarak with a means to dispense summary judgment, imprison, and in some cases execute suspected opponents of the regime.

The radical Islamic groups then turned their fire directly at the government by adopting the tactic of "tourist-terrorism," which attacked the economic base of the regime. The violence culminated in the massacre of 58 tourists at the Hatshepsut Temple opposite Luxor in November of 1997.

Mubarak's repression of the Islamic opposition was supported by liberal intellectuals and politicians, in spite of the apparent disregard for Egyptian judicial processes and international conventions on human rights. On the other hand, the politicians of the Socialist-Labor Party, as well as the Islamic hierarchy at al-Azhar mosque, declared their moral support for the radicals arrested and tried at the military courts. While the Islamic issue politicized and deepened divisions within Egyptian political society, the Islamic groups continued to build popular support. The Islamicists communicated in an Islamic vocabulary that appealed to the Muslim majority, but perhaps more important, to the impoverished. The network of Islamic schools, hospitals, and public services challenged the legitimacy of the Mubarak regime, because Islamicist-run services were provided in social sectors beyond the reach of the government. In 1992 Mubarak sent 14,000 soldiers into the Cairo slums to arrest radicals. This was followed by a massive development project to provide slum residents with paved roads, an effective sewage system, schools, and electricity. The United States Agency for International Development provided tens of millions of dollars to fund this type of urban reconstruction, which had obvious political objectives. While the regime attempted to win popular support, the democratic system itself became more obviously a veil for the autocratic character of the regime. All the political parties participated in the elections of 1995. The results returned record numbers of NDP candidates as Mubarak increased the number of seats in parliament to satisfy his own supporters. The elections were also the most openly corrupt. Regardless, it was generally agreed that by the time of the presidential referendum of 1999 (won by Mubarak) the Islamic opposition had been crushed. However, the fundamental constitutional issues were not resolved. Indeed, the Islamic issue was hardly muted. Meanwhile, the liberal opposition leaders demanded that a "third way" be found between the Islamic and authoritarian alternatives.

Foreign policy provided Mubarak with a more solid pillar to legitimate his rule. Sadat's peace with Israel in 1979 isolated Egypt and united the other Arab states: Egypt was expelled from the Arab League and the Islamic Conference Organization. Nevertheless, by 1981 international relations were transformed by the Iran-Iraq War, which divided the Arab states, notably Syria and Iraq. At the same time Saudi Arabia made a proposal for a negotiated peace with Israel, along lines similar to Camp David. Mubarak emphasized Egyptian stability, which was highly valued by the Arab Gulf states, the United States, and Western Europe. In this international context Egypt rebuilt its stature as a regional leader. For instance, the decision to support the international coalition against Iraq in the Gulf War tended to legitimize Mubarak's foreign policy. It also enhanced his role as a broker in peace negotiations between the Arab states, the Palestinians, and the Israelis. In sum, foreign and domestic crisis in Egypt was allayed, ensuring the survival of Mubarak's regime into the twenty-first century.

JAMES WHIDDEN

Further Reading

Bianchi, R. "The Corporatization of the Egyptian Labor Movement." *The Middle East Journal* 40, no. 3 (1986): 429–444.

Ibrahim, Saad Eddin. *Egypt, Islam, and Democracy*. Cairo: The American University in Cairo Press, 1996.

Moore, C. H. "Money and Power: The Dilemma of the Egyptian Infitah." *The Middle East Journal* 40, no. 4 (1986): 634–660.

Roussillon, A. "Republican Egypt Interpreted: Revolution and Beyond." In *The Cambridge History of Egypt*. Vol. 2, *Modern Egypt from 1517 to the End of the Twentieth Century*, edited by M. W. Daly. Cambridge: Cambridge University Press, 1998.

Springborg, R. *Mubarak's Egypt: Fragmentation of the Political Order*. Boulder, Colo.: Westview Press, 1989.

Tripp, C., and R. Owen, eds. *Egypt under Mubarak*. London: Routledge, 1989.

Waterbury, J., and A. Richards. *A Political Economy of the Middle East: State, Class, and Economic Development*. Boulder, Colo.: Westview Press, 1990.

Egyptology: From Herodotus to the Twentieth Century

The Greek historian Herodotus is usually considered the first Egyptologist, in that he included Egypt in his *Histories*, mostly derived from Egyptian priests and their temple records. The Egyptian priest Manetho compiled a history of Egypt, the *Aegyptiaka*, using similar records some 150 years later, on which is based our arrangement of the Egyptian kings into thirty (-one) dynasties. One of these pharaohs, Amenhotep III (Eighteenth Dynasty), already had conducted "excavations" at Abydos over a thousand years earlier, in search of his ancestors and to ascertain "correct" religious ritual. In more general terms, the ancient Egyptians recorded and revived their own history in an effort to understand themselves and their past, especially in times of uncertainty and for propaganda purposes.

The Romans perceived Egypt as an ancient land, and several histories, geographies and other studies were devoted to its analysis, among the most important being the *Bibliotheca Historica* of Diodorus Siculus and Strabo's *Geography*. The introduction of Christianity altered perspectives, but both Eusebius of Caesarea and Sextus Julius Africanus included an Egyptian history in their respective *Chronicles*. For over the next millennium, however, ancient Egypt became little more than a source of magic, superstition, and lost knowledge that was incompatible with Christian doctrine.

Serious investigation began in the sixteenth century, chiefly focused on recording monumental structures. Ancient artifacts were collected as "exotica" and mummies were gathered for "medical" purposes. The inquisitive scholarly travels of antiquarians made up a significant branch of Egyptology at this point. By the eighteenth-century Enlightenment, numerous attempts already had been made to translate the ancient hieroglyphic (Greek for "sacred carving") inscriptions. In 1822 Jean-François Champollion finally broke the code using the parallel Greek text of the trilingual inscription on the "Rosetta Stone," which enabled Egyptian history to be studied from direct contemporary sources for the first time, rather than relying on the Classical authors who wrote a millennium and more later.

Now in the British Museum, the Rosetta Stone was the preeminent discovery of Napoleon's Egyptian Campaign (1798–1801) when he included numerous *savants* to document the country itself. The resulting *Description de l'Égypte* (1809–1826) fired European imagination and began a flood of activity that was the true beginning of Egyptology as a discipline in its own right. Active acquisition and excavation were conducted on behalf of wealthy private individuals and newly founded public museums, which employed "professionals" (some of whom even became so) such as Giovanni Belzoni (1788–1823) to enhance their collections. By 1850 numerous treasure-hunting "excavations" had produced the Egyptological nucleus of most museums, and then professional museum Egyptologists to administer them. Work focused on accurate observation, recording and copying of both monuments and minutiae, and the resulting publications such as the *Denkamaeler aus Aegypten und Aethiopen* (Monuments of Egypt and Ethiopia, 1849–1859, Karl Richard Lepsius) and *Manners and Customs of the Ancient Egyptians* (1837, Sir Gardner Wilkinson) remain fundamentally important even today. Our detailed typologies and analyses of the monuments, art and artifacts, founded in these early studies and based on art historical and other principles, still continue to illuminate ancient Egyptian attitudes and religion, as well as its chronology.

The Egyptian Antiquities Service was founded in 1858 by the Khedive Saïd, who appointed Auguste Mariette (1821–1881) as its first director. Egyptian antiquities legislation was initiated, and the Museum in

Cairo was founded to house recovered material. Various academic organizations were founded abroad to support research, fieldwork, and publication, such as the Egypt Exploration Fund (later Society) in 1882 in England. Recognition of the importance of accurate "scientific" excavation and its dissemination followed more slowly, to be realized in the person of W. M. Flinders Petrie (1853–1942), beginning in 1880. The "Father of Egyptology" developed his methodology while excavating throughout Egypt, and almost immediately publishing his results, for the next half-century.

Work on Egyptian language and chronology, especially in Germany, developed an historical framework through translation and detailed study of the records, while Egyptian prehistory was revealed by excavation. Egyptology as an organized discipline, working under official auspices and encompassing all its historical phases, was firmly in place by the beginning of the twentieth century. The massive *Wörterbuch der Ägyptische Sprache* (Dictionary of the Egyptian Language, 1926–1953, Adolf Erman and Hermann Grapow) and *Egyptian Grammar* (1927; 1950; 1957, Sir Alan Gardiner) remain unsurpassed as fundamental research tools, based on decades of collaborative analysis. More recent research in collating private documents of the time has done much to clarify problematic periods of Egyptian history for which few official records survive, to the extent that Manetho's history is now considered redundant, although his dynastic framework continues in standard use.

The Aswan Dam constructions and enlargements (1898–1902; 1907–1912; 1929–1932; 1960–1961) initiated a series of surveys in Lower Nubia and spurred further less concentrated work elsewhere, partly due to the potential wealth of information revealed by such broad-based investigation. The twentieth century saw research emphasis gradually turn from the excavation of major individual monuments to settlements and then problem-oriented regional surveys, investigating Egypt's "ordinary" majority as well as its minority elite. Concurrently, investigation expanded beyond the Nile Valley itself to encompass the surrounding desert and its oases, initiated largely by Ahmed Fakhry (1905–1973). Even more recently, research also has extended beyond Egypt's borders to view Egyptian civilization within its wider Mediterranean and African setting, investigating cross-influences and relationships with neighboring cultures and civilizations, in all directions, and challenging previously held "Egypto-centric" perspectives.

While Howard Carter's (1874–1939) excavation of the tomb of Tutankhamun (1922–1932) deservedly caught public imagination, those done by generations of other excavators at Amarna (since 1891), Abydos (since 1895), Hierakonpolis (since 1899) and now Tell el-Dab'a (since 1966), among other sites, have been far more revealing. "Museum excavation" (reanalysis of older site records and stored material), as well as renewed excavation at "old" sites, interdisciplinary research, and increased specialization have begun to illuminate many aspects unconsidered by the original excavators, and to broaden the results of new investigations elsewhere. Use of technological advances in other fields (e.g., satellite photography, forensics, computer simulation) and constantly improving archaeological techniques have revised many traditionally held interpretations and allowed excavation in previously untenable regions, such as the Delta where much current work is being conducted, and from which perspective historical events can now be reconsidered for new insights. While specialists become more specialized, Egyptology increasingly views itself as a collaborative interdisciplinary effort and in a global perspective.

JACKE PHILLIPS

Further Reading

Dawson, W. R., and E. P. Uphill. *Who Was Who in Egyptology*. 3rd rev. ed. Edited by Morris Bierbrier. London: Egypt Exploration Society, 1995.

Herodotus. *The Histories*. Translated by Robert Waterfield and Introduction and Notes by Carolyn Dewald. Oxford: Oxford University Press, 1998.

Lustig, J., ed. *Egyptology and Anthropology: A Developing Dialogue. Monographs in Mediterranean Archaeology* 8. Sheffield: Sheffield Academic Press, 1997.

Salah, M. A. "More than a Century of Archaeological Research in the Sudan." In *Sudan. Ancient Kingdoms of the Nile*, edited by Dietrich Wildung. New York: Flammarion, 1997: pp.1–5.

Yurco, F. J., "Narmer: First King of Upper and Lower Egypt: A Reconsideration of His Palette and Macehead." *Journal of the Society for the Study of Egyptian Antiquities* 25 (1995): 85–95.

Empire: *See* Colonialism: Ideology of Empire: Supremacist, Paternalist.

Engaruka: *See* Sirikwa and Engaruka: Dairy Farming, Irrigation.

Environment, Conservation, Development: Postcolonial Africa

A cursory glance at African environments reveals environmental problems/disasters, weak remedial measures, and ubiquitous ecological threats and challenges. Critical to policymakers has been the issue of how to get Africa out of the vicious cycle of poverty and

Two students feeding the biogas digestor. In the digestor, grass, water, and excrement are transformed into biogas and manure. The biogas is stored in tanks and used for cooking and lighting. Benin. © Enrico Bartolucci/Das Fotoarchiv.

environmental degradation, thus making sustainable development a viable option.

That Africa has been in a state of ecological crisis is not debatable. In Morocco, unsound environmental policies and practices have led to environmental degradation. Farming, overgrazing, and vegetation destruction in marginal lands brought in their wake soil erosion, devegetation, and desertification. Raw sewage contaminated water supplies. Other environmental hazards still confronting Morocco include the pollution of coastal waters and the siltation of reservoirs. Egypt has also encountered environmental problems of high magnitude. The country experienced desertification, increased soil salinization below the Aswan High Dam, marine degradation, and oil pollution. Urbanization and windblown sand led to loss of agricultural land, while intensive irrigation and water-logging engendered soil erosion. Agricultural pesticides, raw sewage, and industrial effluents have caused water pollution. In addition, poor water sanitation has contributed to an increase in water-borne diseases, and population growth has depleted natural resources. Nigeria has also experienced environmental problems such as desertification, deforestation, and soil degradation; poor waste management techniques, oil pollution, and threats to biodiversity have been contributors. The developments in Kenya have been deplorable. There, the problems have been those of desertification, soil erosion, water pollution, and threats to wildlife

populations as a result of poaching. In South Africa, serious environmental problems have been droughts, desertification, soil erosion, acid rain, river pollution, and air pollution.

Africans in both governmental and nongovernmental circles have been part of the global environmental protection movement. On April 22, 1972, they joined their counterparts in marking the first earth day. Promotion of ecology, respect for life on earth, and the dangers of pollution were stressed. In 1972 the United Nations met in Stockholm, Sweden, for a conference on the environment. The outcome of the conference was the establishment of the United Nations environment program (UNEP), which included the Earthwatch, a program designed to monitor the physical and biological resources of the earth. In 1987 negotiators meeting in Montreal, Canada, presented a protocol on substances that deplete the ozone layer there. Industrialized nations were asked to reduce "greenhouse" gas emissions like CFCS (chlorofluorocarbons 11 and 12) and halon, while African states and other developing countries were granted deferrals in such reductions. Developing nations were also promised reimbursement for "all agreed incremental costs" if they complied with the protocol.

Africans also took their seats at the 1992 Earth Summit in Rio de Janeiro, Brazil. The contents of agenda 21 and the Rio Declaration on Environment and Development reflect adequately the aspirations of Africans. Of particular note are principles 7 and 8, which emphasized their earlier call for a new international economic order (NIEO) and their desire for positive developments from the north-south dialogue, such as technological transfer and redistribution of world wealth. The Earth Summit produced pacts on global warming and biodiversity. In 1994 the fifty-three-nation United Nations Commission on Sustainable Development met. It reported that countries were failing to provide the money and expertise necessary for the facilitation of the Rio plans. In December 1997, delegates from 166 countries met in Kyoto, Japan, at the United Nations Climate Change Conference to negotiate actions against global warming. African states participating at the conference insisted that industrialized nations had caused, and were still causing, most global warming, and demanded that the industrialized world bear the brunt of economic sacrifices necessary for the cleanup of the environment. In Bonn, Germany, in 2001, officials from about 180 countries gathered to address the vexing problem of global warming. Carbon dioxide and other "greenhouse" gas emissions were once more identified as culprits for receding glaciers and the rising sea level.

It is pertinent to note that African states have been parties to many international agreements on the environment. They signed agreements that they felt would best serve their specific national environmental needs. These include agreements on climate change, biodiversity, endangered species, hazardous wastes, marine dumping, nuclear test bans, ozone layer protection, tropical timber, desertification, whaling, and marine life conservation.

Internally, African states took certain measures to combat environmental degradation. Agencies and ministries were established to monitor the environment and to execute ecological and conservation programs. In Nigeria, for instance, the Federal Environmental Protection Agency (FEPA) responded to fifteen alerts on toxic chemical in 1994. In the same year, 31,689 metric tons of consignment were inspected to ensure their compliance with FEPA hazardous waste management regulations. A total of 97.7 metric tons of hazardous chemical and recycled wastes were intercepted by FEPA in industrial compliance monitoring in the same year. At the corporate business level, it is important to note the activities of the Shell Petroleum Development Company of Nigeria. The SPDC's environmental spending for 1998 stood at $177.6 million. The company's objective continued to be an end to pollution via facilities and infrastructure upgrades, site remediation, waste management, and environmental studies, as well as an end to gas flaring. Already, the Alakiri flowstation and gas plant has met external certification standards by the International Standards Organization (ISO 14001 standards), and validation per the European Union Eco-Management and Audit Scheme (EMAS) standards.

In the final analysis, in spite of the efforts of African states, in collaboration with external actors, to address the problem of environmental degradation, to conserve natural resources, and attain the goal of sustainable development, the state of the environment remains perilous. Nothing speaks more eloquently of the ugly situation of the environment than the fact that seventeen African countries are currently facing food emergencies due to difficult weather conditions, persistent civil strife, and insecurity. That the remedial measures did not yield the desired results is partly due to the fact that, in some cases, policies were not based on scientifically proven blueprints. The problem was further compounded by eco-politics and official corruption.

PAUL OBIYO MBANASO NJEMANZE

See also: **Debt, International, Development and Dependency; Development, Postcolonial: Central Planning, Private Enterprise, Investment; Geography, Environment in African History; Industrialization and Development; Mining, Multinationals, and Development; Rural Development, Postcolonial.**

Further Reading

Anderson, D., and R. Grove, eds. *Conservation in Africa: People, Policies and Practice.* Cambridge: Cambridge University Press, 1987.

Bell, R. H. V., and E. McShane-Caluzi, eds. *Conservation and Wildlife Management in Africa.* Washington, D.C.: U.S. Peace Corps, 1986.

Central Bank of Nigeria. *Annual Report and Statement of Accounts for the Year Ended 31st December, 1994.* Lagos: Central Bank of Nigeria, 1995.

Choucri, N., ed. *Global Accord: Environmental Challenges and International Responses.* Cambridge, Mass.: The MIT Press, 1993.

Eblen, R. A., and William R. Eblen, eds. *The Encyclopedia of the Environment.* Boston: Houghton Mifflin Company, 1994.

Gibson, C. C. *Politicians and Poachers: The Political Economy of Wildlife in Africa.* New York: Cambridge University Press, 1999.

Laird, B. "6 Ways to Combat Global Warming." *USA TODAY,* July 16, 2001.

Shell Petroleum Development Company. *People and the Environment {Annual Report 1998}.* Lagos: SPDC, 1999.

Timberlake, L. *Africa in Crisis: The Causes, the Cures of Environmental Bankruptcy.* London: Earthscan, 1985.

Epidemics: Malaria, AIDS, Other Disease: Postcolonial Africa

One of the greatest challenges facing Africa is the continuing scourge of deadly epidemics and debilitating disease. According to statistics compiled by the World Health Organization (WHO), a high proportion of Africa's population suffers from a wide variety of illnesses. These include well-known tropical maladies, such as malaria, sleeping sickness, and schistosomiasis, as well as more globally widespread afflictions, such as cholera, tuberculosis, and HIV/AIDS. The high incidence of disease in Africa is partly attributable to environmental conditions. Numerous viruses, bacteria, and parasites thrive in the tropical forests and river valleys, as do the flies and mosquitos that often transmit illnesses to humans. More important, many of Africa's diseases and epidemics are a consequence of widespread poverty. Poor sanitation, contaminated water supplies, malnutrition, and inadequate health care all contribute to the continent's high rate of chronic illness, low life expectancy, and outbreaks of serious epidemics. Although disease prevention efforts have scored some victories, in most cases Africans continue to suffer and die from illnesses that have been successfully controlled or treated in more developed and wealthier regions of the world. Moreover, frequent sickness and high rates of mortality further impoverish families and nations, making them even more vulnerable to future episodes of illness and disease.

Of all tropical diseases, malaria is one of the most serious and widespread. WHO estimates that approximately 270 to 450 million cases occur annually in Africa,

AIDS testing in a hospital in Addis Ababa, Ethiopia, 1999. © Friedrich Stark/Das Fotoarchiv.

and it is difficult to find a family that has not been stricken by the illness. Malaria is caused by four species of *Plasmodium* protozoa that are carried by the anopheline mosquito, which is endemic to most regions of the continent. Children are particularly vulnerable, and in some regions of Africa, as many as half may die from malarial infection before reaching the age of five years. For survivors, malaria can impair physical and mental development and may cause anemia and progressive damage to the liver and other organs. Even when malarial symptoms are less severe, its impact can be great. Outbreaks typically occur during the rainy seasons, the time of greatest agricultural activity in Africa. The loss of farming labor due to fevers and sickness may seriously jeopardize crop production and family income, causing malnutrition, impoverishment, and a greater susceptibility to more serious attacks of malaria and other illnesses. Efforts to control mosquito populations through the use of insecticides have generally been ineffective, and pharmaceutical treatments are often unavailable or too expensive for most households. Additional mosquito-borne illnesses, such as yellow fever and dengue fever, also afflict large numbers of Africans in both rural and urban areas.

Two additional insect-borne diseases, sleeping sickness (trypanosomiasis) and river blindness (onchocerciasis), are transmitted to humans via fly bites. Sleeping sickness is generally restricted to rural areas, particularly in the forest and wooded savanna regions. Long a scourge of cattle and humans alike, the illness is caused by two forms of *Trypanosomia brucei* parasites, both carried by the tsetse fly (*Glossina spp.*). Without treatment, the disease is commonly fatal, although symptoms are difficult to recognize, making early diagnosis difficult. Intensive efforts to reduce tsetse fly infestation, through the clearing of brush and

the use of insecticides, succeeded in bringing the illness under control in many areas by the early 1960s, but the disease reappeared in the 1970s, with periodic flare-ups in west and central Africa. In 1996 some 30,000 new cases were reported, and an additional 55–60 million inhabitants of tsetse fly-infested areas may also be at risk. Sleeping sickness contributes to rural poverty by reducing the work force, cattle production, and the use of animal labor for farming. The loss of cattle herds may also lead to malnutrition, poorer health, and a greater susceptibility to other illnesses and diseases.

Efforts to control river blindness have been more successful. This illness is caused by a filiarial worm carried by a small black fly commonly found in the river valleys of west and central Africa. Once a major illness affecting more than 30 million people in West Africa, river blindness was also a major contributor to rural underdevelopment, as residents fled from the fertile river valleys where the black fly was most prevalent. Beginning in the mid-1970s, African nations and international agencies began an effective program to reduce the black fly population, bringing river blindness largely under control and allowing the resettlement of river basins. The current challenge is to provide African nations the ability and resources to maintain the control programs to prevent a reoccurrence of the disease.

Major diseases spread by contaminated food and water include schistosomiasis, cholera, typhoid, and meningitis. Schistosomiasis (also known as Bilharzia) is a seriously debilitating disease caused by parasites of the genus *Schistosoma* that live in fresh water snails. They enter the human body through the skin and lay their eggs, which often pass back into the water through human waste. The parasitic infection is very painful. It may also cause progressive damage to internal organs, contributing to an early death. For Africa as a whole, it has been estimated that about half the population suffers from schistosomiasis, and in some areas (particularly in the lake and river regions of southern and eastern Africa, and the Nile River Valley), it is estimated that nearly everyone over the age of two is infected. The best preventions against schistosomiasis are clean water supplies and efficient sanitation, but these simple controls—as well as the medicines available for effective treatment—are generally far too expensive for most African countries. In fact, the threat of schistosomiasis may actually be on the rise, as irrigation schemes inadvertently draw water from contaminated rivers and lakes.

Additional illnesses on the rise are cholera and meningococcal meningitis. Cholera is an acute diarrheal illness caused by the infection of the intestine with the bacterium *Vibrio cholera*. It is most commonly transmitted by the ingestion of contaminated food or water, often through municipal water supplies. Persons with severe cases of cholera can die within a few hours due to loss of fluids and salts. Meningococcal meningitis is an inflammation of the lining surrounding the brain and spinal cord, caused by several different bacterium and viruses. In instances where it invades the bloodstream, meningitis can be carried to other organs, including the eyes, heart, lungs, and the central nervous system. Although both of these illnesses have largely disappeared in developed nations, serious epidemics still occur regularly in many regions of Africa.

Of all major illnesses, the HIV/AIDS epidemic is currently the most serious threat to public health and social welfare in Africa. Since the disease was first recognized in the early 1980s, an estimated 34 million people in Sub-Saharan Africa have become infected, a figure which represents about 70 per cent of the world's total cases. More than 11 million Africans, a quarter of them children, have already died as a consequence of AIDS, and the death toll is expected to increase for the foreseeable future. In Africa the primary mode of transmission is through heterosexual intercourse, and surveys have uniformly found the greatest rates of infection in young adults, between the ages of fifteen and forty-five. HIV is also spread perinatally (mother-to-fetus), and as of 1998, there were an estimated 1 million infants and children living with HIV/AIDS. Although all African countries have reported AIDS cases, the epidemic is particularly severe in eastern and southern Africa. In some countries, such as Botswana, Namibia, and Zimbabwe, HIV infection may affect up to 25 per cent of adults.

The high incidence of HIV/AIDS in Africa can be attributed to a variety of factors. Some studies suggest that the virus may have originated in central Africa, and that it spread undetected until fairly recently. Others have found the viral strains of HIV found in eastern and southern Africa to be more virulent than those prevalent in other regions of the world. Another significant factor may be the high incidence of other sexually transmitted diseases, such as gonorrhea and syphilis, which facilitates viral transmission from one individual to another. Social dislocation and economic distress have also contributed to the scope and scale of the epidemic in Africa. Urbanization, rural impoverishment, labor migration, and regional warfare have induced dramatic social changes that, in some cases, have fostered the spread of disease.

Efforts to limit the AIDS epidemic have had mixed results. In the absence of an effective vaccine and lacking the resources to provide the drug therapies available in developed nations, Africans have focused their attention on public awareness and education. In some countries, such as Uganda and Senegal, sustained prevention efforts have yielded reduced rates of HIV infection. But in many other nations, the results have been less successful. In Zimbabwe, for example, AIDS education has succeeded in raising knowledge and awareness of the disease, but risk-reducing behavioral change has lagged behind. Personal denial of risk continues to undermine disease prevention strategies, and the continuing stigma attached to AIDS prevents many sufferers from seeking care and support. As the epidemic increases, so too do other infectious diseases. Particularly worrisome is the merging dual epidemics of AIDS and tuberculosis. People whose immune defenses are weakened by HIV infection have become more vulnerable to other microbes, including the tuberculosis bacillus. In some regions of southern Africa, tuberculosis rates have doubled in the last decade, and approximately one-third of all AIDS deaths are directly attributed to it.

In many African nations, sickness and poverty have become firmly intertwined. Illnesses impair family productivity, creating diminished income, malnutrition, and overall increased impoverishment. In such conditions, individuals may be forced to rely more heavily on unsanitary water or food supplies, or to engage in riskier personal behaviors, such as prostitution, in order to survive. But such measures also increase susceptibility to more sickness, thus continuing the cycle of illness and poverty. A similar trend is observable at the national level. In countries most severely affected by the AIDS epidemic, businesses report dramatically reduced profits as a result of worker absenteeism, caused by sickness or attendance at funerals. Overall, lowered business and family productivity decreases national income, resulting in fewer resources available for health care, improvements in water and sanitation, and consistent insect eradication programs. In a continent already struggling to achieve economic development, malaria, schistosomiasis, HIV/AIDS, and other major maladies seriously hinder efforts to promote social stability and economic growth.

SAMUEL NELSON

Further Reading

Asuni, T. *Mental Health and Disease in Africa*. Ibadan, Nigeria: Spectrum Books, 1994.

Feachem, R, and D. Jamison, eds. *Disease and Mortality in Sub-Saharan Africa*. New York: Published for the World Bank by the Oxford University Press, 1991.

Hartwig, G., and K. D. Patterson, eds. *Schistosomiasis in Twentieth-Century Africa: Historical Studies on West Africa and Sudan*. Los Angeles: Crossroads Press, 1984.

Nelson, S. "Africa Responds to AIDS: The Challenges and Strategies of Disease Prevention." *Journal of Third World Studies* 8, no.2 (fall 1991): 97–126.

Setel, P. W. Milton Lewis, and Maryinez Lyons, eds. *Histories of Sexually Transmitted Diseases and HIV/AIDS in Sub-Saharan Africa*. Westport, Conn.: Greenwood Press, 1999.

Equatorial Africa: *See* **Colonial Federations: French Equatorial Africa; Iron Age (Early): Farming, Equatorial Africa.**

Equatorial Guinea: Colonial Period, Nineteenth Century

The colony that became known as Spanish (after 1963, Equatorial) Guinea took final shape only in the early twentieth century. In the first stage, the islands of Fernando Po (renamed Bioko after independence) and Annobon passed from the Portuguese to the Spanish sphere in 1778. Spain made an initial claim to an area of on the mainland, including parts of modern Nigeria, in 1855; this was whittled down to just over half its original size at the West African Conference of Berlin and fixed at roughly 10,000 square miles (26,000 square kilometers) in 1901, when the boundaries of Río Muni were finally determined. However, Spain effectively occupied this small enclave only in the mid-1920s.

In 1827 Britain became the first European power to establish a physical, albeit unofficial, presence in Fernando Po, which it used as a base to curb the West African slave trade. In the 1840s, the position was regularized when Spain appointed John Beecroft, later British consul for the Bights of Benin and Biafra as its governor over the island, based at Santa Isabel (now Malabo). The first native Spanish governor took office in 1858, to be followed by settlers and Jesuit missionaries. By this time, the island had become an important entrepôt, attracting a mixed population of freed slaves and West African creoles, who settled among the indigenous Bubi and started to produce palm oil for export in the 1840s. However, cocoa, introduced in 1836, became the mainstay of the economy, transforming the island after World War I into a leading continental producer. At times, the industry attracted critical international attention. In the 1920s, the treatment of Liberian migrant workers caused an international scandal and the abrupt termination of their supply in 1930. Thereafter, Nigeria became the most significant provider of labor for the Fernando Po plantations, along with Fang workers from the Río Muni, mainland, part of the colony.

In contrast to this, Río Muni had been treated from the start as an "exploitation" colony, unsuitable for white settlers, initially producing wild rubber and ivory, and when the market for these commodities collapsed, hardwoods for the European market. The actual administration of the mainland area was only finally set in place in the 1920s and operated on a very limited budget, making extensive use of the Fang traditional authorities in a rough and ready form of indirect rule. The vast majority of the Fang were termed *menores* ("minors"), made subject to a different legal system from Spanish citizens, and required also to

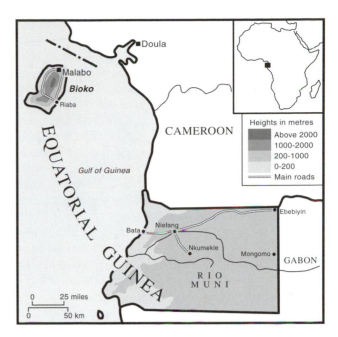

Equatorial Guinea.

perform obligatory labor on plantations and other enterprises. A small number (only about one hundred by the mid-1950s) became *emancipados*, with full rights: a privilege that entailed the acceptance of Christianity and Spanish culture, and the rejection of traditional values. It was a system that offered more to the Westernized creoles and Bubi of Fernando Po (collectively known as the *Fernandinos*) than to the Fang peoples of the economically stagnant and generally neglected mainland. However, the value of these privileges was undermined by General Franco's seizure of power, after his victory in the Spanish Civil War (1936–1939): for the next twenty years, his regime restricted the evolution of political institutions to the local level, and filled them with hand-picked appointees. Black nationalist protests to the United Nations in the mid-1950s were met with official bans on public meetings, the imprisonment of dissidents and reports of their abuse while in detention. Also, the Franco government encouraged European planters to settle in Fernando Po, leading to the gradual displacement of black cocoa producers on the island. However, in contrast to the mainland, the Franco regime succeeded in retaining support there, a circumstance it was able to exploit to its advantage in the early 1960s, when Madrid decided that a limited degree of political advance along carefully controlled channels should be staged.

This process began in 1960, when provincial assemblies were set up in Fernando Po and Río Muni, with political arrangements that favored pro-Spanish and/or conservative elements in the colonial society. Also, for the first time Spanish Guinea was awarded six seats in the Spanish Cortes, all earmarked for supporters of the colonial regime. In response to this, the mainland politician Atanasio Ndongo set up MONALIGE (Movimiento Nacional de Liberacíon de Guinea Ecuatorial) in 1963, winning widespread support in Río Muni. Subsequently, he was edged out by the former civil servant Macías Nguema, who took the party along a more radical path. The growth of MONALIGE on the mainland alarmed the *Fernandinos*, whose traditional support for the colonial power was influenced also by their minority status within the colony (10 per cent of the population), their relative wealth, derived from cocoa production, and the scope of their existing representation in the evolving political structures. They initially opposed a Spanish proposal to give the colony autonomy in 1963 but were won around by an offer of representation in excess of their numbers in a General Assembly for the colony as a whole, and parity with Río Muni on the Governor's Council. Finally, in response to growing international criticism, the Franco regime decided to end its formal control over the colony and convened a constitutional conference in 1967 to prepare for a handover of power. The islanders demanded their own independence, but once again were brought around by an allocation of representation well in excess of their population (15 out of 36 Assembly seats) and similar concessions. In the following year, Macías Nguema won the presidency of Equatorial Guinea on the second ballot and ushered in the era of independence on October 12, 1968.

Although the constitutional road to independence had taken only eight years, it had started from scratch after many years of political repression, and the roots of the new representative institutions were correspondingly shallow, as the rapid move of the Macías Nguema regime towards personal dictatorship was to show. Moreover, the two sections of the new state lacked any fundamental integration, much less a common identity.

MURRAY STEELE

Further Reading

Decalo, S. *Psychoses of Power: African Personal Dictatorships*. Gainsville: Florida University Press, 1998.

Fegley, R. *Equatorial Guinea: An African Tragedy*. New York: Peter Lang, 1989.

Preston, P. *Franco: A Biography*. New York: HarperCollins, 1993.

Sundiata, I. *Equatorial Guinea: Colonialism, State Terror, and the Search for Stability*. Boulder, Colo: Westview Press, 1990.

Equatorial Guinea: Independence to the Present

The comparatively rapid advance of Equatorial Guinea (Río Muni and the islands of Fernando Po [now Bioko] and Annobón) to independence, after many years of authoritarian rule under Franco's Spain, provided insufficient opportunity for the development of a nationalist movement at the grassroots level. It facilitated the emergence of a leader, Francisco Macías Nguema (1924–1979), whose record of repression and violations of basic human rights was matched only by those of Idi Amin and the "emperor" Bokassa. Twenty years of government under his nephew Teodoro Obiang Nguema Mbasogo have seen some limited improvement, but the country still suffers from the dual legacy of colonial and postcolonial despotism.

A former court interpreter under the colonial regime, Macías Nguema was regarded as a "safe" prospect for Spain in the presidential elections preceding independence on October 12, 1968. But within a few months, he had dismayed his former masters by expelling their ambassador and the local Spanish military force, leading to a mass exodus of white settlers. A reign of terror followed, targeting political opponents such as would-be separatists on Bioko Island and dissidents within the ruling party, and manifesting itself in public executions, kidnappings, killing of exiles, "disappearances," and the massacre of whole villages. By 1974, over two-thirds of the original 1968 Assembly members had disappeared. Fegley has estimated that at least 20,000 people were murdered under the Macías regime and at least 100,000 fled the country (about a third of the total population). In 1970 Macías set up PUNT (Sole National Workers' Party), outlawing other political parties; two years later, he declared himself president for life, head of the nation and party, commander in chief of the army, and grand master of education, science, and culture.

Macías distanced himself further from his colonial past by embarking on an idiosyncratic "authenticity" program, involving an anti-Christian campaign that led to the banning of the Roman Catholic Church in 1978, and forbidding the use of Christian names. In its place, he encouraged the traditional Bwiti cult of his Fang group. Other features included the advocacy of traditional medicine and closing down of hospitals, the dismissal of six hundred teachers and the proscription of the term "intellectual" as signifying an alien polluter of African values. The by now habitual excesses accompanied the program: in one incident, a secondary school head was executed and his body exposed after a slashed portrait of the "President for Life" was found in his school entrance. In his final year, Macías seems to have abandoned traditional values as well, possibly influenced by the Eastern-bloc contacts he had started to cultivate, and declared Equatorial Guinea to be "an atheist state."

Meanwhile, the once thriving economy was experiencing severe problems, many of the regime's making. In 1975 police assaults on Nigerian embassy staff at the capital Malabo resulted in the eventual withdrawal of 35,000 Nigerian laborers from the Fernando Po cocoa plantations; they were replaced by Fang laborers, drafted from the mainland under the Compulsory Labor Act (1972), who lacked their skills and failed to sustain production. Ironically, Macías's economic mismanagement made his country more, rather than less, dependent on Spanish financial support, while he continued to blame Spanish imperialism for his plight.

By the later 1970s, Macías was fast losing his faculties and showed unmistakable signs of mania; he was reported to have talked to people he had killed as if they were in the same room with him. However, his authority was total, buttressed by relatives and members of his Esangui clan in positions of trust. It was employed ruthlessly against anyone who dared to complain, much less criticize him. In June 1979, he eventually overreached himself, when a younger brother of his nephew Teodoro Obiang was murdered after protesting about his army pay being in arrears. This threat to the inner circle of power moved Obiang to gather several relatives together and stage a successful coup. After a brief military trial, as it was clear that some of the plotters had been implicated in the excesses of the previous regime, Macías was executed at the end of September 1979.

Obiang's military government took rapid steps to normalize relations with Spain and the Roman Catholic Church, to be rewarded with a papal visit in February 1982. Also, it tried to reach an accommodation with the United Nations Human Rights Commission, which had started investigating the abuses of the Macías regime, in response to Anti-Slavery Society protest, in August 1976. In March 1980, the UN Secretary-General approved the appointment of an expert to help the Obiang government restore human rights. Although lacking the paranoia of his uncle, Obiang's human rights record has been far from perfect, with authenticated cases of extrajudicial murder, torture, and the denial of basic rights to accused persons, compounded by the continuing absence of an independent judiciary and the use of military tribunals to hear cases involving national security. In one such case, a defense counsel was given four hours to prepare a case for an alleged participant in an attempted coup.

Other features of the previous regime have continued, including Esangui clan domination of political structures, and the overriding political and economic authority of the governing Equatorial Guinea Democratic Party (PDGE). Its authority was unaffected by the end of one-party rule in 1992. Elections in 1993 were boycotted by the main opposition parties, while the 1999 elections witnessed short-term detentions of opposition candidates, the alleged removal of known opponents from the voters' roll, and reports that the secret ballot, introduced for the first time in 1999, had been nullified by the lack of privacy in polling booths. Prior to the establishment of multiparty politics, Obiang had taken the precaution of obtaining immunity from prosecution for alleged offenses committed before, during and after his term of office, but this has remained untested. In the 1996 presidential election, he received 98 per cent of the votes cast in a contest again characterized by charges of fraud and intimidation. However, the 1990s were more propitious in other ways for Equatorial Guinea. In 1994 substantial reserves of offshore oil were brought into production, even though the UN Human Rights Commission reported that the benefits accrued to the ruling elite rather than to the people.

After a further crackdown on opponents, Obiang was elected unopposed in the 2002 presidential election, while the oil bonanza gave Equatorial Guinea the highest economic growth rate in Africa.

MURRAY STEELE

Further Reading

Cronjé, S. *Equatorial Guinea—The Forgotten Dictatorship: Forced Labour and Political Murder in Central Africa.* London: Anti-Slavery Society, 1976.

Decalo, S. *Psychoses of Power: African Personal Dictatorships.* Gainsville, Fla.: Florida University Press, 1998.

Fegley, R. *Equatorial Guinea: an African Tragedy.* New York: Peter Lang, 1989.

Sundiata, I. *Equatorial Guinea: Colonialism, State Terror and the Search for Stability.* Boulder, Colo: Westview Press 1990.

United Nations Economic and Social Council Commission on Human Rights. *Report on the Human Rights Situation in the Republic of Equatorial Guinea Submitted by Mr Alejandro Artucio, Social Rapporteur of the Commission.* New York: United Nations, 1998.

Equiano, Olaudah (1745–1797)
Abolitionist

Of Ibo origin, Olaudah Equiano was born in a village near modern Onitsha in about 1745. At approximately eleven years of age, he was kidnapped by slave merchants, and after passing through a number of black owners, was eventually transported to the New World, one of three million Africans extracted from Africa by British slavers in the eighteenth century. He was given the name Gustavus Vassa, probably with ironic purpose, after the Swedish king who had won freedom for his people from Danish rule. It was a name he continued to use after he was emancipated, although usually qualified in print by the words "the African." Spared the brutality of plantation savagery by his own abilities and the fortune of having relatively humane owners, he survived a wide variety of experiences in the West Indies, the American mainland, and England (where he was baptized a Christian in 1759), gaining skills as a domestic servant, barber, sailor (including a period of service in the Seven Years War against France) and as a trader on his own account. His entrepreneurial activities enabled him to accrue sufficient capital (despite frequent cheating by white customers) to secure manumission in 1767.

Equiano settled in London later that year and made a living over the next ten years as a sailor, visiting the Mediterranean and Levant, the West Indies (again), and the Arctic, in one of the abortive attempts to find the North West Passage. He took part in a similarly abortive settlement scheme on the Mosquito Coast of modern Nicaragua. In October 1774, he had a religious experience, receiving a vision of Christ that convinced him that he had been redeemed by divine grace. In 1777 he entered domestic service in London. One employer, impressed by his Christian devotion, suggested missionary work in West Africa, but the Church of England, then unenthusiastic about such work, refused him ordination.

A return to sea in 1784 brought him to Philadelphia, where he made contact with its large free black community, an experience that led to his eventual involvement in the Sierra Leone scheme, inspired by Granville Sharp, with whom Equiano had been in contact since the early 1770s. In 1786 the British government appointed him "Commissary of Provisions and Stores for the Black Poor to Sierra Leone," a post that in practice placed him in the position of trying to satisfy his employers' interests and those of the black settlers themselves. His efforts to safeguard both against the dishonesty of the (white) official in charge of the expedition led to his unjust dismissal in March of the following year.

In 1789 Equiano published his autobiography, *The Interesting Narrative*, under his birth name, relegating his slave name to a subtitle. It achieved massive sales, helped by its author's promotional travels around the country, and ran to nine British editions, the last in 1794, when the tide turned against the abolitionist cause following the French revolutionary terror and Saint Domingue slave revolt.

The Interesting Narrative provides a first-hand account of the violence that underpinned the plantation system: the rapacity of slave traders, the inhumanity of the Middle Passage on slave ships, the savagery of plantation owners, and the treatment of black people (freed as well as enslaved) by whites in the West Indies and American colonies. At the same time, it paints a picture of traditional life in Africa somewhat removed from the idealized and Arcadian notions of many contemporary abolitionists; for example, Equiano refers to the existence of domestic slavery and local warfare in Ibo society. His autobiography is suffused with his passionate and profound evangelical Christianity, attacking slave-owners and slave-traffickers as "nominal Christians" who fail to do to others what they wish to be done to them, corrupted by avarice and wickedness. It forms a worthy supplement to John Wesley's sermons against the evils of slavery. Above all, it is a personal statement by one who had lived the life of a slave. It is written from his own experience; his often-quoted description of the "red faces" of white slavers and the "large furnace" on the ship that took him away from Africa (chap. 3) is etched with the sharp instrument of childhood recollection.

The Interesting Narrative brought Equiano considerable fame in his lifetime. The Prince of Wales (later George IV) and the Duke of York were among its fans. It provided Equiano with a sufficient return to make his final years ones of comfort. On April 7, 1792, he married a white woman, Susanna Cullen, who predeceased him by a year. He died in London on March 31, 1797, and thus did not live to see the Atlantic slave trade abolished. His fame lingered a little thereafter, and then virtually disappeared in the late nineteenth and early twentieth centuries, when chroniclers venerated Wilberforce and his white colleagues for their crusade against slavery and the slave trade, but ignored the contribution made by Equiano and other former black slaves such as Ignatius Sancho and Ottobah Cuguano. The rising interest in black history since the 1960s (especially in the United States) has rectified this imbalance. It has led to the rediscovery of Equiano and his book, which has won "an iconic status" (Walvin 1994) in black diaspora studies. It has also furnished future ages with an authentic and first-hand account of the black experience at the height of the British plantation system in the late eighteenth century.

MURRAY STEELE

Biography

Born in a village near modern Onitsha in about 1745. Kidnapped by slave merchants in about 1756. Regained his freedom and settled in London in 1767. Appointed "Commissary of Provisions and Stores for the Black Poor to Sierra Leone" by the British government in 1786. Dismissed from the post in 1787. Published his autobiography, *The Interesting Narrative*, in 1789. Married Susanna Cullen in 1792. Died in London on March 31, 1797.

Further Reading

Equiano, O. *Equiano's Travels: His Autobiography; The Interesting Narrative of the Life of Olaudah Equiano or Gustavus Vassa the African.* Abridged and edited by Paul Edwards. New York: Praeger, 1967.

———. *The Interesting Narrative and Other Writings*. Edited with an introduction and notes by Vincent Carretta. New York: Penguin, 1995.

Walvin, James. *An African's Life: The Life and Times of Olaudah Equiano, 1745–1797*. New York: Cassell, 1998.

———. *Black Ivory: A History of British Slavery*. Washington, D.C.: Howard University Press, 1994.

Eritrea: Ottoman Province to Italian Colony

Before being unified by the Italians in 1890, Eritrea was formed of different regions that were peripheral areas of diverse imperial states. The presence of the Ottomans dates back to the sixteenth century, when the region that later became known as Eritrea was contended by Ethiopian emperors, the sultan of Harar, known as Ahmed Gran, who occupied the provinces of Seraye, Hamasien, and Akalai Guzai in the highlands, and the Ottomans in the coastal areas. Ahmed Gran was defeated by the Portuguese and the Ethiopian emperor who also drove the Ottomans out of the coast. Nevertheless, the Ottomans reacquired the port of Massawa and neighboring zones in 1557 and established a more secure rule until the nineteenth century. Their control was limited to the coastal area ruled by the *na'ib*, deputy of the Turkish commander who was responsible for the collection of taxes. However, in the nineteenth century, the Egyptians profited from the collapse of the Ottoman Empire, and in 1865 they occupied Massawa and the coastal region. The Egyptians were also able to control the areas of Keren and the Senheit in the west. Thus, two-thirds of Eritrean territory came under Egyptian bureaucratic control. Egyptian influence in a vast part of present-day Eritrea led to collisions with Ethiopian emperor Johannes IV, who succeeded in holding the central highlands. The Hamasien, Akalai Guzai and Seraye regions were connected to the Ethiopian empire to which they paid taxes until the arrival of the Italians in the region. In the nineteenth century the Dankalia region was under the control of local aristocratic rulers.

In 1869, after the opening of the Suez Canal, the Italian shipping company Rubattino purchased the bay of Assab. In 1882 the bay was taken over by the Italian state and declared an Italian colony. Three years later the port of Massawa was incorporated, owing to British diplomatic assistance, and it soon became evident that Italian expansionist policy in the Red Sea was directed toward the acquisition of the Ethiopian highlands' fertile lands. Ethiopia had been always the real objective of Italian colonialism. With the hope of finding more inhabitable lands, the Italians entered the areas located to the northwest of Massawa through military action or stipulating agreements with those local chiefs who were the rivals of Yohannes, emperor of Ethiopia. Italian penetration inland led to an immediate military

Eritrea.

reaction by Emperor Yohannes' troops who defeated a force of five hundred Italians at Dogali in 1887. Later on, Italian penetration into the highlands was facilitated by a period of deep economic and political crisis of the Ethiopian Empire, due to famines, epidemics, and the death of Emperor Yohannes.

In January 1890 the possessed lands in the Red Sea were unified into a political entity called Eritrea. Italy immediately undertook a policy of land alienation against local peasants, particularly between the years 1893 and 1895. However, the colonial administration had to abandon this policy, which caused tensions and rebellions especially in rural areas. Indeed, in 1894 one of the strongest revolts took place in Akalai Guzai, led by *Dejazmach* Bahta Hagos, who had been previously allied to the Italians. The control of rebellious areas became the Italian reasoning behind the invasion of the northern province of Ethiopia, but in 1896 the Italians were defeated by the army of Ras Alula at Adwa.

Italian colonialism in Eritrea lasted almost sixty years, from 1882 to 1941, and during this period it redefined its purposes and designs several times. After the disastrous consequences of the policy of land alienation, Italian administration adopted a policy of consolidation of its colonial rule. The period until the mid-1930s witnessed a gradual transformation of Eritrea. The Italian *colonia primogenita* (first-born colony) of Eritrea was given the first administrative structure and divided into *commissariati* (districts) ruled by Italian officials. Land concessions were given to local and Italian people in both the highlands and lowlands. In the lowlands "capitalist concessions" were introduced.

While the cereal-cultivation of the highlands had to satisfy the consumption needs of the entire population, the cultivation of the lowlands, mainly coffee, was produced primarily for exportation. The construction of primary and secondary roads was also a priority, and a railway was built connecting Massawa to Tessenei. In the urban environment, especially in the capital, Asmara, public works were developed, and the service sector expanded with the opening of shops, restaurants, bars and various businesses which led to mass urbanization.

With the conquest of Ethiopia, Eritrea became the logistical base for the entire Italian Eastern Africa empire and witnessed radical transformation over a very short period. The road network was extended, and a fledgling industrial sector grew rapidly to satisfy the needs of the ever-growing Italian community. According to an economic census of 1939, in Eritrea as a whole, there were more than 2,000 industrial firms involved in construction, transport, repair workshops, chemicals, brick production, furniture, cinematography, graphics, leather tanning, textiles and electricity. Most of them were of course concentrated in the capital Asmara, where the first class of Eritrean entrepreneurs developed. The town of Asmara alone recorded a population of 120,000 in 1934–1941, the Italian community making up half of this figure. Nevertheless, throughout the colonial period recruitment in the colonial army as *askari* ("native" soldier) represented the most stable source of income for the local population. It was calculated in 1939 that out of approximately 617,000 men and women, 40 per cent of men joined the colonial army. *Askari* were recruited for the expansion into Somalia and Libya where opposition to colonialism persisted until 1932.

In the sixty years of Italian domination, a rigid racial policy was applied by the colonial administration. It was only in the 1930s, however, with the massive arrival of Italian settlers, that a regime of apartheid was imposed by the fascist government and institutionalized by laws and governmental decrees that impacted mainly upon the urban milieu of Asmara. During the World War II, Italy had to confront the British army, which entered Eritrea in 1941. Having no design for a future role in Eritrea, the British Military Administration that existed there until 1952 did not really change the structure of Italian colonialism, even if it abolished the regime of apartheid imposed by the Italians.

FRANCESCA LOCATELLI

See also: **Ethiopia: Italian Invasion and Occupation: 1935–1940; Massawa, Ethiopia, and the Ottoman Empire.**

Further Reading

Bereketeab, R. *Eritrea: The Making of a Nation, 1890–1991.* Uppsala: Uppsala University, 2000.

Markakis, J. *National and Class Conflict in the Horn of Africa.* Cambridge: University Press, 1987.

Mesghenna, Y. *Italian Colonialism: A Case Study of Eritrea, 1869–1934.* Lund, Sweden: Studentlitteratur, 1988.

Negash, T. *Italian Colonialism in Eritrea, 1882–1941: Politics, Praxis, and Impact.* Uppsala: Uppsala University, 1987.

Pool, D. *From Guerrillas to Government: The Eritrean People's Liberation Front.* Oxford: James Currey, 2001.

Eritrea: 1941 to the Present

Eritrea, a country of about 119,400 square miles, with a population of about 3.5 million, is located at the southwestern coast of the Red Sea. Modern-day Eritrea, like most African countries, is a creation of nineteenth-century European colonialism. Toward the end of the nineteenth century, Italy was lagging behind in the colonial scramble. The only area open for colonial occupation was the Horn of Africa. Italy first gained a foothold in Eritrea in 1869 when an Italian company bought the Assab Port from a local chief in the name of the Italian government. On January 1, 1890, Eritrea was declared an Italian colony.

Under Italian occupation, Eritrea was converted from a peasant and nomadic state to an industrial and commercial center intended to sustain Italy's colonial ambition in East Africa, while supplying Italy with raw materials and agricultural products. Italy's colonial philosophy was one of maximizing capital returns through exploitative use of fertile lands and local labor. There was little concern for the welfare of Eritreans.

In order to accomplish its exploitative goals, Italy built roads, bridges, canals, railways, cable roads, and a vast administrative bureaucracy. At the end of World War II, Eritrea (along with South Africa, Egypt, and Nigeria) was one of the few industrialized centers in Africa.

Great Britain took possession of Eritrea in 1941, after Italy was defeated in the Horn of Africa. The British Military Administration (BMA) governed Eritrea until 1952. After 1945 the conditions under which the BMA maintained responsibility were stipulated by the United Nations: the administration was to assist Eritrea in the process of making an orderly transition from an occupied territory to full self-determination.

Under British rule, Eritrea experienced political development but suffered economic setbacks. To fulfill the requirements of the "requisitioning" clause of its mandate, the BMA impoverished Eritrea by dismantling and disassembling Eritrean industrial capital. Requisitioning caused massive hardship and economic dislocation.

The British administrative culture, which was based on liberal democratic values, however, promoted political mobilization and freedom of the press. Labor unions in the urban centers, particularly in Asmara, and Massawa were allowed to flourish. Most of all, the BMA opened up opportunities for mass education. Under Italian rule education was limited to the fourth grade level; by contrast, the British introduced primary and secondary education in earnest.

The ten years of British administration had an important effect on the country's political consciousness. The period paved the way for organized political participation, and, for the first time, Eritreans were exposed to the possibilities of political freedom. The dissemination of ideas through the lively press, spearheaded by able Eritreans, boosted political awareness. The urban middle class who served earlier as functionaries of the Italian and British bureaucracies organized themselves into political parties advocating competing programs. Three major political parties emerged during the British occupation: the Muslim League, the Liberal Progressive Party, and the Unionist Party. As the British mandate was approaching an end in 1952, Eritrean political identity was crystallized as a liberal progressive system.

At the end of the British occupation in 1952, Eritrean federation with Ethiopia as mandated by the UN took effect. The federation created an Eritrean parliamentary government with responsibilities for domestic affairs such as police power, education, and health. The mandate called for the Eritrean people to exercise their wish for complete independence or to opt for union with Ethiopia. Complete control of foreign affairs, interstate commerce, the ports, railroads, the national currency, and defense rested on Ethiopia.

Before the referendum could be consummated as planned, Ethiopia maneuvered the Eritrean parliament's activities and subverted the federal provisions, in effect, reducing Eritrea to a mere province of the empire in 1962. Disgruntled Eritreans who resented Ethiopian intervention in Eritrean politics agitated against the Ethiopian government and called for Eritrean independence. In 1961 the Eritrean Liberation Movement (ELM), an underground urban organization, had been born to campaign for Eritrean independence. This organization developed into a guerrilla force calling itself the Eritrean Liberation Front (ELF).

ELF scored military successes against the Ethiopian occupying troops, but it failed to crystallize common ideological programs for Eritrea. The ELF started as a nationalist force, but gradually a large segment of its following harbored conflicting ideologies. Some were Pan-Arabists while others were radical Marxists and nationalists. An internal split resulted in the violent defeat of the Pan-Arabist movement at the hands of the Marxists and the nationalists. In 1977 the Marxists and the nationalists formed a new front called the Eritrean Peoples Liberation Front (EPLF) under the leadership of Issayas Afeworki. In a subsequent showdown between ELF and the EPLF, the ELF was driven out of Eritrea into the refugee camps of Sudan in 1980.

The EPLF started as a nationalist front with radical Marxist inclinations. Its military and political policy relied on strict hierarchy and intense military discipline. Its military energy and discipline enabled the organization to score spectacular victories against the Ethiopian forces. One of these military feats was the 1987 AfaAbbet victory where one-third of the Ethiopian force stationed in Eritrea was defeated. Overnight, Ethiopian troops were forced to abandon their positions in the Eritrean lowlands. They were garrisoned in Asmara, Massawa, and Decamare. In 1990 the EPLF liberated Massawa and encircled the Ethiopian garrison in Decamare. Even though the Ethiopian troops outnumber EPLF forces nearly five to one, the Eritreans were unstoppable. After several months of withering assaults, the Decamare garrison was soundly defeated. On May 24, 1991, EPLF forces marched into Asmara on the heels of a confused Ethiopian retreat. With the capture of Asmara, the capital of Eritrea, the thirty-year war of liberation came to an end. EPLF immediately called for the implementation of the referendum that Haile Selassie's government had undermined in 1962. On May 24, 1993, Eritreans voted for complete independence through internationally supervised referendum.

Ethiopia, under a newly installed regime, became the first country to officially recognize Eritrea's independence.

In May 1998 new border conflicts between Eritrea and Ethiopia climaxed in a full-scale war, resulting in massive carnage. The conflict was formally ended by the brokering of a peace deal in June 2000. However, both nations suffered the loss of thousands of soldiers.

TSEGGAI ISAAC

Further Reading

Gordon, C. *The Horn of Africa.* New York: St. Martin's Press, 1994.

Jordan Gebre-Medhin. *Peasants and Nationalism in Eritrea: A Critique of Ethiopian Studies.* Trenton: N.J.: Red Sea Press, 1989.

Longrigg, S. H. *A Short History of Eritrea.* Oxford: Clarendon Press, 1945.

Pateman, R. *Eritrea: Even the Stones Are Burning.* Trenton: N.J., Red Sea Press, 1998.

Essawira: *See* Morocco: Sidi Muhammad and Foundations of Essawira.

Ethiopia: Muslim States, Awash Valley: Shoa, Ifat, Fatagar, Hadya, Dawaro, Adal, Ninth to Sixteenth Centuries

The spread of Islam in the southern and eastern parts of the Ethiopian region was closely associated with trade. Initially, Muslim merchants established bases at the coast from where they could travel inland, setting up temporary trading posts under the protection of local chieftains. Gradually, as the nomadic peoples occupying the coastal lowlands adopted Islam, if only superficially, these trading posts became permanent settlements. Muslim traders were then able to move further inland, following the course of the Awash River, into Shoa and the kingdoms of the Sidama people in the west. It is unclear exactly when Islam reached these regions but according to tradition a sultanate, ruled by the Makhzumi dynasty, was founded in southeastern Shoa in 896. It was eventually conquered by Ali ibn Wali Asma in 1285 and incorporated into Ifat, which became the paramount Muslim state of the region.

In this way, by the beginning of the fourteenth century, a string of Muslim states circled the southern and eastern borders of the Christian Ethiopian kingdom. Situated on the northern side of the Awash River was Ifat and to its south-west lay Fatagar. On the southern side, the most westerly state was Hadya with Dawaro situated to its east. Further to the south lay Sharka and Bali. Adal, at this time, was a vague term used to refer in general to all the Muslim lowlands east of the Christian kingdom and, more specifically, to the Muslim state of Awssa, situated on the lower course of the Awash River in the Danakil lowlands.

Relations between the Muslim states and the Christian kingdom at this time are often represented in terms of religious enmity and war. The situation was, however, far more complex. While armed conflict did occur, it was seldom directly the result of religious issues, although the call to arms was usually couched in religious terms. The main reasons for military action were territorial expansion, political aggrandizement, and commercial rivalry, especially since the Islamization of the eastern side of the Ethiopian region had effectively cut off the Christian kingdom from direct access to the lucrative southern trade routes and the port of Zeyla. But, despite this focus of contention, there was also considerable cooperation in the field of commerce. Although control of the trade routes to Zeyla was in the hands of the rulers of Ifat, supply and demand for many of the trade items passing along them was generated by the Christian kingdom so that the two were, in effect, bound together by commercial interdependence. On the other hand, while Muslim and Christian could coexist peacefully enough, relations between the Muslim states were plagued by commercial

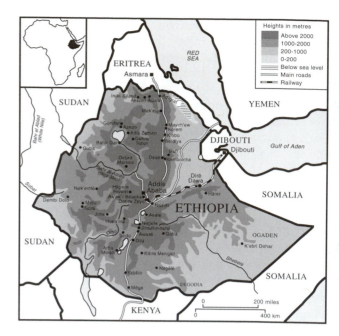

Ethiopia.

competition, internal political disputes, and poor communications, which prevented them from joining together to pose a serious military threat to the Christian kingdom.

The situation was further complicated in the border regions by the fact that the local populations were only superficially Islamized or Christianized. In general, they continued to adhere to their own traditional religious beliefs and could not be relied on to offer military support in case of conflict. Consequently, when fighting did occur, it took the form of limited border raids while more extensive operations, like the conquest envisaged by Muhammad Abu Abd Allah at the very end of the thirteenth century, were short-lived.

The status quo changed during the reign of the militaristic Ethiopian king, Amda Tsiyon (1312–1342). His expansionist policies inevitably led to confrontation with Ifat over control of the trade routes to Zeyla, and, in 1328, tensions finally erupted into war. The Christian side was victorious. The Walasma ruler of Ifat, Haqq ad-Din, was taken prisoner, and Ifat itself was crushed and together with neighboring Fatagar was reduced to a tributary state under the rule of Sabr ad-Din, one of Haqq ad-Din's brothers. Sabr ad-Din, however, quickly renewed plans to attack the Christian kingdom, drawing support from Hadya and Dawaro, as well as from disaffected Agaw regions far to the north. Conflict again erupted in 1332, and again the Muslim forces were defeated, with the result that Amda Tsiyon placed all the hostile Muslim states under one tributary ruler, Jamal ad-Din, yet another of Haqq ad-Din's brothers. The Christian advance then continued eastward, provoking a hostile response from the ruler of Adal, who was also defeated.

The campaigns of 1332 represented a major victory for Amda Tsiyon. The expanding Christian realm, now an empire, had gained the advantage in relation to the Muslim states. Important new tribute-paying territories had been acquired, and control of the southern trade routes had been secured. But the victory was not permanent. In 1376 Ifat rebelled yet again, first under the leadership of Haqq ad-Din II and then under Sa'd ad-Din II, who was eventually forced to take refuge at Zeyla where he was killed in 1415. This event marked the end of Ifat and the emergence of Adal, with a new capital at Dakar, as its successor.

Throughout the fifteenth century, Adal's incursions into Christian-held territories continued to be of concern to the imperial rulers. During the reign of Zara Yaqob (1434–1468), for instance, the sultan of Adal, Ahmad Badlay, launched a series of campaigns into the predominantly Muslim border provinces of the empire. His death in battle in 1445 brought the venture to an end, and Adal was forced to pay tribute in return for peace. This outcome seemed yet again to confirm the ultimate paramountcy of the Christian empire, but the balance of power between the two was, in fact, beginning to change. The region of Adal was far too large and inhospitable for the establishment of direct imperial control and, following the reign of Zara Yaqob, the weakening of imperial government at the center enabled the subjugated peripheral regions to grow more openly rebellious. In comparison, as the power of the empire waned, Adal grew stronger and the way was paved for the Muslim conquest of Christian Ethiopia in the sixteenth century.

CAROLINE ORWIN

See also: **Adal: Ahmad ibn Ibrahim, Conflict with Ethiopia, 1526–1543; Religion, History of.**

Further Reading

Cerulli, E. "Il sultanato dello Scioa nel secolo XIII secondo un nuovo documento storico." Estratto dalla *Rassegna di studi Etiopici1*, no. 1 (January–April 1941).

"Ethiopia's Relations with the Muslim World." In *General History of Africa*. Vol.3, *Africa from the 7th to the 11th Century*. edited by M. el Fasi. Berkeley: University of California Press, 1988.

Cuoq, J. *L'Islam en Ethiopie des origines au XVIe siècle*. Paris: Nouvelles Éditions Latins, 1981.

el Fasi, M. and I. Hrbek. "The Horn of Africa." In *General History of Africa*. Vol. 3, *Africa from the 7th to the 11th Century*, edited by M. el Fasi. Berkeley: University of California Press, 1988.

Taddesse Tamrat., "Ethiopia, the Red Sea and the Horn." In *The Cambridge History of Africa*. Vol. 3, *From c.1050–c.1600*, edited by Roland Oliver. Cambridge: Cambridge University Press, 1977.

Trimingham, J. S. *Islam in Ethiopia*. 2nd ed. London: Frank Cass, 1965.

Ethiopia: Aksumite Inheritance, *c.*850–1150

The civilization of Aksum lasted for the first thousand years of the Christian era. Aksum was a major power of the Red Sea region. It had extensive commercial, diplomatic, and cultural contacts with the Hellenistic, Roman, and Indian Ocean world. It ruled over Yemen. It had a formidable navy, and during the time of King Kaleb (sixth century), sent an expedition to Yemen to repress an uprising against Aksumite rule.

In the eighth century, Aksumite power began to wane. The rise of Islam in the seventh century negatively affected Aksum's role in the Red Sea trade, although it did not stop it completely. During the ninth century, the Aksumite kingdom was confined to the highlands of southern Eritrea, Tigray, Lasta, and Angot. During the same time, some Christian Aksumites moved from Tigray south to Amhara and northern Shawa. In about the middle of the tenth century, a woman identified in the Ethiopian Christian tradition as Yodit Gudit ("Judith the monster") or Esato ("the fiery one") rose to prominence and put an end to the tottering Aksumite state. It seems clear that Aksum, already weakened by successive Beja attacks from the northwest, could not stand Yodit's onslaught. However, her identity is a matter of speculation. It has been suggested that she was from the kingdom of Damot located just south of the Blue Nile gorge or that she was a queen of the Falasha (Ethiopian Jews).

There is a dearth of historical material dealing with the period of the tenth to the twelfth centuries. This was the period between the end of Aksum and the rise of the Zagwe. Reflecting on the bygone days of Aksum's glory, and as if to compensate for their isolation from the outside Christian world, Ethiopians tenaciously held to their Christian religion. Turning to the Old Testament, they rendered Ethiopia as the Second Jerusalem.

Aksumite civilization was reinvigorated in the newly-founded Agaw dynasty, the Zagwe dynasty (c.1150–1270). The seat of the Zagwe dynasty was Lasta, south of Tigray, with its capital at Adafa. It was the immediate inheritor of Aksum's heritage. Aksum left a legacy to Christian Ethiopia in general and to the succeeding Zagwe dynasty in particular. Chief among its legacies are Christianity, architecture, rock-hewn churches, script, literature, and statecraft.

According to Ethiopian and foreign sources, Christianity was introduced into Aksum during the fourth century by Frumentius, a Greco-Phoenician, who became the first head of the church in Ethiopia.. He was instrumental in the conversion of the king of Aksum,

Ezana, who became the first Aksumite king to be converted to Christianity. Aksumite Christianity was derived from Egypt. It followed two of the dominant traits of Coptic Christianity: the monophysite creed (which holds that Jesus Christ had a single, divine nature), and monasticism. Christian Aksum passed on these two legacies to posterity, which still identify Ethiopian Christianity.

In the sphere of architecture, post-Aksumite Ethiopia inherited a distinct Aksumite style of architecture, including the construction of rock-hewn churches. Aksumite architecture used stone, timber, and clay materials. Aksumites built many rock-hewn churches. Two famous ones are the Church of Degum-Sellasse in Guerealta and the Church of Maryam of Berakit, both located in the Aksum area. Of all the heritage bequeathed by Aksum to posterity, none has been as influential to the Zagwe period as the remarkable rock-hewn churches of Lalibela. These churches, built by King Lalibela, have no equal in Christian Ethiopia. They are testimony to what the Zagwe inherited from their Aksumite predecessors as well as the innovative genius of the Zagwe themselves.

The Ge'ez script, also known as the Ethiopic writing system, is one of the most important achievements of Aksumite civilization. The script initially contained consonants only. Some were written from right to left, while others were written in the boustrophedon (plow formation), in which the first line runs from right to left, the second from left to right, and the third back to right to left, and so on. The Ethiopian linguist and scholar Kidane Wald Kifle, in his Ge'ez-Amharic dictionary, *Matshafa Sawasaw Wages Wamazgaba Qalat Haddis*, argued that it was with the introduction of Christianity into Ethiopia that the script took the form it has now, with the addition of vowels and the practice of writing from left to right.

In literature, ecclesiastical works predominated. In statecraft, while some aspects of Aksumite civilization were retained, other new elements were also introduced. The Aksumite state was a tributary state, as were all succeeding states in Ethiopia.

TESHALE TIBEBU

Further Reading

Huntingford, G., W. B. *The Historical Geography of Ethiopia from the First Century AD to 1704*. Edited by Richard Pankhurst. Oxford: Oxford University Press, 1989.

Sergew, Hableselassie. *Ancient and Medieval Ethiopian History to 1270*. Addis Ababa: United Printers, 1972.

Taddesse, Tamrat. *Church and State in Ethiopia, 1270–1527*. Oxford: Clarendon, 1972.

———. "Ethiopia, the Red Sea and the Horn" in *The Cambridge History of Africa*. Vol. 3, *From c.1050– to c.1600*, edited by Roland Oliver. Cambridge: Cambridge University Press, 1977.

Tekle, Tsadik Mekouria. "The Horn of Africa." In *UNESCO General History of Africa*. Vol. 3, *Africa from the Seventh to the Eleventh Century*, edited by M. Elfasi. Berkeley: University of California Press, 1988.

Ethiopia: Zagwe Dynasty, 1150–1270

The period of Zagwe rule in the central Ethiopian highlands was one of the most remarkable in the region's medieval history. The dynasty presided over an energetic Christian expansion through the central Ethiopian plateau, as well as a period of notable commercial and cultural interaction with Egypt and the Middle East; it was also responsible for the creation of some of Ethiopia's most stunning architecture. All of this notwithstanding, however, the Zagwes have been disparaged by the region's subsequent chroniclers, being represented as usurpers of power from the legitimate "Solomonic" line. The Zagwes sought legitimacy by creating the myth that they descended from Moses. They also attempted to assert moral authority with their remarkable architecture. Neither, however, has impressed Ethiopia's royal chroniclers, who have in general depicted the Zagwes as transgressors with no "Israelite" connection, while even Zagwe rock-hewn architecture is actually supposed to have been the work of angels.

Our knowledge of the entire Zagwe period is in fact somewhat limited, while the circumstances of their rise to power are unclear. The Zagwes were originally Agaw-speakers, with their home base in the province of Lasta, an area which had long been part of the Christian kingdom, and which was strategically located to take advantage of north-south trade and communication links. They belonged to an increasingly successful military and political class that had become assimilated into Semitic and Christian culture in the centuries following the decline of Axum, during which period they were integrated into post-Axumite ruling elites. They seized power around 1150 (or 1137, according to Ethiopian tradition), but there is little evidence to suggest that their emergence represented a "revolution" as such, or that there was a dramatic episode at the time of the first Zagwe ruler's accession. It seems, rather, that the assumption of royal powers by the Lasta political class was the culmination of a sociopolitical process dating back at least two centuries and did not represent a significant break with the past. As the state expanded, Christian military leaders, chosen either from among the royal family or those close to it, were appointed as territorial governors with considerable local powers; many members of the Zagwe court were drawn from Lasta and held high ecclesiastical and administrative positions, while military leadership and economic power were also probably awarded to such courtiers. The territorial expansion of the state was attended by Christian missionary activity and, backed by a substantial army, Christian settlement and control were pushed southward, particularly into Gojjam and onto the Shoan plateau.

There was a significant growth in the kingdom's external relations during the era of Zagwe rule. The rise of Fatimid Egypt led to renewed commercial activity along the Red Sea, and the Ethiopian highlands benefited from such trading links. The slave trade in particular expanded, although gold and ivory were also important exports. Textiles and other luxuries from the Islamic world were imported by Muslim merchants through Massawa on the Red Sea coast. In addition to this increased commercial interaction, the Zagwes also strengthened their links with the Egyptian Coptic Church, and strong trading relations between the Ethiopian region and Egypt enabled pilgrims from the highlands to pass through Muslim territories on their way to Jerusalem. Such contacts brought the region once again to the attention of Europe, where in the twelfth century stories began to circulate about a remote but devout and wealthy "kingdom of Prester John."

Visits to the Holy Land may also have been, partly at least, the inspiration behind the remarkable rock-hewn churches of the period. While a tradition of carving churches out of solid rock already existed, the Zagwes raised the architectural form to new heights. The third ruler in the dynasty, Yimrha, is credited with initiating the program of building rock-hewn churches, but it is Lalibela with whom some of Ethiopia's most outstanding architecture is associated. Around the beginning of the thirteenth century, undoubtedly the peak of the Zagwe state, Lalibela presided over what appears to have been an attempt to reconstruct Jerusalem in the central Ethiopian highlands. The stunning results are an indication of the strength of Christianity in the region and represent the Zagwes' determination to demonstrate the primacy of their political and religious order. This was also a period in which, in spite of the links with the Egyptian church, the Ethiopian church developed its own particular characteristics, centered around the idea that it was an outpost of Christianity surrounded by infidels, and that the Christians of the region were God's chosen people. The increasing influence of the Old Testament gave rise to the perception that the Christian kingdom was Israel's true successor.

Despite its considerable achievements, weaknesses in the Zagwe state had begun to appear by the early thirteenth century. Unable to forge regional unity, the Zagwes were also undermined by their own repeated succession disputes, and such internal conflicts encouraged the emergence of anti-Zagwe movements among the Semitic-speaking Tigrayans and Amhara. The most powerful challenge ultimately came from the Christian community in Shoa, which had grown prosperous from the eastbound trade routes and which had the support of the church. The Shoan rebellion under Yekuno Amlak started around 1268 and, after a series of battles across Lasta and Begemedir, the last Zagwe king was killed in 1270, whereupon Yekuno Amlak declared himself ruler. In order to assert its own legitimacy, the new dynasty developed the myth that they descended from King Solomon and Queen Makeda of Saba; the "Solomonic" line claimed that it was now "restored," following the Zagwe usurpation, but it seems fair to say that only insofar as the monarch was once again a Semitic-speaker can Yekuno Amlak's advent to power be considered a "restoration." While the Zagwes were thereafter generally denigrated, Lalibela himself was subsequently canonized by the Ethiopian church, and Zagwe influence continued to be felt in terms of both the architectural and administrative styles of a kingdom, the success of which owed much to Zagwe innovation.

RICHARD REID

See also: **Lalibela and Ethiopian Christianity.**

Further Reading

Gerster, G. *Churches in Rock: Early Christian Art in Ethiopia.* Translated by R. Hosking. London: Phaidon, 1970.

Marcus, H. *A History of Ethiopia.* Berkeley: University of California Press, 1994.

Sergew, Habte Sellassie. *Ancient and Medieval Ethiopian History.* Addis Ababa: United Printers, 1972.

Taddesse, Tamrat, *Church and State in Ethiopia 1270–1527.* Oxford: Clarendon Press, 1972.

Ethiopia: Solomonid Dynasty, 1270–1550

In 1270 a new dynasty came to power in Christian Ethiopia. Founded by Yekuno Amlak, it is traditionally known as the "Solomonid" dynasty because its kings were said to be descended from Solomon and the Queen of Sheba. The advent of this new dynasty is also traditionally referred to as a "restoration," to distinguish it from the preceding Zagwe dynasty, which was claimed to be illegitimate, and to associate it with the renowned rulers of the ancient kingdom of Aksum.

The early decades of the new dynasty were not especially auspicious. Yekuno Amlak's assumption of power was not universally accepted, and after his death a series of disputed successions destabilized the kingdom. It was only when his grandson, Amda Tsiyon (1312–1342), became king that his dynasty was finally able to consolidate its paramountcy within the heartlands of the Christian kingdom and to extend its authority over neighboring regions. Indeed, such was the expansion of the Christian state at this time that it can accurately be termed an empire.

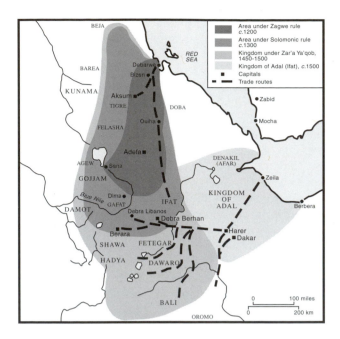

Ethiopia, thirteenth–sixteenth centuries.

Amda Tsiyon's expansionist policies inevitably brought him into conflict with the Muslim states flanking the southern and eastern borders of his realm, and his reign is principally remembered for the campaigns he waged against them. It is important, however, to stress that relations between the two were not always hostile. They were also characterized by a considerable amount of commercial cooperation, which was profitable to both sides. Furthermore, although Amda Tsiyon's military successes ensured that the Christian state gained and maintained the upper hand in relation to its Muslim neighbors, these victories were not in themselves decisive. The Muslim states, benefiting from their contacts with the wider Islamic world, proved to have a remarkable capacity for recovery, and Amda Tsiyon's successors found themselves facing much the same problems. Only in the sixteenth century, when the Muslims, led by Ahmad ibn Ibrahim, declared a full-scale jihad (holy war), did the power struggle between the two reach a crisis point. Between 1529 and 1543, Muslim troops overran almost the entire Christian empire. It was, at least in part, as a result of the growing contacts between Christian Ethiopia and European Christendom, especially the Portuguese, who had dispatched an embassy to Ethiopia in 1520, that the beleaguered king, Galawdewos (1540–1559), was finally able to reverse the situation. With the help of a small, but well-armed, Portuguese contingent, the Christian forces drove the Muslims out of the central highlands. After this destructive conflict Christians and Muslims did not confront each other again in a major war.

Another important theme was the revival of the Ethiopian church, which brought Christianity to the recently subjugated parts of the empire. In many of these areas, however, the process of Christianization was superficial, and the local populations continued to adhere to their old religious beliefs and practices. This gave rise to a religious syncretism or "mixed Christianity" that was at variance with the ordinances of the Alexandrian patriarchate in Egypt but that the poorly organized Ethiopian Church was unable to tackle.

In the central regions, religious life was marked by increasingly bitter theological disputes, particularly over the observance of the Sabbath. The northern-based monastic movement founded by Ewostatewos (c.1273–1352) advocated the observance of the two Sabbaths (Saturday and Sunday), which had been proscribed by the Egyptian church. They were opposed by a strong anti-Sabbath party within the Ethiopian church, especially by the monastic order founded by Takla Haymanot (c.1215–1313) with its base at Debra Libanos in Shoa. The ensuing persecution of the followers of Ewostatewos resulted in their leading an existence almost entirely independent of both the Ethiopian church and the Alexandrian patriarchate, to whose power and prestige their persistent defiance posed a direct and highly embarrassing challenge.

By the reign of Zara Yaqob (1434–1468), the Sabbath controversy was threatening to tear the Ethiopian church apart. Accordingly, in 1450, the king convened the Council of Debra Mitmaq, which attempted to resolve the schism. The issue was decided in favor of the observance of the two Sabbaths, and a reconciliation was effected between the opposing parties. Zara Yaqob also initiated a program of religious reforms, aimed especially at stamping out the "mixed Christianity" of the peripheral regions, with limited success.

The revival of the Ethiopian church was accompanied by a blossoming of Ethiopian literature. Many of the works produced were translated from Arabic, such as the *Senkessar*, a compilation of the lives of the saints. Others were original, including the *Metshafa Berhan* (Book of Light), which is attributed to Zara Yaqob. This deals, in particular, with the Sabbath controversy and expounds the king's religious reforms, offering guidance to the Christian community, refuting heresies and attacking non-Christian practices. Another important literary genre was the royal chronicles, beginning in the reign of Amda Tsiyon with an account of his campaigns against the Muslims. These provide a remarkably rich source for the study of Ethiopian history. But the most important work of this era, although not an original Ethiopian composition, was the *Kebra Nagast* (Glory of the Kings), which was adapted to exemplify Ethiopian concepts of royal legitimacy, linking it not only to an Old Testament heritage, through

496

descent from Solomon and the Queen of Sheba, but also to a New Testament heritage through relationship with Christ.

Thus, under the descendants of Yekuno Amlak, the fundamental characteristics of the Christian Ethiopian state had been established. It had become an expansionist military power, the distinctive nature of Ethiopian Christianity had been defined, and in the political sphere the appropriation of concepts of royal legitimacy, given expression in the *Kebra Nagast*, and the closer identification of church with state, had greatly enhanced the prestige and power of the monarchy. Nevertheless, on the eve of the Muslim conquest, the Solomonid state was to prove surprisingly vulnerable—so much so, in fact, that it was almost completely destroyed.

CAROLINE ORWIN

See also: **Aksum, Kingdom of; Ethiopia: Aksumite Inheritance, *c.*850–1150; Ethiopia: Zagwe Dynasty, 1150–1270; Lalibela and Ethiopian Christianity; Religion, History of.**

Further Reading

Alvarez, F. *Narrative of the Portuguese Embassy to Abyssinia during the Years 1520–1527*. Translated and edited by Lord Stanley of Alderley. 1881. Facsimile reprint, New York: Burt Franklin, 1970.

Budge, Ernest Alfred Wallis, trans. *The Queen of Sheba and her Only Son Menyelek (I): Being the 'Book of the Glory of Kings' (Kebra Nagast)*. London: Oxford University Press, 1932.

Kaplan, S. *The Monastic Holy Man and the Christianization of Early Solomonic Ethiopia*. Wiesbaden: F. Steiner, 1984.

Taddesse, Tamrat. *Church and State in Ethiopia, 1270–1527*. Oxford: Clarendon Press, 1972.

Taddesse, Tamrat. "Ethiopia, the Red Sea and the Horn." *The Cambridge History of Africa*. Vol. 3, *c.*1050–*c.*1600, edited by Roland Oliver. Cambridge: Cambridge University Press, 1977.

Ullendorff, E. "Literature." In *The Ethiopians: An Introduction to Country and People*. 2nd ed. New York: Oxford University Press, 1965.

Ethiopia: Shoan Plateau, Fifteenth and Sixteenth Centuries

The era of the fifteenth and sixteenth centuries witnessed escalating conflict between the Christian state of the Shoan plateau and the increasingly powerful Muslim polity around Harar to the east. Muslim power expanded dramatically into the central and northern Ethiopian highlands and came close to extinguishing the Christian kingdom altogether during an invasion in the early and mid-sixteenth century. The events of the period may be seen as fundamentally shaping the subsequent religious, political, and ethnic history of the region, with the ultimate strengthening, despite the bloody clashes between them, of both Christianity and Islam across much of present-day Ethiopia.

The Christian ruler Zara Yaqob (1434–1468) sought to build on the conquests of his predecessors by creating a more stable and unified kingdom, and by encouraging the further expansion of Christianity, especially in the south. He built a more permanent capital at Debra Berhan in Shoa, and was responsible for reviving the custom of coronation at the town of Axum. In political terms, however, his reign was noted for its brutality and authoritarianism, and in attempting to impose a greater degree of unity he faced the same problems of provincialism which confronted both his predecessors and his successors. In terms of the church, similarly, Zara Yaqob tried to impose orthodoxy, codifying religious practice and attempting to give order to monastic evangelization. The kingdom expanded mainly southward, a combination of military conquest and missionary activity being employed to this end. Christian monasteries were systematically built as centers of conversion. In reality, however, little success was achieved in converting the population of newly conquered districts, particularly in the far south of the kingdom. But there were also commercial considerations behind such expansionism, as the kingdom sought to take advantage of trading networks to the east of the Shoan plateau. This would ultimately bring them into conflict with the Muslims in the area.

Zara Yaqob's death was followed by a relaxing of centralization, in large part because of provincial reaction to the unifying principle; even the capital at Debra Berhan was abandoned. The power of monarchy was undermined to some extent by the fact that the average age of kings at their accession in the late fifteenth and early sixteenth centuries was eleven. This general weakening of the Christian kingdom coincided with the revival of Muslim power to the east. Following Christian military successes in the fourteenth century, Muslim power had relocated to the Harar plateau, where the kingdom of Adal was established. Adal took great advantage of its commercially strategic position between the central Ethiopian highlands and the port of Zeila and united the existing Muslims of the area while converting large numbers of Somalis to Islam. The latter would prove a crucial source of military manpower. The newly unified Islamic state also benefited from Ottoman support, manifest mainly in the import of firearms. Through the fifteenth and early sixteenth centuries, conflict escalated between Christian and Muslim polities, serving to greatly disrupt the commercial system which both sides ultimately sought to control.

The Muslim army commander Ahmad ibn Ibrahim (otherwise known as Gran, "the left-handed") became effective leader of Adal in 1526. Declaring a jihad, he embarked on a systematic attempt to finally destroy the Christian kingdom of the highlands, which by now had become highly decentralized, particularly in southern areas such as Shoa. Invading the kingdom in 1529, Ahmad's forces swept through the Christian highlands, razing churches, seizing captives, and destroying King Lebna Dengel's already fragile administrative infrastructure. Muslim governors were appointed over conquered areas, and many converts to Islam were made. Ahmad was further assisted by the fact that, in addition to the Christian kingdom's weak administration, large numbers of recently conquered Cushitic subjects of the Christian state were only too happy to give expression to their grievances, emanating from the extortions of alien overlords. In areas such as the Shoan plateau, the Christian aristocracy lived virtually independent of central government, and governorships which earlier had been appointed had become in effect hereditary. Ahmad exposed the fundamental weaknesses of the Christian polity.

Ahmad defeated a substantial Christian army at the Battle of Shimbra-Kure in 1529. Over the ensuing decade, the Christian forces were on the defensive, Lebna Dengel constantly retreating to avoid capture and desperately attempting to organize effective resistance as the Muslim army, relying on the zeal of their Somali recruits and the firearms acquired from the Turks, swiftly occupied large areas of the highlands, from Shoa to present-day Eritrea in the north. Out of desperation, Lebna Dengel appealed to Portugal for support against the common enemy of Islam. Lebna Dengel himself did not live to see the outcome of his appeal, but the Portuguese, who had had contact with the Christian state since at least the early 1520s, responded positively, providing a well-equipped force which marched inland from the Red Sea coast and joined up with the remnants of the indigenous Christian army. By this time, Ahmad's forces were severely overstretched, and there had been little effective consolidation of Muslim conquests, while some Somali soldiers, satisfied with their booty, had already begun to return home. Making effective use of his new Portuguese allies, King Galadewos (1540–1559) defeated the Muslim army in 1543; Ahmad himself was killed, whereupon the transience of his "empire" was demonstrated, as the Muslim forces began to disperse eastwards.

Galadewos recovered much of the Shoan plateau through the 1540s and early 1550s. Yet prolonged conflict had depopulated large areas and created a power vacuum in the southern highlands: this facilitated the incursion into the region of Oromo pastoralists from the grasslands adjacent to Lake Turkana. Their rapid occupation of the southern third of present-day Ethiopia was to have profound consequences for the subsequent development of the area. By the end of the sixteenth century, the Oromo, many of whom converted to Christianity and adopted settled agriculture,

had become a significant sector of the population. Others moved onto the Harar plateau where they converted to Islam and became politically as well as demographically prominent. Meanwhile the Christian kingdom, under Sarsa Dengel (1562–1597), sought consolidation and gravitated northward, a move which was at least partly occasioned by the commercial opportunities offered by the Ottoman Turks at Massawa. Both Christianity and Islam had survived the bloody clashes of the fifteenth and sixteenth centuries.

RICHARD REID

Further Reading

Lobo, Father Jerome. *A Voyage to Abyssinia*. Translated by Samuel Johnson. London: Elliot and Kay, 1789.

Marcus, H. *A History of Ethiopia*. Berkeley: University of California Press, 1994.

Pankhurst, R., ed. *The Ethiopian Royal Chronicles*. Addis Ababa: Oxford University Press, 1967.

———. *A Social History of Ethiopia*. Addis Ababa: Institute of Ethiopian Studies, 1990.

Sergew Habte Sellassie. *Ancient and Medieval Ethiopian History*. Addis Ababa: United Printers, 1972.

Taddesse Tamrat. *Church and State in Ethiopia 1270–1527*. Oxford: Clarendon Press, 1972.

———. "Ethiopia, the Red Sea and the Horn." In *The Cambridge History of Africa*. Vol. 3, *From c.1050 to c.1600*, edited by R. Oliver. London: Cambridge University Press, 1977.

Ethiopia: *c.1550–c.1700*

From contemporary sources, the picture that emerges of Ethiopia at the beginning of the sixteenth century is one of internal political stability and prosperity. This picture was to change drastically from the late 1520s as a result of many developments which took place in the country during the sixteenth and seventeenth centuries. These developments included efforts at centralization of power in the hands of the monarch at the expense of the provincial nobility, territorial expansion, attempts at consolidating the power of the state in the conquered areas, political integration, and cultural assimilation of conquered non-Semitic peoples and areas into the culture and religion of the Semitic core. These efforts achieved varying degrees of success during the sixteenth and seventeenth centuries.

Other developments took the form of threats to the survival of the Christian empire, its culture and institutions. The threats came from both internal and external sources. The internal sources included rebellious and separatist tendencies of the regional nobility and the unyielding spirit of the conquered or incorporated peoples. External threats came from the Muslim communities to the east of the Ethiopian plateau and from the Jesuit missionaries from the Iberian countries. A further source of threat was the movement of the

Cushitic Oromo into central and northern parts of the Christian empire.

By about 1550 Ethiopia had recently emerged victorious, thanks to a Portuguese military expedition of 1541–1543, from the most devastating phase of the protracted wars with the Muslims of Adal led by Ahmad Gragn. Gragn's death in 1543 led to the collapse of Adal's hold over Ethiopia, but that did not mean the immediate end of the Muslim threat to the Christian empire, for the wars continued intermittently throughout the 1550s, 1560s, and 1570s. In the 1570s further crushing defeats of the Muslims neutralized the Muslim danger, and by the beginning of the seventeenth century the Muslims were no longer a threat to Christian Ethiopia.

Jesuit missionary activity in Ethiopia took place in the period 1557 to 1632. While it lasted, it threatened not only the unity of the state but also the existence of the Ethiopian Orthodox church as a national institution. By drawing emperor Susneyos into their fold, the Jesuits undermined the traditional ties between the state and the church because the emperor was traditionally the supreme head of the national church and was expected at all times to support and defend the church.

The period *c.*1550–*c.*1700 also saw the migration of the pastoral Oromo into the heartlands of the empire. The Oromo migration altered the demographic picture of highland Ethiopia with the infusion of large numbers of Oromo into the population; it also affected the politics of the empire because, with time, the Oromo began to participate in the politics of the empire at both the imperial court and in the provinces with far-reaching consequences.

Another development in the period 1550–1700 related to the Christian church. Like the state, the Ethiopian church faced a number of challenges that undermined its unity and impaired its effectiveness. The Muslim invasion, the Oromo migration, and the Jesuit missionary activity all posed problems to the church as a national institution. One of these problems was theological disputes, derived in part because the Jesuits challenged several aspects of the monophysite doctrines that were followed by the Ethiopian church. Following the expulsion of the Jesuits and the reconciliation between church and state, emperors Fasiladas (1632–1667) and Yohannes (1667–1682) called a number of councils of church leaders to discuss doctrine. At these councils different interpretations were given to some of the issues in dispute. The disputes were between ecclesiastics from the two leading monastic orders in the empire, the Order of Tekle-Haymanot based at Debra Libanos in Shawa and the Order of Ewostatewos based in Tigre. These disputes led to protracted religious and political schism involving the nobility in the provinces and even the emperor.

This situation continued beyond the seventeenth century into the eighteenth and nineteenth centuries.

Warfare was a major feature of the history of Ethiopia during the sixteenth and seventeenth centuries. Campaigns waged in the first half of the sixteenth century were mainly to resist the invasion of the Muslim soldiers from Adal, but with their defeat subsequent campaigns were directed at restoration, reconstruction, and consolidation of the empire. To these ends campaigns were undertaken to repulse Turkish inroads into the maritime districts of Tigre province against the Agaw, Falasha and Nilotic peoples in the north and northwest, the Sidama and the Oromo in the south. Campaigns by emperors Susneyos, Fasiladas, and Iyasu 1 (1682–1706) finally pacified these areas.

Some of the campaigns waged during the period 1550–1700 were directed against centrifugal forces in the empire. A number of the rulers of this period, especially Gelawdewos, Sarsa Dengel, Susneyos, Fasiladas, and Iyasu I, tried to strengthen imperial authority and centralize political power at the expense of the regional governors by reforming the military and administrative systems in the empire. The reform efforts were invariably opposed by the regional nobility and therefore did not achieve the expected results.

Another development of the period was the transfer of the imperial capital to Gondär by emperor Fasiladas in 1636. Gondär became the permanent capital for the next 200-odd years. Until then the location of the royal court of Solomonid Ethiopia was dictated by the political and or military situation in the empire.

The economy of Ethiopia during this period, as indeed in the centuries before and after, was based on agriculture. The land tenure system in Ethiopia was very complicated and differed, in its specific details, from one province to another and sometimes even within the same province. Basically there were two types of land tenure system: *rest* ownership and *gult* ownership. *Rest* land tended to be owned by families rather than individuals and therefore heritable within the family. *Gult* land, on the other hand, was not inheritable. The holder was entitled to a share of the land's production but did not technically own the land. In terms of land tenure, there were two classes: the land owner/holder class and the landless tenant farmer class (*gabbar*). The former did not participate directly in working on the land but lived off the labor of the *gabbar*.

Besides agriculture, trade, both local and international, was of considerable importance. The emperor participated in the trade through royal agents and also, along with the ruling class, derived revenue from it through taxation. For many centuries Ethiopia traded with Arabia, India, and the Mediterranean world via the Red Sea port of Massawa. Also trade routes developed from the Gulf of Aden to the interior of the Horn of Africa. Despite military turmoil in the area during this period three main trade routes between the coast and the plateau were in use throughout the sixteenth and seventeenth centuries. There were also overland trade routes to Egypt through northern and northwestern Ethiopia. All these international trade routes linked up with internal routes which radiated from southwestern Ethiopia; this area was the main source of nearly all the trade goods originating from Ethiopia.

Trade goods from Ethiopia included slaves, ivory, gold, wax, civet, and coffee; these were exchanged for military items such as swords, helmets, spearheads, muskets, and nonmilitary luxury goods like silk brocades cushions and carpets. The trade was mainly by barter; goods were exchanged for gold, salt bars (*amole*), iron, cloth, and other items. The value of these media of exchange varied from one province to another depending on distance from source of supply. In the sixteenth and seventeenth centuries an indigenous mercantile class did not develop in Ethiopia. For this reason the long-distance trade was in the hands of aliens, mostly Muslims for whom the Islamic religion and the Arabic language served as major assets in dealing with merchants from the Muslim world.

R. H. KOFI DARKWAH

See also: **Ethiopia: Portuguese and, Sixteenth–Seventeenth Centuries; Ethiopia: Solomonid Dynasty, 1270–1550.**

Further Reading

Abir, M. "Ethiopia and the Horn of Africa." In the *Cambridge History of Africa*. Vol. 4, edited by Richard Gray, Cambridge: Cambridge University Press, 1975.

Abir, M. *Ethiopia and the Red Sea: The Rise and Decline of the Solomonic Dynasty and Muslim European Rivalry in the Region*. London: Frank Cass and Company, 1980.

Merid, Wolde Aregay. "Society and Technology in Ethiopia, 1500–1800." *Journal of Ethiopian Studies* 17 (1984).

Hassan, M. *The Oromo of Ethiopia: A History, 1570–1860*. Cambridge: Cambridge University Press, 1990.

Pankhurst, R. *The Ethiopians*. Oxford: Blackwell Publishers, 1998.

Ethiopia: Portuguese and, Sixteenth–Seventeenth Centuries

In the sixteenth and seventeenth centuries Ethiopia established relations with Portugal. There were three aspects to this relationship; diplomatic (1520–1526), military (1541–1543) and religious (1557–1632).

In 1520 a Portuguese diplomatic mission was sent to Ethiopia to establish friendship with its ruler. This was in response to an Ethiopian diplomatic mission sent to the Portuguese in 1512 by Empress Eleni. The background to the Portuguese mission was the European desire to form an alliance with the fabled Prester John, identified at this time with the king of Ethiopia. This alliance was aimed at opposing Muslim control over the Red Sea and the Indian Ocean trade route to the East. With the revival of trade on this route from the fifteenth century, its control by Muslim Turkey became a matter of great concern to Christian Europe, especially Portugal, which by the early sixteenth century had established a trading empire in the East. The sixteenth century also saw the founding of the Jesuit order by Ignatius Loyola, with the goal of resisting Muslim expansion into the Christian world through intensive Catholic missionary activity. Thus commercial interests and a religious crusading spirit combined to pit Christian Portugal against Muslim Turkey in the Red Sea, the Indian Ocean, and the lands bordering these international commercial waterways.

The Portuguese diplomatic mission to Ethiopia in 1520 paved the way for subsequent military and religious contacts. After a stay of six years the embassy returned to Portugal. From then, periodic correspondence passed between the rulers of the two countries. One such correspondence was from Emperor Lebna Dengel of Ethiopia (1508–1540) to King John III of Portugal (1521–1557) asking for military help in his war against Ethiopia's Muslim neighbors. A Portuguese military expedition was sent to Ethiopia in 1540.

The military expedition from Portugal consisted of approximately 400 armed troops. In two engagements in 1541, the Muslim forces were defeated, but the Muslim leader won a crushing victory over the Portuguese in 1542. However, in another engagement at Wayna Daga in Dembiya in February 1843, a combined force of the Portuguese remnants and of the new emperor Gelawdewos (1540–1559) inflicted a devastating defeat on the Muslim troops, leaving their leader, Gragn, among the dead on the battlefield. Gragn's death led to the disintegration of his army and the collapse of his Muslim administration on the highland. In this way the Portuguese expedition helped to save the Christian kingdom from total extinction and ensure its continued survival.

The third element in the Ethiopian-Portuguese relations in the sixteenth and seventeenth centuries was religious and, like the Muslim jihad of Gragn, also threatened the survival of orthodox Christian Ethiopia. This was the attempt by Jesuit missionaries, with the support of Emperor Susneyos (1607–1632), to convert monophysite Ethiopia to the Roman Catholic faith. The diplomatic and military relations between the two countries drew the attention of the Jesuit missionaries to Ethiopia. Some priests had accompanied both the embassy of 1520–1526 and the military expedition of 1540–1543, but serious missionary activity began in

1557 with the arrival in Ethiopia of Andre de Oviedo, appointed bishop of Ethiopia two years earlier. The Jesuit interlude lasted from 1557 to 1632. The Ethiopian emperors of the sixteenth century were sensitive to the disruptive effect the Jesuit activities could have on the established culture of the Ethiopian church and state. For this reason Jesuit missionary efforts received no official encouragement throughout the sixteenth century.

During the reign of Emperor Susneyos (1607–1632), however, the Jesuit missionary activity received official backing from the emperor. Susneyos is portrayed by scholars as a great admirer of learning, and contemptuous of the ignorance and shallowness of the Ethiopian clergy. He was believed to have been attracted to the Jesuits by their learning. Guided by the Jesuit leaders Pedro Paez and Alphonso Mendez, Susneyos encouraged his royal soldiers and court nobles to become Roman Catholic. In 1625 he himself converted to the new faith. He then proceeded to suppress the sacred customs and practices of the Ethiopian church and replaced these with Roman Catholic practices. It has to be remembered that most of the traditional customs that the Jesuits condemned were not just religious practices but in fact formed part of the very basis of the society. To abolish them therefore was to undermine the very foundations of the Ethiopian society. For this reason the emperor's pro-Catholic policy alienated his subjects, clergy, nobility, and ordinary Christians alike. Opposition to the emperor's religious policy expressed itself in widespread rebellions throughout the empire; the country was thus plunged into a bloody civil war, which in the end forced the emperor to reverse his policy and restore the customs and practices he had prohibited. Thus frustrated Emperor Susneyos abdicated his throne in favor of his son Fasiladas.

Fasiladas (1632–1667) restored the Ethiopian church and expelled the Jesuits from the country. Ethiopian converts who persisted in the Catholic faith were persecuted. These measures brought the immediate danger from the Jesuits to an end, though its ripples were felt in the country for the next two centuries. This was because the Jesuit intervention gave a new dimension and intensity to already existing theological disputations in the Ethiopian church. These doctrinal controversies threatened unity in both church and state right into the nineteenth century.

The Jesuit presence in Ethiopia was, however, not all negative in its consequences. Among its positive impacts especially during the time Pedro Paez was bishop (1603–1622) was the stimulation of theological discussion, a challenge that forced the Ethiopian clergy to reach out to the people by operating in Amharic instead of Geez, the official church language, which was hardly understood by the mass of the people.

Shortlived though this was, it stimulated constructive debate between Coptic and Catholic clergy.

Another positive impact connected with the theological debate was the upsurge of literary production by the Ethiopian clergy. Among these were historical accounts of the reigns of emperors Galawdewos (1540–1559), Sartsa Dengel (1563–1597), and Susneyos (1607–1632), as well as *History of the Galla* by the monk Bahrey; there were also theological works, which included *Fekkare Malakot* (Explanation of the Divinity), *Mazgaba Haymanots* (Treasury of Faith), *Sawana Mafs* (Refuge of Soul), and *Haymanot Abaw* (Faith of the Fathers). The first listed of these works discusses the problem of the knowledge of God, while the rest focus on the arguments of the Coptic clergy in favor of the monophysite belief.

Another aspect of the impact was artistic, visual, and architectural in nature and took the form of paintings of church murals and book illuminations depicting religious stories. Many of these were produced in the late sixteenth and early seventeenth centuries; many of them were modeled on foreign ones but adapted to the Ethiopian traditional style of art.

Notwithstanding its positive impact, the Jesuit interlude in Ethiopia is remembered for the divisive destructive civil wars into which it plunged the country in the early decades of the seventeenth century.

R. H. KOFI DARKWAH

See also: **Ethiopia, *c.*1550–*c.*1700; Ethiopia: Shoan Plateau, Fifteenth and Sixteenth Centuries.**

Further Reading

Abir, M. "Ethiopia and the Horn of Africa." In *Cambridge History of Africa*. Vol. 4. Cambridge: Cambridge University Press, 1975.

———. *Ethiopia and the Red Sea*. London: Frank Cass, 1980.

Haberland, E. "The Horn of Africa." In *UNESCO General History of Africa*. Vol 5, edited by B. A. Ogot. Berkeley: University of California Press, 1992.

Tamrat, Taddesse. "Ethiopia, the Red Sea and the Horn." In *Cambridge History of Africa*. Vol. 3, edited by Roland Oliver. Cambridge: Cambridge University Press, 1977.

———. "The Horn of Africa: The Solomonids in Ethiopia and the States of the Horn of Africa." In *UNESCO General History of Africa*. Vol. 4, edited by D. T. Niane. Berkeley: University of California Press, 1984.

Ethiopia: Eighteenth Century

In 1700 Ethiopia was in a period of cultural revival and political vigor. In 1800 it was fragmented and in cultural and political crisis. The middle decades of the century witnessed the political dominance of one of the remarkable women in all of Ethiopian history, the empress, or *yetégé*, Mentewwab.

The century opened with the last years of the reign of Emperor Iyasu I, also known as "the Great." Iyasu had come to the throne in 1682, inheriting it from his father and grandfather in peaceful succession. He was an active, reforming ruler, and very involved in church questions. In 1705 he led a large military expedition south of the Blue Nile, attempting to reassert both Ethiopian rule and Ethiopian Orthodox Christianity in the Gibé region. The expedition was a failure. Not long after, in 1706, he was deposed by one of his sons and then murdered. His death, and the manner of it, introduced a fifteen-year period of confusion and uncertainty.

The Gibé River bounded a number of small kingdoms, with roots centuries back into the past. For hundreds of years it had acted as a collecting point for some of the region's most valuable exports— in those years slaves and the musk of civet cats. It had also provided generous tribute in gold to the Ethiopian emperors. With the Oromo migrations of the sixteenth and seventeenth centuries, its earlier kingdoms disappeared. Iyasu's expedition was designed to re-assert imperial dominance in the region and it failed, leaving the Gibé almost 150 years of autonomous political development. In the course of the eighteenth century, while the fate of the Ethiopian court in Gondär waxed and waned, a number of the Oromo societies of the Gibé slowly developed monarchical institutions. These little states were keenly oriented toward trade, but their rulers also showed themselves equally interested in the wealth which could be extracted from the land. By the end of the eighteenth century, there was a cluster of five states in the Gibé, the best known of which was Jemma.

Iyasu was succeeded by three sons, a brother, and a nephew. Several of them met violent deaths. Gondär, the capital city, was wracked by violent controversies over Christian theology. Bandits and thieves reappeared in the countryside. Three different pretenders laid claim to the throne.

This unstable period came to an end with the succession of Emperor Bäkaffa, a harsh and violent man, in 1721. Bäkaffa, in turn, was succeeded in 1730 by a son, Iyasu II (often known as "the Little," by contrast with his grandfather). Iyasu II ruled for twenty-five years, following which the throne passed peacefully to his son, Iyo'as, who reigned for another fourteen years. The real power in the country during the reigns of Iyasu and Iyo'as was Iyasu's mother, a consort of Bäkaffa called Mentewwab. In a step unprecedented in Ethiopian history, Mentewwab had herself co-crowned with her son and then with her grandson. Behind a façade of demure femininity, Mentewwab had a firm grasp on the organs of state, which she controlled through a web of male relatives. Mentewwab's era saw a second revival of the arts, following that of the seventeenth century, most notably in painting. The empress was an active manipulator of land and founder of churches. Her most important foundation was Débré Séhay Qwesqwam, a magnificent church in Gondér, which set an example of church foundation which was followed for the rest of the century.

In 1752 the Ethiopian court entertained three Franciscan missionaries, but when their presence became publicly known, they were expelled. Ethiopia was still suffering under the trauma created by the Jesuit intervention of the early seventeenth century. Iyasu's nephew, Yostos (r.1711–1716), had harbored three Roman Catholic missionaries, who, when their presence was discovered, were stoned to death.

Ethiopia found it difficult to deal with foreign Christians in part because its own Christian community was so divided. From the 1660s onward a series of increasingly acrimonious councils were held to resolve questions of Christian doctrine provoked by the preaching of the Jesuits. These controversies were important in the assassination both of Iyasu the Great and of his son and successor. There were two main parties in the seventeenth century, but, in the latter years of Mentewwab, a third party joined them. Church quarrels took on political significance through the regional attachments of their leaders in the great monasteries. Orthodox Christianity, one of the constituents of the Ethiopian state throughout the Solomonic period, was no longer a source of unity, but rather of division and conflict.

The era of Mentewwab ended violently. The empress herself was shunted aside into retirement, but her grandson, Iyo'as, was assassinated in 1769. The year is conventionally taken as the start of the "Era of the Princes," a period likened by the Ethiopian chroniclers to the era of the biblical judges, "when there was no king in Israel." Emperor followed emperor, made and unmade by powerful regional nobles, none of whom proved strong enough to impose his will on all the others. Emperor Téklé Giyorgis, who ruled no fewer than six times between 1779 and 1800, received the nickname "Ender of the Kingdom." From about 1780 to 1855, when the period ended, the nominal Solomonic rulers were shadow kings, without dignity, wealth, comfort, or substance.

The kingdom was now in the hands of the great lords. Some of them descended from provincial lineages of considerable antiquity. The dominant group, however, was of Oromo origin. Mentewwab had married her son, Iyasu, to an Oromo woman from the province of Wéllo, on the eastern side of the highlands, and on coming to the court she brought her relatives with her. They proved unsuccessful in the civil wars of the 1770s and 1780s, but another Oromo group, led by one Ali, from a neighboring territory, did prevail. From the 1780s to the 1850s Ali and his descendants dominated the Ethiopian kingdom from their new capital at Débré Tabor.

DONALD CRUMMEY

See also: **Ethiopia, c.1550–c.1700; Ethiopia: Early Nineteenth Century; Massawa, Ethiopia, and the Ottoman Empire.**

Further Reading

Abir, M. "Ethiopia and the Horn of Africa." *Cambridge History of Africa.* Vol. 4 (1975).

Crummey, D. *Land and Society in the Christian Kingdom of Ethiopia: From the Thirteenth to the Twentieth Century.* Urbana: University of Illinois Press, 1999.

Ethiopia: Early Nineteenth Century

Ethiopia entered the nineteenth century more divided than it had been for many centuries. The Solomonic kings who traced their dynasty back to 1270 and beyond it to biblical origins were now powerless puppet kings, without authority. Instead of a national royal court, the country was now ruled by a number of competing regional lords, whose relations were precariously balanced and who often fell to fighting the one with the other.

The church was similarly divided. Controversies over the nature of Christ had arisen in the seventeenth century, in the aftermath of a twenty-year period of intensive exposure to Portuguese Jesuit missionaries. These controversies slowly formed themselves into distinct schools, each of which was particularly strong within one or other of the country's two major monastic traditions. Many church councils were held during the seventeenth and early eighteenth centuries to resolve the controversies, but without effect. In 1763 a third sectarian party appeared. These theological divisions undermined the authority of the bishops of the church and reinforced the divisive competition of the regional lords. For three decades this state of division and weakness had few strategic consequences. However, in the 1830s Ethiopia began to feel the pressure of a modernizing, expanding Egypt; and Ethiopians soon became aware of the transformations which were taking place in Europe, which presented both opportunities and challenges to their country.

In 1800 the most powerful man in Ethiopia was *Ras* Gugsa, a representative of the Wérréshék dynasty, which had originated on the eastern edge of the plateau in Yéjju province, and whose power drew on the neighboring, Muslim province of Wéllo. The Wérréshék were Christians, but as their collective name (shék = shaykh or sheikh) and the names of some of their rulers

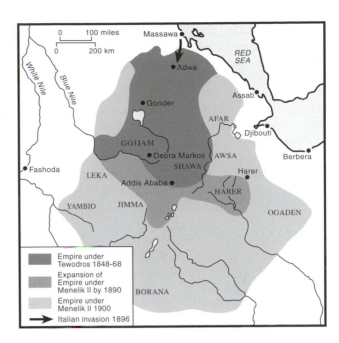

Ethiopia, nineteenth century.

(Ali) suggest, they were much influenced by Islam. Conservative Christians viewed this as a threat to the country's cultural legacy. The Wérréshék ruled from Débré Tabor in the central highlands, and they controlled the puppet rulers of Gondér. Their dominance was challenged by a number of rivals. The most enduring were to the north and the south. To the north the rulers of Tigre province maintained a degree of independence, as, to a lesser extent, did the rulers of Gojjam to the south. Both Tigre and Gojjam viewed themselves as Christian heartland. Still other rivals appeared in the regions to the west and north of Gondér. One prince of the early nineteenth century, *Däjjazmach* Maru, created a very large fiefdom which was known for many years after his death as *YäMaru Qemes*, "What Maru tasted."

These regional rivalries came together in two climactic battles: at Débré Abbay in southwestern Tigre in 1831 and at Débré Tabor in 1842. Tens of thousands of men participated in these battles in which the principal weapons were spears and swords. Cavalry was important and firearms were also used. However, in these years Ethiopians were still using outdated muskets, of uncertain reliability and effectiveness. Both these battles involved all the major lords of the day, and, although both the Wérréshék ruler and his Tigre rival died at Débré Abbay, neither of them fundamentally shifted the balance of power. However, Ethiopian rulers were increasingly turning to external sources to buttress their positions and promote their ambitions. Preparing for the Battle of Débré Abbay, *Däjjazmach* Webé arranged for the patriarch of

Alexandria to send him a bishop, *Abunä* Sélama, who made propaganda on his behalf, denouncing the Wérréshék as Muslim usurpers. The gambit failed and Webé lost the battle.

Webé's overture to Egypt was not the only action involving Egypt in Ethiopian affairs. In the 1820s Egypt had conquered Sudan, and their enlarging rule there brought them in the mid-1830s to the Ethiopian borderlands. Frontier tussles created alarm in some conservative Christian circles in Ethiopia and a general awareness that the strategic isolation which Ethiopia had known for two hundred years was now coming to an end.

Europeans were also now making themselves known again in Ethiopia. Portuguese Jesuits had been of great influence in the years from 1603 to 1632. They had succeeded in converting the royal court, which plunged the country into bitter civil war. In reaction, the Jesuits were expelled and contacts with Europeans were strictly controlled. However, by the early nineteenth century those controls no longer obtained. Sustained contact between Ethiopia and western Europe started in 1830 with the arrival of the Protestant missionary Samuel Gobat and in 1839 with the arrival of the Roman Catholic missionary Justin de Jacobis. While neither of these missionaries had striking evangelical success, both became involved in promoting relations between their respective protecting powers, Britain and France, and Ethiopia. The number of European travelers climbed steadily through the 1830s and 1840s, some of the travelers producing reports of value even today. Various Ethiopian lords protected and promoted the travelers in the hopes of benefiting from their knowledge and contacts.

Given the multiple rivalries involved (Ethiopian lords with one another, European powers with one another) and Egypt's continual growth as a regional power, the situation was one of increasing danger for Ethiopia's national integrity and independence. A number of Ethiopian lords began to think of promoting themselves as new national leaders. For example, *Däjjazmach* Webé, undaunted by his failure in the Battle of Débré Tabor, aspired to make himself king (*negus* in the Amharic). While this would not fully have restored the Solomonic order, it would have placed him on a footing that none of his rivals could claim. This ambition, too, was frustrated.

The period of disunity ended suddenly. *Däjjazmach* Kassa, one of the lords of Ethiopia's western frontier, who had confronted directly the Egyptians, and who was connected to the heirs of *YäMaru Qemes*, in a dramatic series of battles between 1852 and 1855, defeated all the other great lords of the central highlands. His last victim was Webé, and, immediately following his defeat of Webé, Kassa had himself crowned as

Téwodros II, in the church that Webé had probably built for his own coronation. But unlike Webé, Kassa was crowned as king of kings, thereby claiming the Solomonic legacy.

DONALD CRUMMEY

See also: **Ethiopia: Eighteenth Century.**

Further Reading

Abir, M. Ethiopia. *The Era of the Princes: The Challenge of Islam and the Re-unification of the Christian Empire 1769–1855.* London: Longman, 1968.

Crummey, D. *Priests and Politicians: Protestant and Catholic Missions in Orthodox Ethiopia 1830–1868.* Oxford: Clarendon Press, 1972.

Rubenson, S. "Ethiopia and the Horn." *Cambridge History of Africa.* Vol. 5 (1976).

———. *The Survival of Ethiopian Independence.* London: Heinemann, 1976.

Rubenson, Sven. Getatchew Haile, and John Hunwick, eds. *Acta Æthiopica*: Vol. 1, *Correspondence and Treaties 1800–1854.* Evanston, Ill.: Northwestern University Press, 1987.

Ethiopia: Tewodros II, Era of (1855–1868)

Emperor Tewodros fought his way to the throne and, ultimately, proved unable to find a peaceful basis for his rule. He committed suicide at his fortress retreat of Mäqdäla rather than surrender to a British expeditionary force sent to free Europeans he had taken as hostages. By that point, his effective rule had been limited to the immediate vicinity of his army.

His rise to power and his early years of rule were dramatic. In a succession of battles starting in 1852, he defeated all the major lords in Ethiopia, and following the last of those battles had himself crowned by the bishop of the Ethiopian Orthodox Church, *Abunä* Sélama. The suddenness and completeness of his rise amazed contemporaries. So, too, did the aura of reform with which he surrounded himself. His chosen throne name referred to a medieval prophecy that foretold the coming of a king called Tewodros, who would do mighty deeds and usher in an era of prolonged peace. His early reforms were morality-based. He attacked the decadence into which Ethiopia had fallen during the previous century. He also promised to restore Ethiopia's national institutions, monarchy and church, and to recover ancient national territory. The British consul in Ethiopia, Walter Plowden, gave a secular interpretation to the reforms, claiming that the emperor intended to "end the feudal system," to institute a regular system for paying for his administration and army, and to open relations with Europe in the interest of importing European technology.

Tewodros did pursue European technology. In 1856 he received the first of a small group of Protestant missionaries. He installed them at a place called Gafat, not far from Débré Tabor, where he frequently resided himself, and set them to road building and metal casting. His interest increasingly narrowed to military technology. The missionaries forged for him a giant mortar, which he dragged across country to Méqdéla, where it may still be seen.

The emperor's complex relations with the church demanded time and attention. The church was central to his vision of a renewed Ethiopia, but it was in need of leadership. Normally it was headed by one bishop, a Copt appointed by the patriarch of Alexandria, and its faith was the faith of Alexandria. However, following a seventeenth–century encounter with European Roman Catholic Jesuits, new schools of thought began to develop within the church. These eventually crystallized into three parties, the smallest of which identified itself with the bishop. Relations between the parties were often rancorous and occasionally violent. As a result of his efforts to impose Alexandrian doctrine, Sélama had been roughly expelled from Gondér in 1846. One of the emperor's first political acts in 1854, even before he was crowned, was to recall the bishop from his exile to the national capital, Gondér. Together they pronounced uniformity of doctrine and an end to sectarianism. Tewodros also gave Sélama a degree of administrative authority within the church, which none of his predecessors had enjoyed for a long time.

These happy relations between church and state did not last long. By 1856 emperor and bishop had fallen into public acrimony. The issue was church land. During the Gondér period (1632 to late eighteenth century) a good deal of land had passed into the hands of the church as grants from national and regional rulers. These grants were endowments for individual churches intended to provide an income to support the material needs of the churches, as well as the upkeep of the clergy. Some of these lands had previously been under military tenures. The emperor wanted to recover the lands to generate the revenues necessary to support his army. On this issue there could be no agreement between the emperor and the bishop. It appears that around 1860 the emperor tried to limit to each church the amount of land necessary to support the minimal number of clergy required to perform the Mass. For some churches, which had well over two hundred clergy attached to them, this meant quite a reduction. It is unclear what practical effect this measure had, although it did deeply alienate the bishop from the emperor and must have turned the clergy into very active opponents of the crown.

The emperor needed a large army, because establishing and maintaining his rule proved difficult. Shortly after his coronation he embarked on an expedition through the provinces of Wéllo and Shéwa designed to bring these two provinces back under imperial control. They presented different problems. The province now known as Wéllo had, in the thirteenth century, been the homeland of the Amhara people and the Solomonic dynasty. However, migrations and settlement of the Oromo people in the sixteenth and seventeenth centuries resulted in the prolonged alienation of the province from national control and its conversion from Christianity to Islam. Wéllo was also the base for the dynasty which controlled the central provinces during the late decades of the period of national division. Shéwa, by contrast, had survived as a Christian, Amhara territory, but beyond imperial control, because of the buffer created by the Oromo. In the short term, the expedition was a resounding success, but it was a long-term failure. Tewodros seems never to have had a firm grip on Wéllo and frequently had to return there for bitter campaigning. Given his distractions with the church and the continuing problems of control in Wéllo, other provinces also raised the banner of rebellion, and the reign of Tewodros, far from being the prophesied millennium of peace, was turning into a period of violence.

The emperor continued to hope for productive, progressive relations with Europe, particularly Britain, but when the British neglected to respond to a formal overture of his in 1862, he began to make hostages of the British-protected foreigners in Ethiopia. The result was the British expedition that created the circumstances of his death in April 1868. He left behind an Ethiopia divided and unreformed.

DONALD CRUMMEY

See also: **Ethiopia: Johannes IV, Era of; Ethiopia: Menelik II, Era of.**

Further Reading

Crummey, D. *Priests and Politicians. Protestant and Catholic Missions in Orthodox Ethiopia 1830–1868.* Oxford: Clarendon Press, 1972.

Pankhurst, R. "Ethiopia and Somalia." *In General History of Africa.* Vol. 6, *Africa in the Nineteenth Century until the 1880s.* Cambrigde: Cambridge University Press, 1989.

Rubenson, Sven. *King of Kings: Tewodros of Ethiopia.* Addis Ababa: Haile Selassie I University Press, 1966.

———. "Ethiopia and the Horn." In *Cambridge History of Africa.* Vol. 5. Cambridge: Cambridge University Press, 1976.

———. *The Survival of Ethiopian Independence.* London: Heinemann, 1976.

———. Amsalu Aklilu and Merid Wolde Aregay, eds. *Acta Æthiopica.* Vol. 2, *Tewodros and His Contemporaries 1855–1868.* Addis Ababa: Addis Ababa University Press, 1994.

Ethiopia: Johannes IV, Era of (1868–1889)

Three great emperors ruled Ethiopia in the second half of the nineteenth century: Tewodros II (1855–1868), Johannes IV (1872–1889), and Menilik (1889–1913). Their policies revived the imperial power and authority.

Emperor Tewodros's death in 1868 was followed by a power struggle from which *Dajazmach* Kasa Mercha of Tigre province emerged victorious, thanks to the firearms he received from Lord Napier after defeating Tewodros, and was crowned as Emperor Johannes IV in January 1872. He remained emperor until his death in March 1889.

Johannes' reign was marked by reforms and warfare against both internal and external threats to his government and country. In domestic political affairs Johannes' goal was to strengthen imperial authority against provincial nobles and maintain the hegemony of Tigre, his native province, in the country. In religious matters Johannes was an ardent supporter of the Ethiopian Orthodox Church, encouraging unity of religion and uniformity of doctrine. His foreign policy aimed to safeguard the sovereignty of his empire. His strategies for achieving his aims differed in some important respects from those employed by Tewodros. For example, unlike Tewodros, he did not seek to achieve his domestic political objective through centralization of power. Instead he established a loose federation in which, in return for recognition of his suzerainty and payment of tribute, considerable autonomy was given to the provinces of Shawa and Gojjam. However, to realize his domestic political and external objectives Johannes engaged in many military campaigns against both domestic and external foes.

Johannes spent the first three years of his reign consolidating his authority in Tigre. He needed a strong united Tigre as the power base of his imperial government. This involved him and his faithful general, Ras Alula, in campaigns against ambitious local nobility and troublesome district governors. Typical examples of such people were *Dajjach* Walda Mikael Solomon, governor of Hamasen, *Dajjach* Dabbab Araya, Johannes' own cousin, and *Dajjach* Sebhat Aregawi of Agame. By 1875 Johannes had secured his authority in Tigre, Amhara, Bagemder, and the rest of the northern heartland of the empire. He had also received the allegiance of Ras Adal Tasamma, ruler of Gojjam province, whom he later elevated as *negus* Takla Haymanot.

Between 1875 and 1878 Johannes made at least two attempts to secure the allegiance of Menilik, the ruler of Shaw, but on each occasion he had to abandon the projected attack to attend to threats to his authority in Tigre. Menilik was the greatest domestic threat to Johannes' position as emperor; he was the strongest ruler in the empire besides Johannes and had imperial ambitions himself. Although from 1868 to 1872 he did not compete seriously for the throne, mainly because of his relative military weakness against the other contestants, he styled himself "King of Kings" and was believed to be conspiring with Egypt and later Italy against Johannes. Moreover, he conquered Wallo province to the north of Shawa and expanded his territory southward into Oromo-occupied areas. These conquests increased Menilik's power and resource base within the empire. Menilik's imperial ambitions threatened Johannes' position.

In 1877 Johannes marched to Shawa to force the province into submission. This time he was successful. In March 1878 Menilik made a formal submission to Johannes, recognized the emperor's suzerainty, and agreed to pay tribute. In return Johannes officially crowned Menilik as n*egus* of Shawa and confirmed his conquests in Wallo and the south.

However, Menilik did not abandon his imperial ambitions. He intensified his conquests in the south; at the Battle of Embabo in June 1882, Menilik defeated and captured the *negus* of Gojjam, with whom he had competed for the southwestern territories. This was a setback for Emperor Johannes, who in 1881 had crowned Ras Adal of Gojjam as *Negus* Takla Haymanot of Gojjam and Kafa to counterbalance the growing strength of Menilik. Johannes imposed peace on his two rival subjects and confiscated from Menilik not only the Gojjamese weapons he had captured but also the province of Wallo. But as a conciliatory gesture Johannes married his (young) son, Ras Araya Sellasie, to Menilik's (even younger) daughter, Zawditu in 1883. From then until his death in March 1889 Johannes lived in a state of uneasy peace with Menilik.

In 1878 Emperor Johannes, as a strong supporter of the Ethiopian Orthodox Church, convened a religious conference to settle doctrinal disputes within the church. The conference affirmed one Ethiopian Orthodox Church, imposed doctrinal uniformity by recognizing the *Qarra Haymanot* (two-birth) doctrine as Orthodox teaching, and decreed that within five years all non-Christians in the empire should convert to Christianity. A year later, Johannes ordered the expulsion of Catholic missionaries from Shawa.

In his dealings with outside powers, Johannes' main concern was to safeguard the independence and frontiers of his empire against foreign encroachment. Such encroachments came from Egyptians, Italians, and Mahdist Sudan.

In 1868 Egypt took over from the Ottomans the Red Sea port of Massawa and others in the Gulf of Aden and began to expand into Ethiopian territory, occupying Bogos and other areas. This brought Egypt into conflict with Emperor Johannes. In 1875 Egypt sent three expeditions into Ethiopia, one from Massawa towards Tigre and two from the Somali coast towards Harar and Shawa respectively. The one to Harar successfully reached and occupied the town in October, but the one to Shawa ended disastrously before reaching its destination. The one from Massawa led to two battles at Gundat in November 1875 and Gura in March 1876, both of which Johannes won. After 1876 uneasy peace existed between Ethiopia and Egypt until the Treaty of Adwa (1884) led to Egyptian withdrawal from Massawa, Bogos and other occupied areas in the Red Sea and Somali territories.

Johannes' efforts to establish friendly relations with European powers yielded little positive results. Italy, for example, had colonial ambitions in the Red Sea and Somali region and was secretly encouraged by Britain to occupy Massawa in 1885 on the withdrawal of the Egyptians. From Massawa the Italians, like the Egyptians before them, advanced inland occupying places in Ethiopian's coastal district. This brought them into conflict with Ras Alula, Johannes' governor of the district, who annihilated Italian troops at Dogali in January 1887. The Italian problem was not resolved before Johannes died in March 1889.

Mahdist Sudan was another intruder against whom Johannes had to defend his western frontiers. After their overthrow of Egyptian rule, the Mahdists launched a jihad against Christian Ethiopia. Between 1885 and 1889 a number of battles were fought between the two countries on their common border areas. In one such battle, fought at Matamma in March 1889, Ethiopia was victorious, but Emperor Johannes was mortally wounded; he died from his wounds a few days later.

Probably the least innovative of Ethiopia's three great nineteenth-century rulers, Johannes nevertheless oversaw modest reforms. For example, in the area of scientific medicine, mercury preparations for treatment of syphilis and vaccine inoculation against smallpox were introduced during his reign. In other areas, modern firearms came into more extensive use during his reign. Johannes successfully asserted the authority of the imperial government at home, restored unity to the Ethiopian Orthodox Church, and managed to hold foreign intruders at bay. In these and other ways Johannes prepared the ground for Menilik's successful reign.

R. H. Kofi Darkwah

See also: **Ethiopia: Menelik II, Era of; Ethiopia: Tewodros II, Era of.**

Further Reading

Erlich, H. *Ras Alula and the Scramble for Africa: A Political Biography: Ethiopia and Eritrea 1875–1897.* Lawrenceville, N.J.: The Red Sea Press, 1996.
Gabre-Selassie, Zewde. *Johannes IV Of Ethiopia: A Political Biography.* Oxford: Clarendon Press, 1975.
Marcus, H. G. *A History of Ethiopia.* Berkeley: University of California Press, 1994.
Pankhurst, R. *The Ethiopians.* Oxford: Blackwell Publishers, 1998.
Rubenson, S. *The Survival of Ethiopian Independence.* London: Heinemann, 1976.
Zewde, B. *A History of Modern Ethiopia 1855–1974.* Athens: Ohio University Press, 1991.

Ethiopia: Menelik II: Era of

The nineteenth century in Africa began with processes of African state formation throughout the continent and ended with European colonial conquest. Africans could neither sustain their newly created states (such as the states born out of the Mfecane in Southern Africa) or rejuvenated ones (like Egypt), nor keep European imperialism at bay. By the time Africa was under the colonial occupation of seven European powers at the beginning of the twentieth century, only Ethiopia and Liberia remained sovereign African states. Sliced and mutilated by France and Britain, Liberia entered the twentieth century as a diminished sovereign state. Ethiopia, under the leadership of Emperor Menelik II, not only withstood the colonial onslaught of Italy by coming out victorious at the Battle of Adwa, but doubled its territory by the beginning of the twentieth century.

Menelik's Ethiopia consisted of three major parts that were brought under his overall authority. First was the Ethiopia of the Ge'ez civilization marked by the tripartite distinction of *beta mangest* (house of state), *beta kehenat* (house of clergy), and *gabbar* (tribute-paying peasant). The second component of Menelik's Ethiopia was the southern highlands, the area inhabited mostly by the Oromos, who practiced mixed economy of agriculture and pastoralism. Some Oromos had become Muslims while others have had their own "traditional" religion. Lastly was the hot lowlands of eastern Ethiopia inhabited by Muslims, mainly the Somali. It was these three major areas, alongside the cultural complex of southern Ethiopia and the long region bordering the Sudan, that were brought under central rule by Emperor Menelik.

The mountains near Adowa, Ethiopia. © Das Fotoarchiv.

There are three main reasons that enabled Ethiopia to withstand the colonial onslaught: religion, statehood, and diplomacy. In the sphere of religion, the established Judeo-Christian culture, and the sense of uniqueness and of being God's chosen people, together with the ideology of a monophysite Christian island surrounded by religious enemies, helped cement a distinct unifying identity. This Christian nationalism was critical in mobilizing the population against foreign invasion.

Declarations of war mobilizations against foreign invasions invoked three sacred causes to die for: religion, land, and wife. The enemy was described as one that came from afar to destroy the religion, occupy the land, and defile the honor of wives. The view that Ethiopia is the land of a unique Christianity, a second Jerusalem, was a powerful force in cementing national consensus for mobilization against foreign invaders, including the Italians at the Battle of Adwa. Another key factor was that Ethiopia possessed the longest indigenous history of statehood in Africa. This state was based on a professional class of armed men specializing in the art of war-making, the *watadar* or *chawa*. Also, Menelik's genius in the diplomatic and military field helped Ethiopia avert the colonial "Scramble." By playing European powers off against each other, and by importing a large quantity of arms from various sources, Menelik was able to create the largest and best-equipped army in Africa. At the 1902 military parade held in Addis Ababa to commemorate the Battle of Adwa, 600,000 troops armed with modern weapons were present. Of these, 90,000 belonged to the imperial standing army. There were an additional 100,000 troops that did not participate at the parade, bringing Ethiopia's total military strength to 700,000. Menelik's Ethiopia was the best-armed and most organized African state of its time. It was this formidable force that saved Ethiopia from falling victim to the "Scramble."

Of the many accomplishments of Emperor Menelik II, his victory over the Italians at the Battle of Adwa in March 1896 stands out. The victory came in the midst of the great famine, *kefu qan* (bad times), that killed many people and consumed over 90 per cent of the cattle population. The rinderpest epidemic introduced into Massawa in 1885 by the Italians ravaged the cattle population of the eastern part of Africa from the Red Sea to South Africa.

As king of Shawa, Menelik was on friendly terms with the Italians. After the death of Emperor Yohannes IV on March 10, 1889, at the Battle of Matamma (against the Mahdist forces), Menelik signed the Treaty of Wuchale with the Italians on May 2, 1889. Controversy soon emerged on the interpretation of article 17 of the treaty. While the Amharic text reads that Menelik could, if he wished, call upon the services of the Italian authorities in his communications with other powers, the Italian version made this obligatory, thereby making Ethiopia in effect a protectorate of Italy. The Italians crossed the river Marab, the boundary separating their colony of Eritrea from Ethiopia, and occupied the town of Adwa in January 1890. The Italian move was meant to put pressure on Emperor Menelik to accept their interpretation of the Treaty of Wuchale. Menelik refused to accept the Italian interpretation. Finally, on February 12, 1893, Menelik denounced the Treaty of Wuchale. He declared national mobilization on September 17, 1895. On March 1, 1896, the Battle of Adwa took place, the result of which was a spectacular Ethiopian victory over Italian forces. After Menelik's victory at Adwa, the Italians signed the Treaty of Peace on October 26, 1896, at Addis Ababa which annulled the Wuchale treaty. In the treaty, the Italians recognized the independence of Ethiopia. Menelik recognized the Italian colony of Eritrea. The Marab River was reaffirmed as the boundary separating Italian Eritrea from Ethiopia.

Ethiopia was transformed under Emperor Menelik. The major signposts of modernization were put in place. Schools, hospitals, roads, railway lines, telephones, a postal system, telegraphs, banks, hotels, and a ministerial cabinet were established during his reign. Menelik II was a modernizer, following in the footsteps of the early modernizer and unifier of Ethiopia, Emperor Tewodros II (r.1855–1868). The political map of today's Ethiopia is Menelik's creation.

TESHALE TIBEBU

See also: **Ethiopia: Tewodros II, Era of; Mfecane; Monophysitism, Coptic Church, 379–640.**

Further Reading

Bahru Zewde. *A History of Modern Ethiopia, 1855–1974.* Athens: University of Ohio Press, 1991.
Berkeley, G. F. H. *The Campaign of Adowa and the Rise of Menelik.* New York: Negro University Press, 1969.
Donham, D., and W. James, eds. *The Southern Marches of Imperial Ethiopia.* Cambridge: Cambridge University Press, 1986.
Marcus, H. *The Life and Times of Menelik II: Ethiopia 1844–1913.* Oxford: Clarendon, 1975.
Teshale Tibebu. *The Making of Modern Ethiopia, 1896–1974.* Lawrenceville, N.J.: Red Sea Press, 1995.

Ethiopia: Italian Invasion and Occupation: 1935–1940

The Italian attempts to invade Ethiopia date back to the end of the nineteenth century, following the establishment of the first Italian colony, Eritrea. Over-ambitious colonial plans led Italy to an excruciating defeat at Adwa in 1896, which forced the Italian government to radically change its political attitudes towards Ethiopia and to undertake a more reliable and realistic colonial policy. At the beginning of the twentieth century, the Italian "empire" was limited to Libya, Eritrea, and Somalia.

However, the advent of the fascist regime in Italy in 1922 represented the beginning of a new phase for Italian colonialism. Expansionist ambitions toward Ethiopia were caused by the need to solve the problem of an ever-growing population and increasing unemployment in Italy, which tripled between 1926 and 1928. The myth of the Italian "race," the cult of the motherland, and a perceived Italian moral duty to construct an empire rooted in Roman times constituted the foundations of Mussolini's ideological framework, which he used to justify his colonial policy. The fascist regime prepared the colonizers through the activities of government bodies, institutions, and organs of propaganda that were set up with the aim of forming a "colonial consciousness," which Italian policy had been so far lacking. In 1935 with Mussolini's motto "imperialism is the eternal and unchangeable law of life," Italy inaugurated her new colonial campaign.

As early as December 1934, Italy occupied a territory fallen within the Ethiopian side of the borderline between Ethiopia and Italian Somalia. This event, known as the "Walwal incident," is considered the starting point of the Italo-Ethiopian war, and occurred with the implied consent of France and Britain. In autumn 1935, military operations were carried out in northeast and southern Ethiopia. On May 5, 1936, Italian troops entered Addis Ababa, thanks to their superior numbers, to a widespread use of mustard-gas, which had been banned in 1925 by the Geneva Convention of the International Committee of the Red Cross, and to the weak policy of the League of Nations. In May 1936 the Ethiopian emperor, Haile Sellasie, chose exile in Bath, England. Reactions to the Italian invasion of Ethiopia were worldwide, from African countries to Europe. Among international public opinion, Ethiopia was seen as the only independent African country and became the symbol of the Pan-African movement.

It was only through the constant use of violence and repression that the Italians seemed to be able to control the situation in Ethiopia. Indeed, widespread Ethiopian resistance generated frustration and strain among the Italian soldiers. Fear and "shame" of the possibility of losing Ethiopia was to such an extent that Mussolini ordered Graziani, the viceroy, to establishing a "regime of absolute dread." That year (1937) was one of the most difficult and violent years for the Italian army in Ethiopia. It culminated with one of the cruelest episodes in Ethiopian history: the attempt on Graziani's life in February 1937. During a ceremony, Viceroy Graziani was wounded by seven hand grenades thrown by the partisans. The executors of the plot were two Eritreans, Abraham Deboch and Mogos

Asghedom, working for the Italian administration. Fascist reprisals came immediately: many huts in Addis Ababa were set ablaze, people killed in the streets, many partisans arrested and deported in the Italian prisons or executed. Furthermore, many partisans' heads and corpses were publicly displayed in order to terrify the population. It has been calculated that in three days approximately 3,000 to 6,000 people were killed in Addis Ababa alone. The attempt on Graziani's life is widely regarded as the turning point in the history of Ethiopian resistance; for it marks the beginning of a stronger and more organized guerrilla warfare, mostly concentrated in the regions of Shawa, Gojjam, and Bagemder and armed mainly with ammunition captured from the enemy and provided by deserters. Particularly remarkable was the participation of Ethiopian women in the resistance, also caused by a reaction to the fact that the rape of women and girls was a systematic policy of domination for the fascist army.

In 1941 Ethiopia was liberated, thanks to the Ethiopian resistance movement and the intervention of the British army. As a matter of fact, Mussolini's entry into World War II as Germany's ally clarified the composition of the two fronts involved in the war. Britain and Italy were actually enemies and the necessity of attacking the enemy everywhere led to important changes in British policy regarding the "Ethiopia case." Emperor Haile Selassie, who had been living for a long time completely isolated in Bath, was now considered as an ally, and full military support was provided to allow him to lead the liberation war against the fascist occupation. On May 5, 1941, exactly five years since the Italian occupation of Addis Ababa, Haile Selassie entered the capital victorious and was welcomed by thousands of Ethiopians.

In the five years of occupation, the Italian impact on the socioeconomic structure of Ethiopia was of marginal extent, and guerrilla warfare prevented the Italian colonial administration from implementing the fascist projects of mass Italian settlement, construction of infrastructures, and exploitation of natural resources. The results of five years of occupation basically consisted of the development of a top-heavy bureaucracy and system of corruption. As reported by historians Del Boca and Barhu Zewde, the viceroy Duca d'Aosta himself defined this bureaucracy "formed as 50 per cent by unsuited people and 25 per cent by thieves." Corruption seemed to be the deepest rooted and widespread phenomenon in the Italian Eastern Africa Empire, and it favored big public and private companies and the military and civil ruling-class.

FRANCESCA LOCATELLI

See also: **Eritrea: Ottoman Province to Italian Colony; Haile Selassie I.**

Further Reading

Sbacchi, A. *Legacy of Bitterness. Ethiopia and Fascist Italy 1935–1941.* Lawrenceville, N.J.: Red Sea Press, 1997

Zewde, B. *A History of Modern Ethiopia, 1885–1991.* 2nd ed. Oxford: James Currey, 2001.

Ethiopia: Land, Agriculture, Politics, 1941–1974

Ethiopia gained back its independence from Italian occupation on May 5, 1941, five years to the day of the fall of Addis Ababa to the Italian fascist forces. Ethiopian society prior to the revolution of 1974, and even more so in the pre-Italian occupation period, consisted of three social orders: the *Beta Mangest* (House of State), *Beta Kehenat* (House of Clergy/Church), and *Balagar* or *Gabbar* (peasant or tribute-payer).

The land tenure system in Ethiopia consisted of three different arrangements. In the Christian north and north-central parts of the country, the *rist* system of landholding was predominant. In the southern highlands, large landed property and widespread peasant tenancy were prevalent. In the eastern and western lowland border-lands, nomadic and communal land ownership patterns, respectively, prevailed. In terms of population ratio, most of Ethiopia was either under the *rist* system or large landed property alongside peasant tenancy.

The *rist* system was an arrangement in which Christians of both sexes had the right to claim, possess, inherit, and pass on to their children land by virtue of belonging to the same cognatic-descent kin group. This right entitles anyone born into the kinship network of the lineage pedigree to possess a piece of the land that belongs to the kinship. Those belonging to the kinship were called *zemed* (relatives). As *zemed*, they were entitled to land sharing. Muslims and craftspeople (weavers, tanners, smiths) were excluded from belonging to the *rist* arrangement; instead, they became tenants paying rent to the Christian *rist* owners.

In the southern highland regions, in the aftermath of the military conquest during Menelik's time, the *naftagna* (gun-bearers) became landlords with extensive holdings turning the peasantry into tenants of the warrior class. The relationship between the military overlords and the peasants came to be known as the *naftagna-gabbar* system. These *naftagnas* eventually transformed themselves into big landed property owners, thereby turning the peasants into tenants.

In both the *rist* and large landed property holdings of the highlands, there was also an arrangement called *gult*. *Gult* was the right of tribute appropriation from peasants granted by the emperor to the various ranks of the warrior class, the church, and other people in return for military, administrative, and religious services rendered to the emperor by the *gult* grantees. *Gult* was

granted on a temporary basis and could be revoked anytime by the emperor when the grantee failed to live up to the patron-client social norm. In some cases, especially *gult* grants to the church, *gult* became *rist* called *rist-gult*.

In the post-Italian occupation period, *gult* rights, especially in the southern regions, were transformed into large private property holdings. Known as *gasha meret* (shield land), former notables who were granted extensive landholdings as *gult* now became agrarian entrepreneurs transforming their land into capital. Accordingly, large estates of coffee plantations and large farms replaced the earlier arrangement of tribute extraction from the *gabbar* (tribute-paying peasants).

The transformation in land tenure relations as a result of the *naftagna* becoming large landed estates resulted in the extensive commercialization of both land and labor. Alongside the rise of an agrarian capitalist class emerged a part-time proletarianized labor force, while those who could not find employment in agriculture left the countryside and headed for the towns. Peasants were evicted from the land to give space for coffee plantations, cattle ranches, and large farms. Small peasants were further squeezed from competition from large farms. Accompanied by periodic droughts, the net result of commercialized agriculture was extreme rural poverty. In regions like the Awash Valley, foreign firms like the Dutch HVA were offered large tracts of land for sugar plantations and a sugar factory at Wonji. The seminomadic inhabitants of the area were evicted, adding more to the problem of rural poverty.

Peasant discontent grew as a result of land alienation. When extreme rural poverty is added to natural calamities like the 1972–1973 drought, the result was mass famine that claimed the lives of hundreds of thousands of people.

The transformation in land tenure relations in Ethiopia during the period 1941–1974 took place simultaneously with that of a political and military transformation in the state structure. After the restoration to his throne on May 5, 1941, Emperor Haile Selassie continued with an increased tempo his earlier policy of state centralization, which had been temporarily disrupted during the Italian occupation.

In an attempt to undermine and eventually destroy the political and military power of the regional notables, the *telek sawach* ("big men"), the emperor pursued a policy of transforming the once-formidable regional notables from being political, economic, military powerhouses into being economic powers with reduced political weight and no military force of their own. In old Ethiopia before Haile Selassie, each regional notable had huge *gult* holdings, an army of his own, and rules over his regional domain. Although this triple power depended on the good will of the *negusa nagast* ("king of kings"), the latter was also careful not to upset the balance of power between himself as the overlord of the whole country and the many regional notables under his rule. The state modernization process that Haile Selassie carried out for the first time in Ethiopian history took away the regional armies of the notables and created an all-Ethiopian armed forces under his direct command. Haile Selassie awarded the notables with important government posts and grants of large tracts of land. What they did not have were military forces of their own. The emperor appointed provincial administrators called *endarasie* ("like myself") who were in charge of ruling the provinces in the name of and on behalf of the emperor. Thus the big men were reduced to mere shadows of their former selves. The position they were appointed to could be taken away from them anytime by the emperor, no questions asked. The process was known as *shum/shir* (appoint/demote), and it was an age-old practice in Ethiopian political history.

Overall, during the period between the restoration of Ethiopian independence in 1941 and the revolution of 1974, Ethiopian society was transformed in ways never before attained. The pace of social change was slow; nevertheless, it was constant. The emperor, who was perhaps one of the most progressive princely notables pushing for the modernization of Ethiopia, was found later to be the principal obstacle in the path of Ethiopia's progress. The revolution of 1974 that deposed Haile Selassie was meant to clear the way for the development of Ethiopian society along modern lines.

TESHALE TIBEBU

See also: **Ethiopia: Italian Invasion and Occupation: 1935–1940; Haile Selassie I.**

Further Reading

Bahru, Zewde. *A History of Modern Ethiopia, 1855–1974.* Athens: Ohio University Press, 1991.

Clapham, C. *Haile Selassie's Government.* New York: Praeger, 1969.

Gilkes, P. *The Dying Lion: Feudalism and Modernization in Ethiopia.* New York: St. Martin's Press, 1975.

Mantel-Niecko, J. *The Role of Land Tenure in the System of Ethiopian Imperial Government in Modern Times.* Warsaw, 1980.

Markakis, J. *Ethiopia: Anatomy of a Traditional Polity.* Oxford: Clarendon, 1974

Teshale, Tibebu. *The Making of Modern Ethiopia, 1896–1974.* Lawrenceville, N.J.: Red Sea Press, 1995.

Ethiopia: Famine, Revolution, Mengistu Dictatorship, 1974–1991

The year 1974 was a turning point in modern Ethiopian history. It was the year of the Ethiopian revolution, which brought down Emperor Haile Selassie I, the last Christian monarch of the oldest Christian monarchy in the world. As world-renowned as Haile Selassie was, the country he ruled was one where a handful of men monopolized power and wealth while the majority lived in poverty.

The 1973 Wallo famine precipitated the downfall of Selassie. The government attempted to downplay the famine and hide it from the public, as officials were busy preparing for the eightieth birthday celebration of the emperor, to be observed July 23, 1973. The famine and the 1973 oil crisis, which resulted in higher gasoline prices, increased discontent against the imperial order. From February 1974, there were spontaneous protests, demonstrations, and strikes in many parts of the country, as individuals from all walks of life joined in demanding justice and equality. The most serious challenge to the imperial order came from the military. Starting with the arrest of senior officers in Nagalle, dissent in the army spread rapidly.

The Ethiopian Students Movement (ESM), both inside the country and abroad, played the most critical role in exposing the injustices of the monarchical order. Informed by Marxist ideas, students challenged what they called a semifeudal, semicolonial system. They condemned the ruling classes and the Western powers that supported them, primarily the United States. They identified feudalism, imperialism, and bureaucratic capitalism as the three main enemies of the Ethiopian people. The students advocated a Chinese-style revolution as the panacea for the ills of the society.

It was on the fertile ground of protest plowed by the ESM that the *Dergue* (council or committee) came into the historical scene. The *Dergue* was a council made up of 120 men elected from the various branches of the armed forces. Through the summer of 1974, the *Dergue* assumed *de facto* state power, arresting key government officials and making the newly formed Endalkachaw cabinet ineffective. On September 12, 1974, the *Dergue* deposed Selassie and assumed state power under the name Provisional Military Administrative Council (PMAC). It declared its rule provisional and promised to go back to its barracks once the "cleansing" of the old order was accomplished. That was not to be. With its slogan *Ityopya Teqdam* (Ethiopia First), the *Dergue* called all citizens to rally behind its version of a bloodless revolution. In March 1975, the *Dergue* carried out its most radical measure: the nationalization of all rural land. Rural land became state property, while peasants were granted usufructuary rights. Shortly afterward, urban land and extra houses were also nationalized. Major foreign-owned firms had been brought under state control earlier.

In its seventeen-year rule (1974–1991), the *Dergue* went through an ideological transformation, from *Ityopya Teqdam* to scientific socialism. *Ityopya Teqdam* was an ideology of military state nationalism articulated by the *Dergue* elite. Scientific socialism grew out of the influence of Marxist organizations, principally the All Ethiopian Socialist Movement (MEISON, in the Amharic acronym). In its foreign policy, the *Dergue* supported radical movements like the PLO, ZANU, and the ANC. It closely allied itself with the Soviet Union and the socialist countries of Eastern Europe. In the last year of its rule, however, the *Dergue* retreated from scientific socialism.

Within the PMAC, General Aman Andom was appointed head of state and chairman of the *Darg*, while Major Mengustu Haile Mariam was elected first vice chairman of the *Dergue* and Colonel Atnafu Abate second vice chairman. Mengustu had Andom and another official, Tafari Banti, killed. Some sixty top officials of Haile Selassie's government were executed in November 1974. Mengustu killed other high-ranking *Dergue* officials, including Abate. Mengustu ruled as a dictator, eliminating adversaries and crushing opposition.

The *Dergue* was faced with major challenges to its rule, including Eritrean and Tigrayan nationalism, the rise of the Ethiopian Peoples Revolutionary Party (EPRP), and the Somali invasion of 1977. The *Dergue* engaged in military warfare with Eritrean, Tigrayan, and Somali nationalist armies, while also conducting a campaign of terror against EPRP and its sympathizers. (The EPRP, a Marxist political party, called for the replacement of the *Dargue* by a Provisional Peoples Government (PPG) composed of all sectors of society, including the military. It called the *Dergue*'s regime a fascist dictatorship.) "Revolutionary Motherland or Death" was the slogan used against Eritrean and Somali nationalism, while the urban campaign of terror against the EPRP was meant to eliminate "anarchists and counter-revolutionaries."

The *Darg*'s urban terror campaign relied on *natsa ermeja* (unlimited action). It referred to the right granted to security forces to shoot anyone they suspected of being a counterrevolutionary. Legal procedure was disregarded. The Urban Dwellers Association (*qabales*), created after the nationalization of urban land and extra houses in 1975, played a key role in carrying out the terror campaign, alongside the security forces and the AESM cadres. Thousands of young people died during the campaign. Corpses of the young were left in public places like squares, churches, and mosques, and parents were denied the right to mourn for their dead children. In some cases, parents paid "bullet price" to get the bodies of their deceased children back. Mass terror and fear gripped the nation from 1977 through 1979.

Ethiopia was wracked by disaster and civil unrest throughout the 19080s. In 1984–1985, another famine gripped the country. This was the worst famine to affect Ethiopia in the twentieth century, and hundreds of thousands perished. The Workers Party of Ethiopia (WPE) was formed, under the leadership of Mengustu, while the official name of the country was changed to the People's Democratic Republic of Ethiopia (PDRE) in 1987. In May 1991, the Eritrean and Tigrayan movements entered Asmara and Addis Ababa, respectively. Two years later, Eritrea became a sovereign state. Mengustu fled to Zimbabwe in defeat in May 1991.

TESHALE TIBEBU

See also: **Haile Selassie I.**

Further Reading

Andargachew, T. *The Ethiopian Revolution, 1974–1987: A Transformation from an Aristocratic to a Totalitarian Society.* Cambridge: Cambridge University Press, 1993.

Halliday, F., and M. Molyneux. *The Ethiopian Revolution.* London: New Left Books, 1981.

Jansson, K., M. Harris, and Angela Penrose. *The Ethiopian Famine.* Atlantic Highlands, N.J.: Zed Books, 1987

Markakis, J. *National and Class Conflict in the Horn of Africa.* Cambridge: Cambridge University Press, 1987.

Teferra Haile Selassie. *The Ethiopian Revolution, 1974–1991: From a Monarchical Autocracy to a Military Oligarchy.* New York: Kegan Paul International, 1997.

Ethiopia: Civil War and Liberation (to 1993)

Ethiopia existed in a state of continual warfare from 1961 to 1991, due to the secessionist war with Eritrea, the insurrection of the Tigrayan People's Liberation Front, and the second, lesser insurrection of the Oromo people in the south and east of the country. In addition to these three insurrections, Ethiopia was embroiled in the 1977–1978 Ogaden War with Somalia.

British forces had liberated Eritrea and Ethiopia from Italian occupation in 1941 when Haile Selassie returned from exile to resume his throne in Addis Ababa. In September 1952 the United Nations decided that Eritrea should be federated with Ethiopia; by 1958 it had become clear that Haile Selassie meant to integrate Eritrea into Ethiopia, and this led Eritrean opponents of integration to form the Eritrean Liberation Front (ELF).

The first shots in what was to be a thirty-year Eritrean war of liberation were fired in September 1961. Resistance to the central government during the 1960s was spasmodic and uneven. At the end of the decade, a split in the leadership of ELF led to the formation of a more radical movement, the Eritrean People's Liberation Front (EPLF). The two movements cooperated during much of the 1970s, but their differences gradually grew more pronounced, and following some brutal fighting between them (1979–1981), the EPLF emerged as the main Eritrean liberation movement in 1981, replacing the ELF, which later disintegrated.

A revolution in Addis Ababa, meanwhile, had transformed Ethiopia into a Marxist state. The Sahel drought of 1973 had a deep impact on Ethiopia and government mishandling of drought relief measures hastened the downfall of Haile Selassie. Hewas was forced to abdicate in 1974 and was replaced by a military Dergue. Haile Mengistu Mariam emerged as its leader and soon turned to the USSR for military assistance (Moscow had switched its support from Somalia to Ethiopia in 1975). By that year ELF forces, which numbered between 15,000 and 25,000, controlled most of Eritrea. By 1977, which turned out to be a climactic year, Ethiopian forces had been confined to four towns in Eritrea; however, at that point the differences between the ELF and EPLF exploded into warfare just when an Eritrean victory seemed possible. Meanwhile, in July 1977 Somali forces crossed the Ethiopian border and by November were besieging the town of Harar, only to run out of military supplies. The Cubans, who had been supporting the Eritrean war of secession, switched their allegiance to the Ethiopian government, sending 16,000 troops to fight the Somalis in the Ogaden War, while the USSR airlifted an estimated $1 billion worth of arms to the Mengistu government. As a result, by March 1978, the Somalis had been forced to withdraw and Mengistu could turn his full attention to the war in Eritrea.

A second nationalist insurrection, by the people of Tigre province, would eventually ensure the collapse of the Mengistu government. Tigre had long been a part of the Ethiopian Empire in which it had enjoyed a high degree of autonomy. A Tigrayan, Yohannis IV, had been emperor from 1871 to 1889. Haile Selassie had faced several Tigrayan revolts during his reign, and after his downfall in 1974 the Tigre People's Liberation front (TPLF) was formed. The TPLF became significant in military terms at the end of the 1970s, when the war against the Eritreans was reaching a climax. In alliance, the TPLF amd EPLF together would present a formidable challenge to the Mengistu government through the 1980s.

By the early 1980s the Tigrayan revolt was widespread and the TPLF was inflicting heavy casualties upon the Ethiopian army, while the TPLF and EPLF were coordinating their tactics. By 1988 government forces only controlled the Tigre regional capital of Makele, while the TPLF commanded 20,000 battle-hardened troops.

A third more spasmodic and limited insurrection had occurred among the Oromo peoples of the south (who represent 40% of the population) although they were more scattered and less coordinated than either the Eritreans or Tigrayans. From 1963 to 1970, under the leadership of Wako Gutu, they had revolted under the banner of the Oromo Liberation Front (OLF). They sought better treatment by the central government rather than secession, and in 1970, when Gutu himself accepted a government appointment, the first revolt came to an end. A second Oromo revolt followed the fall of Haile Selassie, but this was dependent on Somali support and petered out following the Somali defeat of 1978.

At the beginning of 1989 the TPLF formed a coalition, the Ethiopian People's Revolutionary Democratic Front (EPRDF), with the Ethiopian People's Democratic Movement, and in combination with the EPLF mounted the last major campaign of the war. The combined forces of the EPRDF and EPLF swept all before them in the early months of 1991, and the collapse of the Mengistu regime came in May. Mengistu fled Addis Ababa to Zimbabwe and the EPRDF forces entered the capital. Meles Zenawi, the Tigrayan leader who had also commanded the EPRDF, became interim president of Ethiopia. The EPLF established an autonomous administration in Asmara and the EPLF leader, Issaias Afewerke, formed a provisional Eritrean government. The EPLF refused to be a part of the interim government in Addis Ababa, emphasizing that it saw the future of Eritrea as separate from that of Ethiopia. The EPRDF had agreed that the EPLF should hold a referendum on independence from Ethiopia, and this was held in April 1993, monitored by the United Nations. There was a 98.2 per cent turnout and a 99.8 per cent vote in favor of independence. On May 24, 1993, Eritrea became formally independent and was recognized as such by the international community. Issaias Afewerke became its first president. Asmara became the capital of the new state, which had a population of 3.5 million.

During 1991 and 1992, the EPRDF asserted its authority over the whole of Ethiopia. A new constitution was drafted, while about 100 political parties emerged. Elections to a constituent assembly were held in 1994, and the EPRDF and its allies triumphed. It was the first stage in the creation of the Federal Democratic Republic of Ethiopia, which came into being following elections to a new federal parliamentary assembly of May 1995.

GUY ARNOLD

Further Reading

Clapham, C. *Transformation and Continuity in Revolutionary Ethiopia*. Cambridge: Cambridge University Press, 1988.

Giorgis, D. W. *Red Tears: War, Famine and Revolution in Ethiopia*. Trenton, N.J.: Red Sea Press, 1989.

Henze, P. B. *Ethiopia and Eritrea: The Defeat of the Derg and the Establishment of New Governments*. Washington, D.C.: United States Institute of Peace, 1993.

Lefebvre, J. A. *Arms for the Horn: US Security Policy in Ethiopia and Somalia 1953–1991*. Pittsburgh: University of Pittsburgh Press, 1991.

Tiruneh, A. *The Ethiopian Revolution 1974–1987: A Transformation from an Aristocratic to a Totalitarian Autocracy.* Cambridge: Cambridge University Press, 1993.

Ethiopia: 1991 to the Present

A new chapter in Ethiopia's history opened when the Dergue was overthrown in May 1991 by the peoples of Ethiopia, led by the armed forces of the Ethiopian Peoples' Revolutionary Democratic Front (EPRDF). The former military dictator Mengistu fled to Zimbabwe, and the EPRDF entered Addis Ababa, forming an interim government. Faced with the immense problem of bringing peace and economic reconstruction to the war-torn country, the EPRDF called a National Conference of over twenty organizations in order to immediately establish a Transitional Government of Ethiopia (TGE). The National Conference also approved a National Charter guaranteeing basic democratic rights and outlining the main tasks of the TGE: to establish peace, democracy, and economic development in Ethiopia. Meles Zenawi, the leader of the EPRDF was elected president of the TGE and chairman of the transitional Council of Representatives.

The TGE was a coalition of political organizations led by the EPRDF and initially included the Oromo Liberation Front (OLF), another opponent of the Dergue. However, the OLF refused to relinquish the armed struggle in accordance with the aims of the National Charter, despite its role in the new government, and finally withdrew from the TGE in June 1992, vowing to continue to fight for the creation of an independent state of Oromia. It has remained one of the most determined opponents of Ethiopian governments since 1991, and in 1999 launched military attacks on Ethiopia from neighboring Somalia.

One of the first measures taken by the TGE to bring peace to the country was the successful demobilization and retraining of the Dergue's army, one of the largest in Africa, and its replacement initially with EPRDF fighters and subsequently with a new army drawn from all of Ethiopia's nationalities. The Ethiopian government, with international assistance, also began the process of bringing to trial those who had committed human rights violations under the regime of the Dergue. After lengthy preparations the first 'war crimes trials began in 1995.

One of the most important tasks of the TGE was to establish modern democratic structures and procedures in a country that hitherto had known no popularly elected democratic government or legislature and where democratic freedoms had been severely restricted. Within a few years over sixty different political parties and a free press were established, and although there have continued to be some allegations of human rights abuses, Ethiopia has made a remarkably rapid transition to a multi-party democracy.

Regional elections, held in 1992, established locally elected representatives for communities and districts throughout Ethiopia. From 1993 a lengthy process was begun to involve the population in drafting a constitution. Countrywide debates were held even at village level on the draft constitution, and in June 1994 a Constituent Assembly was elected. This body finally ratified the new constitution in December 1994. General elections monitored by international observers followed in May 1995, at which the EPRDF won a landslide victory. Meles Zenawi was elected prime minister of the renamed Federal Democratic Republic of Ethiopia.

The constitution established a new federal structure for Ethiopia, with a great amount of autonomy for the nine states. These regional states have their own constitutions, can levy taxes, and have budgetary and other responsibilities. The federal structure took into account the cultural and ethnic diversity of the country, and the people in a particular region are even able to choose the official state language. The states are able to safeguard and foster the identities, languages and cultures of the many Ethiopian nationalities that were previously ignored or suppressed. The nations and nationalities are also represented, according to the size of their population, in the House of Federation, one part of the bicameral parliament, and the constitution accords every nation and nationality in Ethiopia the right to self-determination including the right to secession.

When the Dergue was overthrown, Ethiopia was on the verge of bankruptcy, its foreign currency reserves were barely adequate to finance imports for one month, and its foreign debt was nearly $9 billion. Large parts of the country were short of food, and there was massive dislocation of people due to the many years of war. The TGE therefore acted quickly to liberalize and rapidly develop the economy. Ethiopia was forced to join the Structural Adjustment Program, but unlike other African governments it presented the World Bank with its own plans for economic reforms and continued negotiations for some eighteen months until satisfactory agreement was reached. Ethiopia's governments have maintained their opposition to privatizing some key areas of the economy and have refused to make land a commodity. From 1992 to 1996 the Ethiopian economy grew yearly at the rate of 7.6 per cent. Inflation fell to less than 1 per cent by 1996, and much of the foreign debt has been canceled. In May 1995 the EPRDF government introduced a Five-Year Plan aimed at creating an economic infrastructure throughout the country and at developing the health service, education and in particular agriculture. In 1997 Ethiopia actually became self-sufficient in food and began exporting maize to neighboring countries, although problems of drought and famine still exist in some areas of the country.

The TGE quickly established good relations with Ethiopia's neighbors and signed agreements of friendship and cooperation with the neighboring countries of Sudan, Djibouti, and Kenya. Ethiopian governments have continued to play an important role in efforts to bring peace to Somalia and hosted many of the meetings that culminated in the formation of the National Salvation Council of Somalia in January 1997. Initially, Ethiopia also had good relations with Eritrea and fully supported the independence of Eritrea and the right of the Eritrean people to decide their own future in the referendum held in that country in April 1993. There were also strong economic ties between two countries; until 1998, they shared the same currency. However, in May 1998 Eritrean military forces invaded border areas of Ethiopia. Despite efforts by the Organization of African Unity and other countries to mediate, a state of war has existed between the two countries since that time.

HAKIM ADI

See also: **Ethiopia: Famine, Revolution, Mengistu Dictatorship, 1974–1991.**

Further Reading

Abraham, K. *Ethiopia from Bullets to the Ballot Box: The Bumpy Road to Democracy and the Political Economy of Transition.* Lawrenceville, N.J.: Red Sea Press, 1994.

Hammond, J. *Fire from the Ashes: A Chronicle of the Revolution in Tigray, Ethiopia, 1975–1991.* Lawrenceville, N.J.: Red Sea Press, 1999.

Vaughan, S. *The Addis Ababa Transitional Conference of 1991: Its Origins, History, and Significance.* Edinburgh: Edinburgh University Centre of African Studies Occasional Paper, 1994.

Young, J. "Ethnicity and Power in Ethiopia" *Review of African Political Economy* 70 (1996): 531–542.

Young, J. *Peasant Revolution in Ethiopia: The Tigray Peoples' Liberation Front 1975–1991.* Cambridge: Cambridge University Press, 1997.

Ethiopianism and the Independent Church Movement

By the late 1800s white missionaries' ingrained paternalism had become evident to their African congregants. The white missionaries' persistent denial of church leadership roles to Africans resulted in "Ethiopian" breakaways. For aspiring pastors from a prospering mission-educated middle class, Scripture translation had encouraged the Protestant "open Bible" approach, providing their early Africanism with a biblical lineage in the symbol of an unconquered imperial Ethiopia.

Inspired by African-American examples, this religious independency also incubated a political reaction to the mounting oppression of Africans countrywide after 1900. Ethiopians became key organizers, in particular against white settler interests impeding the emergence of their class. Meanwhile in the slums and hostels, a grassroots reaction to migrancy's hardships was spreading, taking charismatic and utopian forms in "spirit" or "indigenized" healing churches.

No independent churches appeared before 1880. By the early 1900s, with industrialization and labor migrancy taking hold, about twenty had been founded, all Ethiopian reactions to mission rooted in the early nineteeth century Xhosa prophet Ntsikana. Thousands of mission converts had sided with the rebels during the last Cape Frontier War (1879). Ethnic sentiment resulted in the first such church, founded in 1884 by the Wesleyan Nehemiah Tile, being only an ethnic "Thembu Church." But in 1892, another Wesleyan, Reverend Mangena Mokone, fathered Pan-African Ethiopianism by forming the first nationwide nonethnic indigenous church, Ibandla laseTopiya, the Ethiopian Church.

Under James Dwane, another Wesleyan who became leader in 1896, the church came under American Methodist Episcopal influence, becoming their fourteenth district and soon expanding to over 10,000 members. However, in 1900 Dwane, a Gcaleka Xhosa from a chiefly line, broke away to found an Order of Ethiopia that confined itself to his ethnic community. Again, when P. J. Mzimba, United Free Church of Scotland pastor, left in 1898 to form the African Presbyterian Church, only his fellow Mfengu followed him.

By 1893, however, a Pan-African vision had largely infused Ethiopianism, so that it began securing widespread support among different ethnicities. By 1902 its name was in use with everyone from urban workers to chiefs and headmen, to the mission bourgeoisie and wealthy peasantry, to denote "a whole range of the black man's efforts to improve his religious, educational and political status in society" (Chirenje 1987). For whites hostile to its perceived political agenda, it meant the entire indigenous church "peril": Natal's governor attributed the 1906 antipoll tax uprising of Bhambhatha not to oppressive taxation policies, but to "Ethiopian agitators" and their program of "Africa for the Africans."

When the 1910 Union and 1913 Land Act made South Africa a "white man's country," Ethiopians moved directly into political activism. The churches waned accordingly, but although Ethiopianism's classical period had ended by the 1930s, intellectuals seeking a broader African nationalist ideology continued to invoke its notion of spiritual nationhood, and Mussolini's 1935–1936 invasion of Ethiopia gave impetus to its Pan-Africanism.

Although the Ethiopians upheld some African customs (chiefly polygamy), they had remained largely orthodox, only covertly African in ethos compared with the charismatic indigenous spirit churches that emerged around 1900. Zionism came to South Africa when an American teaching (from John Dowie's Zion City, Illinois, theocracy, founded 1896) that prayer alone could heal persuaded Pieter le Roux, Afrikaner missionary to the Zulu, to break from the Dutch Reformed Church. Among postconquest Zulu converts, sentiment against diviners was already strong, so that Le Roux's congregation followed him, although when he broke from Dowie in 1908 to join a Pentecostal mission, they remained "in Zion," and were soon introducing innovations (prophecy, trance-dancing, use of white robes, and healing staves).

"In Zion" signified a New Testament church carrying on John the Baptist's work. Where Ethiopians longed for a free Christian African nation under a "Lion of Judah," the mythological focus for this new religion of the poor was the Holy Land itself. Cosmological events such as Halley's Comet of 1910 were regarded as portents, and during the devastating Spanish Influenza of 1919, many stricken laborers felt they had died and been with Jesus, who returned them as his envoys to the troubled earth.

Before World War II, the "Zion City" type of spirit church arose on the Dowie model, prioritizing land purchase and capital accumulation in order to achieve a degree of separation from a profaned world and working toward communal self-sufficiency. Often allied to their local royalty, these movements' leaders used alternative readings of the Bible to revitalize moribund traditional forms and values. What Ethiopian secession was to the literate elite—namely, a response to political and economic dispossession—these Zion City "homes" were for the rural underclass and their chiefs. But following the state's 1921 massacre of Enoch Mgijima's Israelites, although Zionism spread in the poorer areas, it remained politically quiet.

After the war, in response to intensified urbanization and its privations, the "Zion-Apostolic" church type appeared, drawing Rand migrant worker and rural pauper alike into small prophet-led healing bands. Here the powers of both the Holy Spirit and ancestor spirits operated within a context of richly indigenized liturgy and biblical symbolism. Low wages and unemployment were met with prayer-healing and speaking in tongues, while taoo observances and purification rites protected the group.

Protestant missiologists (Sundkler 1961) at first proclaimed the Zionist church a mere "syncretist sect" and a "bridge back to heathenism." Anthropologists counter (Kiernan 1992) that the Zionist prophet is in fact a genuine Christian replacement of the diviner, his ritualizations having "inculturated" divine healing to African needs.

Ethiopian-type churches formed the majority of African-initiated congregations until the mid-twentieth century, but by 1970 the charismatic churches of Zion were almost twice as numerous. They presently number between 3,000 and 6,000 congregations. Despite continuous influence from American Pentecostals arriving since the 1910s, those who today call themselves Christian Zionists have become a minority; a range of New Jerusalem charismatics currently "raid Christianity from without, capturing features selectively" (Kiernan).

ROBERT PAPINI

See also: **Religion, Colonial Africa: Independent, Millenarian/Syncretic Churches.**

Further Reading

Anderson, A. *Zion and Pentecost: The Spirituality and Experience of Pentecostal and Zionist/Apostolic Churches in South Africa.* Pretoria: University of South Africa Press, 2000.

Chirenje, J. M. *Ethiopianism and Afro-Americans in Southern Africa 1883–1916.* Baton Rouge: Louisiana State University Press, 1987.

———. *Havens of Health in a Zulu City: The Production and Management of Therapeutic Power in Zionist Churches.* Lewiston: Edwin Mellen Press, 1990.

———. "The Herder and the Rustler: Deciphering the Affinity between Zulu Diviner and Zionist Prophet." *African Studies* 51, no. 2 (1992).

———. "Variations on a Christian Theme: the Healing Synthesis of Zulu Zionism." In *Syncretism/Anti-Syncretism: The Politics of Religious Syncretism*, edited by C. Stewart. and R. Shaw. New York: Routledge, 1994.

———. "The African Independent Churches." In *Living Faiths in South Africa*, edited by M. Prozesky and J. de Gruchy. Cape Town and Johannesburg: David Philip, 1995.

Sundkler, B. G. M. *Bantu Prophets in South Africa.* Oxford: Oxford University Press, 1961.

———. *Zulu Zion and Some Swazi Zionists.* London: Oxford University Press, 1976.

Sundkler, Bengt, and Christopher Steed. *A History of the Church in Africa.* London: Oxford University Press, 2000.

Europe: Explorers, Adventurers, Traders

Between about 1770 and 1880, exploration of Africa made possible accurate maps and publishable information on the continent. Although Portuguese navigators had charted the coasts by 1500, the interior remained almost wholly unknown to Europeans up until the late eighteenth century. Maps were available earlier, based on classical, Arab or Portuguese information, but such material was discarded by the great French cartographer D'Anville in 1749. Serious exploration involved a few private adventurers, seldom traders, more frequently Christian missionaries, but, most important, official or quasi-official expeditions often led by servicemen. Malarial fever, rapids on rivers, and, occasionally, unwelcoming people demanded reasonably well-organized endeavors. At least until the 1870s, geographical societies, especially the Royal Geographical Society of London (RGS), missionary societies, or governments claimed to be motivated by science or religion and eschewed any political designs. Nevertheless, explorers directly or indirectly served those who wanted to change Africa, by acquiring its resources or access to its markets, by ending the slave trade, or by introducing the Gospel. The explorers responded by describing a continent in need of Europe's expertise, technology and moral superiority, whether or not this implied political change. Africans themselves made the expeditions possible by acting as porters, interpreters, and guides. The reception of explorers depended on the current local political situation.

The Scottish landowner James Bruce traveled in Ethiopia from 1768 to 1773 and visited the source of the Blue Nile. In 1788 a group of aristocrats founded the African Association to achieve for Africa what Captain Cook had for the Pacific. Interest centered on the kingdoms of the Western Sudan, as stories of its wealth and magnificence had long filtered through to Europe. This region was watered by the Niger. Whether it flowed west to the Atlantic, east to the Nile, or into the sands of the desert was unknown. The Association's first expeditions followed Saharan trade routes from the Mediterranean, with the first German explorer of Africa, Friedrich Konrad Hornemann, reaching Bornu before dying in 1800. The alternative starting point was the Atlantic coast, from which the young Scottish surgeon and child of the Enlightenment, Mungo Park, reached the Niger in 1796, "glittering to the morning sun, as broad as the Thames at Westminster and flowing slowly to the eastward." Park was sent back in 1805 to find out where it actually flowed by a government concerned to forestall any French activity and to aid the search for markets. He died at Bussa, far down the river in 1806 but his fate was long unknown.

René Caillé began a long French association with the western part of the region when, in 1827, he reached the (to Europeans) mysterious city of Timbuktu. Meanwhile, British expeditions from the Mediterranean pushed toward the middle of the Niger; Hugh Clapperton gained Sokoto but not the river in 1824. He died on a return trip, but in 1830 his former servant, Richard Lander, showed that the Niger debouched into the Gulf of Guinea. Attempts were now made to send steamboats up the river and a British-financed German, Heinrich Barth, completed the exploration of the Sudanic kingdoms in the early 1850s.

In South Africa there was progressive settlement by Afrikaaner farmers from the Cape along the south and east coastal regions, while on the plateau inland, travelers such as Gordon, Paterson, Burchell, and the missionary Robert Moffat penetrated to Botswana by the 1840s. Moffat's son-in-law, David Livingstone, reached the Zambesi in 1851. Livingstone came to believe that he must open up a new route to the interior for commerce and the Gospel; the Zambesi seemed to be the answer. He reached the west coast at Luanda in 1854 and then, in his greatest feat, crossed the continent to the mouth of the Zambesi in 1856 having visited the Victoria Falls on the way. Livingstone's *Missionary Travels and Researches* of 1857 was to be one of the best-sellers of the century combining, as it did, excellent science, exciting adventures, exotic scenes, and a strong moral message.

Like the Niger, the Zambesi did not prove an easy route inland for steamboats as Livingstone himself discovered between 1858 and 1864 when the government sent him to lead an expedition to follow up his ideas, much to the dismay of the Portuguese, as their Dr. Lacerda (in 1798) and Majors Monteiro and Gamitto (in the 1830s) had penetrated the region northward of the Zambesi. Although Livingstone reached Lake Malawi in 1859, his steamboat could not get to the lake or far up the Zambesi.

Meanwhile, rumors of other lakes further north and news of snow-covered mountains seen by the German Lutheran missionaries Johann Ludwig Krapf and Rebmann of the Anglican Church Missionary Society (CMS) had attracted enormous interest, not least because somewhere in the region, it was surmised, must lie the source of the Nile. The RGS sent Richard Burton with John Speke from the east coast to discover Lake Tanganyika in 1858. Speke diverted north to find Lake Victoria and claimed it as the Nile source. This he proved in July 1862 and then followed the river down to Egypt. Samuel Baker reached Lake Albert in 1864. However, he accidentally shot himself dead before a scheduled debate with Burton. Doubts existed about Speke's Nile claims; they were still unresolved in 1873 when Livingstone died, in public eyes a martyr to the slave trade but actually seeking the Nile further south. He was really at the sources of the Zaïre (Congo). Verney Cameron, sent to find Livingstone, met his body but went on to cross the Congo basin in 1874–1876. It was Henry Stanley, made famous after finding Livingstone in October 1871, who solved the remaining problems in 1874–1877. Having confirmed Speke's Nile source, he followed the Zaïre to the Atlantic. Well-financed, Stanley was ruthless and efficient. The milder Joseph Thomson traveled peacefully through Kenya in the early 1880s.

Attempts were now being made to follow up the explorers' work. Egypt tried to found an empire on the upper Nile, and Emin Pasha was stranded there after the Mahdist revolt. The greatest effect was on King Leopold of the Belgians who set up an "International

Association," ostensibly to reform Africa. He employed Stanley who, in 1886–1890, proceeded up the Zaïre and through the great forest to "rescue" Emin Pasha. The Ruwenzori range and other new features were put on the map, but essentially, this was an imperialist venture in the developing contest between Belgian, British, and German interests.

Even if indirectly, the explorers did shape situations and attitudes as Africans came to terms with the encroaching Western world. On the whole, popular accounts of the exploits of explorers and missionaries tended to underestimate the difficulties of introducing European technology and trade, while ignoring or dismissing the interests and abilities of the people they encountered.

ROY BRIDGES

See also: **Livingstone, David; Stanley, Leopold II, "Scramble"; Timbuktu.**

Further Reading

Bridges, R. C. "Africa from the Eighteenth Century." In *The Times Atlas of World Exploration*, edited by Felipe. Fernandez-Armesto. London: HarperCollins, 1991.
———. "Towards the Prelude to the Partition of East Africa." In *Impreialism, Decolonization, and Africa*, edited by Felipe Fernandez-Armesto. London: Harper Collins, 1991.
Hallett, R. *The Penetration of Africa. European Enterprise and Exploration principally in Northern and Western Africa up to 1830*. London: Routledge, 1965.
Heintze, B., and A. Jones, eds. *European Sources for Sub-Saharan Africa before 1900: Use and Abuse*. Stuttgart: Steiner, 1987.
Moorehead, A. *The White Nile*. London: Hamish Hamilton, 1960.
Simpson, D. *Dark Companions. The African Contribution to the European Exploration of East Africa*. London: Elek, 1975.
Youngs, T. *Travelers in Africa. British Travelogues, 1850–1900*. Manchester: Manchester University Press, 1994.

Europe: Industrialization and Imperialism

Of the many developments that took place in Europe during the nineteenth century, two had far-reaching consequences for Africa in particular and the non-European world in general: European industrialization and imperialism.

The industrialization of Europe was the result of the Industrial Revolution, a term generally used to refer to the rapid economic and technological innovations which transformed Europe from an agrarian and mercantile society to an industrial society. The Industrial Revolution started in Britain in the last quarter of the eighteenth century and continued there steadily until approximately the middle of the nineteenth century, when it reached its peak. From Britain it gradually spread to Western European countries and the United States. The most notable features of the Industrial Revolution were the changes that came about in the production of goods and in the distribution of the produce. These changes led to the replacement of handicraft production with production by machines.

In Britain the innovations began with the introduction of machines in the textile and wool industries; other innovations took place in power production with the invention of the steam engine, and in iron manufacturing. Inventions and improvements in one area impacted, and resulted in, corresponding improvements in other areas. For example, initially machines were made of wood; improvement in the iron industry resulted in the replacement of wooden tools with iron tools which improved the quality of machines used in the factories. Similarly, invention of the steam engine and the harnessing of steam power resulted in efficient operation of machines, and also made it possible to locate industries virtually anywhere. Moreover, the steam engine was applied to the transportation sector and resulted in the development of canals and railways which made possible cheap and fast freight transportation. The combined effect of these various innovations was massive increases in manufactured goods, which in turn led to other economic and social changes in areas such as finance, markets, labor, and urbanization among others. By the 1850s, as a result of its lead in the Industrial Revolution, Britain had become the "workshop of the world," and a major world power.

As the Industrial Revolution spread to other European countries and the United States, it had similar economic and social consequences. This impacted relations between European nations, particularly in the search for markets and raw materials for the expanding industrial output as well as for capital investment. The resulting competition went beyond the boundaries of Europe into overseas territories in the form of European imperialism in Asia, the Pacific region, and Africa.

There is dispute among scholars as to the precise meaning of the term "imperialism," as well as its origins, nature, manifestation, and consequences. The word is used here to refer to European expansion into areas of the world previously not inhabited by Europeans in the nineteenth and early twentieth centuries, resulting in empire building or the acquisition of overseas colonies by the major European powers.

With reference to Africa, European imperialism took place from the 1870s to about 1914 and lasted until the 1960s in most parts of Africa, the 1970s and 1980s in the remaining areas. This is not to say that Europe did not have interest or territorial holdings in Africa before the 1870s, but such holdings as there were, except in a few isolated spots such as Algeria and the southern tip of Africa, were mainly trading or coaling and refueling posts. The Europeans did not directly rule or govern these holdings and did not have to do so in order to safeguard their interests or exert influence. From the 1870s, however, competition among European nations for colonies in Africa intensified to such an extent that by 1914 virtually all of the continent, except Morocco and Ethiopia, had been parceled out as colonies/protectorates among the main European powers (Britain, France, Germany, Italy, Portugal, Spain, and Belgium). These colonies were directly governed or administered by the European powers through structures set up by them in the colonies.

Scholars are not agreed on the motives behind European imperialism in Africa. Some scholars have pointed to economic motivation and have argued that the search for new and guaranteed markets for the ever increasing output of European industries, new sources of raw materials to feed the industries, new areas for capital investment, and cheap and reliable labor force was the driving force behind colonial acquisition. Others have pointed to noneconomic reasons and have argued that nationalism, the pursuit of international power, security, and strategic—even humanitarian considerations—were the primary motivation. These seemingly divergent views are not necessarily mutually exclusive. All these factors were at play in varying combinations at different times in the calculation of the various imperial powers. While the economic motives were probably foremost in the thinking of the imperial powers none of the other considerations can be ruled out as either unimportant or irrelevant. Imperialism was a complex phenomenon, as were its motivation, its nature, its manifestation and its impact on the colonized territories. Each of the various motives was connected in one way or another with the industrialization of Europe.

The nineteenth century was not only a century of European industrialization and imperialism but also of nationalism in Europe, a phenomenon as complex and difficult to define as imperialism. There was a connection between all three phenomena, as each added to and reinforced the others. For example, industrialization sharpened the nationalist sentiment among leaders and other opinion makers in various European nations and either led to or intensified competition among the nations in terms of political power, overseas trade, international stature and national security among others. This kind of competition was a major factor in unleashing European imperialism on Africa and Asia in the nineteenth century.

R. H. KOFI DARKWAH

See also: **Colonial European Administrations: Comparative Survey; Colonialism: Impact on African Societies.**

Further Reading

Berlanstein, L. R., ed. The *Industrial Revolution and Work in 19th Century Europe*. London: Routledge, 1992.
Fieldhouse, D. K. *Colonialism 1870–1945: An Introduction*. London: Macmillan Press, 1983.
———. *Economics and Empire, 1830–1914*. London: Macmillan Publishers, 1984.
Gollwitzer, H. *Europe in the Age of Imperialism, 1880–1914*. London: Thames and Hudson, 1969.
Hobsbawm, E. J. *The Age of Empire 1875–1914*. London: Weidenfeld and Nicolson, 1987.
Porter, Andrew. *European Imperialism, 1860–1914*. London: Macmillan Press, 1994.

European Union: *See* **Maghrib Unity, European Union and.**

Ewe: *See* **Aja-speaking Peoples: Aja, Fon, Ewe, Seventeenth and Eighteenth Centuries.**

Ewuare: *See* **Benin, Empire: Oba Ewuare, Trade with the Portuguese.**

Eyadèma, Gnassingbe: *See* **Togo: Eyadèma, Gnassingbé, Life and Era of.**

F

Faidherbe, Louis: *See* Senegal: Faidherbe, Louis and Expansion of French Senegal, 1854–1855.

Famine: *See* Drought, Famine, Displacement; Ethiopia: Famine, Revolution, Mengistu Dictatorship, 1914–1991.

Fante: *See* Akan States: Bono, Denkyira, Wassa, Akyem, Akwamu, Fante, Fifteenth to Seventeenth Centuries.

Farming: Stone Age Farmers of the Savanna

Farming in much of Sub-Saharan Africa is based on management of animal herds, together with cultivation of a range of indigenous savanna crops. These savanna crops include a wide range of small-seeded grasses (various millet species), sorghum, African rice, as well as pulses native to the savanna-forest margins (cowpea, hyacinth bean, Bambara groundnuts). These species, however, represent numerous distinct domestication events in different regions across the Sub-Saharan savanna belt. The full process of the domestication of these species, from their wild exploitation by foragers to cultivation and morphological change, is incompletely documented.

Important precursors to savanna farming are to be found in the foraging societies of Sahara under wetter conditions, 7,000–4,000BCE. Sites from the Western Desert of Egypt (such as the Nabta Playa cultural complex) and southwest Libya (the Early Acacus to Early Pastoral tradition) provide ample evidence for the exploitation of wild harvested grasses. With the exception of wild sorghum from sites in western Egypt, the grasses exploited at this time were not species subsequently domesticated, but their exploitation attests to a delayed-return foraging economy that probably included storage, an essential prerequisite for the development of cultivation. These societies began to manufacture pottery, much of which shared dotted-wavy line decoration, which suggests wide-ranging contacts among these mobile societies. It is also among these hunter-foragers of the Saharan grasslands that pastoralism became established. The spread of sheep and goats of Near Eastern origins occurred rapidly by the sixth millennium BCE, while cattle that spread during this period may have derived from indigenous domestication in the eastern Sahara as much as a millennium or two earlier. These societies would have been seasonally mobile and focused on perennial oasis water sources in the dry season, where use of cached wild grains would also have been important. As climate change caused the desertification of the Sahara, such groups would have been increasing forced southwards or into the Nile Valley. Evidence from Nabta Playa in southern Egypt and from southwest Libya both indicate that the desert had been abandoned by around 3,000BCE.

It is during this period of aridification that food production was adopted in the Sudanese Nile Valley. While the Early Khartoum tradition, which included dotted-wavy line ceramics, had subsisted by fishing, hunting, and foraging, the Shaheinab Neolithic, which emerged in the region north of Khartoum from around 4,000BCE, added evidence for domestic herd animals. Evidence from ceramic plant impressions and common quernstones attest to the use of wild grains, including wild sorghum. These communities were seasonally mobile, exploiting the Nile during the dry season and ranging into adjacent savannas during the wet season. Increasing reliance on pastoral production by these communities provided a basis for systems of wealth and hierarchy, which is evident in burials beginning in the later fourth millennium BCE. While some scholars have argued that it was among these communities that sorghum was first cultivated, the available evidence is inconclusive, and these archaeological traditions end around 3,000BCE without subsequent evidence for settlements with cultivation in this area. The earliest finds of domesticated sorghum are not until the first millennium BCE on sites well established by sedentary farmers further north in Nubia. From the third millennium, the village to urban tradition of Kerma emerged, but it remains unclear whether this was based solely on the production of introduced wheat and barley cultivation in the Nile flood plain or also included summer cultivation of sorghum.

In West Africa, semisedentary communities of cultivators emerged in the early second millennium BCE among pastoralists who had retreated south from the drying Sahara. One such tradition emerged in the palaeolake and wadi systems of southeast Mauretania in the Tichitt Tradition. Here ceramics begin around 2,000BCE and incorporate chaff-temper from the local processing of domesticated pearl millet from around 1700BCE. Large communities are indicated by stone remains of town and village sites with large domestic compounds focused on water sources. While summer cultivation and storage probably focused on these settlements, pastoral mobility remained important, as indicated by surface scatters of campsites. In the Niger bend regions, the sites of Karkarichinkat South and Winde Koroji indicate established village farming traditions with pearl millet by the mid-second millennium BCE. Further south in northnern Buriko Fao, the sites of Orusi and Ti-n-Akof indicate the establishment of millet cultivation and pastoral production on stabilized sand dunes of northern savanna. Genetic evidence suggests that southwest Mauretania and these Niger bend sites could relate to two distinct domestications of wild pearl millet populations. The currently available dates from these sites, however, provide only the minimum age for the end of the domestication process, as equivalent or slightly older dates are available beyond the wild pearl millet range, including finds from India.

The Kintampo culture, known archaeologically from Ghana, indicates the adoption of savanna agropastoralism among forest margin hunter-gatherers. Evidence for domesticated pearl millet from around 1700BCE, as well as domestic fauna, at Birimi in northern Ghana attests to the importance of millet cultivation among some groups, while Kintampo sites further south in Ghana lack millet but have yielded abundant evidence for oil palm exploitation from the forest edge environment as well as probable early cowpea.

Pastoralism, possibly accompanied by some crop cultivation, also spread eastward and southward from the Sudan from the mid- to late third millennium BCE. The Nderit ceramic tradition of the Lake Turkana region is associated with evidence for domesticated sheep and goats, while contemporary Eburran tradition hunter-gatherer sites further south have produced small quantities of ceramics and sheep/goat bones. The slow spread of domestic fauna in this region during the second millennium BCE is due in part to the presence of disease threats to domesticates, as well as established hunter-gatherer adaptations. In the mid-first millennium BCE, Pastoral Neolithic societies were much more widespread and domesticates had begun to spread into southern Africa. On present evidence it is unclear the extent to which cultivated crops played a role in these eastern African food production economies. Similarly requiring further research is the establishment of food production in more coastal East Africa, where some sites with ceramics may also date back to as early as the mid-third millennium BCE. In the uplands of Ethiopia, evidence from Gobedra and Lake Besaka for domesticate cattle dates from the mid- to late second millennium BCE, while early crop evidence remains elusive. In southern Africa domestic livestock were adopted among Khoisan-speaking groups, perhaps in Namibia and the Zambezi River Valley in the last centuries BCE, with subsequent dispersal southward. Later iron-using farmers made a more noticeable impact. Evidence for plant cultivation comes from the third century CE, when pearl millet is known from Silver Leaves in eastern South Africa.

The patchy evidence for early farmers in African savannas contrasts with traditional models of the beginnings of farming developed from Near Eastern archaeology. While in the Near East sedentary hunter-gatherers took up cultivation, then animal domestication and then pottery, in Africa ceramics first occur among mobile foragers, and animal herding preceded plant cultivation and sedentary settlement.

DORIAN Q. FULLER

Further Reading

D'Andrea, A. C., and J. Casey. "Pearl Millet and Kintampo Subsistence." *African Archaeological Review*. 19(2002): 147–173.

Barker, G. "Transitions to Farming and Pastoralism in North Africa." In *Examining the Farming/language Dispersal Hypothesis*, edited by Peter Bellwood and Colin Renfrew. Cambridge: McDonald Institute for Archaeological Research, 2003.

Blench, R. M., and K. C. MacDonald, eds. *The Origins and Development of African Livestock: Archaeology, Genetics, Linguistics, and Ethnography*. London: UCL Press, 2000.

Clark, J. D., and S. A. Brandt, eds. *From Hunters to Farmers: The Causes and Consequences of Food Production in Africa*. Berkeley: University of California Press, 1984.

Marshall, F., and E. Hildebrand. "Cattle before Crops: The Beginnings of Food Production in Africa." *Journal of World Prehistory* 16(2002): 99–143.

Farming: Tropical Forest Zones

The history of farming in Africa's tropical forest zones is a persistent research challenge. Direct archaeological evidence, especially of plant remains but also of animal bones, is rare, and many of the species of particular importance would be difficult to identify archaeologically even if they were present. As a result, our understanding of past farming in these zones remains extremely patchy and is inferred largely from indirect evidence, ethnographic models, and historical linguistics.

A number of important crop species are native to the forests or forest margins of Africa, and their modern distributions provide clues to their regions of origin. There are several tuber species, which have played a limited role in agriculture outside the forest or forest margin zones. African yams (*Dioscorea cayenensis* complex and *D. bulbifera*) are taxonomically complex and could have multiple domestications across Africa. Other tubers like the hausa potato (*Plectranthus excultentus*), yampea (*Sphenostylis stenocarpa*), and piasa (*Solenostemon rotundifolius*) are all likely domesticates of the west-central Africa forest zone. In addition to possibly native yams, the forests of southwest Ethiopia provided early cultivators with ensete, cultivated for its starchy "stems." While guinea millet (*Brachiaria deflexa*) is native to the West African forest margin, other cereals cultivated in the forest zone, such as pearl millet and sorghum, were introduced from savanna agriculture. In Ethiopia, finger millet, tef, and the oilseed noog may have been domesticated in forest margin zones.

Important pulses of West Africa include cowpea, Kersting's groundnut, and Bambara groundnut, while in East Africa the hyacinth bean is a probable forest margin domesticate. Important tree crops include the akee apple (*Blighia sapida*), the oil palm (*Elaeis guineensis*), and the incense tree (*Canarium schweinfurthii*) in West Africa. Additional crops include okra (*Abelmoschus esculentus*) and the fluted gourd (*Telfaira occidentalis*). Both West Africa and Ethiopia also have native stimulant species, with cola nuts and robusta coffee in West Africa and arabica coffee and chat in Ethiopia. Many species important to the agriculture of this zone today have been introduced from overseas. Bananas and probably taro/cocoyam and Asian yams were introduced in antiquity from across the Indian Ocean, while cassava/manioc, the sweet potato, and peanuts/groundnuts were introduced in post-Columbian times from South America.

None of the livestock that are important in the forest zone are native but were introduced via savanna zones.

The ungulates (sheep, goat, and cattle) all show special adaptation to this environment through dwarfism, which can be identified through metrical analysis of archaeological bone, and provides an intriguing parallel to human pygmy groups in this zone. As with other parts of equatorial Africa, the presence of endemic tsetse flies in this zone creates a potential disease barrier to the successful colonization by pastoralists.

The origins of agriculture in the west-central African forests lie in the interaction between native hunter-gatherers and early savanna agropastoralists. Such interactions appear to be represented by the Kintampo archaeological culture of Ghana. Lithic traditions and distinctive artifacts known as "terracotta cigars" suggest development of this ceramic-using tradition from local precursors. The northern range of this tradition is found in the savannas of northern Ghana from the early second millennium BCE, where pearl millet was cultivated, as indicated at Birimi. Further south, in more wooded environments, archaeobotanical evidence points to use of wild fruits, including incense tree nuts and oil palm, as well as pulses, including cowpea. Kintampo sites have produced evidence for cattle and goats, and some of the goat remains have been attributed to a dwarf breed. Linguistic evidence suggests that among the early cultivators of these forest crops were Benue-Congo speakers.

It was a subsection of the Benue-Congo language, the Bantu languages, which appear to have been spread by the early cultivators in central Africa, a process which could have begun as early as the second millennium BCE, although hard evidence for dating this process is elusive. Anthropogenic impacts on vegetation in West Africa are more readily apparent from the early to mid-first millennium BCE, which suggests that food-producing populations had reached some critical mass. Bantu speakers spread in two directions: eastward along forest margins, where other language groups may also have practiced agriculture and millet cultivation was added to the tuber crops, while another direction was south and east in central Africa carrying yam cultivation and livestock, while practicing fishing and mollusk collecting. The northern savanna route brought them to the great lakes region, where savanna food-producers were probably already established, and where the addition of ironworking promoted more intensive food production.

During the Iron Age, characterized by Urewe ceramics into the first centuries CE, the vegetation in this region registers the impact of widespread agriculture. Here perhaps in this period dwarf, humped cattle may have been adopted, which included genetic input from Indian zebu. The dispersal in the forest zone is thought to have followed river corridors, the west coastal zone, and possible savanna corridors favored for forest margin cultivation. Population densities are likely to have been limited in part due to disease factors, and symbiosis of specialized hunter-gatherer groups may have been important. The minimum age for dispersal may be provided by the Ngovo tradition, with ceramics and groundstone axes, known from the lower Zaire River south of the central Africa rainforest, and dating from the end of the first millennium BCE, although present faunal data lacks livestock. Further south in Namibia and Zimbabwe to the east, livestock may have been adopted by Khoesaan-speaking communities in the last centuries BCE. Among the widespread words in Bantu languages are words for banana and possibly taro/cocoyam. Evidence for banana in the form of archaeological phytoliths comes from Nkang, Cameroon, from the mid- to late first millennium BCE. This indicates that bananas had spread westward from the East African coast by this time.

Early farming in equatorial Africa was a complex mosaic and raises important issues about the interaction between different systems of food production, persistent hunting and gathering, and between different cultural traditions. Developments drew on traditions from the African savannas, as well as species introduced to Africa via long-distance Indian Ocean trade

DORIAN Q. FULLER

Further Reading

Blench, R. M., and K. C. MacDonald, eds. *The Origins and Development of African Livestock: Archaeology, Genetics, Linguistics, and Ethnography.* London: UCL Press, 2000.

Marshall, F., and E. Hildebrand. "Cattle before Crops: The Beginnings of Food Production in Africa." *Journal of World Prehistory* 16 (2002): 99–143.

Mbida, C. M., W. Van Neer, H. Doutrelepont, and L. Vrydaghs. "Evidence for Banana Cultivation and Animal Husbandry during the First Millennium BC in the Fioest of southern Cameroon." *Journal of Archaeological Science* 27 (2000): 151–162.

Sutton, J., ed. "The Growth of Farming Communities in Africa from the Equator Southwards." *Azania,* journal volumes X Nairobi: British Institute in Eastern Africa, 1996.

Fatagar: *See* Ethiopia: Muslim States, Awash Valley: Shoa, Ifat, Fatagar, Hadya, Dawaro, Adal, Ninth to Sixteenth Centuries.

Fatimid Caliphate: *See* Egypt: Fatimid Caliphate.

Fatimid Empire: Maghrib, 910–1057

Early in the tenth century, Abu Abdallah, a Shi'ite propagandist, instigated an uprising against Ifriqiya's Aghlabid rulers. After defeating them in 910, he gave his support to Ubaidallah al-Mahdi, a messianic figure whose goal was to establish Shi'ite control throughout the Muslim world. By claiming the title of caliph (successor to Muhammad), Ubaidallah openly challenged the legitimacy of the Abbasid family, which had held the position for over a century. To stress their descent from Fatima, Muhammad's daughter and the wife of Ali, whom the Shi'a acknowledged as Muhammad's true heir, Ubaidallah and his family called themselves Fatimids.

The Kutama Berbers who had formed the nucleus of Abu Abdallah's army fell out with the Fatimids when the new rulers refused to allow the plundering of the province. Other Fatimid practices also disillusioned potential allies. The taxes needed to finance a large army proved burdensome, and the new regime's insistence on such Shi'ite tenets as the primacy of the descendants of Ali irked the egalitarian Berbers. Their disillusion boiled over into open revolt when Ubaidallah ordered the assassination of Abu Abdallah in 911.

Other opponents of the Fatimids—among them merchants aggrieved by the dynasty's acquisition of control over their lucrative trade routes and an Aghlabid pretender in Sicily—joined the rebels. Ubaidallah quelled the uprising with the assistance of Berbers whose loyalty was bought with promises of looting. The ensuing sack of the religious center of Qairawan, whose leaders had shown no inclination to renounce Sunni traditions, assured the Fatimids of the enduring enmity of that city. Nor did Shi'ite Islam make significant gains among the population at large. The hostility of Qairawan and the Fatimids' desire to carry their revolution beyond Ifriqiya explain Ubaidallah's decision to construct a new capital, Mahdiyya, on a peninsula on the province's eastern coast. Thus the Shi'ite rulers replaced Qairawan, originally founded to facilitate expansion farther west, with a coastal city looking eastward to the Muslim heartlands where the Fatimids hoped to organize their ideal state.

Nevertheless, the Fatimids did not ignore the lands to their west. Campaigns to bring other areas of the Maghrib under their rule provided an outlet for the militancy of Ifriqiya's Berbers and enhanced the Fatimid economy by securing control over additional North African termini of the trans-Saharan trade in the mid-tenth century. But the determination of the Umayyad rulers of the Iberian peninsula to halt Fatimid expansion turned much of the Maghrib into a battlefield contested by Berber proxies of both the Fatimid and Spanish Umayyad dynasties.

A resurgence of Kharajism, an egalitarian Muslim doctrine that had earlier attracted considerable support in North Africa, coincided with this period of Fatimid expansion. A populist figure named Abu Yazid led a Kharaji insurrection in the vicinity of Tozeur shortly after Ubaiadallah's death in 934. The Fatimids arrested Abu Yazid, but he escaped and renewed the rebellion a decade later, capturing Tunis and Qairawan. His failure to take Mahdiyya broke the revolt and he was executed in 947. Abu Yazid's death ended the Kharaji threat in Ifriqiya, but the difficulties he had caused spurred the Fatimid leaders to begin planning the complicated process of transplanting their regime to the east.

Successful military thrusts into the Nile Valley enabled the Fatimids to transfer their capital to the newly created city of al-Qahira (Cairo) in 969. They did not, however, renounce their interests in the Maghrib, but appointed Buluggin ibn Ziri, a Berber tribal leader and long-time Fatimid ally, as governor of the area. His primary task was to hold the line against the Spanish Umayyads and their Zanata Berber allies. Buluggin and his successors engaged their former masters in a cat-and-mouse game, testing the limits of their independence. The Fatimids were unwilling to incur heavy expenses in curbing Zirid ambitions, but neither were they prepared to hand over their former territories to their vassals. Instead, they encouraged the Kutama Berbers to revolt, preventing the Zirids from focusing too sharply on their relationship with Cairo. On Buluggin's death in 984, his relatives divided the extensive Fatimid inheritance. His son Hammad received the lands of the central Maghrib west of Ifriqiya, where he carved out an independent state by the early eleventh century. Hammad's kinsmen in Ifriqiya resented his ambition but recognized that he provided them with a barrier against Zanata and Spanish Umayyad attacks.

As the threat of direct Fatimid intervention in North Africa waned, the Zirids found themselves in control of a thriving agricultural and commercial economy. Their commitment to maintaining stability in Ifriqiya and effectively controlling the caravan routes won them the support of urban artisans and businessmen dependent on agriculture and commerce for their livelihoods, particularly those of Mansuriyya, a suburb of Qairawan, which became the Zirids' economic and political hub. Early in the eleventh century, however, the trans-Saharan trade began to decline. The Zirids proved unable to provide the same measure of stimulation for this trade as had the Fatimids, who demanded its gold and other luxury items to finance their ambitious plans and its slaves to fill the ranks of their army. Equally responsible for the trade's decline, however, were the rise of the Almoravid confederation in the western Maghrib and the continuing Sub-Saharan commercial interests of the Fatimids themselves, both of which diverted caravan routes from Ifriqiya.

Spurred on as much by these economic considerations as by political motives, the Zirid ruler Muiz formally severed his links with the Fatimids in 1049. Ifriqiya no longer figured prominently in the Fatimids'

plans, but they were enraged by the disloyalty of their vassals. To punish them, they forced a number of Arab bedouin groups to move from Egypt to the Maghrib, fully aware that so massive a nomadic influx would wreak havoc there. In a pitched battle at Haidaran, northwest of Qairawan, in 1052, the bedouins routed the Zirid forces. Five years later, they sacked Qairawan, finalizing their hold over the interior of the province. The Zirids retreated to the coastal fortress of Mahdiyya, from which they maintained a tenuous grip on Ifriqiya's coastal regions for the next century.

KENNETH J. PERKINS

Further Reading

Brett, M. "The Fatimid Revolution (861–973) and Its Aftermath in North Africa." In *Cambridge History of Africa.* Vol. 2. Cambridge: Cambridge University Press, 1978.

Halm, H. *The Empire of the Mahdi: The Rise of the Fatimids.* Leiden: E. J. Brill, 1996.

Hrbek, I. "The Emergence of the Fatimids." In *General History of Africa.* Vol. 3, *Africa from the Seventh to the Eleventh Century,* edited by M. El Fasi. Berkeley: University of California Press, 1988.

Fatimids: *See* Egypt: Fatimids, 1073–1171; Egypt: Fatimids, Later (1073–1171): Army and Administration.

Administration; Egypt: Fatimids, Later: World Trade.

Federations and Unions, Postcolonial

The pace of independence of African colonies in the 1950s and 1960s ensured that the structure of some colonial unions and federations continued into the new era relatively intact. Others, formed for the administrative convenience of the appropriate European power, were broken up into their constituent parts, which then became sovereign entities. Differing attitudes to federal structures also determined the form, means, and success of unions and federations in each of the imperial systems of Africa.

The oldest federal structure in imperial Africa was the Union of South Africa, created in 1910 out of the self-governing British colonies of Cape Colony and Natal and the recently annexed former Afrikaner republics, the Orange Free State and Transvaal. Designed along the lines of the Dominion of Canada and the Commonwealth of Australia, it nevertheless vested dominant authority in the Union Government in Pretoria and relatively little in the states. This tendency to centralization was reinforced in the republican constitutions of 1961 and 1984, although some provincial autonomy was restored in the postapartheid constitution in 1996 that increased the number of states from four to nine.

Elsewhere in British Africa, unions and federations were attempted with more limited success. Nigeria, unified under one administration in 1914, was an obvious test case for a federal structure during the colonial administrative reforms of the 1940s and 1950s. The "Richards" and "Macpherson" constitutions of 1947 and 1951 gradually extended the powers of regional assemblies and of the central legislature. Full internal self-government followed in the constitution of 1954, leading to a federal independent constitution in 1961. Nigeria's repeated difficulties with military rule and the secessionist Biafran regime of the late 1960s saw a tendency toward centralization at the expense of the states, a pattern familiar in many parts of the continent.

The post-1945 era saw two further efforts to create colonial federations out of geographically contiguous colonies in British Africa, neither of which survived the transition to independence. Efforts to bring about "partnership" between the European and African inhabitants of Northern and Southern Rhodesia and Nyasaland resulted in the Central African Federation of the three colonies, which lasted from 1953 to 1963. The dominance of the federal government by the small white minority (as well as the preponderance of white-minority-ruled Southern Rhodesia economically and politically) raised the ire of African nationalists in all three territories. The federation was dissolved pending the independence of the three as separate states in 1964–1965. A similar experiment had long been posited for Kenya, Tanganyika, and Uganda, where the idea of multiracial "partnership" was also attractive to officials. However, federation only went as far as the East African High Commission of 1948 to coordinate common services; suspicion of further integration, the Mau Mau crisis, and Tanganyika's unique position as a United Nations (UN) Trust Territory made any federal plans impossible. The three states achieved independence in 1961–1963, and in 1964 Zanzibar joined Tanganyika to form Tanzania.

In general, British efforts to maintain some degree of regional autonomy within newly independent states amounted to quasi-federal constitutions in Kenya, Uganda, and Ghana, but in all cases these were denounced within a short time by the national leaders in the name of "national unity." Within British Africa, only Nigeria retained its federal structure beyond the early years of independence.

Federal structures were organized by the French at the turn of the century to ease their administration of the vast territories acquired in Sub-Saharan Africa. French West Africa (AOF) and French Equatorial Africa (AEF) each had a resident governor general and centralized administrative apparatus, and a governor and other officials at the level of each constituent territory (Mauritania; Senegal; Guinea; Côte d'Ivoire [Ivory Coast]: Dahomey; Sudan: Upper Volta; Niger: AEF: Congo; Oubangui-Chari; Chad). In the Fourth Republic constitution of 1946, each territory was granted a local assembly and was represented in the French National Assembly. This territorial autonomy was further enhanced by the *loi cadre* (enabling law) reforms of 1956, although executive authority at the federal level remained in the hands of the governors general. The short-lived Gaullist French Community arrangements of 1958 accelerated the pace toward independence, which came in 1960, at which time the AEF and AOF ceased to exist. The new republics that emerged from French Africa were for the most part unitary states with a strong executive presidency, although Mali (formerly French Sudan) and Senegal did form a brief federal republic in the aftermath of independence. This collapsed in August 1960 because of the very different populations and political cultures of the two territories. Elsewhere, Gabon, Congo-Brazzaville, the Central African Republic, Chad, and the former UN Trust Territory of Cameroon formed a customs union.

Cameroon was a separate case because prior to independence it was a League of Nations Mandate (later UN Trust Territory) administered by France, although a smaller portion adjoining Nigeria was administered by Britain. Part of British Cameroon joined independent Nigeria in 1960, whereas the southern part was federated with now-independent French Cameroon in the following year. The two parts made up the Federal Republic of Cameroon with separate parliaments and ministries in addition to the federal government structure until a May 1972 referendum abolished the federation in favor of a United Republic.

In the former Belgian Congo, a federal constitution was promulgated in May 1960 in which the six colonial provinces would enjoy certain autonomies. Ultimate power lay with the central government, and in the disintegration that followed, provinces gained power that was affirmed in a new federal constitution in 1964. This was short-lived, and in October 1966 President Mobutu Sese Seko abolished provincial autonomy.

In order to settle the fate of the former Italian colonies after World War II, the UN attached Eritrea to Ethiopia in a federal arrangement in 1952. Eritrea enjoyed its own democratically elected government and constitution and was in theory equal to Ethiopia at the federal level until the territory was formerly annexed into a unitary state by Ethiopia in 1962.

DAVID DEVEREUX

See also: **Colonial Federations: British Central Africa; Colonial Federations: French Equatorial Africa; Colonial Federations: French West Africa.**

Further Reading

Ansprenger, F. *The Dissolution of the Colonial Empires.* London: Routledge, 1989.

Chabal, P., ed. *Political Domination in Africa: Reflections on the Limits of Power.* London: Cambridge University Press, 1986.

Hodder-Williams, *An Introduction to the Politics of Tropical Africa.* London: Allen and Unwin, 1984.

Tordoff, W. *Government and Politics in Africa.* Bloomington: Indiana University Press, 1984.

Young, C. *Ideology and Development in Africa.* New Haven: Yale University Press, 1982.

FIDES: *See* Fonds d'Investment pour le Développement Economique et Social (FIDES).

Firestone: *See* Liberia: Firestone.

FNLA: *See* Angola: MPLA, FNLA, UNITA, and the War of Liberation, 1961–1974.

Fon: *See* Aja-speaking Peoples: Aja, Fon, Ewe, Seventeenth and Eighteenth Centuries.

Fonds d'Investissement pour le Développement Economique et Social (FIDES)

Created by a law of April 30, 1946, the Fonds d'Investissement pour le Développement Economique et Social (FIDES [Investment Fund for Economic and Social Development]) was established to finance and coordinate the provision of facilities for the French overseas territories. It was placed at the service of France's new colonial policy after World War II, becoming the favored financial instrument by which a large part of French public-sector investment in these colonial territories was transmitted between 1946 and the attainment of independence by the former colonies.

Indeed, this radical change in policy on public-sector investment was the major innovation in the French colonies after the war. Breaking with the principles implicit in the *Pacte Colonial* (Colonial Pact), which had imposed self-financing on the colonial territories, the metropolitan power now accepted that it would have to invest public-sector capital directly into its colonies. This injection of capital was carried out within the framework of plans for modernizing and providing infrastructure for the *Union Française* (French Union) as a whole. In this way, a new vision of colonial development was formulated, within the context of the postwar emergence of "technocrats," so that there was a transposition to the overseas territories of the French planning system inaugurated by the Monnet Plan; and this within the broader framework of the Marshall Plan, which secured an inflow of capital aimed at reconstruction.

FIDES was, therefore, a crucial financial organism for the colonial "New Deal." While a related organism, the Caisse Centrale de la France d'Outre-Mer (CC-FOM [Central Fund for the French Overseas Territories]) was responsible for the provision of loans to such territories, FIDES provided direct grants. In doing so, it broke away from the logic that had been accepted before the war, when the colonies had been expected essentially to develop their own infrastructures with borrowed funds.

In fact, legally speaking, FIDES was simply one account held at the CCFOM, which was entrusted with the management of its funds, but the bulk of resources originating from the public sector and allocated for the implementation of infrastructure and development programs were transmitted through FIDES. Its leading personnel took part in drawing up, financing, and carrying out infrastructure plans and submitted long-term programs to the Ministère de la France d'Outre-Mer (Ministry for the French Overseas Territories), the government body that had responsibility for FIDES.

From the beginning, the moneys received by FIDES came from several sources, including both budgetary allocations by the metropolitan government and contributions from each of the colonial territories. In practice, it was the metropolitan power that, taking the insurmountable problems of local budgets into account, provided the bulk of the moneys for FIDES from the beginning of the 1950s. As a result, it may be said that these postwar investments prefigured the policy of bilateral aid that was to be developed between France and its former colonies once they had gained their independence.

FIDES conducted its operations through two principal divisions, the *section générale* (general section) and the *section d'outre-mer* (overseas section). The former was responsible for distributing state grants for studies and research of general interest and was authorized to take shares in public-sector companies, or companies with mixed public-private ownership, that operated in the colonies. The overseas section allocated grants to the whole range of specific development programs, such as those for roads, bridges, health facilities, educational institutions, town planning, and housing.

The definition and distribution of these investments was entrusted to a Guiding Committee, which was in effect the executive of FIDES. The committee was chaired by the minister for the French overseas territories, and its members included the director of the CCFOM, leading officials from the Ministères du Plan et de l'Economie (Ministries for the Plan and the Economy), individuals from the world of business, and a small number of parliamentarians. This committee had all the powers of decision over the financing and implementation of FIDES programs, and it followed that the local assemblies and governors lost some of their prerogatives: infrastructure policy for the colonies was essentially defined in Paris.

In addition, the work of FIDES was largely beyond the control of the French parliament. FIDES was not required to observe the strictly annual framework of the budgetary process, and the parliament, having allocated block credits to it, had no right to anything more than a fairly distant supervision over the allocation of its capital. Increasingly, therefore, the colonial domain seemed to be a sector set apart from the French government machine, even though, in principle, the local colonial authorities took part in drawing up its plans.

Two plans for modernizing the colonies were brought into operation between 1947 and 1959. One historian, Jacques Marseille, has calculated that, in real terms, the volume of capital invested in French Africa during these years was larger than the total invested throughout the sixty-five years preceding them. The investments by FIDES, in cities and countryside alike, produced significant results: hospitals, educational institutions, roads, ports, hydraulic and electrical infrastructure, and many other forms of infrastructure were introduced during the 1950s.

The infrastructure drive mounted by France between 1946 and 1959 appeared to be a delayed, if determined, attempt to modernize its colonial territories. However, many of the schemes that were implemented were no more than investments in catching up, which were incapable of meeting the needs of fast-growing populations. FIDES was also criticized for doing a great deal to serve the interests of French enterprises, which were certain to find protected markets in the colonies. Moreover, little of the capital provided by FIDES was devoted to industrialization or to lasting development; many of its investments helped to accentuate the indebtedness and dependent status of the colonies, for they did not promote self-sufficient development.

Following the attainment of independence by the colonies, the Fonds d'Aide et de Coopération (FAC [Aid and Cooperation Fund]) was created in 1960 as a channel for French bilateral aid. FAC was cast in the same mould as FIDES and took over most of its characteristics.

SOPHIE DULUCQ

Further Reading

La France et l'Outre-Mer: Un siècle de relations monétaires et économiques. Paris: CHEF-Ministère de l'Economie, 1998.
Marseille, Jacques. *Empire colonial et capitalisme français: Histoire d'un divorce.* Paris: Albin Michel, 1984.

Forest Peoples: Sierra Leone, Liberia and Côte d'Ivoire (Ivory Coast): History of to 1800

The western end of the Upper Guinea forest block, unlike the east, has yet to yield evidence of early civilization. Scholars believe that for a long period, only isolated human groups subsisting by hunting and gathering were found in the western forests. Further development, beginning with permanent settlement, rice cultivation, and ironworking, are attributed to the growth of interregional trade—malaguetta pepper grown in the forests of present-day Liberia found its way to medieval Europe via trans-Saharan networks— and immigration from the savanna and eastern forests. The region remained a periphery of African states and empires, especially the Mande civilization of the upper Niger basin, until Europeans arrived on the coast in the fifteenth century.

Data on the early history of the region are scarce. Excavations at Kamabai rock shelter in northern Sierra Leone yielded iron artifacts dating from the eighth century, the earliest yet known for the region. These artifacts were deposited with a new type of pottery found throughout the savanna. This pottery has been excavated from other sites in Sierra Leone and western Liberia, and its appearance suggests that savanna trading empires were penetrating the western end of the region by this time. Iron tools must have facilitated forest clearance, allowing shorter fallow cycles and higher population densities. Present-day techniques of rain-fed rice agriculture, which require heavy seasonal labor inputs, may therefore have developed as a result of these trading contacts, spreading southward and eastward across the region. Indeed, some groups living at the eastern end of the region, notably the Gagou of the Côte d'Ivoire, combined hunting and gathering with a secondary dependence on low-intensity root-crop agriculture as recently as the late nineteenth century.

Data on sickle-cell gene frequencies lend further support to the view that agriculture is long established in the west of the region (Sierra Leone) but a more recent development in the east (southeast Liberia-Côte d'Ivoire). The sickle-cell gene confers immunity to malaria. High rates of exposure to malaria may select for the gene, and this is more likely to occur among densely settled farming populations than isolated bands of hunters and gatherers inhabiting closed-canopy forest. Sickle-cell gene frequencies among modern populations of the region are substantially higher in the west than in the east. Furthermore, several modern groups, notably the Mende of Sierra Leone and Guéré of Côte d'Ivoire, have legends that their ancestors met a race of dwarfs when they first settled. No other evidence of an aboriginal race of West African pygmies has emerged, but the strongly bimodal distribution of heights among modern forest populations has led some scholars to argue that this reflects the intermarriage of short forest aborigines with taller immigrants from the savanna.

Linguistic evidence lends further support to the view that external agents played a key role in the historical development of the region. Today, representatives of three language families are present. Speakers of Kwa languages (Dei, Belle, Gbassa, Krahn, Grebo, Kru, Bété, Dida, Guéré, Agni-Baoulé, and the lagoon peoples) preponderate in the east (Côte d'Ivoire-eastern Liberia), while speakers of Mel languages (Temne, Bolem, Bom, Krim, Kissi and Gola) cluster in the west (Sierra Leone-western Liberia). Speakers of Mande languages form a middle cluster. They include representatives of Northern (Kono, Vai), Southern (Mano, Gio), and Southwestern (Mende, Kpelle, Gbandi, Loma, Dan, Gouro, and Gagou) Mande linguistic subdivisions.

Scholars have argued that local Kwa speakers, whose languages are related to those spoken in the Lower Niger basin, represent a vanguard of westward migration along the Guinea coast. This may in fact have involved shifts in language use as well as physical movement of people and may be linked to trade network expansion generated by state formation in Lower Guinea (Igbo Ukwu, Ife, Benin) and later, among the Akan of Asante. The Mande speakers are likewise seen as descendants of immigrants from the savanna and/or local populations drawn into savanna trade networks. Indeed, the Kono and Vai, speaking languages closely related to those spoken in the Upper Niger basin, may represent the ethnolinguistic imprint of an ancient trading system linking that region to the coast. The Southwestern Mande group may be the product of an even older and more geographically diffuse penetration from the area around Mount Nimba.

The Mel languages are specific to the Upper Guinea coast. Ancient stone figurines (*nomoli*) have been unearthed by local farmers in areas either currently inhabited by Mel-speaking Bolem and Kissi, or from which these peoples may have been displaced by Mande-speaking groups in the recent past. Some scholars have suggested that these figurines may be all

that remains of a lost forest civilization, of which the Bolem and Kissi, and perhaps Mel-speakers generally, are modern descendants. However, modern inhabitants of the region have no knowledge of the origin and purpose of these figurines.

It is significant that ethnographic data point to extensive and historically deep-seated processes of cultural convergence within the region. Even groups speaking unrelated languages tend to share the same cultural features. These include institutions that either facilitate social accommodation between groups of diverse origin (e.g., Islam, Mande, and European linguistic creoles, Mande clan names and secret societies), or reflect such accommodation (e.g., bilateral kinship). Historic forest culture seems to have focused less on conserving local identities and traditions than on building communities from whatever human and material resources were at hand.

The arrival of Europeans led savanna states to extend their power and influence toward the coast. Some forest groups (the Kissi in particular) were probably subject to intensified raiding in response to the European demand for slaves. In general, however, frontier conditions persisted in the Upper Guinea forests throughout the Atlantic trade era. European traders tapped into a regional trade and alliance system already built upon complex accommodations between local African rulers and resident agents of external commercial and political interests.

RICHARD FANTHORPE

See also: **Sahara: Trans-Saharan Trade; Slavery: Atlantic Trade: Effects in Africa and the Americas.**

Further Reading

Atherton, J. H. "Early Economies of Sierra Leone and Liberia: Archaeological and Historical Reflections." In *Essays on the Economic Anthropology of Sierra Leone and Liberia*, edited by Vernon Dorjahn and Barry Issac. Philadelphia: Institute of Liberian Studies, 1979.

D'Azevedo, Warren. "Some Historical Problems in the Delineation of a Central West Atlantic Region." *Annals of the New York Academy of Sciences* 96 (1962): 512–538.

Brooks, G. E. *Landlords and Strangers: Ecology, Society, and Trade in Western Africa, 1000–1630.* Boulder, Colo.: Westview Press, 1993.

Person, Y. "Les Kissi et leurs statuettes de pierre dans le cadre d'histoire ouest-Africaine." *Bulletin de l'Institut Français d'Afrique Noire* 23, nos. 1–2 (1961): 1–59.

Richards, P. "Forest Indigenous Peoples: Concept, Critique, and Cases." *Proceedings of the Royal Society of Edinburgh* 104B (1996): 349–365.

Rodney, W. *A History of the Upper Guinea Coast, 1545–1800.* London: Oxford University Press, 1970.

Fort Jesus: *See* **Swahili: Mombasa, Fort Jesus, the Portuguese, 1589–1698.**

Four Communes: *See* **Senegal: Colonial Period: Four Communes: Dakar, Saint-Louis, Goré, and Rufisque.**

Francophonie, Africa and the

La francophonie is defined as the unique and distinct group of countries that identify with a greater, French-speaking community of nations whose cultural center is France. Twenty-five countries from all regions of the African continent constitute the African portion of *la francophonie*: Burundi, Cameroon, Central African Republic, Chad, Congo-Brazzaville, Gabon, Rwanda, and the Democratic Republic of Congo (Congo-Kinshasa) in central Africa; Djibouti in East Africa; Comoros, Madagascar, Mauritius, and Seychelles in the Indian Ocean; Algeria, Morocco, and Tunisia in North Africa; and Benin, Burkina Faso, Côte d'Ivoire, Guinea, Mali, Mauritania, Niger, Senegal, and Togo in West Africa.

The preservation and further strengthening of *la francophonie* remains one of the bedrock principles of most francophone African countries. The resilience of this cultural attachment is demonstrated by the continued importance of French as at least one of the official languages of government activity, as well as by the self-classification of local elites as comprising part of a larger French-speaking community. The most vigorous proponents of this culturally based foreign policy during the early years of the postcolonial era were President Félix Houphouët-Boigny of Côte d'Ivoire, and President Léopold Sédar Senghor of Senegal, the leaders of the two most economically and politically influential countries in francophone West Africa. Although the once- privileged status of French is gradually being eroded in several countries by "national languages" movements intent upon making indigenous languages more integral to government business, as well as by the increasing number of elite children who are learning English as a second language both at home and at universities abroad, the commitment of francophone African elites to the linguistic component of *la francophonie* remains strong.

The foreign policy dimension of *la francophonie* is best demonstrated by the regular Franco-African summits attended by the presidents of France and their francophone counterparts throughout Africa. Launched in Paris, France, on November 13, 1973, these summits have been described as the "centerpiece" of Franco-African cultural relations, primarily because they are perceived as "family reunions" designed to strengthen already close personal relationships between the French president and his francophone African counterparts. The careful nurturing of close, high-level personal ties is the cornerstone of each gathering; moreover, it is equally important in regard to the day-to-day decision making related to French foreign policy toward Africa. In addition to the eleven Franco-African summits (1973, 1976, 1978, 1980, 1981, 1983, 1985, 1987, 1990, 1994, and 1998) that have been held in France, nine additional summits have been held on francophone African soil: Central African Republic (1975), Senegal (1977), Rwanda (1979), Congo-Kinshasa (1982), Burundi (1984), Togo (1986), Morocco (1988), Gabon (1992), and Burkina Faso (1996).

The worldwide francophone summit also serves as an important diplomatic platform for the promotion and strengthening of *la francophonie*. As is the case with the more regionally focused Franco-African summit, francophone African nations perceive the hosting of this conference as an important diplomatic achievement. It is precisely for this reason, for example, that President Nicéphore Soglo successfully sought to make Cotonou, Benin, the site of the sixth summit, which was held in December 1995. The holding of the meeting in Cotonou not only conferred a significant amount of prestige on President Soglo, but in essence served to anoint Benin's special status as the most successful case of democratic transition in francophone West Africa. It is important to note, however, that the worldwide summit does not serve as intimate a role as its Franco-African counterpart due to the attendance of non-African francophone states and the existence of leadership tensions between France, Canada, and to a lesser degree Belgium.

A firm commitment to regional cooperation and economic integration serves as an important pillar of *la francophonie*. One of the most important rationales for regional integration—the promotion of self-reliant development capable of reducing dependence on foreign bodies and sources—nonetheless has served as a point of dissension among francophone African countries due to its obvious focus on France as the former colonial power. During the 1950s, for example, two extreme versions of this argument were evident: President Houphouët-Boigny embraced the strengthening of economic ties with France, leading some to denounce him as "more French than African," with the Guinean president, Ahmed Sékou Touré, emerging as the most critical opponent of what he perceived as the perpetuation of French neo-colonialism in Africa. The majority of francophone African leaders placed themselves in between these two positions, although with a strong tilt toward maintaining close ties with France.

The inclusion of thirteen former French colonies and Equatorial Guinea in the franc zone serves as one of the most enduring economic outgrowths of *la francophonie*. Created in 1947, the franc zone constituted a supranational financial system in which France served as the central bank and a common currency, the Communauté

Financière Africaine (CFA) franc, was tied to the French franc and guaranteed by the French treasury. By wedding its fiscal policy to the franc zone, France sought to preserve monetary stability and French influence throughout francophone Africa. The negative implications of deferring monetary policy to France was sharply felt for the first time in 1994, when French policymakers took the extraordinary step of devaluing the CFA franc by 50 per cent. The sensitivity associated with France's decision to undertake such a drastic measure with no forewarning was clearly demonstrated at the 1996 Franco-African summit held in Burkina Faso. The only significant point of dissension at this summit occurred when French President Jacques Chirac sought to allay the fears of his franc zone counterparts by proclaiming that France would never again devalue the CFA franc, even though the further implementation of the Maastricht Treaty calls for the creation of a common European currency in 1999. The response of the assembled franc zone leaders was both guarded and lighthearted, with President Pascal Lissouba of Congo-Brazzaville taking the lead in demanding that Chirac place this promise "in writing," a clear reference to earlier promises obviously not kept when France devalued the CFA franc in 1994.

The role of France is critical to any complete understanding of francophone Africa's relationship to *la francophonie*. Indeed, France is the only former colonial power that has sought to maintain and expand its presence throughout Africa, most notably in francophone Africa. Regardless of whether France has been led by the socialists of François Mitterrand or the more conservative partisans of Charles de Gaulle or Jacques Chirac, French policy makers consistently have claimed that historical links and geographical proximity justify placing francophone Africa within France's sphere of influence. The implicit assumption of what has been described as the French version of the Monroe Doctrine is that francophone Africa constitutes France's *domaine réservé* (natural preserve), and therefore is "off limits" to other great powers.

France's self-appointed leadership role as the cultural center of *la francophonie* has been the target of rising criticisms among some francophone African countries. Questions have emerged not only from a new generation of democratically elected francophone African elites less enamored of past French support for their authoritarian predecessors, but from traditional, often authoritarian allies who fear that a diminished France will be either unwilling or unable to maintain previous commitments. Equally important, France's financial support for *la francophonie* appears to be waning, and at best seems diminished by priorities elsewhere. The policy-making elite is preoccupied with the implications of European integration and the enlargement of the European security zone. The French public is particularly prone to question French financial commitments to maintaining *la francophonie* in Africa in an era of economic stagnation at home. The uglier side of this public shift is growing intolerance for francophone African immigrants (most notably those from North Africa) who historically have looked upon France as the land of opportunity.

PETER J. SCHRAEDER

See also: **Colonial Federations: French Equatorial Africa; Colonial Federations: French West Africa; Colonialism: Inheritance of: Postcolonial Africa; Houphouët-Boigny, Félix, 1905–1993; Senghor, Léopold Sédar.**

Further Reading

Clark, J. F. and D. E. Gardinier, eds. *Political Reform in Francophone Africa*. Boulder, Colo.: Westview, 1997.

Martin, G. "Continuity and Change in Franco-African Relations." *Journal of Modern African Studies* 33, no. 1 (March 1995): 1–20.

Martin, G. "Francophone Africa in the Context of Franco-African Relations." In *Africa in World Politics*, edited by John W. Harbeson and Donald Rothchild. 2nd ed. Boulder, Colo.: Westview, 1995.

Schraeder, P. J. "From Berlin 1884 to 1989: Foreign Assistance and French, American & Japanese Competition in Francophone Africa." *Journal of Modern African Studies* 33, no. 4 (1996): 539–567.

Vaillant, J. G. *Black, French, and African: A Life of Léopold Sédar Senghor*. Cambridge, Mass.: Harvard University Press, 1990.

Freedom Charter: *See* South Africa: Defiance Campaign, Freedom Charter, Treason Trials: 1952–1960.

Freetown

The capital of Sierra Leone, Freetown has a population of 2.5 million residents (2002 estimate), up from approximately 1 million just a decade earlier, a result of mass immigration to the city during the nation's civil war. This seaport city is located on the northern tip of the country's Western Province, four miles from the estuary of the Sierra Leone River. It has a tropical climate, with temperatures averaging 80 degrees Fahrenheit (27 degrees Centigrade) and rainfalls totaling 150 inches (381 centimeters) a year. Initially comprising freed slaves, Maroons, Nova Scotians, and liberated Africans, Freetown's population now includes large numbers of other ethnic groups from the provinces as well as foreigners.

In 1779 two Scandinavians, Carl Bernhard Wadström and Anders Johansen, initiated the idea of building a refuge for freed black slaves in Freetown. However, Granville Sharp, an English philanthropist and abolitionist, became the first person to implement such a plan when he settled about 400 freed slaves on land where Freetown now stands. The settlers suffered from hunger, disease, and warfare, and the settlement almost perished. In 1791 Wadström and Johansen decided to work with the British-owned Sierra Leone Society and took part in its second attempt to establish a functioning settlement in Freetown. The town plan for that second try was drawn by the two Scandinavians, who also calculated the cost of the houses to be built.

In September 1794 the Freetown settlement was attacked and destroyed by a French naval squadron. After it was rebuilt, it was again attacked in 1801 and 1802 by the neighboring Temne in alliance with some dissident Nova Scotians.

Due to its excellent natural harbor, the Freetown port was seen as an easy target by ships plying the west coast of Africa at the height of the transatlantic slave trade. After the British Parliament made the slave trade illegal in 1807, it declared the Sierra Leone peninsula (Freetown and its environs) a British Crown Colony the following year. Freetown was used by the British naval squadron as its base of operations against slave ships as well as the seat of the British Mixed Commission Courts. The Vice-Admiralty Court, which was set up in Freetown in 1808, tried the captains of slave ships captured by the British naval squadron patrolling the west coast of Africa. The squadron's operations were hampered because it could not legally examine foreign ships for slaves, unless permitted by treaty with the foreign countries involved. Nonetheless, it did manage to free many slaves from the slave ships of many nations and settled the recaptives in the colony.

During the second half of the nineteenth century, Freetown was gloriously described as the "Athens of West Africa" for its highly westernized buildings, services, enterprises, educational institutions, and civic life. And in both World War I (1914–1918) and World War II (1939–1945), Freetown was utilized as a major naval base by the British.

The glorious image of Freetown was drastically altered in January 1999 when a contingent of rebels from the Revolutionary United Front (RUF), which had engaged in a protracted civil war with various Sierra Leonean civilian and military regimes for eight years, attacked the city. The attack resulted in more than 5,000 deaths, about 7,000 newly registered refugees in neighboring Guinea, and tens of thousands being prevented from crossing into Guinea and Liberia by troops from regional governments of the Economic Community of West Africa (ECOMOG) and by the RUF rebels. An estimated 65 to 85 per cent of the capital was destroyed after the slaughter, looting, and arson that took place.

ABDUL KARIM BANGURA

See also: **Sierra Leone.**

Further Reading

Allie, Joe A. D. *A New History of Sierra Leone.* New York: St. Martin's Press, 1990.

American University. *Area Handbook for Sierra Leone.* Washington, D.C.: United States Government Printing Office, 1976.

Cities of the World. Vol. 1, Africa. 5th ed. Detroit: GALE, 1990.

Foray, C. P. *Historical Dictionary of Sierra Leone.* Metuchen, N. J.: Scarecrow Press, 1977.

Höjer, S. *Slav Stig Upp* [Slave Rise!]. Stockholm: P. A. Norstedt & Söners Förlag, 1961.

Milsome, J. *Sierra Leone* [Let's Visit Places and Peoples of the World Series]. New York: Chelsea House, 1988.

Frelimo: *See* Mozambique: Frelimo and the War of Liberation, 1962–1975.

French Equatorial Africa: *See* Colonial Federations: French Equatorial Africa.

French Protectorate: *See* Morocco: French and Spanish Protectorates, 1903–1914; Morocco: Lyautey, General Hubert, and Evolution of French Protectorate, 1912–1950; Tunisia: French Protectorate, 1878–1900.

French West Africa: *See* Colonial Federations: French West Africa.

Front Line States: *See* Zimbabwe: Second Chimurenga, 1966–1979.

Fulani: *See* Fulbe/Fulani/Peul: Cattle Pastoralism, Migration, Seventeenth and Eighteenth Centuries; Fulbe/Fulani/Peul: Origins; Sokoto Caliphate: Hausa, Fulani and Founding of.

Fulbe/Fulani/Peul: Origins

The Fulbe are one of the most widespread ethnic groups in West Africa and have played a prominent role in West African history. Known primarily for their expertise as cattle pastoralists, the Fulbe, over the past 1,000 years, have spread across 2,000 miles of savanna, from Senegambia in the west to Cameroon in the east. They are easily the most significant pastoralist group in all of West Africa. They were also the single most instrumental black African group in spreading Islam, the dominant religion, throughout much of the savanna region of West Africa. Today they number about ten million in many different countries. They are still the dominant pastoralist group in the Sahel and savanna regions of West Africa.

Because of their widespread geographic distribution across anglophone and francophone countries, the Fulbe have been known by a variety of names in the literature. Arbitrary distinctions between Muslim and non-Muslim, and nomadic and sedentary Fulbe have caused variations in terminology. Even today there is considerable confusion about what term to use, and who is actually Fulbe. All Fulbe speak the language of Fulfulde, which has numerous dialects, depending on location. The Fulbe of Senegambia call themselves *Haalpulaar'en* (speakers of Pulaar, the local dialect of Fulfulde). In addition, Fulbe in Futa Toro are often called Futankobe or Futanke, while those of Futa Bundu are known as Bundunkobe. During the colonial period, the French divided the *Haalpulaar'en* of Senegal into "Toucouleur" or "Tukolor," whom they considered primarily agricultural and centered in Futa Toro, and "Peul" or "Peuhl," using the Wolof term for primarily pastoral peoples inhabiting the upper river region and the Casamance. The French also mistakenly labeled the so-called Tukolor as radical anti-French Muslims and considered the Peuls as docile non-Muslims.

The government of Senegal, many Senegalese, and some scholars continue to differentiate between Tukolor and Peul to the present, inaccurately treating them as separate ethnic and linguistic groups. Many Senegalese, especially the Wolof, refer to the Fulfulde language as Tukolor. Guinea Fulbe are often called Pula Futa, after their center of concentration in Futa Djallon. In northern Nigeria, the Fulbe are called Fulani, borrowing the Hausa term, and in Sierra Leone and Gambia, the Malinke term, Fula, is most often used to refer to local Fulbe. In Niger, the Fulbe are labeled Woodabe, or "red" Fulbe, because of their apparently lighter complexion than other groups. Some Europeans, especially in anglophone regions, divided the Fulbe into "town" Fulani, who mostly farmed, and "cattle" Fulani, who were more pastoralist and usually non-Muslim.

Hence, a people with an essentially similar language, culture, and identity are found in the literature under a confusing variety of names. Scholarship now confirms that all these groups are essentially Fulbe, and that the term *Fulbe* (or *Fuulbe*) is the most accurate designation. The term *Haalpulaar'en*, which many Fulbe use for themselves, is also acceptable.

The origins of the Fulbe have caused considerable speculation among early European ethnographers and have continued to puzzle later Western anthropologists, linguists, and historians. Fulbe oral traditions suggest an origin in Egypt or the Middle East, a common theme in West African Muslim traditions. According to these origin myths, the Fulbe then migrated westward until they reached the Atlantic Ocean. They then moved south into the highlands of central Guinea. Based on these traditions, some early ethnographers ascribed an Egyptian, Arab, or even Jewish origin to the Fulbe who appeared to be lighter-skinned, taller, and more "Caucasoid" than other West African groups. Some commentators claimed that the Fulbe were not African at all but a Semitic people. These ethnographers also concluded that the Fulbe spread from North Africa and then east to west, finally drifting southward in a deliberate and calculated pattern.

Linguistic evidence suggests that the Fulfulde language belongs to the West Atlantic subgroup and is closely related to Wolof and Serer, both spoken originally in western Senegambia. Therefore, the modern Fulbe and their language, Fulfulde, originated in Senegambia, probably in the northern river area of Futa Toro. The original Fulbe may have descended from a pastoral group inhabiting the Western Sahara in the Chadian wet phase 5,000 to 10,000 years ago, before moving into the Mauritanian Adrar as the Sahara dried up. Later they may have gradually filtered down to the lower and middle Senegal River valley, the area known as Futa Toro, and intermarrying with local groups. From Futa Toro, the Fulbe most likely spread into the Sahel zone along the Senegal and Niger Rivers, and then further east. They also migrated south from Futa Toro into the upper Senegal River valley, the upper Casamance region, and eventually into the Futa Djallon highlands of Guinea. Existing landowners throughout West Africa had no reason to treat the pastoralists as competitors for resources and did not hinder their spread. Occasionally clashes did occur between the migratory Fulbe and settled farmers, but more often the interaction was peaceful cooperation. It is also likely that the Fulbe migrated to areas that were suited to cattle herding and that did not require considerable defense from farmers. The migratory process was not a single set mass movement but a series of short and long-distance moves, sometimes temporary and sometimes permanent, occurring at various intervals over hundreds of years.

The Fulbe have always maintained a strong sense of identity separate from other West African groups. They have consistently been aware of their occupational specialty and distinctive appearance. In fact, many Fulbe may feel "racially" superior to their agricultural neighbors and have incorporated some of the early European ideas about a North African or Middle Eastern origin into their traditions. The Fulbe have also emphasized their independence and mobility, in comparison to their settled neighbors.

ANDREW F. CLARK

See also: **Futa Jalon; Futa Toro.**

Further Reading

Clark, A. F. "The Fulbe of Bundu: From Theocracy to Secularization." *International Journal of African Historical Studies* 29 (1996): 1–23.

Curtin, P. *Economic Change in Precolonial Africa: Senegambia in the Era of the Slave Trade.* Madison: University of Wisconsin Press, 1975.

Horton, R. "Stateless Societies in the History of West Africa." In *History of West Africa: Volume One,* edited by J. Ade Ajayi and Michael Crowder. New York: Columbia University Press, 1972.

Stenning, D. *Savannah Nomads.* London: Oxford University Press, 1959.

Fulbe/Fulani/Peul: Cattle Pastoralism, Migration, Seventeenth and Eighteenth Centuries

The search for the origin of the Fulani is not only futile, it betrays a position toward ethnic identity that strikes many anthropologists as profoundly wrong. Ethnic groups are political action groups that exist, among other reasons, to benefit their members. Therefore, by definition, the social organization, as well as cultural content, will change over time. Moreover, ethnic groups, such as the Fulani, are always coming into, and going out of, existence. Rather than searching for the legendary eastern origins of the Fulani, a more productive approach might be to focus on the meaning of Fulani identity within concrete historical situations and analyze the factors that shaped Fulani ethnic identity and the manner in which people used it to attain particular goals.

The people whom historians identify as Fulani entered present-day Senegal from the north and east. It is certain that they were a mixture of peoples from northern and Sub-Saharan Africa. These pastoral peoples tended to move in an eastern direction and spread over much of West Africa during the tenth century. Their adoption of Islam increased the Fulani's feelings of cultural and religious superiority to surrounding peoples. That adoption became a major ethnic boundary marker.

Toroobe, a branch of the Fulani, settled in towns and mixed with the ethnic groups there. They quickly became outstanding Islamic clerics, joining the highest ranks of the exponents of Islam, along with Berbers and Arabs. Fulani Sirre, or town Fulani, never lost touch with their relatives, however, often investing in large herds themselves. Cattle remain a significant symbolic repository of Fulani values.

The Fulani movement in West Africa tended to follow a set pattern. Their first movement into an area tended to be peaceful. Local officials gave them land grants because their products, including fertilizer, were highly prized. The number of converts to Islam increased over time. With that increase Fulani resentment at being ruled by pagans or imperfect Muslims increased.

That resentment was fueled by the larger migration that occurred during the seventeenth century, in which the Fulani migrants were predominantly Muslim. These groups were not so easily integrated into society as earlier migrants had been. By the beginning of the eighteenth century, revolts had broken out against local rulers. Although these revolts began as holy wars (jihads), after their success they followed the basic principle of Fulani ethnic dominance.

The situation in Nigeria was somewhat different from that elsewhere in West Africa in that the Fulani entered areas that are more settled and developed than those in other West African lands did. At the time of their arrival, in the early fifteenth century, many Fulani settled as clerics in Hausa city-states such as Kano, Katsina, and Zaria. Others settled among the local peoples during the sixteenth and seventeenth centuries. By the seventeenth century, the Hausa states had begun to gain their independence from various foreign rulers, with Gobir becoming the predominant Hausa state.

The urban culture of the Hausa was attractive to many Fulani. These town or settled Fulani became clerics, teachers, settlers, and judges and in many other ways filled elite positions within the Hausa states. Soon they adopted the Hausa language, many forgetting their own Fulfulde languages. Although Hausa customs exerted an influence on the town Fulani, they did not lose touch with the cattle or bush Fulani.

These ties proved useful when their strict adherence to Islamic learning and practice led them to join the jihads raging across West Africa. They tied their grievances to those of their pastoral relatives. The cattle Fulani resented what they considered an unfair cattle tax, one levied by imperfect Muslims. Under the leadership of the outstanding Fulani Islamic cleric, Shehu Usman dan Fodio, the Fulani launched a jihad in 1804. By 1810 almost all the Hausa states had been defeated.

Although many Hausa joined dan Fodio after victory was achieved, the Fulani in Hausaland turned their religious conquest into an ethnic triumph. Those in Adamawa, for instance, were inspired by dan Fodio's example to revolt against the kingdom of Mandara. After their victories, the Fulani generally eased their Hausa collaborators from positions of power and forged alliances with fellow Fulani.

For the fully nomadic Fulani, the practice of transhumance (the seasonal movement in search of water) strongly influences settlement patterns. The basic settlement, consisting of a man and his dependents, is called a *wuru.* It is social but ephemeral, given that many such settlements have no women and serve simply as shelters for the nomads who tend the herds.

There are, in fact, a number of settlement patterns among Fulani. Since the late twentieth century, there has been an increasing trend toward livestock production and sedentary settlement, but Fulani settlement types still range from traditional nomadism to variations on sedentarism. As the modern nation-state restricts the range of nomadism, the Fulani have adapted ever increasingly complex ways to move herds among them. Over the last few centuries, the majority of Fulani have become sedentary.

Those Fulani who remain nomadic or seminomadic have two major types of settlements: dry-season and wet-season camps. The dry season lasts from about November to March, the wet season from about March to the end of October. Households are patrilocal and range in size from one nuclear family to more than one hundred people. The administrative structure, however, crosscuts patrilines and is territorial. Families tend to remain in wet-season camp while sending younger males—or, increasingly, hiring non-Fulani herders to accompany the cattle to dry-season camps.

FRANK A. SALAMONE

See also: **Hausa Polities: Origins, Rise Ibn Khaldun: History of the Berbers; 'Uthman dan Fodio.**

Further Reading

Hogben, S. J., and Anthony Hamilton Millard Kirk-Greene. *The Emirates of Northern Nigeria.* London: Longman, 1966.

Eguchi, P. K., and Victor Azarya, eds. *Unity and Diversity of a People.* Senri Ethnological Studies, no. 35. Osaka: National Museum of Ethnology, 1993.

Riesman, P. *Freedom in Fulani Social Life.* Translated by Martha Fuller. Chicago: University of Chicago Press, 1977.

Salamone, F. A. "Colonialism and the Emergence of Fulani Ethnicity." *Journal of Asian and African Studies* 20(1985): 170–201.

Stenning, D. J. *Savannah Nomads.* London: International African Institute; Oxford University Press, 1959.

Funj Sultanate, Sixteenth to Eighteenth Centuries

The Sinnar sultanate dominated much of the northern Nile Valley Sudan from about 1500 to 1821, last in the long sequence of precolonial kingdoms that comprise one of the world's most ancient and resilient traditions of civilized statecraft. At its greatest extent the sultanate extended from the Ottoman Egyptian border at the Third Cataract southward to the Ethiopian highlands and the Sobat River, and from the Red Sea westward across the Nile to include the Nuba Mountains and Kordofan. The sultanate arose from the ruins of the medieval Nubian kingdoms of Makuria and Alodia after more than a century of troubles during which invaders from Egypt introduced Islam and Arabic

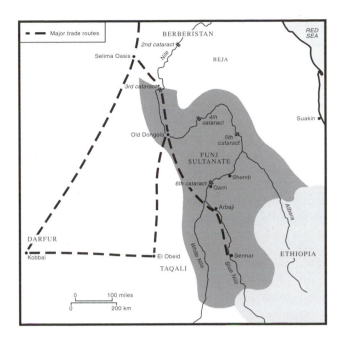

Funj sultanate, sixteenth–seventeenth centuries.

speech to the Nubian world; the kings of Sinnar thus embraced Islam as religion of state and Arabic as language of administration while reestablishing their realm according to traditional African principles. In addition to a northern and central core of Nubian speakers the sultanate came to incorporate wide eastern, western and southern peripheries of ethnically diverse subject peoples.

The hereditary ruling elite of Sinnar, the Funj, defined themselves as offspring through the female line of a remote legendary ancestress. A royal court of titled high officials elected the king from among the sons of Funj noblewomen by previous rulers. Unless a nobleman won the hand of a princess his status died with him; the quest for and the bestowal of noble Funj wives thus constituted a fundamental idiom of statecraft. There arose a hierarchy of noble status and governmental offices within which each successful lord owed political responsibilities to the superior from whom he received a Funj wife as well as his title and office, while remaining forever socially subordinate to his maternal uncle. For example, it was the king's maternal uncle's responsibility to execute him if rejected and deposed by the royal court. Subordinate lords in turn donated female kin of Funj descent as wives to their superiors; thus the king had about 600 noble wives, a senior nobleman about 200, and a lesser lord about 30.

Sinnar was primarily an agricultural society; most forms of wealth derived from the land, which in theory belonged to the king. The pyramid of kinship relations among the Funj nobility also served to structure the territorial subdivision of the realm into major provincial and subordinate district governates. The monarch, having reserved some estates as a personal demesne, apportioned the bulk of the realm to a number of his kinsmen as provincial governates; they in turn reserved demesnes and subdivided their provinces as district governates among their kinsmen. Lesser lords not only obeyed and served their superiors politically but also paid tribute to them in the form of quality goods derived from their estates such as cloth, tobacco, gold, ivory, horses, medicines, spices, and perfumes. Superior noblemen redistributed among their subordinates exotic forms of wealth acquired through activities monopolized by the central government, notably slaves taken through judicial process or warfare and foreign luxury goods imported from abroad by royal trading expeditions. Subjects were legally bound to the estate of their lord, whom they supported through the delivery of substantial levies upon grain cultivation and animal husbandry supplemented by a wide variety of fees and obligations payable in kind or in labor services. Strict sumptuary laws maintained social distance between noblemen and subjects, and severe forms of deviance such as leaving one's estate without permission or being the offspring of an illicit mixed liaison were punished by enslavement.

Over most of its history the Sinnar sultanate enjoyed peaceful relations with its neighbors, but a chronicle of decisive events must inevitably highlight the exceptions. During the sixteenth century Sinnar struggled to contain the ambitions of the Ottoman Empire, both along the Nile in the north and, with the collaboration of imperial Ethiopia, at the Red Sea coast. The seventeenth century witnessed a deterioration in relations with Ethiopia as the Funj pressed southward up the Blue Nile to annex the gold-producing land of Fazughli; major Ethiopian invasions were repulsed in 1618–1619 and again in 1744. During the eighteenth century an increasingly bitter struggle developed between Sinnar and her Fur-speaking western neighbors over the vast gold-producing region of Kordofan that lay between the respective heartlands of the two kingdoms. First the Musabba'at, a defeated and exiled faction of the royal family of Dar Fur, settled in Kordofan and used it as a base for attempted re-conquest of their homeland; after 1785 the Dar Fur sultans themselves struck eastward to impose their rule at the expense of both Funj and Musabba'at. By the early decades of the nineteenth century Sinnar was exhibiting signs of internal weakness that attracted renewed acquisitive attention from the Turkish government of Egypt.

The Funj kingdom reached its apogee during the reigns of the great seventeenth-century monarchs Rubat I, Badi II, and Unsa II, who opened diplomatic and commercial relations with the Islamic heartlands, established at Sinnar the first fixed urban capital for their hitherto-agrarian realm, and built this new city into a large and cosmopolitan metropolis through the dispatch of royal caravans to attract foreigners with valuable goods and skills. Yet these more intimate contacts with the outside world could not fail to expose features of Funj society, notably noble matrilinearity and royal dominance over foreign commerce, that would inevitably appear controversial from a Middle Eastern cultural perspective. As the eighteenth century passed, intrusive alien concepts found ever-larger native constituencies: demographically superfluous male Funj princes, individuals who aspired to Islamic piety and learning, governors excluded from royal trade, and would-be merchants themselves. Cultural dissidence expressed itself in the rise of towns, whose numbers increased from one in 1700 to about thirty by 1821, and in accelerating political chaos; royal matrilinearity was abandoned in 1719, a military strongman reduced the king to a puppet in 1762, and by 1800 the urbanized fragments of the old agrarian realm had lapsed into interminable civil war. Many dissidents welcomed the Turkish invaders from Egypt who swept over the kingdom in 1820–1821, and the remaining defenders of the old order were easily overwhelmed.

JAY SPAULDING

See also: **Nubia: Banu Kanz, Juhayna, and the Arabization of the Nilotic Sudan.**

Further Reading

Holt, P. M., ed., *The Sudan of the Three Niles: The Funj Chronicle, 910–1288/1504–1871.* Leiden: Brill, 1999.

Spaulding, J. L., and R. S. O'Fahey. *Kingdoms of the Sudan.* London: Methuen, 1974.

Spaulding, Jay. *The Heroic Age in Sinnar.* East Lansing: African Studies Center, Michigan State University, 1985.

Spaulding, Jay, and Muhammad Ibrahim Abu Salim, eds. *Public Documents from Sinnar.* East Lansing: Michigan State University Press, 1989.

Yusuf Fadl Hasan, ed. *Kitab al-Tabaqat . . . ta'lif Muhammad al-Nur b. Dayf Allah.* [The Book of Biographies of the Religiously Distinguished written by Muhammad al-Nur b. Dayf Allah]. Khartoum: University of Khartoum Press, 1970.

Futa Jalon to 1800

Futa Jalon, or Djalon (also spelled "Foutah Djallon" in countries of French expression) is an extensive mountainous area located in Guinea, with outlying areas reaching into Sierra Leone and Liberia. With an average height of 3,000 feet (914 meters), Futa Jalon forms the second highest land in West Africa, the highest being Mount Cameroon.

The first settlers of the kingdom were a group of Susu who migrated to the west coast of Africa from the banks of the Falama River, a southern tributary of the Senegal, arriving in Futa Jalon about 1400. These migrants had been part of the Soninke kingdom, which was itself part of the kingdom of Ghana, until 1076 when the Almoravids overran the Soninke capital. Before and during the nineteenth century, Futa Jalon was renowned for its jihads (holy wars), its trade, and its educational institutions.

The jihad in Futa Jalon can be traced back to the reign of the great king of the Songhai Empire, Askia Mohammed. Upon returning from his pilgrimage to Mecca in 1497, Askia attacked and forcibly converted to Islam his neighbors: Fulani/Fulbe/Peul, Koranko, and Mandingo. His successors continued his crusade; and before 1559, they had already begun to drive the Koranko back across the Niger toward Sierra Leone where they soon occupied the eastern provinces of Limba country. The last act of this jihad began just before 1600 when the Muslims of Futa Jalon, who were Fulani and Mandingo, drove the remnants of the Mende, across the frontier into Sierra Leone.

In about 1725 Alpha Ba of Koranko, proclaiming himself *alimamy*, instead of taking the usual title of military leaders who were known as *siratiks*, declared a jihad against the non-Muslims of Futa Jalon, mainly Susu and Yalunka. When he died, the holy war was continued under the theologian and soldier, the former Alpha Ibrahima of Timbo (the capital of Futa Jalon), usually referred to as Karamoko Alpha. By 1786 the Muslims had fought from Futa Jalon to the headwaters of the Moa River in the southeastern region, but encountered no Mende people. The fighting in the Niger district must have driven the Mende south. By the end of the eighteenth century, Futa Jalon had become an Islamic state.

The war dispersed many Susu, converted or unconverted, south and west. Small groups settled among the Limba, at first peaceably, conquering them later, or driving them east. Other Susu groups moved to the coast to dominate the Baga, Temne, and Bulom north of the Scarcies River. Susu immigrants whom Temne kings allowed to build a town opposite Port Loko at Sendugu gradually wrested power from the Temne. Eventually, the Sanko family, Muslims of Sarakulé origin, replaced them altogether.

At first, the Yalunka accepted Islam. However, as the Fula grew powerful, the Yalunka renounced the religion, fought against them, and they were driven from Futa Jalon. The Yalunka found their new capital Falaba in the mountains near the source of the Rokel River. The rest of the Yalunka went further into the mountains to settle among the Koranko, Kissi, and Limba.

Some Muslim adventurers in Futa Jalon also dispersed. The Loko invited a Mandingo from Kankan to be their king. A Fula styled *Fula Mansa* became the ruler of Yoni country south of the Rokel River. Some Temne

living in the area fled to found Banta country near the Jong River; they became known as the Mabanta Temne. Non-Limba kings ruled the Limba. Muslim Mandingo traders also spread through the country, singly or in groups, from the hinterland. Interested mainly in trading, they also spread the teachings of Islam.

It did not take long for the Europeans to notice the lucrative trade in Futa Jalon. At first, many in England, especially the African Association founded (with William Wilberforce a member) in 1788 to encourage exploration, knew very little about the interior of Sierra Leone. However, early in 1794, James Watt and Dr. Thomas Winterbottom's brother, Mathew Winterbottom, set off for Futa Jalon, sailing up the coast to the Rio Nunez, then overland to Timbo. The residents of Futa Jalon received them warmly and sent a delegation with them to Freetown to arrange regular trade. The following year, Watt and John Gray, the Sierra Leone Company's accountant, traveled up the Kamaranka and Bumpe Rivers to visit a Muslim Mandingo king who wanted to trade with the Freetown Colony.

While Christian Europe was gaining a foothold on the Freetown peninsula, Islam was still spreading south and west from Futa Jalon. The Baga, Bulom and other coastal peoples along the Northern Rivers— Malakori, Bereira, Rio Pongas, Rio Nunez, and their sluggish, interpenetrating tributaries—were gradually conquered by Muslims from Futa Jalon. They settled at Forekaria, which became known as "Mandingo country." Meanwhile, the French on Gambia Island sent the Bunduka, a group of aristocratic Fula, into Temne country as trading agents. The Bunduka stayed and won themselves the Mafonda chiefdom, which is situated south of the Small Scarcies River.

The Freetown colony's small trade with the interior in gold, ivory, and hides depended on the Fula caravans being able to pass safely along the paths to the coast. In 1820 the king of Futa Jalon wrote requesting that Governor Sir Charles MacCarthy, whose fame had reached the interior, mediate in a war in the Northern Rivers that inhibited their trade outcome. Early in the subsequent year Dr. Brian O'Beirne, an army surgeon, was sent to Timbo with a friendly message, overland from Port Loko, to open a new trade route. He traveled on horseback through Limba country, returning the same way, encouraging traders in Futa Jalon to do the same.

The end of the Temne wars in 1840 prompted the Fula to revive the gold trade with the colony. When Freetown merchants suggested sending a mission to Timbo, the government would only contribute £200. Instead, Governor Dr. William Fergusson persuaded them to subscribe themselves. Three recaptives, Carew, Wilhelm and William Jenkins, subscribed. Cooper Thompson, the Christian Missionary Society linguist, led the mission, starting off in December 1841 with his twelve-year-old-son. They were well received upon their arrival in Timbo.

In 1863 French Governor Louis-Léon César Faidhèrbe embarked upon linking the Senegal to the Niger in order to secure the entire West African hinterland for France. By the time Dr. Valesius Skipton Gouldsbury, administrator of the Gambia, reached Futa Jalon in 1881, he found French agents had preceded him. The king of Futa Jalon denied having sold the French land, but in France it was claimed that Futa Jalon was now under the aegis of France. Expecting to earn profits from their investment in Futa Jalon, the French declared a virtual monopoly in that territory's trade. The British government was forced to extend its influence inland, not by assuming administrative responsibilities, but by trade treaties.

In 1873 Dr. Edward Wilmot Blyden, one of the most erudite of educated Africans at the time, traveled to Timbo and signed a treaty with the king for a £100 annual stipend and tried to reconcile him with his non-Muslim neighbors at Falaba. Blyden urged the British government to extend its influence over these inland kingdoms, highlighting the French encroachment, and suggesting that a consular agent be stationed in Timbo.

Governor Sir Samuel Rowe had planned to encircle the French and unite Gambia to Sierra Leone through the interior. In 1879 he sent messengers to Timbo, ignored (and stipend unpaid) since Blyden's visit. Rowe also urged Gouldsbury to take an expedition in 1881 up the River Gambia, overland to Futa Jalon, and on to Freetown.

That Futa Jalon had an excellent reputation as a place for higher learning is hardly a matter of dispute. In 1769, as a king in Sierra Leone sent one son to Lancaster to learn Christianity, he also sent another son to Futa Jalon to learn Islam. Mohamadu Savage, the Muslim Aku leader at Fourah Bay, bought ships for the sole purpose of trading. Instead of allowing his children to attend Christian school, this wealthy man sent them to Futa Jalon to study. Harun al-Rashid of Fourah Bay, educated at the Grammar School (as Henry Valesius King), continued his studies at Futa Jalon and Fez. He later went to Mecca, the first pilgrim from the colony to do so. Upon his return from Mecca, al-Rashid, with the title of *al-Haji*, taught Arabic for one year at Fourah Bay College. He then worked as a private teacher until his death in 1897.

With an admiration for Islam, William Winwood Read (author of books such as *Savage Africa; The Last Negroes; The African Sketch-book*; and *The Martyrdom of Man*) was quite pleased when he got to know Mohamed Sanusie, an Aku Muslim and highly respected product of Futa Jalon education, who showed him a collection of Islamic works composed in Futa Jalon and other parts of West Africa. Sanusie served as an interpreter for the colonial government. He was highly skilled in Arabic, able to speak it fluently and to write it sufficiently well. Blyden himself thought that Sanusie's Arabic library was very respectable. His English, moreover, was excellent, and he knew the Bible better than most missionaries knew the Qur'an.

ABDUL KARIM BANGURA

See also: **Fulbe/Fulani/Peul.**

Further Reading

Blyden, E. W. "Report on the Expedition to Timbo." In Hollis R. Lynch, ed. *Selected Letters of Edward Wilmot Blyden.* New York: Kto Press, 1978.

Harris, J. E. "The Kingdom of Fouta Djallon." Ph.D. diss., Northwestern University, 1965.

Howard, A. M. "Big Men, Traders, and Chiefs: Power, Commerce and Special Change in the Sierra Leone, Guinea Plain." Ph.D. diss. University of Wisconsin, 1972.

Jamburia, O. "The Story of the Gihad or Holy War of the Foulahs." *Sierra Leone Studies* 3 (1919): 30–34.

Marty, P. *L'Islam en Guinée, le Fouta Djallon.* Paris: Leroux, 1921.

McGowan, W. F. "The Development of European Relations with Fuuta Jallon and French Colonial Rule 1794–1896." Ph.D. diss., School of Oriental and African Studies, London, 1972.

Rodney, W. *A History of the Upper Guinea Coast 1545 to 1800.* Oxford: Clarendon Press.

Winterbottom, T. *An Account of the Native African in the Neighbourhood of Sierra Leone.* 2nd ed. 2 vols. London: Frank Cass, 1969.

Futa Jalon: Nineteenth Century

The Futa Jalon was a Muslim theocracy located in West Africa that extended from Côte d'Ivoire to Mauritania and Mali. It contributed to the Islamic renaissance in West Africa during the seventeenth, eighteenth, and nineteenth centuries. From a political standpoint, the first half of the nineteenth century in Futa Jalon was characterized by a deep crisis of succession, starting toward the close of the eighteenth century after the demise of the forerunners, Karamoko Alfa and Almami Sory Mawdho. While some (the *Alfaya*) acknowledged the right of succession of the descendants of Karamoko Alfa, the constitutional monarch, others (the *Soriya*) upheld the claims of the descendants of his successor, Almami Sory Mawdho, in view of the vital role the latter played in the consolidation of the state. This ultimately led to a compromise consisting of a bicephalous system, whereby two *Almami* were appointed to run the federation: one from *Alfaya* and the other, from *Soriya*, ruling alternately for a two-year mandate.

This early compromise, however, was only effective at the beginning of the second half of the nineteenth century, when the *Hubbu* uprising in Fitaba southeast of Timbo threatened the kingdom with disintegration.

Hence, much of the first half of the nineteenth century was dominated by internecine wars between the two parties. The effect of this protracted war was the emergence of a state of anarchy that weakened the central power, tarnishing its image in the eyes of the orthodox theocracy. Toward the end of the nineteenth century, enforcement of the law helped secure the stability of the central organ of power, which, as a result, wielded greater control over the provinces, particularly those located in the "Rivers of the South" area, and engaged in new conquests, the most important of which was the Ngabou, which was the most powerful centrally organized state in the region. The only instance of failure occurred during the war against the *Hubbu* dissidents, who would not have been conquered without Samori Touré's intervention in the early 1880s.

The nineteenth–century Futa Jalon lived on a subsistence economy with a predominance of agriculture and animal husbandry, drawing most of its labor force from the slave class. This economy satisfied most of the country's needs, along with a dynamic foreign trade with Sudan and the Atlantic coast that benefited the ruling class. Though well organized, its tax system was implemented so abusively that it gave rise to the insurrection that became known as the *Hubbu* movement.

Nineteenth–century Futa Jalon witnessed a consolidation of the changes initiated in the eighteenth century, including the passage from a patriarchal, egalitarian type of animist society to a hierarchical one dominated by the aristocracy that emerged from the Islamic conquests. Underlying the social order were religious considerations that made a distinction between Muslims and non-Muslims, the former enjoying the full rights of free people and the latter being subjected to slavery. This differentiation led to the division of society into two main groups: the *rimbhè*, designating the order of free individuals, and the *jiyabhè*, referring to the slave class. Each class had its internal hierarchy depicting relations of inequality and exploitation. As regards the division of labor, there emerged a society where some (members of the aristocracy) concentrated the administration of political power and religion—court life, holy wars, intellectual and spiritual life—whereas those in the lower class (ordinary free men, artisans and slaves) were committed to manual labor and services. In this regard, nineteenth–century society in the Futa Jalon was a hierarchical, non-egalitarian, and segregationist society.

In the field of religion and culture, the nineteenth century is said to have witnessed the golden age of Islam in the Futa Jalon. It was the century of great scholars and the growth of Islamic culture. All the disciplines of the Quran were known and taught: translation, the hadiths, law, apologetics, the ancillary sciences such as grammar, rhetoric, literature, astronomy, local works in *Pular* and Arabic, and mysticism. Nineteenth-century European visitors were highly impressed by the extent of the Islamization, which was visible in the large number of mosques and schools at all levels, the degree of scholarship, the richness of the libraries, and the widespread practice of Islamic worship. All this seems to have been facilitated by the use of the local language, *Pular*, as a medium of teaching and popularization of Islamic rules and doctrine. This intense intellectual and religious activity made Futa Jalon a leading religious center in nineteenth–century West Africa. In the same way as it attracted disciples from all parts of the region, its own scholars visited the Moorish shaykhs or renowned scholars in Futa Toro, Macina and Bhundu to supplement their education.

European interest in Futa Jalon was intensified during the course of the nineteenth century. The process that started from the end of the eighteenth century with the Sierra Leone Company continued throughout the nineteenth century and ended with actual European occupation of the region. Visits to the region were made mainly by French and English emissaries under various pretexts. Fascinated by reports about the country's real or alleged wealth, these European powers sent explorers, followed by trade missions with thinly disguised political motives, and finally, the conquerors who took advantage of the internal squabbles caused by the fight for succession to overrun the country in 1896.

ISMAEL BARRY

Further Reading

Diallo, Th. *Les institutions politiques du Fuuta Djalon au XIXè s.* Dakar: IFAN, 1972.

Harris, J. E. "The Kingdom of Fouta-Djalon." Ph.D. diss. Northwestern University, 1965.

McGowan, W. F. "Fula Resistance to French Expansion into Fuuta Jallon, 1889–1896." *Journal of African History* 22 (1981): 245–261.

Futa Toro

Futa Toro is the region situated along the middle valley of the Senegal River in West Africa, immediately south of the Sahara Desert. The north bank lies in Mauritania, while the south bank is in Senegal. The Senegal River was a link, not a divide, between the north and south banks. The river also served as the central focus of the region, linking east and west.

Futa is the general name that the Fulbe, the area's dominant ethnic group, gave to the areas where they lived, while Toro is the province with the oldest identity in the middle valley; it lies in the western portion around the towns of Podor and Njum. The area never extended more than approximately ten miles on either bank of the river, and stretched for about 250 miles along the length of the Senegal River. The linguistic evidence strongly suggests that Futa Toro may be the birthplace of the Fulbe people, and many Fulbe oral traditions cite Futa Toro as their homeland. The Fulbe of Futa Toro and elsewhere in the river valley now call themselves *Haalpulaar'en*, or "those who speak Pulaar," the local dialect of the Fulfulde language. In Wolof, French, and general Senegalese usage, the Fulbe of Futa Toro are called *Toucouleur*, derived from the name of the ancient state of Takrur (or Tekrur).

Futa Toro's predecessor was ancient Takrur, situated on both banks of the middle Senegal River and contemporary with the Ghana Empire. Takrur may have been founded as early as 100CE, reaching its height in the ninth and tenth centuries. The dominant ethnic group was Fulbe (sometimes called Fulani or Peul), with minority populations of Wolof, Berber, and Soninke. The rulers apparently became Muslims in the 1030s. The region was situated just beneath the Western Sahara and on trans-Saharan caravan routes, which were developed well before the tenth century.

The state also had the advantage of being on a river that flowed from the south, permitting people to live very close to the desert edge. Berbers operated the trade routes through the desert to Morocco, exporting some gold from Bambuk, further up the Senegal River, which was exchanged in Takrur. The people also grew millet and cotton and manufactured cotton textiles, which were traded to the desert nomads. While Takrur received some salt from desert traders, most of its salt came from the evaporating salt pans at the mouth of the Senegal River. Takrur defended itself successfully against several Moroccan raids in the eleventh century but was in decline by the twelfth century, owing primarily to local power struggles and competition for resources.

Several dynasties and groups attempted but failed to rule the middle valley after the decline of Takrur. The main obstacle was the length of Futa Toro along the river. In the period from about 1490 until 1776, however, most of Futa Toro was ruled by the Denanke dynasty founded by Koly Tengela Ba. Futa Toro came into limited contact with Portuguese traders in the early sixteenth century, supplying some slaves, usually captives from non-Muslim states, for the transatlantic slave trade. Later the French, who used the Senegal River as a trade conduit into the interior, became Futa Toro's dominant European trading partners. From the sixteenth to the eighteenth centuries, Futa Toro, like its predecessor Takrur, was often the subject of raids by Moroccan forces eager to expand the influence of their state and acquire the wealth in gold and slaves from the Western Sudan. Futa Toro was able to maintain its independence from invading armies, but the constant attacks weakened the central state. By the sixteenth century, the Denanke rulers and a significant portion of the population were

Muslims. A clerical diaspora from Futa Toro helped spread Islam throughout Western Africa.

The inhabitants of Futa Toro practiced mixed farming, combining agriculture and livestock herding. The summer rains watered the highland crops and raised the river level, which spilled over the banks of the middle valley. After the waters receded in December, the moist floodplain could then be planted with millets, sorghum, and maize for a dry season harvest.

This double harvest made Futa Toro a food-exporting region and also drew migrant farmers from the surrounding areas. Cattle raising was also an important part of the Fulbe of Futa's early economy and identity. Fulbe herders practiced seasonal migration, staying near permanent sources of water in the dry season, then moving out with the rains, and finally returning when the water holes and pastures dried up. Futa pastoralists moved in regular patterns, either to the steppe north of the river and close to the Sahara Desert, or south into the steppe called the Ferlo between Futa Toro and the Gambia River. In Futa Toro, two groups of Fulbe emerged, including sedentary farmers and migratory herders. The herders were dependent on the farmers of all ethnic groups for agricultural goods and water during the dry season while the herders supplied milk and meat for the farmers. Raiding periodically disrupted the exchange of goods and services, but cooperation generally characterized farmer-herder interactions. There was also some fishing and craft production, especially leatherwork, blacksmithing, and weaving. Finally, *griots* or praise singers lived at court and performed many diplomatic and judicial functions in addition to their public performance. Much of what is known about the early history of Futa Toro derives from oral traditions preserved by *griots*.

In 1776 indigenous Muslims, led by Suleyman Bal, took advantage of the weak Denanke dynasty and launched a successful and influential Islamic revolution, creating the *almamate* of Futa Toro. They instituted a new ruling class, the *torodbe*. The most effective *almamate* ruler, Abdul Kader Kan, extended the borders of Futa to the west and southeast. However, the defeat of his forces by the Wolof state of Kajoor, signaled the decline of the *almamate* until its dominance by the French in the mid-nineteenth century.

ANDREW F. CLARK

See also: **Fulbe/Fulani/Peul.**

Further Reading

Barry, B. *Senegambia and the Atlantic Slave Trade.* Cambridge: Cambridge University Press, 1998.

Kane, M., and D. Robinson. *The Islamic Regime of Fuuta Tooro.* East Lansing: Michigan State University Press, 1984.

Robinson, D. *Chiefs and Clerics: Abdul Bokar Kan and Futa Toro, 1853–1891.* Oxford: Clarendon Press, 1985.

Robinson, D., P. Curtin, and J. Johnson. "A Tentative Chronology of Futa Toro from the Sixteenth through the Nineteenth Centuries." *Cahiers d'Etudes Africaines* 12 (1972): 555–592.

Willis, J. R. "The Torodbe Clerisy: A Social View." *Journal of African History* 19 (1978): 195–212.

Futa Toro: Early Nineteenth Century

Three changes marked the history of early nineteenth-century Senegal: the decline and end of the Atlantic slave trade, the continuation of a Muslim religious revolution, and the development of commodity production. These events were all related and contributed to the making of modern Senegal.

At the beginning of the century, there were two European island bases in Senegal: St. Louis in the mouth of the Senegal River, and Gorée in what is now Dakar harbor. Both had been bases in the slave trade for centuries, but during the eighteenth century, slave exports from Senegambia declined while the sale of gum and supplies for shipping became more important. As part of its struggle with Napoleon Bonaparte, Britain occupied Gorée in 1803 and St. Louis in 1809. Thus, when Britain abolished the slave trade in 1807, the act was implemented in Senegal. Before Senegal was returned to the French, the restored French monarchy had to agree to abolition. France did not enforce its abolition ordnance rigorously until 1831, but the Atlantic slave trade was effectively over in Senegambia. This created difficulties for the Wolof and Sereer states that bordered the French ports. They all had strongly militarized state structures in which slave raiding and slave trading played an important role.

Islam was well established in Senegal, but from at least the seventeenth century there were deep divisions between an orthodox Muslim minority that supported schools and maintained strict standards of religious observance and a more lax majority. The courts were marked by heavy drinking and conspicuous consumption. The majority of commoners mixed Islam and traditional religious observance. Muslims first turned to resistance in 1673, when a Mauritanian *marabout*, Nasr Al Din, led a jihad directed both at the warrior tribes of Mauritania and the Wolof states south of the border. Nasr Al Din's appeal was in part to peoples threatened by slave-raiding. With the aid of the French, the traditional elites defeated Nasr Al Din, but some of his disciples founded a state in upper Senegal, Bundu, and his ideas remained important.

The *torodbe* clerics of the Futa Toro maintained ties with Bundu, with their Wolof brethren and with the Fulbe elites that were creating a Muslim state in the Futa Jalon of central Guinea during the eighteenth century.

The Futa Toro was a narrow strip of land on both sides of the Senegal River, which was vulnerable to attack by Mauritanian nomads. The insecurity engendered by these raids and the inability of the *denianke* rulers to protect local populations led people to turn for leadership to the *torodbe*. Their victory in 1776 was followed by a prohibition of the slave trade down the Senegal river and in 1785, an agreement under which the French promised not to sell Muslim slaves. The French also agreed to generous customs payments to the new Futa state.

The first *Almamy*, Abdul Kader, tried to extend his control. He defeated the Mauritanian emirates of Trarza and Brakna, but when he sought to extend his control over the Wolof states of Kajoor and Waalo, he was defeated and taken prisoner. The battle gave rise to a ballad that is still sung by Wolof bards. Though Abdul Kader was freed, his defeat also ended the Futa's efforts to impose its version of Islam on its neighbors. By time he died in 1806, the élan was gone from the revolution, and the Futa was transformed into a state dominated by a small number of powerful *torodbe* aristocratic families. The egalitarian ideals of the revolutionaries remained alive. Umar Tall, a young cleric of modest *torodbe* origins, left the Futa in about 1827 to make the pilgrimage to Mecca. He returned only in 1846 to recruit support for a new jihad.

With the end of the export slave trade, the commercial populations looked for new commodities to trade. In St. Louis, local merchants expanded the gum trade. Gum was used in France to provide dyes for high quality textiles and to produce medicines. Between 1825 and 1838, gum exports came close to tripling. The gum was produced by slaves from acacia trees in southern Mauritania. The trade thus provided a continuing market for slaves. Slaves were also imported into Mauritania for herding and the cultivation of dates. Other parts of the river produced a grain surplus, which fed St. Louis, the Moors, and their slaves. These linkages also seem to have stimulated the cultivation of cotton, the mining of gold, and the production of textiles and gold jewelry.

Gorée survived on a trade in wax and hides. Its salvation came when French chemists determined how to use peanut oil to make a high quality soap. In 1833 a small purchase was made in the Gambia. In 1841 a little over a ton was purchased in Senegal, a quantity that rose in 1854 to about 5,500 tons. These changes strained social relationships. Peanuts were a smallholder's crop. The cultivation of peanuts in the Wolof states and grain in the Futa Toro provided ordinary farmers the resources to buy weapons and consumer goods. The most industrious peasants tended to be Muslim. At the same time, there were intermittent conflicts all over Senegal. In 1827 Njaga Issa revolted against Kajoor. A year later, Hamme Ba in the western Futa Toro revolted, and in 1830, the *marabout*, Diile Fatim Cam, revolted in Waalo.

All of these revolts were suppressed, but they reveal tensions that were to erupt in the second half of the century. In 1852 Al Hajj Umar Tal began a jihad that eventually created a series of Umarian states across the western Sudan. He did not succeed in incorporating his native Senegal in his domains, but only because a new French governor, Major Louis Faidherbe, appointed in 1854, established French control over key areas on the mainland and blocked Umar's efforts to incorporate the Futa Toro in his state. The second half of the century saw increased conflict as Muslim forces established their hegemony in much of Senegambia, but were eventually forced to yield political control to the French.

MARTIN A. KLEIN

See also: **Futa Jalon: Nineteenth Century.**

Further Reading

Barry, B. *Senegambia and the Atlantic Slave Trade.* Translated from the French by Ayi Kwei Armah. Cambridge: Cambridge University Press, 1998.

Robinson, D. *The Holy War of Umar Tal: The Western Sudan in the Mid-Nineteenth Century.* Oxford: Clarendon Press, 1985.

Robinson, D. "The Islamic Revolution of Futa Toro." *International Journal of African Historical Studies* 8 (1975): 185–221.

Searing, J. *West African Slavery and Atlantic Commerce: The Senegal River Valley, 1700–1860.* Cambridge: Cambridge University Press, 1993.

G

Gabon: Nineteenth Century: Precolonial

Three main events dominated the history of Gabon in the nineteenth century: the French establishment in the Gabon estuary, the French exploration of the Como, Rembwe, and Ogooué Rivers, and the Fang migrations throughout the Ogooué basin. The French occupation of the Gabon estuary started with a treaty signed by the French naval officer Bouet-Willaumez and the Mpongwe leader Denis Rapontchombo in 1839. The signing of this treaty allowed France to have access to a small piece of land in the left bank of the Gabon estuary, and in return Rapontchombo benefited from French "protection." This establishment was used by France as a basis to combat the slave trade in the west coast of Africa. In 1842 American missionaries established a mission at Baraka, and a year later the French post was moved to the right bank of the Gabon estuary, with the agreement of Mpongwe chiefs. The French helped Roman Catholic missionaries to settle in the Gabon estuary in 1844.

This new establishment became known as the Comptoir du Gabon (Syndicate/Cartel of Gabon) and was used by the French not only to capture slave ships, but also to challenge the British and German domination of trade in the region. But the creation of this post led to tensions between the people of Glass and the French navy. After settling these tensions with Britain and suppressing the rebellion in the village of Glass, France became engaged in the organization of its comptoir between 1845 and 1859. This organization was marked by the construction of the Fort d'Aumale, which in 1850 was moved from the seashore to the Okolo plateau, an elevated site considered more hygienic. Nonetheless, this French establishment experienced difficulties, as food was not abundant, disease was rampant among French colonists, and the comptoir faced a shortage of manpower. French commerce was unable to compete with British trade, which was flourishing. As an effort to spread the French culture, the village of Libreville was created in 1849, to resettle fifty recaptured slaves from the slave ship *Elizia*. Libreville later became the capital of the French Congo and the capital of independent Gabon.

Despite these early difficulties, the French became engaged in territorial exploration, marked by the signing of treaties with local populations in the Gabon region. These treaties stipulated the abandonment of sovereignty by local leaders and provided commercial and political advantages to France. Between 1845 and 1885, France organized a much more aggressive territorial expansion to widen its zone of influence. In June 1846 Pigeard explored the Como and Rembwé and signed a treaty with the Mpongwe and Seke chiefs. In 1848 a treaty was signed between the naval officer Roger and the Bakele chief Kianlowin, and in 1852 the Benga of Cape Esterias and Corisco were placed under French "protection." In 1853 Baudin explored the Como area and established direct contacts with the Fang. In 1862 Payeur-Didelot reached and signed a treaty with the Orungou chief Ndebulia. The same year Serval and Griffon du Bellay explored the Lower-Ogooué and established relations with the Orungou, Vili, Galwa, and Bakele population of the interor. In 1873 Alfred Marche and the Marquis de Compiègne, after exploring lakes Onangué, Oguemoué, and the lower-Ngounié, explored the Ogooué River and reached Lopé in 1874. They experienced firsthand the hostility of the Fang-Meke when arriving in the mouth of the Ivindo River, and returned to the Gabon estuary.

But the most famous explorer of all was Pierre Savorgnan de Brazza. He made his first exploration trip to the Ogooué River in November 1875. Accompanied by Ballay, he reached the Alima River in 1878 and returned to the Gabon estuary. Between 1879 and 1882 de Brazza made another exploratory trip in the Ogooué

Gabon.

Region and founded the post of Franceville in 1880. Between 1883 and 1885, he was asked by the French government to make a third trip on the Ogooué River, known as the Mission de l' Ouest Africain (Mission of West Africa). This mission opened up the Ogooué and Congo basin to French influence. In 1886 de Brazza was nominated Haut Commandant du Congo-Français (High Commander of the French Congo). The same year his brother Jacques de Brazza left the post of Maddiville (Lastourville) to explore the Ivindo region in the northeast.

In 1888 Paul Crampel visited the north and northwestern part of the Ogooué and reached the Ntem River, while Alfred Fourneau explored the northern Gabon in 1889. The upper Ogooué was explored by agents of the Société du Haut-Ogooué (SHO), such as Bravard and Chaussé, at the end of the nineteenth century. At the turn of the century, the whole Gabonese territory had already been explored by Westerners. Their explorations allowed the French to come into contact with local populations and sign treaties of sovereignty with them, thus permitting French domination over the entire Ogooué River basin.

While the French penetrated interior regions, the Fang left their northern settlements to migrate in different areas of the Ogooué River basin. These Fang were trying to position themselves as middlemen in the growing trade that was taking place not only in the coastal areas, but also in strategic economic zones throughout the Ogooué basin. Trading with the Europeans was very important to the Fang, because European manufactured goods were necessary for dowries and provided prestige

in society. Leaving the Woleu-Ntem region, the Fang migrated in the Gabon region where they occupied the Como and Rembwé regions between 1840 and 1860. At the time of their occupation Ningue-Ningue island was the main trading center.

Leaving the Crystal Mountains area, the Fang moved to the mid-Ogooué River between 1860 and 1875. They were attracted to the region by Hattonand Cookson factories installed in Samkita. Some of these Fang clans moved to the Lower-Ogooué in the southern lakes between 1875 and 1900, where English, German, and American firms were active. The Fang-Mekey attracted by trade in 1875 settled in the Ndjolé post, while the Fang-Nzaman who occupied the Ogooué-Ivindo moved toward the trading center of Lopé between 1860 and 1900. The Fang came into contact with the Kwele, occupied the Djaddié, and established trading contacts with other Fang clans in the Lower-Ivindo and the Okande of Lopé. During these migrations the Fang displaced other ethnic groups across the Ogooué River basin. But throughout the nineteenth century, trade in the Ogooué region was dominated by the English, German, and American firms, which forced the French authorities to reorganize commerce by creating concessionary companies, which became active in Gabon at the beginning of the twentieth century.

FRANÇOIS NGOLET

See also: **Concessionary Companies.**

Further Reading

Ambouroue-Avaro, J. *Un Peuple Gabonais à l'Aube de la Colonisation: Le Bas Ogooué au 19eme Siècle.* Paris: Karthala, 1981.
Chamberlin, C. "The Migration of the Fang into Central Gabon during the Nineteenth Century: A New Interpretation." *International Journal of Historical African Studies* 11, no. 3 (1978): 429–456.
Gardinier, D. *Historical Dictionary of Gabon.* Lanhan, Md.: Scarecrow Press, 1994.
———. *L'implantation Coloniale au Gabon. Résistance d'un Peuple.* Paris: L'Harmattan, 1979.
Mbokolo, E. *Noirs et Blancs en Afrique Equatoriale.* Paris: La Haye-Mouton, 1981.

Gabon: Colonial Period: Administration, Labor and Economy

Throughout the nineteenth century, trade in the Ogooué River basin was mainly dominated by British firms. The beginning of the twentieth century was marked by an aggressive policy of the French colonial authority to reverse the situation by introducing concessionary companies. This economic regime allowed the creation of forty companies throughout the French Congo, while ten companies divided the whole Gabonese territory into zones of exploitation. The largest was the Société du Haut-Ogooué (SHO), and the smallest was the Société du Bas-Ogooué (SBO). These companies did not make any serious investment in the country. They simply became involved in the exploitation of natural resources, such as rubber and ivory. In order to increase revenues, concessionary companies submitted local populations to cruel and brutal exploitation. Local products were purchased at a low price, while the value of manufactured goods was overestimated by company agents.

These abuses and injustices did not encourage the local population to work for concessionary companies. Rather, they led to widespread revolt in many parts of the country. In the first quarter of the twentieth century, these revolts prompted the colonial administration to implement administrative structures to assert full control over the territory. Forced labor was introduced to coerce native people to work for concessionary companies, which would allow them to gain money to pay for a head tax. In 1905 five *régions* were created and subdivided into cerles and postes. In 1909 these terms were abandoned and the country was divided into twenty *circonscriptions*: sixteen were civilian and four were military. When French Equatorial Africa (AEF) was created in 1910, Gabon was headed by a lieutenant governor who was under the authority of the general-governor who resided at Brazzaville (Congo). This political reform was followed with a clearer territorial organization, because *circonscriptions* were divided into thirty-eight subdivisions. Although this territorial and administrative division was still unstable in 1920, it, nonetheless, allowed the French colonial administration to exercise control over the population of Gabon. This control was increased by a better organization of colonial troops, the national guards and the militia, which were enforcing the law throughout the land. One of these laws was the indigénat, which allowed colonial administrators to jail the natives without trial for fifteen days and make them pay a 100 franc fine for any minor offense. While the French colonial administration asserted its control over local populations, it also defined Gabon's southern border with Leopold II, king of Belgium and the Congo Free State (1918), and agreed with Spain and Germany on the northern border (1919).

The timber industry eventually replaced the disastrous concessionary regime. The rise of the timber industry along the lagoons, the coast, and lakes near Lambaréné, and the upper Komo and Rembwe regions salvaged the colonial economy, attracting thousands of wood-cutters from the southern and eastern regions of Gabon. These woodcutters cut down the trees and chopped the logs, which were then floated down creeks and rivers. They were mainly transported from the interior to the coast, particularly Port-Gentil and Cape-Lopez, which had main ports from the timber export. World War I disturbed the timber industry. It was only after the war that the timber exploitation started again, attracting thousands of men from the Ngounié region, and activated the economy of towns such as Lambaréné, Port-Gentil, and Libreville. Labor conditions were particularly difficult because of the fact that the timber industry was not mechanized. The cutting of the trees and sawing of logs were done by hand. The most arduous task was the moving of logs over rough forest clearings to reach the Decauville rail, which was transporting lumber from inland to the coast (1927–1930). Up to seventeen men were employed in moving a single log. This was dangerous and accidents were frequent. Labor recruiting also provoked the neglect of village plantations, thus causing food shortages. The timber industry experienced a period of crisis in 1930 and picked up again between 1932 and 1939. Administrative demands for labor to work for infrastructure projects like the building of the roads often led to serious crisis. This forced the colonial administration to recruit workers in Chad and other parts of French Equatorial Africa.

After World War II, administrative and territorial reorganization was introduced in Gabon. Gabon was now going to be headed by a governor and no longer by a lieutenant governor, which had been a designation retained since 1910. This governor was assisted by territorial administrators. The Gabon territory was divided into nine regions, which were subdivided into districts. In 1946 the Upper-Ogooué region was attached to Gabon, giving to the country its present international boundaries. While these administrative and territorial reconfigurations were taking place, labor unions were fighting for better working conditions for the people of Gabon. Together with nationalist leaders, such as Jean Hilaire Aubame, Paul Gondjout, and Léon Mba, these trade unions fought to obtain the end of forced labor and the end of the worst abuses of colonialism. These developments were also accompanied by important changes in the timber industry; for example, the Decauville rails were abandoned. It was now the Grumier tractor trail that carried and cut the logs, which made the transportation of the logs a year-round activity. The French colonial administration also built the largest timber factory in the world (CFG), which attracted thousands of workers in Port-Gentil.

The colonial economy was reinvigorated by the exploitation of oil wells of Ozouri and the exploitation of manganese, uranium, and iron in the 1950s. These natural resources gave a new momentum to the Gabonese economy and provided support for the expansion of roads and ports. These economic changes

545

completely transformed the nature of labor in Gabon during the colonial and postcolonial periods.

FRANÇOIS NGOLET

See also: **Colonial Federations: French Equatorial Africa; Concessionary Companies.**

Further Reading

Gardinier, D. *Historical Dictionary of Gabon.* Latham, Md.: Scarecrow Press, 1994.
Chris, G., and F. Ngolet. "Lambaréné, Okoumé and the Transformation of Labor along the Middle Ogooué (Gabon)." *Journal of African History*, 40 (1999): 87–107.
Pourtier, R. *Le Gabon, T. II: Etats et développement.* Paris: L'Harmattan, 1989.

Gabon: Colonial Period: Social Transformation

Social transformation during the colonial period (1843–1945) resulted mainly from the policies and practices of the French administration and the responses of the indigenous peoples to them. To a lesser extent, transformation came about through the interaction of Western traders and Christian missionaries with the Africans.

The French occupation brought under a single administration several hundred thousand Africans scattered sparsely over an area half the size of France. Three quarters of this territory were covered by dense tropical rainforest, and most of the rest by grasslands. The Africans lived in several thousand villages usually composed of extended families and their slaves. Only the Fang people, who formed perhaps 30 per cent of the population and were spreading out over the northern half of the country, ordinarily possessed few slaves and did not pursue inter-group warfare to obtain slaves. Most of Gabon's forty or so different Bantu-speaking peoples lived from hunting, gathering and subsistence farming.

Many of the interior peoples were linked by commercial networks to coastal peoples, such as the Mpongwe along the Gabon River estuary in the north, the Orungu at the mouths of the Ogooué River near Cape Lopez, and the Vili and others in the far south, all of whom became middlemen traders between Western manufactures and inland residents.

Between 1815 and 1830, the estuary and Cape Lopez exported several thousand slaves annually to the New World. Although these numbers were small in comparison to the slave trade in the Niger and Congo river basins, the ensuing labor shortages and the constant disruption resulting from warfare and raiding had destructive results for the African societies. During the 1860s and 1870s, France put an end to the slave trade.

Though it did not attempt to abolish domestic slavery immediately, it sought to prevent mistreatment of slaves and to cooperate with private agencies in their liberation.

The economic and financial dimensions of French rule, however, had mainly negative social consequences. From the 1840s on, the French administration used military force to take control of the main trade routes from the coasts through waterways into the interior. After the introduction in 1865 of the steamboat on the Ogooué River, whose watershed covers 80 per cent of the country, Western traders gained access to most of the commercial networks. The African middlemen were eliminated. Some became agents for the large French, British, and German firms that now dominated commerce. The French met strong and often prolonged resistance from the peoples who had previously controlled trade through their lands. The French also encountered opposition when, during the 1880s, they began to impose burdensome head taxes, food requisitions, and forced labor on all able-bodied adults. Even more devastating were official attempts at economic development through monopolistic concessionary companies between 1893 and 1914. The toll of flight, death, and destruction led to a demographic decline from which Gabon did not begin to recover until the mid-1950s.

During World War II, French recruitment of soldiers and porters led to neglect of food crops, particularly among the Fang of the far north, where thousands died from famines between 1918 and 1920 while several thousand more, weakened by malnutrition, succumbed to Spanish flu epidemics. These situations, along with the perennial health problems of the equatorial regions, caused further demographic stagnation. Thus the census of 1921 showed a population of 389,000, and that of 1959 only 416,000.

In the meantime, the timber industry had become the most important employer of African wage labor as well as the largest source of public revenue. Although the timber camps provided employment for thousands of men, their absence from home for months at a time hindered food production while spreading venereal diseases and malaria.

The most common route for African advancement during the colonial period was not economic activity but acquisition of a Western-style education. American Protestant and French Roman Catholic missionaries, who arrived in the estuary in the early 1940s, educated a new class of literate Mpongwe and Fang youths who became employees of Western companies and the colonial administration. Smaller numbers became catechists, teachers, pastors, and priests. Girls also received instruction, including in health care and sanitation. As a result of the imposition of a French primary curriculum in 1883, the Americans transferred their mission to French Protestants in 1893. The first public schools enrolled 457 pupils, Protestants 680, and Catholics 2,100, for a total of 3,237 pupils, that is, less than 1 per cent of the population.

French policy discouraged postprimary instruction for fear of creating an unemployable intelligentsia. French colonial education after 1900 produced a tiny elite strongly attached to the French language, culture, and lifestyle but critical of colonialism and desirous of equality with the French. By 1945 a majority of the Africans had become at least nominal Christians, with Catholics outnumbering Protestants three to one. A revived Fang sect, Bwiti, syncretized both Catholic and traditional elements.

DAVID E. GARDINIER

Further Reading

Bucher, H. H. "The Atlantic Slave Trade and the Gabon Estuary: The Mpongwe to 1860." In *Africans in Bondage: Studies in Slavery and the Slave Trade*, edited by Paul E. Lovejoy. Madison: African Studies Program, University of Wisconsin Press, 1986.

Gardinier, D. E. "Education in French Equatorial Africa, 1842–1945." In *Proceedings of the French Colonial Historical Society* 3 (1978): 121–137.

Gardinier, D. E. "The American Board (1842–1870) and Presbyterian Board (1870–1892) Missions in Northern Gabon and African Responses." *Africana Journal* 17 (1997): 215–234.

Gardinier, D. E. "The Schools of the American Protestant Mission in Gabon (1842–1870)." *Revue française d'histoire d'outremer* 75, no. 2 (1988): 168–184.

Headrick, R. *Colonialism, Health & Illness in French Equatorial Africa, 1888–1935*. Atlanta, Ga.: African Studies Association, 1995.

Patterson, K. D. *The Northern Gabon Coast to 1875*. Oxford: Clarendon Press, 1975.

Vansina, J. *Paths in the Rainforest: Toward a History of Political Traditions in Equatorial Africa*. Madison: University of Wisconsin Press, 1990.

Gabon: Decolonization and the Politics of Independence, 1945–1967

World War II was a turning point in the history of Gabon. The French held the Brazzaville Conference (January–February 1944) that initiated the decolonization of French black Africa. There they decided to promote self-rule for the Africans, and rapid economic and social advancement through assimilation rather than separation from France.

As a result, the French provisional government headed by General de Gaulle (1944–1946) and the two Constituent Assemblies (1945–1946) abolished many of the oppressive aspects of colonial rule such as forced labor, the prestation (labor tax), travel controls, and the indigénat (administrative justice). The constitution of October 1946 offered Africans greater participation in their own administration, but under the continued domination of France. Voting at first was restricted to a tiny fraction of Africans, mainly the educated elite and war veterans. A system of two electoral colleges gave the few thousand Frenchmen living in the territory one-third of the representation.

Between 1946 and 1956 the electorate was widened to include all adults. In 1956 the French lost special representation. By 1956 pressures throughout Francophone Africa for self-government and independence, together with the failures of French integrationist policies in Indochina and North Africa, led France to abandon the policy of assimilation. As a result, Gabon experienced a rapid decolonization generated almost entirely by forces elsewhere, including by this time British Africa, whose territories were achieving self-government and independence. Thus, in April 1957 Gabon acquired a legislative assembly and an executive council. In March 1959 it became an autonomous republic entirely outside the new Fifth French Republic but a member of the French Community, which controlled its external affairs. Then on August 13, 1960, Gabon gained independence, and in 1961 the community ceased to function.

The reforms of April 1957 had monumental importance for the future of Gabon. They allowed Gabonese representatives not only to legislate and direct executive departments but also to seek separation from FEA. Gabon had been administratively attached to Congo (Brazzaville) since 1886 and to all of FEA since 1910. Taxes on Gabon's timber became FEA's largest source of revenues. The funds were used for infrastructure, such as the Congo-Ocean Railway (1921–1934), and public facilities in Brazzaville, while Gabon lacked even all-season roads, among other things. The Gabonese leaders were able to end this drain in 1957 and prevent continuation of the federation after the collapse of the Fourth Republic in 1958. Henceforth, Gabon was able to use its growing revenues for development of its own economy and society.

Between 1946 and 1958 France spent $25 million, mainly for infrastructure to permit expansion of production, particularly timber production, as well as for improved ports and airfields, and a plywood factory. Lesser sums went toward schools and a hospital. From the 1950s France sought investments from Western nations to develop Gabon's manganese, petroleum, and iron industries (which proved unviable for lack of transport). The French also aimed to provide primary schooling for both sexes and further education for the most talented. The curriculum was that of France, entirely in French, with African material added. Primary enrollments increased from 9,082 (1945–1946) to 50,545 (1959–1960). In 1959–1960 there were 2,036 secondary students. During 1957–1958, 87 Gabonese studied in French universities. At independence only a handful of Gabonese had completed the entire secondary programs or higher education. This situation meant that independent Gabon continued to depend upon French personnel to staff the higher levels of the bureaucracy, economy, and education. The country would also depend on France for investment capital and development aid.

From 1945 to 1947 leaders emerged from the educated elite to compete for public office. They organized political parties based in Libreville that had ties with notables in the nine provinces. The most important leaders were Jean-Hilaire Aubame (1912–1989) and Léon M'Ba (1902–1967). Aubame served as the African voters' deputy to the French National Assembly (1946–1958). He had support from the far northern Fang, Christian missionaries and administration. M'Ba led the Estuary Fang and originally had ties with the far Left. From March 1952 M'Ba was an important figure in the Territorial Assembly, first elected mayor of Libreville in November 1956, then executive council head, prime minister, and president of the republic (1961–1967). M'Ba gained national office in 1957 because French lumbermen shifted their support to him.

President M'Ba believed that Gabon could not survive as an independent state without French aid and assistance as well as protection. As prime minister he negotiated the fifteen cooperation agreements of July 15, 1960, which provided for these needs but perpetuated dependence and French control of the economy. Following difficulties with a parliamentary system of government, Gabon adopted a system modeled after that of de Gaulle's Fifth French Republic, with M'Ba as president, in February 1961. After repeated conflicts with other leaders of his own party and of Aubame's, M'Ba pressured them in 1963 to join a single party under his direction. His actions provoked resistance and in their turn repression and new conflicts, which culminated in a military coup, February 17–20, 1964. Although the coup toppled M'Ba, De Gaulle sent troops who restored him to power. M'Ba was thus able, despite growing popular discontent, to establish a regime that eliminated opponents, violated civil liberties, and ended Gabon's democratic experiment.

DAVID E. GARDINIER

Further Reading

Ballard, J. A. "Four Equatorial States" In *National Unity and Regionalism in African States*, edited by Gwendolyn Carter. Ithaca, N.Y.: Cornell University Press, 1966.

Bernault, F. *Démocraties Ambigües en Afrique Centrale: Congo-Brazzaville, Gabon, 1940–1965*. Paris: Karthala, 1996.

Gardinier, D. E. "France in Gabon since 1960." *Proceedings of the French Colonial Historical Society* 6–7 (1982): 65–75.

———. *Historical Dictionary of Gabon*. 2nd ed. Lanham, Md.: Scarecrow Press, 1994.

M'Bokolo, E. "French Colonial Policy in Equatorial Africa in the 1940s and 1950s" In *The Transfer of Power in Africa: Decolonization, 1940–1960*, edited by Prosser Gifford and Wm. Roger Louis. New Haven, Conn.: Yale University Press, 1982.

Weinstein, B. *Gabon: Nation-Building on the Ogooué*. Cambridge, Mass.: MIT Press, 1966.

Gabon: Bongo, Omar, and the One-Party State, 1967 to the Present

Omar Bongo (b.1935) became president of Gabon on November 28, 1967, following the death of President Léon M'Ba, who had selected him for that position on recommendation of agents from French President de Gaulle's office. Bongo was chosen because he was expected to protect French interests in Gabon while promoting reconciliation and stability in the aftermath of M'Ba's troubled presidency. As a member of the Téké, a small people in the southeast, he stood outside the ethnic rivalries (Myènè vs. Fang, intra-Fang) that had long troubled political life. Though young, he had a sound education in business administration and a decade of government experience, including several years in M'Ba's office. Yet he had not been personally involved in the rivalries or repression of the M'Ba presidency. Bongo released M'Ba's opponents from prison, allowing them to reenter government service or return to private life. Thereafter, in March 1968, in cooperation with an assembly composed only of member from M'Ba's party, Bongo established a single party, the Parti Démocratique Gabonais (PDG). He justified such action on the grounds that the existing parties represented ethnic and regional interests that hindered effective government and national unity. Although during the early years of Bongo's presidency a good deal of discussion and debate took place within the PDG, ultimately the president made the important decisions himself.

While the single-party system gave Gabon new stability, it also provided the president and ruling class a means for perpetuating themselves in office without much regard for the needs of the people. Revolt would have been futile, because France was ready to intervene militarily, under the defense cooperation agreement, to keep Bongo in power. Beginning in April 1969, Bongo began to curb the independence of the trade unions; by 1973 he had forced them to join a single federation under government control. Illegal strikes, work stoppages, and slowdowns periodically revealed the workers' dissatisfaction. Criticism by a handful of Marxist professors and students at the new university in Libreville concerning the undemocratic nature of the regime and financial corruption resulted in 1972 in harsh prison terms for the offenders.

Greater possibilities for the ruling class to enrich themselves resulted from a period of economic expansion that coincided with Bongo's accession to the presidency. Based on petroleum, manganese, uranium, and timber, that expansion multiplied the revenues hitherto available to the government. Between 1973 and 1985, revenues mainly from increased petroleum at higher prices increased eighteen-fold. Assuming that oil reserves would ultimately become depleted, the government used the bulk of the additional funds to promote development that would decrease dependence on petroleum. To this end, between 1974 and 1986, it constructed the Trans-Gabonais Railway between Owendo on the estuary, where a new port was built, and Franceville on the upper Ogooué River. It thereby sought to reach the forest and mineral riches of the interior. The government also created forty-six corporations, in seventeen of which private investors held shares, in order to give Gabon greater control of its industrial and commercial sectors. Unfortunately, most of the businesses proved a drain on the treasury because of nepotism, financial corruption, and mismanagement.

The political elite also diverted funds from public works and services, as well as income from 25 per cent of petroleum sales. As a result, by the late 1980s 2 per cent of the population held 80 per cent of all personal income. The elite had transferred to foreign bank accounts 28 billion French francs, a sum double the national debt created by their actions.

After a prolonged downturn starting in 1986 halved government income, froze salaries, and increased unemployment, popular discontent burgeoned. By 1990 three-fifths of the population was living in cities, mainly in Libreville and Port-Gentil, center of the timber and petroleum industries. They had relocated there to obtain better opportunities for salaried employment, health care, and education, and because of regime neglect of agriculture.

Popular demonstrations and strikes between January and June 1990 forced the Bongo regime to ease some financial restrictions. Bongo then summoned a national conference to deal with the country's problems, which led to the return of a multiparty system and freer exercise of the freedoms of speech, communication, and association. In May 1990 the death of an opposition leader in suspicious circumstances sparked violence that led to French military intervention to protect French citizens and petroleum facilities in Port-Gentil. Intervention had the effect of propping up the regime until its forces could regain control of the situation.

Although opposition parties functioned throughout the 1990s, they never maintained a united front against Bongo and the PDG. The Bongo regime, through vote-rigging, repression, and support from both Center-Right and Socialist regimes in France, won the parliamentary elections of 1990 and 1996, and the presidential elections of 1993 and 1998. The rigged election of December 1993, together with the French-initiated devaluation of the franc by 50 per cent in January 1994 sparked protests in the cities, during which as many people were killed as in the French intervention of 1964. The regime thereafter granted modest salary increases and placed controls on soaring prices of basic commodities, 85 per cent of which were now being imported.

During the 1990s the new Rabi-Kounga oil field, south of Port-Gentil, provided additional revenues for the state budget, 40 per cent of which went toward the international debt. France continued to aid Gabon by canceling and rescheduling debts while loaning funds to support its Structural Adjustment Program. The IMF's insistence that Gabon privatize state corporations and eliminate diversion of petroleum revenues threatened to reduce the wealth and influence of the ruling class. At the same time ordinary citizens were discouraged by the continued decrease in living standards and the impossibility of peaceful political change.

DAVID E. GARDINIER

Further Reading

Decalo, S. *The Stable Minority: Civilian Rule in Africa.* Gainesville, Fla: Florida Academic Press, 1998.

Gardinier, D. E. "France and Gabon during the Mitterand Presidency: The Evolution of a PostColonial Relationship." *Proceedings of the 18th Meeting of the French Colonial Historical Society FCHS* 18 (1993): 91–101.

———. *Historical Dictionary of Gabon.* 2nd ed. Lanham, Md.: Scarecrow Press, 1994.

Gardinier, David E. "France and Gabon since 1993: The Reshaping of a Post-Colonial Relationship." In *Essays in French Colonial History.* East Lansing, Mich.: Michigan State University Press, 1999.

———. "The Development of a Petroleum-Dominated Economy in Gabon." *Essays in Economic and Business History* 17 (1999): 1–15.

Gaddafi: *See* Libya: Foreign Policy under Qaddafi; Libya: Gaddafi (Qadhdhafi) and Jamahiriyya (Libyan Revolution).

Gambia, The: Nineteenth Century to Independence

By 1800 the British were the dominant European traders on the Gambia River, but individual merchants, rather than the government, maintained the British presence. The area was politically dominated by Wolof and Mande kingdoms on both banks of the river. Nine Mande kingdoms dominated the southern bank of the river, while five kingdoms with large Wolof populations controlled the northern bank. Each of the Mande

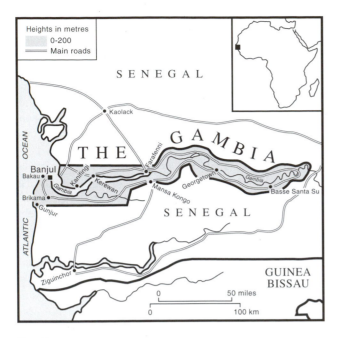

Gambia.

states was ruled by a king, or mansa, who had advisers and an armed force to defend the state as well as keep order within the state. Inhabitants included Mande, Wolof, some Diola and Serer, as well as some Fulbe, especially in the kingdoms on the upper Gambia River. To the north of the Gambian region were the large Wolof and Serer kingdoms, which were increasingly dominated in the nineteenth century by the French, who sometimes intervened in the affairs of the kingdoms on the northern bank of the Gambia River.

The abolition of the slave trade by the British in 1808 meant that a part of the British navy needed harbor facilities in West Africa, and the mouth of the Gambia River was chosen as the site. In 1816 Captain Alexander Grant purchased the sand banks of Bamboo Island, later named Saint Mary's Island, adjacent to the south bank of the river, from Tumani Bojang, the Mande king of Kombo. The garrison constructed administration buildings, harbor facilities and a barracks, forming the nucleus of the town of Bathurst (later Banjul) named after Lord Henry Bathurst, the British Colonial Secretary. Wolof merchants as well as newly liberated African slaves increased the local population. In 1821 the new Crown Colony's administration was given to the governor of Freetown, Sierra Leone, and the colony was attached to the British West African Federation. In 1823 the acquisition of MacCarthy Island and some other concessions from local Mande rulers augmented the colony's size and population. The establishment of the new colony had some economic impact on neighboring Mande and Wolof kingdoms, but no political or military implications. The African states traded on a

small scale with the British, but maintained their independence. In the early 1830s the British introduced peanut cultivation, which soon spread to neighboring kingdoms. Within a decade, peanuts had become the colony's dominant export, and the British presence increased.

The most important changes in the nineteenth century, however, developed out of conflicts between the traditional Wolof and Mande kingdoms and Muslim reform leaders, beginning in the 1850s and lasting until about 1900, and affecting all areas of the Gambia River. These so-called Soninke-Marabout wars (which is a misnomer, as they did not involve the Soninke) destroyed most of the existing kingdoms and created several new states, dominated by Muslims. The British did not intervene to support the traditional Mande and Wolof authorities. The conflicts were part of a series of Muslim reform movements that swept across the entire Senegambian region in the second half of the nineteenth century, destroying traditional ethnic polities and establishing new states with an Islamic identity. Most of the Gambian population also adopted Islam during this turbulent period. The most famous and influential Muslim reformers were Ma Ba, Alfa Molloh Balde, and Fode Kabba Dumbuya, all of whom created new states in the Gambia River area. Many of the conflicts involved nearby areas under French control, and the reform leaders often took refuge on the other side of the border. Ma Ba, in particular, envisioned a united theocracy in Senegambia, but this was never achieved.

During the conflicts, the British intervened militarily in a few instances when their economic interests appeared threatened, but most of the conflicts occurred in areas beyond the British sphere of influence. The wars interfered with trade along the river, causing some decline in revenues. The British Parliament increasingly questioned the wisdom of investing in such a region, and some encouraged selling the territory to the French, who were aggressively expanding their control over Senegal and were interested in acquiring the Gambia River area.

Despite some calls in Britain for selling the area to the French, a conference in 1889 finally secured French agreement to British control of the Gambia River and eventually the establishment of the present-day boundaries. In 1894 the colony was declared a Protectorate. By 1900 Britain had imposed indirect rule on Gambia, dividing it into thirty-five chiefdoms, although the real power remained with the governor and his staff at Bathurst. The area was divided into the colony and protectorate areas, depending on the distance from Bathurst. Obviously, the British presence was felt most strongly in the colonial area around Bathurst. While there was some sporadic resistance to British rule, the inhabitants were exhausted from the recent conflicts and apparently welcomed peace.

Because of their limited presence and financial resources in the colony, the British did not interfere in local political or religious matters. Muslim authorities cooperated with colonial officials, and peasants grew peanuts to pay their taxes. In 1906 slavery was officially abolished throughout the area, but this had little impact on peanut production, which continued to expand rapidly.

Colonial economic policy in Gambia centered on the production and export of peanuts. The administration sought to collect taxes and duties on trade, and to maintain peace and stability to encourage peanut production. Gambia was Britain's smallest and poorest colony in West Africa and received very little development assistance. The taxable value of peanuts was barely sufficient to meet local government costs. Some harbor and transportation and communication improvements were made in Bathurst, and some missionary groups set up schools. The rest of the protectorate was sorely neglected, with no all-weather roads, and only one secondary school and one hospital. The river continued to be the main link between Bathurst and the remainder of the protectorate, and also the main transport route for peanuts from interior to coast. Even on the river, transport facilities remained basic.

After World War II, European colonial powers began to take small steps toward decolonization. In Gambia, however, political parties were slow in forming, and moves toward greater autonomy were very gradual, especially when compared to the other colonies in British West Africa. Ghana, formerly the Gold Coast, received full independence in 1957, and Nigeria became independent in 1960, with Sierra Leone following in 1961. These three countries achieved independence after long preparations and well before Gambia. There was some question about the viability of Gambia as an independent country, given its lack of resources, tiny land mass, and geographic location as an enclave within French-speaking Senegal, which many assumed would take control over the area and incorporate it into an independent Senegal or Senegambia. There was also the lack of an educated elite who could eventually take over the reins of power. For the majority of people in the area, their ethnic solidarity was considerably stronger than any sense of national identity or allegiance to a political party. Chiefs still dominated local political affairs.

Even after some concessions to greater Gambian participation in government in the 1950s, the governor and higher administrative officers, all British, wielded tremendous power. The protectorate was dominated by district officers and officially sanctioned chiefs who benefited from the status quo and were reluctant for change. The constitution was revised in 1954 and again in 1960, allowing for political parties to contest elections, but without setting a timetable for independence.

Several small political parties were formed in Gambia in the 1950s, most notably the Protectorate People's Party, established in 1959 by David Jawara and his associates. The results of the 1960 elections caused a stalemate in the government, and Jawara and his partners resigned, calling for more constitutional changes. New elections in 1962 were won by Jawara and his renamed People's Progressive Party. The party won 62 of the vote and Jawara became prime minister. In 1963 Gambia became self-governing, and discussions began on the method and date for complete independence. While opposition parties sought a new election at independence, Jawara and his party convinced the British that new elections were not necessary. On February 18, 1965, Gambia became an independent country within the British Commonwealth, with Jawara as prime minister. In 1966 Jawara was knighted and changed his name to Dawda Jawara. Gambia became a republic on April 24, 1970.

ANDREW F. CLARK

See also: **Diouf, Abdou; Senegal: Casamance Province, Conflict In.**

Further Reading

Gailey, H. A. *Historical Dictionary of the Gambia.* Metuchen, N.J.: Scarecrow Press, 1987.

Gamble, D., *The Gambia: A Bibliography.* Oxford: Clio Press, 1988.

Swindell, K. "Serawoollies, Tillibunkas and Strange Farmers: The Development of Migrant Groundnut Farming along the Gambia River, 1848–1895." *Journal of African History* 21 (1980): 221–250.

Wright, D. *The Early History of Niumi: Settlement and Foundation of a Mandinka State on the Gambia River.* Athens, Ohio: Ohio University Press, 1977.

Wright, D. *The World and a Very Small Place in Africa.* Armonk, N.Y.: M.E. Sharpe, 1997.

Gambia, The: Independence to Present

At independence in February 1965, the Republic of The Gambia was headed by Prime Minister Dawda Jawara and dominated by his political party, the People's Progressive Party (PPP). Jawara had converted to Islam in 1965 and changed his name from David to Dawda. He was knighted in 1966, and thereafter was commonly known as Sir Dawda Jawara. The name of the capital, Bathurst, was changed to Banjul in 1973. The Gambian economy, as it had been during colonial rule, was based on the production and export of peanuts. The new government, with its limited resources, embarked on a program of development, including the construction of the trans-Gambian all-weather road, improved river transport, and the encouragement of rice cultivation. Jawara faced little political opposition, owing primarily to the lack of divisive national issues.

He consolidated his power and in 1970, voters approved his plan to make The Gambia a republic. Jawara became the first president, with extended powers. He was handily reelected in 1972 and again in 1977, with the PPP winning over 70 per cent of the popular vote in both elections.

During the 1970s, Jawara emerged as an articulate leader and a voice of moderation in Africa, active in several international organizations while maintaining a democracy. The economy, however, was in crisis. The Gambian agriculture, already marginal at best, was severely affected by the Sahelian drought of the 1970s, especially in the middle and upper river areas. Peanut production declined, as did the international price for peanuts. More youth began to migrate to Banjul in search of employment, contributing to a declining labor force in the rural areas and increased unemployment in the urban center. The country had to depend on large amounts of foreign assistance and substantial loans to meet its budget. There was increased talk of a merger with Senegal, but Jawara and others felt that The Gambia would be overwhelmed by its considerably larger French-speaking neighbor. The two countries discussed joint economic development programs, although Senegal, with its southern province of Casamance physically isolated on the other side of The Gambia, was more eager to cooperate.

In July 1981, while Jawara was in Britain, an attempted military coup d'etat disrupted the general stability of the country. The rebels briefly seized power in Banjul. Jawara called on a 1967 mutual defense treaty signed with Senegal and with the aid of Senegalese forces, he was returned to power. Over 600 people died in the aborted coup attempt. The Senegalese troops were then asked to stay to maintain order and discourage any further unrest. In the rebellion's aftermath, Jawara and President Abdou Diouf of Senegal agreed to form the Confederation of Senegambia in late 1981. The two countries pledged to integrate their foreign policy as well as economic and military resources, but maintain their independence in most other areas. Diouf was named president, with Jawara designated vice president. An executive and legislature were also set up, but progress toward further integration was slow, with each side blaming the other for lack of progress. Many Gambians felt they were simply being absorbed by Senegal and were relieved when the arrangement began to dissolve. The confederation was officially abolished in 1989.

By early 1985, The Gambia again faced serious economic troubles. Foreign aid donors began to refuse requests for further funds. Food and fuel shortages, common in the rural areas, began to affect Banjul. The government declared a series of austerity measures in line with structural adjustment programs of the International Monetary Fund. Reforms included abolition of price controls, elimination of interest rate and credit controls, floating of the exchange rate, privatization of several state-owned enterprises, and a more disciplined fiscal and monetary policy. The reform program improved The Gambia's overall economic outlook, and foreign assistance once again returned to the country. For the vast majority of peasant farmers, however, there was virtually no change in their harsh economic plight. Bad harvests and falling prices for peanuts continued throughout the 1980s. Jawara and the PPP easily won reelection in 1987 and 1992, although opposition parties gained some support.

In July 1994 a group of young officers from the Gambian National Army, led by Captain (later Colonel) Yahya Abdul Jammeh, staged a bloodless coup d'état which successfully overthrew the Jawara government. The Senegalese government did not intervene as it had done in 1981. Jawara went into exile in the United Kingdom. The new military government justified the coup by citing the corruption and malpractice of Jawara and the PPP, as well as The Gambia's economic troubles. The military leaders continually promised a return to civilian rule once corruption had been rooted out of government. The government ruled by proclamation, and dissent was brutally repressed. Political activity was banned until August 1996, and elections were held in late 1996 and early 1997. Four political parties officially contested the elections. Jammeh, who had retired from the military, was elected president with over 55 per cent of the vote, and his political party, the Alliance for Patriotic Reorientation and Construction (APRC), dominated the national assembly. A new constitution came into effect in January 1997. The return to civilian rule improved The Gambia's international reputation and aid organizations once again assisted the country. The Gambia has worked on improving relations with Senegal, although a portion of the border on the upper river remains disputed. The next national elections were held in 2001; President Jammeh was elected to another term. In the January 2002 parliamentary elections, the APRC won all but three seats.

The Gambian economy continues to be characterized by traditional subsistence agriculture, primarily in peanuts, which employs 75 per cent of the labor force. Fisheries and tourism are also foreign exchange earners, although tourism declined precipitously with the 1994 coup. Since 1998, however, The Gambia has enjoyed consistent growth. In July 2002 the government presented a Poverty Reduction Strategy Paper (PRSP) to the International Monetary Fund (IMF) and World Bank, in which it outlined plans for economic diversification and the implementation of a supplementary technical assistance program in the years to come.

ANDREW F. CLARK

Further Reading

Hughes, A., ed. *The Gambia: Studies in Society and Politics.* Birmingham, UK: Birmingham University African Studies Series, 1991.

McPherson, M., and S. Radelet, eds. *Economic Recovery in the Gambia: Insights for Adjusment in Sub-Saharan Africa.* Cambridge, Mass.: Harvard Institute for International Development, 1995.

Sallah, T. M. "Economics and Politics in the Gambia." *Journal of Modern African Studies* 28 (1990): 621–648.

Wiseman, J. "Military Rule in the Gambia: An Interim Assessment." *Third World Quarterly* 17 (1996): 917–940.

Wright, D. *The World and a Very Small Place in Africa.* Armonk, N.Y.: M. E. Sharpe, 1997.

Gambia, The: Relations with Senegal

The Gambia, except for a short coastline on the Atlantic Ocean, is an enclave surrounded by Senegal. It is a strip of land 15 to 20 miles wide on either side of the Gambia River and extends for 295 miles into the interior. The Gambia River begins in Guinea-Conakry, then flows through Senegal before reaching the country of The Gambia. The nation's unusual size and shape are a direct result of nineteenth-century territorial compromises between Britain and France, and in particular the Anglo-French Convention of 1889, which officially established the borders between the two colonies.

Prior to independence in 1965, there was some discussion of establishing a political union, or at least a closely cooperative alliance, between Gambia and Senegal in order to increase the economic prosperity of both countries. One of the reasons Great Britain agreed to the colony's eventual independence was the belief that The Gambia would amalgamate with Senegal. A treaty of association was signed in the early 1960s, but no serious progress was made toward closer association besides a mutual defense treaty signed in 1967. The ruling Gambian party, the People's Progressive Party (PPP) feared domination by French-speaking Senegal, with its very close ties to France. In addition, with the improvement in The Gambia's economic outlook in the late 1960s, there was no urgency for closer union with Senegal. The Sahelian drought of the 1970s hit Senegal much harder than The Gambia, further contributing to The Gambian reluctance to move toward closer integration. Continued smuggling from The Gambia, where prices were lower, into Senegal benefited The Gambian traders, but it did not cause a serious rift between the two countries. Occasionally, border searches were increased, but the smuggling continued, and there were no confrontations between the two nations.

Relations between the two countries were dramatically altered in July 1981 when a coup against President Jawara was initiated by a group of self-proclaimed African Marxists. The rebels briefly took control of the government, and Jawara fled to Dakar. Jawara, citing the 1967 defense treaty, was restored by Senegalese troops. President Abdou Diouf of Senegal, who had come to power only one year before with the resignation of Leopold Senghor, feared the creation of a radical Marxist regime in The Gambia. The coup in The Gambia, if successful, likewise posed a threat to the Diouf regime.

By December 1981 Senegal and The Gambia had signed an agreement to create the Confederation of Senegambia, which went into effect in February 1982. A joint executive was declared, with Abdou Diouf as president and Jawara as vice president. The confederation was a clear victory for Diouf and Senegal, although the coup had encouraged some Gambians to consider the prospect of a closer union with their neighbor more favorably.

The confederation agreement was an ambitious document, creating the theoretical infrastructure for a single government. A common federal legislature was planned, with Senegal controlling two-thirds of the seats. A Senegambian council of ministers, dominated by Senegalese, and the confederal assembly met for the first time in January 1983. The two nations agreed to recognize and respect the unique aspects of each country. They also pledged to consult and cooperate on economic, defense, communications and foreign affairs policies. A gendarmerie equipped by France and trained by Senegal replaced the defunct Gambia Field Force. Other attempts at integrating defense and security forces mainly resulted in an increased Senegalese military presence in The Gambia. The proposed economic and financial integration was slow in forthcoming, with each side blaming the other for lack of progress.

By the mid-1980s, Gambian politicians had begun to revert to the rhetoric of the 1970s, claiming Senegal was absorbing The Gambia and forcing the country to give up its independence, the English language, its ties to Britain, and its cultural identity. Plans to finance and construct a Trans-Gambian Highway and bridge exacerbated tensions. The Gambians saw the project as benefiting only Senegal, which sought to link its southern province of the Casamance with the rest of Senegal by building a highway through The Gambia and a bridge across the river. Ferries were being used, and the roads through The Gambia linking Senegal and the Casamance were in serious disrepair. Senegal wanted The Gambia to pay most of the costs, since the project would occur on Gambian soil, but The Gambia strongly resisted. The project never moved past the planning stages; Diouf was increasingly preoccupied with domestic political and economic problems and did not force the issue. The confederation was not working as planned, and by the time it was abandoned in September 1989 it had ceased functioning. By necessity, Senegal and The Gambia maintained cordial relations and many economic links, but there were no further efforts at unity or closer integration.

Relations between The Gambia and Senegal reverted to their previous cordial but stagnant state until July 1994, when a group of young officers from the Gambian National Army, led by Captain (later Colonel) Yahya Abdul Jammeh, staged a bloodless coup which successfully overthrew the Jawara government. Jawara, who was in the United Kingdom, vowed to return to power but he remained in exile. Senegalese troops did not intervene as they had done during the 1981 coup. Apparently, the Senegalese government did not fear the new military regime in Banjul, which promised to root out corruption and to hold elections in the near future. Senegal remained neutral throughout the coup and transition period. There were some tensions over poorly defined borders in upper Gambia, but there were no confrontations. The new government did not shut down the ferries across the river and insisted it sought good relations with Senegal. In elections in 1997, Jammeh, who retired from the military, was elected president. Relations between Gambia and Senegal remain cordial. During the 1998–1999 rebellion in Guinea-Bissau, when Senegalese troops intervened, The Gambia was instrumental in coordinating peace talks and the withdrawal of Senegalese troops. There is no discussion of a renewal of the confederation or closer political ties in progress.

ANDREW F. CLARK

See also: **Diouf, Abdou; Senegal: Casamance Province, Conflict in.**

Further Reading

Clark, A. F., and L. C. Phillips. *Historical Dictionary of Senegal.*, Metuchen, N.J.: Scarecrow Press, 1994.

Hughes, A. "The Collapse of the Senegambian Confederation." *Journal of Commonwealth and Comparative Politics* 30 (1992): 200–222.

Proctor, J. "The Gambia's relations with Senegal: The Search for Partnership." *Journal of Commonwealth Political Studies* 5 (1967): 143–160.

Schraeder, P. "Senegal's Foreign Policy: Responding to Internal and International Pressures for Change." In *African Foreign Policies*, edited by Stephen Wright. Boulder, Colo.: Westview Press, 1999.

Gandhi: *See* South Africa: Gandhi, Indian Question.

Gao: *See* Songhay Empire, Gao and Origins of.

Garamantes: Early Trans-Saharan Trade

At the beginning of the first millennium BCE, the Maghreb was inhabited by sedentary Berber groups, the ancestors of the Moors of western regions, the Numids of current eastern Algeria and High Plains, the Getulians of the Predesert, and the Garamantes of the Fezzan. Two important events precipitated the inclusion of the Maghreb into the world of the Mediterranean empires: the founding of Carthage around 750BCE by Phoenicians from Tyre and that of Cyrena in 631BCE by Greeks from Thera.

Carthage occupied the rich coastal plains of present-day Tunisia and Tripolitania but had no interest in spreading westward or southward, toward mountains or desert steppes. Its domain was on the seas, off Sicily, Sardinia, the Balearic Islands, Andalusia, and in her ports along the African coast up to Gibraltar and Mogador. Its power eventually led to the clash with Rome: the Punic Wars concluded in 146BCE with the destruction of Carthage.

Cyrena, although erected on African soil, was an ordinary Greek city, famed only for its chariot-racing. As it exploited the narrow coastal strip of Cyrenaica and Marmarica, it was continually embroiled in conflict with raiding desert nomads and occasionally Egypt. It remained independent until its conquest by Alexander (331BCE) and was incorporated into the Roman Empire in 96BCE.

Toward the beginning of the Christian era, the whole coastal Maghrib and Egypt were Romanized.

The Garamantes are already mentioned in the fifth century BCE by Herodotus. He describes them as people chasing the "Ethiopians on their four-horse chariots," which attests that the Garamantes, like all their Mediterranean contemporaries, used horses and chariots. The Garamantes were sedentary agriculturists, mainly settled in the fertile Wadi el-Agial, a huge oasis, and throughout the whole southwestern corner of present-day Libya, between Tibesti and Ghadames. The Romans regarded them as half-legendary, nevertheless disquieting, "an ungovernable tribe," as Tacitus writes, "unceasingly engaged in brigandage actions against its neighbors," too distant to be conquered. Germa (the Geramantes' capital city) had a stormy relationship with Rome. Sometimes the Garamantes attacked Mediterranean cities, and Rome frequently launched punitive expeditions against them. In other periods, peace prevailed. The Garamantes were still in existence as a political unit, independent from Rome and Byzantium, at the time of the Islamic conquest around 640.

During the first millennium, the climactic episode of the Actual Arid Phase was being established south of the Maghrib. The break between the Sahara and Egypt was absolute, as the Libyan Desert was a daunting barrier. However, from the Mediterranean countries some innovations found their way to the central Sahara. The horse and the chariot were introduced there. Some technical markers (two-pole chariots, trigas, and quadrigas) give a clue for dating this innovation: all the Saharan chariots date to after 700BCE. This is the time of the "Horse Period" or "Caballine Period" in the Saharan rock art sequence. Another new item, the throwing spear, was now replacing the bow, the traditional weapon of the Saharan neolithic groups. Some centuries later the sword and the shield also appeared.

But the major novelty is certainly the introduction of the camel, shortly before the Christian era. The dromedary had been domesticated in the Middle East, then introduced into Egypt by the Assyrians when they conquered Egypt in the seventh century BCE. From there the animal reached first the Maghrib, where it was used as a draught animal for agricultural labor, then the central Sahara. It is plentifully represented in the "Camel Period" of the rock art. The Saharan populations quickly realized the importance of this "ship of the desert."

During the first centuries of the Christian era, keeping horses in a severe desert became too difficult. They could be maintained only in some regions, on the Sahelian fringes (Air, Adrar des Iforas, Mauritania) or in the Maghrib countries. Anywhere else the camel replaced the horse as a pack animal. Above all, it made raids easier to carry out.

It was also toward the beginning of the camel period that caravan trade was being established. At this time, typical African products, such as the Guinean gold from Bambuk, began to regularly arrive at the Mediterranean coasts, and items of Punic origin then arrived in southern Morocco or Mauritania. The beginning of this trans-Saharan trade could only happen after the introduction of the camel into central and western Sahara.

The rock art of the central Sahara (that is, of the current Tuareg country) shows no discontinuity in the evolution from the horse period to the camel period, and the latter continued until the present. Therefore, the introduction of the horse, the chariot, the throwing spear, the camel and writing can be attributed to the Tuareg or their immediate ancestors, who were already settled in the central Sahara, at least since the beginning of the first millennium BCE. This is at variance with oral traditions of the Tuareg, which claim that they arrived at Air already Islamicized.

ALFRED MUZZOLINI

See also: **Carthage; North Africa: Roman Occupation, Empire; Rock Art, Saharan; Sahara: Trans-Saharan Trade.**

Further Reading

Daniels C. M. *The Garamantes of Southern Libya.* Stoughton: Oleander Press, 1970.

Daniels C. M. "Excavation and Fieldwork amongst the Garamantes." *Libyan Studies* 20 (1989): 45–61.

Muzzolini, A. "The Chariot-Period of the Rock-Art Chronology in the Sahara and the Maghreb: A Critical Reappraisal of the Traditional Views." In *Rock Art in the Old World*, edited by M. Lorblanchet. Papers of AURA Congress (Darwin), New-Delhi: Indira Gandhi Nal Centre of Arts 1992.

Norris H. T. *The Tuaregs. Their Islamic Legacy and its Diffusion in the Sahel.* London: Aris and Phillips, 1975.

Garang, John, and the Sudan Peoples' Liberation Party (SPLA)

John Garang de Mabior was born into a family of Tuic pastoralists, of the Dinka people of the Upper Nile in South Sudan in about 1945. In 1968 he joined the Anyanya movement, which fought the first round of civil war between north and south Sudan (1955–1972). When the first north-south war ended in an agreement signed in Addis Ababa, Ethiopia, in 1972, between the then-president of Sudan, Jaafer Nimeiri and the southern rebels, the Anyanya forces were absorbed into the Sudan Peoples' Armed Forces, and Garang was made a captain. Shortly thereafter, he was appointed by President Nimeiri as deputy director of Military Research in the Sudan Army General Head Quarters in Khartoum.

In 1981 Garang was awarded a doctorate in agricultural economics by Iowa State University. Upon return to Sudan, he took up teaching positions at Khartoum University and at the Sudan Military College, in addition to his post at the military research unit. At both institutions, his radical ideas about the political participation (or lack thereof) of what he called "the marginalized areas" inspired many students.

During his tenure at the Sudan Military College and the Army General Head Quarters, Garang moved up to the rank of a colonel in the Sudan army, although he was growing increasingly dissatisfied with Nimeiri's government policies concerning the south. Plans to exploit southern oil resources, maltreatment of southern labor migrants in the north, extraction of forest reserves by military personnel working in the south, the policy to redesign the north-south boundaries, mass imprisonment of southern politicians, and attempts to undermine the Addis Ababa agreement, all drove Garang to formulate his ideas into a different brand of nationalist thinking.

Garang advocated a system of dispersed authority. He believed that the political leadership should not be concentrated in the capital, especially in such a vast and diverse country like Sudan. He argued that the political leadership in such a country should be widely distributed geographically in order to stay in touch with the people at large. Such thinking appealed to groups in underrepresented regions such as the Nuba, the Fur, the Nubians of the far north, the people of the southern Blue Nile, and the Beja of eastern Sudan.

On May 16, 1983, Garang joined an army revolt against the central government. The revolt occurred in the southern town of Bor and was led by Kerabino Kuanyin Bol, another former Anyanya soldier and a high-ranking officer in the Sudan army. The revolt was a result of consultation among the former Anyanya officers in the Sudan army who were disenchanted with Nimeiri. These officers, along with some politicians, realized that the people of the south had reached a stalemate in their struggle to implement the 1972 Addis Ababa agreement. Many southern army officers were disappointed with the agreement and claimed they were coerced into signing it by their superiors, chiefly Joseph Lagu, head of the Anyanya movement. They argued that they could not trust the northerners and that a return to war was inevitable.

Toward the end of 1983, Garang and colleagues founded the Sudan Peoples' Liberation Army (SPLA) with Garang as the commander-in-chief, and its political wing, the Sudan Peoples' Liberation Movement (SPLM) under his chairmanship as well. The liberation struggle was launched with a different ideology. Unlike the first round of north-south war, which called for secession, the SPLA postulated the goal of liberating the whole country and creating a "New Sudan" that would be freed from any discrimination based on race, ethnicity, religion, or culture.

Garang insisted that the idea of independence for the south must be dropped, which earned him favor among moderate people in the north and the support of other countries that oppose the breakup of Sudan. Garang was the first to propose the idea that the conflict in Sudan should no longer be referred to as the "southern problem," as the south was not the only region that suffered from northern domination and injustice. In order to implement a lasting solution, the conflict had to be viewed as a national problem and could only be resolved in the context of a constitutional conference involving all sectors of the society, its political organizations, and its trades unions. To force Nimeiri's government into recognizing the importance of such a conference, he called upon all the people of the "marginalized areas" to take up arms in order to end the dictatorship and to set up a "united democratic secular Sudan."

Garang's ideas were perceived as tantamount to a reversal of Arab-Islamic domination in favor of a more African identity for the country. Garang rejected the popular southern wish for secession and instead declared a socialist liberation movement, in a bid to win external support from socialist/communist nations. His pro-unity stance, however, was eventually perceived by many both within and outside Sudan as a euphemistic disguise of separatist aspirations.

Garang popularized his line of thinking through an SPLA manifesto, which portrayed the SPLA as a socialist organization attempting to enforce unity, but only in a state built upon the recognition of its diversity and equal representation of all cultural groups. To this end, he sought the help of Haile Mariam Mengistu of Ethiopia with arms and training. Help also came from Muammar Gaddafi of Libya. Both men were quietly pleased by the revival of the southern Sudanese civil war, which they viewed primarily as an insurrection against Nimeiri. Within a few months and well into the middle of 1980s, thousands of young Nuer and Dinka, the two largest ethnic groups in the south, flocked to western Ethiopia for military training. The SPLA trained and deployed many battalions that captured scores of towns in Upper Nile and Equatoria, victories that resulted in more recruits from different ethnic groups in the south. In 1984 the SPLA set up a radio station in Ethiopia to broadcast into Sudan called Radio SPLA. Garang gave his first radio address on March 3, 1984, calling "upon all the Sudanese people to abolish the divisions among them that the oppressor has imposed through the policy of divide and rule."

With more gains on the military front came political achievements in the north, and the public became more agitated against Nimeiri's government. While Nimeiri was visiting the United States in 1985, a popular uprising occurred in Khartoum and his sixteen-year military rule was brought to an end. The SPLA, under the leadership of Garang, took much of the credit for the fall of Nimeiri. A transitional military council took power and called on Garang to return to the country to participate in a government to be elected after the transitional period, but Garang rejected the request, arguing that overthrowing Nimeiri had not translated into a change in the system. His beliefs were confirmed shortly afterward, when Sadiq al Mahdi came to power in 1986 as prime minister through an elected government. Elections were not held in much of the south due to war, and the Khartoum government recruited militia forces to destabilize the civilian population in the south. The SPLA regarded the so-called democratic period as another northern dictatorship, and the war raged on until a military coup brought an Islamist government to power in June 1989 headed by President Lieutenant General Umar Hasan Ahmad al-Bashir. Since then the government has put significant pressure on the SPLA and Garang, despite the fact that it is the first government in Sudan to come under heavy international pressure for its dismal human rights record, terrorism, and religious intolerance.

Under the leadership of John Garang, the SPLA is considered by the majority of the people of the south, the Nuba Mountains, and Southern Blue Nile as the only hope in ending their perceived domination by the Islamist, Arabized north. This support helped the SPLA survive a near-fatal split in August 1991, when a group of commanders, disgruntled with Garang's leadership, broke away with an attempt to overthrow him. The coup was rebuffed and the splinter group formed a separate organization called the SPLA-Nasir, under the leadership of Riek Machar, while Garang's group became known as SPLA-Mainstream. Since 1991 SPLA-Nasir has evolved into various organizations including SPLA-United, the Southern Sudan Independence Army (SSIA), and finally the Southern Sudan Defense Force (SSDF). In 1996 Riek and his Nuer followers signed an agreement with the northern government.

As of 2004, Garang's SPLA controls most of the south, including some territory in central and eastern Sudan.

JOK MADUT JOK

See also: **Sudan: Nimeiri, Peace, the Economy; Sudan: Sadiq Al-Mahdi Regime, 1980s; Sudan: Civil War: 1990s.**

Further Reading

Burr, M., and R. Collins. *Africa's Thirty Years' War: Chad, Libya, and the Sudan 1963–1993*. Boulder, Colo.: Westview Press, 1993.
Garang, J. *John Garang Speaks*. Edited by Mansour Khalid. Kegan Paul International, 1987.
———. *The Call for Democracy in Sudan*. Kegan Paul International.
Nyaba, P. A. T*he Politics of Liberation in South Sudan: An Insider's View*. Kampala: Fountain Publishers, 1997.
Wright, R. *Sacred Rage: The Wrath of Militant Islam*. New York: Simon and Schuster, 1986.

Gaza State: *See* **Soshangane, Umzila, Gungunhane and the Gaza State.**

Gender and Migration: Southern Africa

Much of the academic literature on labor migration in southern Africa that has emerged since the late 1970s has been devoted almost exclusively to the movement of men (e.g.,. Crush, Jeeves, and Yudelman 1991; Jeeves 1985). The word "migrant" typically denoted a male person. The titles of these studies indicate that the literature on migration has focused primarily on migration to the South African mines, a system of migrancy that was exclusively male. However, as Belinda Bozzoli pointed out in her seminal 1983 article, there was an intimate connection between male migration to the mines and female migration to other sectors. She emphasized, in addition, that male migration had a profound impact on the status of rural women and that underlying the dominant historiography was a set of subtle assumptions and misconceptions about the "place" and the role of rural women. The paradoxical

image of women as both essential producers (laboring in the fields and nurturing future generations) and as morally degenerative agents was questioned. In the 1980s, therefore, with the growth of feminist approaches, there was a concurrent growing awareness that a historiography devoid of women leads to distorted views of society, and that the evolution of entire academic paradigms focused solely on men's experiences is profoundly androcentric.

This realization triggered a shift from studies focused exclusively on men's migration to studies of men's migration that mentioned women. More specifically, the late 1970s and early 1980s witnessed a barrage of studies on the effects of the (male) migrant labor system on women in the rural areas. Unfortunately, the "add-women-and-stir" methods of this literature did not seriously challenge or undermine the male bias of previous research. Men were assumed to be the migrants while women were passive victims "left behind" in the rural areas. Women were typically portrayed not as active participants in social change, but as victims of the migrant labor system. These victims suffered from both economic insecurity (male migrants' irregular remittances and rural impoverishment) and social dislocation (the breakdown in the traditional family structure, a high prevalence of depressive illness, and the growth of female-headed households). Women were also viewed as essentially passive, an assumption rooted in colonial discourse and perpetuated in these studies.

Women migrants, studied primarily by feminist scholars, entered the academic literature in southern Africa in the 1980s as a separate and legitimate focus of analysis. Researchers analyzed gender (the social construction of men and women and masculinity and femininity) rather than sex (the biological differences between females and males). They recognized that gender was an essential tool for unlocking the migration process. Feminist scholars criticized the gender-blindness of the migrant labor literature. These (mostly female) scholars have called for a new research agenda with women situated at the forefront of the analysis.

Migrant labor had generated an extensive literature and a plethora of theoretical approaches drawn from other contexts. Western feminist theory had not been systematically applied to the study of migration and relatively little of the literature addressed feminist theoretical concerns. In contrast, much of the new 1980s literature on women's migration in southern Africa was written by white, Western, well-educated women, very familiar with the Marxist and socialist feminism of the 1970s and early 1980s. It is not surprising, therefore, that it was this variant of Western feminist theory that was particularly evident in early theorizing about women's migration. The African literature was more noted for its empirical strengths than its theoretical sophistication, as field studies got underway on women migrants throughout southern Africa.

Feminist analysis of gender and migrancy in southern Africa has, for the most part, adopted either a socialist or a Marxist feminist theory rather than any of the other strands of Eestern feminism (such as radical, liberal, postmodern, or poststructural feminism). Marxist feminists view the female migrant as part of a vast "reserve" pool, forced to move to acquire cash to meet the needs of the state. Wages paid to women in the formal sector are unfairly low since it is assumed that they are either unmarried, or their husband will earn the wages. Socialist feminists perceive (migrant) women's oppression stemming from both capitalism and patriarchal gender relations. Further, they argue that this oppression can be challenged through collective political struggle against capitalism and patriarchy. Poststructural and postmodern approaches to migration and gender tend to explore issues of identity and power, on the understanding that social identities such as gender identities serve as an important influence on peoples' migrant behavior. Some studies (e.g., Cockerton 1995) examine how, through the migration process, migrants challenge and reconstruct their gender identities. In her analysis of female migration in Africa, Wright (1995) identifies a common thesis (or even trope) of female migrancy:

> In spite of, or perhaps because of, the best endeavors of chiefly and colonial powers alike, a small but very visible number of African women did migrate, breaking out of their role in the rural hinterland. In many cases women were seeking to escape the oppression of male control, which had reached an intolerable intensity in their lives (Wright, p. 786).

Women's migration is typically understood as flight from male control or patriarchal oppression, a function of male controls, the (male) migrant labor system, or men in general, but some research challenges these assumptions. Although a growing number of studies on women migrants in southern Africa adopted feminist insights in the 1980s, this was less true of research on men migrants. Little of the extensive literature on the (male) migrant labor system or migrant men uses gender as a critical tool for untangling the migration process.

CAMILLA COCKERTON

Further Reading

Bozzoli, B. "Marxism, Feminism, and South African Studies." *Journal of Southern African Studies* 9, no. 2 (1983): 139–171.

Cockerton, C. "'Running away' from the 'Land of the Desert': Women's Migration from Colonial Botswana to South Africa, 1885–1966." Ph.D. diss., Queen's University), 1995.

Crush, J., A. Jeeves, and D.Yudelman. *South Africa's Labor Empire: A History of Black Migrancy to the Gold Mines.* Boulder, Colo.: Westview Press, 1991.

Fairhurst, J., Ingrid Booysen, and Phillip Hattingh, eds. *Migration and Gender: Place, Time and People Specific.* Pretoria: Department of Geography, University of Pretoria, 1997.

Jeeves, A. *Migrant Labour in South Africa's Mining Economy.* Kingston: McGill-Queen's University Press, 1985.

Wright, C. "Gender Awareness in Migration Theory: Synthesizing Actor and Structure in Southern Africa." *Development and Change* 26 (1995): 771–791.

Geography, Environment in African History

The history of Africa, like that of any other continent, has been fundamentally shaped by geographical and environmental influences, just as Africans, like people elsewhere, have in turn shaped the landscapes and ecological contexts in which they live. Historians have debated the character and relative influence of this human–environment relationship, moving over the course of decades from a set of crude assumptions and stereotypes, to a more subtle and nuanced view of environmental history. Environmental history combines the techniques of two academic disciplines, history and ecology (or biology in a broader sense), using the data of "hard" science to interpret the past as it relates to human interactions with the diverse landscapes they inhabit. Environmental historians try to "read" landscapes; that is, they try to collect information about humans and their environments at given points in time, and then detect the historical dynamics affecting these ecological relationships.

During much of the twentieth century, the debate on African environmental history alternated between two extremes. On one side were scholars who conceived of a primitive precolonial Africa, where people lived in a constant state of war against nature, until they were introduced to modern agriculture and industry through the imposition of Western science and technology. This view, which developed from the writings of colonial observers, has proved resilient, appearing in modified forms to the present day. Other scholars argued that precolonial Africans lived in harmony with their surroundings, and that colonialism robbed them of their natural wealth and abundant resources. A modified form of this "Merrie Africa" thesis, that precolonial Africans had successfully tamed their harsh environments before the colonial intrusion, was especially popular during the nationalist phase of African historiography. But most scholars now agree that both of these views are simplistic, because they neglect the fact that humans have always lived in constantly changing relationships with their environments. Learning how to "read" landscapes properly, then, requires both an understanding of ecological relationships and the ability to interpret them within a dynamic historical context.

The current, more nuanced view of African environmental history has been deeply influenced by the work of pioneering non-Africanist environmental historians, such as Alfred Crosby, whose work traces the global biological impact of European expansion, and William Cronon, who has detailed the effects of colonialism in North America. One of the earliest Africanist works to signal the development of environmental history as a discipline in its own right was John Ford's 1971 book on trypanosomiases, an exhaustively researched account of the spread of the tsetse fly continentwide during the colonial era. Since then, more localized studies have added greatly to the subtlety and depth of environmental history, such as the work of James Fairhead and Melissa Leach on the Guinean forests, James McCann on Ethiopian agriculture, and William Beinart on South Africa. Perhaps most impressive in range and depth has been the work on East Africa's environmental history, which began in earnest with the 1975 conference of the Historical Association of Kenya, "Ecology and History in East Africa," and since then has attracted a strikingly large number of scholars, including David Anderson, James Giblin, Helge Kjekshus, Peter Little, Gregory Maddox, Thomas Spear, and Richard Waller. James McCann has attempted to synthesize these localized studies from a continentwide perspective, perhaps an indication of similar efforts to come.

Environmental historians ground their work in an understanding of ecology, the study of relationships between organisms and their surroundings, or environments. Ecologists previously thought of "good" environments as having some sort of internal balance or stability, but these days it is widely accepted that all environments are constantly changing, and not necessarily in one particular direction or towards any culminating "climax" state. A crucial component of current ecological thinking is biodiversity, meaning the number and variety of species and habitats in an environment. Biodiversity involves both the total number of species in an area and their complex interactions; like the environment itself, biodiversity is constantly changing. Biodiversity is an unusual quantitative concept because it is impossible to quantify with any sort of precision, but ecologists generally agree that greater biodiversity is an important indicator of a healthy environment.

Human beings are an integral part of this biodiversity. We now know that humans have dramatically modified their environments for thousands of years, in ways that both positively and negatively affect biodiversity. Human activity makes a significant impact upon soil composition and vegetation patterns, as well as the distribution and diversity of animal populations. Humans modify their environments through subsistence practices such as hunting, gathering, fishing, herding, and farming; through increases and decreases in population size and density; and through technological development, such as the use of iron tools. Many of the landscapes once considered "natural" are actually the result of human modification: the great African savannas, for instance, would simply be overgrown woodlands without the continual grazing of cattle and the occasional brush-fires set by human inhabitants to maintain the rolling grasslands.

In some obvious ways, humans are subject to overriding geographical and environmental influences beyond their control. In Africa these influences include long-term and short-term fluctuations in climate. Over very long time spans, Africa, like other continents, has been shaped by slow climate changes, such as alternating eras of heavy or sparse rainfall, which have produced dramatic changes in African landscapes. For example, researchers in the Sahara Desert, which now covers almost a third of the continent's surface, have unearthed tools, jewelry, paintings, and fossilized agricultural products, indicating that the desert was once a rolling grassland that supported substantial human populations. Over the past four thousand years, long-term climate change has produced the desert we see today, slowly but significantly altering the human history of the entire continent.

In addition to these long-term influences, short-term climate variations can impose stark limitations on human communities, spurring them to adapt creatively in order to survive. Most of the African continent is characterized by a "bimodal" seasonal pattern: the year is divided into wet and dry seasons, rather than the four seasons of the earth's more temperate zones. Thus, while many parts of Africa receive nearly as much rainfall as European countries, the precipitation in Africa tends to occur within the span of a four-month rainy season, leaving a lengthy dry spell during which riverbeds can often dry up completely. African communities have adapted to these dry conditions in creative and diverse ways. Agriculturalists rotate their crops in a careful pattern to conserve water and soil, and pastoralists maintain a high level of mobility in order to make use of a wider zone of watering points and grasslands. Such human adaptations are usually the result of individual decisions in response to immediate concerns. Over the long term, a series of such decisions often develops into a noticeable historical trend, an incremental process with eventual large-scale effects.

Other geographical considerations have also influenced the history of human migration and settlement in Africa and exploration outward from its periphery. The rift valleys that scar the eastern half of the continent have guided north-south migration for thousands of years, and the deep lakes in those valleys have been focal points of human settlement since earliest times. Likewise, the oceans have shaped the direction of human movement. The Atlantic Ocean, whose trade winds blow in a steadily southward direction, made sailing near the western coast of Africa quite difficult, but the more favorable monsoon winds of the Indian Ocean have allowed East Africans since ancient times to maintain contacts with Arabia, India, and even China. From this point of view, Africa is not historically an isolated continent, but rather has been interacting with the broader world for an extraordinarily long time.

This interaction involved not only the exchange of trade items and intellectual ideas, but also an ecological exchange of plant and animal species dating back at least thirty million years. Africans incorporated many species from elsewhere and made them their own. Domesticated cattle were adapted to local African environments perhaps seven thousand years ago, and not long after that wheat and barley were worked into African agriculture. Perhaps two thousand years ago, Africans borrowed bananas from Southeast Asia and made them a staple of many African diets. More recently, important crops such as manioc (cassava) and maize (corn) were brought to Africa from across the Atlantic Ocean. African peoples used all of these ecological exchanges to dramatically modify their landscapes and the biodiversity of their environments.

Africans also interacted with their environment through the different ways in which they organized their social and economic lives. Precolonial Africa consisted of a vast network of communities in diverse environmental settings, linked together by markets, urban centers, and far-flung trading routes. In addition, different communities were often linked by ties of reciprocal obligation, through kinship or marriage alliances. All of these economic, political, and social connections provided ways by which Africans could cope with environmental adversity and shape the landscapes they inhabited. During times of severe ecological stress, such as famines or outbreaks of disease, these complex networks of human interaction were often disrupted and restructured, so that environmental history is closely intertwined with the history of African political and social institutions. Historians have even suggested that the development of many of Africa's powerful empire states, such as Mali, Aksum, and Great Zimbabwe, might have been deeply affected by the influence of long-term climate changes. At the same time, these kingdoms in turn played a large part in modifying, sometimes dramatically, the environment of precolonial Africa.

The development of the Asante Empire in central Ghana illustrates many of the ideas introduced above. Akan kingdoms predated Asante in the frontier area between the Upper Guinea forest along the coast and the interior savanna. Akan settlement and state building were fueled by two processes that dramatically altered the ecology of the area: the refinement of a forest fallow system of agriculture; and the heavy involvement of Akan in the emerging Atlantic mercantile system from the sixteenth century onward. The Akan forest fallow system involved the removal of the high forest canopy to let sunlight down onto fields, combined with careful management of the succession of forest regrowth to improve farming conditions. At the same time, the Atlantic exchange was transporting humans, food crops, and diseases among Africa, Europe, and the "New World." One byproduct of this exchange was that Akan farmers began to experiment with cassava and maize imported to West Africa aboard Portuguese ships from the Americas. These new crops proved well suited to forest agriculture, and soon provided the foundation for an expanding population. The Asante Empire, which rose in the eighteenth century, built upon these earlier legacies, so that by the reign of Osei Bonsu in the early nineteenth century, the landscape of central Ghana was hardly "natural" at all, but rather the result of careful human manipulation over the course of several hundred years.

The environmental history of precolonial Africa is not merely the result of the impacts from large-scale kingdoms and empires. Stateless, decentralized societies have also played an important role in shaping Africa's diverse landscapes. The broad savannas of East Africa, for example, are largely a product of human manipulation. Pastoralists have been in East Africa for at least four thousand years, and the continual grazing of their cattle, combined with occasional brush fires, has helped to maintain the grasslands that support wildlife. The Maasai, who came to prominence during the nineteenth century, practiced a highly sophisticated form of transhumant pastoralism, in which small groups of stock-owning families move in seasonal and yearly cycles across a wide stretch of land. Maasai range management techniques included the rotation of grazing patterns, the use of dry-season reserves, and the use of special grazing areas near homesteads for calves. They were keen observers of their environments, recognizing distinctions between several types of grasses and their nutritional value for livestock, and using trees and other plants for fencing, medicine, building materials, and a variety of other purposes. The Maasai also established wide-ranging trade linkages, acquiring agricultural produce, iron implements, clothes, and ornaments in exchange for goods produced from their cattle.

Coinciding with the colonial expansion into Africa in the late nineteenth century, a catastrophic wave of disease and famine swept across the eastern side of the continent. These disasters set the context in which many of the early colonial conquests were undertaken, and deeply influenced their outcomes. Between 1888 and 1892, for example, a triple disaster of rinderpest, drought, and infestation by locusts and caterpillars swept across Ethiopia, demolishing the country's agricultural system and leading to a time remembered as the "Great Famine." The Italians took advantage of the famine to advance unopposed into northern Ethiopia, but Emperor Menelik rallied his people by radically altering the form of agricultural production and distribution, eventually defeating the Italians and bringing several southern peripheral areas under Ethiopian control. In this case, environmental disaster had actually led to a consolidation of African state power and military strength. In other areas, such as the Mahdist state in Sudan, quite the opposite occurred: the ecological disaster crippled any possibility of military resistance to the colonial intrusion.

During the colonial era, Africans continued to interact with and modify their environments as they had before, but they were now acting within the overarching political context of colonial administration. European imperialists came to Africa with their own ideas of what Africa should look like, and when reality did not meet their expectations, colonial policy was often enacted to reshape Africa into the romantic image of the continent held by Europeans. At the same time, colonial administrations were primarily concerned with economic profit, and environmental policy had to be crafted to best suit maximum production. Within the new structure of power created by colonial occupation, Europeans to a certain extent were able to take over the role of modifying African landscapes, but without the benefit of the detailed environmental knowledge and experience Africans had gained during the past several centuries. Colonial policies and European cultural attitudes relating to wildlife conservation, forestry, agriculture, and soil erosion were often inherited by subsequent independent African governments and development agencies, and continue to affect Africa's environments to the present day.

CHRISTIAN JENNINGS

See also: **Neolithic, Pastoral: Eastern Africa; Rinderpest and Smallpox: East and Southern Africa.**

Further Reading

Adams, J. S., and T. O. McShane, *The Myth of Wild Africa: Conservation Without Illusions.* Berkeley: University of California Press, 1996.

Anderson, D., and R. Grove, eds. *Conservation in Africa: People, Policies, and Practice.* Cambridge: Cambridge University Press, 1987.

Beinart, W., and P. Coates. *Environment and History: The Taming of Nature in the USA and South Africa.* London: Routledge, 1995.

Fairhead, J., and M. Leach. *Misreading the African Landscape: Society and Ecology in a Forest-Savanna Mosaic.* Cambridge: Cambridge University Press, 1996.

Ford, J. *The Role of the Trypanosomiases in African Ecology: A Study of the Tsetse Fly Problem.* Oxford: Clarendon Press, 1971.

Johnson, D. H., and D. M. Anderson, eds. *The Ecology of Survival: Case Studies from Northeast African History.* London: Lester Crook, 1988.

Kjekshus, H. *Ecology Control and Economic Development in East African History.* London: James Currey, 1996.

Maddox, G., J. Giblin, and Isaria N. Kimambo, eds. *Custodians of the Land: Ecology & Culture in the History of Tanzania.* London: James Currey, 1996.

McCann, J. C. *Green Land, Brown Land, Black Land: An Environmental History of Africa, 1800–1990*, Portsmouth, N.H.: Heinemann, 1999.

Ogot, B. A., ed. *Hadith 7: Ecology and History in East Africa.* Nairobi: Kenya Literature Bureau, 1979.

German South West Africa: *See* Namibia, (Southwest Africa): German Colonization, 1893–1896.

Ghana Empire: Historiography of Origins

As long as Leo Africanus and Luis del Mármol Carvajal were the principal sources for early West African history, European scholars believed that state-formation in Sudanic Africa had been initiated by North African Arabs together with the Saharan Berber nomads who had conquered much of the region in the late eleventh century. In 1821 the British geographer James MacQueen, for example, described Ghana as the richest and most important kingdom that the Arabs ruled in the interior of Africa. This picture began to change when medieval Arabic sources for West African historical geography became available to European scholars. These sources proved that the kingdoms of Sudanic Africa were much older than Leo Africanus and Mármol had claimed. Friedrich Stüwe, who published in 1836 a study on the long distance trade of the Arabs in the Middle Ages, suggested (relying in this matter upon the recently discovered work of al-Bakrī) that black Africans had established their first kingdoms, such as Ghana and Takrur, independently before their contacts with the Islamic civilization through trans-Saharan trade in the tenth century.

The medieval Arabic sources are, however, silent concerning the actual founders of Ghana and the other early kingdoms of the Sudanic zone. These sources merely confirm that the kingdom of Ghana existed at the time of the Arab conquest of North Africa in the late seventh century and that it was already then ruled by a pagan black monarch. Therefore, William Desborough Cooley, who established the modern historiography of Western Africa, left the question on the origins of Ghana unanswered. Cooley seems to have shared implicitly Stüwe's view that the state formation in Sudanic Africa had begun independently, for he believed that black

Africans had, in a remote past, extended their domination much deeper into the Sahara than nowadays. Moreover, Cooley considered that the Berber nomads of the Sahara were incapable of establishing and maintaining any large political units.

The first European scholar to seriously speculate on the origins of Ghana was Heinrich Barth who had found a copy of *Ta'rīkh al-Sūdān* during his travels in Hausaland. According to this chronicle, the earliest state in Sudanic West Africa had been the powerful empire of Kayamagha, which, according to Barth, was the Ghana of the medieval Arabic authors. This identification seemed plausible because the capital of Kayamagha was called "Gana." Twenty-two rulers had reigned in the empire of Kayamagha before the *hijra* (622) and twenty-two after that. No other dates are given for Kayamagha. On the basis of this information Barth concluded that the empire of Kayamagha (that is, ancient Ghana) had been established around 300. The founders of Kayamagha had been (according to *Ta'rīkh al-Sūdān*), "white," although nothing was known of their ethnicity. Barth concluded that they had been either the Berbers of the Sahara or the Fulani. The first choice was supported by al-Bakrī's mention of the matrilinear inheritance followed by the kings of Ghana. The matrilinear inheritance was typical for the nomads of the Sahara, and Barth believed that it was introduced to the black kings of Ghana by their Berber ancestors. The latter choice, the Fulani, was backed by the indisputable fact that the Fulani had recently conquered much of Sudanic Africa from Senegal to the borders of Bornu, thus proving their skill in forming large political units. Furthermore, the Fulani were not considered true blacks; although European scholars could not agree on their ancestry, all agreed that they were more intelligent and civilized than other peoples of western Africa, thanks to their claimed Semitic inheritance.

Belief in the non-African origins of Ghana strengthened at the turn of the nineteenth century. There were three reasons for this. The first was the new ideology which emphasized the inequality of races. According to the colonial historians, the seeds of civilization in Sub-Saharan Africa had been planted by more advanced "white" peoples from the Mediterranean (at present this task was carried on by the colonial powers), whereas the blacks were capable of only serving their "white" masters. The second reason was the discovery of West African oral historical traditions, following the colonial conquest of Sudanic Africa. Many of these traditions trace the origins of the ruling Sudanese dynasties either to the companions of Prophet Muhammad or to Jemeni warriors. The purpose of these genealogies was to link the dynasties to the sacred history of Islam, but the colonial historians, who were eager to find white founders for the ancient Sudanese empires, took the

oral traditions literally, as if the genealogies were historical records. The third reason was the more general hypothesis of cultural diffusion in world history. It was believed that no nation could civilize itself, but it had to learn the basic elements of civilization—such as agriculture, pottery, and metallurgy—from outsiders. The cultural diffusion could only take place through migration. Of course, there had to be a place where the basic elements of civilization were developed for the first time. According to European historians, this cradle was Mesopotamia, whence civilization had gradually spread to other parts of the "Old World."

Following this ideological context, several fantastic theories on the origins of Ghana were proposed by Western authors. In 1896 the French reporter Felix Dubois (1862–1943), who followed in the footsteps of the French army from Senegal to Timbuktu, searched for the origins of the Sudanese civilization in the Nile Valley. He toyed with the idea that Jenne might originally have been an ancient Egyptian colony. Dubois's hypothesis sounded reasonable. Already Heinrich Barth had considered it possible that the Niger bend area had received its civilization from ancient Egypt. Evidence for Dubois's hypothesis on the connection between the middle Niger Valley and Egypt were the architectural parallels that Dubois found in the houses of Jenne and the tombs of pharaonic Egypt.

Dubois's hypothesis was elaborated by the British journalist Flora Shaw (Lady Lugard, 1852–1929) who in 1905 wrote that Ghana was established by a white people whose ancestry was in Mesopotamia and Persia. She assumed that this people descended from the soldiers who had belonged to the unfortunate army that Great King Cambyses of Persia sent to conquer Ethiopia in 525. Her hypothesis was in accordance with the theory, which she considered the most logically supported, that the Fulani originated from India.

In 1906 the French lieutenant Desplagnes published a book in which he claimed that the founders of Ghana were descendants of Carthaginian settlers. A proof for his hypothesis was the resemblance between the two names, "Ganna" (as he called Ghana) and the Punic family name of "Hanno." Another proof was the custom among the Bozo and the Sorko, who were considered to be the oldest inhabitants of the Niger inland delta, of burying their dead in vast jars; a similar custom had also existed in Carthage. Furthermore, the old men of Hombori had told Desplagnes that red conquerors from the east had brought the civilization to the middle Niger Valley.

The most popular theory on the founders of Ghana was expressed in 1912 by Maurice Delafosse in his influential *Haut-Sénégal-Niger*, which dominated the historiography of western Africa until the early 1960s. According to Delafosse, ancient Ghana had been established by a group of Jewish refugees who escaped the Roman revenge from Cyrenaica after their unsuccessful revolt in 117. Led by their chief Kara, the refugees arrived in the Niger inland delta in about 150. They were the ancestors of the present Fulani. Having finally settled in the western Sahel, the descendants of Kara subjugated the local blacks and established the empire of Ghana around the year 300 (actually the city of Ghana had been established by the blacks around 200BCE). This empire flourished under the Judeo-Syrian dynasty until the year 790, when the black subjects revolted and massacred their Semitic lords. During this chaos, Kaya-Maghan Sissé, the ruler of the neighboring kingdom of Wagadu, conquered Ghana. This conquest finally created the black empire of Ghana, which is familiar to us from the medieval Arabic sources. Delafosse cited no explicit sources for his story of the Judeo-Syrian founders of Ghana, which is, in fact, a skillful construction based on Fulani oral traditions concerning their Middle Eastern origins and on various unconnected hypotheses expressed in previous works dealing with the early history of Sudanic West Africa. Delafosse's hypothesis survived, as it corresponded exactly with the ideology of colonialism.

PEKKA MASONEN

Further Reading

Barth, H. *Travels and Discoveries in North and Central Africa Being a Journal of an Expedition Undertaken under the Auspices of H.B.M's Government in the Years 1849–1855*. London: Frank Cass, 1965.

Cooley, W. D. *The Negroland of the Arabs Examined and Explained; or An Inquiry into the Early History and Geography of Central Africa*. 1841. 2nd ed., with a bibliographical introduction by John Ralph Willis, London: Frank Cass, 1966.

Delafosse, M. *Haut-Sénégal-Niger*. 3 vols. Paris, 1912.

Desplagnes, L. *Le Plateau Central Nigérien: Une mission archéologique et ethnographique au Soudan Français*. Paris, 1907.

Dubois, F. *Tombouctou la mysterieuse*. Paris, 1896.

MacQueen, J. *A Geographical and Commercial View of Northern Central Africa: Containing a Particular Account of the Course and Termination of the Great River Niger in the Atlantic Ocean*. Edinburgh, 1821.

Masonen, P. *The Negroland Revisited. Discovery and Invention of the Sudanese Middle Ages*. Helsinki: Finnish Academy of Science and Letters, 2000.

Mounkaïla, F. "Ancestors from the East in Sahelo-Sudanese Myth: Dinga Soninké, Zabarkane Zarma, and Other." *Research in African Literatures* 24 (1993): 13–21.

Shaw, F. *A Tropical Dependency. An Outline of the Ancient History of the Western Sudan with an Account of the Modern Settlement of Northern Nigeria*. London, 1905.

Ghana, Empire of: History of

The ancient kingdom of Ghana was founded in the western part of the savanna region of West Africa. Arabs who conquered North Africa in the seventh and eighth centuries referred to the area as *Bilad-al-Sudan* ("Land of Black People"), hence the modern name of Sudan.

The largest group of indigenous inhabitants, the Soninke, was involved in subsistence farming and pastoralism. They grew a variety of crops, but the primary food crop was millet. The location of the kingdom, between the fertile upper sections of the Senegal and Niger Rivers, facilitated farming.

Given that most of the West African savanna was free of the tsetse fly, the Soninke practiced pastoralism, keeping cattle, sheep, and goats for their meat, milk and skins. Ghana was also endowed with plentiful mineral deposits, especially iron ore and gold. Ghana was the first state in the western Sudan to acquire iron technology.

By at least 400, the Soninke had acquired knowledge of iron smelting. The Soninke were therefore able to produce iron implements such as hoes, knives, axes, and iron-headed arrows.

However, the most important mineral in terms of Ghana's power as a kingdom was gold. It was produced in the Wangara region in the southern part of the Kingdom. This was alluvial gold that was washed down from the highlands by the Niger and Senegal Rivers and their tributaries. From the Wangara region, gold was transported by porters to Kumbi-Saleh, the capital town of the kingdom further north. In Kumbi-Saleh, gold was sold to North African traders, the Berbers and Arabs, who transported it to North Africa. Some of this gold was sold to consumers in North Afria and the rest was exported to Europe and the Middle East.

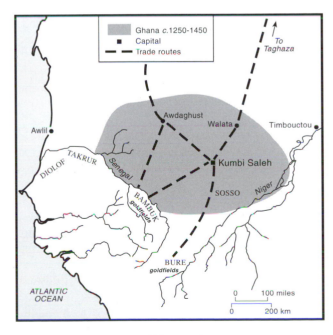

Ghana Empire, eighth–twelfth centuries.

Ghana was widely known because of its large deposits of gold, which made ancient Ghana a rich kingdom.

The kingdom's location in the savannah region enabled it to develop commercial relations with both North Africa and the forest region in the south, and thus play a major role in the trans-Saharan trade. Since Ghana was located in a plain, traders found it easy to traverse its territories during their trading activities. The western trans-Saharan trade route, which started from Sijilmasa in Morocco and passed through Taghaza and Awdoghast in the Sahara desert, had Kumbi-SAleh as its southern terminal. Goods from North Africa were exchanged for goods from the forest region further south in the towns of Ghana. Using revenue collected from the trans-Saharan trade, the rulers of Ghana were able to meet the expenses of administering the kingdom.

Kumbi-Saleh was both the capital and main commercial center of Ghana. It was located in the southeastern part of the modern state of Mauritanian, and lay about two hundred miles north of Bamako (capital of modern Mali). It was composed of two sections lying about six miles apart. One of these sections was called "Al Ghaba" ("forest"), due to the thicket around it. This section, where the majority of the Soninke residents lived, was primarily made up of grass-thatched huts with mud walls. The government was located in this section; the *Gāna* (king of Ghana) lived here in a stone palace fitted with glass windows and surrounded by a fence, thus showing the influence of North African Muslims, who had introduced this style of building. The Soninke employees of the government of Ghana lived in this section of the town as well.

Although Ghanian monarchs had not embraced Islam before 1076, as they practiced traditional religions, they allowed a mosque to be constructed near the palace for the use of Muslim ambassadors and North African Muslims who were employed as civil servants at the court because they were literate in Arabic and thus helped the kings communicate with the outside world.

The other section of Kumbi-Saleh was known as the Muslim section. It was composed of well-constructed stone buildings; their architectural style was introduced by North African Muslim traders. This was the commercial and educational center of Kumbi-Saleh. It had many Quranic schools and about twelve mosques. Young Muslim converts were taught Islamic theology as they read and wrote in Arabic and recited the Qur'an. This neighborhood was the center from which Islam spread to other parts of Ghana and western Sudan. The North African Muslim traders interacted freely with Muslim traders from other African regions and took African women as wives or concubines, converting them and their offspring to Islam.

Kumbi-Saleh played a major role in the trans-Saharan trade. It was one of the leading commercial centers in the western Sudan. Goods from North Africa and the Sahara desert were exchanged with goods from western Sudan and the forest states further south. The Arab and Berber merchants from North Africa brought goods such as mirrors, horses, silk cloth, glasses, palm dates, razor blades, and salt and exchanged these goods with the Soninke and other southern African traders. The southern African traders provided goods such as gold, kola nuts, ostrich feathers, and slaves. Some of the slaves offered for sale at Kumbi-Saleh had been captured during the wars of conquest, as the Soninke of Ghana invaded the neighboring territories, and the rest were captured during the raids in the forest states. The commercial transactions that were conducted in Kumbi-Saleh were based on barter trade.

The North African traders used some of the Soninke in Kumbi-Saleh as their agents for carrying on trade throughout the year. The Soninke agents made arrangements for the accommodation of the North African traders during their stay in Kumbi-Saleh. In addition to this, they ensured that the North African traders maintained goods relations with the rulers of Ghana. The Soninke agents advised the North African traders to give gifts to the rulers of Ghana so that the latter would not interfere with trade.

However, the trans-Saharan trade was not always beneficial to Ghana, for it provoked resentment and envy from its neighbors. For example, the Saharan Berbers based at the town of Awdoghast, north of Kumbi-Saleh, were envious of Ghana's prosperity. They wanted to control the trans-Saharan trade and make Awdoghast the southern terminal of the western trans-Saharan route instead of Kumbi-Saleh. It was partly with the aim of controlling the thriving trans-Saharan trade that in 1076, a group of Saharan Berbers called the Almoravids invaded Ghana, sacked its capital, and imposed their control over the kingdom. The chaos that followed the Almoravid invasion disrupted trade and weakened Ghana's position as a major participant in the trans-Saharan trade. Active trade henceforth shifted further east, where there were strong governments to offer protection to traders and their merchandise. The Almoravids ruled Ghana until they were finally driven out by the Soninke in 1087.

SEWANYANA SENKOMAGO

See also: **Sahara: Salt: Production, Trade; Sahara: Trans-Saharan Trade; Yusef ibn Tashfin: Almoravid Empire: 1070–1147.**

Further Reading

Ajayi Ade, J. F. and M. Crowder, eds. *History of West Africa.* Vol. 1. London: Longman, 1976.

Ajayi Ade, J. F., and I. Espie, eds. *A Thousand Years of West Africa History.* University of Ibandan Press, 1969.

Boahen, A. A. *Topics in West African History.* London: Longman, 1966.

Crowder, M., and G. Abdullahi. *A History of West Africa A.D. 100 to the Present.* London: Longman, 1979.

Mauny, R. A. "The Question of Ghana." *Africa.* 24, no. 3 (1954).

Ghana (Republic of): 1800–1874

By the beginning of the nineteenth century, the people of the Gold Coast were connected through the intricacies of trade and the political structure of Asante. The only area free of Asante suzerainty was the Fante region, but this changed in 1807, when Asante conquered the area. The major areas under Asante rule in the north included Banda, Bron, Dagomba, Gonja, Guasso, Gyaman, Nkoransa, Nsoko, and Takyiman; in the southeast there were the Ga and Adanme, and in the eastern region were the Assin, Sehwi, Denkyera, Wassaw, and Nzima.

In 1807 Asante finally conquered the Fante states in order to gain a direct trade access to the coast and to punish the Fante for providing shelter for two Assin chiefs, Kwadwo Tsibu and Kwaku Aputae. The Asante consolidated their defeat of the Fante in further engagements in 1809, 1810, 1811, and 1814–1816. Following these campaigns, Fante chiefs who were deemed disloyal to Asante were replaced by ones who were favorably disposed toward Asante.

Following Asante's conquest of the Fante, the Fante provinces were expected to pay tribute and taxes, but with the encouragement of the British, the Fante refused to pay and to acknowledge Asante authority. Fante unwillingness to accept Asante rule, and the reluctance of the British to hand over the notes on the castles to Asante, and to pay rent for the land on which the castles were situated, led the British to dispatch missions to the

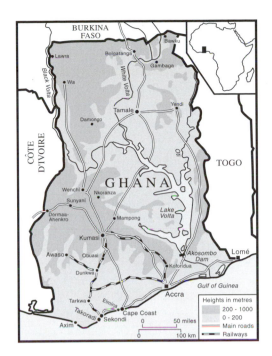

Ghana.

Asantehene in 1816 and 1819. According to the treaty resulting from these mission, Asante retained sovereignty over the Fante, but the British assumed administrative and judicial jurisdiction over the Fante. When Britain failed to ratify the treaty, the Asantehene ordered his ambassador to leave Cape Coast, the seat of British government on the Gold Coast, and placed it under blockade in 1821. In this same year, the administration of British forts and possessions on the Gold Coast were transferred from the African company of merchants to the British governor of Sierra Leone, Sir Charles MacCarthy. The governor who arrived on the Gold Coast in March 1821 provoked hostilities with Asante by his lack of understanding of the Asante problem and his failure to recognize the position of the Asantehene. Conflict between the British and Asante resulted in an invasion of the southern states in 1824.

MacCarthy lost his life in an encounter with the Asante in 1824. Later in 1824, Asante suffered serious setbacks in their conflict with the British and their allies and suffered serious reversals that culminated in heavy defeat in 1826 in the Battle of Katamanso. The victory of 1826 secured independence from Asante for the southern states of the Gold Coast. The period following Asante's defeat marked a period of decline and disintegration for the state and the growth of the power of Asante war chiefs.

While Asante's relations with the southern provinces of the Gold Coast were more chaotic, Asante kings achieved a measure of stability in the north and were

The Cape Coast slave fort in Ghana. © Henning Christoph/Das Fotoarchiv.

able to maintain tributary arrangements and trade regulations. For most of the nineteenth century the major northern provinces of Asante-Banda, Bron, Dagomba, Gonja, Guasso, Gyaman, Nkoransa, Nsoko, and Takyiman maintained some association with it in line with the vigorous northern policy that was laid during the reign of Asantehene Osei Kwadwo (1764–1777) and further developed by Asantehene Osei Kwame (1777–1798). The Asantehene Osei Bonsu (1800–1823) also pursued a rigorous northern policy and advanced Asante trading interests in the north.

The year of Asante's invasion to the coast was also the year the British abolished the slave trade. Although the slave trade persisted after abolition, it made most of the trade on the Gold Coast illegal and the Europeans on the coast–Great Britain, Holland and Denmark–and their African partners had to find alternate trading staples. The interest of Holland and Denmark in the Gold Coast during this period was declining. Denmark was to leave the country in 1850 and Holland in 1872. Thus much of the active interaction of the people during this period was with the British. Following the abolition of the slave trade, Europeans focused their economic activities on the natural products of the country and hoped that trade in staple items like gold dust and ivory would increase. The European traders also made efforts to establish plantations and to encourage the indigenous people to grow and export cotton and coffee. But it was not until the last two decades of the nineteenth century that the bulk of the plantation efforts yielded results.

In 1828 the British settlements on the Gold Coast, which had been administered by the monarchy, were relinquished and entrusted to a committee of London merchants. Much of the responsibility for administering the settlements fell upon George Maclean, who was appointed governor in 1830. The significant political and economic expansion that took place under Maclean can be regarded as an important phase of British involvement on the Gold Coast. Maclean negotiated a peace treaty between Asante and the coastal states, and this peace led to trade expansion and prosperity. Fante traders traveled inland to Asante, and Asante state traders under the direction of the *Gaasewahene* who functioned as head of the exchequer and the *Batahene* or chief of trade, ventured south and north to trade. Some of the southern states like Akuapem and Krobo were also able to expand their palm oil plantations, and the export of palm oil increased. The British crown resumed the control of the Gold Coast settlements in 1843 following investigation of British merchants trading with Portuguese and Spanish slave ships.

The growing trade and prosperity on the gold Coast from the 1830s resulted in the rise of an African merchant class that actively participated in the import and export trade. This trade was enhanced by London merchants like Forster, Smith, and Swanzy, which sent quantities of goods on credit to correspondents on the Gold Coast to be sold on commission. The formation of the African Steamship Company in 1852 for trade in West Africa both regularized and shortened the journey between England and the Gold Coast. By the 1850s, however, the prevailing system of credit and intense competition from European traders began to affect the commercial operations of the African merchants, and a large number of them went bankrupt.

While the economic and political power of Africans declined, the power of the British on the Gold Coast increased. In 1850, the British separated the administration of the Gold Coast from that of Sierra Leone; this created a need for increased government staff and greater expense. It was the need to meet the increasing expense of the government that led to the Poll Tax Ordinance in 1852. In spite of opposition from educated, urban Africans, the ordinance went into effect. Efforts to collect the taxes resulted in riots, and in 1854 there were riots in Accra that led to the bombardment of Labadi, Teshi, and Christiansburg. In the Krobo area, they refused to pay the tax, which led to a fine of £8,125 which was to be paid in oil to an African agent who had paid the original fine. The increase in British authority was also resisted by some of the coastal chiefs like Chief John Aggrey of Cape Coast. When in 1866 Aggrey wrote protesting British interference in his affairs, he was arrested, deposed, and exiled to Sierra Leone.

In 1863 developments on the Gold Coast were affected by the resumption of hostilities between Asante and the British. The immediate cause of the hostilities was the refusal of the British to hand over two Asante fugitives. The disastrous campaign that the British waged against Asante shook the confidence of the people of the southern states. The war with Asante in 1863 brought the question of defending the southern states to the fore. Rumors of a British departure following the parliamentary select committee of 1865 report made the problem of defense urgent. The British did not withdraw in 1865, but following an exchange of forts between the English and the French, educated Fante and their chiefs met at Mankessim to form the Fante Confederation. In spite of hostile British attitude toward the movement, the Fante drew up a document for self-government and self-defense. However, another war between the southern states in 1873–1874 shifted the focus of the people to preparation for war. When the war ended in 1874, Britain declared the southern area of the Gold Coast a protectorate and abolished domestic slavery in the country.

EDWARD REYNOLDS

Further Reading

Arhin, K. *West African Traders in Ghana in the Nineteenth Century*. London: Longman, 1979.

McCarthy, M. *Social Change and Growth of British Power in the Gold Coast Fante States 1807–1874*. New York: University Press of America, 1988.

Reynolds, E. *Trade and Economic Change on the Gold Coast, 1807–1874*. London: Longman, 1974.

Wilks, I. *Asante in the Nineteenth Century*. Cambridge: Cambridge University Press, 1970.

Ghana (Republic of): Colonization and Resistance, 1875–1901

Although Europeans have been in contact with the peoples of Ghana since the late fifteenth century, the actual colonization of that country did not really begin until the 1830s, during the administration of George Maclean, who was appointed by the committee of British merchants operating on the coast. The process, however, proceeded by fits and starts. Indeed, it was not until July 1874 that, after inflicting a decisive defeat on the Asante, Great Britain decided to convert the area south of the Pra-Ofin confluence into a British crown colony and protectorate. From that time, the colonization of the country went through two phases, from 1875 to 1890 and from 1890 to 1901.

The first phase of colonization of the country (1875 to 1890) proceeded in the same reluctant, hesitant, and almost absent-minded manner as before. From 1874 to 1879, Britain demonstrated a certain amount of enthusiasm for colonization, with the annexation of the coastal areas east of the Volta as far as Anlo and Aflao, and inland as far as Agbosome, mainly with a view to checking the smuggling that was going on in those areas. This enthusiasm soon dried up. However, in 1884, in response to the sudden annexation of the coast of Togo by Germany signaling the beginning of the "Scramble" for West Africa, Britain rushed east of the Volta to conclude treaties with the Ewe states of Anlo, Mafi, Vume, Tefle, and Krepi in 1884; Akwamu in 1886; and Anum in 1888. Britain also signed an agreement with Germany in 1888 declaring the area from Yeji to Yendi to the northeast as a neutral zone. In 1890 Britain and Germany signed a treaty that divided Eweland into two, the eastern half including Anlo, Some, Klikor, Peki, and Tongu falling to the British and becoming part of the Gold Coast Colony, while the rest of Eweland fell to Germany and became Togo. In 1899 the neutral zone was also finally divided, splitting the kingdom of Dagomba into British and German zones.

Nothing illustrates the reluctant and hesitant nature of British colonization during this period better than the fact that, in spite of its invasion and conquest of Asante in 1874, Britain left the region alone. For the most part it was not until 1889 that, partly to checkmate French expansion northward and eastward from Côte d'Ivoire, and partly to prevent the revival of the power of Asante, Britain sent its first mission to conclude treaties of protection with Gyaaman and Atebubu, states north of Asante, in 1889 and 1890, respectively. It followed this up with a mission by the Fante, George Ekem Ferguson, in April 1892 who succeeded in concluding similar treaties of protection with the chiefs of Bole, Daboya, Dagomba, and Bimbila between 1893 and 1894, and others with Mossi, Mamprusi, and Chakosi chiefs. In 1895 the British rushed north in a very hot race with the French to occupy Bole in the northwest and Gambaga in the northeast. The Anglo-German treaties of 1885 and 1890 defined the eastern boundaries of Ghana, while the Anglo-French treaties of 1889 and 1898 delineated the present northern and western boundaries.

Even more hesitant and reluctant was the British colonization of Asante. It was not until 1891 that Britain really embarked on the colonization of Asante with an offer of a treaty of protection. When this was firmly rejected, it was not until 1894 that British repeated that offer and undertook to pay the Asante chiefs a monthly stipend if they would agree to accept a British resident in Kumasi. But this was also firmly rejected. In 1895, however, alarmed by the possibility of a French occupation, and more especially by the successful outcome of the negotiation for an alliance between Prempe, the Asantehene, and the great Mandingo leader, Almami Samori, the new secretary of states for colonies, Joseph Chamberlain, an arch-imperialist, ordered the invasion and conquest of Asante. The British army entered Kumasi in January 1896 without firing a shot since Prempe had decided not to fight to save his kingdom from utter destruction and the Golden Stool from sequestration. In spite of this, he was arrested together with his mother, father, brother, and some Kumasi chiefs and exiled first to Sierra Leone in 1896 and then to the Seychelles in 1900. This ended the territorial colonization of the country.

The Ghanaian traditional rulers and their peoples did not sit down unconcerned to watch their sovereignty and culture being trampled upon, but they resorted to all sorts of strategies first to oppose the imposition of colonization, including direct confrontation armed conflicts and rebellions. Thus, from 1874 onward, the Anlo rebelled and attacked the British forces under Glover, but they were defeated and forced to sign a treaty to accept British occupation. But they continued the resistance to the exercise of British jurisdiction in their area. In 1878 the people of Denu burned down the factory of Messrs Alexander Millers Brothers and Company. In 1884–1885, with the assistance of Geraldo de Lima, a great trader, the Anlo again rebelled and led by their chiefs Tsigui of Anyako and Tenge Dzokoto, they attacked the police escort sent to arrest de Lima and released him. But he was recaptured and detained at the Elmina Castle from May 1885 to November 1893. With an army of 3,000, the Anlo attacked the district commissioner of Keta fourteen miles west of Keta during which the he was seriously wounded and two Hausa soldiers were killed. The armed rebellion, nevertheless, continued until 1889 when it was suppressed. The people of Tavieve also took up arms in 1888 to prevent being subjected to the rule of Peki by the British.

But the most determined and protracted resistance during the period was put up by the Asante. As has already been pointed out, when the British abandoned their hesitant attitude and offered protection to the Asantehene in 1891, Prempe turned the offer down firmly but politely. When the British repeated this offer in 1894, Prempe again rejected it and sent a delegation to England to plead his cause of ensuring the continued sovereign existence of his kingdom. This powerful delegation left Kumasi in November 1894 and arrived in England in April 1895. Though it remained in London till November, the British government refused to receive it. Indeed, it was while the delegation was in England that the secretary of state ordered the invasion and conquest of Asante. As indicated already, although Prempe refused to put up any resistance, he was arrested with others and exiled first to Sierra Leone in 1896 and to the Seychelles in 1900.

It was this most unexpected arrest and above all the highly provocative and irreverent request by the governor for the Golden Stool, that sacred symbol of the soul and unity of the Asante on which even the Asantehene never sits, to be surrendered to him so that he could sit on, which touched off the Asante rebellion of 1900 under the leadership of Yaa Asantewaa, the old queen of Edweso of about sixty years of age, to expel the British from Asante. This rebellion began with the siege of the governor in the Kumasi fort in April with a force of 6,000 men that lasted till June when the Governor was compelled to leave the fort for the coast "to hazard death from rebel bullets in preference to death by starvation," and he and his detachment fought their way through rebel forces before he reached the coast in July 1900.

Using the new method of stockades, which they built all over the place, the Asante were able to harass and resist all the relief columns and reinforcements sent into Asante from the coast. It was not until November that the rebellion was suppressed. Yaa Asantewaa and the other rebel leaders were arrested and deported to join Prempe in the Seychelles where Yaa Asantewaa, then very old, died on October 17, 1921. Having crushed this rebellion, the British completed the colonization of the country with the passing of three orders-in-council

in September 1901 constituting Asante, Northern Territiories, and the Crown Colony and Protectorate into the British colony of the Gold Coast, now Ghana.

In the areas south of the Pra where colonization had been entrenched since 1874, the traditional rulers and their people also put up strong resistance but not to drive out the imperialists but to oppose or reform or seek participation in the new colonial measures and institutions that were introduced for the administration and economic exploitation of the country such as new legislative and executive councils, native jurisdiction ordinances, land bills, and direct taxation. The strategies that they resorted to here consisted less and less of armed conflicts and more and more of peaceful rallies, demonstrations, the press and literary campaigns, and petitions and demonstrations to the local colonial administration or to the home government in London. These strategies were originally organized at the local level by the traditional rulers, but from the 1860s onward nationally by the protonationalist movements and societies formed and led by the traditional rulers and the rising educated and professional elite. These movements included the Fante Confederation and the Accra Native Confederation of the 1860s and early 1870s, the *Mfantsi Amanbuhu Fekuw* (Fante National Society) of the 1880s, which was converted into the Aborigines' Rights Protection Society (ARPS) of the 1890s. Using newspapers such as the *Gold Coast Times*, the *Western Echo*, the *Gold Coast Chronicle*, and through petitions such as the one sent by the *Mfantsi Amanbuhu Fekuw* to the colonial secretary in 1889, and deputations sent to London in 1898 by the ARPS, the societies demanded representation on the legislative council. They vehemently opposed the introduction of direct taxation, and the appropriation of all so-called empty lands by the government as well as the condemnation of African culture-names, dressing, religion, and traditions. These protonationalist movements only won a few concessions such as direct taxation, land ownership by Ghanaians, and token representation on the legislative council, but they could not fundamentally alter the exploitative, unrepresentative, and culturally arrogant aspects of colonization until the 1950s and 1960s.

A. ADU BOAHEN

Further Reading

Agbodeka, F. *African Politics and British Policy in the Gold Coast, 1868–1900*. London: Longman, 1971.

Boahen, A. A. *Ghana: Evolution and Change in the Nineteenth and Twentieth Centuries*. London: Longman, 1975.

Crowder, M., ed. *West African Resistance: The Military Response to Colonial Occupation*. London: Hutchinson Library for Africa, 1971.

Kimble, D. *A Political History of Ghana: The Rise of Gold Coast Nationalism, 1850–1928*. Oxford: Clarendon Press, 1963.

Ward, W. E. F. *A History of Ghana.* London: George Allen and Unwin, 1967.

Ghana (Republic of) (Gold Coast): Colonial Period: Administration

As British authority increased on the Gold Coast (the colonial name of Ghana) in the 1860s, administrators were intolerant of any challenge to their authority, as evidenced by Governor Conran's deportation of King Aggrey of Cape Coast in 1866 and Governor Ussher's deportation of King Kobena Gyan of Elmina in 1872. At the same time, they recognized the need for local authority figures if they were to carry out even limited sanitary improvements in the coastal towns. The war against the Asante in 1873–1874, and the need for porters further underscored the need for chiefly support. Neither did British administrators want to alienate the chiefs and have them make common cause with the "educated natives" of the coast to challenge British rule as had happened during the short-lived Fante Confederation from 1868 to 1873. Most of all, they recognized that there were not enough British judges to maintain law and order. Traditionally, this was one of the chief's main functions.

In 1878 there was a first attempt to pass an ordinance "to facilitate and regulate the exercise in the Protected Territories of certain powers and jurisdiction by Native Authorities," but in anticipation of chiefly protest over the lack of stipends to be paid to them this legislation was never implemented. The gold-mining boom in the Tarkwa area made it imperative to recognize some sort of native authority, and in 1883 Governor Rowe enacted the 1878 legislation with the major modification that decisions by native tribunals could be appealed in the British courts. Initially this ordinance was applied to only six head chiefs in the Protectorate area outside the coastal settlement. Even so there were many officials who felt that it was only a short-term expedient and that the chiefs would eventually lose their power.

However, the Supreme Court's ruling in the 1887 case of *Oppon v. Ackinie* that the Supreme Court ordinance had "in no way impaired the judicial powers of native kings and chiefs, and that...[no] other ordinance had taken them away" boosted chiefly power. King Ackinie, who had appealed the decisions of lower courts, was a chief in the protectorate, but the long-term significance of this ruling was that the distinction between the colony and the protected territories was breaking down. At the turn of the century there were also a number of governors who had served in some of Britain's Far Eastern colonies who were enthusiastic supporters of what Governor Sir William Maxwell described as "decentralization." The annexation of Asante and the orders in council that defined the boundaries of the Northern Territories, Asante, and the Gold Coast Colony allowed the governor to claim that the ambiguous relationship with the chiefs that the bond of 1844 had defined had been superseded by a new arrangement which signified that chiefly powers were not inherent but derived from the Crown. Indicative of this attitude was the government's creation in 1902 of a new department known as the secretariat of native affairs "to secure greater consistency in the administration of native affairs."

Apart from the issue of inherent jurisdiction, the equally controversial issue was which arm of government should have control over the chiefly courts, the judiciary or the political administration, and who would be responsible for the codification of "customary law." The struggle over these issues delayed the passage of a new native jurisdiction bill until 1910. Significantly, this bill extended chiefly courts to the entire colony, defined their jurisdiction, and established the fees and fines they could charge, and most importantly placed these native tribunals, as they were called, under the supervision of the district commissioners. Appeals from them went first to his court or to the provincial commissioner's court if land was in dispute.

The attractiveness of government recognition was a powerful incentive for chiefs to seek inclusion under the terms of the new Native Jurisdiction Act. The recognition of the chiefly order also provoked a response from the educated elite, who felt that the government was following a divide and rule policy. In 1916 Governor Clifford appointed three chiefs, or what were now officially referred to as *amanhin*, from the colony's three provinces to the Legislative Council and exacerbated these tensions. Further attempts to define the relationship between head chiefs and their subordinates met with considerable opposition, and not until the administration of Sir Gordon Guggisberg was legislation passed that sought to increase the integration of the chiefly order into the colony's administration. The incorporation of the chiefs of northern Nigeria into colonial administration played an important role in influencing what many historians have considered this second "interventionist" phase of indirect rule in the Gold Coast. The return of the exiled Prempe I to Kumasi in 1924 also stimulated an indirect rule policy for the Ashanti region. In addition, the policy was extended to the Northern Region, but here there was considerable difficulty finding suitable native authorities among people who were predominantly noncentralized.

In 1925, as part of the colony's new constitution, three Provincial Councils of head chiefs were established, and they were given the right to elect six of their members to sit on the expanded Legislative Council. As an indication of the greater role that the Guggisberg administration intended the chiefs to play, they were given the opportunity to introduce a new native administration ordinance. This 1927 ordinance strengthened the powers of head chiefs by giving their courts more civil and criminal jurisdiction, made them responsible for hearing stool disputes, and defined more precisely the question of their "inherent versus derived jurisdiction." It was extremely controversial and accentuated the rift that had been developing between what was then called the "intelligentsia" and the "natural leaders." The leadership of the Cape Coast-based Gold Coast Aborigines' Rights Protection Society became the most uncompromising opponents of the new ordinance and tried to prevent chiefs from attending the Provincial Councils.

Native affairs in the 1930s were characterized by bitter struggles to control chiefly positions, with the native tribunals an important prize. To prevent this and to better regulate the financial affairs of the native states, the government tried to establish state treasuries, but not until 1939 was it able to enact the Native Administration Treasuries Ordinance. Shortly afterward the native tribunals were subjected to a highly critical examination and were restructured as native courts by the Native Courts Ordinance of 1944. They had to be constituted by order of the governor, they were graded into four categories, appeal was to the Magistrates' Courts, their number was reduced, and more than 50 per cent were no longer presided over by chiefs.

This new native authority system, however, enjoyed only a short life as the pace of constitutional change quickened in the early 1950s. The British government decided to abandon the policy of indirect rule in favor of local elected government. Local authorities were to have chiefs as presidents, but the post was merely ceremonial.

ROGER GOCKING

See also: **Ghana (Republic of) (Gold Coast): Colonial Period: Economy; Ghana (Republic of): Colonization and Resistance, 1875–1901.**

Further Reading

Busia, K. A. *The Position of the Chief in the Modern Political System of Ashanti: A Study of the Influences of Contemporary Social Changes on Ashanti Political Institutions.* 1951. Reprint, London: Frank Cass and Company, 1968.

Crook, R. C. "Decolonization, the Colonial State, and Chieftaincy in the Gold Coast." *African Affairs* 85 (1986): 75–105.

Crowder, M., and Obaro Ikime, eds. *West African Chiefs.* New York: Africana Publications Corporation, 1970.

Gocking, R. *Facing Two Ways: Ghana's Coastal Communities under Colonial Rule.* Lanham, Md.: University Press of America, 1999.

Hailey, W. M. *An African Survey.* Rev. ed. 1956. London: Oxford University Press, 1957.

Kimble, D. *A Political History of Ghana 1850–1928.* London: Oxford University Press, 1963.

Lugard, F. J. *The Dual Mandate in British Tropical Africa.* 1923. Reprint, London: Frank Cass and Company, 1965.

Ghana (Republic of) (Gold Coast): Colonial Period: Economy

From the earliest period of European contact (fourteenth century), the economy of Ghana was based on gold and kola nuts. During the colonial period, cocoa farming and mining became the major industries, aided by the transport development of the early twentieth century. The result was a revolutionary transformation of the economy during the colonial period.

From its humble beginnings in 1858, cocoa became the major export of Ghana by 1911. The Basel missionaries imported cocoa seedlings from Surinam in 1858 for propagation, but the experiment was a futile exercise. A second experiment by Tete Quashie, who returned from Fernado Po with cocoa beans and planted tham at Mampon-Akwapem in 1879, yielded better results. This experiment attracted other farmers, and in 1885, 121 pounds of cocoa were exported overseas. Governor William Griffith also promoted cocoa cultivation by starting a nursery at the Aburi Botanical Gardens in 1890 to produce seedlings for distribution.

Cocoa cultivation spread rapidly throughout Akuapem and Akyem Abuakwa (1890); Asante and Brong Ahafo (1900); and other parts of Ghana after 1912. Production rose from a modest 80 pounds in 1891 to 88.9 million pounds by 1911, as energetic farmers from Akwapim migrated in bands to buy land elsewhere for cocoa production. In 1906 the industry got a further boost when William Cadbury started buying cocoa for chocolate production. Even though from 1911 onward farmers experienced hardships due to cocoa diseases, by 1951, cocoa production had risen to 300,000 tons, almost two-thirds of the country's export earnings.

This phenomenal development of the cocoa industry was an exclusively Ghanaian enterprise. The capitalistic outlook and equipment of kola farmers were transferred to cocoa production. Paradoxically, the success of cocoa was a constant source of anxiety for the colonial government. Consequently, the industry did not receive direct sustained support.

Wartime licensing created problems for cocoa farmers who suspected attempts by European purchasing companies to prevent them from shipping their cocoa directly to Europe and the United States. From 1914 growers associations were formed to fight for better prices and to ship cocoa directly to Europe and the United States and to circumvent middlemen. From 1929 cooperatives were formed for the same purpose. The struggle between farmers and middlemen led to the famous cocoa "hold-up" in 1937. A "Buying Agreement," which combined twelve cocoa purchasing firms, was perceived by farmers as an attempt to introduce monopolistic conditions into cocoa purchase. On the other hand, the 1948 Gold Coast disturbances arising out of the directive to cut down cocoa trees was a by-product of the fear that the colonial government was attempting to destroy the cocoa industry. Though not necessarily valid, farmers perceived the directive as a manifestation of the systematic opposition of the colonial government to the progress of the cocoa industry.

The changes that were taking place affected trade as well. Until the 1860s and 1870s, import-export business was a joint activity of Ghanaian merchant princes, businessmen, and overseas firms. In the last decade of the nineteenth century, however, European, Syrian, and Lebanese firms gradually took over the business sector of the country. After the consolidation of British rule over Asante in 1900, many overseas firms opened branches in Asante and later, the northern regions. Ghanaian businessmen continued to participate actively in the import-export trade, but the depression of the 1920s and European competition in the 1930s and 1940s drove many out of business. Trade in the colonial period consisted of the export of agricultural products and importation of textiles, liquor, machinery, tobacco, sugar, beads, building material and provisions.

These developments went hand in hand with the development of mining in Ghana. The gold trade had been the centerpiece of European commerce with West Africa. Gold was obtained mainly through the traditional methods of washing or panning and light digging. In the 1860s, the first steps were taken toward modern mining when one Thomas Hughes of Cape Coast used heavy machines in Western Wassa. The Wassa chief purportedly stopped him from further operations after he struck a very rich gold vein in 1861.

In 1877 the French trader J. Bonnat made another attempt at introducing machinery into gold mining. He formed the African Gold Coast Company, acquired a concession in Tarkwa in 1878, and commenced operations first at Awudua and later at Tarkwa. Encouraged by reports of gold finds, Ghanaians working by themselves or in partnership with Europeans rushed to Tarkwa, but by 1882, most of the mining companies had collapsed, leaving only six in business.

A mining revolution occurred in Ghana when E. A. Cade bought a lease at Obuasi from three Fante businessmen (J. E. Ellis, J. E. Biney, and J. P. Brown) in 1895 and formed the Ashanti Goldfields Corporation (AGC) in 1897 to operate what became one of the richest gold mines in the world. By 1901 foreign capitalists reorganized the gold industry, which had been in African hands. The success of AGC set off another gold rush in other parts of Asante and Akyem. Aided by the Sekondi-Tarkwa railway line (1898), gold production expanded dramatically between 1901 and 1911—from 60,000 ounces in 1901 to 280,000 ounces in 1911—becoming the second most important export earner for Ghana.

A geological survey in 1914 revealed quantities of manganese deposits near Nsuta. The Wasaw Exploring Syndicate, later the African Manganese Company, started mining the Dagwin-Nsuta deposits and made the first shipment of ore in September 1916. Production increased from 30,000 tons in 1918 to 527,036 in 1937.

The first major diamond deposits were found at Abomosu, and, in 1920, the newly formed Diamond Fields of Eastern Akim Limited exported the first ores from the Birim Valley near Kibi. Several European companies joined the search for diamonds at Atiankama, Akwatia, and Oda near Kade. In 1922 diamonds were also found at Bonsa but since the deposits were not large enough for commercial mining, Ghanaians flocked to the area and started digging and panning. From a few hundred carats in 1923, diamond exports reached over 750,000 carats in 1933.

The expanding economy and the concomitant increase in cocoa production and mining necessitated improvement in roads, harbors, and railways. Consequently, an inspector of roads was appointed in 1890. Added to this, in 1894, the Trade Roads Ordinance empowered chiefs to recruit their people to provide labor for six days in each quarter. Proposals for a light tramway from Cape Coast to the river were abandoned after the Wolseley expedition of 1874. Governor Brandford Griffith, the British Chamber of Commerce, and several Gold Coast towns similarly abandoned other schemes for railway lines despite suggestions in the 1890s. The biggest revolution in transportation was the construction of a deep-water harbor at Takoradi and the construction of railway lines. In 1898 the West Coast railway line was began at Sekondi. The line reached Tarkwa in May 1901, Obuasi in December 1902, and Kumasi in October 1903. In 1904 the railway line carried 91,000 passengers. In 1912 the Eastern Line from Accra ended at Mangoase. The Accra-Kumasi (started in 1909 and abandoned during the war) was completed in 1923, and by 1956, Takoradi was linked to Accra by rail. The rapid development of mining and railways brought about a considerable inflow of capital and encouraged exports between 1892 and 1910. Motor cars had been introduced in 1909, but it was not until the use of the light Ford chassis that a veritable transportation revolution took place in the Gold Coast.

In Ghana during the colonial period, the economy was marked by revolutionary changes in cocoa farming, mining, trade, and transportation.

EDMUND ABAKA

See also: **Ghana (Republic of) (Gold Coast): Colonial Period: Administration; Ghana (Republic of): Colonization and Resistance, 1875–1901.**

Further Reading

Boahen, A. *Adu, Ghana: Evolution and Change in the 19th and 20th Centuries*. London: Longman, 1975.

Cardinal, A. W. *The Gold Coast*. Accra: Government Printer, 1931.

Coombs, D. *The Gold Coast, Britain and the Netherlands 1850–74*. London: Oxford University Press, 1963.

Dickson, K. B. *A Historical Geography of Ghana*. Cambridge: Cambridge University Press, 1969.

Genoud, R. *Nationalism and Economic Development in Ghana*. New York: Praeger, 1969.

Hill, P. *Studies in Rural Capitalism in West Africa*. Cambridge, 1970.

Kay, G. B. *The Political Economy of Colonialism in Ghana: A Collection of Documents and Statistics 1900–1960*. Cambridge: Cambridge University Press, 1972.

Kimble, D. *A Political History of the Ghana. The Rise of Gold Coast Nationalism 1850–1928*. Oxford: Clarendon Press, 1963.

Macmillan, A, *The Red Book of West Africa: Historical and Descriptive, Commercial and Industrial Facts, Figures, and Resources*. London: Frank Cass, 1968.

Ghana (Republic of) (Gold Coast): Guggisberg Administration, 1919–1927

In the summer of 1928, Brigadier-General Gordon F. Guggisberg was assigned the governorship of British Guyana. Just eight months after arriving at his post, he became ill and was returned to England, where he died in 1930. From 1919 through 1927, however, Guggisberg served as governor of the Gold Coast (Ghana), and in the history of that country, he is described most favorably. In fact, in the most detailed biography, the author R. E. Wraith described Guggisberg as the "founder of the modern Gold Coast as surely Nkrumah was the founder of the modern Ghana."

There are important factors to which the administration's success can be attributed. Guggisberg's prior experience in the colony where he first arrived in 1902 for the survey of the Gold Coast and Ashanti has been cited. Seconded by the Royal Engineers to this special employment under the Colonial Office, he traveled the territories and under the aegis of the Mines Survey Department, he worked toward addressing the problem of mapping the Gold Coast. In 1906 he was appointed director of survey. Later survey work in southern Nigeria brought Guggisberg additional African experiences. Furthermore, Governor Hugh Clifford, whose position Guggisberg inherited in 1919, was said to have laid solid foundation upon which his successor could make rapid progress. For example, there was the "Clifford Constitution of 1916" by which the first Africans were allowed on the legislative council. Furthermore, the administration discussed the need for a deep-water harbor, laid some rail lines to the gold-mining regions, and also supported the establishment of elementary schools by the various Christian missions.

While the dedication with which England, and therefore the Clifford administration, assessed colonial affairs may have been retarded by World War I in Europe (1914–1917), Guggisberg arrived at his appointed post at war's end. In addition to past African experiences, the new governor inherited a budget surplus to finance parts of his development ideas. Most important, however, it was his professional training as Royal Engineer and Surveyor that allowed him the ability to understand the ramifications of the construction programs he advocated. Guggisberg was convinced that progress in the Gold Coast was dependent on the good physical health of its people. It was in light of this that the first comprehensive medical institution at Korle Bu was undertaken. Also, to exploit resources of the colony for the financing of the many construction projects, the government saw the need for an improved transportation system. The existing school system was also thought to be inadequate to sustain future developments. In his agenda for education, Guggisberg saw a central role for the colonial state. This was a radical departure from previous administrations that had not seen any need for the colonial government to become an aggressive provider of education let alone to waste resources in the funding of postelementary schooling. Guggisberg's Prince of Wales College for boys and girls, now Achimota College, was indeed a grand trophy of the government's educational policy.

Only a month after arriving at his post in 1919, Guggisberg presented a ten-year program in which his development policies were outlined. Many have lamented about how previous British governors resisted pressures to open up the hinterlands.

Thus, the start of rail construction in the beginning of the 1900s was considered overdue; nevertheless, to aggressively pursue the expansion of road, railway services, and a deep-water harbor in the colony as Guggisberg did was indeed radical. In a September 1919 *Preliminary Report on Transportation in the Gold Coast Colony,* the newly appointed governor made his vision clear to the Colonial Office. Hence, under his stewardship, a deep-water harbor at Takoradi commenced; over 230 miles of railway were laid, and about 260 miles of tarred roads were constructed. As a result of this opening up of the hinterlands, the colony was able to increase its exports of timber, gold, manganese, and cocoa with relative ease than in previous years. The benefits of Guggisberg's construction policies were evident by 1927 when 82 per cent of the colony's foreign earning came from cocoa exports alone.

Central to the policies of the government was the conviction that Africans in the Gold Coast were capable of becoming involved in the administration of the colony. Most important, the governor was of the view that developments must be applicable to local needs. It was for this reason that he advocated technical education as well as the study of the local vernaculars. Those who were suspicious of the insistence on this kind of education, however, accused him of advocating an inferior education for Africans compared to that which could be earned at London. The accomplishments of students from Achimota College, nonetheless, have proved otherwise. This same practicality was evident in the manner the governor sought to place Africans in responsible administrative positions.

While the 1916 Clifford Constitution allowed "three paramount chiefs and three other Africans" on the Gold Coast legislative council, the 1925 changes introduced by Governor Guggisberg made it possible for the number of Africans in positions of responsibility to increase. For example, at the time of his appointment as governor, there were only three Africans holding positions in the civil service, but the number increased to thirty-eight by 1927. The administration, supported by a network of provincial and district commissioners, made it a responsibility to improve the native courts. Detailed record keeping was encouraged at all levels, and to ensure fairness in the enforcement of laws, the district commissioner's courts abrogated to itself the right to review cases from the native courts. Entries in the diaries of Duncan-Johnstone, the district commissioner of Ashanti-Akim, are indicative of the efforts made to bring progress to the people at all levels of society. In fact, an effective native administration system was perceived as critical to the goal of involving Africans in the management of their own affairs. Hence, the 1925 legislative changes allowed the establishment of provincial councils of chiefs. From these councils, elected members served on the colony's legislative council. While the process made it possible for educated personalities as E. J. P. Brown, T. Hutton Mills, and J. Casely Hayford to become legislative council members, Guggisberg preferred reliance on traditional chiefs—a policy that was consistent with the British colonial idea of indirect rule.

But for the stability and administration of the colony, the governor was conservative and deliberate in certain policy matters. For example, even though a Kumase council petition seeking the return of the ex-Asantehene from the Seychelles was submitted in 1919, the governor recommended that the former King Prempeh I be allowed back at a later date (1924) and only as a private citizen. Two years later, however, the former Asantehene was installed as Kumasihene. The governor's caution was with regard to the effective introduction of his policy on native administration. But this occasional conservatism notwithstanding, the government laid a solid foundation for the "Africanization" of the Gold Coast administration and gave impetus to the rise of nationalism in the Gold Coast. It was not surprising then that the Gold Coast (Ghana) was to become the first colony in black Africa to gain political independence from colonial rule in 1957.

DAVID OWUSU-ANSAH

See also: **Ghana (Republic of): Nationalism, Rise of, and the Politics of Independence; Nkrumah, Kwame.**

Further Reading

Agbodeka, Francis. *Achimota in the National Setting: A Unique Educational Experiment in West Africa*, Accra: Afram Publications, 1977.

Dumett, Raymond E. *El Dorado in West Africa: The Gold-Mining Frontier, African Labor, and Colonial Capitalism in the Gold Coast, 1875–1900*, Athens: Ohio University Press, and Oxford, James Curry, 1998.

Gold Coast Committee on Prince of Wales. College, Report of the Committee Appointed in 1938 by the Governor of the Gold Coast Colony to Inspect the Prince of Wales' College, Achimota, Accra, Government Printing Office, 1939.

Goodall, L.B. *Beloved Imperialist: Sir Gordon Guggisberg, Governor of the Gold Coast.* Bath: George Wishart and Associates, 1998.

Guggisberg, Decima Moore, and F.G. Guggisberg. *We Two in West Africa.* London: Heinemann, 1909.

Kimble, David. *A Political History of Ghana: The Rise of Gold Coast Nationalism, 1850–1928.* Oxford: Clarendon Press, 1965.

Owusu-Ansah, David and McFarland Daniel Miles, Entry on Gordon Frederick Guggisberg in *Historical Dictionary of Ghana.* Metuchen, N.J.: Scarecrow Press, 1995.

Setse, Theo K. *Foundations of Nation-Building: The Case of Achimota School.* Legon, s.n., 1974.

Tashjian, Victoria B. "The Diaries of A.C. Duncan-Johnstone: A Preliminary Analysis of British Involvement in the 'Native Court' of the Gold Coast." *Ghana Studies*, 1 (1998): 135–150.

Wraith, R.E. *Guggisberg.* London: Oxford University Press, 1967.

———. *Local Government in West Africa.* London: George Allen and Unwin Ltd., 1972.

Ghana (Republic of): Nationalism, Rise of, and the Politics of Independence

On March 6, 1957, the people of Ghana gained their independence. As the first European colony in Sub-Saharan Africa to win its freedom, Ghana launched a march to self-government and independence that proved a catalyst for the overthrow of European imperialism throughout much of Africa. Capturing this larger significance of the achievement, the new prime minister, Kwame Nkrumah, told the jubilant independence day crowd, "Our independence is meaningless unless it is linked with the total liberation of the African continent."

Ghanaian nationalists won their independence in a largely peaceful, democratic, and constitutional process following World War II. The success of this approach reflects the country's history, the tactics of the independence movement's leadership, and the character of the British colonial reaction.

The growth of modern Ghanaian nationalism sprang from deep historical roots. One source was resistance to British imperialism by Ghanaians under their traditional leaders. The Asante, for example, provoked by the unreasonable demands of the British governor, rose in revolt in 1900 under the leadership of Yaa Asantewaa. Military force had contained this primary resistance to colonial rule, but colonialism itself produced a second fount of discontent: a Western-educated African middle class. Small in numbers, but often articulate, this group included lawyers and journalists capable of challenging the British authorities with their own ideals, such as a people's right to self-determination. J. E. Casely Hayford, a member of this new elite, organized the National Congress of British West Africa in 1920. This movement, often seen as a predecessor to modern nationalism and Pan-Africanism, faltered because of the physical separation of Britain's colonies, lack of a strong mass base, and political competition between the traditional and Western-educated elites.

After World War II, British officials still regarded the Gold Coast, as Ghana was then known, as a "model colony." They believed harmony could be achieved in a system that shared power largely between British officials and the chiefs, with a secondary role for the Western-educated middle class. In 1946 Governor Sir Alan Burns introduced a new constitution that actually established an African majority on the legislative council, but time had run out for Britain's gradualist measures. New forces were about to remake the colony's politics.

In 1947 members of the colony's Western-educated elite established the United Gold Coast Convention (UGCC). Its leaders, such as J. B. Danquah, were mostly lawyers who sought self-government in "the shortest time possible" and greater representation for their class on the legislative council. As general secretary for the party, they recruited Kwame Nkrumah. After twelve years overseas, Nkrumah returned to the Gold Coast, having lived the life of an impoverished foreign student in the United States and Britain. In a remarkable political achievement, he became head of the government in four years.

Nkrumah's success rested in part on his ability to expand the appeal of the nationalist movement. Soon discontented young people, especially those with limited Western educations but few employment opportunities in colonial society, became some of his most enthusiastic supporters. He also gained essential backing from cocoa farmers who were angered by the colonial administration's efforts to control their crop's swollen shoot disease by cutting down affected trees.

To these elements of his coalition he added support among low-level civil servants, teachers, market women, and the working class.

In 1948 the heavy-handed British response to protests in Accra radicalized politics in the colony. High prices had led to a consumer boycott of foreign-owned stores, when a British officer fired on the veterans' march to the governor's residence. Rioting broke out and spread to other towns. With Cold War fears of communism on their minds, British officials arrested the top six leaders of the UGCC. The British soon released them, but their detention already had made them popular heroes and increased the membership of the party. With one exception, however, the leaders were men of property and unlikely revolutionaries. They were willing to accept the initiative of the new British governor, Sir Arden-Clarke, to work out a moderate program of constitutional reform.

Nkrumah, the exception, broke with this gradualist approach of his colleagues, whom he now denounced as men of "property and standing." In June 1949 he launched the rival Convention People's Party (CPP). It's clear and uncompromising slogan, "Self-Government NOW," soon captured the imagination of the masses. The following January, he initiated a campaign of strikes and boycotts, known as "positive action," designed to force the colonial administration to concede immediate self-government. Nkrumah's subsequent arrest and sentence to three years in jail transformed him into a martyr.

When elections for the new Legislative Assembly were held in 1951, the CPP swept the elected seats, winning thirty-four out of thirty-eight. Recognizing this undeniable victory, Arden-Clarke performed an amazing about-face, releasing Nkrumah from prison and asking him to become leader of government business. Nkrumah and his followers had adopted white caps as symbols of solidarity with India's nonviolent struggle for freedom. When they emerged from prison, they proudly inscribed P.G., for "prison graduate," on their caps.

Over the next six years, Nkrumah pressed for and won increasing powers of self-government leading to independence. The British responded in a largely cooperative fashion to this transfer of power. The CPP won elections in 1954 and 1956, providing Nkrumah with the ability to establish a unitary state rather than the federal constitution preferred by some of his regional opponents. After independence, Nkrumah's government would be marred by authoritarian tendencies and economic mismanagement, but as a nationalist leader and visionary Nkrumah has remained a hero of African liberation.

The choice of the country's new name at the time of independence in 1957 referred back to the medieval

West African empire of Ghana and reflected pride in the state's African identity. From Mali to Zimbabwe, other African nationalists would follow this example. Many also would recognize the lessons and achievement of the Ghanaian struggle: the popular support for an uncompromising demand for freedom, the power of a mass party, and the vision of independence achieved.

BRIAN DIGRE

See also: **Colonialism, Overthrow of: Nationalism and Anticolonialism; Colonialism, Overthrow of: Sub-Saharan Africa; Nkrumah, Kwame.**

Further Reading

Apter, David. *Ghana in Transition.* 2nd rev. ed. Princeton: Princeton University Press, 1972.

Austin, Dennis. *Politics in Ghana, 1945–60.* Oxford: Oxford University Press, 1964.

Birmingham, David. *Kwame Nkrumah: The Father of African Nationalism.* Rev. ed. Athens: Ohio University Press, 1998.

Nkrumah, Kwame. *Ghana: The Autobiography of Kwame Nkrumah.* London: Thomas Nelson and Sons, 1957.

Padmore, George. *The Gold Coast Revolution.* London, Dennis Dobson, 1953.

Rooney, David. *Kwame Nkrumah: The Political Kingdom in the Third World.* New York: St. Martin's Press, 1989.

Ghana, Republic of: Social and Economic Development: First Republic

At the time of independence from Britain in 1957, Ghana (formerly the Gold Coast) was one of Africa's wealthiest former colonies. Ghana's economy and society were widely seen to embody characteristics that were considered advantageous for modern economic development, including: a high per capita income by the standards of Sub-Saharan Africa, an impressive number of existing and potential export commodities (cocoa, gold, diamonds, manganese, bauxite), and a good transportation system of roads and railways. With respect to human resources, Ghana's relatively well-developed educational system had by the 1950s produced a large number of educated people. The new state was endowed with an efficient, professional public service bureaucracy. In short, Ghana's developmental prospects were considered favorable.

During the late 1950s the economy grew quite rapidly, with over 5 per cent growth in gross national product (GNP) annually between 1955 and 1960. Prices were relatively stable and the cost of living was rising only slowly. Between 1960 and 1966, following an attempt at state-led, "socialist" economic growth, the economy performed much more poorly, while living standards for most Ghanaians declined. Led by Kwame Nkrumah and his Convention Peoples Party (CPP) government, the country's failure in this regard

was attributed to the government's program of centrally planned economic and social development. This was ironic given that the victory of Nkrumah and the CPP in 1957 had appeared to represent the epitome of Africa's anticolonial revolution, a triumph of the principle of self-determination and racial equality over the baleful effects of European tutelage and paternalism. But the government, disappointed by what it saw as slow progress, attempted to transform Ghana into an industrialized country by state-led development strategies. To the government, "socialism" implied central planning in order to ensure that the entire resources of the state, both human and material, were employed in the best interests of all Ghanaians

Such planning involved a strong commitment to state-led industrial development, protected by high trade barriers to speed up the growth process so that Ghana might "catch up" both with the West and the Soviet Union. The strategy involved extensive state intervention both in extractive industries and agricultural production. However, the economic grounds for reallocation of resources through state intervention in Africa were unproved, and, over time, the lack of success of such policies became clear. Under the regime of state-led growth, private capitalist investment was discouraged, whether Ghanaian or foreign. Ghanaian enterprises were limited mainly to small-scale concerns. The direct participation of the state in production was to be achieved by setting up new enterprises rather than by nationalizing private concerns, and socialist goals to be achieved by maximizing the growth of the public sector. Legislative controls in a number of strategic areas—including imports, capital transfers, the licensing of industrial production, the minimum wage, prices, levels of rents, trade union activities—were used to try to effect state-directed growth, but with limited success. In sum, Nkrumah's government not only failed to transform Ghana into an industrialized, socialist state but under its control the economy declined rapidly, paving the way for the country's descent into penury.

Six years of central planning (1960–1965) resulted in severe shortages of basic commodities, soaring price inflation, plummeting real incomes, and producer prices for Ghana's highly important cocoa farmers. Politically the period saw the incarceration of hundreds of the government's political opponents and a crackdown on the opposition press. Nkrumah and the CPP government's ousting from power in February 1966 seemed to be welcomed by most ordinary Ghanaians. The very ease with which the regime was overthrown belied the contemporary conventional scholarly view of the CPP as a strong, well-organized mass party. It appears that the CPP's organizational and mobilization capacity was based on little more than patrimonial authority, built on a network of material incentives and rewards that provided the motive force for the political system. CPP leaders were by and large a gang of opportunists who combined a rhetorical identification with the longings of ordinary Ghanaians for economic well-being with a near total surrender to the graft and corruption within which they immersed themselves.

But in this environment of politics as a means to reward, Nkrumah enjoyed a virtual monopoly of power. Assisting him were a cabal of foreign socialists who saw him and his regime as an instrument of their own designs to create a worldwide socialist-revolutionary movement. Partly as a result of their influence, Nkrumah was led to proclaim the pursuit of socialist development strategy, with predictably disastrous results given the political and economic realities of Ghana.

The major policy shift toward increased state control and regulation of the economy from the early 1960s owed a great deal to the urgent political need to satisfy the aspirations of the ruling party's supporters, to offset burgeoning urban unemployment, and to speed up industrialization as the only way, the government believed, to increase national income speedily. The results, however, were disappointing. Per capita GNP grew by only 0.2 per cent a year between 1960 and 1965, much slower than the rate of population increase at around 3 per cent per annum. As a result, many people's living standards declined quite badly during the first half of the 1960s.

The central figure in the formulation of development strategy was Nkrumah himself, a man whose personal ideology was influenced strongly by Leninism. Nkrumah had three main goals: Ghana's political independence, economic growth providing the means for his country's development, and Africa's overall political and economic unity. It was necessary for the continent's international standing, he argued, to form a third power bloc after the United States of America and the Soviet Union and their allies. Nkrumah believed that Ghana's underdevelopment and reliance on the export of cocoa beans were attributable to the structure of imperialist monopoly capitalism. To break free from this stranglehold required not merely political independence but also economic self-reliance, a goal that necessarily implied, to Nkrumah's way of thinking, a socialist development strategy. If Ghanaians were to be delivered from poverty, inequality, ill-health and ignorance—in other words, if development was to be achieved—then this desirable set of goals could not be accomplished on the basis of a backward, dependent economy. Instead, Ghana's trading and raw material-producing economic structure had to be transformed into a productive unit capable of bearing a superstructure of modern agriculture and industry, entailing public

ownership of the means of production, the land, and its resources; through such a transformation, progressive, industrialized, socialist Ghana would be forged.

African political and economic unity was conceived as an integral part of Ghana's industrialization program in that the "essential industrial machine which alone can break the vicious cycle of Africa's poverty can only be built on a wide enough base to make the take-off realistic, if it is planned on a continental scale" (Kwame Nkrumah, *Africa Must Unite*, p.167). In this respect, Nkrumah was a kind of African developmentalist Trotsky, in as much as he believed in the necessity of permanent revolution to achieve his goals. African unity was the political framework within which the process of erasing neocolonialism from the continent could proceed, while socialism symbolized the new order that had to replace the imperialist system of colonialism, neo-colonialism, racism, and apartheid. Together Pan-Africanism and socialism would coalesce into a progressive ideology for building a new Ghana and a new, post-colonial Africa. For both political entities, the new political system had to be "scientifically" formulated and vigorously propagated.

Many Ghanaians believed that Nkrumah spent too much time and energy struggling for a nonachievable goal—African unity—and not enough in ensuring Ghana's well-being. Certainly, the economic policies his government adopted after 1960 did not achieve their goals. Import-substitution industrialization was a failure, often providing substandard goods at inflated prices. The government spent more than it could afford on prestigious public buildings, state-owned enterprises, such as Ghana Airways and the Ghana National Construction Corporation, and on providing employment for the growing number of Ghanaians. The country's currency, the cedi, was maintained at an artificially high rate of exchange in order to offset excessive public spending and so encouraged imports and discouraged exports. The Cocoa Marketing Board paid such low prices to cocoa farmers for their produce that output declined greatly, while government used the surplus extracted to finance public expenditures that primarily benefited the urban areas. To meet accelerating deficits on both domestic budgets and the balance of payments, the CPP government borrowed heavily abroad, resulting in a high level of public debt.

The military and police officers who overthrew Nkrumah in 1966 proclaimed that they had felt compelled to oust him and his government because of the combined weight of economic failure—so serious that Ghana's development was severely stunted for decades—and a political repression which, in the way that it silenced and imprisoned opponents, had all the hallmarks of the Soviet system that Nkrumah professed to admire. Following the coup, the CPP was banned and disbanded. Nkrumah fled to Guinea, eventually dying in Romania in 1972.

JEFF HAYNES

See also: **Nkrumah, Kwame.**

Further Reading

Apter, David. *Ghana in Transition.* New York: Atheneum Press, 1963.

Austin, David. *Ghana Observed.* London: Oxford University Press, 1976.

Bretton, Henry. *The Rise and Fall of Kwame Nkrumah.* London: Pall Mall Press, 1967.

Chazan, Naomi. *Ghanaian Politics: Managing Political Recession, 1969–82.* Boulder, Colo.: Westview, 1983.

Davidson, Basil. *Black Star. A View of the Life and Times of Kwame Nkrumah.* London: Allen Lane, 1973.

Nkrumah, Kwame. *Africa Must Unite.* London: Panaf Books, 1963.

Ghana, Republic of: Coups d'état, Second Republic, 1966–1972

On February 24, 1966, the civilian administration of the Convention People's Party (CPP) that ruled Ghana under the leadership of President Kwame Nkrumah was overthrown in a coup d'état. Colonel E. K. Kotoka, Major A. A. Afrifa, and the other coup leaders established the National Liberation Council (NLC) to rule the nation, until the beginning of the second republic in 1969.

Knowing very well the ramifications of this first military interference in civil administration, Major Afrifa (later to rise to the rank of general) wrote in defense of the security forces in staging the coup. He blamed Kwame Nkrumah for the politicization of the armed forces when Ghanaian troops were sent to the Congo in the early 1960s. According to Afrifa, the Congo crisis, as well as the nationalist struggles in Southern Rhodesia (now Zimbabwe) for which preparations were underway to send more troops, were internal affairs in which Nkrumah had no right to intervene. The president was described as overly ambitious in his quest to become the first head of a dreamed United States of Africa.

On the domestic front, Nkrumah was accused of dictatorial behavior. The introduction of the 1958 Preventive Detention Act, which allowed political opponents to be imprisoned without trial, was among the examples cited. The establishment of the republican constitution of 1960 also placed enormous power in the hands of Nkrumah as president. Because of changes in the constitution, the president was able to force opponents such as K. A. Busia into exile. Another challenger, J. B. Dankwa, was detained and died in 1965 as prisoner. Because of these acts, the president was accused of recklessly endangering the nation at the same time as he blocked all constitutional means to challenge his powerful grip over national affairs.

While acknowledging that the CPP used repression to consolidate power, intellectuals of the left such as Bob Fitch and Mary Oppenheimer explained Ghana's problems differently. In their *Ghana: End of an Illusion,* they pointed to the inability of the administration, in the first half of its tenure (1957–1961), to reconstruct the economic institutions left to it by the colonial government. By nurturing a neocolonial economic system in the immediate postindependence years, Ghana lost critical momentum to becoming truly free. While Fitch and Oppenheimer thought of the 1961 socialist "Seven Year Plan for Work and Happiness" as the more realistic policy for the nation's self-sufficiency, the scholars were of the view that Ghana's break with its colonial past was tentative.

Notwithstanding such opposing interpretations, the coup leaders found Nkrumah's economic centralization as outlined in the seven-year plan to be problematic. Those socialist policies were reversed by the NLC, and pro-Western private sector initiatives were pursued with vigor. In fact, in his *Ghana under Military Rule, 1966–1969,* Robert Pinkley argued that Ghana's economic problems were seen by the NLC to be symptomatic of a larger predicament—political dictatorship of the former administration. The answer laid in the establishment of a duly constituted civilian administration.

Only three days after seizing power, the NLC announced its intentions to return power to an appropriately elected government. In the meantime, however, Nkrumah's Preventive Detention Act was revoked, and the NLC solicited public opinions on governance. During the three years it remained in office, the military governed with the support of a network of advisory committees, numerous commissions, and committees of inquiry. A commission was also created to submit proposals for a constitution under which the nation was returned to civilian administration in 1969. But while the NLC commitment to reestablish constitutional rule may have been impressive, it must be noted that the effort to address national problems through committees and commission was responsible for the emergence of many powerful pressure groups with which the next administration had to contend. Furthermore, under NLC rule, military and police officers were increasingly appointed to public positions hitherto held by civilians—the official politicization of the Ghana Armed Forces had indeed occurred.

The constitution of the second republic was approved in August of 1969. Under this liberal arrangement, the president acted as a ceremonial head of state. The prime minister was the head of government and had the power to select his own ministers. A house of chiefs was also approved. In all, powers that were hitherto held by the president became broadly distributed. Thus, when the second republic commenced in October 1969, it was agreed by many that a parliamentary democracy had again been established in Ghana.

Elected as prime minister in the 1969 election was K. A. Busia, who also served in the earlier years of the first republic as leader of the opposition United Party (UP). As head of the ruling progress Party (PP), Busia's international acclaim as scholar per excellence as well as his pro-Western leanings were thought to bring external support in solving Ghana's mounting economic problems. Above all, with 105 of the 140 parliamentary seats in PP control, the ruling party was expected to rapidly address national problems. In fact, with democracy reestablished, the public's attention turned to the nation's dire economic conditions which they required the government to address in the shortest possible time.

To create more jobs and open up the private sector to citizens, the government ordered the expulsion of all illegal aliens from Ghana just a month after taking office. American and European creditors were also called upon to consider new arrangements by which Ghana could address its foreign debts. In its efforts to restructure the public sector, the administration purged 568 employees from the civil service. University students, who had enjoyed free tuition and board under Nkrumah's liberal education policy, were also asked to pay for their schooling. In July 1971 the government introduced an austerity budget that called for the removal of benefits but raised taxes. The inability of the government to convince the nation that these were necessary actions led many to question the logic of such policies. Two of the nation's powerful pressure groups, the National Union of Ghana Students (NUGS) and the Trade Union Congress (TUC), protected the economic actions vehemently. In certain circles, Nkrumah was missed.

In response to the emerging crisis, any direct or indirect mention of Nkrumah and the CPP was outlawed by the administration. Firm actions were also announced to prevent the TUC from protesting the austerity budget by strike actions. While many may have been frustrated or even disappointed by the harsh economic conditions that prevailed in the country, the announcement on January 13, 1972, that the military had seized power took most by surprise. Listing the economic crisis and the decline in benefits for the armed forces as justification, Colonel I. K. Achaempong and his National Redemption Council abolished the constitution of the second republic and began the next phase of military rule in Ghana.

DAVID OWUSU-ANSAH

See also: **Nkrumah, Kwame.**

Further Reading

Afrifa, A. A. *The Ghana Coup, 24th February 1966.* London: Frank Cass, 1967.
Alexander, H. T. Major General. *African Tightrope: My Two Years as Nkrumah's Chief of Staff.* New York: Praeger Publishers, 1965.
Amonoo, Benjamin. *Ghana, 1957–1966: Politics of Institutional Dualism.* London: George Allen and Unwin, 1981.
Chazan, Naomi. *An Anatomy of Ghanaian Politics: Managing Political Recession, 1969–1982.* Boulder, Colo.: Westview Press, 1983.
Fitch, Bob, and Oppenheimer. *Ghana: End of an Illusion.* New York: Monthly Review Press, 1966.
Jones, Trevor. *Ghana's First Republic 1960–1966: The Pursuit of the Political Kingdom.* London: Methuen and Company, 1976.
LeVine, Victor. *Political Corruption: The Case of Ghana.* Stanford, Calif.: Hoover Institution Press at Stanford University, 1975.
Pinkney, Robert. *Ghana under Military Rule, 1966–1969.* London: Methuen and Company, 1972.
Shillington, Kevin. *Ghana and the Rawlings Factor.* London: Macmillan Press, 1992.

Ghana, Republic of: Acheampong Regime to the Third Republic, 1972–1981

On January 13, 1972, Colonel Ignatius Kutu Acheampong toppled the government of Kofi Abrefa Busia. He had been planning a coup six months into the Busia administration. Whatever Acheampong's plan might have been, it was clear that the country, under Busia, was facing major difficulties, including huge foreign debts, shortages of goods, and a declining agricultural sector. Busia's attitude toward the Trade Union Congress and the National Union of Ghanaian Students alienated these groups. Busia cut military personnel and their allowance, and in December 1971 devalued the Ghanaian cedi by 48.6 per cent and imposed a 5 per cent national development levy on the people. Acheampong charged the Busia administration with corruption, arbitrary dismissals, economic mismanagement, and the implementation of policies designed to lower the army's morale.

Acheampong was born in Kumasi on September 23, 1931. He enrolled in the army in March 1959 after officer cadet training at Mons, England. He was the commanding officer of the Fifth Battalion of the Ghana army at the time of the coup. Acheampong's time in office can be divided into the periods 1972–1974 and 1975–1978. Acheampong initially set up the National Redemption Council, which consisted largely of the people who had planned the original coup, but in 1975 he introduced the Supreme Military Council, which was made up of the commanders of the various military services.

The early years of the Acheampong regime proved to be very popular, even though there were people who felt that there was no justification for the coup. During the first phase of his administration he abolished some of the harsh economic measures introduced by the Busia administration. He revalued the cedi and restored some benefits to the military and civil servants. He tried to correct the image of the beggar nation which had been created by the Busia administration. His speech "Yentua" (We won't pay), which repudiated some of the country's debts, was well received.

One of Acheampong's early major achievements included Operation Feed Yourself and Operation Feed your Industries, which were aimed at increasing the production of local food crops like rice and maize and cash crops like rubber, sugar cane, cotton, groundnuts, and cashew. Rice production rose from 11,000 tons in 1971 to 61,000 tons in 1973, and maize production from 53,000 in 1971 to 430,000 tons in 1973. The program died out after 1975, however, when the government was confronted with severe economic difficulties. There was a drop in the export of cocoa, gold, timber, and diamonds, and the low prices the government paid farmers for their cocoa crops led to large-scale smuggling to the neighboring countries of Côte d'Ivoire and Togo. These problems were compounded by the rise of oil prices, droughts, and bush fires.

The country experienced dramatic economic decline two years into the Acheampong regime, and a period of unprecedented corruption ensued. The profiteering, cheating, and corruption that the country witnessed between 1974 and 1979 became known as *kalabule* (from the Hausa "kere kabure," "keep it quiet"). Chits were issued, especially to young women, who obtained import licenses; they often resold the licenses for over three times the value. These corrupt women who obtained licenses maintained an ostentatious life style. Besides *kalabule*, the country experienced a period of high inflation; the inflation level, which was 10.1 per cent in 1972 rose to 116.5 per cent in 1977. In 1974 the money supply rose by 2.4 per cent and in 1976 by 44.3 per cent. Faced with such a grim economic situation, many Ghanaians, especially academics and professionals emigrated to Nigeria, Côte d'Ivoire, Europe, the United States, and other countries. The country also began to experience unprecedented strikes and industrial unrest. Among the most formidable opponents to the government was the People's Movement for Freedom and Justice, which included leaders like General A. A. Afrifa, William Ofori Atta, and Komla Gbedemah. The Third Force under Dr. J. K. Bilson, and the Front for the Prevention of Dictatorship under Kwame Safo-Adu and Victor Owusu also opposed the Acheampong regime.

On September 23, 1976, the Ghana Bar Association met in Kumasi and called for a return to a civilian and constitutional government no later than 1978. The Bar Association also demanded the abolition of military tribunals and unlawful detentions. It was clear at this point that Acheampong could not hold on to power, and so in January 1977, he proposed a system which he called Union Government (UNIGOV). This government was to be composed of soldiers, policemen and civilians. The army would be dominant, however, and Acheampong would have had a significant role. Despite opposition from students and professional associations, there was civilian support from the organizers' council, patriots, the African Youth Command, and others. In the vote on Union Government held at the end of March 1978, only 43 per cent of the people voted, and, despite obvious manipulation on the part of the Acheampong regime, there was only a 54 per cent majority voting for the measure.

Massive strikes followed the Union Government vote, and on July 5, 1978, Lieutenant General FWK Akuffo staged a palace coup and forced Acheampong to resign and retire from the military. Akuffo's government, known as the Supreme Military Council II (SMC II), was doomed from the beginning because the military was totally discredited in the view of the people at this point. The SMC II under Akuffo released people who had been detained during the referendum, but the new government did not have support for UNIGOV and strikes continued. With growing opposition, the government set up a constituent assembly in December 1978 to draw up a constitution and lifted the ban on political parties on January 1, 1979. Akuffo's SMC II, which included civilians, tried to deal with Ghana's declining economy. In September 1978 the cedi was effectively devalued by 58 per cent, and in March 1979, new cedi notes replaced the old ones. Although bank accounts were exchanged on the rate of one to one, currency notes were exchanged for a fraction of their value.

From January to March 1979, the constituent assembly drafted a new constitution with an executive president and a 140-member national assembly. Elections were scheduled to be held on June 18, 1979, but on May 15, 1979, there was an attempted mutiny led by Flight Lieutenant Jerry J. Rawlings. Rawlings was imprisoned and put on trial for treason, but on June 4, 1979 the lower ranks rebelled, sprang Rawlings from prison, and overthrew Akuffo's SMC II.

Rawlings set up an Armed Forces Revolutionary Council which launched a so-called house cleaning exercise to tackle profiteering and corruption, especially within the military. Eight prominent military men were publicly executed by firing squad, including three former heads of state: Acheampong, Akuffo, and General A. A. Afrifa.

In spite of this, the elections went on as scheduled. The election proved to be a contest between two main parties, the People's National Party (PNP) and the Popular Front Party (PFP), which had a lot of the United Party (UP) and Progressive Party (PP) tendencies. The PNP under H. Limann won seventy-one seats, and the PFP under Victor Owusu won forty-two seats. The rest of the seats were taken by other smaller parties like the United National Convention, the Action Congress Party, and the Social Democratic Front.

Limann beat his rival Owusu in the election for president on July ninth. On September 24, 1979, Rawlings handed over power to the newly elected government of Hilla Limann, which established the third republic of Ghana. The third republic would be overthrown in twenty-eight months on December 31, 1981, once again by Jerry Rawlings.

EDWARD REYNOLDS

Further Reading

Boahen, Albert, and Adu. *The Ghanaian Sphinx, Reflections on the Contemporary History of Ghana 1972–1987.* JB Danguah Memorial Lectures,Twenty-first Series. Accra, 1989.

Chazan, Naomi. *An Anatomy of Ghanaian Politics.* Boulder, Colo.: Westview, 1983.

Frimpong, Ansah Jonathan H. *The Vampire State in Africa: The Political Economy of Decline in Ghana.* London: James Curry, 1991.

Oquaye, Mike. *Politics in Ghana, 1972–1979.* Accra: Tornado, 1980.

Shillington, Kevin. *Ghana and the Rawlings Factor.* New York: St. Martin's Press, 1992.

Ghana: Revolution and Fourth Republic, 1981 to Present

On New Year's eve, 1982, Lt. Jerry John Rawlings launched the December 31 Revolution, formed a new government—the Provisional National Defence Council (PNDC), to replace the PNP (People's National Party)—and vowed to establish a new system of "popular democracy." To this end, Peoples Defense Committees (PDCs) and Workers Defense Committees (WDCs) were formed as the basis for grassroots mobilization programs for development. Rawlings called for a revolution that would transform the social and economic structure of Ghana. Citizens Vetting Committees (CVCs) were set up to probe tax evasion by the rich, corruption in state corporations, banking, and the civil service. Finally, tribunals were set up to provide quick and simple alternatives to the complex and expensive legal system that purportedly served the elite and the rich. On May 15, 1982, the December 31 Women's Movement was founded to involve women and mobilize their support for the revolution.

The PNDC embarked on participatory activities like land clearing, community work, and desilting drainage to mobilize Ghanaians for self-help projects. It also focused on revenue collection, antismuggling, and anticorruption operations. Various groups—students, radical intellectuals, workers, trade unionists, and farmers—became the vanguard of PNDC support. On the other hand, opposition to the PNDC coalesced around the Ghana Bar Association, the Catholic Bishops Conference, the Protestant Christian Council, and a London-based campaign for democracy group who opposed the "revolutionary organs" as facades for extrajudicial dictatorial power.

In 1982–1983 some PDCs and WDCs were accused of acts of terrorism and profiteering. Power to the people in some cases became power to the brutal and violent in society as people used the PDCs and WDCs to settle scores. In addition, there was indiscipline, rowdiness, and arbitrary use of power by soldiers, border guards, and policemen during the early years of the revolution.

The anticorruption, antismuggling stance of the PNDC, and the stress on accountability and probity in public affairs, appealed to students who, in an unprecedented move, offered to help carry cocoa and other agricultural commodities from remote farming communities to the ports for export. In a little over six weeks, hundreds of thousands of bags of cocoa were carted to the Tema port for export. The students also participated in mass education, to educate people about the aims and objectives of the Revolution. The success of the student task force provided a lot of credibility to the government in its first crucial months in office.

In an attempt to alleviate the plight of workers, the PNDC introduced a system of price controls and seized goods of traders who flouted the price control laws. These activities created serious shortages of basic consumer goods, and empty shelves became the most common sight in many department stores. The excessive abuse of power by soldiers and policemen in enforcing price control laws shocked the nation, but the abduction and murder of three high court judges and a retired army major in early July 1982 caused serious consternation. The three judges had apparently undone punishments meted out by the Armed Forces Revolutionary Council in 1979. The perpetrators were tried, and Amartey Kwei, a PNDC member, was executed in one of the most politically and emotionally charged trials in Ghana.

The initial anti-Western, anti-imperialist rhetoric of the PNDC government gave way in 1982 to negotiations with Western donors. In a period of shortages in foreign exchange, industrial raw materials, basic consumer commodities, hyper inflation and economic stagnation, the PNDC began negotiations with the International Monetary Fund (IMF). Some revolutionary organs such as the June Fourth Movement and the New Democratic Movement were opposed to the size of the devaluation and the nature of the IMF package.

Students also opposed the IMF package, especially since it called for downsizing the whole educational system, a reduction in funding for education, and retrenchment of both academic and nonacademic staff at the universities.

The 1982 Economic Recovery Program (ERP) was designed as a program for reconstruction and development to improve infrastructure and increase production especially in agriculture and industry. The finance secretary, Kwesi Botwey, announced a four-year program of prepricing for imports due to the high domestic cost of production and the over-valuation of the cedi. The ERP was launched in a tough 1983 budget at a time when the economy was crippled by shortfalls in agricultural production due to scanty rainfall, and a gradual desiccation of the Sahel which caused an inflow of immigrants from Sahel into Ghana. The government drew attention to the critical state of the economy, foreign exchange scarcities, an unprecedented drop in export earnings and fall in production, and flooding of the economy by excess money supply about thirty times the amount in circulation. The latter led to a withdrawal of the largest currency denominations, the fifty-cedi note.

In the midst of these crises, professionals and skilled personnel left the country in large numbers, thus exacerbating a problem of brain drain that had started half a decade earlier. The economic problems of the time were exacerbated by the expulsion of about 1.2 million Ghanaians from Nigeria. In spite of ECOWAS protocols, the Shehu Shagari government ordered "illegal immigrants" out of Nigeria, and against a backdrop of transportation problems, oil shortage, and lack of spare parts, the PNDC undertook a two-week repatriation exercise on a scale unprecedented in the nation's history. Utilizing Ghana Air Force and Airways planes, Black Star Line Vessels, and an armada of haulage trucks, the government repatriated Ghanaians stuck in Nigerian ports and other border crossings between Nigeria and Ghana.

The PNDC also implemented a number of educational reforms designed to make education more socially and economically relevant to the Ghanaian situation. A new education structure "6:3:3:4" years (primary, junior secondary school, senior secondary school, university) was adopted in place of the former "9:7:3" system. However, the piecemeal manner that attended this reform was opposed by faculty, students, the Ghana National Association of Teachers (GNAT), and other professional bodies that accused the government of hurriedly implementing the junior secondary school reforms to meet the demands of donor countries like England. Clashes erupted between students protesting against the ad hoc reforms and the security agencies culminating in the closure of the country's universities.

In 1983 the universities were closed for a year due to confrontations between students and government. In 1986 and 1987 student–government clashes flared up again. The PNDC commissioned a University Rationalization Study as part of its education reform program, and the Committee recommended a new tertiary system of education made up of three groups: universities and university colleges, the polytechnics, and similar institutions (two new universities at Winneba and Tamale subsequently were created). To finance the new system, the URC recommended the privatization and commercialization of some university activities and services: health, sanitary, catering, and transport facilities for students and staff. In addition, student halls were to be converted into self-financing hostels. It also recommended different types of financial support for students, such as scholarships and loan schemes for all students, but the amounts indicated were deemed to be woefully inadequate by students. Universities were closed down and some students were dismissed from the universities for participation in those demonstrations.

The ERP began to yield results as signs of economic recovery began to show in 1984. The government paid higher prices for exports, and inflation fell from 120 per cent in 1983 to 10.4 per cent in 1985. Economic activity was revived in all sectors, especially mining and the timber industry, and the government was able to implement phase two of the economic recovery program: divestiture of state corporations and institutions that were a drain on the economy. This was closely followed by the introduction of "forex bureaus," a system of weekly auction of foreign exchange, designed to cripple the black market for foreign currency. At the same time the government undertook a major rehabilitation of the communications infrastructure of the country—notably the ports of Tema and Takoradi, major trunk roads, bridges, and railway lines. Tata buses and railway engines and coaches were imported from India to augment public transportation and rail services. A Malaysian company currently holds majority shares in the telephone system in Ghana.

In 1990, when the government paid off in full the $600 million of foreign exchange arrears that had accumulated before the ERP, Ghana became the "darling boy" of the International Monetary Fund and international donor agencies pledged more money. Cocoa, timber, and mining output all continued to increase. The PNDC also pursued an active policy of diversification of the economy and encouraged the production of non-traditional exports such as banana, pineapples, shea butter, lime, and yam. Unfortunately, life continued to be difficult for the average Ghanaian, and the government launched the Program of Action to Mitigate the Social Cost of Adjustment (PAMSCAD) in 1989 to help with local community initiatives. It later grew to incorporate supplementary feeding programs for new mothers in remote areas.

The PNDC took steps toward the institutionalization of parliamentary government when it lifted the ban on political activity in 1992. Between May and November, 1992, an array of clubs and friendship societies metamorphosed into political parties: the New Patriotic Party (led by Professor Adu Boahen), the Progressive Alliance (National Democratic Congress, National Convention Party and Egle Party, led by Jerry Rawlings), the NIP (led by Kwabena Darko) and the PHC (led by Hilla Limann). In spite of a report of fairly contested elections on November 2 by observer groups from the Commonwealth, the Carter Center of Emory University, and the Organization of African Unity, the opposition parties accused Rawlings of rigging the elections to secure victory. Thus, the fourth republic was inaugurated amid a cloud of uncertainty.

The NDC continued the program of recovery (ERP II) launched by the PNDC. Mass infrastructure programs have been continued, including road construction, rural electrification, free press (private television, radio and newspapers), and improvements in the transport, telecommunication, and mining sector. The popularity of these projects can be gauged from the fact that, in 1996, Rawlings and the NDC won another general election— a victory the opposition grudgingly conceded. Nevertheless, life continues to be difficult for the average Ghanaian, as school fees are high, health services are expensive, and salaries are low.

EDMUND ABAKA

See also: **Rawlings, Jerry John; World Bank, International Monetary Fund, and Structural Adjustment.**

Further Reading

Chazan, Naomi, and Deborah Pellow. *Ghana: Coping with Uncertainty.* Boulder, Colo.: Westview Press, 1986.

Gyimah-Boadi, Emmanuel, ed. *Ghana under PNDC Rule.* Dakar: CODESRIA, 1993.

Hansen, Emmanuel, and Kwame A. Ninsin, eds. *The State, Development, and Politics in Ghana.* London: CODESRIA, 1989.

Nugent, Paul. *Big Men, Small Boys, and Politics in Ghana: Power, Ideology, and the Burden of History, 1982–1994.* New York: Printer, 1995.

Rothchild, Donald, ed. *Ghana: The Political Economy of Recovery.* Boulder, Colo.: Lynne Rienner, 1991.

Shillington, Kevin. *Ghana and the Rawlings Facto.* New York: St. Martin's Press, 1992.

Skalnik, Peter. "Rawlings Revolution in Ghana: Countrywide and District Levels." *Asian and African Studies* 1 (1992).

Toye, John. "Ghanas Economic Reforms, 1983–1987: Origins, Achievements and Limitations." In *Towards Economic Recovery in Sub-Saharan Africa: Essays in Honour of Robert Gardiner,* edited by James Pickett and Hans Singer. New York: Routledge, 1990.

Giriama: *See* Kenya: Mekatilele and Giriama Resistance, 1900–1920.

Globalization, Africa and

Political independence and the formation of nation-states swept the African continent in the 1960s. A central goal of the governments of the new states, and of the handful of previously independent countries, was to implement a development policy that would integrate the national economies into the global system of trade and finance in a manner to foster the structural transformations associated with economic modernization. As this process unfolded through the second half of the twentieth century, one could identify several important themes: (1) attempts to industrialize largely agrarian economies, (2) to reduce dependence on primary products by extending industrialization into the export sector, and (3) via the first two to facilitate national sovereignty in policy making. The last was especially important, both ideologically and practically, because prior to the 1960s most of the continent had been directly or indirectly dominated by colonial powers, which organized and implemented a strategy of integration to the world market designed primarily to serve the needs of those powers.

As the tables on page 584 demonstrate, the levels of development in North Africa and the Sub-Saharan region were quite different. In the mid-1960s the per capita income of the North African countries averaged about 14 per cent of that of the developed market economies (i.e., the Organization of Economic Cooperation and Development countries), while the average for the Sub-Saharan countries was less than 4 per cent. Notwithstanding the higher average level of income and economic development in the North African countries, their degree of industrialization was only slightly higher than the Sub-Saharan average in the 1960s. To varying degrees, governments of the Sub-Saharan countries sought to foster structural change through industrial policy, frequently (and inaccurately) called "import substitution."

Through a combination of import restrictions, partial or complete state ownership, and encouragement of foreign investment, governments attempted to stimulate manufacturing, which had been so singularly underdeveloped during the colonial period. The strategy anticipated a long transitional period during which primary product exports would finance the import of machinery and inputs for manufacturing. If policy were successful, this period would be followed by a shift to manufactured exports as the sector matured and became international competitive. From the perspective of the end of the twentieth century, one can judge industrial policy to have been unsuccessful for the sub-Sahara as a whole. While some progress was made in raising the share of manufacturing in national income through the 1970s, by the 1990s it was only marginally greater than twenty years before. In part this lack of success can be attributed to weaknesses of industrial policy in many countries. Lack of success was also the consequence of a regional shift in the strategy of world market integration in the 1980s. In North Africa a significant increase in industrialization was achieved in Egypt, Morocco, and Tunisia, though not in the oil-exporting countries (Algeria and Libya). The manifest failure of the oil economies in North Africa to use effectively their petroleum revenues to transform their economies was an outcome characteristic of the entire continent (e.g., Cameroon, Gabon, and Nigeria), though in the case of Angola this might be attributed to war rather than economic policy.

Along with unsuccessful industrialization went a failure to diversify exports. In the mid-1960s, 93 per cent of exports from the Sub-Saharan region were primary products (agriculture, mining, and petroleum), and the share hardly changed to the end of the century. For the petroleum exporters of North Africa, the result was the same. In Morocco and Tunisia the primary product share fell below 50 per cent by the end of the 1990s. With these exceptions, at the end of the century the countries of the continent were integrated into the world trading system in much the way they had been at independence.

For the Sub-Saharan countries, along with a failure to achieve structural change of domestic economies went a dependence on official development assistance. In the 1980s and 1990s, "foreign aid" accounted for just over 8 per cent of national income, a percentage considerably more than double that for Latin America and Asia. Because of the higher per capita income of the North African countries, their aid inflows were less, with the exception of Egypt, whose large inflows reflected U.S. geopolitical priorities. While the Sub-Saharan region received relatively low private capital inflows, the region accumulated considerable debt through official flows. From about 5 per cent of export earnings, debt service rose to 13 per cent in the 1980s and 1990s. Because of the concessionary nature of official lending, the level of debt service understated debt accumulation, which by the 1990s had reached 90 per cent of national income.

This debt accumulation reflected an increasing dependence of the Sub-Saharan countries on official development assistance, and an increasing involvement of international agencies in domestic policy formation, both occurring in the context of a general crisis of development in the region. During the 1960s, the per capita income of the Sub-Saharan countries as a whole increased at slightly over 2 per cent per annum. While this was less than for all other developing regions

(including North Africa), it represented an improvement upon performance during the late colonial period. In the 1970s growth rates across the region declined to hardly more than 1 per cent. This decline in growth was associated with falling export earnings, despite a substantial increase in export prices from 1972 through 1981. The slowdown in growth, the result of structural constraints to export expansion in the Sub-Saharan region, overlapped in the early 1980s with the international debt crisis, which primarily affected the Latin American countries. In response to the debt crisis, the International Monetary Fund (IMF) and the World Bank initiated programs of policy-based lending, in which short-term balance of payments support was conditional upon governments adopting a specific set of policy conditionalities (stabilization and structural adjustment programs). These conditionalities involved what came to be called "neoliberal" policies, deregulation of domestic markets, and liberalization of foreign trade.

The problems of the Sub-Saharan region were quite different from those of the highly indebted countries; that is, the former was not characterized by debt insolvency, high inflation, or severe balance of payment disequilibrium. Nonetheless, the IMF and World Bank programs were applied to the region much as they had been designed for the highly indebted countries. By the end of the 1980s, virtually every Sub-Saharan government had entered into policy-based lending with both the IMF and the World Bank, and in several countries policy making was shaped by multilateral conditionality virtually without interruption during the 1980s and 1990s (e.g., Central African Republic, Côte d'Ivoire, Kenya, and Tanzania). Thus, in the Sub-Sahara, more than any other region, the autonomy of economy policy was constrained by external intervention during these two decades.

The evidence suggests that the stabilization and structural adjustment programs were not successful in rejuvenating growth in the Sub-Saharan countries. After slow per capita growth in the 1970s, incomes fell in the 1980s, and again in the 1990s. On average, per capita incomes in the Sub-Saharan region at the end of the century were approximately at their level of the mid-1960s. To a great extent, falling per capita incomes in the region during the 1980s and 1990s were the result of a severe deterioration in the international terms of trade. From 1981 through 1992, the composite price index of Sub-Saharan exports fell almost 100 per cent compared to the index of imports. The stabilization and adjustment programs were not well designed to cope with such a problem. Trade liberalization, their principal focus in the trade field, if it would stimulate exports at all, would tend to do so for products currently exported, rather than stimulating new exports. To achieve the latter would require investment expenditures, both by the private and public sectors, to adjust the production structure to changing demand in the world economy. Over the period of policy-based lending the growth rate of investment was negative, an outcome associated with such lending programs in other regions as well.

At the end of the twentieth century, the world economy was quite different from what it had been four decades before, when most African countries gained independence. In terms of trade and financial flows, the continent did not adjust to world market changes. This was especially the case for petroleum-exporting countries. Almost two decades of market-oriented policies across the continent had not, apparently, altered the manner of integration into the world market, either for petroleum exporters or for the other countries. At the end of the century African governments remained in search of a successful strategy of world market integration, in a global context considerably less favorable to their autonomy and development than at the time of independence.

JOHN WEEKS

See also: **Development, Postcolonial: Central Planning, Private Enterprise, Investment; Oil; World Bank, International Monetary Fund, and Structural Adjustment.**

Indicators of Development and Integration into the World Economy, the Sub-Sahara, 1960–1997*

Indicator/ decade	1960s	1970s	1980s	1990s
Growth of Per Capita Income (PCY)	2.2	1.1	−.7	−.9
PCY as % of Developed Countries	3.4	2.7	2.2	1.6
Manufacturing as % of GDP	7.6	9.3	11.1	10.3
Exports as % of GDP	25.4	26.6	27.7	28.7
Primary Products as % of merchandise exports	93.1	90.0	88.3	90.3
Foreign Direct Investment As % of GDP	na	.8	.6	1.4
Official Development Aid as % of GDP	na	na	8.1	8.1
Debt Service as % of Exports	na	4.8	13.5	13.0
Debt as % of GDP	na	17.3	44.8	69.8

*South Africa excluded.
Source: World Bank, World Development Indicators 1999 (CD-ROM)

Indicators of Development and Integration into the World Economy, North Africa, 1960–1997*

Indicator/ decade	1960s	1970s	1980s	1990s
Growth of Per Capita Income*	3.0	4.0	1.7	1.0
PCY as 0% of Developed Countries*	13.7	15.7	13.6	8.6
Manufacturing as % of GDP*	10.9	11.2	13.2	17.5
Exports as % of GDP	25.8	30.8	31.0	33.1
Primary Products as % of merchandise exports	77.2	77.0	74.6	64.7
Foreign Direct Investment as % of GDP	na	.4	.8	1.1
Official Development Aid as % of GDP	na	4.8	2.4	3.1
Debt Service as % of Exports*	na	14.8	30.9	29.7
Debt as % of GDP*	na	32.0	63.8	60.0

*No data for Libya.
Source: World Bank, World Development Indicators 1999 (CD-ROM)

Further Reading

Jamal, Vali, and John Weeks. *Africa Misunderstood: or Whatever Happened to the Rural-Urban Gap?* London: Macmillan, 1993.

Mosley, Paul, and John Weeks. "Has Recovery Begun? 'Africa's Adjustment in the 1980s' Revisited." *World Development* 21, no. 10 (1993): 1583–1606.

Mosley, Paul, Turan Subasat, and John Weeks. "Assessing Adjustment in Africa." *World Development* 23, no. 9 (1995): 1459–1472.

Sender, John. "Africa's Economic Performance: Limitations of the Current Consensus." *Journal of Economic Perspectives* 13, no. 3 (1999): 89–114.

United Nations Conference on Trade and Development. "African Development in a Comparative Perspective." In *Trade and Development Report, 1998.* Geneva: United Nations Conference on Trade and Development, 1998.

World Bank. *Adjustment in Africa: Results, Reforms and the Road Ahead.* Oxford: Oxford University Press, 1994.

Gold: Akan Goldfields: 1400 to 1800

A vital segment in the economic history—and even of the political and social history—of what is today Ghana can be conveyed in terms of gold. Though mining for the glittering yellow metal in West Africa is undoubtedly of great antiquity, no one will ever know for certain when the first grains of gold were mined from the hills or gathered from river sands by the people of the Akan forest zone and adjacent savanna regions.

Modern research confirms that gold from the Upper Volta River region was one of the three main sources for the trans-Saharan gold trade from at least the fourteenth century onward; and there is speculation that knowledge of the overland trade and of mining itself could have been brought south to the Akan region in medieval times by Manding peoples from the bend of the Niger. Scattered references in early Portuguese sources provide information on the coastal ports where gold first was traded to Europeans, for example, Axim in the district of Ahanta, Samaa (Shama) in the kingdom of Yabi, and Acomane (Kommnda). In addition, Afuto (Fetu), Fanti, Agonna, and Accra were clearly identified as early gold-exporting coastal towns; but we have scant information on the locations of interior gold mines, let alone details on exactly how the gold was mined, partly because Akan chiefs kept such information secret from interloping adventurers. By the late seventeenth century, as state formation evolved, European travelers were regularly listing Wassa, Denkyera, Akyem, Asante, and Gyaman as the main Akan gold mining kingdoms; but these same sources stated that some gold retrieval took place in almost every Akan state.

The major gold-bearing zone in Ghana begins approximately forty miles inland from the southwestern coast and extends in a rectangular form for about two hundred miles in a northeasterly direction through the heart of the forest zone to the Kwahu Escarpment. Gold in Ghana can be classified according to three main types: (1) alluvial or placer gold; (2) hard rock, also known as lode or vein gold; and (3) subsurface soil and outcrop gold. The most important geological strata are the Birimian and the Tarkwaian, both formed in the Precambrian period; and it is in these strata that the major intrusions of gold have occurred. Of lode or vein gold deposits there were basically two types in Ghana: (a) banket formations and (b) quartz reef formations. Most of the richer banket deposits of the Wassa-Fiase state in southwestern Ghana, particularly Tarkwa and Aboso, were found in one of the basic Tarkwaaian substrata known as the Banket Series, whereas the main quartz reef gold formations, found mainly in Asante and also in the Heman-Prestea west of the River Ankobra, derived mainly from the older and deeper Birimian strata. Much of the quartz vein gold existed in a free state and could be easily milled; but some was embedded in sulfide ores which required complex mechanized techniques for separation.

Early European sources attest that the Akan were "a nation of born gold finders"; and recently gathered evidence demonstrates that the search for and mining for gold occupied much more time in the life of Akan men and women in many locales than was formerly recognized by historians. Thus, the main economic pursuits of the peoples of Wassa in the southwest and of Akyem in the eastern Gold Coast were listed as farming, hunting and fishing, trading, foraging, and gold mining, with the latter predominating. Traditional gold mining tended to be a seasonal activity, with alluvial or placer mining taking place mainly during the rainy season along the seashore and the banks of streams, with pit or reef gold mining concentrated in the dry months of the year between the planting and harvesting seasons, when the water table was low. Akan gold miners were amazingly skilled and inventive. The perfection of gold-finding techniques (one of which was known as "loaming"), the cracking of rock by fire-setting, indigenous development of specialized iron tools, and the digging and reinforcement of deep shafts, with occasional timbering and lagging, were among their many innovations over the centuries. The most common form of mine was the open pit or shaft, dug from the top or side of a hill; and these might assume a variety of shapes and sizes, with some running as deep as 200 feet. There were clear-cut divisions of labor among Akan miners, mainly along lines of sex: underground mining for gold embedded in quartz or banket reefs was almost exclusively a male activity; while panning for river gold, plus pulverization and separation of reef gold in the final stages, were mainly the tasks of women and young girls. Slaves were sometimes used in mining, but mainly as adjuncts to the small family work unit, rather than as the components of a separate and central slave-based mining work force.

Gold mining, and the overland as well as the seaborne gold trades, were also important for state building among the Akan. It is generally recognized that the earliest Akan state was Bono-Manso in the Brong-Ahafo region northwest of Kumase. Early gold mining sites were located near the present-day villages of Bamboi, Jugboi, and Wasipe on the eastern side of the Black Volta River. It was from Bono-Mansu that the system of divine kingship and the use of the golden regalia—the sword, the mace and, above all, the royal throne (or stool)—evolved and diffused southward to later developing Akan states. Of the people of the central forest zone who first brought gold dust to Europeans on the coast in the sixteenth and seventeenth centuries, the most important were the Accany (the term is almost synonymous with "traders"), who came from the heartland territory known by the same name. And their original homeland, in the basin between the Pra-Offin and Birim Rivers, is generally regarded as the seedbed for southern Akan state formation.

There continues to be some scholarly debate over the degree of involvement and intervention by precolonial Akan kings and chiefs in the actual mining process. The scholarly consensus is that the main connection between mining and the state lay in revenue collection, and that digging, crushing, and panning were carried on mainly by solitary individuals, or by family labor under direction of the head of household. Kings and chiefs could skim off a portion of the proceeds from family mining, either under the traditional *abusa* share system (a kind of seigniorage) or through a system of corvee, or compulsory labor, in which villages would be expected to work on a certain day of the week or month on behalf of the king or local ruler In theory all nuggets discovered by miners became the property of the state. The resplendent yellow metal—in the form of ingots, gold dust currency, ornamentation for the ruling class and jewelry for ordinary people—became the touchstone for the commercial wealth, social status, and the measurement for state power among the later great kingdoms of the Akan forest zone, including Akwamu, Denkyera, Wassa, Gyaman, Akyem, and, above all, Asante. Taxes in gold dust on the estates of all deceased persons, court fines and fees on slaves purchased for shipment to the coast, a tax on every subordinate chief paid in proportion to the increase in his gold ornamentation, and a customs duty paid in gold by all traders returning from the coast provided (along with profits from the trade in slaves and kola nuts) the main foundations for the enormous economic surplus of the great Asante kingdom. Added to this were the great sums derived every year from the tributes levied, paid partly in gold, but also in slaves, and other products, imposed on conquered states within the "Greater Asante" Empire.

Any attempt to put forward estimates, either for the gold exports, let alone, annual gold production of the Gold Coast/Ghana during particular centuries, faces innumerable difficulties. Over the years, several scholars have ventured broad estimates on the total amount of gold exported from the Gold Coast since the beginning of the European contact to about 1900. Timothy Garrard, in a conservative reckoning, puts the figure at 9,350,000 ounces from 1871 to 1900, with an average at 21,750 ounces per year. But such figures derive from the customs reports of European importing countries only, and they fail to account for smuggling and the wide variations between bumper years to decades when scarcely any gold exports were reported at the coastal stations. The overseas shipment of gold took a sharp drop in the early 1700s, and the export of slaves replaced it for the remainder of the century as the number one export from the Akan coast. Exports of gold overseas from traditional mining picked up again in 1850 and continued fairly steady until the end of the nineteenth century. As such guesses do not include the immense quantities of gold retained for local internal use, whether as jewelry, as gold dust currency for saving, for the overland trade, or skimmed off as taxation by the state, the annual amount of gold actually produced by Akan indigenous farmer-miners can never be known.

RAYMOND E. DUMETT

See also: **Akan and Asante; Asante Kingdom.**

Further Reading

Dumett, Raymond E. *El Dorado in West Africa: The Gold Mining Frontier, African Labor, and Colonial Capitalism in the Gold Coast.* Athens, Ohio: 1998.

Garrard, Timothy. *Akan Weights and the Gold Trade.* London, 1980.

Kesse, G. O. *The Mineral and Rock Resources of Ghana.* Boston, 1985.

Gold Coast: *See* Ghana (Republic of) (Gold Coast): Colonial Period: Administration

Gold: Mining Industry of Ghana: 1800 to the Present

The modern gold industry of the Gold Coast and Asante commenced with the gold boom of 1877–1883, which, although called a European "gold rush," was in fact orchestrated in large part by a coterie of educated African coastal merchants hoping to attract new capital to a stagnant mid-nineteenth-century West African economy based mainly on the export of palm products. Three of the African leaders of these pioneering efforts at mechanized mining were Ferdinand Fitzgerald, Dr. James Africanus Horton, and most importantly W. E. "Tarkwa" Sam, a trained mining engineer, known as the father of the Ghanaian mining industry. Unfortunately, mechanized mining during these pioneering decades was plagued by a number of difficulties, including poor sanitary and health conditions, for both Africans and Europeans, rudimentary extraction machinery, lack of engineering skills, inexperienced management, insufficient capital, and inadequate support by the colonial government. Transportation was the main problem. Until 1900, huge machines weighing several tons had to be fragmented into sections of 100 to 200 pounds for conveyance forty to fifty miles up-country by a combination of canoe transport up the Ankobra River and human porterage overland. Out of some thirty-seven registered companies, ten engaged in active mining operations, and just three produced substantial quantities of gold. Until 1898 successive British governments refused to fund railways on grounds of expense. The result was frequent breakage and extreme malfunction of those machines that even reached their destinations.

The decision of the British imperial government to build a railway from the port of Sekondi northward to the mining centers of Tarkwa (Wassa state) in 1901, to Obuasi in Asante in 1903, and to Prestea in 1910 constituted major turning points in the creation of a modern mining industry. Establishment of this modern transport infrastructure, which made possible the installation of the most up-to-date heavy machinery, was followed by a second gold rush and speculative investment euphoria, known as the "jungle boom," even greater than that of twenty years earlier. As early as 1901, some thirty-three companies had exhibited an interest in as many as 2,325 separate concessions in the Gold Coast and Asante. By 1904 at the end of the boom a total of 3,500 concessions had been leased out to more than 200 companies, with a total invested capital of over four million pounds sterling. The main beneficiary of the government railway was the giant Ashanti Goldfields Corporation (AGC), founded by Edwin A. Cade and Frederick Gordon, with strong backing from London investors. During its peak years of twentieth-century production, the AGC returned over eight ounces of gold for every ten tons of ore that was excavated.

Gold production for all the mines of the Gold Coast and Asante remained high and steady from 1905 through 1919 with an average of 300,149 ounces valued at £1,275,070 per year. The major decline and slowdown came less during the two world wars than in the 1920s. Total gold output accelerated again in the early 1930s, owing to a fall in the gold price of the major world currencies. Gold Coast production reached its highest levels in the first four years of World War II, when there was a heavy demand for gold for a wide variety of uses related to war-related production. From 1930 to 1950, gold production averaged 557,519 ounces, valued at £2,363,529 per annum for all mines. During this same twenty year period, the size of the Gold Coast African mines labor force grew from 7,165 in 1930–1931 to 31,072 personnel. Of this total, about 50 per cent were recruited from the Northern Territories of the Gold Coast and the neighboring French colonial territories of Upper Volta and Côte d'Ivoire. With this expansion came trade union organization.

The modern organizational structure of gold mining in Ghana dates from the 1960s when, following Ghana's independence in 1957, a majority of Ghana's gold mines—with the notable exception of Ashanti Goldfields—having become unprofitable operations, were absorbed into the new Ghana State Mining Corporation. In 1969 the Ashanti Goldfields Corporation was taken over by the Lonrho Group, a major multinational conglomerate. Subsequently, a joint management agreement was reached between the AGC and the Ghana government concerning direction, investment strategies, development, and the distribution of profits.

RAYMOND E. DUMETT

See also: **Ghana: Nationalism, Rise of, and the Politics of Independence; Gold: Production and Trade: West Africa.**

Further Reading

Dumett, Raymond E. *El Dorado in West Africa: The Gold Mining Frontier, African Labor, and Colonial Capitalism in the Gold Coast.* Athens, Ohio: Crisp, 1998.
Crisp, Jeff. *The Story of an African Working Class: Ghanaian Miners' Struggles, 1870–1980.* London, 1984.
Stockwell, S.E. *The Business of Decolonization: British Business Strategies in the Gold Coast.* New York, 2000.
Wilks, Ivor. *Asante in the Nineteenth Century.* Cambridge, 1975.

Gold: Production and Trade: West Africa

Gold was an important staple in the trans-Saharan trade. The lure of gold spurred the Portuguese exploration down the African coast. But long before the Portuguese began exploring, gold from West Africa had reached Europe and the Middle East through the trans-Saharan trade. The exact location of gold mines often remained a secret, because middlemen tried to prevent foreigners from reaching them. Gold and gold mining were also traditionally associated with legend and myth. For example, when Mansa Musa (1312–1337), the ruler of the Sudanese kingdom of Mali, visited Egypt, he described two plants in his country whose roots contained pure gold.

Although gold from West Africa had reached Europe and the Middle East for centuries, its flow from West Africa dramatically increased from the middle of the eighth century. From the eighth century until the

Lobi women washing for gold, southwest Burkina Faso (Upper Volta), 1930s. This work was done entirely by women, each of whom was paid one franc per day. © SVT Bild/Das Fotoarchiv.

twelfth century, most of the gold coming from West Africa remained in the Muslim world. In the centuries before 1200, Western Europe had abandoned gold as the basis for its currency, as most of the gold at the time had been drained through an adverse balance of trade with the East. However, from the second half of the thirteenth century and the beginning of the fourteenth century, European countries returned to the gold standard, and the demand for, as well as the volume of gold, once more increased.

Gold from West Africa came from four principal fields: Bambuhu, between the Senegal and the Faleme Rivers, Bure on the Upper Niger, Lobi, southeast of the Bure fields, and the Akan gold fields in present-day Ghana and Côte d'Ivoire.

The Bambuhu fields were mined when Ghana was at its apogee. The king of Ghana ruled that gold nuggets found in the mines of his country should be reserved for him and his people could have only the gold dust.

During the eleventh and twelfth centuries Sudanese traders ventured south and opened the Bure gold fields. This shift of gold sources in effect coincided with the decline of Ghana. Ghana had actually controlled the gold fields, but it turned out that whenever the area of production was conquered and controlled, gold production in the area declined or stopped completely.

The rise of Mali in the thirteenth century was associated with the development of the Bure gold fields. The king of Mali did not control the gold fields, however, for fear that gold production would be interrupted. Mali was content to extract tribute from the gold-bearing regions. It was gold from this region that the Mali ruler Mansa Musa (1312–1337) distributed on a lavish scale during his pilgrimage to Mecca. Mansa Musa reputedly arrived in Egypt with camels loaded with gold bars and bags of gold dust. He spent and gave away so much gold that it depressed the currency exchange for twelve years.

The kings of the Songhay Empire, which was further away from the Bure and Akan gold fields, did not control the production of gold either, but they too benefited from the gold passing through their empire.

The gold that was produced and traded in West Africa was also used as currency in the commercial centers of north Africa and the western Sudan. Even in the sixteenth century, commercial centers such as Jenne and Timbuktu continued using gold as currency for larger transactions. Before the fifteenth century, gold and the production of gold were in the hands of Africans and African merchants.

When the Portuguese arrived on the west African coast during the fifteenth century, they sought to secure a share of the gold trade that had previously reached Europe through the north African ports on the Mediterranean Sea. In 1448 the Portuguese built a fort at Arguin, hoping that it might divert some of the trans-Saharan gold trade to the adjacent African coast, but very little gold flowed to that trading post. When Portugal reached the area of Senegambia in the 1450s, it was able to secure some gold coming mainly from the gold fields of Bure and Bambuhu. In fact, it was their interest in gold that led the unsuccessful effort by the Portuguese to interfere in the affairs of the Jolof by attempting to unseat Bumi Jelen as their ruler in the late fifteenth century. The Portuguese interest in gold further led them to establish the first European post in the African interior, in Bambuhu, in the sixteenth century. The English also advertised the Gambia region as the source of the gold trade in the seventeenth century. Meanwhile, the French focused their trading plans on the Senegal on both gold and slaves.

In 1471 when the Portuguese reached the Gold Coast, Mande merchants were already active in the area and the Portuguese found themselves competing with the Mande for the gold from the Akan gold fields. Despite the presence of the Mande, the Portuguese did profitable business in gold and maintained a monopoly on this trade for one hundred and fifty years, until they were dislodged by the Dutch. Their desire to protect the gold trade led the Portuguese to build the Elmina castle. Not only did the Portuguese build a castle, they also brought slaves from the area of Benin to the Gold Coast to work in the mines.

Annual Portuguese gold exports from the Akan gold fields between 1481 and 1521 are estimated at between 20,000 and 25,000 ounces. There was, however, a drastic decline after 1550. Gold mining was a peacetime activity, and the competition from the slave trade and the method of procuring slaves no doubt affected gold exports. Export volume was further affected when most of the alluvial layer was exhausted and deep mining was required. In the Akan area, it was clear by the second decade of the eighteenth century that the so-called Gold Coast had become primarily concerned in slave trading. Gold exports declined after 1550 and did not recover until the middle of the nineteenth century.

EDWARD REYNOLDS

Further Reading

Curtin, Philip D. *Economic Change in Precolonial Africa.* Madison: University of Wisconsin Press, 1975.

Dumett, Raymond E. *El Dorado in West Africa: The Gold-Mining Frontier, African Labor, and Colonial Capitalism in the Gold Coast, 1875–1900.* Athens: Ohio University Press, 1998.

Gerrard, Timothy F. *Akan Weights and the Gold Trade.* London: Longman, 1980.

Sundstrom, Lars. *The Trade of Guinea.* Upsala, Oslo, 1965.

Wilks, Ivor. *Forest of Gold: Essays on the Akan and the Kingdom of Asante.* Athens: Ohio University Press, 1993.

Goré: *See* **Senegal: Colonial Period: Four Communes: Dakar, Saint-Louis, Goré, and Rufisque.**

Gore-Browne, Stewart (1890–1967)
Politician

Sir Stewart Gore-Browne was one of the most important settler politicians in Northern Rhodesia (Zambia). He led the white Legislative Council between 1939 and 1946, and represented African interests in the Legislative Council until 1951. He was a firm believer in the African nationalist cause, as evidenced by his sponsorship of legislation favorable to Africans.

Gore-Browne was active in settler politics, but with a keen interest in the affairs of the African population. When he was elected to the Legislative Council, he immediately demonstrated a clear understanding of the Africans, especially those in the rural areas. He was opposed to racial segregation and championed the cause for cooperation between the races in the running of the country as early as the late 1930s. It was on the basis of these views that, in 1938, he was selected to represent African interests in the council. Gore-Browne used his new position to initiate the creation of Urban Courts and African Advisory Councils, first on the Copperbelt and later in the rest of the urban areas of the country. The African Advisory Councils gave Africans in Northern Rhodesia an opportunity to participate in local urban politics.

He learned to speak *iciBemba* very well and was therefore able to communicate with the local people in the Northern Province. This gave him the advantage of being able to discuss problems and political issues with Africans in a language they understood. He also ensured that Europeans listened to educated Africans as well as African chiefs. Because of his position as representative for African interests in the Legislative Council, and also because of his interest in the affairs of Africans, he often spoke to African Welfare Societies and deliberately encouraged the development of nationalist movements. He genuinely sought to integrate the two nations while fighting against the oppression of Africans. Throughout his political career he worked for a steady increase in African political, social and economic rights.

Although he was considered a friend of Africans and one who understood them, he sometimes made mistakes and proposed ideas which were opposed by Africans. In 1948 he proposed the partition of Northern Rhodesia into an African-controlled area and a European area. His argument was that Africans would attain self-rule in their area without European opposition. The idea was not acceptable to Africans because the proposed African area was the lesser developed, while the European area included the Copperbelt and other areas along the line of rail. His proposal angered African nationalists who saw him as serving European interests. Undoubtedly, Gore-Browne was inspired by the existing white rule in Southern Rhodesia. African nationalists, including Kenneth Kaunda, condemned his attitude. African nationalists at a meeting in July at Munali School confirmed their opposition to the renomination of Gore-Browne as representative for African interests in the Legislative Council.

Yet Gore-Browne was usually in conflict with Europeans because of his desire to see African self-rule in Northern Rhodesia. Europeans who favored amalgamation with Southern Rhodesia were not happy with his call for African self-rule. Gore-Browne found himself in a position where neither the African nationalists nor European settlers were happy with him. He further alienated African nationalists when he called for African self-rule within the Federation of Rhodesia and Nyasaland. His support for the creation of the federation, which he believed to be a compromise that would help both races, made African suspicious of his motives.

In 1961 Gore-Browne officially joined the United National Independence Party (UNIP), led by Kenneth David Kaunda, who was to become the first president of the Republic of Zambia. As a member of UNIP, in April 1962 he accompanied Kaunda to New York where Kaunda delivered a speech to the United Nations' Commission on Colonialism. When Legislative Council elections were called for October 1962, he stood on a UNIP ticket but was not elected despite African support. As Zambia was approaching independence, Gore-Browne was again very close to African nationalists, especially given that he was one of few European settlers who officially joined the nationalist party.

Gore-Browne remained in Zambia after independence until his death on August 4, 1967. President Kaunda declared a state funeral for Gore-Browne in honor of his support for the African nationalist cause.

BIZECK JUBE PHIRI

See also: **Kaunda, Kenneth; Zambia (Northern Rhodesia): Federation, 1953–1963; Zambia: Nationalism, Independence.**

Biography

Sir Stewart Gore-Browne (1890–1967) was born into an upper-class British family in Great Britain. He first came to Northern Rhodesia in 1911 as an army officer with the joint Anglo-Belgian Commission, which set the Congo-Rhodesian border. After the commission's work he returned to Britain, but in 1921 he returned to Northern Rhodesia and started a farm at Shiwa

Ng'andu in the northern part of the country among the Bemba people. As a wealthy landowner, he married Lorna Goldman, with whom he had two daughters. Together in the late 1920s and early 1930s, they developed the estate at Shiwa Ng'andu. They divorced in 1950. Gore-Browne died in Zambia on August 4, 1967.

Further Reading

Davidson, James W. *The Northern Rhodesia Legislative Council.* London: Oxford University Press, 1948.

Gann, Louis H. *A History of Northern Rhodesia: Early Days to 1953.* London: Chatto and Windus Press, 1964.

Rotberg, Robert I. *The Rise of Nationalism in Central Africa: The Making of Malawi and Zambia 1873–1964.* New Haven, Conn.: Yale University Press, 1965.

Rotberg, Robert I. *Black Heart: Gore-Browne and the Politics of Multiracial Zambia.* Berkeley: University of Carlifornia Press, 1977.

Scannell, Theodore D. "Profile: Sir Stewart Gore-Browne." *Horizon* 6, no. 7 (July 1964): 16–19.

Stabler, John B. "Northern Rhodesian Reaction to 1948 Responsible Government Proposals: The Role of Sir Stewart Gore-Browne." *Journal of South African Affairs* 3, no. 3 (July 1978): 295–317.

Gowon Regime: *See* Nigeria: Gowon Regime, 1966–1975.

Great Lakes Region: Growth of Cattle Herding

Cattle herding was to become one of the major social divides in the later kingdoms of the Great Lakes region, and the supposed basis for twentieth-century rivalries between Tusi and Hutu in Rwanda and Burundi and Hima and Iru in southwestern Uganda.

The evidence for the origins of cattle herding in the Great Lakes region is meager. Livestock had definitely been introduced to East Africa by 2000BCE, and many sites have been excavated in the Rift Valley, being given the name of the (Savanna) Pastoral Neolithic. These were stone tool and pottery-using societies, which maintained both smaller livestock and cattle.

In the entire Great Lakes Region itself, prior to 1000, the evidence for livestock is restricted to two sites from Rwanda, associated with Urewe pottery, with unspecified finds of cattle teeth. This absence is partially an issue of bone preservation. Histories based on the comparative linguistics of the region do shed considerably more light on the issue. The initial iron- and pottery-using, Bantu-speaking farmers, who emerged from the forests to the west in the first millennium BCE, would not have had access to either cattle or grain agriculture. It is no coincidence that the Urewe settlement is confined to the forested margins of Lake Victoria and the highlands of the Western Rift. While sites with Urewe pottery represent virtually the only

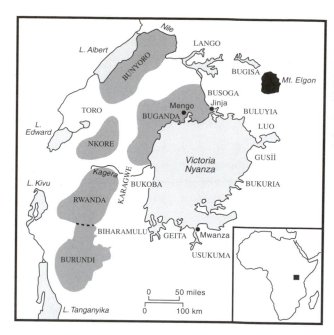

The Great Lakes region, *c*.1800.

archaeologically recognized phenomena for this time period, comparative linguistics indicate that the drier interior areas, termed the Karagwe Depression, would have been inhabited by stone tool-using pastoralists, speaking both Sudanic and Cushitic languages. Most notably, the words for cattle, sorghum, and finger millet in Great Lakes Bantu languages today can all be demonstrated to have either Sudanic or Cushitic origins. The linguistic record further indicates that in the ensuing 1,000 years of contact, up to around the year 500, these societies assimilated into a single society with a multilingual base.

From around 800 there are radical changes apparent in the linguistic record. Shifts of population are evident with major relocations in the drier interior grasslands. New terminologies for political authority indicate that there were also developments toward more centralized leadership, based on health and ritual healing. Most significantly, there is an "explosion" of terms associated with specialized cattle herding. In particular, these represent a proliferation of terms used to differentiate horn shapes, skin colors, and skin patterns; elements that are key in the emphasis and maintenance of recent pastoralist culture. The linguistic record indicates that this development of pastoralist tendencies came from within the Great Lakes region and were not the product of a migration or invasion by pastoralists from far to the north. For instance, all the new terms for describing cattle have demonstrably Great Lakes Bantu roots.

Archaeological evidence for these developments has been derived from the site of Ntusi, southwestern Uganda. From 1000 to 1400 a large settlement flourished at this site. The animal bone remains recovered from throughout the occupation of the site indicate a uniform preference for cattle over small livestock and wild animals, with between 80 and 90 per cent of assemblages comprising cattle. Furthermore, mortality profiles for these cattle, based on tooth eruption and wear and on long-bone fusion criteria, indicate that the assemblages are dominated by young animals, suggesting large herds and relatively sophisticated livestock management strategies. While this archaeological data clearly indicates a new habitation of the central grasslands—and there is a uniform change in pottery use throughout the Great Lakes region associated with this new settlement—these changes can be interpreted as representing radical changes in political and economic structures rather than a simple migration into the region of a new population. Importantly, the occupation of Ntusi is not simply pastoralist; it also had a visible and extensive agricultural contribution. This is evidenced by grain-harvesting knives, grinding stones, storage pits, and by pottery that can be directly associated with the cooking of grains. Most notably, one location at Ntusi appears to have been a livestock enclosure associated with several houses, but also storage pits, grinding stones, and harvesting knives. Furthermore, 33 per cent of the pottery assemblage recovered from this location can be associated with grain preparation. What this evidence indicates is that in the fourteenth century, agriculture and cattle-herding were still in association at the household level, and that the exclusive and specialized pastoralism, and therefore the pastoral elites, of the later kingdoms had not yet emerged.

On the basis of this archaeological evidence it can be argued that gender roles would also have changed, with the emphasis on cattle herding leading to a lessening of female contribution to select household economies. This suggestion is further strengthened by the evidence for altered gender roles and values that appear at this time in the linguistic record. Such gender relations culminated in the total exclusion of women from pastoralist production.

These conclusions on political authority and social divisions concur with recent revisions of history based on oral traditions. These revisions emphasize the late development of kingdoms from chiefdoms in the seventeenth and eighteenth centuries, and the formalization of social divisions, in part based on economic practice. It is from these times that pastoralist ideologies will have emerged, establishing the ethnic differences between pastoralists and agriculturalists and promoting exclusive pastoralist diets. These ideologies would also have helped to formulate new constructions of history which projected the authority of cattle-keepers into the past.

The association between cattle keeping and political authority is well demonstrated at two later archaeological sites. Both Bweyorere, a seventeenth- and nineteenth-century Nkore capital, and Ryamurari, an eighteenth-century Ndorwa site, consist of a main enclosure with large middens ringing their lower edges and with smaller enclosures radiating out from these centers. Each enclosure clearly emulated a cattle kraal, and the animal bone from the sites appears to have been dominated by cattle remains. Nevertheless, it is important to remember that the kings who inhabited such capitals ultimately stood above the pastoralist-agriculturalist divide and in their rituals emphasized both livestock and agriculture.

Thus, the combined archaeological, linguistic and historical evidence currently suggests that the growth of cattle herding was a gradual process, which took place over a long period of time and which had its roots within the Great Lakes region.

ANDREW REID

Further Reading

Posnansky, M. "The Excavation of an Ankole Capital Site at Bweyorere." *Uganda Journal* 32 (1968): 165–182.

Reid, A. "Ntusi and the Development of Social Complexity in Southern Uganda." In *Aspects of African Archaeology: Papers from the 10th Congress of the Pan African Association for Prehistory and Related Studies*, edited by G. Pwiti and R. Soper. Harare: University of Zimbabwe Press, 1996.

Robertshaw, P. T. *Early Pastoralists of South-western Kenya.* Nairobi: British Institute in Eastern Africa, 1990.

Schoenbrun D. L. *A Green Place, A Good Place. Agrarian Change, Gender, and Social Identity in the Great Lakes Region to the 15th Century.* Portsmouth, N.H.: Oxford: James Currey, 1998.

Steinhart, E. I. "Herders and Farmers: The Tributary Mode of Production in Western Uganda." In *Modes of Production in Africa: The Precolonial Era*, edited by D. E. Crummey and C. C. Stewart. London: Sage, 1981.

Sutton J. E. G. "The Antecedents of the Interlacustrine Kingdoms." *Journal of African History* 34 (1993): 33–64.

Great Lakes Region: Karagwe, Nkore, and Buhaya

Karagwe, Nkore, and Buhaya formed small neighboring states to the major kingdoms of Bunyoro and Buganda in the Great Lakes region. Karagwe and Nkore were individual polities, while Buhaya refers to an area along the western side of Lake Victoria in which seven small states were recognized: Kiamutwara, Kiziba, Ihangiro, Kihanja, Bugabo, Maruku, and Missenye.

Although this entry only deals with the period up to the end of the eighteenth century, it is essential to recognize that the earlier histories of these polities and the detail with which they have been recorded are a direct product of nineteenth- and twentieth-century history and the circumstances which befell them. Nkore (Ankole in colonial times) found itself within the British Protectorate of Uganda and became a cornerstone of Protectorate policy, being one of the four main kingdoms and enjoying a considerably enlarged territorial status under the Protectorate than it had done in precolonial times. It was also served well by various missionaries, ethnographers, anthropologists, and historians. Buhaya was moderately well served, partly through expedient politics in the early colonial era and the siting of the regional colonial administrative center in Bukoba. By contrast, Karagwe fell from being one of the most powerful of the nineteenth century states in the Great Lakes, a position it had largely attained through its domination of early Indian Ocean–Great Lakes trade routes, to total collapse and obscurity by 1916. Writers on Karagwe have been sporadic and have failed to provide the rich array of texts that are available for Nkore, its northern neighbor. In independent Tanzania, under Nyerere, there was little place for such overtly unequal, precolonial political formations.

Not surprisingly, the earliest farming settlements appeared in the wet coastal littoral of Buhaya, on the western shores of Lake Victoria. Archaeological research has indicated extensive activity, most notably in terms of iron smelting, from the last few centuries BCE. These societies exploited the extensive rainforests that were available at the time and, after initial cultivation of yams and other forest crops, presumably became proficient in the exploitation of bananas. Linguistic and archaeological evidence in Karagwe and Nkore on the other hand, indicates occupation around the beginning of the second millennium, based upon the increasing exploitation of cattle, supported by grain crops. From these bases, the core elements of the polities undoubtedly developed, although there is little evidence, as yet, to document the process.

The actual origins of the dynasties that came to dominate are also unclear, being dependent on the interpretation of oral traditions. At face value, in all areas, dynasties claimed origin back to the Cwezi persona, Wamara. Subsequently, power fell into the hands of Ruhinda, and descent was directly drawn to him by many of the royal clans, known as Abahinda. Reinterpretations of these oral traditions suggest that characters such as Wamara and Ruhinda may well have been charismatic chiefs, who, after their deaths, became important spirits controlled by mediums tied to political power. Shrines to Wamara and Ruhinda were specifically associated with the manipulation and control of fertility.

A further integral component of these polities was clans. Each polity was an amalgamation of clans, and each clan contributed important components to the polity. Clans involved in the polity at an earlier stage tended to be regarded with a higher status. Clans were also associated with specialized activity, such as cattle-herding,

iron-smelting, and regulating rituals. The royal clan sat atop this confederation and carefully maintained the status quo, by allocating particular offices to specific clans and by accepting wives for the king from the different clans. Thus, the mother of the king and her clan were very powerful in each individual reign, and this power helps to explain the regularity of succession disputes revealed by oral traditions. Particularly in drier Karagwe and Nkore, there was also an increasing importance in the distinction between cattle-herding Bahima and farmers. In later years, these economic pastimes became almost mutually exclusive and were the foundations of class formation. It is significant, however, that although kings generally leaned toward pastoralism as an ideal lifestyle, even in the later centuries the king stood above the cattle–agriculture dichotomy, practicing rituals which were integral to both economic forms. Most notably, every month kings conducted the New Moon rituals which ensured the fertility of the land and the fecundity of cattle. Furthermore, at least some kings were also regarded as iron smiths (but not smelters). The best-known example of this was the incorporation of iron-working hammers into the royal regalia of Karagwe, generally associated with *Omukama* Ndagara in the early nineteenth century.

These fairly simplistic reconstructions, of course, mask the major tensions and conflicts that existed within these states. An insight into such political intrigue has been provided by the historical work focusing on the Kaijja shrine, within the Maruku kingdom, twenty kilometers south of Bukoba. The site is the *gashani*, or jaw-bone shrine, of the seventeenth- and eighteenth-century king, Rugomora Mahe, who is said to have occupied the site and to have overseen iron-working there. The site is also an important shrine to the Cwezi spirit, Wamara. All the Buhaya states record a change from Hinda to Bito rulers around the seventeenth century, referring to the extension of Bito dynastic influence from Bunyoro. Significantly, Rugomora Mahe was an early Bito ruler, and his association with the shrine is interpreted as an integral part of the ritual conflict between Hinda followers and their spirits, and the new Bito rulers. At broadly similar times oral traditions in Karagwe and Nkore record incursions and even lengthy occupations by forces from Bunyoro, but emphasize ultimate victory over the invaders.

In Nkore, it has been possible to identify sites associated with political authority, extending several centuries back into the past. The locations of these sites indicate that the early core Nkore area was in a restricted highland area, Isingiro, twenty kilometers south of the modern center of Mbarara. The suggestion is therefore that these were initially very localized political formations, some of which gradually expanded. Military power was initially realized in terms of numbers.

The Buhaya states were all small and do not appear to have had a significant military capability. Karagwe does appear to have had military strength, and this may have been due to its greater population size. Nkore, from its small base, does not appear to have had expansionist pretensions, or more importantly, capability, until key changes in its military organization. The creation of permanent levies of troops, known as *Emitwe*, allowed both the conquest of territory such as Mpororo and Buhweju and also the protection of its increasing herds from powerful neighbors to the north.

It is important to emphasize that, in their early stages, all these polities were small and vulnerable. In particular, they appear to have been susceptible to succession disputes, which seem to have been the main cause of conflict. More detailed histories of significant changes in structure and organization only really begin to emerge toward the end of the eighteenth century, when some polities started looking beyond their frontiers for new territories and resources to control.

ANDREW REID

See also: **Buganda: To Nineteenth Century; Bunyoro; Nyerere, Julius; Uganda: Colonial Period: Administration, Economy.**

Further Reading

Karugire, S. R. *A History of the Kingdom of Nkore in Western Uganda to 1896*. Oxford: Clarendon Press, 1971.

Katoke, I. K. *The Karagwe Kingdom: A History of the Abanyambo of North-West Tanzania*. Nairobi: East Africa Publishing House, 1975.

Reid, D. A. M., and R. MacLean. "Symbolism and the Social Contexts of Iron Production in Karagwe." *World Archaeology* 27, no. 1 (1995): 144–161.

Reid, D. A. M., and P. T. Robertshaw. "A New Look at Ankole Capital Sites." *Azania* 22 (1987): 83–88.

Roscoe, J. *The Banyankole*. Cambridge: Cambridge University Press, 1923.

Schmidt, P. R. *Historical Archaeology: A Structural Approach in an African Culture*. Westport, Conn.: Greenwood, 1978.

Schoenbrun, D. L. *A Green Place, a Good Place. Agrarian Change, Gender, and Social Identity in the Great Lakes Region to the 15th Century*. Oxford: James Currey, 1998.

Steinhart, E. I. "Herders and Farmers: The Tributary Mode of Production in Western Uganda." In *Modes of Production in Africa: The Precolonial Era*, edited by D. E. Crummey and C. C. Stewart. London: Beverley Hills, Calif.: Sage, 1981.

Great Lakes Region: Kitara and the Chwezi Dynasty

The Chwezi are an enigmatic people, their legacy marked by a blend of myth and history. Their legends are so well woven and compelling as to make them seem authentic, yet the little available evidence, at least at this time, does not seem to bear out the historical myths that surround them.

The Chwezi are legendary figures said to have ruled over a vast empire known as Bunyoro-Kitara in the interlacustrine region of East Africa, with a short-lived dynasty lasting from 1350 to 1500. This empire is thought to have covered the territory extending from Bunyoro in western Uganda, as delineated by the southern banks of the Nile, to the central Nyanza district of Kenya among the Wanga people. Then, within the north-south latitudes, the empire is said to have stretched from the Albert Nile in the north covering all the Sesse Islands and then on to the kingdoms of northwestern Tanzania of Ukerewe, Usukuma, Karagwe, as well as Rwanda and Burundi to the southwest of Uganda and finally into the Mboga region of the Democratic Republic of Congo. In some sources, writers have even argued that Bunyoro-Kitara could have covered the whole of modern Uganda and parts of southern Sudan.

Many theories have been advanced, all attempting to establish the identity and nature of the Chwezi. They are said to have been of a relatively light complexion and to have arrived from "the north." Some writers have described the Chwezi as having been of Caucasian stock, an off-shoot of Caucasian Egyptians, who had sailed up the Nile into the interlucustrine region, especially into Bunyoro and Buganda. Some of these claims mesh well with explorer Hannington Speke's "hamitic hypothesis" of a highly civilized Caucasian group which colonized the blacks of Central Africa and set up the well-organized interlucustrine kingdoms, which the early explorers encountered in the nineteenth century. However, this hypothesis has been discredited since the 1970s.

For the origins of the Chwezi, legend provides a link between the Chwezi and the Batembuzi rulers through Nyinamwiru, a daughter of Bukuku from the Batembuze period. This tradition mentions a dynasty of only three Chwezi kings. These were Ndahura, his half-brother Mulindwa, and his son Wamara. The Chwezi took over the kingdom from equally mystical figures, the Batembuze (pioneers), through a matrilineal connection, the mother of Ndahura having been a Mutembuzi clanswoman, daughter of Bukuku from the Batembuze period.

A dynasty with three rulers (two brothers and a son) could only cover two to three generations, covering perhaps fifty or sixty years at most of Chwezi rule. Yet oral tradition has claimed a period of about 250 years for the Chwezi's rule. This is not possible; the available facts simply do not match the claimed time span.

The end of the Chwezi rule over Bunyoro-Kitara, which occurred around 1500, is as unclear as the beginning. Legend conveniently explains that the Chwezi simply "disappeared" from Bunyoro-Kitara because of a bad omen that had been cast against them. However, not wanting to leave a political vacuum, they sent word to descendants of Kyomya (a Muchwezi) with Nyatwor, a Mukidi woman, to come to Bunyoro-Kitara and "take over the kingdom of their Batembuze forefathers." These descendants were the Babiito who, we now know, are of Lwo origin, from across the Nile River in Acholiland and Lango.

The Palwo of Pawir in the Karuma falls area (Otada, or Sir Samuel Bakers' BaChopi), who are unmistakably Lwo, have direct ethnic links with the Babiito of Bunyoro. The Palwo Babiito themselves belong to the Lobiito clan. Both families in Bunyoro and Karuma (Otada) participate in each other's royal installation ceremonies and cannot complete their own rituals without the participation of the other.

The turbulent years of Amin rule in Uganda adversely affected research in all fields. The history of Uganda has therefore not been revised or reassessed in light of new evidence since the hotchpotch reconstructions of the colonial administrator-cum-missionary-cum-anthropologists from a mixture of myth and fiction. Many of these imaginative reconstructions have already been recycled into "historical traditions" and are being passed on as part of authentic oral tradition. Bunyoro-Kitara history is similarly riddled with many such untested hypotheses.

A number of sites such as Kibengo, Kagogo, Kansonko, Bigo bya Mugenyi, and Mubende Hill all in western Uganda have been named as centers of Bachwezi's power. Chwezi are said to have lived and ruled from Bigo bya Mugenyi, a two-square-kilometer earthworks site in Mawogola county, near Masaka. There is, however, no evidence to support the presence of a powerful monarchy at Bigo bya Mugenyi, apart from the earthworks, the constructors of which must have had access to vast labor reserves. Many archaeologists working in the region have been seriously questioning the authenticity and existence of the Chwezi.

The Chwezi's mysterious departure and the seemingly peaceful takeover of their kingdom by the Babitto is also suspect. Popular rulers, as we are told the Chwezi were, normally simply do not up and leave without resisting or being defended by their loyal subjects. But present Bunyoro traditions strongly support this peaceful withdrawal. It is a version which proves that the current Babiito rulers of Bunyoro were the natural inheritors of the Chwezi kingdom, a convenient justification or legal charter of their take over of Bunyoro-Kitara kingdom.

The reality of the Chwezi is apparent today in the Chwezi cult, *Embandwa*, a spirit possession cult. The *Embandwa* cult has a pantheon of gods including Mugasa, Mulindwa, Wamala, and Ndahura. These are now recognized, revered, and accepted in the entire Lake Victoria littoral and in the lake archipelago. People in these areas have always sought—and still seek—assistance for various ailments and wishes from these powerful gods through a number of spirit mediums. Some of these mediums are resident at specific shrine locations, others are constantly itinerant, while some ordinary people in western Uganda, northwestern Tanzania, Rwanda, and Burundi occasionally suffer possession by these Chwezi *embandwa*.

DAVID KIYAGA-MULINDWA

Further Reading

Apuuli, D. Kihumuro. *A Thousand Years of Bunyoro-Kitara Kingdom: The People and the Rulers.* Kampala: Fountain Publishers 1994.

Berger, I. "Deities, Dynasties, and Oral Tradition: The History and Legend of the Abacwezi." In *The African Past Speaks*, edited by J. C. Miller. Folkestone: Dawson, 1980.

Oliver, R. "A Question about the Bachwezi." *Uganda Journal* 22, no. 1 (1957).

Posnansky, M. "Toward an Historical Geography of Uganda." *East African Geographical Review*, 1963.

Posnansky, M. "Kingship, Archaeology and Historical Myth." *Uganda Journal*. 30, no. 1 (1986).

Robertshaw, P., and Kamuhangire, E. "The Present to the Past: Archaeological Sites, Oral Traditions, Shrines, and Politics in Uganda." In *Aspects of African Archaeology*, edited by G. Pwiti and R. Soper. Harare: University of Zimbabwe Press, 1996.

Great Lakes Region: Ntusi, Kibiro, and Bigo

Large archaeological sites have been recognized in western Uganda since the beginning of the twentieth century. These sites, which in some cases feature extensive ditch systems, were associated with oral traditions relating to Bacwezi—variously recognized as spirits, heroes, or historical characters—and in particular the sites were linked with the now discredited construct of the Bacwezi Empire. More recent archaeological work, in combination with revisions of history derived from oral traditions, indicates the importance of examining the archaeological record separately from other sources and generating robust archaeological constructs before comparing the diverse results.

Archaeological survey and excavation now show that the area in which these sites are found was not previously occupied by the early farming Urewe tradition. All of these sites are associated with roulette-decorated pottery which appeared at around or slightly before 1000. This new pottery tradition seems to have been widely adopted across the entire Great Lakes region but can be interpreted as reflecting a new organization of society rather than a migration of a new population into the region, an interpretation consistent with the reconstruction of history based on comparative linguistics.

The earliest of these new sites for which comprehensive evidence has been produced is Ntusi. Radiocarbon dates from the site indicate occupation between 1000 and 1400. The site covers an area of one square kilometer.

Although it is impossible at present to determine how much of the site was occupied at any one point in time, excavations suggest that many parts of the site were occupied in the thirteenth and fourteenth centuries. Archaeological survey of the Mawogola area, immediately around Ntusi, revealed the presence of numerous smaller sites. The size difference implies a hierarchy resulting from political dominance of Ntusi over its hinterland. The range of located sites suggests a comparatively small polity with centralized power but little administrative delegation of this power to local centers. The polity has therefore been interpreted as a small chiefdom.

All the Mawogola sites reveal a preponderance of cattle in the animal bone remains recovered. The outlying sites and certain locations at Ntusi itself are interpreted as cattle enclosures. Furthermore, mortality profiles of these remains indicate that the majority of animals slaughtered were very young, suggesting the presence of large herds and relatively sophisticated herd management strategies. An important component at all sites is also, however, evidence for agriculture. Grinding stones, storage pits, harvesting knives, and pottery damaged in cooking grain, all testify to the considerable significance of agriculture in the subsistence economy.

Best known of the western Ugandan sites are those with ditch networks. There are three principal sites in this category: Bigo, Munsa, and Kibengo. Bigo was investigated in the late 1950s. It comprises a network of ditches extending more than ten kilometers in length across several hillsides on the southern side of the Katonga River, only thirteen kilometers north of Ntusi. The radiocarbon dating for the site is problematic but suggests occupation in the fifteenth or sixteenth century and later. The features and artifacts produced in the excavations were little understood at the time but begin to make more sense in the light of recent archaeological work. The economy appears to be similar to that at Ntusi, with a mixture of cattle herding and agriculture.

Recent work has concentrated on the other two earthwork sites, Munsa and Kibengo. These two sites are situated in wetter terrain to the north and northwest of Bigo. Both sites again indicate a mixture of herding and grain agriculture in their subsistence strategies. Extensive excavation at Munsa has revealed that the main hilltop, around which the ditches concentrate, saw a range of different activities from 1200 to 1500. These activities include extensive burials, an iron-smelting furnace, and a huge pit, possibly for centralized grain storage. This careful work at Munsa indicates that there are likely to have been complex histories at all sites, which are unavailable to us due to the limitations of radiocarbon dating.

In all three cases the ditch networks remain enigmatic. They are clearly not simple defensive systems, since there are many points of ingress and often the inside bank of the ditch is markedly lower then the outside. The ditches, which are up to four meters in depth, may have been designed to keep cattle in, or alternatively to keep cattle or wildlife, such as elephants, out, possibly to protect crops. When freshly dug into the bright red subsoil, the ditches stand out very clearly within the well-vegetated green landscape. No doubt this visual impression was important. It is also worth noting that at Kasonko, six kilometers northeast of Bigo, a ditch system was created around a hilltop that has no obvious archaeological deposits, and so these sites were not always occupied. There is, therefore, little that can be said definitively about these earthworks. It has been noted that Kibengo, Munsa, and Bigo are located roughly equidistant from one another, approximately fifty kilometers apart, which suggests competing centers of similar influence. Again, the archaeological interpretation has been that these sites represent the centers of small chiefdoms that flourished and then disappeared prior to the kingdoms which arose later in the millennium. Elements of ritual and authority also seem to have been an important component at these centers.

A very different kind of site has been examined at Kibiro, on the shores of Lake Rwitanzige (Albert). Historically, Kibiro has been an important salt-producing center, and salt is still produced there today. Salt production is self-sustaining since it relies on salt-bearing springs saturating soil marked off in "gardens," water being poured through this soil, and finally the solution being boiled and reduced. Archaeological investigations have indicated that there has been continuous settlement at the site since the thirteenth century. Given that Kibiro lies in the rain shadow beneath the imposing escarpment of the east side of the lake, crop production is as unlikely to have been possible in the past as it is today. It is therefore likely that from the very beginnings of the settlement, apart from lake fish, communities would have been dependent on trading salt to acquire their subsistence needs.

Historical work has suggested that precolonial markets in the Great Lakes region would have featured trade in a wide range of produce including iron, salt, pottery, barkcloth, dried bananas, and grain. While many of these products are not likely to be preserved on archaeological sites, some early evidence for trade and exchange can be adduced. On a grand scale, the settlements at Ntusi and Kibiro represent populations moving into previously marginal areas and exploiting new forms of resources—cattle and salt—both of which would ultimately have required support from societies in other parts of the region. The presence of trade is also indicated by the recovery of glass Indian Ocean trade beads at Ntusi, Kibiro, Munsa, and Bigo and cowrie shells at Ntusi and Kibiro. These items are present in small quantities and they do not indicate direct contact between the Great Lakes region and the coast. Rather they can be seen as a testament to the attractive power of the Great Lakes markets, sucking in items from distant locations.

These archaeological sites therefore confirm that important advances in the regional political economy had occurred by the middle of the second millennium, with both the development of chiefdoms and the flourishing of trade and exchange. These conclusions tally well with reconstructions of oral history for the area, which emphasize the existence of short-term, charismatic leadership during this period. Comparative linguistics also indicate new forms of centralized authority at this time.

ANDREW REID

Further Reading

Connah, G.E. *Kibiro: The Salt of Bunyoro, Past and Present*, Nairobi: British Institute in Eastern Africa, Memoir 14, 1996.

Posnansky, M. "Bigo bya Mugenyi." *Uganda Journal* 33 (1969): 125–150.

Reid, A. "Ntusi and the Development of Social Complexity in Southern Uganda," in *Aspects of African Archaeology: Papers from the 10th Congress of the Pan African Association for Prehistory and Related Studies*, edited by G. Pwiti and R. Soper. Harare: University of Zimbabwe Press, 1996.

Robertshaw, P.T. "Munsa Earthworks: A Preliminary Report." *Azania*, 32 (1997): 1–20.

Robertshaw, P.T. "Seeking and Keeping Power in Bunyoro-Kitara, Uganda," in *Beyond Chiefdoms: Pathways to Complexity in Africa*, edited by S.K. McIntosh, Cambridge: Cambridge University Press, 1999.

Schmidt, P.R. "Oral Traditions, Archaeology and History: A Short Reflective History," in *A History of African Archaeology*, edited by P.T. Robertshaw. London: James Currey, 1990.

Schoenbrun, D.L. *A Green Place, A Good Place. Agrarian Change, Gender, and Social Identity in the Great Lakes Region to the 15th Century*. Portsmouth, NH: Heinemann and Oxford: James Currey, 1998.

Sutton, J. E. G. "The Antecedents of the Interlacustrine Kingdoms," *Journal of African History*, 34 (1993): 33–64.

Tantala, R.L. "The Early History of Kitara in Western Uganda: Process Models of Religious and Political Change." Ph.D. dissertation, University of Wisconsin at Madison, 1989.

Uzoigwe, G.N. "Precolonial Markets in Bunyoro Kitara," *Hadith*, 5 (1976): 24–66.

Great Rebellion: *See* Madagascar: Great Rebellion, 1947–1948.

Great Trek: *See* Boer Expansion: Interior of South Africa.

Great Zimbabwe: Colonial Historiography

Great Zimbabwe was first seen by a European who recorded his experiences in 1871. Karl Mauch immediately identified the site as King Solomon's biblical Ophir (1 Kings 9: 26–28). Mauch was a German traveler who had imbibed myths of a golden Ophir lying in the African interior. Stories of interior wealth had long circulated, disseminated by the Portuguese, who had established themselves along the East African coast and the Zambezi River from the fifteenth century. Myths of Great Zimbabwe's non-African origins were established in canonical form by Rider Haggard's 1886 novel *King Solomon's Mines*.

From the late nineteenth century, the British overtook the Portuguese in myth making, as in colonizing. So amazed by the sophistication of Great Zimbabwe were the new colonizers that, inspired by Rider Haggard's acquaintance, Cecil John Rhodes, they (like Mauch) denied Africans credit for such monumental architecture. Rhodes's motives for colonizing were commercial and imperial. Consequently, mythmaking about Great Zimbabwe, which Rhodes's pioneers visited in 1890, spread quickly by commercial promotion of settler enterprise.

Inspired by what they took for Great Zimbabwe's extraneous origins, Rhodes's settlers, known as Rhodesians, called the hill ruin at Great Zimbabwe the Acropolis (after ancient Greece), and the valley ruin—following their suppositions about Near Eastern religious ceremonies in the valley—the Temple. Despite evidence to the contrary adduced by archaeologists David Randall McIver (1906), Gertrude Caton Thompson (1931), and Roger Summers (1958), local belief in Great Zimbabwe's exotic origins remained an article of settler faith.

Early attempts to prove Great Zimbabwe's alien pre-Christian origins led Rhodesians to dig up and discard evidence of the site's indigenous builders. Despite such destruction, archaeological finds at Great Zimbabwe included Persian bowls, Chinese celadon dishes, and Near Eastern glassware. As Rhodesians contended, these items indicated ancient, outside settlement prior to the arrival of local Africans (*c*.400). In fact, such twelfth- to fifteenth-century goods (radio-carbon techniques settled disputed datings after 1945) merely validated the Shona-Indian Ocean trading links that brought luxury items to Great Zimbabwe.

Another interesting insight on amateur settler interpretation of Great Zimbabwe lies in the sequencing Rhodesians gave to the site's dry stone walling. To them, walling styles ran chronologically from coursed and dressed, to dressed and piled-and-wedged. In other words, from "best" to "worst," showing how native labor degenerated as imagined alien influences weakened. This interpretation matched colonial fears of white degeneration by interracial contact. Randall McIver, however, illustrated how Great Zimbabwe's walling progressed from piled-and-wedged, to dressed, and then on to dressed and coursed. Thus, the actual progression was from simpler to more complex styles, thus revealing how African builders at Great Zimbabwe mastered the materials available to them.

Nonetheless, Rhodesians erroneously attributed hill and valley ruins to Phoenicians, Jews, and Arabs: anyone, in fact, but the site's historical Shona builders. "Shona" is the popularly accepted name for related peoples speaking mutually intelligible languages, subdivided into Zezuru, Manyika, Korekore, and Karanga peoples living in Mozambique as well as Zimbabwe. Fifteen miles from Masvingo (once Ft. Victoria), Great Zimbabwe lies in a Karanga, Shona-speaking area.

Attracting as it has polemical dispute, Great Zimbabwe has drawn attention away from the multiplicity of Zimbabwes ("houses of stone") scattered across southeast Africa. These lesser Zimbabwes reveal the extent of interregional trading in precolonial southern, eastern, and central Africa. Today's archaeologists concern themselves with this inland-coastal trading network of which Great Zimbabwe was a part, a fifteenth-century network reaching to the Kongo kingdom (modern Angola) and across the Indian Ocean to China and India.

Rhodesians, however, needed to believe that Great Zimbabwe was unconnected to indigenous African genius. They had come from South Africa into what became Southern Rhodesia (1890–1965), Rhodesia (1965–1979), and finally majority-ruled Zimbabwe to make their fortunes. Of mixed South African and British stock, they believed themselves to be opening up central Africa to civilization. Such was their credo until Rhodesia disappeared with Zimbabwean independence (1980). In the dim light of racial prejudice and archaeological ignorance, most whites found it inconceivable that Africans could have built Great Zimbabwe.

A host of local diggers—Theodore Bent, R. M. Swan, and R. N. Hall—bolstered early mythmaking about the site that became a defining characteristic of colonial worldviews. In his book *The Ruined Cities of Ancient Rhodesia* (1906), Hall argued that Phoenicians were responsible for Great Zimbabwe's construction. Ancient Semites had provided the organizational skills and the intelligence without which the Shona could never have built their architectural marvels. Such myths mutated throughout the colonial period (1890–1979), as Rhodesians directing African labor had a vested interest in perpetuating them.

The stakes were raised after 1965 when, from a desire to protect rather than reform their racially privileged lifestyles, whites declared themselves independent of the British Commonwealth, whose scientists and historians had long proclaimed Great Zimbabwe's African origins. Now more than ever, colonial myths about Great Zimbabwe exemplified for whites what outside genius might achieve in Africa.

Such white defiance of archaeological evidence and political liberation provoked a defiant African response.

To African nationalist movements of the 1960s and 1970s, Great Zimbabwe proved what most whites sought to deny: that blacks had, could, and would create a great nation. From the early twentieth century, there never was any doubt about the site's African origins: colonial mythmaking was believed by those who needed or wanted to believe it.

DAVID LEAVER

See also: **Rhodes, Jameson, and the Seizure of Rhodesia.**

Further Reading

Bent, Theodore. *The Ruined Cities of Mashonaland.* London: Longman's, Green and Co., 1893.

Chanaiwa, David. *The Zimbabwe Controversy: A Case of Colonial Historiography.* Syracuse, N.Y.: Syracuse University Press, 1973.

Garlake, Peter. *Great Zimbabwe.* London: Thames and Hudson, 1973.

Hall, R. N., and Neal, W. G. *The Ancient Ruins of Rhodesia.* London: Methuen, 1904.

Henige, David. *The Shona and Their Neighbours.* Oxford: Blackwell, 1994.

Randell-MacIver, David, *Mediaeval Rhodesia.* London: Macmillan, 1906.

Summers, Roger. *Zimbabwe: A Rhodesian Mystery.* London: Nelson, 1963.

Great Zimbabwe: Origins and Rise

Great Zimbabwe is the name given to the largest site of ruins in Africa, covering a span of approximately 1800 acres. Evidence from Portuguese travelers in the sixteenth century reported that Shona kings lived in these stone fortifications, which were the center of a flourishing gold trade across the Indian Ocean. The monuments were built between 1100 and 1450, when they were abandoned due to multiple factors, including a long drought, internecine warfare, and an influx of a warlike people who plundered and destroyed everything in their wake.

The site is also intimately associated with the independence of the modern nation of Zimbabwe. The national shrine on the hill complex was the home of the spirit mediums whose main duty was to act as the conscience of the Zimbabwe confederation and to preserve the traditions of the founding fathers, Chaminuka, Chimurenga, Tovera, Soro-rezhou, and others. Different clans shared in this sacred trust, beginning with the Dziva-Hungwe priesthood, which by lineage was more ancient than the Shona themselves and in whose country Chigwagu Rusvingo had set up the confederation of Zimbabwe. The Hungwe totem bird (fish eagle) has been the symbol of the Zimbabwe state since it gained independence in April 1980.

Eurocentric colonial scholarship assumed that Great Zimbabwe could not have been built by the Shona people, despite the testimonies of the Portuguese travelers who confirmed the Shona as the builders.. Even those who were sympathetic to the African origin of the monument, because of their inadequate grasp of the African cultures, did not quite appreciate the significance of the facts at their disposal. European scholars placed undue emphasis on the economic development at Great Zimbabwe and tried to explain all other developments as corollaries to that central development.

There is plenty of oral evidence for the idea that the first builder saw the inadequacy of a kingdom built entirely on an economic foundation. The genius of the succeeding developers was that power was based not entirely on force or on economic enterprise, but on religion. Great Zimbabwe became a center of the divine. The system of checks and balances, whereby the *Monomutapa* (king) lived in the hill complex, while the priests lived nearby in the cave complex, were blurred in favor of a priestly monarchy. Although the two authorities were separate, to the common man the Monomutapa was a divine ruler who presided over harvest festivals and rain making ceremonies.

The first white men who visited southern Zambesia (now Zimbabwe) were the Portuguese, in the sixteenth century. The colonial Europeans arrived in the nineteenth century. By that time, the Shona civilization had deteriorated beyond recognition from the days of its medieval splendor. It was unthinkable then to entertain the idea that the Shona were the builders of these ancient monuments.

The most vexing question for the early European travelers and archaeologists was the origin of these edifices. One of the arguments advanced by R N. Hall, author of *Great Zimbabwe Mashonaland, Rhodesia: An Account of Two Years Examination Work in 1902–4 on Behalf of the Government of Rhodesia* (1969) in favor of a Himyartic (Arab) origin was that the Karanga were not associated with the gold and copper artifacts found at Great Zimbabwe. Hall wrote that he saw gold scorifers in the lower floors of the ruins and that these were produced and worked "by very old Kafir (black) people" and that the Portuguese records clearly showed that the "medieval Makalanga, not only produced gold but manufacture it, especially into gold wire" (p.3).

Despite the evidence, Hall could not conceive of a situation in which the simple Shona-Karanga, who were then "blessed" by British rule, could have been the originators of a once flourishing civilization. His own archaeological research had shown that, even as far down as the fifth layer of occupation, the artifacts were no different from those of the Shona-Karanga found at the top layer. This is the argument on which Dr. Randall-MacIver was to base his native origin theory later.

Archaeological evidence at Great Zimbabwe shows that settlements there can be traced to as far back as 200BCE. We know that the Khoi and the San preceded the Shona by thousands of years. Professor R. Dart has argued convincingly that the tambootie tree, found in the wall of the Great Zimbabwe, shows evidence, thanks to carbon dating, of human life much earlier than the generally accepted date of 1200. Oral evidence points to the fact that the Shona occupied Southern Zambesia much earlier than 1200.

Written records about the Shona can be found in the journals of the Arab traveler Ibu Said (1214–1286), who wrote about a "Soyouna" (i.e., Shona) people inhabiting southern Zambesia. Another traveler and geographer, by the name of Janson, recorded on his 1639 map of Zambazia the name of people living there as "Sajona."

When the Shona crossed the Zambezi on their southward migration around 1000, they settled in the iron district of Wedza. Because of the religious significance of Great Zimbabwe, which came from the prestige of the Hungwe spirit mediums and the Dzimbahwe fortress, it was fitting that all the future kings of this dynasty resided at Great Zimbabwe. The name Mwene-Mutapa means "owner of the land," a title assumed by all Zimbabweasn kings resident at Great Zimbabwe. From Great Zimbabwe, the Mwene-Mutapa family spread its influence to the Limpopo River in the south and to the Zambezi River in the north. In some cases they subjugated neighboring tribes, left them intact, and named a "royal" representative as chief. In other cases they intermarried. They dominated the whole of Zambesia to such as extent that no chief was legitimate until confirmed in office at Great Zimbabwe.

By 1490 Great Zimbabwe had been deserted. The direct descendants of the builders of Great Zimbabwe can still be found in the district of Mwenezi on the border with South Africa; they are called the BaVenda. These people trace their lineage beyond the BaRozi mambos to the Mwene-mutapa. They also practice ancient rainmaking rituals and circumcision, formerly associated with Great Zimbabwe but not practiced among modern-day Shona.

The BaVenda continued to build enclosures well into the twentieth century. The tradition today is that their art dated from the great king at Dzimbahwe. BaVenda architecture is very similar to that of Dzimbahwe, very often placed in inaccessible places. The BaVenda built their fortresses and divided them into two sections, the political and the sacrificial shrine. The BaVenda priests go up to their fortresses and there pray for rain, the same procedure followed at Great Zimbabwe. Occasionally, the BaVenda have placed a gigantic monolith at a village entrance, for no specific reason but merely to imitate their ancestors. These monoliths are very common at Great Zimbabwe.

The BaVenda possess beads and divining bowls similar to those found at Great Zimbabwe. A motif on a divining bowl at Great Zimbabwe shows a sacred bull, a crocodile, spindle whorls, a lizard, and some doll-like figurines. Similar motifs can be found on wooden BaVenda bowls. While the flourishing civilization of Great Zimbabwe has long since come to an end, its legacy thrives even today.

KENNETH MUFUKA

See also: **Iron Age (Later): Southern Africa: Leopard's Kopje, Bambandyanalo, and Mapungubwe; Iron Age (Later): Southern Africa: Toutswemogala, Cattle, and Political Power.**

Further Reading

Huffman, T. N., *Snakes & Crocodiles: Power and Symbolism in Ancient Zimbabwe.* Johannesburg: Witwatersrand University Press, 1996.

Mufuka, K. *Dzimbahwe: Life and Politics in the Golden Age.* Harare Publishing House, 1983.

Guèye: *See* **Diagne, Guèye, and Politics of Senegal, 1920s and 1930s.**

Guggisberg: *See* **Ghana (Republic of) (Gold Coast): Guggisberg Administration, 1919–1927.**

Guinea: Colonial Period

Guinea is a crescent-shaped country, the result of the arbitrary amalgamation of various regions by colonial conquest. The practice of dividing Guinea into four geopolitical regions dates to this period, but it also reflects both precolonial features (states and peoples) and the very process of colonial conquest. The four regions comprise coastal or lower Guinea, the highlands of Futa Jalon, Upper Guinea, and the forest region.

Initially an administrative dependency of Senegal, thus known as the "Rivières du Sud" ("Southern Rivers"), French Guinea became a colony with its own governor in 1893. Its territory was progressively broadened, beginning in the 1860s, with commercial expansion on the coast. In 1896, after more than a decade of negotiation and protectorate treaties with the Muslim state of Futa Jalon, the military conquest of central Guinea took place. Starting in 1882, severe fighting erupted between the forces led by Samori Touré and the French military. Over the next decade, parts of Touré's former empire were gradually annexed into French Sudan. In 1899 this region was incorporated in French Guinea. Due to long-lasting resistance in the numerous forest chiefdoms, the eastern extremity remained under military control as late as 1911–1912.

After some hesitation and compromises with former paramount chiefs, such as Alpha Yaya Diallo, head

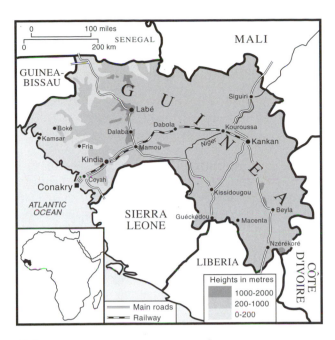

Guinea.

of Labé Province in the Futa Jalon, the administration of Guinea adopted the policy applied elsewhere in French West Africa: the colony was divided into administrative units known as "circles." Africans were used as intermediaries serving as "chefs de canto" (a new administrative position) and as village headmen. Former chiefs who demonstrated their loyalty to French authority were kept in power, especially in Central Guinea. However, the power of these auxiliaries was controlled, and their tasks included collecting taxes, recruiting manpower for forced labor or military service, carrying out judicial responsibilities, and transmitting economic policy to the local level.

As elsewhere in colonial Africa, most borders were arbitrary. Of greatest significance for their impact on the local population were the boundaries between French and foreign territories, for they disrupted established trading and social networks. As a result of the crescent shape of Guinea, some regions were much farther from the capital, Conakry, than from two other international harbors: Freetown, Sierra Leone and Monrovia, Liberia. This has an impact even today in terms of smuggling or cross-boundary strategies. A coercive policy was therefore necessary to attract exports from far-away regions to Conakry. This was effected through the construction of roads and a railway, and the imposition of taxes and high customs duties.

Agriculture (mainly cash crops) was the basis of the economy and the main source of revenue until the 1950s, when some mineral ores began to be exported in significant quantities. Guinea went through successive economic cycles. The first product to be exported on a large scale, and one of the driving forces behind the colonization of the hinterland was wild rubber, from central and upper Guinea. Collecting the latex required long hours of hard work. A railway line alleviated the difficult task of portage: it linked Conakry to Mamou (about 186 miles from the capital) in 1908 and reached Kouroussa in 1910 and Kankan in 1914 (a total of 414 miles). Rubber exports peaked in 1909–1912, with 1,700 to 2,100 tons per year. Rubber provided an average of 73 per cent of Guinea's exports by value between 1892 and 1913. After the turn of the century, Guinean wild rubber was in competition with plantation rubber from Indonesia and later Brazil. After two crises in 1907 and 1911, the market for wild rubber collapsed in 1913. The following year, exports dropped to 914 tons, representing only 28 per cent of exports by value. Despite low prices, rubber continued to be exported, as it represented the only product for some regions, and hence the only means of procuring sufficient funds to pay taxes.

The rubber cycle was followed by a long depression, until the colony started to export bananas from lower Guinea in the 1930s. This production was encouraged by the government through preferential customs duties. The introduction of refrigerated ships in 1935 accelerated the process. Most plantations were European-owned: the expatriates benefited from their access to capital and from the support of an administration that recruited manpower through forced labor. Some Africans were nevertheless able to enter the banana industry. Exports grew steadily: 114 tons in 1920, more than 20,000 in 1933, and 52,800 tons in 1938. Guinea was the main banana producer in French West Africa, with 80 per cent of total exports. Exports reached a peak of 98,000 tons in 1955 but then declined because of a leaf disease. Besides this main product, Guinea also exported palm products, cola nuts, hides, and cattle, and, after World War II, coffee and pineapples. The exploitation of minerals started in the 1950s, although some diamonds had been exported from the forest region as early as 1936. Iron ore was extracted near Conakry beginning in 1953, by the Compagnie Minière de la Guinée française, with partial American capital. It peaked at 1 million tons in 1957, but mining ceased in 1966. Bauxite was to become the main export after independence, but exploitation only started in the early 1950s, at three different mines: Kassa (1952–1974), Kindia-Friguiabgé, and the main site, Fria-Boké. In 1958, bananas and coffee still provided 80 per cent of exports by value.

Colonization brought with it severe social disruption. Slavery was a major problem, particularly in Futa Jalon. There, slaves were estimated at more than 50 per cent of the population, as opposed to 40 per cent in the colony as a whole, according to a 1904 report. The formal abolition of this status in 1905 did not change immediately the captives' social position. Former slaves were the first to be sent to the army or to forced labor projects, and their ex-masters used Islamic religious knowledge to dominate them. But colonization also implied demographic movements between the hinterland and the capital city or other new economic regions, such as the coastal region (basse-côte). The urban population was estimated at 6 per cent in 1958, half of which was concentrated in Conakry (80,000 to 100,000 people). The total population grew from about 1.8 million in 1910 to 2.6 million in 1956. Population growth accelerated after 1945, although medical equipment was still deficient with three hospitals (two in the capital) and ninety-nine dispensaries. The education system was also underdeveloped.

Colonization introduced changes in the relationships between elders and family members of lower social status, especially "younger brothers" who could seek wage labor and therefore partly escape the elders' authority. The absence of cash crops combined with French-imposed taxation pushed young men to migrate to more promising economic zones, such as the groundnut fields of Senegal in the 1920s–1930s, or the diamond mines of Sierra Leone from the 1940s.

Formal political activity was highly restricted until 1946, as in other French colonies. Political parties and trade unions were not authorized; only a few associations promoting leisure or solidarity, sometimes on a regional basis, were allowed. Some of these associations later became the starting point for larger unions, such as the "Union du Mandé" or the "Union forestiére." Other forms of political expression existed, including exodus to neighboring countries, and strikes among the few wage workers (dock workers, civil servants). In 1946, associations—political parties, labor unions, and cultural groups—were authorized. The nation witnessed the birth of many political parties at that time. Some representatives from Guinea helped found the Rassemblement Démocratique Africain (RDA) party in Bamako in 1946, and the following year the Guinean branch was started; it was renamed the Parti Démocratique de Guinée (PDG) in 1950. Under the leadership of Sekou Touré, who became its secretary general in 1952, the party grew rapidly. (In 1945 Touré had initiated the first trade union, followed by a confederation a year later.)

Other parties were also formed, some, such as the Union Franco-Africaine, under the auspices of French colonizers, who hoped to control the election results. After 1945 several legislative elections were held, and the first municipal elections occurred in 1956. In that year Sekou Touré became the first mayor of Conakry. The PDG was first successful in the forest region and upper Guinea, later along the coast. Central Guinea, the last region to vote for the PDG, was long dominated by two local parties, the Démocratie Socialiste de Guinée and the Bloc Africain de Guinée. The first semiautonomous government, formed in 1957 as a result of the *loi cadre* (a decree instituting decentralization and devolution for French-administered regions) was headed by Sékou Touré. Saéfoulaye Diallo, number two in the party, was elected president of the Territorial Assembly, which immediately took significant measures, such as the abolition of headmanship in December 1957, replacing this unpopular institution with elected councils.

Responding to President Charles de Gaulle of France on August 25, 1958, Sékou Touré proclaimed in a speech that his country preferred poverty in freedom to opulence in slavery. The PDG advocated a "no" vote in the referendum of September 28, 1958. As a result, an overwhelming 95 per cent rejected the French Community. Independence was proudly declared on the second of October, abruptly severing all links with France. Guinea was the first French Sub-Saharan colony to achieve independence.

ODILE GOERG

See also: **Guinea: Decolonization, Independence; Guinea: Touré, Ahmed Sékou, Era of.**

Further Reading

Iffono A. G. *Lexique historique de la Guinée-Conakry.* Paris: L'Harmattan, 1992.

Lamp F. *La Guinée et ses héritages culturels.* Conakry: Service d'information et de Relations culturelles de l'Ambassade des Etats-Unis en Guinée, 1992.

Nelson H., et al. *Area Handbook for Guinea.* Washington, D.C.: Foreign Area Studies of the American University, 1975.

O'Toole, T. E. *Historical Dictionary of Guinea (Republic of Guinea/Conakry).* Metuchen, N.J., 1995.

Guinea: Decolonization, Independence

Guinea, a country in West Africa, is the result of the colonial partition of that region at the end of the nineteenth and the beginning of the twentieth centuries. After nearly sixty years of French rule, the decolonization of Guinea took place within the wider context of the disintegration of European colonial dominions in Africa and Asia after World War II. It should be emphasized that this decolonization process was, to a large extent, contingent upon this favorable context, which prevailed in the wake of the war, and accounts, to a large extent, for the speed with which the colonies succeeded in ridding themselves of the subjection they suffered.

Political awareness in Guinea, as in other French African colonies, was facilitated by a series of reforms initiated by France from 1944 to meet the expectations of the colonial people. These reforms were in keeping with the recommendations of the Brazzaville Conference of January–February 1944, at which the French colonial authorities in Africa fully realized the need to bring about changes in their colonial approaches, while paradoxically asserting their desire to safeguard the existing colonial order. These reforms included granting the colonies certain rights and freedoms, such as union rights, the right of association, the right to vote and to participate in the local and metropolitan houses of representatives, the latter being newly established institutions.

In Guinea this new political context found expression in the creation of ethnic or geographically based associations (S. K Kéita 1978, vol. 1, pp.171–172). It was also translated into the emergence of political and ideological parties and circles. The activities of these associations gave rise to a brisk nationalistic trend. Of the parties that came into being between 1946 and 1954, three engaged in the competition for political leadership in the territory: the Bloc Africain de Guinée (BAG), the Parti Démocratique de Guinée (PDG), and the Démocratie Socialiste de Guinée (DSG). Until 1956 Barry Diawadou's BAG, backed by the colonial administration and drawing the bulk of its membership from the feudal class and the influential members of society, defeated the other political parties at the successive polls. Nevertheless, since then, the PDG, the Guinean section of the Rassemblement Démocratique Africain (RDA) under Sékou Touré, pulled itself up to the first position, the hostility of the colonial authorities notwithstanding. This process was crowned with the latter party's momentous victory at the territorial elections of March 31, 1957, winning fifty-seven out of the sixty seats in the colony's territorial assembly, a feat that afforded it preeminence in the country and pushed the competing parties to the background.

The PDG owed this new position on the political scene to several factors. One such factor was the economic and social situation prevailing in Guinea at the time of the colony's political awakening. It was an underdeveloped state, compared to its other neighbors in French West Africa. This state of underdevelopment showed mainly in the predominance of trade in raw commodities and the scarcity of industries. This condition contributed to the radicalization of the nationalist movement in Guinea. The PDG realized that it could politically turn the situation to its advantage.

Another factor was the particularly inspiring topics discussed during the PDG's campaigning with regard to the colony's economic situation. These topics were mainly focused on the castigation of the old and new methods of colonial exploitation and suppression meted out to the people. The PDG was also boosted by a sound organization at the national and local levels, buttressed by a highly efficient trade union movement, and the exceptional oratory skills of its leader, Sékou Touré.

In April 1957, when the French government promulgated the decrees on enforcement of the Gaston Deferre Outline Law, which granted the colonies a semiautonomous status, the PDG had already secured such a strong position that it was readily called upon to form the first government. Sékou Touré became vice president, with the position of president going to the colonial governor. The PDG efficiently consolidated its positions by carrying out the reforms the people were yearning for. It settled its scores with the feudal class by abolishing traditional chieftaincy (Niane D. T. 1998, p.81). This increased its popularity as compared to the contending parties, the BAG and the DSG, which, though weakened, still remained active on the political arena.

It was against this background that French President de Gaulle put forward a proposal to the French colonies in Africa. They could opt for full independence, or accept the French offer of the creation of a new community, at a referendum to be held on November 28, 1958. Unlike in most of the colonies involved, in Guinea the referendum was held in a context where the full implementation of the Outline Law revealed its weaknesses with regard to the Guineans' quest for self-rule. From January 1958, Sékou Touré was of the view that the opportunities offered by the proposed reforms had elapsed. Consequently, de Gaulle's initiative was generally welcomed by the political actors, including those considered to be siding with the colonial administration. They took an official stand in favor of independence, even before the PDG and its leader made their views known on September 14, 1958, at the party's convention.

Of all the French colonies in Africa, Guinea alone voted for independence, which was proclaimed on October 2, 1958. This result was the outcome of the concurrent action of all the political forces on the scene, particularly the PDG, whose control over the country was so strong that, in the view of the colonial governor on the eve of the referendum, any voting directive issued by its leadership would unquestionably be followed by 95 per cent of the electorate, whatever that directive might be (Kaba, p.87).

Guinea's example was contagious and resulted in the independence, in succession, of the other African countries, which cost France its painstakingly fashioned community.

ISMAEL BARRY

See also: **Guinea: Touré, Ahmed Sékou, Era of.**

Further Reading

Ademolekun, L. *Sékou Touré's Guinea.* London: Panaf, 1978.
DuBois, V. *The Guinean Vote for Independence.* New York: American Universities Field Staff Reports, 1962.
Morgenthau, Ruth S. *Political Parties in French-speaking West Africa.* Oxford: 1964.
Niane, D. T. *La République de Guinée.* Conakry, Guinea: S.A.E.C., 1998.

Guinea: Touré, Ahmed Sékou, Era of

Two distinctive and contrasting symbols can summarize Ahmed Sékou Touré's (1922–1984) Guinea: independence and the Boiro Camp. Political leader of decolonization, hero of the first colony to achieve independence in French Sub-Saharan Africa, Sékou Touré, like Kwame Nkrumah, was among the most eminent African leaders to oppose imperialism. He was welcomed in Guinea after the military coup in 1966 and was named vice president. But after the enthusiasm of independence and high hopes for the future of the country, things changed, through a combination of internal factors, external pressure, and Sékou Touré's own personality. Sékou Touré became a dictator, eliminating opposition to his power and resorting to the worst methods of oppression, while radicalizing his discourse and practice in terms of both local and foreign policy. Three schematic phases can be distinguished in Touré's regime: initial accommodation and negotiation (to *c.*1965), radicalization (*c.*1965–1975) and, from around 1975, a gradual softening of his hard-line policies.

Independence was proclaimed on October 2, 1958, and Guinea was admitted to the United Nations in December 1958. Guinea's then-representative was Diallo Telli. After holding various other high official positions, including being the first secretary general of the Organization of the African Unity (OAU), he would become a target of Sékou Touré's suspicion, and one of the most famous victims of the Boiro Camp, the concentration camp located in a Conakry suburb.

A series of plots, real or faked, starting in 1960, was followed by increased repression. The repression peaked after the November 22, 1970, attempt by Portuguese and exiled Guinean forces both to liberate Portuguese soldiers (Guinea was a strong supporter of the liberation movement of Guinea Bissao and Cape Verde [PAIGC]) and overthrow Sékou Touré. Many people were arrested, including several ministers and ambassadors, high military officers, and Monsignor Tchidimbo, the archbishop of Conarky. Following a trial in January 1971, eight people were publicly hanged under the Tumbo bridge, in Conakry. Altogether 10,000 to 30,000 people were victims of the regime.

After the massive "no" vote in the 1958 referendum, France left with all its technicians and equipment and withdrew its aid, trying to block Guinea's international contacts. Responding to the rigid French attitude, Guinea established its own money in 1960, the Guinean franc or *sily* (the elephant), symbol of the party and its leader. The sily was nonconvertible, which gave the state an efficient means to control the economy. Diplomatic relationships with France were finally terminated in 1965. They were reestablished only ten years later, on July 14, 1975. Guinea turned to the Eastern bloc, to the Soviet Union and to China, for diplomatic and economic support (trade agreements were signed as early as 1958–1959). But, by 1961, some distance had been taken from the Soviet Union, accused of perverting the student movement. As a general rule, Guinea always tried not to depend too heavily on one partner, as demonstrated by its economic policy.

Guinea had rich assets: various ecological regions, sufficient water supply, mineral resources, and skilled labor. During colonization, this potential had not been fully utilized, but new projects were underway in the 1950s such as the exploitation of bauxite and iron and the building of a dam on the Konkouré river (finally inaugurated in 1999). In 1958 Guinea was the third colony in French West Africa in terms of economic value. These assets attracted foreign investment: French (despite the political problems), American, and Soviet. Investment was mainly aimed at the exploitation of bauxite: at Fria (the French Company Péchiney combined with North American capital), Boké (American-controlled international consortium), Kindia-Friguiagbé (a joint venture between the Guinean State and the Soviet Union), and from 1952 to 1974 at Kassa. Because of its nationalistic orientation, Guinea was partially able to impose its own terms and negotiate more favorable contracts. The example of the transformation of bauxite in Guinea itself illustrates this policy, but the aluminum factory in Fria, an intermediate stage in the processing of aluminum, shows the limits of negotiation with international trusts. Despite the agreement, Guinea failed to have an aluminum factory built to take advantage of the surplus value created by this industrial stage. The production at Fria went rapidly from 185,000 tons in 1960 to 460,000 two years later and 700,000 in the 1980s. A 145-kilometer-long railway was built from Fria to Conakry while the harbor of Kamsar was the outlet for Boké mines whose exports started in 1973. Guinea was the second largest world bauxite producer, and this product was responsible for over 90 per cent of its hard currency earnings. Diamonds were another important resource, whose small-scale exploitation was strictly controlled and even forbidden in 1975–1980, in order to prevent smuggling toward Freetown.

Resorting to Marxist phraseology, Sékou Touré applied a policy of nationalization and centralization. The 1962 congress of the PDG proclaimed the adoption of the noncapitalist mode of development. The regime aimed at creating a unified Guinean nation, without class or ethnic divisions. The nationalization of industries, which started in 1959, was broadened with the passage of a new fundamental law in 1964 which repressed corruption and private enterprise. Guinea was basically an agricultural country (although most of its monetary resources came from mining), and there, too, a similar policy was applied: collective farming was organized and received much public financial help. (The final stage was the FAPA, or *fermes agro-pastorales d'Arrondissement*, in 1978.) Students spent one year at the end of their curriculum working in the countryside and " educating" the masses. In addition, foreign trade was nationalized and private trade forbidden for some time.

The state also controlled all political and intellectual activity. Some parties spontaneously rallied to the PDG, but most of them were forbidden, resulting in the establishment of the one-party state. As a result, the whole country was organized under the leadership of the PDG. In 1967 Guinea was divided into 7 "Commissariats généraux de la Révolution," 33 administrative regions, 350 districts, and at the village or neighborhood level 2,500 "Pouvoirs révolutionnaires locaux" (PRL). The organization of the party (in which membership was compulsory at the age of seven and required the payment of dues, a substitute for direct taxation) reproduced the same scheme. Attending party meetings was also an obligation. The party aimed at controlling all activities; it organized the population, mainly the workers (CNTG/Confédération nationale des travailleurs de Guinée), the youth (JRDA/Jeunesse de la Révolution démocratique africaine), and women (URFG/Union révolutionnaire des femmes de Guinée). The state also controlled public opinion through the school system and censorship of the media.

Mottos espousing revolution, anti-imperialism, and egalitarianism were particularly attractive in a country characterized by discrimination, be it by age, gender, or socioeconomic status (slaves, castes). Campaigns were organized against so-called mystical practices. Feudalism, in Marxist terms, was attacked: the old chief system, used by colonization, was abolished in 1957, and captivity, which still existed in indirect ways, was repressed in an attempt to change attitudes. This was mainly aimed at the Fula aristocraty and led to multifold repression. But despite his Marxist discourse, Sékou Touré was able to gain the support of Muslim leaders and to attract Arab capital. A Friday mosque was built on the outskirts of Conakry.

In the mid-1970s, Guinea gradually opened up again and balanced its relations between the Western and the Eastern bloc. Trade and agriculture were progressively liberalized, and reconciliation was proclaimed with several European and African countries. As a result, the borders reopened and negotiations started with the European Economic Community (Guinea signed the Lomé Agreement) and international organizations (IMF). Sékou Touré assumed again the figure of a Pan-Africanist and nonaligned leader after he personally attended the Organization of African Unity (OAU) summit in Monrovia in 1978 (where Guinea reconciled with Senegal and Côte d'Ivoire). Previously, in 1968, he had encouraged the founding of the Organization of the States Bordering the Senegal River (Organisation des Etats riverains du Sénégal) whose treaty had been signed in Guinea; but it broke up in 1971 because of conflicts between Guinea and its neighbors following the 1970 Portuguese aggression. Similarly he favored the foundation of other regional organizations (Gambia River, Mano River, Niger). He also served as mediator for various conflicts (Chad, Western Sahara). This role was supposed to attain its apogee with the organization of the twentieth OAU summit in Conakry in 1984. Sékou Touré's death interrupted the preparations.

Sékou Touré's regime, which lasted almost unchallenged from 1958 to his natural death on March 26, 1984, had profound consequences for Guinea. It accelerated a migration process started under colonization. This resulted in the exodus of about 25 per cent of the total population, and the death or flight of most intellectuals. At the same time the radicalization of the ideology created economic problems in a country whose resources were promising. After some hesitation and competition between Prime Minister Béavogui and Ismaël Touré, Sékou Touré's half-brother, the army took over on April 3, 1984, under the leadership of Colonels Lansana Conté and Diarra Traoré who formed the CMRN (Comité militaire de redressement national). The second republic was proclaimed, and the PDG and its institutions were abolished.

ODILE GOERG

See also: **Guinea: 1984 to the Present; Nkrumah, Kwame.**

Further Reading

Adamolekun, L. *Sékou Touré's Guinea: An Experiment in Nation Building.* London: Methuen and Co., 1976.

Nelson, H., et al. *Area Handbook for Guinea.* Washington, D.C.: Foreign Area Studies of the American University, 1975.

O'Toole, T. E. *Historical Dictionary of Guinea (Republic of Guinea/Conakry).* 3rd ed. Metuchen, N. J., 1995.

Rivière, C. *Classes et stratifications sociales en Afrique: Le cas guinéen.* Paris: Ed ° Marcel Rivière et Cie, 1978.

Guinea: 1984 to the Present

During the night of March 25, 1984, the president of Guinea, Sékou Touré, "Responsable Suprême de la Révolution" (Supreme Chief of the Revolution), died at age sixty-two of a heart attack in a hospital in Cleveland, Ohio. His death provoked a harsh struggle for succession and an atmosphere of political insecurity. One week later, the Guinean army seized power by force in order to avoid civil war. An official statement, read on Radio-Conakry during the morning of April 3, proclaimed the creation of a Comité Militaire de Redressement National (CMRN; Military Committee of National Recovery), and so dissolved the Parti Démocratique de Guinée (Democratic Party of Guinea), of which Sékou Touré had been the political leader. It also dissolved the National Assembly and suspended the constitution. The army's eruption onto the political scene ousted the two potential successors of the deceased president, Lansana Béavogui, who, since 1972, had been the prime minister for Sékou Touré, and Ismael Touré, the half-brother of the ex-president. The CMRN, composed of eighteen members, set up a new government with Colonel Lansana Conté (born in 1943 in Loumbayah-Moussayah), the former chief of the land forces at its head. The statement "Guinean People, you are free now!" was repeated endlessly on national radio.

Sékou Touré was undoubtedly the "homme africain décisif" (decisive African man) as described by Aimé Césaire (an avant-garde poet born in Martinique in the French Caribbean and advocate of *négritude*). Famous for the "no!" he gave General Charles de Gaulle in 1958, he led the country to national independence and opposed colonialism. However, his socialist regime had been marked by his acutely personal and harsh form of dictatorship. Sékou Touré left behind him a country facing a number of problems. The national economy was undeveloped and unproductive, while corruption was rampant. The Guinean state was forced to rely on its centralized and omnipotent party. Favorably disposed toward Malinké populations, the regime had encouraged ethnic rivalries and the emergence of a corrupt bourgeoisie. Isolated from the international scene but remaining close to Communist countries, Sékou Touré had led a paranoid government obsessed with plot and conspiracy. (Between 1960 and 1984 Sékou Touré fabricated thirteen plots to legitimize the elimination of his opponents.) Human rights and individual freedom were both highly controlled, and thousands of opponents of the regime (intellectuals, officers, and traders) were killed or tortured in the Boirot Camp. These political acts of violence led many Guineans to flee their country, resulting in a broad Guinean diaspora around the world.

In the aftermath of April 3, the CMRN inaugurated the second republic and initiated a decollectivization policy. Taxes on production were suppressed and the production cooperatives were closed. The new government fostered a liberal policy and committed itself to the development of the private sector. In 1985 the Guinean franc replaced the sily, the monetary unit of Sékou Touré's regime. Guinea attempted to escape its economic isolation; agreements were signed with the International Monetary Fund, and in 1986 the first Structural Adjustment Program was established. At the same time, the CMRN promised to lead the country to democracy. The Boirot Camp was closed, and a committee was commissioned to write the *Loi Fondamentale* (Fundamental Law) recognizing a multiparty system. Parties such as the Parti de l'Unité et du Progrès (Party of Unity and Progress), the Rassemblement du Peuple Guinéen (People's Assembly of Guinea), and the Union pour la Nouvelle République (Union for the New Republic) entered the political arena. In 1993, for the first time in Guinean history, presidential elections were held: Lansana Conté received 50.93 per cent of the vote and established the Third Republic.

However, these promising changes took place in an atmosphere of increasing economic precariousness, political insecurity, and corruption. Since 1984, the economic situation has remained fragile despite the natural richness of the country, and the educational and juridical systems are equally insecure. Health care is generally inaccessible, and administration is inefficient. During the 1990s, Guinea suffered the repercussive effects of the civil wars in Liberia and Sierra Leone, receiving a huge influx of refugees from the two countries (500,000). The situation in the early 2000, is threatened by heightened political tensions colored by ethnic rivalries. General-President Lansana Conté is accused of privileging people from his own ethnic group, the Susu. In February 1996, when Malinké Diarra Traoré was arbitrarily relegated from the position of prime minister to that of state minister, a few officers launched a coup. The rebellion failed, but only after the officers had successfully bombarded the national palace.

After the 1998 presidential elections, Alpha Condé, the leader of the RPG (Rassemblement du Peuple Guinéen), was accused of conspiracy and thrown in jail for more than two years. The border conflicts between Guinea and rebels from Sierra-Leone and Liberia, who are supposedly allied with Guinean opponents plotting against the regime, allowed the government to reinforce its politicomilitary control over the population.

General President Lansana Conteé—nicknamed "fori" (the "old man")—has been in power since 1984. A referendum, which was denounced by the opposition parties, was held on November 11, 2001, and a 98 per cent majority was obtained in favor of the removal of the two-term limit, which would have forced him to retire in 2003. According to the opposition, the vote was in flagrant disregard of the constitution and essentially ensures that he will remain president for life.

DAVID BERLINER

See also: **Guinea: Touré, Ahmed Sékou, Era of; World Bank, International Monetary Fund, and Structural Adjustment.**

Further Reading

Devey, Muriel. *La Guinée.* Paris: Karthala, 1997.
Césaire, Aimé. "La pensée politique de Sékou Touré." *Présence Africaine* 29 (1960): 65–74.
Goerg, Odile. "Guinée: l'après Sékou Touré." *Politique Africaine* 36 (1989).
Lansiné, Kaba. "Guinea: Myth and Reality of Change." *Africa Report* 26 (1981): 53–57.
Niane, Djibril Tamsir. *La République de Guinée.* Conakry, Guinea: SAEC, 1998.
O'Toole, Thomas. *Historical Dictionary of Guinea.*, Meluchen, N. J., 1995.

Guinea-Bissau: Nineteenth Century to 1960

With approximately twenty-five different populations living within a territory of about 14,000 square miles, the history of Guinea-Bissau is primarily regional. However, four factors have affected the country as a whole and have in some way contributed to its shaping: colonial conquest, the end of the slave trade, the rise of the peanut trade, and the fall of the Gabounke Empire.

From an administrative point of view, Portuguese Guinea consisted originally of two *capitanias* (Cacheu and Bissau) joined as districts in 1852, yet annexed to Cape Verde until 1879, at which time it became administratively independent. Besides Cacheu and Bissau, "Guinea" was composed of the enclaves of Ziguinchor on the Casamance River, Bolor at the mouth of the Rio Cacheu (to counter French advancement),

Gabon.

605

Ganjarra and Fa (minor trading posts), Farim and Geba (commercial gateways to the Mandinka trade), and the island of Bolama, a source of dispute with Britain until 1868.

Honório Pereira Barreto (1813–1859) was made the first true governor of colonial Portuguese Guinea in 1845. The first half of the nineteenth century was marked by the repeated insurrections of the *grumetes* (a term used originally to designate the sailors working on the Portuguese ships and later extended to all accultured individuals), as well as by the uprisings of a garrison composed primarily of convicts. The Portuguese clashed frequently with neighbors (Papel, Manyak, Biafada) and were the target of systematic piracy from the Bijagos. It was only from 1880 on, and with great difficulty, that colonization began to spread beyond the trading posts. The process of colonization was completed by 1920 for continental Guinea and by 1935 for the islands of Bijagos.

Until 1800 Cacheu and Bissau were the main slave entrepôts on the Southern Rivers, from which more than four thousand slaves were exported yearly. From 1810 on, England coerced Portugal into accepting a series of treaties to end the slave trade and included, in 1842, its assimilation to piracy. Although slavery was abolished in 1858, the newly liberated slaves continued working for their masters until 1874, when a new decree set them effectively free. In the late 1840s when the slave trade ended, the Guinean economy was dominated by slave traders who were associated with *Nhara* (women of matrilineal communities who played an intermediary role between African societies and the European merchants). Consequently, when the local economy shifted from slave to pelt and peanut trade, Bissau, but especially Cacheu and Ziguinchor, missed out on the opportunity to participate in this economic transformation. The French, meanwhile, developed the post of Sédhiou. From there, the French Resident composed the first long text concerning Guinea (E. Bertrand-Bocandé, "Notes sur la Guinée Portugaise ou Sénégambie méridionale," *Bulletin de la Société de Géographie*, 1849).

The introduction of peanut cultivation was a major event. Peanuts became the major export item of Guinea until overtaken by cashew nuts in the early 1980s. Peanut cultivation began in the Bijagos Islands in about 1840 and spread to Grande de Buba and Foreah around 1847. These previously neglected regions thus experienced a sudden development that ended abruptly when warfare erupted in 1868. The end of the slave trade dealt the final blow to the animistic Mandinka Empire of Gabu, confederating forty-seven provinces during the nineteenth century. Challenged for more than fifty years by the theocratic Pulaar (or Fula) state of Fuuta Jalon (present-day Guinea Conakry)

mainly for the control of commercial networks, the Gabu Empire did not substitute the slave trade by the exploitation of its labor force. The Fula were soon engaged largely in peanut production, while the Gabunka ignored it. By the time the slave trade reached its end, the Fula had created the *runde* (villages of slaves dedicated to the production of peanuts), whereas the noblemen and soldiers of the Gabunka Empire, unable to adapt to the new situation and deprived of resources, became looters. In 1851 the Fula gained a hold on several Gabunka provinces. Blockaded in Kansala sometime between 1864 and 1867, the *Mansa-Ba* (emperor) and his followers committed suicide by igniting their remaining barrels of powder. This was the end of the great Gabu.

The fall of the empire brought about a state of violence that was to last approximately thirty years. The Gabunka, the FulaKunda, and Balanta migrated en masse to the south, where the Biafada accepted them in exchange for a yearly tribute, which they refused to pay shortly thereafter. This led to the war of Foréah, which broke out in 1868 and lasted for the next twenty years, leaving the Biafada chiefdoms defeated. Competing constantly for control, these chiefdoms previously submissive to the confederation were now in permanent conflict—a situation from which the Portuguese profited by supporting one group or another, according to their own interests.

The agreement signed by the Portuguese and the French in 1889 exchanged the zone of the Cassini River (over which the chiefs had accepted a French protectorate in 1857) for the area of Ziguinchor, which, although dominated by French merchants, had been the seat of a Portuguese mission since 1770. Between 1888 and 1905 five campaigns were launched to establish the borders. Casamance, Naloutaye, and Foréah were henceforth divided lengthwise.

With the advent of the Portuguese Republic (1910), da Silva Gouveia was elected the first deputy of Guinea in 1911. In 1912 Governor de Almeida Pereira created a department of public works and a postal service. He banned the arms trade and built the first road suitable for automobiles.

Thirteen days after the rebellion of Madère against the dictatorship of Salazar (April 4, 1931), the governor was expelled by a junta, which promptly disappeared when the uprising was crushed on May 4.

Exportation remained almost entirely in the hands of foreign enterprises until the advent of the *Estado Novo* when, by means of the exportation taxes that he had put into effect in 1927, Salazar established the quasi-monopoly *Companhia Uniao Fabril-Gouveia*. Thus, by 1930, 70 per cent of all exports were bound for Portugal. In 1943 the capital city was transferred from Bolama to Bissau. In 1951 the term "colony" was dropped in favor of "overseas province," and the Colonial Act was revoked. However, the low level of education among the colonists (30% were illiterate), coupled with the inability of the fascist regime to mobilize capital, contributed to a state of economic stagnation.

GÉRALD GAILLARD (TRANSLATED BY NARDA ALCANTARA)

See also: **Slavery: Atlantic Trade: Abolition: Philanthropy or Economics?**

Further Reading

Bowman, Joye Hawkins. "Conflict, Interaction, and Change in Guinea-Bissau: Fulbe Expansion and Its Impact, 1850–1900." Ph.D. diss., University of California, 1980.
Books, George. "Peanuts and Colonialism: Consequences of the Commercialization of Peanuts in West Africa, 1830–1870." *Journal of African History* 15, no. 1 (1975): 29–54.
Pélissier, René. *Naissance de la Guinée, Portugais et Africains en Sénégambie (1841–1936).* Orgeval: Pélissier, 1989.

Guinea-Bissau: Cabral, Amílcar, PAICG, Independence, 1961–1973

Amílcar Cabral (1924–1973) was born in Guinea in 1924. His parents had emigrated from Cape Verde during one of the periodical famines striking the islands, only to return in 1931. Cabral set off for Lisbon in 1945 to study agricultural engineering. There he met Agostinho Neto and Mario de Andrade, future leaders of the Liberation Movement of Angola. Cabral and de Andrade created the *Centro de Estudos Africanos* in 1951 with the aim of "reafricanizing the mind."

With a degree in engineering (granted in 1950), Cabral was hired by the National Institute of Agriculture to conduct the agricultural census of Guinea. Parallel to his study of the agrarian social and economic structures, he created the African Peoples' Sports and Leisure Association (1954). The association was banned by the colonial authorities, and Cabral was exiled to a sugar cane plantation in Angola, with permission to visit his family once a year. During one of these visits, on September 19, 1956, Cabral and five other Cape Verdians, including Aristide Pereira (future president of Cape Verde), Luis Cabral (Amílcar's half-brother), and Fernando Fortes, created the African Party for Independence (PAI), renamed two years later PAIGC (African Party for the Independence of Guinea and Cape Verde).

Although Guinea and Cape Verde were politically and economically interdependent, the inhabitants had never subscribed to the idea of unifying their territories as the PAIGC anticipated.

In 1959 the workers of the port of Bissau (Pidgiguiti) gathered in a general uprising. A shoot-out ensued with fifty-eight deaths officially reported. This event surprised the leaders of the PAIGC who had considered it possible to attain independence without armed conflict, as had been the case with the English and French colonies south of the Sahara.

Cabral returned to Bissau, and during the meeting of September 19, 1959, the leaders of the PAIGC decided to engage the rural masses and start an armed offensive. The group led by Rafael Barbosa, Aristide Pereira, and Fernando Fortes remained in charge of expanding the influence of the party in the countryside, while the group with Cabral, Carlos Correia, and Francisco Mendes went to Conakry to establish a party school. Cabral taught history, geography, and international relations and at the same time engaged in intense diplomatic negotiations to obtain arms.

However, the Portuguese would adamantly refuse a peaceful transition to independence. In the case of the French and English colonies, the nineteenth-century scheme of progressive assimilation was given up not only because of the political history (the role played by Africa in World War II) but also for economic reasons. For France and England, the transition to neocolonialism appeared then more profitable than the integration of their colonies in the metropolis. This was not the case of Portugal, a country which had not participated in World War II and had a less progressive economy.

In 1962 three independence movements based in Dakar united to form the FLING (Nationale Front for the Liberation of Guinea) and proposed a negotiated decolonization. The PAIGC took a more aggressive position, initiating a series of attacks before declaring open conflict in February 1963. Six months later, the southern regions of Geba and Corubal were liberated, and a new front opened in the north of Bissau. The objective was the strengthening of the PAIGC in order to challenge the position of the FLING, which had already been recognized by the Organization of African Unity (OAU). Operating from military bases in the liberated zones, they systematically destroyed the production of peanuts and the warehouses of the Portuguese company *Companhia união fabril*.

The military brilliance of Cabral was based in his immediate understanding of which societies the movement had to approach first. The Balanta, for instance, with a horizontal social structure were of a more revolutionary tendency, while the Fula, the Mandinka, and the Biafada, vertically and hierarchically organized, were not. In 1964 Portugal mobilized three thousand men to take the island of Como, a strategic platform necessary for the eventual recovery of the south. After seventy-five days of combat, however, the expedition had to acknowledge defeat.

In the midst of intense combat, the PAIGC held its first congress at Cassaca in February 1964. The party founded regional organizations such as village committees, schools (164 between 1964 and 1973) and "people's stores." These stores bought rice from the farmers at a higher price than the Portuguese offered and sold tools at a lower price. Outstanding students were sent to Conakry to be trained as intellectual leaders of the party. The Congress also handled complaints about the behavior of commanders. Following an inquiry, several were imprisoned or executed. The Organization of African Unity recognized the PAIGC in 1965 as "the only organization fighting for the people of Guinea." By 1966 the party controlled two-thirds of the territory.

The Portuguese, with some 15,000 to 20,000 soldiers, brought together the villages still under their control. They bombed the liberated regions, destroying the rice paddies of the Balanta, but the conflict only intensified.

Originally opposed to armed struggle, and supporting the anti-PAIGC organizations, Léopold-Sédar Senghor (president of Senegal) authorized the creation of a center for casualties of war in 1967, in Ziguinchor. Later, he accepted the existence of military bases. However, one of the main bases was in the south. The southern zone was placed under the leadership of Nino Vieira (future president of Guinea Bissau) and was supported by the forces of Guinea Conakry, under the command of Lanzana Conté (who in turn was to become president of Guinea Conakry).

The year 1970 was marked by important diplomatic accomplishments for the PAIGC. Cabral met with several heads of state, including Pope Paul VI.

General Antonio de Spinosa, appointed in 1968, declared that "subversive war cannot be won by military force" and launched a campaign for "a better Guinea." He opened 160 schools in strategic villages and made promises to the opponents of the PAIGC. Spinosa stabilized the military front and undertook operations such as the attempt to assassinate Sékou Touré (then president of Guinea) in 1970.

In 1972 the PAIGC called for elections in the liberated zones, which led to the formation of the first national assembly. Shorly afterward, on January 20, 1973, Amílcar Cabral was assassinated in Conakry by a naval officer of the PAIGC. To this day no light has been shed on this affair. Beginning in 1973, the Soviet Union provided the PAIGC with anti-air missiles, henceforth changing the military odds.

On September 24, 1973, the National Popular Asembly (ANP) led by Nino Vieira proclaimed the independence of Guinea-Bissau—"an African nation forged in combat"—in Madina do Boé, near Kandiafara. The United Nations immediately recognized the new state. The large cities, however, remained under Portuguese control and had to be maintained with imported rice. The colonial war had taken a heavy toll on the Portuguese nation, which maintained 35,000 young men overseas who were no longer willing to die in a distant country. It was precisely within the garrisons of Guinea that the Movement of Captains was born that overthrew the Portuguese dictatorship on April 25, 1974. Portugal recognized the independence of Guinea in September and that of Cape Verde in 1975. The PAIGC held control of the state for a long time. Luis Cabral ruled the country until 1981, when his government was overthrown by his army chief Joao Vieira. Although elected to the presidency in 1994, he was ousted four years later after he dismissed his own army chief, a series of events which set off a civil war. Foreign intervention led to a truce. Elections were held in 2000, resulting in the election of Kumba Yalla as president.

GÉRALD GAILLARD

Further Reading

Cabral, Amílcar. *Unity and Struggle.* London: Heinemann, 1980.

Chabal, Patrick. *Amícal Cabral: Revolutionary Leadership and People's War.* New-York, 1983.

Dadha, Mustaphah. *Warriors at Work: How Guinea Was Really Set Free.* Niwot: University Press of Colorado, 1993.

Forrest, J. B. *Guinea-Bissau : Power, Conflict, and Renewal in a West African Nation.* Boulder, Colo.: 1992.

Lopes, Carlos. *Guinea-Bissau: From Liberation Struggle to Independent Statehood.* Boulder, Colo.: Westview Press, 1987.

Guinea-Bissau: Independence to the Present

Final victory over Portugal in September 1974 brought no solutions to increasingly entrenched ethnic, political, and economic problems in Guinea-Bissau. Independence compounded factionalism in the vanguard party, the Partido Africano da Independencia da Guiné-Bissau e Cabo Verde (PAIGC), the government, and the army. Political ambition in the context of a one-party state relied on the development of strong clientelist bonds, as an erstwhile revolutionary army moved into a government and administration position. Corruption became endemic.

A central issue was the future relationship between Guinea-Bissau and Cape Verde. Although Cape Verde achieved independence following elections in June 1975, there was no settled plan for unification of the two countries. As a result, a Cape Verdean, Aristides Pereira, occupied a dual role as head of state of Cape Verde and PAIGC secretary general. Luis Cabral, half-brother to the assassinated former leader of the PAIGC Amílcar Cabral, assumed the presidency of Guinea-Bissau. The PAIGC's most successful military leader, Joao "Nino" Vieira, became commissar of the armed forces and, later, prime minister. However, non-Cape Verdeans emained very much in the minority in the upper echelons of the party, the government, and the armed forces.

The party proved incapable of controlling the new government. Party workers found difficulty assuming peacetime administrative procedure. Public servants had often worked for the Portuguese and were not naturally sympathetic to the PAIGC. Individual commissioners or ministers soon became preoccupied with assuring funds, usually from external sources, for their ministries. Links with the party structure assumed secondary importance. As the PAIGC demobilized, the ministries manifested an impulse toward *clientelismo*. Although ministers remained as part of the PAIGC, party and government moved apart on a functional and organizational level.

At the same time, the party was distancing itself from its grassroots support. At independence the party leadership and many middle-ranking personnel moved to Bissau. As well as a perceived need to exercise command in a city that the PAIGC never took by force, militants felt that their long sacrifices in the bush warranted a period of relative urban comfort. Village committees suffered from a lack of resources and commitment. Electoral exercises were conducted in 1972 and 1976, but neither was an authentic process. Elections were held to reassert party authority in those regions hostile to the PAIGC during the war of liberation, to give the impression of legitimacy in the country, and, thus, to increase economic aid for Guinea-Bissau in the international community, especially the European Union. An increasingly authoritarian environment prevailed. Mass organizations, created at independence, were emasculated.

The level of disaffection throughout the country was unsustainable. The agent for change was Nino Vieira, who benefited from a long-standing anticolonial alliance with the largest ethnic group, and the backbone of the army, the Balanta. By 1979 Vieira and Luis Cabral had built up rival power bases. Vieira won support from the army and in rural areas, while public servants in the towns were behind the resident. Balanta and Papel backed Vieira and Cape Verdeans Cabral. In a tense political environment, Cabral resorted to authoritarian methods. Vieira's removal as army commander, followed by the incorporation of prime ministerial powers in the hands of the resident, prompted the army to move. Vieira assumed power on November 14, 1980.

All top-level government officials of Cape Verdean origin were dismissed or demoted. Relations between Praia and Bissau were severed in January 1981. The PAIGC in Cape Verde reformed as the Partido Africano da Independencia da Cabo Verde (PAICV). The PAIGC in Bissau maintained its original title but expelled all members of the PAICV, including Pereira. Coup attempts or rumors of coup attempts, the arrest of alleged conspirators and their rehabilitation, execution,

and imprisonment became a recurrent cycle during the Vieira era. Balanta faith in Vieira soon dissipated. A growing perception that insufficient Balanta were receiving high-ranking posts in the army and government led to a series of conspiracies. Vieira responded in 1985 by arresting a swath of alleged conspirators, in the most part Balanta. After a dubious judicial process, six people were executed.

Factionalism endured. Vieira's retention of power was based on the recasting of the PAIGC as a hierarchical, vanguard party. The containment of infighting continued to require a deft political touch. Individuals were removed and resuscitated as Vieira attempted to countercheck each faction. There were increasing calls for genuine democracy. Elections in 1984 were manipulated, and 1989 elections saw voter numbers drop to 53 per cent of the registered electorate. Economic liberalization, initiated in 1983, led to a structural adjustment program financed by external aid totaling $46.4 million. In a climate of political conditionality, émigré opposition groups grasped the opportunity to agitate for pluralism in Bissau.

Guinea-Bissau embarked on a constitutional transition process in 1991. Defunct and exiled parties were revived and new parties formed. Elections were held in two rounds in July and August 1994. The PAIGC won a clear majority in the National Assembly. Vieira narrowly defeated Koumba Yalla of the Partido da Renovação Social (PRS) for the presidency. Yalla objected, citing voting irregularities, and the country descended into economic and political disarray. Entry into the Franc Zone in 1997 resulted in a sharp rise in food prices and a reduction of purchasing power, causing widespread unrest.

A secessionist rebellion in neighboring Casamance, led by the Mouvement des forces démocratiques de la Casamance (MFDC), influenced relations with Senegal throughout the 1990s. Vieira attempted to allay Senegalese fears that the MFDC was receiving weapons and support from Bissauan sources. In June 1998 veteran army commander Ansumane Mané was dismissed for alleged arms trafficking. A large majority of the disaffected army and veterans of the war of liberation rallied behind the popular Mané, who proclaimed himself leader of an interim military junta. A civil war that precipitated the destruction of Bissau, significant carnage, and large-scale internal displacement ensued. Vieira requested, and received, military support from Senegal and Guinea. For Senegal the intervention was an opportunity to assault MFDC rear bases. The conflict also saw a brief return to colonial power politics, with France supporting Vieira and Senegal, while Portugal gave tacit backing to the rebels. However, by October, loyalist forces were contained in a small area of central Bissau. The Economic Community of West African States (ECOWAS) brokered a ceasefire and peace agreement.

609

In March 1999 Senegalese and Guinean troops were replaced by a 600-strong ECOWAS monitoring group (ECOMOG) acting as a peacekeeping interposition force, which ultimately proved ineffectual. On May 6 Mané launched a final assault on the loyalist stronghold. Vieira was forced to seek asylum in Portugal.

The speaker of the National Assembly and member of the PAIGC, Malam Bacai Sanha, was appointed interim president, and a government of national unity was installed. Guinea-Bissau's first authentic elections were conducted in November 1999 and January 2000. Kumba Yalla, a former teacher, defeated Sanha for the presidency, and the PAIGC lost its preeminent position in parliament to the PRS. Although Mané kept his promise not to undermine the process, the military junta retained the potential to influence the governance of the country. With a view to conciliation, the National Assembly tabled a bill in April 2000 proposing the creation of a national security council, to include members of the junta, whose members would hold ministerial rank. In 2001 the junior members of Yalla's governing coalition deserted their posts in protest because they claimed they had not been consulted about a reshuffling of the cabinet. Guinea-Bissau remains one of the poorest countries in the world.

SIMON MASSEY

See *also*: **Economic Community of West African States (ECOWAS); Senegal: Casamance Province, Conflict in.**

Further Reading

Forrest, Joshua B. *Guinea-Bissau: Power, Conflict, and Renewal in a West African State*. Boulder, Colo.: Westview Press, 1992.

Forrest, Joshua. "Guinea-Bissau Since Independence: A Decade of Domestic Power Struggles." *Journal of Modern African Studies* 25 (1987).

Galli, Rosemary E., and Jocelyn Jones. *Guinea-Bissau: Politics, Economics, and Society*. London: Frances Pinter, 1987.

Lobban, Richard, and Peter Karibe Mendy. *Historical Dictionary of the Republic of Guinea-Bissau*. Lanham, M.D.: Scarecrow Press, 1997.

Lopes, Carlos. *Guinea-Bissau: From Liberation Struggle to Independent Statehood*. N.J.: Zed Books, 1987.

Rudebeck, Lars. "'To Seek Happiness': Development in a West African Village in the Era of Democratisation." *Review of African Political Economy* 71(1997).

Gun War: *See* **Lesotho (Basutoland): Colonization and Cape Rule, 1868–1884.**

Gungunhane: *See* **Soshangane, Umzila, Gungunhane, and the Gaza State.**